O|S Ordnance Survey

STREET ATLAS
West
Yorkshire

Contents

Explanation of street index reference system

Key to town, village and rural locality abbreviations in index

Key to map symbols

Key to map pages

Administrative and post code boundaries

Street maps

Index of hospitals, railway stations, schools, shopping centres, street names and universities

PHILIP'S

First colour edition published 1996
Reprinted 1996, twice 1997, 1998 by

Ordnance Survey® and George Philip Ltd
Romsey Road,   an imprint of Reed Consumer
Maybush,   Books Ltd
Southampton   Michelin House, 81 Fulham Road,
SO16 4GU   London SW3 6RB
                     and Auckland and Melbourne

ISBN 0-540-06328-2 (pocket edition)

To the best of the Publishers' knowledge, the information in
this atlas was correct at the time of going to press. No
responsibility can be accepted for any errors or their
consequences.

The representation in this atlas of a road, track or path is
no evidence of the existence of a right of way.

**The mapping between pages 1 and 200 (inclusive) in
this atlas is derived from Ordnance Survey® OSCAR®**

D0348929

EXPLANATION OF THE STREET INDEX REFERENCE SYSTEM

Street names are listed alphabetically and show the locality, the Post Office Postcode District, the page number and a reference to the square in which the name falls on the map page.

Example: Rutland St. Han ST4.....................................57 D3 8

Rutland St	This is the full street name, which may have been abbreviated on the map.
Han	This is the abbreviation for the town, village or locality in which the street falls.
ST4	This is the Post Office Postcode District for the street name.
57	This is the page number of the map on which the street name appears.
D3	The letter and figure indicate the square on the map in which the centre of the street falls. The square can be found at the junction of the vertical column carrying the appropriate letter and the horizontal row carrying the appropriate figure.
8	In congested areas numbers may have been used to indicate the location of a street. In certain circumstances, the number used to represent a street will follow the reference in the gazetteer entry.

ABBREVIATIONS USED IN THE INDEX
Road Names

Approach	App	Corner	Cnr	Heights	Hts	Road	Rd
Arcade	Arc	Cottages	Cotts	Industri al Estate	Ind Est	Roundabout	Rdbt
Avenue	Ave	Court	Ct	Interchange	Intc	South	S
Boulevard	Bvd	Courtyard	Ctyd	Junction	Junc	Square	Sq
Buildings	Bldgs	Crescent	Cres	Lane	La	Stairs	Strs
Business Park	Bsns Pk	Drive	Dr	North	N	Steps	Stps
Business Centre	Bsns Ctr	Drove	Dro	Orchard	Orch	Street,Saint	St
Bungalows	Bglws	East	E	Parade	Par	Terrace	Terr
Causeway	Cswy	Embankment	Emb	Park	Pk	Trading Estate	Trad Est
Centre	Ctr	Esplanade	Espl	Passage	Pas	Walk	Wlk
Circle	Circ	Estate	Est	Place	Pl	West	W
Circus	Cir	Gardens	Gdns	Precinct	Prec	Yard	Yd
Close	Cl	Green	Gn	Promenade	Prom		
Common	Comm	Grove	Gr	Retail Park	Ret Pk		

Key to abbreviations of Town, Village and Rural locality names used in the index of street names.

Aberford	Aber	64	E7	Cullingworth	Cull	52	C6
Ackworth Moor Top . Ack M T		163	E6	Darrington	Dar	147	C5
Addingham	Add	6	E8	Dearne	Dearne	194	D1
Adwick Le Street	Ad Le S	184	E2	Denby Dale	D Dale	192	B6
Arthington	Arth	25	D6	Denholme	Denh	52	D1
Askwith	Ask	9	F5	Denshaw	Densh	167	B3
Bacup	Bacup	106	B4	Denton	Denton	9	A6
Badsworth	Bad	164	E2	Dewsbury	Dew	139	C7
Baildon	Bail	38	C3	Diggle	Diggle	185	B4
Bardsey	Bard	28	D4	Draughton	Draug	1	D5
Barnsley	Barn	178	F1	Dunford Bridge	Dun Br	199	D1
Barwick in Elmet	B in Elm	63	E7	East Ardsley	E Ard	120	B7
Batley	Batley	118	C4	East Carlton	E Carl	23	D3
Beal	Beal	127	F6	East Keswick	E Kes	28	C6
Beamsley	Beam	2	F5	Eccup	Eccup	25	F1
Bickerton	Bick	15	C7	Elland	Elland	134	E6
Bingley	Bing	37	C4	Embsay	Embsay	1	A8
Birkenshaw	Birk	96	B5	Emley	Emley	175	C6
Birkin	Birkin	127	D7	Fairburn	Fair	105	B4
Blackshaw Head	B Head	87	F4	Farnhill	Farnh	4	D1
Bolton Abbey	B Abby	2	E8	Farnley	Farnley	11	D4
Boston Spa	B Spa	30	D7	Featherstone	Feath	145	C7
Bradford	Brad	74	E8	Flockton	Floc	157	C2
Bramham	Bramham	30	E3	Garforth	Gar	83	B5
Bramhope	Bramho	24	D3	Gildersome	Gild	97	D8
Brierley	Bri	181	A3	Glusburn	Glu	16	C6
Brighouse	Brig	115	B2	Great Houghton	G Hou	194	A3
Brodsworth	Brod	195	F2	Grimethorpe	Grim	181	B1
Brotherton	Broth	126	D8	Guiseley	Guise	39	C8
Burghwallis	Burg	184	E4	Halifax	Hali	113	E7
Burley in Wharfdale	Bur in W	9	D1	Halton East	Hal E	1	A3
Burton Salmon	B Sal	105	E3	Hampole	Ham	184	B1
Byram	Byram	126	E7	Harden	Harden	36	B1
Carlecotes	Carl	200	B3	Harewood	Hare	27	A7
Castleford	Castle	124	F8	Haworth	Haw	51	B7
Castley	Cast	25	B8	Hazlewood	Hazl	3	B8
Cawthorne	Caw	193	D4	Hebden Bridge	Heb Br	89	B3
Clayton	Clay	194	C4	Hemsworth	Hem	181	C8
Clayton West	Clay W	175	F2	Heptonstall	Hep	67	C2
Cleckheaton	Clec	116	C6	High Hoyland	H Hoy	176	C1
Clifton	Clift	10	E5	Hillam	Hillam	105	F7
Collingham	Coll	29	B8	Holme	Holme	197	F8
Cononley	Con	4	A3	Holme Chapel	H Chap	85	B6
Cowling	Cowl	32	C7	Holmfirth	Holmfi	189	B5
Cridling Stubbs	C Stub	127	D1	Honley	Honley	171	E4
Crigglestone	Crig	159	E5	Hooton Pagnell	H Pag	195	C5
Crofton	Crof	143	F1	Horbury	Hor	141	B2
Cudworth	Cud	180	B1	Horsforth	Hors	41	A2
Huddersfield	Hud	154	C6	Royston	Roy	179	D3
Hunger Hill	H Hill	8	B8	Ryhill	Ryhill	162	B1
Ilkley	Ilkley	8	C4	Saxton	Saxton	65	E8
Ingbirchworth	Ing	191	E1	Scarcroft	Scar	45	D8
Keighley	Keigh	35	D6	Shafton	Shaf	180	B3
Kexbrough	Kex	177	A1	Shelf	Shelf	93	D6
Kippax	Kippax	83	B2	Shepley	Shep	190	F8
Kirk Deighton	K Deig	13	C8	Sherburn in Elmet	S in Elm	65	E1
Kirk Smeaton	K Smea	166	D5	Shipley	Ship	55	B7
Kirkburton	Kirkb	173	E6	Sicklinghall	Sickl	12	C5
Kirkheaton	Kirkhe	137	C1	Silkstone	Silk	193	F1
Knottingley	Knot	127	B4	Silsden	Sil	5	E1
Leathley	Leath	24	C8	Skelmanthorpe	Skel	175	B2
Ledsham	Ledsh	104	D8	Skipton	Skip	1	A4
Ledston	Ledst	103	E6	Slaithwaite	Slai	152	A1
Leeds	Leeds	79	A7	South Elmsall	S Elm	183	A2
Lepton	Lepton	155	E3	South Hiendley	S Hie	180	D6
Lindley	Lind	11	E7	South Kirkby	S Kirk	182	C1
Littleborough	Litt	129	B2	South Milford	S Mil	84	E3
Liversedge	Liver	117	A6	Sowerby Bridge	Sow Br	112	C3
Lofthouse Gate	Loft G	121	D6	Spofforth	Spof	12	C8
Low Bradley	L Brad	4	D5	Steeton	Stee	17	D5
Mapplewell	Mapp	178	C1	Stutton	Stut	48	C5
Marsden	Mars	168	E3	Sutton-in-Craven	S-in-Cra	16	E5
Meltham	Mel	170	E3	Swillington	Swil	82	B1
Menston	Men	22	A4	Tadcaster	Tad	31	E3
Micklefield	M'field	84	A7	Thorner	Thorner	45	E5
Mickletown	M'town	102	D3	Thornton	Thorn	72	E6
Middleton	Midd	99	D4	Thorp Arch	Th Arch	14	F1
Mirfield	Mir	138	A6	Thorpe Audlin	Th Aud	165	B4
Monk Fryston	M Fry	105	E8	Tintwistle	Tint	197	A2
Morley	Morley	98	C3	Todmorden	Tod	108	C6
Nesfield	Nes	7	C8	Trawden	Traw	32	A2
Netherton	Neth	158	E6	Upton	Upton	183	A8
Normanton	Nor	123	B1	Wadsworth Moor	Wad M	68	E6
Northowram	Northo	93	B2	Wakefield	Wake	142	E5
Norton	Norton	166	F1	Walton	Walton	161	B6
Notton	Notton	178	F6	West Bretton	W Bret	176	E8
Ossett	Ossett	140	E6	West Hardwick	W Har	145	A3
Otley	Otley	23	B8	Wetherby	Weth	13	C6
Oxenhope	Oxen	51	D2	Whitley Common	Wh Com	200	E7
Penistone	Pen	192	E1	Whitworth	Whit	106	E1
Pontefract	Pont	146	B6	Wighill	Wig	15	C5
Pool	Pool	24	D7	Wilsden	Wil	53	D5
Pudsey	Pudsey	76	D7	Womersley	Wom	147	F3
Queensbury	Queen	72	C5	Woolley	Wool	177	F7
Ripponden	Rip	132	D4	Worsthorne	Worst	66	A4
Rothwell	Roth	100	E5	Yeadon	Yeadon	40	D5

Key to map symbols

Motorway

Primary Routes (Dual carriageway and single)

A Roads (Dual carriageway and single)

B Roads (Dual carriageway and single)

C Roads (Dual carriageway and single)

Minor Roads

Roads under construction

County boundaries

All Railways

Track or private road

Gate or obstruction to traffic (restrictions may not apply at all times or to all vehicles)

All paths, bridleways, BOAT's, RUPP's, dismantled railways, etc.

The representation in this atlas of a road, track or path is no evidence of the existence of a right of way

174 Adjoining page indicator

Acad	Academy	Mon	Monument
Cemy	Cemetery	Mus	Museum
C Ctr	Civic Centre	Obsy	Observatory
CH	Club House	Pal	Royal Palace
Coll	College	PH	Public House
Ex H	Exhibition Hall	Resr	Reservoir
Ind Est	Industrial Estate	Ret Pk	Retail Park
Inst	Institute	Sch	School
Ct	Law Court	Sh Ctr	Shopping Centre
L Ctr	Leisure Centre	Sta	Station
LC	Level Crossing	TH	Town Hall/House
Liby	Library	Trad Est	Trading Estate
Mkt	Market	Univ	University
Meml	Memorial	YH	Youth Hostel

British Rail station

Private railway station

Bus, coach station

Ambulance station

Coastguard station

Fire station

Police station

Casualty entrance to hospital

Churches, Place of worship

H Hospital

i Information Centre

P Parking

Post Office

Public Convenience

Important buildings, schools, colleges, universities and hospitals

River Soar Water Name

Stream

River or canal (minor and major)

Water Fill

Tidal Water

Woods

Houses

0		¼		½		¾		1 mile
0	250m	500m	750m	1 Kilometre				

The scale of the maps is 3.92 cm to 1 km (2½ inches to 1 mile)

The small numbers around the edges of the maps identify the 1 kilometre National Grid lines

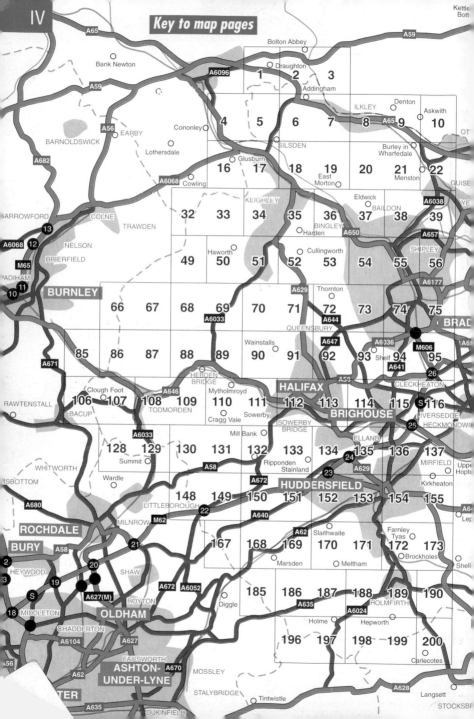

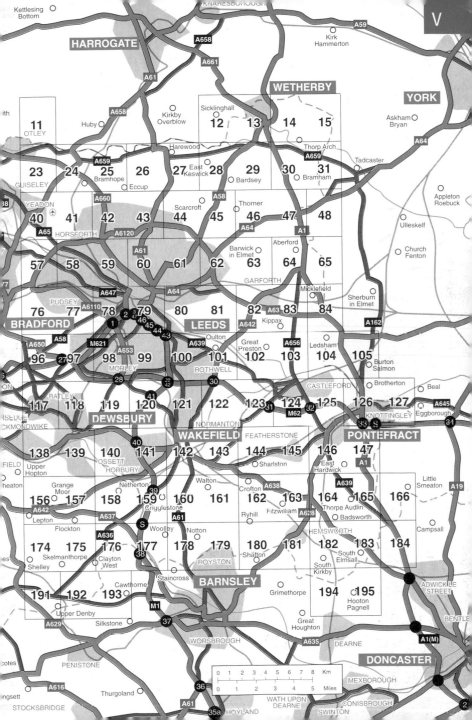

Major administrative and post code boundaries of West Yorkshire

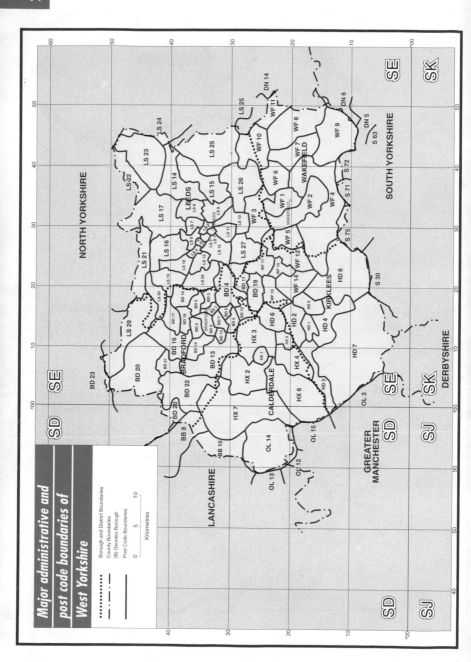

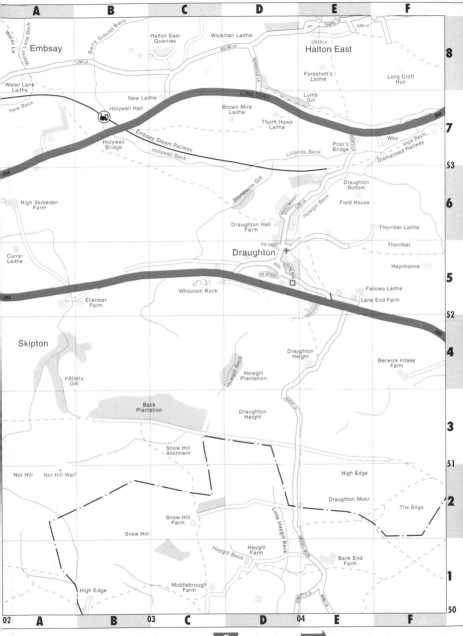

A B C D E F

Water La
Water Lane Beck
Embsay
Berry Ground Beck
Halton East Quarries
Wickman Laithe
HOLME LA
CHAPEL LA
GAW LA
GREEN LA
Halton East
8
LOW LA
Water Lane Laithe
New Laithe
Foreshott's Laithe
Long Croft Hull
Haw Beck
Holywell Halt
LONG CSWY
Brown Mire Laithe
Lumb Gill
A59
7
Holywell Bridge
Embsay Steam Railway
Thorn Haws Laithe
Wks
Ings Back
Holywell Beck
Lillands Beck
Prior's Bridge
Dismantled Railway
53
Stonsacre Gill
Draughton Bottom
High Skibeden Farm
MEADSWORTH
LOW LA
Howgill Beck
Field House
6
Draughton Hall Farm
Thornber Laithe
Currer Laithe
THE CROFT
Draughton
Thornber
Haynholme
THE SPINNEY
5
A55
Wheolam Rock
Fallows Laithe
Lane End Farm
Ellenber Farm
52
Skipton
Draughton Height
Berwick Intake Farm
4
Potters Gill
Howgill Beck
Howgill Plantation
HEIGHT LA
Back Plantation
Draughton Height
3
Snow Hill Allotment
51
Nor Hill
Nor Hill Well
High Edge
Draughton Moor
2
Snow Hill Farm
Little Haygill Beck
The Bogs
Snow Hill
Haygill Beck
Haygill Farm
HAYGILL MOOR
Bank End Farm
1
High Edge
Middlebrough Farm
FORRETS LA
BANK LA
50
A B C D E F
02   03   04

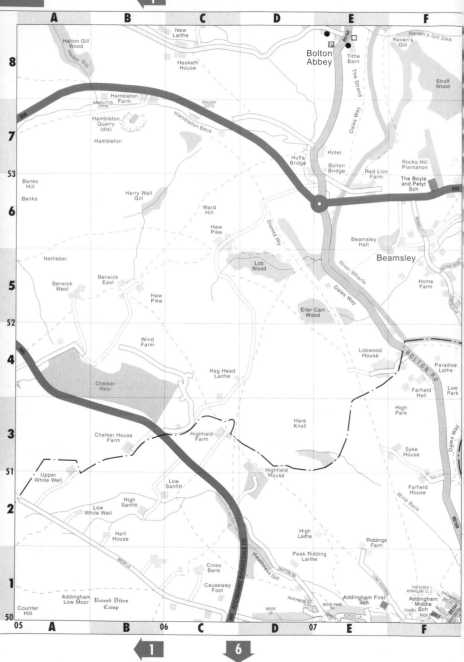

| A | B | C | D | E | F |

8

Halton Gill Wood
Halton Gill
New Laithe
Hesketh House
Bolton Abbey
B6160
Tithe Barn
Raven's Gill Dike
Raven's Gill
Struff Wood
P
The Strand

7

A59
Hambleton Farm
HAMBLETON COTTS
Hambleton Quarry (dis)
Hambleton
Hambleton Beck
RAILWAY COTTS
Huffa Bridge
Hotel
Bolton Bridge
Dales Way
Red Lion Farm
Rocks Hill Plantation
The Boyle and Petyt Sch
A59

53

Banks Hill
Banks
Harry Wall Gill
Ward Hill
BEAMSLEY LA

6

Haw Pike
Dismd Rly
Beamsley Hall
Beamsley
LANGBAR BANK

Nettleber
Berwick East
Lob Wood
River Wharfe
Home Farm
LOWER GATE

5

Berwick West
Haw Pike
Dales Way
Eller Carr Wood

52

Wind Farm
Lobwood House
BOLTON RD
Paradise Lathe

4

M6
Chelker Resr
Hag Head Laithe
Farfield Hall
Low Park
Dales Way

3

Chelker House Farm
Highfield Farm
Hare Knoll
High Park
Syke House
Farfield House
Wine Beck

51

Upper White Well
Low Sanfitt
Highfield House

2

Low White Well
High Sanfitt
Hart House
B6160

1

MOOR LA
Cross Bank
Causeway Foot
Heatherness Gill
High Laithe
Peak Ridding Laithe
Riddings Farm
MR ADDINGHAM WHARFEDALE RD
SKIPTON RD
Addingham First Sch
THE ACRES 1
AYNHOLME CL 2
SPRINGFIELD
MT PLEASANT
Addingham Middle Sch
CHAPEL ST
BACK BECK
LOW MILL

50

Counter Hill
Addingham Low Moor
Round Dikes Camp
MOOR LA
HEATHERNESS RD
MOOR PARK DRI
GREEN LA
SCHOOL LA

| A | 06 | B | C | 07 | D | E | F |

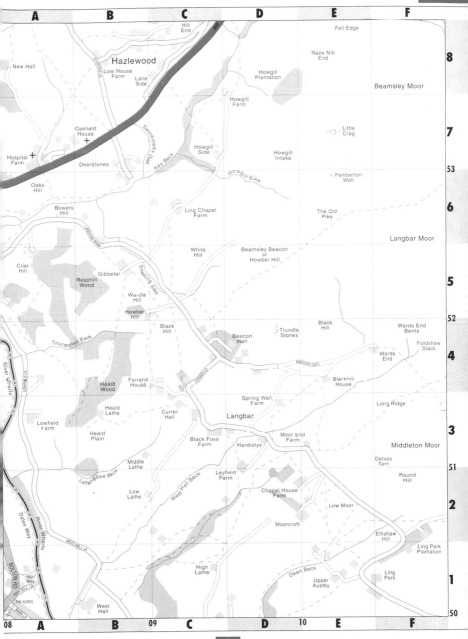

A   B   C   D   E   F

Hill
End

Fell Edge

8

Naze Nib
End

Hazlewood

Beamsley Moor

New Hall

Low House
Farm

Lane
Side

Howgill
Plantation

Howgill
Farm

Little
Crag

7

Oakfield
House

Howgill
Side

Howgill
Intake

Hospital
Farm

Deerstones

Pemberton
Well

53

Oaks
Hill

Howgill Sike

Bowers
Hill

Ling Chapel
Farm

The Old
Pike

6

Langbar Moor

White
Hill

Beamsley Beacon
or
Howber Hill

Crier
Hill

Gibbeter

Resphill
Wood

Wardla
Hill

5

Howber
Hill

52

Black
Hill

Trundle
Stones

Black
Hill

Wards End
Bents

Thurstones Beck

Beacon
Hall

Foldshaw
Slack

4

BADGERS GATE

Wards
End

Heald
Wood

Farrand
House

Blackhill
House

River Wharfe

Heald
Lathe

Currer
Hall

Spring Well
Farm

Long Ridge

Langbar

3

Lowfield
Farm

Heald
Plain

Black Foss
Farm

Hardistys

Moor End
Farm

Middleton Moor

Delves
Tarn

51

Middle
Lathe

Leyfield
Farm

Round
Hill

Low
Lathe

Chapel House
Farm

Low Moor

2

Moorcroft

Dales Way

Ellishaw
Hill

Ling Park
Plantation

West Hall Beck

High
Lathe

Dean Beck

Ling
Park

1

BOLTON RD

High
Mill

Upper
Austby

THE ACRES

West
Hall

50

08   A   B   09   C   D   10   E   F

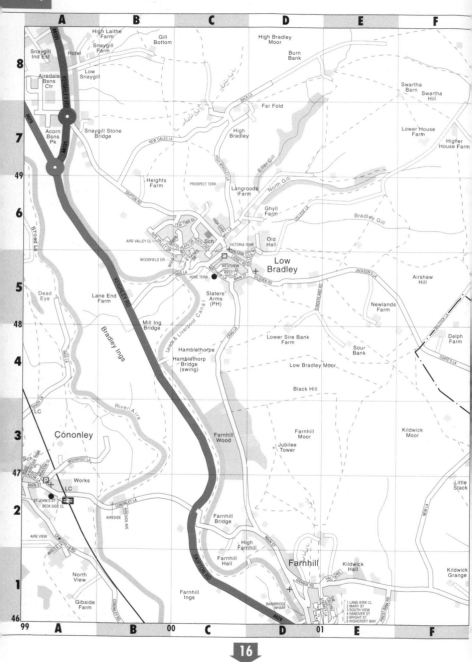

8

Snaygill Ind Est

Airedale Bsns Ctr

Hotel

High Laithe Farm

Snaygill Farm

Low Snaygill

Gill Bottom

High Bradley Moor

Burn Bank

Swartha Barn

Swartha Hill

7

Acorn Bsns Pk

Snaygill Stone Bridge

NEW DALES LA

High Bradley

Far Fold

Lower House Farm

Higher House Farm

49

Heights Farm

PROSPECT TERR

Langroods Farm

North Gill

Eller Gill

Bradley Gill

6

YEW TREE CL

Sch

Ghyll Farm

COLLEGE LA

AIRE VALLEY CL

VICTORIA TERR

Old Hall

Low Bradley

WOODFIELD DR

WESTVIEW

JACKSON'S LA

Airshaw Hill

5

ROBE TERR

MAIN ST

Slaters' Arms (PH)

SILSDEN RD

Newlands Farm

Dead Eye

Lane End Farm

SUNDERLAND RD

Delph Farm

48

Mill Ing Bridge

Leeds & Liverpool Canal

Hamblethorpe

Lower Sire Bank Farm

Sour Bank

COATE'S LA

4

Bradley Ings

Hamblethorp Bridge (swing)

Low Bradley Moor

Black Hill

3

Cononley

River Aire

Farnhill Wood

Farnhill Moor

Jubilee Tower

Kildwick Moor

Sch

MOORFOOT LA

47

Works

Little Stack

P

LC

2

ST JOHN'S ST

BECK SIDE CL

MAIN ST

CONONLEY LA

AIRESIDE AVE

Farnhill Bridge

SKIPTON RD

MAIN ST

AIRE VIEW

High Farnhill

Farnhill Hall

Farnhill

Kildwick Hall

GRANGE RD

Kildwick Grange

1

North View

Farnhill Ings

BAINBRIDGE WHARF

PRIEST BANK RD

1 LANG KIRK CL
2 MARY ST
3 SOUTH VIEW
4 HANOVER ST
5 BRIGHT ST
6 HIGHCROFT WAY

Gibside Farm

CONONLEY RD

46

99 A | B **00** C | D **01** E | F

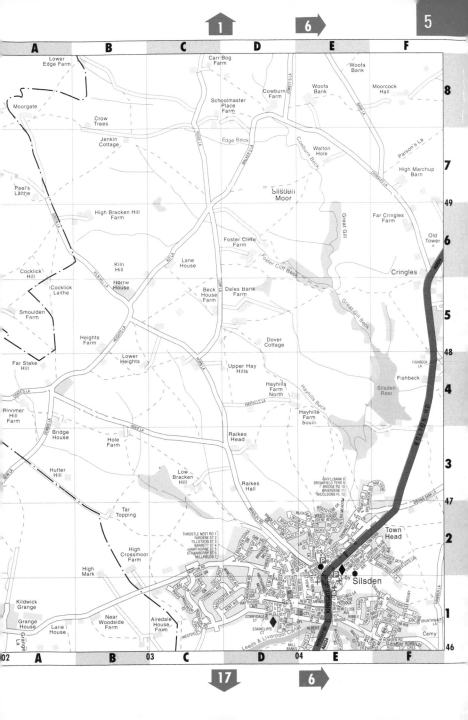

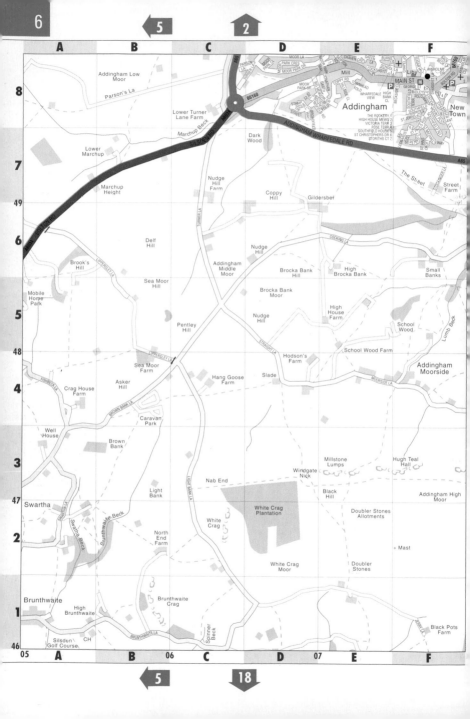

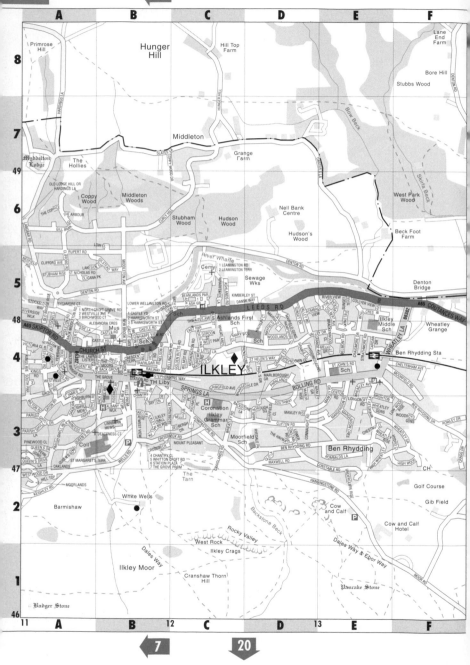

ILKLEY

Hunger Hill

Primrose Hill

Lane End Farm

Bore Hill

Stubbs Wood

Middleton

Middleton Lodge

The Hollies

Grange Farm

West Park Wood

Old Lodge Hill or Hardings La

Coppy Wood

Middleton Woods

Nell Bank Centre

Beck Foot Farm

Stubham Wood

Hudson Wood

Hudson's Wood

Denton Bridge

River Wharfe

1 LEAMINGTON RD
2 LEAMINGTON TERR

Cemy

Sewage Wks

LEEDS RD

RIVER VIEW

COLLYER VIEW

Ilkley Middle Sch

Wheatley Grange

COUTANCES WAY

Ashlands First Sch

1 NORTH CROFT GROVE RD
2 WESTVILLE AVE
3 BIRCHWOOD CT

LOWER WELLINGTON RD

BEANLANDS PAR

KIMBERLEY ST

1 CASTLE YD
2 HAWKSWORTH ST
3 HAWKSWORTH ST

Mus

CHURCH ST

Ben Rhydding Sta

ILKLEY

St HELEN'S WAY

St JOHN'S RD
Sch

CHELTENHAM AVE

SPRINGS LA

BOLLING RD

Coronation Ilkley Grammar Sch

Moorfield Sch

Ben Rhydding

4 CHANTRY CL
5 WHITTON CROFT RD
6 STATION PLAZA
7 THE GROVE PROM

The Tarn

Golf Course

Gib Field

White Wells

Cow and Calf

Cow and Calf Hotel

Barmishaw

Backstone Beck

Rocky Valley

West Rock

Ilkley Crags

Dales Way & Ebor Way

Ilkley Moor

Dales Way

Cranshaw Thorn Hill

Pancake Stone

Badger Stone

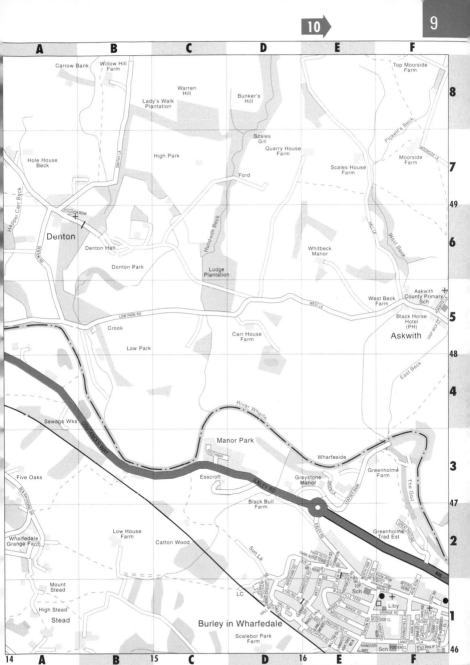

8

Carrow Bank
Willow Hill Farm
Top Moorside Farm

Warren Hill
Lady's Walk Plantation
Bunker's Hill
Pickett's Beck

7

Hole House Beck
High Park
Scales Gill
Quarry House Farm
Scales House Farm
Moorside Farm
MOORSIDE LA

Hopper Carr Beck
CHURCH ROW
Ford
49

Denton
Denton Hall
Whitbeck Manor
West Beck

6

Donton Park
Lodge Plantation
WEST LA
West Beck Farm
Askwith County Primary Sch

LOW PARK RD
Crook
HALL LA
Black Horse Hotel (PH)
5

Low Park
Carr House Farm
Askwith
EAST BECK LA

48
East Beck

River Wharfe
4

Sewage Wks
SOUTHMOSS WAY
Manor Park
SOUTHWAY
Wharfeside
Greenholme Farm
The Goit

Five Oaks
Esscroft
ILKLEY RD
Greystone Manor
GREEN LA
LEATHLEY LANE
Greenholme Trad Est

3

Black Bull Farm
47

Wharfedale Grange Farm
Low House Farm
Catton Wood
Sun La
Greenholme Trad Est
A65
2

Mount Stead
LC
FARR ROYD TERR
1

High Stead
Stead
HALL
Sch
Liby
GRANGE RD

Burley in Wharfedale
Scalebor Park Farm
HANOVER WAY
Sch
FOSTER
ST PHILIP'S
46

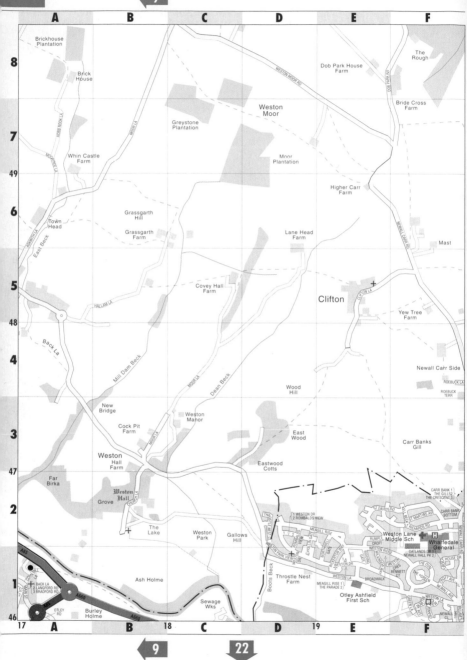

A B C D E F

8

Brickhouse
Plantation

Brick
House

HOBB NOOK LA

MOOR LA

7

Whin Castle
Farm

MOOR LA

49

Greystone
Plantation

Weston
Moor

WESTON MOOR RD

Dob Park House
Farm

The
Rough

RD PARK RD

Bride Cross
Farm

Moor
Plantation

Higher Carr
Farm

NEWALL CARR RD

Mast

6

Town
Head

East Beck

Grassgarth
Hill

Grassgarth
Farm

Lane Head
Farm

5

HALLAM LA

Covey Hall
Farm

Clifton

CLIFTON LA

Yew Tree
Farm

48

Back La

Mill Dam Beck

MOOR LA

Dean Beck

Wood
Hill

Newall Carr Side

ROEBUCK LA

ROEBUCK
TERR

4

New
Bridge

Cock Pit
Farm

MOOR LA

Weston
Manor

East
Wood

Carr Banks
Gill

3

Weston
Hall Farm

Far
Birka

Weston
Grove

CUCKHILL

Weston
Hall

The
Lake

Weston
Park

Gallows
Hill

Eastwood
Cotts

CARR BANK 1
THE GILLS 2
THE CRESCENT 3

CARR BANK
BOTTOM

ST DAVIDS RD

ST MARTINS AVE

ST RICHARDS RD

Weston Lane
Middle Sch

Wharfedale
General

2

A65

A65

Ash Holme

1 WESTON DR
2 ROMBALDS VIEW

MEAGILL RISE

RUMPLE
CROFT

WESTON RIDGE

WESTON DR

WESTON LA

BROADWALK

OATLANDS DR
NEWALL HALL PK

THE OAK

OREF
BENNETT

HOUSE DR

1

A65

BACK LA
LANGFORD RD
BRADFORD RD

OTLEY RD

A65

Burley
Holme

Throstle Nest
Farm

Boots Beck

MEAGILL RISE 1
THE PARADE 2

Otley Ashfield
First Sch

WESTON LA

GREEN LA

NEWALL MOUNT

WK CL

NEWALL
CL

46

Sewage
Wks

17 A 18 B C D 19 E F

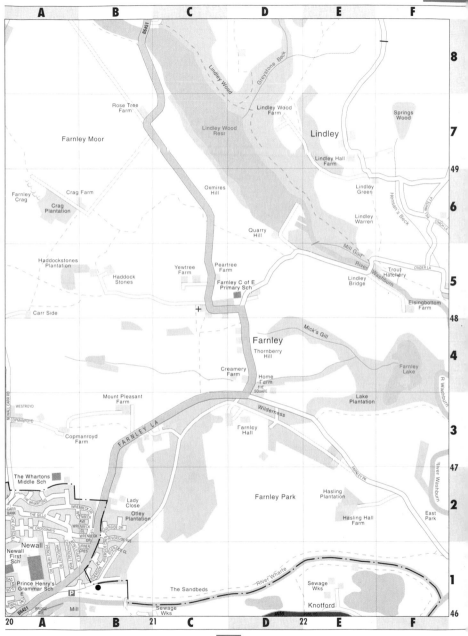

Lindley

Springs Wood

Lindley Wood

Greystone Beck

Lindley Wood Farm

Rose Tree Farm

Farnley Moor

Lindley Wood Resr

Lindley Hall Farm

Lindley Green

Oxmires Hill

Farnley Crag

Crag Farm

Crag Plantation

Lindley Warren

Hirsain's Beck

WHITE LA

COACH LA

Quarry Hill

Mill Golf

River Washburn

CINDER LA

Trout Hatchery

Haddockstones Plantation

Yewtree Farm

Peartree Farm

Farnley C of E Primary Sch

Lindley Bridge

Elsingbottom Farm

Haddock Stones

Carr Side

Farnley

Mick's Gill

Thornberry Hill

Creamery Farm

Home Farm THE SQUARE

Farnley Lake

Lake Plantation

R Washburn

Wilderness

Mount Pleasant Farm

WESTROYD

COPMANROYD

Copmanroyd Farm

FARNLEY LA

Farnley Hall

Farnley Park

Lake Plantation

Hasling Plantation

FARNLEY LA

R Washburn

NEWALL CARR RD

The Whartons Middle Sch

THE WHARTONS

GARR BANK

THE GILLS

THE CROSSWAYS

Newall First Sch

WRENBECK DR

WRENBECK AVE

WRENBECK DR

Lady Close

Otley Plantation

HARECROFT RD

PRINCE HENRY RD

TURNER CRES

RIVERSIDE AVE

RIVERSIDE CL

Hasling Hall Farm

East Park

Prince Henry's Grammar Sch

P

BRIDGE AVE

B6451

Mill

The Sandbeds

River Wharfe

Sewage Wks

Sewage Wks

Knotford

B6451

20 21 22

46 47 48 49

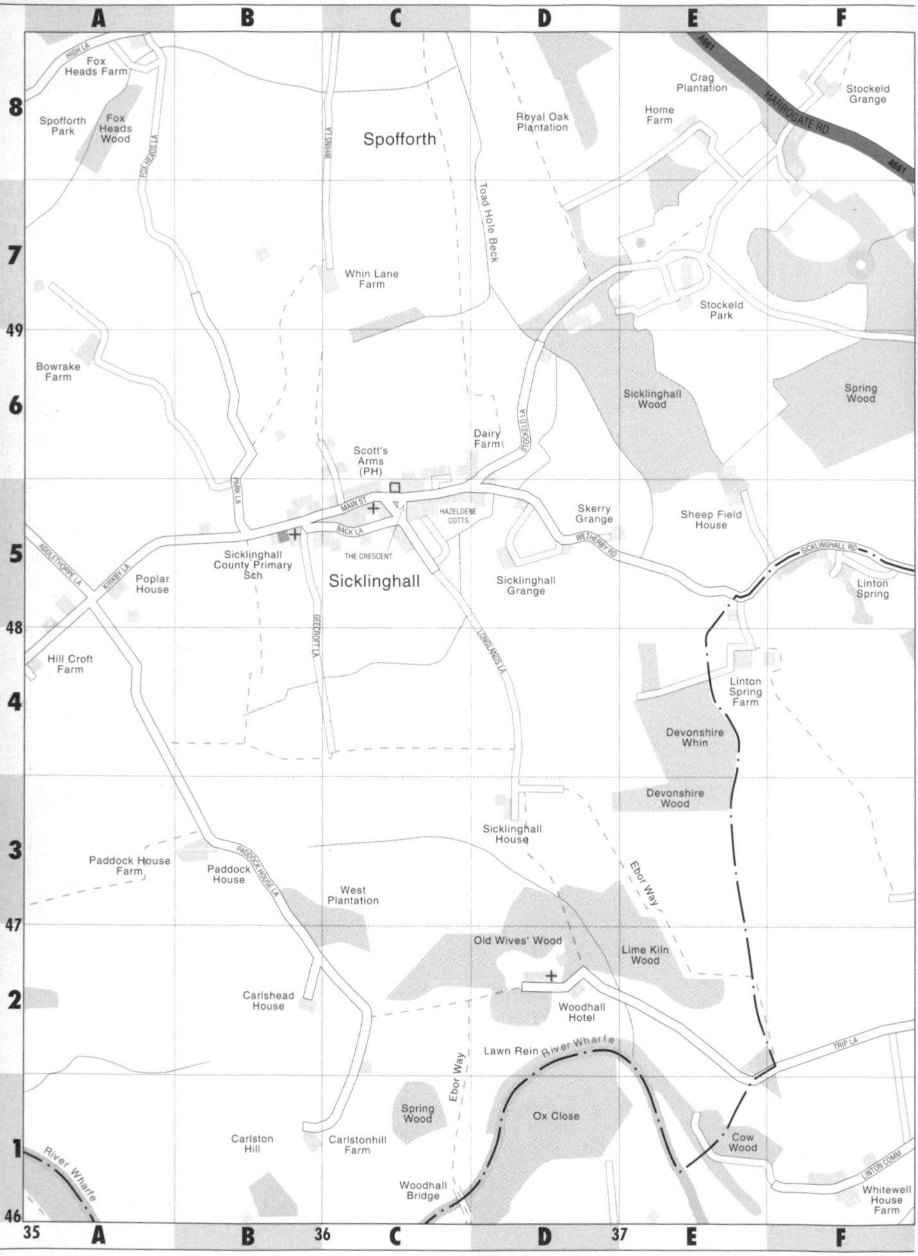
A
B
C
D
E
F
8
7
49
6
5
48
4
3
47
2
1
46
35
36
37
HIGH LA
Fox Heads Farm
Spofforth Park
Fox Heads Wood
FOX HEADS LA
WHINS LA
Spofforth
Royal Oak Plantation
Crag Plantation
Home Farm
A661
HARROGATE RD
Stockeld Grange
Toad Hole Beck
Whin Lane Farm
Stockeld Park
Bowrake Farm
Sicklinghall Wood
Spring Wood
Dairy Farm
STOCKELD LA
Scott's Arms (PH)
PARK LA
MAIN ST
HAZELDENE COTTS
Skerry Grange
Sheep Field House
BACK LA
WETHERBY RD
SICKLINGHALL RD
THE CRESCENT
ADDLETHORPE LA
KIRKBY LA
Sicklinghall County Primary Sch
Poplar House
Sicklinghall
Sicklinghall Grange
Linton Spring
GEECROFT LA
LONGLANDS LA
Hill Croft Farm
Linton Spring Farm
Devonshire Whin
Devonshire Wood
Sicklinghall House
Paddock House Farm
Paddock House
PADDOCK HOUSE LA
Ebor Way
West Plantation
Old Wives' Wood
Lime Kiln Wood
Carlshead House
Woodhall Hotel
Lawn Rein
River Wharfe
TRIP LA
Ebor Way
Spring Wood
Ox Close
Carlston Hill
Carlstonhill Farm
Cow Wood
River Wharfe
Woodhall Bridge
LINTON COMM
Whitewell House Farm

28

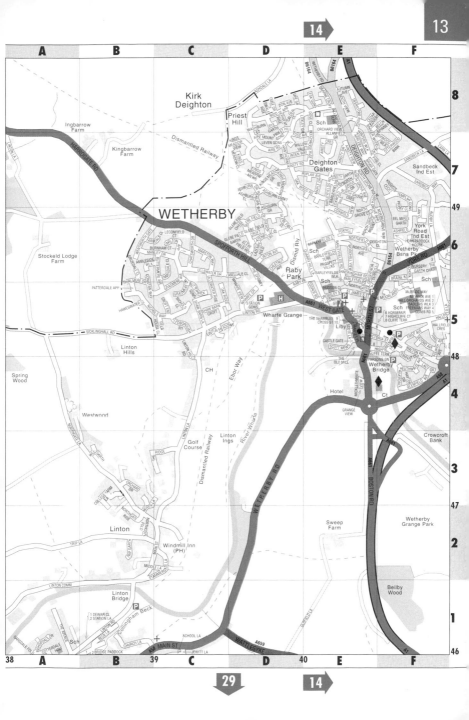

A   B   C   D   E   F

Broad Wath
Ingmanthorpe Park
8
Sandbeck House
SANDBECK LA
Swinnow Hill
Moss Carrs Farm
B1224

Sandbeck Wood
Sand Beck
Cockshot Wood
Swinnow Park
YORK RD

7
HM Young Offender Inst
Sand Bridge
Champagne Whin
Works
THE ROWANS
49
B1224
Ind est
SPRINGS LA

6
Wetherby Race Course
Sykes House Farm
The Rampart
AR TRUCK AVE
HALL ORCHARDS
FREEMANS WAY
SYKE RD
Stables
Springs Wood

5
Hallfield Cemy
THIRD AVE
SPRING LA
MOOR LA

48
A1
WALTON RD
Dismantled Railway

4
A58
Park Hill Farm
WATERSIDE LA
WETHERBY RD
SCHOOL LA

Heuthwaite La
Ebor Way
Flint Mill Grange
West Field

3
Crowcroft Bank
Sewage Works
FLOUTH LA
MOOR LA
Thorparch Grange Sch

47
Wray Wood

Wetherby Grange
River Wharfe

2
Wetherby Grange Park
LEYS LA
Whin Covert
New Springs
Middle Field

The Leys
Hall Farm
Hall Wood
Thorparch Hall
The Pax Inn (PH)
Lady Elizabeth Hastings C of E Sch
DOWKELL LA

1
Gunter Wood
WEST LA
WEST DALE
Thorparch Park
PEAR TREE ACRE
THE VILLAGE
Thorp Arch
WHINS LA

46
41   A   B   42   C   West Park   D   43   E   F

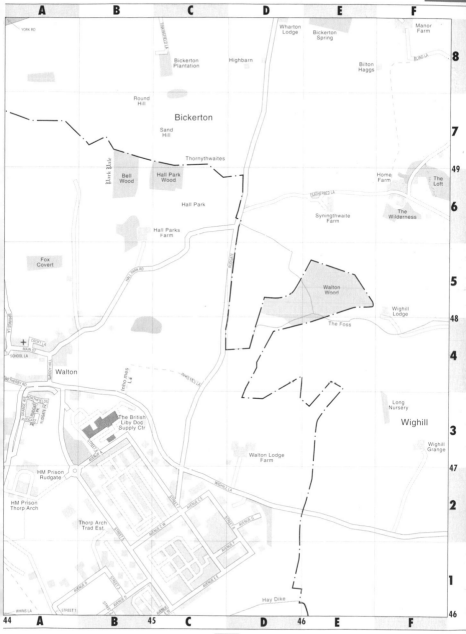

YORK RD

Wharton
Lodge

Bickerton
Spring

Manor
Farm

BLIND LA

8

Bickerton
Plantation

Highbarn

Bilton
Haggs

TINNINGFIELD LA

Round
Hill

Bickerton

Sand
Hill

7

Park Dale

Thornythwaites

49

Bell
Wood

Hall Park
Wood

Home
Farm

FEATHERBED LA

The
Loft

Hall Park

Syningthwaite
Farm

The
Wilderness

6

Hall Parks
Farm

Fox
Covert

HALL PARK RD

RUDGATE

Walton
Wood

5

Wighill
Lodge

48

The Foss

SPRING LA

CROFT LA

MAIN ST

4

SCHOOL LA

Walton

Inholmes La

THORP ARCH LA

Long
Nursery

WETHERBY RD

GRANGE AV

NORTHFIELDS

RUDGATE
PK

WOOD HILL

STREET A

AVENUE A

The British
Liby Doc
Supply Ctr

Wighill

Wighill
Grange

3

HM Prison
Rudgate

STREET B

AVENUE B

STREET C

47

Walton Lodge
Farm

WIGHILL LA

HM Prison
Thorp Arch

AVENUE C W

AVENUE D

STREET D

AVENUE C E

2

Thorp Arch
Trad Est.

STREET E

AVENUE F

AVENUE E E

AVENUE B

STREET F

AVENUE D

STREET G

AVENUE E E

1

WHINS LA

STREET T

AVENUE D

AVENUE C

Hay Dike

46

44

45

46

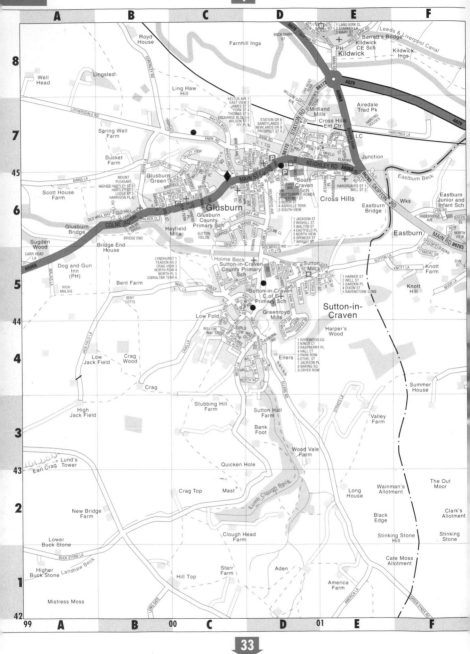

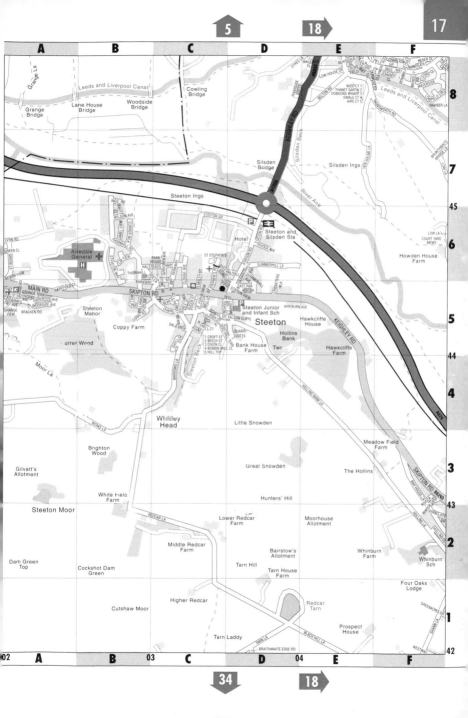

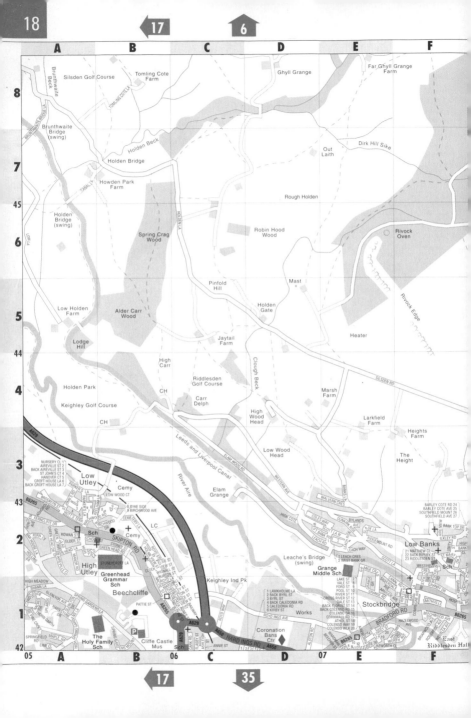

A   B   C   D   E   F

8

Silsden Golf Course
Tomling Cote Farm
Ghyll Grange
Far Ghyll Grange Farm

Brunthwaite Beck

Brunthwaite Bridge (swing)

Holden Beck

7

Holden Bridge

Dirk Hill Sike

Out Laith

45

Howden Park Farm

Rough Holden

Holden Bridge (swing)

Rivock Oven

6

Spring Crag Wood

Robin Hood Wood

Rivock Edge

Pinfold Hill

Mast

5

Low Holden Farm

Alder Carr Wood

Holden Gate

Heater

Rivock Edge

Lodge Hill

Jaytail Farm

44

High Carr

Riddlesden Golf Course

Clough Beck

Silsden Rd

4

Holden Park

Carr Delph

CH

Marsh Farm

Keighley Golf Course

CH

High Wood Head

Larkfield Farm

Heights Farm

Leeds and Liverpool Canal

Low Wood Head

The Height

3

NURSERY CL 1
AIREVILLE ST 2
BACK AIREVILLE ST 3
ST JOHN'S ST 4
HANOVER CT 5
CROFT HOUSE LA 6
BACK CROFT HOUSE LA 7

Low Utley

Cemy

River Aire

Elam Grange

43

B6265

LOW WOOD CT

8 BYKE SIDE
9 BIRCHWOOD AVE

LC

BARLEY COTE RD 24
BARLEY COTE AVE 25
SOUTHFIELD MOUNT 26
SOUTHFIELD AVE 27

2

Sch

SKIPTON RD

Cemy

Low Banks

21 MATTHEW CT
22 BACK RIPLEY ST
23 RIDDLESDEN ST

Sch

High Utley

Greenhead Grammar Sch

GREEN HEAD RD

1 LEACH CRES
2 WEST BANK DR

Leache's Bridge (swing)

Grange Middle Sch

Westfield

Beechcliffe

1

The Holy Family Sch

Cliffe Castle Mus

PATTIE ST

Sch

A629

ANNIE ST

HARD INGS RD

A650

1 LAWKHOLME LA
2 BACK BYRL ST
3 BYRL ST
4 BACK CALEDONIA RD
5 CALEDONIA RD
6 KIRBY ST

Works

LAKE ST 7
VALE ST 8
FORD ST 9
POOL ST 10
RIVER ST 11
CROSS RIVER ST 12
DALE ST 13
BACK FLORIST ST 14
BACK COLENSO RD 15
CORNWALL RD 16
COLENSO ST 18
COLENSO WAY 19
COLENSO MOUNT 20

Stockbridge

Coronation Bsns Ctr

BRADFORD RD

B6265

East Riddlesden Hall

42
05   A   06   B   C   D   07   E   F

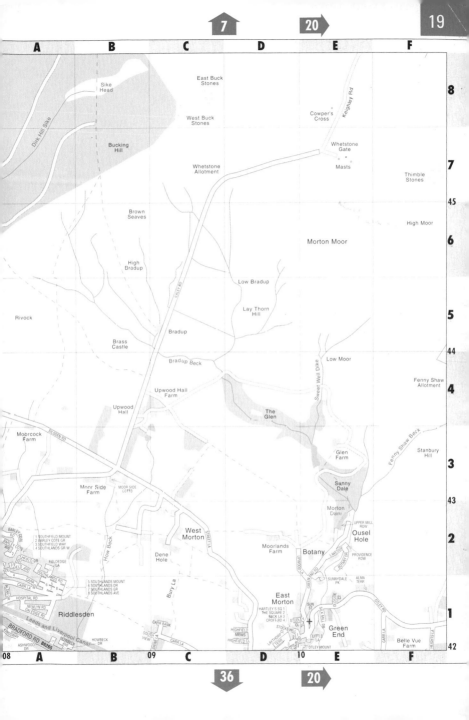

A B C D E F

8

Sike
Head

East Buck
Stones

Cowper's
Cross

Keighley Rd

West Buck
Stones

Whetstone
Gate

Bucking
Hill

Dirk Hill Sike

7

Whetstone
Allotment

Masts

Thimble
Stones

45

Brown
Seaves

High Moor

High
Bradup

Morton Moor

6

Low Bradup

Rivock

Lay Thorn
Hill

5

ROYD RD

Bradup

44

Brass
Castle

Sweet Well Dike

Bradup Beck

Low Moor

Upwood Hall
Farm

Fenny Shaw
Allotment

Upwood
Hall

The
Glen

4

Fenny Shaw Beck

Moorcock
Farm

NILSDEN RD

Glen
Farm

Stanbury
Hill

3

Sunny
Dale

Moor Side
Farm

MOOR SIDE
COTTS

Morton
Dam

43

West
Morton

STREET LA

UPPER MILL
ROW

Ousel
Hole

2

Moorlands
Farm

LAKE RD

Botany

PROVIDENCE
ROW

Dene
Hole

HOW BECK

GREEN RD

SUNNYDALE
PK

ALMA
TERR

BARLEY
RD

1 SOUTHFIELD MOUNT
2 BURLEY COTE GR
3 SOUTHFIELD WAY
4 SOUTHLANDS GR W

OLDSIDE RD

5 SOUTHLANDS MOUNT
6 SOUTHLANDS DR
7 SOUTHLANDS GR
8 SOUTHLANDS AVE

East
Morton

SUN
ST

HARTLEY S SQ 1
THE SQUARE 2
BACK LA 3
CROFT RD 4

ST JOILS
CL

BURY LA

HOSPITAL RD

Green
End

HEIGHTS LA

NEWLYN RD

DALESIDE RD

Riddlesden

CARR BANK

HIGHFIELD
MEWS

STOCKS HILL

LITTLE
LA

Belle Vue
Farm

ILKLEY RD

BRADFORD RD

Leeds and Liverpool Canal

B6265

SOUTH
VIEW

HOWBECK
DR

CARR LA

HIGHFIELD CL

LACK HIND
TERR

OTLEY MOUNT

42

ASHWOOD
DR

08 A B 09 C D 10 E F

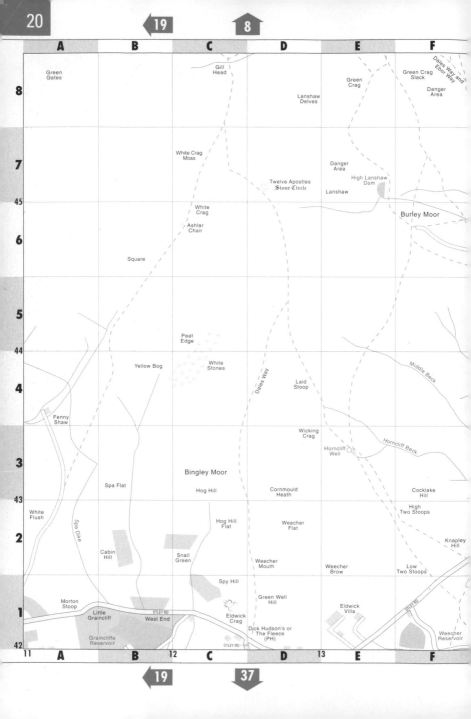

	A	B	C	D	E	F

8

Green Gates

Gill Head

Lanshaw Delves

Green Crag

Green Crag Slack

Danger Area

Dales Way and Ebor Way

7

White Crag Moss

Danger Area

Twelve Apostles Stone Circle

High Lanshaw Dam

45

White Crag

Lanshaw

Burley Moor

6

Ashlar Chair

Square

5

Peat Edge

44

Yellow Bog

White Stones

Middle Beck

4

Dales Way

Laid Stoop

Fenny Shaw

Wicking Crag

Horncliff Beck

3

Horncliff Well

Bingley Moor

Spa Flat

Hog Hill

Cornmould Heath

Cocklake Hill

43

White Flush

Spa Dike

Hog Hill Flat

Weecher Flat

High Two Stoops

2

Cabin Hill

Snail Green

Weecher Mouth

Weecher Brow

Low Two Stoops

Knapley Hill

1

Morton Stoop

Little Graincliff

OTLEY RD

West End

Spy Hill

Eldwick Crag

Green Well Hill

Dick Hudson's or The Fleece (PH)

Eldwick Villa

OTLEY RD

Weecher Reservoir

42

Graincliffe Reservoir

OTLEY RD

11	A	B	12	C	D	13	E	F

8

7

45

6

5

44

4

3

43

2

1

42

A   B   15   C   D   16   E   F

14

Stead Crag

Woofa Bank

Roes Farm

Moor House

Rushy Beck

Scalebor Park

Southfield Rd

West Lodge

Hanover St Philip's Way
St Michael's Oak Way
Prospect Rd
Sch Peasborough View

Coldstone Beck

MOOR RD

MOOR LA

Hag Farm Rd

Greenfield

Holme La

Hill Cres

Jubilee Trees

Barks Crags

Rose Garth

The Hermit (PH)

Carr Beck

Castle Dr

45

Lower Lanshaw Dam

Carr Bottom Resr

Crag Top

Prospect Row

Spring Bank Farm

Reevadale

Westbourne

Carr Beck

Burley Woodhead

STONEY LA

GREEN LA

York View Farm

Hag Farm

Bleach Mill

Southpiece Cottage

Whiddon

Victoria Ave

Danger Area

Stocks Hill

Oates Way & Ebor Way

BLEACH MILL LA

MOOR LA

Mount Pleasant

Craven Hall Hill

Rifle Range

Heather Bank

Gynest

Hill Top

Croft Cl

Sch

Hawksworth Shaw

Black Beck

Reva Hill

Matthew Dike

Derry Hill Farm

Derry Hill

Hillside

Hawksworth Dr

Sch

Hawksworth Moor

Middle Beck

BINGLEY RD

Horncliff Beck

White Flush

Intake Gate Farm

ST INGLA LA

43

Leedale Farm

OLD WOOD LA

BINGLEY RD

Whin Hills

High Royds Hall

Knapley-Ing Farm

Old Wood Farm

Reva Resr

DELFS RD

Old Wood La

Old Wood

GOOSE LA

Jum Beck

New Dam

Hawksworth Quarry

Odda Hill

West Wood

Storth House

Jum Bridge

Old La 1
Mill La 2

ODDA LA

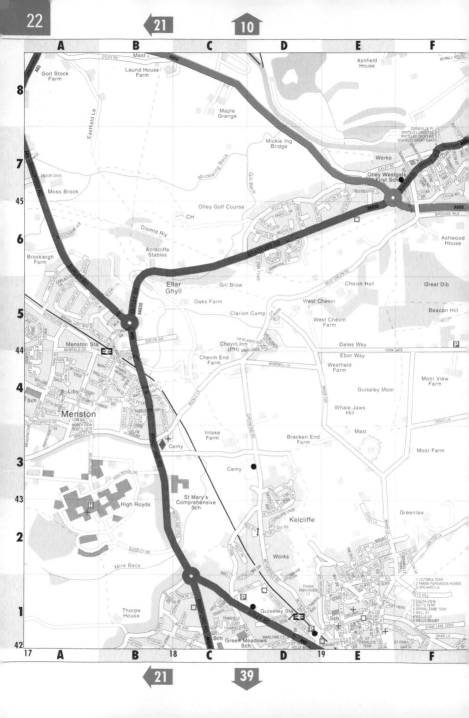

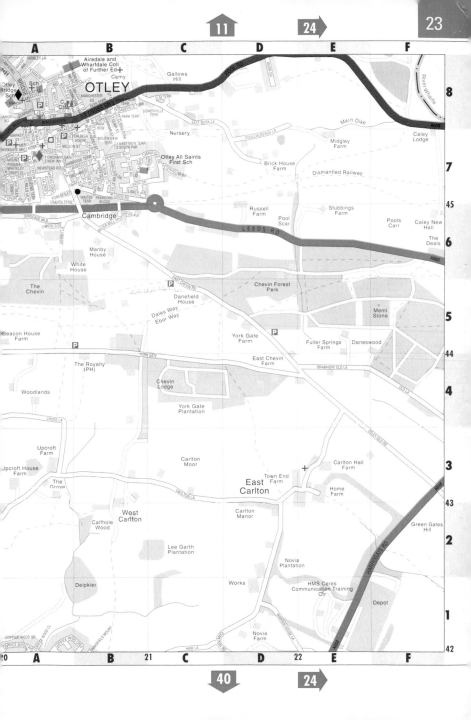

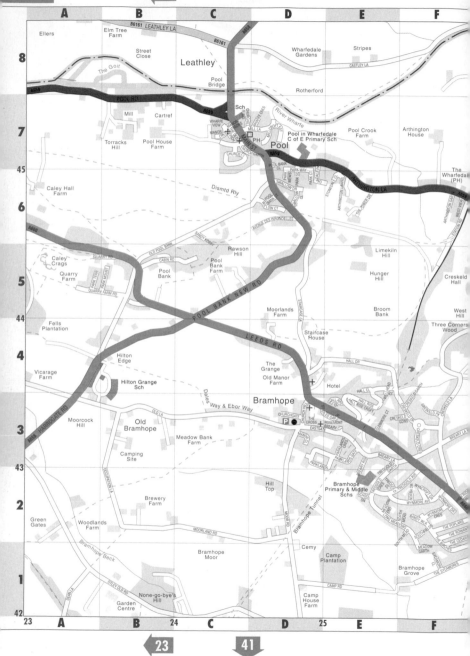

25

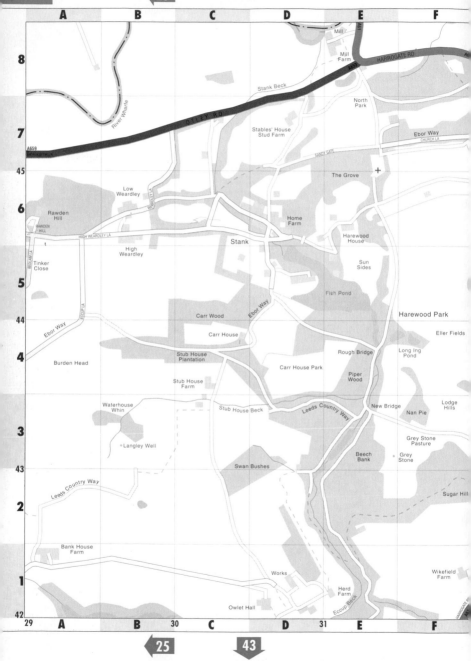

8

Harewood Castle
(rems of)

Willow
Garth

PITTS LA
Ebor Way

Stockton

Hill Climb
Course

Stockton
Farm

Middlefield
Farm

Farfield
Farm

Moor End
Farm

Harewood

SPRING GDNS
CASTLE WOOD CL
Hotel

Stockton
Grange
Farm

7

Harewood C of E
(controlled)
Primary Sch

THE SQUARE

HARROGATE GATE

CHURCH LA

HAREWOOD AVE

A659

45

THE A TRACK

A659

Gateways Girls'
Preparatory and High
Sch

SLEIGHTS LA

Cemy

Vicarage
Farm

MOOR LA

6

Moor Hill
Farm

New Laithe
Farm

Vicar's Whin

5

Wall Side
Plantation

HARROGATE RD

Burn's
Farm

44

Hollin
Hall

Cut Whin
Wood

4

Lofthouse
Grange

Hollin Hall
Ponds

Spring
Wood

Gateon House
Farm

Lodge Hills
Plantation

3

Lofthouse
Farm

Wike
Wood

WIKE LA

Rigton Moor
Farm

43

Cote
Hill

Leeds Country Way

Biggin
Farm

WIKE LA

2

Low Green
Farm

Fortshot
House

FORTSHOT LA

Hillcrest
Farm

Grace Beck

Camp Site

Gill Beck

Grace
Bridge

BACKSTONE GILL LA

Manor
Farm

Whinside
Farm

1

Wike

School Lane
Farm

EDGE LA

SCHOOL LA

GOAL RD

Wike
Whin

CH

42

A   B   33   C   D   34   E   F

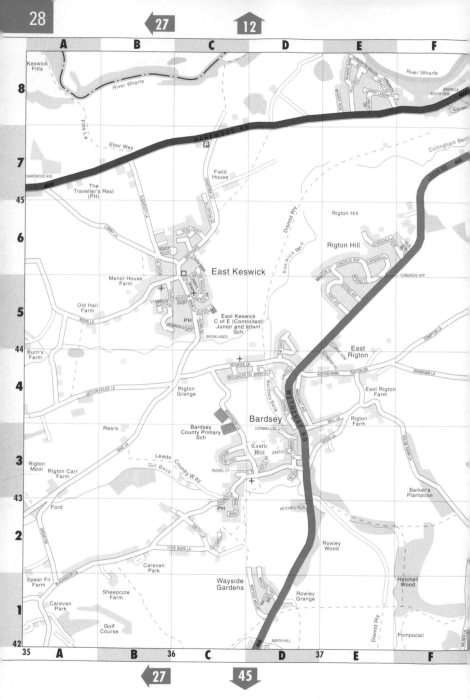

27

12

A B C D E F

8

Keswick
Fitts

River Wharfe

River Wharfe

Fitts La

Ebor Way

LANGWITH VALLEY
WHARFE RISE
UNITY ST
UPPER LANGWITH
WHARFE VIEW
LANGWITH

GREEN LA
SOUTH VIEW
ROSE WAY
A659

Collingham Beck

7

HAREWOOD RD

HAREWOOD AVE
A659

P

Field
House

Dismtd Rly

LEEDS RD
A4

45

The
Traveller's Rest
(PH)

CLEBURT'S LA
CHARTREE LA
ALLERTON DR

Rigton Hill

6

LIBERTY LA

SOUTH
MOUNT
THE GROVE

ROSS CROFT

WHITAKER
NORTH VIEW

Keswick Beck

Rigton Hill

MEADOW CL
CONGREVE WAY
SCARSDALE LA
JACKSON LA
MILL LA

Congreve App

East Keswick

CONGREVE APP

Manor House
Farm

CHURCH LA
ST MARY'S
ST BARTH'S

THE PADDOCK
MEADOW CROFT

ECONEY AVE
KINGS CT
GREY LANE

Old Hall
Farm

MOOR LA

PH

SCHOOL LA
LUMB LANE

East Keswick
C of E (Controlled)
Junior and Infant
Sch

5

KESWICK GRANGE

BROOKLANDS

44

Burn's
Farm

KESWICK LA

WOODACRE GN
BANKFIELD
Bardsey Beck

MARGOSET AVE
WINDSOR LA

COLSHAW VIEW
RETHER RD

RIGTON BANK
RIGTON GN

COMPTON LA

East
Rigton

BRAMHAM LA

4

GATEON HOUSE LA

Rigton
Grange

THE DRIVE

WETHERBY RD

MILL LA

East Rigton
Farm

Resrs

Bardsey
County Primary
Sch

CORNMILL CL
CASTLE CRES

Bardsey

CASTLE CL
PRIEST LA

WOOD LA

Rigton
Farm

3

Rigton
Moor

Rigton Carr
Farm

WIKE LA

Leeds
Country Way

Gill Beck

RUSSEL CT

Castle
Hill

HETCHELL VIEW

Barker's
Plantation

43

Ford

PH

CHURCH LA
MAIN ST
PIMS

2

SPEAR FIR

TITHE BARN LA

SMITHY LA
THE CL

Rowley
Wood

Spear Fir
Farm

BLACKMOOR LA

Caravan
Park

Sheepcote
Farm

WAYSIDE CRES
WAYSIDE MOUNT

Wayside
Gardens

Rowley
Grange

Hetchell
Wood

1

Caravan
Park

Golf
Course

NORTH HILL

Dismtd Rly

Pompocali

42

35 A B 36 C D 37 E F

27

45

A B C D E F

8

1 LANGWITH MEWS
2 COVERDALE GARTH
3 BISHOPDALE DR
4 COTTERDALE HOLE
5 LINTON RD
6 DEWAR CL
7 STATION LA

8 HASTINGS CT
9 ELIZABETH CT

Collingham

Collingham
Fields

Cow Moor

Howcroft
Wood

Collingham
Moor

7

Compton Grove

Compton La

Mast

45

Waver Spring
Pond

Compton

Dalton
Parlours

6

5

44

West
Woods

4

Lund
Wood

Lady
Wood

Dalton
Hill

Spring
Wood

Old Pickhill
Rash

Hope
Hall

3

43

Holme
Farm

HOLME FARM LA

THORNER LA

2

Wothersome

Stubbing
Moor

Ragdale
Plantation

Bramham
Beck

Bramham
Park

Lendrick
Hills

1

Stubbing Moor
Plantation

Terry
Lug

KENNELS
LA

Milner Beck

42

38 A B 39 C D 40 E F

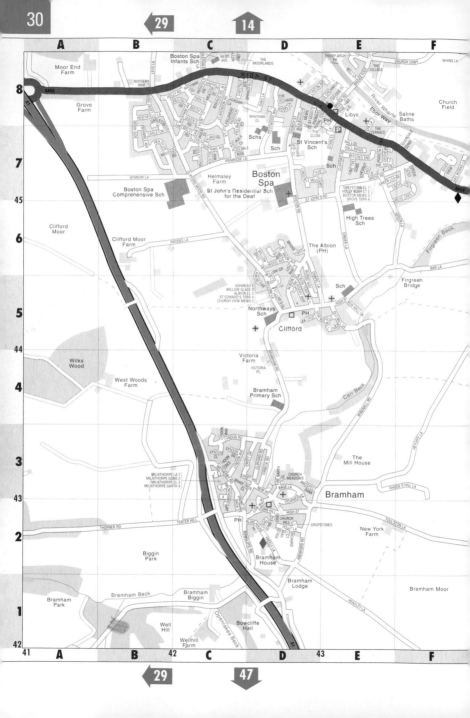

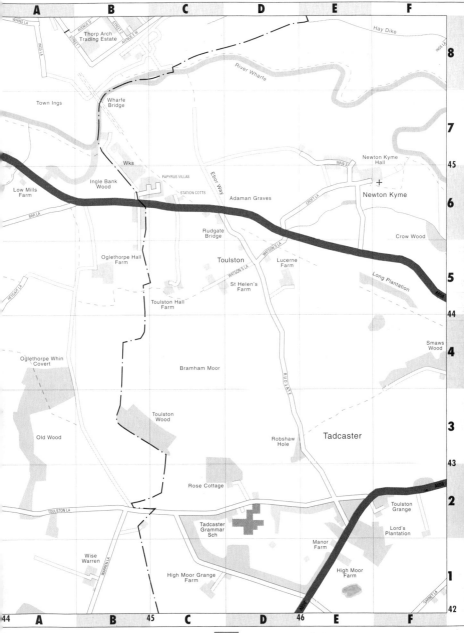

8

WHINS LA
INGS LA

Thorp Arch
Trading Estate

AVENUE D
STREET 2
STREET 1
AVENUE E W

Hay Dike

INGS LA

River Wharfe

Town Ings

Wharfe
Bridge

7

Wks

45

Ingle Bank
Wood

PAPYRUS VILLAS

STATION COTTS

Ebor Way

Newton Kyme
Hall

MAIN ST

Newton Kyme

Low Mills
Farm

BAR LA

Adaman Graves

CROFT LA

6

Rudgate
Bridge

Crow Wood

Oglethorpe Hall
Farm

Toulston

WATSON S LA

Lucerne
Farm

Long Plantation

A58

5

HEYGATE LA

WATSON S LA

St Helen's
Farm

44

Toulston Hall
Farm

Smaws
Wood

4

Oglethorpe Whin
Covert

Bramham Moor

RUD GATE

Toulston
Wood

Tadcaster

3

Old Wood

Robshaw
Hole

43

Rose Cottage

A659

Toulston
Grange

2

TOULSTON LA

WARREN LA

Tadcaster
Grammar
Sch

Lord's
Plantation

Manor
Farm

Wise
Warren

High Moor Grange
Farm

High Moor
Farm

A659

GARNET LA

1

42

44

A

B

45

C

D

46

E

F

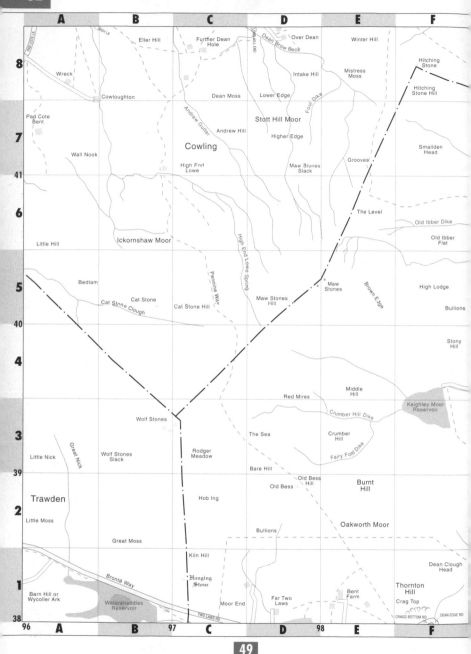

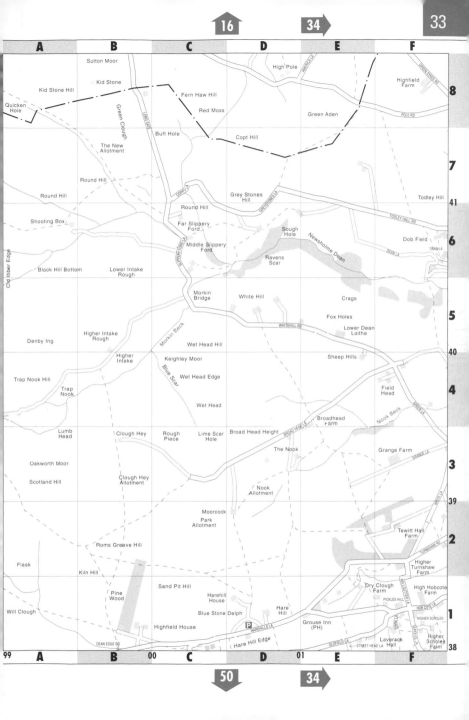

A   B   C   D   E   F

Sutton Moor

High Pole

Highfield Farm

Kid Stone

Kid Stone Hill

8

Quicken Hole

Green Clough

Fern Haw Hill

Red Moss

Green Aden

POLE RD

AMBER LA

GREEN EDGE RD

7

Buft Hole

The New Allotment

Copt Hill

Round Hill

Round Hill

Grey Stones Hill

Todley Hill

41

Round Hill

Round Hill

GREYSTONE LA

TODLEY HALL RD

Shooting Box

Far Slippery Ford

Sough Hole

Newsholme Dean

Dob Field

6

Cld Ibber Edge

Middle Slippery Ford

SLIPPERY FORD LA

Ravens Scar

DEAN LA

DEAN LA

Black Hill Bottom

Lower Intake Rough

Morkin Bridge

White Hill

Crags

5

Higher Intake Rough

Morkin Beck

Fox Holes

Lower Dean Laithe

WHITEHILL RD

Denby Ing

Wet Head Hill

40

Higher Intake

Keighley Moor

Sheep Hills

Trap Nook Hill

Blue Scar

Wet Head Edge

Field Head

4

Trap Nook

Wet Head

Broadhead Farm

Nook Beck

GREEN LA

Lumb Head

Clough Hey

Rough Piece

Lime Scar Hole

Broad Head Height

BROAD HEAD LA

The Nook

Grange Farm

GRANGE LA

3

Oakworth Moor

Clough Hey Allotment

Nook Allotment

39

Scotland Hill

HEY LA

Moorcock Park Allotment

Tewitt Hall Farm

2

Roms Greave Hill

TURNSHAW RD

Higher Turnshaw Farm

Flask

Kiln Hill

Sand Pit Hill

Harehill House

Dry Clough Farm

PICKLES HILL

High Hobcote Farm

PICKLES HILL LA

HOB COTE LA

Pine Wood

Blue Stone Delph

Hare Hill

Grouse Inn (PH)

SCROLES LA

HIGHER SCROLES

1

Will Clough

Highfield House

P

HAREHILLS LA

Hare Hill Edge

OLDFIELD LA

Laverack Hall

Higher Scroles Farm

DEAN EDGE RD

STREET HEAD LA

38

99 A   B   00 C   D   01 E   F

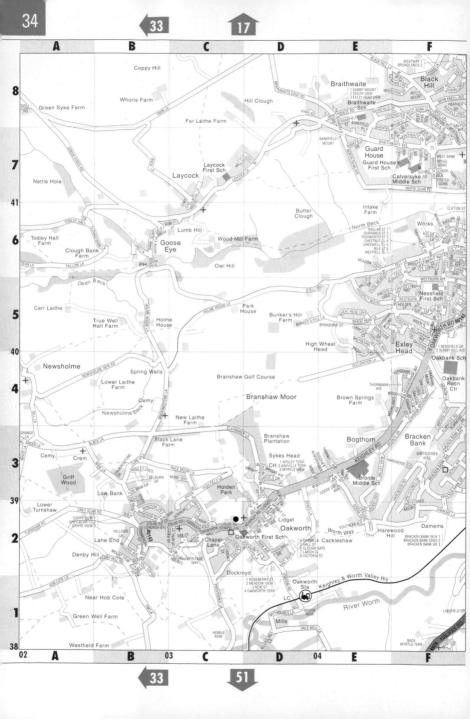

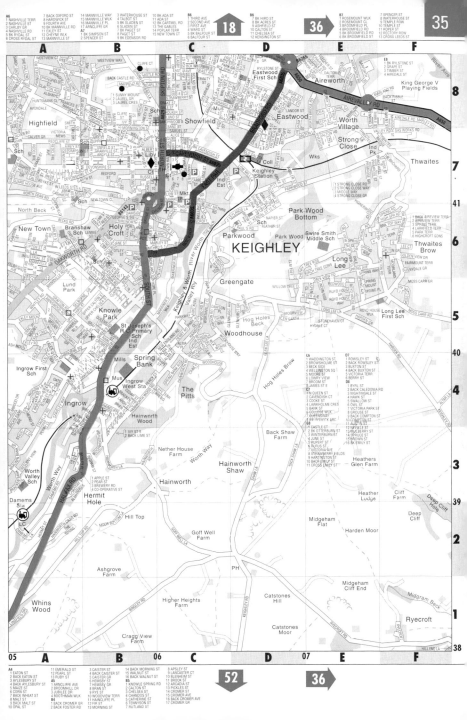

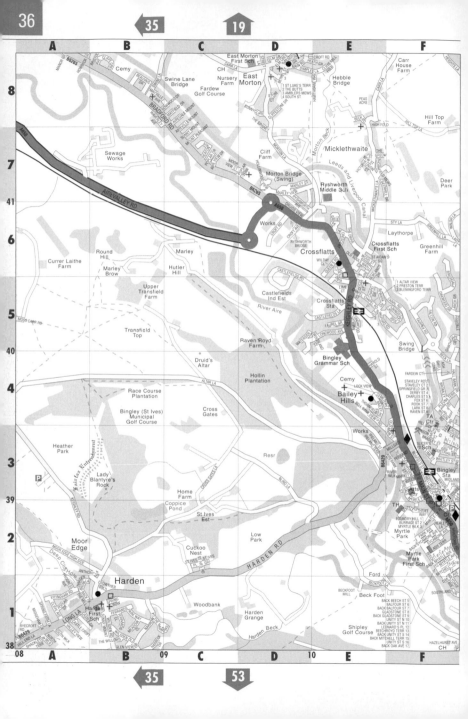

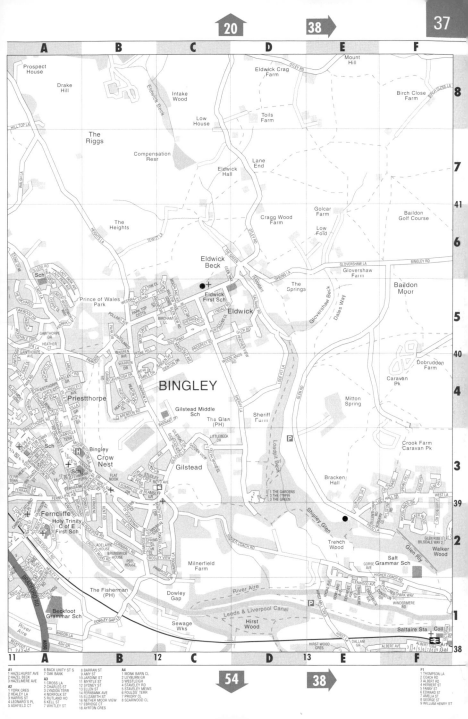

41

A1
1 HAZELHURST AVE
2 HAZEL BECK
3 HAZELMERE AVE

A2
1 YORK CRES
2 HEALEY LA
3 HARRIS ST
4 LEONARD'S PL
5 ASHFIELD CT

6 BACK UNITY ST S
7 OAK BANK

1 CROSS LA
2 CHARLES ST
3 LYNDON TERR
4 NORFOLK ST
5 RUTLAND RD
6 KELL ST
7 WHITLEY ST

8 BARRAN ST
9 AMY ST
10 JARDINE ST
11 MYRTLE ST
12 SYDNEY ST
13 ELLEN ST
14 FERNBANK AVE
15 ELIZABETH ST
16 NETHER MOOR VIEW
17 EBRIDGE CT
18 AYRTON CRES

A4
1 MONK BARN CL

A3
1 LEYBURN GR
2 WESTLEIGH
3 STAVELEY RD
4 STAVELEY MEWS
5 FOULDS TERR
6 PRIORY CL
7 PRIORY CL
8 SCARWOOD CL

F1
1 THOMPSON LA
2 COACH RD
3 ALBERT RD
4 HERBERT ST
5 FANNY ST
6 EDWARD ST
7 AMELIA ST
8 GEORGE ST
9 WILLIAM HENRY ST

8

7

41

6

5

40

4

3

39

2

1

38

A B C D E F

Faweather Grange

West Wood

BIRCH CL

Hawksworth

Hawksworth Hall Sch

Intake Side Farm

TAVERNDALE

Hawksworth C of E Primary Sch

OLD LA

MILL LA

JUM BECK

Round Hill

Birkin Hill

Ash House Farm

Potter Brow Bridge

Honey Joan Hill

Gill Beck

Low Springs

Bradford Golf Course

Hall Croft

Pennythorn Hill

Sconce Crag

Low Hill

Low Springs Farm

Hawkaworth Spring

Baildon Golf Course

Bracken Hill

LOW HILL

The Whitehouse

Lunds Farm

Windy Hill

Acrehowe Hill

BINGLEY RD

Low Plain

Plain Side

Baildon Moor

Baildon Hill

Hazel Head Wood

Ladderbanks Middle Sch

Tong Park

Hope Hill

C4
1 HIGHFIELD MEWS
2 ROCKLANDS AVE
3 ROCKLANDS PL
4 AMBLERS MEWS
5 TENTER CROFT
6 SOUTH VIEW TERR

7 STRAITS
8 TOWNGATE
9 BINNSWELL FOLD
10 DELPH HILL
11 WANT ED
12 PADGUM

D4
1 PERSEVERANCE ST
2 ANGEL ST
3 FLOWER MOUNT

Baildon CE First Sch

Church Sch

Church Hill

Hope Farm

Dove Hall

BAILDON

The Beeches

Low Baildon

Baildon Sta

Tong Park First Sch

Buck Mill La

Sandal First Sch

Belmont Middle Sch

Baildon Bank

Kirklands Ct

Hartlington

Hoyle Court First Sch

Charlestown

Wks

River Aire

Midgeley Wood

Baildon Green

A2
1 WESTLEIGH WAY
2 DEEPDALE CL
3 WESTLEIGH CL
4 BRANSDALE CL
5 ROSEDALE CL
6 BEECHTREE CT

WOOD VIEW

Ferniehurst First Sch

B2
1 KNOLL VIEW
2 LOWER GREEN
3 BANKSIDE TERR
4 GREEN MOUNT
5 UPPER GREEN

The Oval

Glenaire First Sch

Baildon Wood Bottom

5 OXFORD PL
6 UNION ST
7 OXFORD TERR

Leeds and Liverpool Canal

Ind Est

Wks

Wks

Baildon Homes

HIGHER COACH RD

River Aire

Dales Way

Leeds & Liverpool Canal

Mills

Rec Ctr

BRACKENDALE DR 1
CYPRUS DR 2
CHERRY TREE GDNS 3
COTE FARM COTTS 4

Perkin

14 15 16

A B C D E F

C1
1 ADELAIDE RISE
2 ALBERT ST
3 VICTORIA ST
4 WOOD ST
5 QUEEN ST
6 GEORGE ST

D2
1 IVY BANK CT
2 ROSEMONT LA
3 OAKROYD TERR
4 AIREDALE TERR

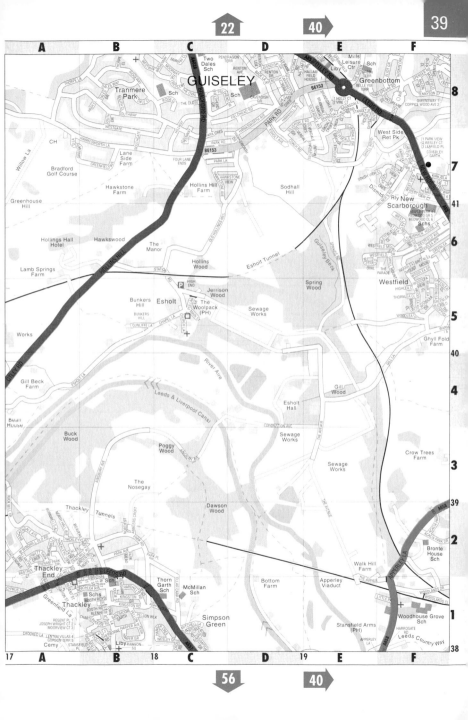

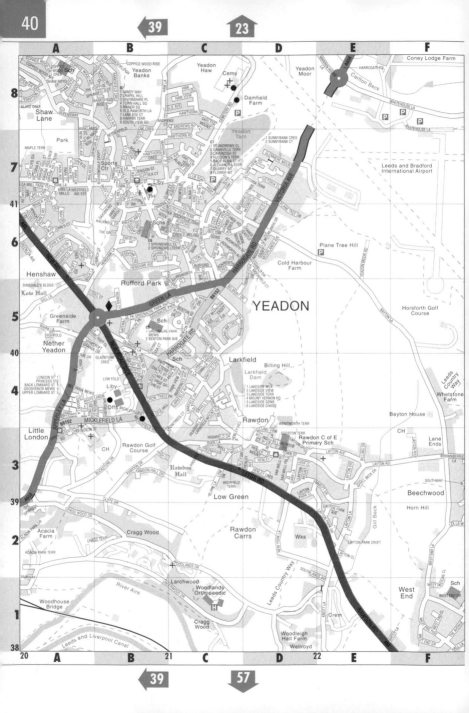

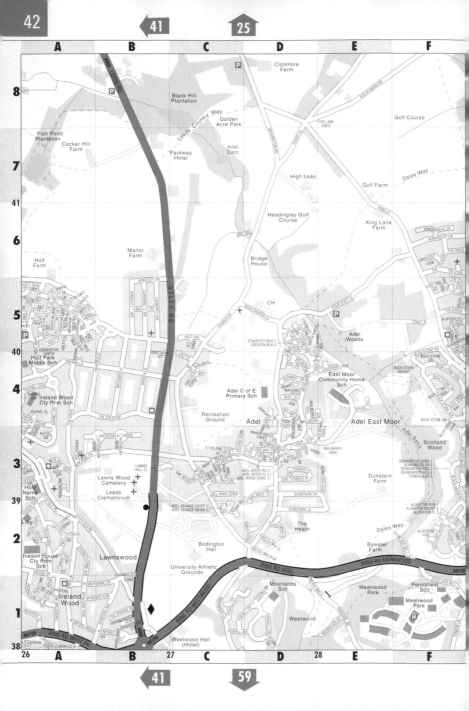

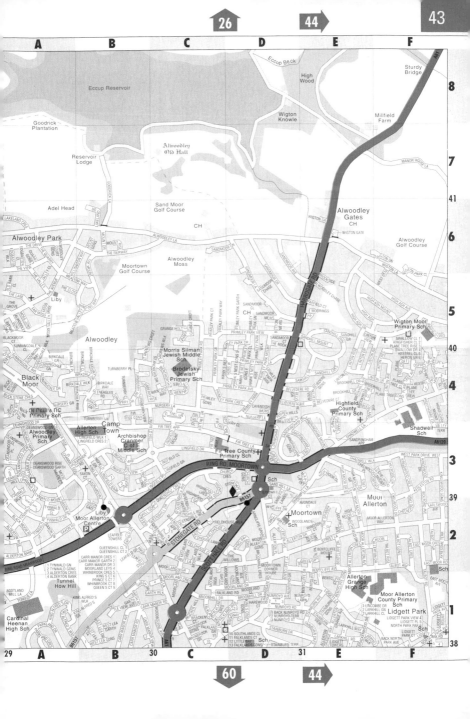

A **B** **C** **D** **E** **F**

8

SCHOOL LA

Leeds Golf
Centre

Collier Beck

CH

Golf Course

7

Wike Ridge

Brandon La

Blackmoor
Farm

LING LA

Wike Ridge
Farm

WIKE RIDGE RD

Sturdy Beck

COAL RD

BRANDON CRES

41

Shaw
Hill

TARN LA

Wigton Heath
Farm

ST HELENS WAY

Wigton Moor
Whin

Brandon
Hall

Hall
Farm

Nursery

BRANDON CRES

6

Wigton Moor

Alwoodley
Golf Course

Brandon

Brandon Grange
Farm

Low Brandon
Farm

Brandon Drain

Golf Course

Brandon
Royd

BRISTOL PATH RD

CHASE

WIKE RIDGE MT

WIKE RIDGE

WIGTON LA

BRANDON CT

Slaid Hill

4 LONGWOOD WAY
5 SLAID HILL CT
6 CHARTWELL CT
7 BRANDON TERR
8 HARROGATE VIEW

CH

HOLYWELL LA

5

CARLTON GARTH 1
OVERDALE AVE 2
RAYGILL CL 3

PLANTATION AVE

SILVERDALE
AVE

HIGH ASH AVE

PLANTATION GDNS

BARFIELD
CRES

Middlethorne
Middle Sch

SHADWELL PARK
AVE

SHADWELL PARK
GDNS

Liby

MAIN ST

ASH HILL GDNS
ASH HILL DR
ASH HILL GARTH

STRICKLAND
AVE

40

OAKDENE WAY

ELMHURST

OAKDENE VALE

Park Lane
Mews

SHADWELL PARK
DR

CH

GATELAND DR

CHURCHFARM
GARTH

ASH HILL LA

HERON
GR

OAKDENE CT

WOODLEA

SHADWELL

SHADWELL PARK
GR

BLIND LA

COLLIERS LA

Manor
Farm

Shadwell
Primary Sch

STRICKLAND
CL

4

9 WOODTHORNE CROFT
10 BEECHCROFT MEAD
11 ROCHESTER WYND
12 OAKDENE CT

Shadwell
Grange
Farm

SHADWELL LA

PARK CT

Shadwell

BRADLEY
TERR

Blackwood

Oakhill

BROADGATE LA

HIGHTHORNE
GR

VALLEY
TERR

BIRCHWOOD AVE

Ferndale

CHARVILLE
GDNS

HORSFORTH LA

A6120

RING RD MOORTOWN

KINGSWOOD
AVE

WEST PARK
CHASE

Woodhouse
Farm

3

WEST PARK DR W

KEDLESTON RD

WEST PARK CL

WEST PARK DR

WEST PARK GR

WHINMOOR LA

39

VALE AVE

SUMMERHILL
PL

ROMAN AVE

Great Heads Beck

RING RD SHADWELL

ELMETE LA

BACK NORMAN
PL

NORMAN TERR

EARLSWOOD
AVE

THOMAS ST

2

AYRE HILL AVE

DEVONSHIRE
AVE

Parkview

BACK ROMAN PL

1 SUMMERHILL GDNS
2 BACK ROMAN ST
3 ROMAN PL
4 BACK ROMAN PL
5 ROMAN ST
6 ROMAN MOUNT
7 WEST PARK GDNS
8 CROSS INGLEDEW CRES
9 BACK INGLEDEW CRES
10 INGLEDEW CRES

Golf
Course

Redhall
House

SHAFTSBURY AVE

PRINCE'S AVE

THE AVENUE

THE CARRIAGE DR

RED HALL LA

DEVONSHIRE
AVE

Ram Wood

Cobble
Hall

RED HALL GDNS

1

EAST
MOOR
DR

NORTH PARK AVE

FERNWOOD

PARK
COTTS

P

Upper
Lake

Castle

Cobble Hall
Farm

Cobble Hall
Golf Course

Wellington
Hill

Mansion Hotel

COUNCIL VIEW

THE WESTERN

13 FERNWOOD
14

Roundhay
Park

Waterloo
Lake

KINGSMEAD
DR

38

NORTH PARK AVE

PRINCE'S AVE

LIDGETT PARK RD

St
Edmund's
Sch

Park
Villas

11 PARK VILLA CT
12 ROBINWOOD CT
13 FERNWOOD CT
14 WEDGEWOOD CT

GARDEN
LANE

15 WEDGEWOOD GR
16 WEDGEWOOD DR

A **B** **C** **D** **E** **F**

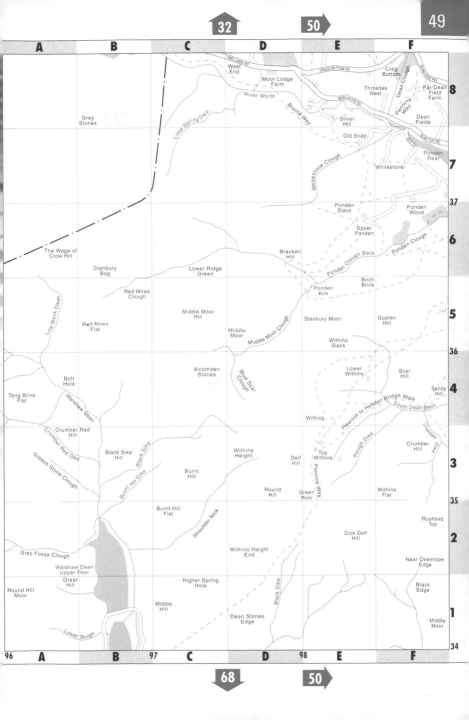

West End

TWO LAWS RD

CRAGG BOTTOM RD

Crag Bottom

CROW EDGE RD

8

Moor Lodge Farm

Throstles Nest

Dean Clough

Far Dean Field Farm

River Worth

NEW LAITHE RD

Pennine Way

Dean Fields

Grey Stones

Little Spring Dike

Brontë Way

Silver Hill

Old Snap

SCAR TOP RD

Ponden Resr

7

Whitestone Clough

Whitestone

37

Ponden Slack

Ponden Wood

The Wage of Crow Hill

Stanbury Bog

Lower Ridge Green

Bracken Hill

Upper Ponden

Ponden Clough

6

Ponden Clough Beck

Red Mires Clough

Ponden Kirk

Birch Brink

Low Slack Dike

Red Mires Flat

Middle Moor Hill

Stanbury Moor

Goaten Hill

5

Middle Moor

Middle Moor Clough

Withins Slack

36

Boft Hole

Alcomden Stones

Blue Scar Clough

Lower Withins

Scar Hill

Sandy Hill

4

Tang Brink Flat

Walshaw Dean

Haworth to Hebden Bridge Walk

South Dean Beck

Crumber Dike

Crumber Red Hill

Withins

Crumber Red Dike

Black Sike Hill

Black Sike

Withins Height

Delf Hill

Top Withins

Rough Dike

Crumber Hill

3

Greave Stone Clough

Burnt Hill Dike

Burnt Hill

Pennine Way

Round Hill

Green Hole

Withins Flat

35

Burnt Hill Flat

Shoulder Nick

Dick Delf Hill

Rushbed Top

2

Grey Fosse Clough

Withins Height End

Near Oxenhope Edge

Walshaw Dean Upper Resr

Great Hill

Higher Spring Hole

Black Dike

Black Edge

Round Hill Moor

Middle Hill

Middle Moor

1

Lower Sough

Dean Stones Edge

34

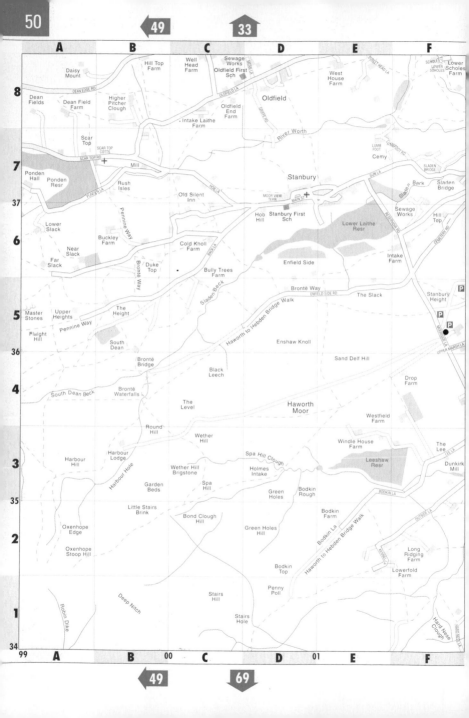

A **B** **C** **D** **E** **F**

8

Daisy
Mount

Hill Top
Farm

Well
Head
Farm

Sewage
Works
Oldfield First
Sch

West House
Farm

Lower
Scholes
Farm

SCHOLES
LOWER
SCHOLES

Dean
Fields

Dean Field
Farm

Higher
Pitcher
Clough

DEAN EDGE RD

OLDFIELD LA

Oldfield

Oldfield
End
Farm

SPITFIELD RD

GREEN LA

SYPELY HEAD LA

Intake Laithe
Farm

River Worth

LUMB
FOOT

LAMPPOST RD

Scar
Top

SCAR TOP
COTTS

Cemy

SLADEN
BRIDGE

7

Mill

SCAR TOP RD

Stanbury

SUN LA

Sladen
Beck

Slaeden
Bridge

RESERVOIR RD

Ponden
Hall

Ponden
Resr

Rush
Isles

Old Silent
Inn

HOB LA

MOOR VIEW
TERR

MAIN ST

Stanbury First
Sch

Slack
Bank

Sewage
Works

Hill
Top

37

FLASS LA

Pennine Way

Hob
Hill

Lower
Slack

Buckley
Farm

Cold Knoll
Farm

Lower Laithe
Resr

Intake
Farm

CEMETERY RD

6

Near
Slack

Duke
Top

BACK LA

Enfield Side

Far
Slack

Bully Trees
Farm

Bronté Way

Stanbury
Height

P

Bronté Way

ENFIELD SIDE RD

The Slack

P

Master
Stones

Upper
Heights

The
Height

Sladen Beck

Haworth to Hebden Bridge Walk

MOORSIDE LA

P

P

5

Pennine Way

Enshaw Knoll

Flaight
Hill

South
Dean

UPPER MARSH LA

36

Bronté
Bridge

Black
Leech

Sand Delf Hill

Drop
Farm

4

South Dean Beck

Bronté
Waterfalls

The
Level

Haworth
Moor

Westfield
Farm

The
Lee

Round
Hill

Wether
Hill

Windle House
Farm

LEE LA

Harbour
Hill

Harbour
Lodge

Wether Hill
Brigstone

Spa Hill Clough

Holmes
Intake

Leeshaw
Resr

Dunkirk
Mill

3

HARBOUR HOLE

Garden
Beds

Spa
Hill

Green
Holes

Bodkin
Rough

BODKIN LA

35

Little Stairs
Brink

Bond Clough
Hill

Green Holes
Hill

Bodkin
Farm

Bodkin La

Haworth to Hebden Bridge Walk

OUTSIDE LA

Long
Ridging
Farm

2

Oxenhope
Edge

Oxenhope
Stoop Hill

Bodkin
Top

Penny
Poll

Lowerfold
Farm

KEBB LA

1

Robin Dike

Deep Nitch

Stairs
Hill

Stairs
Hole

Hard Nese
Clough

HARD NESE LA

34

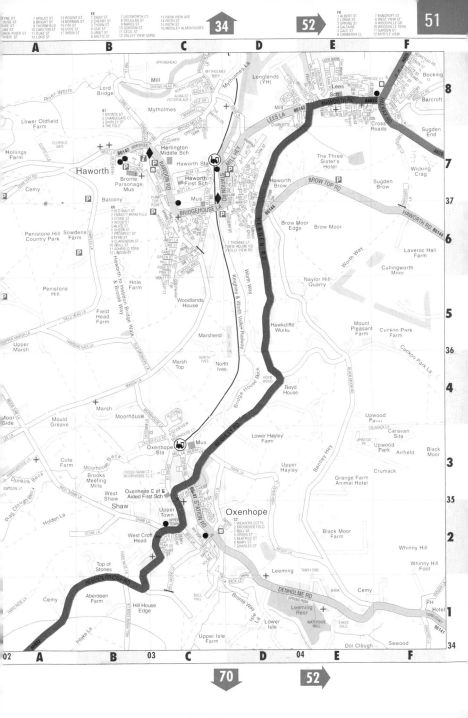

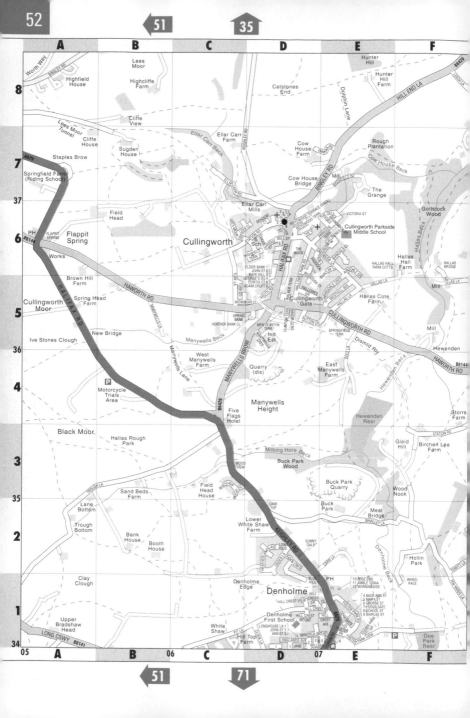

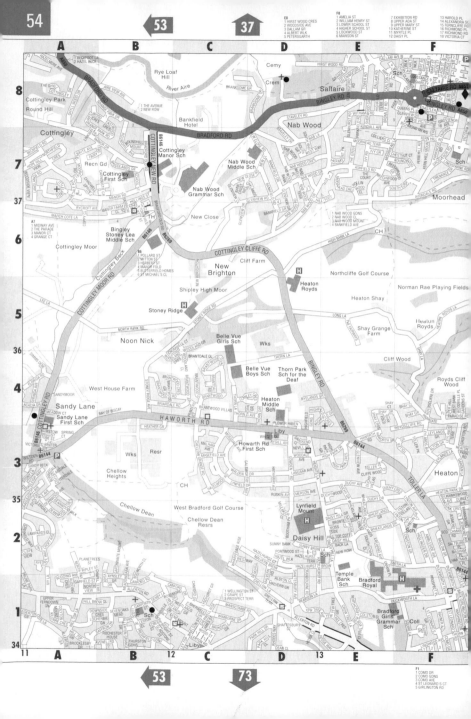

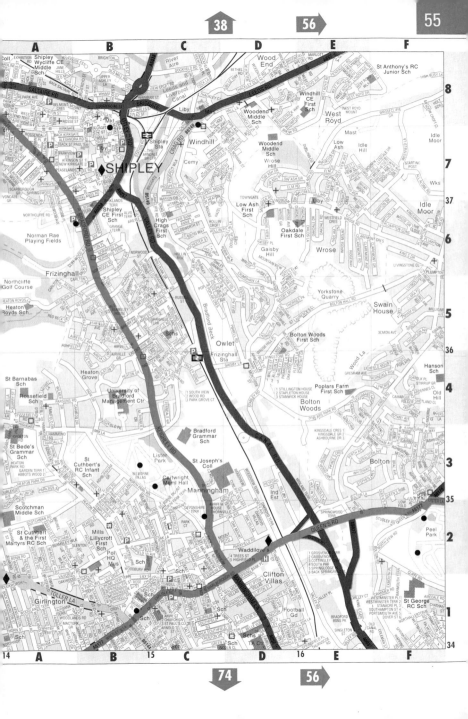

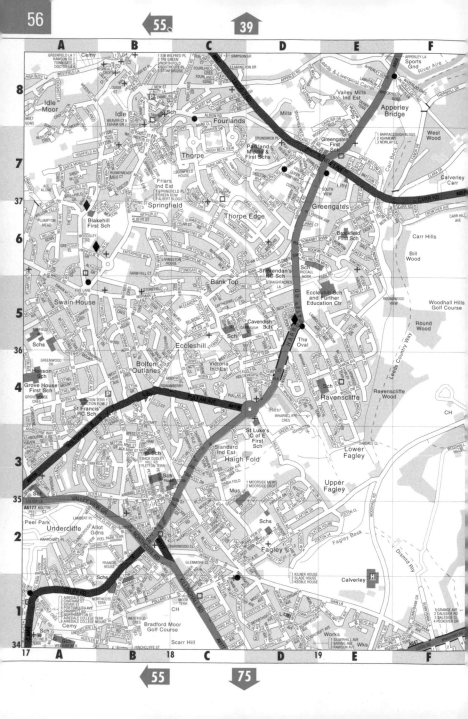

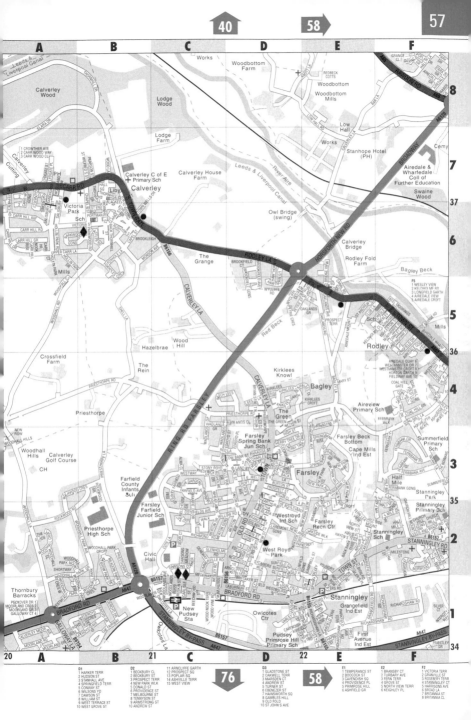

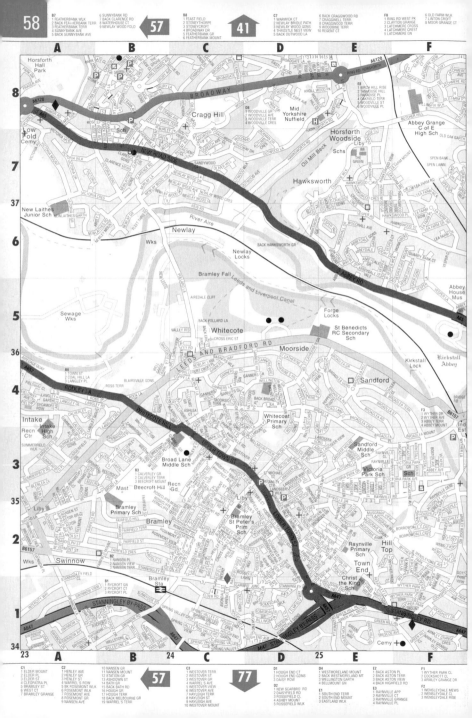

58

57 ← / 41

B7
1 FEATHERBANK WLK
2 BACK FEATHERBANK TERR
3 FEATHERBANK TERR
4 SUNNYBANK AVE
5 BACK SUNNYBANK AVE
6 SUNNYBANK RD
7 BACK CLARENCE RD
8 WATERHOUSE CT
9 NEWLAY WOOD FOLD

B8
1 FEAST FIELD
2 STONEYTHORPE
3 STONEYCROFT
4 BROADWAY DR
5 FEATHERBANK GR
6 FEATHERBANK MOUNT

C7
1 WARWICK CT
2 NEWLAY BRIDLE PATH
3 NEWLAY WOOD GDNS
4 THROSTLE NEST VIEW
5 BACK OUTWOOD LA
6 BACK CRAGGWOOD RD
7 CRAGGWELL TERR
8 CRAGGWOOD TERR
9 WOODVINE TERR
10 REGENT CT

F8
1 RING RD WEST PK
2 CLAYTON GRANGE
3 LATCHMERE CROSS
4 LATCHMERE CREST
5 LATCHMERE DN
6 OLD FARM WLK
7 LINTON CROFT
8 MOOR GRANGE CT

Map references:
A B C D E F
8 7 37 6 5 36 4 3 35 2 1 34
23 A B 24 C D 25 E F

Horsforth Hall Park
Low Fold Cemy
A6120 / A65
BROADWAY
Cragg Hill
Mid Yorkshire Nuffield
Horsforth Woodside
Abbey Grange C of E High Sch
NEW ROAD SIDE
Hawksworth
New Laithes Junior Sch
River Aire
Newlay
Newlay Locks
Back Hawksworth Gr
Bramley Fall
Leeds and Liverpool Canal
Airedale Cliff
Sewage Wks
Abbey House Mus
Whitecote
Forge Locks
St Benedicts RC Secondary Sch
Moorside
LEEDS AND BRADFORD RD
Kirkstall Lock
Kirkstall Abbey
Sandford
Intake Recn Ctr
Intake High Sch
RODLEY LA
WHITECOTE LANE
Whitecoat Primary Sch
Sandford Middle Sch
Broad Lane Middle Sch
Beecroft Hill
Victoria Park Sch
Bramley Primary Sch
Bramley
Bramley St Peter's Prim Sch
Raynville Primary Sch
Hill Top
Swinnow
Town End
Christ the King Sch
Bramley Sta
STANNINGLEY BY-PASS
A647 / A6120
A47
Cemy

C1
1 ELDER MOUNT
2 ELDER PL
3 ELDER ST
4 CLEOPATRA PL
5 BRAMLEY ST
6 WEST CT
7 BRAMLEY GRANGE

C2
1 HENLEY AVE
2 HENLEY GR
3 HENLEY ST
4 WARRELS ROW
5 BK ROSEMONT WLK
6 ROSEMONT WLK
7 ROSEMONT AVE
8 ROSEMONT GR
9 NANSEN AVE
10 NANSEN GR
11 NANSEN MOUNT
12 STATION GR
13 ASHDOWN ST
14 BATH GR
15 BACK BATH RD
16 HOUGH GR
17 HOUGH TERR
18 BACK MELBOURNE GR
19 WARRELS TERR

C3
1 WESTOVER TERR
2 WESTOVER ST
3 WESTOVER GR
4 WARRELS AVE
5 WESTOVER VIEW
6 WESTOVER AVE
7 HAYLEIGH TERR
8 HAYLEIGH ST
9 HAYLEIGH AVE
10 WESTOVER MOUNT

D1
1 HOUGH END CT
2 HOUGH END GDNS
3 DAISY ROW

D2
1 NEW SCARBRO RD
2 DAISYFIELD RD
3 ROSSEFIELD CL
4 ASHBY MOUNT
5 ROSSEFIELD WLK

D4
1 WESTMORELAND MOUNT
2 BACK WESTMORELAND MT
3 WELLINGTON GARTH
4 BELLMOUNT GN

E1
1 SOUTH END TERR
2 SOUTH END MOUNT
3 EASTLAND WLK

E2
1 BACK ASTON TERR
2 BACK ASTON VIEW
3 BACK ASTON VIEW
4 BACK HIGHFIELD RD

E3
1 RAYNVILLE APP
2 RAYNVILLE CT
3 RAYNVILLE GRANGE
4 RAYNVILLE GR

F1
1 WYTHER PARK CL
2 COCKSHOTT CL
3 ARMLEY GRANGE DR

F2
1 WENSLEYDALE MEWS
2 WENSLEYDALE AVE
3 WENSLEYDALE RISE

F3
1 WYTHER DR
2 WYTHER AVE
3 ABBEY TERR
4 ABBEY MOUNT

A4
1 TOWN ST
2 COAL HILL LA
3 LANGLEY PL

B3
1 CALVERLEY GR
2 CALVERLEY TERR
3 BEECROFT MOUNT

B1
1 RYCROFT GN
2 RYCROFT CT
3 RYCROFT PL

B2
1 NANSEN PL
2 NANSEN TERR
3 NANSEN GR

57 ← / 77

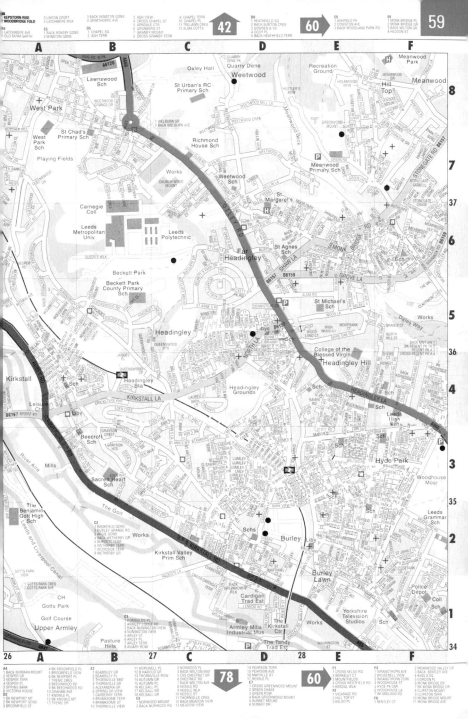

B5
KEPSTORN RISE
WOODBRIDGE FOLD

B6
LATCHMERE AVE
OLD FARM GARTH

3 LINTON CROFT
4 LATCHMERE WLK

C5
2 BACK ROKEBY GDNS
3 WINSTON GDNS

D5
1 CHAPEL SQ
2 ASH TERR

3 ASH VIEW
4 CROSS CHAPEL ST
5 ARISDALE CTR
6 GRANBURY ST
7 GRANBY MOUNT
8 CROSS GRANBY TERR

9 CHAPEL TERR
10 CHAPEL PL
11 TRELAWN CRES
12 ALMA COTTS

42

D6
1 HEATHFIELD SQ
2 BACK BURTON CRES
3 SOWDEN S YD
4 DEOY PL
5 BACK HEATHFIELD TERR

60

E5
1 ASHFIELD PK
2 CONISTON AVE
3 BACK WOODLAND PARK RD

E6
1 MONK BRIDGE PL
2 MONK BRIDGE RD
3 BACK WINSTON GR
4 HEDDON ST

59

26 A B **27** C D **28** E F **34**

A4
1 BACK NORMAN MOUNT
2 VESPER GR
3 VESPER TERR
4 VESPER PL
5 SPRING BANK
6 VICTORIA HOUSE

D3
7 BK NEWPORT MT
8 BK NEWPORT GDNS
9 BROMFIELD ST

4 BK BROOMFIELD PL
5 BROOMFIELD VIEW
6 BK NEWPORT PL
7 TRENIC CRES
8 BEECHWOOD RD
9 BK BEECHWOOD RD
10 GRAHAM AVE
11 KNOWLE PL
12 BK KNOWLE MT
13 TRENIC DR

E2
1 BEAMSLEY GR
2 BEAMSLEY PL
3 THORNVILLE MNT
4 THORNVILLE GR
5 ALEXANDRA GR
6 SPRING GR VIEW
7 CARBERRY TERR
8 BRANKSOME TERR
9 BRANKSOME ST
10 THORNVILLE VIEW

11 HOPEWELL PL
12 HAROLD GR
13 THORNVILLE ROW
14 AUTUMN GR
15 AUTUMN PL
16 KELSALL PL
17 KELSALL RD
18 KELSALL GR

E3
1 NORWOOD MOUNT
2 BACK NORWOOD PL

3 NORWOOD PL
4 BACK WELTON MNT
5 CSS CHESTNUT GR
6 BACK WELTON AVE
7 HESSLE RD
8 HESSLE WLK
9 HESSLE ST
11 THORNVILLE CRES
12 BACK MEADOW VIEW
13 MEADOW VIEW

14 FEARSON TERR
15 PEARSON AVE
16 MAYVILLE ST
17 HESSLE PL

78

60

E1
1 CROSS GREENWOOD MOUNT
2 GREEN CHASE
3 GREEN ROW
4 BACK GREENWOOD MOUNT
5 SUNSET MOUNT
6 SUNSET DR

F1
1 CROSS KELSO RD
2 BERKELEY CT
3 MOUNTFIELDS
4 CROSS WESTFIELD RD
5 KENDAL WLK

F2
1 VICARAGE RD
2 HILL TOP ST
3 KELSO RD

F3
1 WRANGTHORN AVE
2 BRUDENELL VIEW
3 WRANGTHORN TERR
4 WOODHOUSE ST
5 THORNTON GR

F4
1 HYDE PK CNR
2 WOODHOUSE LA
3 CLIPSTON MOUNT

F5
1 CLIPSTON TERR

F6
1 BENTLEY CT

2 MEANWOOD VALLEY GR
3 BACK BENTLEY AVE
4 KING S SQ
5 MONK BRIDGE DR
6 MONK BRIDGE ST
7 BK MONK BRIDGE DR
8 CLIPSTON AVENUE
9 CLIPSTON TERR
10 MONK BRIDGE MOUNT
11 MONA BRIDGE RD

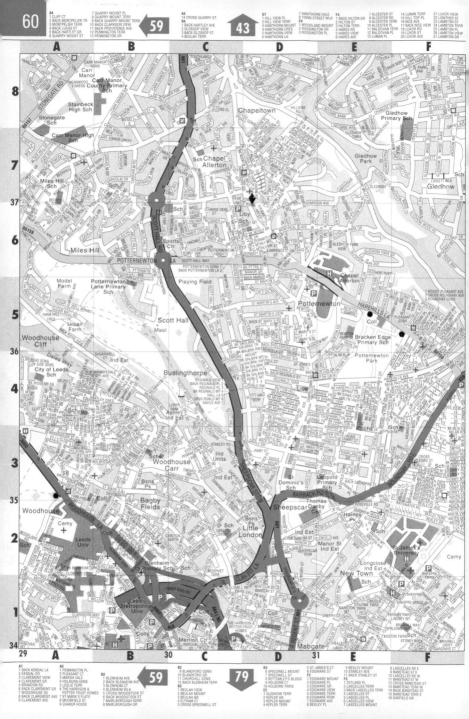

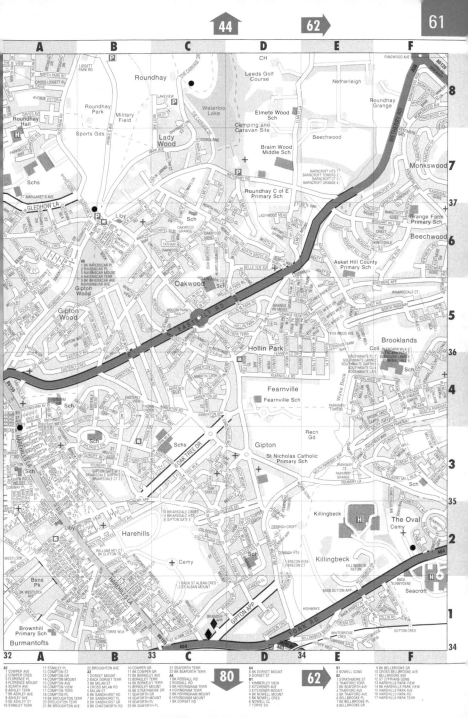

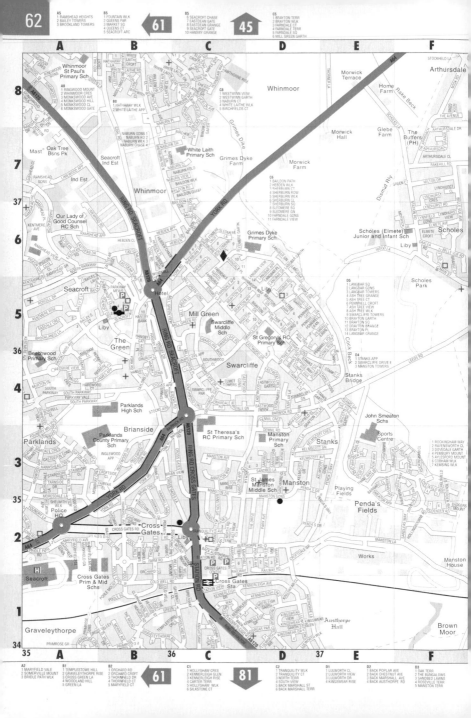

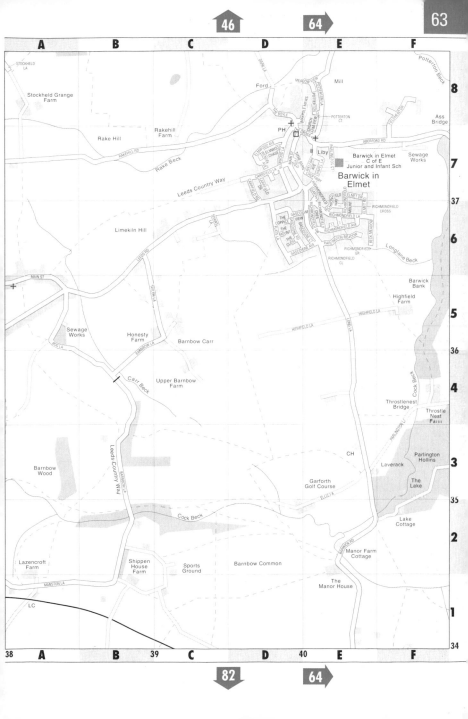

8

STOCKHELD LA

Stockheld Grange Farm

Rake Hill

Rakehill Farm

RAKEHILL RD

Rake Beck

DARK LA

Ford

MEADOW VIEW

POTTERTON LA

JOFFRE WAY

Mill

MAYPOLE MEWS

THE BOYLE

PH

Potterton Ct

POTTERTON CT

Potterton Beck

Ass Bridge

ABERFORD RD

VETERANS WAY

Liby

Barwick in Elmet C of E Junior and Infant Sch

Barwick in Elmet

7

Sewage Works

37

Leeds Country Way

CARRFIELD RD

ELMWOOD LA

ELMWOOD CHASE

ELM TREE WAY

KIPPAX RD

SPRINGHEAD

GASCOIGNE RD

ELMET DR

ELMET RD

Richmondfield La

BECK MEADOW

LONG LA

RICHMONDFIELD LA

Richmondfield Cross

Limekiln Hill

THE COPPICE

VIEW

THE MOUNT

THE CLOSE

GASCOIGNE AVE

PAUL ROYSTON MEADOW

Richmondfield Gr

RICHMONDFIELD CL

Longlane Beck

6

+

MAIN ST

LEEDS RD

ROTH LA

Barwick Bank

Highfield Farm

5

Sewage Works

BELLE LA

Honesty Farm

BARNBOW LA

Barnbow Carr

HIGHFIELD LA

HIGHFIELD LA

LONG LA

36

Carr Beck

Upper Barnbow Farm

Cock Beck

4

Throstlenest Bridge

Throstle Nest Farm

PARLINGTON LA

Barnbow Wood

Leeds Country Way

BARNBOW LA

CH

Laverack

Parlington Hollins

3

The Lake

Garforth Golf Course

ELLCLA

35

Lake Cottage

Cock Beck

2

Lazencroft Farm

Shippen House Farm

Sports Ground

Barnbow Common

BARNBOW RD

Manor Farm Cottage

MANSTON LA

The Manor House

1

LC

A B C D E F

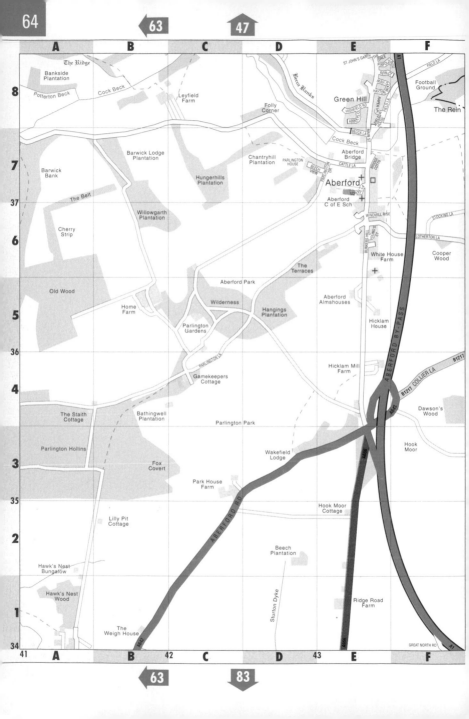

63
47

| | A | B | C | D | E | F |

8
The Ridge
Bankside Plantation
Potterton Beck
Cock Beck
Leyfield Farm
Folly Corner
Becca Banks
ST. JOHN'S GARTH
Green Hill
Football Ground
The Rein

7
Barwick Bank
Barwick Lodge Plantation
Hungerhills Plantation
Chantryhill Plantation
PARLINGTON HOUSE
Cock Beck
Aberford Bridge
Aberford
CATTLE LA

37
The Bell
Willowgarth Plantation
Aberford C of E Sch
WINDMILL RISE
STOCKING LA
LOTHERTON LA

6
Cherry Strip
White House Farm
Cooper Wood

5
Old Wood
Home Farm
Wilderness
Aberford Park
Hangings Plantation
The Terraces
Aberford Almshouses
Hicklam House
ABERFORD BY-PASS

36
Parlington Gardens
PARLINGTON LA
Hicklam Mill Farm
COLLIER LA
B1217

4
Gamekeepers Cottage
Dawson's Wood

3
The Staith Cottage
Bathingwell Plantation
Parlington Hollins
Fox Covert
Parlington Park
Wakefield Lodge
Hook Moor
ABERFORD RD

35
Park House Farm
Hook Moor Cottage

2
Lilly Pit Cottage
Beech Plantation

1
Hawk's Nest Bungalow
Hawk's Nest Wood
Sturton Dyke
Ridge Road Farm

34
The Weigh House
GREAT NORTH RD
A1

| 41 | A | 42 | C | D | 43 | E | F |

63
83

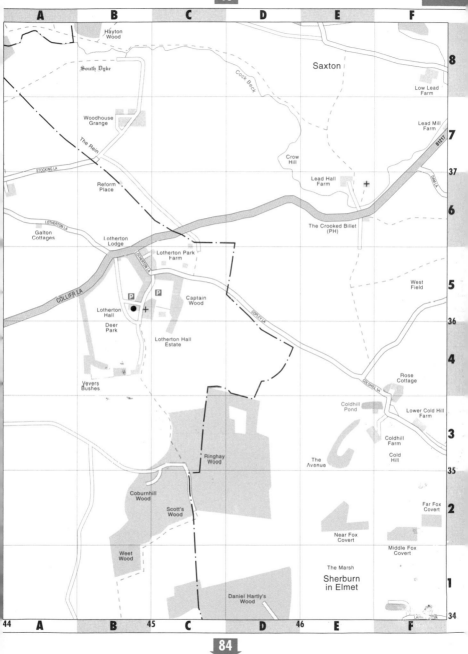

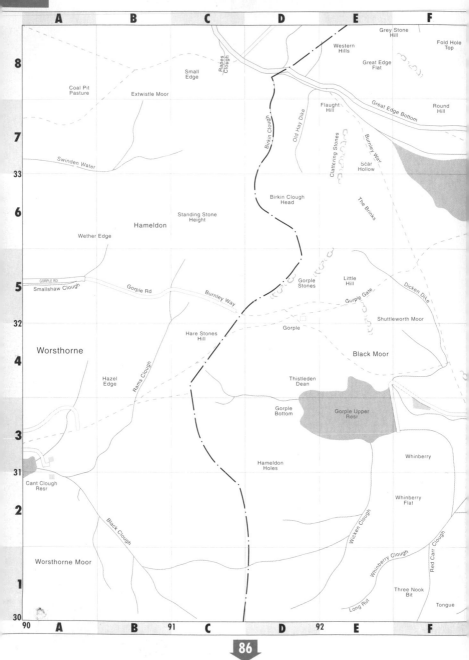

A **B** **C** **D** **E** **F**

8

Grey Stone Hill

Fold Hole Top

Western Hills

Great Edge Flat

Small Edge

Raps Clough

Coal Pit Pasture

Extwistle Moor

7

Birkin Clough

Old Hay Dike

Flaught Hill

Great Edge Bottom

Round Hill

Clattering Stones

Burnley Way

Scar Hollow

Swinden Water

33

Birkin Clough Head

The Brinks

6

Standing Stone Height

Hameldon

Wether Edge

5

GORPLE RD

Gorple Rd

Smallshaw Clough

Burnley Way

Gorple Stones

Little Hill

Gorple Gate

Dicken Dike

32

Hare Stones Hill

Gorple

Shuttleworth Moor

Worsthorne

Black Moor

4

Hazel Edge

Rams Clough

Thistleden Dean

Gorple Bottom

Gorple Upper Resr

3

Hameldon Holes

Whinberry

31

Cant Clough Resr

Whinberry Flat

2

Wicken Clough

Red Carr Clough

Black Clough

Whinberry Clough

Worsthorne Moor

1

Three Nook Bit

Tongue

Long Rut

30

A 90 **B** 91 **C** **D** 92 **E** **F**

A B C D E F

8
Lady Bower
Great Round Hill
The Greave
Greave Height
Shaw Dike

Greave Dike Flat
Hudson Greave
Little Round Hill
The Scout
Greave Clough
7
Greave Pasture
Back Shaw

Higher Houses
Pisser Clough
Pisser Hill
Pisser Rough
33

Pig Hole Dike
Widdop Lodge
New Hey
6
Slack Stones
Sutcliffe Rough

Widdop Resr
Wicking Slack
The Notch
Clough Foot

Cludders Slack
Alcomden
5
Flask
Brown Scout

Holme Ends
Alcomden Water
32

Dicken Rocks
Graining Water
Pennine Way
The Rough
Pack Horse (PH)
Paller End Slade
4
Ridge Nook

Gorple Lower Resr
Ridge Rough
Blake Dean

Black Rut
Gorple Cottages
Ridge Scout
3
King Common Rough

Clegg Foot
Great Rough Hey
Reaps Coppy
Low Moor
31

Raistrick Greave
The Plain
Ox Holes
2
King Common
Heptonstall

Rushy Sikes
Reaps Level

Clegg Rough
Reaps Bottom
Heptonstall Moor
Reaps Edge
Reaps Cross (remains of)
Standing Stone Hill
Ling Hollow
1
Clough Head Hill

Raistrick Greave Hill
30

93 A B 94 C D 95 E F

67
49

8

Shaw Dike Hill
Walshaw Dean Middle Resr
Fenny Lees
The Lodge
Lower Fold Hill
Black Clough
Black Clough Hill
Novich Brink
White Swamp
Hole Head
Hole Head Rushes

Pennine Old Dike

7

Old Dike Hill

Walshaw Dean Lower Resr

White Hill

Flaight Hill

Stony Dike

33

Black Nursery

Rushy Dike

Calf Hey Clough

6

The Grough

Dean Gate

High Rakes

Round Hill

Wadsworth Moor

Crumper Hill

White Hill

Haworth to Hebden Bridge Walk

Hare Edge

Shackleton Moor

5

Hoar Nib

Delf Brink

Rowshaw Clough

Lower Edge

Higher Edge

Navvy Head

32

BABY HOUSE HILL LA

Jack Allotment

Knoll Flat

Hardibut Clough

4

New Laithe Moor

New Laithes Farm

New Cote

Horodiddle

WAL SHAW LA

Rowshaw

Shackleton Knoll

Nook

COPPY LA

Coppy

SUNNY BANK RD

Black Dean

Over Wood

Hebden Dale

Walshaw

COWLING LA

3

Widdop Gate

Stony Edge

Dole

Abel Cross

Laithe

Charles Rough

High Laithe

Hebden Water

31

Ferny Beds

Coppy

High Greenwood House

Black Hill

Haworth to Hebden Bridge Walk

Crimsworth Dean Beck

2

High Greenwood Farm

Walshaw Wood

Lady Royd Edge

Kid Stones

Hamlet

Turn Hill

Abel Cote Wood

ABEL SPINK

CRIMSWORTH DEAN BRIDLEWAY

Hoar Royd

Pisser Clough

Lady Royd Farm

Abel Cote

1

White Mires

Mould Grain

Hardcastle Crags

Lady Royd

Clough Head Hill

Boothroyd Farm

30

96 **A** **B** 97 **C** **D** 98 **E** **F**

67
88

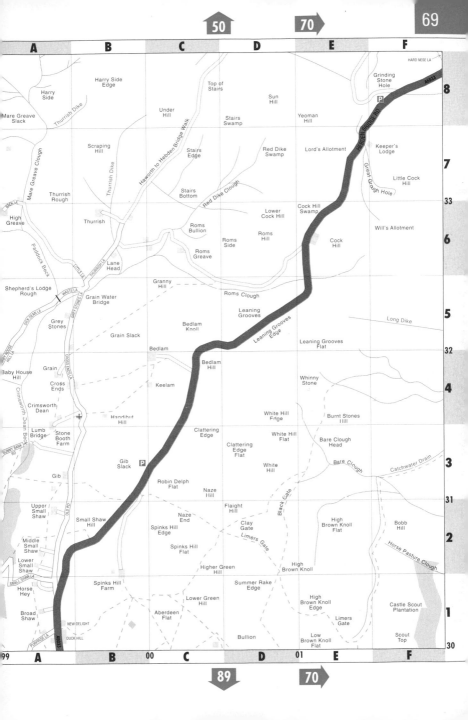

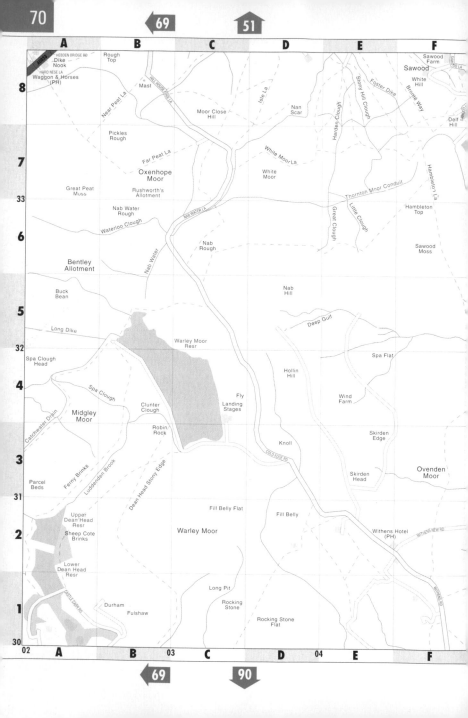

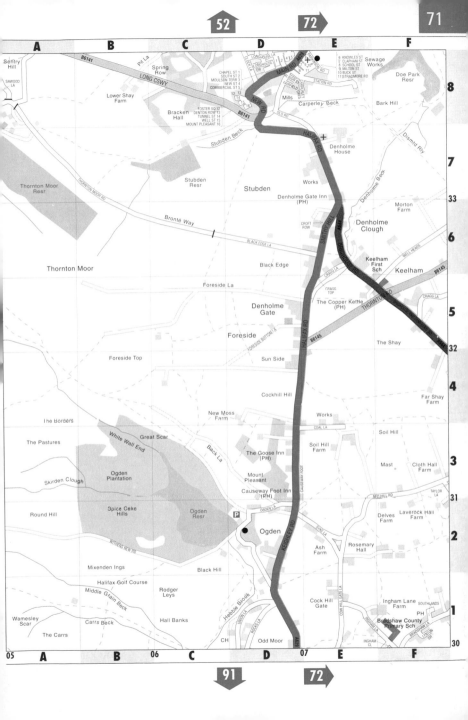

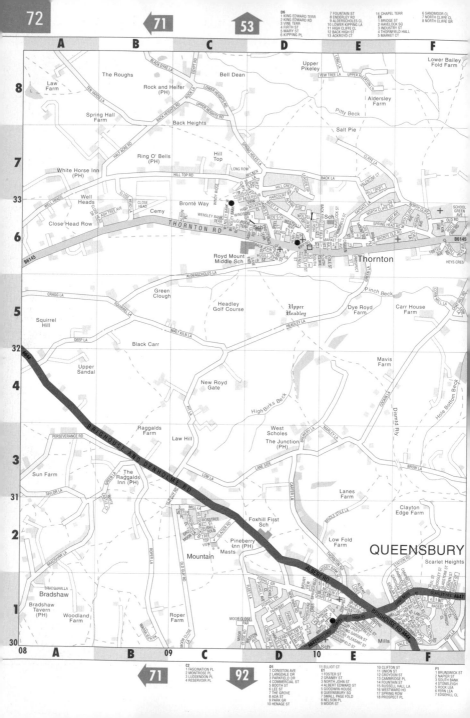

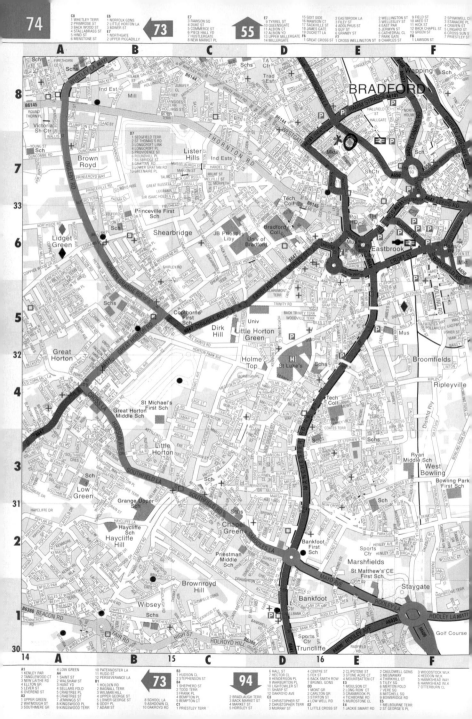

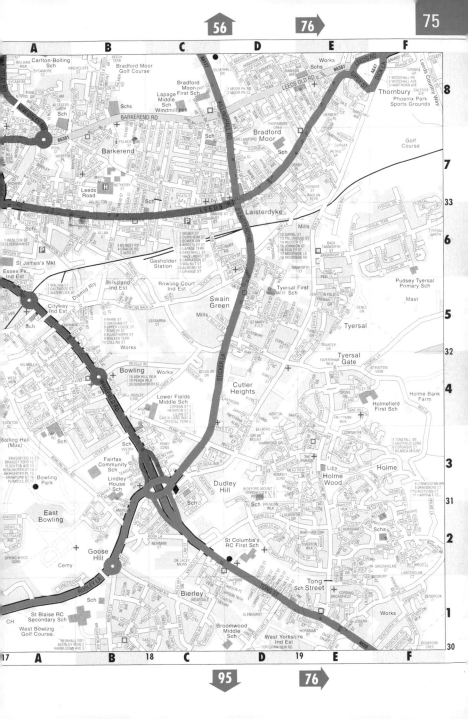

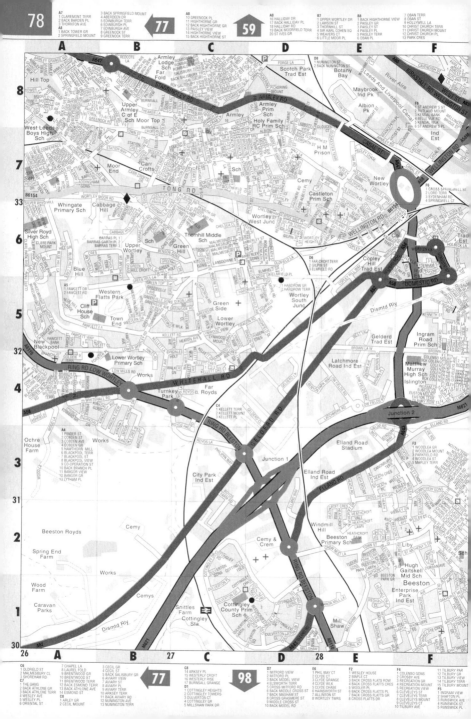

INGRAM CT
MEYNELL SQ
MEYNELL WLK
ST MATTHEW'S ST
HOLBECK TOWERS
GAITSKELL GRANGE
7 GAITSKELL CT
8 CROSBY RD
9 CROSBY VIEW
10 BERTRAND ST

B8
1 LEIGHTON PL
2 PORTLAND CRES
3 VICTORIA SQ
4 CROSS FOUNTAINE ST
5 SOMERS PL
6 BOND CT

C7
1 REGENT CT
2 CLOTH HALL ST
3 CORN EXCHANGE
4 BACK NEW YORK ST
5 ASSEMBLY ST
6 BLAYD'S YD
7 BLAYD'S MEWS

C8
1 CROSS BELGRAVE ST

C8
2 GRAND ARC
3 DORTMUND SQ
4 THORNTON'S ARC
5 QUEEN'S ARC
6 QUEEN VICTORIA ST
7 EBENEZER ST

60

D8
1 BELL ST
2 CROSS BELL ST
3 BRIDGE ST
4 LADY BECK CL
5 BACK GEORGE ST
6 MILLGARTH ST

80

E8
1 THEALBY PL
2 CROMWELL HTS
3 NASEBY PL
4 NASEBY GRANGE
5 NASEBY GDNS
6 NASEBY VIEW

F8
1 HASLEWOOD CT
2 HASLEWOOD GN
3 SAVILLE GN
4 APPLETON CT
5 APPLETON CL
6 APPLETON SQ

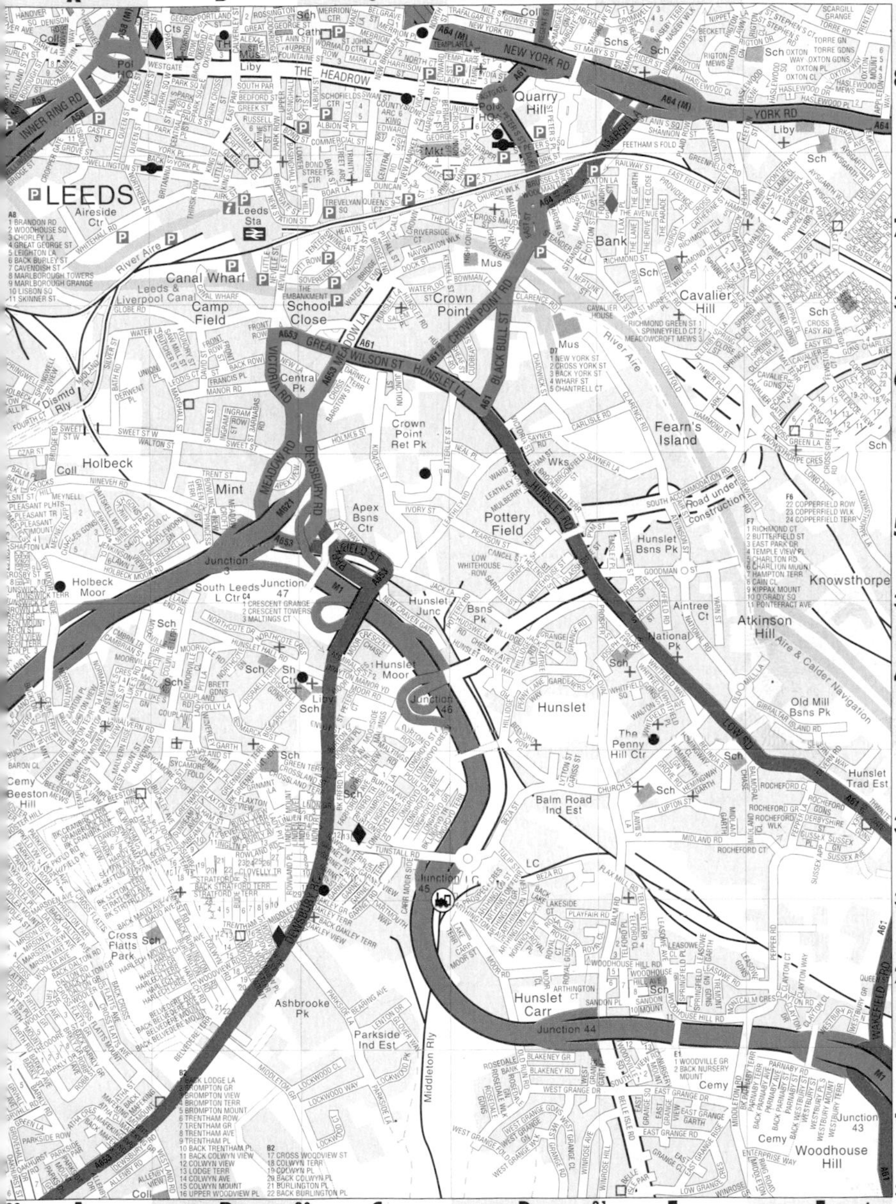

A B C D E F
8 7 33 6 5 32 4 3 31 2 1 30
29 30 31
LEEDS
Aireside Ctr
River Aire
Canal Wharf
Leeds & Liverpool Canal
Camp Field
School Close
Crown Point
Quarry Hill
THE HEADROW
NEW YORK RD
YORK RD
INNER RING RD
GREAT WILSON ST
HUNSLET LA
CROWN POINT RD
BLACK BULL ST
VICTORIA RD
MEADOW LA
DEWSBURY RD
MEADOW RD
Central Pk
Crown Point Ret Pk
Holbeck
Mint
Dismtd Rly
Apex Bsns Ctr
Pottery Field
Junction 3
Junction 47
South Leeds L Ctr
Holbeck Moor
Hunslet Junc
Bsns Pk
Hunslet Moor
Junction 46
Hunslet
The Penny Hill Ctr
Balm Road Ind Est
Junction 45
Hunslet Bsns Pk
National Pk
Aintree Ct
Atkinson Hill
Fearn's Island
Cavalier Hill
Knowsthorpe
Old Mill Bsns Pk
Aire & Calder Navigation
Hunslet Trad Est
LOW RD
Road under construction
Cemy
Beeston Hill
Cross Flatts Park
Ashbrooke Pk
Parkside Ind Est
Middleton Rly
Hunslet Carr
Junction 44
Junction 43
Woodhouse Hill
WAKEFIELD RD
M1
A61
A64 (M)
A653
A58

29 **A** **B** **30** **C** **D** **31** **E** **F**

A1
1 BARKLY PL
2 BARKLY PAR
3 BACK BARKLY PAR
4 OAKHURST MOUNT
5 BACK GROVEHALL AVE
6 OAKHURST AVE
7 BACK GROVEHALL DR

A2
1 WOOLER RD
2 CROSS FLATTS DR
3 BACK CROSS FLATTS GR
4 WOOLER ST
5 FIRTH VIEW
6 BACK CROSS FLATTS MOUNT
7 BARKLY TERR
8 BACK BARKLY TERR

A3
1 BACK MIDDLETON VIEW
2 BACK TEMPEST RD
3 WOOD PL
4 PARKFIELD RD
5 BACK PARKFIELD PL
6 BACK PARK VIEW
7 HARDY VIEW
8 HARDY GR

A4
1 RECREATION ROW
2 RECREATION CRES
3 RECREATION AVE
4 BACK ST LUKE'S CRES
5 MALVERN VIEW
6 ST LUKE'S VIEW

B3
1 FLAXTON GDNS
2 FLAXTON CL
3 FULHAM PL
4 GREENMOUNT CT
5 FULHAM SQ
6 STEWART PL
7 ELLIS PL
8 HARDY TERR
9 SUNBEAM GR
10 INGLETON CL
11 INGLETON GR
12 INGLETON ST
13 BEVERLEY MOUNT
14 MAUD PL
15 BACK TEMPEST RD
16 MARIAN GR
17 CATHERINE GR
18 FRANCIS GR
19 WESTBOURNE ST
20 WESTBOURNE AVE
21 WESTBOURNE PL
22 WESTBOURNE MNT
23 CLOVELLY ROW
24 CLOVELLY GR

99

25 CLOVELLY AVE
26 CLOVELLY PL
27 BACK CLOVELLY PL
28 BROMPTON ROW
29 TRENTHAM TERR

C3
1 COCKBURN WAY
2 BK CROSSLAND TERR
3 BACK LINDEN GR
4 LINDEN PL
5 CROSS LINDEN TERR
6 LINDEN GDNS
7 ROWLAND TERR
8 BACK ROWLAND TERR
9 CAMBERLEY ST
10 BACK CAMBERLEY ST
11 BACK STRATFORD ST
12 BACK BURTON TERR
13 BURTON TERR

E2
1 TELFORD GDNS
2 TELFORD WLK
3 WHINCUP GDNS
4 TELFORD ST
5 WOODHOUSE HILL TR
6 BRAITHWAITE ROW
7 WOODHOUSE HILL PL
8 WOODHOUSE HILL GR
9 LEASOWE CT
10 SANDON GR
11 EBOR TERR
12 NURSERY MOUNT RD
13 KEARSLEY TERR

F6
1 THORNLEIGH GR
2 THORNLEIGH VIEW
3 THORNLEIGH MOUNT
4 THORNLEIGH ST
5 CAVALIER CL
6 BACK CROSS GN CRES
7 CROSS GREEN CRES
8 BACK CROSS GREEN LA
9 CROSS GREEN AVE
10 CROSS GREEN GR
11 ST HILDA'S RD
12 ST HILDA'S PL
13 ST HILDA'S MOUNT
14 ST HILDA'S AVE
15 ST HILDA'S GR
16 ST HILDA'S CRES
17 COPPERFIELD GR
18 COPPERFIELD VIEW
19 COPPERFIELD PL
20 COPPERFIELD CRES
21 COPPERFIELD DR

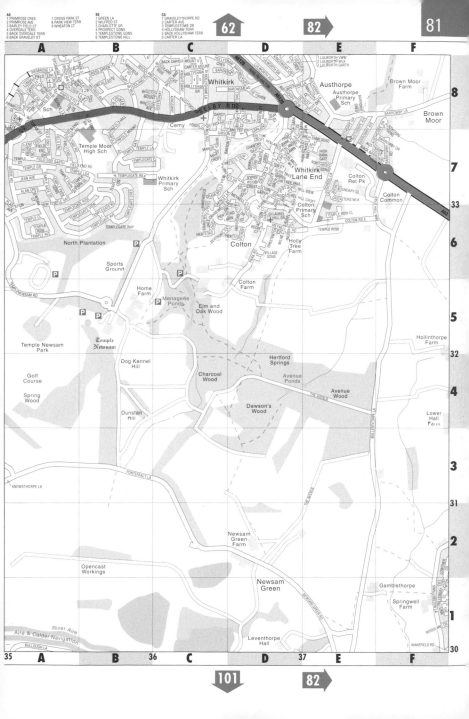

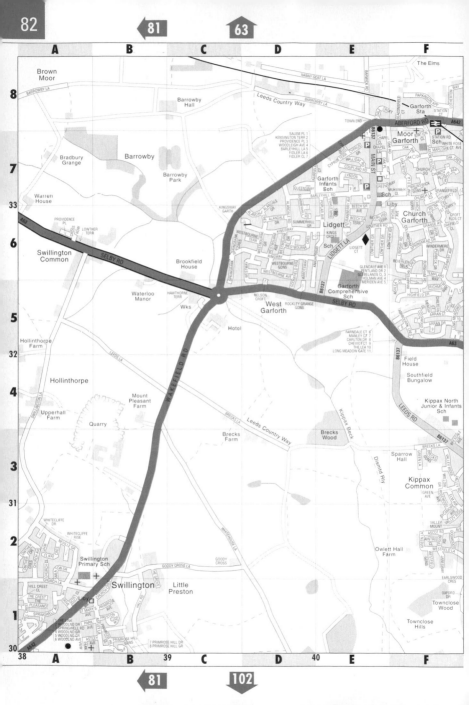

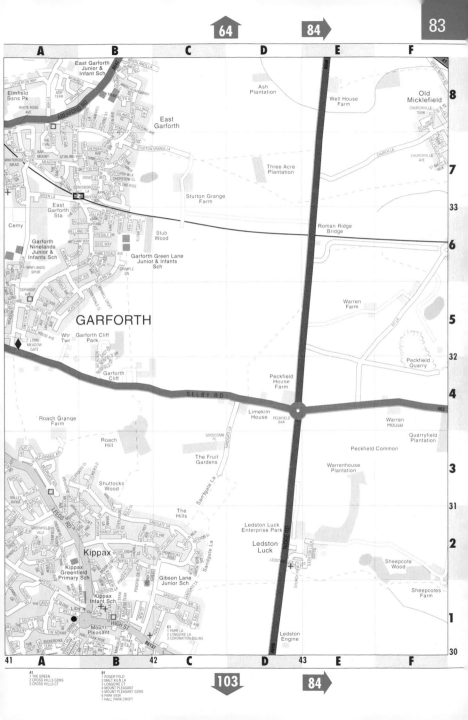

A   B   C   D   E   F

8

Elmfield
Bsns Pk

WHITE ROSE
AVE

LOTHERTON WAY

East Garforth
Junior &
Infant Sch

ABERFORD RD

BRIERLANDS LA

Ash
Plantation

Well House
Farm

A656

GREAT NORTH RD A1

Old
Micklefield

CHURCHVILLE
TERR

7

WHITEHOUSE
MEAD

THE
OVAL

BAR
MOUNT

STIRLING WAY

MEADOW RD

SKIPTON DR
DOVER ST

CONISBOROUGH
LA

East
Garforth

STURTON GRANGE LA

CHEPSTOW CL

ATHLONE RISE

Three Acre
Plantation

CHURCH LA

CHURCHVILLE
AVE

ST MARY'S
WLK

33

East
Garforth
Sta

Cemy

GREEN LA

CHURCH LA

HILLSIDE

INVERNESS CL

RIVENDALE DR

APPLEBY

Sturton Grange
Farm

Garforth
Ninelands
Junior &
Infants Sch

NINEFIELDS
SPUR

WELLAND

AIREDALE DR

WITHAM WAY

FOSSE WAY

ELDER GATE

RIBBLESDALE AVE

Stub
Wood

Garforth Green Lane
Junior & Infants
Sch

Roman Ridge
Bridge

6

DERWENT
AVE

LONG
MEADOWS

BRENT AVE

CASTLEWOOD

ACASTER DR

CRIMPLE
GN

GARFORTH

Warren
Farm

5

Wtr
Twr

LONG
MEADOW
GATE

Garforth Cliff
Park

LEE HOUSE AVE

Garforth
Cliff

NEW STH DR

Peckfield
Quarry

32

Roach Grange
Farm

SELBY RD

Limekiln
House

Peckfield
House
Farm

PECKFIELD
BAR

Warren
House

A63

4

LEEDS RD

Roach
Hill

Shuttocks
Wood

GOODCOMB
PL

SANDGATE

The Fruit
Gardens

Peckfield Common

Quarryfield
Plantation

3

VALLEY
RIDGE

GREENFIELD
VALE

The
Hills

Sandgate La

Warrenhouse
Plantation

31

Kippax

MOORLEIGH

Kippax
Greenfield
Primary Sch

Kippax
Infant Sch

GIBSON LA

PEMBROKE RISE

Sandgate La

Gibson Lane
Junior Sch

MERTON

Ledston Luck
Enterprise Park

Ledston
Luck

RIDGE RD

CHURCH LA

KLINGSTON
COTTS

LEDSTONE

2

Mount
Pleasant

LIDY
WELL LA

HIGH ST

SOUTH RIDGE

PARK RISE

HALL PARK

INTAKE

B6137

C1
1 PARK LA
2 LONGDIKE LA
3 CORONATION BGLWS

THE
CRESCENT

BICKERDIKE
TERR

THE INTAKE

Ledston
Engine

Sheepcote
Wood

Sheepcotes
Farm

1

41   A   B   42   C   43   D   E   F   30

A1
1 THE GREEN
2 CROSS HILLS GDNS
3 CROSS HILLS CT

B1
1 ROGER FOLD
2 MALT KILN LA
3 LONGDIKE CT
4 MOUNT PLEASANT
5 MOUNT PLEASANT GDNS
6 PARK VIEW
7 HALL PARK CROFT

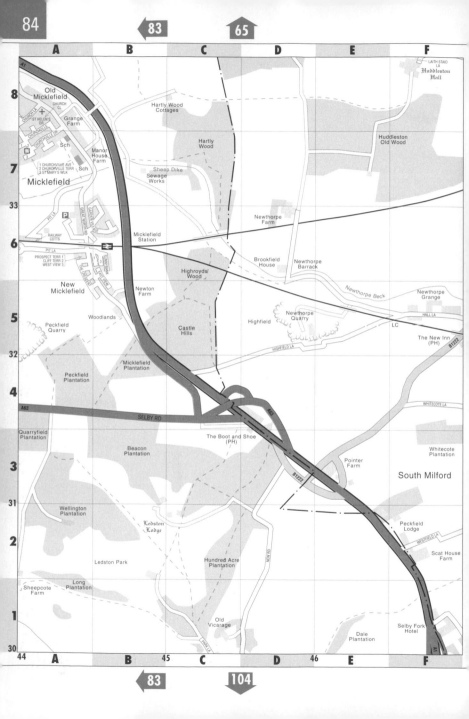

A B C D E F

8

LAITH STAID LA
Huddleston
Hall

Old
Micklefield
CHURCH CL
ST HELEN'S DR
Grange
Farm

Hartly Wood
Cottages

Hartly
Wood

Huddleston
Old Wood

7

Manor
House
Farm
1 CHURCHVILLE AVE
2 CHURCHVILLE TERR
3 ST MARY'S WLK
Sch
Sch

Micklefield

Sheep Dike
Sewage
Works

Newthorpe
Farm

33

RAILWAY
COTTS
P
PIT LA
GREAT NORTH RD
LEEDS ROAD

Micklefield
Station

Brookfield
House

Newthorpe
Barrack

6

PIT LA
PROSPECT TERR 1
CLIFF TERR 2
WEST VIEW 3
SUNNYBANK

Highroyds
Wood

Newthorpe
Beck

Newthorpe
Grange

New
Micklefield

Newton
Farm

Highfield

Newthorpe
Quarry

HALL LA

5

Peckfield
Quarry

Woodlands

Castle
Hills

HIGHFIELD LA

LC

The New Inn
(PH)

B1222

32

Peckfield
Plantation

Micklefield
Plantation

4

A63

SELBY RD

A63

WHITECOTE LA

Quarryfield
Plantation

The Boot and Shoe
(PH)

B1222

Pointer
Farm

Whitecote
Plantation

3

Beacon
Plantation

South Milford

31

Wellington
Plantation

Ledston
Lodge

Peckfield
Lodge

WESTFIELD LA

2

Ledston Park

Hundred Acre
Plantation

NEW RD

Scat House
Farm

Long
Plantation

1

Sheepcote
Farm

PARK LA

Old
Vicarage

Dale
Plantation

Selby Fork
Hotel

30

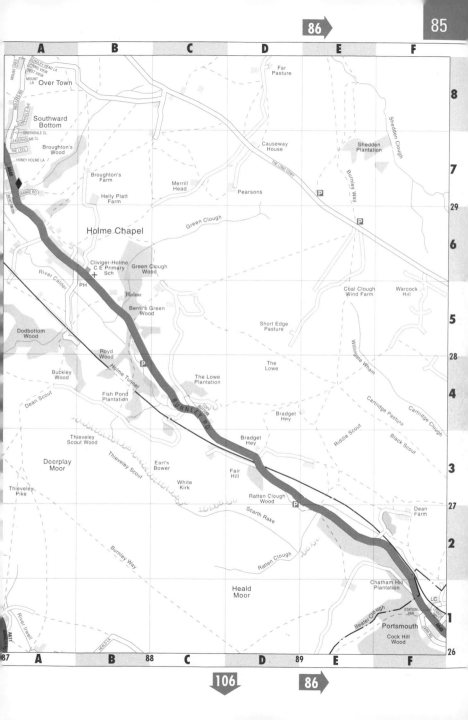

85
66

	A	B	C	D	E	F

Sheddon Edge

Sheddon Top

White Hill

Hoar Side

8

Black Hameldon

Crooker Hill

North Grain

Hoar Side Top

7

Rush Candle Clough

Hoof Stones Height

29

The Lead Mine

Noah Dale Water

Stiperden Moor

Lead Mine Clough

6

Stiperden Bar House

Stiperden Slack

Moss Crop

THE LONG CAUSY

Moss Crop Hill

5

Bent's Pasture

Cold Soil

Stansfield Moor

28

Stiperden House Farm

Stiperden Bank

Hoppet

NEW RD

Coal Clough

Paul Clough

Burnley Way

Bank Top Farm

4

Burnt Edge Pasture

Lower Mount Farm

Upper Mount

Sportsman's Arms (PH)

Coal Clough Farm

Ford

Pudsey Clough

MOUNT LA

Cross Hill

Higher Intake

KEBB RD

Hawks Stones

Keb Bridge

3

BANK LA

Redmires Water

Nant Wood

COAL CLOUGH

Reddish Shore Rocks

Higher Green End

DELF LA

GAIL LA

Dyke Farm

CAUSAL LA

Orchan House Farm

27

Shore Law

BLUE BELL LA

Bride Stones

Whitaker Naze

Dawk Hole Wood

Mount Pleasant Farm

Shore

Hudson Bridge

2

PUDSEY RD

Pudsey

Blue Bell Farm

Mast

Hartley Royd Farm

Hudson Moor

STONEY LA

STATION RD

Cornholme Junior & Infants Sch

Liby

PARKSIDE

BOBBIN MILL LA

ACKROYD ST

BURNLEY RD

BROOKFIELD ST

Vale

Back Wood

Clunters

Calderdale Way

Kit Hill How Gate

1

Cornholme

River Calder

Cat Hole

JUMPS LA

26

90	A	B	91	C	D	92	E	F

1 DURN ST
2 GARRFIELD VILLAS

85
107

81
1 BROWN BIRKS ST
2 DAISY BANK ST
3 PEAR PL
4 PEAR ST
5 SPRING VILLAS
6 STANSFIELD TERR
7 CORNHOLME TERR
8 OAKLEIGH TERR
9 SUNNY BANK TERR
10 GLADSTONE ST

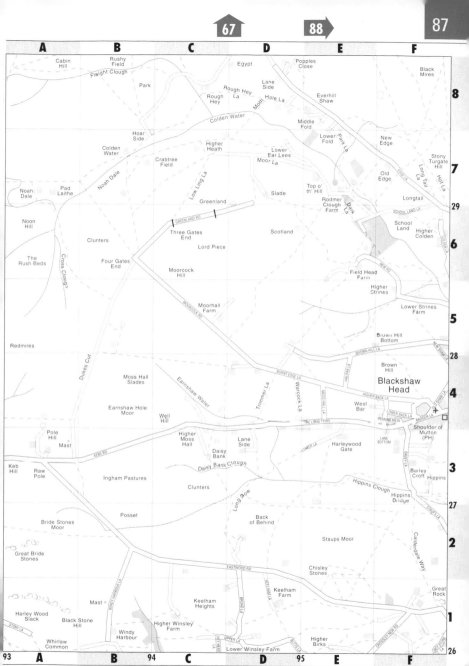

Grid references along right edge (top to bottom): 8, 7, 29, 6, 5, 28, 4, 3, 27, 2, 1, 26

Grid columns (top): A, B, C, D, E, F

Cabin Hill
Rushy Field
Flaight Clough
Egypt
Popples Close
Black Mires
Park
Rough Hey La
Lane Side
Hole La
Everhill Shaw
Rough Hey
Moth
Colden Water
Middle Fold
Hoar Side
Lower Fold
Park La
New Edge
Colden Water
Higher Heath
Lower Ear Lees
Top o' th' Hill
Old Edge
Stony Turgate Hill
Long Tail La
Hol La
Crabtree Field
Moor La
Noah Dale
Slade
Rodmer Clough Farm
Dark La
Longtail
Noah Dale
Pad Laithe
Low Ling La
Greenland
School Land La
School Land
Higher Colden
Noon Hill
Clunters
Greenland Rd
Three Gates End
Scotland
Colden La
The Rush Beds
Four Gates End
Lord Piece
Field Head Farm
Cross Clough
Moorcock Hill
Higher Strines
Redmires
Moorhall Farm
Lower Strines Farm
Dukes Cut
Moss Hall Slades
Earnshaw Water
Burnt Edge La
Brown Hill Bottom
New Shaw La
Brown Hill La
Half Mile La
Brown Hill
Moss Hall La
Blackshaw Head
Higher Back La
Pole Hill Mast
Earnshaw Hole Moor
Well Hill
Trimmer La
Warcock La
West Bar
Lower Back La
Badger La
Shoulder of Mutton (PH)
Kebs Rd
Higher Moss Hall
Lane Side
The Long Henry
Pennine View
Lane Bottom
Keb Hill
Raw Pole
Daisy Bank
Daisy Bank Clough
Lower La
Harleywood Gate
Davey La
Barley Croft
Hippins
Ingham Pastures
Clunters
Long Row
Hippins Clough
Hippins Bridge
Strines La
Bride Stones Moor
Posset
Back of Behind
Calderdale Way
Great Bride Stones
Staups Moor
Eastwood Rd
Chisley Stones
Keelham Farm
Great Rock
Mast
Keelham Heights
Windy Harbour La
Brian La
Keelham La
Harley Wood Slack
Black Stone Hill
Higher Winsley Farm
Windy Harbour
Pye Nest La
Upper La
Lower Winsley Farm
Butts La
Higher Birks
Crossley New Rd
Stony La
Whirlaw Common
Calf La

93   94   95   26

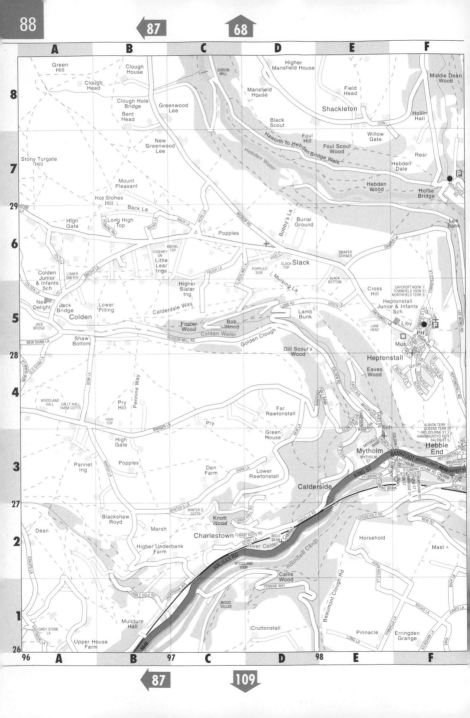

8

7

29

6

5

28

4

3

27

2

1

26

A B C D E F

Purprise

Bent Head

Higher Crimsworth

Lower Crimsworth

Pecket Well

Middle Dean Wood

War Meml

Kitling Bridge

Midgehole

Spring Wood

Lee Mill Bridge

Lee Wood

Fearney Fields

Old Town

Ibbotroyd Farm

Wood End

Nutclough

Birchcliffe

Dodd Naze

HEBDEN BRIDGE

Machpelah

Fairfield

Hebden Bridge Sta

Crow Nest Wood

Old Chamber

Great Jumps

Hill Top

Mill

Cemy

Robin Hood Inn (PH)

Far Shaw Croft

Moor Side

Wall Stones Flat

Wainsgate

Resr

Hurst

Carrs

Snow Booth

Great Burlees Farm

Falling Royd

Wood Top

Stubb Clough

Delf End

Slack House

Weather House

Bog Eggs Edge

Bog Eggs

Old Laithe

Old Town Junior & Infant Sch

Chiserley

Hare & Hounds (PH)

Far Nook

High Royd Farm

Raw Farm

Rochdale Canal

Clog Sole Works

Broad Bottom Farm

Hawks Clough

Great Stubb

Nest Estate

Delf End Flat

Tom Tittiman

Old Hold Edge

Old Hold

Dick Ing

Claytone

Nook

Little Moor

Mount Skip Inn (PH)

Burlees Wood

Long Royds

Deer Stones Edge

Blacks

Calderdale Way

Commons Farm

Latham La

Poppies La

Dike La

CH

Mount Skip Golf Course

Cock Hill

Owlers

Bethesda Row

Hobart Bldgs

Burnley Road Jun & Inf Sch

Ashton Rd

Low Brown Knoll

Low Brown Knoll Hollow

Collon Flat

Keelam

Keelam Edge

Wicken Hill

Hill House Farm

Sewage Works

White Houses

Shore End Top

Shore End

Shore End Wood

Back Clough

Dimmin Dale

Hough Dean

Dimmin Dale Edge

Sheep Stones Edge

High Rough

Foster Clough Bridge

Wadsworth Banks Farm

Throstle Bower Farm

Wadsworth Banks Fields

Ray Gate

Foster Clough

Raw La

Calder High Sch

A 99 B 00 C D 01 E F

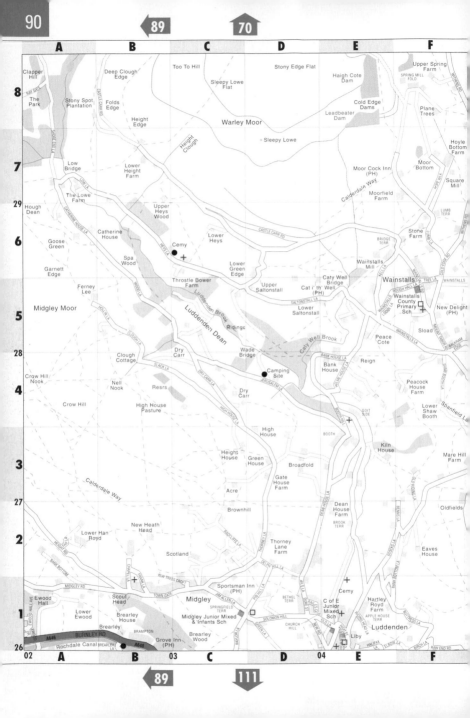

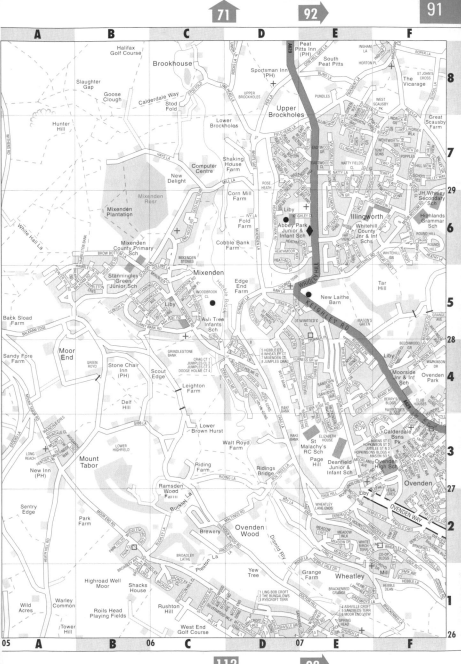

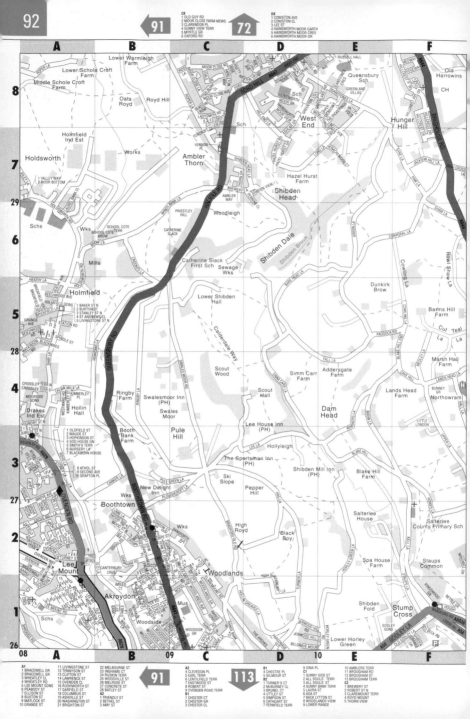

91 72

C8
1 OLD GUY RD
2 MOOR CLOSE FARM MEWS
3 CLARENDON PL
4 SUNNY VIEW TERR
5 MYRTLE GR
6 OXFORD RD

D8
1 CONISTON AVE
2 CONISTON CL
3 LEE ST
4 HAINSWORTH MOOR GARTH
5 HAINSWORTH MOOR CRES
6 HAINSWORTH MOOR DR

Lower Warmleigh Farm
Lower Schole Croft
Middle Schole Croft Farm
Holdsworth
Holmfield Ind Est
Works
Oats Royd
Royd Hill
RUSSELL HALL
Queensbury Sch
GREENLAND VILLAS
Old Harrowins
CH
West End
Hunger Hill
Ambler Thorn
Hazel Hurst Farm
Shibden Head
1 VALLEY WAY
2 MOOR BOTTOM
Woodleigh
PRIESTLEY HILL
AMBLER WAY
Wks
SCHOOL COTE TERR
SCHOOL COTE BROW
Catherine Slack
Shibden Dale
Shibden Brook
Mills
Catherine Slack First Sch
Sewage Wks
Dunkirk Brow
Holmfield
1 BAKER ST N
2 BURTONST
3 STANLEY ST N
4 ST ANDREWS CL
5 LIVINGSTONE ST N
BEECHWOOD AVE
HOLMFIELD GDNS
STATION RD
SPINDLE ST
Lower Shibden Hall
Barns Hill Farm
Cut Teal La La
GRANGE AVE
Calderdale Way
Marsh Hall Farm
CROSSLEY TERR N
CROSSLEY TERR S
MOORSIDE GDNS
Scout Wood
Simm Carr Farm
Addersgate Farm
Lands Head Farm
BUNNEY GR Northowram
Ringby Farm
Swalesmoor Inn (PH)
Swales Moor
Scout Hall
Dam Head
Lands Head Farm
LITTLE LONDON
Hollin Hall
Drakes Ind Est
FOUNDRY ST
1 OLDFIELD ST
2 MAUDE ST
3 HOPKINSON ST
4 SOD HOUSE GR
5 SMITH'S TERR
6 NURSERY LA
7 BLACKBORN HOUSE
Booth Bank Farm
Pule Hill
Lee House Inn (PH)
Hollyleigh
Shibden Mill Inn (PH)
Blake Hill Farm
8 ATHOL ST
9 SECOND AVE
10 GRAFTON PL
The Sportsman Inn (PH)
New Delight Inn
Ski Slope
Pepper Hill
Salterlee House
Salterlee County Primary Sch
Boothtown
Wks
High Royd
Black Boy
Spa House Farm
Staups Common
Lee Mount
Woodlands
CANTERBURY CRES
WELLS RD
Akroydon
Mus
Shibden Fold
Stump Cross
Schs
Woodside
Woodside GR
WOODSIDE TERR
GODLEY GDNS
Lower Horley Green
BELGRAVE MOUNT
GODLEY LA
NETHLEY GR

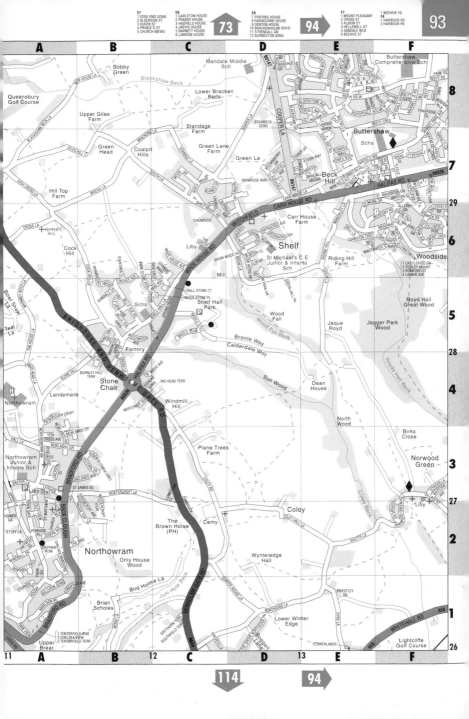

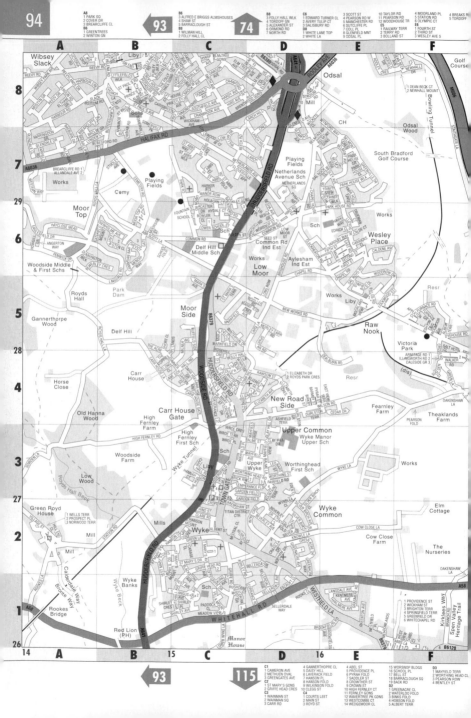

93

74

93

115

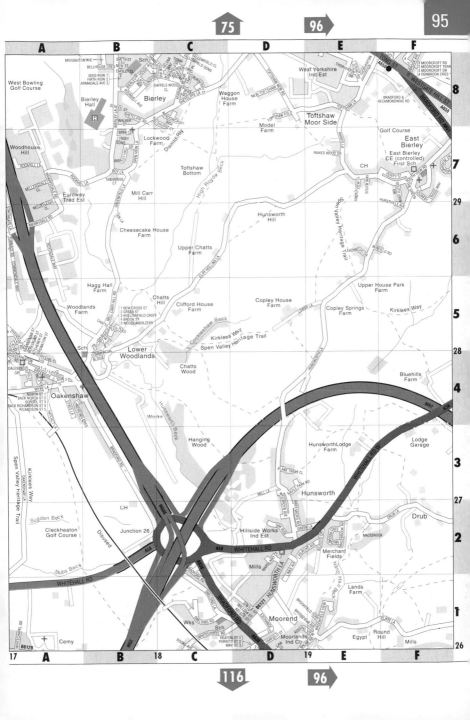

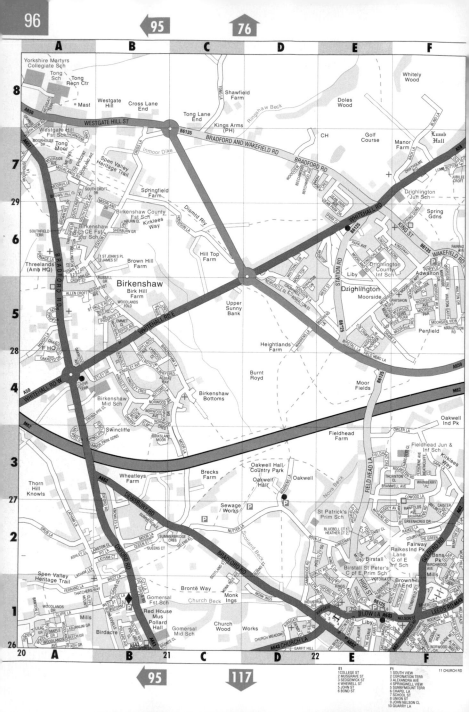

E1
1 COLLEGE ST
2 MUSGRAVE ST
3 SEDGEWICK ST
4 WHEWELL ST
5 JOHN ST
6 BOND ST

F1
1 SOUTH VIEW
2 CORONATION TERR
3 ALEXANDRA AVE
4 SPRINGWELL VIEW
5 SUNNYMOUNT TERR
6 THORNTON ST
7 SCHOOL ST
8 UNION ST
9 JOHN NELSON CL
10 QUARRY LA

11 CHURCH RD

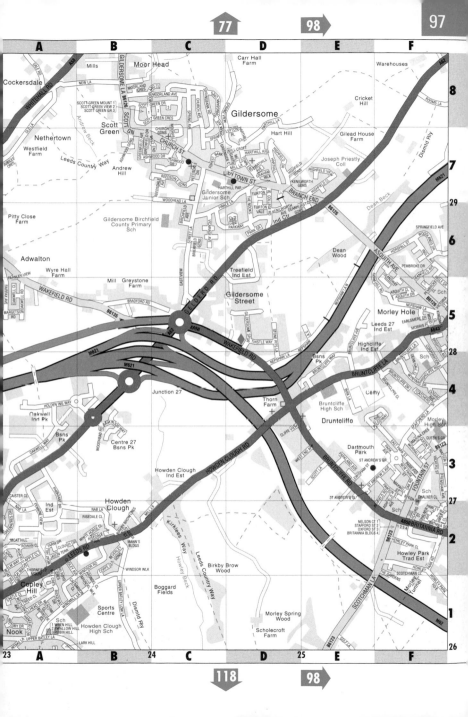

A B C D E F

8

Cockersdale

WHITEHALL RD

Mills

Moor Head

GILDERSOME LA

Carr Hall Farm

Warehouses

NEW LA

MOORLAND GDNS
SCOTT GREEN MOUNT 1
SCOTT GREEN VIEW 2
SCOTT GREEN GR 3
MOORLAND AVE
MOORLAND GDNS
SCOTT GREEN DR
SCOTT GREEN CRES

Cricket Hill

Gildersome

Netherton

Scott Green

Andrew Beck

CHURCH ST

SPRING AVE

CHURCH AVE

Hart Hill

Gilead House Farm

Dismd Rly

M62

8

Westfield Farm

Leeds Country Way

Andrew Hill

ASHWOOD DR
GRAHAM GR

HARTHILL RISE
MILL CROFT

Liby TOWN ST

HARTHILL PAR

Joseph Priestly Coll

Highfield View

M621

7

Pitty Close Farm

REEDSDALE GDNS

WOODHEAD LA

Gildersome Junior Sch

TURTON GN

TURTON VALE

KENILWORTH GDNS

BRANCH END

B6126

Dean Beck

29

Adwalton

Gildersome Birchfield County Primary Sch

THE HOOKS

PARKWAY

FRONT ST

Ind Ctr

SPRINGFIELD AVE

6

Wyre Hall Farm

FARNLEY VIEW

Mill

Greystone Farm

EAST VIEW

GELDERD RD

Treefield Ind Est

Dean Wood

ASQUITH AVE

B6126

Sch

WAKEFIELD RD

BRADFORD RD

B6135

DAWSHAW TER

GILDERSOME LA

Gildersome Street

NEPSHAW LA

Morley Hole

Leeds 27 Ind Est

A643

5

M621

A62

A650

WAKEFIELD RD

THISTLE WAY

NEPSHAW LA

Bsns Pk

Highcliffe Ind Est

28

Junction 27

Oakwell Ind Pk

OAKWELL WAY

Bsns Pk

WOODKIRK

Centre 27 Bsns Pk

Thorn Farm

BRUNTCLIFFE WAY

Bsns Pk

Cemy

BRUNTCLIFFE LA

BRUNTCLIFFE LA

4

Bruntcliffe High Sch

Druntcliffe

Morley High Sch

QUEEN'S GR

B6123

CLIFFE DENE

WEST END LA

Howden Clough Ind Est

HOWDEN CLOUGH RD

BRUNTCLIFFE RD

Dartmouth Park

ST ANDREW'S GR

St Andrew's Gr

FOUNTAIN ST

Sch

CHALNER CL

3

27

Caister Cl

Ind Est

Howden Clough

NAB LA

RISEDALE CL

WHITE HORSE LA

RISEDALE CL

Kirklees Way

Howley Beck

ST ANDREW'S Cl

NELSON CT 1
STAFFORD ST 2
OXFORD ST 3
BRITANNIA BLDGS 4

A650 BRITANNIA RD

B6123

Howley Park Trad Est

2

MANN'S BLDGS

Windsor Wlk

Birkby Brow Wood

Leeds Country Way

HOWLEY PARK RD

SCOTCHMAN LA

THE GARDENS

Morley Tunnel

Copley Hill

Boggard Fields

Dismd Rly

Morley Spring Wood

SCOTCHMAN LA

M62

1

Nook

Sch
1 WREN HILL
2 SWALLOW HILL
3 ROBIN HILL

LEEDS RD

Sports Centre

Howden Clough High Sch

LARK HILL

Scholecroft Farm

B6123

26

97
78

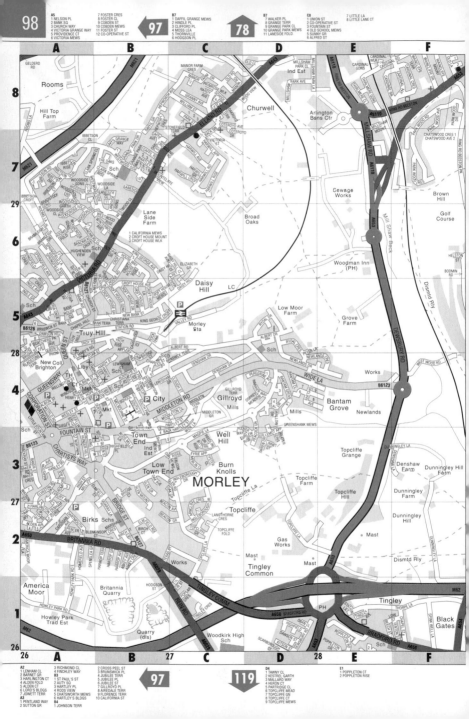

97
119

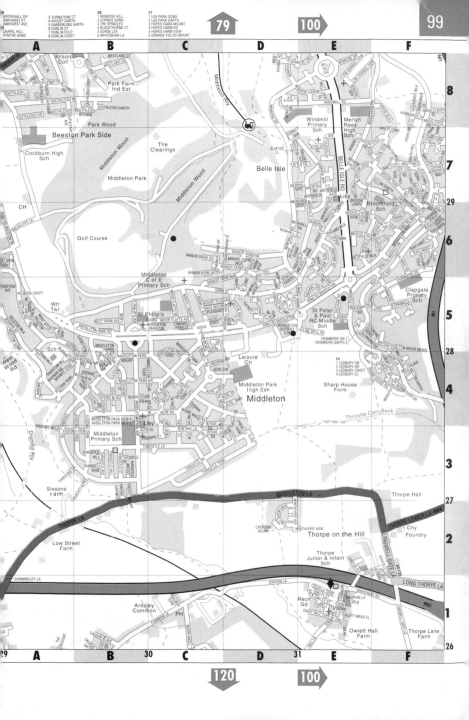

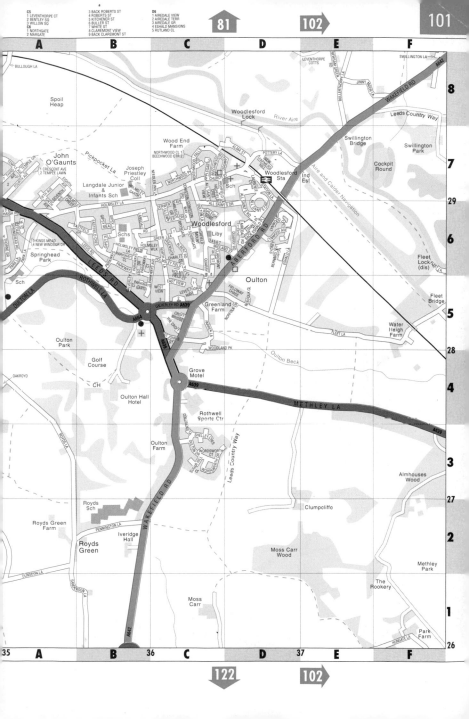

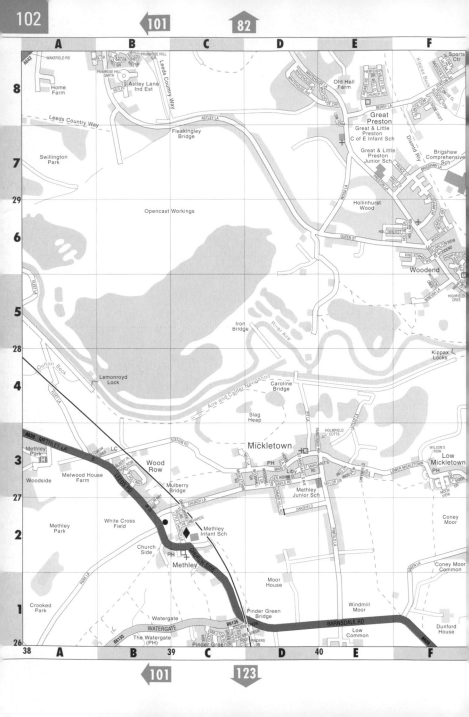

	A	B	C	D	E	F

8

Park House Farm

Plaster Pits

Park Lane Farm

Hastings Plantation

Hill Top Farm

ST JOHN'S HOSPITAL (ALMSHOUSES)

Lady E Hastings Sch

PH

Ledsham

HOLY ROOD LA

Wormstall Wood

7

Capon Hill

CLAYPIT LA

Horselock Dale

Madbanks

29

Lambkin Plantation

Lambkin Hill

6

BACK NEWTON LA

Newfield Farm

Newfield Plantation

Newfield La

Caudle Hill Plantation

5

Haugh Hill Plantation

Beckfield House

Newton Farm

28

Newton

NEWTON LA

P

CAUDLE HILL

4

Newton Abbey

Fairburn Ings Nature Reserve

3

Newton Ings

Fairburn Ings

River Aire

New Fryston

Aire Bridge

27

Spoil Heap

P
P

BRIGG

NORTH ST

WINDHILL ST

Sewage Works

Spoil Heap

2

Wheldale Ings

Sewage Works

WHELDON RD

Wheldale Farm

SOUTH VIEW

WHELDALE LA

Well Wood

KESWICK DR

Hall Farm

Water Fryston

1

Wheldale

STANSFIELD DR

PEMBERTON RD

STANSFIELD

FOSS WLK

NIDD DR

FRISTON RD

PRESCOTT DR

SMAWTHORNE LA

PARK DALE

LANSBURY'S RD

LANCASTER CRES

LANGDALE TERR

SCHOLES LA

Sch

ASKHAM RD

FAIRFIELD CL

GRANGE RD

CHAMBERS HOUSE CT

BRANDWOOD CL

ROSECLIFFE

Fryston Hall

Whin Covert

26

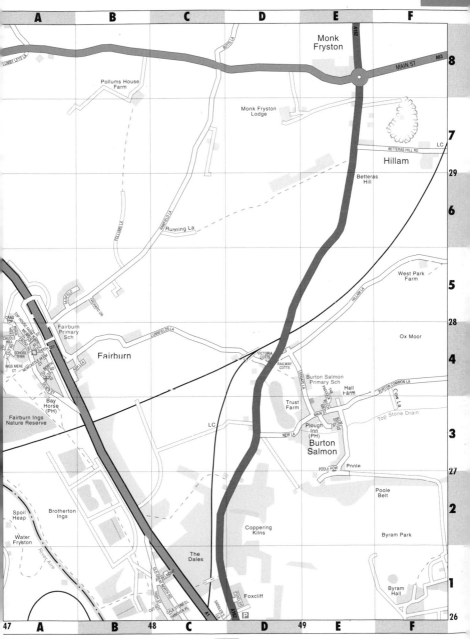

A B C D E F

Monk
Fryston

MAIN ST

LUMBY LEYS LA

Pollums House
Farm

Monk Fryston
Lodge

8

7

Hillam

BETTERAS HILL RD

LC

29

Betteras
Hill

Running La

6

West Park
Farm

5

28

Ox Moor

Fairburn
Primary
Sch

HILLAM LA

Fairburn

LUMBFIELDS LA

VICTORIA
COTTS

RAILWAY
COTTS

Burton Salmon
Primary Sch

4

BURTON COMMON LA

Hall
Farm

COW LA

Bay
Horse
(PH)

Trust
Farm

MAIN ST

Top Stone Drain

Fairburn Ings
Nature Reserve

LC

Plough
Inn
(PH)

NEW LA

TOP
STONE
CL

3

Burton
Salmon

Poole

27

POOLE ROW

Poole
Belt

Spoil
Heap

Brotherton
Ings

2

Water
Fryston

River Aire

Coppering
Kilns

Byram Park

The
Dales

1

Byram
Hall

Foxcliff

P

26

47 A B 48 C D 49 E F

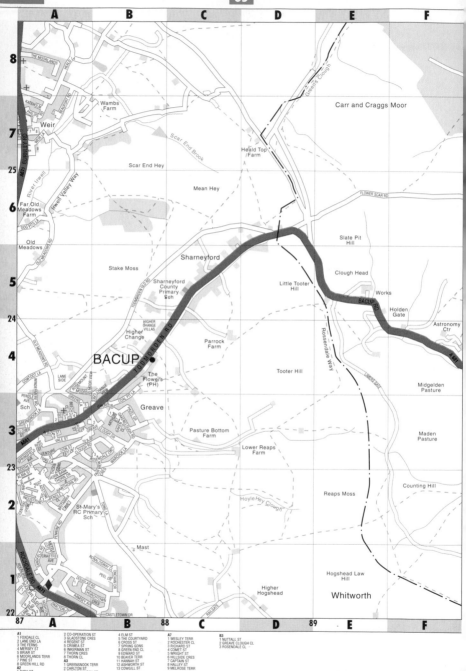

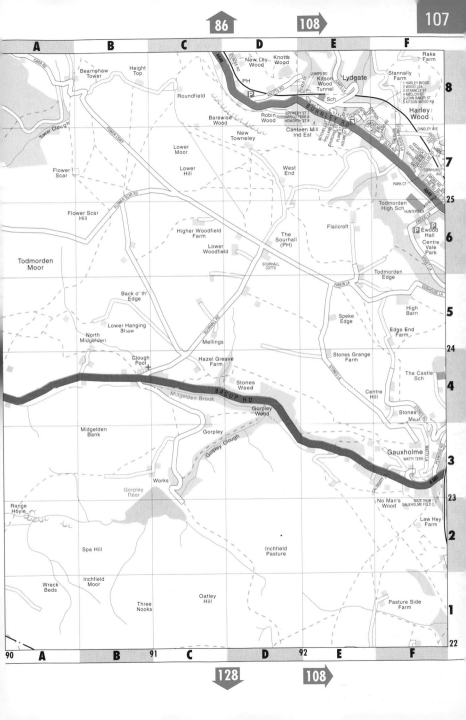

86 108

A B C D E F

Rake Farm

New Ley Wood Knotts Wood

Bearnshaw Tower

Height Top

Stannally Farm

1 HARLEY WOOD
2 WOOD LEA
3 STANMLEY ST
4 MELLOR ST
5 JOHN BAKER ST
6 KITSON WOOD RD

8

Roundfield

PH

Lydgate

Kitson Wood Tunnel

Sch

Harley Wood

CARR RD

Tower Clough

Barewise Wood

Robin Wood

New Towneley

Canteen Mill Ind Est

BURNLEY RD

DINELEY AVE

7

Lower Moor

COWHURST AVE

Flower Scar

Lower Hill

West End

PARK CT

25

Todmorden High Sch

HUNTERS LEA

Flower Scar Hill

Higher Woodfield Farm

Flailcroft

EWOOD LA

P Ewood Hall

Centre Vale Park

6

FLOWER SCAR RD

Lower Woodfield

The Sourhall (PH)

SOURHALL COTTS

Todmorden Moor

PARKIN LA

Todmorden Edge

DOGHOUSE LA

Back o' th Edge

Speke Edge

High Barn

Edge End Farm

5

Lower Hanging Shaw

SOURHALL RD

North Midgelden

Mellings

Stones Grange Farm

STONES LA

24

Clough Foot

Hazel Greave Farm

The Castle Sch

4

Stones Wood

BACUP RD

Centre Hill

Stones Meal

Midgelden Brook

Gorpley Wood

Midgelden Bank

Gorpley

WATTY LA

Gauxholme

WATTY TERR

3

Gorpley Clough

Works

Gorpley Moor

CALDERBROOK RD

PLYMOUTH ST

R DET

23

No Man's Wood

NAZE VIEW

GAUXHOLME FOLD 2

Range Hoyle

Law Hey Farm

2

Spa Hill

Inchfield Pasture

Wreck Beds

Inchfield Moor

Three Nooks

Oatley Hill

Pasture Side Farm

1

22

A B C D E F

90 91 92

128 108

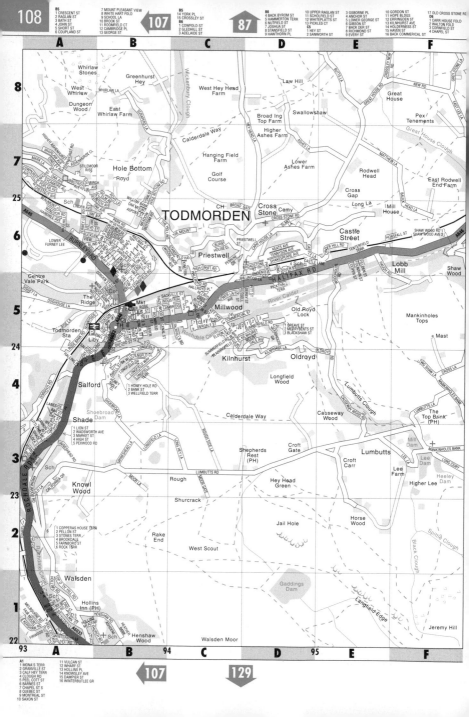

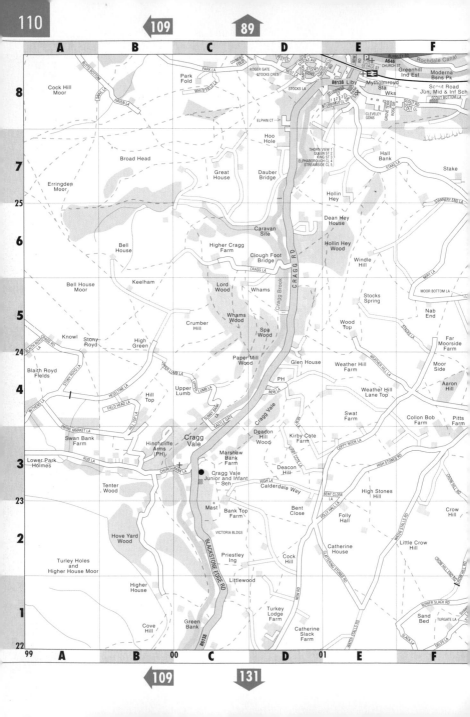

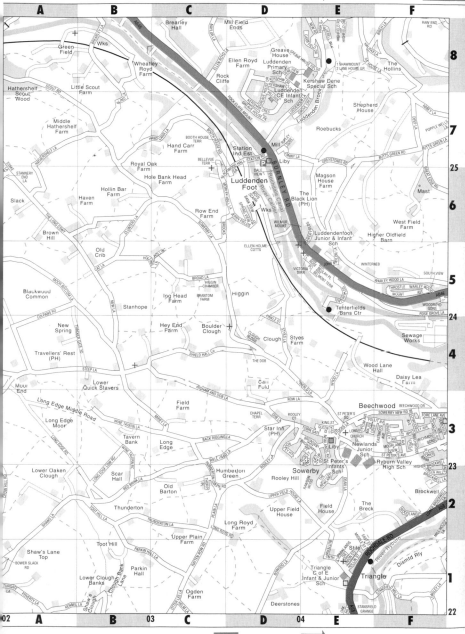

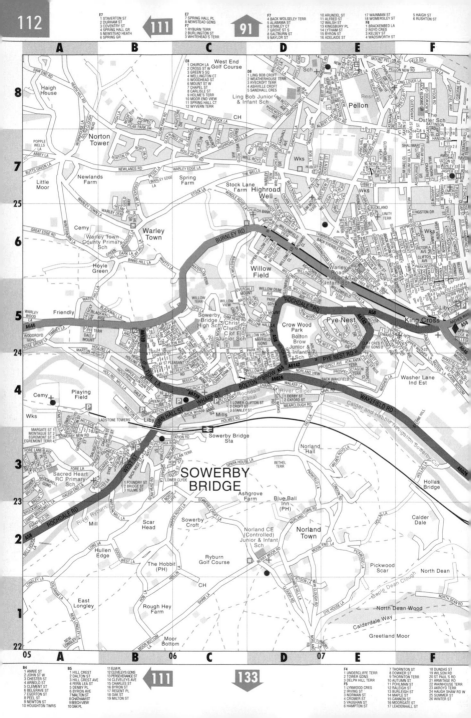

111
91

111
133

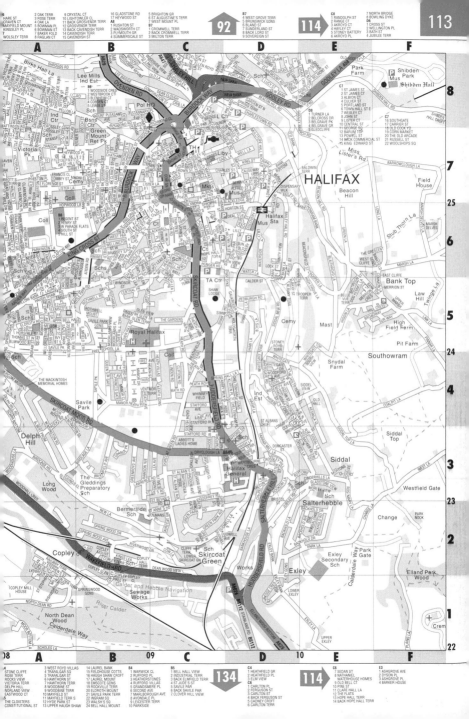

HALIFAX

94

116
1 WICKHAM ST
2 BRIGHTON TERR
3 WALKER ST
4 TABBS LA
5 NAYLOR S BLDGS
6 GREENFIELD DR

7 WHITECHAPEL RD
8 ACER WAY
9 COWDRAY DR
10 UPPER GREEN AVE
11 LOWER GREEN AVE
12 THE PADDOCK
13 INDUSTRIAL ST

115

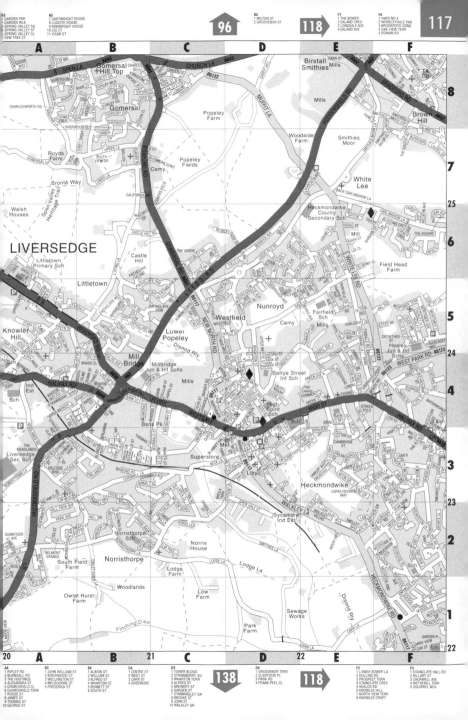

C5
1 CHURCHFIELD ST
2 HENRIETTA ST
3 BK HENRIETTA ST
4 BK PROVIDENCE ST
5 MARKET SQ
6 BRUNSWICK ST

7 HUME CREST
8 COBDEN CL
9 BAYLDONS PL
10 WARDS HILL CT

A   B   C   D   E   F

8

Wilton Park
Brookroyd
1 EALAND CRES
2 EALAND AVE

Bagshaw
Mus
Obsy

Howley Park
Quarry
Howley Hall
Golf Course

7

Batley
Grammar
Sch

Upper Batley

Old Hall
Mews
Batley Hall

25
Carlinghow
Princess Royal
Junior, Infant Sch
Carlinghow

Batley
High Sch

Howley Park
Farm

Batley
Bsns Ctr

6
Batley
Enterprise
Ctr
Victoria
Mills
Carlinghow
Mills
St Mary's
Sch

Lady Anne
Crossing

Lady Anne
Bsns Pk

Lower Soothill

Batley Parish
Sch

Cemy

Bank Foot

5

Library

Lydgate County
Primary Sch

24
HEALEY LA

BATLEY

Batley
Sta

GRANGE RD
Mills

4
Mount Pleasant

1 BONACCORD TERR
2 BONACCORD SQ
3 BACK PURWELL LA

Zakira
High Sch

Staincliffe
Junior Sch

3
Hyrstmount
Junior Sch

Mill Lane
Sch

Batley
Carr

Chapel Fold

Hyrstlands
Park

Warwick
Road Sch

23

Dewsbury
District

St Joseph's
Primary Sch

Hanging Heaton
C of E Sch

Hanging
Heaton Golf
Course

2

Birkdale
High Sch

Birkdale
High Sch

Westborough

Bywell C of E
Middle Sch

1

The
General

Crackenedge

Eastborough

CH

22
St John Fisher
RC High Sch

23   A   B   24   C   D   25   E   F

A1
1 SCHOOL CRES
2 BACK LEATHAM ST
3 GLADSTONE CT
4 HANOVER CT
5 FAIRFIELD CRES
6 FIR BANK
7 STAINCLIFFE CL

B2
1 TOP OF CARR
2 NORTH VIEW TERR
3 MITCHELL AVE
4 SOUTH VIEW TERR
5 MARLBRO TERR

C1
1 LOWER CROSS ST
2 UPPER CROSS ST
3 BRIGHT ST
4 SPINKWELL RD

D1
1 UPPER PEEL ST
2 DEWSBURY RING RD
3 ERNEST ST
4 BACK MARRIOT ST

D3
1 MOUNT AVE
2 BACK MOUNT AVE
3 CROSS RINK ST
4 RINK TERR
5 RINK PAR

E1
1 ALFRED ST
2 JOHN ST
3 WELL ST
4 HOLLINROYD RD
5 VICTORIA BLDGS
6 MOOR PARK CT

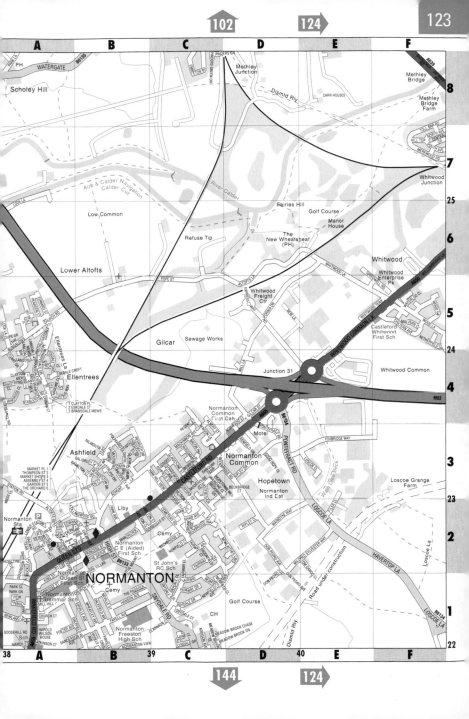

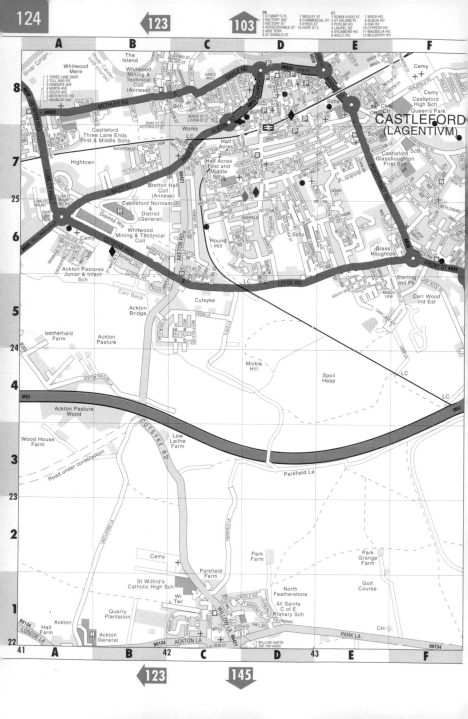

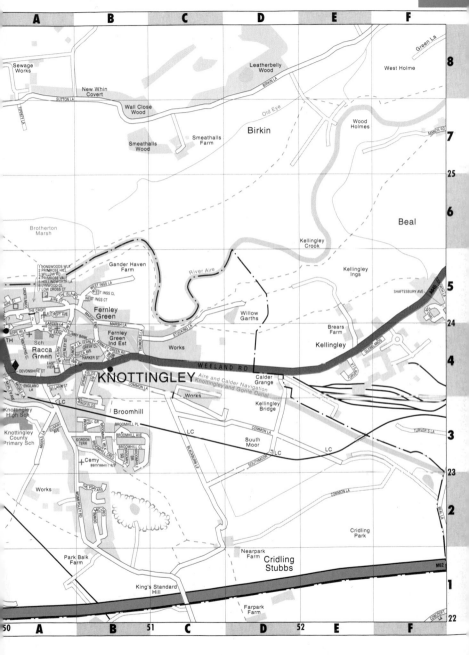

A B C D E F

8

New Whin
Covert

Sewage
Works

Leatherbelly
Wood

West Holme

Green La

SUTTON LA

Wall Close
Wood

Old Eye

BIRKIN LA

Wood
Holmes

7

Smeathalls
Wood

Smeathalls
Farm

Birkin

MANOR RD

TIPPITY LA

25

Brotherton
Marsh

Beal

6

Gander Haven
Farm

River Aire

Kellingley
Crook

Kellingley
Ings

1 LONGWOODS WLK
2 PRIMROSE HILL
3 WILLOW RD
4 PRIMROSE VALE
5 HOLLINGWORTH LA
6 LYNWOOD CL
7 LOW CROSS CT

WEST INGS LA

WEST INGS CL

WEST INGS CT

Willow
Garths

SHAFTESBURY AVE

A645

5

Fernley
Green

Fernley
Green Ind Est

Works

Brears
Farm

Kellingley

24

MARSH LA

THUNDER LA

STOCKING LA

Racca
Green

DEVONSHIRE CT

WEELAND RD

Calder
Grange

BYRAM INGS

4

KNOTTINGLEY

Aire and Calder Navigation
Knottingley and Goole Canal

Works

Kellingley
Bridge

TURVER'S LA

ENGLAND LA

COMMON LA

Kellingley
Bridge

TURVER'S LA

Broomhill

LC

South
Moor

COMMON LA

LC

3

Knottingley
High Sch

QUARRY AVE

Knottingley
County
Primary Sch

GORDON
TERR

BROOMHILL AVE

BROOMHILL CL

LC

BLACKSMITH LA

SOUTHMOOR

LC

COMMON LA

23

Cemy

Works

THE POPLARS

Cridling
Park

2

Park Balk
Farm

Nearpark
Farm

Cridling
Stubbs

COMMON LA

M62

B611

1

King's Standard
Hill

Farpark
Farm

CONDUIT LA

22

50 A B 51 C D 52 E F

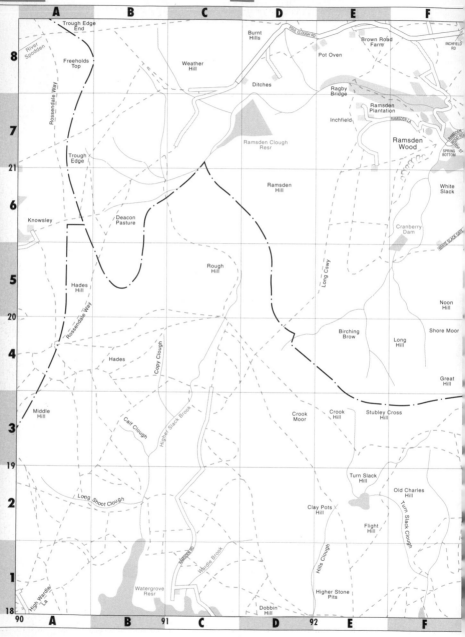

A   **B**   **C**   **D**   **E**   **F**

River Spodden

Trough Edge End

Freeholds Top

Rossendale Way

Burnt Hills

TOLL CLOUGH RD

Brown Road Farm

INCHFIELD RD

8

Weather Hill

Pot Oven

Ditches

Ragby Bridge

Ramsden Plantation

Inchfield

RAMSDEN LA

LUMBDEN WOOD RD

Ramsden Wood

SPRING BOTTOM

7

Trough Edge

21

Ramsden Clough Resr

Ramsden Hill

White Slack

6

Knowsley

Deacon Pasture

Cranberry Dam

WHITE SLACK GATE

Rough Hill

Long Causeway

5

Hades Hill

Rossendale Way

Noon Hill

20

Birching Brow

Shore Moor

Long Hill

4

Hades

Copy Clough

Higher Slack Brook

Great Hill

Middle Hill

Cail Clough

Crook Moor

Crook Hill

Stubley Cross Hill

3

19

Turn Slack Hill

Old Charles Hill

Long Shoot Clough

2

Clay Pots Hill

Flight Hill

Turn Slack Clough

RAMSDEN RD

Whirle Brook

Hills Clough

1

High Wardle La

Watergrove Resr

Higher Stone Pits

18

Dobbin Hill

90   **A**   **B**   **91**   **C**   **D**   **92**   **E**   **F**

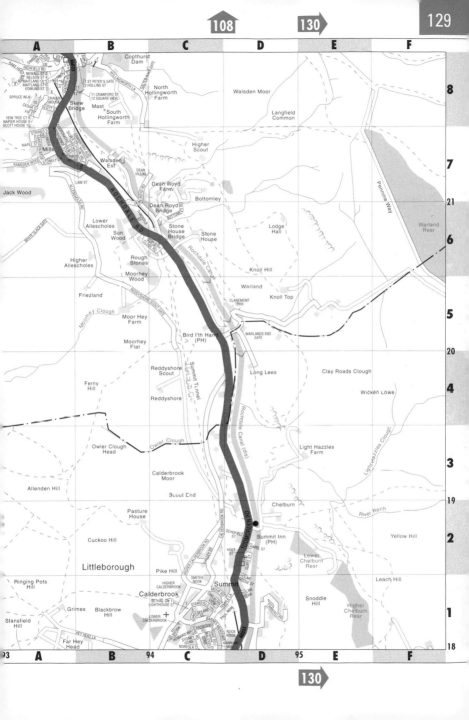

129
109

| A | B | C | D | E | F |

8

Warland Drain

Warland Drain

Bird Nest Hill

Turley Holes and Higher House Moor

7

Blake Moor

21

Little Dove Lowe

White Holme Drain

6

White Holme Moss

Turvin Clough

Round Hills

Light Hazzles Resr

5

Little Moor Clough

B6138

Saw Gill Hollow

BLACKSTONE EDGE RD

20

White Holme Resr

Little Moor

Round Hill

4

Captains Mark Hill

Chelburn Moor

Pennine Way

Light Hazzles Edge

Farther Hill

Soyland Moor

Knave Holes Hollow

3

Toad La

Middle Hill

Cold Laughton Drain

Knave Holes Hill

19

Utley Edge

Byron Edge

Nigher Hill

TURVIN RD

2

Head Drain

Black Castle Drain

Rush Bed Hill

Cow Head

A58

1

Blackstone Edge Resr

Black Castle Hill

ROCHDALE RD

Fairy Hill

B6138

HALIFAX RD

A58

Slate Pit Hill

18

| 96 | A | B | 97 | C | D | 98 | E | F |

129
148

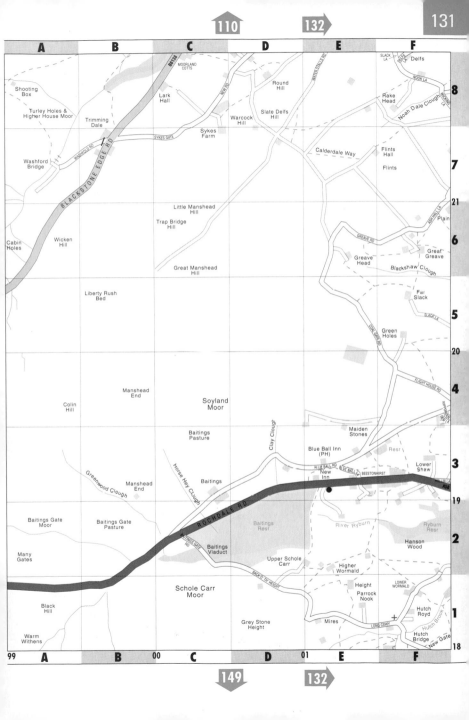

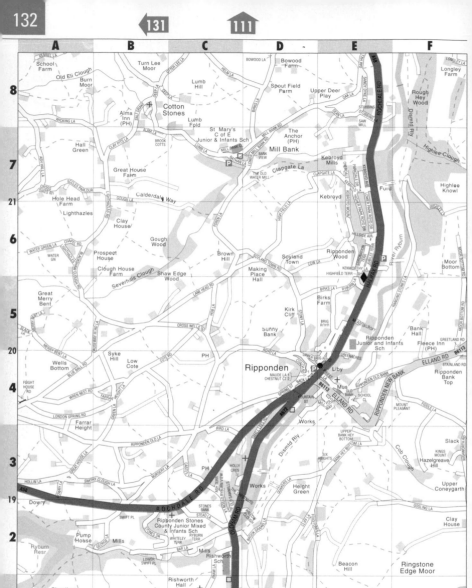

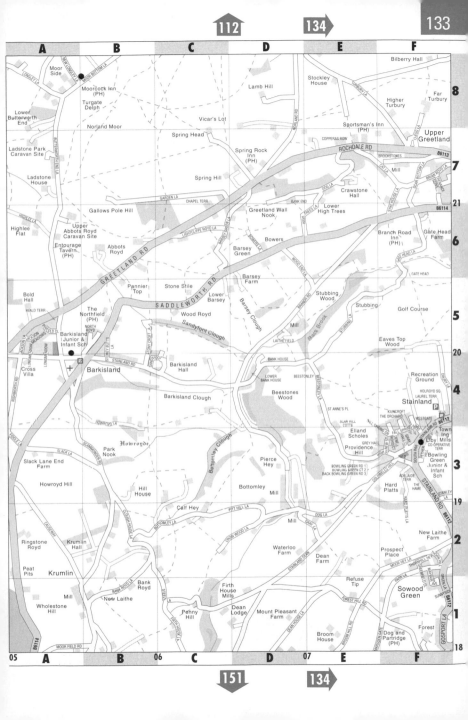

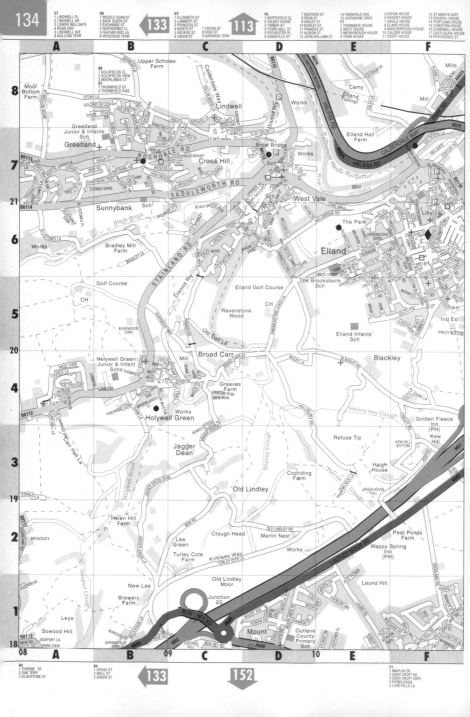

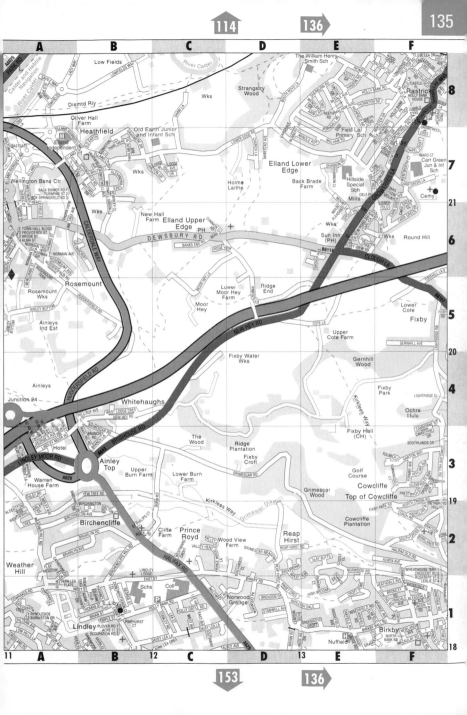

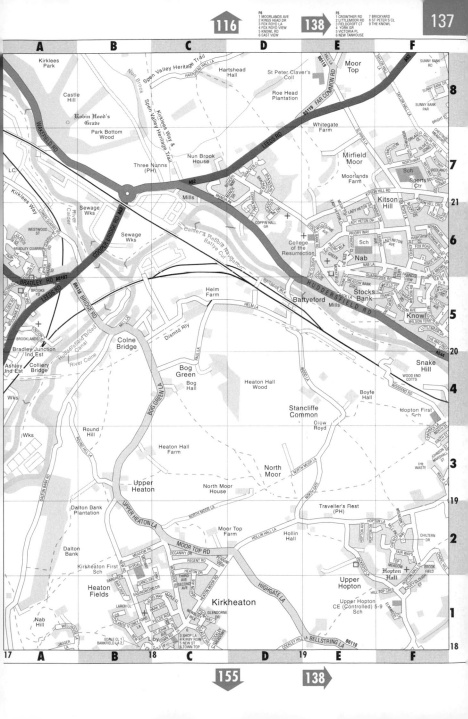

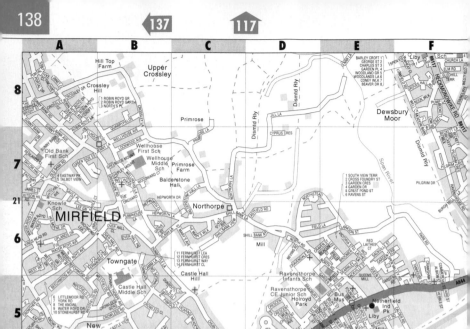

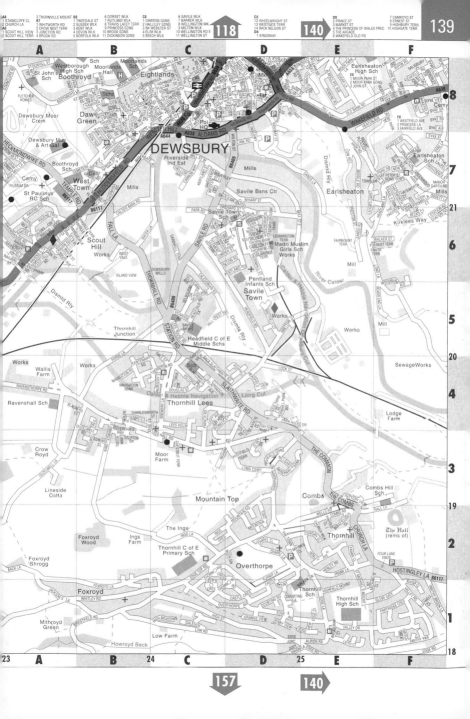

OSSETT

Chickenley

Ossett Street Side

Chickenley Heath Farm

Heath House

Lodge Hill Farm

Lodge Hill

Owlers Farm

Flushdyke

WAKEFIELD RD

Cemy

Mills

Schs

Paleside

Sandbeds Trad Est

Ashley Ind Est

Town End

Longlands Trad Est

Recn Gd

Holy Trinity C of E Sch

Works

The Bungalows

Mills

Sch

Golf Course

Westfield Cres

Liby

Dismtd Rly

Mitchell Laithes Farm

Works

Runtlings

Sewage Works

Kirklees Way

Granary Farm

Dimple Well Infant Sch

Drill Hall

Fairfield Terr

Schs

South Ossett Infant Sch

The Rookery Farm

Healey Old Mills

River Calder

St Ignatius Jun & Inf Sch

Mills

South Ossett

Ossett Sch

Sowood Farm

Works

Healey

Netherend Brow

Storrs Hill

Rock House

Clifton Infant Sch

Dismtd Rly

Long Cut

Calder & Hebble Navigation

Horbury Cut

Mills

Dismtd Rly

Healey Mills Sidings

Manorfield Dr

WESTFIELD RD

HOSTINGLEY LA

Hostingley Farm

Smithy Brook

Smithy Brook Farm

Works

Quarry Hill Ind Est

Horbury Bridge

Parklands Cres

QUARRY HILL

BRIDGE RD

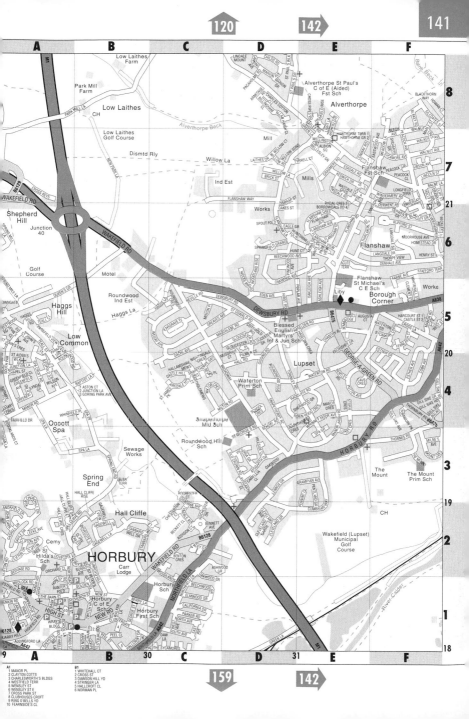

A1
1 MANOR PL
2 CLAYTON COTTS
3 CHARLESWORTH'S BLDGS
4 WESTFIELD TERR
5 WENSLEY ST
6 WENSLEY ST E
7 CROSS PARK ST
8 CLUBHOUSES CROFT
9 RING O'BELLS YD
10 FEARNSIDE'S CL

B1
1 WHITEHALL CT
2 CROSS ST
3 DAWSON HILL YD
4 STRINGER LA
5 HALLCROFT CL
6 NORMAN PL

C6
1 GILL ST
2 BARSTOW SQ
3 TAMMY HALL ST
4 CHANCERY LA
5 GEORGE & CROWN YD
6 SILVER ST

C6
7 RADCLIFFE PL
8 TALBOT AND FALCON YD
9 SMALLPAGE YD
10 WESTMORLAND HOUSE
11 TEALL ST
12 THE SPRINGS

C6
13 MARYGATE
14 BREAD ST
15 CROSS SQ
16 NORTHGATE
17 SAW YD
18 WHEATER HOUSE

C6
19 FIRTH HOUSE
20 CARR HOUSE
21 CATHEDRAL WLK
22 WARREN HOUSE
23 TUDOR HOUSE
24 GREENWOOD HOUSE

C7
1 CLARENDON CT
2 CLARENDON ST
3 RICHARD ST
4 INDUSTRIAL ST
5 BACK HAMBLETON ST
6 HAMBLETON ST

D6
1 VICARAGE ST S
2 LOWER WARRENGATE
3 TRINITY HOUSE
4 MANOR HOUSE
5 HARDY CROFT
6 INGWELL CT

D6
7 CRYSTAL PL
8 BRUNSWICK GR
9 BRUNSWICK STREET BGLW
10 JOHNSTON ST
11 PINCHEON ST
12 UPPER WARRENGATE

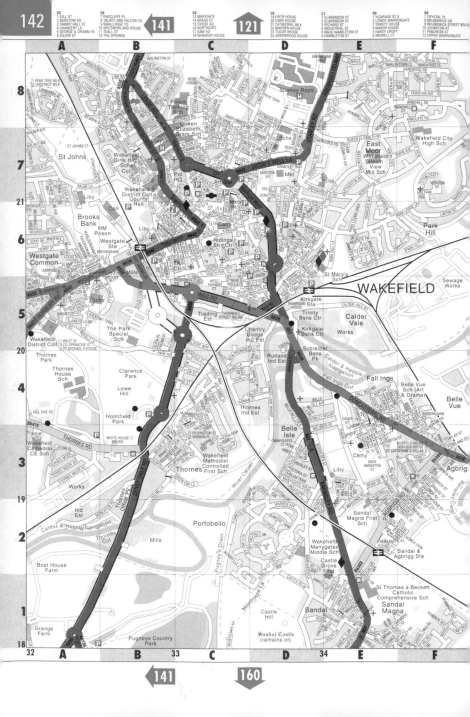

WAKEFIELD

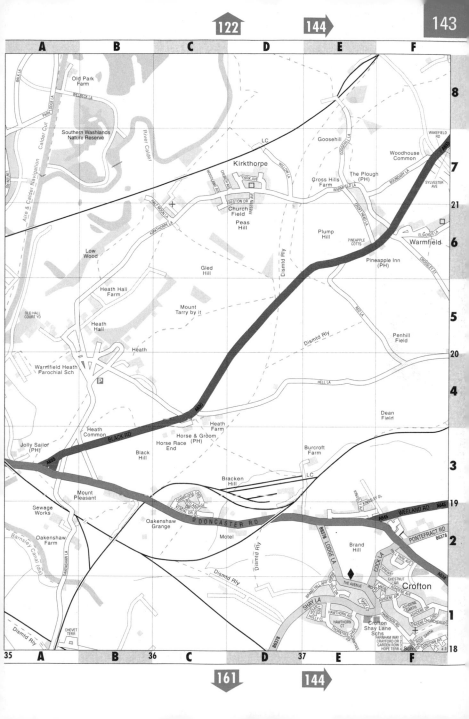

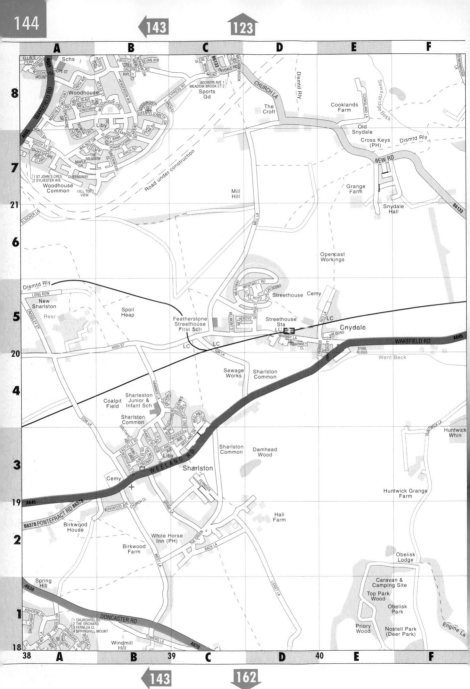

143
123

A **B** **C** **D** **E** **F**

Ellin's Terr
Schs
Pope St
Woodhouse
Bevan Ave
Dalefield Rd
Ripley St
Addison Ave 1
Meadow Brook Ct 2
Sports Gd

8

Church La
Dismtd Rly

The Croft
Cooklands Farm
Old Snydale
Cross Keys (PH)
Dismtd Rly

7

Liby
The Meadow
Queensway

New Rd

Woodhouse Common
1 St John's Cres
2 Sylvester Ave
Hill Top View

Grange Farm

21

Mill Hill

Snydale Hall

6

Opencast Workings

Dismtd Rly
Long Row

New Sharlston

Resr

Spoil Heap

Went Well Rd
Crescent
Royd
Streethouse
Cemy

5

High St

Featherstone Streethouse First Sch

Streethouse Sta
LC

Snydale
LC

Wakefield Rd
A645

LC
Side La
LC
Whinby La
Whinney Cl

Went Gdns
Dyas Bloggs
Went Beck

20

Corn La
Coalpit Field

Sewage Works
Sharlston Common

4

Sharlston Junior & Infant Sch
Sharlston Common

Huntwick Whin

Weeland Rd
Liby
Sharlston
Sharlston Common
Damhead Wood

3

Huntwick Grange Farm

Cemy

Pontefract Rd B6378
B6378
A645

Birkwood Ave
Church Cl

19

Hall Farm

Birkwood House
Birkwood Farm

White Horse Inn (PH)
Back La

2

Obelisk Lodge

Caravan & Camping Site
Top Park Wood
Obelisk Park

Spring Hill
A638

1 Churchfield
2 The Orchard
3 Fernlea Cl
4 Springhill Mount

Doncaster Rd
A638

Windmill Hill

Priory Wood
Nostell Park (Deer Park)
Obelisk Park
Engine La

1

18

38 **A** **B** 39 **C** **D** 40 **E** **F**

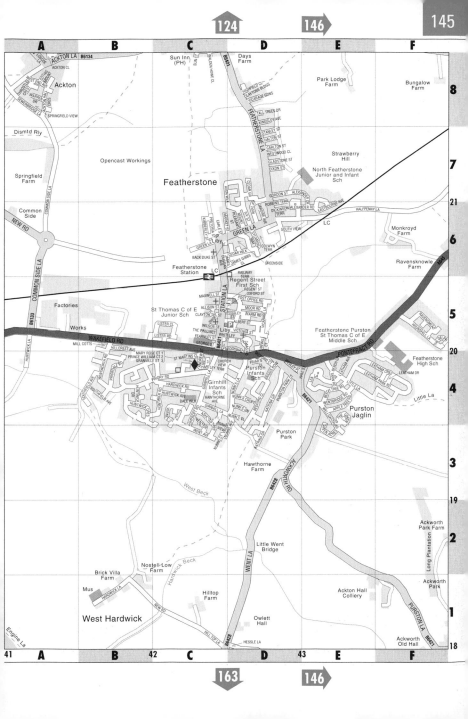

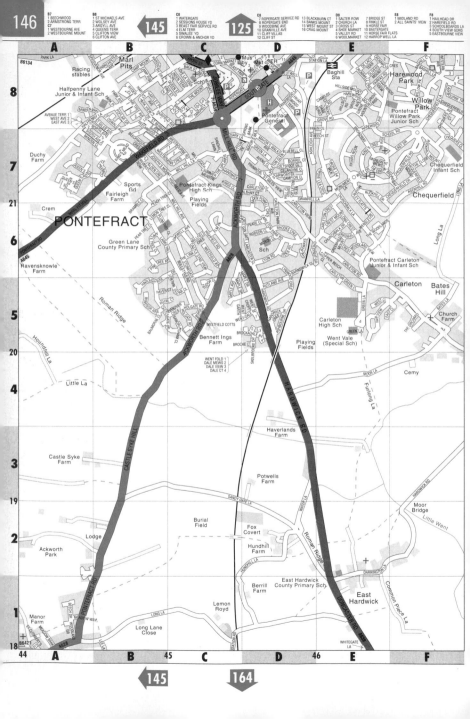

130

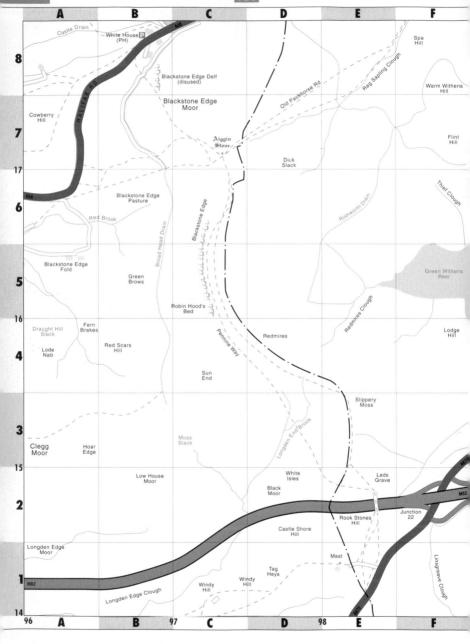

A B C D E F

8

Castle Drain

White House
(PH) P

A58

Blackstone Edge Delf
(disused)

Spa
Hill

Old Packhorse Rd

Rag Sapling Clough

Warm Withens
Hill

Blackstone Edge
Moor

HALIFAX RD

7

Cowberry
Hill

Flint
Hill

17

Aiggin
Stone

Dick
Slack

A58

6

Blackstone Edge
Pasture

Blackstone Edge

Thief
Clough

Red Brook

Broad Head Drain

Rishworth Drain

5

Blackstone Edge
Fold

Green
Brows

Green Withens
Resr

16

Draught Hill
Slack

Fern
Brakes

Robin Hood's
Bed

Redmires Clough

Lodge
Hill

4

Lode
Nab

Red Scars
Hill

Pennine Way

Redmires

Sun
End

3

Clegg
Moor

Hoar
Edge

Moss
Slack

Longden End Brook

Slippery
Moss

15

Low House
Moor

White
Isles

Lads
Grave

M62

A672

2

Black
Moor

Rook Stones
Hill

Junction
22

Longden Edge
Moor

Castle Shore
Hill

Mast

Linsgreave Clough

1

M62

Tag
Heys

Windy
Hill

Windy
Hill

Longden Edge Clough

A672

14

96 A B 97 C D 98 E F

Grey Stone Edge

Lench House

Flat Hill

Black Hill Clough

LONG CSWY

8

Dry Moss

Blackwood

Lower End

Nook End

Cat Moss

White Isles

Blackwood Common

7

Cat Stones

Old Scar

Blackwood Edge

Rishworth Moor

Dog Hill

Sandal Scar

White Hill

17

Green Withens Edge

Cut Stones Hill

Whinny Nick

Blackwood Edge Rd.

Booth Moor

Pike End Gate

6

Green Withens Moss

Joiner Stones Hill

Hasket Hill

Sam Hill

Stoney Lane Head

Green Withens Clough

Furrow Brink

5

Little Wolden Edge

Castle Dean

Booth Dean

A672

Wolden Edge Clough

Oxygrains

Resrs

Humphrey Shore Rocks

16

Lodge Clough

Oxygrains Old Bridge

Spa Clough

Small Clough

Burn Clough Grains

M62

4

Great Wolden Edge

Broad Shaw Clough

Spa Clough Resr

Hunger Hill

Long Clough

3

Linsgreave Brink

Burn Clough

Burn Moss

15

Moss Moor

Broad Shaw Flat

Small Clough

Lodge Hole

2

Broad Shaw Graining

Burn Clough Flat

Linsgreave

Great Groove Holes

Middle Scars

1

Way Stone Edge

Way Pit Holes

Moss Moor Edge

Way Stone

14

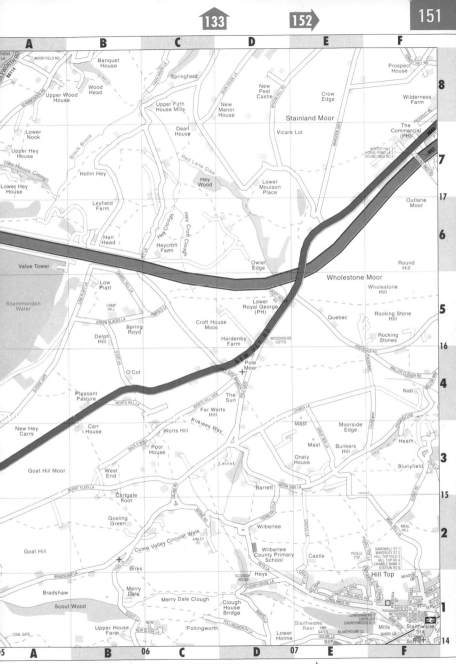

133
152

A　　B　　C　　D　　E　　F

8

WITHENS LA
MOOR FIELD RD
Banquet House
Springfield
New Peel Castle
Crow Edge
Prospect House
Wilderness Farm

B611
SCAMMONDEN RD
Upper Wood House
Wood Head
Upper Firth House Mills
New Manor House
Stainland Moor
Vicars Lot
The Commercial (PH)

7

Lower Nook
Dean House
WINTER HILL LA
HORSE POND LA 2
ROUND INGS RD 3
M62

Upper Hey House
Black Brook
Hollin Hey
Red Lane Dike
Hey Wood
Lower Moulson Place
Outlane Moor

17

Hey House Clough
Lower Hey House
Leyfield Farm
Hey Clough
Hey Croft Clough

6

Han Head
Heycroft Farm
Owlet Edge
Wholestone Moor
Round Hill

Valve Tower
Low Platt
CHAPEL HILL LA
Lower Royal George (PH)
Wholestone Hill

5

Scammonden Water
CAMP HILL
PINFOLD LA
Croft House Moor
Quebec
Rocking Stone Hill

GREEN SLACKS LA
Spring Royd
Hardenby Farm
WOODHOUSE COTTS
ROCHDALE RD
Rocking Stones

16

Delph Hill
NEW HEY RD
POLE GATE BRIDGE LA
Pole Moor
WALLER CLOUGH RD

O'Cot
MELFOR RD

4

Pleasant Pasture
WORTS HILL LA
WORTS HILL SIDE
The Sun
Far Worts Hill
CRIMEA LA
Nab

SLEDGE GATE
New Hey Carrs
BACK O'TH'L
Carr House
Worts Hill
KAYLEES WAY
Mast
GREAT BELL LA
Moorside Edge
Heath

Poor House
Onely House
Mast
Bunkers Hill
Stonyfield

3

Goat Hill Moor
LAUND RD
West End
J AINT
MOOR SIDE LA

BURNT PLATS LA
Cartgate Foot
Barrett

15

Gosling Green
Wilberlee
CASTLE LA

Goat Hill
Coine Valley Circular Walk
AINLEY PL
Wilberlee County Primary School
Castle
PICKLE TOP
SANDWELL ST 1
WAVERLEY ST 2
HILL TOP FOLD 3
HILL TOP RD 4
CRIMBLE BANK 5
STATION RD 6

2

Birks
Heys
Hill Top
MEADOW

BRADSHAW LA
SCOUT LA
Merry Dale
Merry Dale Clough
CLOUGH HOUSE LA
LONGROYD CRES
PRETORIA RD

Bradshaw
Scout Wood
Clough House Bridge
LONGLANDS RD
MILNS LA

1

Coal Gate
Upper House Farm
NEW CL
NEW CLOSE LA
FOLLINGWORTH LA
Follingworth
Slaithwaite Resr
Lower Holme
LEWISHAM RD 1
CHURCHWOOD CL 2
Slaithwaite Sta

14

169
152

05　　A　　B　　06　　C　　D　　07　　E　　F

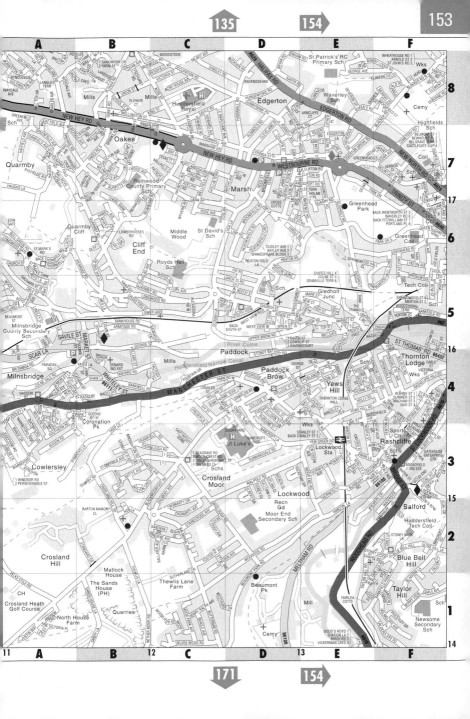

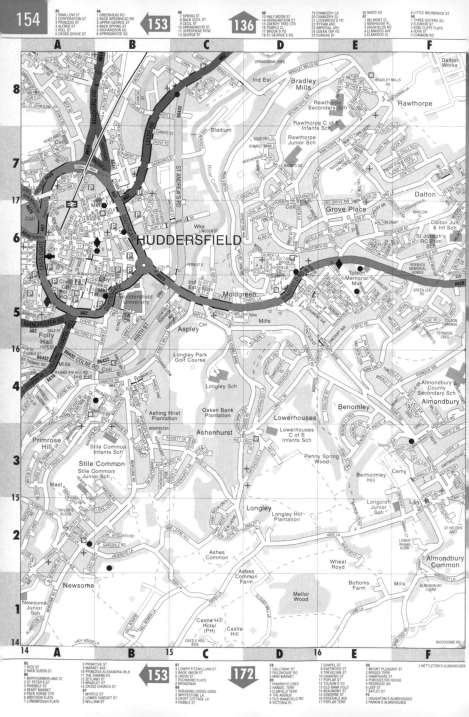

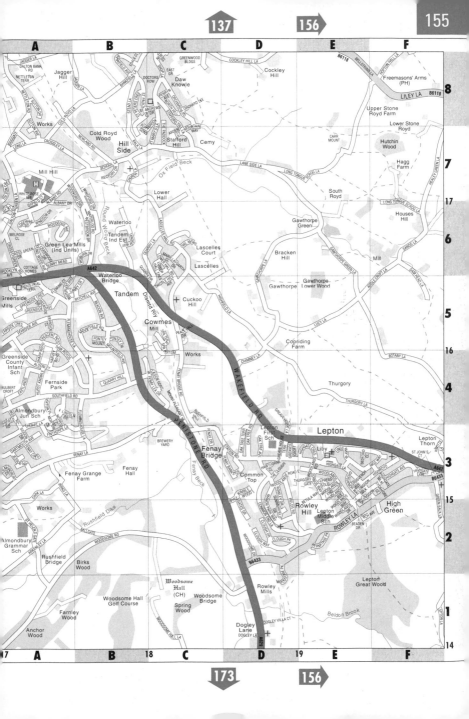

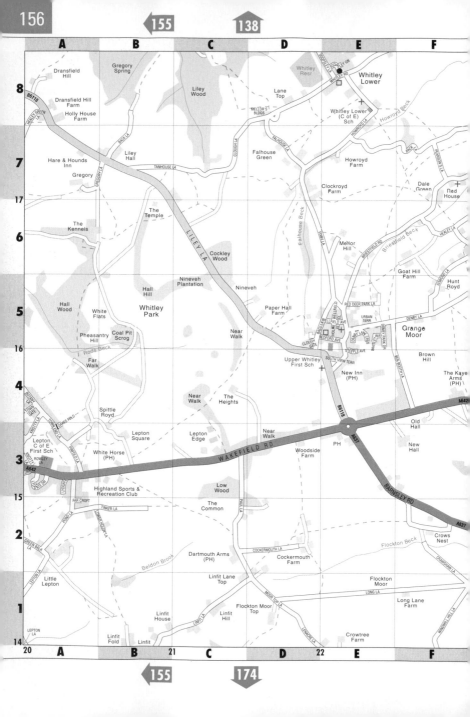

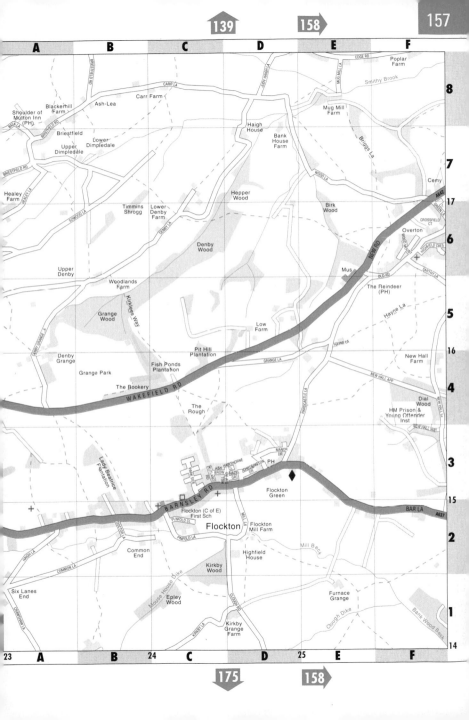

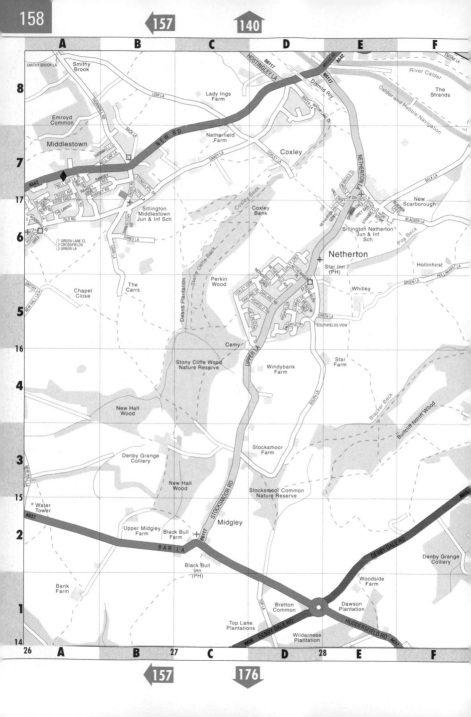

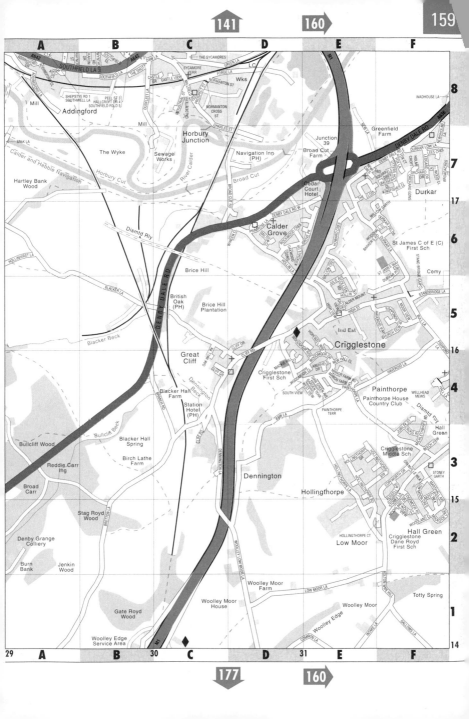

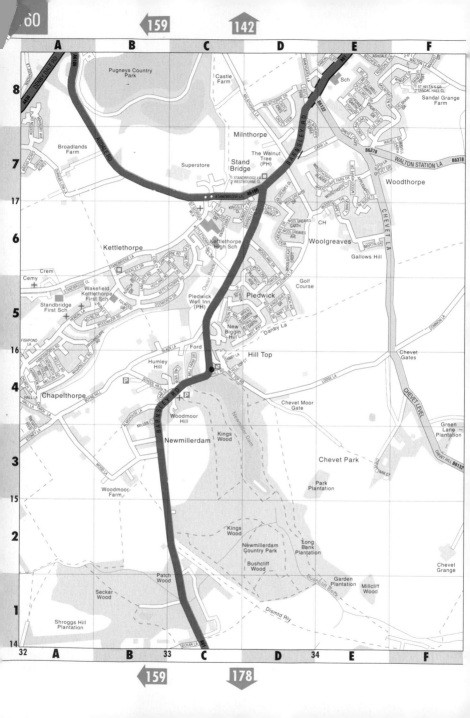

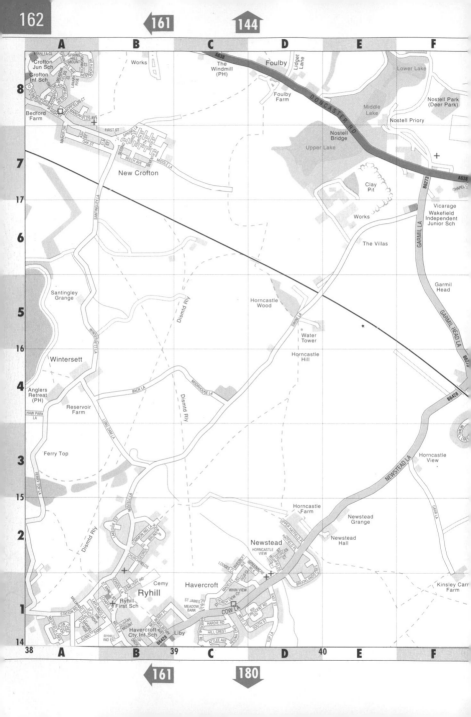

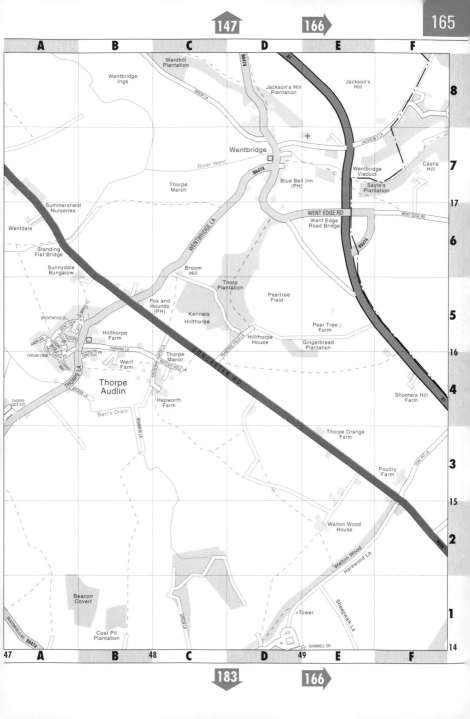

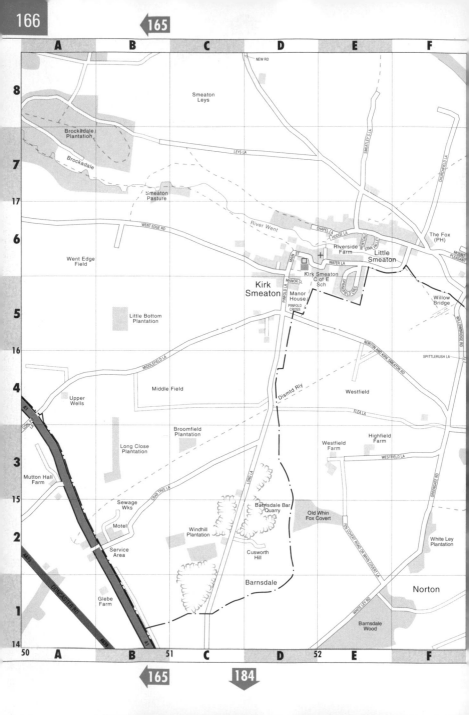

New Rd

Smeaton
Leys

Brockadale
Plantation

Leys La

Brockadale

Smeaton
Pasture

River Went

Went Edge Rd

Went Edge
Field

Chapel La
Hodge La
Westfield La
Stan Pit
The Fox
(PH)
Mount
Pleasant
Riverside
Farm
Little
Smeaton
Main St
Water La
Kirk Smeaton
C of E
Sch
Kirk
Smeaton
Manor Cl
Manor
House
Pinfold
Cross
Willow
Bridge

Little Bottom
Plantation

Pinfold La

Norton And Kirk Smeaton Rd
Spittlerush La

Middlefield La

Middle Field

Dismtd Rly

Westfield

Flea La

Upper
Wells

A1(M)
Gorse La

Broomfield
Plantation

Long Close
Plantation

Westfield
Farm

Highfield
Farm

Westfield La

Mutton Hall
Farm

Crab Tree La

Doncaster Rd

Sewage
Wks

Long La

Barnsdale Bar
Quarry

Old Whin
Fox Covert

Fox Covert Road Or White Covert

White Ley
Plantation

Motel

Windhill
Plantation

Cusworth
Hill

Service
Area

Barnsdale

Norton

A1(M)
A638

White Ley Rd

Glebe
Farm

Barnsdale
Wood

8

7

17

6

5

16

4

15

3

2

14

1

50

51

52

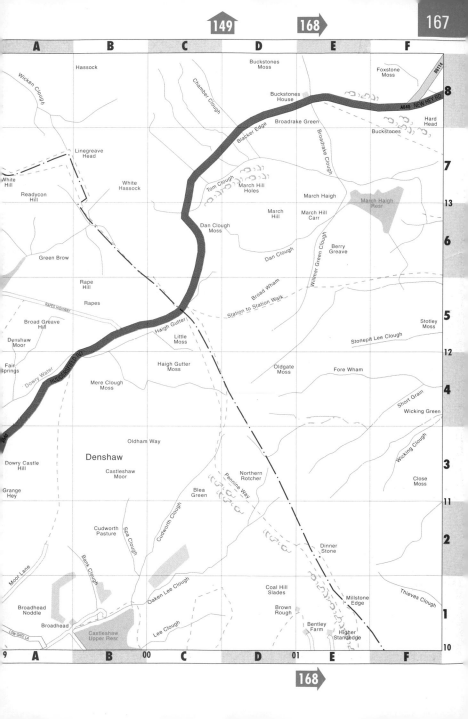

A | B | C | D | E | F

8

Hassock

Wicken Clough

Buckstones Moss

Foxstone Moss

Chamber Clough

Buckstones House

A640 NEW HEY RD

M6141

Broadrake Green

Blacker Edge

Hard Head

Linegreave Head

Buckstones

White Hill

White Hassock

7

Readycon Hill

Tom Clough

March Hill Holes

March Haigh

March Haigh Resr

13

Dan Clough Moss

March Hill

March Hill Carr

6

Green Brow

Dan Clough

Willmer Green Clough

Broadrake Clough

Berry Greave

Rape Hill

Broad Wham

Rapes

RAPES HIGHWAY

Station to Station Walk

5

Broad Greave Hill

Haigh Gutter

Little Moss

Stotley Moss

Denshaw Moor

Stonepit Lee Clough

12

Fair springs

Dowry Water

HUDDERSFIELD RD

Haigh Gutter Moss

Oldgate Moss

Fore Wham

4

Mere Clough Moss

Short Grain

Wicking Green

A640

Oldham Way

Wicking Clough

3

Denshaw

Dowry Castle Hill

Castleshaw Moor

Blea Green

Northern Rotcher

Pennine Way

Close Moss

11

Grange Hey

Cudworth Pasture

Spa Clough

Cudworth Clough

2

Moor Lane

Bank Clough

Dinner Stone

Thieves Clough

Oaken Lee Clough

Coal Hill Slades

Broadhead Noddle

Brown Rough

Millstone Edge

1

Broadhead

LOW GATE LA

Castleshaw Upper Resr

Lee Clough

Bentley Farm

Higher Standedge

10

9 | A | B | 00 | C | D | 01 | E | F

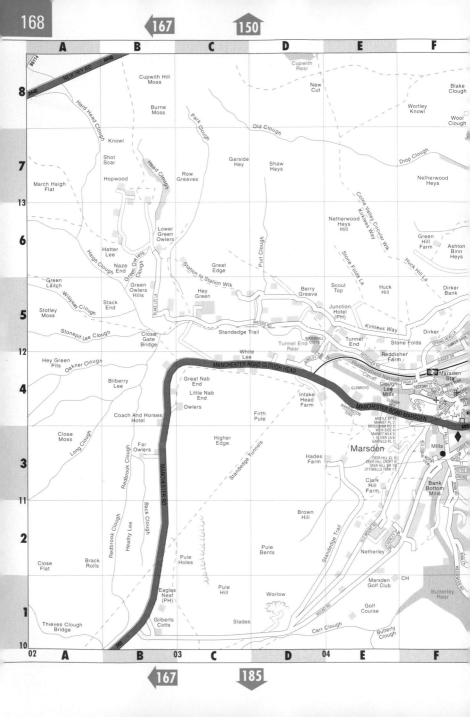

167
150

B6114
NEW HEY RD
A640
A640
Hard Head Clough

Cupwith Hill Moss

Cupwith Resr

New Cut

Blake Clough

Wortley Knowl

Wool Clough

8

Burne Moss

Park Clough

Old Clough

Knowl

Shot Scar

Head Clough

Garside Hey

Shaw Heys

Drop Clough

Netherwood Heys

7

March Haigh Flat

Hopwood

Row Greaves

13

Lower Green Owlers

Colne Valley Circular Wlk

Kirklees Way

Netherwood Heys Hill

Green Hill Farm

Ashton Binn Heys

6

Hatter Lee

Naze End

Green Owlers Clough

Haigh Clough

Great Edge

Purll Clough

Stone Folds La

Huck Hill La

Huck Hill

Dirker Bank

Green Laitch

Willykay Clough

Green Owlers Hills

Station to Station Wlk

BLAKE LEY LA

Hey Green

Berry Greave

Scout Top

Junction Hotel (PH)

Dirker

5

Stotley Moss

Stack End

Stonepit Lee Clough

Close Gate Bridge

WATERS RD

Standedge Trail

WATERFALL COTTS

Tunnel End Resr

Tunnel End

Kirklees Way

Stone Folds

SPRING HEAD LA

DINKER DR

12

Hey Green Pits

Oakner Clough

White Lee

MANCHESTER ROAD CLOUGH HEAD

AINLEY LA

Huddersfield Narrow Canal

REDDISHER RD

Reddisher Farm

HIGH LEA

DURKER DR

Marsden Sta

4

Bilberry Lee

Great Nab End

Little Nab End

Owlers

Intake Head Farm

WARRINGTON TERR

MANCHESTER ROAD MARSDEN N

GLENROYD

Clough Lee Mills

CLOUGH

RECTORY CL

GREEN

Coach And Horses Hotel

Close Moss

Long Clough

Far Owlers

Redbrook Clough

MANCHESTER RD

Higher Edge

Firth Pule

Standedge Tunnels

Hades Farm

ARGYLE ST 1
MARKET PL 2
BROUGHAM RD 3
WEIR SIDE 4
MARKET WLK 5
OLIVER LA 6
GARFIELD PL 7

Marsden

Mills

CARRS

SPRING

3

DEER HILL CL 8
DEER HILL CROFT 9
DEER HILL DR 10
OTTIWELLS TERR 11

Clark Hill Farm

Bank Bottom Mills

ROYDS

11

Back Clough

Heathy Lee

Redbrook Clough

Brown Hill

Standedge Trail

OLD MOUNT RD

Netherley

PICKLE LA

Marsden Golf Club

CH

BINNS

WESSENDEN HEAD RD

2

Brack Rolls

Pule Holes

Pule Bents

Worlow

MOUNT RD

Golf Course

Butterley Resr

1

Close Flat

Eagles Nest (PH)

Pule Hill

Slades

Carr Clough

Butterly Clough

Thieves Clough Bridge

Gilberts Cotts

A62

10

167
185

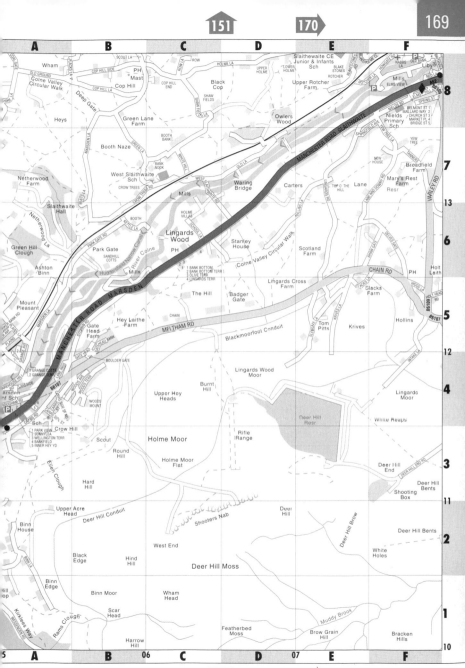

169
152

Liby Mills
River Colne
Kitchen Clough
Colne Valley Circular Walk
Heywoods Farm
Green Head
High House
Black Rock Mills
Lower Clough
Crosland Heath Golf Course
Height
Upper Clough
Bate's Square
Winter Hill
Jerusalem Farm
Lower Hey Farm
Bradley Brook
Bethany Farm
Blackmoorfoot
Bulls Head (PH)
Jubilee Quarries (dis)
Hey
Blackmoorfoot Resr
Holt Head
Green Gate
Black Moor
Cottage Home Farm
Edge Moor
Moortop Farm
Meltham Edge
Cop End Farm
Orange Wood
Will's O'Nat's (PH)
Helme
Laund Farm
Meltham Cop
Far Fields
Queen Mary's Farm
Laund
Helme CE (Aided) Junior & Infant Sch
Blackmoorfoot Conduit
Helme Hall
Hall Heys Wood
Upper Hey Farm
Upper Hey
Lower Hey Farm
Meltham Grange Farm
Travellers' Rest (PH)
Hassocks Rd
Meltham
Meltham Primary Sch
Dismtd Rly
Catchwater Drain
Deer Hill Bents
Britain
Town Gate
Meltham Hall
New Bridge
Albion Mills
Golcar Brow
Meltham Mills Ind Est
Mill
Brow Grains Dike
Hotel
Halfroods Farm
Legards Slack
Oldfield Hill
Thick Hollins
Calmlands
Royd Edge Sch
SLAITHWAITE RD
HUDDERSFIELD RD
HOLMFIRTH RD
B6107
B6108
B6109
A62
A B C D E F
08 09 10

169
187

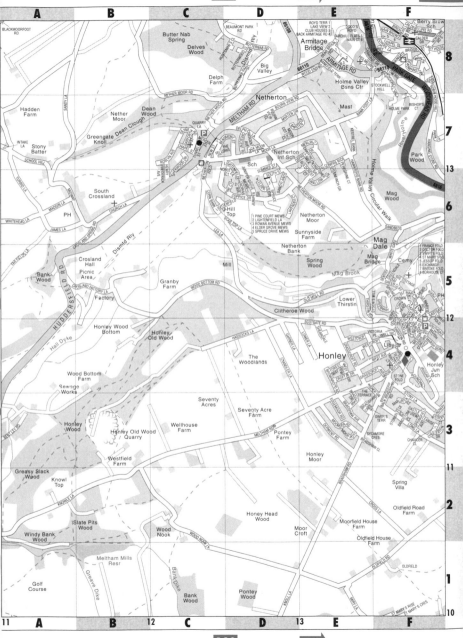

A B C D E F

8

7

13

6

5

12

4

11

3

2

1

10

BLACKMOORFOOT RD

Butter Nab Spring

Delves Wood

BEAUMONT PARK RD

ROYD TERR 1
LAKE VIEW 2
CLUB HOUSES 3
BACK ARMITAGE RD 4

Berry Brow Sch

FAREHILL FLATS 5
WAIN CT 6

Armitage Bridge

ARMITAGE RD

CALDER DR

LAST HOLME LA

Big Valley

Delph Farm

NETHER MOOR RD

MELTHAM RD

Netherton

Holme Valley Bsns Ctr

Mast

Holme Valley Circular Walk

Park Wood

River Holme

Hadden Farm

Nether Moor

Dean Wood

Greengate Dean Clough

QUARRY LA

BOURN VIEW RD

Netherton Int Sch

KESTREL BANK

STOCKWELL HILL

BISHOP'S CT

INTAKE LA

Stony Batter

SCHOOL HILL

SANDY LA

South Crossland

Knoll

Sch

SUMMER ST

Netherton Moor

Mag Wood

WHITEHEAD LA

MAGUM LA

CHURCH LA

JAMES LA

PH

Hill Top

1 PINE COURT MEWS
2 LIGHTENFIELD LA
3 ROWAN AVENUE MEWS
4 ELDER GROVE MEWS
5 SPRUCE DRIVE MEWS

Netherton Moor

Sunnyside Farm

Mag Dale

1 FRANCE FOLD
2 DOCTOR FOLD
3 SWIFTS FOLD
4 ST MARY'S FOLD
5 JESSOP FOLD
6 EXCHANGE
7 BROOKE FOLD
8 BURHOUSE CT

Crosland Hall Picnic Area

Dismtd Rly

HUDDERSFIELD RD

Netherton Bank

Spring Wood

Mag Brook

Mag Bridge

Cemy

HALL DYKE

Bank Wood

Factory

WOODS MILL FACTORY LA

Granby Farm

WOOD BOTTOM RD

Mill

Lower Thirstin

Sch

PH

Honley Wood Bottom

Honley Old Wood

Clitheroe Wood

HASSOCKS LA

SCOTGATE RD

Honley

Liby

Honley Jun Sch

Wood Bottom Farm

The Woodlands

MELTHAM ROW

CHANGE LA

LONG LA

STONE FOLD

Sewage Works

Honley Wood

Honley Old Wood Quarry

Wellhouse Farm

Seventy Acres

Seventy Acre Farm

Pontey Farm

Honley Moor

Westfield Farm

SYCAMORE CRES

CHAUCER CT

Greasy Slack Wood

Knowl Top

KNOWL LA

Spring Villa

Oldfield Road Farm

Honey Head Wood

Moor Croft

Moorfield House Farm

CROSS LA

Windy Bank Wood

Slate Pits Wood

Wood Nook

WOOD NOOK LA

Pontey Wood

Oldfield House Farm

OLDFIELD RD

OLDFIELD

Golf Course

Meltham Mills Resr

Greave Dike

Bank Dike

Bank Wood

ST MARY'S RISE
ST MARY'S CRES

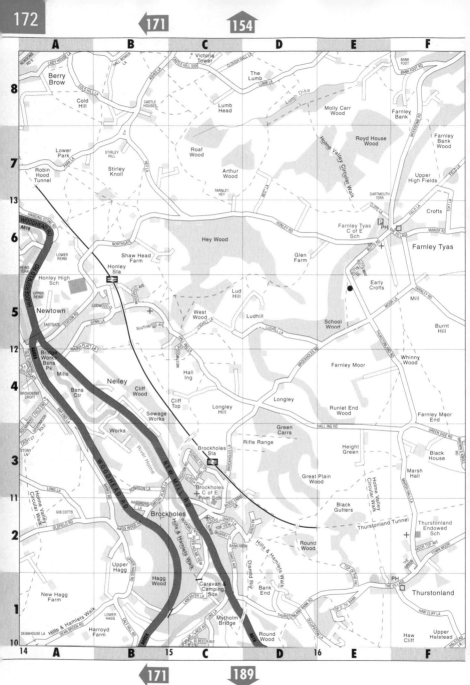

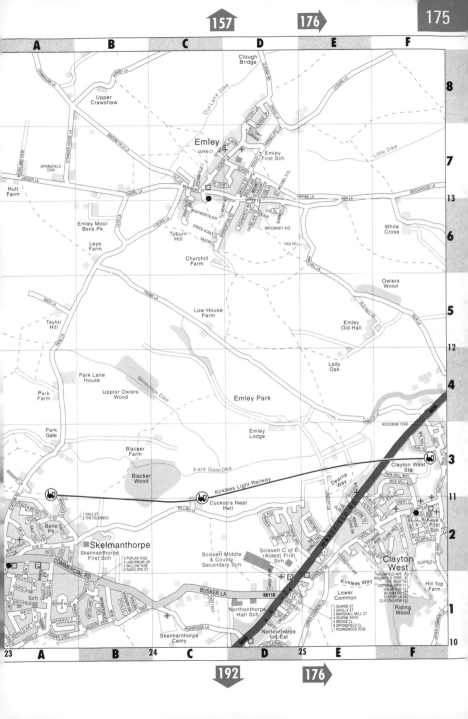

8
7
13
6
5
12
4
3
11
2
1
10

A B C D E F

Clough
Bridge

Upper
Crawshaw

Emley

Emley
First Sch

Little Dike

Springfield
Terr

Hutt
Farm

White
Cross

Emley Moor
Bsns Pk

Leys
Farm

Tyburn
Hill

Churchill
Farm

Broomhey Ave

Hag Hill

Owlers
Wood

Taylor
Hill

Back La

Low House
Farm

Emley
Old Hall

Lady
Oak

Park Lane
House

Upploor Owlers
Wood

Nineclogs Dike

Emley Park

Woodbine Terr

Park
Farm

Park
Gate

Blacker
Farm

Emley
Lodge

Clayton West
Sta

Blacker
Wood

Park Gate Dike

Kirklees Light Railway

Dearne
Way

1 DALE ST
2 THE FOLDINGS

Cuckoo's Nest
Halt

PILLING LA

Vinery Cl

Kaye's
First Sch

Bsns
Pk

Skelmanthorpe

Skelmanthorpe
First Sch

3 POPLAR RISE
4 LABURNUM GR
5 WILLOW RISE
6 RADCLIFFE ST

Scissett Middle
& County
Secondary Sch

Scissett C of E
(Aided) First
Sch

Clayton
West

Hill Top
Farm

HOLMFIELD AVE
HOLMFIELD TERR
THE INGS
VICTORIA TERR
HOLMFIELD ST
BILHAM ROAD
CHERRY LA
CLIFTON VIEW

COMMERCIAL RD

Sch

BUSKER LA

Kirklees Way

Riding
Wood

B6116

Lower
Common

Northonthorpe
Hall Sch

Northonthorpe
Ind Est

1 DEARNE ST
2 SAVILLE ST
3 MARSHALL MILL CT
4 DEARNE ROYD
5 BRIDGE CL
6 SPRINGFIELD CL
7 RIDINGWOOD RISE

Skelmanthorpe
Cemy

A643

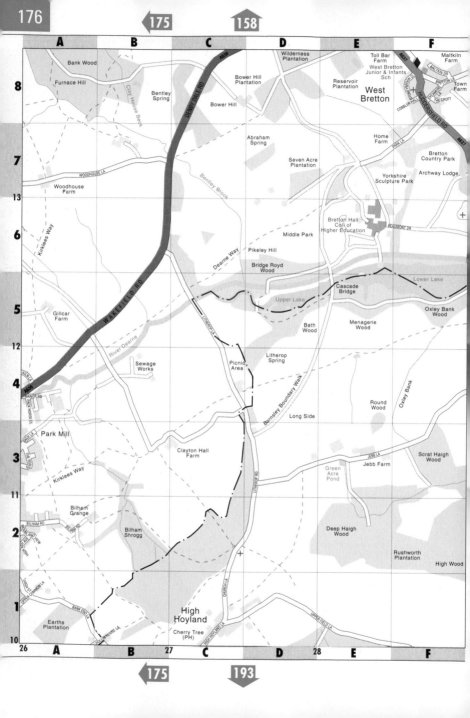

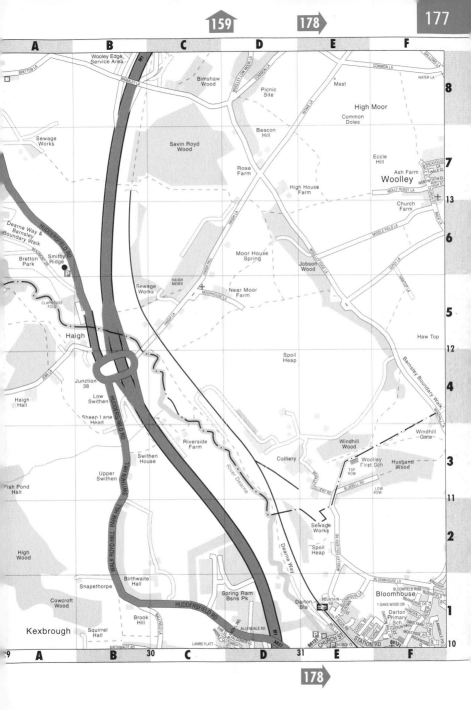

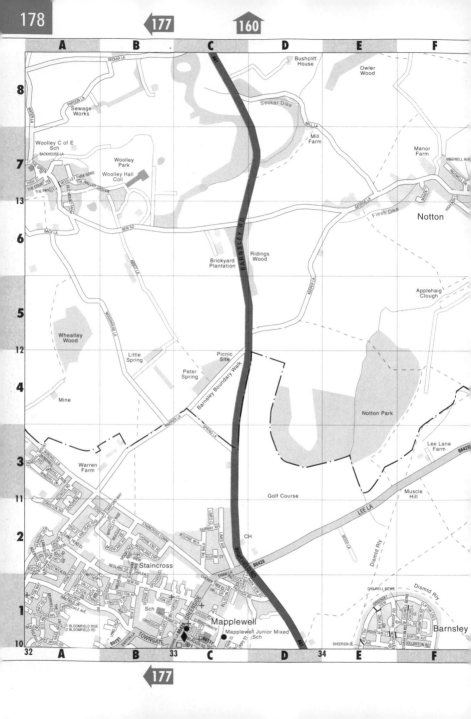

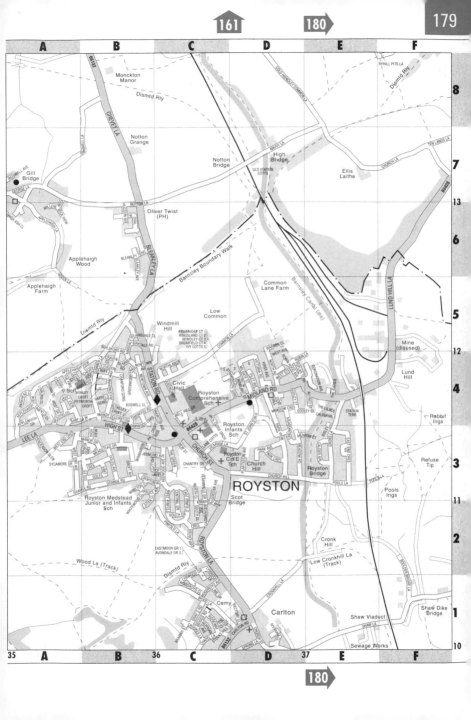

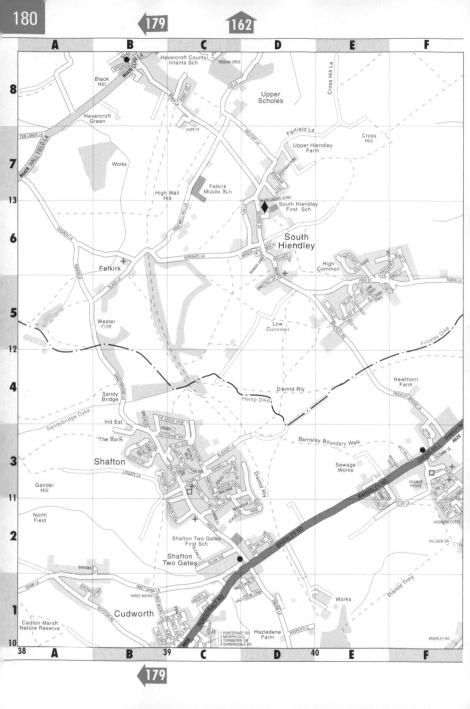

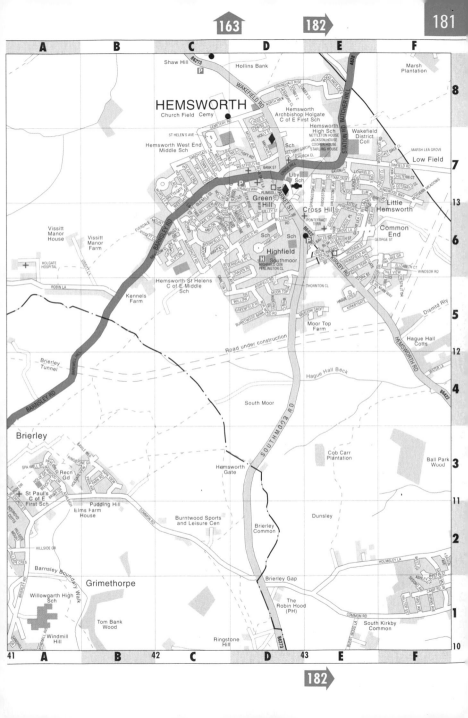

HEMSWORTH

Shaw Hill
Hollins Bank
Marsh Plantation
WAKEFIELD RD
SPRINGSIDE RISE
NORTH WLK
NETTLE CL

Church Field Cemy
Hemsworth Archbishop Holgate C of E First Sch

Hemsworth High Sch
NETTLETON HOUSE
JACKSON HOUSE
COOPER HOUSE
STARLING HOUSE

Hemsworth Wakefield District Coll

ST HELEN'S AVE
MARSH LEA GROVE

Hemsworth West End Middle Sch
CROSS LA
HOLLY LA

Low Field

CEMETERY RD
OWFIELD RD
LOWFIELD RD
CHILTERN CT

WESTFIELD RD
BANK ST
RECTORY GARTH
CHURCH CL
EATON RD

Liby Sch
COTTAM CROFT
LOWER MEADOWS

Green Hill
PLIMSOLL
GREEN ST
Cross Hill
PONTEFRACT TERR
Little Hemsworth

Vissitt Manor House
EVERDALE MOUNT
BULLENSHAW RD
BARNSLEY RD
Common End

Vissitt Manor Farm
GEORGE ST

Holgate Hospital
VICTORIA ST

ROBIN LA
Hemsworth St Helens C of E Middle Sch
WINDSOR RD

Kennels Farm
MOOR TOP
THORNTON CL
Highfield
Southmoor HIGHFIELD CEN PENLINGTON CL

WILLOW
Sch
Sch
ELIZABETH CT
VALE VIEW

GREENFIELD RD
BURNTWOOD BANK
MOOR RD
Moor Top Farm

Dismtd Rly

Brierley Tunnel
Road under construction
Hague Hall Beck
Hague Hall Cotts

HEMSWORTH RD
WINTER LA

BARNSLEY RD
South Moor
SOUTHMOOR RD

Brierley

Cob Carr Plantation
Ball Park Wood

SPA WELL GR
BAILIE WLK
RINGSTONE GR
PINFOLD

Recn Gd
Hemsworth Gate

St Paul's C of E First Sch
Pudding Hill
Elms Farm House
Burntwood Sports and Leisure Cen
Dunsley

COMMON RD
HILLSIDE GR
HOLMSLEY LA

Barnsley Boundary Walk
Brierley Common

Grimethorpe
Brierley Gap

Willowgarth High Sch
The Robin Hood (PH)
South Kirkby Common

Tom Bank Wood
Windmill Hill
Ringstone Hill
COMMON RD

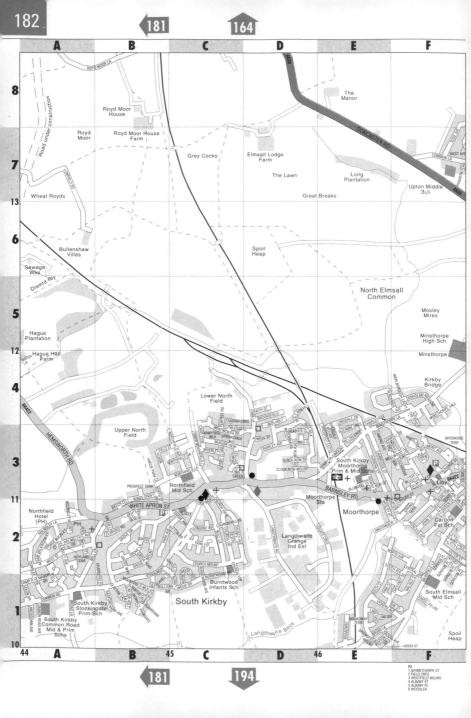

F2
1 GRIMETHORPE ST
2 FIELD CRES
3 WESTFIELD BGLWS
4 ALBANY ST
5 ALBANY PL
6 WOODLEA

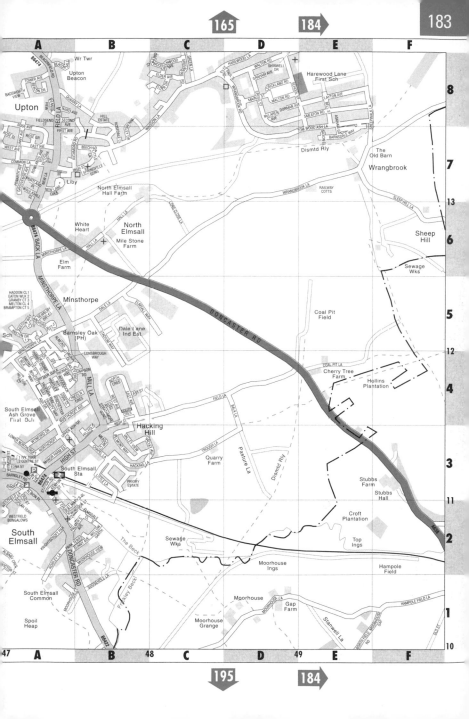

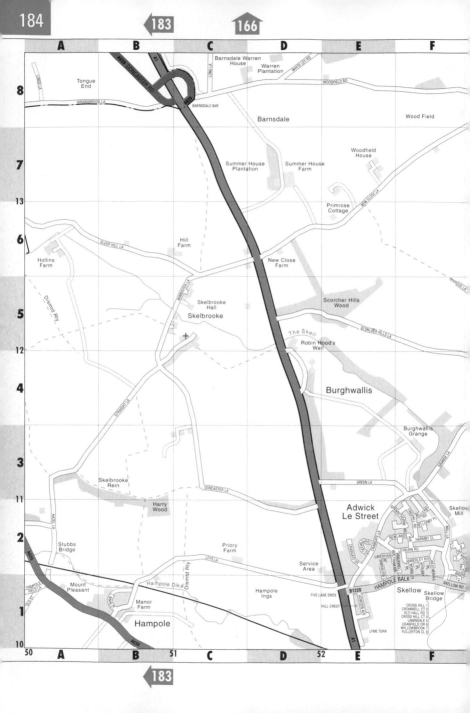

Barnsdale Warren House

Warren Plantation

WHITE LEY RD

WOODFIELD RD

Tongue End

LONGS LA

WRANGBROOK LA

M18 DONCASTER RD

A1

A638

BARNSDALE BAR

Barnsdale

Wood Field

Woodfield House

MOW CLOSE LA

Summer House Plantation

Summer House Farm

Primrose Cottage

Hill Farm

SLEEP HILL LA

New Close Farm

Hollins Farm

Scorcher Hills Wood

Dismid Dike

Skelbrooke Hall

BARNSDALE LA

Skelbrooke

The Skell

SCORCHER HILLS LA

Robin Hood's Well

Burghwallis

Burghwallis Grange

GRANGE LA

Skelbrooke Rein

STRAIGHT LA

DONCASTER LA

Harry Wood

GREEN LA

Adwick Le Street

Skellow Mill

MILL LA

Stubbs Bridge

HAZEL LA

Priory Farm

LEYS LA

Service Area

NEWLANDS

HARMBY CL

BELLAMY PL

LAVENHAM PL

KIMBERLEY RISE

Skellow

Mount Pleasant

Manor Farm

Dismid Dike

Hampole Dike

Hampole Ings

FIVE LANE ENDS

HILL CREST

B1220

HAMPOLE BALK

SKELLOW RD

Skellow Bridge

CROSS HILL 1
CROMWELL CT 2
OLD HALL RD 3
CROSS HILL CT 4
LAWNDALE 5
CRANFIELD DR 6
WILLOWBROOK 7
FULLERTON CL 8

LYME TERR

Hampole

M18

A639

HAMPOLE FIELD LA

TOLL ST

50   51   52

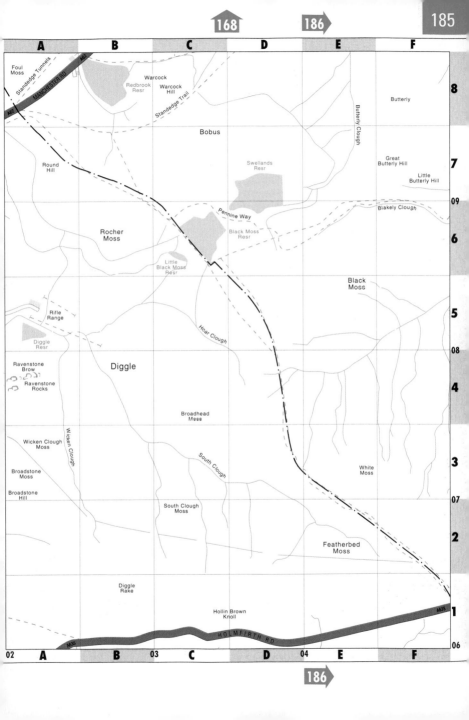

| A | B | C | D | E | F |

8

Foul Moss

Standedge Tunnels

MANCHESTER RD

A62

Warcock

Redbrook Resr

Warcock Hill

Standedge Trail

Butterly Clough

Butterly

Bobus

7

Round Hill

Swellands Resr

Great Butterly Hill

Little Butterly Hill

09

Pennine Way

Blakely Clough

Rocher Moss

Black Moss Resr

6

Little Black Moss Resr

Black Moss

5

Rifle Range

Hoar Clough

08

Diggle Resr

Ravenstone Brow

Ravenstone Rocks

Diggle

4

Broadhead Moss

Wicken Clough

South Clough

White Moss

3

Wicken Clough Moss

Broadstone Moss

South Clough Moss

07

Broadstone Hill

Featherbed Moss

2

Diggle Rake

Hollin Brown Knoll

1

A635

HOLMFIRTH RD

A635

| 02 | A | B | 03 | C | D | 04 | E | F |

06

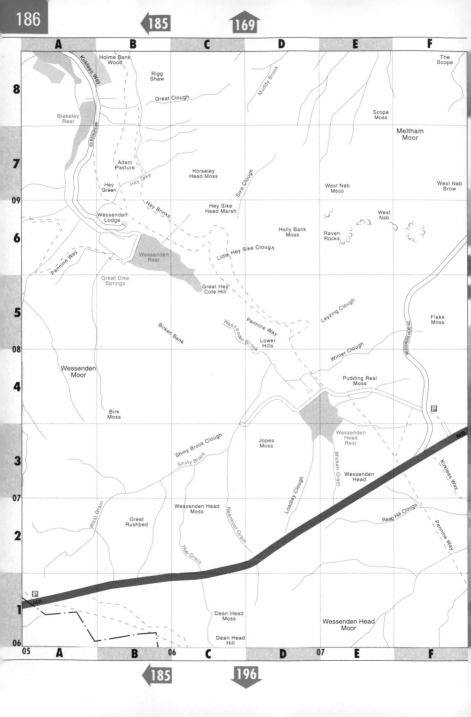

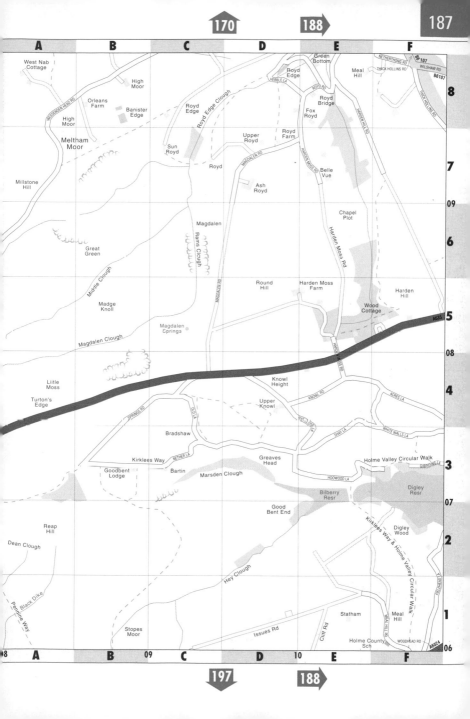

A B C D E F

West Nab Cottage

NETHERTHONG RD
WILSHAW RD
THICK HOLLINS RD
B6107
B6107

8

High Moor

Green Bottom
Royd Edge
Meal Hill

WESSENDEN HEAD RD

Orleans Farm
Royd Edge
HEBBLE LA
Royd Bridge
Royd Royd
Fox Royd

Banister Edge

High Moor

Sun Royd
Royd Edge Clough
Upper Royd
Royd Farm
Belle Vue

HARDEN HILL RD

7

Meltham Moor

Royd
MAGDALEN RD
Ash Royd

HARDEN MOSS RD

09

Millstone Hill

Magdalen
Rams Clough

Chapel Plot

6

Great Green

Middle Clough

Madge Knoll

Round Hill
Harden Moss Farm
Harden Hill

MAGDALEN RD

Magdalen Clough
Magdalen Springs

Wood Cottage

A635

5

Little Moss

HARDEN MOSS RD

08

Turton's Edge

SPRINGS RD

Knowl Height

Upper Knowl
KNOWL RD
ACRES LA

4

Bradshaw

GO LA
HILL LA END
SHAFT LA
WHITE WALLS LA

NETHER LA

Kirklees Way
Bartin
Greaves Head
Holme Valley Circular Walk
GIBRIDING LA

3

Goodbent Lodge
Marsden Clough
HOOWOOD LA

Bilberry Resr
Digley Resr

07

Reap Hill

Good Bent End

Digley Wood

2

Dean Clough

Kirklees Way & Holme Valley Circular Walk

Hey Clough

Black Dike

Pennine Way

Statham
Meal Hill
MEAL HILL LA
WOODHEAD RD

1

Stopes Moor

Issues Rd
Cliff Rd

Holme County Sch
A6024

06

A B C D E F

09 10

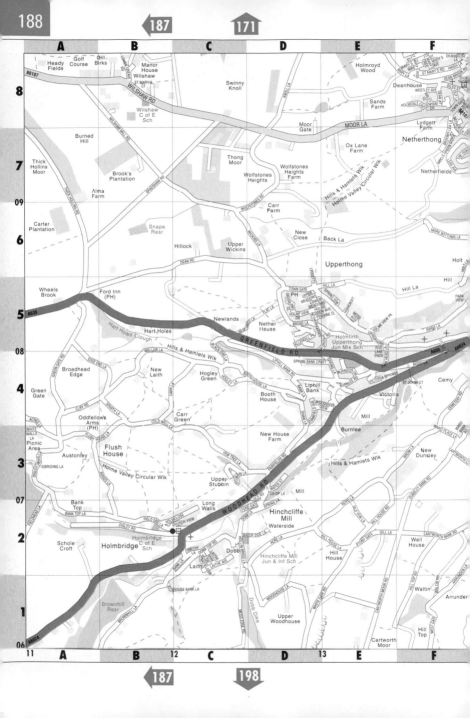

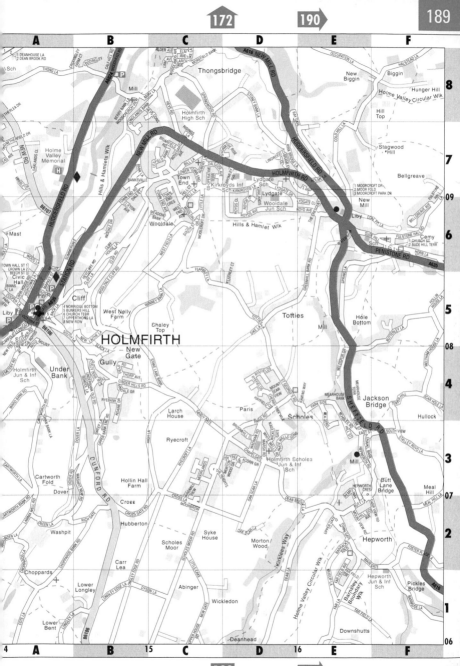

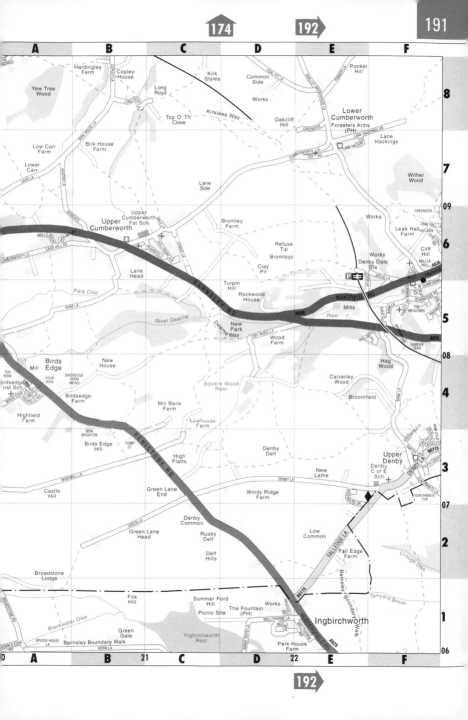

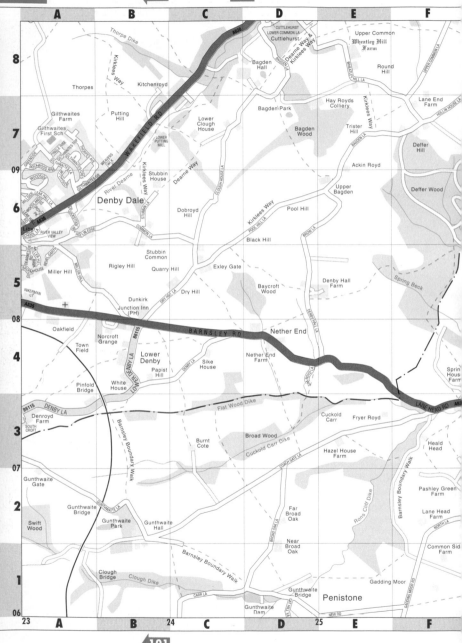

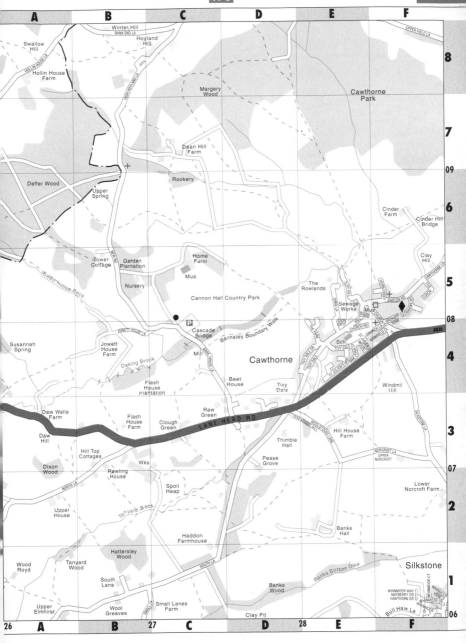

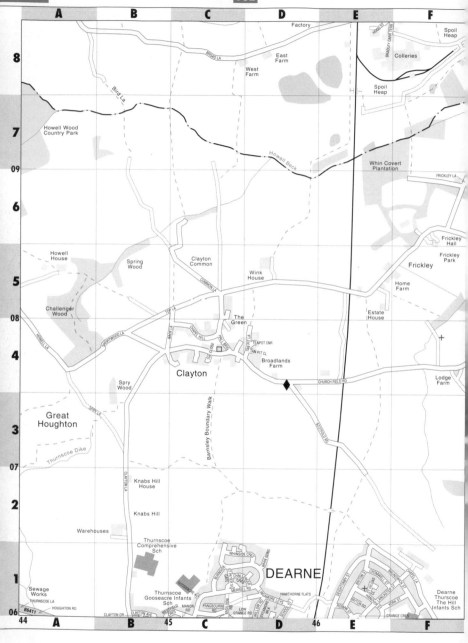

A | B | C | D | E | F

8

Factory
Broad La
West Farm
East Farm
Colleries
Spoil Heap
Bradley Gars Terr
Honey St

Bird La

7

Howell Wood Country Park

09

Howell Beck

Whin Covert Plantation
Frickley La

6

Howell House
Spring Wood
Clayton Common
Wink House
Frickley Hall
Frickley Park
Frickley

5

Challenger Wood
Common La
Top La
Home Farm
Estate House

08

Shirtwood La
Morrell La
Back La
Chapel Hill
The Close
Tan Pit Cl
The Green
Pry Mill La
Teapot Cnr
Broadlands Farm

4

Spry Wood
Clayton
Church Field Rd
Lodge Farm

Great Houghton
Spry La
Barnsley Boundary Walk
Westfield Rd

3

Thurnscoe Dike

07

Clayton La
Knabs Hill House

2

Knabs Hill
Warehouses
Thurnscoe Comprehensive Sch
Whinside Cres

1

Sewage Works
Thurnscoe La
Houghton Rd
Thurnscoe Gooseacre Infants Sch
Broadway
Manor Rd
Pangbourne Rd
Merrill Rd
Low Grange Rd
DEARNE
Hawthorne Flats
Cromwell St
Cross St
Chapel La
Dearne Thurscoe The Hill Infants Sch
Grange Cres

06

B6411

44 | A | B | 45 | C | D | 46 | E | F

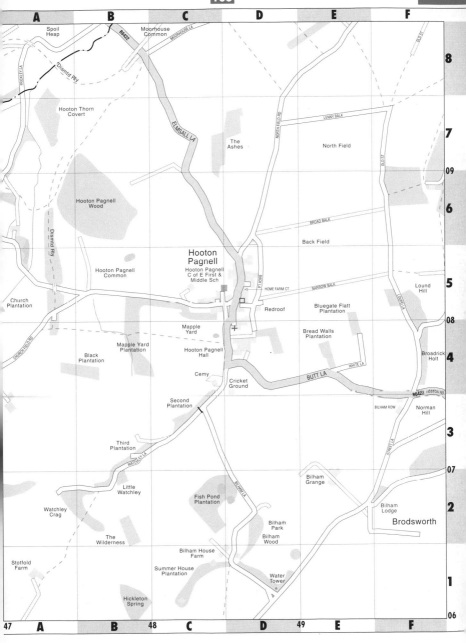

Spoil Heap

Moorhouse Common

B6422

Froxley La

Dismtd Rly

Hooton Thorn Covert

MOORHOUSE LA

ELMSALL LA

The Ashes

NORTH FIELD RD

LENNY BALK

North Field

OLD ST

Hooton Pagnell Wood

Dismtd Rly

BROAD BALK

Back Field

Hooton Pagnell Common

Hooton Pagnell

Hooton Pagnell C of E First & Middle Sch

BACK LA

HOME FARM CT

NARROW BALK

Lound Hill

LOUND LA

OLD ST

Church Plantation

CHURCHFIELD RD

Redroof

Bluegate Flatt Plantation

Mapple Yard

Mapple Yard Plantation

Hooton Pagnell Hall

Bread Walls Plantation

Broadrick Holt

Black Plantation

Cemy

Cricket Ground

BUTT LA

WHITE LA

B6422

HOOTON RD

Second Plantation

BILHAM ROW

Norman Hill

STREET LA

Third Plantation

WATCHLEY LA

Little Watchley

Fish Pond Plantation

BILHAM LA

Bilham Grange

Bilham Lodge

Watchley Crag

The Wilderness

Bilham Park

Bilham Wood

Brodsworth

Stotfold Farm

Bilham House Farm

Summer House Plantation

Water Tower

Hickleton Spring

186

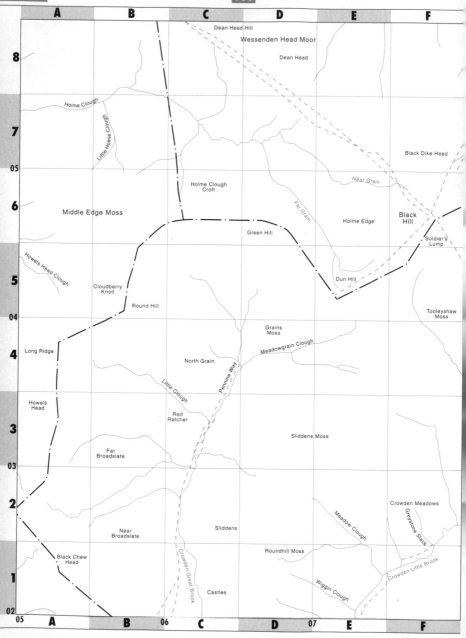

Dean Head Hill
Wessenden Head Moor
Dean Head

Holme Clough
Little Home Clough

Black Dike Head

Near Grain

Holme Clough
Croft

Middle Edge Moss

Far Grain

Holme Edge

Black
Hill

Green Hill

Soldier's
Lump

Howels Head Clough

Cloudberry
Knoll

Round Hill

Dun Hill

Tooleyshaw
Moss

Long Ridge

Grains
Moss

Meadowgrain Clough

North Grain

Pennine Way

Little Clough

Howels
Head

Red
Ratcher

Far
Broadslate

Sliddens Moss

Crowden Meadows

Greystone Slack

Meadow Clough

Near
Broadslate

Sliddens

Crowden Little Brook

Black Chew
Head

Crowden Great Brook

Roundhill Moss

Wiggin Clough

Castles

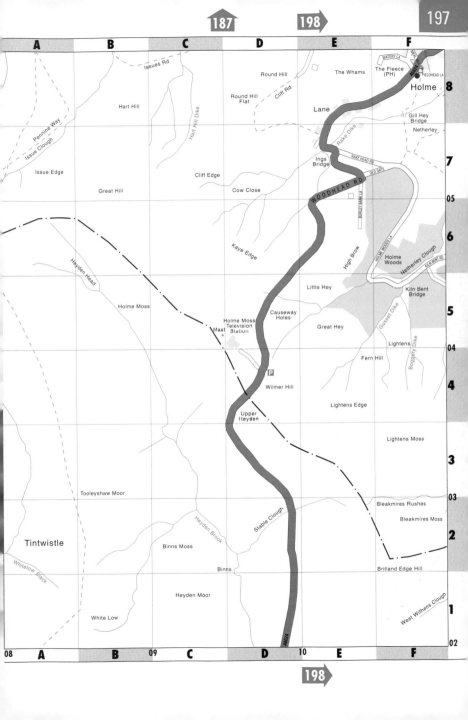

187
198

	A	B	C	D	E	F	

Issues Rd

Round Hill

The Whams

WATERY LA

The Fleece (PH)

FIELDHEAD LA

Holme

8

Hart Hill

Round Hill Flat

Cliff Rd

Lane

Gill Hey Bridge

Netherley

Pennine Way

Hart Hill Dike

Rake Dike

Issue Clough

RAKE HEAD RD

Issue Edge

Cliff Edge

Ings Bridge

WOODHEAD RD

OLD GATE

7

Great Hill

Cow Close

05

BURLEY BANK LA

Kaye Edge

High Brow

HOLME WOODS LA

Holme Woods

Netherley Clough

6

KILN BENT RD

Holme Moss

Little Hey

Kiln Bent Bridge

Heyden Head

Causeway Holes

Great Hey

Gusset Dike

5

Holme Moss Television Station

Mast

Lightens

04

Fern Hill

Boggery Dike

Wilmer Hill

Lightens Edge

4

Upper Heyden

Lightens Moss

3

Tooleyshaw Moor

Bleakmires Rushes

03

Bleakmires Moss

Heyden Brook

Stable Clough

Tintwistle

Binns Moss

2

Whitelow Slack

Binns

Britland Edge Hill

Heyden Moor

1

White Low

West Withers Clough

02

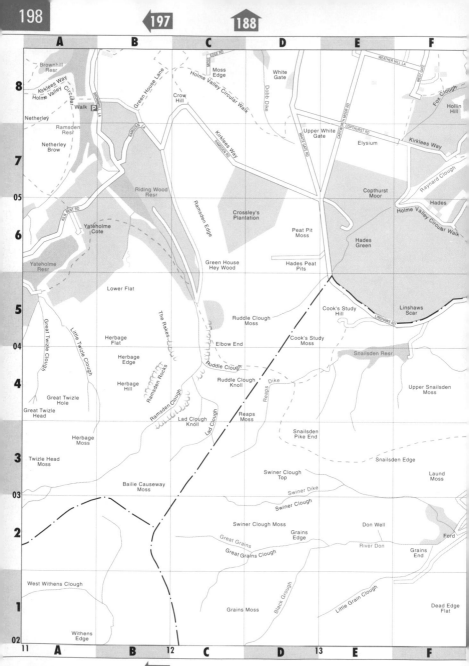

A **B** **C** **D** **E** **F**

8

Brownhill
Resr

Kirklees Way
Holme Valley Circular
Walk

Netherley

Ramsden
Resr

Netherley
Brow

Green House Lane

Crow
Hill

Moss
Edge

Holme Valley Circular Walk

White
Gate

Dobb Dike

Upper White
Gate

Elysium

WEATHER HILL LA

COPTHURST RD

Kirklees Way

Fox Clough

Hollin
Hill

Raynard Clough

7

05

Riding Wood
Resr

Kirklees Way

Ramsden Edge

Crossley's
Plantation

Copthurst
Moor

Hades

Holme Valley Circular Walk

6

Yateholme
Cote

Green House
Hey Wood

Peat Pit
Moss

Hades
Green

Yateholme
Resr

Hades Peat
Pits

5

Lower Flat

Great Twizle Clough

Little Twizle Clough

The Rakes

Ruddle Clough
Moss

Elbow End

Cook's Study
Hill

Cook's Study
Moss

Linshaws
Scar

LINSHAWS RD

04

Herbage
Flat

Herbage
Edge

Ramsden Clough

Ramsden Rocks

Ruddle Clough

Ruddle Clough
Knoll

Snailsden Resr

4

Herbage
Hill

Lad Clough

Reaps Dike

Upper Snailsden
Moss

Great Twizle
Hole

Great Twizle
Head

Ramsden Clough

Lad Clough
Knoll

Reaps
Moss

Snailsden
Pike End

3

Herbage
Moss

Twizle Head
Moss

Bailie Causeway
Moss

Snailsden Edge

Laund
Moss

03

Swiner Clough
Top

Swiner Dike

Swiner Clough

2

Swiner Clough Moss

Grains
Edge

Great Grains

Great Grains Clough

Don Well

River Don

Grains
End

Ferd

1

West Withens Clough

Black Grough

Grains Moss

Little Grain Clough

Dead Edge
Flat

02

Withens
Edge

11 **A** **12** **B** **C** **D** **13** **E** **F**

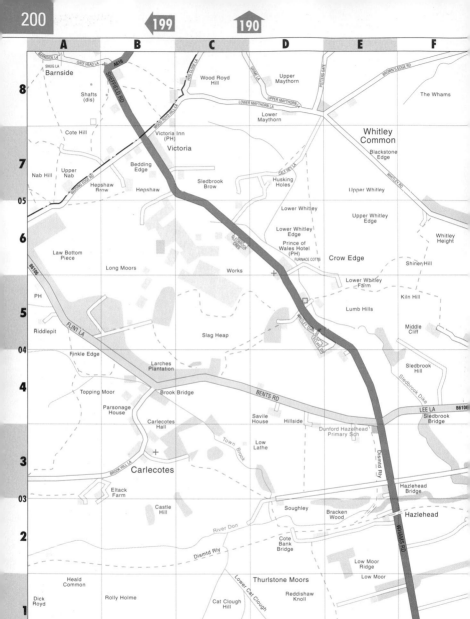

A **B** **C** **D** **E** **F**

BARNSIDE LA
SNUG LA
GATE HEAD LA
Barnside
Shafts
(dis)
Cote Hill
Upper
Nab
Nab Hill
Hepshaw
Brow
Hepshaw
Bedding
Edge
Victoria Inn
(PH)
Victoria
Wood Royd
Hill
Upper
Maythorn
UPPER MAYTHORN LA
LOWER MAYTHORN LA
Lower
Maythorn
SHEFFIELD RD
A616
WOOD ROYD HILL LA
WOOD ROYD LA
GRIME LA
POTTERS GATE
BROWN'S EDGE RD
The Whams
Whitley
Common
Blackstone
Edge
Sledbrook
Brow
Husking
Holes
CALF HEY LA
WHITLEY RD
Upper Whitley
Law Bottom
Piece
Long Moors
Lower Whitley
Lower Whitley
Edge
Prince of
Wales Hotel
(PH)
Upper Whitley
Edge
Whitley
Height
PH
Riddlepit
FLINT LA
Finkle Edge
Topping Moor
Works
Crow Edge
Shiner Hill
FURNACE COTTS
Lower Whitley
Farm
Kiln Hill
Lumb Hills
Middle
Cliff
Slag Heap
Larches
Plantation
SLEDBROOK DIKE
WHITLEY TOP LA
CROW EDGE
Sledbrook
Hill
Sledbrook
Dike
Brook Bridge
BENTS RD
Savile
House
Hillside
Dunford Hazlehead
Primary Sch
LEE LA
B6106
Sledbrook
Bridge
Parsonage
House
Carlecotes
Hall
Low
Lathe
Dismd Rly
Hazlehead
Bridge
BROOK HILL LA
Carlecotes
Eltack
Farm
Town Brook
Castle
Hill
Soughley
Bracken
Wood
Hazlehead
WHAMS RD
River Don
Cote
Bank
Bridge
Low Moor
Ridge
Low Moor
Dismtd Rly
Heald
Common
Dick
Royd
Rolly Holme
Lower Cat Clough
Cat Clough
Hill
Thurlstone Moors
Reddishaw
Knoll
Wogden Moor
Cat Clough
Head

A 17 **B** 18 **C** **D** 19 **E** **F**

A1 Bsns Pk. Knot ... 126 C3
Aachen Way. Hali HX1 ... 113 A5
Abb Scott La. Brad BD12, BD6 ... 94 B6
Abbey Cl. Hali HX3 ... 113 D7
Abbey Ave. Leeds LS5 ... 58 F3
Abbey Cl. Add LS29 ... 7 A8
Abbey Cl. Hud HD2 ... 199 B7
Abbey Cl. Hors LS18 ... 58 B6
Abbey Dr. Shep HD8 ... 173 F1
Abbey Farm Dr. Shep HD8 ... 190 F8
Abbey Gorse. Leeds LS5 ... 59 A5
Abbey Grange CE High Sch. Leeds ... 58 F8
Abbey House Mus. Leeds ... 58 F5
Abbey La. Hali HX2 ... 111 F7
Abbey Lea. Brad BD15 ... 73 C8
Abbey Mount. Leeds LS5 ... 58 F3
Abbey Park Jun & Inf Sch. Hali ... 91 D6
Abbey Rd. Batley WF17 ... 117 F4
Abbey Rd. Hud HD2 ... 136 B1
Abbey Rd. Leeds LS5 ... 58 E6
Abbey Rd N. Shep HD8 ... 173 F1
Abbey Rd S. Shep HD8 ... 190 F8
Abbey Rd. Shep HD8 ... 174 A8
Abbey St. Leeds LS3 ... 78 F8
Abbey Terr. Leeds LS5 ... 58 F3 3
Abbey View. Leeds LS5 ... 58 F3
Abbey Wlk. Hali HX3 ... 113 C4
Abbey Wlk. Leeds LS5 ... 58 F5
Abbeydale Garth. Leeds LS5 ... 58 E6
Abbeydale Gdns. Leeds LS5 ... 58 E6
Abbeydale Gr. Leeds LS5 ... 58 E6
Abbeydale Mount. Leeds LS5 ... 58 E6
Abbeydale Oval. Leeds LS5 ... 58 E6
Abbeydale Vale. Leeds LS5 ... 58 E6
Abbeydale Way. Leeds LS5 ... 58 E6
Abbot La. Wool WF4 ... 178 B6
Abbot St. Hud HD1 ... 153 E7
Abbots Pl. Hud HD2 ... 136 F5
Abbots Wood. Brad BD9 ... 55 C8
Abbotside Cl. Brad BD10 ... 56 C6
Abbotsway. Gar LS25 ... 82 D6
Abbott Cl. Leeds LS12 ... 78 D8
Abbott Rd. Leeds LS12 ... 78 D8
Abbott Terr. Wake WF1 ... 142 D7
Abbott View. Leeds LS12 ... 78 D8
Abbott's Ladies Home. Hali HX3 ... 113 C3
Abbotts Cl. Ader LS25 ... 64 E8
Abel St. Brad BD12 ... 94 C4 4
Abelia Mount. Brad BD7 ... 73 F6
Aberdeen Dr. Leeds LS12 ... 78 A8
Aberdeen Gr. Leeds LS12 ... 78 A8
Aberdeen Pl. Brad BD7 ... 74 A5
Aberdeen Rd. Leeds LS12 ... 78 A8
Aberdeen Terr. Brad BD14 ... 71 74
Aberdeen Terr. Brad BD7 ... 74 A6
Aberdeen Wlk. Leeds LS12 ... 78 A7
Aberfield Bank. Midd LS10 ... 99 E5
Aberfield Cl. Midd LS10 ... 99 E7
Aberfield Cres. Midd LS10 ... 99 E6
Aberfield Crst. Midd LS10 ... 99 E7
Aberfield Dr. Crig WF4 ... 159 E4
Aberfield Gate. Midd LS10 ... 99 E6
Aberfield Mount. Midd LS10 ... 99 E6
Aberfield Rd. Midd LS10 ... 99 E6
Aberfield Rise. Midd LS10 ... 99 E6
Aberfield Wlk. Midd LS10 ... 99 E6
Aberford Cl. Midd LS10 ... 99 E7
Aberford Rd. Aber LS25 ... 64 E8
Aberford Rd. B'ton LS15 ... 63 E7
Aberford Rd. Brad BD8 ... 71 A8
Aberford Rd. Bramham LS23 ... 30 D2
Aberford Rd. Gar LS25 ... 83 A8
Aberford Rd. Loft W WF1 ... 121 F3
Aberford Rd. Roth LS26 ... 101 D6
Aberford Rd. Wake WF1 ... 142 E8
Abingdon St. Brad BD8 ... 55 B1
Abraham Hall. Roth LS26 ... 101 A4
Abraham Ormerod Day Hospl. Tod ... 108 B5
Abram St. Brad BD5 ... 74 E4
Acacia Cl. Castle WF10 ... 125 D6
Acacia Dr. Brad BD15 ... 54 A4
Acacia Dr. Brig HX3 ... 115 A7
Acacia Dr. Castle WF10 ... 125 D6
Acacia Gr. Pont WF8 ... 125 F1
Acacia Gr. Heb Br HX7 ... 89 F1
Acacia Gr. Shaf S72 ... 180 C2
Acacia House. Castle WF10 ... 124 E7
Acacia Park Dr. Yeadon BD10 ... 39 F2
Acacia Park Terr. Yeadon LS19 ... 40 A2
Acacia Wlk. Knot WF11 ... 126 D3
Acacia Cl. S Elm WF9 ... 183 A4
Acaster Dr. Brad BD12 ... 94 C4
Acaster Dr. Gar LS25 ... 82 D7
Accommodation Rd. Leeds LS7 ... 60 A7
Acer Way. Brig BD19 ... 115 F8
Ackroyd Ct. Thorn BD13 ... 72 D6
Ackroyd St. Morley LS27 ... 98 A4
Ackroyd St. Tod OL14 ... 86 B1
Ackton Cl. Feath WF7 ... 145 A8
Ackton General Hospl. Feath ... 124 C1
Ackton Hall Cres. Feath WF7 ... 145 A8
Ackton La. Feath WF7 ... 124 C1
Ackton Pasture La. Castle WF7 ... 124 B4
Ackton Pastures Jun & Inf Sch. Castle ... 124 A6
Ackw Ave. Yeadon LS19 ... 40 C6
Ackworth Bell Lane Fst Sch. Ack M T ... 164 D8
Ackworth Bridle Rd. Ack M T WF8 ... 164 E6
Ackworth Cres. Yeadon LS19 ... 40 C6
Ackworth Dr. Yeadon LS19 ... 40 C6
Ackworth House Cl. Ack M T WF7 ... 164 A8
Ackworth Mid Sch. Ack M T ... 163 F4
Ackworth Rd. Feath WF7 ... 145 D3
Ackworth Rd. Pont WF7, WF8 ... 146 C5
Ackworth Sch. Ack M T ... 164 C2
Ackworth St. Brad BD5 ... 74 E4
Acme Terr. Wake WF1 ... 142 D3
Acorn Bsns Pk. Brad ... 94 B5
Acorn Cl. Leeds LS14 ... 62 C8
Acorn Gr. Holmfl HD7 ... 189 D3
Acorn Pk. Hud HD7 ... 38 E2
Acorn St. Hali HX1 ... 203 E3
Acorn St. Keigh BD21 ... 35 B5
Acre Ave. Brad BD2 ... 56 B5
Acre Cir. Midd LS10 ... 99 C4
Acre Cl. Brad BD2 ... 56 B5

Acre Cl. Midd LS10 ... 99 B3
Acre Cres. Brad BD2 ... 56 B5
Acre Cres. Midd LS10 ... 99 C4
Acre Dr. Brad BD2 ... 56 B5
Acre Fold. Add LS29 ... 6 E8
Acre Gr. Brad BD2 ... 56 B5
Acre House Ave. Hud HD3 ... 153 C8
Acre La. Brad BD2 ... 56 B4
Acre La. Brad BD6 ... 74 C1
Acre La. Haw BD22 ... 51 C7
Acre La. Hep HX7 ... 88 C6
Acre La. Holmfl HD7 ... 188 D2
Acre La. Holmfl HD7 ... 190 B6
Acre La. Mel HD7 ... 170 F1
Acre Mount. Midd LS10 ... 99 C4
Acre Pl. Midd LS10 ... 99 C4
Acre Rd. Midd LS10 ... 99 C4
Acre Rise. Bail BD17 ... 38 C4
Acre Sq. Midd LS10 ... 99 C4
Acre St. Hud HD3 ... 153 C8
Acre St. Midd LS10 ... 99 D4
Acre Terr. Midd LS10 ... 99 C4
Acre Villas. Heb Br HX7 ... 89 E1 1
Acrehowe Rise. Bail BD17 ... 38 E4
Acres Hall Ave. Pudsey LS28 ... 77 A6
Acres Hall Cres. Pudsey LS28 ... 77 A6
Acres Hall Dr. Pudsey LS28 ... 77 A6
Acres La. Hep HX7 ... 88 C6
Acres La. Holmfl HD7 ... 187 F4
Acres Rd. Loft G WF3 ... 121 C8
Acres St. Keigh BD21 ... 35 B6
Acres The. Add LS29 ... 7 A8
Acres The. Beam LS29 ... 3 A1
Acres The. S in Cra BD20 ... 16 C6
Acton Flat La. Hud HD3 ... 135 A3
Acton St. Brad BD3 ... 75 C7
Acute Terr. Wake WF2 ... 141 E6
Ada St. Bail BD17 ... 38 B7
Ada St. Hali HX3 ... 92 C1 6
Ada St. Keigh BD21 ... 35 A7 11
Ada St. Keigh BD21 ... 72 D1 8
Ada St. Shep BD18 ... 54 F8
Ada's Pl. Pudsey LS28 ... 57 F2
Adam Croft. Cull BD13 ... 52 D6
Adam Ct. Hud HD3 ... 135 B1
Adam St. Brad BD4 ... 81 B1 7
Adam St. Brad BD7 ... 74 D3
Adams Gr. Leeds LS15 ... 62 E4
Addersgate Fst & Mid Sch. Castle ... 125 C7
Addingford Cl. Horb WF4 ... 141 C5
Addingford Dr. Horb WF4 ... 159 A8
Addingford Gdns. Leeds LS12 ... 78 F7
Addingford La. Horb WF4 ... 159 A8
Addingham Fst Sch. Adel ... 7 F1
Addingham Gdns. Leeds LS12 ... 78 F7
Addingham Mid Sch. Add ... 2 F1
Addison Ave. Nor WF6 ... 123 C1
Addison Ct. Hor WF4 ... 141 C2
Addison La. Leeds LS15 ... 81 D6
Addle Croft La. Lepton HD8 ... 155 F5
Adeltherpe La. Sid LS22 ... 13 A3
Addy Cres. S Elm WF9 ... 182 F3
Adel CE Sch. Hors ... 42 D4
Adel Garth. Hors LS16 ... 42 D4
Adel Grange Cl. Hors LS16 ... 42 C2
Adel Grange Croft. Hors LS16 ... 42 C2
Adel Grange Mews. Hors LS16 ... 42 C2
Adel La. Hors LS16 ... 42 D4
Adel Mead. Hors LS16 ... 42 D4
Adel Mill. Eccup LS16 ... 42 D6
Adel Park Cl. Hors LS16 ... 42 C5
Adel Park Croft. Hors LS16 ... 42 C5
Adel Park Ct. Hors LS16 ... 42 C5
Adel Park Dr. Hors LS16 ... 42 C5
Adel Park Gdns. Hors LS16 ... 42 C5
Adel Pasture. Hors LS16 ... 42 C5
Adel Vale. Hors LS16 ... 42 D3
Adel Wood Cl. Hors LS16 ... 42 D4
Adel Wood Dr. Hors LS16 ... 42 D4
Adel Wood Gdns. Hors LS16 ... 42 D4
Adel Wood Gr. Hors LS16 ... 42 D4
Adel Wood Pl. Hors LS16 ... 42 D4
Adel Wood Rd. Hors LS16 ... 42 D4
Adelaide House. Bing BD16 ... 37 B2
Adelaide Rise. Bail BD17 ... 38 A3
Adelaide St. Brad BD5 ... 74 E4 3
Adelaide St. Hali HX1 ... 112 F7 16
Adelaide St. Hud HD1 ... 153 F4
Adelaide St. Tod OL14 ... 108 B6 3
Adelaide Terr. Elland HX4 ... 133 F3
Adelphi Rd. Hud HD3 ... 153 C7
Adgil Cres. Hali HX3 ... 114 A4
Administration Rd. Leeds LS9 ... 80 C7
Admiral St. Leeds LS11 ... 79 C4 6
Adolphus St. Brad BD1 ... 74 F6 4
Adowsley Cl. Ack M T WF7 ... 163 E6
Adwalton Cl. Birk BD11 ... 96 D5
Adwalton Gr. Birk BD11 ... 96 D5
Adwick Cl. Wake WF2 ... 160 A7
Adwick Gr. Wake WF2 ... 160 A7
Adwick Pl. Leeds LS4 ... 59 C1
Adwick Terr. Pont WF8 ... 146 B6 3
Aeron Wilkinson Ct. S Kirk WF9 ... 182 A2
Agar St. Brad BD8 ... 55 B1 6
Agar Terr. Brad BD8 ... 55 B1 6
Agbrigg Gr. Wake WF2 ... 142 E2
Agbrigg Rd. Wake WF1, WF2 ... 142 E2
Agincourt Dr. Nor WF6 ... 123 C3
Agnes St. Keigh BD20 ... 18 C1
Agnes Stewart CE High Sch. Leeds ... 79 E8
Aike La. Hali HX2 ... 90 E1
Aimbry Ct. Hud HD5 ... 154 F2
Ainley Bottom. Elland HX5 ... 135 A5
Ainley Rd. Hud HD3 ... 153 A5
Ainley St. Mars HD7 ... 151 C1 2
Ainley Rd. Hud HD3 ... 135 A1
Ainley Pl. Mars HD7 ... 151 C1
Ainsbury Ave. Brad BD10 ... 39 A3
Ainsdale Gr. Brad BD14 ... 73 B4
Ainsdale Gr. Cull BD13 ... 52 E6
Ainsley La. Wals HD7 ... 179 B5
Ainsdale Gr. Cull BD13 ... 52 E6
Ainsley La. Wals HD7 ... 179 B5
Ainsty Cres. Weth LS22 ... 13 E7
Ainsty Dr. Weth LS22 ... 13 E7
Ainsty Garth. Weth LS22 ... 13 E7
Ainsty Rd. Weth LS22 ... 13 E7
Ainsty View. Weth LS22 ... 13 E7
Aintree Cl. Kippax LS25 ... 82 F2
Aintree Ct. Leeds ... 79 E4

Air St. Leeds LS10 ... 79 E5
Aire and Calder Cotts. Wake WF3 ... 122 B2
Aire Cl. Bail BD17 ... 38 B1
Aire Cres. Glu BD20 ... 16 E6
Aire. Sil BD20 ... 17 E8
Aire St. Glu BD20 ... 40 C6
Aire Mount. Weth LS22 ... 13 D7
Aire Rd. Weth LS22 ... 13 D7
Aire St. Bing BD16 ... 36 E6
Aire St. Brad BD10 ... 39 A1
Aire St. Brig HX6 ... 115 B1
Aire St. Castle WF10 ... 124 D7
Aire St. Dew WF13 ... 138 F5
Aire St. Glu BD20 ... 16 E6
Aire St. Haw BD22 ... 51 D7 3
Aire St. Keigh BD21 ... 35 D8
Aire St. Knot WF11 ... 127 A5
Aire Terr. Castle WF10 ... 103 D1
Aire Valley Cl. L Brad BD20 ... 4 B6
Aire Valley Dr. L Brad BD20 ... 4 A8
Aire View. Ave. Ship BD16 ... 54 B8
Aire View. Ave. Ship BD18 ... 55 A8
Aire View. Broth WF11 ... 126 C8
Aire View. Inf Sch. Sil ... 5 E1
Aire View. Keigh BD20 ... 5 F8
Aire View. Knot WF11 ... 126 D5
Aire View. Sil BD20 ... 5 E1
Aire View. Yeadon LS19 ... 40 C6
Aire Way. Bail BD17 ... 38 A1
Airebank. Bing BD16 ... 36 F3
Aireborough L Dr. Guise ... 39 E8
Aireburn Ave. Stee BD20 ... 17 D5
Airedale Ave. Ship BD16 ... 54 A7
Airedale Band Ctr. L Brad ... 4 A8
Airedale Cliff. Leeds LS13 ... 58 C5
Airedale College Mount. Brad BD3 ... 56 A1
Airedale College Rd. Brad BD3 ... 56 A1
Airedale College Terr. Brad BD3 ... 56 A1
Airedale Cres. Brad BD3 ... 56 A1
Airedale Croft. Pudsey LS13 ... 57 F5 5
Airedale Ct. Leeds LS14 ... 61 F5
Airedale Dr. Castle WF10 ... 104 C2
Airedale Dr. Hors LS18 ... 57 F8
Airedale Gr. Hors LS18 ... 57 F8
Airedale Gr. Leeds LS13 ... 58 C5
Airedale Gr. Roth LS26 ... 100 E5
Airedale General Hospl. Stee ... 17 A6
Airedale Gr. Hors LS18 ... 57 F8
Airedale Gr. Roth LS26 ... 101 D6 3
Airedale High Sch. Castle ... 125 D7
Airedale Hts. Wake WF2 ... 141 C4
Airedale Mews. Sil ... 5 E1
Airedale Mount. Keigh BD20 ... 36 A8
Airedale Mount. Pudsey LS13 ... 57 F5
Airedale Quay. Leeds LS13 ... 58 A5
Airedale Rd. Brad BD3 ... 75 E1
Airedale Rd. Castle WF10 ... 125 B7
Airedale Rd. Roth LS26 ... 101 D6
Airedale St. Bing BD16 ... 36 F3
Airedale St. Brad BD10 ... 39 A1
Airedale Terr. Bail BD17 ... 38 B4
Airedale Terr. Bing BD16 ... 36 F3
Airedale Terr. Morley LS27 ... 98 B4
Airedale Terr. Yeadon LS19 ... 40 C7
Airedale Trad Pk. Glu ... 16 D7
Airedale View. Glu BD20 ... 16 D7
Airedale View. Roth LS26 ... 101 D6 1
Airedale Wharf. Pudsey LS13 ... 57 F4
Airedale & Wharfdale Coll of F Ed. Otley ... 23 A8
Aireside. Con BD20 ... 4 B2
Aireside Ctr. Leeds ... 211 D3
Aireside Terr. Con BD20 ... 4 A3
Airevalley Rd. Keigh BD21 ... 36 B7
Aireview Cres. Bail BD17 ... 38 B1
Aireview Prim Sch. Pudsey ... 57 F4
Aireview Terr. Keigh BD21 ... 35 B5
Aireville Ave. Ship BD18 ... 55 B5
Aireville Cl. Ship BD18 ... 55 B4
Aireville Cres. Ship BD18 ... 55 B5
Aireville Cres. Stee BD20 ... 5 F1
Aireville Dr. Ship BD18 ... 55 B5
Aireville Grange. Ship BD18 ... 55 B5
Aireville Mount. Bail BD20 ... 5 F1
Aireville Rd. Ship BD9 ... 55 B5
Aireville Rise. Brad BD9 ... 54 D2
Aireville St. Keigh BD20 ... 18 E1
Aireville Terr. Bur in W LS29 ... 21 F8
Aireworth Cl. Keigh BD21 ... 35 D8
Aireworth Gr. Keigh BD21 ... 18 E1
Aireworth Rd. Keigh BD21 ... 35 E8
Aireworth St. Keigh BD21 ... 35 C8
Airey St. Keigh BD21 ... 35 A7
Airlie Ave. Leeds LS8 ... 60 F4
Airlie Pl. Leeds LS8 ... 60 F4

Albany St. Brad BD5 ... 74 E4
Albany St. Hali HX3 ... 113 D5
Albany St. Hud HD1 ... 153 F4
Albany St. Leeds LS12 ... 78 A7
Albany St. S Elm WF9 ... 182 F2
Albany Terr. Hali HX3 ... 113 D5
Albany Terr. Leeds LS12 ... 78 A7
Albany Wlk. Ilkley LS29 ... 8 B3
Albert Ave. Brad BD10 ... 56 C8
Albert Ave. Hali HX2 ... 112 E8
Albert Ave. Wake WF2 ... 141 D7
Albert Bldgs. Brad BD10 ... 56 C8
Albert Cl. Batley WF17 ... 118 C2
Albert Cres. Birk BD11 ... 96 B4
Albert Cres. Queen BD13 ... 72 E2
Albert Ct. Hali HX2 ... 112 E8
Albert Dr. Hali HX2 ... 112 E8
Albert Dr. Morley LS27 ... 98 D5
Albert St. & Queen BD13 ... 72 E1
Albert Gdns. Hali HX2 ... 112 E8
Albert Gr. Leeds LS6 ... 59 D6
Albert La. Tod OL14 ... 108 B6
Albert Pl. Brad BD3 ... 75 E8
Albert Pl. Hors LS18 ... 41 C1
Albert Pl. M'town LS26 ... 102 B3
Albert Prom. Hali HX3 ... 113 A1
Albert Rd. Clay W HD8 ... 175 E2
Albert Rd. Glu BD20 ... 16 D6
Albert Rd. Hali HX3 ... 113 A1
Albert Rd. Morley LS27 ... 98 C5
Albert Rd. Queen BD13 ... 72 E2
Albert Rd. Ship BD18 ... 54 F8
Albert Rd. Sil BD20 ... 5 D1
Albert Sq. Yeadon LS19 ... 40 C7
Albert St. Bail BD17 ... 38 C4
Albert St. Brad BD10 ... 56 B6
Albert St. Brad BD14 ... 73 B4
Albert St. Brig HD6 ... 115 C2
Albert St. Castle WF10 ... 124 D8
Albert St. Clec BD19 ... 116 D8
Albert St. Curf S72 ... 180 C1
Albert St. Elland HX5 ... 134 F6
Albert St. Feath WF7 ... 145 D5
Albert St. Heb Br HX7 ... 89 A3
Albert St. Hud HD1 ... 153 D5
Albert St. Keigh BD21 ... 35 D7
Albert St. Liver WF15 ... 117 A4
Albert St. Queen BD13 ... 72 E1
Albert St. Yeadon LS19 ... 40 C7
Alberta Ave. Leeds LS7 ... 60 E7
Albion Arc. Leeds ... 211 F4 3
Albion Cl. B Spa LS23 ... 30 D5
Albion Croft. Ossett WF5 ... 140 E6
Albion Ct. Brad BD1 ... 201 B2
Albion Ct. Brad BD10 ... 56 C8
Albion Ct. Hali HX1 ... 203 F2
Albion Fold. Brad BD15 ... 53 C4
Albion Pk. Leeds ... 212 A3
Albion Pl. Brig HD6 ... 115 A3
Albion Pl. Guise LS20 ... 39 E8
Albion Pl. Leeds LS1 ... 211 F3
Albion Pl. Pont WF8 ... 125 D2
Albion Rd. Brad BD10 ... 56 C8
Albion Rd. Dew WF12 ... 139 C4
Albion Rd. Pudsey LS28 ... 76 F8
Albion St. Bail BD17 ... 38 C4
Albion St. Batley WF17 ... 118 C5
Albion St. Birk BD11 ... 96 C3
Albion St. Brad BD1 ... 201 B2
Albion St. Brig HD6 ... 115 B2
Albion St. Castle WF10 ... 124 C8
Albion St. Clec BD19 ... 116 D7
Albion St. Dew WF13 ... 118 C1
Albion St. Elland HX5 ... 134 F7
Albion St. Hali HX1 ... 203 F3
Albion St. Heck WF16 ... 117 C4
Albion St. Leeds LS1 ... 211 F3
Albion St. Liver WF15 ... 117 B3
Albion St. Mir WF14 ... 138 A4
Albion St. Morley LS27 ... 98 B4
Albion St. Oaken OL15 ... 129 C1
Albion St. Ship BD18 ... 54 F8
Albion St. Thorn BD13 ... 72 E6
Albion Terr. Brad BD12 ... 94 D2 4
Albion Terr. S Elm WF9 ... 182 F3
Albion Terr. Wake WF1 ... 142 D8
Albion Way. Leeds LS12 ... 210 A2
Alcester Garth. Brad BD3 ... 56 A1
Alcester Pl. Leeds LS8 ... 207 F1
Alcester Rd. Leeds LS8 ... 207 F1
Alcester Terr. Leeds LS8 ... 204 A1
Aldams Rd. Dew WF12 ... 139 D4
Alden Ave. Morley LS27 ... 97 F2
Alden Cl. Morley LS27 ... 97 F2
Alden Ct. Morley LS27 ... 98 A2
Alder Ave. Keigh BD21 ... 35 A8
Alder Carr. Bail BD17 ... 38 D2
Alder Cl. Mapp S75 ... 178 A1
Alder Dr. Pudsey LS28 ... 76 D8
Alder Garth. Pudsey LS28 ... 76 C7
Alder Gr. Hali HX2 ... 112 C7
Alder Hill Ave. Leeds LS6 ... 59 F4
Alder Hill Gr. Leeds LS6 ... 59 F4

Alder St. Hud HD1, HD2 ... 136 B1
Aldermanbury. Brad BD1 ... 74 F2
Alderney Rd. Batley WF12 ... 118 F2
Aldersholes La. Thorn BD13 ... 72 D6 9
Aldershot Cl. Thorn BD13 ... 72 C6
Aldersholes La. Thorn BD13 ... 72 C5
Alderson St. Brad BD6 ... 93 E7 2
Alderstone Rise. Hud HD3 ... 135 A2
Alderside. Batley WF17 ... 96 E1
Alderson Rd. Wake WF2 ... 142 C7
Alderton Bank. Leeds LS17 ... 43 A2
Alderton Cres. Leeds LS17 ... 43 A2
Alderton Hts. Leeds LS17 ... 42 F2
Alderton Mount. Leeds LS17 ... 42 F2
Alderton Pl. Leeds LS17 ... 42 F2
Alderton Rise. Leeds LS17 ... 42 F2
Aldonley. Hud HD5 ... 155 A4
Alegar St. Brig HD6 ... 115 C2
Alexander Cres. Pont WF7 ... 145 E7
Alexander Rd. Feath WF7 ... 145 E6
Alexander St. Brad BD10 ... 73 B4 10
Alexander St. Brad BD6 ... 94 B8 5
Alexander St. Leeds LS1 ... 79 B8
Alexandra Ave. Hali HX3 ... 113 A2
Alexandra Cres. Dew WF13 ... 118 A2
Alexandra Cres. Ell HX4 ... 135 B7
Alexandra Cres. Ilkley S29 ... 8 A4
Alexandra Dr. Nor WF6 ... 144 B7
Alexandra Gr. Leeds LS6 ... 59 E2 5
Alexandra Gr. Pudsey LS28 ... 76 D6
Alexandra Rd. Brad BD2 ... 56 C5
Alexandra Rd. Heb Br HX7 ... 89 A3 8
Alexandra Rd. Hors LS18 ... 58 C8
Alexandra Rd. Hud HD3 ... 153 C5
Alexandra Sq. Ship BD18 ... 54 F8 14
Alexandra St. Brad BD7 ... 74 C5
Alexandra St. Hali HX1 ... 113 A4
Alexandra St. Liver WF15 ... 117 A4 4
Alexandra St. Queen BD13 ... 72 E1
Alexandra Terr. Leeds LS19 ... 40 C7 6
Alford Terr. Brad BD7 ... 74 A7
Alfred E Briggs Almshouses. Brad BD12 ... 94 B3 3
Alfred St. Batley WF17 ... 118 B4
Alfred St. Brig HD6 ... 115 A3
Alfred St. Dew WF13 ... 118 C1 1
Alfred St E. Hali HX1 ... 113 D7
Alfred St. Elland HX4 ... 134 D7
Alfred St. Hali HX1 ... 203 F1
Alfred St. Keigh BD21 ... 35 A8
Alfred St. Liver WF15 ... 117 B4 3
Alfred St. Roy S71 ... 179 C4
Alfred's Way. Batley WF17 ... 118 C5
Alice St. Brad BD8 ... 74 D8
Alice St. Clec BD19 ... 116 D8 2
Alice St. Haw BD22 ... 51 C6
Alice St. Keigh BD21 ... 35 C7
Alioncoate St. Keigh BD21 ... 35 C6
All Alone. Brad BD10 ... 56 A7
All Saints C of E Jun Sch. Otley ... 22 D8
All Saints' Dri. Roth LS26 ... 101 D6
All Saints CE Jun Sch. Otley ... 22 D8
All Saints CE Jun & Inf Sch. Hali HX3 ... 113 D5
All Saints CE Prim Sch. Leeds ... 79 E8
All Saints Comp Sch. Hud ... 136 C5
All Saints Cl. B Spa LS23 ... 30 D5
All Saints' Ind Pk. Wake WF1 ... 142 B8
All Saints' Rd. Brad BD7 ... 74 C5
All Saints' View. Roth LS26 ... 101 D6
All Souls' Rd. Hali HX3 ... 92 C1 3
All Souls' St. Hali HX3 ... 92 C1
All Souls' Terr. Hali HX3 ... 92 C1
All Saints CE Prim Sch. Wake ... 141 E5
Allan St. Brad BD3 ... 75 B6
Allan Terr. Sow B HX6 ... 112 B3
Allandale Ave. Brad BD6 ... 94 A7
Allandale Rd. Brad BD6 ... 94 A7
Allanfield Terr. Weth LS22 ... 13 B3
Allen Croft. Brad BD11 ... 96 A5
Allenby Cres. Leeds LS11 ... 99 B7
Allenby Dr. Leeds LS11 ... 99 B7
Allenby Gdns. Leeds LS11 ... 99 B7
Allenby Gr. Leeds LS11 ... 99 B7
Allenby Pl. Leeds LS11 ... 99 B7
Allenby Rd. Leeds LS11 ... 99 B7
Allenby View. Leeds LS11 ... 99 B7
Allendale Rd. Mapp S75 ... 178 A1
Allergill Pk. Holmfl HD7 ... 189 D2
Allerton Bank. Leeds LS17 ... 43 A3
Allerton Bywater Jnr Sch. Kippax ... 103 B5
Allerton Bywater Prim Sch. Kippax ... 103 B5
Allerton Cl. Brad BD15 ... 53 D5
Allerton Dr. Leeds LS17 ... 43 A2
Allerton Grange Ave. Leeds LS17 ... 43 E1
Allerton Grange Cl. Leeds LS17 ... 43 E1
Allerton Grange Cres. Leeds LS17 ... 43 E1
Allerton Grange Croft. Leeds LS8 ... 61 D8
Allerton Grange Dr. Leeds LS17 ... 43 E1
Allerton Grange Gdns. Leeds LS17 ... 43 E1
Allerton Grange High Sch. Leeds ... 43 D1
Allerton Grange Rise. Leeds LS17 ... 43 D1
Allerton Grange Vale. Leeds LS17 ... 43 E1
Allerton Grange Way. Leeds LS17 ... 43 E1
Allerton Grange Wlk. Leeds LS17 ... 43 D1
Allerton High Sch. Leeds ... 43 B3
Allerton Hill. Leeds LS7 ... 60 C7
Allerton La. Thorn BD13, BD15 ... 72 E8
Allerton Pk. Leeds LS7 ... 60 C6
Allerton Pl. Hali HX1 ... 113 A7
Allerton Rd. Brad BD15, BD8 ... 54 D1
Allerton Rd. Leeds LS17 ... 43 A3
Allerton St. Leeds LS4 ... 59 D2
Allescholes Rd. Tod OL14 ... 106 F3
Allinson St. Leeds LS12 ... 78 E6 7
Allison Dr. Hud HD4 ... 154 A4
Allison La. Brad BD2 ... 56 C2
Allison Dr. Hud HD4 ... 136 B2

202 All - Ash

Allison La. Ship BD2 55 D4
Allison St. Feath WF7 145 C5
Allison Terr. Wake WF2 120 B2
Alloe Field View. Hali HX2 91 E6
Allott Cl. S Elm WF9 182 F3
Allums La. Arth LS21 25 F5
Alma Cl. Pudsey LS28 57 C3
Alma Cotts. Leeds LS6 59 D5 12
Alma Dr. Hud HD5 154 D6
Alma Gr. Leeds LS9 60 F2
Alma Gr. Ship BD18 55 D8
Alma La. Batley WF16 117 D6
Alma La. Rip HX6 132 B7
Alma Pl. Keigh BD21 35 C5
Alma Pl. Leeds BD3 60 E2
Alma Rd. Leeds LS6 59 E5
Alma Rd. Tod OL14 108 A1
Alma St. Bacup OL13 106 A2
Alma St. Brad BD4 75 D3
Alma St. Brad BD4 75 D5
Alma St. Elland HX5 135 A6
Alma St. Haw BD22 51 C8
Alma St. Keigh BD21 35 C5
Alma St. Leeds LS9 60 F1
Alma St. Queen BD13 72 D1
Alma St. Roth LS26 101 D7
Alma St. Ship BD18 55 D8
Alma St. Tod OL14 108 A1
Alma St. Yeadon LS19 40 C7
Alma Terr. Keigh BD20 19 E1
Alma Terr. Keigh BD21 35 C5
Alma Terr. Roth LS26 100 D6
Almhouses. Keigh BD21 35 A3
Almond Cl. S Elm WF9 183 A5
Almond St. Brad BD3 75 C6
Almond Way. Batley WF17 96 F1
Almondbury Bank. Hud HD5 154 E5
Almondbury Cl. Hud HD5 155 A3
Almondbury Comm. Hud HD4 154 F1
Almondbury Cty Jun Sch. Hud 155 A4
Almondbury Cty Sec Sch. Hud 154 F4
Almondbury Gram Sch. Hud 155 A2
Almondroyd. Liver WF16 117 C5
Almscliffe Ave. Dew WF12 139 E8
Almshouse Hill. Bramham LS23 30 D2
Almshouse La. Crig WF2 160 B4
Almshouse La. Wake WF1 142 C6
Alpha St. Keigh BD21 35 D6
Alpine Cl. Batley WF17 118 B4
Alpine Rise. Thorn BD13 72 D6
Alpine Terr. Roth LS26 100 D6
Alston Cl. Brad BD9 54 D1
Alston La. Leeds LS14 62 A3
Alston Rd. Keigh BD21 18 D1
Altar Dr. Brad BD9 55 A3
Altar Dr. Keigh BD20 19 A1
Altar La. Harden BD16 36 C4
Altar View. Bing BD16 36 E5
Althorpe Gr. Brad BD10 56 A6
Altinkool St. Wake WF1 142 F2
Altofts Hall Rd. Nor WF6 122 F4
Altofts La. Castle WF10 123 D5
Altofts Lodge Dr. Nor WF6 122 E3
Altofts Mid Sch. Nor 122 F3
Altofts Rd. Nor WF6 123 A2
Alton Ave. Hud HD5 154 F7
Alton Gr. Brad BD9 54 F3
Alton Gr. Ship BD18 55 B5
Alton Way. Mapp S75 178 A1
Alum Ct. Brad BD9 55 A3
Alum Dr. Brad BD9 55 A3
Alvanley Ct. Brad BD8 73 D8
Alverthorpe Rd. Wake WF2 141 F6
Alverthorpe St Paul's CE (Aided)
Fst Sch. Wake 141 E8
Alvo Terr. Ship BD18 55 B6
Alwen Ave. Hud HD2 135 F2
Alwoodley Chase. Leeds LS17 43 E5
Alwoodley Court Gdns. Leeds LS17 . 43 A6
Alwoodley Ct. Leeds LS17 42 F5
Alwoodley Gdns. Leeds LS17 43 A5
Alwoodley Golf Course. Leeds 43 F6
Alwoodley La. Leeds LS17 43 C6
Alwoodley Prim Sch. Leeds 43 A3
Amber St. Batley WF17 118 A6
Amberley Ct. Brad BD3 75 C6
Amberley Gdns. Leeds LS12 78 C6
Amberley Rd. Leeds LS12 78 C6
Amberley Rise. Ad Le S DN6 184 F2
Amberley St. Brad BD3 75 C7
Amberley St. Leeds LS12 78 D6
Amberton App. Leeds LS8 61 C4
Amberton Cl. Leeds LS8 61 C5
Amberton Cres. Leeds LS8 61 C4
Amberton Garth. Leeds LS8 61 C4
Amberton Gdns. Leeds LS8 61 C4
Amberton Gr. Leeds LS8 61 C4
Amberton La. Leeds LS8 61 C4
Amberton Mount. Leeds LS8 61 C4
Amberton Pl. Leeds LS8 61 B4
Amberton Rd. Leeds LS8, LS9 61 C4
Amberton St. Leeds LS8 61 C4
Amberton Terr. Leeds LS8 61 C5
Amble Tonia. Denh BD13 52 E1
Ambler St. Brad BD8 55 C1
Ambler St. Castle WF10 124 E7
Ambler St. Keigh BD21 35 D7
Ambler Way. Queen BD13 92 C7
Amblers Croft. Brad BD10 39 B2
Amblers Ct. Pudsey LS28 76 E6
Amblers Mews. Bail BD17 38 C4 4
Amblers Mews. Keigh BD20 36 D8
Amblers Terr. Hali HX3 92 C1 10
Ambleside Ave. Brad BD9 54 F2
Ambleside Dr. Walton WF2 161 A6
Ambleside Gdns. Pudsey LS28 76 C7
Ambleside Gr. Roth LS26 101 C6
Ambleside Rd. Castle WF10 104 E1
Ambleside Wlk. Weth LS22 13 B6
Amelia Way. Queen BD13 92 C8
Amelia St. Ship BD18 54 F8 1
America La. Brig HD6 115 C2
America La. S in Cra BD20 16 E1
America Moor La. Morley LS27 98 A2
Amisfield Rd. Brig HX3 114 D8
Amos St. Hali HX1 112 F7
Amport Cl. Brig HD6 115 B1
Amundsen Ave. Brad BD2 56 A5
Amy St. Bing BD16 37 A3 9
Amy St. Hali HX3 92 A2 3
Amyroyce Dr. Ship BD18 55 E7
Anaheim Dr. Loft G WF1 121 D5
Ancaster Cres. Leeds LS16 59 B7
Ancaster Rd. Leeds LS16 59 B7
Ancaster View. Leeds LS16 59 B7
Anchor Pl. Brig HD6 136 D8
Anchor St. Hud HD1 154 B7
Anchor St. Tod OL14 108 C5 4
Anderson Ave. Leeds LS8 60 E2
Anderson House. Bail BD17 38 B1
Anderson Mount. Leeds LS8 60 E2
Anderson St. Brad BD8 55 C1
Anderson St. Pont WF8 125 C1
Anderson St. Wake WF2 142 A6
Anderton St. Glu BD20 16 D7
Anderton St. Wake WF1 142 E3
Andover Gn. Brad BD4 75 E4
Andrew Cl. Hali HX3 114 A4
Andrew Cres. Hud HD4 153 A1
Andrew Cres. Loft G WF1 121 B5
Andrew St. Feath WF7 145 C4
Andrew St. Pudsey LS28 57 D2 10
Andrew St. Pudsey LS28 57 D3 4
Andrew St. Wake WF1 142 B8
Andrews Gr. Ack M T WF7 163 F6
Anerley St. Brad BD4 75 B2
Angel Rd. Hali HX1 113 A8
Angel Row. Roth LS26 100 B5
Angel St. Bail BD17 38 D4
Angel Way. Brad BD7 74 D6
Angerton Way. Brad BD6 94 A6
Anglers Country Park. Ryhill 161 F5
Angus Ave. Brad BD12 94 C1
Anlaby St. Brad BD4 75 D5
Ann Pl. Brad BD5 74 E5
Ann St. Denh BD13 52 D1
Ann St. Haw BD22 51 D7
Ann St. Keigh BD21 35 B6
Annat Royd La. Ingb S30 191 D1
Anne Cres. S Hie S72 180 E5
Anne Gate. Brad BD1 74 F7
Anne St. Batley WF17 118 A7
Anne St. Brad BD7 73 F3
Anne's Ct. Hali HX3 114 A4
Annie St. Hali HX6 112 B4 1
Annie St. Haw BD22 51 F8
Annie St. Hem WF9 163 A4
Annie St. Keigh BD21 18 C1
Annie St. Loft G WF1 121 B4
Annie St. Morley LS27 98 B4
Annie St. Ship BD18 55 C6
Annison St. Brad BD3 75 A7
Annottes Croft. Hud HD5 154 F7
Anroyd St. Dew WF13 118 A1
Anson Gr. Brad BD7 73 F2
Anston Dr. S Elm WF9 183 A5
Anthony La. Harden BD16 36 B2
Antony Cl. Hud HD3 134 D1
Anvil Ct. Brad BD8 55 B1
Anvil St. Brad BD8 55 B1
Anvil St. Brig HD6 115 A3
Apex Bsns Ctr. Leeds 79 C5
Apex View. Leeds LS11 79 B5
Apex Way. Leeds LS11 79 C5
Apperley Gdns. Brad BD10 56 E8
Apperley La. Yeadon BD10 39 F2
Apperley La. Yeadon LS19 40 A4
Apperley Rd. Brad BD10 56 D8
Apple Cl. Batley WF17 97 A2
Apple House Terr. Hali HX2 90 E1
Apple St. Keigh BD21 35 A3
Apple St. Oxen BD22 51 C2
Apple Tree Cl. E Ard WF3 120 C8
Apple Tree Cl. Pont WF8 146 B6
Apple Tree Ct. E Ard WF3 120 C7
Apple Tree Gdns. Ilkley LS29 7 F4
Apple Tree Rd. Feath WF7 145 E4
Appleby La. Gar LS25 83 B7
Appleby Pl. Ad Le S DN6 184 F2
Appleby Pl. Leeds LS15 80 E8
Appleby Way. Morley LS27 98 B4
Appleby Way. Weth LS22 13 E7
Appleby Wlk. Leeds LS15 80 E8
Applegarth. Roth LS26 101 C7
Applegarth. Wake WF2 160 E7
Applehaigh Gr. Roy S71 179 A4
Applehaigh La. Notton WF4 159 A6
Applehaigh View. Roy S71 179 A4
Appleshaw Cres. Wake WF2 120 F3
Appleton Cl. Bing BD16 37 B5
Appleton Cl. Brad BD12 94 F5
Appleton Cl. Leeds LS9 79 F8 5
Appleton Ct. Leeds BD13, LS9 79 F8 4
Appleton Gr. Leeds LS9 79 F8
Appleton Sq. Leeds LS9 79 F8 6
Appleton Way. Leeds LS9 79 F8
Appletree Cl. B Spa LS23 30 D7
Appleyard Rd. Heb Br HX7 89 F1
Approach The. B in Elm LS15 62 F7
April Ct. Liver WF15 117 A2
Aprilia Ct. Brad BD14 73 D5
Apsley Cres. Brad BD8 55 C1
Apsley St. Haw BD22 34 D3
Apsley St. Haw BD22 51 D7 7
Apsley St. Keigh BD21 35 B5 8
Apsley Terr. Haw BD22 34 D3
Aquamarine Dr. Hud HD2 136 C2
Aquila Way. Clec WF15 116 D5
Arborary La. Mel HD4 170 F6
Arbour The. Ilkley LS29 8 A6
Arcade The. Dew WF12 139 D8 5
Arcade The. Knot WF11 126 E4
Arcadia St. Keigh BD21 35 B5 12
Archbell Ave. Brig HD6 136 B8
Archbishop Cranmer CE Mid Sch.
Leeds 43 B3
Archer Rd. Brig HD6 115 D1
Archer St. Castle WF10 124 C6
Archery Pl. Leeds LS2 60 B2
Archery Rd. Leeds LS2 60 B2
Archery St. Leeds LS2 60 B2
Archery Terr. Leeds LS2 60 B2
Arches St. Hali HX1 113 B6
Arches The. Hali HX3 92 D1
Archibald St. Brad BD7 74 C7
Arctic Par. Brad BD7 74 A4
Arctic St. Haw BD22 51 E8 6
Arctic St. Keigh BD20 18 B1
Arden Ct. Hor WF4 159 A8
Arden Ct. Kirkhe HD5 155 C7
Arden Rd. Brad BD8 73 C7
Arden Rd. Hali HX1 113 B6
Ardennes Cl. Brad BD2 55 F4
Ardsley Cl. Brad BD4 75 F2
Argent Way. Brad BD4 75 F2
Argie Ave. Leeds LS4 59 B3
Argie Gdns. Leeds LS4 59 C2 3
Argie Rd. Leeds LS4 59 C2
Argie Terr. Leeds LS4 59 C2
Argyl Mews. E Kes LS17 28 C5
Argyle Rd. Knot WF11 126 C5
Argyle Rd. Leeds LS9 79 D8
Argyle St. Brad BD4 75 B4
Argyle St. Keigh BD21 35 B7
Argyle St. Mars HD7 168 F4
Argyle St. Ship BD18 55 B6
Argyle St. Wake WF1 142 E4
Argyll Ave. Pont WF8 146 B8 3
Argyll Cl. Bail BD17 38 E2
Argyll Cl. Hors LS18 41 B4
Ark St. Leeds LS9 79 E6
Arkendale Mews. Brad BD7 73 E3 5
Arkenley La. Hud HD4 155 A2
Arkenmore. Hud HD5 154 F7
Arksey Pl. Leeds LS12 78 C8 14
Arksey Terr. Leeds LS12 78 C8 10
Arkwright House. Liver WF15 117 A5 9
Arkwright St. Brad BD14 73 B4
Arkwright St. Brad BD4 75 E6
Arkwright St. Leeds LS12 78 E8
Arlesford Rd. Brad BD4 75 E2
Arley Cl. Holmfi HD7 188 F8
Arley Gr. Leeds LS12 78 C8 1
Arley Pl. Leeds LS12 78 C8
Arley St. Leeds LS12 59 C1 5
Arley Terr. Leeds LS12 78 C8
Arlington Bsns Ctr. Morley 98 E8
Arlington Cres. Hali HX2 112 D4
Arlington Gr. Leeds LS8 61 B5
Arlington Rd. Leeds LS8 61 B5
Arlington St. Brad BD3 75 B6
Arlington St. Wake WF1 142 B8
Armadale Ave. Brad BD4 95 B8
Armgill La. Ship BD2 55 D4
Armidale Way. Brad BD2 55 F3
Armitage Ave. Brig HD6 136 B8
Armitage Bldgs. E Ard WF12 119 B6
Armitage Rd. Brad BD12 94 F4
Armitage Rd. Hali HX1 112 F5 21
Armitage Rd. Hud HD2 135 F1
Armitage Rd. Hud HD3 153 B5
Armitage Rd. Hud HD4 171 E8
Armitage Rd. Wake WF2 141 D8
Armitage Sq. Pudsey LS28 76 D6 2
Armitage St. Castle WF10 124 C8
Armitage St. Dew WF13 138 D5
Armitage St. Hud HD4 154 A4
Armitage St. Roth LS26 100 E4
Armley Grange Ave. Leeds LS12 78 A8
Armley Grange Cres. Leeds LS12 58 F1
Armley Grange Dr. Leeds LS12 77 F8
Armley Grange Mount. Leeds LS12 . 77 F8
Armley Grange Oval. Leeds LS12 58 F1
Armley Grange Rise. Leeds LS12 77 F8
Armley Grange View. Leeds LS12 78 A8
Armley Grange Wlk. Leeds LS12 78 A8
Armley Grove Pl. Leeds LS12 78 D7
Armley Lodge Rd. Leeds LS12 78 C8
Armley Lodge Sch. Leeds 78 C8
Armley Mills Ind Mus. Leeds 59 D1
Armley Park Rd. Leeds LS12 59 C1
Armley Prim Sch. Leeds 78 C8
Armley Rd. Leeds LS12 78 E7
Armley Ridge Cl. Leeds LS12 78 A8
Armley Ridge Rd. Leeds LS12 59 A1
Armley Ridge Rd. Leeds LS12 78 B8
Armoury Ave. Mir WF14 138 A5
Armstrong Cl. Nor WF6 123 A4
Armstrong St. Brad BD4 75 D6
Armstrong St. Pudsey LS28 57 D2 9
Armstrong Terr. Pont WF8 146 B7 2
Armytage Cres. Hud HD1 153 F3
Armytage Rd. Brig HD6 115 D1
Armytage Way. Brig HD6 115 D1
Armytage Wlk. S Kirk WF9 182 C3
Arncliffe Ave. Keigh BD22 35 A5 1
Arncliffe Cres. Brig HD6 135 E8
Arncliffe Cres. Morley LS27 98 C2
Arncliffe Ct. Hud HD1 153 E7
Arncliffe Dr. Knot WF11 126 C4
Arncliffe Garth. Pudsey LS28 57 D2 11
Arncliffe Gdns. Batley WF17 118 B5
Arncliffe Gr. Keigh BD22 35 A6 17
Arncliffe Grange. Leeds LS17 43 D2
Arncliffe Rd. Batley WF17 118 B5
Arncliffe Rd. Keigh BD22 35 A6
Arncliffe Rd. Leeds LS16 59 A8
Arncliffe Rd. Wake WF1 142 F8
Arncliffe St. Pudsey LS28 57 D2
Arncliffe Terr. Brad BD7 74 B6
Arndale Ctr. Leeds LS6 59 D5 5
Arndale Gr. Holmfi HD7 189 B4
Arndale Sh Ctr The. Ship BD18 55 B7
Arnford Cl. Brad BD3 74 F8
Arnold Ave. Hud HD2 135 F1
Arnold Pl. Brad BD8 74 C8
Arnold Royd. Brig HD6 135 E7
Arnold St. Brad BD8 55 C1
Arnold St. Hali HX6 112 B4 4
Arnold St. Hali HX1 113 A7
Arnold St. Hud HD2 135 F1
Arnold St. Liver WF15 117 A4
Arnside Ave. Keigh BD20 18 E1
Arnside Cl. Castle WF10 125 D8
Arnside Cres. Castle WF10 125 D8
Arnside Rd. Brad BD5 74 E2
Arran Cl. Hud HD7 152 D5
Arran Ct. Gar LS25 82 F5
Arran Dr. Gar LS25 82 F5
Arran Dr. Hors LS18 41 B4
Arrunden La. Holmfi HD7 188 F2
Arthington Ave. Leeds LS10 79 D2
Arthington Cl. E Ard WF3 119 D7
Arthington Ct. Leeds LS10 79 D2
Arthington Garth. Arth LS21 24 F6
Arthington Gr. Leeds LS10 79 D2
Arthington La. Arth LS21 25 D6
Arthington La. Pool LS21 24 E6
Arthington Lawns. Pool LS21 24 E6
Arthington Pl. Leeds LS10 79 D2
Arthington Rd. Eccup LS16 25 C2
Arthington Sch. Arth 25 B6
Arthington St. Brad BD8 74 C8
Arthington St. Leeds LS10 79 D2
Arthington Terr. Leeds LS10 79 D2
Arthington View. Leeds LS10 79 D2
Arthur Ave. Brad BD8 73 D7
Arthur Gr. Batley WF17 117 F8
Arthur St. Bacup OL13 106 B3
Arthur St. Bing BD16 36 F3
Arthur St. Brad BD10 56 B6
Arthur St. Brig HD6 115 C2
Arthur St. Haw BD22 34 C2
Arthur St. Hud HD7 152 E4
Arthur St. Pudsey LS28 57 D2
Arthur St. Pudsey LS28 57 E2
Arthur St. Wake WF1 142 E3
Arthursdale Cl. B in Elm LS15 62 F7
Arthursdale Dr. B in Elm LS15 62 F7
Arthursdale Grange. B in Elm LS15 . 62 F7
Artillery St. Batley WF16 117 D3
Artist St. Leeds LS12 78 E7
Arum St. Brad BD5 74 C3
Arundel Cl. Batley WF17 97 B2
Arundel Cl. Wake WF1 142 C7
Arundel St. Gar LS25 83 B8
Arundel St. Hali HX1 112 F7 10
Arundel St. Wake WF1 142 C7
Arundel Wlk. Batley WF17 97 B1
Ascot Ave. Brad BD7 73 E2
Ascot Dr. Brad BD7 73 E2
Ascot Gdns. Brad BD7 73 E2
Ascot Gr. Brig HD6 135 E8
Ascot Par. Brad BD7 73 E2
Ascot Rd. Kippax LS25 82 F2
Ascot Terr. Leeds LS9 79 F7
Asdale Rd. Crig WF2 160 B7
Asdale Rd. Wake WF2 160 B7
Ash Ave. Leeds LS6 59 D5
Ash Brow. Floc WF4 157 C3
Ash Brow Rd. Hud HD2 136 B3
Ash Cl. Brig HX3 114 D8
Ash Cl. Ilkley LS29 7 E4
Ash Cl. Ossett WF5 140 D5
Ash Cres. Leeds LS6 59 D5
Ash Cres. Loft G WF3 121 F5
Ash Croft. Brad BD6 94 A8
Ash Ct. Brig BD19 115 F8
Ash Gdns. Leeds LS6 59 D5
Ash Ghyll Gdns. Bing BD16 36 F4
Ash Gn. Pont WF8 125 F1
Ash Gr. Bing BD16 37 A1
Ash Gr. Birk BD11 96 A6
Ash Gr. Brig HD6 115 C2
Ash Gr. Clec BD19 96 A1
Ash Gr. Clec BD19 116 B6
Ash Gr. Dar WF8 147 C5
Ash Gr. Hors LS18 41 C2
Ash Gr. Ilkley LS29 8 C5
Ash Gr. Keigh BD21 35 B4
Ash Gr. Leeds LS6 59 F3
Ash Gr. Loft G WF3 121 F2
Ash Gr. Otley LS21 22 F7
Ash Gr. Pudsey LS28 76 E6
Ash Gr. S Elm WF9 183 A4
Ash Gr. S in Cra BD20 16 D5
Ash Gr. Stee BD20 17 D5
Ash Grove Rd. Holmfi HD7 188 E5
Ash Grove Terr. Brig HD6 115 A1 6
Ash Hall La. Rip HX6 132 A7
Ash Hill Dr. Thorner LS17 44 F4
Ash Hill Garth. Thorner LS17 44 F4
Ash Hill Gdns. Thorner LS17 44 F4
Ash Hill La. Thorner LS17 44 F4
Ash Hill Wlk. Brad BD4 75 B4
Ash La. Emley HD8 175 E7
Ash La. Gar LS25 83 A8
Ash Lea. Fair WF11 105 B4
Ash Lea. Loft G WF3 121 F3
Ash Meadow Cl. Hud HD2 136 C3
Ash Mount. Brad BD7 74 B5
Ash Mount. Keigh BD21 35 A5
Ash Rd. Leeds LS6 59 C5
Ash Rd. Shaf S72 180 D2
Ash St. Clec BD19 116 C7
Ash St. Crof WF4 162 A7
Ash St. Glu BD20 16 D6
Ash St. Hud HD1 154 A8
Ash St. Ilkley LS29 8 C5
Ash St. Loft G WF3 121 F2
Ash St. Oxen BD22 51 C3
Ash Terr. Bing BD16 36 F2
Ash Terr. Gar LS25 83 A8
Ash Terr. Leeds LS6 59 D5 2
Ash Terr. Rip HX6 132 C3
Ash Tree App. Leeds LS14 62 D4
Ash Tree Ave. Thorn BD13 72 B6
Ash Tree Bank. Leeds LS14 62 D5
Ash Tree Cl. Leeds LS14 62 D5
Ash Tree Ct. Leeds LS14 62 D5 5
Ash Tree Gdns. Hali HX2 91 C5
Ash Tree Gdns. Leeds LS14 62 D5
Ash Tree Gdns. Nor WF6 122 F3
Ash Tree Gr. Leeds LS14 62 D4
Ash Tree Grange. Leeds LS14 62 D5 4
Ash Tree Inf Sch. Hali 91 C5
Ash Tree Rd. Hali HX2 91 C5
Ash Tree View. Leeds LS14 62 D5 7
Ash Tree Wlk. Bur in W LS29 9 E1
Ash Tree Wlk. Leeds LS14 62 D5 8
Ash View. E Ard WF3 120 C7
Ash View. Leeds LS6 59 D5 3
Ash Wlk. Hud HD7 152 E5
Ashbourne Ave. Brad BD2 55 F3
Ashbourne Ave. Clec BD19 116 D6
Ashbourne Bank. Brad BD2 55 F3
Ashbourne Cl. Brad BD2 55 F4
Ashbourne Cres. Brad BD2 55 F3
Ashbourne Cres. Gar LS25 82 F5
Ashbourne Cres. Queen BD13 72 D1
Ashbourne Croft. Clec BD19 116 D6
Ashbourne Dr. Brad BD2 55 F3
Ashbourne Dr. Clec BD19 116 D6
Ashbourne Dr. Pont WF8 146 D5
Ashbourne Garth. Brad BD2 56 A4
Ashbourne Gdns. Brad BD2 55 F3
Ashbourne Gdns. Clec BD19 116 D6
Ashbourne Gr. Brad BD2 55 F3
Ashbourne Gr. Hali HX1 112 F7
Ashbourne Haven. Brad BD2 55 F3
Ashbourne Mount. Brad BD2 55 F3
Ashbourne Oval. Brad BD2 55 F3
Ashbourne Rd. Brad BD2 55 F3
Ashbourne Rd. Keigh BD21 35 A5
Ashbourne Rise. Brad BD2 55 F3
Ashbourne View. Clec BD19 116 D6
Ashbourne Way. Brad BD2 55 F3
Ashbourne Way. Clec BD19 116 D6
Ashbrook Cl. Ossett WF5 140 D7
Ashbrooke Pk. Leeds 79 C2
Ashbrow Cty Prim Sch. Hud 136 C3
Ashbrow Inf Sch. Hud 136 B3
Ashburn Cl. Weth LS22 13 D7
Ashburn Croft. Weth LS22 13 D7
Ashburn Dr. Weth LS22 13 D7
Ashburn Gr. Bail BD17 38 C4
Ashburn Gr. Weth LS22 13 D7
Ashburn Pl. Ilkley LS29 8 A3
Ashburn Way. Weth LS22 13 D7
Ashburnham Gr. Brad BD9 55 B3
Ashbury Chase. Loft G WF1 121 A5
Ashby Ave. Leeds LS13 58 D1
Ashby Cl. Liver WF15 116 F1
Ashby Cres. Leeds LS13 58 D1
Ashby Mount. Leeds LS13 58 D2 4
Ashby Sq. Leeds LS13 58 D2
Ashby St. Brad BD4 75 A4
Ashby Terr. Leeds LS13 58 D2
Ashby View. Leeds LS13 58 D2
Ashcombe Dr. Knot WF11 126 F3
Ashcroft Ave. Feath WF7 145 C4
Ashcroft Rd. Feath WF7 145 C4
Ashdale La. Weth LS22 13 D8
Ashdale. Wake WF2 142 E1
Ashday La. Brig HX3 114 B3
Ashday La. Hali HX3 114 B3
Ashdene App. Crof WF4 143 F1
Ashdene Ave. Crof WF4 143 F1
Ashdene Cl. Pudsey LS28 76 E5
Ashdene Cres. Crof WF4 143 F1
Ashdene Cres. Pudsey LS28 76 E5
Ashdene Ct. Cull BD13 52 D6
Ashdene Dr. Crof WF4 143 F1
Ashdene Garth. Crof WF4 143 F1
Ashdene. Gild LS12 77 D3
Ashdene Gr. Pont WF8 125 F4
Ashdene. Tod OL14 108 B1
Ashdown Cl. Brad BD6 74 B1 9
Ashdown Cl. Hali HX2 112 D6
Ashdown Ct. Ship BD18 55 A7
Ashdown Rd. Wake WF1 142 E3
Ashdown St. Leeds LS13 58 C2 13
Ashenhurst Ave. Hud HD4 154 C3
Ashenhurst Cl. Hud HD4 154 B3
Ashenhurst Cl. Tod OL14 108 A7
Ashenhurst Rd. Hud HD4 154 B3
Ashenhurst Rd. Tod OL14 108 A7
Ashenhurst Rise. Hud HD4 154 B3
Ashes La. Hud HD4 154 C1
Ashes La. Tod OL14 108 D7
Ashfield Ave. Morley LS27 97 F3
Ashfield Ave. Ship BD18 55 B5
Ashfield Ave. Skel HD8 175 A1
Ashfield. Brad BD4 75 D1
Ashfield Cl. Hali HX3 91 F2
Ashfield Cl. Leeds LS15 62 D4
Ashfield Cl. Leeds LS12 77 F4
Ashfield Cres. Bing BD16 37 A2
Ashfield Cres. Pudsey LS28 57 E1
Ashfield Ct. Bing BD16 37 A2 5
Ashfield. Dew WF12 139 D4
Ashfield Dr. Bail BD17 38 D3
Ashfield Dr. Hali HX3 92 A2
Ashfield Dr. Ship BD18, BD9 55 B5
Ashfield Gr. Pudsey LS28 57 E1 6
Ashfield Gr. Ship BD9 55 B5
Ashfield. Leeds LS12 77 F4
Ashfield Pk. Leeds LS6 59 E5 1
Ashfield Pl. Brad BD2 56 D2
Ashfield Rd. Batley WF17 97 A2
Ashfield Rd. Brad BD10 39 C1
Ashfield Rd. Elland HX4 134 B7
Ashfield Rd. Hem WF9 181 D5
Ashfield Rd. Hud HD2 135 E1
Ashfield Rd. Morley LS27 97 F3
Ashfield Rd. Pudsey LS28 57 E1
Ashfield Rd. Ship BD18 54 E7
Ashfield Rd. Thorn BD13 72 D6
Ashfield St. Hud HD2 136 B2
Ashfield St. Keigh BD21 35 B6 9
Ashfield St. Nor WF6 123 C3
Ashfield Terr. Brad BD12 94 D4
Ashfield Terr. Clec BD19 116 E7 10
Ashfield Terr. Elland HX4 134 B8
Ashfield Terr. Haw BD22 51 C6 11
Ashfield Terr. Leeds LS15 62 D4
Ashfield Terr. Midd WF3 99 F2
Ashfield Way. Leeds LS12 77 F4
Ashfield. Weth LS22 13 F6
Ashford Ct. Kirkb HD8 173 F7
Ashford Dr. Pudsey LS28 76 F6
Ashford Gn. Brad BD6 73 F1
Ashford Pk. Hud HD7 152 D5
Ashgap La. Nor WF6 123 B3
Ashgrove Ave. Hali HX3 113 E3 1
Ashgrove. Brad BD2 56 C3
Ashgrove. Brad BD10 56 E7
Ashgrove. Brad BD7 74 D6
Ashgrove Cres. Kippax LS25 83 B3
Ashgrove Croft. Kippax LS25 83 B2
Ashgrove Mews. Pudsey LS13 57 F4
Ashgrove Mount. Kippax LS25 83 A3
Ashgrove Pl. Hali HX3 113 E3 3
Ashgrove Rd. Hud HD2 136 F2
Ashgrove Rd. Keigh BD20 18 A2
Ashington Cl. Brad BD2 56 D3
Ashlands Fst Sch. Ilkley 8 C5
Ashlands Rd. Ilkley LS29 8 C5
Ashlar Gr. Castle WF10 124 F6
Ashlar Gr. Queen BD13 92 D8
Ashlea Ave. Brig HD6 136 B8
Ashlea Cl. Brig HD6 136 B8
Ashlea Cl. Gar LS25 82 F5
Ashlea Ct. Leeds LS13 58 C3
Ashlea Dr. Brig HD6 136 B8
Ashlea Gate. Leeds LS13 58 C3
Ashlea Gn. Leeds LS13 58 C3
Ashleigh Ave. Pont WF8 146 D7
Ashleigh Ave. Wake WF2 141 E5
Ashleigh. Bri S72 181 A3
Ashleigh Cl. Shep HD8 173 F2
Ashleigh Dale. Hud HD2 135 E1
Ashleigh Gdns. Roth LS26 101 C6
Ashleigh Rd. Leeds LS16 59 A8
Ashleigh St. Keigh BD21 35 C8
Ashley Ave. Leeds LS9 61 A2 7
Ashley Cl. Clec BD19 96 A2
Ashley Cl. Wake WF2 120 F2
Ashley Croft. Roy S71 179 B4
Ashley Ct. S Kirk WF9 181 F1
Ashley Gr. Heb Br HX7 89 E1
Ashley Ind Est. Hud 137 A4
Ashley Ind Est. Leeds 60 C4
Ashley Ind Est. Ossett 140 E7
Ashley La. Ship BD17 55 B8
Ashley Rd. Bing BD16 37 A2
Ashley Rd. Brad BD12 94 C2
Ashley Rd. Leeds LS9 61 A2
Ashley Rd. Leeds LS12 78 B6
Ashley St. Hali HX1 112 F7
Ashley St. Ship BD17 55 B8
Ashley Terr. Leeds LS9 61 A2 6
Ashmead. B Spa LS23 30 D5
Ashmead. Batley WF17 118 A3
Ashmere Gr. Hud HD2 136 C2
Ashmews. Brad BD10 56 E7
Ashmore Dr. Ossett WF5 119 C1
Ashmount. Brad BD14 73 D4
Ashroyd. Roth LS26 100 F4
Ashtofts Mount. Guise LS20 22 E1
Ashton Ave. Brad BD7 73 E5
Ashton Ave. Leeds LS8 60 F3

Ashton Clough Rd. Liver WF15 .... 117 A4
Ashton Cres. Roth WF3 .... 100 D3
Ashton Ct. Leeds LS8 .... 61 A3
Ashton Gr. Leeds LS8 .... 60 F2
Ashton Pl. Leeds LS8 .... 61 A2
Ashton Rd. Leeds LS8 .... 60 F2
Ashton Rd. Castle WF10 .... 124 D6
Ashton Rd. Ind Est. Leeds LS8 ... 61 A3
Ashton St. Brad BD1 .... 74 D7
Ashton Terr. Leeds LS8 .... 61 A2
Ashton View. Leeds LS8 .... 60 F2
Ashtree Dr. Brad BD7 .... 73 F3
Ashtree Gr. Kippax LS25 .... 83 B1
Ashville Ave. Leeds LS6 .... 59 E3
Ashville Croft. Hali HX2 .... 112 D8 4
Ashville Gdns. Hali HX2 .... 112 D8
Ashville Gr. Hali HX2 .... 91 D1
Ashville Gr. Leeds LS6 .... 59 D3
Ashville Rd. Hali HX2 .... 91 D1
Ashville Rd. Leeds LS6 .... 59 E3
Ashville St. Hali HX3 .... 92 A1 19
Ashville Terr. Glu BD20 .... 16 D6
Ashville Terr. Leeds LS6 .... 59 D3
Ashville Terr. Pudsey LS28 .... 76 D7
Ashville Terr. Pudsey LS28 .... 57 D2 14
Ashville View. Leeds LS6 .... 59 E2
Ashwell Cl. Shar S72 .... 180 C3
Ashwell La. Ship BD9 .... 55 C6
Ashwell Rd. Brad BD8 .... 55 B1
Ashwell Rd. Brad BD9 .... 55 A4
Ashwell St. Brad BD8 .... 55 B1
Ashwood Cl. Hud HD2 .... 136 C3
Ashwood Dr. Gild LS27 .... 97 C7
Ashwood Dr. Keigh BD20 .... 19 A1
Ashwood Gdns. Gild LS27 .... 97 C7
Ashwood Gr. Gild LS27 .... 97 C7
Ashwood Gr. Hor WF4 .... 141 C2
Ashwood La. Keigh BD20 .... 19 A1
Ashwood St. Brad BD4 .... 75 B1
Ashwood Terr. Leeds LS6 .... 59 F4
Ashwood Villas. Leeds LS6 .... 59 F4
Ashworth Cl. Dew WF13 .... 139 C8
Ashworth Gdns. Dew WF13 .... 139 C8
Ashworth Pl. Brad BD6 .... 94 C7
Ashworth Rd. Dew WF13 .... 139 C8
Ashworth Rd. Bacup OL13 .... 106 A3 12
Askam Ave. Pont WF8 .... 125 F4
Asket Ave. Leeds LS14 .... 61 F5
Asket Cl. Leeds LS14 .... 61 F5
Asket Cres. Leeds LS14 .... 61 E5
Asket Garth. Leeds LS14 .... 61 F5
Asket Gdns. Leeds LS8 .... 61 D6
Asket Gn. Leeds LS14 .... 61 E6
Asket Hill City Prim Sch. Leeds .. 61 E5
Asket Hill. Leeds LS8 .... 61 E6
Asket Pl. Leeds LS14 .... 61 E5
Asket Wlk. Leeds LS14 .... 61 E5
Askey Ave. Morley LS27 .... 98 B2
Askey Cres. Morley LS27 .... 98 B2
Askham Gr. Upton WF9 .... 183 E7
Askham Rd. Castle WF10 .... 104 D1
Askrigg Dr. Brad BD2 .... 56 C2
Askwith Cty Prim Sch. Ask 9 F5
Askwith La. Ask LS21 .... 9 D4
Aspden St. Tod OL14 .... 108 B6
Aspect Gdns. Pudsey LS28 .... 76 D8
Aspect Terr. Pudsey LS28 .... 76 D8
Aspen Cl. Wake WF2 .... 120 E2
Aspen Cl. Emley HD8 .... 175 D7
Aspen Ct. Emley HD8 .... 175 C7
Aspen Mount. Morris LS16 .... 41 C2
Aspen Rise. Brad BD15 .... 53 F4
Aspinall St. Hali HX1 .... 112 F6
Aspinall St. Heb Br HX7 .... 89 E1
Aspinall Rd. Hali HX1 .... 154 B6
Asquith Ave. Morley LS27 .... 97 F5
Asquith Cl. Morley LS27 .... 97 F5
Asquith Dr. Morley LS27 .... 97 F5
Asquith St. Batley WF17 .... 97 C7
Assembly St. Leeds LS1 .... 211 F3
Assembly St. Nor WF6 .... 123 A2
Astley La. Swil LS26 .... 102 B8
Astley Lane Ind Est. Swil 102 B8
Astley Way. Swil LS26 .... 102 B8
Aston Ave. Leeds LS13 .... 58 E2
Aston Cl. Liver WF15 .... 116 F2
Aston Cres. Leeds LS13 .... 58 E2
Aston Ct. Leeds LS13 .... 58 E2
Aston Dr. Leeds LS13 .... 58 E2
Aston Gr. Leeds LS13 .... 58 E2
Aston Mount. Leeds LS13 .... 58 E2
Aston Pl. Leeds LS13 .... 58 E2
Aston Rd. Brad BD5 .... 74 C3
Aston Rd. Leeds LS13 .... 58 D2
Aston St. Leeds LS13 .... 58 D2
Aston Terr. Leeds LS13 .... 58 E2
Aston View. Leeds LS13 .... 58 E2
Astor Gr. Leeds LS13 .... 58 B3
Astor St. Leeds LS13 .... 58 B3
Astral Ave. Brig HX3 .... 114 D8
Astral View. Brad BD6 .... 74 A2
Atalanta Terr. Hali HX2 .... 112 C4
Atha Cl. Leeds LS11 .... 79 A1
Atha Cres. Leeds LS11 .... 79 A1
Atha St. Leeds LS11 .... 79 A1
Athelstan La. Otley LS21 .... 11 A1
Atherstone Dr. Hud HD4 .... 154 A1
Atherton La. Brad BD15 .... 73 B7
Atherton La. Brig HD6 .... 136 D8
Athlone Dr. Batley WF12 .... 119 A5
Athlone Gr. Leeds LS12 .... 78 C7
Athlone Rise. Gar LS25 .... 83 B7
Athlone St. Leeds LS12 .... 78 C7
Athlone Terr. Leeds LS12 .... 78 C7
Athol Cl. Hali HX3 .... 92 A3
Athol Cres. Hali HX3 .... 92 A3
Athol Gdns. Hali HX3 .... 92 A3
Athol Gn. Hali HX3 .... 92 A3
Athol Rd. Hali HX3 .... 92 A3
Athol St. Hali HX3 .... 92 A3
Athol St. Keigh BD21 .... 35 C8
Atholl Cl. Hud HD4 .... 153 F1
Atholl Dr. Ossett WF5 .... 140 F5
Atkinson Ct. Nor WF6 .... 123 A1
Atkinson La. Pont WF8 .... 125 F2
Atkinson St. Leeds LS10 .... 80 A7
Atkinson St. Ship BD18 .... 55 B8
Atlanta St. Leeds LS13 .... 58 A2
Atlas Fst Sch. Brad 74 C8

Atlas Mill Rd. Brig HD6 .... 115 A2
Atlas St. Brad BD8 .... 55 B1
Attlee Ave. Ryhil WF4 .... 162 C1
Attlee Cres. Wake WF2 .... 160 E8
Attlee Gr. Loft G WF1 .... 121 C4
Attlee St. Nor WF6 .... 144 B8
Auckland Rd. Brad BD6 .... 74 A1
Audby La. Weth LS22 .... 13 F6
Audrey St. Ossett WF5 .... 140 E4
Audsley's Yd. Hor WF4 .... 140 E1
Augusta Ct. Wake WF2 .... 141 F5
Aurelia House. Brad BD6 .... 74 A1
Austhorpe Ave. Leeds LS15 ...... 81 E7
Austhorpe Ct. Leeds LS15 .... 81 E7
Austhorpe Dr. Leeds LS15 .... 81 E7
Austhorpe Gdns. Leeds LS15 .... 81 E8
Austhorpe Gr. Leeds LS15 .... 81 E8
Austhorpe La. Leeds LS15 .... 62 D1
Austhorpe Prim Sch. Leeds 81 E8
Austhorpe Rd. Leeds LS15 .... 81 E8
Austin Ave. Brig HD6 .... 114 F4
Austin Rd. Castle WF10 .... 125 D8
Austwick Cl. Mapp S75 .... 178 A2
Authorpe Rd. Leeds LS6 .... 59 F6
Autumn Ave. Leeds LS6 .... 59 E2
Autumn Ave. Weth LS22 .... 13 E8
Autumn Cres. Hors LS18 .... 58 D7
Autumn St. Hali HX1 .... 112 F5 10
Autumn St. Leeds LS6 .... 59 E2
Autumn Terr. Leeds LS6 .... 59 E2
Auty Cres. Loft G WF3 .... 121 F5
Auty Sq. Morley LS27 .... 98 B3 2
Avenel Rd. Brad BD15 .... 73 B8
Avenham Way. Brad BD3 .... 75 A8
Avenue Cl. Brad BD8 .... 73 D7
Avenue A. T Arch LS23 .... 15 B3
Avenue B. Th Arch LS23 .... 15 B1
Avenue C E. Th Arch LS23 .... 15 C2
Avenue C W. Th Arch LS23 .... 15 C2
Avenue Cres. Leeds LS8 .... 60 F4
Avenue Des Hirondelles. Pool LS21 24 D6
Avenue E E. Th Arch LS23 .... 15 D1
Avenue E W. Th Arch LS23 .... 15 C1
Avenue F. Th Arch LS23 .... 15 D1
Avenue G. Th Arch LS23 .... 15 D2
Avenue Gdns. Leeds LS17 .... 43 A5
Avenue Hill. Leeds LS8 .... 60 F4
Avenue Lawns. Leeds LS17 .... 42 F5
Avenue No 2. Brig HD6 .... 115 A1
Avenue Rd. Brad BD5 .... 74 F3
Avenue Rd. Wake WF2 .... 142 E1
Avenue St. Brad BD4 .... 75 C7
Avenue Terr. Otley LS21 .... 22 F7
Avenue Terr. Pudsey LS28 .... 57 B6
Avenue The. B in Elm LS15 .... 62 F8
Avenue The. Batley WF17 .... 96 E1
Avenue The. Batley WF17 .... 117 F3
Avenue The. Brad BD14 .... 73 C4
Avenue The. Bur W LS29 .... 9 E1
Avenue The. Coll LS22 .... 13 A1
Avenue The. Crof WF4 .... 143 E1
Avenue The. E Ard WF3 .... 120 A8
Avenue The. Guise BD10 .... 39 D2
Avenue The. Hare LS17 .... 27 B6
Avenue The. Hors LS18 .... 40 F1
Avenue The. Hud HD5 .... 154 D5 4
Avenue The. Leeds LS8 .... 44 A1
Avenue The. Leeds LS15 .... 62 D3 2
Avenue The. Leeds LS17 .... 44 A4
Avenue The. Loft G WF1 .... 121 B4
Avenue The. Roy S71 .... 179 E4
Avenue The. Shin ND14 .... 5 C8
Avenue Victoria. Leeds LS8 ...... 61 A8
Averingcliffe Rd. Brad BD10 ..... 56 D6
Avery Tulip Ct. Brad BD10 .... 56 C6
Aviary Gr. Leeds LS12 .... 78 C8
Aviary Mount. Leeds LS12 .... 78 C8
Aviary Rd. Leeds LS12 .... 78 C8
Aviary Row. Leeds LS12 .... 78 C8 7
Aviary St. Leeds LS12 .... 78 C8
Aviary Terr. Leeds LS12 .... 78 C8 6
Aviary View. Leeds LS12 .... 78 C8
Avison Rd. Hud HD4 .... 153 A3
Avison Yd. Wake WF1 .... 142 D6
Avocet Cl. Brad BD8 .... 73 C7
Avocet Garth. Midd LS10 .... 99 D5 4
Avon Cl. Thorner LS17 .... 44 A4
Avon Ct. Thorner LS17 .... 44 B5
Avon Dr. Gar LS25 .... 83 A5
Avon Wlk. Feath WF7 .... 145 D7
Avondale Cres. Ship BD18 .... 55 A8
Avondale Dr. Wake WF2 .... 142 A7
Avondale Gr. Loft G WF3 .... 121 E5
Avondale Dr. Roy S71 .... 179 C1
Avondale Mount. Ship BD18 .... 55 A8
Avondale Rd. Wake WF1 .... 142 F3
Avondale St. Leeds LS13 .... 58 C1
Avondale Way. Wake WF2 .... 142 C4
Aydon Way. Shelf HX3 .... 93 E7
Aygill Ave. Brad BD9 .... 54 D3
Aylesbury St. Keigh BD21 .... 35 A5
Aylesford Mount. Leeds LS14 ... 62 B4
Aylesham Ind Est. Brad 94 D6
Aynholme Cl. Sil LS29 .... 6 F8
Aynholme Dr. Sil LS29 .... 6 F8
Aynsley Gr. Brad BD15 .... 54 A2
Aysgarth Cl. Brad BD4 .... 75 B4
Aysgarth Cl. Leeds LS15 .... 61 E1
Aysgarth Cres. Hali HX2 .... 112 C4
Aysgarth Dr. Leeds LS15 .... 61 E1
Aysgarth Dr. Wake WF2 .... 141 E5
Aysgarth Pl. Leeds LS15 .... 61 E1
Aysgarth Rd. Batley WF17 .... 118 A5
Aysgarth Wlk. Leeds LS15 .... 61 E1
Ayton Cl. Brad BD3 .... 75 A8

Ayton Rd. Hud HD3 .... 152 E6
Azealea Ct. Brad BD3 .... 75 B8
Baby House Hill La. Wad M HX7 .. 69 A4
Bachelor La. Hors LS18 .... 41 A4
Back Acres St. Keigh BD21 .... 35 B6 8
Back Ada St. Keigh BD21 .... 35 A7 10
Back Aireview Terr. Keigh BD21 .. 35 E6
Back Aireville St. Keigh BD20 ..... 35 A5
Back Albert Gr. Leeds LS6 .... 59 D6
Back Albert Terr. Leeds LS6 ...... 59 E1
Back Allerton Terr. Leeds LS7 .... 60 F3
Back Anna St. Yeadon LS19 ...... 40 C7
Back Anderton St. Wake WF1 .... 142 E3
Back Ann St. Denh BD13 .... 52 E1
Back Archery Pl. Leeds LS2 .... 60 B2
Back Archery Rd. Leeds LS2 ...... 60 B2
Back Archery St. Leeds LS2 .... 60 B2
Back Archery Terr. Leeds LS2 .... 60 B2
Back Armitage Rd. Hud HD4 ..... 171 E8
Back Ash Gr. Leeds LS6 .... 59 F3
Back Ashgrove (W). Brad BD7 ... 74 D6
Back Ashley Ave. Leeds LS9 ...... 61 A2 8
Back Ashley St. Leeds LS9 .... 61 A2 9
Back Ashville Ave. Leeds LS6 ..... 59 E3
Back Ashville Rd. Leeds LS6 ...... 59 E3
Back Ashville Terr. Leeds LS6 .... 59 D3
Back Ashwood Terr. Leeds LS6 .. 59 E3
Back Aston Rd. Leeds LS13 ...... 58 D2
Back Aston St. Leeds LS13 ...... 58 D2
Back Aston Terr. Leeds LS13 .... 58 E2
Back Athlone Ave. Leeds LS12 .. 78 C7
Back Athlone Gr. Leeds LS12 .... 78 C7 3
Back Athlone Terr. Leeds LS12 .. 78 C7
Back Atlanta St. Leeds LS13 ..... 58 A2
Back Aviary Rd. Leeds LS12 ..... 78 C8
Back Baker St. Ship BD18 .... 55 A8
Back Balfour St. Keigh BD21 ..... 35 B6 5
Back Bank St. Castle WF10 ...... 124 D8
Back Bank Terr. Pudsey LS28 .... 57 E2
Back Banstead St. Leeds LS8 .... 60 F3 14
Back Barden Pl. Leeds LS12 ..... 78 A7 2
Back Barkly Gr. Leeds LS11 ...... 79 A2
Back Barkly Parade. Leeds LS11 . 79 A1 3
Back Barkly Terr. Leeds LS11 .... 79 A1
Back Barrowby View. Leeds LS15 81 B7
Back Bath Rd. Leeds LS13 .... 58 C2 15
Back Beacon St. Hud HD7 .... 116 A1
Back Beamont St. Batley WF17 . 118 C3
Back Beech St. Hud HD7 .... 136 A2
Back Beechwood Gr. Leeds LS4 . 59 D3
Back Beechwood Rd. Leeds LS4 . 59 D3 9
Back Bellbrooke Gr. Leeds LS9 .. 61 B2 9
Back Bellbrooke Pl. Leeds LS9 ... 61 B2 7
Back Bellbrooke Terr. Leeds LS9 . 61 B2 6
Back Belvedere Ave. Leeds LS11 . 79 B2
Back Belvedere Mount. Leeds LS11 79 B2
Back Bentley Ave. Leeds LS6 .... 59 F6 3
Back Bentley Gr. Leeds LS6 ...... 59 F6
Back Berkeley Ave. Leeds LS8 ... 61 A3
Back Berkeley Terr. Leeds LS8 ... 61 A3 14
Back Beverley Terr. Leeds LS11 .. 78 F2
Back Blackwood Gr. Hali HX1 ... 112 F8
Back Blenheim Ave. Leeds LS2 .. 60 A4
Back Blenheim Mount. Brad BD8 55 C2
Back Blenheim Terr. Leeds LS2 .. 60 B2 12
Back Bower Rd. Eland HX5 ...... 135 A7
Back Bowling Green Rd.
  Elland HX4 .... 133 F3
Back Bowman St. Wake WF1 .... 142 D3
Back Branch Pl. Leeds LS12 ..... 78 A4 10
Back Breary Ave. Hors LS18 ..... 41 B4
Back Breary Terr. Hors LS18 ..... 41 B4
Back Briggate. Sil BD20 .... 5 E2
Back Broad La. Leeds LS13 ...... 58 D4
Back Broomfield Cres. Leeds LS6 59 D3
Back Broomfield Pl. Leeds LS6 ... 59 D3 8
Back Broomfield Rd. Keigh BD21 35 B7 5
Back Broomfield St. Keigh BD21 . 35 A7 4
Back Broughton Ave. Leeds LS9 . 61 A2 21
Back Broughton Terr. Leeds LS9 . 61 A2 20
Back Brudenell Gr. Leeds LS6 ... 59 F2
Back Brudenell Mount. Leeds LS6 59 F2
Back Brudenell Rd. Leeds LS6 ... 59 F2
Back Brunswick St. Dew WF13 .. 118 A1
Back Burchett Pl. Leeds LS6 ..... 60 A4
Back Burley Hill. Leeds LS4 ...... 59 C3
Back Burley St. Leeds LS3 .... 79 A8
Back Burlington Pl. Leeds LS11 .. 79 B2 2
Back Burlington Rd. Leeds LS11 . 79 B2
Back Burton Cres. Leeds LS6 .... 59 D6
Back Burton Terr. Leeds LS11 ... 79 C2
Back Buxton St. Keigh BD21 ..... 35 D7 4
Back Byrl St. Keigh BD21 .... 18 F1
Back Byron St. Tod OL14 .... 108 A3
Back Caister St. Keigh BD21 ..... 35 A5
Back Camberley St. Leeds LS11 . 79 C3 10
Back Carlinghow La. Batley WF17 117 D8
Back Cartmel Rd. Keigh BD21 ... 35 A7 12
Back Castle Rd. Keigh BD21 ..... 35 A7
Back Cavendish Rd. Brad BD10 . 56 B6
Back Cavendish St. Keigh BD21 . 35 A7
Back Cecil St. Hud HD3 .... 153 A4
Back Chapel La. Leeds LS6 ...... 59 F2
Back Chapel St. Brad BD6 .... 74 B1
Back Charles St. Brig HD6 .... 115 A3 10
Back Chatsworth Rd. Leeds LS8 . 61 C4
Back Chestnut Ave. Leeds LS15 . 62 A2
Back Chestnut Gr. Leeds LS6 .... 59 D3 5
Back Christ Church View.
  Leeds LS12 .... 78 B8
Back Church La. Leeds LS16 ..... 42 D3
Back Church La. Leeds LS16 ..... 42 D3
Back Church View. Wake WF1 ... 142 A8
Back Claremont Ave. Leeds LS3 . 60 A2
Back Claremont Gr. Leeds LS3 .. 60 A2
Back Claremont Terr. Leeds LS12 78 B8 3
Back Claremount Terr.
  Leeds LS11 .... 79 A1 6
Back Clarence St. Hali HX1 ...... 113 B7
Back Clarendon Pl. Hali HX1 .... 113 A6

Back Clarkson View. Leeds LS6 .. 60 A4 10
Back Clayton St. Roth LS26 ...... 100 F5
Back Cliff Mount. Leeds LS6 ..... 60 A4
Back Clifton Rd. Hud HD1 .... 153 E7
Back Clifton Rd. Hud HD1 .... 153 E7
Back Clipston Ave. Leeds LS6 ... 59 F6
Back Clough. Northo HX3 .... 93 A2
Back Clovelly Pl. Leeds LS11 .... 79 B3 27
Back Coldcotes Ave. Leeds LS9 . 61 B2
Back Colenso Mount. Leeds LS11 78 F3
Back Colenso Rd. Keigh BD21 ... 18 E1
Back Colenso Rd. Leeds LS11 ... 78 F4
Back Colne Rd. Glu BD20 .... 16 A6
Back Colton Rd. Leeds LS12 ..... 78 C7
Back Colwyn Pl. Leeds LS11 ..... 79 B2 20
Back Colwyn View. Leeds LS11 .. 79 B2 11
Back Commercial St. Hali HX1 .. 113 C7 14
Back Commercial St. Tod OL14 . 108 C5 16
Back Compton St. Keigh BD21 .. 35 D8 9
Back Conway St. Leeds LS8 ..... 60 F3
Back Cowper Gr. Leeds LS8 ..... 61 A3 11
Back Cowper St. Leeds LS7 ...... 60 E3
Back Craggwood Rd. Hors LS18 58 E8
Back Cranbrook Ave. Leeds LS11 79 A1
Back Cranbrook Terr. Leeds LS11 79 A3
Back Croft House La. Keigh BD20 18 A4
Back Croft Rd. Bing HX6 .... 132 C1
Back Cromer Ave. Keigh BD21 ... 35 B5 16
Back Cromer Gr. Keigh BD21 .... 35 B4 1
Back Cromer Terr. Leeds LS2 .... 60 A2
Back Cromwell Terr. Hali HX1 ... 113 B7 2
Back Cross Flats Ave. Leeds LS11 79 F2 3
Back Cross Flats Gr. Leeds LS11 . 79 F2
Back Cross Flats Rd. Leeds LS11 79 F2 4
Back Cross Flats Mount.
  Leeds LS11 .... 79 A2 6
Back Cross Flatts Pl. Leeds LS11 . 79 F6
Back Cross Green La. Leeds LS9 . 80 B8 3
Back Cross La. Elland HX5 .... 134 E6
Back Crossland Terr. Leeds LS11 79 F2
Back Dalton Ave. Leeds LS11 .... 79 A2
Back Dalton Rd. Leeds LS11 ..... 79 A2
Back Dargai St. Leeds LS7 .... 60 E3
Back Dawlish Ave. Leeds LS9 .... 80 B8 3
Back Dawlish Mount. Leeds LS9 80 B8 2
Back Dawlish Rd. Leeds LS9 ..... 80 B8
Back De Lacy Mount. Leeds LS5 . 59 A5
Back Delph Mount. Leeds LS6 .. 60 A4
Back Der St. Tod OL14 .... 108 C5 7
Back Devonshire La. Leeds LS8 .. 44 A2
Back Dorset Mount. Leeds LS8 . 61 A4 7
Back Dorset Rd. Leeds LS8 ...... 61 A3 2
Back Dudley Hill Rd. Brad BD2 .. 56 B2
Back Duke of York St. Wake WF1 142 D4
Back Duke St. Feath WF7 .... 145 C6
Back Dunbar St. Wake WF1 ..... 142 D4
Back East Park Rd. Leeds LS9 ... 80 A7 10
Back Eaton St. Keigh BD21 ...... 35 A4 2
Back Ecclesburn Gr. Leeds LS9 . 88 B7 1
Back Edensor Rd. Keigh BD21 ... 35 A5
Back Edinburgh Rd. Leeds LS12 . 78 A8
Back Eldon Rd. Hud HD1 .... 153 D7
Back Elford Pl. Leeds LS8 .... 61 A7
Back Elmfield Terr. Hali HX1 .... 113 B5
Back Elsworth St. Leeds LS12 ... 78 C7
Back Emily St. Keigh BD21 ...... 35 D8 16
Back Esmond Terr. Leeds LS12 .. 78 C7 12
Back Estcourt Ave. Leeds LS6 ... 59 C4
Back Estcourt Terr. Leeds LS6 ... 59 C4
Back Eversley Mount. Hali HX2 . 112 D6
Back Fairford Pl. Leeds LS11 ..... 79 B1
Back Featherbank Terr. Hors LS18 58 C7
Back Ferguson St. Hali HX1 ..... 113 C7 4
Back Field Ct. Thorn BD13 ...... 72 D6
Back Fitzwilliam St. Hud HD1 ... 153 F6
Back Florist St. Keigh BD21 ..... 35 A4
Back Fold. Brad BD14 .... 73 C4
Back Foster Rd. Keigh BD21 ..... 35 A4
Back Garden St. Wake WF10 .... 124 D6
Back Garton Rd. Leeds LS9 ...... 80 A7
Back Gathorne St. Leeds LS8 ... 61 A6
Back George St. Leeds LS2 ...... 79 D8 5
Back Gerrard St. Hali HX1 .... 113 B7
Back Gillett La. Roth LS26 .... 100 F5
Back Girlington Rd. Brad BD8 ... 54 F1
Back Gladstone St. Bing BD16 .. 36 F2
Back Glebe Terr. Leeds LS16 .... 59 D6
Back Glen Terr. Hali HX1 .... 113 B6
Back Glenthorpe Terr. Leeds LS9 80 B7
Back Glossop St. Leeds LS6 ..... 60 A4
Back Gooder La. Brig HD6 .... 115 B1
Back Gordon St. Wake WF1 ..... 142 F2
Back Gordon Terr. Leeds LS6 .... 59 D6
Back Graham Gr. Leeds LS4 ..... 59 C3
Back Grange Ave. Leeds LS7 .... 60 E5
Back Grange Cres. Leeds LS7 ... 60 F5
Back Grange Terr. Leeds LS7 .... 60 E5
Back Grange View. Leeds LS7 ... 60 E5
Back Grant St. Keigh BD21 ...... 35 B4 1
Back Grantham Terr. Leeds LS9 . 80 B8
Back Granville St. Eland HX5 .... 135 B7
Back Gt Russell St. Brad BD7 ... 74 D7
Back Greaves St. Brad BD5 ...... 74 D4
Back Greenhead Rd. Hud HD1 .. 154 A6
Back Greenmount Terr.
  Leeds LS11 .... 79 E1
Back Greenwood Mount.
  Leeds LS6 .... 59 F6
Back Grosvenor Terr. Hali HX1 .. 113 A7 11
Back Grosvenor Terr. Leeds LS6 . 60 A3
Back Grouse St. Keigh BD21 ..... 35 C7
Back Grove Gdns. Leeds LS6 .... 59 E3
Back Grove Rd. Leeds LS6 .... 59 E3
Back Grovehall Dr. Leeds LS11 .. 79 A1 7
Back Haigh Ave. Roth LS26 ...... 100 C7
Back Haigh St. Roth LS26 .... 100 C7
Back Haigh View. Roth LS26 ..... 100 C7
Back Halliday Pl. Leeds LS12 .... 59 C1
Back Halliday Gr. Leeds LS12 .... 59 C1
Back Hambleton St. Wake WF1 . 142 E4
Back Hamilton Ave. Leeds LS7 .. 60 F6
Back Hamilton View. Leeds LS7 . 60 F6

Back Harehills Park View.
  .... 61 B2 14
Back Hares Mount. Leeds LS8 ... 60 E4
Back Harold Gr. Leeds LS6 ...... 59 E2 12
Back Hartley Ave. Leeds LS6 .... 60 B4 1
Back Hartley Gr. Leeds LS6 ...... 60 A4 5
Back Hartley St. Morley LS27 ... 98 C5
Back Hatfield St. Leeds LS7 ..... 142 C7
Back Hawksworth Gr. Leeds LS5 58 E5
Back Headingley Ave. Leeds LS6 59 C5
Back Headingley Mount. Leeds LS6 59 C5
Back Heathfield Terr. Leeds LS6 . 59 D6 5
Back Heddon Pl. Leeds LS6 ..... 59 E4
Back Heddon St. Leeds LS6 ..... 59 E4
Back Heights Rd. Wils BD13 ..... 72 B8
Back Henrietta St. Batley WF17 . 118 C5 3
Back Hessle Ave. Leeds LS6 ..... 59 E3
Back Hessle Mount. Leeds LS6 .. 59 E3
Back Hessle Terr. Leeds LS6 ..... 59 E3
Back Hessle View. Leeds LS6 .... 59 E3
Back High St. Thorn BD13 .... 72 D6 12
Back Highbury Terr. Leeds LS6 .. 59 E3
Back Highfield Rd. Leeds LS13 .. 58 E2 4
Back Highgate Gdns. Leeds LS13 78 B8 7
Back Highthorne Gr. Leeds LS12 77 A3 4
Back Highthorne St. Leeds LS12 77 A8 15
Back Highthorne St. Leeds LS12 77 A8
Back Hillcrest Ave. Leeds LS7 ... 60 F4
Back Hillcrest View. Leeds LS7 .. 60 F4
Back Hilton Gr. Leeds LS8 .... 61 A6 1
Back Hilton Pl. Leeds LS8 .... 61 A6
Back Hilton Rd. Leeds LS8 ...... 61 A6
Back Hollyshaw Terr. Leeds LS15 81 C8 5
Back Honoria St. Hud HD1 ...... 136 A1
Back Hope Hall Terr. Hali HX1 .. 113 C6 14
Back Hovingham Gr. Leeds LS8 . 61 A4
Back Hovingham Mount. Leeds LS8 61 A4 3
Back Hovingham Terr. Leeds LS8 61 A4 4
Back Hyde Gr. Keigh BD21 ...... 35 A4
Back Hyde Terr. Leeds LS2 ...... 60 A1
Back Ibbetson Pl. Leeds LS2 .... 60 B1
Back Ingledew Cres. Leeds LS8 . 44 A2
Back Ivy Ave. Leeds LS9 .... 80 A8 11
Back Ivy Gr. Leeds LS9 .... 80 B8 2
Back Ivy Mount. Leeds LS9 ...... 80 A8
Back Ivy St. Leeds LS9 .... 80 A8 12
Back John St. Thorn BD13 .... 72 D6
Back Karnac Rd. Leeds LS8 ..... 61 A1
Back Kendal La. Leeds LS3 ...... 60 A1
Back Kennerleigh Wlk. Leeds LS15 62 C1
Back Kensington St. Brad BD8 .. 55 C8
Back Kensington Terr. Leeds LS6 59 F2
Back Kirby St. Keigh BD21 ...... 35 D8
Back Kirkgate. Ship BD18 .... 55 A7
Back Kitson St. Leeds LS9 .... 80 A7
Back Knowl Rd. Mir WF14 .... 137 F6
Back Knowle Mount. Leeds LS6 . 59 D3 12
Back La. Bad WF9 .... 164 E2
Back La. Birk BD11 .... 96 F7
Back La. Brad BD10 .... 56 B8
Back La. Bramham LS23 .... 30 D3
Back La. Bur in W LS29 .... 9 F1
Back La. Clay W HD8 .... 176 A1
Back La. Crof WF4 .... 144 C2
Back La. Dew WF12 .... 139 C3
Back La. Emley HD8 .... 175 A5
Back La. Flock WF4 .... 156 F5
Back La. Guise LS20 .... 22 D8
Back La. H Pag DN5 .... 195 D5
Back La. Hali HX3 .... 91 D5
Back La. Hep HX7 .... 88 F4
Back La. Holmfi HD7 .... 189 A7
Back La. Keigh BD20 .... 19 D1
Back La. Kippax WF10 .... 103 A4
Back La. Leeds LS13 .... 58 A1
Back La. Lepton WF4 .... 156 F7
Back La. Mir WF14 .... 137 E5
Back La. Ossett WF5 .... 140 D5
Back La. Otley LS29 .... 10 C8
Back La. Ryhil WF4 .... 162 B4
Back La. Shep HD8 .... 174 A3
Back La. Ship BD9 .... 55 A4
Back La. Sickl LS22 .... 12 C5
Back La. Skelm BD23 .... 3 D2
Back La. Thorn BD13 .... 72 E6
Back La. W Bret WF4 .... 176 F7
Back La. Wad M HX7 .... 88 C3
Back La. Wils BD15 .... 53 D5
Back Laisteridge La. Brad BD7 .. 74 D6
Back Landseer Terr. Leeds LS13 . 58 C1
Back Landseer View. Leeds LS13 58 C1
Back Langdale Terr. Leeds LS6 .. 59 C1
Back Laurel Mount. Leeds LS7 .. 60 F3 3
Back Leatham St. Dew WF13 .... 139 A5
Back Leeming. Denh BD13 ...... 71 C6
Back Lodge La. Leeds LS11 ..... 79 D1
Back Lombard St. Yeadon LS19 . 40 A4
Back Lord St. Hali HX1 .... 113 B7
Back Low La. Hors LS18 .... 58 C7
Back Lucas St. Leeds LS6 .... 60 A3
Back Lunan Pl. Leeds LS8 .... 61 A7
Back Lunan Terr. Leeds LS8 ..... 61 A7
Back Mackinson Ave. Leeds LS11 79 E1
Back Manor Dr. Leeds LS6 ...... 59 E4

Bark House La. Shep HD8 — 174 C3
Bark La. Add LS29 — 7 A2
Barker Cl. Hali HX3 — 113 E3
Barker Ct. Hud HD2 — 135 E1
Barker House. Hali HX3 — 113 E3 4
Barker Pl. Leeds LS13 — 58 D1
Barker Rd. Hor WF4 — 140 F2
Barker St. Liver WF15 — 117 B4
Barker St. Cl WF3 — 122 B6
Barker St. Tod OL14 — 108 B6
Barker's Rd. Crig WF4 — 159 E6
Barkerend Fst Sch. Brad — 75 A8
Barkerend Rd. Brad BD1, BD3 — 75 B8
Barkisland Jun & Inf Sch. Rip — 133 A5
Barkly Ave. Leeds LS11 — 79 A1
Barkly Dr. Leeds LS11 — 79 A1
Barkly Gr. Leeds LS11 — 79 A1
Barkly Par. Leeds LS11 — 79 A1 2
Barkly Pl. Leeds LS11 — 79 A1 1
Barkly Rd. Leeds LS11 — 79 A1
Barkly St. Leeds LS11 — 79 A1
Barkly Terr. Leeds LS11 — 79 A2 8
Barlbro' Pl. Hud HX4 — 153 A4
Barlby Way. Leeds LS8 — 61 C6
Barley Cote Ave. Keigh BD20 — 19 A2
Barley Cote Gr. Keigh BD20 — 19 A2
Barley Cote Rd. Keigh BD20 — 19 A2
Barley Croft. Dew WF13 — 138 F8
Barley Field Ct. Leeds LS15 — 81 A8 3
Barley Mews. Roth WF3 — 100 B3
Barley St. Keigh BD22 — 35 A8
Barleycorn Cl. Wake WF3 — 121 E1
Barleyfield Cl. Wake WF1 — 142 E8
Barleyfields Cl. Weth LS22 — 13 E6
Barleyfields Ct. Weth LS22 — 13 E6
Barleyfields La. Weth LS22 — 13 E6
Barleyfields Rd. Weth LS22 — 13 E7
Barleyfields Terr. Weth LS22 — 13 E6
Barleyfields Wlk. Weth LS22 — 13 E6
Barleyhill Cres. Gar LS25 — 82 E6
Barleyhill La. Gar LS25 — 82 E7
Barleyhill Rd. Gar LS25 — 82 E7
Barlow Rd. Keigh BD21 — 35 B8
Barm Side. St. Brad BD3 — 75 B7
Barmby Cl. Ossett WF5 — 141 A4
Barmby Cres. Ossett WF5 — 141 A4
Barmby Fold. Ossett WF5 — 140 F4
Barmby Pl. Brad BD2 — 56 B1
Barmby Rd. Brad BD2 — 56 B1
Barmby St. Brad BD12 — 94 D4
Barmouth Terr. Brad BD3 — 55 F2
Barn Cl. Men LS29 — 21 F4
Barn St. Oxen BD22 — 51 C2
Barnaby Rd. Bing BD16 — 37 C4
Barnard Cl. Leeds LS15 — 62 E3
Barnard Rd. Brad BD4 — 75 E3
Barnard Way. Leeds LS15 — 62 E3
Barnbow Fold. Ossett WF5 — 140 F4
Barnbow La. B in Elm LS15 — 63 B5
Barnbow La. Leeds LS15 — 63 A5
Barnbrough St. Leeds LS4 — 59 C2
Barnby Road. Hud HD5 — 154 F7
Barncliffe Hill. Shelf HD8 — 174 C1
Barncroft Cl. Leeds LS14 — 61 E6
Barncroft Ct. Leeds LS14 — 61 E6
Barncroft Dr. Leeds LS14 — 61 E7
Barncroft Gdns. Leeds LS14 — 61 E6
Barncroft Grange. Leeds LS14 — 61 E6
Barncroft Hts. Leeds LS14 — 61 E7
Barncroft Mount. Leeds LS14 — 61 E6
Barncroft Rd. Leeds LS14 — 61 E7
Barncroft Rise. Leeds LS14 — 61 F6
Barncroft Towers. Leeds LS14 — 61 E6
Barnes Ave. Wake WF1 — 121 B3
Barnes Meadows. Litt OL15 — 129 C1
Barnes Rd. Brad BD8 — 73 F7
Barnes Rd. Castle WF10 — 124 D6
Barnes St. Tod OL14 — 108 A1 6
Barnet Gr. Morley LS27 — 98 A2 2
Barnet Rd. Leeds LS12 — 78 D7
Barnett House. Brad BD6 — 93 E8 3
Barnsdale Est. Castle WF10 — 124 B6
Barnsdale Rd. Kippax WF10 — 103 D4
Barnsdale Rd. M'town LS26 — 102 E3
Barnsdale Way. Upton WF9 — 183 E7
Barnsdale La. Holmfi HD7 — 189 F1
Barnsley Beck Gr. Bail BD17 — 37 F1
Barnsley Rd. Bri WF2 — 161 A4
Barnsley Rd. Bri S72 — 181 B2
Barnsley Rd. Bri S72 — 181 B3
Barnsley Rd. Clay W HD8 — 175 E1
Barnsley Rd. Crig WF1, WF2, WF4 — 160 C5
Barnsley Rd. D Dale HD8 — 191 C5
Barnsley Rd. Floc WF4 — 157 A3
Barnsley Rd. Hem WF9 — 181 C5
Barnsley Rd. Notton WF4 — 178 E5
Barnsley Rd. S Kirk WF9 — 182 C3
Barnsley Rd. S Kirk WF9 — 182 E3
Barnsley Rd. Wake WF1, WF2 — 142 E2
Barnsley Rd. Wake WF1, WF2, WF4 — 160 C5
Barnsley Rd. Wool WF4 — 178 C6
Barnstone Vale. Wake WF1 — 121 E1
Barnswick Cl. Pont WF8 — 146 D6
Barnswick View. Hors LS16 — 41 E4
Baron Cl. Leeds LS11 — 79 A4
Baronscourt. Leeds LS15 — 81 D8
Baronsway. Leeds LS15 — 81 D8
Barr St. Hud HD1 — 154 C8
Barrack Rd. Leeds LS7 — 60 D3
Barrack St. Leeds LS7 — 60 D8
Barracks Fold. Holmfi HD7 — 189 D2
Barracks St. Liver WF15 — 117 C4
Barraclough Bldgs. Brad BD10 — 56 E7
Barraclough Sq. Brad BD12 — 94 C4 18
Barraclough St. Brad BD12 — 94 B6 5
Barran Ct. Leeds LS8 — 60 F2
Barran St. Bing BD16 — 37 A3 8
Barras Garth Pl. Leeds LS12 — 78 B6
Barras Garth Rd. Leeds LS12 — 78 B5
Barras Pl. Leeds LS12 — 78 B6
Barras St. Leeds LS12 — 78 B6
Barras Terr. Leeds LS12 — 78 B6
Barratt's Rd. Wake WF1 — 145 C8
Barrett St. Sil BD20 — 5 D1
Barrington Cl. Hali HX3 — 114 A4
Barrington Par. Clec BD19 — 117 A8
Barrowby Ave. Leeds LS15 — 62 E2
Barrowby Cl. Men LS29 — 22 B4
Barrowby Cres. Leeds LS15 — 81 E8
Barrowby Dr. Leeds LS15 — 81 E8
Barrowby La. Gar LS25 — 82 D8
Barrowby La. Leeds LS15 — 81 F8
Barrowby La. Swil LS15, LS25, LS26 — 82 A8
Barrowby Rd. Leeds LS15 — 81 F7

Barrowclough La. Hali HX3 — 113 F7
Barrows La. Stee BD20 — 17 C4
Barrowstead. Skel HD8 — 175 B1
Barry St. Brad BD1 — 74 E7
Barsey Green La. Rip HX4 — 133 C6
Barstow Sq. Wake WF1 — 142 C6 2
Barthorpe Ave. Leeds LS17 — 60 B8
Barthorpe Cl. Brad BD4 — 75 F2
Barthorpe Cres. Leeds LS17 — 60 C8
Bartle Cl. Brad BD7 — 73 F3
Bartle Fold. Brad BD7 — 74 A4
Bartle Gill Dr. Bail BD17 — 38 E4
Bartle Gill Rise. Bail BD17 — 38 E4
Bartle Gill View. Bail BD17 — 38 E4
Bartle Gr. Brad BD7 — 73 F3
Bartle La. Brad BD7 — 73 F3
Bartle Pl. Brad BD7 — 73 F3
Bartle Sq. Brad BD7 — 74 A4
Barton Ave. Barn S71 — 178 F1
Barton Cl. Leeds LS15 — 81 D7
Barton Ct. Leeds LS15 — 81 E7
Barton Hill. Leeds LS11 — 79 A4
Barton Manor Cl. Hud HD4 — 153 B2
Barton Manor Cl. Leeds LS11 — 79 A4
Barton Pl. Leeds LS11 — 79 A4
Barton Rd. Leeds LS11 — 79 A4
Barton St. Brig HD6 — 115 A3 17
Barton Terr. Leeds LS11 — 79 A4
Barton View. Leeds LS11 — 79 A4
Barton Way. S Elm WF9 — 183 A5
Barum Top. Hali HX1 — 113 C7 12
Barwick Gn. Brad BD6 — 73 F3
Barwick in Elmet CE Jun & Inf Sch. B in Elm — 63 E7
Barwick Rd. B in Elm LS15, LS25 — 62 E2
Barwick Rd. Leeds LS15, LS14, LS15 — 62 D4
Basford St. Wake WF2 — 142 A5
Basil St. Brad BD5 — 74 B3
Basil St. Hud HD4 — 153 D4
Basildon Rd. Dearne S63 — 194 C1
Baslow Gr. Brad BD9 — 54 F2
Bassenthwaite Wlk. Knot WF11 — 126 E2
Batcliffe Dr. Leeds LS6 — 59 C6
Batcliffe Mount. Leeds LS6 — 59 C5
Bateman Cl. Shaf S72 — 180 B2
Bateman St. Brad BD8 — 55 D1
Bates Ave. Sow B HX6 — 111 F3
Bates La. Pont WF8 — 146 F5
Bateson St. Brad BD10 — 56 B7
Bath Cl. Leeds LS13 — 58 C2
Bath Gr. Leeds LS13 — 58 C2 14
Bath La. Leeds LS13 — 58 C2
Bath Pl. Clec BD19 — 116 D7
Bath Pl. Hali HX3 — 92 B1
Bath Rd. Batley WF16 — 117 D4
Bath Rd. Clec BD19 — 116 D7
Bath Rd. Hali HX3 — 113 B4
Bath Rd. Leeds LS11 — 79 A4 1
Bath St. Bacup OL13 — 106 A2 1
Bath St. Batley WF17 — 118 D5
Bath St. Brad BD3 — 75 A7
Bath St. Dew WF13 — 118 C1
Bath St. Elland HX5 — 134 F6
Bath St. Hali HX1 — 113 D6 3
Bath St. Hud HD1 — 153 F3
Bath St. Ilkley LS29 — 8 C5
Bath St. Tod OL14 — 108 B5 3
Batley Ave. Hud HD1 — 153 F6
Batley Bsns Ctr. Batley — 118 B6
Batley Enterprise Ctr. Batley — 118 B6
Batley Field Hill. Batley WF17 — 118 C6
Batley Gram Sch. Batley — 118 B7
Batley High Sch. Batley — 118 C6
Batley Manorfield Inf Sch. Batley — 118 A4
Batley Parish CE (Aided) Sch. Batley — 118 C6
Batley Rd. Batley WF16 — 117 D4
Batley Rd. E Ard FW3 — 119 E5
Batley Rd. Wake WF2 — 120 B2
Batley St. Hali HX3 — 92 A1 28
Batley St. Hud HD1 — 153 F6
Batley Sta. Batley — 118 D4
Battinson Rd. Hali HX1 — 112 D8
Battinson St. Hali HX3 — 113 E5
Battye Ave. Hud HD4 — 153 B3
Battye St. Brad BD4 — 75 D6
Battye Street Inf Sch. Batley — 117 D4
Battyeford CE (C) Jun & Inf Sch. Mir — 137 E6
Baulk Head La. Tod OL14 — 108 B4
Bavaria Pl. Brad BD8 — 55 B1
Bawn App. Leeds LS12 — 77 F5
Bawn Ave. Leeds LS12 — 77 F5
Bawn Dr. Leeds LS12 — 77 F5
Bawn Gdns. Leeds LS12 — 77 F6
Bawn La. Leeds LS12 — 77 F6
Bawn Vale. Leeds LS12 — 77 F6
Bawn Wlk. Leeds LS12 — 77 F6
Bawson Ct. Clec BD19 — 96 A1
Baxandall St. Brad BD5 — 74 D3
Baxter La. Northa HX3 — 93 A3
Baxter Wood. Glu BD20 — 16 C7
Baxtergate. Pont WF8 — 146 D8 10
Bay Cl. Hud HD3 — 152 D5
Bay Horse Ct. Leeds LS7 — 60 C7
Bay Horse La. Scar LS14 — 45 A5
Bay Horse La. Thorner LS17 — 45 B4
Bay of Biscay. Brad BD9 — 54 B4
Bayford Cl. Holmfi HD7 — 199 B8
Bayldons Pl. Batley WF17 — 118 C5 9
Bayswater Gr. Brad BD2 — 56 B3
Bayswater Terr. Hali HX3 — 92 A1
Bayton La. Horsf LS18, LS19 — 40 F5
Beacon Ave. Morley LS27 — 97 F2
Beacon Brow. Brad BD6 — 73 D2
Beacon Gr. Brad BD6 — 73 D2
Beacon Gr. Morley LS27 — 98 A2
Beacon Hill Rd. Hali HX3 — 113 E7

Beacon Hill. Upton WF9 — 183 A8
Beacon Pl. Brad BD6 — 73 E1
Beacon Rd. Brad BD6 — 73 E2
Beacon Rise. Ilkley LS29 — 7 E4
Beacon St. Add LS29 — 7 A8
Beacon St. Brad BD7 — 73 E2 1
Beacon St. Dew WF13 — 138 E6
Beacon St. Hud HD2 — 136 A1
Beaconsfield Rd. Brad BD14 — 73 D4
Beaconsfield St. Hali HX3 — 113 E6
Beaconsfield St. Tod OL14 — 108 C5
Beaden Ave. Hud HD5 — 155 B5
Beagle Ave. Hud HD4 — 153 C1
Beal La. Knot DN14 — 127 F2
Beamsley. S Kirk WF9 — 182 B1
Beamsley Gr. Bing BD16 — 37 B3
Beamsley Gr. Ship BD18 — 55 B5
Beamsley Mount. Leeds LS6 — 59 E2
Beamsley Pl. Leeds LS6 — 59 E2 1
Beamsley Rd. Bing BD16 — 37 B3
Beamsley Rd. Ship BD18 — 55 B5
Beamsley Terr. Leeds LS6 — 59 E2 2
Beamsley View. Ilkley LS29 — 7 F4
Beamsley Wlk. Brad BD9 — 55 A2
Bean St. Elland HX5 — 135 C6
Beancroft Rd. Castle WF10 — 124 D7
Beancroft St. Castle WF10 — 124 D7
Beanlands Dr. Glu BD20 — 16 C6
Beanlands Par. Ilkley LS29 — 8 C5
Beanlands Pl. Glu BD20 — 16 C7
Beast Fair. Pont WF8 — 146 C8
Beast Fair Service Rd. Pont WF8 — 146 C8 3
Beast Market. Hud HD1 — 154 B6 4
Beatrice St. Keigh BD21 — 18 D1
Beaufort Gr. Brad BD2 — 56 A3
Beaufort Rd. Bacup OL13 — 106 A7
Beaumont Ave. Hud HD5 — 154 D5
Beaumont Cl. Loft G WF3 — 121 F5
Beaumont Dr. W Bret WF4 — 176 F6
Beaumont Park Rd. Hud HD4 — 153 D2
Beaumont Pl. Batley WF17 — 117 F3
Beaumont Rd. Brad BD8 — 55 B1
Beaumont St. Batley WF17 — 118 D5 8
Beaumont St. Castle WF10 — 125 D5
Beaumont St. Hali HX3 — 113 A3
Beaumont St. Hud HD4 — 153 D4
Beaumont St. Liver WF15 — 117 C3
Beaver Dr. Dew WF13 — 138 F7
Beaver Terr. Bacup OL13 — 106 A7
Becca La. Aber LS25 — 64 E7
Beck Bottom. Pudsey LS28 — 56 E6
Beck Bottom. Wake WF2 — 120 C3
Beck Hill. Brad BD6 — 93 E8
Beck La. Bing BD16 — 37 A4
Beck La. Coll LS22 — 13 B1
Beck Meadow. B in Elm LS15 — 63 B6
Beck Rd. Keigh BD21 — 35 B6
Beck Rise. Hem WF9 — 181 D7
Beck Side Cl. Keigh BD20 — 18 E1
Beck St. Keigh BD21 — 35 C8
Beckbridge Cl. Nor WF6 — 123 C3
Beckbridge Gn. Nor WF6 — 123 C3
Beckbridge La. Nor WF6 — 123 C2
Beckbridge Rd. Nor WF6 — 123 C3
Beckbridge Way. Nor WF6 — 123 C3
Beckbury St. Pudsey LS28 — 57 D2 2
Beckenham Pl. Hali HX1 — 112 D7
Becket Cres. Dew WF12 — 138 F8
Beckett Ct. Leeds LS15 — 81 D6
Beckett La. Dew WF12 — 139 A8
Beckett Park Cty Prim Sch. Leeds — 59 B5
Beckett Rd. Nor WF6 — 144 A8
Beckett St. Batley WF17 — 118 D4
Beckett's Park Cres. Leeds LS6 — 59 B5
Beckett's Park Dr. Leeds LS6 — 59 C5
Beckett's Park Rd. Leeds LS6 — 59 C5
Beckett Wlk. Dew WF13 — 138 F7
Becketts Cl. Hep HX7 — 88 F4
Beckfield Rd. Ship BD16 — 54 B5
Beckfoot Grammar Sch. Bing — 37 A1
Beckfoot La. Harden BD16 — 36 E1
Beckfoot Mill. Harden BD16 — 36 E1
Beckford St. Batley WF17 — 118 D3
Beckhill App. Leeds LS7 — 60 C6
Beckhill Ave. Leeds LS7 — 60 C6
Beckhill Chase. Leeds LS7 — 60 C6
Beckhill Cl. Leeds LS7 — 60 C6
Beckhill Dr. Leeds LS7 — 60 C6
Beckhill Fold. Leeds LS7 — 60 C6
Beckhill Garth. Leeds LS7 — 60 C6
Beckhill Gate. Leeds LS7 — 60 C6
Beckhill Gdns. Leeds LS7 — 60 C6
Beckhill Gn. Leeds LS7 — 60 C6
Beckhill Gr. Leeds LS7 — 60 C6
Beckhill Lawn. Leeds LS7 — 60 C6
Beckhill Row. Leeds LS7 — 60 C6
Beckhill Vale. Leeds LS7 — 60 C6
Beckhill View. Leeds LS7 — 60 C6
Beckhill Wlk. Leeds LS7 — 60 C6
Becks Ct. Dew WF12 — 139 F6
Beckside Cl. Add LS29 — 7 F8
Beckside Gdns. Hud HD5 — 155 C4
Beckside La. Brad BD7 — 74 A3
Beckside Rd. Brad BD7 — 74 A5
Beckwith Dr. Brad BD10 — 56 D5
Bedale Ave. Brig HD6 — 135 E8

Bedale Ave. Skel HD8 — 174 F1
Bedale Dr. Brad BD6 — 73 F1
Bedale Dr. Skel HD8 — 174 F1
Bedale. E Ard WF3 — 119 D8
Bedale Wlk. Shaf S72 — 180 C3
Bedding Edge Rd. Holmfi HD7 — 200 A7
Bede Ct. Wake WF1 — 142 C8
Bede House. Wake WF1 — 142 C8
Bede's Cl. Thorn BD13 — 72 E6
Bedford Ave. Floc WF4 — 156 E5
Bedford Cl. Crof WF4 — 162 A8
Bedford Cl. Lepton HD8 — 155 E3
Bedford Cl. Hors LS16 — 41 E3
Bedford Ct. Leeds LS8 — 61 C6
Bedford Dr. Hors LS16 — 41 E3
Bedford Garth. Hors LS16 — 41 E3
Bedford Gdns. Hors LS16 — 41 E3
Bedford Mount. Hors LS16 — 41 E2
Bedford Row. Leeds LS10 — 79 D4
Bedford St. Brad BD4 — 74 F6
Bedford St. Keigh BD21 — 35 B6
Bedford St. Clec BD19 — 116 C7
Bedford St. Elland HX5 — 134 F6 7
Bedford St. Hali HX1 — 113 A2
Bedford St. Sow B HX6 — 111 F3
Bedford St. N. Hali HX1 — 113 A3
Bedivere Rd. Brad BD8 — 73 D7
Bedlam La. Arth LS21 — 25 F4
Beech Ave. Crof WF4 — 162 A8
Beech Ave. Denh BD13 — 52 C3
Beech Ave. Hali HX6 — 112 B5
Beech Ave. Hud HD5 — 154 F5
Beech Ave. Leeds LS12 — 78 C8
Beech Ave. Loft G WF3 — 121 F4
Beech Ave. Tod OL14 — 108 B6
Beech Ave. Wake WF2 — 141 F7
Beech Cl. Bacup OL13 — 106 A3
Beech Cl. Brad BD3 — 56 E1
Beech Cl. Leeds LS14 — 62 A4
Beech Cl. Liver FW15 — 117 C5
Beech Cres. Bail BD17 — 38 C2
Beech Cres. Castle WF10 — 125 D5
Beech Cres. Leeds LS9 — 59 D3
Beech Croft. Leeds LS12 — 58 B3 3
Beech Gr. Cl. Keigh BD21 — 35 B5
Beech Gr. Gar LS25 — 82 E6
Beech Gr. Hali HX1 — 113 A4
Beech Gr. Hor WF4 — 141 C1
Beech Gr. Ilkley LS29 — 8 D3
Beech Gr. Keigh BD21 — 35 B5
Beech Gr. Pont WF8 — 146 B7
Beech Grove Ave. Gar LS25 — 82 E6
Beech Grove Terr. Gar LS25 — 82 E6
Beech La. Leeds LS9 — 61 E8
Beech Lees. Pudsey LS28 — 57 C1
Beech Mount. Leeds LS9 — 61 E8
Beech Pl. Leeds LS9 — 59 D3
Beech Rd. Brad BD6 — 94 A7
Beech Rd. Castle WF10 — 124 F6
Beech Rd. Dew WF13 — 138 E5
Beech Rise. Leeds LS14 — 62 A4
Beech Sq. Brad BD14 — 73 C4
Beech St. Bacup OL13 — 106 B3
Beech St. Bing BD16 — 37 A3
Beech St. Brad BD14 — 73 C4
Beech St. Castle WF10 — 124 C7
Beech St. Hali HX3 — 113 A3
Beech St. Harden BD16 — 36 B1
Beech St. Keigh BD21 — 35 B5
Beech St. Morley LS27 — 98 A3
Beech St. S Elm WF9 — 183 A4
Beech Terr. Brad BD3 — 56 E1
Beech View. Aber LS25 — 64 D7
Beech Way. Batley WF17 — 118 A4
Beechcroft Cl. Leeds LS11 — 78 E2
Beechcroft Mead. Leeds LS17 — 43 E4
Beechcroft View. Leeds LS11 — 78 E2
Beechcroft. Weth LS22 — 13 E4
Beechdale Ave. Batley WF17 — 118 A4
Beeches End. B Spa LS23 — 30 E3
Beeches The. Bing BD16 — 36 F3
Beeches The. Shelf HX3 — 93 B5
Beechmount Cl. Bail BD17 — 38 C4

Beechroyd. Pudsey LS28 — 76 E6
Beechroyd Terr. Brad BD16 — 36 F2
Beechtree Ct. Bail BD17 — 38 A2
Beechwood Ave. Birk BD11 — 96 D7
Beechwood Ave. Brad BD6 — 74 B2
Beechwood Ave. Hali HX2, HX3 — 92 A5
Beechwood Ave. Keigh BD20 — 18 F1
Beechwood Ave. Leeds LS4 — 59 D3
Beechwood Ave. Ship BD18 — 54 D8
Beechwood Ave. Shelf HX3 — 93 B5
Beechwood Cl. Bird LS14 — 45 A1
Beechwood Cl. Hors LS18 — 41 B3
Beechwood Cl. Hors LS16 — 41 E2
Beechwood Cres. Hali HX2 — 91 F4
Beechwood Cres. Leeds LS4 — 59 D3
Beechwood Cres. Pont WF8 — 146 B7
Beechwood Cres. Sow B HX6 — 111 D4
Beechwood Dale. Ack M T WF7 — 164 B7
Beechwood Dr. Brad HX6 — 111 E3
Beechwood Dr. Sow B HX6 — 111 F3
Beechwood Gr. Birk BD11 — 96 D7
Beechwood Gr. Brad BD6 — 74 B2
Beechwood Gr. Hali HX2 — 91 F4
Beechwood Gr. Hor WF4 — 141 C1
Beechwood Gr. Leeds LS4 — 59 D3
Beechwood Mount. Leeds LS4 — 59 D3
Beechwood Pl. Leeds LS4 — 59 D3
Beechwood Prim Sch. Leeds — 62 A4
Beechwood Rd. Brad BD6 — 74 B2
Beechwood Rd. Hali HX2 — 91 F4
Beechwood Rd. Hor WF4 — 141 C1
Beechwood Row. Leeds LS4 — 59 D3
Beechwood St. Leeds LS4 — 59 D3
Beechwood St. Pudsey LS28 — 57 E1
Beechwood Terr. Leeds LS4 — 59 D3
Beechwood View. Leeds LS4 — 59 D3
Beechwood Wlk. Leeds LS4 — 59 D3
Beecroft Cl. Leeds LS13 — 58 B3 3
Beecroft Cres. Leeds LS13 — 58 B3
Beecroft Gdns. Leeds LS13 — 58 B3
Beecroft Mount. Leeds LS13 — 58 B3
Beecroft Prim Sch. Leeds — 58 B3
Beecroft St. Keigh BD21 — 35 D7
Beecroft St. Leeds LS5 — 59 B3
Beecroft Wlk. Leeds LS13 — 58 B3
Beehive St. Leeds LS11 — 79 A3
Beeston Park Croft. Leeds LS11 — 78 E2
Beeston Park Garth. Leeds LS11 — 78 E2
Beeston Park Gr. Leeds LS11 — 78 E2
Beeston Park Pl. Leeds LS11 — 78 E2
Beeston Park Terr. Leeds LS11 — 78 E2
Beeston Prim Sch. Leeds — 78 E2
Beeston Rd. Leeds LS11 — 79 A3
Beeston Royds Ind Est. Leeds — 78 C4
Beestonley La. Elland HX4 — 133 E4
Beestonley La. Stainl HX4 — 133 E4
Belcross Dr. Hali HX3 — 113 B4
Beldon La. Brad BD7 — 73 F2
Beldon Park Ave. Brad BD7 — 73 E2
Beldon Park Cl. Brad BD7 — 73 E2
Beldon Pl. Brad BD2 — 56 B3
Beldon Rd. Brad BD7 — 73 F2
Belfast St. Hali HX1 — 112 F5
Belford Cl. Brad BD4 — 95 B8
Belfry The. Yeadon LS19 — 40 C7
Belgrave Ave. Ossett WF5 — 140 F4
Belgrave Cl. Hali HX3 — 113 D8
Belgrave Cres. Hali HX3 — 113 D8
Belgrave Dr. Hali HX3 — 113 D8
Belgrave Gdns. Hali HX3 — 113 D8
Belgrave Mount. Hali HX3 — 113 D8
Belgrave Mount. Wake WF1 — 142 E8
Belgrave Pk. Hali HX3 — 113 D8
Belgrave Rd. Keigh BD21 — 35 B8
Belgrave Rd. Kippax WF10 — 103 A5
Belgrave St. Leeds LS2 — 206 C2
Belgrave St. Ossett WF5 — 140 E4
Belgrave St. Wake WF1 — 142 E8
Belinda St. Leeds LS10 — 80 A2
Bell Bank View. Bing BD16 — 36 F2
Bell Dean Rd. Brad BD15 — 73 C8
Bell Hall Mount. Hali HX1 — 113 A5 24
Bell Hall Terr. Hali HX1 — 113 A5 1
Bell House Ave. Brad BD4 — 75 E1
Bell La. Ackw WF7 — 164 D8
Bell La. Leeds LS13 — 58 D3
Bell Isle Ave. Wake WF1 — 142 E4
Bell Isle Dr. Leeds LS10 — 80 A1
Bell Isle Rd. Leeds LS10 — 80 A1
Bell St. Brad BD13 — 72 D6
Bell St. Hali HX3 — 113 B4
Bell St. Leeds LS9 — 207 F4
Bell Vue Ave. B in Elm LS15 — 62 F6

Belle Vue Ave. Leeds LS8 61 D6
Belle Vue Boys Sch. Brad 54 C4
Belle Vue. Brad BD8 55 D1
Belle Vue Cres. Hud HD2 136 C3
Belle Vue Cres. Shelf HX3 93 B5
Belle Vue Dr. Pudsey LS28 57 C3
Belle Vue Est. B in Elm LS15 62 F6
Belle Vue Fst Sch. Brad 55 D1
Belle Vue Girls Sch. Ship 54 C5
Belle Vue. Ilkley LS29 8 C3
Belle Vue. Queen BD13 92 E7
Belle Vue Rd. B in Elm LS15 62 F6
Belle Vue Rd. Leeds LS3 59 F1
Belle Vue Rd. Shelf HX3 93 B5
Belle Vue Rd. Wake WF1 142 E2
Belle Vue Sch (Art & Drama). Wake 142 F4
Belle Vue St. Batley WF17 117 F5
Belle Vue Terr. Guise LS20 39 E8
Belle Vue Terr. Hali HX3 113 E5
Bellerby Brow. Brad BD6 73 E1
Bellerby Pl. Ad Le S DN6 184 F2
Bellerby Rd. Ad Le S DN6 184 F2
Bellevue Terr. Sow Br HX2 111 C7
Bellgreave Ave. Holmfi HD7 189 F6
Bellhouse Cres. Brad BD4 95 B8
Bellmont Cres. Hem WF9 181 E6
Bellmount Cl. Leeds LS13 58 D3
Bellmount Gdns. Leeds LS13 58 C4
Bellmount Gn. Leeds LS13 58 D4 4
Bellmount Pl. Leeds LS13 58 D4
Bellmount View. Leeds LS13 58 D3
Belloe St. Brad BD5 74 D4
Bellshaw St. Brad BD8 73 E7
Bellstring La. Mir WF14 137 E1
Bellwood Ave. B Spa LS23 30 D6
Belmont Ave. Bail BD17 38 B3
Belmont Ave. Brad BD12 94 E7
Belmont Ave. Otley LS21 10 F1
Belmont. Broth WF11 105 C1
Belmont Cl. Bail BD17 38 B3
Belmont Cl. Hud HD1 154 A7 1
Belmont Cres. Brad BD12 94 E7
Belmont Cres. Ship BD18 55 A8
Belmont Gdns. Brad BD12 94 D7
Belmont Gr. Brad BD6 94 D7
Belmont Gr. Leeds LS2 60 A1
Belmont Gr. Yeadon LS19 40 C5
Belmont Grange. Liver WF15 117 A2
Belmont Mid Sch. Bail 38 B3
Belmont Pl. Hali HX1 113 A6
Belmont Rd. Ilkley LS29 8 E4
Belmont Rise. Bail BD17 38 B3
Belmont Rise. Brad BD12 94 E7
Belmont St. Brad BD2 56 C5
Belmont St. Feath WF7 144 C5
Belmont St. Hali HX6 112 C4
Belmont St. Hali HX3 113 E8
Belmont St. Hud HD1 154 A7
Belmont St. Slai HD7 169 F8
Belmont St. Wake WF1 142 B8
Belmont Terr. Hali HX2 111 E5
Belmont Terr. Midd WF3 99 F2
Belmont Terr. Ship BD18 55 A8
Belmont Way. S Elm WF9 183 B3
Belton Cl. Brad BD7 74 A3
Belton Gr. Hud HD3 135 B2
Belton Rd. Sil BD20 17 E8
Belton St. Hud HD5 154 E5
Belvedere Ave. Leeds LS17 43 D4
Belvedere Ave. Leeds LS11 79 B2
Belvedere Cl. Shaf S72 180 C2
Belvedere Ct. Leeds LS17 43 E4
Belvedere Gr. Leeds LS17 43 D4
Belvedere Mount. Leeds LS11 79 B2
Belvedere Rd. Batley WF17 118 B4
Belvedere Rd. Leeds LS17 43 D4
Belvedere Terr. Brad BD8 74 B8
Belvedere Terr. Leeds LS11 79 B2
Belvedere View. Leeds LS17 43 E4
Belvoir Dr. Knot WF11 126 E4
Belvoir Gdns. Hali HX3 113 C3
Bembridge Ct. Wake WF2 141 E5
Bempton Ct. Brad BD7 74 B4 5
Bempton Gr. Batley WF17 96 F2
Bempton Pl. Brad BD7 74 B4 4
Ben Booth La. Floc WF4 156 F4
Ben Rhydding Dr. Ilkley LS29 8 F3
Ben Rhydding Rd. Ilkley LS29 8 D3
Ben Rhydding Sta. Ilkley 8 E4
Benbow Ave. Brad BD10 56 E5
Bendigo Rd. Dew WF12 118 F1
Benjamin Gott High Sch The. Leeds 59 A2
Benjamin St. Liver WF15 117 B3
Benjamin St. Wake WF2 142 A7
Benn Ave. Brad BD7 73 F4
Benn Cres. Brad BD7 73 F4
Benn La. Hud HD3 152 F6
Bennet Ct. Leeds LS15 81 D8
Bennett Ave. Hor WF4 141 C2
Bennett Ct. Otley LS21 10 F1
Bennett House. Brad BD15 73 B7 8
Bennett La. Batley WF12 118 F2
Bennett Rd. Leeds LS6 59 D5
Bennett St. Hali HX3 113 D6
Bennett St. Liver WF15 117 B4 5
Benns La. Hali HX2 90 F2
Benny La. Slai HD7 152 B3
Benny Parr Cl. Batley WF17 118 E5
Benomley Cres. Hud HD5 154 E4
Benomley Dr. Hud HD5 154 E3
Benomley Rd. Hud HD5 154 E3
Benroyd Terr. Elland HX4 134 C4
Benson Gdns. Leeds LS12 78 B6
Benson Gdns. Nor WF6 123 C3
Benson La. Nor WF6 123 C3
Benson St. Leeds LS7 60 D2
Bent Close La. Heb Br HX7 110 E3
Bent Cotts. S in Cra BD20 16 B5
Bent La. Holmfi HD7 199 B8
Bent La. S in Cra BD20 16 C5
Bent Lea. Hud HD2 136 F6
Bent Ley Rd. Mel HD7 171 A3
Bent Rd. Holmfi HD7 199 D7
Bent St. Hud HD4 154 B4
Bentcliff Wlk. Brad BD15 73 B7 1
Bentcliffe Ave. Leeds LS17 43 E2
Bentcliffe Cl. Leeds LS17 43 E1
Bentcliffe Ct. Leeds LS17 43 E1
Bentcliffe Dr. Leeds LS17 43 E2
Bentcliffe Gdns. Leeds LS17 43 E1
Bentcliffe Gr. Leeds LS17 43 E1
Bentcliffe La. Leeds LS17 43 D2
Bentcliffe Mount. Leeds LS17 43 E1
Bentfield Cotts. Brad BD14 73 C5
Bentham Way. Mapp S75 178 A2
Bentley Ave. Brig HX3 115 A7
Bentley Cl. Bail BD17 38 B4
Bentley Ct. Leeds LS6 59 F6 1
Bentley Gr. Leeds LS6 59 F6
Bentley La. Leeds LS6, LS7 59 F6
Bentley Mount. Hali HX6 112 D5
Bentley Mount. Leeds LS6 59 F6
Bentley Par. Leeds LS6 59 F6
Bentley Prim Sch. Leeds 59 F6
Bentley Rd. Wake WF2 141 E4
Bentley Sq. Roth LS26 101 C5 2
Bentley St. Brad BD12 94 D3 4
Bentley St. Hud HD1 153 E3
Benton Cres. Hor WF4 141 C2
Benton Park Ave. Yeadon LS19 40 C5 2
Benton Park Cres. Yeadon LS19 40 C5
Benton Park Dr. Yeadon LS19 40 C5
Benton Park Rd. Yeadon LS19 40 C5
Benton Park Sch. Yeadon 40 B5
Bents La. Mars HD7 169 B6
Bents La. Wils BD15 53 A6
Bents Rd. Carl S30 200 D4
Benyon Park Way. Leeds LS12 78 D4
Beresford Rd. Brad BD6 94 B7
Beresford St. Brad BD12 95 A5
Berkeley Ave. Leeds LS8 61 A3
Berkeley Cres. Leeds LS8 61 A3
Berkeley Croft. Roy S71 179 B4
Berkeley Ct. Leeds LS3 59 F1 2
Berkeley Gr. Leeds LS8 61 A3
Berkeley Mount. Leeds LS8 61 A3 15
Berkeley Rd. Leeds LS8 61 A3
Berkeley St. Leeds LS8 61 A3
Berkeley Terr. Leeds LS8 61 A3 13
Berkeley View. Leeds LS8 61 A3
Berking Ave. Leeds LS9 79 F8
Bermerside Sch. Hali 113 B2
Bermondsey St. Otley LS21 23 B8
Bernard St. Hud HD2 136 E3
Bernard St. Leeds LS2 79 C8
Bernard St. Roth LS26 101 D6
Berne Gr. Wake WF1 142 C7
Berners St. Wake WF1 142 D6
Berry Bank La. Holmfi HD7 189 B8
Berry Brow Inf Sch. Hud 171 F8
Berry Croft. Honley HD7 171 F5
Berry La. Hali HX3 113 D7
Berry La. Hor WF4 141 B1
Berry La. Keigh BD21 35 B6
Berry La. Swil LS26 102 E8
Berry Moor Rd. Sow Br HX6 112 D2
Berry Rd. Mel HD7 170 C3
Berry St. Keigh BD21 35 D7 6
Berry View. Hud HD4 153 F1
Berry's Bldgs. Hali HX2 91 F4
Berry's Yd. Hor WF4 141 B2
Bertha St. Keigh BD21 35 C7
Bertha St. Pudsey LS28 57 D2
Bertie St. Brad BD4 75 C3
Bertram Dr. Bail BD17 38 B2
Bertram Rd. Brad BD8 55 C2
Bertrand St. Leeds LS11 79 A5 10
Berwick Ave. Batley WF16 117 D6
Berwick St. Hali HX1 113 D7
Bescaby Gr. Bail BD17 38 E3
Besha Ave. Brad BD12 94 D6
Besha Gr. Brad BD12 94 D6
Bessingham Gdns. Brad BD6 93 F8
Best La. Kirkb HD4 172 D7
Best La. Oxen BD22 51 C2
Beswick Cl. Brad BD3 75 D7
Beswick St. Tod OL14 129 A7
Bethal Gn. Litt OL15 129 C1
Bethel Rd. Ship BD18 55 D8
Bethel St. Brig HD6 115 B2
Bethel St. Hali HX3 92 A2 2
Bethel St. Keigh BD20 36 D8
Bethel Terr. Hali HX2 90 D1
Bethel Terr. Sow Br HX6 112 D3
Bethesda Row. Heb Br HX7 89 D1
Betteras Hill Rd. Hillam LS25 105 F7
Betula Way. Lepton HD8 155 E3
Beulah Gr. Leeds LS6 60 B3 3
Beulah Mount. Leeds LS6 60 B3 2
Beulah Pl. Hali HX2 111 E5
Beulah St. Leeds LS6 60 B3
Beulah Terr. Leeds LS6 60 B4 4
Beulah Terr. Leeds LS15 62 C2
Beulah View. Leeds LS6 60 B3 1
Bevan Ave. Nor WF6 144 B8
Bevan Pl. Wake WF2 141 C4
Bevedere Gdns. Leeds LS17 43 E4
Beverley Ave. Brad BD12 94 D2
Beverley Ave. Leeds LS11 79 B3
Beverley Cl. Elland HX5 135 B7
Beverley Ct. Hud HD2 136 B2
Beverley Dr. Brad BD12 94 D2
Beverley Dr. Dew WF12 139 F8
Beverley Garth. Ack M T WF7 164 A5
Beverley Gdns. Batley WF17 97 B2
Beverley Mount. Leeds LS11 79 B3 13
Beverley Pl. Hali HX3 92 B1
Beverley Rise. Ilkley LS29 7 E4
Beverley St. Brad BD4 75 D5
Beverley Terr. Hali HX3 92 B1
Beverley Terr. Leeds LS11 79 B3
Beverley View. Leeds LS11 79 B3
Beverley Wlk. Gar LS25 82 F6
Bevin Cl. Loft G WF1 121 C5
Bevin Cres. Loft G WF1 121 C5
Bevor Cres. Batley WF16 117 D6
Bewdley Ct. Roy S71 179 D4
Bewerley Cres. Brad BD6 94 A6
Bewerley Street Prim Sch. Leeds 79 B4
Bewick Gr. Midd LS10 99 F7
Bexhill Cl. Pont WF8 125 F2
Bexley Ave. Leeds LS8 60 F2
Bexley Gr. Leeds LS8 60 F2
Bexley Mount. Leeds LS8 60 F2 9
Bexley Pl. Leeds LS8 60 F2 8
Bexley Rd. Leeds LS8 60 F3
Bexley Terr. Leeds LS8 60 F2
Bexley View. Leeds LS8 60 F2
Beza Rd. Leeds LS10 79 D3
Beza St. Leeds LS10 79 D3
Bickerdike Pl. Kippax WF10 103 B4
Bickerdike Terr. Kippax LS25 83 A1
Bickerton Way. Otley LS21 10 E1
Biddenden Rd. Leeds LS15 62 F2
Bideford Ave. Leeds LS8 43 F2
Bideford Mount. Brad BD4 75 E3
Bierley CE Fst Sch. Brad 75 B1
Bierley Hall Gr. Brad BD4 95 B7
Bierley Hall Hospl. Brad 95 B8
Bierley House Ave. Brad BD4 75 C1
Bierley La. Brad BD4 95 B8
Bierley View. Brad BD4 75 C1
Big Meadow Dr. Sil LS29 6 D8
Bilham La. H Pag DN5 195 D2
Bilham Rd. Clay W HD8 176 A2
Bilham Row. H Pag DN5 195 F3
Bill La. Holmfi HD7 189 C7
Billam's Hill. Otley LS21 10 F1
Billey La. Leeds LS12 77 E4
Billing Ct. Yeadon LS19 40 D3
Billing Dr. Yeadon LS19 40 E3
Billing View. Brad BD10 56 C7
Billing View. Yeadon LS19 40 D3
Billingbauk Dr. Leeds LS13 58 D1
Billingham Cl. Wake WF2 141 D8
Billingsley Terr. Brad BD4 75 B4
Billingwood Dr. Yeadon LS19 40 D3
Billy La. Wad M HX7 89 C5
Bilsdale Grange. Brad BD6 93 F8
Bilsdale Way. Bail BD17 38 A2
Bilton Pl. Brad BD8 74 C8
Bingley Bank. Bard LS17 28 C2
Bingley CE Fst Sch. Bing 36 F3
Bingley Grammar Sch. Bing 36 E4
Bingley Hospl. Bing 37 A3
Bingley Rd. Bail BD17 38 B6
Bingley Rd. Brad BD9 54 D4
Bingley Rd. Cull BD13 35 B1
Bingley Rd. Cull BD13 52 E7
Bingley Rd. Guise LS29 21 C2
Bingley Rd. Men LS29 21 F3
Bingley Rd. Ship BD18 54 E8
Bingley St. Brad BD8 74 A7
Bingley (St Ives) Municipal Golf Course. Harden 36 B4
Bingley St. Leeds LS3 78 F8
Bingley Sta. Bing 36 F3
Bingley Stoney Lea Mid Sch. Ship 54 B6
Binham Rd. Hud HD2 153 D8
Binks Fold. Brad BD12 94 D2 3
Binks St. Loft G WF1 121 C4
Binn La. Mars HD7 169 A2
Binn Rd. Mars HD7 168 F3
Binn. Slai HD7 170 A7
Binnie St. Brad BD3 75 B7
Binns Hill La. Hali HX2 112 B6
Binns La. Brad BD7 73 F5
Binns La. Glu BD20 16 A6
Binns La. Holmfi HD7 188 F5
Binns St. Bing BD16 37 A3
Binns Top La. Hali HX3 114 B2
Binswell Fold. Bail BD17 38 C4 9
Birch Ave. Brad BD5 74 F2
Birch Ave. Leeds LS15 81 A8
Birch Ave. Lepton HD8 155 E2
Birch Ave. Rip HX6 132 C1
Birch Ave. Tod OL14 108 A7
Birch Cl. Brad BD5 74 F2
Birch Cl. Brig HD6 115 C3
Birch Cliff. Bail BD17 38 B2
Birch Close La. Bail BD16 37 F8
Birch Cres. Leeds LS15 81 A8
Birch Ct. Morley LS27 98 D2
Birch Dr. Kippax LS25 83 A3
Birch Gn. Pont WF8 125 F1
Birch Gr. Batley WF17 118 A8
Birch Gr. Brad BD5 74 E1
Birch Gr. Castle WF10 125 D6
Birch Gr. Hud HD7 152 E5
Birch Gr. Keigh BD21 35 B4
Birch Gr. Kippax LS25 83 A3
Birch Hill Rise. Hors LS18 58 E8 1
Birch House. Castle WF10 124 E7 7
Birch La. Brad BD5 74 E3
Birch La. Brad BD5 74 F2
Birch La. Hali HX2 111 F8
Birch Pk. Honley HD7 172 D2
Birch Rd. Hud HD4 171 F8
Birch Rd. Kippax LS25 83 A3
Birch Rd. Nor WF6 144 B7
Birch St. Brad BD8 74 A8
Birch St. Morley LS27 98 B2
Birch St. Wake WF1 142 F4
Birch Tree Gdns. Keigh BD21 35 E6
Birch Way. Brad BD5 74 F2
Bircham Cl. Bing BD16 37 C5
Birchcliffe Rd. Heb Br HX7 89 A3
Birchdale. Bing BD16 36 F5
Birchen Ave. Ossett WF5 140 C6
Birchen Hills. Ossett WF5 140 C5
Birchencliffe Hill Rd. Hud HD3 135 B2
Birchenlee Cl. Heb Br HX7 89 F1
Birches The. Bramho LS16 24 F2
Birches The. Guise LS20 22 E2
Birchfield Ave. Gild LS27 97 C6
Birchfield Garth. Leeds LS14 62 C8
Birchfield Gr. Skel HD8 175 A1
Birchfields Ave. Leeds LS14 62 C8
Birchfields Cl. Leeds LS14 62 C7
Birchfields Cres. Leeds LS14 62 C8
Birchfields Ct. Leeds LS14 62 C8 5
Birchfields Rise. Leeds LS14 62 C8
Birchington Ave. Hud HD3 135 B2
Birchington Cl. Hud HD3 135 B2
Birchington Dr. Hud HD3 135 A2
Birchlands Ave. Wils BD15 53 B6
Birchlands Gr. Wils BD15 53 B6
Birchroyd. Roth LS26 100 F4
Birchtree Cl. Wake WF1 142 F8
Birchtree Way. Hors LS16 41 E2
Birchtree Wlk. Knot WF11 126 D3
Birchwood Ave. Batley WF17 96 F2
Birchwood Ave. Keigh BD20 18 B2
Birchwood Ave. Leeds LS17 44 A3
Birchwood Cl. Hud HD2 135 D2
Birchwood Ct. Ilkley LS29 8 A4
Birchwood Ct. Liver WF15 117 B3 2
Birchwood Dr. Keigh BD20 18 B2
Birchwood Hill. Leeds LS17 44 A4
Birchwood Mount. Leeds LS17 44 A4
Birchwood Rd. Keigh BD20 18 A2
Bird La. Rip HX6 132 C3
Birdale Field La. Coll LS22 29 D8
Birdcage Hill. Hali HX3 113 A3
Birdcage La. Hali HX3 113 B3
Birdcage Wlk. Otley LS21 23 A6
Birds Edge La. D Dale HD8 190 F4
Birds Royd La. Brig HD6 115 C1
Birdsedge Farm Mews. D Dale HD8 191 A4
Birdsedge Fst Sch. D Dale 191 A4
Birdsnest La. Wh Com HD7 190 D2
Birdswell Ave. Brig HD6 115 D3
Birfed Cres. Leeds LS4 59 B3
Birk House La. Shep HD8 191 B8
Birk La. Morley LS27 97 E4
Birk Lea St. Brad BD5 74 F4
Birkby Brow Cres. Batley WF17 97 B2
Birkby Hall Rd. Hud HD2 135 E1
Birkby Haven. Brad BD6 93 E8
Birkby Jun Sch. Hud 136 A1
Birkby La. Brig HD6 115 D7
Birkby Lodge Rd. Hud HD2 153 F8
Birkby Rd. Hud HD2 135 D1
Birkby St. Brad BD12 94 D4
Birkdale Ave. Hud HD3 153 A8
Birkdale Cl. Cull BD13 52 E6
Birkdale Cl. Leeds LS17 43 B4
Birkdale Dr. Leeds LS17 43 B4
Birkdale Gn. Leeds LS17 43 B4
Birkdale Gr. Dew WF13 118 A1
Birkdale Gr. Hali HX2 91 F7
Birkdale Gr. Leeds LS17 43 A4
Birkdale High Sch. Dew 118 A2
Birkdale High Sch. Dew 118 B2
Birkdale Mount. Leeds LS17 43 B4
Birkdale Pl. Leeds LS17 43 A4
Birkdale Rd. Dew WF13 118 B1
Birkdale Rd. Roy S71 179 B5
Birkdale Rise. Leeds LS17 43 A4
Birkdale Way. Leeds LS17 43 B4
Birkdale Wlk. Leeds LS17 43 A4
Birkenshaw CE Fst Sch. Birk 96 A6
Birkenshaw Cty Fst Sch. Birk 96 B6
Birkenshaw La. Birk BD11 96 C4
Birkenshaw Mid Sch. Birk 96 B4
Birkett St. Clec BD19 116 D8
Birkhead St. Batley WF16 117 E3
Birkhill. Castle WF10 125 C8
Birkhill Cres. Birk BD11 96 B5
Birkhouse La. Brig HD6 115 D6
Birkhouse La. Hud HD1, HD4 153 E5
Birkhouse La. Hud HD5 154 E5
Birkhouse Rd. Brig HD6 115 C6
Birkin La. Birkin WF11 127 D8
Birklands Rd. Hud HD2 135 F2
Birklands Rd. Ship BD18 55 B7
Birklands Terr. Ship BD18 55 B7
Birks Ave. Brad BD7 73 F5
Birks Fold. Brad BD7 73 F6
Birks Hall St. Hali HX1 113 A8
Birks Hall Terr. Hali HX1 113 A8
Birks La. Hud HD4 155 A3
Birks La. Kirkb HD8 173 D3
Birks La. Rip HX6 132 E5
Birks La. Sow Br HX6 132 D8
Birks La. Tod OL14 129 B8
Birks Rd. Hud HD3 153 A5
Birkshall La. Brad BD4, BD3 75 B6
Birkshead. Wils BD15 53 D5
Birksland Ind Est. Brad 75 B5
Birksland Moor. Birk BD11 96 B3
Birksland St. Brad BD3 75 B6
Birkwith Cl. Leeds LS14 62 B8
Birkwood Ave. Crof WF4 144 B2
Birkwood Rd. Nor WF6 122 C3
Birmingham La. Mel HD7 170 C3
Birnam Gr. Brad BD4 75 A4
Birr Rd. Brad BD9 55 B3
Birstall Cty Jun & Inf Sch. Batley 96 F1
Birstall La. Birk BD11 96 E5
Birstall St Peter's CE Prim Sch. Batley 96 E2
Birthwaite Rd. Kex S75 177 B1
Bishop St. Brad BD9 55 B2
Bishop Way. E Ard WF3 119 F8
Bishop's Ct. Hud HD4 171 F7
Bishopdale Dr. Coll LS22 13 A1
Bishopdale Holme. Brad BD6 93 E8
Bishopgate St. Leeds LS1 79 B7
Bishops Way. Mel HD7 170 E2
Bishops Way. Mir WF14 137 D7
Bisley Cl. Roy S71 179 E4
Bismarck Dr. Leeds LS11 79 B4
Bismarck St. Leeds LS11 79 B4
Bittern Rise. Morley LS27 98 C3
Black Abbey La. Glu BD20 16 C6
Black Brook Way. Elland HX4 134 C6
Black Bull St. Leeds LS10 79 D6
Black Dyke La. Wils BD13 53 B1
Black Edge La. Denh BD13 71 D6
Black Gates Ct. E Ard WF3 119 F8
Black Gates Rise. E Ard WF3 119 F8
Black Hill La. Eccup LS16 25 D1
Black Hill La. Keigh BD20 17 E1
Black Hill Rd. Arth LS21 25 C5
Black Hill. Wad M HX7 89 B8
Black La. Mel HD7 170 E7
Black Moor Rd. Leeds LS17 43 A2
Black Moor Rd. Oxen BD22 51 E4
Black Rd. Crof WF4 143 B3
Black Sike La. Holmfi HD7 188 C5
Black Wlk. Pont WF8 125 E2
Black Wood Gr. Hors LS16 41 D3
Black Wood Mount. Hors LS16 41 D3
Black Wood Rise. Hors LS16 41 D3
Blackbird Gdns. Brad BD8 73 B7 11
Blackburn Bldgs. Brig HD6 115 C2
Blackburn Cl. Brad BD8 73 D7
Blackburn Cl. Hali HX3 91 F3
Blackburn Ct. Pont WF8 146 C8 13
Blackburn Ct. Roth LS26 100 F5
Blackburn House. Hali HX3 92 A3
Blackburn La. Knot WF11 127 C3
Blackburn Pl. Batley WF17 118 D5
Blackburn Rd. Batley WF17 96 E1
Blackburn Rd. Brig HD6 115 A4
Blacker Cres. Neth WF4 158 E6
Blacker La. Neth WF4 159 B5
Blacker La. Shaf S72 180 C3
Blacker Rd. Hud HD1, HD2 153 F8
Blacker Rd. Mapp S75 178 C1
Blacker Rd N. Hud HD1, HD2 153 F8
Blackers Ct. Dew WF12 139 B4
Blackett St. Pudsey LS28 57 B7
Blackgates Cres. E Ard WF3 119 F8
Blackgates Dr. E Ard WF3 119 F8
Blackgates Fold. E Ard WF3 119 F8
Blackgates Inf Sch. E Ard 98 E1
Blackgates Jun Sch. E Ard 119 F8
Blackhouse Rd. Hud HD2 136 B2
Blackledge. Hali HX1 113 D7
Blackley Rd. Elland HX5 134 E4
Blackman La. Leeds LS2 60 B2
Blackmires. Hali HX2 92 A5
Blackmoor Ct. Leeds LS17 42 F5
Blackmoor La. Bard LS17 28 A1
Blackmoorfoot Rd. Hud HD4 153 E4
Blackmoorfoot Rd. Slai HD7 170 D7
Blackpool Gr. Leeds LS12 78 A4
Blackpool Pl. Leeds LS12 78 A4
Blackpool St. Leeds LS12 78 A4 7
Blackpool Terr. Leeds LS12 78 A4 6
Blackpool View. Leeds LS12 78 A4 8
Blackshaw Beck La. Shelf BD13 93 A8
Blackshaw Clough Rd. Rip HX6 132 A6
Blackshaw Dr. Brad BD6 93 D8
Blackshaw St. Tod OL14 108 D5
Blacksmith Fold. Brad BD7 74 A4
Blacksmith La. Eccup LS16 25 F1
Blacksmiths Fold. Hud HD5 154 F3
Blackstone Ave. Brad BD12 94 C2
Blackstone Edge Rd. Heb Br HX7 131 B7
Blackstone Edge Rd. Rip HX6 130 F5
Blackthorn Way. Wake WF2 142 A8
Blackthorne Ct. Midd LS10 99 D8 4
Blackwall. Hali HX1 113 C6
Blackwall La. Hali HX6 112 B5
Blackwall Rise. Hali HX6 112 B5
Blackwood Ave. Hors LS16 41 D3
Blackwood Gdns. Hors LS16 41 D3
Blackwood Gr. Hali HX1 112 F8
Blackwood Hall La. Hali HX2 111 D7
Blacup Moor View. Clec BD19 116 D7
Blagden La. Hud HD4 153 F1
Blairsville Gdns. Leeds LS13 58 B4
Blairsville Gr. Leeds LS13 58 C4
Blaith Royd La. Heb Br HX7 109 F4
Blaithroyd La. Hali HX3 113 E6
Blake Cres. Guise LS20 39 F8
Blake Gr. Leeds LS7 60 D6
Blake Hall Dr. Mir WF14 138 C4
Blake Hall Rd. Mir WF14 138 C4
Blake Hill End. Northo HX3 92 F5
Blake Hill. Northo HX3 92 E3
Blake Law La. Brig WF15 115 F2
Blake Law La. Liver HD6 116 A2
Blake Lee La. Mars HD7 168 B5
Blake Stones. Slai HD7 169 F8
Blakehill Ave. Brad BD2 56 C2
Blakehill Fst Sch. Brad 56 A6
Blakehill Terr. Brad BD2 56 C2
Blakeholme Cl. Slai HD7 169 E8
Blakelaw Dr. Brig HD6 115 D3
Blakeley Gr. Wake WF2 141 F6
Blakeney Gr. Midd LS10 79 D1
Blakeney Rd. Midd LS10 79 D1
Blakeridge La. Batley WF17 118 B5
Blakestones Rd. Slai HD7 169 E8
Blakey Rd. Wake WF2 141 F8
Blamires Pl. Brad BD7 73 F3
Blamires St. Brad BD7 73 F3
Blanche St. Brad BD4 75 D6
Bland St. Hali HX1 113 B7 6
Bland St. Hud HD1 153 F4
Bland's Cl. Castle WF10 124 E7
Blandford Gdns. Leeds LS2 60 B2 9
Blandford Gr. Leeds LS2 60 B2 10
Blands Ave. Kippax WF10 103 A5
Blands Cres. Kippax WF10 103 A5
Blands Gr. Kippax WF10 103 A5
Blands Terr. Kippax WF10 103 A5
Blanket Hall St. Liver WF16 117 D3
Blayd's Mews. Leeds LS1 79 C7 7
Blayd's Yd. Leeds LS1 79 C7 6
Blayds St. Leeds LS9 79 F7
Bleach Mill La. Men LS29 21 E5
Bleak Ave. Shaf S72 180 C2
Bleak St. Clec BD19 117 C8
Bleak St Lower. Clec BD19 117 C8
Bleakley Ave. Notton WF4 179 B6
Bleakley Cl. Shaf S72 180 C2
Bleakley La. Notton WF4 179 B6
Bleakley Terr. Notton WF4 179 B6
Bleasdale Ave. Hud HD2 135 F1
Bleasdale Ave. Knot WF11 126 F4
Blencarn Cl. Leeds LS14 61 F4
Blencarn Garth. Leeds LS14 61 F4
Blencarn Lawn. Leeds LS14 61 F4
Blencarn Path. Leeds LS14 61 F4
Blencarn Rd. Leeds LS14 61 F4
Blencarn View. Leeds LS14 61 F4
Blencarn Wlk. Leeds LS14 61 F4
Blenheim Ave. Leeds LS2 60 B2 1
Blenheim Cl. Knot WF11 126 C4
Blenheim Cres. Leeds LS2 60 B2
Blenheim Ct. Hali HX1 113 B8
Blenheim Ct. Leeds LS2 60 B2 3
Blenheim Dr. Batley WF17 118 C6
Blenheim Dr. Dew WF13 118 A1
Blenheim Gr. Leeds LS2 60 B2
Blenheim Hill. Batley WF17 118 D7
Blenheim Mid Sch. Leeds 60 B3
Blenheim Mount. Brad BD8 55 C2
Blenheim Pl. Brad BD10 39 B1
Blenheim Prim Sch. Leeds 60 B2
Blenheim Rd. Brad BD8 55 C2
Blenheim Rd. Wake WF1 142 B8
Blenheim Sq. Batley WF17 118 C6
Blenheim Sq. Leeds LS2 60 B2
Blenheim St. Heb Br HX7 89 B3
Blenheim St. Keigh BD21 35 B5 10
Blenheim Terr. Leeds LS2 60 B2
Blenheim View. Leeds LS2 60 B2
Blenheim Wlk. Leeds LS2 60 B2 4
Blenkinsop Ct. Morley LS27 98 B2
Blessed English Martyrs' Inf & Jun Sch. Wake 141 D5
Blind La. Bick LS24 15 F8
Blind La. Birk BD11 96 F8
Blind La. E Ard WF3 120 A5
Blind La. Hali HX2 91 E8
Blind La. Harden BD16 36 D3
Blind La. Heb Br HX2 111 B7
Blind La. Thorner LS17 44 E4
Blind La. Tod OL14 108 B6
Bloomfield Rd. Mapp S75 177 F1
Bloomfield Rise. Mapp S75 177 F1
Bloomhouse La. Mapp S75 177 F1
Blucher St. Brad BD4 75 D6
Blue Ball La. Rip HX6 131 E3
Blue Ball Rd. Rip HX6 131 D3
Blue Bell Hill. Hud HD4 153 F2
Blue Bell La. Tod OL14 86 D2
Blue Butts. Ossett WF5 140 D5
Blue Hill Cres. Leeds LS12 78 A6
Blue Hill. Denh BD13 52 D1
Blue Hill Gr. Leeds LS12 78 A6
Blue Hill Grange. Leeds LS12 78 A5
Blue Hill La. Leeds LS12 78 A6
Bluebell Cl. Pont WF8 146 D7
Bluebell Ct. Batley WF17 96 E2
Bluebell Rd. Wool S75 177 E3
Bluebell Wlk. Hali HX2 111 E8
Blundell St. Leeds LS1 60 B1
Blundell St. S Elm WF9 182 E3
Blythe Ave. Brad BD8 74 A8
Blythe St. Brad BD7 74 D7
Boar La. Leeds LS1 79 C7
Boardman St. Tod OL14 108 B6
Boat La. Kippax WF10 103 B3

Boat La. M'town WF10 ...... 103 A3
Boathouse La. Mir WF14 ...... 138 C3
Bob La. Hali HX2 ...... 112 D7
Bobbin Mill Cl. Stee BD20 ...... 17 C5
Bobbin Mill Ct. Tod OL14 ...... 86 B1
Bobbin Mill Ct. Stee BD20 ...... 17 C5
Bobbin St. Tod OL14 ...... 86 C1
Bodiham Hill. Gar LS25 ...... 83 B8
Bodington Hall. Hors 42 C2
Bodkin La. Oxen BD22 ...... 50 B3
Bodley Terr. Leeds LS4 ...... 59 D1
Bodmin App. Midd LS10 ...... 99 A5
Bodmin Ave. Dup BD18 ...... 55 F7
Bodmin Cres. Midd LS10 ...... 99 B5
Bodmin Croft. Midd LS10 ...... 99 B4
Bodmin Dr. Nor WF6 ...... 123 B3
Bodmin Garth. Midd LS10 ...... 99 A4
Bodmin Gdns. Midd LS10 ...... 99 A4
Bodmin Pl. Midd LS10 ...... 99 A4
Bodmin Rd. Midd LS10 ...... 99 A4
Bodmin Sq. Midd LS10 ...... 99 A4
Bodmin St. Midd LS10 ...... 99 A4
Bodmin Terr. Midd LS10 ...... 99 A4
Bog Green La. Kirkhe HD5 ...... 137 C2
Bog La. B in Elm LS15 ...... 63 A5
Boggart Hill Cres. Leeds LS14 ...... 61 E6
Boggart Hill Dr. Leeds LS14 ...... 61 E6
Boggart Hill Gdns. Leeds LS14 ...... 61 E6
Boggart La. Skel LS14 ...... 61 E6
Boggart Hill Rd. Leeds LS14 ...... 61 E6
Boggart La. Skel HD8 ...... 175 A3
Boggart La. Now Br HX6 ...... 112 B3
Boland Cres. Haw BD22 ...... 34 E3
Boldgrove St. Dew WF12 ...... 140 A6
Boldmere Rd. Leeds LS15 ...... 80 E7
Boldron Holt. Brad BD6 ...... 93 F8
Boldshay St. Brad BD3 ...... 75 B8
Bolehill Pk. Brig HD6 ...... 114 E6
Bolingbroke St. Brad BD5 ...... 74 D2
Bolland St. Brad BD12 ...... 94 C3
Bolling Hall (Mus). Brad 74 E3
Bolling Rd. Brad BD4 ...... 74 F5
Bolling Rd Fst Sch. Ilkley 8 E6
Bolling Rd. Ilkley LS29 ...... 8 D4
Bolsover Cl. Gar LS25 ...... 83 B7
Bolstermoor Rd. Slai HD7 ...... 152 B4
Boltby La. Brad BD6 ...... 93 E8
Bolton Bridge Rd. Ilkley LS29 ...... 8 A4
Bolton Brow. Hali HX6 ...... 112 C4
Bolton Brow Jun & Inf Sch. Hali 112 C4
Bolton Cres. Brad BD2 ...... 56 C2
Bolton Ct. Brad BD2 ...... 56 A2
Bolton Dr. Brad BD2 ...... 56 B4
Bolton Gdns. Yeadon LS19 ...... 40 C6
Bolton Gr. Brad BD2 ...... 56 B3
Bolton Hall. Hali HX2 ...... 91 E7
Bolton Hall Rd. Brad BD2 ...... 55 E5
Bolton Hall Rd. Ship BD2 ...... 55 E5
Bolton La. Brad BD2 ...... 55 E3
Bolton Lane Fst Sch. Brad 55 F3
Bolton Rd. add LS29 ...... 2 F4
Bolton Rd. Brad BD2, BD3 ...... 55 F2
Bolton Rd. Brnug LS29 ...... 2 F4
Bolton Rd. Sil BD20, LS29 ...... 5 F4
Bolton Royd Prim Sch. Pudsey 76 A8
Bolton St. Brad BD3 ...... 75 A7
Bolton St. Brad BD2 ...... 94 C6
Bolton Tarr. Sp BD22 ...... 5 E2
Bolton Way. B Spa LS23 ...... 30 C7
Bolton Wife Hill. Crig WF4 ...... 159 F1
Bolton Woods Fst Sch. Ship 55 D4
Bolus Cl. Loft G WF1 ...... 121 C4
Bolus La. Loft G WF1 ...... 121 C4
Bonaccord Sq. Batley WF17 ...... 118 C4
Bonaccord Terr. Batley WF17 ...... 118 C4
Bond Cl. Leeds LS1 ...... 78 B8
Bond St. Batley WF17 ...... 96 E1
Bond St. Brad BD5 ...... 74 D4
Bond St. Brig HD6 ...... 115 B3
Bond St Tnw WF1 ...... 119 C8
Bond St. Hali HX1 ...... 113 B6
Bond St. Heb Br HX7 ...... 89 A3
Bond St. Leeds LS2 ...... 78 A8
Bond St. Tront WF8 ...... 125 E2
Bond St. Tod OL14 ...... 108 B5
Bond St. Wake WF1 ...... 142 B7
Bond Street Ctr. Leeds 79 C7
Bondgate. Hare LS17 ...... 27 A7
Bondgate. Otley LS21 ...... 23 B7
Bondgate. Pont WF8 ...... 125 E1
Bonegate Ave. Brig HD6 ...... 115 B3
Bonegate Rd. Brig HD6 ...... 115 B3
Bonn Rd. Brad BD9 ...... 55 A2
Bonwick Mall. Brad BD6 ...... 93 E7
Boocock St. Pudsey LS28 ...... 57 E1
Bookers Cl. Clec DB19 ...... 117 C7
Bookers Field. Clec BD19 ...... 117 C7
booth stank. Mars HD7 ...... 169 C7
Booth. Hali HX2 ...... 90 E8
Booth Hall La. Hali HX2 ...... 90 E8
Booth House La. Holmfi HD7 ...... 188 C6
Booth House Rd. Sow Br HX2 ...... 111 C7
Booth St. Dew WF13 ...... 138 D6
Booth. Mars HD7 ...... 169 B1
Booth Royd. Brad BD10 ...... 39 B1
Booth Royd Dr. Brad BD10 ...... 39 B1
Booth Royd La. Brig HD6 ...... 135 D8
Booth St. Brad BD10 ...... 39 B1
Booth St. Bur in W LS29 ...... 9 E8
Booth St. Castle WF10 ...... 124 C8
Booth St. Queen BD13 ...... 72 D1
Booth St. Ship BD18 ...... 55 D7
Boothroyd Dr. Leeds LS13 ...... 58 D2
Boothroyd. Dew WF13 ...... 138 D5
Boothroyd Dr. Dew WF13 ...... 138 D5
Boothroyd La. Dew WF13 ...... 139 B8
Boothroyd Lane Fst Sch. Dew 139 A8
Boothtown Rd. Hali HX3 ...... 92 B1
Border Cl. Hud HD3 ...... 134 F1
Borough Marret. Hali HX1 ...... 113 C7
Borough Rd. Wake WF2 ...... 142 A5
Boroughgate. Otley LS21 ...... 23 A8
Borough's Bldgs. Brig HD6 ...... 115 B3
Borrough View. Leeds LS8 ...... 60 E8
Borrowdale Cres. Leeds LS12 ...... 58 D2
Borrowdale Croft. Yeadon LS19 ...... 40 B7
Borrowdale Dr. Castle WF10 ...... 104 D1
Borrowdale Terr. Leeds LS14 ...... 61 F3

Boston Hill. Wad M HX7 ...... 89 B6
Boston Mews. B Spa LS23 ...... 30 E7
Boston Rd. B Spa LS23 ...... 30 D6
Boston Spa Cl. B Spa 13 E3
Boston Spa CE Prim Sch. B Spa 30 E7
Boston Spa Comp Sch. B Spa 30 D7
Boston Spa Inf Sch. B Spa 30 C8
Boston Spa Jun Sch. B Spa 30 D7
Boston St. Castle WF10 ...... 124 E8
Boston St. Hali HX1 ...... 112 F7
Boston St. Sow Br HX6 ...... 112 A3
Boston Towers. Leeds LS9 ...... 60 E1
Boston St. Brad BD5 ...... 93 F8
Boswell Cl. Roy S71 ...... 179 B4
Bosworth Ave. Nor WF6 ...... 122 E4
Bosworth Cl. Brad BD6 ...... 93 E7
Botany Ave. Brad BD2 ...... 55 F4
Botany Dr. Keigh BD20 ...... 19 E2
Botany La. Lepton HD8 ...... 155 F6
Bothom Hall Rd. Hud HD3 ...... 152 F5
Bottom Boat Rd. Loft G WF3 ...... 122 D6
Bottomley La. Rip HX4 ...... 133 C2
Bottomley Rd. Tod OL14 ...... 129 C6
Bottomley St. Brad BD5 ...... 74 D4
Bottomley St. Brad BD6 ...... 93 F7
Bottomley's Bldgs. Leeds LS6 ...... 60 B3
Bottoms. Hali HX3 ...... 113 D3
Boulder Bridge La. Roy S71 ...... 179 F1
Boulder Gate. Mars HD7 ...... 169 B4
Boulevard The. Brad BD6 ...... 93 E8
Boulevard The. Pudsey LS28 ...... 57 D2
Boundary Ave. Glu BD20 ...... 16 D6
Boundary Cl. Leeds LS15 ...... 81 E7
Boundary Farm Rd. Leeds LS17 ...... 43 A3
Boundary La. Crof WF6 ...... 143 F7
Boundary Pl. Leeds LS7 ...... 60 E2
Boundary Rd. Batley WF13 ...... 117 F2
Boundary Rd. Leeds LS7 ...... 60 E2
Boundary St. Liver WF16 ...... 117 C4
Bourbon Cl. Brad BD6 ...... 94 B8
Bourn View Cl. Hud HD4 ...... 171 D7
Bourn View Rd. Hud HD4 ...... 171 D7
Bourne Ct. Maps S75 ...... 178 C2
Bourne St. Brad BD10 ...... 39 B2
Bourne Wlk. Mapp S75 ...... 178 C2
Bow La. B Head HX7 ...... 88 A4
Bow St. Keigh BD21 ...... 35 C7
Bow St. Hud HD1 ...... 153 F5
Bowater Rd. Brad BD3 ...... 56 C7
Bowbridge Rd. Brad BD5 ...... 56 D6
Bowcliffe Rd. Bramham LS23 ...... 30 D2
Bower Gn. Brad BD3 ...... 75 C7
Bower La. Ratley WF13 ...... 117 F3
Bower Rd. Leeds LS15 ...... 62 D7
Bower Slack Rd. Sow Br HX7 ...... 110 F1
Bower St. Brad BD5 ...... 74 E4
Bower The. Batley WF17 ...... 117 F1
Bowers La. Rip HX4 ...... 133 D6
Bowes Rd. Sil BD20 ...... 5 E1
Bowfell Cl. Leeds LS14 ...... 62 A4
Bowland Ave. Bail BD17 ...... 37 F1
Bowland Cl. Leeds LS15 ...... 80 E7
Bowling Alley. Brig HD6 ...... 136 A8
Bowling Ave. Wake WF2 ...... 120 B8
Bowling Back La. Brad BD4 ...... 75 B5
Bowling Court Ind Est. Brad 75 C5
Bowling Dyke. Hali HX1 ...... 113 C8
Bowling Green Cl. Hud HD3 ...... 152 E7
Bowling Green Jun & Inf Sch.
Elland 133 E3
Bowling Green Rd. Elland HX4 ...... 133 F3
Bowling Green Terr. Leeds LS11 ...... 79 B3
Bowling Hall Rd. Brad BD4 ...... 75 A3
Bowling Old La. Brad BD5 ...... 74 B2
Bowling Old La. Brad BD5 ...... 74 E4
Bowling Park Dr. Brad BD4 ...... 74 F3
Bowling Park Fst Sch. Brad 74 F3
Bowling St. Hud HD4 ...... 153 A4
Bowman Ave. Brad BD6 ...... 94 B7
Bowman Gr. Brad BD6 ...... 94 B7
Bowman La. Leeds LS10 ...... 79 D7
Bowman Pl. Hali HX1 ...... 113 A7
Bowman Rd. Brad BD6 ...... 94 B7
Bowman Terr. Hali HX1 ...... 142 F3
Bownas Rd. B Spa LS23 ...... 30 D8
Bowness Ave. Brad BD10 ...... 56 D4
Bowness Ave. Castle WF10 ...... 104 E1
Bowness Dr. Hud HD5 ...... 154 D7
Bowood Ave. Leeds LS7 ...... 60 A6
Bowood Cres. Leeds LS7 ...... 60 A6
Bowood La. Sow Br HX6 ...... 111 C4
Bowwood Dr. Keigh BD20 ...... 36 D7
Box Tree Cl. Brad BD8 ...... 54 F1
Box Trees La. Hali HX2 ...... 91 D3
Boxhill Rd. Elland HX5 ...... 134 F7
Boxwood Rd. Elland HX5 ...... 134 F5
Boy La. Brad BD4 ...... 95 B7
Boy La. Hali HX3 ...... 92 A2
Boycott St. Ask M T WF7 ...... 145 A4
Boycott Way. S Elm WF9 ...... 183 A4
Boyd Ave. Brad BD3 ...... 56 E1
Boyle & Petyt Sch The. Beam 2 F6
Boyne Dr. Wake WF2 ...... 160 A5
Boyne Hill. Wake WF2 ...... 160 A5
Boynton House. Brad BD15 ...... 73 B8
Boynton St. Brad BD5 ...... 74 E3
Boynton Terr. Brad BD5 ...... 74 E3
Boys La. Hali HX3 ...... 113 C2
Boys' Scarr. Hali HX2 ...... 111 D6
Bracewell Ave. Brad BD15 ...... 73 C8
Bracewell Bank. Hali HX3 ...... 92 A2
Bracewell Dr. Hali HX3 ...... 92 A1
Bracewell Gr. Hali HX3 ...... 92 A2
Bracewell Mid Sch. Brad 73 C8
Bracewell Rd. Hali HX3 ...... 170 C1
Bracewell St. Keigh BD21 ...... 35 B6
Bracken Bank Ave. Keigh BD22 ...... 34 F3
Bracken Bank Cres. Keigh BD22 ...... 34 F3
Bracken Bank Gr. Keigh BD22 ...... 34 F3
Bracken Bank Way. Keigh BD22 ...... 34 F3
Bracken Bank Wlk. Keigh BD22 ...... 34 F3
Bracken Cl. Brig HD6 ...... 115 B3
Bracken Cl. Mir WF14 ...... 137 D5
Bracken Ct. Leeds LS17 ...... 43 C1

Bracken Edge. Brad BD10 ...... 56 C7
Bracken Edge. Leeds LS8 ...... 60 F5
Bracken Edge Prim Sch. Leeds 60 E5
Bracken Ghyll Dr. Sil BD20 ...... 5 D2
Bracken Gr. Hud HD2 ...... 136 B4
Bracken Gr. Mir WF14 ...... 137 D7
Bracken Hall. Hud HD2 ...... 136 C3
Bracken Hill. Leeds LS17 ...... 43 C1
Bracken Hill. Ack M T WF7 ...... 163 A4
Bracken Hill. S Kirk WF9 ...... 182 C3
Bracken Mount. Sil BD20 ...... 5 D2
Bracken Pk. Scar LS14 ...... 45 A7
Bracken Rd. Brig HD6 ...... 115 A5
Bracken Rd. Keigh BD22 ...... 35 A4
Bracken Sq. Hud HD2 ...... 136 C4
Bracken St. Keigh BD21 ...... 35 B4
Brackenbeck Rd. Brad BD7 ...... 73 F4
Brackenbed Grange. Hali HX2 ...... 91 E1
Brackenbed La. Hali HX2 ...... 91 F1
Brackendale Ave. Brad BD10 ...... 39 A2
Brackendale Dr. Brad BD10 ...... 38 F2
Brackendale Dr. Brad BD10 ...... 38 F2
Brackendale Gr. Brad BD10 ...... 38 F2
Brackenhall Fst Sch. Brad 73 F3
Brackenholme Royd. Brad BD6 ...... 93 E8
Brackenwood Cl. Ilkley LS29 ...... 8 E4
Brackenwood Cl. Leeds LS8 ...... 60 E7
Brackenwood Ct. Loft G WF1 ...... 121 D5
Brackenwood Dr. Leeds LS8 ...... 60 E8
Brackenwood Gn. Loft G WF1 ...... 121 D5
Bradbeck Rd. Brad BD7 ...... 73 E4
Bradburn Rd. Roth WF3 ...... 100 A3
Bradbury St. Dew WF13 ...... 138 E5
Bradcliff Rd. Hud HD4 ...... 171 A7
Braddford Cl. Brad BD6 ...... 93 F7
Bradford and Heckmondwike Rd.
Birk BD4 ...... 95 F8
Bradford and Wakefield Rd.
Birk BD4, BD11 ...... 96 C7
Bradford Bsns Pk. Brad 55 E1
Bradford City Tech Coll. Brad 74 D7
Bradford City Tech Coll. Brad 74 E4
Bradford Coll. Brad 74 D6
Bradford Forster Sq Sta. Brad 54 F1
Bradford Girls' Grammar Sch. Brad 54 E1
Bradford Golf Course. Guise 39 A7
Bradford Grammar Sch. Brad 55 C3
Bradford & Ilkley Community Coll.
Ilkley 8 C6
Bradford Ind Mus. Brad 56 C3
Bradford Interchange Sta. Brad 74 F6
Bradford La. Oxen BD22 ...... 51 C3
Bradford Moor Fst Sch. Brad 75 C8
Bradford Moor Golf Course. Brad 56 E4
Bradford Rd. Bail BD17 ...... 37 F1
Bradford Rd. Birg BD19 ...... 95 E1
Bradford Rd. Batley WF17 ...... 118 C5
Bradford Rd. Brad BD12 ...... 94 F5
Bradford Rd. Brig HD6 ...... 115 B2
Bradford Rd. Clec BD19 ...... 116 E8
Bradford Rd. Elland HX4 ...... 133 D5
Bradford Rd. Gild LS27 ...... 97 E7
Bradford Rd. Keigh BD21 ...... 35 D5
Bradford Rd. Leeds LS28 ...... 58 A3
Bradford Rd. Liver WF15 ...... 117 B4
Bradford Rd. Loft G WF1 ...... 121 C6
Bradley Ave. Silk S75 ...... 178 C1
Bradley Carr Terr. S Elm WF9 ...... 194 E8
Bradley Dr. Hud HD2 ...... 136 B4
Bradley Grange Gdns. Hud HD2 ...... 136 F6
Bradley Junction Ind Est. Hud 136 F4
Bradley La. Elland HX4 ...... 134 B6
Bradley La. Pudsey LS28 ...... 76 D7
Bradley Mills La. Hud HD5 ...... 154 C8
Bradley Park Golf Course. Hud 136 D6
Bradley Quarry Cl. Hud HD2 ...... 137 A6
Bradley Rd. Hud HD2 ...... 136 E6
Bradley Rd. Sil BD20 ...... 5 D2
Bradley Rise. Sil BD20 ...... 5 D2
Bradley St. Hud HD1 ...... 154 A6
Bradley St. Shep BD9 ...... 55 A1
Bradley Way. Liver WF16 ...... 117 C4
Bradshaw Ave. Honley HD7 ...... 171 E3
Bradshaw Cl. Honley HD7 ...... 171 F4
Bradshaw Cres. Honley HD7 ...... 171 E3
Bradshaw Dr. Honley HD7 ...... 171 F3
Bradshaw La. Hali HX2 ...... 91 B7
Bradshaw La. Honley HD7 ...... 171 E4
Bradshaw Rd. Mel HD7 ...... 188 B8
Bradshaw Rd. Tod OL14 ...... 108 B4
Bradstock Gdns. Morley LS27 ...... 98 B4
Bradstock Gr. Morley LS27 ...... 98 A4
Brae Ave. Brad BD2 ...... 55 E5
Braemar Croft. S Hie S72 ...... 180 D7
Braemar Dr. Gar LS25 ...... 83 B8
Braemar Rise. S Hie S72 ...... 180 D7

Brafferton Arbor. Brad BD6 ...... 93 E8
Braim Wood Mid Sch. Leeds 61 D7
Braine Rd. Weth LS22 ...... 13 F6
Braithwaite Ave. Keigh BD22 ...... 34 F7
Braithwaite Cres. Keigh BD22 ...... 34 F7
Braithwaite Dr. Keigh BD22 ...... 34 F7
Braithwaite Edge Rd. Keigh BD22 ...... 34 D8
Braithwaite Gr. Keigh BD22 ...... 34 F7
Braithwaite Rd. Keigh BD22 ...... 34 E8
Braithwaite Row. Leeds LS10 ...... 79 E2
Braithwaite St. Keigh BD22 ...... 34 F8
Braithwaite St. Leeds LS11 ...... 78 B8
Braithwaite St. Leeds LS11 ...... 79 B8
Braithwaite St. Mapp S75 ...... 178 C1
Braithwaite St. Leeds LS11 ...... 34 F7
Bramble Ave. B Spa LS23 ...... 30 B7
Bramble Ct. Wake WF2 ...... 160 B5
Bramble Gr. Wake WF2 ...... 160 B5
Bramble St. Roy S71 ...... 179 C1
Bramble Pl. Leeds LS14 ...... 62 D8
Bramble Wlk. Batley WF17 ...... 96 F1
Brambles The. Ilkley LS29 ...... 7 F4
Bramham Dr. Bail BD17 ...... 38 D4
Bramham La. Bard LS23 ...... 28 E3
Bramham Park. Bramham 47 A7
Bramham Prim Sch. Bramham 30 D4
Bramham Rd. B Spa LS23 ...... 30 D4
Bramham Rd. Castle WF10 ...... 124 A6
Bramham Rd. Thorner LS14 ...... 46 C7
Bramhope Old La. Otley LS21 ...... 23 E4
Bramhope Prim & Mid Schs.
Bramhope 24 E2
Bramleigh Dr. Morley LS27 ...... 98 A6
Bramleigh Gr. Morley LS27 ...... 98 A6
Bramley Cl. Holmfi HD7 ...... 189 D7
Bramley Cres. Loft G WF1 ...... 121 D6
Bramley Ctr. Leeds 58 D3
Bramley Fold. Brig HX3 ...... 114 D8
Bramley Fst Sch. Leeds LS13 ...... 58 D2
Bramley Gdns. Leeds LS14 ...... 45 C1
Bramley Grange Coll. Leeds 45 C1
Bramley Grange. Leeds LS14 ...... 58 C1
Bramley Hill Prim Sch. Leeds 58 D2
Bramley La. Brig HX3 ...... 114 D8
Bramley La. W Bret WF4 ...... 177 B8
Bramley Sta. Leeds 58 C3
Bramley Sta. Leeds 58 C3
Bramley View. Brig HX3 ...... 114 F8
Brampton Ct. S Hie WF9 ...... 183 A5
Brampton Heb Br HX2 ...... 90 F7
Bramston Ave. Leeds LS13 ...... 58 A3
Bramston Cl. Leeds LS13 ...... 58 A3
Bramston St. Brig HD6 ...... 115 A3
Bramston Rectr Crn. Leeds 58 A4
Bramston St. Brig HD6 ...... 115 A1
Bran St. Keigh BD21 ...... 35 B4
Brancepeth Pl. Leeds LS12 ...... 78 E7
Branch Cl. Leeds LS12 ...... 78 B4
Branch End. Gild LS27 ...... 97 E7
Branch La. Hud HD2 ...... 135 B3
Branch Pl. Leeds LS12 ...... 78 B4
Brandon Ct. Batley WF17 ...... 118 C5
Brandon La. Roth LS17 ...... 44 C5
Brandon Cl. Leeds LS17 ...... 44 A5
Brandon Cres. Scar LS17 ...... 44 E5
Brandon La. Scar LS17 ...... 44 E5
Brandon La. Leeds LS17 ...... 60 A1
Brandon Rd. Leeds LS3 ...... 78 F6
Brandon St. Brad BD7 ...... 74 C6
Brandon Terr. Leeds LS17 ...... 44 C5
Brandon Way. Leeds LS7 ...... 60 D5
Brandy Carr Rd. Wake WF2 ...... 120 E5
Branksome Cres. Brad BD9 ...... 54 F2
Branksome Ct. Brad BD9 ...... 55 A2
Branksome Dr. Ship BD18 ...... 54 F8
Branksome Gr. Ship BD18 ...... 54 F8
Branksome Pl. Leeds LS6 ...... 59 E2
Branksome St. Leeds LS6 ...... 59 E2
Branksome Terr. Leeds LS6 ...... 59 E2
Bransby Cl. Pudsey LS28 ...... 57 D2
Bransby Ct. Pudsey LS28 ...... 57 D2
Bransby Rise. Pudsey LS28 ...... 57 D2
Bransdale Ave. Nor WF6 ...... 123 A1
Bransdale Cl. Bail BD17 ...... 38 A2
Bransdale Cl. Nor WF6 ...... 123 A1
Bransdale Clough. Brad BD6 ...... 73 E1
Bransdale Gdns. Guise LS20 ...... 39 E8
Bransdale Garth. Guise LS20 ...... 39 E8
Bransdale Gr. Nor WF6 ...... 123 A1
Bransdale Mews. Nor WF6 ...... 123 A1
Bransdale Wlk. Nor WF6 ...... 123 A1
Branshaw Dr. Keigh BD22 ...... 34 F6
Branshaw Golf Course. Keigh 34 D6
Branshaw Gr. Keigh BD22 ...... 34 F6
Branshaw Mount. Keigh BD22 ...... 34 F6
Branshaw Sch. Keigh 34 E6
Branstone Gr. S Elm WF9 ...... 182 F2
Brant Ave. Hali HX2 ...... 91 F4
Brant Bank La. Nes LS29 ...... 7 B8
Brantcliffe Dr. Bail BD17 ...... 38 C4
Brantcliffe Way. Bail BD17 ...... 38 D4
Brantdale Cl. Brad BD9 ...... 54 B5
Brantdale Rd. Brad BD9 ...... 54 B5
Brantford St. Leeds LS7 ...... 60 D6
Branwell Ave. Brad BD18 ...... 37 A1
Branwell Dr. Haw BD22 ...... 51 C7
Brathay Gdns. Leeds LS14 ...... 62 A4
Bray Cl. Brad BD7 ...... 73 D2
Braybrook Ct. Brad BD8 ...... 55 C3
Brayshaw Dr. Brad BD7 ...... 73 D2
Brayshaw Rd. E Ard WF3 ...... 120 C7
Brayside Ave. Hud HD2 ...... 135 F2
Brayton App. Leeds LS14 ...... 62 C5
Brayton Cl. Leeds LS14 ...... 62 C5
Brayton Garth. Leeds LS14 ...... 62 D510
Brayton Gn. Leeds LS14 ...... 62 C5
Brayton Grange. Leeds LS14 ...... 62 D5
Brayton Pl. Leeds LS14 ...... 62 D513
Brayton Sq. Leeds LS14 ...... 62 D511
Brayton Terr. Leeds LS14 ...... 62 C5
Brayton Wlk. Leeds LS14 ...... 62 C5 2
Brazil St. Castle WF10 ...... 124 E8
Bread St. Wake WF1 ...... 142 C514
Break Neck. Hali HX3 ...... 114 A8
Breakmoor Ave. Sil BD20 ...... 5 E3
Breaks Rd. Brad BD12 ...... 94 E6
Brearcliffe Cl. Brad BD6 ...... 94 A8
Brearcliffe Dr. Brad BD6 ...... 94 A7
Brearcliffe Gr. Brad BD6 ...... 94 A7
Brearcliffe Rd. Brad BD6 ...... 94 A7
Brearcliffe St. Brad BD6 ...... 94 A7
Brearley La. Heb Br HX2 ...... 111 B8
Brearley St. Batley WF17 ...... 118 B4
Breary Ave. Hors LS18 ...... 41 D1
Breary Ct. Bramho LS16 ...... 24 E3
Breary La. Bramho LS16 ...... 24 E3
Breary La E. Bramho LS16 ...... 24 F3
Breary Rise. Bramho LS16 ...... 24 E3
Breary Terr. Hors LS18 ...... 41 D1
Breary Wlk. Hors LS18 ...... 41 D1
Breck Lea. Sow Br HX6 ...... 112 A3
Breck Willows. Sow Br HX6 ...... 111 F2
Brecks Gdns. Kippax LS25 ...... 82 F3
Brecks La. Kippax LS25 ...... 82 F3
Brecks La. Swil LS26 ...... 82 C4
Brecks Rd. Brad BD14 ...... 73 D5
Brecon Ave. Dew WF12 ...... 139 F1
Brecon App. Leeds LS9 ...... 61 D1
Brecon Cl. Brad BD10 ...... 56 E6
Brecon Cl. Leeds LS9 ...... 61 D1
Brecon Rise. Leeds LS9 ...... 61 D1
Bredon Ave. Ship BD18 ...... 55 F7
Bredon Cl. Hem WF9 ...... 181 F7
Breighton Adown. Brad BD6 ...... 93 D8
Bremner St. Otley LS21 ...... 23 B8
Brendan Ct. Brad BD10 ...... 56 D6
Brendon Ct. Brad BD4 ...... 75 F3
Brendon Dr. Mir WF14 ...... 137 F2
Brendon Wlk. Brad BD4 ...... 75 E3
Brentford Rd. Brad BD12 ...... 94 C6
Brentlea Ave. Wake WF2 ...... 142 A3
Brentwood Cl. Batley WF17 ...... 118 E5
Brentwood Ct. Th Aud WF8 ...... 166 A6
Brentwood Gdns. Brad BD6 ...... 94 B8
Brentwood Gr. Leeds LS12 ...... 78 C710
Brentwood St. Leeds LS12 ...... 78 C711
Brettel Ct. Dew WF12 ...... 139 D5
Brett Gdns. Leeds LS11 ...... 79 B4
Brettegate. Hem WF9 ...... 181 C7
Bretton Country Pk. W Bret 176 F7
Bretton Hall Coll (Annexe).
Castle 124 C7
Bretton Hall Coll of Higher Education.
W Bret 176 F6
Bretton La. W Bret WF4 ...... 159 F2
Bretton La. Midd WF4 ...... 159 B2
Bretton St. E Ard WF3 ...... 119 E3
Brewerton La. Batley WF13 ...... 117 F2
Brewery Ln. Hull HX4 ...... 133 E4
Brewery La. Dew WF12 ...... 139 E6
Brewery La. Knott WF11 ...... 126 E2
Brewery La. Queen BD13 ...... 92 C7
Brewery Rd. Ilkley LS29 ...... 8 C4
Brewery Rd. Keigh BD21 ...... 35 A3
Brewery Rd. Wake WF2 ...... 142 D3
Brewery St. Batley WF16 ...... 117 D4
Brewery St. Keigh BD21 ...... 35 A4
Brewery St. Tod OL14 ...... 107 E8
Brewery Wharf. Leeds 79 F7
Brexdale Ave. Kippax LS25 ...... 82 F3
Brian Ave. Hud HD5 ...... 155 A4
Brian Cres. Leeds LS15 ...... 62 B3
Brian Pl. Leeds LS15 ...... 62 B3
Brian Royd La. Elland HX4 ...... 133 E3
Brian St. Hud HD3 ...... 135 A1
Brian View. Leeds LS15 ...... 62 C3
Briar Ave. Wake WF1 ...... 142 F2
Briar Bank. Hem WF9 ...... 163 A2
Briar Cl. Dew WF13 ...... 139 B8
Briar Cl. Pudsey LS28 ...... 57 D3
Briar Dr. Batley WF13 ...... 117 F2
Briar Gate. Men LS29 ...... 22 A5
Briar Rose. Bramho LS16 ...... 24 F3
Briar Wood. Ship BD18 ...... 55 C8
Briarfield Ave. Brad BD10 ...... 56 E7
Briarfield Cl. Brad BD10 ...... 56 E7
Briarfield Cl. Men LS29 ...... 21 F5
Briarfield Gdns. Gild LS12 ...... 77 D3
Briarfield Gdns. Ship BD18 ...... 55 B5
Briarfield Gr. Leeds LS15 ...... 80 E7
Briarfield Rd. Leeds LS15 ...... 80 E7
Briarlea Cl. Yeadon LS19 ...... 40 C4
Briarlyn Ave. Hud HD3 ...... 135 A2
Briarlyn Rd. Hud HD3 ...... 135 A2
Briarmains Rd. Birs WF17 ...... 96 F1
Briarsdale Ct. Leeds LS8 ...... 61 B6
Briarsdale Garth. Leeds LS8 ...... 61 A6
Briarsdale Gn. Leeds LS8 ...... 61 B6
Briarsdale Heights. Leeds LS9 ...... 61 B6
Briarwood Ave. Brad BD6 ...... 94 B7
Briarwood Ave. Keigh BD20 ...... 18 E1
Briarwood Cl. Ossett WF5 ...... 141 A3
Briarwood Cres. Brad BD6 ...... 94 B7
Briarwood Dr. Brad BD6 ...... 94 B7
Briarwood Gr. Brad BD6 ...... 94 A7
Brick & Tile Terr. Brig HD6 ...... 115 A1
Brick Mill Rd. Pudsey LS28 ...... 76 F6

Brick Row. Brad BD12 .... 94 C3
Brick St. Clec BD19 .... 116 C7
Brick St. Leeds LS9 .... 79 D7
Brick St. Wake WF2 .... 141 D7
Brick Terr. Brig HD6 .... 115 B1
Brickbank. Hud HD5 .... 154 F3
Brickfield Gr. Hali HX2 .... 92 A5
Brickfield La. Hali HX2 .... 92 A5
Brickfield Terr. Hali HX2 .... 92 A5
Brickyard. Mir WF14 .... 137 F5 7
Bride St. Tod OL14 .... 108 B6
Bride Ave. Otley LS21 .... 23 A8
Bridge Cl. B Spa LS23 .... 30 E8
Bridge Cl. Clay W HD8 .... 175 E2
Bridge Cl. Hor WF4 .... 140 E1
Bridge Cotts. Aber LS25 .... 64 E7
Bridge Croft. Hud HD3 .... 153 B4
Bridge Ct. Hem WF9 .... 163 A2
Bridge Ct. Morley LS27 .... 98 B3
Bridge End. Brig HD6 .... 115 A1
Bridge End. Glu BD20 .... 16 B6
Bridge End. Leeds LS1 .... 79 C7
Bridge End. Tod OL14 .... 86 C1
Bridge Fold. Leeds LS5 .... 59 A4
Bridge Foot. Th Arch LS23 .... 30 E8
Bridge Garth. B Spa LS23 .... 30 E8
Bridge Gate. Heb Br HX7 .... 89 A3
Bridge La. Holmfi HD7 .... 189 A6
Bridge La. Ilkley LS29 .... 8 A4
Bridge La. Oxen BD22 .... 51 C6
Bridge La. Shelf HX3 .... 93 B7
Bridge La. Th Aud WF8 .... 165 B4
Bridge Lanes. Heb Br HX7 .... 88 F3
Bridge Paddock. Coll LS22 .... 13 B1
Bridge Rd. B Spa LS23 .... 30 E8
Bridge Rd. Brig HD6 .... 115 A2
Bridge Rd. Hud HD2 .... 137 B5
Bridge Rd. Leeds LS5 .... 59 A4
Bridge Rd. Leeds LS11 .... 79 B8
Bridge Rd. Pudsey LS13 .... 57 E5
Bridge Rd. S in Cra BD20 .... 16 D5
Bridge St. Sil BD20 .... 5 E2
Bridge St. Batley WF17 .... 118 E8
Bridge St. Brad BD1 .... 74 F6
Bridge St. Castle WF10 .... 124 D8
Bridge St. Haw BD22 .... 34 B2
Bridge St. Hud HD4 .... 153 F3
Bridge St. Hud HD4 .... 171 F8
Bridge St. Keigh BD21 .... 35 B6
Bridge St. Leeds LS2 .... 79 D8 3
Bridge St. Liver WF16 .... 117 C4
Bridge St. Mapp S75 .... 177 C1
Bridge St. Morley LS27 .... 98 B2
Bridge St. Nor WF6 .... 123 C3
Bridge St. Otley LS21 .... 23 A8
Bridge St. Slai HD7 .... 152 A1
Bridge St. Sow Br HX6 .... 112 C5
Bridge St. Thorn BD13 .... 72 E6
Bridge St. Tod OL14 .... 108 B5
Bridge St. Wake WF1 .... 142 D4
Bridge Terr. Hali HX2 .... 91 F6
Bridge View. Pudsey LS13 .... 57 E6
Bridge Wood Cl. Hors LS18 .... 41 D2
Bridge Works Bsns Pk. Horsley 172 A4
Bridgegate Way. Brad BD10 .... 56 D6
Bridgehouse La. Haw BD22 .... 51 C6
Bridgewater Ct. Leeds LS6 .... 59 F5
Bridgewater Park Dr. Ad Le S DN6 .... 184 F2
Bridgewater Rd. Leeds LS9 .... 79 F5
Bridgeway. Brad BD4 .... 75 D3
Bridgland Ave. Men LS29 .... 22 A5
Bridgwater Rd. Brad BD9 .... 55 A3
Bridle Ave. Ossett WF5 .... 140 C8
Bridle Cl. Neth WF4 .... 158 E7
Bridle Dene. Shelf HX3 .... 93 C5
Bridle La. Neth WF4 .... 158 F7
Bridle Path Rd. Hare LS17 .... 44 E5
Bridle Path Wlk. Leeds LS15 .... 62 A3
Bridle Pl. Ossett WF5 .... 140 D8
Bridle Stile La. Queen BD13 .... 72 E2
Bridle Stile. Shelf HX3 .... 93 C5
Bridley Brook. Slai HD7 .... 170 A5
Bridge La. Brad BD4 .... 75 D6
Brier Hy Cl. Heb Br HX7 .... 89 F1
Brier Hey La. Heb Br HX7 .... 89 F1
Brier La. Crig WF4 .... 159 E4
Brier Hill View. Hud HD2 .... 136 E5
Brier La. Brig HD6 .... 114 E2
Brier La. Ryhill WF4 .... 180 C8
Brier La. Ryhill WF4 .... 162 A1
Brier St. Keigh BD21 .... 35 B4
Brierdene. Sil BD20 .... 5 E2
Brierfield Gdns. Gild LS27 .... 97 C6
Brierley Cl. Glu BD18 .... 55 C6
Brierley Cres. S Kirk WF9 .... 182 C3
Brierley Rd. One S72 .... 181 A1
Brierley Rd. S Hie S72 .... 180 E5
Brierley Rd. Shaf S72 .... 180 B5
Briery Cl. Ilkley LS29 .... 7 E4
Briery Field. Ship BD18 .... 55 A7
Briery Gr. Mir WF14 .... 138 A2
Briery La. Mir WF14 .... 138 A2
Brig Royd. Rip HX6 .... 132 E5
Brigg Gdns. Keigh BD22 .... 34 F7
Brigg's Way. Castle WF10 .... 124 D6
Briggate. Brig HD6 .... 115 A2
Briggate. Elland HX5 .... 134 F7
Briggate. Hud HD5 .... 155 A7
Briggate. Leeds LS1 .... 79 D8
Briggate. Ship BD17 .... 55 B8
Briggate. Sil BD20 .... 5 E2
Briggland Ct. Wilsd BD15 .... 53 C5
Briggs Ave. Brad BD6 .... 74 A1
Briggs Ave. Castle WF10 .... 124 F6
Briggs Pl. Brad BD6 .... 74 A1
Briggs Rd. Roy S71 .... 179 C1
Briggs Row. Feath WF7 .... 145 D4
Briggs St. Queen BD13 .... 72 E1
Brighouse and Clifton CE (Aided) Prim Sch. Brig 115 E2
Brighouse and Denholme Gate Rd. Northo HX3 .... 93 B4

Brighouse and Denholme Gate Rd. Queen HX3 .... 92 F6
Brighouse and Denholme Gate Rd. Shelf HX3 .... 93 B4
Brighouse and Denholme Rd. Queen BD13 .... 72 B3
Brighouse Cemy. Brig 115 A5
Brighouse Eastfield Sec Sch. Brig 114 F7
Brighouse F Ed Ctr. Brig 115 A3
Brighouse High Sch. Brig 114 F5
Brighouse High Sch. Brig 115 A2
Brighouse Hill. Leeds LS7 .... 115 A3
Brighouse Rd. Brad BD12 .... 94 D6
Brighouse Rd. Brig HX3 .... 114 D7
Brighouse Rd. Denh BD13 .... 71 B6
Brighouse Rd. Hud HD3 .... 135 B3
Brighouse Rd. Queen BD13 .... 92 F7
Brighouse Rd. Shelf BD13, HX3 .... 92 F7
Brighouse Wood La. Brig HD6 .... 114 F3
Brighouse Wood Row. Brig HD6 .... 114 F3
Brighouse Woodhouse Jun & Inf Sch. Brig 136 B8
Bright St. Brad BD15 .... 54 B1
Bright St. Brad BD4 .... 73 B4
Bright St. Clec BD19 .... 118 C1 3
Bright St. E Ard WF3 .... 120 E8
Bright St. Farnh BD20 .... 4 D1
Bright St. Hali HX6 .... 112 B5
Bright St. Haw BD22 .... 51 D7 8
Bright St. Mir WF14 .... 138 A8
Bright St. Morley LS27 .... 98 A4
Bright St. Pudsey LS28 .... 57 E2
Bright St. Queen BD13 .... 72 F1
Bright St. Tod OL14 .... 108 A3
Brighton Ave. Morley LS27 .... 97 F5
Brighton Cl. Batley WF17 .... 117 E6
Brighton Cliff. Leeds LS13 .... 58 C2
Brighton Gr. Hali HX1 .... 113 A8 5
Brighton Gr. Leeds LS13 .... 58 C2
Brighton Rd. Otley LS21 .... 23 E8
Brighton St. Batley WF16 .... 117 D4
Brighton St. Brad BD10 .... 39 A1
Brighton St. Hali HX1 .... 92 A21
Brighton St. Ship BD17 .... 55 B8
Brighton St. Tod OL14 .... 86 C1
Brighton St. Wake WF2 .... 142 A5
Brighton Terr. Brig BD19 .... 116 C7
Brignall Croft. Leeds LS9 .... 60 F1
Brignall Garth. Leeds LS9 .... 60 F1
Brignall Way. Leeds LS9 .... 60 F1
Brigshaw Comprehensive Sch. Kippax 102 F7
Brigshaw Dr. Kippax WF10 .... 102 F6
Brigshaw La. Kippax LS25, WF10 .... 103 A8
Brindley Gr. Brad BD7 .... 73 C7
Brindley Rd. Sil BD20 .... 17 E7
Brindley Way. Loft G WF2 .... 120 F4
Brindley Way. Loft G WF2 .... 121 A4
Brisbane Ave. Brad BD2 .... 55 E3
Briscoe La. Elland HX4 .... 134 B7
Bristfield Rd. Dew WF12 .... 157 A8
Bristol La. Leeds LS7 .... 60 A8
Bristol St. Leeds LS7 .... 113 D3
Britannia Ave. Bacup OL13 .... 106 A2
Britannia Bldgs. Morley LS27 .... 97 F2
Britannia Cl. Pudsey LS28 .... 57 F2 8
Britannia Ct. Pudsey LS13 .... 57 A8
Britannia Rd. Hud HD3, HD7 .... 152 F4
Britannia Rd. Morley LS27 .... 98 A2
Britannia St. Slai HD7 .... 169 F8
Britannia St. Leeds LS1 .... 79 A7
Britannia St. Ship BD16 .... 37 A3
Britannia St. Brad BD5 .... 74 F6
Britannia St. Leeds LS1 .... 79 B8
Briton Libury Document Supply Ctr The. Th Arch 14 F2
Briton Sq. Dearne S63 .... 194 E1
Briton St. Dearne S63 .... 194 E1
Briton St. Liver BD19 .... 116 F6
Broad Acres. Crig WF4 .... 146 A7
Broad Balk. H Pag DN5 .... 195 E6
Broad Carr La. Elland HX4 .... 133 F3
Broad Carr La. Holmfi HD7 .... 190 C8
Broad Cut Rd. Crig WF4 .... 159 D7
Broad Gate. Tod OL14 .... 108 D6
Broad Gate. Tod OL14 .... 108 D6
Broad Head La. Haw BD20 .... 33 D3
Broad Ings Way. Shelf HX3 .... 93 C5
Broad La. Brad WF3 .... 100 C1
Broad La. Heb Br HX7 .... 88 F1
Broad La. Heb Br HX7 .... 89 F1
Broad La. Hep HX7 .... 88 B6
Broad La. Holmfi HD7 .... 188 D5
Broad La. Leeds LS13 .... 58 D4
Broad La. S Kirk WF9 .... 182 C3
Broad La. Sow Br HX6 .... 111 C5
Broad La. Sow Br HX6 .... 112 A5
Broad Oak. Hud HD7 .... 152 E2
Broad Oak La. Brig HD6 .... 114 D6
Broad Oak La. Ingb S30 .... 192 D2
Broad Oak Pl. Brig HX3 .... 114 D6
Broad Oak St. Hud HX3 .... 114 D6
Broad St. Brad BD1 .... 74 F7
Broad St. Dew WF13 .... 139 C8
Broad St. Hali HX1 .... 113 C7
Broad St. Pudsey LS28 .... 57 C3
Broad St. Tod OL14 .... 108 B6
Broad View. Dew WF13 .... 139 B8
Broad View. Ossett WF5 .... 140 F5
Broadacre Way. Brad BD10 .... 56 B8
Broadbent Croft. Honley HD7 .... 172 A6
Broadcroft Chase. E Ard WF3 .... 119 E7
Broadcroft Dr. E Ard WF3 .... 119 E7
Broadcroft Way. E Ard WF3 .... 119 E7
Broadfield Cl. Brad BD4 .... 75 E1
Broadfield Ind Est. Hud 153 F3
Broadfield Way. Sil LS29 .... 6 E8
Broadfolds. Brad BD14 .... 73 C4
Broadgate Ave. Hors LS18 .... 41 C1
Broadgate Cres. Hors LS18 .... 41 C1
Broadgate Ct. Hud HD5 .... 154 D4
Broadgate Dr. Hors LS18 .... 41 C1
Broadgate Inf Sch. Hors 41 C1
Broadgate Jun Sch. Hors 41 C1
Broadgate La. Hors LS18 .... 41 C1

Broadgate. Ossett WF5 .... 140 E5
Broadgate Rise. Hors LS18 .... 58 D8
Broadgate Wlk. Hors LS18 .... 58 C8
Broadlands. Neth BD20 .... 35 A8
Broadlands Rd. Mel HD7 .... 170 D3
Broadlands St. Brad BD4 .... 75 C2
Broadlea Ave. Leeds LS13 .... 58 E4
Broadlea Cl. Leeds LS13 .... 58 E4
Broadlea Cres. Brad BD5 .... 74 F3
Broadlea Cres. Leeds LS13 .... 58 E4
Broadlea Gdns. Leeds LS13 .... 58 E4
Broadlea Gr. Leeds LS13 .... 58 E4
Broadlea Hill. Leeds LS13 .... 58 E4
Broadlea Mount. Leeds LS13 .... 58 F3
Broadlea Oval. Leeds LS13 .... 58 E4
Broadlea Pl. Leeds LS13 .... 58 E4
Broadlea Rd. Leeds LS13 .... 58 E4
Broadlea Terr. Leeds LS13 .... 58 E4
Broadlea View. Leeds LS13 .... 58 D4
Broadley Ave. Hali HX2 .... 91 B2
Broadley Cres. Hali HX2 .... 91 C1
Broadley Lathe. Hali HX2 .... 91 C2
Broadley Gr. Leeds LS13 .... 58 C2
Broadley La. Hali HX2 .... 91 C2
Broadley Rd. Hali HX2 .... 91 C1
Broadmead. Castle WF10 .... 124 A8
Broadmeadows. Loft G WF1 .... 121 D5
Broadmeadows. Wake WF2 .... 140 A8
Broadowler La. Ossett WF5 .... 140 F5
Broadstone Rd. D Dale HD8 .... 190 F3
Broadstone St. Ingb S30 .... 191 A1
Broadstone St. Tod OL14 .... 108 D6
Broadstone Way. Brad BD4 .... 75 E2
Broadwalk. Otley LS21 .... 10 E1
Broadway Ave. Brad BD5 .... 74 D2
Broadway Ave. Leeds LS6 .... 59 E2
Broadway Cl. Shelf HX3 .... 93 E8
Broadway Cl. Sow Br HX6 .... 111 E3
Broadway Dr. Hors LS18 .... 58 B4
Broadway. Guise LS20 .... 39 C8
Broadway. Hali HX3 .... 113 F5
Broadway. Hors LS18 .... 58 B4
Broadway. Hud HD1 .... 154 B7
Broadway. Leeds LS15 .... 80 F7
Broadway. Mapp S75 .... 178 B1
Broadway. Pont WF8 .... 146 E7
Broadway. Sow Br HX6 .... 111 E3
Broadway. Sow Br HX6 .... 111 E3
Broadway Terr. S Elm WF9 .... 182 E1
Broadway. Wake WF1 .... 142 D4
Broadwell Rd. Ossett WF5 .... 140 F5
Broadwood Ave. Hali HX2 .... 91 C1
Brock Bank. Hud HD5 .... 154 F7
Brockadale Ave. Pont WF8 .... 146 D5
Brockholes CE Prim Sch. Honley 172 C3
Brockholes La. Honley HD7 .... 172 C3
Brockholes La. Honley HD4 .... 172 C3
Brockholes Rd. Kirkh HD4 .... 172 C3
Brockholes Sta. Honley 172 C2
Brocklesby Dr. Brad BD15 .... 73 B8
Brocklesby La. Leeds LS10 .... 99 E4
Brockstones. Elland HX4 .... 133 F3
Brockswood Cl. Walton WF2 .... 161 C5
Brockwell Gdns. Sow Br HX6 .... 112 A3
Brockwell La. Sow Br HX6 .... 111 F2
Brockwell La. Sow Br HX6 .... 111 F2
Brodetsky Jewish Prim Sch. Leeds 43 C4
Brodrick Ct. Leeds LS6 .... 59 D5
Broken Cross. Hud HD5 .... 154 E2
Broken Way. Brad BD5 .... 74 D2
Bromet Pl. Brad BD2 .... 56 C2
Bromfield Ct. Roy S71 .... 179 C4
Bromford Rd. Brad BD4 .... 75 B3
Bromley Ct. Keigh BD20 .... 18 A2
Bromley Gr. Keigh BD20 .... 18 A2
Bromley Mount. Wake WF1 .... 142 D4
Bromley Rd. Brig BD16 .... 36 F4
Bromley Rd. Hud HD2 .... 136 A3
Bromley Rd. Ship BD18 .... 54 E8
Bromley St. Batley WF17 .... 118 C3
Brompton Ave. Brad BD4 .... 75 B4
Brompton Gr. Leeds LS11 .... 79 B2 5
Brompton Mount. Leeds LS11 .... 79 B2 5
Brompton Rd. Brad BD4 .... 75 B4
Brompton Row. Leeds LS11 .... 79 B2
Brompton Terr. Leeds LS11 .... 79 B2
Brompton View. Leeds LS11 .... 79 B2
Bronshill Gr. Brad BD15 .... 73 B8
Bronte Ave. Wood WF11 .... 126 B4
Bronte Cl. Brad BD9 .... 54 E2
Bronte Cl. Dew WF13 .... 138 D5
Bronte Cl. Hud HD4 .... 153 D3
Bronte Dr. Keigh BD20 .... 19 D1
Bronte Gr. Mir WF14 .... 138 C4
Bronte House Sch. Yeadon 39 F5
Bronte Old Rd. Thorn BD13 .... 72 E6
Bronte Parsonage Mus. Haw 51 B7
Bronte Pl. Thorn BD13 .... 72 E6
Bronte Rise. Mir WF14 .... 138 C4
Bronte St. Haw BD22 .... 51 C7
Bronte St. Keigh BD21 .... 35 D8
Bronte Villas. Hali HX2 .... 112 D7
Brook Cotts. Rip HX6 .... 132 B7
Brook Dr. Liver WF15 .... 116 F4
Brook Field. Dew WF12 .... 139 E8
Brook Gdns. Dew WF12 .... 139 B8
Brook Grain Hill. Brig HD6 .... 136 B8
Brook Grains La. Rip HX6 .... 132 F3
Brook Hill. Bail BD17 .... 37 E3
Brook La. Clec WF15 .... 116 D4
Brook La. Crof WF4 .... 144 B3
Brook La. Dew WF12 .... 139 E8
Brook Lane Ind Sch. Leeds 62 F6
Brook Rd. Shelf HX3 .... 93 E7
Brook St. Batley WF17 .... 118 C4
Brook St. Brig HX3 .... 115 A7
Brook St. Clec BD19 .... 116 D7
Brook St. Dew WF13 .... 139 C8
Brook St. Elland HX5 .... 134 F7
Brook St. Hali HX1 .... 113 C7
Brook St. Haw BD22 .... 51 C6
Brook St. Hud HD1 .... 154 B6
Brook St. Ilkley LS29 .... 8 B4
Brook St. Keigh BD20 .... 35 B11
Brook St. Leeds LS9 .... 79 E7

Brook St. Nor WF6 .... 122 F3
Brook St. Ossett WF5 .... 140 D5
Brook St. Tod OL14 .... 108 B5 10
Brook St. Wake WF1 .... 142 C6
Brook Terr. Slai HD7 .... 90 E2
Brook Terr. Slai HD7 .... 152 A2
Brook The. Liff OL15 .... 129 C1
Brook's Yd. Hud HD1 .... 154 A6 17
Brookdale Ave. Ossett WF5 .... 119 B3
Brookdale. Tod OL14 .... 108 A2
Brooke Ct. Pont WF8 .... 146 D5
Brooke St. Batley WF16 .... 117 D3 8
Brooke St. Brig HX6 .... 115 A1
Brooke St. Clec BD19 .... 116 E7
Brookfield Ave. Brad BD3 .... 75 A8
Brookfield Ave. Clec BD19 .... 95 E1
Brookfield Ave. Leeds LS8 .... 43 F1
Brookfield Ave. Pudsey LS13 .... 57 D6
Brookfield Ave. Ship BD18 .... 55 D8
Brookfield Ct. Nor WF6 .... 123 A3
Brookfield Gdns. Leeds LS13 .... 57 D6
Brookfield Pl. Leeds LS6 .... 59 E3
Brookfield Rd. Leeds LS6 .... 59 E3
Brookfield Rd. Ship BD18 .... 55 D8
Brookfield St. Leeds LS10 .... 79 F5
Brookfield Terr. Leeds LS6 .... 59 E3 4
Brookfield Terr. Leeds LS10 .... 80 A7
Brookfield View. Clec BD19 .... 95 E1
Brookfield. Bing BD16 .... 36 A2
Brookfoot Ave. Birk BD11 .... 96 A5
Brookfoot La. Brig HD6 .... 115 A4
Brookhill Ave. Leeds LS17 .... 43 E4
Brookhill Cl. Leeds LS17 .... 43 E4
Brookhill Cres. Leeds LS17 .... 43 E4
Brookhill Dr. Leeds LS17 .... 43 E4
Brookhill Gr. Leeds LS17 .... 43 E4
Brookhouse Gdns. Brad BD10 .... 56 F8
Brookland Towers. Leeds LS14 .... 62 A3 3
Brooklands Ave. Elland HX4 .... 134 B4
Brooklands Ave. Leeds LS14 .... 62 A4
Brooklands Cl. Leeds LS14 .... 61 F4
Brooklands Cres. Leeds LS14 .... 61 F4
Brooklands Cres. Ryhill WF4 .... 162 D1
Brooklands Ct. Leeds LS14 .... 62 A4
Brooklands Ct. Yeadon LS19 .... 40 B6
Brooklands Dr. Leeds LS14 .... 61 F4
Brooklands Dr. Yeadon LS19 .... 40 B6
Brooklands La. Leeds LS14 .... 62 A4
Brooklands La. Men LS29 .... 22 B5
Brooklands View. Leeds LS14 .... 62 A4
Brooklands View. Walton WF2 .... 161 A7
Brooklands Wlk. Men LS29 .... 22 B5
Brooklands. Walton WF2 .... 161 A7
Brooklands Wlk. Men LS29 .... 22 B5
Brooklyn Ave. Hud HD5 .... 155 C6
Brooklyn Ave. Leeds LS12 .... 78 B4
Brooklyn Pl. Leeds LS12 .... 78 B4
Brooklyn St. Keigh BD21 .... 18 A2
Brooklyn St. Leeds LS12 .... 78 B4
Brooklyn Terr. Leeds LS12 .... 78 B4
Brooks Yd. Dew WF13 .... 139 C8
Brooksbank Ave. Brad BD7 .... 74 A4
Brooksbank Dr. Leeds LS15 .... 80 E8
Brooksbank Gdns. Elland HX5 .... 134 F6
Brooksbank Sch The. Elland 134 F6
Brookside. Coll LS22 .... 29 A8
Brookside. D Dale HD8 .... 191 F6
Brookside. Heb Br HX7 .... 89 A4
Brookside. Hebd HX7 .... 87 A8
Brookside. Mir WF14 .... 137 E7
Brookside. Ship BD18 .... 54 F8
Brookside Terr. S Elm WF9 .... 182 F3
Brookway. Mapp LS29 .... 22 C5
Broom Cl. Brad BD6 .... 93 E8
Broom Cres. Leeds LS10 .... 99 E7
Broom Cross. Leeds LS10 .... 99 E7
Broom Gdns. Leeds LS10 .... 99 F7
Broom Hill. Batley WF16 .... 117 C4
Broom Hill. Batley WF17 .... 117 F8 3
Broom La. Leeds LS10 .... 99 F7
Broom Mount. Leeds LS10 .... 99 F7
Broom Nook. Leeds LS10 .... 99 F7
Broom Pl. Leeds LS10 .... 99 F7
Broom Rd. Leeds LS10 .... 99 E7
Broom St. Brad BD4 .... 75 C5
Broom St. Keigh BD21 .... 35 C7
Broom Terr. Leeds LS10 .... 99 F7
Broom Wlk. Leeds LS10 .... 99 F7
Broombank. Hud HD2 .... 135 F1
Broome Ave. Pont WF8 .... 125 D2
Broome Cl. Pont WF8 .... 125 D1
Broome Ct. Brad BD2 .... 56 B2
Broomer St. Dew WF13 .... 139 C8
Broomfield. Baghill WF7 .... 147 A6
Broomfield Ave. Hali HX3 .... 113 A2
Broomfield Bsns Pk. Hud 154 D7
Broomfield Cres. Leeds LS6 .... 59 D5
Broomfield. Elland HX5 .... 134 F6
Broomfield Gdns. Hud HD2 .... 135 F1

Broomfield. Hors LS16 .... 42 B4
Broomfield Pl. Brad BD14 .... 73 A3
Broomfield Pl. Keigh BD21 .... 35 B7 3
Broomfield Rd. Leeds LS6 .... 59 D3
Broomfield Rd. Hud HD1, HD2 .... 136 A6
Broomfield Rd. Hud HD1, HD2 .... 153 D6
Broomfield Rd. Keigh BD21 .... 35 B7 4
Broomfield Rd. Leeds LS6 .... 59 D3
Broomfield Sch. Hud 99 F7
Broomfield St. Keigh BD21 .... 35 B7
Broomfield St. Leeds LS6 .... 59 D3 3
Broomfield Terr. Hud HD1 .... 153 D7
Broomfield Terr. Leeds LS6 .... 59 D3
Broomhill Ave. Clec BD19 .... 95 E1
Broomhill Ave. Keigh BD21 .... 35 A5
Broomhill Ave. Knot WF11 .... 127 B3
Broomhill Cl. Hud HD2 .... 136 E5
Broomhill. Castle WF10 .... 125 A6
Broomhill Cres. Leeds LS17 .... 43 D2
Broomhill Cres. Knot WF11 .... 127 B3
Broomhill Cres. Leeds LS17 .... 43 D2
Broomhill Dr. Keigh BD21 .... 35 A5
Broomhill Dr. Knot WF11 .... 127 B3
Broomhill Gr. Knot WF11 .... 127 B3
Broomhill Mount. Keigh BD21 .... 35 A5
Broomhill Pl. Knot WF11 .... 127 B3
Broomhill Sq. Knot WF11 .... 127 B3
Broomhill St. Keigh BD21 .... 35 A4
Broomhill Terr. Batley WF17 .... 118 D4
Broomhill Terr. Knot WF11 .... 127 B3
Broomhill Wlk. Keigh BD21 .... 35 A5
Broomhouse Cl. D Dale HD8 .... 192 A6
Broomroyd. Hud HD2 .... 153 F7
Brooms La. Ripponden WF17 .... 118 C5
Broomwood Mid Sch. Brad 75 D1
Broomy Lea La. Holmfi HD7 .... 188 F7
Broster Ave. Keigh BD22 .... 34 F4
Brotherton Ave. Wake WF1 .... 142 E7
Brotherton Prim Sch. Broth 126 C7
Brougham Rd. Hali HX3 .... 92 C1 11
Brougham St. Mars HD7 .... 169 A4
Brougham St. Hali HX3 .... 92 C1 12
Brougham Terr. Hali HX3 .... 92 C2 13
Broughton Ave. Brad BD4 .... 75 B3
Broughton Ave. Leeds LS9 .... 61 A2 22
Broughton St. Heb Br HX7 .... 89 A4
Broughton Terr. Leeds LS9 .... 61 A2 19
Broughton Terr. Pudsey LS28 .... 76 E8 7
Broughtons Yd. Knot WF11 .... 126 C5
Brow Bottom La. Hali HX2 .... 111 D6
Brow Grains Rd. Mel HD7 .... 170 B2
Brow La. D Dale HD8 .... 192 D6
Brow La. Hali HX3 .... 93 A1
Brow La. Northa HX3 .... 93 A4
Brow La. Shelf HX3 .... 93 B6
Brow Quarry Ind Est. Brig 114 D6
Brow Rd. Haw BD22 .... 51 B7
Brow Rd. Hud HD1 .... 153 E5
Brow St. Keigh BD21 .... 35 D6
Brow Top Rd. Haw BD22 .... 51 B7
Brow Wood Cres. Brad BD2 .... 55 E3
Brow Wood Rise. Shelf HX3 .... 93 C6
Browcliff. Sil BD20 .... 5 E2
Browfoot. Ship BD18 .... 55 D8
Browfoot Dr. Hali HX3 .... 92 A2
Browgate. Bail BD17 .... 38 C4
Brown Ave. Leeds LS11 .... 78 E1
Brown Bank La. Sil BD20 .... 6 B4
Brown Bank Terr. Glu BD20 .... 16 E7
Brown Birks St. Tod OL14 .... 86 B1 1
Brown Hill Ave. Leeds LS9 .... 61 A1
Brown Hill Cl. Birk BD11 .... 96 A5
Brown Hill Cres. Leeds LS9 .... 61 A2
Brown Hill Terr. Leeds LS9 .... 61 A1
Brown La E. Leeds LS11 .... 78 C5
Brown La W. Leeds LS11, LS12 .... 78 B5
Brown Lee La. Wils BD15 .... 53 A4
Brown Pl. Leeds LS11 .... 78 E1
Brown Rd. Leeds LS11 .... 78 E1
Brown Royd Ave. Hud HD5 .... 154 D8
Brown Royd Dr. Gild LS27 .... 97 C7
Brown St. Mir WF14 .... 137 F5
Brown's Edge Rd. Wh Com S30 .... 200 A8
Brown's Knoll Rd. Kirkh HD4 .... 173 A4
Brown's Pl. Batley WF17 .... 118 B4
Brown's St. Batley WF17 .... 118 B4
Brownberrie Ave. Hors LS18 .... 41 C3
Brownberrie Cres. Hors LS18 .... 41 B4
Brownberrie Dr. Hors LS18 .... 41 C3
Brownberrie Gdns. Hors LS18 .... 41 B3
Brownberrie La. Hors LS18 .... 41 A3
Brownberrie Wlk. Hors LS18 .... 41 C3
Brownhill Cl. Birk BD11 .... 96 B5
Browning Ave. Hali HX3 .... 113 D4
Browning Ave. Pont WF8 .... 146 D8
Browning Rd. Hud HD2 .... 136 C2
Browning St. Brad BD3 .... 75 A7
Brownings The. Brig HX3 .... 114 C7
Brownlea Cl. Yeadon LS19 .... 40 B4
Brownroyd Hill Rd. Brad BD6 .... 74 B1
Brownroyd Rd. Honley HD7 .... 171 F4
Brownroyd St. Brad BD8 .... 74 C8
Brownroyd Wlk. Brad BD6 .... 74 A1
Brownsmuir Terr. Brad BD2 .... 55 F4
Brubeck Cl. Wake WF1 .... 142 E7
Bruce Gdns. Leeds LS12 .... 78 E4
Bruce Lawn. Leeds LS12 .... 78 E4
Brudenell Ave. Leeds LS6 .... 59 F4
Brudenell Gr. Leeds LS6 .... 59 F4
Brudenell Mount. Leeds LS6 .... 59 F4

Brudenell Prim Sch. Leeds ... 59 E3
Brudenell Rd. Leeds LS6 ... 59 E3
Brudenell St. Leeds LS6 ... 59 F3
Brudenell Vw. Leeds LS6 ... 59 F3 2
Brunel Cl. Brad BD9 ... 55 A2
Brunel Ct. Hali HX3 ... 82 B2 3
Brunel Gdns. Brad BD5 ... 74 C3 7
Brunel Rd. Loft G WF2 ... 120 F4
Brunswick Arc. Keigh BD21 ... 35 C7 8
Brunswick Ct. Leeds LS2 ... 60 D1
Brunswick Dr. Wake WF1 ... 118 A1
Brunswick Gdns. Gar LS25 ... 82 F7
Brunswick Gdns. Hali HX1 ... 113 B7 5
Brunswick Gr. Wake WF1 ... 142 D6 8
Brunswick House. Bing BD16 ... 37 B2
Brunswick Pl. Brad BD10 ... 56 D7
Brunswick Pl. Morley LS27 ... 98 B4 3
Brunswick Rd. Brad BD10 ... 56 D7
Brunswick Rd. Pudsey LS28 ... 76 E8
Brunswick Row. Leeds LS2 ... 60 D1
Brunswick. Ryhill WF4 ... 162 B2
Brunswick St. Batley WF16 ... 117 D3
Brunswick St. Bubley WF17 ... 118 C5 6
Brunswick St. Bing BD16 ... 37 B3
Brunswick St. Cull BD13 ... 52 E6
Brunswick St. Dearne S63 ... 194 F1
Brunswick St. Dew WF13 ... 118 A1
Brunswick St. Heb Br HX7 ... 88 F3
Brunswick St. Hud HD1 ... 154 A6
Brunswick St. Morley LS27 ... 98 A5
Brunswick St. Queen BD13 ... 72 F1 1
Brunswick St. Wake WF1 ... 142 D6
Brunswick Street Bglws. Wake WF1 ... 142 D6 9
Brunswick Terr. Leeds LS2 ... 60 C1
Brunswick Terr. Morley LS27 ... 98 B4
Bruntcliffe Ave. Morley LS27 ... 97 F4
Bruntcliffe Cl. Morley LS27 ... 97 F4
Bruntcliffe Dr. Morley LS27 ... 97 F4
Bruntcliffe La. Morley LS27 ... 97 E4
Bruntcliffe La. Morley LS27 ... 97 F4
Bruntcliffe Rd. Morley LS27 ... 97 E3
Bruntcliffe Way. Morley LS27 ... 97 E4
Brunthwaite Bridge La. Sil BD20 ... 18 A8
Brunthwaite La. Sil BD20 ... 6 B1
Brussels St. Leeds LS9 ... 79 D7
Bryan Cl. Castle WF10 ... 124 A8
Bryan Rd. Elland HX5 ... 134 D6
Bryan Rd. Hud HD1 ... 135 D1
Bryan St. Brig HD6 ... 115 A1 5
Bryan St. Pudsey LS28 ... 57 D4
Bryan Terr. Hud HD7 ... 152 E6
Bryanstone Rd. Brad BD4 ... 75 D3
Bryer St. Dew WF13 ... 139 C8
Bryngate. Roth LS26 ... 101 C6
Bryony Ct. Midd LS10 ... 99 F5
Buck La. Bail BD17 ... 38 F3
Buck Mill La. Brad BD10 ... 39 A2
Buck St. Brad BD3 ... 75 A6
Buck St. Denh BD13 ... 71 E8
Buck Stone Ave. Leeds LS17 ... 42 F4
Buck Stone Cl. Leeds LS17 ... 43 A4
Buck Stone Cr. Leeds LS17 ... 43 A4
Buck Stone Cres. Leeds LS17 ... 42 F4
Buck Stone Gdns. Leeds LS17 ... 42 F4
Buck Stone Gn. Leeds LS17 ... 42 F4
Buck Stone Gr. Leeds LS17 ... 42 F4
Buck Stone La. Ln Cra BD20 ... 16 A1
Buck Stone Mount. Leeds LS17 ... 42 F4
Buck Stone Oval. Leeds LS17 ... 42 F4
Buck Stone Rd. Leeds LS17 ... 42 F4
Buck Stone Rise. Leeds LS17 ... 42 F4
Buck Stone View. Leeds LS17 ... 42 F4
Buckden Cl. Sil BD20 ... 5 E2
Buckden Rd. Hud HD3 ... 153 D8
Buckfast Ct. Brad BD10 ... 56 B7
Buckingham Ave. Leeds LS6 ... 59 E4
Buckingham Cres. Brad BD14 ... 73 D5
Buckingham Cl. Wake WF1 ... 110 F1
Buckingham Ct. Leeds LS6 ... 59 E4
Buckingham Dr. Wake WF1 ... 142 F3
Buckingham Gr. Leeds LS6 ... 59 E4
Buckingham Mount. Leeds LS6 ... 59 E4
Buckingham Pl. Leeds LS6 ... 59 E4
Buckingham Way. Byram WF11 ... 126 E8
Buckingham Way. Roy S71 ... 179 B4
Buckland Pl. Hali HX1 ... 112 E6
Buckland Rd. Brad BD8 ... 73 F8 3
Buckle La. Men LS29 ... 22 C4
Buckle La. Nor WF6 ... 123 A2
Buckley Ave. Leeds LS11 ... 79 B3
Buckley La. Hali HX2 ... 91 C2
Buckley View. Tod OL14 ... 108 A6
Buckrose St. Hud HD1 ... 136 A1
Buckstone Dr. Yeadon LS19 ... 40 B3
Buckthorne Ct. E Ard WF3 ... 120 D8
Buckthorne Cl. E Ard WF3 ... 120 D8
Buckthorne Dr. E Ard WF3 ... 120 D8
Buckthorne Fold. E Ard WF3 ... 120 D8
Buckton Cl. Leeds LS11 ... 79 A4
Buckton Mount. Leeds LS11 ... 79 A4
Buckton View. Leeds LS11 ... 79 A4
Bude Rd. Brad BD5 ... 74 F1
Bude Rd. Leeds LS11 ... 79 B3
Bugler Terr. Hor WF4 ... 140 E1
Bula Cl. Kippax LS25 ... 83 A1
Bulay Rd. Hud HD1 ... 153 F4
Bull Close La. Hali HX1 ... 113 C6
Bull Gn. Hali HX1 ... 113 C7
Bull Green Rd. Hud HD3 ... 152 F6
Bull Hill. Oxen BD22 ... 51 C1
Bull La. Crig WF4 ... 159 F5
Bull Ring. Wake WF1 ... 142 C6
Bull Royd Ave. Brad BD8 ... 73 C8
Bull Royd Cres. Brad BD8 ... 73 C8
Bull Royd Dr. Brad BD8 ... 73 B8
Bull Royd La. Brad BD8 ... 73 C8
Bullace Trees La. Liver WF15 ... 116 E4
Bullenshaw Rd. Hem WF9 ... 181 D6
Buller Cl. Leeds LS9 ... 61 C1
Buller Ct. Leeds LS9 ... 61 C1
Buller Gr. Leeds LS9 ... 61 C1
Buller St. Brad BD4 ... 75 D5
Buller St. Roth LS26 ... 100 C6 6
Bullerthorpe La. Leeds LS15,LS26 ... 81 E4
Bullfield The. Harden BD16 ... 36 B1
Bullfields Cl. Dew WF12 ... 139 E2
Bullough La. Leeds LS26 ... 81 A1
Bullroyd Dr. Brad BD8 ... 73 C8
Bullytde Rd. Pont WF8 ... 146 C6
Bungalow Rd. Glu BD20 ... 16 C5
Bungalows The. Clay W HD8 ... 175 F2
Bungalows The. Hali HX1 ... 91 D1
Bungalows The. Hali HX3 ... 92 A2

Bungalows The. Hali HX3 ... 113 E2
Bungalows The. Leeds LS15 ... 62 D3
Bungalows The. Nor WF6 ... 123 A5
Bungalows The. Ossett WF5 ... 140 C6
Bunker's Hill La. Keigh BD22 ... 34 D5
Bunkers Hill. Aber LS25 ... 64 E6
Bunkers Hill. Guise BD17 ... 39 B5
Bunkers Hill. Holmfi HD7 ... 189 A5
Bunkers Hill. Wake WF2 ... 120 F2
Bunkers La. Batley WF17 ... 117 F4
Bunney Gr. Northo HX3 ... 92 F4
Burbeary Rd. Hud HD1 ... 153 E3
Burberry Cl. Brad BD4 ... 95 C8
Burchett Gr. Leeds LS6 ... 60 A4
Burchett Pl. Leeds LS6 ... 60 A4
Burchett Terr. Leeds LS6 ... 60 B4
Burcote Dr. Elland HD3 ... 134 B1
Burdale P. Brad BD7 ... 74 B6
Burdett Terr. Leeds LS4 ... 59 C2 5
Burdock Way. Hali HX1 ... 113 B7
Burfitts Rd. Hud HD3 ... 153 B7
Burgh Mill La. Dew WF13 ... 139 A7
Burhouse Ct. Honley HD7 ... 171 F4
Burkill St. Wake WF1 ... 142 D2
Burking Rd. Dew WF13 ... 139 B8
Burleigh St. Hali HX1 ... 89 C3
Burley La. Hors LS18 ... 58 F5 13
Burley Bank La. Holme HD7 ... 197 E6
Burley C Fst Sch. Bur in W ... 9 E1
Burley Ct. Stee BD20 ... 17 C5
Burley Grange Rd. Leeds LS4 ... 59 C2 2
Burley Hill Cres. Leeds LS4 ... 59 B3
Burley Hill Dr. Leeds LS4 ... 59 B3
Burley La. Hors LS18 ... 58 B7
Burley La. Men LS29 ... 21 F5
Burley Lodge Pl. Leeds LS6 ... 59 E1
Burley Lodge Rd. Leeds LS6 ... 59 E1
Burley Lodge St. Leeds LS6 ... 59 E1
Burley Lodge Terr. Leeds LS6 ... 59 E1
Burley Mews. Stee BD20 ... 17 C5
Burley St. Leeds LS11 ... 99 H
Burley Park Sta. Leeds ... 59 D3
Burley Pl. Leeds LS4 ... 59 B2
Burley St W. Brad BD3 ... 75 A8
Burley Rd. Men LS29 ... 22 A6
Burley St. Elland HX5 ... 134 F6 10
Burley St. Leeds LS3 ... 78 F8
Burley St Matthias' Sch. Leeds ... 59 D2
Burley St. Shlp BD2 ... 55 D4
Burley Wlk. Batley WF17 ... 118 B5
Burley Wood Cres. Leeds LS4 ... 59 C2
Burley Wood La. Leeds LS4 ... 59 C2
Burley Wood Mount. Leeds LS4 ... 59 B3
Burley Wood View. Leeds LS4 ... 59 C3
Burley & Woodhead CE Sch. Bur in W ... 21 F8
Burlington Ave. Brad BD3 ... 56 A1
Burlington Mews. Leeds LS13 ... 79 B2 21
Burlington St. Brad BD8 ... 55 D1
Burlington St. Hali HX1 ... 112 F7 2
Burlington Works. Brad ... 56 A1
Burn Rd. Hud HD2, HD3 ... 135 C3
Burned Gr. Shelf HX3 ... 93 C7
Burned Rd. Shelf HX3 ... 93 D7
Burneston Gdns. Brad BD6 ... 93 E8 12
Burnett Ave. Brad BD5 ... 74 D3
Burnett Pl. Brad BD5 ... 74 D3
Burnett Rise. Queen BD13 ... 92 C8
Burnett St. Brad BD1 ... 74 E7
Burnham Ave. Brad BD4 ... 75 C1
Burnham Ave. Mapo S75 ... 178 B1
Burnham Ct. Weth LS22 ... 13 E5
Burnham Rd. Gar LS25 ... 82 F6
Burnhill La. Brad WF9 ... 164 B8
Burniston Cl. Wils BD15 ... 53 C4
Burniston Dr. Hud HD3 ... 153 A8
Burlewood Cl. Hud HD4 ... 171 D8
Burnlee Gr. Holmfi HD7 ... 188 F4
Burnley Rd. Hali HX2, HX6 ... 112 A4
Burnley Rd. Hali HX2, HX6 ... 111 C6
Burnley Rd. Sower Br HX6 ... 111 C6
Burnley Rd. Tod OL14 ... 85 B1
Burnleyville. Clec BD19 ... 96 B1
Burnroyd Ave. Glu BD20 ... 16 D6
Burns Ave. S Kirk WF9 ... 182 C1
Burns Ct. Wake WF2 ... 96 D2
Burns Hill. Sil LS29 ... 6 E8
Burns Rd. Hali HX1 ... 93 C3
Burns Way. E Spo LS23 ... 30 D5
Burnsall Ave. Batley WF17 ... 118 A5
Burnsall Croft. Leeds LS12 ... 78 B8
Burnsall Ct. Leeds LS12 ... 78 B8
Burnsall Gdns. Leeds LS12 ... 78 B8
Burnsall Grange. Leeds LS12 ... 78 C8 17
Burnsall Rd. Batley WF17 ... 118 A5
Burnsall Rd. Brad BD3 ... 75 B6
Burnsall Rd. Liver WF15 ... 116 F4
Burnside. Brad BD15 ... 54 A3
Burnside Ave. Shelf HX3 ... 93 A1
Burnside Cl. Batley WF17 ... 97 A1
Burnside. Dearne S63 ... 194 C1
Burnside Dr. Holmfi HD7 ... 188 E4
Burnt Acres La. Heb Br OL14 ... 109 B8
Burnt Edge La. B Head HX7 ... 87 D4
Burnt House Cl. Tod OL14 ... 108 B4
Burnt Plats La. Mars HD7 ... 168 F5
Burnt Side Rd. Leeds LS12 ... 77 D3
Burnt Wood Cres. S Kirk WF9 ... 182 C2
Burnt Wood La. S Kirk WF9 ... 182 A2
Burntwood Ave. Hem WF9 ... 181 D5
Burntwood Bank. Hem WF9 ... 181 D5
Burntwood Cres. Roy S71 ... 179 E1
Burntwood Dr. S Elm WF9 ... 182 F3
Burntwood Gr. S Kirk WF9 ... 182 B1
Burntwood Mount. Hem WF9 ... 181 D7
Burntwood Pk. Hem WF9 ... 181 D6
Burntwood Rd. Hem WF9 ... 181 D6
Burntwood Sports & Ltr. Brn ... 181 C7
Burntwood St. Brad BD5 ... 74 C4
Burnup Gr. Clec BD19 ... 116 C7
Burnwells Ave. Brad BD10 ... 39 A2
Burnwells Cl. Brad BD10 ... 39 A2
Burr Tree Dri. Leeds LS15 ... 81 E7
Burr Tree Garth. Leeds LS15 ... 81 E7
Burr Tree Vale. Leeds LS15 ... 81 E7
Burrage St. Bing BD16 ... 36 F3
Burras Ave. Otley LS21 ... 22 F7
Burras La. Otley LS21 ... 22 F7
Burras Rd. Brad BD4 ... 75 B2
Burrell Cl. Weth LS22 ... 13 F4
Burrell St. Wake WF1 ... 142 D6
Burrow Hills. Brad BD15 ... 74 A8
Burrowes St. Batley WF17 ... 117 F7
Burrows The. Batley WF17 ... 117 F7
Burrwood Terr. Elland HX4 ... 134 B5

Burnwood Way. Elland HX4 ... 134 B5
Burton Acres Dr. Kirkb HD8 ... 173 E7
Burton Acres La. Kirkb HD8 ... 173 F7
Burton Acres Mews. Kirkb HD8 ... 173 E7
Burton Acres Way. Kirkb HD8 ... 173 E7
Burton Ave. Leeds LS11 ... 79 C3
Burton Common La. B Sal LS25 ... 106 C6
Burton Cres. Leeds LS6 ... 59 D6
Burton Cross. Kirkb HD8 ... 173 E8
Burton Mews. Leeds LS17 ... 43 D5
Burton Row. Leeds LS11 ... 79 C4
Burton Royd La. Kirkb HD8 ... 174 A7
Burton Salmon Prim Sch. B Sal ... 105 E3
Burton St. Brad BD4 ... 75 A4
Burton St. Hali HX3 ... 92 A5
Burton St. Keigh BD20 ... 18 B2
Burton St. Leeds LS11 ... 79 C4
Burton St. Pudsey LS28 ... 57 D3
Burton St. S Elm WF9 ... 182 F2
Burton St. Wake WF1 ... 142 B7
Burton Terr. Leeds LS11 ... 79 C3
Burton Way. Leeds LS9 ... 61 A1
Burwood Rd. Hud HD3 ... 153 C8
Busfield St. Bing BD16 ... 36 F3
Busfield St. Brad BD4 ... 75 B3
Bushey Bank. Hem WF9 ... 181 E6
Bushill Fold. Queen BD13 ... 72 C2
Busker La. Skel HD8 ... 175 C1
Buslingthorpe Gn. Leeds LS7 ... 60 C3
Buslingthorpe La. Leeds LS7 ... 60 C4
Buslingthorpe Vale. Leeds LS7 ... 60 C4
Bussey Ct. Leeds LS6 ... 60 A3
Busy La. Ship BD18 ... 38 E1
Butcher Hill. Hem WF9 ... 181 E8
Butcher Hill. Leeds LS16, LS18 ... 58 F8
Butcher La. Roth LS26 ... 100 E5
Butcher St. Brad BD7 ... 74 D7
Butcher St. Leeds LS11 ... 79 F8
Bute Ave. Brig HD6 ... 115 A5
Butler La. Bail BD17 ... 38 D4
Butler St E. Brad BD3 ... 75 A7
Butler St W. Brad BD3 ... 75 A8
Butt Hill. Kippax LS25 ... 83 A1
Butt La. Brad BD10 ... 56 B8
Butt La. H Pag DN5 ... 195 E4
Butt La. Leeds LS12 ... 77 C4
Butt La. Holmfi HD7 ... 189 E2
Butt La. Leeds LS12, LS13 ... 77 D6
Butterbowl Dr. Leeds LS12 ... 77 F5
Butterbowl Gdns. Leeds LS12 ... 77 F5
Butterbowl Gr. Leeds LS12 ... 77 F5
Butterbowl Lawn. Leeds LS12 ... 77 F5
Butterbowl Mount. Leeds LS12 ... 77 F5
Butterbowl Rd. Leeds LS12 ... 77 F5
Butterfield Homes. Bing BD16 ... 36 F3
Butterfield Homes. Brad BD9 ... 54 B6 5
Butterfield Homes. Wils BD15 ... 53 B6
Butterfield St. Leeds LS9 ... 79 F7
Butterley La. Holmfi HD7 ... 189 F5
Butterley St. Leeds LS10 ... 79 C6
Buttermere Ave. Weth LS22 ... 13 D8 13
Buttermere Croft. Walton WF2 ... 161 A6
Buttermere Rd. Brad BD2 ... 56 D3
Buttermere Rd. Hud HD5 ... 154 D6
Butternab Rise. Hud HD4 ... 171 D8
Butternab Rd. Hud HD4 ... 171 D8
Buttershaw Comp Sch. Brad ... 93 F6
Buttershaw Dr. Brad BD6 ... 73 E1
Buttershaw First Sch. Brad ... 93 F7
Buttershaw La. Brad BD6 ... 94 B8
Buttershaw La. Clec WF15 ... 116 B5
Buttershaw Mid Sch. Brad ... 93 F6
Butterwick Gdns. Weth LS22 ... 13 C5
Butterwood Cl. Hud HD4 ... 171 D8
Butterworth End La. Sower Br HX6 ... 132 A7
Butterworth Hill. Slai HD3 ... 152 A7
Butterworth La. Sower Br HX6 ... 111 E1
Buttholme Gate. Brad BD6 ... 93 F8
Button Hill. Leeds LS7 ... 60 D4
Button Pk. Pont WF8 ... 146 C7
Buttress La. Hali HX2 ... 90 F3
Butts Cl. Kirkb HD4 ... 172 E6
Butts Ct. Leeds LS1 ... 79 C8
Butts Garth. Thorner LS14 ... 45 F5
Butts Garth View. Thorner LS14 ... 45 F5
Butts Green La. Hali HX2 ... 112 A7
Butts Green Rd. Hali HX2 ... 111 F7
Butts Hill. Clec BD19 ... 117 C8
Butts La. Guise LS20 ... 22 E5
Butts La. Kirkb HD8 ... 173 D4
Butts La. Tod OL14 ... 108 E8
Butts Mount. Leeds LS12 ... 78 D7
Butts Rd. Kirkb HD8 ... 173 D4
Butts Terr. Guise LS20 ... 22 E1
Butts The. Pont WF8 ... 125 D1
Butts The. Keigh BD20 ... 19 D5
Buxton Ave. Ship BD9 ... 55 C4
Buxton La. Ship BD9 ... 55 C4
Buxton Pl. Wake WF1 ... 142 B8
Buxton St. Hali HX3 ... 92 A1 8
Buxton St. Keigh BD21 ... 35 D6
Byeway. Guise LS20 ... 22 D1
Byland Cl. B Spa LS23 ... 30 C7
Byland Gr. Brad BD15 ... 53 F1
Byland. Hali HX2 ... 91 E7
Byram Arc. Hud HD1 ... 154 A6 22
Byram Park Ave. Byram WF11 ... 126 E8
Byram Park Rd. Byram WF11 ... 126 E8
Byrom St. Brad BD5 ... 74 C3
Byron Ave. Brad WF8 ... 125 E2
Byron Ct. Knott WF11 ... 126 D8
Byron St. Brad BD3 ... 75 B8
Byron St. Hali HX3 ... 92 A1 4
Byron St. Leeds LS2 ... 79 E8
Byways The. Pont WF8 ... 146 D6
Bywell CE JC Mid Sch. Dew ... 118 F1
Bywell Rd. Dew WF12 ... 140 A8
Bywell Rd. Dew WF12 ... 118 F1

Cabb La. S Kirk WF9 ... 182 D4
Cabbage Hill. Leeds LS12 ... 78 B6

Cabin Rd. Pool LS21 ... 24 B5
Cable St. Hud HD1 ... 154 A4
Cad Beeston Mews. Leeds LS11 ... 79 A3
Cadney Croft. Hali HX1 ... 113 C6 5
Cadogan Ave. Hud HD3 ... 153 B8
Caenarvon Cl. Batley WF17 ... 97 A1
Caernarvon Ave. Gar LS25 ... 83 B7
Cain Cl. Leeds LS9 ... 79 F7 8
Cain La. Hali HX3 ... 114 A4
Cairns Cl. Brad BD2 ... 55 F3
Caister Cl. Batley WF17 ... 97 A2
Caister Gr. Keigh BD21 ... 35 B4 5
Caister St. Keigh BD21 ... 35 B4 3
Caister Way. Keigh BD21 ... 35 B4
Calde Ct. Brad BD12 ... 94 E6
Caldene Ave. Brad BD12 ... 94 E6
Caldene Ave. Heb Br HX7 ... 89 D1
Calder High Sch. Heb Br ... 89 F1
Calder House. Mirnf HX5 ... 134 F7 10
Calder House. Mir WF14 ... 138 A4
Calder Mount. Crig WF4 ... 159 F5
Calder Rd. Dew WF13 ... 138 F5
Calder Rd. Mir WF14 ... 138 A3
Calder St. Brig HD6 ... 115 C1
Calder St. Castle WF10 ... 124 D7
Calder St. Elland HX4 ... 134 D7
Calder St. Hali HX4 ... 113 D6
Calder St. Tod OL14 ... 108 B5
Calder St. Wake WF1 ... 142 D4
Calder Terr. Elland HX3 ... 113 A1
Calder Terr. Heb Br HX7 ... 88 F3
Calder Terr. Hor WF4 ... 141 C6
Calder Vale Rd. Wake WF1 ... 142 E5
Calder View. Brig HD6 ... 115 A1
Calder View. Crig WF4 ... 159 F5
Calder View. Ossett WF5 ... 140 B5
Calder Way. Sil BD20 ... 17 E8
Calderbrook Rd. Litt OL15 ... 129 C2
Calderdale Bsns Pk. Hali ... 91 F3
Calderdale Ind Mus. Hali ... 113 D6
Caldercroft. Elland HX5 ... 135 B6
Calderdale Way. Elland HX5 ... 135 B6
Calderstone Ave. Brad BD6 ... 93 E8
Caldervale. Roy S71 ... 179 E4
Caldicott Cl. Tod OL14 ... 86 C2
Caledonia Ct. Wake WF2 ... 120 B2
Caledonia Rd. Batley WF17 ... 118 D5
Caledonia Rd. Keigh BD21 ... 35 D8
Caledonia St. Brad BD4, BD5 ... 74 E5
Caledonian Rd. Dew WF12 ... 139 C5
Calf Hey La. Wh Com S30 ... 200 D7
Calf Hey Terr. Tod OL14 ... 108 A1 3
Calf Hill Rd. Holmfi HD7 ... 172 B1
Calgary Cres. E Ard WF3 ... 119 F7
Calgary Pl. Leeds LS7 ... 60 D6
California Dr. Castle WF10 ... 124 D8
California Dr. Wor WF4 ... 141 C1
California St. Morley LS27 ... 98 A3
California St. Tod OL14 ... 108 A3
California Terr. Morley LS27 ... 98 A3
Call La. Leeds LS1 ... 79 C7
Calls The. Leeds LS2 ... 79 C7
Cally Hall Farm Cotts. B Head HX7 ... 88 A4
Calmlands Rd. Mel HD7 ... 170 D1
Calpin Cl. Brad BD10 ... 56 B8
Calton Gr. Keigh BD21 ... 35 A6
Calton Rd. Keigh BD21 ... 35 A6
Calton St. Hud HD1 ... 154 B8
Calton St. Keigh BD21 ... 35 A6 3
Calver Ave. Keigh BD21 ... 35 A8
Calver Gr. Keigh BD21 ... 35 A8
Calverley Ave. Brad BD3 ... 75 E8
Calverley Ave. Leeds LS13 ... 58 B3
Calverley CE Prim Sch. Pudsey ... 57 B6
Calverley Cl. Leeds ... 57 B6
Calverley Ct. Leeds LS13 ... 58 B3 2
Calverley Cutting. Pudsey BD10 ... 56 F8
Calverley Dr. Leeds LS13 ... 58 B3
Calverley Garth. Leeds LS13 ... 58 A4
Calverley Gdns. Leeds LS13 ... 58 A3
Calverley Gr. Leeds LS13 ... 58 B3 1
Calverley La. Hors LS18 ... 58 A8
Calverley La. Leeds LS13 ... 57 F5
Calverley La. Pudsey LS28 ... 57 C7
Calverley Moor Ave. Pudsey LS28 ... 76 C7
Calverley Parkside Cty Prim Sch. Pudsey ... 57 B6
Calverley Rd. Leeds LS26 ... 100 E5
Calverley St. Leeds LS1 ... 60 D1
Calverley Terr. Leeds LS13 ... 58 B3 2
Camargue Fold. Brad BD2 ... 56 E4
Camberley Cl. Pudsey LS28 ... 76 E5
Camberley Mount. Brad BD4 ... 75 E3 9
Camberley St. Leeds LS11 ... 79 B3
Camberley Way. Pudsey LS28 ... 76 E5
Camborne Dr. Hud HD2 ... 136 F4
Camborne Way. Keigh BD22 ... 34 F7
Cambrian Bar. Brad BD12 ... 94 C6
Cambrian St. Leeds LS11 ... 79 B3
Cambrian Terr. Leeds LS11 ... 79 B3
Cambridge Cl. Morley LS27 ... 98 A3
Cambridge Cres. Hud HD2 ... 136 F5
Cambridge Ct. Morley LS27 ... 98 A3
Cambridge Dr. Leeds LS13 ... 58 C1
Cambridge Dr. Otley LS21 ... 23 B7
Cambridge Gdns. Leeds LS13 ... 58 C1
Cambridge Gn. Leeds LS13 ... 58 C1
Cambridge Pl. Brad BD3 ... 56 A1
Cambridge Pl. Otley LS21 ... 23 B7
Cambridge Rd. Batley WF17 ... 117 F5
Cambridge Rd. Hud HD1 ... 154 B4
Cambridge Rd. Leeds LS7 ... 60 E6
Cambridge St. Brad BD14 ... 73 B4
Cambridge St. Brad BD4 ... 74 D4
Cambridge St. Castle WF10 ... 124 D7
Cambridge St. Guise LS20 ... 22 E1
Cambridge St. Nor WF6 ... 123 A1
Cambridge St. Otley LS21 ... 23 B7
Cambridge St. S Eln WF9 ... 182 F1 13
Cambridge St. Tod OL14 ... 108 C5
Cambridge Terr. Otley LS21 ... 23 B7
Cambridge Way. Otley LS21 ... 23 B7
Camden St. Castle WF10 ... 125 D8
Camden St. Sow W HX6 ... 112 C5
Camden Terr. Brad BD8 ... 55 B1
Camela La. S Kirk WF9 ... 181 B1
Camellia Cl. Wake WF2 ... 141 D3
Camellia Mount. Brad BD7 ... 73 E6
Camelot Ct. Pont WF8 ... 146 E8
Cameron Ave. Brad BD12 ... 94 C5
Camerton Gn. Brad BD5 ... 74 F2
Camilla Ct. Dew WF12 ... 139 F7
Camm La. Mir WF14 ... 138 B6
Camms Terr. Dews S63 ... 194 B1
Camp Hill. Mars HD3 ... 151 B5
Camp Mount. Pont WF8 ... 146 C6
Camp Rd. Bramho LS16 ... 24 E1
Camp Rd. S Kirk WF9 ... 181 F1
Camp Rise. Pont WF8 ... 146 B8
Camp Sq. Thorner LS14 ... 45 F5
Campbell St. Brad BD13 ... 72 F1
Campbell St. Glu BD20 ... 16 D7
Campbell St. Pudsey LS28 ... 57 E2
Campbell St. Queen BD13 ... 72 F1
Campden Rd. Heb Br HX7 ... 89 A3
Campinot Vale. Slai HD7 ... 151 F1
Campion Cl. Pont WF8 ... 146 D7
Campus Rd. Brad BD7 ... 74 C6
Camroyd St. Dew WF13 ... 118 D1
Canada Cres. Yeadon LS19 ... 40 C4
Canada Dr. Yeadon LS19 ... 40 C5
Canada Rd. Yeadon LS19 ... 40 C5
Canada Terr. Yeadon LS19 ... 40 C4
Canal Cl. Loft G WF3 ... 121 D6
Canal La. Loft G WF3 ... 121 D6
Canal La. Sil BD20 ... 18 A7
Canal Pl. Leeds LS12 ... 78 F7
Canal Rd. Bing BD16 ... 36 F5
Canal Rd. Brad ... 55 C1
Canal Rd. Hali HX1 ... 112 F4
Canal Rd. Keigh BD20 ... 18 E1
Canal Rd. Leeds LS12 ... 78 F8
Canal Rd. Pudsey LS13 ... 57 E5
Canal Wlk. Bing BD16 ... 37 A3
Canal St. Brig HD6 ... 115 B3
Canal St. Hali HX4 ... 113 C3
Canal St. Tod OL14 ... 108 B5
Canal Wharf. Leeds LS11 ... 79 F6
Canal Wlk. Loft G WF3 ... 121 F6
Canberra Cl. Clec BD19 ... 116 D8
Canberra Dr. Haw BD22 ... 51 F8 6
Canby Gr. Hud HD5 ... 155 B5
Cancel St. Leeds LS10 ... 79 D5
Canford Dr. Brad BD15 ... 54 C1
Canford Gr. Brad BD15 ... 54 C1
Canford Rd. Brad BD15 ... 54 B1
Canker La. Hali HX3 ... 113 B4
Canning Ave. Wake WF2 ... 141 D8
Cannon Gr. Batley WF16 ... 117 D5
Cannon Hall Cl. Brig HD6 ... 115 D2
Cannon Hall Country Pk. Caw ... 193 D5
Cannon St. Brig HD6 ... 115 A2
Cannon St. Castle WF10 ... 124 E8
Cannon St. Hud HD1 ... 154 B4
Canonbury Terr. Leeds LS11 ... 78 F3
Canterbury Ave. Brad BD5 ... 74 E2
Canterbury Ct. Brad BD5 ... 74 D4
Canterbury Cres. Hali HX1 ... 92 F1
Canterbury Dr. Leeds LS6 ... 59 E3
Canterbury Rd. Leeds LS6 ... 59 E3
Cardan Dr. Liver WF15 ... 117 B3
Cardigan Ave. Morley LS27 ... 98 B6
Cardigan Cl. Batley WF17 ... 97 A3
Cardigan Ct. Leeds LS6 ... 59 E4
Cardigan Fields Rd. Leeds LS4 ... 59 D2
Cardigan La. Leeds LS4, LS6 ... 59 E3
Cardigan La. Ossett WF5 ... 141 A3
Cardigan Rd. Leeds LS6 ... 59 E4
Cardigan Terr. E Ard WF3 ... 120 B7
Cardinal Ave. Leeds LS11 ... 98 F8
Cardinal Cres. Leeds LS11 ... 98 F8
Cardinal Gdns. Leeds LS11 ... 98 F8
Cardinal Gr. Leeds LS11 ... 98 F8
Cardinal Rd. Leeds LS11 ... 98 F8
Cardinal Sq. Leeds LS11 ... 79 A1
Cardinal Wlk. Leeds LS11 ... 98 F8
Carilinco Mews. Loft G WF2 ... ...
Carisbrooke Cres. Brad BD6 ... 93 F6
Carisbrooke La. Gar LS25 ... 82 F6
Carisbrooke Rd. Leeds LS16 ... 59 A6
Cark Rd. Keigh BD21 ... 35 B7
Carlby Gr. Keigh BD22 ... 35 A6 3
Carlby St. Keigh BD22 ... 35 A6
Carleton Cl. Pont WF8 ... 146 B5
Carleton Cres. Pont WF8 ... 146 B6
Carleton Dr. Pont WF8 ... 146 C6
Carleton Gate. Pont WF8 ... 146 C6
Carleton Glen. Pont WF8 ... 146 B5
Carleton Gn. Pont WF8 ... 146 B6
Carleton Green Cl. Pont WF8 ... 146 B5
Carleton High Sch. Pont ... 146 E5

Carlton House. Brad BD6 .... 93 E8 1
Carlton Park Ave. Pont WF8 ...... 146 D6
Carlton Park Dr. Pont WF8 .... 146 D6
Carlton Park Prim Sch. Pont 146 D6
Carlton Park Rd. Pont WF8 .... 146 D6
Carlton Pont WF8 .... 146 D6
Carltile St. Mel HD7 .... 170 E7
Carlton St. Keigh BD20 .... 18 C1
Carlton View. Pont WF8 .... 146 D6
Carlinghow La. Batley WF17 ...... 118 A7
Carlinghow La. Batley WF17 ...... 117 F6
Carlinghow Mills. Batley 118 B6
Carlinghow Princess Royal Jun &
  Inf Sch. Batley 118 A7
Carlisle Ave. Yeadon LS19 .... 40 C6
Carlisle Cl. Dew WF13 .... 118 C2
Carlisle Dr. Pudsey LS28 .... 76 D6
Carlisle Gr. Pudsey LS28 .... 76 D6
Carlisle Pl. Brad BD8 .... 55 C1
Carlisle Rd. Brad BD8 .... 55 C1
Carlisle Rd. Pudsey LS28 .... 76 D6
Carlisle Rd. Brad BD8 .... 55 C1
Carlisle St. Hali HX2 .... 112 E8 8
Carlisle St. Keigh BD21 .... 35 D7
Carlisle St. Pudsey LS28 .... 57 C1
Carlisle Terr. Brad BD8 .... 55 C1
Carrayne La. Men LS29 .... 22 A5
Carlton App. Weth LS22 .... 13 C6
Carlton Ave. Batley WF17 .... 118 B3
Carlton Ave. Castle WF10 .... 124 F7
Carlton Ave. Pudsey LS28 .... 76 E7
Carlton Ave. Ship BD18 .... 54 F8
Carlton Carr. Leeds LS7 .... 60 C2
Carlton Cl. Cleck BD19 .... 116 D7 1
Carlton Cl. Hem WF9 .... 181 C5
Carlton Cl. Leeds LS7 .... 60 C2
Carlton Cl. Nor WF6 .... 123 B2
Carlton Croft. Leeds LS7 .... 60 C2
Carlton Croft. Wake WF2 .... 160 D6
Carlton Ct. Bail BD17 .... 38 C4
Carlton Dr. Gar LS25 .... 82 F5
Carlton Dr. Guise LS20 .... 22 F2
Carlton Dr. Ship BD18 .... 55 A5
Carlton Dr. Ship BD18 .... 55 B4
Carlton Fst Sch. S Elm 182 F2
Carltdn Garth. Leeds LS17 .... 44 A5
Carltdn Garth. Leeds LS7 .... 60 C2
Carltdn Gate. Leeds LS7 .... 60 C2
Carltdn Gdns. Leeds LS7 .... 60 C2
Carltdn Gdns. S Elm WF9 .... 182 F3
Carlton Gr. Brad BD5 .... 74 D3 2
Carlton Gr. Elland HX5 .... 135 C7
Carlton Gr. Leeds LS7 .... 60 C2
Carlton Gr. Ship BD18 .... 55 B5
Carlton Hill. Leeds LS2, LS7 ...... 60 C2
Carlton House Terr. Hali HX1 .... 113 A3
Carlton Jun & Inf Sch. Dew 118 B2
Carlton Jun & Inf Sch. Roth 100 D3
Carlton La. C Gar LS19 .... 23 C3
Carlton La. Guise LS20 .... 23 C3
Carlton La. Guise LS20 .... 100 C1
Carlton La. Roth LS26 .... 100 C4
Carlton Marsh Nature Reserve.
  Cud 180 A1
Carlton Moor Mews. Midd LS10 .. 99 F5
Carlton Mount. Yeadon LS19 ..... 40 C6
Carlton Pl. Hali HX1 .... 113 C6 1
Carlton Pl. Leeds LS7 .... 60 C2
Carlton Rd. Batley WF16 .... 117 C6
Carlton Rd. Dew WF13 .... 118 C1
Carlton Rd. Liver WF15 .... 117 B4
Carlton Rd. Roy S71 .... 179 D1
Carlton Rd. S Elm WF9 .... 182 F3
Carlton Rise. Leeds LS7 .... 78 A8
Carlton Rise. Pudsey LS28 .... 76 E7
Carlton Row. Leeds LS12 .... 78 A7
Carlton St. Bacup OL13 .... 106 A3
Carlton St. Brad BD2 .... 74 D6
Carlton St. Castle WF10 .... 124 D8
Carlton St. Hali HX1 .... 113 C6 1
Carlton St. Haw BD22 .... 51 D7
Carlton St. Heb Br HX7 .... 89 A3
Carlton St. Nor WF6 .... 123 C2
Carlton St. Otley LS21 .... 23 B7
Carlton St. Wake WF1 .... 216 A1
Carlton Terr. Batley WF17 .... 118 A3
Carlton Terr. Dew WF12 .... 139 D6
Carlton Terr. Hali HX1 .... 113 C6 6
Carlton Terr. Pudsey LS28 .... 76 E8 2
Carlton Terr. Yeadon LS19 .... 40 C7
Carlton View. Kippax WF10 ...... 102 F6
Carlton Wlk. Ship BD18 .... 55 B5
Carlton-Bolling Sch. Brad 56 A1
Carlyle Cres. Castle WF10 .... 125 A2
Carlyle Rd. Castle WF10 .... 125 B7
Carmel Rd. Hali HX3 .... 92 C2
Carmine Cl. Hud HD5 .... 154 F4
Carmona Ave. Ship BD18 .... 55 B5
Carmona Gdns. Ship BD18 .... 55 B5
Carnaby Rd. Brad BD7 .... 73 E2
Carnegie Cell. Leeds 59 B6
Carnegie Dr. Ship BD18 .... 55 C6
Carnlea Gr. Wake WF2 .... 142 C3
Carnoustie Gr. Ship BD16 .... 54 B7
Caroline St. Hud HD7 .... 152 D5
Caroline St. Ship BD18 .... 55 B8
Carperby Ct. Leeds LS16 .... 42 D3
Carr Bank. Otley LS21 .... 10 F2
Carr Bank. Keigh BD20 .... 19 C1
Carr Bank. Otley LS21 .... 11 A2
Carr Bottom Ave. Brad BD5 ...... 74 C2
Carr Bottom Fold. Brad BD5 ..... 74 D2
Carr Bottom Gr. Brad BD5 .... 74 D2
Carr Bottom Rd. Brad BD5 .... 56 E7
Carr Bottom Rd. Brad BD5 .... 74 D2
Carr Bridge Ave. Hors LS16 .... 41 D3
Carr Bridge Cl. Hors LS16 .... 41 D3
Carr Bridge Dr. Hors LS16 .... 41 D3
Carr Bridge View. Hors LS16 ..... 41 D3
Carr Cl. Yeadon LS19 .... 40 D3
Carr Crofts Dr. Leeds LS12 .... 77 D7
Carr Crofts. Leeds LS12 .... 77 D7
Carr Field Dr. Hali HX2 .... 111 E8
Carr Gate Cres. Loft G WF2 .... 120 D5
Carr Gate Dr. Loft G WF2 .... 120 D5
Carr Gate Mount. Loft G WF2 .... 120 D5

Carr Gr. Keigh BD20 .... 19 A1
Carr Green Ave. Brig HD6 .... 135 F6
Carr Green Cl. Brig HD6 .... 135 F6
Carr Green Dr. Brig HD6 .... 135 F6
Carr Green La. Brig HD6 .... 135 F6
Carr Green La. Brig & Sch. Brig .. 135 F7
Carr Green La. Brig HD6 .... 135 F7
Carr Green La. Hud HD5 .... 154 D6
Carr Hall La. Elland HX4 .... 134 A4
Carr Hall Rd. Brad BD12 .... 94 B6
Carr Head La. S in Cra BD20 ...... 16 A4
Carr Hill Ave. Pudsey LS28 .... 57 A6
Carr Hill Dr. Pudsey LS28 .... 57 A6
Carr Hill Gr. Pudsey LS28 .... 57 A6
Carr Hill Nook. Pudsey LS28 ..... 57 A6
Carr Hill Rd. D Dale HD8 .... 191 A6
Carr Hill Rd. Pudsey LS28 .... 57 A6
Carr Hill Rise. Pudsey LS28 .... 57 A6
Carr House Fold. Tod OL14 .... 129 D1
Carr House Gate. Brad BD12 ..... 94 C4
Carr House La. Brad BD12 .... 94 C4
Carr House Gr. Brad BD12 .... 94 C4
Carr House La. Brad BD12 .... 94 C4
Carr House La. Shelf HX3 .... 93 D7
Carr House La. Tod OL14 .... 108 D6
Carr House Mount. Brad BD12 ... 94 C4
Carr House Rd. Holmfi HD7 ...... 189 A5
Carr House Rd. Shelf HX3 .... 93 D7
Carr House. Wake WF1 .... 142 C6
Carr Houses. M'town LS26 .... 123 D8
Carr La. Bing BD16 .... 36 E8
Carr La. Brad BD12 .... 94 D5
Carr La. Castle WF10 .... 124 F5
Carr La. Denh BD13 .... 52 E2
Carr La. Dew WF16 .... 117 E1
Carr La. Dew WF12, WF13 .... 157 C8
Carr La. Hem WF4 .... 162 F2
Carr La. Holmfi HD7 .... 188 B4
Carr La. Ingb S30 .... 192 C1
Carr La. Keigh BD20 .... 19 A1
Carr La. Keigh BD20 .... 36 C8
Carr La. Neth WF4 .... 158 A4
Carr La. Roth WF3 .... 100 E3
Carr La. Shep HD8 .... 190 F6
Carr La. Ship BD18 .... 55 A7
Carr La. Slai HD7 .... 152 A1
Carr La. Thorner LS14 .... 45 D5
Carr La. Wake WF2 .... 160 E7
Carr La. Wake WF2 .... 141 C6
Carr Lane Ave. Castle WF10 .... 124 E5
Carr Manor Ave. Leeds LS17 ...... 43 B1
Carr Manor Cty Prim Sch. Leeds .. 60 B8
Carr Manor Cres. Leeds LS17 ..... 43 B1
Carr Manor Croft. Leeds LS17 .... 60 B8
Carr Manor Dr. Leeds LS17 .... 43 B1
Carr Manor Gdns. Leeds LS17 .... 60 B8
Carr Manor Garth. Leeds LS17 ... 43 B1
Carr Manor Gr. Leeds LS7 .... 60 A8
Carr Manor Gr. Leeds LS17 .... 60 B8
Carr Manor Mount. Leeds LS17 .. 60 B8
Carr Manor Par. Leeds LS17 ...... 60 B8
Carr Manor Pl. Leeds LS17 .... 60 B8
Carr Manor Rd. Leeds LS17 .... 60 B8
Carr Manor View. Leeds LS17 .... 60 B8
Carr Moor Side. Leeds LS11 .... 79 C3
Carr Moor St. Leeds LS10 .... 79 D2
Carr Mount. D Dale HD8 .... 191 A6
Carr Rd. Brad BD12 .... 94 C3
Carr Rd. Pudsey LS28 .... 57 A7
Carr Rd. Tod OL14 .... 107 A8
Carr Side Cres. Batley WF17 ...... 118 C2
Carr St. Batley WF17 .... 96 E1
Carr St. Batley WF15 .... 117 C4 3
Carr St. Batley WF17 .... 118 C2
Carr St. Brad BD5 .... 74 D2
Carr St. Brig HD6 .... 115 B4
Carr St. Cleck BD19 .... 116 D7
Carr St. Hud HD3 .... 153 A4
Carr St. Keigh BD20 .... 35 C7
Carr St. Liver WF15 .... 117 B3
Carr Top Cl. Batley WF17 .... 118 B2
Carr Top La. Hud HD7 .... 152 D4
Carr View Rd. Holmfi HD7 .... 189 F2
Carr View. S Kirk WF9 .... 182 C3
Carr Wood Cl. Pudsey LS28 .... 57 A7
Carr Wood Gdns. Pudsey LS28 ... 57 A7
Carr Wood Ind Est. Castle 124 F5
Carr Wood Rd. Castle WF10 ...... 124 F5
Carr Wood Way. Pudsey LS28 .... 57 A7
Carr's Cl. Batley WF13 .... 117 F3
Carrbottom Rd. B in Elm LS15 ... 63 D7
Carfield La. B in Elm LS15 .... 63 D7
Carfield Rd. B in Elm LS15 .... 63 D7
Carfield Villas. Tod OL14 .... 108 A1
Cargate. Hem WF9 .... 163 B2
Carholm Cres. Leeds LS7 .... 60 B7
Carholm Dr. Leeds LS7 .... 60 B7
Carholm Mount. Leeds LS7 .... 60 B7
Carholm View. Leeds LS7 .... 60 B7
Carlidge Dr. Hali HX1 .... 113 A6
Carriage Dr The. Elland HX4 ..... 134 A4
Carriage Dr The. Leeds LS8 .... 61 A6
Carriage Dr The. Elland HX4 ..... 134 C8
Carriers Cl. Brad BD12 .... 94 E6
Carrier's La. Hali HX1 .... 113 C7 17
Carrington St. Brad BD3 .... 75 C7
Carrington Terr. Guise LS20 ...... 39 D8
Carroll Ct. S Elm WF9 .... 182 E3
Carrs Side St No 1. Mars HD7 .... 169 A4
Carrs Side St No 2. Mars HD7 .... 169 A4
Carrs St. Mars HD7 .... 169 A4
Carter Ave. Leeds LS15 .... 81 C8
Carter La. Leeds LS15 .... 81 C8
Carter La. Queen BD13 .... 72 D7
Carter Mount. Leeds LS15 .... 81 C8
Carter St. Brad BD4 .... 75 C7
Carter Terr. Leeds LS15 .... 81 C8
Carter's La. B in Elm LS15 .... 62 C1 4
Cartmel Rd. Keigh BD21 .... 35 B8
Cartmell Dr. Leeds LS15 .... 80 D7
Cartwell House. Brad BD3 .... 75 D7 7
Cartworth La. Holmfi HD7 .... 189 A3
Cartworth Moor Rd. Holmfi HD7 . 189 A2
Cartworth Rd. Holmfi HD7 .... 189 A4
Cartwright Memorial Hall. Brad .. 55 D2

Cartwright St. Liver BD19 .... 116 F6
Carver St. Cleck BD19 .... 116 D8
Caryl Rd. Brad BD4 .... 75 A3
Cashmere Cl. Keigh BD21 .... 35 A7
Cashford Snowthorne Inf Sch.
  Castle 124 D6
Casson Ave. E Ard WF3 .... 99 B1
Casson Dr. E Ard WF3 .... 120 B8
Casson Gr. E Ard WF3 .... 99 B1
Casterton Gdns. Leeds LS14 ...... 62 A3
Castle Ave. Brig HD6 .... 135 F8
Castle Ave. Hud HD4 .... 154 A1
Castle Ave. Wake WF2 .... 142 D2
Castle Carr Rd. Hali HX2 .... 90 D6
Castle Cl. Meth WF4 .... 70 A1
Castle Cl. Batley WF17 .... 118 D3
Castle Cl. Hali HX3 .... 113 A3
Castle Croft. Harden BD16 .... 36 A1
Castle Croft. Keigh BD21 .... 35 C8 1
Castle Croft. Meth WF4 .... 85 C3
Castle Gate. Keigh BD21 .... 35 C8
Castle Gate. Ilkley LS29 .... 8 B4
Castle Gate. Loft G LS26 .... 122 A8
Castle Gate. Weth LS22 .... 13 C5
Castle Gr. Bard LS17 .... 28 D3
Castle Gr. Harden BD16 .... 36 A1
Castle Grove Ave. Leeds LS6 ..... 59 D6
Castle Grove Dr. Leeds LS6 .... 59 D6
Castle Grove Fst Sch. Wake 142 E2
Castle Head Cl. Meth WF3 .... 100 C1
Castle Head La. Loft G WF3 ...... 121 A6
Castle Head. Wake HD6 .... 135 F8
Castle Hill. Ilkley LS29 .... 8 B4
Castle Hill Jun & Inf Sch. Tod 108 D6
Castle Hill Side. Hud HD4 .... 172 C6
Castle Hill View. Batley WF16 ... 117 F3
Castle Hill. Wake WF2 .... 141 C4
Castle Ings Cl. Leeds LS12 .... 77 A7
Castle Ings Dr. Leeds LS12 .... 77 A7
Castle Ings Gdns. Leeds LS12 ..... 77 A7
Castle Ings Gdns. Gild LS12 ...... 77 D2
Castle La. Rip HX6 .... 132 C3
Castle La. Slai HD7 .... 151 C8
Castle La. Tod OL14 .... 108 D6
Castle Mount. Wake WF2 .... 142 D2
Castle One Cl. Tod OL14 .... 108 D6
Castle Pl. Brig HD6 .... 135 F8
Castle Rd. Ilkley LS29 .... 8 B4
Castle Rd. Keigh BD21 .... 35 C8
Castle Rd. Roth LS26 .... 100 C5
Castle Rd. W. Wake WF2 .... 142 D2
Castle Rd. Wake WF2 .... 142 E1
Castle Sch The. Tod 107 F4
Castle St. Brad BD5 .... 74 D5
Castle St. Castle WF10 .... 125 C7
Castle St. Hali HX1 .... 203 F3
Castle St. Leeds LS1 .... 211 D4
Castle Syke Hill. Ack M T WF8 .. 146 B3
Castle Syke View. Pont WF8 ...... 146 B3
Castle Terr. Wake WF2 .... 160 D6
Castle View. Horkley HD7 .... 171 F3
Castle View. Leeds LS17 .... 43 A3
Castle View. Meth WF4 .... 138 B5
Castle View. Pont WF8 .... 146 B3
Castle Wood Cl. Hare LS17 .... 27 D6
Castle Wood Cl. Hors LS18 .... 58 D8
Castle Yd. Ilkley LS29 .... 8 B4
Castlefield Cl. Castle WF10 .... 124 B7
Castlefield Rd. Bing BD16 .... 36 F5
Castlefields Dr. Bing BD16 .... 36 E5
Castlefields Ind Est. Bing 36 D5
Castlefields La. Bing BD16 .... 36 F5
Castlefields Rd. Bing BD16 .... 36 E5
Castleford Glasshoughton Fst Sch.
  Castle 124 F7
Castleford High Sch. Castle 124 F7
Castleford La. Feath WF7 .... 124 B2
Castleford La. Feath WF7 .... 145 D5
Castleford Normanton & District
  Hospl (General). Castle 124 A8
Castleford Oyster Park Jun Sch.
  Castle 125 D8
Castleford Rd. Nor WF6 .... 123 C2
Castleford Sta. Castle 124 D7
Castleford Three Lane Ends Fst &
  Mid Schs. Castle 124 A8
Castleford Whitwood Fst Sch.
  Castle 123 F5
Castlegate Dr. Pont WF8 .... 146 C6
Castlegate. Hud HD1 .... 154 B6
Castle Syke Hill. Elland HX5 ..... 134 F7
Castlegate Loop. Hud HD1 .... 154 A6
Castlegate Slip. Hud HD1 .... 154 A6
Castlemere Rd. Bail BD17 .... 38 D7
Castlerigg Bn. Brad BD6 .... 93 F6
Castleton Cl. Leeds LS12 .... 78 D7
Castleton Dr. Bacup OL13 .... 106 B3
Castleton Rd. Leeds LS12 .... 78 D7
Cat Hill La. Pen S30 .... 192 D1
Cat La. Dew WF13 .... 138 B5
Cathedral St. Elland HX5 .... 134 F7
Cather Wks. Elland HX5 .... 134 F6

Catherine St. Hem WF9 .... 163 A4
Catherine St. Keigh BD21 .... 35 B5 5
Catlow St. Castle WF10 .... 124 C7
Cattle Market St. Otley LS21 ..... 23 A8
Cattle La. Aber LS25 .... 64 E7
Cattlelaith La. Knot WF11 .... 126 D2
Caudle Hill. Fair WF11 .... 104 F4
Caulms Wood Rd. Dew WF13 ..... 118 E4 2
Causeway Cres. Slai HD7 .... 152 D1
Causeway Gdns. Leeds LS14 ...... 62 A3
Causeway Garth La. Th Aud WF8 . 165 C4
Causeway Head La. Rip HX6 ...... 113 D7
Causeway Head La. Rip HX6 ...... 132 B5
Causeway. Rip HX6 .... 133 A2
Causeway Side. Slai HD7 .... 152 D1
Causeway. Slai HD7 .... 151 F4
Cautley Rd. Leeds LS9 .... 80 B6
Cavalier App. Leeds LS9 .... 79 F6
Cavalier Cl. Leeds LS9 .... 79 F6
Cavalier Ct. Leeds LS9 .... 79 F6
Cavalier Dr. Brad BD10 .... 56 E8
Cavalier Gate. Leeds LS9 .... 79 F6
Cavalier Gdns. Leeds LS9 .... 79 F6
Cavalier Gr. Leeds LS9 .... 79 F6
Cave Cres. Wake WF2 .... 141 E4
Cave La. E Ard WF3 .... 120 C7
Cave Hill. Northo HX3 .... 92 F4
Cave La. E Ard WF3 .... 120 C7
Cavendish Ct. Brad BD10 .... 56 C5
Cavendish Dr. Guise LS20 .... 39 D8
Cavendish Dr. Guise LS20 .... 39 D8
Cavendish Fst Sch. Brad 56 D5
Cavendish Gr. Guise LS20 .... 39 D8
Cavendish Mews. Leeds LS17 .... 43 U4
Cavendish Pl. Pudsey LS28 .... 57 E1
Cavendish Rd. Brad BD10 .... 56 C5
Cavendish Rd. Guise LS20 .... 39 D8
Cavendish Rd. Leeds LS3 .... 60 B2
Cavendish Rise. Pudsey LS28 ..... 77 A7
Cavendish Sq. Pudsey LS28 .... 57 E1
Cavendish St. Keigh BD21 .... 35 C7 2
Cavendish St. Yeadon LS19 .... 40 C7 3
Cavendish St. Leeds LS3 .... 78 C8
Cavewell Cl. Ossett WF5 .... 140 E3
Cavewell Gdns. Ossett WF5 ...... 140 F3
Cawcliffe Dr. Brig HD6 .... 115 A4
Cawcliffe Rd. Brig HD6 .... 115 A5
Cawood Garth. Batley WF16 ..... 117 E3
Cawley La. Batley WF16 .... 117 E3
Cawood Haven. Brad BD6 .... 93 E8
Cawthorne Ave. Hud HD2 .... 136 C5
Cawthorne CE Prim Sch. Caw 193 F6
Cawthorne Ct. Wake WF2 .... 160 A6
Cawthorne La. Caw S75 .... 193 F5
Cawthorne Rd. Wake WF2 .... 160 B6
Caxton Rd. Otley LS21 .... 22 E7
Caxton St. Weth LS22 .... 13 E6
Caynott Nook. Hap HX7 .... 88 F5
Caygill Terr. Hali HX1 .... 203 E2
Cayton La. Wyke WF2 .... 141 A4
Cayton Wlk. Brad BD10 .... 56 B6
Cecil Ave. Bail BD17 .... 38 D4
Cecil Ave. Hali HX3 .... 91 F3
Cecil Gr. Leeds LS12 .... 78 C8 3
Cecil Mount. Leeds LS12 .... 78 C8 5
Cecil Rd. Leeds LS12 .... 78 C8
Cecil St. Haw BD22 .... 51 C6
Cecil St. Hud HD1 .... 154 A5 6
Cecil St. Leeds LS12 .... 78 C8 4
Cedar Ave. Hud HD1 .... 153 F7
Cedar Ave. Leeds LS12 .... 78 C8 7
Cedar Ave. Ossett WF5 .... 140 E4
Cedar Cl. Hud HD7 .... 152 D1
Cedar Cl. Leeds LS12 .... 78 C8 1
Cedar Cl. Pont WF8 .... 146 D5
Cedar Ct. Elland HX4 .... 134 D7
Cedar Ct. Feath WF7 .... 145 D7
Cedar Dr. Gar LS25 .... 82 F6
Cedar Dr. S Elm WF9 .... 182 F4
Cedar Gr. Bacup OL13 .... 106 A2
Cedar Gr. Elland HX4 .... 134 A4
Cedar Gr. Hem WF9 .... 181 D8
Cedar Mount. Hud HD1 .... 153 F7
Cedar Mount. Leeds LS12 .... 78 C8 2
Cedar Pl. Leeds LS12 .... 78 C8 6
Cedar Rd. Dew WF12 .... 139 C8
Cedar Rd. Leeds LS12 .... 78 C8
Cedar Rd. Nor WF6 .... 144 A8
Cedar Ridge. Gar LS25 .... 82 F6
Cedar St. Bing BD16 .... 37 A3
Cedar St. Hali HX1 .... 112 F6
Cedar St. Hud HD1 .... 153 F7
Cedar St. Keigh BD21 .... 35 B5
Cedar St. Leeds LS12 .... 78 C8
Cedar St. Tod OL14 .... 108 B5
Cedar Terr. Leeds LS12 .... 78 C8
Cedar Way. Clec BD19 .... 117 C8
Cedars The. Bramho LS16 .... 24 F2
Celandine Ave. Hud HD3 .... 153 B8
Celandine Cl. Pont WF8 .... 146 D7
Celandine Dr. Hud HD3 .... 153 B8
Cemetery La. Hali HX4 .... 112 A4
Cemetery La. Knot WF11 .... 127 B4
Cemetery Rd. Batley WF17 .... 118 C6
Cemetery Rd. Brad BD7 .... 74 A5
Cemetery Rd. Dew WF13 .... 139 B7
Cemetery Rd. Leeds LS11 .... 79 A3
Cemetery Rd. Pudsey LS28 .... 76 F7
Cemetery Rd. Ryhill WF4 .... 162 A1
Cemetery Rd. Yeadon LS19 .... 40 B5
Centenary Rd. Bing BD16 .... 37 A2
Centenary Sq. Brad BD1 .... 201 B2
Centenary Way. Brad BD24 .... 55 B7
Central Arc. Clec BD19 .... 116 F7
Central Ave. Bail BD17 .... 38 C1
Central Ave. Brad BD5 .... 74 D4
Central Ave. Hud HD7 .... 152 E8
Central Ave. Ship BD18 .... 55 B7

Central Ave. Keigh BD22 .... 34 F3
Central Ave. S Elm WF9 .... 182 F2
Central Ave. Ship BD18 .... 55 B7
Central Cl. Hud HD2 .... 136 B3
Central Dr. Castle WF10 .... 124 A7
Central Dr. Castle WF10 .... 124 A7
Central Dr. Hud HD2 .... 136 B3
Central Dr. Keigh BD22 .... 34 F3
Central Par. Leeds LS9 .... 80 C8
Central Par. Clec BD19 .... 116 E7 6
Central Pk. Hali HX1 .... 113 A5
Central Pl. Leeds LS9 .... 79 B6
Central Rd. Hud HD2 .... 136 B3
Central Rd. Leeds LS2 .... 211 F3
Central St. Dew WF13 .... 139 C8
Central St. Hali HX1 .... 113 C7 10
Central St. Leeds LS1 .... 211 E3
Central View. Bacup OL13 .... 106 A2
Centre 27 Bsns Pk. Batley 97 B3
Centre St. Brad BD5 .... 74 C3 4
Centre St. Hem WF9 .... 181 D8
Centre St. Hali HX1 .... 117 C4 1
Centre St. S Elm WF9 .... 183 A3
Centre St. Dew WF13 .... 139 C8
Century Rd. Elland HX5 .... 134 F7
Ceres Rd. Weth LS22 .... 14 A5
Chaddlewood Cl. Hors LS18 ...... 41 C1
Chadwell Springs. Shop BD16 ... 54 A7
Chadwick La. Mir WF14 .... 137 F3
Chadwick St. Leeds LS10 .... 79 D6
Chadwick St. Leeds LS10 .... 212 C2 6
Chaffinch Wlk. Hud HD4 .... 171 E7
Chain. Mars HD7 .... 169 C5
Chain. Mel HD7 .... 170 A5
Chain Rd. Mel HD7 .... 169 F6
Chain St. Brad BD1 .... 74 D7
Chain St. Castle WF10 .... 124 C8
Chain St. Castle WF10 .... 124 C8
Chalcroft Cl. Batley WF16 .... 117 E3
Chald La. Wake WF2 .... 142 B5
Chalfont Rd. Leeds LS16 .... 59 B8
Chalice Cl. Midd LS10 .... 99 E7
Challenge Way. Batley WF12 ..... 119 A3
Challenger Cres. Dearne S63 ..... 194 D1
Challis Gr. Brad BD5 .... 74 E3
Chalner Ave. Morley LS27 .... 97 F2
Challenger Dr. Leeds LS16 .... 97 F2
Chalwood. Hud HD2 .... 136 F4
Chancellor St. Leeds LS6 .... 60 C3
Chancery Cl. Hud HD1 .... 154 A6 19
Chancery La. Hali HX1 .... 154 A4
Chancery La. Wake WF1 .... 142 C6 4
Chancery Rd. Ossett WF5 .... 140 D6
Chandler Cl. Batley WF17 .... 96 E1
Chandler La. Honley HD7 .... 171 D4
Chandlers Cl. Loft G WF1 .... 121 A5
Chandlers The. Leeds LS22 .... 79 D7
Chandos Ave. Leeds LS8 .... 60 E6
Chandos Fold. Leeds LS8 .... 61 A6
Chandos Garth. Leeds LS8 .... 60 E6
Chandos Gdns. Leeds LS8 .... 61 A5
Chandos Gr. Leeds LS8 .... 60 E6
Chandos Pl. Leeds LS8 .... 61 A6
Chandos St. Brad BD4 .... 75 B4
Chandos St. Keigh BD21 .... 35 B5 4
Chandos Terr. Leeds LS8 .... 61 A6
Chandos Wlk. Leeds LS8 .... 61 A6
Change Way. Bacup OL13 .... 106 B4
Changegate Ct. Haw BD22 .... 51 B7
Changegate. Haw BD22 .... 51 B7
Channing Way. Brad BD1 .... 74 E7
Chantry Bridge Ind Est. Wake .. 142 D5
Chantry Cl. Ilkley LS29 .... 8 D3
Chantry Croft. Leeds LS15 .... 81 D7 8
Chantry Cl. Pont WF8 .... 146 B7
Chantry Dr. Ilkley LS29 .... 8 D4
Chantry Garth. Leeds LS15 .... 81 D7
Chantry Gr. Roy S71 .... 179 C3
Chantry La. Stut LS24 .... 48 F5
Chapel Allerton Hospl. Leeds 60 D6
Chapel Allerton Prim Sch. Leeds . 60 D6
Chapel Ave. Batley WF16 .... 117 E3
Chapel Bank. Holmfi HD7 .... 189 A3
Chapel Cl. Brad BD10 .... 56 C7
Chapel Cl. Brad BD10 .... 56 C8
Chapel Cl. Gar LS25 .... 82 F7
Chapel Cl. Hud HD7 .... 152 D1
Chapel Cl. Loft G WF1 .... 121 B5
Chapel Cl. Wake WF4 .... 162 B2
Chapel Cl. W Har WF9 .... 183 A6
Chapel Ct. Leeds LS15 .... 81 D7 9
Chapel Ct. Hal E BD23 .... 1 C4
Chapel Fold. Batley WF17 .... 118 B5
Chapel Fold. Brad BD6 .... 74 C1
Chapel Fold. Brad BD6 .... 93 F7 1
Chapel Fold. Brad BD7 .... 74 B6
Chapel Fold. Loft G WF1 .... 121 B5
Chapel Fold. Hud HD7 .... 152 C1 2
Chapel Garth. Ack M T WF7 ..... 164 A6
Chapel Gn. Pudsey LS28 .... 76 E7 8
Chapel Gr. Bing BD16 .... 36 E5
Chapel Gr. Grid LS12 .... 77 D3
Chapel Hill. Brad BD12 .... 94 C1
Chapel Hill. Clay W HD8 .... 175 F2
Chapel Hill. Hud HD1 .... 154 A5
Chapel Hill. Leeds LS6 .... 59 E5
Chapel Hill. Mir WF14 .... 138 A5
Chapel Hill. Sch HX6 .... 112 C5
Chapel Hill. Skel HD8 .... 175 A1
Chapel Hill. Yeadon LS19 .... 40 A5
Chapel House. Brad BD12 .... 94 C1
Chapel La. B Spa LS23 .... 30 D7
Chapel La. Birken BD11 .... 96 B5
Chapel La. Brad BD15 .... 54 A2
Chapel La. Gar LS25 .... 82 F7
Chapel La. Guise LS20 .... 22 E1
Chapel La. Hali HX3 .... 113 B4
Chapel La. Hali HX3 .... 92 A3
Chapel La. Hd Gr LS29 .... 9 E1
Chapel La. Hebden HX7 .... 88 F5
Chapel La. Hud HX1 .... 113 E1
Chapel La. Leeds LS6 .... 59 F5
Chapel La. Leeds LS12 .... 77 D3
Chapel La. Ledst WF10 .... 103 E6
Chapel La. Mapp S75 .... 178 C1
Chapel La. Midd LS10 .... 99 B5
Chapel La. Mir WF14 .... 138 A5
Chapel La. Yeadon LS19 .... 40 B6

Central Ave. Keigh BD22 .... 34 F3
Central Ave. S Elm WF9 .... 182 F2
Central Ave. Ship BD18 .... 55 B7
Central Ave. Keigh BD22 .... 34 A7
Central Dr. Castle WF10 .... 124 A7
Central Dr. Hud HD2 .... 136 B3
Central Dr. Keigh BD22 .... 34 F3
Central Par. Leeds LS9 .... 80 C8
Central Pk. Hali HX1 .... 113 A5
Central Rd. Leeds LS2 .... 211 F3
Central St. Hali HX1 .... 113 C7 10
Central St. Leeds LS1 .... 211 E3
Centre St. Hem WF9 .... 181 D8
Chadwick St S. Leeds LS10 .... 212 C2
Chapel Pl. Leeds LS6 .... 59 F5
Chapel Rd. Ship BD18 .... 55 A8
Chapel Row. Brad BD12 .... 94 E3
Chapel Royd Ave. Oss WF5 .... 140 E4
Chapel Sq. Leeds LS6 .... 59 E5
Chapel St. B Spa LS23 .... 30 C7
Chapel St. Batley WF17 .... 118 C5
Chapel St. Bing BD16 .... 37 A3
Chapel St. Birken BD11 .... 96 B5
Chapel St. Brad BD1 .... 201 C2
Chapel St. Brad BD15 .... 54 A3
Chapel St. Brad BD12 .... 94 C1
Chapel St. Brig HD6 .... 115 B2
Chapel St. Castle WF10 .... 124 C8
Chapel St. Cleck BD19 .... 116 E7
Chapel St. Dew WF13 .... 118 C1
Chapel St. E Ard WF3 .... 120 D8
Chapel St. Elland HX4 .... 134 B7
Chapel St. Guise LS20 .... 22 E1
Chapel St. Hali HX3 .... 92 A3
Chapel St. Heb Br HX7 .... 89 A3
Chapel St. Holmfi HD7 .... 189 A4
Chapel St. Hud HD1 .... 154 A5
Chapel St. Hud HD4 .... 171 D7
Chapel St. Knot WF11 .... 127 B4
Chapel St. Liver WF15 .... 117 B3
Chapel St. Liver WF15 .... 117 B4
Chapel St. Low U WF3 .... 121 B5
Chapel St. Mel HD7 .... 170 A1
Chapel St. Mir WF14 .... 138 A5
Chapel St. Morley LS27 .... 98 B4
Chapel St. Oaken WF8 .... 166 C6
Chapel St. Queen BD13 .... 72 E1
Chapel St. Roy S71 .... 179 C3
Chapel St. S Elm WF9 .... 182 F3
Chapel St. Slai HD7 .... 152 A1
Chapel St. Thornt BD13 .... 72 E6
Chapel St. Yeadon LS19 .... 40 B6
Chapeltown. Pudsey LS28 .... 76 E8
Chapeltown Rd. Leeds LS7 .... 206 C1
Chapman St. Brad BD4 .... 75 B5
Chapman St. Leeds LS9 .... 80 B7
Charles Ave. Brad BD3 .... 75 D7
Charles Ave. Hali HX3 .... 113 E7
Charles Ave. Hud HD5 .... 155 A4
Charles Ave. Leeds LS9 .... 80 B7
Charles Ct. Haw BD22 .... 51 C6
Charles Gr. Roth LS26 .... 100 D6
Charles Jones Ct. Wake WF1 .... 142 F3
Charles St. Batley WF17 .... 118 C5
Charles St. Bing BD16 .... 37 A3
Charles St. Brad BD12 .... 94 C3
Charles St. Brig HD6 .... 115 B2
Charles St. Castle WF10 .... 124 C8
Charles St. Cleck BD19 .... 116 D8
Charles St. Denholme BD13 ...... 52 E1
Charles St. Elland HX5 .... 134 F7
Charles St. Haw BD22 .... 51 C6
Charles St. Holmfi HD7 .... 189 A4
Charles St. Hud HD1 .... 154 B6
Charles St. Liver WF15 .... 117 A4
Charles St. Morley LS27 .... 98 B3
Charles St. Pudsey LS28 .... 76 E7
Charles St. Queen BD13 .... 72 E1
Charles St. S Elm WF9 .... 182 F3
Charles St. Shipley BD18 .... 55 B7
Charles St. Wake WF1 .... 216 B2
Charlesworth Cl. Hud HD5 .... 154 D6
Charlesworth Ct. Ossett WF5 .... 140 E3
Charlesworth Gr. Hali HX2 .... 112 B7
Charlesworth Pl. Hali HX3 .... 113 A3
Charlesworth St. Knot WF11 ..... 127 A4
Charlesworth Terr. Hali HX2 ..... 112 B7
Charlesworth Way. Wake WF2 ... 216 A1
Charlotte Cl. Hali HX3 .... 113 A3
Charlotte Ct. Haw BD22 .... 51 E7
Charlotte Gr. Leeds LS15 .... 81 B7
Charlotte St. Wake WF1 .... 216 C3
Charlton Gr. Leeds LS9 .... 80 B7
Charlton Mount. Leeds LS9 ...... 80 B7
Charlton Pl. Leeds LS9 .... 80 B7
Charlton Rd. Leeds LS9 .... 80 B7
Charlton St. Leeds LS9 .... 80 B7
Charnley Dr. Leeds LS7 .... 60 C6
Charnock House. Leeds LS15 .... 81 A8
Charnwood Bank. Mir WF14 ..... 137 F8
Charnwood Cl. Brad BD2 .... 56 C4
Charnwood Gr. Brad BD2 .... 56 C4
Charnwood Rd. Brad BD2 .... 56 C4
Charterhouse Rd. Brad BD10 .... 56 E8
Charteris Rd. Brad BD8 .... 73 C7
Chartists Way. Morley LS27 ..... 98 A4
Chase The. Gar LS25 .... 82 F6
Chase The. Leeds LS17 .... 43 D4
Chase The. Otley LS21 .... 23 B8
Chase The. Roy S71 .... 179 C1
Chase The. Shep HD8 .... 190 E8
Chase The. Ship BD18 .... 55 A6
Chase The. Wake WF2 .... 141 E4
Chassum Gr. Brad BD9 .... 54 F2
Chatham St. Brad BD3 .... 75 B7
Chatham St. Hali HX3 .... 92 A1
Chatsworth Ave. Pudsey LS28 ... 76 D6
Chatsworth Cl. Leeds LS8 .... 61 A6
Chatsworth Cres. Pudsey LS28 .. 76 D6
Chatsworth Dr. Pudsey LS28 .... 76 D6
Chatsworth Dr. Weth LS22 .... 13 F6
Chatsworth Fall. Pudsey LS28 ... 76 D6
Chatsworth Mews. Morley LS27 . 98 D6
Chatsworth Pl. Brad BD7 .... 74 A4
Chatsworth Rd. Leeds LS8 .... 61 A6
Chatsworth Rd. Pudsey LS28 .... 76 D6
Chatsworth Rise. Pudsey LS28 .. 76 D6
Chatsworth St. Keigh BD21 ...... 35 B5
Chatsworth Terr. Leeds LS12 .... 209 D4
Chatts Wood Fold. Brad BD12 ... 94 F7
Chaucer Ave. Pudsey LS28 .... 76 F5
Chaucer Gdns. Pudsey LS28 ..... 76 F5
Chaucer Gr. Pudsey LS28 .... 76 F5

Colliers Cl. Ship BD18 ... 54 E7
Colliers La. Thorner LS17 ... 44 E4
Collin Moor La. Elland HX4 ... 134 C8
Collin Rd. Leeds LS14 ... 61 F1
Collindale Cl. Brad BD10 ... 56 E6
Collinfield Rise. Brad BD6 ... 93 F8
Collingham Ave. Brad BD6 ... 93 E8
Collingham Dr. Gar LS25 ... 82 F6
Collingwood Rd. Mor WF6 ... 123 B2
Collins St. Brad BD7 ... 74 A3
Collins St. Brad BD4 ... 75 B4
Collinson St. Clec BD19 ... 116 D8
Collyer View. Ilkley LS29 ... 8 E5
Colmore Gr. Leeds LS12 ... 78 D6
Colmore Rd. Leeds LS12 ... 78 D6
Colne Hurst. Hud HD2 ... 136 E4
Colne Rd (Chapel La). Haw BD22 ... 34 C2
Colne Rd (Church St). Haw BD22 ... 34 B2
Colne Rd. Glu BD20 ... 16 B6
Colne Rd (Goodley). Haw BD22 ... 34 C2
Colne Rd. Hud HD1 ... 154 A4
Colne St. Hud HD1 ... 153 E4
Colne St. Hud HD1 ... 153 E4
Colne Vale Rd. Hud HD3 ... 153 A4
Colne Valley Bsns Pk. Slai ... 152 D1
Colne Valley Marsden Cty Jun Sch. Mars ... 169 A4
Colonel's Wlk. Pont WF8 ... 125 C1
Colston Cl. Brad BD8 ... 54 E1
Colton Croft. Leeds LS15 ... 81 D7
Colton Garth. Leeds LS15 ... 81 D7
Colton La. Leeds LS15 ... 81 D7
Colton Prim Sch. Leeds ... 81 E6
Colton Rd E. Leeds LS15 ... 81 E6
Colton Rd. Leeds LS15 ... 81 D6
Colton Rd. Leeds LS15 ... 81 C7
Colton Ret Pk. Leeds ... 81 E7
Colton St. Leeds LS15 ... 81 D6
Coltsfoot Cl. Pont WF8 ... 146 D7
Columbus St. Hali HX3 ... 92 A118
Colville Terr. E ard WF3 ... 99 E1
Colville Terr. Leeds LS11 ... 79 B4
Colwyn Ave. Leeds LS11 ... 79 B2 14
Colwyn Mount. Leeds LS11 ... 79 B2 15
Colwyn Pl. Leeds LS11 ... 79 B2 17
Colwyn Rd. Leeds LS11 ... 79 B2
Colwyn St. Hud HD1 ... 153 D7
Colwyn Terr. Feath WF7 ... 145 D6
Colwyn Terr. Leeds LS11 ... 79 B2 18
Colwyn View. Leeds LS11 ... 79 B2 12
Colyton. Brad BD15 ... 54 A1
Combs Hill Sch. Dew ... 139 F3
Combs The. Dew WF12 ... 139 E3
Combs The. Dew WF12 ... 139 E3
Comet St. Bacup OL13 ... 106 A4 4
Comet St. Hali HX3 ... 203 F4 5
Commercial Bdgs. Brad BD12 ... 95 B4
Commercial Rd. Dew WF13 ... 118 C1
Commercial Rd. Leeds LS5 ... 59 A3
Commercial Rd. Skel HU8 ... 175 A2
Commercial St. Batley WF16 ... 117 D4
Commercial St. Batley WF17 ... 118 C5
Commercial St. Brig HD6 ... 115 B2
Commercial St. Castle WF10 ... 124 D8 8
Commercial St. Clec BD19 ... 116 E7
Commercial St. Denh BD13 ... 71 D8
Commercial St. Dew WF13 ... 138 F6
Commercial St. Dew WF12 ... 139 C7
Commercial St. Hali HX1 ... 113 C7
Commercial St. Heb B HX7 ... 89 A3
Commercial St. Hud HD1 ... 154 B5
Commercial St. Leeds LS1 ... 79 B7
Commercial St. Morley LS27 ... 98 B4
Commercial St. Queen BD13 ... 72 D1 4
Commercial St. Roth LS26 ... 100 F5
Commercial St. Ship BD18 ... 55 B8
Commercial St. Slai HU7 ... 169 D8
Commercial St. Tod OL14 ... 108 D6
Commercial Vills. Pudsey LS28 ... 76 D6
Common End La. Lepton HD8 ... 155 E3
Common Holme La. Nes LS29 ... 7 C6
Common Ing La. Kippa LS25 ... 83 D8
Common La. Dar WF8 ... 147 C6
Common La. D Dale HD8 ... 192 B6
Common La. E Ard WF3 ... 99 C1
Common La. Emley HD8 ... 174 E2
Common La. Hali HX3 ... 113 F5
Common La. Knot WF11 ... 127 B4
Common La. Roy S71 ... 179 C5
Common La. Th aud WF8 ... 165 B3
Common Rd. Batley WF17 ... 96 F1
Common Rd. Wilsd ... 177 D8
Common Rd. Batley WF17 ... 117 C4
Common Rd. Brad BD12 ... 94 C5
Common Rd. Bri S72 ... 181 B2
Common Rd. Elland HX5 ... 135 C6
Common Rd. Hem WF9 ... 163 A2
Common Rd. Hud HD1 ... 154 A8 5
Common Rd. S Kirk WF9 ... 181 E1
Common Road Ave. S Kirk WF9 ... 182 A3
Common Road End. Brad ... 94 D6
Common Side La. Feath WF7 ... 164 A6
Common Terr. Brig HD6 ... 115 A1
Common The. Dew WF12 ... 139 E3
Commondale Way. Brad BD4 ... 95 B8
Commonside. Batley WF17 ... 118 C3
Commonside. Liver FW15 ... 116 E2
Como Ave. Brad BD8 ... 54 F1 3
Como Dr. Brad BD8 ... 54 F1 2
Como Gdns. Brad BD8 ... 54 F1
Como Gr. Brad BD8 ... 54 F1 2
Compeigne Ave. Keigh BD21 ... 18 F1
Compton Ave. Leeds LS9 ... 61 A2
Compton Cres. Leeds LS9 ... 61 A2
Compton La. Bard LS22 ... 28 A6
Compton Mount. Leeds LS9 ... 61 A2
Compton Pl. Leeds LS9 ... 61 A2
Compton Rd. Leeds LS9 ... 61 A2
Compton Row. Leeds LS9 ... 61 A2
Compton St. Keigh BD21 ... 35 D8
Compton St. Leeds LS9 ... 61 A2
Compton Terr. Leeds LS9 ... 61 A2
Concord St. Leeds LS2 ... 60 D1
Concordia St. Leeds LS1 ... 79 C7
Concrete St. Hali HX3 ... 92 A1 27

Conduit St. Brad BD8 ... 55 C1
Coney La. Keigh BD21 ... 35 C7
Coney Moor Gr. M'town LS26 ... 102 F3
Coney Warren La. Loft G WF3 ... 121 E8
Coney Wlk. Dew WF13 ... 138 F8
Conference Gr. Leeds LS12 ... 78 A7
Conference Pl. Leeds LS12 ... 78 A7
Conference Rd. Leeds LS12 ... 78 A7
Conference Terr. Leeds LS12 ... 78 A7
Congress Mount. Leeds LS12 ... 78 A7
Congress St. Leeds LS12 ... 78 A7
Congreve App. Bard LS17 ... 28 E6
Congreve Way. Bard LS17 ... 28 E6
Conisborough La. Gar LS25 ... 83 B7
Coniston Ave. Hud HD5 ... 154 D6
Coniston Ave. Leeds LS6 ... 59 E5 2
Coniston Cl. Elland HX5 ... 135 B7
Coniston Cl. Queen BD13 ... 92 D7
Coniston Ct. Elland HX5 ... 135 B7
Coniston Dr. Castle WF10 ... 125 E7
Coniston Gr. Bail BD17 ... 37 F1
Coniston Gr. Brad BD9 ... 54 F2
Coniston House. Brook LS14 ... 134 F7 15
Coniston Pl. Knot WF11 ... 126 E1
Coniston Rd. Batley WF12 ... 118 E7
Coniston Rd. Brad BD7 ... 73 E3 4
Coniston Rd. Mel HD7 ... 170 E1
Coniston Rd. Roth LS26 ... 101 C6
Coniston Way. Wsett LS22 ... 13 B5
Conistone Cres. Wake WF1 ... 142 E8
Connaught Fold. Hud HD2 ... 136 E5
Connaught Rd. Ilkley LS29 ... 8 D3
Cononley Cty Prim Sch. Con ... 4 A3
Cononley La. Con BD20 ... 4 B2
Cononley Rd. Glu BD20 ... 16 B8
Consort St. Leeds LS3 ... 59 F1
Consort Terr. Leeds LS3 ... 59 F1
Consort View. Leeds LS3 ... 59 F1
Consort Wlk. Leeds LS3 ... 59 F1
Constable Gr. Loft G WF3 ... 121 E6
Constable Rd. E arsd WF3 ... 119 F8
Constable Rd. Ilkley LS29 ... 8 E3
Constance Way. Brad BD8 ... 54 F8
Constitutional St. Hali HX1 ... 143 A5 2
Convent Ave. S Kirk WF9 ... 182 C2
Conway Ave. Leeds LS8 ... 60 F3
Conway Cres. Batley WF17 ... 118 C2
Conway Dr. Leeds LS8 ... 60 F3
Conway Gr. Leeds LS8 ... 60 F3
Conway House. Brad BD15 ... 73 B7 2
Conway Mount. Leeds LS8 ... 60 F3
Conway Pl. Leeds LS8 ... 61 A3
Conway Rd. Leeds LS8 ... 61 A3
Conway St. Wake WF2 ... 141 E7
Conway St. Brad BD4 ... 74 F5
Conway St. Hali HX1 ... 113 A6
Conway Terr. Leeds LS8 ... 60 F3
Cook La. Liver WF16 ... 117 C4
Cooke Cres. Clec BD19 ... 117 B8
Cooke La. Keigh BD21 ... 35 C7 3
Cooke St. Keigh BD21 ... 35 C7 2
Cookridge Ave. Hors LS16 ... 41 F5
Cookridge Cty Prim Sch. Hors ... 41 F5
Cookridge Dr. Hors LS16 ... 41 F5
Cookridge Gr. Hors LS16 ... 41 F5
Cookridge Hospl. Hors ... 41 E2
Cookridge La. Hors LS16 ... 41 E8
Cookridge St. Leeds LS2 ... 79 B8
Cookson Cl. Castle WF10 ... 125 D5
Cookson St. Brig HD6 ... 114 F3
Coombe Rd. Hud HD3 ... 135 B1
Coombe Rd. I lud BD3 ... 75 D5
Cooper Bridge Rd. Hud WF14 ... 137 B6
Cooper Cl. Bing BD16 ... 37 B2
Cooper Fields. Hali HX2 ... 111 E6
Cooper Gr. Chelf HX3 ... 93 D7
Cooper Hill. Pudsey LS28 ... 76 F5
Cooper La. Brad BD6 ... 93 D6
Cooper La. Shelf BD6, HX3 ... 93 D6
Cooper Lane Fst Sch. Brad ... 93 C6
Cooper St. Weth LS22 ... 13 F1
Cooperative St. Tod OL14 ... 108 C6
Cop Hill End. Mars HD7 ... 169 C6
Cop Hill La. Mars HD7 ... 169 B8
Cop Hill Side. Mars HD7 ... 169 C6
Copeworth Dr. Crig WF4 ... 159 F3
Copgrove Cl. Brad BD4 ... 75 E3
Copgrove Ct. Brad BD4 ... 75 E3
Copgrove Rd. Brad BD4 ... 75 E3
Copgrove Rd. Leeds LS8 ... 61 C7
Copley Ave. Hali HX2 ... 112 F5
Copley Ave. Mel HD7 ... 170 C2
Copley Bank Rd. Slai HD7 ... 152 A6
Copley Cl. Hali HX3 ... 113 B3
Copley Glen. Hali HX3 ... 113 B3
Copley Hall St. Hali HX3 ... 113 B3
Copley Hill. Batley WF17 ... 118 C3
Copley Hill. Leeds LS12 ... 78 E6
Copley La. Terr. Hali HX3 ... 113 B3
Copley La. Kippax LS26 ... 102 E4
Copley La. Leeds LS12 ... 78 E6
Copley La. Aber LS25 ... 65 B2
Copley La. Shelf HX3 ... 93 C1
Copley La. Saxton LS25 ... 65 B2
Copley La. Shelf BD6, HX3 ... 93 D1
Copley Mill View. Elland HX3 ... 113 B3
Copley Mount. Hali HX3 ... 113 B3
Copley St. Batley WF17 ... 118 C3
Copley St. Leeds LS12 ... 78 E6
Copley Terr. Hali HX3 ... 113 B3
Copley View. Hali HX3 ... 113 B3
Copmanroyd. Otley LS21 ... 11 A1
Copper Beech Cl. Pont WF8 ... 146 E6
Copperas House Terr. Tod OL14 ... 108 A7
Copperas Row. Elland HX4 ... 133 F3
Copperfield Ave. Leeds LS9 ... 79 F6

Copperfield Cres. Leeds LS9 ... 79 F6 20
Copperfield Dr. Leeds LS9 ... 79 F6 21
Copperfield Gr. Leeds LS9 ... 80 A6 4
Copperfield Mount. Leeds LS9 ... 80 A6 3
Copperfield Pl. Leeds LS9 ... 79 F6 22
Copperfield Row. Leeds LS9 ... 79 F6 23
Copperfield Terr. Leeds LS9 ... 80 A6
Copperfield View. Leeds LS9 ... 79 F6 18
Copperfield Wlk. Leeds LS9 ... 79 F6 23
Coppice Cl. Wake WF1 ... 142 E8
Coppice Dr. Hud HD4 ... 171 D6
Coppice Dr. B in Elm LS15 ... 63 D6
Coppice The. Glu BD20 ... 16 C6
Coppice The. Hud HD2 ... 136 B4
Coppice The. Ilkley LS29 ... 8 A6
Coppice The. Mir WF14 ... 138 A8
Coppice The. Yeadon LS19 ... 39 F5
Coppice The. Yeadon LS19 ... 40 B8
Coppice View. Brad BD10 ... 56 B6
Coppice Way. Leeds LS8 ... 61 A6
Coppice Wood Ave. Brad BD7 ... 74 A6
Coppice Wood Cl. Guise LS20 ... 23 A1
Coppice Wood Cres. Yeadon LS19 ... 23 C1
Coppice Wood Gr. Brad BD7 ... 74 A6
Coppice Wood Gr. Yeadon LS20 ... 40 A8
Coppice Wood Rise. Yeadon LS19 ... 40 A8
Coppies The. Brad BD12 ... 94 B4
Coppin Hall Gr. Mir WF14 ... 137 D6
Coppin Hall La. Mir WF14 ... 137 D6
Copp Cl. Ship BD16 ... 54 A6
Coppy La. Haw BD22 ... 33 C7
Coppy La. Leeds LS13 ... 58 C4
Coppy La. Wad M BB10 ... 68 F3
Coppy Rd. Sut Cr BD20 ... 5 A1
Coppy Rd. Stee BD20 ... 17 B5
Copse The. Bing BD16 ... 37 B3
Copse The. Brad BD19 ... 115 F7
Copse The. Feath WF7 ... 124 C1
Copt Royd Gr. Yeadon LS19 ... 40 A7
Copthorne Fst Sch. Brad ... 74 C5
Copthorne Gdns. Hud HD2 ... 136 B5
Copthurst Rd. Holme HD7 ... 198 E7
Copy Bottom. H Chap BB10 ... 85 C2
Corban St. Brad BD4 ... 75 C3
Corby St. Hud HD2 ... 136 A1
Cordingley Cl. Brad BD4 ... 75 E1
Cordingley St. Brad BD4 ... 75 E1
Corfe Cl. Batley WF17 ... 97 B2
Corn Bank. Hud HD4 ... 171 C6
Corn Exchange. Leeds LS1 ... 79 C7 3
Corn Market. Hali HX1 ... 113 C7 19
Corn Market. Pont WF8 ... 146 C8
Corn Mill Ct. Leeds LS13 ... 77 C7
Corn Mill La. Otley BD20 ... 10 A3
Corn Mill La. Thorn BD13 ... 72 F5
Corn Mill. Men LS29 ... 22 A4
Corn. St. Keigh BD21 ... 35 A4 6
Cornfield Ave. Hud HD3 ... 153 A4
Cornfield St. Tod OL14 ... 108 D6
Cornforth Gr. Keigh BD22 ... 34 F5
Cornholme Terr. Tod OL14 ... 86 A1
Cornmill Ave. Liver WF15 ... 117 C3
Cornmill Cl. Bard LS17 ... 28 D3
Cornmill Cres. Liver WF15 ... 117 B2
Cornmill La. Bard LS17 ... 28 D3
Cornmill La. Liver WF15 ... 117 B3
Cornrace View. Hud HD4 ... 154 B4
Cornus Gdns. Midd LS10 ... 99 D8 2
Cornwall Cl. Roth LS26 ... 101 C5
Cornwall Cres. Bail BD17 ... 38 B4
Cornwall Cres. Roth LS26 ... 101 C5
Cornwall House. Elland HX5 ... 134 F7 16
Cornwall Pl. Brad BD8 ... 55 D1
Cornwall Rd. Bing BD16 ... 37 B2
Cornwall Rd. Keigh BD21 ... 35 B4
Cornwall Terr. Brad BD8 ... 55 D1
Coronation Ave. Guise BD10 ... 39 D4
Coronation Ave. Hali HX3 ... 113 D4
Coronation Ave. Nor WF6 ... 122 F3
Coronation Bglws. Kippax LS25 ... 83 C1 3
Coronation Bglws. Mel HD7 ... 170 E1
Coronation Hospl. Ilkley ... 8 C3
Coronation Mount. Keigh BD22 ... 34 F7
Coronation Par. Leeds LS15 ... 80 E7
Coronation Rd. Crof WF4 ... 144 B4
Coronation Rd. Hali HX3 ... 113 D4
Coronation St. Cast WF10 ... 124 C7
Coronation St. Castle ... 124 C7
Coronation Terr. Batley WF17 ... 96 F1 2
Coronation Terr. Brad BD6 ... 94 A1
Coronation Terr. Silsden BD20 ... 5 E1
Coronation Way. Keigh BD22 ... 34 F7
Corporal La. Hali HX3 ... 113 A4
Corporation St. Dew WF13 ... 139 C8
Corporation St. Hali HX1 ... 203 F3
Corpus Christi High Sch. Leeds ... 62 A2
Corpus Christi RC Prim Sch. Leeds ... 61 F2
Cote Farm Cotts. Brad BD10 ... 38 F1
Cote La. Brad BD15 ... 54 A4
Cote La. Hud HD3 ... 153 D6
Cote La. Oxen BD13 ... 51 C2
Coteroyd Ave. Morley LS27 ... 98 B6
Coteroyd Dr. Morley LS27 ... 98 B6
Cotefields Ave. Pudsey LS28 ... 57 C3
Cotewall Rd. Brad BD5 ... 74 C3
Cotswold Ave. Ship BD18 ... 55 D8
Cotswold Cl. Roth LS26 ... 100 D6

Cotswold Mews. Kirkb HD8 ... 173 F7
Cotswold Rd. Roth LS26 ... 100 E6
Cotswold Way. Wake WF2 ... 141 D5
Cottage Gn. Brad BD8 ... 73 F8 12
Cottage Homes. Hud HD5 ... 155 A6
Cottage Rd. Brad BD10 ... 56 D7
Cottage Rd. Leeds LS6 ... 59 D6
Cottage The. Honley HD7 ... 171 F5
Cottage Rd. Leeds LS6 ... 74 B6
Cottam Ave. Brad BD7 ... 74 A7
Cottam Croft. Hem WF9 ... 181 E7
Cottam Terr. Brad BD7 ... 74 B6
Cotterdale. Brad BD15 ... 54 A3
Cotterdale Holt. Coll LS22 ... 13 A1
Cotterdale View. Leeds LS15 ... 80 E6
Cotterill Rd. Knot WF11 ... 126 D3
Cottingley App. Morley LS11 ... 78 D1
Cottingley Chase. Morley LS11 ... 78 D1
Cottingley Cliffe Rd. Ship BD16 ... 54 C6
Cottingley Cty Prim Sch. Morley ... 78 C1
Cottingley Cres. Morley LS11 ... 78 D1
Cottingley Dr. Morley LS11 ... 78 C2
Cottingley Gdns. Morley LS11 ... 78 D1
Cottingley Gn. Morley LS11 ... 78 D1
Cottingley Gr. Morley LS11 ... 78 D1 4
Cottingley Heights. Morley LS11 ... 78 D1 1
Cottingley Manor Sch. Ship ... 54 B7
Cottingley Moor Rd. Ship BD16 ... 54 A5
Cottingley New Rd. Ship BD16 ... 54 B7
Cottingley Rd. Brad BD15 ... 54 A4
Cottingley Rd. Morley LS11 ... 78 C2
Cottingley Sta. Morley ... 78 C1
Cottingley Terr. Brad BD8 ... 55 D1
Cottingley Towers. Morley LS11 ... 78 D1 2
Cottingley Vale. Morley LS11 ... 78 D1
Cotton St. Leeds LS9 ... 79 D7
Cotton St. Wake WF2 ... 142 C4
Couford Gr. Hud HD2 ... 136 F4
Coule Royd. Hud HD5 ... 154 D6
Coultas Cl. Men LS29 ... 22 B4
Coupe Gr. Wor WF6 ... 122 F5
Coupland Pl. Leeds LS11 ... 79 B4
Coupland Rd. Gar LS25 ... 82 C7
Coupland Rd. Leeds LS11 ... 79 B4
Coupland St. Leeds LS11 ... 79 B3
Coupland St. Leeds LS11 ... 79 B3 5
Coupland St Tod OL14 ... 108 B5 6
Court Dr. Leeds LS5 ... 58 D6
Court La. Hali HX2 ... 112 D7
Court No 6. Batley WF17 ... 118 C4
Court The. Leeds LS17 ... 42 F5
Court The. Liver WF15 ... 116 E4
Court Yd. The. Wool WF4 ... 178 A7
Courtenay Cl. Brad BD3 ... 75 D7
Courtyard The. Bacup OL13 ... 106 A3 5
Courtyard The. Batley WF17 ... 96 D8
Courts Leet. Brad BD12 ... 94 C4
Courtyard The. Hud WF14 ... 138 C4 1
Cousen Ave. Brad BD7 ... 73 F5
Cousen Rd. Brad BD7 ... 74 A4
Cousin La. Hali HX2 ... 91 E4
Coutances Way. Ilkley LS29 ... 8 F5
Coverdale Garth. Coll LS22 ... 29 B1
Coverdale Way. Bail BD17 ... 38 E4
Covert The. Wake WF2 ... 160 E6
Covey Clough Ct. Mir WF14 ... 138 A7
Cow Close Gr. Leeds LS12 ... 78 A4
Cow Close La. Brad BD12 ... 94 D3
Cow Close La. Leeds LS12 ... 78 A4
Cow Gate. Hud HD3 ... 152 E6
Cow Gn. Hali HX1 ... 203 E3
Cow Heys. Hud HD5 ... 154 E4
Cow La. Hud HD4 ... 153 D4
Cow La. Brig HD3 ... 114 D4
Cow La. Crof WF4 ... 144 A4
Cow La. Crof WF4 ... 144 A4
Cow La. Knot WF11 ... 127 A4
Cow La. Ripp HX6 ... 132 C3
Cow La. Wad M HX7 ... 88 A7
Cow Rake La. Ilkley LS29 ... 8 C5
Cowcliff Hill. Holmfi HD7 ... 199 D8
Cowcliffe Hill Rd. Hud HD2 ... 136 C4
Cowdray Dr. Clec BD19 ... 116 C7
Cowdrey Cl. Dew WF12 ... 139 D2
Cowell Gdns. Hud HD4 ... 153 F3
Cowfold St. Tod OL14 ... 108 A1
Cowgate. Hud HD2 ... 136 B4
Cowgate. Leeds LS6 ... 59 C5
Cowgill St. Bacup OL13 ... 106 A3 13
Cowgill St. Haw BD22 ... 51 E8
Cowhurst Ave. Tod OL14 ... 108 A4
Cowhurst Ave. Tod OL14 ... 108 A4
Cowley Cres. Brad BD9 ... 54 C4
Cowley Rd. Leeds LS13 ... 58 D4
Cowlersley Cty Jun & Inf Sch. Hud ... 152 F4
Cowlersley La. Hud HD4 ... 152 F4
Cowley Cres. Brad BD9 ... 54 C4
Cowpe Rd. Pudsey LS13 ... 57 D1
Cowpasture Rd. Ilkley LS29 ... 8 C3
Cowper Ave. Leeds LS9 ... 61 A2 1
Cowper Cres. Leeds LS9 ... 61 A2 4
Cowper Gr. Leeds LS9 ... 61 A2 3
Cowper Mount. Leeds LS9 ... 61 A2 A10
Cowper Rd. Leeds LS9 ... 61 A2
Cowper St. Leeds LS7 ... 60 C5
Cowper St. Leeds LS9 ... 61 A2 1
Cowper Terr. Leeds LS9 ... 61 A2 2
Cowroyd Pl. Hali HX3 ... 113 D4 2
Cowslip St. Hud HD1 ... 153 D6
Cowslip St. Hud HD1 ... 153 D6
Coxley Cres. Netherton WF4 ... 158 B6
Coxley La. Neth WF4 ... 158 C6
Coxley View. Neth WF4 ... 158 B6
Coxwold View. Weth LS22 ... 13 F6
Coxwold Vale. Weth LS22 ... 13 F6
Crab Hill. Pont WF8 ... 146 F7
Crab La. Crig WF2 ... 160 C3
Crab La. Leeds LS12 ... 78 A8
Crab Tree La. K Smea WF8 ... 166 A8
Crabgate Dr. Ad LS Smea ... 166 D5
Crabgate La. Ad l S Smea ... 166 D5
Crabtree Ave. Bacup OL13 ... 106 A3
Crabtree Ave. Batley WF16 ... 117 E5

Crabtree Gn. Coll LS22 ... 29 B7
Crabtree Gr. Coll LS22 ... 29 B8
Crabtree La. E kes LS17 ... 28 C7
Crabtree La. Shad ... 62 C7
Crabtree Pl. Brad BD7 ... 74 A4 5
Crabtree St. Hali HX1 ... 112 F7
Crabtree Way. E ard WF3 ... 119 F7
Crack La. Wils BD15 ... 53 D5
Crackenedge La. Dew WF13 ... 118 D1
Crackenedge Terr. Dew WF13 ... 118 D1
Cracoe Rd. Brad BD3 ... 75 B6
Crag Cl. Hali HX2 ... 91 D4
Crag Cl. S in Cra BD20 ... 16 C5
Crag Ct. Hali HX2 ... 91 D4
Crag Gdns. Bramham LS23 ... 30 D2
Crag Hill Ave. Hors LS16 ... 41 E6
Crag Hill Rd. Brad BD10 ... 39 A2
Crag La. Hali HX2 ... 91 D3
Crag La. Hud HD5 ... 154 C7
Crag La. Leeds LS17 ... 42 F5
Crag La. S in Cra BD20 ... 16 C4
Crag Mount. Pont WF8 ... 146 C8 16
Crag Pl. Keigh BD21 ... 35 C4
Crag Rd. Ship BD18 ... 55 C7
Crag The. Bramham LS23 ... 30 D2
Crag Top. Fair WF11 ... 105 A4
Crag Vale Terr. Glu BD20 ... 16 C6
Crag View. Brad BD10 ... 56 D6
Crag View. S in Cra BD20 ... 16 C5
Cragg Ave. Hors LS18 ... 58 C8
Cragg Bottom Rd. Haw BD22 ... 49 E8
Cragg Dr. Ilkley LS29 ... 8 F3
Cragg Hill. Hors LS18 ... 58 C8
Cragg La. Brad BD7 ... 74 A3
Cragg La. Denh BD13 ... 71 E6
Cragg Rd. Heb Br HX7 ... 110 D6
Cragg Rd. Hors LS18 ... 58 C8
Cragg St. Brad BD7 ... 74 A3
Cragg Terr. Brad BD7 ... 74 A3
Cragg Terr. Hors LS18 ... 58 B8
Cragg Terr. Yeadon LS19 ... 40 B2
Cragg Vale Jun & Inf Sch. Heb Br ... 110 A4
Cragg Wood Dr. Yeadon LS19 ... 40 A2
Craggwell Terr. Hors LS18 ... 58 C7
Craggwood Cl. Hors LS18 ... 58 C7
Craggwood Rd. Hors LS18 ... 58 C7
Craggwood Terr. Hors LS18 ... 58 C7 8
Cragside. Brad BD10 ... 38 F1
Cragside Cl. Leeds LS5 ... 58 F7
Cragside Cres. Leeds LS5 ... 58 F7
Cragside Gdns. Leeds LS5 ... 58 F7
Cragside Gr. Leeds LS5 ... 58 F7
Cragside Pl. Leeds LS5 ... 58 F7
Cragside Wlk. Leeds LS5 ... 58 F7
Craig Cl. Batley WF17 ... 118 C6
Craig House. Brad BD15 ... 73 B8 6
Craig-y-don. Dew WF12 ... 139 F7
Craiglands. Brig HD6 ... 114 D8
Craiglands Rd. Ilkley LS29 ... 8 D3
Craigmore Ct. Brad BD4 ... 75 F2
Craigmore Dr. Ilkley LS29 ... 8 F2
Cranberry Ave. Tod OL13 ... 106 A1
Cranbourne Rd. Brad BD9 ... 54 D1
Cranbrook Ave. Brad BD6 ... 94 B8
Cranbrook Ave. Leeds LS11 ... 79 E4 3
Cranbrook Pl. Brad BD5 ... 74 E4
Cranbrook St. Brad BD5 ... 74 E4 4
Cranbrook View. Pudsey LS28 ... 77 A5
Cranbrook St. Clec BD19 ... 116 E7
Cranewells Dr. Leeds LS15 ... 81 C6
Cranewells Gn. Leeds LS15 ... 81 C6
Cranewells Rise. Leeds LS15 ... 81 C6
Cranewells Vale. Leeds LS15 ... 81 C6
Cranewells View. Leeds LS15 ... 81 C5
Cranfield Cl. Silsden BD20 ... 5 C1
Cranford Gdns. Roy S71 ... 179 C4
Cranford Pl. Wils BD15 ... 53 C5
Cranleigh Mount. Keigh BD21 ... 35 A5
Cranmer Bank. Leeds LS17 ... 43 B3
Cranmer Cl. Leeds LS17 ... 43 B3
Cranmer Gdns. Leeds LS17 ... 43 B3
Cranmer Gdns. Mel HD7 ... 170 F2
Cranmer Rd. Brad BD3 ... 55 F1
Cranmer Rd. Leeds LS17 ... 43 A3
Cranmer Rise. Leeds LS17 ... 43 A3
Cranmore Cres. Midd LS10 ... 99 E5
Cranmore Dr. Midd LS10 ... 99 E5
Cranmore Gdns. Midd LS10 ... 99 E5
Cranmore Gn. Midd LS10 ... 99 E5
Cranmore Gr. Midd LS10 ... 99 E5
Cranmore La. Midd LS10 ... 99 E5
Cranmore Rd. Midd LS10 ... 99 E5
Cranmore Rise. Midd LS10 ... 99 E5
Cranwood Dr. Hud HD5 ... 155 A6
Craven Ave. Sil BD20 ... 5 E1
Craven Cl. Oakw BD22 ... 34 C8
Craven Ct. Roth LS26 ... 100 A5
Craven Rd. Keigh BD21 ... 35 A5
Craven St. Brad BD4 ... 75 A4

Cure Hill. Haw BD22 ... 34 B3
Curlew Ct. Castle WF10 ... 124 D6
Curlew Cl. Ilkley LS29 ... 7 E4
Curlew Rise. Morley LS27 ... 98 D3
Curlew St. Brad BD5 ... 74 C3
Curly Hill. Ilkley LS29 ... 8 B6
Currer Ave. Brad BD4 ... 75 B1
Currer La. Nes LS29 ... 3 C4
Currer St. Brad BD1 ... 74 F7
Currer Wlk. Stee BD20 ... 17 B6
Curwen Cres. Batley WF16 ... 117 E6
Curzon Rd. Brad BD3 ... 75 A7
Curzon St. Hud HD2 ... 137 A6
Cut Rd. Broth WF11 ... 105 C1
Cut Rd. Fair WF11 ... 105 A4
Cuthberts Cl. Queen BD13 ... 92 D8
Cutler Heights La. Brad BD4 ... 75 D3
Cutler La. M'town LS26 ... 102 E4
Cutler Pl. Brad BD4 ... 75 D4
Cutsyke Ave. Castle WF10 ... 124 B5
Cutsyke Crest. Castle WF10 ... 124 B5
Cutsyke Hill. Castle WF10 ... 124 B6
Cutsyke Rd. Castle WF10 ... 124 B5
Cutsyke Rd. Feath WF7 ... 124 C5
Cypress Fold. Lepton HD8 ... 155 E3
Cypress House. Castle WF10 ... 124 E7
Cypress Rd. Nor WF6 ... 144 C8
Cyprus Ave. Brad BD10 ... 38 F1
Cyprus Ave. Wake WF1 ... 142 A8
Cyprus Cres. Wkr WF14 ... 138 D7
Cyprus Dr. Brad BD10 ... 39 A1
Cyprus Gr. Gar LS25 ... 82 E7
Cyprus Gr. Wake WF1 ... 142 A8
Cyprus Mount. Wake WF1 ... 142 A8
Cyprus Rd. Gar LS25 ... 82 E7
Cyprus St. Wake WF1 ... 142 B8
Cyprus Terr. Gar LS25 ... 82 E7
Czar St. Leeds LS11 ... 79 A6

Dacre Ave. Wake WF2 ... 141 C4
Dacre Cl. Liver WF15 ... 116 F5
Daffels Wood Cl. Brad BD4 ... 95 B8
Daffil Ave. Morley LS27 ... 98 B7
Daffil Gr. Morley LS27 ... 98 B7 1
Daffil Grange Mews. Morley LS27 ... 98 B7
Daffil Grange Way. Morley LS27 ... 98 B7
Daffil Rd. Morley LS27 ... 98 B7
Dagenham Rd. Brad BD4 ... 75 C3
Daisy Bank. Holi HX1 ... 203 D4
Daisy Bank St. Tod OL14 ... 86 B1 2
Daisy Ct. Batley WF17 ... 96 F2
Daisy Croft. Sil BD20 ... 5 F1
Daisy Gn. Stav HD7 ... 170 C7
Daisy Hill Ave. Morley LS27 ... 98 C6
Daisy Hill Back La. Brad BD9 ... 54 E2
Daisy Hill Cl. Morley LS27 ... 98 C5 5
Daisy Hill Cl. Morley LS27 ... 98 C6
Daisy Hill. Dew WF13 ... 139 C8
Daisy Hill. Gr Brad BD9 ... 54 E2
Daisy Hill La. Brad BD9 ... 54 E2
Daisy Hill Mid Sch. Brad ... 54 E2
Daisy Hill. Morley LS27 ... 98 C5
Daisy Hill. Sil BD20 ... 5 F1
Daisy Lea. Elland HD3 ... 152 A8
Daisy Lea La. Hud HD3 ... 135 C1
Daisy La. Holmfi HD7 ... 199 C7
Daisy Mount. Halo HX6 ... 112 A5
Daisy Pl. Shilp BD18 ... 54 F8 12
Daisy Rd. Brg HD6 ... 136 B8
Daisy Row. Leeds LS13 ... 58 D1 3
Daisy Royd. Hud HD4 ... 154 C6
Daisy St. Brad BD7 ... 74 A3
Daisy St. Brig HD6 ... 115 A1
Daisy St. Hali HX1 ... 203 D6
Daisy St. Haw BD22 ... 51 E8 1
Daisy Vale Terr. E Ard WF3 ... 119 E7
Daisyfield Rd. Leeds LS13 ... 58 D2 2
Dalby Ave. Brad BD3 ... 56 C1
Dalby St. Brad BD3 ... 75 C8
Dalcross Gr. Brad BD5 ... 74 E4
Dalcross St. Brad BD5 ... 74 F4
Dale Ave. Tod OL14 ... 108 D5
Dale Cl. Batley WF17 ... 118 C3
Dale Cl. D Dale HD8 ... 191 F5
Dale Cl. Guise LS20 ... 22 E7
Dale Croft. Gar LS25 ... 82 E8
Dale Croft. Ilkley LS29 ... 7 E4
Dale Croft Rise. Brad BD15 ... 54 A2
Dale Cl. Start. HD8 ... 175 A2
Dale Ct. Holmfi HD7 ... 172 E1
Dale Ct. Pont WF8 ... 146 D5
Dale Garth. Bail BD17 ... 38 B3
Dale La. Batley WF16 ... 117 E5
Dale La. S Elm WF9 ... 183 B5
Dale Lane Ind Est. S Elm ... 183 B5
Dale Park Ave. Hors LS16 ... 41 D4
Dale Park Cl. Hors LS16 ... 41 D4
Dale Park Gdns. Hors LS16 ... 41 D4
Dale Park Rise. Hors LS16 ... 41 D4
Dale Park View. Hors LS16 ... 41 D4
Dale Rd. Gild BD11 ... 97 A8
Dale St. Brad BD1 ... 201 B3
Dale St. Dew WF12 ... 139 C4
Dale St. Hali HX6 ... 112 B4
Dale St. Hud HD1 ... 154 A5
Dale St. Keigh BD21 ... 35 B8
Dale St. Ossett WF5 ... 140 E7
Dale St. Skel HD8 ... 175 A2
Dale St. Tod OL14 ... 108 B6
Dale Stone Cl. Broth WF11 ... 105 C1
Dale. The. Aber LS25 ... 47 E1
Dale View Cl. Keigh BD21 ... 35 A6
Dale View. Hali HX3 ... 92 B1
Dale View. Hali HX3 ... 113 A4
Dale View. Hem WF9 ... 181 F6
Dale View. Pont WF8 ... 146 D5
Dale View Rd. Keigh BD21 ... 35 A6
Dale View. Wilsd BD15 ... 53 C5
Dale Way. Batley WF17 ... 118 C3
Dalefield Ave. Nor WF6 ... 123 A1
Dalefield Rd. Nor WF6 ... 144 B8
Dales Dr. Guise LS20 ... 39 B8
Dales Way. Guise LS20 ... 39 B8
Daleside Ave. Pudsey LS28 ... 76 A8
Daleside Cl. Brad BD18 ... 56 F1
Daleside. Dew WF12 ... 139 C1
Daleside. Elland HX4 ... 134 A7

Daleside Gr. Brad BD12 ... 94 F4
Daleside Gr. Pudsey LS28 ... 76 A7
Daleside Rd. Keigh BD20 ... 19 A1
Daleside Rd. Pudsey LS28 ... 75 F8
Daleside Rd. Ship BD18 ... 55 E8
Daleside Wlk. Brad BD5 ... 74 F2
Daleside Cl. Northo HX3 ... 93 A3
Dalesway. Bing BD16 ... 37 B5
Daleview Ct. Bard BD17 ... 38 A2
Dallam Ave. Ship BD18 ... 54 E8 3
Dallam Gr. Ship BD18 ... 54 E8
Dallam Rd. Ship BD18 ... 54 F8
Dallam Wlk. Ship BD18 ... 54 F8
Dalmeny Ave. Hud HD4 ... 153 C3
Dalmeny Cl. Hud HD4 ... 153 C3
Dalton Ave. Leeds LS11 ... 79 A2
Dalton Bank Rd. Hud HD5 ... 137 A3
Dalton Clowes. Hud HD5 ... 154 E7
Dalton Fold Rd. Hud HD5 ... 154 D7
Dalton Green La. Hud HD5 ... 155 A6
Dalton Jun & Inf Sch. Hud ... 154 F6
Dalton La. Coll LS23 ... 29 E3
Dalton La. Keigh BD21 ... 35 E7
Dalton Rd. Keigh BD21 ... 35 E7
Dalton Rd. Leeds LS11 ... 79 A2
Dalton St. Hali HX6 ... 112 B5 2
Dalton St. Tod OL14 ... 108 B5
Dalton Terr. Brad BD8 ... 74 B8
Dalton Terr. Castle WF10 ... 124 D7
Dalton Terr. Keigh BD21 ... 35 E8
Dalton Works. Hud ... 136 F1
Dam Head La. Lepton HD8 ... 155 F5
Dam Head Rd. Hali HX6 ... 112 C5
Dam Hill. Shep HD8 ... 173 E3
Dam La. Leeds LS25 ... 66 A6
Dam La. Yeadon LS19 ... 40 C7
Damask St. Hali HX1 ... 113 B8
Damems La. Keigh BD22 ... 35 A2
Damems Rd. Keigh BD21 ... 35 A3
Damon Ave. Brad BD10 ... 56 E4
Dampier St. Tod OL14 ... 108 A1
Damside. Keigh BD21 ... 35 B6
Danby La. Wake WF2 ... 160 C4
Danby Wlk. Leeds LS9 ... 79 F7
Dandy Mill Ave. Pont WF8 ... 125 F2
Dandy Mill Croft. Pont WF8 ... 125 F2
Dane Hill Dr. Brad BD4 ... 75 E3
Danebury Rd. Brg HD6 ... 115 B1
Danecourt Rd. Brad BD4 ... 75 F3
Danefield Terr. Otley LS21 ... 23 B8
Danehurst. Pont WF8 ... 146 E8
Danella Cres. Wake WF2 ... 120 F3
Danella Gr. Wake WF2 ... 120 F2
Danes La. Neth WF4 ... 158 B6
Danesleigh Dr. Neth WF4 ... 158 B6
Daniel Ct. Brad BD4 ... 75 F2
Daniel St. Brad BD3 ... 75 D7
Danny La. Hali HX2 ... 111 C6
Dansk Way. Ilkley LS29 ... 8 D5
Danum Dr. Bail BD17 ... 38 C1
Darbyfields. Hud HD7 ... 152 E6
Darcey Hey La. Hali HX2 ... 112 C5
Darcy Ct. Leeds LS15 ... 81 C8
Darfield Ave. Leeds LS8 ... 61 A3
Darfield Cres. Leeds LS8 ... 61 A3
Darfield Gr. Leeds LS8 ... 61 A3
Darfield Pl. Leeds LS8 ... 61 A3
Darfield Rd. Leeds LS8 ... 61 A3
Darfield St. Brad BD1 ... 201 A3
Darfield St. Leeds LS8 ... 61 A3
Dark La. B Head HX7 ... 88 C3
Dark La. B In Elm LS15 ... 63 D8
Dark La. Batley WF17 ... 96 F1
Dark La. Batley WF17 ... 118 B4
Dark La. Caw S75 ... 193 E5
Dark La. Hali HX2 ... 91 C2
Dark La. Haw BD22 ... 33 E1
Dark La. Hud HD4 ... 155 A3
Dark La. Oxen BD22 ... 51 D3
Dark La. Pont WF8 ... 146 C4
Darkfield La. Pont WF8 ... 125 F4
Darkwood Cl. Leeds LS17 ... 44 A4
Darkwood Way. Leeds LS17 ... 44 A4
Darley Ave. Leeds LS10 ... 99 D7
Darley Rd. Liver WF15 ... 116 F5
Darley St. Batley WF16 ... 117 D4
Darley St. Brad BD1 ... 74 F7
Darley St. Keigh BD20 ... 18 B1
Darnell Terr. Leeds LS11 ... 79 C6
Darnes Ave. Hali HX2 ... 112 B4
Darning La. Th Aud WF8 ... 165 B5
Darnley Ave. Wake WF2 ... 142 A6
Darnley Cl. Mel HD7 ... 170 E1
Darnley La. Leeds LS15 ... 81 E6
Darren St. Brad BD4 ... 75 E6
Darrington CE Jun & Inf Sch. Dar ... 147 D5
Darrington La. Dar WF8 ... 147 C5
Darrington La. Went WF4 ... 147 C5
Dartmouth Ave. Hud HD5 ... 155 A3
Dartmouth Ave. Morley LS27 ... 98 A3
Dartmouth Mews. Morley ... 97 F3
Dartmouth Terr. Kirkb HD4 ... 172 E6
Dartmouth Way. Leeds LS11 ... 79 C6
Darton Hall Dr. Mapp S75 ... 177 F1
Darton Hall Dr. Mapp S75 ... 177 F1
Darton La. Mapp S75 ... 178 B1
Darton Mapplewell Cty Inf Sch. Mapp ... 178 B1
Darton Prim Sch. Mapp ... 177 F1
Darton Rd. Caw S75 ... 193 F5
Darton St. Oak S75 ... 193 F1
Darwin St. Brad BD5 ... 74 C3
Davey La. B Head HX7 ... 88 C3
Davey La. Dew WF13 ... 118 C2
David St. Castle WF10 ... 124 B7
David St. Leeds LS11 ... 79 F8
Davids St. Pudsey LS28 ... 57 D2
Davies Ave. Leeds LS8 ... 44 A1
Davies Ave. Leeds LS8 ... 61 A8
Daw Green Ave. Crig WF4 ... 159 E5
Daw La. Crig WF4 ... 159 D4
Daw La. Hor WF4 ... 159 D4
Daw Royds. Hud HD5 ... 155 A4
Dawlish Ave. Leeds LS9 ... 80 B8
Dawlish Gr. Leeds LS9 ... 80 B8
Dawlish Mount. Leeds LS9 ... 80 B8
Dawlish Pl. Leeds LS9 ... 80 B8 1
Dawlish Rd. Leeds LS9 ... 80 B8
Dawlish Row. Leeds LS9 ... 80 B8

Dawlish St. Leeds LS9 ... 80 B8
Dawlish Terr. Leeds LS9 ... 80 B8
Dawnay Rd. Brad BD5 ... 74 C4
Dawson Ave. Brad BD6 ... 94 C8
Dawson Gdns. Dew WF13 ... 139 C8 1
Dawson Hill. Hor WF4 ... 141 A5
Dawson Hill Hd. Hor WF4 ... 141 B8 3
Dawson La. Birk BD4 ... 76 E2
Dawson La. Brad BD4 ... 75 C1
Dawson La. Roth LS26 ... 100 E6
Dawson Mount. Brad BD4 ... 75 C1
Dawson Pl. Brad BD4 ... 75 C1
Dawson Pl. Keigh BD21 ... 35 C5
Dawson Rd. Hud HD4 ... 154 B3
Dawson Rd. Keigh BD21 ... 35 C5
Dawson St. E Ard WF3 ... 120 C8
Dawson St. Pudsey LS28 ... 57 D1 7
Dawson Terr. Brad BD4 ... 75 C1
Dawson Way. Keigh BD21 ... 35 C5
Dawson's Corner. Pudsey LS28 ... 57 C2
Dawsons Meadow. Pudsey LS28 ... 57 C2
Dawtrie Cl. Castle WF10 ... 125 D7
Dawtrie St. Castle WF10 ... 125 D7
Day St. Hud HD1 ... 154 C5
De Lacey Mews. Brad BD4 ... 75 C2
De Lacy Ave. Brad BD4 ... 75 C2
De Lacy Ave. Feath WF7 ... 124 C1
De Lacy Mount. Leeds LS5 ... 59 A4
De Lacy Terr. Pont WF8 ... 146 D5
Deaconess Ct. Ilkley LS29 ... 8 C4
Deacon Cl. Mel HD7 ... 170 E2
Deaconess Ct. Ilkley LS29 ... 8 C4
Deadmanstone. Hud HD4 ... 171 F8
Deal St. Hali HX1 ... 113 D6
Deal St. Keigh BD21 ... 35 E8
Dealburn Rd. Brad BD12 ... 94 E4
Dean Ave. Holmfi HD7 ... 188 F8
Dean Beck Ave. Brad BD6 ... 74 F1
Dean Beck Ct. Brad BD6 ... 94 F8
Dean Bridge La. Holmfi HD7 ... 189 E2
Dean Brook Rd. Holmfi HD7 ... 172 A1
Dean Brook Rd. Hud HD4 ... 172 A1
Dean Ct. Brad BD8 ... 54 D1
Dean Cl. Wake WF2 ... 120 F2
Dean Clough. Hali HX1 ... 113 C8
Dean End. Elland HX4 ... 133 F3
Dean Hall Cl. Morley LS27 ... 97 F4
Dean Head. Hors LS18 ... 41 A8
Dean House La. Hali HX2 ... 90 E2
Dean La. E Carl LS16 ... 24 D2
Dean La. Guise LS20 ... 38 F8
Dean La. Holmfi HD7 ... 189 F4
Dean La. Sow B HX6 ... 111 B3
Dean Park Ave. Birk BD11 ... 96 E7
Dean Pk Dr. Birk BD11 ... 96 E6
Dean Rd. Brad BD6 ... 94 B8
Dean Rd. Holmfi HD7 ... 188 C6
Dean Rd. Elland HX4 ... 134 D7
Dean St. Elland HX4 ... 134 F6 8
Dean St. Hud HD3 ... 153 B8
Dean St. Ilkley LS29 ... 8
Dean Villas. Tod OL14 ... 86 B1
Dean Wood View. Hali HX3 ... 113 C2
Deane. The. Leeds LS15 ... 80 D7
Deanery Gdns. Brad BD10 ... 56 C5
Deanfield Ave. Morley LS27 ... 97 F6
Deanhurst Gdns. Gild LS27 ... 97 E6
Deanhurst Ind Ctr. Gild LS27 ... 97 E6
Deanroyd Rd. Tod OL14 ... 129 B7
Deanstones Cres. Queen BD13 ... 92 E8
Deanstones La. Queen BD13 ... 92 E8
Deanswood Cl. Leeds LS17 ... 43 A3
Deanswood Dr. Leeds LS17 ... 43 A3
Deanswood Garth. Leeds LS17 ... 43 A3
Deanswood Gdns. Leeds LS17 ... 43 A3
Deanswood Gn. Leeds LS17 ... 42 F3
Deanswood Hill. Leeds LS17 ... 43 A3
Deanswood Pl. Leeds LS17 ... 43 A3
Deanswood Rise. Leeds LS17 ... 43 A3
Deanswood View. Leeds LS17 ... 43 A3
Deanwood Ave. Brad BD15 ... 54 A4
Deanwood Cres. Brad BD15 ... 54 A4
Deanwood Wlk. Brad BD15 ... 54 A4
Dearden St. Hali HX6 ... 112 B5
Dearden St. Ossett WF5 ... 140 D7
Dearne Croft. Weth LS22 ... 13 E8
Dearne Dike La. D Dale HD8 ... 190 E5
Dearne Fst Sch. Denb ... 192 A1
Dearne Pk. Clay W HD8 ... 175 F2
Dearne Royd. Clay W HD8 ... 175 E2
Dearne St. Clay W HD8 ... 175 D1
Dearne St. Mapp S75 ... 177 F1
Dearne Terr. S Hien S72 ... 180 C6
Dearne Thurscoe The Hill Jnr Sch. Denb ... 194 F1
Dearneside Rd. D Dale HD8 ... 191 F6
Dearnfield. D Dale HD8 ... 191 C6
Dearnley St. Dew WF13 ... 138 D6
Deben Cl. Brad BD2 ... 56 D2
Deep La. B Spa LS23 ... 30 E7
Deep La. Brig HD6 ... 114 F8
Deep La. Hali HX2 ... 91 E7
Deep La. Hali HX3 ... 92 E2
Deep La. Nor WF6 ... 122 E3
Deep La. Sow B HX6 ... 132 B8
Deepdale. B Spa LS23 ... 30 E7
Deepdale Cl. Brad BD15 ... 54 A1
Deepdale La. B Spa LS23 ... 30 E7
Deepdale La. Brad BD15 ... 54 A1

Defarge Ct. Brad BD5 ... 74 E3
Deffer Rd. Wake WF2 ... 160 C6
Degamay Dr. Kirkhe HD5 ... 137 C2
Deighton Cl. Weth LS22 ... 13 F6
Deighton Cty Jun Sch. Hud ... 136 D4
Deighton Cty Sec Sch. Hud ... 136 D4
Deighton Gates Jun & Inf Sch. Weth ... 13 E8
Deighton La. Batley WF17 ... 118 A4
Deighton Rd. Hud HD2 ... 136 E3
Deighton Rd. Weth LS22 ... 13 E7
Deighton Sta. Hud ... 136 E3
Delacy Cres. Castle WF10 ... 104 D1
Delamere St. Brad BD5 ... 74 D2
Delf Hill. Brig HD6 ... 135 E7
Delf Hill Mid Sch. Brad ... 94 C6
Delf La. Tod OL14 ... 86 D3
Delf La. Wad W HX7 ... 89 C8
Delf Pl. Brg HD6 ... 135 E7
Delfs La. Sow Br HX7 ... 110 F7
Delius Ave. Brad BD10 ... 56 E5
Dell Cl. Brad BD13 ... 73 A6
Dell. The. Bard LS17 ... 28 D3
Dell. The. Cull BD13 ... 52 D6
Dell. The. Hud HD2 ... 136 F3
Dell. The. Leeds LS6 ... 60 A4
Delmont Cl. Batley WF17 ... 117 E6
Delph Cres. Brad BD14 ... 73 B4
Delph Ct. Leeds LS6 ... 60 A4
Delph Dr. Brad BD14 ... 73 B4
Delph Gr. Brad BD14 ... 73 B4
Delph Hill. Bail BD17 ... 38 C4 10
Delph Hill. Hali HX2 ... 113 A4 5
Delph Hill. Leeds LS13 ... 58 D1
Delph Hill La. Hali HX2 ... 112 A6
Delph Hill Rd. Hali HX2 ... 112 A6
Delph Hill Terr. Hali HX2 ... 112 F4 3
Delph La. Hud HD2 ... 171 D7
Delph La. Leeds LS6 ... 60 A4
Delph Mount. Leeds LS6 ... 60 A4
Delph St. Hali HX1 ... 113 B6
Delph Terr. Brad BD14 ... 73 B4
Delph The. Feath WF7 ... 145 F5
Delph View. Leeds LS6 ... 60 A4
Delph Wood Cl. Bing BD16 ... 37 C3
Delverne Gr. Brad BD2 ... 56 C3
Delves Gate. Slai HD7 ... 169 F4
Delves Wood Ris. Hud HD4 ... 153 E3
Denard Ind Est. Hud ... 153 B4
Denbigh App. Leeds LS9 ... 61 D2
Denbigh Croft. Leeds LS9 ... 61 D2
Denbigh Hts. Leeds LS9 ... 61 D2
Denbrook Ave. Brad BD4 ... 75 F1
Denbrook Cl. Brad BD4 ... 75 F1
Denbrook Cres. Brad BD4 ... 75 F1
Denbrook Way. Brad BD4 ... 75 F1
Denbrook Wlk. Brad BD4 ... 75 F1
Denby Cl. Batley WF17 ... 96 F1
Denby Cl. Liver WF15 ... 117 A4
Denby Dale Rd. Crig WF4 ... 159 F3
Denby Dale Rd. Dew WF12 ... 139 F1
Denby Dale Rd E. Wake WF2 ... 160 D5
Denby Dale Rd. Nor WF6 ... 159 F7
Denby Dale Rd. Wake WF2 ... 142 B3
Denby Dale Sta. D Dale ... 191 F5
Denby Dr. Bail BD17 ... 38 C1
Denby Grange La. Flo WF4 ... 157 A5
Denby Hall La. D Dale HD8 ... 191 D5
Denby Hill Rd. Haw BD22 ... 34 A5
Denby La. Brad BD15 ... 54 A1
Denby La. D Dale HD8 ... 191 C4
Denby La. Up Cumb BD13 ... 52 C2
Denby Mount. Oxen BD22 ... 51 C2
Denby Pl. Hali HX6 ... 112 B5
Denby Rd. Keigh BD21 ... 35 E5
Denby St. Brad BD8 ... 55 B1
Dene Bank. Bing BD16 ... 37 A5
Dene Cl. Elland HX5 ... 134 E5
Dene Cres. Brad BD7 ... 73 E3
Dene Gr. Sil BD20 ... 5 E2
Dene Hill. Bail BD17 ... 37 E3
Dene Mount. Brad BD15 ... 54 C1
Dene Pl. Hali HX1 ... 113 A7
Dene Rd. Brad BD6 ... 93 F6
Dene Rd. Skel HD8 ... 174 F1
Dene Royd Cl. Sow B HX4 ... 133 F5
Dene Royd Ct. Sow B HX4 ... 133 F5
Denecliffe. Hud HD4 ... 155 C1
Denefield Pl. Brad BD12 ... 94 C1
Denehill. Brad BD9 ... 54 E3
Deneside. Ossett WF5 ... 140 C7
Deneside Mount. Brad BD5 ... 74 C2
Deneside Terr. Brad BD5 ... 74 C2
Denesway. Gar LS25 ... 82 F6
Denesway. Mir WF14 ... 137 E5
Denfield Ave. Hali HX3 ... 91 F3
Denfield Cres. Hali HX3 ... 91 F3
Denfield Edge. Hali HX3 ... 91 F3
Denfield Gdns. Hali HX3 ... 91 F3
Denfield La. Hali HX3 ... 91 F3
Denfield Sq. Hali HX3 ... 91 F3
Denham Dr. Holmfi HD7 ... 188 F8
Denham St. Brad BD4 ... 75 B4
Denham St. Brig HD6 ... 115 A3
Denhale Ave. Wake WF2 ... 120 F3
Denholme Clough. Holmfi HD7 ... 189 F5
Denholme Dr. Ossett WF5 ... 140 C7
Denholme Gate Rd. Hali HX3 ... 114 C8
Denholme Meadow. S Elm WF9 ... 182 F3
Denholme Rd. Oxen BD22 ... 51 C3
Denison Rd. Brad BD8 ... 55 D1
Denison Rd. Leeds LS3 ... 211 D4
Dennil Cres. Leeds LS15 ... 62 E1
Dennil Rd. Leeds LS15 ... 81 E8
Dennington La. Crig WF4 ... 159 E2
Dennis La. Sil BD20 ... 5 D4
Dennison Fold. Brad BD4 ... 75 E5
Dennistead Cres. Leeds LS6 ... 59 D5
Denshaw Dr. Morley LS27 ... 98 B4
Denshaw Gr. Morley LS27 ... 98 B4
Denshaw La. E Ard WF3 ... 98 F1
Denshaw La. Midd WF3 ... 98 F1

Dent Dr. Wake WF1 ... 142 F8
Dent St. Leeds LS9 ... 79 F7
Denton Ave. Leeds LS8 ... 60 F8
Denton Dr. Bing BD16 ... 37 C4
Denton Gdns. Ack M T WF7 ... 164 A5
Denton Gdns. Leeds LS8 ... 60 F8
Denton Rd. Denton BD16 ... 93 E8 9
Denton Rd. Denton LS29 ... 9 F8
Denton Rd. Denton LS29 ... 9 A6
Denton Rd. Ilkley LS29 ... 9 D5
Denton Row. Denb BD13 ... 71 D8
Denton Row. Elland HX4 ... 134 C4
Denton Terr. Castle WF10 ... 124 E8
Denwell Terr. Pont WF8 ... 125 D1
Der St. Tod OL14 ... 108 C5
Derby Rd. Brad BD3 ... 75 D7
Derby Rd. Brad BD3 ... 75 D7
Derby Rd. Yeadon LS19 ... 40 B4
Derby St. Bing BD16 ... 36 F3
Derby St. Brad BD12 ... 94 B3
Derby St. Brad BD7 ... 74 B4
Derby St. Hali HX6 ... 112 D4
Derby St. Queen BD13 ... 72 D1
Derby St. Tod OL14 ... 108 D5
Derry Hill. Men LS29 ... 21 F4
Derry Hill Gdns. Men LS29 ... 21 F4
Derwent Ave. Bail BD17 ... 38 C4 10
Derwent Ave. Gar LS25 ... 82 F6
Derwent Ave. Wils BD15 ... 53 C4
Derwent Cl. Heb Br HX7 ... 89 A4
Derwent Ct. Sil BD20 ... 17 E8
Derwent Dr. Castle WF10 ... 104 E1
Derwent Dr. Hors LS16 ... 42 D4
Derwent Dr. Hud HD5 ... 154 D7
Derwent Dr. Wake WF2 ... 141 F6
Derwent Pl. Knot WF11 ... 127 A4
Derwent Pl. Leeds LS11 ... 79 A6
Derwent Rd. Batley WF12 ... 118 F2
Derwent Rd. Brad BD2 ... 55 F4
Derwent Rd. Huns HD7 ... 171 C1
Derwent Rd. Mel HD7 ... 170 D1
Derwent Rd. Wake WF2 ... 141 F6
Derwentwater Gr. Leeds LS6 ... 59 D5
Derwentwater Terr. Leeds LS6 ... 59 D5
Derwin Ave. Kirkb HD4 ... 173 C2
Detroit Ave. Leeds LS15 ... 81 E8
Detroit Dr. Leeds LS15 ... 81 E8
Deveron Gr. Ossett WF5 ... 140 C4
Devon Cl. Leeds LS2 ... 60 B8
Devon Gr. Ossett WF5 ... 140 C4
Devon Rd. Leeds LS2 ... 206 A2
Devon St. Hali HX1 ... 202 C1
Devon Way. Bring HD6 ... 115 B6
Devon Wlk. Dew WF13 ... 139 B8 4
Devonshire Ave. Leeds LS8 ... 44 A1
Devonshire Cl. Leeds LS8 ... 44 A1
Devonshire Cl. Knot WF11 ... 127 A4
Devonshire Cres. Leeds LS8 ... 44 A1
Devonshire Gdns. Leeds LS2 ... 60 B8
Devonshire La. Leeds LS8 ... 44 A1
Devonshire Pl. Yeadon LS19 ... 40 B7 3
Devonshire St. Keigh BD21 ... 35 A7
Devonshire St W. Keigh BD21 ... 35 A7
Devonshire Terr. Bar L ... 59 B5
Dewar Cl. Coll LS22 ... 13 E1
Dewhirst Cl. Bail BD17 ... 38 D2
Dewhirst Pl. Brad BD4 ... 75 E6
Dewhirst Rd. Bail BD17 ... 38 D2
Dewhirst Rd. Brg HD6 ... 114 F4
Dewhurst Rd. Hud HD2 ... 136 B2
Dewsbury and Batley Tech & Art Coll. Batley ... 118 C5
Dewsbury and Batley Tech & Art Coll. Dew ... 139 D8
Dewsbury District Golf Course. Mir ... 138 D3
Dewsbury District Hospl. Batley ... 118 A2
Dewsbury Gate Rd. Dew WF13 ... 117 F1
Dewsbury Mkts. Dew WF12 ... 139 D7
Dewsbury Moor Crem. Dew ... 139 A8
Dewsbury Moor Jnr Sch. Dew ... 139 B8
Dewsbury Moor Sch. Dew ... 117 F1
Dewsbury Rd. Brig WF15 ... 117 B4
Dewsbury Rd. Cle BD19 ... 96 B5
Dewsbury Rd. Dew WF12 ... 118 F1
Dewsbury Rd. E Ard WF3 ... 119 D7
Dewsbury Rd. Gomer WF16 ... 117 B4
Dewsbury Rd. Hud HD1 ... 154 B4
Dewsbury Rd. Leeds LS11 ... 214 B3
Dewsbury Rd. Liver WF15 ... 117 B4
Dewsbury Rd. Mir WF14 ... 137 E4
Dewsbury Rd. Nor WF6 ... 123 C1
Dewsbury Rd. Ossett WF5 ... 140 F5
Dewsbury Rd. Wake WF2 ... 141 E4
Deyne Rd. Hud HD4 ... 171 C1
Diadem Dr. Leeds LS14 ... 61 F1
Dial St. Leeds LS9 ... 212 C1
Diamond Ave. S Elm WF9 ... 182 E1
Diamond St. Batley WF17 ... 118 C5
Diamond St. Brad BD1 ... 201 C2
Diamond St. Hali HX1 ... 113 A4
Diamond Terr. Hali HX1 ... 113 A4
Dian St. Haw BD22 ... 51 F8
Dib Cl. Leeds LS8 ... 61 D6
Dib La. Leeds LS8 ... 61 D7
Dibb La. Yeadon LS19 ... 39 F8
Dick Dean La. Wad W HX7 ... 69 A5
Dick La. Brad BD3 ... 75 C5
Dick La. Leeds BD3 ... 75 C5
Dick's Garth Rd. Men LS29 ... 22 A4
Dickens St. Brad BD5 ... 74 D4
Dickens St. Keigh BD22 ... 35 A4
Dickinson Ct. Wake WF1 ... 142 E4
Dickinson St. Hors LS18 ... 41 C1
Dickinson Terr. Feath WF7 ... 145 D6
Dickson Fold. Liver WF15 ... 116 F4
Digby Rd. Men LS29 ... 22 A4
Dirkhill Rd. Brad BD7 ... 74 C5
Digley Rd. Holmfi HD7 ... 188 A2
Digley Royd La. Holmfi HD7 ... 188 B3
Dimple Gdns. Ossett WF5 ... 140 D4
Dimple Well Inf Sch. Ossett ... 140 D4
Dimple Wells Cl. Ossett WF5 ... 140 D4

Dimple Wells La. Ossett WF5 — 140 D4
Dimple Wells Rd. Ossett WF5 — 140 D4
Dimples La. Haw BD22 — 51 B6
Dimples La. Keigh BD20 — 36 D8
Dineley Ave. Tod OL14 — 108 A7
Dingle Rd. Hud HD1 — 153 D6
Dingley Rd. Hud HD3 — 153 C8
Dinsdale's Bldgs. Yeadon LS19 — 40 A6
Dirker Ave. Mars HD7 — 169 A5
Dirker Bank Rd. Mars HD7 — 168 F5
Dirker Dr. Mars HD7 — 168 F4
Dirkhill Rd. Brad BD7 — 74 C5
Dirkhill St. Brad BD7 — 74 B5
Discovery Rd. Hali HX1 — 113 D6
Dish Hill Fly-over. Broth WF11 — 126 D8
Disney Cl. Hud HD4 — 153 D3
Dispensary Wlk. Hali HX1 — 113 D7
Disraeli Gdns. Leeds LS11 — 79 B4
Disraeli Terr. Leeds LS11 — 79 B4
Dixon Ave. Brad BD7 — 73 F5
Dixon Cl. Elland HX4 — 134 B8
Dixon Cl. Stee BD20 — 17 C5
Dixon La. Leeds LS12 — 78 C8
Dixon Lane Rd. Leeds LS12 — 78 C5
Dixon St. Feath WF7 — 145 D7
Dixon St. S in Cra BD20 — 16 E5
Dixon's Yd. Wake WF1 — 142 D6
Dob La. Sow Br HX6 — 111 D3
Dob Park Rd. Clift LS21 — 10 E8
Dob Royd. Shep HD8 — 190 D7
Dob The. Sow Br HX6 — 111 D3
Dobb La. Holmfi HD7 — 188 C2
Dobb Top Rd. Holmfi HD7 — 188 C2
Dobroyd Rd. Tod OL14 — 108 A5
Dobson Ave. Leeds LS11 — 79 C3
Dobson Gr. Leeds LS11 — 79 C3
Dobson Pl. Leeds LS11 — 79 C3
Dobson Terr. Leeds LS11 — 79 C3
Dobson View. Leeds LS11 — 79 C3
Dobsons Wharf. Sil BD20 — 17 E8
Dock La. Shipl BD17,BD18 — 55 C8
Dock St. Leeds LS10 — 79 C7
Dockery. Hud HD1 — 153 F3
Dockfield Pl. Ship BD17 — 55 C8
Dockfield Rd. Ship BD17 — 55 C8
Dockfield Terr. Ship BD17 — 55 C8
Dockroyd La. Haw BD22 — 34 D2
Doctor Fold. Honley HD7 — 171 F5
Doctor Hill. Brad BD10 — 56 A6
Doctor Hill. Hali HX2 — 91 E6
Doctor Hill. Hali HX2 — 91 E1
Doctor La. Floc WF4 — 157 B2
Doctor La. Mir WF14 — 138 A5
Doctor La. Shep HD8 — 174 A3
Dodd's Royd. Hud HD4 — 171 E8
Dodge Holme Ct. Hali HX2 — 91 D4
Dodge Holme Dr. Hali HX2 — 91 D4
Dodge Holme Gdns. Hali HX2 — 91 D4
Dodgeholme Cl. Hali HX2 — 91 D4
Dodgson Ave. Leeds LS7 — 60 E3
Dodlee La. Hud HD3 — 152 E7
Dodsworth Cres. Nor WF6 — 144 A8
Dodworth Dr. Wake WF2 — 160 B5
Dog Hill Dr. Shaf S72 — 180 C3
Dog Hill. Shaf S72 — 180 C3
Dog Kennel Bank. Hud HD5 — 154 C4
Dog Kennel Hill. Caw S75 — 193 E3
Dog La. Elland HX4 — 133 E5
Dog La. Elland HX4 — 133 E2
Dog Pits La. Bacup OL13 — 106 A8
Doghouse La. Tod OL14 — 108 A5
Dogley La. Lepton HD4 — 155 D1
Dogley Villa Ct. Lepton HD8 — 155 D1
Doldram La. Sow Br HX6 — 112 A1
Dole La. Heb Br HX7 — 89 A1
Dole St. Thorn BD13 — 72 E6
Doles Ave. Roy S71 — 179 B3
Doles Cres. Roy S71 — 179 B3
Dolfin Pl. Hud HD2 — 136 F5
Doll La. Cull BD13 — 52 D1
Dolly La. Leeds LS9 — 60 E2
Dolphin La. Midd WF3 — 99 F2
Dolphin St. Leeds LS9 — 80 A7
Dombey St. Hali HX1 — 113 A7
Domestic Rd. Leeds LS12 — 78 F5
Domestic St. Leeds LS11 — 78 F5
Domestic Street Ind Est. Leeds — 78 F6
Dominion Ave. Leeds LS7 — 60 D7
Don Pk. Brig — 114 C8
Don Ave. Weth LS22 — 13 E6
Don Ct. Sil BD20 — 5 E1
Don Pedro Ave. Nor WF6 — 123 D2
Don Pedro Cl. Nor WF6 — 123 D2
Don St. Keigh BD21 — 35 B6
Don View. Dun Br S30 — 199 D1
Donald Ave. Brad BD6 — 94 C8
Donald St. Pudsey LS28 — 57 D2
Doncaster La. Ham DN6 — 184 C2
Doncaster Rd. Ackw WF7 — 163 F4
Doncaster Rd. Crof WF4 — 143 D2
Doncaster Rd. Dar WF7 — 164 A8
Doncaster Rd. Hems WF9 — 183 D5
Doncaster Rd. Knot WF11 — 126 C4
Doncaster Rd. S Elm WF9 — 183 D5
Doncaster Rd. Upton WF9 — 166 A1
Doncaster Rd. Upton WF9 — 182 E7
Doncaster Rd. W Har WF9 — 163 A6
Doncaster Sq. Knot WF11 — 126 D5
Doncaster St. Hali HX3 — 113 D3
Donisthorpe St. Leeds LS10 — 79 E5
Dorchester Ave. Pont WF8 — 146 D5
Dorchester Cres. Brad BD4 — 75 E2
Dorchester Cres. Pont WF8 — 146 D5
Dorchester Ct. Brad BD14 — 75 E3
Dorchester Dr. Hali HX2 — 91 E7
Dorchester Dr. Yeadon LS19 — 40 E1
Dorchester Rd. Hud HD2 — 136 B5
Dore Rd. Grot WF9 — 183 C6
Dorman Ave. Upton WF9 — 183 D8
Dorothy St. Keigh BD21 — 35 A3
Dorset Ave. Leeds LS8 — 61 A4
Dorset Cl. Brad BD5 — 74 E3
Dorset Gr. Pudsey LS28 — 76 E6
Dorset Mount. Leeds LS8 — 61 A3
Dorset Rd. Leeds LS8 — 61 A3

Dorset St. Brad BD5 — 74 D3
Dorset St. Hud HD1 — 153 F8
Dorset St. Leeds LS8 — 61 A4
Dorset Terr. Leeds LS8 — 61 A3
Dortmund Sq. Leeds LS2 — 79 C8
Doubting La. Dew WF12 — 139 D1
Doubting Rd. Dew WF12 — 139 D1
Douglas Ave. Batley WF17 — 118 F5
Douglas Ave. Hud HD3 — 153 B6
Douglas Cres. Ship BD18 — 55 D6
Douglas Dr. Brad BD4 — 75 C4
Douglas Rd. Bacup OL13 — 106 A1
Douglas Rd. Brad BD4 — 75 C4
Douglas St. Dew WF12 — 139 C4
Douglas St. Hali HX3 — 92 B2
Douglas St. Haw BD22 — 51 E8
Dove Cl. Weth LS22 — 13 C6
Dove Dr. Castle WF10 — 125 B8
Dove St. Haw BD22 — 51 D7
Dove St. Keigh BD21 — 35 B7
Dove St. Ship BD18 — 54 F8
Dovecote Cl. Hor WF4 — 141 B2
Dovecote Dr. Ledst WF10 — 103 E6
Dovecote La. Hor WF4 — 141 A2
Dovedale Cl. Crof WF4 — 144 A1
Dovedale Cl. Shelf HX3 — 93 B6
Dovedale Garth. Leeds LS15 — 62 F3
Dovedale Gdns. Leeds LS15 — 62 F3
Dovelands. S in Cra BD20 — 16 C6
Dover La. Holmfi HD7 — 189 B3
Dover Rd. Holmfi HD7 — 189 A3
Dover St. Brad BD3 — 56 A1
Dover St. Gar LS25 — 82 B7
Dover St. Tod OL14 — 108 D5
Dovesdale Gr. Brad BD5 — 74 D2
Dovesdale Rd. Brad BD5 — 74 D2
Dowkell La. Th Arch LS23 — 14 F1
Dowker St. Hali HX1 — 112 F5
Dowker St. Hud HD3 — 153 B5
Dowley Gap La. Bing BD16 — 37 B1
Downham St. Brad BD3 — 75 B7
Downing Cl. Brad BD3 — 75 B7
Downing St. Slai HD7 — 152 A3
Downland Cres. Knot WF11 — 127 B2
Downside Cres. Brad BD15 — 54 A1
Downy La. Rip HX6 — 132 A3
Dracup Ave. Brad BD7 — 73 F3
Dracup Rd. Brad BD7 — 73 F3
Dradishaw Rd. Sil BD20 — 5 D1
Dragon Cres. Leeds LS12 — 78 D5
Dragon Dr. Leeds LS12 — 78 D5
Dragon Rd. Leeds LS12 — 78 D5
Drake La. Birk BD11 — 96 E5
Drake Rd. Litt OL15 — 129 C1
Drake St. Brad BD1 — 74 F6
Drake St. Keigh BD21 — 35 C8
Drakes Ind Est. Hud — 154 B7
Draper Corner. Hep HX7 — 88 E6
Draper La. Hep HX7 — 88 F6
Draughton Gr. Brad BD5 — 74 D1
Draughton St. Brad BD5 — 74 D1
Dray Haw. Batley WF12 — 117 F2
Draycott Wlk. Brad BD4 — 75 E2
Drayton Manor Yd. Leeds LS11 — 79 C4
Drewry Rd. Keigh BD21 — 35 B7
Drewton Rd. Brad BD1 — 74 E7
Driftholme Rd. Birk BD11 — 96 F7
Drighlington Cty Inf Sch. Birk — 96 E6
Drighlington Jun Sch. Birk — 96 F7
Drill Dr. Brad BD8 — 55 D1
Drill St. Haw BD22 — 51 C8
Drive The. Bard LS17 — 28 D5
Drive The. Batley WF17 — 118 A6
Drive The. Bing BD16 — 36 E6
Drive The. Brad BD10 — 56 D6
Drive The. Brig HX3 — 114 D8
Drive The. Bur in W LS29 — 21 E8
Drive The. Heb Br HX7 — 89 A3
Drive The. Kippax LS25 — 83 A1
Drive The. Leeds LS17 — 43 A6
Drive The. Leeds LS8 — 61 C6
Drive The. Leeds LS8 — 62 D2
Drive The. Nor WF6 — 123 B1
Drive The. S Elm WF9 — 182 F3
Drive The. Swil LS26 — 82 C2
Driver St. Leeds LS12 — 78 E6
Driver Terr. Leeds LS12 — 78 E6
Driver Terr. Sil BD20 — 5 E1
Drivers Row. Pont WF8 — 146 B7
Drub La. Cleck BD19 — 95 F2
Druggist La. Sil LS29 — 6 F8
Druids St. Brad BD14 — 73 C4
Druids View. Bing BD16 — 36 D6
Drummer La. Slai HD7 — 152 B4
Drummond Ave. Leeds LS16 — 59 C6
Drummond Cl. Leeds LS16 — 59 C5
Drummond Mid Sch. Brad — 55 C1
Drummond Rd. Brad BD8 — 55 C1
Drummond Rd. Leeds LS16 — 59 C5
Drummond Trad Est. Brad — 74 D8
Drury Ave. Hors LS18 — 58 C8
Drury Cl. Hors LS18 — 58 B8
Drury La. Hors LS18 — 58 B8
Drury La. Nor WF6 — 122 F3
Drury La. Wake WF1 — 142 D5
Dry Carr La. Hali HX2 — 90 C4
Dry Hill La. D Dale HD8 — 192 B5
Dryclough La. Hali HX3 — 113 C2
Dryclough La. Hud HD4 — 154 A3
Dryclough Rd. Hud HD4 — 153 F3
Dryden St. Bing BD16 — 36 F3
Dryden St. Brad BD1 — 74 D7

Dudley Hill Rd. Brad BD2 — 56 B3
Dudley Rd. Hud HD1 — 153 D6
Dudley St. Brad BD4 — 75 B3
Dudley St. Brad BD4 — 75 C3
Dudley St. Brad BD4 — 75 E5
Dudwell Ave. Hali HX3 — 113 C2
Dudwell Gr. Hali HX3 — 113 C2
Dudwell La. Hali HX3 — 113 C2
Dufton App. Leeds LS14 — 62 A3
Duich Rd. Brad BD6 — 93 E6
Duinen St. Brad BD5 — 74 F5
Duke of York Ave. Wake WF2 — 142 D1
Duke of York St. Wake WF2 — 142 D1
Duke of York St. Wake WF1 — 142 F1
Duke St. Brad BD1 — 74 E7
Duke St. Castle WF10 — 124 D8
Duke St. Dew WF13 — 138 E5
Duke St. Elland HX5 — 134 F6
Duke St. Hali HX1 — 90 D1
Duke St. Haw BD22 — 51 D7
Duke St. Hem WF9 — 163 A3
Duke St. Keigh BD20 — 18 C1
Duke St. Leeds LS9 — 79 F7
Duke St. Liver WF15 — 117 B3
Duke Wood Rd. Clay W HD8 — 175 F2
Dulverton Cl. Morley LS11 — 78 D1
Dulverton Ct. Morley LS11 — 78 D1
Dulverton Garth. Morley LS11 — 78 C1
Dulverton Gdns. Morley LS11 — 78 D1
Dulverton Gn. Morley LS11 — 78 C1
Dulverton Gr. Brad BD4 — 75 D5
Dulverton Gr. Morley LS11 — 78 D1
Dulverton Pl. Morley LS11 — 78 C1
Dulverton Sq. Morley LS11 — 78 D1
Dumb La. Dew WF12 — 118 C1
Dunbottle Cl. Mir WF14 — 138 C5
Dunbottle La. Mir WF14 — 138 B6
Duncan Ave. Otley LS21 — 22 D6
Duncan Ave. Wake WF2 — 142 E2
Duncan St. Brad BD5 — 74 D4
Duncan St. Leeds LS1 — 79 C7
Dunce Park Cl. Elland HX5 — 134 F6
Duncombe Rd. Brad BD8 — 74 A7
Duncombe St. Brad BD8 — 74 A7
Duncombe St. Leeds LS1 — 79 B7
Duncombe Way. Brad BD8 — 74 A7
Dundas St. Hali HX1 — 112 F5
Dundas St. Keigh BD21 — 35 D8
Dundee Rd. Tod OL14 — 107 D8
Dunderdale Cres. Castle WF10 — 125 A2
Dunford Rd. Holmfi HD7 — 189 D4
Dunford Rd. Dun Br HD7 — 199 D2
Dunford Townhead Sch. Dun Br — 199 F2
Dungeon La. Roth LS26 — 101 A1
Dunhill Cres. Leeds LS9 — 80 E8
Dunhill Rise. Leeds LS9 — 80 E8
Dunkirk Gdns. Hali HX1 — 112 D6
Dunkirk Hill. Leeds LS12 — 78 C4
Dunkirk La. Hali HX1 — 112 D6
Dunkirk Rise. Keigh BD21 — 18 E2
Dunkirk St. Hali HX1 — 112 D6
Dunkirk Terr. Hali HX1 — 112 D6
Dunlin Cl. Midd LS10 — 99 D5
Dunlin Croft. Midd LS10 — 99 D5
Dunlin Dr. Midd LS10 — 99 D5
Dunlin Fold. Midd LS10 — 99 D5
Dunlin Way. Brad BD8 — 73 D7
Dunn Cl. Wake WF2 — 120 F3
Dunningley La. Midd WF3 — 99 F2
Dunningley La. Ting WF3 — 99 F2
Dunnington Wlk. Brad BD6 — 94 A6
Dunrobin Ave. Gar LS25 — 83 B8
Dunsford Ave. Brad BD4 — 75 E3
Dunsil Villas. S Elm WF9 — 182 F1
Dunsley Bank Rd. Holmfi HD7 — 188 D2
Dunsley Terr. S Kirk WF9 — 182 A2
Dunstan Cl. Ossett WF5 — 140 F8
Dunstarn Dr. Leeds LS16 — 42 D3
Dunstarn Gdns. Leeds LS16 — 42 E3
Dunstarn La. Leeds LS16 — 42 E3
Durban Ave. Leeds LS11 — 78 F2
Durban Cres. Leeds LS11 — 78 F2
Durham Rd. Brad BD8 — 74 A8
Durham St. Castle WF10 — 124 E6
Durham St. Hali HX2 — 112 C7
Durham Terr. Brad BD8 — 74 A8
Durkar Fields. Crig WF4 — 159 F6
Durkar La. Crig WF4 — 159 F6
Durkar Low La. Crig WF4 — 159 E6
Durkar Rise. Crig WF4 — 159 F6
Durley Ave. Brad BD9 — 54 E2
Durling Dr. Ship BD18 — 55 C7
Durn St. Tod OL14 — 86 A1
Durrance St. Keigh BD22 — 34 F4
Durrant Cl. Weth LS22 — 13 E7
Dutton Gn. Leeds LS14 — 62 A4
Dutton Way. Leeds LS14 — 62 A4
Duxbury Rise. Leeds LS7 — 79 F8
Dyehouse Dr. Brad BD12 — 94 C1
Dyehouse La. Brig HD6 — 114 F4
Dyehouse La. Pudsey LS28 — 76 E6
Dyehouse Rd. Brad BD12 — 95 A4
Dyer St. Leeds LS2 — 79 D7
Dyke Bottom. Shep HD8 — 174 B3
Dyke Cl. Mir WF14 — 138 A8
Dymond Gr. Liver WF15 — 117 B2
Dymond Rd. Liver WF15 — 117 B2
Dymond View. Liver WF15 — 117 B2
Dyson Pl. Hali HX3 — 113 C2
Dyson Rd. Hali HX1 — 112 F7
Dyson St. Brad BD1 — 74 D7
Dyson St. Brad BD9 — 55 A3
Dyson St. Hud HD1 — 153 F8
Dyson's Mill. Honley HD7 — 171 E5

Eagle St. Keigh BD21 — 35 B7
Eagle St. Tod OL14 — 108 B6
Eaglesfield Dr. Brad BD6 — 94 A6
Ealand Ave. Batley WF17 — 118 A7
Ealand Cres. Batley WF17 — 118 A7
Ealand Rd. Batley WF17 — 117 F7
Ealand Rd. Batley WF17 — 118 A7
Ealing Cl. Batley WF17 — 118 A6
Earl Cowper Mid Sch. Leeds — 60 E4
Earl St. Dew WF12 — 140 B8
Earl St. Haw BD22 — 51 C6
Earl St. Hem WF9 — 163 A3
Earl St. Keigh BD21 — 35 B8
Earl St. Wake WF1 — 142 D7
Earl Terr. Hali HX3 — 113 A3
Earle St. Feath WF7 — 145 C6
Earles Ave. Hud HD5 — 154 E5
Earls View. S in Cra BD20 — 16 C4
Earlsheaton High Sch. Dew — 139 E8
Earlsheaton Inf Sch. Dew — 139 F7
Earlsmere Dr. Morley LS27 — 97 F5
Earlswood Ave. Leeds LS8 — 43 F2
Earlswood Chase. Pudsey LS28 — 76 E6
Earlswood Mead. Pudsey LS28 — 76 E6
Easby Ave. Batley WF17 — 117 F6
Easby Cl. Ilkley LS29 — 7 F4
Easby Dr. Ilkley LS29 — 7 F4
Easby Rd. Brad BD7 — 74 D5
Easdale Cl. Leeds LS14 — 61 F5
Easdale Cres. Leeds LS14 — 62 A5
Easdale Mount. Leeds LS14 — 62 A5
Easdale Rd. Leeds LS14 — 61 F5
Easingwood Dr. Kirkhe HD5 — 137 B1
East Acres. Byram WF11 — 126 D7
East Ardsley Prim Sch. E Ard — 120 D8
East Ave. Glu BD20 — 16 D6
East Ave. Horbury WF4 — 141 C1
East Ave. Hud HD5 — 154 C5
East Ave. Keigh BD21 — 35 C8
East Ave. Upton WF9 — 183 A7
East Bath St. Batley WF17 — 118 C4
East Bolton. Hali HX2 — 91 E7
East Busk La. Otley LS21 — 23 C8
East Byland. Hali HX2 — 91 E7
East Causeway Cl. Leeds LS16 — 42 D4
East Causeway Cres. Leeds LS16 — 42 D4
East Causeway. Leeds LS16 — 42 D4

East Chevin Rd. Otley LS21 — 23 C5
East Cl. Hud HD2 — 136 B2
East Cl. Pont WF8 — 146 E6
East Dale Cl. Hem WF9 — 181 F7
East Dene. Keigh BD20 — 18 E1
East Dene. Sil BD20 — 5 D1
East Down. Castle WF10 — 125 A8
East End Cres. S Elm WF9 — 182 F3
East Field St. Leeds LS9 — 80 B7
East Garforth Cty Prim Sch. Gar — 83 B8
East Grange Cl. Leeds LS10 — 79 F1
East Grange Dr. Leeds LS10 — 79 F1
East Grange Garth. Midd LS10 — 79 F1
East Grange Gdns. Leeds LS10 — 79 F1
East Grange Rd. Midd LS10 — 79 F1
East Grange Rise. Leeds LS10 — 79 F1
East Grange Sq. Leeds LS10 — 79 F1
East Grange View. Leeds LS10 — 79 F1
East Hardwick Cty Prim Sch. Dar — 146 A2
East Keswick CE Jun & Inf Sch. E Kes — 28 C5
East Lee La. Tod OL14 — 109 F8
East Leeds High Sch. Leeds — 62 C5
East Moor Ave. Leeds LS8 — 43 F1
East Moor Community Home Sch. — 42 E4
East Moor Cres. Leeds LS8 — 43 F1
East Moor Dr. Leeds LS8 — 44 A1
East Moor La. Kirkhe HD5 — 137 C8
East Moor Rd. Leeds LS8 — 44 A1
East Mount Pl. Brig HD6 — 115 A3
East Mount. Brig HD6 — 115 A3
East Par. Ilkley LS29 — 8 A4
East Par. Keigh BD21 — 35 C7
East Par. Leeds LS1 — 79 B8
East Par. Men LS29 — 22 A4
East Par. Shipl BD18 — 55 B7
East Park Dr. Leeds LS9 — 80 A7
East Park Gr. Leeds LS9 — 80 A7
East Park Mount. Leeds LS9 — 80 A7
East Park Par. Leeds LS9 — 80 A7
East Park Pl. Leeds LS9 — 80 A7
East Park Rd. Brad BD4 — 75 B4
East Park Rd. Hali HX3 — 92 A1
East Park Rd. Leeds LS9 — 80 A7
East Park Rd. Spen BD19 — 116 D7
East Park St. Leeds LS9 — 80 A7
East Park St. Morley LS27 — 98 B4
East Park Terr. Leeds LS9 — 80 A7
East Park View. Leeds LS9 — 80 A7
East Pinfold. Roy S71 — 179 C2
East Rd. Brad BD12 — 94 C6
East Royd. Haw BD22 — 34 D2
East Squire La. Brad BD8 — 55 C1
East St. Batley WF17 — 118 C4
East St. Brig HD6 — 115 B1
East St. Heb Br HX7 — 89 A3
East St. Hud HD1 — 154 B6
East St. Leeds LS9 — 79 F7
East St. Loft WF1 — 121 B2
East St. S Elm WF9 — 183 A4
East St. S Kirk WF9 — 182 B2

East View. M'field LS25 — 84 B6
East View. Mir WF14 — 137 F5
East View. Ossett WF5 — 140 E3
East View. Pudsey LS28 — 76 E5
East View Rd. Yeadon LS19 — 40 C5
East View. Roth LS26 — 101 C5
East View. Sil BD20 — 5 E2
East View Terr. Otley LS21 — 23 B7
East View. Yeadon LS19 — 40 C6
East-Thorpe Pl. Mir WF14 — 138 B4
Eastborough Cres. Dew WF13 — 118 B1
Eastborough Jun & Inf Sch. Dew — 139 D8
Eastbourne Ave. Feath WF7 — 145 E6
Eastbourne Cl. Feath WF7 — 145 E6
Eastbourne Cres. Pont WF8 — 147 A8
Eastbourne Dr. Pont WF8 — 147 A8
Eastbourne Rd. Ship BD9 — 55 B5
Eastbourne Terr. Pont WF8 — 147 A8
Eastbourne View. Pont WF8 — 147 A8
Eastbrook Well. Brad BD1 — 74 F7
Eastbury Ave. Brad BD6 — 93 E7
Eastburn Jun & Inf Sch. Stee — 16 F6
Eastcliffe. Brad BD13 — 72 D6
Eastdean Bank. Leeds LS14 — 62 A6
Eastdean Dr. Leeds LS14 — 62 A6
Eastdean Gate. Leeds LS14 — 62 B5
Eastdean Gdns. Leeds LS14 — 62 B6
Eastdean Gr. Leeds LS14 — 62 B6
Eastdean Grange. Leeds LS14 — 62 A6
Eastdean Rd. Leeds LS14 — 62 A6
Eastdean Rise. Leeds LS14 — 62 B6
Easterly Ave. Leeds LS8 — 61 B4
Easterly Cl. Leeds LS8 — 61 B3
Easterly Cres. Leeds LS8 — 61 B4
Easterly Cross. Leeds LS8 — 61 B4
Easterly Garth. Leeds LS8 — 61 A4
Easterly Gr. Leeds LS8 — 61 B4
Easterly Mount. Leeds LS8 — 61 B4
Easterly Rd. Leeds LS8 — 61 B4
Easterly Sq. Leeds LS8 — 61 B4
Easterly View. Leeds LS8 — 61 B4
Eastfield Ave. Knot WF11 — 126 F3
Eastfield Cres. Roth LS26 — 101 B6
Eastfield Dr. Kirkb HD8 — 173 E7
Eastfield Dr. Pont WF8 — 125 F1
Eastfield Dr. Roth LS26 — 101 B6
Eastfield Gdns. Brad BD4 — 75 E3
Eastfield La. Castle WF10 — 124 E8
Eastfield Pl. S in Cra BD20 — 16 D5
Eastfield Rd. Mir WF14 — 138 D6
Eastfield. Shep HD8 — 190 F8
Eastgate. Elland HX5 — 134 F7
Eastgate. Hem WF9 — 181 E7
Eastgate. Honley HD7 — 171 F5
Eastgate. Leeds LS2 — 79 C8
Eastland Wlk. Leeds LS13 — 58 E1
Eastleigh Dr. E Ard WF3 — 120 A8
Eastleigh Gr. Wake WF2 — 141 F5
Eastmoor Pk. Mir WF14 — 138 A4
Eastway. Mir WF14 — 137 F7
Eastway Pk. Mir WF14 — 138 A7
Eastwood Ave. Brad BD6 — 74 A1
Eastwood Cl. Crig WF4 — 159 F7
Eastwood Dr. Leeds LS8 — 61 D5
Eastwood Garth. Leeds LS14 — 62 D4
Eastwood Gdns. Leeds LS14 — 62 D4
Eastwood La. Leeds LS14 — 62 D4
Eastwood Nook. Leeds LS14 — 62 D4
Eastwood St. Brad BD4 — 74 F5
Eastwood St. Brig HD6 — 114 F3
Eaton Hill. Leeds LS16 — 42 C2
Eaton Mews. Midd LS10 — 99 D4
Eaton Pl. Hem WF9 — 181 E7
Eaton Rd. Ilkley LS29 — 8 A3
Eaton Sq. Midd LS10 — 99 D4
Eaton St. Keigh BD21 — 35 A7
Ebenezer St. Brad BD1 — 74 D7
Ebenezer St. Pudsey LS28 — 57 D3
Ebony St. Keigh BD21 — 18 F1
Ebor Ct. Batley WF17 — 118 D4
Ebor Gardens Cty Prim Sch. Leeds — 79 F8
Ebridge Ct. Bing BD16 — 37 A3
Ebson House La. Wils BD15 — 53 C5
Ebury Cl. Batley WF17 — 118 D6
Ebury St. Batley WF17 — 118 D6
Ecclesburn Ave. Leeds LS9 — 80 B7
Ecclesburn Rd. Leeds LS9 — 80 B7
Ecclesburn St. Leeds LS9 — 80 B7
Ecclesburn Terr. Leeds LS9 — 80 B7
Eccup Moor Rd. Eccup LS16 — 26 E3
Edale Cl. Kirkhe HD5 — 137 B1
Edale Gr. Queen BD13 — 92 C8

Edale Way. Hors LS16 .... 41 F3
Eddercliff Cres. Liver WF15 ...... 117 A6
Edderthorpe St. Brad BD3 .... 75 A6
Eddison Cl. Hors LS16 .... 42 D5
Eddison St. Pudsey LS28 .... 57 D2
Eddison Wlk. Hors LS16 .... 42 D5
Eddystone Rise. Knot WF11 ...... 126 D3
Edenham Gr. Wake WF2 .... 160 F8
Eden Ave. Ossett WF5 .... 140 D6
Eden Ave. Wake WF2 .... 141 D5
Eden Cl. Brad BD12 .... 94 D3
Eden Cres. Leeds LS4 .... 59 B4
Eden Dr. Leeds LS4 .... 59 B4
Eden Gdns. Leeds LS4 .... 59 B3
Eden Gr. Leeds LS4 .... 59 B3
Eden Mount. Leeds LS4 .... 59 B3
Eden Rd. Leeds LS4 .... 59 B4
Eden Way. Leeds LS4 .... 59 B3
Edendale. Castle WF10 .... 124 F8
Edensor Rd. Keigh BD21 .... 35 A7
Ederoyd Ave. Pudsey LS28 ...... 57 B1
Ederoyd Cres. Pudsey LS28 ...... 57 B1
Ederoyd Dr. Pudsey LS28 ...... 57 B1
Ederoyd Gr. Pudsey LS28 ...... 57 B1
Ederoyd Mount. Pudsey LS28 .... 57 B1
Ederoyd Rise. Pudsey LS28 ...... 57 A1
Edgar St. Brad BD14 .... 73 D3
Edgbaston Cl. Leeds LS17 .... 43 A1
Edgbaston Wlk. Leeds LS17 ...... 43 A1
Edge Ave. Dew WF12 .... 139 D1
Edge Cl. Dew WF12 .... 139 E1
Edge Hill Rd. 152 E4
Edge End. Denh BD13 .... 52 E1
Edge End Gdns. Brad BD6 .... 93 E7
Edge End La. Holmfi HD7 .... 188 A4
Edge Hill Cl. Hud HD5 .... 154 D7
Edge Junc. Dew WF12 .... 139 D1
Edge La. Dew WF12 .... 139 F1
Edge La. Hep HX7 .... 87 F7
Edge Rd. Dew WF12 .... 139 F1
Edge Terr. Hud HD3 .... 152 F7
Edge Top Rd. Dew WF12 .... 139 C1
Edge View. Dew WF12 .... 139 E1
Edge View. Hud HD7 .... 152 E4
Edgebank Ave. Brad BD6 .... 93 F8
Edgehey Gn. Hep HX7 .... 88 B6
Edgehill Cl. Queen BD13 .... 72 H6 6
Edgehill Rd. Mapp S75 .... 178 B2
Edgeholme La. Hali HX2 .... 112 A7
Edgemoor Cl. Hali HX2 .... 91 B4
Edgemoor Rd. Crig WF4 .... 159 F2
Edgemoor Rd. Honley HD7 ...... 171 E3
Edgerton Garth. Hud HD1 .... 153 E7
Edgerton Gr. Hud HD1 .... 153 E7
Edgerton Grove Rd. Hud HD1 .... 153 E7
Edgerton La. Hud HD1 .... 153 E7
Edgerton Rd. Leeds LS16 .... 59 B8
Edgeware Rd. Hud HD5 .... 154 D5
Edgware Ave. Leeds LS8 .... 60 F2 7
Edgware Gr. Leeds LS8 .... 60 F2
Edgware Mount. Leeds LS8 ...... 60 F2 2
Edgware Pl. Leeds LS8 .... 60 F2 3
Edgware Row. Leeds LS8 .... 60 F2 4
Edgware St. Leeds LS8 .... 60 F2 5
Edgware Terr. Leeds LS8 .... 60 F2 6
Edgware View. Leeds LS8 .... 60 F2 8
Edinburgh Ave. Leeds LS12 ...... 78 A8
Edinburgh Gr. Leeds LS12 ...... 78 A8
Edinburgh Pl. Gar LS25 .... 83 B7
Edinburgh Rd. Leeds LS12 ...... 78 A8
Edinburgh Rd. Leeds LS12 ...... 78 A8
Edinburgh Terr. Leeds LS12 .... 78 A8
Edington Cl. Brad BD4 .... 75 E3
Edmund Campion R C Sch. Brad ... 73 D8
Edmund St. Brad BD5 .... 74 D6
Edmund St. Tod OL14 .... 129 B7
Edna St. S Elm WF9 .... 183 A3
Edrich Cl. Brad BD11 .... 96 F7
Edroyd Pl. Pudsey LS28 .... 57 D3
Edroyd St. Pudsey LS28 .... 57 D3
Education Rd. Leeds LS7 .... 60 C3
Edward Cl. Hew HX3 .... 114 A4
Edward Cl. Mir WF14 .... 117 C5
Edward Dr. W W WF1 .... 121 C5
Edward St. Bacup OL13 .... 106 A3
Edward St. Brad BD4 .... 74 F6
Edward St. Brad BD4 .... 75 E1
Edward St. Brig HD6 .... 115 C2
Edward St. Hali HX6 .... 112 A4
Edward St. Heb Br HX7 .... 89 A3
Edward St. Liver WF15 .... 117 A5
Edward St. Wake WF1 .... 142 D7
Edward Turner Cl. Brad BD12 .... 94 C6 1
Edwards Rd. Hali HX2 .... 112 C5
Edwin Rd. Leeds LS6 .... 59 F5
Eel Holme View St. Keigh BD20 ... 18 B2
Eel Mires Garth. Weth LS22 ...... 13 F6
Effingham Rd. Harden BD16 ...... 36 A1
Egerton St. Brad BD1 .... 84 F7
Egerton St. Hali HX6 .... 112 B4
Egerton Terr. Rodley LS19 ...... 40 D3
Eggleston Dr. Brad BD4 .... 75 E1
Eggleston St. Leeds LS13 ...... 58 C2
Egglestone Sq. B Spa LS23 ...... 30 C7
Egham Gn. Brad BD10 .... 56 E6
Egmanton Rd. Barn S71 .... 178 F1
Egremont Cres. Brad BD6 ...... 93 F6
Egremont St. Sow Br HX6 ...... 112 C3
Egremont Terr. Sow Br HX6 ...... 112 C3
Egypt Rd. Wils BD13 .... 72 C8
Eiffel Bldgs. Heb Br HX7 .... 89 A3
Eiffel St. Heb Br HX7 .... 89 A3
Eighth Ave. Dew WF13 .... 118 D4
Eighth Ave. Leeds LS12 .... 78 E6
Eighth Ave. Roth LS26 .... 101 C6
Eightlands Ave. Leeds LS13 ...... 58 D2
Eightlands La. Leeds LS13 ...... 58 D2
Eightlands Rd. Dew WF13 ...... 139 C8
Elam Wood Rd. Keigh BD20 ...... 18 C3
Eland House. Elland HX5 .... 134 F7 8
Elba Terr. Ossett WF4 .... 141 B2
Elbow La. Brad BD2 .... 56 A3
Elbow La. Hali HX2 .... 91 E1
Elder Ave. Upton WF9 .... 183 C8
Elder Ave. Wake WF2 .... 160 C3
Elder Bank. Cull BD13 .... 52 D6
Elder Cl. Batley WF17 .... 96 F2
Elder Croft. Leeds LS13 .... 58 C1

Elder Dr. Dew WF12 .... 139 D3
Elder Dr. Upton WF9 .... 183 C8
Elder Garth. Gar LS25 .... 83 B6
Elder Gr. Wake WF2 .... 142 A7
Elder Gr. Hud HD4 .... 171 D6
Elder Gr. Wake WF2 .... 142 A7
Elder Grove Mews. Hud HD4 ...... 171 D6
Elder La. Hud HD4 .... 137 A5
Elder Mount. Leeds LS13 .... 58 C1 1
Elder Pl. Leeds LS13 .... 58 C1 2
Elder Rd. Leeds LS13 .... 58 C1
Elder St. Brad BD10 .... 56 E7
Eldon Pl. Brad BD1 .... 74 D8
Eldon Pl. Clec BD19 .... 116 E7
Eldon St. Batley WF16 .... 117 D4
Eldon St. Hali HX1 .... 113 C8
Eldon St. Ossett WF5 .... 140 C8
Eldroth Mount. Hali HX1 .... 113 A5 20
Eldwick Fst Sch. Bing 37 C5
Eleanor Dr. Pudsey LS28 .... 76 F7
Eleanor St. Brig HD6 .... 115 A1
Eleventh Ave. Clec WF15 .... 116 C5
Elford Gr. Leeds LS8 .... 60 F3
Elford Pl E. Leeds LS8 .... 60 F3
Elford Pl W. Leeds LS8 .... 60 F3
Elford Rd. Leeds LS8 .... 60 F3
Elgar Wlk. Loft G WF3 .... 121 E6
Elgin Cl. Hud HD4 .... 153 C6
Eli St. Brad BD5 .... 74 F3
Elia St. Keigh BD21 .... 35 D8
Elim Wlk. Dew WF13 .... 139 C8 4
Eliot Gr. Guise LS20 .... 39 F8
Elizabeth Ave. Brad BD12 ...... 94 D4
Elizabeth Ave. S Hie S72 .... 180 E5
Elizabeth Cres. Brad BD12 ...... 94 D4
Elizabeth Ct. Castle WF10 ...... 125 C8
Elizabeth Dr. Hem WF9 .... 181 E6
Elizabeth Ct. Coll LS22 .... 29 A8
Elizabeth Dr. Hem WF9 .... 181 E6
Elizabeth Dr. Castle WF10 ...... 125 C8
Elizabeth Gdns. Morley LS27 .... 147 C7
Elizabeth Jer. Morley LS27 ...... 98 C5
Elizabeth House. Hali HX2 ...... 91 E3
Elizabeth St. Bing BD16 .... 37 C3
Elizabeth St. Brad BD5 .... 74 E5
Elizabeth St. Brad BD12 .... 94 D4
Elizabeth St. Elland HX4 .... 134 D7 1
Elizabeth St. Hem WF9 .... 181 E6
Elizabeth St. Haw BD22 .... 51 C6
Elizabeth St. Hud HD4 .... 154 A3
Elizabeth St. Liver WF15 .... 116 F4
Elizabeth St. Leeds LS8 .... 61 E2
Elizabethan Ct. Pont WF8 ...... 125 E2
Ella St. Hem WF9 .... 163 A4
Elland Bridge. Elland HX5 ...... 134 F7
Elland CE S. Elland 134 F7
Elland Golf Course. Elland 134 A4
Elland Independent Hospl. Elland .. 135 A7
Elland Inf Sch. Elland 134 E5
Elland La. Elland HX5 .... 135 A7
Elland Rd. Hali HD6, HX5 .... 114 E2
Elland Rd. Morley LS27 .... 78 E3
Elland Rd. Morley LS11 .... 78 E3
Elland Rd. Rip HX6 .... 132 E4
Elland Road Ind Est. Leeds 78 F1
Elland Road Stadium. Leeds 78 F1
Elland St. Castle WF10 .... 103 F1
Elland Way. Leeds LS11 .... 78 F1
Elland Wood Bottom. Hali HX3, HX5 .... 113 D1
Elland-Riorges' Link. Elland HX5 .... 135 A7
Ellar Carr Rd. Cull BD10 ...... 39 C1
Ellar Carr Rd. Cull BD13 .... 52 C7
Ellen Holme Cotts. Hali HX2 .... 111 C5
Ellen Royd La. Hali HX2 .... 111 C8
Ellen Royd St. Hali HX3 .... 113 C8
Ellen St. Bing BD16 .... 37 A3 13
Ellenthorpe Rd. Bail BD17 ...... 37 F2
Ellerby La. Leeds LS9 .... 79 E6
Ellerby Rd. Leeds LS9 .... 79 E7
Ellercroft Ave. Brad BD7 ...... 74 A6
Ellercroft Rd. Brad BD7 .... 74 A6
Ellercroft Terr. Brad BD7 ...... 74 A6
Ellerker La. Thorner LS14 ...... 46 B5
Ellerker La. Thorner LS14 ...... 46 B5
Ellers Gr. Leeds LS8 .... 60 F4
Ellers Rd. Leeds LS8 .... 60 F4
Ellers Rd. S in Cra BD20 .... 16 D4
Ellerton St. Brad BD3 .... 75 A6
Ellicott Ct. Men LS29 .... 22 A4
Ellin's Terr. Nor WF6 .... 144 A8
Ellinthorpe St. Brad BD4 .... 75 B1
Elliot Ct. Queen BD13 .... 72 D1 1
Elliott St. Sil BD20 .... 5 D1
Elliott St. Sil BD20 .... 5 D1
Ellis Pl. Leeds LS11 .... 79 B3 7
Ellis St. Brad BD5 .... 65 A1
Ellison St. Hali HX4 .... 92 A1 7
Elliston Ave. Mapp S75 .... 178 C1
Ellistones Gdns. Elland HX4 .... 134 A4
Ellistones La. Elland HX4 ...... 134 A6
Ellmont Ave. Emley HD8 .... 175 D7
Ellwood Cl. Leeds LS7 .... 43 A1
Elm Ave. Holmfi HD7 .... 189 C8
Elm Ave. Hud HD1 .... 153 F5
Elm Ave. Tod OL14 .... 129 A7
Elm Ave. Tod OL14 .... 108 B6
Elm Cl. Ossett WF5 .... 140 E4
Elm Cres. Keigh BD20 .... 18 A1
Elm Croft. Leeds LS14 .... 62 A3
Elm Ct. Birk BD11 .... 96 B6
Elm Gdns. Castle WF10 .... 125 C8
Elm Gr. Bur in Wf LS29 .... 9 E1
Elm Gr. Keigh BD21 .... 35 B4

Elm Gr. Liver WF16 .... 117 C5
Elm Gr. S Elm WF9 .... 182 F3
Elm Gr. Shelf HX3 .... 93 H6
Elm Gr. Ship BD18 .... 55 E7
Elm Gr. Sil BD20 .... 5 D1
Elm Pk. Pont WF8 .... 146 C6
Elm Pl. Hali HX6 .... 112 B5 11
Elm Rd. Dew WF13 .... 138 E5
Elm Rd. Nor WF6 .... 144 B7
Elm Rd. S in Cra BD20 .... 16 C5
Elm Rd. Ship BD18 .... 55 D7
Elm St. Bacup OL13 .... 106 A3
Elm St. Crof WF4 .... 162 C6
Elm St. Elland HX4 .... 134 A4
Elm St. Hud HD4 .... 154 B4
Elm St. Leeds LS6 .... 60 B4
Elm St. Oxen BD22 .... 51 C2
Elm St. Skel HD8 .... 175 A2
Elm Terr. Brig HD6 .... 115 B5
Elm Terr. Otley LS21 .... 23 B8
Elm Terr. Pont WF8 .... 146 C6
Elm Tree Ave. Brad BD6 .... 94 C8
Elm Tree Cl. Batley WF15 .... 117 C2
Elm Tree Cl. Keigh BD21 .... 35 D6
Elm Tree Gdns. Brad BD6 .... 94 C8
Elm Tree St. Wake WF1 .... 142 F4
Elm View. Hali HX3 .... 113 C4 3
Elm View. Stee BD20 .... 17 C5
Elm Way. Batley WF17 .... 97 A2
Elm Wood St. Brig HD6 .... 115 B4
Elmet Dr. B in Elm LS15 .... 63 E6
Elmet Rd. B in Elm LS15 .... 63 E6
Elmet Towers. Leeds LS14 ...... 62 C4
Elmete Ave. B in Elm LS15 ...... 62 F6
Elmete Ave. Leeds LS8 .... 61 C7
Elmete Cres. Leeds LS8 .... 61 D6
Elmete Croft. B in Elm LS15 .... 62 F6
Elmete Ct. Leeds LS8 .... 61 C6
Elmete Dr. Leeds LS8 .... 61 D6
Elmete Grange. Men LS29 ...... 22 A4
Elmete Hill. Leeds LS8 .... 61 C6
Elmete La. Leeds LS8 .... 44 E2
Elmete Mount. Leeds LS8 ...... 61 D6
Elmete Wlk. Leeds LS8 .... 61 D6
Elmete Way. Gild LS27 .... 77 D3
Elmfield Bsns Pk. Gar 83 A4
Elmfield Ct. Morley LS27 ...... 98 B3
Elmfield Dr. Brad BD6 .... 94 A7
Elmfield Dr. Skel HD8 .... 175 A1
Elmfield Pl. Leeds LS12 .... 78 C6
Elmfield Rd. Hud HD2 .... 136 B1
Elmfield Rd. Leeds LS12 .... 78 C6
Elmfield Terr. Hali HX1 .... 78 B8
Elmfield Terr. Leeds LS12 ...... 78 C6
Elmfield Way. Leeds LS13 ...... 58 C1
Elmhurst Cl. Leeds LS17 .... 44 A5
Elmhurst Gdns. Leeds LS17 ..... 44 A5
Elmroyd. Roth LS26 .... 100 F4
Elms The. Guise LS20 .... 39 D8
Elms View. Slai HD7 .... 169 F8
Elmsall La. H Pag DN6 .... 195 C7
Elmsall St. Brad BD8 .... 55 A1
Elmsall Way. S Elm WF9 .... 183 B3
Elmsdale Cl. S Elm WF9 .... 183 B2
Elmsley St. Stee BD20 .... 17 D5
Elmton Cl. Midd LS10 .... 99 D7
Elmtree La. Leeds LS10 .... 99 E7
Elmwood Ave. B in Elm LS15 .... 63 B6
Elmwood Ave. Walton WF2 ...... 161 A7
Elmwood Chase. B in Elm LS15 .. 63 B6
Elmwood Cl. Hud HD1 .... 154 A6
Elmwood Dr. Brig HD6 .... 114 E7
Elmwood Dr. Keigh BD22 ...... 34 F5
Elmwood Dr. Walton WF2 ...... 161 A7
Elmwood Garth. Walton WF2 .... 161 A7
Elmwood Gr. Batley WF17 ...... 118 D5
Elmwood La. B in Elm LS15 ...... 63 B6
Elmwood La. Leeds LS2 .... 206 B3
Elmwood Rd. Keigh BD22 ...... 34 F5
Elmwood Rd. Leeds LS2 .... 206 B3
Elmwood St. Hali HX1 .... 202 C4
Elmwood Terr. Dew WF13 ...... 138 E5
Elmwood Terr. Keigh BD22 ...... 34 F5
Elphaborough Cl. Heb Br HX7 .... 89 A1
Elphin Ct. Heb Br HX7 .... 89 A1
Elsdon Gr. Brad BD5 .... 74 E3
Elsham Terr. Leeds LS4 .... 59 C2
Elsicker La. Croft WF1 .... 143 F1
Elsie St. Haw BD22 .... 51 C7
Elsie St. Keigh BD20 .... 18 A1
Elsinore Ave. Elland HX5 .... 134 E6
Elstone Ct. Elland HX5 .... 134 F6
Elstow House. Brad BD15 .... 73 A7
Elsworth Terr. Leeds LS12 ...... 59 C1
Elsworth Terr. Leeds LS12 ...... 59 C1
Eltham Ct. Leeds LS6 .... 59 F5
Eltham Dr. Leeds LS6 .... 59 F5
Eltham Gdns. Leeds LS6 .... 59 F5
Eltham Gr. Brad BD6 .... 93 E7
Eltham Rise. Leeds LS6 .... 59 F5
Elvaston Rd. Morley LS27 ...... 97 F2
Elvey Cl. Brad BD2 .... 56 B2
Elwell St. Loft G WF3 .... 121 F5
Elwell St. E ard WF3 .... 120 B8
Elwell St. Ward WF3 .... 120 B8
Ely St. Castle WF10 .... 124 D8
Ely St. Elland HX4 .... 134 A7
Embankment The. Leeds LS1 .... 211 D3
Embleton Rd. M'town LS26 ...... 102 A6
Embsay Steam Rly. Hal 1 C8
Emerald St. Batley WF17 .... 118 C5
Emerald St. Hud HD4 .... 153 D4
Emerald St. Keigh BD22 .... 35 A7
Emerson Ave. Brad BD9 .... 54 D3

Emily St. Keigh BD21 .... 35 D8
Emley Fst Sch. Emley 175 D7
Emley Moor Bsns Pk. Emley 175 D7
Emm La. Brad BD9 .... 55 B3
Emmanuel Terr. Hud HD4 ...... 153 F2
Emmanuel Trad Est. Leeds 78 F6
Emmeline Cl. Brad BD10 .... 56 B8
Emmet Cl. Birk BD11 .... 96 B5
Emmfield Dr. Ship BD9 .... 55 A4
Emmott Dr. Yeadon LS19 ...... 40 E3
Emmott Farm Fold. Haw BD22 .. 51 C6 2
Empsall Row. Brig HD6 .... 115 B3 4
Emscote Ave. Hali HX1 .... 113 A5
Emscote Gdns. Hali HX1 .... 113 A5 A518
Emscote Gr. Hali HX1 .... 113 A5
Emscote Pl. Hali HX1 .... 113 A5
Emscote St S. Hali HX1 .... 113 A5
Emsley Cl. Brad BD4 .... 95 B8
Emsley Pl. Leeds LS10 .... 79 E5
Emville Ave. Leeds LS17 .... 44 C5
Enderley Rd. Thorn BD13 ...... 72 D6
Endor Cres. Bur in W LS29 ...... 21 F7
Endor Gr. Bur in W LS29 .... 21 F7
Endsleigh Pl. Brad BD14 .... 73 A5
Enfield Ave. Leeds LS7 .... 60 E2
Enfield Cl. Batley WF17 .... 117 F6
Enfield Dr. Batley WF17 .... 117 F6
Enfield Par. Brad BD6 .... 74 A1
Enfield Rd. Baildon BD17 ...... 38 C2
Enfield Side Rd. Haw BD22 ...... 50 A1
Enfield St. Keigh BD21 .... 35 B7
Enfield St. Leeds LS7 .... 60 E2
Enfield Terr. Leeds LS7 .... 60 E2
Enfield Wlk. Brad BD6 .... 74 A1
Enfield. Yeadon LS19 .... 40 B6
Engine La. Hor WF4 .... 162 B7
Engine La. Staf S72 .... 180 D1
Engine La. W Har WF4 .... 163 A4
Englefield Cres. Brad BD4 ...... 75 E2
Ennerdale Ave. Batley WF12 .... 118 E2
Ennerdale Cl. Weth LS22 .... 13 C6
Ennerdale Cres. Batley WF12 .... 118 E2
Ennerdale Dr. Brad BD2 .... 56 B3
Ennerdale Dr. Knot WF11 ...... 126 D3
Ennerdale Rd. Batley WF12 ...... 118 E2
Ennerdale Rd. Dew WF12 .... 139 D7
Ennerdale Rd. Wake WF2 .... 141 F7
Ennerdale Way. Gild LS12 ...... 77 D3
Enoch La. Hud HD4 .... 153 F3
Enterprise Park Ind Est. Leeds ... 79 D3
Enterprise Way. Brad BD10 ...... 56 C5
Enterprise Way. Castle WF10 .... 124 C8
Enterprise Way. Wald LS10 ...... 79 F1
Envoy St. Leeds LS11 .... 79 B3
Epsom Rd. Kippax LS25 .... 82 F2
Epsom Way. Knotw HD5 .... 137 C1
Epworth Pl. Leeds LS10 .... 79 D4
Eric St. Keigh BD21 .... 35 C6
Eric St. Leeds LS13 .... 58 C5
Eric St. S Elm WF9 .... 183 B8
Ernest Gn. Dew WF13 .... 138 B8
Ernest St. Tod OL14 .... 86 L1
Errington St. Heb Br HX7 ...... 88 D6
Errington Terr. Heb Br HX7 ...... 88 C12
Escroft Cl. Brad BD12 .... 94 C6
Eshald La. Roth LS26 .... 101 D6
Eshald Mansions. Roth LS26 .... 101 D6 4
Esholt Ave. Guise LS20 .... 39 E8
Esholt La. Bail BD17 .... 38 F4
Esholt La. Guise LS20 .... 38 F4
Eshton Ct. Mapp S75 .... 178 A2
Eshton Ave. Brad BD12 .... 94 C1
Esk Gdns. Weth LS22 .... 13 F8
Eskdale Ave. Nor WF6 .... 123 A1
Eskdale Ave. Shelf HX3 .... 93 A5
Eskdale Cl. Batley WF12 .... 118 E3
Eskdale Cl. Guise LS20 .... 22 E1
Eskdale Cl. Nor WF6 .... 123 A1
Eskdale Croft. Guise LS20 ...... 22 E1
Eskdale Croft. Nor WF6 .... 123 A1
Eskdale Gr. Gar LS25 .... 83 B8
Eskine Par. Brad BD6 .... 74 A1
Esmond St. Brad BD7 .... 74 A5
Esmond Terr. Leeds LS12 .... 78 B4
Essex St. Brad BD4 .... 75 A5
Essex St. Hali HX1 .... 112 F6
Estcourt Ave. Leeds LS6 .... 59 D5
Estcourt Dr. Dar WF8 .... 147 C2
Estcourt Gr. Brad BD7 .... 74 A3
Estcourt Rd. Dar WF8 .... 147 C2
Estcourt Rd. Brad BD7 .... 74 A3
Estcourt Terr. Leeds LS6 .... 59 D5
Esther Ave. Wake WF2 .... 141 F4
Esther Gr. Wake WF2 .... 141 F4
Esthwaite Gdns. Leeds LS15 .... 80 E6
Eton Ave. Hud HD5 .... 154 F6
Eton St. Heb Br HX7 .... 89 A3
Eton St. Hali HX1 .... 113 B4
Euden Edge Rd. Slai HD7 .... 151 F2
Eunice La. Dale HD8 .... 191 C5
Euroway Trad Est. Brad 95 A7
Euston Gr. Leeds LS11 .... 79 A4
Euston Mount. Leeds LS11 ...... 79 A4
Euston Terr. Leeds LS11 .... 79 A4
Evanston Ave. Leeds LS4 .... 59 B3
Evelyn Ave. Brad BD3 .... 56 A1
Evelyn Pl. Leeds LS12 .... 78 B4
Everard St. Hud HD4 .... 171 E8
Everdale Mount. Hem WF9 ...... 181 D6
Everest Ave. Ship BD18 .... 55 D7
Everleigh St. Leeds LS9 .... 80 B7
Eversley Dr. Brad BD4 .... 75 A2
Eversley Mount. Hali HX2 ...... 112 C7
Eversley Pl. Hali HX2 .... 112 C7
Eversley View. Shadw LS14 ...... 45 E7
Ewart Pl. Brad BD7 .... 74 C6
Ewart St. Brad BD7 .... 74 C6
Ewart St. Queen BD13 .... 72 D1
Ewood Dr. Heb Br HX7 .... 90 A1

Ewood Hall Ave. Heb Br HX7 .... 89 F1
Ewood La. Tod OL14 .... 107 F6
Exchange Bldgs. Gildersome 16 D7
Exchange. Honley HD7 .... 171 F5
Exchange St. Clec BD19 .... 95 D1
Exchange St. Elland HX4 .... 134 D6 3
Exchange St. Nor WF6 .... 123 A2
Exchange St. S Elm WF9 .... 182 F3
Exeter Dr. Midd LS10 .... 99 E8
Exeter St. Hali HX6 .... 112 C4
Exeter St. Leeds LS13 .... 113 D3
Exhibition Rd. Ship BD18 .... 54 F8 7
Exley Ave. Keigh BD21 .... 35 A4
Exley Bank. Hali HX3 .... 113 D3
Exley Bank Top. Hali HX3 .... 113 D3
Exley Cres. Keigh BD21 .... 35 A5
Exley Gr. Keigh BD21 .... 35 A5
Exley La. Elland HX5 .... 134 E8
Exley La. Elland HX5 .... 134 E8
Exley Mount. Keigh BD21 .... 35 A5
Exley Rd. Keigh BD21 .... 35 A5
Exley St. Keigh BD21 .... 35 A511
Exley Way. Keigh BD21 .... 35 A4
Exmoor St. Hali HX1 .... 202 C1
Exmouth Pl. Brad BD3 .... 55 F1
Express Way. Castle WF10 ...... 123 D5
Exton Pl. Leeds LS15 .... 80 E7
Eyre St. Batley WF12 .... 118 D4
Eyre St. Dew WF12 .... 139 D8
Eyres Ave. Leeds LS12 .... 78 C8
Eyres Gr. Leeds LS12 .... 78 C8
Eyres Mill Side. Leeds LS12 .... 78 B8
Eyres St. Leeds LS12 .... 78 C8
Eyres Terr. Leeds LS12 .... 78 C8
Eyrie App. Morley LS27 .... 98 C3

Factory La. Brad BD4 .... 75 B2
Factory La. Hud HD1 .... 153 B4
Factory St. Brad BD4 .... 75 B2
Fagley Cres. Brad BD2 .... 56 D2
Fagley Croft. Brad BD2 .... 56 D2
Fagley La. Brad BD2 .... 56 D2
Fagley Pl. Brad BD2 .... 56 D2
Fagley Rd. Brad BD2 .... 56 D2
Fagley Terr. Brad BD2 .... 56 D2
Fair Bank. Ship BD18 .... 55 C6
Fair Lea Rd. Hud HD4 .... 153 C4
Fair Mount. Tod OL14 .... 108 A1
Fair Rd. Brad BD6 .... 94 B8
Fair St. Hud HD1 .... 153 F4
Fair View Cres. Bacup OL13 .... 106 A3
Fair View. Pont WF8 .... 146 D5
Fairbank Rd. Brad BD8 .... 55 A1
Fairbank Terr. Brad BD8 .... 55 A1
Fairbourne House. Brad BD6 .... 93 F8
Fairburn Ct. Gar LS25 .... 83 A6
Fairburn Dr. Gar LS25 .... 83 A6
Fairburn Gdns. Brad BD2 .... 56 A4
Fairburn Ings Nature Reserve.
  Ledsh 104 B4
Fairburn Prim Sch. Fair 105 A4

Fairfax Ave. Batley WF17 .... 118 D5
Fairfax Ave. Brad BD4 .... 95 B8
Fairfax Ave. Feath WF7 .... 124 C1
Fairfax Cl. Leeds LS14 .... 62 A4
Fairfax Cres. Brad BD4 .... 95 B8
Fairfax Cres. Hali HX3 .... 114 C8
Fairfax Flats. Norm 119 F1
Fairfax Gdns. Men LS29 .... 22 A4
Fairfax Gr. Yeadon LS19 .... 40 A7
Fairfax House. Brad BD4 .... 95 B8
Fairfax Rd. Brad BD13 .... 72 E6
Fairfax Rd. Bur in Wf LS29 ...... 9 F1
Fairfax Rd. Leeds LS11 .... 79 B1
Fairfax St. Brad BD4 .... 95 B8
Fairfax St. Haw BD22 .... 51 C6
Fairfax St. Otley LS21 .... 23 B7
Fairfax St. Silsden BD20 .... 5 E1
Fairfax View. Netherton WF4 .... 158 A5
Fairfax View. Thornt BD13 ...... 71 D8
Fairfield Ave. Brad BD6 .... 94 D8
Fairfield Ave. Knot WF11 .... 127 A4
Fairfield Ave. Leeds LS13 .... 58 B2
Fairfield Ave. Norm WF6 .... 123 B2
Fairfield Ave. Ossett WF5 .... 140 D4
Fairfield Cl. Leeds LS13 .... 58 B2
Fairfield Cl. Roth LS26 .... 100 F5
Fairfield Cres. Leeds LS13 ...... 58 B2
Fairfield Ct. Bail BD17 .... 38 E3
Fairfield Ct. Brad 94 D8
Fairfield Dr. Bail BD17 .... 38 E3
Fairfield Dr. Ossett WF5 .... 140 D4
Fairfield Gr. Leeds LS13 .... 58 B2
Fairfield Gr. Roth LS26 .... 100 F5
Fairfield Hill. Leeds LS13 .... 58 B2
Fairfield La. Roth LS26 .... 100 F5
Fairfield Mount. Leeds LS13 .... 58 B2
Fairfield Rd. Brad BD8 .... 73 F8
Fairfield Rd. Dew WF12 .... 139 D6 9
Fairfield Sch. Batley 118 D5
Fairfield St. Brad BD4 .... 75 A5
Fairfield St. Leeds LS13 .... 58 B2
Fairfield Terr. Clec BD19 .... 116 E7
Fairfield Terr. Leeds LS13 ...... 58 B2

Fairfield Terr. Ossett WF5 ... 140 E4
Fairfield Wlk. Ossett WF5 ... 140 F4
Fairfields. Castle WF10 ... 125 E7
Fairfields. D Dale HD8 ... 191 F3
Fairfields Rd. Holmfi HD7 ... 188 D3
Fairford Ave. Leeds LS11 ... 79 C3
Fairford Terr. Leeds LS11 ... 79 C3
Fairhaven Gn. Brad BD10 ... 56 C7
Fairlea Ave. Hud HD4 ... 153 E1
Fairlea Cotts. Hud HD4 ... 153 E1
Fairleigh Cres. E Ard WF3 ... 119 F8
Fairleigh Cres. E Ard WF3 ... 120 A8
Fairlegh Rd. E Ard WF3 ... 120 A8
Fairless Ave. Brig HX3 ... 115 A7
Fairmoor Way. Batley WF17 ... 117 E5
Fairmount. Brad BD9 ... 55 C2
Fairmount Pk. Ship BD18 ... 54 E7
Fairmount Terr. Keigh BD21 ... 35 B6
Fairview Ave. Batley WF17 ... 117 F6
Fairview Cl. Bail BD17 ... 38 B1
Fairview Rd. Batley WF17 ... 118 A6
Fairview Terr. Hali HX3 ... 92 B1
Fairway App. Nor WF6 ... 123 C2
Fairway Ave. Brad BD7 ... 73 F1
Fairway Ave. Nupps S75 ... 178 C2
Fairway Ave. Nor WF6 ... 123 C2
Fairway. Brad BD7 ... 73 F1
Fairway Cl. Brad BD7 ... 73 F1
Fairway Cl. Guise LS20 ... 39 C8
Fairway Cl. Nor WF6 ... 123 C1
Fairway Cres. Haw BD22 ... 51 C6
Fairway Dr. Brad BD7 ... 73 F2
Fairway Dr. Nor WF6 ... 123 C1
Fairway Gr. Brad BD7 ... 74 A2
Fairway. Guise LS20 ... 22 C1
Fairway Pk. Batley ... 96 F2
Fairway. Nor WF6 ... 123 C1
Fairway. Ship BD18 ... 54 F7
Fairway The. Feath WF7 ... 124 D1
Fairway The. Hali HX2 ... 91 F7
Fairway The. Hud WF12 ... 136 A4
Fairway The. Leeds LS17 ... 43 A5
Fairway The. Pudsey LS28 ... 57 B1
Fairway Wlk. Brad BD7 ... 73 F2
Fairway. Yeadon LS19 ... 40 A2
Fairways The. Ship BD9 ... 54 E5
Fairweather Green Mid Sch. Brad ... 73 E7
Fairweather Mews. Brad BD8 ... 73 E7
Fairy Dell. Ship BD16 ... 37 A4
Fairy Hill La. Castle WF8 ... 125 D5
Faith St. S Kirk WF9 ... 182 D4
Falcon Cl. Otley LS21 ... 23 A7
Falcon Cliffe. Stee BD20 ... 12 D1
Falcon Dr. Castle WF10 ... 124 C6
Falcon Knowl Ing. Kex S75 ... 177 D1
Falcon Mews. Brad BD8 ... 73 C8
Falcon Mews. Morley LS27 ... 98 C3
Falcon Rd. Bing BD16 ... 36 F5
Falcon St. Brad BD7 ... 74 D7
Falcon St. Hali HX3 ... 113 D3
Falcon St. Hud HD4 ... 153 F2
Falconer Cl. Kex S75 ... 177 C1
Falconers Ride. Hud HD4 ... 171 E1
Falhouse La. Dew WF4 ... 156 D7
Falkland Cres. Leeds LS17 ... 43 C1
Falkland Ct. Leeds LS17 ... 43 C1
Falkland Gr. Leeds LS17 ... 43 C1
Falkland Mount. Leeds LS17 ... 43 C1
Falkland Rd. Brad BD10 ... 56 D6
Falkland Rd. Leeds LS17 ... 43 C1
Falkland Rise. Leeds LS17 ... 43 C1
Falklands. Leeds LS17 ... 43 C1
Fall Ings Rd. Wake WF1 ... 142 E4
Fall La. Dew WF13 ... 139 B6
Fall La. E Ard WF3 ... 120 D8
Fall La. Hali HX6 ... 112 D3
Fall La. Liver WF15 ... 116 D1
Fall La. Mars HD7 ... 168 F3
Fall La. Northo HX3 ... 92 E4
Fall Mill. Mir WF14 ... 137 F5
Fall Spring Gdns. Elland HX4 ... 133 F3
Fall Spring Gn. Elland HX4 ... 133 F3
Fall Wood St. Haw BD22 ... 51 D6
Falledge La. D Dale HD8 ... 191 F7
Fallow Croft. Hud HD2 ... 136 F5
Fallow La. Keigh BD22 ... 34 A6
Fallowfield Cl. Brad BD4 ... 75 C1
Fallowfield Dr. Brad BD4 ... 75 C1
Fallowfield Gdns. Brad BD4 ... 75 C1
Fallswood Gr. Leeds LS13 ... 58 D4
Falmouth Ave. Brad BD3 ... 75 F6
Falmouth Ave. Nor WF6 ... 123 B3
Falmouth Cres. Nor WF6 ... 123 B3
Falsgrave Ave. Brad BD2 ... 56 D2
Faltis Sq. Brad BD10 ... 56 C6
Fanny Moor Cres. Hud HD4 ... 154 C2
Fanny Moor La. Hud HD4 ... 154 C2
Fanny St. Keigh BD21 ... 35 B6
Fanny St. Ship BD18 ... 37 F1
Far Bank. Shep HD8 ... 174 B3
Far Common Rd. Mir WF14 ... 137 E8
Far Croft. Lepton HD8 ... 156 A2
Far Croft Terr. Leeds LS12 ... 78 D6 1
Far Dene. Kirkb HD8 ... 173 F6
Far Field Ave. Holmfi HD7 ... 189 E1
Far Field La. Holmfi HD7 ... 189 E1
Far Fields La. Mel HD7 ... 170 F1
Far Fields La. Mel HD7 ... 171 A5
Far La. Holmfi HD7 ... 189 E1
Far La. Holmfi HD7 ... 189 C4
Far Moss. Leeds LS17 ... 43 A5
Far Reef Cl. Hors LS18 ... 41 C2
Far Richard Cl. Ossett WF5 ... 140 D7
Far View Bank. Hud HD5 ... 154 F4
Far View Cres. Hud HD5 ... 154 F4
Far View. Hali HX2 ... 91 E6
Far Well Fold. Yeadon LS19 ... 41 A2
Far Well Rd. Yeadon LS19 ... 40 A8
Faraday Sq. Hud HD1 ... 153 F4
Farcliffe Pl. Brad BD8 ... 55 B1
Farcliffe Rd. Brad BD8 ... 55 B1
Farcliffe Terr. Brad BD8 ... 55 B1
Fardene St. Stee BD20 ... 17 B5
Fardew Ct. Bing BD16 ... 36 F3
Farfew Golf Course. Keigh ... 36 C3
Farehill Flats. Hud HD7 ... 171 F8
Farehill Rd. Hud HD4 ... 171 F8

Farfield Ave. Batley WF17 ... 117 F6
Farfield Ave. Brad BD6 ... 93 E2
Farfield Ave. Pudsey LS28 ... 57 C3
Farfield Cres. Brad BD6 ... 93 F7
Farfield Ct. Leeds LS17 ... 43 C4
Farfield Dr. Pudsey LS28 ... 57 C2
Farfield Gr. Brad BD6 ... 93 F7
Farfield Gr. Pudsey LS28 ... 57 C3
Farfield Rd. Bail BD17 ... 38 D2
Farfield Rd. Brad BD6 ... 94 A2
Farfield Rd. Hud HD5 ... 154 F3
Farfield Rd. Ship BD18 ... 55 A4
Farfield Rise. Pudsey LS28 ... 57 C3
Farfield St. Brad BD9 ... 55 A2
Farfield St. Cleck BD19 ... 95 D1
Farfield Terr. Brad BD9 ... 55 A2
Farm Ct. Leeds LS15 ... 62 B2
Farm Gdns. Feath WF7 ... 144 F5
Farm Hill Cres. Leeds LS7 ... 60 A6
Farm Hill Ct. Brad BD10 ... 56 B5
Farm Hill Mount. Leeds LS7 ... 97 F5
Farm Hill Rise. Leeds LS7 ... 60 A5
Farm Hill S. Leeds LS7 ... 60 A5
Farm Hill Way. Leeds LS7 ... 60 A5
Farm La. Hem WF9 ... 163 A3
Farm Mount. Leeds LS15 ... 62 C2
Farm Pond Dr. Brig HD6 ... 114 E5
Farm Rd. Feath WF7 ... 145 C5
Farm Rd. Leeds LS15 ... 62 B2
Farmfield Dr. Hem WF9 ... 163 A3
Farmstead Rd. Brad BD10 ... 56 D5
Farnboro St. Tod OL14 ... 108 A2
Farndale App. Leeds LS14 ... 62 C5
Farndale Cl. Leeds LS14 ... 62 C6
Farndale Gdns. Leeds LS14 ... 62 C6 10
Farndale Pl. Leeds LS14 ... 62 C6
Farndale Rd. Bail BD17 ... 38 A2
Farndale Rd. Wils BD15 ... 53 C4
Farndale Sq. Leeds LS14 ... 62 C5 5
Farndale Terr. Leeds LS14 ... 62 C5 5
Farne Ave. Wake WF2 ... 141 F6
Farnham Cl. Bail BD17 ... 38 D4
Farnham Cl. Leeds LS14 ... 45 B1
Farnham Croft. Leeds LS14 ... 45 B1
Farnham Fst Sch. Brad ... 74 B5
Farnham Rd. Brad BD7 ... 74 B5
Farnham Way. Covf WF4 ... 143 F1
Farnlee. Hud HD3 ... 135 B1
Farnley CE Prim Sch. Farnley ... 11 D5
Farnley Cres. Haw BD22 ... 34 D8
Farnley Cres. Leeds LS12 ... 77 B5
Farnley Hey. Kirkb HD4 ... 172 C7
Farnley La. Farnley LS21 ... 11 B3
Farnley La. Otley LS21 ... 11 B3
Farnley Park High Sch. Leeds ... 77 B4
Farnley Pk. Farnley LS21 ... 11 B3
Farnley Rd. Kirkb HD4 ... 172 F5
Farnley Tyas CE Sch. Kirkb ... 172 E6
Farnley View. Birk BD11 ... 97 A6
Farr Boyd. Bur in W LS29 ... 9 F2
Farr Royd Terr. Bur in W LS29 ... 9 F2
Farra St. Oxen BD22 ... 51 C2
Farrar Ave. Mir WF14 ... 137 F7
Farrar Ct. Hors LS16 ... 42 A4
Farrar Height La. Ripp HX6 ... 132 F6
Farrar La. Hors LS16 ... 42 A4
Farrar Mill La. Hali HX3 ... 113 D3
Farriers Ct. Brad BD14 ... 73 C4
Farriers Croft. Brad BD2 ... 55 F4
Farrington Cl. Brad BD4 ... 75 E4
Farrington Ct. Brad BD4 ... 75 E4
Farrow Bank. Leeds LS12 ... 77 E7
Farrow Gn. Leeds LS12 ... 77 E7
Farrow Rd. Leeds LS12 ... 77 E7
Farrow Vale. Leeds LS12 ... 77 E7
Farside Gr. Brad BD6 ... 74 C1
Farside Grn. Brad BD5 ... 74 C2
Farsley Farfield Jun Sch. Pudsey 57 D3
Farsley Springbank Jun Sch. Pudsey 57 D3
Fartown Cl. Pudsey LS28 ... 76 E5
Fartown Green Rd. Hud HD2 ... 136 B2
Fartown High Sch. Hud ... 136 B1
Fartown. Pudsey LS28 ... 76 E5
Fartown. Brad BD4 ... 75 B2
Fascination Pl. Queen BD13 ... 72 C1 1
Faugh La. Hep HX7 ... 88 C6
Favell Ave. Nor WF6 ... 123 B1
Faversham Wlk. Brad BD4 ... 75 F3
Fawcett Ave. Leeds LS12 ... 78 B3
Fawcett Bank. Leeds LS12 ... 78 A3
Fawcett Cl. Leeds LS12 ... 78 A3
Fawcett Ct. Holmfi HD7 ... 189 D5
Fawcett Dr. Leeds LS12 ... 78 A3
Fawcett Gdns. Leeds LS12 ... 78 A3
Fawcett La. Leeds LS12 ... 78 A3
Fawcett Pl. Brad BD4 ... 95 C8
Fawcett Rd. Leeds LS12 ... 78 A3
Fawcett St. Wake WF2 ... 142 A6
Fawcett Vale. Leeds LS12 ... 78 A3
Fawcett View. Leeds LS12 ... 78 A3
Fawcett Way. Leeds LS12 ... 78 A3
Faxfleet St. Brad BD5 ... 74 D2
Fearnley Ave. Ossett WF5 ... 140 E6
Fearnley Cl. Leeds LS12 ... 78 D7
Fearnley Ct. Holmfi HD7 ... 189 D5
Fearnley Pl. Leeds LS12 ... 78 D7
Fearnsides St. Brad BD8 ... 55 A1
Fearnsides Terr. Brad BD8 ... 55 A1
Fearnville Ave. Leeds LS8 ... 61 D4
Fearnville Cl. Leeds LS8 ... 61 E4
Fearnville Dr. Brad BD4 ... 75 C2
Fearnville Dr. Leeds LS8 ... 61 E4
Fearnville Gr. Leeds LS8 ... 61 E4
Fearnville Mount. Leeds LS8 ... 61 E4
Fearnville Pl. Leeds LS8 ... 61 E4

Fearnville Rd. Leeds LS8 ... 61 D4
Fearnville Sch. Leeds ... 61 D4
Fearnville Terr. Leeds LS8 ... 61 E4
Fearnville View. Leeds LS8 ... 61 D4
Feast Field. Hors LS18 ... 41 B1
Feather Bed La. Elland HX4 ... 134 D6 5
Feather Rd. Brad BD3 ... 75 B7
Feather St. Keigh BD21 ... 35 D6
Featherbank Ave. Hors LS18 ... 58 B7
Featherbank Gr. Hors LS18 ... 58 B8 5
Featherbank Mount. Hors LS18 ... 58 B8 6
Featherbank Terr. Hors LS18 ... 58 B7 3
Featherbank Wlk. Hors LS18 ... 58 B7 1
Featherbed Cl. Elland HX4 ... 134 D6 4
Featherbed La. Birk LS24 ... 15 E6
Featherbed La. Wig LS24 ... 15 E6
Featherstone High Sch. Feath ... 145 D4
Featherstone La. Feath WF7 ... 145 D7
Featherstone Purston St Thomas
  CE Mid Sch. Feath ... 145 C6
Featherstone Sch. Feath ... 145 C6
Featherstone Streethouse Fst
  Sch. Feath ... 144 C5
Federation St. Brad BD5 ... 74 F2
Feethan's Fold. Leeds LS7 ... 60 A7
Felbrigg Ave. Keigh BD22 ... 35 A6
Felcote Ave. Hud HD5 ... 154 E6
Felcourt Dr. Brad BD4 ... 75 C2
Felkirk Mid Sch. S Hie ... 180 C7
Felkirk View. Shaf S72 ... 180 B3
Felks Stile Rd. Hud HD4 ... 153 A1
Fell Cres. Keigh BD22 ... 34 F6
Fell Gr. Hud HD2 ... 136 C2
Fell Gr. Keigh BD22 ... 34 F6
Fell Graeve Cres. Hud HD2 ... 136 C4
Fell Greave Rd. Hud HD2 ... 136 C4
Fell La. Keigh BD22 ... 34 F6
Fellows The. Hud HD4 ... 171 C7
Fellowsides La. Ossett WF5 ... 140 E5
Fellside. Tod OL14 ... 109 B5
Fellwood Ave. Haw BD22 ... 51 E8
Fellwood Cl. Haw BD22 ... 51 E8
Felnex Cres. Leeds LS9 ... 80 C6
Felnex Rd. Leeds LS9 ... 80 C5
Felnex Sq. Leeds LS9 ... 80 B5
Felnex Way. Leeds LS9 ... 80 B5
Fenay Bankside. Lepton HD8 ... 155 D3
Fenay Bridge Rd. Lepton HD8 ... 155 C3
Fenay Cres. Hud HD5 ... 155 A5
Fenay Dr. Lepton HD8 ... 155 C3
Fenay La. Hud HD5 ... 155 B3
Fenay La. Hud HD5 ... 155 C4
Fenby Ave. Brad BD4 ... 75 C2
Fenby Cl. Brad BD4 ... 75 C2
Fenby Gdns. Brad BD4 ... 75 C2
Fencote Cres. Brad BD2 ... 56 D3
Fender Rd. Brad BD6 ... 93 F6
Fenny Royd Est. Brig HX3 ... 114 B8
Fenton Cl. S Kirk WF9 ... 182 B1
Fenton Rd. Hali HX1 ... 117 F5
Fenton Rd. Holmfi HD7 ... 153 F3
Fenton Sq. Hud HD1 ... 153 F5
Fenton St. Bur in W LS29 ... 9 F1
Fenton St. Leeds LS2 ... 79 C6
Fenton St. Mir WF14 ... 138 A4
Fentonsgate. Roth WF3 ... 100 C1
Fenwick Dr. Brad BD6 ... 94 A6
Ferguson St. Hali HX1 ... 203 D3
Fern Ave. Mel HD7 ... 170 C3
Fern Bank. Otley LS21 ... 23 B8
Fern Chase. Scar LS14 ... 45 A7
Fern Cl. Batley WF17 ... 118 A6
Fern Croft. Clec WF15 ... 116 C4
Fern Ct. Keigh BD20 ... 18 A1
Fern Ct. Wake WF2 ... 120 D3
Fern Gdns. Ilkley LS29 ... 8 A3
Fern Hill Ave. Ship BD18 ... 54 F7
Fern Hill Gr. Ship BD18 ... 54 F7
Fern Hill Mount. Ship BD18 ... 54 F7
Fern Hill Rd. Ship BD18 ... 54 F7
Fern La. Flats. Hud HD3 ... 153 A6
Fern Lea. Queen BD13 ... 72 F1
Fern Lea Rd. Hud HD3 ... 135 A1
Fern Lea St. Brad BD4 ... 75 D3
Fern St. Brad BD4 ... 75 D3
Fern St. Haw BD22 ... 51 C6
Fern St. Hud HD1 ... 154 A6
Fern St. Keigh BD21 ... 35 C8
Fern Terr. Dew WF13 ... 118 C1
Fern Way. Scar LS14 ... 45 A7

Fernlea Cl. Crof WF4 ... 162 A8
Fernlea Gr. Hud HD7 ... 152 E3
Fernlea. Roth LS26 ... 100 F6
Fernleigh Ct. Wake WF2 ... 141 F5
Fernley Gdns. Brad BD12 ... 94 C6
Fernley Green Cl. Knot WF11 ... 127 B4
Fernley Green Ind Est. Knot ... 127 B4
Fernley Green Rd. Knot WF11 ... 127 B4
Ferney Hill Dr. Nor WF6 ... 123 B1
Ferns The. Bacup OL13 ... 106 A1 3
Fernside Ave. Hud HD5 ... 154 F4
Fernside Cl. Hud HD5 ... 155 A5
Fernside Cres. Hud HD5 ... 155 A5
Fernside. Crof WF4 ... 144 C3
Fernwood Cl. Leeds LS8 ... 44 A1
Fernwood. Leeds LS8 ... 44 A1
Ferrand Ave. Brad BD4 ... 95 C8
Ferrand La. Bing BD16 ... 36 F3
Ferrand La. Clec BD19 ... 116 E7
Ferrand St. Bing BD16 ... 37 A3
Ferrands Cl. Harden BD16 ... 36 B1
Ferrands Park Way. Harden BD16 ... 36 B1
Ferriby Cl. Brad BD2 ... 56 D3
Ferriby Towers. Leeds LS9 ... 60 E1
Ferry La. Loft U WF3 ... 121 E2
Ferry Top La. Ryhill WF4 ... 162 A3
Ferrybridge By-Pass. Knot WF11 ... 126 C3
Ferrybridge Power Sta. Castle ... 126 B7
Ferrybridge Rd. Castle WF10 ... 124 F7
Ferrybridge Rd. Knot WF11 ... 126 C5
Ferrybridge Rd. Pont WF8 ... 125 F3
Festival Ave. Ship BD18 ... 55 D8
Feversham St. Brad ... 201 D3
Fewston Ave. Leeds LS9 ... 79 F6
Fewston Ave. Wake WF1 ... 142 F8
Fewston Ct. Leeds LS9 ... 79 F6
Fiddle La. Rip HX6 ... 132 F4
Fiddler Hill. Dew WF12 ... 139 B4
Fidler Cl. Gar LS25 ... 82 F7
Fidler La. Gar LS25 ... 82 E7
Field Cl. Batley WF16 ... 117 D6
Field Cres. S Elm WF9 ... 182 F2 2
Field Ct. Thorn BD13 ... 72 E6
Field End Cl. Leeds LS15 ... 81 A7
Field End Cres. Leeds LS15 ... 81 A7
Field End Ct. Leeds LS15 ... 81 A7
Field End Garth. Leeds LS15 ... 81 A7
Field End Gdns. Leeds LS15 ... 81 A7
Field End Gr. Leeds LS15 ... 81 A7
Field End. Holmfi HD7 ... 188 D4
Field End La. Holmfi HD7 ... 172 A4
Field End Mount. Leeds LS15 ... 81 A7
Field End Rd. Leeds LS15 ... 81 A7
Field Head. Hud HD7 ... 152 D5
Field Head La. Batley WF17 ... 96 E1
Field Head La. Haw BD22 ... 51 A5
Field Head La. Oxen BD22 ... 51 A5
Field Head Way. Hali BD13 ... 73 B7
Field House Cl. Weth LS22 ... 13 F7
Field House. Bar LS23 ... 15 A3
Field La. Batley WF17 ... 118 D4
Field La. Brig HD6 ... 115 A3
Field La. Kirkb HD8 ... 173 F7
Field La. Leeds LS25 ... 83 B6 3
Field La. Loft WF1 ... 121 C3
Field La. Upton WF9 ... 183 A8
Field Lane Jun & Inf Sch. Batley ... 118 D4

Fifth St. Brad BD12 ... 94 E6
Fifth St. Crof WF4 ... 162 B7
Filbert St. Hud HD1 ... 136 A1
Filey Ave. Roy S71 ... 179 C1
Filey St. Batley WF17 ... 74 F6 3
Filey St. Brad BD1 ... 75 A6
Filley Royd. Clec BD19 ... 116 A6
Fillingfir Dr. Leeds LS16 ... 58 F8
Fillingfir Rd. Leeds LS16 ... 58 F8
Fillingfir Wlk. Leeds LS16 ... 58 F8
Finch Ave. Wake WF2 ... 160 D5
Finch St. Brad BD5 ... 74 D4
Finching Gr. Mir WF14 ... 138 A8
Finchley St. Brad BD5 ... 74 D3
Finchley Way. Morley LS27 ... 98 A3 4
Findon Terr. Brad BD10 ... 56 E4
Fine Garth Cl. Bramham LS23 ... 30 D3
Finghall Rd. Ad Le S DN6 ... 184 F2
Finkil St. Brig HD6 ... 114 F5
Finkin Ave. Pudsey LS28 ... 76 E6
Finkin Croft. Loft U WF3 ... 121 E2
Finkin La. Loft U WF3 ... 121 E2
Finkle Cl. Wool WF4 ... 177 F7
Finkle La. Morley LS27 ... 98 A3
Finkle St. Sowt WF9 ... 183 A4
Finkle St. Wool WF4 ... 177 F7
Finsbury Dr. Brad BD2 ... 55 F3
Finsbury Rd. Leeds LS1 ... 211 F4
Finthorpe La. Hud HD5 ... 155 A3
Fir Ave. Dew WF13 ... 138 D6
Fir Bank. Dew WF13 ... 118 A1 6
Fir Par. Dew WF13 ... 138 D5
Fir Rd. Hud HD1 ... 153 D6
Fir St. Haw BD22 ... 51 C6
Fir St. Keigh BD21 ... 35 B4 12
Fir Tree Ave. Leeds LS17 ... 43 C3
Fir Tree Cl. Leeds LS17 ... 43 C3
Fir Tree Cty Prim Sch. Leeds ... 43 C3
Fir Tree Gdns. Brad BD10 ... 56 D7
Fir Tree Gdns. Leeds LS17 ... 43 B4
Fir Tree Gn. Leeds LS17 ... 43 C3
Fir Tree La. Leeds LS17 ... 43 D3
Fir Tree Rise. Leeds LS17 ... 43 C3
Fir Tree Vale. Leeds LS17 ... 43 C3
Fir Wlk. Dew WF13 ... 138 D5
Firbank Gn. Brad BD2 ... 56 B6
Firbank Gr. Leeds LS15 ... 80 E6
Firbeck. Harden BD16 ... 53 B8
Firbeck Rd. Bramham LS23 ... 30 D3
Firbeck Rd. Leeds LS14 ... 62 A8 1
Firs The. Roy S71 ... 179 A4
First Ave. Bard LS17 ... 28 E5
First Ave. Clec WF15 ... 116 C5
First Ave. Hali HX3 ... 113 A4
First Ave. Hor WF4 ... 140 F1
First Ave. Hud HD7 ... 152 E3
First Ave. Keigh BD21 ... 35 B6 3
First Ave. Leeds LS12 ... 78 D7
First Ave. Loft U WF1 ... 121 C3
First Ave. Roth LS26 ... 100 F7
First Ave. Roy S71 ... 179 C1
First Ave. Weth LS22 ... 13 F5
First Ave. Yeadon LS19 ... 40 C5
First Avenue Ind Est. Pudsey ... 57 E1
First St. Brad BD12 ... 94 E6
Firth Cl. Loft G WF3 ... 121 A2
Firth House La. Brig HD6 ... 136 C1
Firth Mount. Leeds LS11 ... 99 A8
Firth Rd. Brad BD9 ... 55 A3
Firth Rd. Leeds LS11 ... 99 A8
Firth St. Brig HD6 ... 115 B1
Firth St. Holmfi HD7 ... 189 A5
Firth St. Hud HD1 ... 154 B5
Firth St. Thorn BD13 ... 72 D6
Firth Terr. Leeds LS7 ... 207 A2 5
Firth View. Leeds LS11 ... 99 A8

Fifth Ave. Loft G WF3 ... 121 A2
Fitts La. Bard LS17 ... 28 E5
Fitzgerald St. Brad BD5 ... 74 D5
Fitzroy Dr. Leeds LS8 ... 61 B6 3
Fitzwilliam St. Hem WF9 ... 181 C6
Fitzwilliam St. Hud HD1 ... 154 B6
Fitzwilliam St. Leeds LS9 ... 212 A3
Five Acres. Hem WF9 ... 163 A4
Five Lane Ends. Ad Le S DN6 ... 184 F1
Five Lane Ends. Holmfi HD7 ... 188 D5
Five Oaks. Bail BD17 ... 38 E3
Flasby Ave. Hali HX2 ... 112 A5
Flasby Cty Prim Sch. Hud ... 136 A4

Fixby La. Dew WF4 ... 156 E6
Fixby Park Dr. Hud HD2 ... 135 F2
Fixby Rd. Hud HD2 ... 136 A5
Fixby View Rd. Brig HD6 ... 135 E6
Flanshaw Cres. Wake WF2 ... 141 E6
Flanshaw Cres. Wake WF2 ... 141 E6
Flanshaw Fst Sch. Wake ... 141 F7
Flanshaw Gr. Wake WF2 ... 141 E6
Flanshaw La. Wake WF2 ... 141 E6
Flanshaw Rd. Wake WF2 ... 141 E6
Flanshaw St Michael's C E Sch. Wake ... 141 E5
Flanshaw St. Wake WF2 ... 141 E6
Flanshaw View. Wake WF2 ... 141 E6
Flanshaw Way. Wake WF2 ... 141 D7
Flappit Spring. Coll BD13 ... 52 A6
Flasby St. Keigh BD21 ... 35 C5
Flash La. Mir WF14 ... 138 B6
Flass La. Castle WF10 ... 124 C5
Flat House. Slai HD7 ... 170 C8
Flat La. Holmfi HD7 ... 188 D5
Flat Nook. Bing BD16 ... 37 B3
Flats La. B in Elm LS15 ... 63 E6
Flats The. Hali HX1 ... 113 C6 12
Flavell Cl. S Kirk WF9 ... 182 B1
Flawith Dr. Brad BD2 ... 56 D2
Flax Meadow. Hud HD3 ... 135 A2
Flax Mill Rd. Leeds LS10 ... 79 E3
Flax Pl. Leeds LS9 ... 79 E7
Flaxton Cl. Leeds LS11 ... 79 B3 2
Flaxton Gdns. Leeds LS11 ... 79 B3 1
Flaxton La. Brad BD2 ... 56 D2
Flaxton Pl. Brad BD7 ... 74 B6
Flaxton St. Leeds LS11 ... 79 B3
Flaxton View. Leeds LS11 ... 79 B3
Flea La. Norton WF8 ... 166 E4
Fledborough Rd. Weth LS22 ... 13 C5
Fleece St. Brad BD6 ... 93 F7
Fleece St. Keigh BD21 ... 35 C7
Fleet La. M'town LS26 ... 102 A4
Fleet La. Queen BD13 ... 72 D1
Fleet La. Roth LS26 ... 101 E5
Fleet St. Clay W HD8 ... 175 D1
Fleet Thro Rd. Hors LS18 ... 58 B6
Fleming Ct. Hud HD5 ... 155 A5
Fleming House. Brad BD15 ... 73 A7 6
Fleming St. Batley WF17 ... 118 C5
Flemingshouse La. Hud HD5 ... 155 A5
Fletcher Ave. Sil BD20 ... 5 E1
Fletcher Cres. Brig HD6 ... 135 E6
Fletcher Homes. Dew WF13 ... 139 A8
Fletcher La. Ship BD2 ... 55 E4
Fletcher Rd. Brad BD6 ... 74 B1
Fletton Terr. Brad BD2 ... 56 B2
Flexbury Ave. Morley LS27 ... 98 A3
Flight Hill. Dun Br HD7 ... 199 C5
Flight House Rd. Rip HX6 ... 131 F4
Flint La. Carl HD7, S30 ... 200 A5
Flint St. Hud HD1 ... 154 B6
Flintmill La. Th Arch LS23 ... 14 D3
Flinton Gr. Brad BD2 ... 56 D3
Flockton Ave. Brad BD4 ... 75 A4
Flockton (*)*) Fst Sch. Flee WF7 ... 157
Flockton Cl. Brad BD4 ... 75 A4
Flockton Cres. Brad BD4 ... 75 A4
Flockton Dr. Brad BD4 ... 75 A4
Flockton Gr. Brad BD4 ... 75 A4
Flockton Rd. Brad BD4 ... 75 A4
Floral Ave. Leeds LS7 ... 60 C6
Florence Ave. Leeds LS9 ... 61 A2
Florence Ave. Wils BD15 ... 53 B6
Florence Gr. Leeds LS9 ... 61 A2
Florence Mount. Leeds LS9 ... 61 A2
Florence Pl. Leeds LS9 ... 61 A2
Florence St. Brad BD3 ... 75 C5
Florence St. Castle WF10 ... 124 D8
Florence St. Hali HX1 ... 113 A7
Florence St. Leeds LS9 ... 61 A2
Florence Terr. Morley LS27 ... 98 B4
Flora Kai Rd. Brad BD17 ... 54 A4
Florist St. Keigh BD21 ... 18 E1
Flounders Hill. Ack M T WF7 ... 163 E4
Flower Acre. Elland HX5 ... 134 F6
Flower Bank. Brad BD2 ... 55 F4
Flower Bank. Sow Br HX6 ... 111 F3
Flower Cl. Yeadon LS19 ... 40 A7
Flower Croft. Keigh BD21 ... 34 F5
Flower Garth. Brad BD10 ... 56 D6
Flower Haven. Brad BD9 ... 54 F4
Flower Hill. Brad BD9 ... 54 F4
Flower Mount. Baild BD17 ... 38 D4
Flower Mount. Yeadon LS19 ... 40 C7 8
Flower Scar Rd. Tod OL14 ... 107 B7
Flowerlands. Brig HX3 ... 114 A8
Floyd St. Brad BD5 ... 74 B3
Flush House La. Holmfi HD7 ... 188 A3
Flush. Liver FW15 ... 117 C2
Fold La. Hep HD7 ... 88 A6
Fold The. Haw BD22 ... 51 B7 4
Fold The. Leeds LS15 ... 62 E4
Foldings Ave. Brig BD19 ... 115 F8
Foldings Cl. Brig BD19 ... 115 E8
Foldings Ct. Brig BD19 ... 115 E8
Foldings Gr. Brig BD19 ... 115 E8
Foldings Par. Brig BD19 ... 115 E8
Foldings Rd. Brig BD19 ... 115 E8
Foldings The. Shel HD8 ... 175 A2
Foljambe St. Wake WF1 ... 142 C4
Folkestone St. Brad BD3 ... 75 C7
Folkton Holme. Brad BD2 ... 56 E2
Follett Ave. Hud HD4 ... 153 F2
Follingworth La. Slai HD7 ... 152 D1
Follingworth Rd. Batley WF17 ... 118 F5
Folly Hall Ave. Brad BD6 ... 94 B8
Folly Hall Cl. Brad BD6 ... 94 B8 2
Folly Hall Gdns. The. Brad BD6 ... 94 B8
Folly Hall. Hud HD1 ... 154 A4
Folly Hall La. Heb H HX7 ... 110 F2
Folly Hall Mount. E Ard WF3 ... 119 E8
Folly Hall Rd. Brad BD6 ... 94 B8
Folly Hall Rd. E Ard WF3 ... 119 E8
Folly La. Bramham LS23 ... 30 D2
Folly La. Leeds LS11 ... 79 B4
Folly View. Brantham LS23 ... 30 D2
Folly View Rd. Haw BD22 ... 51 D6
Fontmell Cl. Brad BD4 ... 95 B8
Foodall. Yeadon LS19 ... 40 C4
Forber Gr. Brad BD4 ... 75 E5
Ford Dr. Mir WF14 ... 137 E6
Ford Gate. Holmfi HD7 ... 188 D7
Ford Hill. Queen BD13 ... 72 D1
Ford House Sch. Leeds ... 59 E4
Ford. Queen BD13 ... 92 C8
Ford St. Hem WF9 ... 163 B1

Ford St. Keigh BD21 ... 18 E1
Fore La. Sow Br HX6 ... 112 A3
Fore Lane Ave. Sow Br HX6 ... 112 A3
Foreside Bottom La. Denh BD13 ... 71 D5
Forest Ave. Hali HX2 ... 91 E4
Forest Bank. Gild LS27 ... 97 D7
Forest Cl. Wake WF1 ... 121 F1
Forest Cres. Hali HX2 ... 91 E4
Forest Gate. Otley LS21 ... 23 A7
Forest Gn. Hali HX2 ... 91 E4
Forest Hill Gdns. Elland HD3 ... 152 A8
Forest Hill Rd. Elland HD3 ... 133 E1
Forest Rd. Hud HD5 ... 154 E5
Forest Way. Honley HD7 ... 171 E4
Forge Hill La. Knot WF11 ... 126 E4
Forge La. Batley WF15 ... 117 C2
Forge La. Hud HD4 ... 171 F8
Forge La. Leeds LS12 ... 78 C4
Forge La. Liver LS17 ... 27 D1
Forge La. Hor WF4 ... 159 C8
Forge La. Leeds LS12 ... 78 C4
Forge La. Tingley WF3 ... 117 B3
Forge Row. Gild LS12 ... 77 D3
Forge View. Stee BD20 ... 17 C5
Forman's Dr. Roth WF3 ... 100 A3
Formby Ave. Hud HD2 ... 135 F3
Forrest Ave. Hud HD1 ... 153 D7
Forrester Cl. Wake WF2 ... 159 E6
Forrester Ct. Hem WF9 ... 163 A3
Forster Ct. Brad BD1 ... 74 F7
Forster Dr. Batley WF16 ... 117 E3
Forster Pl. Leeds LS12 ... 78 A4
Forster Sq. Brad BD1 ... 74 F7
Forster St. Leeds LS10 ... 79 E5
Forsythia Ave. E Ard WF3 ... 120 C7
Fort Ann Rd. Batley WF17 ... 118 F4
Fortis Way. Hud HD3 ... 152 E8
Fortshot La. Hare LS17 ... 27 B7
Forum View. Th Auf WF8 ... 165 A5
Foss Ave. Weth LS22 ... 13 D7
Foss Wlk. Castle WF10 ... 104 B1
Fosse Way. Gar LS25 ... 83 B6
Foster Ave. Hud HD4 ... 153 C2
Foster Ave. Nor WF6 ... 123 A1
Foster Ave. Sil BD20 ... 5 D2
Foster Ave. Thorn BD13 ... 72 F6
Foster Beaver Coll The. Brad ... 54 F1
Foster Cl. Bur in W LS29 ... 9 F1
Foster Cl. Morley LS27 ... 98 A5 8
Foster Cres. Morley LS27 ... 98 A5
Foster Gdns. Keigh BD22 ... 34 F7
Foster La. Heb Br HX7 ... 89 A4
Foster Park Gr. Denh BD13 ... 52 E1
Foster Park Rd. Denh BD13 ... 52 E1
Foster Park View. Denh BD13 ... 52 E1
Foster Pk. Denh BD13 ... 52 E1
Foster Place La. Holmfi HD7 ... 189 F7
Foster Rd. Keigh BD21 ... 35 B4
Foster Sq. Denh BD13 ... 71 D8
Foster St. Morley LS27 ... 98 A5 11
Foster St. Queen BD13 ... 72 E1 1
Foston Cl. Brad BD2 ... 56 E2
Foston La. Brad BD2 ... 56 E2
Fothergill Ave. Ack M T WF7 ... 163 E6
Foul Clough Rd. Tod OL14 ... 128 D8
Foulcauseway La. Otley LS21 ... 23 D7
Foulds' Terr. Bing BD16 ... 37 A4 6
Foundry App. Leeds LS9 ... 61 D1
Foundry Ave. Leeds LS8, LS9 ... 61 D3
Foundry Dr. Leeds LS9 ... 61 D3
Foundry Hill. Bing BD16 ... 36 F3
Foundry La. Knot WF11 ... 127 A4
Foundry La. Leeds LS14, LS9 ... 61 D3
Foundry Mill Cres. Leeds LS14 ... 61 E3
Foundry Mill Dr. Leeds LS14 ... 61 E3
Foundry Mill Gdns. Leeds LS14 ... 61 E2
Foundry Mill Mount. Leeds LS14 ... 61 E3
Foundry Mill St. Leeds LS14 ... 61 E3
Foundry Mill Terr. Leeds LS14 ... 61 E3
Foundry Pl. Leeds LS9 ... 61 D3
Foundry St. N. Hali HX3 ... 91 F3
Foundry St. Sow Br HX6 ... 112 B3
Foundry Terr. Clec BD19 ... 108 A4
Foundry Terr. Clec BD19 ... 116 E7
Fountain Cl. Liver WF15 ... 116 F1
Fountain Dr. Liver WF15 ... 116 F1
Fountain St. Mapp S75 ... 177 E1
Fountain St. Barn S71 ... 178 C1
Fountain St. Brad BD1 ... 74 D7
Fountain St. Denh BD13 ... 71 D7
Fountain St. Hali HX1 ... 203 E3
Fountain St. Liver WF15 ... 117 A1
Fountain St. Hud HD1 ... 153 E4
Fountain St. Hud HD4 ... 154 A4
Fountain St. Liver WF15 ... 116 F1
Fountain St. Mir WF14 ... 138 A4
Fountain St. Morley LS27 ... 98 B4
Fountain St. Tod OL14 ... 108 A6
Fountain Terr. Brad BD12 ... 94 D3
Fountain Way. Ship BD18 ... 55 D7
Fountains Ave. Batley WF17 ... 96 F1
Fountains Way. Wake WF1 ... 121 F1
Four Acres. Mir WF14 ... 138 B6 4
Four Gates End. Tod OL14 ... 108 A2 1
Four Lane Ends. Gar WF12 ... 139 F2
Four Lanes. Brad BD9 ... 54 F3
Fourlands Ct. Brad BD10 ... 56 D6
Fourlands Cres. Brad BD10 ... 56 D6
Fourlands Dr. Brad BD10 ... 56 D6
Fourlands Gdns. Brad BD10 ... 56 D6
Fourlands Gr. Brad BD10 ... 56 D6
Fourlands Rd. Brad BD10 ... 56 D6
Fourteenth Ave. Leeds LS12 ... 78 D6
Fourth Ave. Brad BD3 ... 75 E7
Fourth Ave. Clec WF15 ... 116 B5
Fourth Ave. Halit WF15 ... 116 B5
Fourth Ave. Keigh BD21 ... 35 E8
Fourth Ave. Leeds ... 61 D1
Fourth Ave. Roth LS26 ... 101 A7
Fourth Ave. Weth LS22 ... 13 F5

Fourth Ct. Leeds LS11 ... 79 A6
Fourth St. Brad BD12 ... 94 E6 1
Fourth St. Crof WF4 ... 162 B7
Fowler St. Brad BD4 ... 75 B5
Fowler's Pl. Pudsey LS28 ... 57 C2
Fox Cl. Emley HD8 ... 175 D6
Fox Covert Road or Wnn Covert
    La. Norton WF8 ... 166 E2
Fox Ct. Crig WF4 ... 159 F7
Fox Ct. Elland HX4 ... 134 D2
Fox Heads La. Spoff LS22 ... 12 A8
Fox Hollies Rd. Hud HD2 ... 136 F5
Fox La. Crig WF4 ... 159 F7
Fox La. Wake WF1 ... 121 A1
Fox Royd Ave. Mir WF14 ... 137 F6
Fox Royd Dr. Mir WF14 ... 137 F6
Fox Royd La. Mir WF14 ... 137 F6 3
Fox Royd. Shep HD8 ... 173 F1
Fox Royd View. Mir WF14 ... 137 F6 4
Fox St. Batley WF17 ... 118 D4
Fox St. Brad BD5 ... 74 C4
Fox St. Clec BD19 ... 116 D7
Fox St. Elland HX3 ... 138 D5
Fox St. Hud HD1 ... 154 A6
Fox Terr. Pont WF8 ... 125 E1
Fox View. Batley WF13 ... 118 A3
Fox Wood Ave. Leeds LS8 ... 61 E5
Fox Wood Cl. Leeds LS8 ... 61 E5
Fox Wood Gr. Leeds LS8 ... 61 E5
Fox Wood Rise. Leeds LS8 ... 61 E5
Fox Wood Wlk. Leeds LS8 ... 61 E5
Foxbridge Way. Feath WF6 ... 123 D1
Foxcliff. Leeds LS14 ... 105 D1
Foxcroft Cl. Leeds LS6 ... 59 C6
Foxcroft Ct. Queen BD13 ... 92 C7
Foxcroft Dr. Brig HD6 ... 114 F6
Foxcroft Gn. Leeds LS6 ... 135 F8
Foxcroft Rd. Leeds LS6 ... 59 B5
Foxcroft Way. Leeds LS6 ... 59 B5
Foxdale Cl. Bacup OL13 ... 106 A1 1
Foxen La. Rip HX6 ... 132 E4
Foxglove Ave. Leeds LS8 ... 61 C6
Foxglove Rd. Batley WF17 ... 96 E2
Foxglove Way. Hud HD5 ... 154 E4
Foxhill. Aws Leeds LS16 ... 42 D1
Foxhill. Queen BD13 ... 38 B3
Foxhill Ave. Keigh BD21 ... 35 A8
Foxhill Cl. Leeds LS16 ... 42 D1
Foxhill Cres. Leeds LS16 ... 42 D1
Foxhill Dr. Leeds LS16 ... 42 D1
Foxhill Fst Sch. Queen ... 72 D2
Foxhill Gn. Leeds LS16 ... 42 D1
Foxhill Gr. Leeds LS16 ... 42 D1
Foxhill Gr. Queen BD13 ... 72 D1
Foxhill. Leeds LS27 ... 13 E6
Foxhole La. Pudsey LS28 ... 57 B6
Foxholes Cres. Pudsey LS28 ... 57 B6
Foxholes La. Nor WF6 ... 123 C3
Foxlow Ave. Hud HD5 ... 154 E8
Foxroyd La. Dew WF12 ... 139 B1
Foxstone Rise. Bail BD17 ... 38 B3
Foxstones La. Rip HX6 ... 132 D2
Foxwood Farm Way. Leeds LS6 ... 61 F3 5
Foxwood Wlk. Weth LS22 ... 13 F7
Fram Cl. Pont WF8 ... 146 E7
France Fold. Honley HD7 ... 171 E1
France St. Batley WF17 ... 118 E4
Frances Ave. Hud HD4 ... 153 C2
Frances Rd. Dew WF13 ... 139 A7
Frances St. Ack M T WF7 ... 163 D5
Frances St. Elland HX5 ... 134 F6
Frances St. Keigh BD21 ... 35 A8
Frances St. Pudsey LS28 ... 57 D3
Francis Ave. Hud HD3 ... 153 B4
Francis Catholic Prim Sch. Morley ... 97
Francis Cl. Hali HX1 ... 111 A7
Francis Ct. Leeds LS7 ... 60 D3
Francis House. Brad BD2 ... 55 D2
Francis St. Ack M T WF7 ... 163 D5
Francis View. Mir WF14 ... 137 F5
Frank Cl. Dew WF12 ... 139 E2
Frank La. Dew WF12 ... 139 E2
Frank Parkinson Ct. Guise LS20 ... 22 E1
Frank Parkinson Homes.
    Guise LS20 ... 22 E1
Frank Peel Cl. Batley WF16 ... 117 D4
Frank Pl. Brad BD7 ... 74 B4
Frank St. Brad BD7 ... 74 B4
Frank St. Hali HX1 ... 113 A6
Frankland Gr. Leeds LS7 ... 60 E8
Frankland Pl. Leeds LS7 ... 60 E8
Franklin House. Leeds LS6 ... 41 E2
Fraser Ave. Hors LS18 ... 41 C1
Fraser House. Brad BD6 ... 93 E8 2
Fraser Rd. Brad BD6 ... 93 F8
Fraser St. Brad BD8 ... 55 C1
Fraser St. Leeds LS9 ... 60 F1
Freakfield La. Liver WF15 ... 116 F1
Fred St. Keigh BD21 ... 35 B6
Frederick Ave. Leeds LS9 ... 80 B8
Frederick Ave. Hud HD5 ... 154 D5
Frederick Cl. Brad BD10 ... 38 F1
Frederick St. E Ard WF3 ... 120 A8 2
Frederick St. Keigh BD21 ... 18 E1
Frederick St. Liver WF15 ... 117 B3
Frederick St. Leeds LS2 ... 62
Frederick Walker Gdns. Batley
    WF17 ... 118 C4
Freehold La. Hali HX3 and LS ... 113 C5
Freeman St. Brad BD4 ... 95 B8
Freeman Way. Heck WF16 ... 117 A3
Freemont St. Leeds LS13 ... 58 C1
Freeston Ct. Nor WF6 ... 123 D3
Freeston Dr. Nor WF6 ... 123 D3
Freestone Way. Nor WF6 ... 122 E4

Fremantle Gr. Brad BD4 ... 75 E5
Fremantle Pl. Leeds LS15 ... 80 E7
French Ave. Morley LS27 ... 97 F3
Frensham Dr. Brad BD7 ... 73 D3
Frensham Gr. Castle WF10 ... 125 D6
Frensham Gr. Brad BD7 ... 73 D3
Frensham Way. Brad BD7 ... 73 D3
Freshfield Gdns. Brad BD15 ... 54 A1
Freston Ave. Crof WF1 ... 143 D7
Freston Dr. Crof WF1 ... 143 D7
Friar La. Brad BD10 ... 56 C6
Friendly St. Hali HX3 ... 136 B2
Friar's Cl. Feath WF7 ... 145 D4
Friars Ind Est. Brad ... 56 B7
Friars Nook. Pont WF8 ... 146 E7
Friarwood La. Pont WF8 ... 146 D8
Frickley Bridge La. Bri S72 ... 180 F4
Frickley La. Clay WF9 ... 195 A8
Frickley La. S Elm WF9 ... 195 A8
Friedhurst Rd. Tod OL14 ... 86 C1
Friendly St. Hali HX6 ... 112 A5
Friendly Fold Rd. Hali HX3 ... 92 A2
Friendly St. Hali HX3 ... 92 A2 1
Friendly St. Castle WF10 ... 124 C6
Friendly St. Thorn BD13 ... 72 D6
Friends Adult Sch. Morley ... 98 B4
Frimley Dr. Brad BD5 ... 74 C2
Frith House. Brig HD6 ... 136 C7
Frith St. Haw BD22 ... 51 E8
Frizinghall Fst Sch. Ship ... 55 C5
Frizinghall Mid Sch. Ship ... 55 C5
Frizinghall Rd. Ship BD9 ... 55 C4
Frizinghall Sta. Ship ... 55 C4
Frobisher Gdns. Ship BD9 ... 55 C4
Frobisher Gr. Wake WF2 ... 141 E5
Frobisher Rd. Liet DL15 ... 129 C1
Frognaor Ave. Brad BD7 ... 94 F5
Front Row. Leeds LS11 ... 79 B6
Front St. Bramham LS23 ... 30 C2
Front St. Leeds LS11 ... 79 B6
Front St Leeds LS11 ... 79 B6
Front St. Leeds LS11 ... 79 B6
Frost Hill. Liver WF15 ... 116 E4
Fruit St. Keigh BD21 ... 35 E8
Fryergate. Wake WF2 ... 141 F7
Fryston La. Castle WF11 ... 125 F7
Fryston La. Castle WF10 ... 125 F8
Fulford La. Hud HD4 ... 171 F4
Fulford St. Castle WF10 ... 124 D6
Fulford Cl. Mapp S75 ... 178 A1
Fulford St. Castle WF10 ... 124 C7
Fulford Wlk. Brad BD2 ... 56 A1
Fulham Pl. Leeds LS11 ... 79 B3 3
Fulham Sq. Leeds LS11 ... 79 B3 5
Fulham St. Leeds LS11 ... 79 B3
Fullerton Cl. Ad Le S DN6 ... 184 F2
Fullerton St. Brad BD4 ... 75 A6
Fullwood Dr. Hud HD7 ... 152 D4
Fulmar Cl. Mold LS10 ... 99 D8
Fulmar Ct. Brad BD8 ... 73 C7 6
Fulmar Mews. Brad BD8 ... 73 C7 8
Fulneck Boys' Sch. Pudsey ... 76 C6
Fulneck Cl. Hud HD2 ... 135 F3
Fulneck Girls' Sch. Pudsey ... 76 D6
Fulneck Golf Course. Pudsey ... 76 D4
Fulneck. Pudsey LS28 ... 76 C6
Fulstone Hall La. Holmfi HD7 ... 190 A7
Fulstone Rd. Kirkb HD4 ... 173 C1
Fulwood Gr. Wake WF2 ... 160 E7
Furnace Cofts. Wth Com S30 ... 200 D6
Furnace Gr. Brad BD12 ... 95 A4
Furnace Inn St. Brad BD4 ... 75 C5
Furnace La. Birk BD11 ... 96 A5
Furnace Rd. Brad BD12 ... 94 F5
Furness Ave. Hali HX2 ... 91 C4
Furness Ave. Wake WF2 ... 120 E1
Furness Cres. Hali HX2 ... 91 C4
Furness Dr. Hali HX2 ... 91 C4
Furness Dr. Wake WF2 ... 120 E1
Furness Gdns. Hali HX2 ... 91 C4
Furness Gr. Hali HX2 ... 91 C4
Furness Pl. Hali HX2 ... 91 C4
Fusden La. Clec BD19 ... 96 A1
Fusden La. Liver WF15 ... 96 A1
Fyfe Cres. Baild BD17 ... 38 C2
Fyfe Gr. Baild BD17 ... 38 C2
Fyfe La. Baild BD17 ... 38 C2

Gable The. Keigh BD21 ... 35 A7 13
Gadding Moor Rd. Caw S30 ... 192 F1
Gaggewell Dr. Hor WF4 ... 141 B2
Gaggewell La. Hor WF4 ... 141 B2
Gaggewell View. Hor WF4 ... 141 B2
Gain La. Brad BD3 ... 56 D1
Gain La. Brad BD3 ... 56 D1
Gairloch Cl. Brad BD7 ... 74 A3
Gaisby La. Ship BD18 ... 55 B6
Gaisby Mount. Ship BD18 ... 55 B6
Gaisby Pl. Ship BD18 ... 55 B6
Gaitskell Grange. Leeds LS11 ... 79 A5 6
Gaitskell Wlk. Leeds LS11 ... 79 A5 4
Gale St. Haw BD22 ... 51 F8 5
Gale St. Keigh BD21 ... 35 B6
Galefield Gn. Brad BD6 ... 93 F6
Gall La. Tod OL14 ... 86 A1
Gallon Croft. S Elm WF9 ... 183 A6
Galloway Ct. Pudsey LS28 ... 76 A8 3
Galloway La. Pudsey LS28 ... 57 A1
Galloway Rd. Brad BD10 ... 39 A2
Gallows Hill. Castle WF10 ... 125 D7
Gallows Hill. Nc (or) ... 159 F1
Galsworthy Ave. Brad BD8 ... 73 B7
Gamble Hill Chase. Leeds LS13 ... 77 D8
Gamble Hill Cl. Leeds LS13 ... 77 D8
Gamble Hill Cross. Leeds LS13 ... 77 D8
Gamble Hill Dr. Leeds LS13 ... 77 D8
Gamble Hill Grange. Leeds LS13 ... 77 D8
Gamble Hill Lawn. Leeds LS13 ... 77 D8
Gamble Hill Path. Leeds LS13 ... 77 D8
Gamble Hill Rise. Leeds LS13 ... 77 D8

Gamble Hill Vale. Leeds LS13 ... 77 D8
Gamble Hill Wlk. Leeds LS13 ... 77 D8
Gamble La. Leeds LS12 ... 77 C6
Gambles La. Leeds LS12 ... 77 C6
Gamel View. Stee BD20 ... 17 B6
Gang The. Leeds LS12 ... 78 C7 1
Ganners Cl. Leeds LS13 ... 58 C4
Ganners Gn. Leeds LS13 ... 58 C4
Ganners Gr. Leeds LS13 ... 58 D4
Ganners Hill. Leeds LS13 ... 58 D4
Ganners La. Leeds LS13 ... 58 C4
Ganners Mount. Leeds LS13 ... 58 C4
Ganners Rd. Leeds LS13 ... 58 C4
Ganners Way. Leeds LS13 ... 58 C4
Ganners Wlk. Leeds LS13 ... 58 C4
Gannerthorpe Cl. Brad BD12 ... 94 C3 4
Gannet Cl. Nor WF6 ... 124 C6
Ganny Rd. Brig HD6 ... 115 B2
Ganton Cl. Leeds LS6 ... 60 B4
Ganton Way. Hud HD2 ... 136 F4
Gaol La. Hali HX1 ... 113 D7
Garden Ave. Liver WF15 ... 117 A6
Garden Cl. Brad BD12 ... 94 C6
Garden Cl. Glu BD20 ... 16 B6
Garden Cl. Liver WF15 ... 117 A5
Garden Cl. Ossett WF5 ... 140 E3
Garden Cres. Dew WF13 ... 138 E8
Garden Dr. Leeds LS12 ... 78 B4
Garden Field. Brad BD12 ... 94 D3
Garden Fold. Brig HX3 ... 114 C8
Garden House. Mtown LS26 ... 102 D3
Garden House La. E Ard WF3 ... 120 A8
Garden La. Brad BD9 ... 54 F3
Garden La. Knot WF11 ... 127 C4
Garden La. Hali HX6 ... 131 C7
Garden Par. Liver WF15 ... 117 A5 1
Garden Pl. Leeds LS15 ... 117 F1
Garden Pl. S in Cra BD20 ... 16 B6
Garden Rd. Brig HD6 ... 115 A4
Garden St. Ack M T WF7 ... 163 D5
Garden St. Bir BD11 ... 117 D3 6
Garden St. Baile BD ... 54 D8
Garden St. Castle WF10 ... 124 D6
Garden St. Castle WF10 ... 125 A6
Garden St. Hali HX1 ... 153 F4
Garden St. Hud HD1 ... 51 E8 11
Garden St. Liver WF15 ... 79 D7
Garden St. N. Hali HX3 ... 113 A4
Garden St. Nor WF6 ... 123 B2
Garden Terr. Leeds LS7 ... 60 E7
Garden Terr. Brad BD8 ... 55 D1 2
Garden Terr. Crig WF4 ... 159 E4
Garden Terr. D Dale HD8 ... 191 F5
Garden Terr. Hali HX3 ... 113 A4
Garden View. Bing BD16 ... 37 C3
Garden View. Liver WF15 ... 117 A6
Garden Row. Brad BD4 ... 75 B3
Garfield Ave. Brad BD8 ... 55 B2
Garfield Pl. Mirs HD7 ... 168 B4
Garfield St. Hali HX3 ... 92 A11 2
Garfield St. Brad BD15 ... 73 C7
Garfield St. Hali HX1 ... 113 B4
Garfield St. Tod OL14 ... 86 A1
Garfield Terr. Ship BD18 ... 55 A8
Garfit Hill. Hud HD7 ... 152 A6
Garforth Barleyhill Inf Sch. Gar ... 82 F7
Garforth Cl. Nor WF6 ... 122 E3
Garforth Golf Course. B in Elm ... 63 B8
Garforth Green Lane Jun & Inf
    Sch. Gar ... 82 E7
Garforth Ninelands Jun & Inf
    Sch. Gar ... 83 A6
Garforth Rd. Keigh BD21 ... 35 B8
Garforth Rd. Hud HD1 ... 171 C7
Garforth St. Hud HD4 ... 171 C7
Garforth St. Leeds ... 78 B4
Gargrave App. Leeds LS9 ... 80 A1
Gargrave Cl. Brig HD6 ... 135 D7
Gargrave Cres. Hem WF9 ... 181 C6
Gargrave Ct. Leeds LS9 ... 80 A1
Gargrave Pl. Leeds LS9 ... 60 F1 1
Garibaldi St. Brad BD3 ... 75 F7
Garlic St. Brig HD6 ... 81 D8
Garland Dr. Leeds LS15 ... 81 D8
Garmont Mews. Leeds LS7 ... 60 D6
Garmont Rd. Leeds LS7 ... 60 D6
Garnet Ave. Leeds LS11 ... 79 D3
Garnet Cres. Leeds LS11 ... 79 D3
Garnet Gr. Leeds LS11 ... 79 D3
Garnet La. Hare LS17 ... 28 B4
Garnet Pl. Leeds LS11 ... 79 D3
Garnet Rd. Leeds LS11 ... 79 D3
Garnet Terr. Leeds LS11 ... 79 D3
Garnet View. Leeds LS11 ... 79 D3
Garsdale Ave. Brad BD10 ... 56 D5
Garsdale Cres. Baild BD17 ... 38 B1
Garsdale Rd. Hud HD4 ... 171 C7
Garsdale Wlk. Leeds LS12 ... 77 C4 3
Garth Ave. Leeds LS17 ... 43 C1
Garth Ave. Nor WF6 ... 144 A8
Garth Barn Cl. Ship BD9 ... 55 A4

Garth Dr. Leeds LS17 .... 43 B1
Garth End. Coll LS22 .... 29 B8
Garth Gr. Men LS29 .... 22 A4
Garth Land Way. Brad BD4 .... 75 C3
Garth St. Leeds LS17 .... 43 B1
Garth St. Castle WF10 .... 124 C6
Garth St. Keigh BD21 .... 35 A7
Garth The. Coll LS22 .... 29 B8
Garth The. Gar LS25 .... 83 C7
Garth The. Leeds LS9 .... 79 E7
Garth Wlk. Leeds LS17 .... 43 C1
Garthwaite Mount. Brad BD15 ..... 54 B2
Garton Ave. Leeds LS9 .... 80 A6
Garton Dr. Brad BD10 .... 56 D5
Garton Gr. Leeds LS9 .... 80 A7
Garton St. Leeds LS9 .... 80 A7
Garton Terr. Leeds LS9 .... 80 A7
Garton View. Leeds LS9 .... 80 A7 9
Garvey View. Brad BD5 .... 74 E4
Garwick Terr. Elland HX4 .... 134 D7 9
Gas The. Haw BD22 .... 51 D7 4
Gas Works La. B Spa LS23 .... 30 F7
Gas Works La. Elland HX5 .... 134 F7
Gas Works Rd. Hali HX6 .... 112 D4
Gas Works Rd. Keigh BD21 .... 35 F7
Gascoigne Ave. B in Elm LS15 ...... 63 D6
Gascoigne Ct. B in Elm LS15 .... 63 E6
Gascoigne Rd. B in Elm LS15 ...... 63 D6
Gascoigne Rd. E Ard WF3 .... 99 C1
Gascoigne View. B in Elm LS15 .... 63 D6
Gaskell Dr. Hor WF4 .... 141 A2
Gaskell St. Wake WF2 .... 142 A5
Gasson St. Hud HD3 .... 153 A4
Gasworks St. Hud HD1 .... 154 B7
Gasworks St. Liver WF15 .... 117 B4
Gate Foot La. Holmfi HD8 .... 190 C5
Gate Head. Elland HX4 .... 133 F6
Gate Head La. Elland HX4 .... 133 F6
Gate Head. Mars HD7 .... 200 A8
Gate Way Dr. Yeadon LS19 .... 40 A6
Gatefield Mount. Brad BD6 .... 94 B6
Gatehead Bank. Mars HD7 .... 169 B5
Gatehouse Enterprise Ctr. Hud .. 153 F3
Gateland Dr. Thorner LS17 .... 44 E4
Gateland La. Thorner LS17 .... 44 E4
Gateon House La. Bard LS17 .... 28 B4
Gatesgarth Cres. Hud HD3 .... 153 A5
Gateside View. Leeds LS15 .... 80 E6
Gateways Girls' Prep & High Sch.
Hare 27 A6
Gateways. Loft G WF1 .... 121 C5
Gathorne Ct. Leeds LS8 .... 60 F3
Gathorne St. Brad BD7 .... 74 B4
Gathorne St. Brig HD6 .... 115 B3
Gathorne St. Leeds LS8 .... 60 E3
Gathorne Terr. Leeds LS8 .... 60 E3
Gauk St. Ryhi WF11 .... 126 C8
Gaukroger La. Hali HX3 .... 113 D5
Gauldine Hill. Todd OL14 .... 107 F3
Gaw La. Hal E BD23 .... 1 B7
Gawcliffe Rd. Ship BD18 .... 55 C8
Gawthorpe Ave. Bing BD16 .... 37 A5
Gawthorpe Ave. Bing BD16 .... 37 A5
Gawthorpe Green La. Lepton HD8 155 D6
Gawthorpe La. Bing BD16 .... 37 A4
Gawthorpe La. Kirkhe HD6 .... 155 D6
Gawthorpe La. Ossett WF5 .... 119 C1
Gawthorpe Prim Sch. Ossett 119 C1
Gay La. Otley LS21 .... 23 B7
Gaynor St. Brad BD8 .... 74 D8
Gaythorn Terr. Brig HX3 .... 93 C1
Gaythorne Rd. Brad BD2 .... 56 C2
Gaythorne Rd. Brad BD5 .... 74 E4
Gaythorne Terr. Brad BD14 .... 73 C4
Geecroft La. Sickl LS22 .... 12 B4
Geelong Cl. Brad BD2 .... 55 C7
Gelder Rd. Leeds LS12 .... 78 C3
Gelder Terr. Hud HD5 .... 154 C5
Gelderd Cl. Leeds LS12 .... 78 D4
Gelderd Pl. Leeds LS12 .... 78 E6
Gelderd Rd. Batley WF17 .... 97 C5
Gelderd Rd. Birst WF17 .... 96 F3
Gelderd Rd. Leeds LS12 .... 78 E6
Gelderd Trad Est. Leeds 78 E5
General Hospl The. Dew 118 B1
General Infmy at Leeds The. Leeds 60 B1
Geneva Gr. Wake WF1 .... 142 A6
Genista Dr. Midd LS10 .... 99 D8
George and Crown Yd. Wake WF1 142 C6 5
George Ave. Hud HD2 .... 153 E8
George Buckley Ct. S Kirk WF9 ... 182 A2
George La. Norton WF4 .... 178 E6
George Sq. Hali HX1 .... 132 B2
George St. Bail BD17 .... 38 C4
George St. Bat HX3 .... 113 C7 11
George St. Batley WF16 .... 117 D4
George St. Brig HX3 .... 114 D7
George St. Brig HD6 .... 115 A1
George St. Brig HD6 .... 115 B2
George St. Cleck BD19 .... 116 D8
George St. Denh BD13 .... 52 E1
George St. Dew WF13 .... 139 C8
George St. Dew WF13 .... 138 F8
George St. Elland HX4 .... 134 A7
George St. Feath WF7 .... 145 D8
George St. Feath WF7 .... 145 C5
George St. Hali HX1 .... 113 A1
George St. Hali HX1 .... 132 C4
George St. Hem WF9 .... 181 D6
George St. Hor WF4 .... 141 A1
George St. Hud HD1 .... 153 D5
George St. Hud HD1 .... 154 A6
George St. Hud HD1 .... A4 12
George St. Kirkb HD8 .... 173 F6
George St. Leeds LS2 .... 79 E8
George St. Loft G WF1 .... 121 C4
George St. Mapp S75 .... 178 A1
George St. Nor WF6 .... 122 F3
George St. Ryhil WF4 .... 162 B1
George St. S Hie S72 .... 180 D6
George St. S Kirk WF9 .... 18 F4
George St. Sow Br HX6 .... 112 B3

George St. Thorn BD13 .... 72 D6
George St. Tod OL14 .... 108 B5 13
George St. Wake WF1 .... 142 C6
George St. Yeadon LS19 .... 40 B4
George's Sq. Hud HD3 .... 52 D6
George's Sq. Keigh BD21 .... 35 B6
George's St. Hali HX3 .... 91 F3
George-a-green Rd. Wake WF2 ... 141 E4
Georgia Mews. Ossett WF5 .... 140 F4
Geraldton Ave. Brad BD2 .... 55 E3
Gerard Ave. Morley LS27 .... 97 F4
Gernhill Ave. Brig HD2 .... 135 F5
Gerrard St. Hali HX1 .... 113 B7
Gervase Rd. Hor WF4 .... 141 A2
Ghyll Beck Dr. Otley LS21 .... 22 D6
Ghyll Beck Dr. Yeadon LS19 .... 40 C3
Ghyll Cl. Stee BD20 .... 17 C5
Ghyll Mews. Ilkley LS29 .... 8 A3
Ghyll Mount. Yeadon LS19 .... 39 F6
Ghyll Rd. Leeds LS6 .... 59 A6
Ghyll Royd. Guise LS20 .... 39 E7
Ghyll Royd Sch. Ilkley 7 F3
Ghyll The. Hud HD2 .... 136 A4
Ghyll The. Ship BD16 .... 54 A8
Ghyll Way. Ship BD16 .... 54 A8
Ghyll Wood. Ilkley LS29 .... 7 E3
Ghyllbank. Sil BD20 .... 5 E2
Ghyllroyd Ave. Birk BD11 .... 96 B5
Ghyllroyd Dr. Birk BD11 .... 96 B4
Gib Cotts. Honley HD7 .... 172 A2
Gib La. Skel HD8 .... 175 A2
Gibb La. Hali HX2 .... 91 B3
Gibbet St. Hali HX1, HX2 .... 112 E7
Gibraltar Ave. Hali HX1 .... 112 E6
Gibraltar Island Rd. Leeds LS10 .. 79 F4
Gibraltar Rd. Hali HX1 .... 117 F4
Gibraltar Rd. Pudsey LS28 .... 76 B7
Gibraltar Terr. S in Cra BD20 ...... 16 C5
Gibriding La. Holmfi HD7 .... 187 F3
Gibson Ave. Wake WF2 .... 141 F7
Gibson Cl. Wake WF2 .... 142 A7
Gibson Dr. Leeds LS15 .... 81 C7
Gibson La. Kippax LS25 .... 83 B2
Gibson La. Pon Kipp 83 B2
Gibson Mill. Hep HX7 .... 88 C8
Gibson St. Brad BD3 .... 75 B6
Gibson St. Hud HD3 .... 153 B5
Gibson St. Tod OL14 .... 108 C5 6
Gilbert Chase. Leeds LS5 .... 59 A3
Gilbert Cl. Leeds LS5 .... 59 B3
Gilbert Gr. Hud HX4 .... 153 D3
Gilbert Mount. Leeds LS5 .... 59 A3
Gilbert St. Pudsey LS28 .... 57 D2
Gilcar St. Nor WF6 .... 123 D4
Gilderome Birchfield Cty Prim
Sch. Gild 97 C6
Gildersome Junc Sch. Gild 97 C7
Gildersome Spur. Gild LS27 .... 77 B1
Gildersome Spur. Gild LS27 .... 97 B7
Gilead Rd. Hud HD3 .... 152 E7
Giles Hill La. Shelf HX3 .... 93 A7
Gill St. Brad BD4 .... 75 A4
Gill St. Brad BD5 .... 74 D5
Gill St. Holmfi HD7 .... 188 F8
Gill Beck Rd. Ilkley LS29 .... 8 F4
Gill La. Guise LS19 .... 39 F4
Gill Sq. Leeds LS17 .... 188 E2
Gill La. Keigh BD22 .... 34 A4
Gill La. Yeadon LS19 .... 40 A5
Gill Sike Ave. Wake WF2 .... 141 F4
Gill Sike Bglws. Wake WF2 .... 141 F4
Gill Sike Gr. Wake WF2 .... 141 F4
Gill Sike House. Wake WF2 .... 141 F4
Gill Sike Rd. Wake WF2 .... 141 F4
Gill St. Wake WF1 .... 142 C6 1
Gill's Bldgs. Wake WF2 .... 142 A5
Gill's Yd. Wake WF1 .... 142 C7
Gillann St. Knot WF11 .... 127 A4
Gillett Dr. Roth LS26 .... 100 F5
Gillett La. Roth LS26 .... 100 F5
Gilling Ave. Gar LS25 .... 83 B8
Gillingham Gn. Brad BD4 .... 75 E3
Gillion Cres. Crig WF4 .... 159 E6
Gillrene Ave. Wils BD15 .... 53 C5
Gilroyd La. Hud HD7 .... 170 D8
Gilpin Pl. Leeds LS12 .... 78 B4
Gilpin St. Brad BD3 .... 75 C7
Gilpin St. Leeds LS12 .... 78 B4
Gilpin Terr. Leeds LS12 .... 78 B4
Gilpin View. Leeds LS12 .... 78 B4
Gilroyd Rise. Brad BD7 .... 74 B7
Gilstead Dr. Bing BD16 .... 37 B3
Gilstead La. Bing BD16 .... 37 C4
Gilstead Way. Ilkley LS29 .... 8 B5
Gilthwaites Cres. D Dale HD8 ..... 192 A7
Gilthwaites Gr. D Dale HD8 .... 192 A6
Gilthwaites First Sch. D Dale 192 A7
Gilthwaites La. D Dale HD8 .... 192 A7
Gilthwaites Top. D Dale HD8 ...... 192 A7
Gilynda Cl. Brad BD8 .... 73 C7
Gin La. Crof WF7 .... 144 E4
Ginnel The. Bard LS17 .... 28 C6
Gipsy La. Leeds LS26 .... 99 A3
Gipsy La. Leeds LS11 .... 99 A1
Gipsy La. Roth LS26 .... 99 A3
Gipsy La. Wake WF2 .... 160 E5
Gipsy Mead. Roth LS26 .... 101 B6
Gipton Ave. Leeds LS8 .... 61 A1
Gipton App. Leeds LS9 .... 61 D1
Gipton Gate E. Leeds LS9 .... 61 C1
Gipton Gate W. Leeds LS9 .... 61 B1
Gipton Sq. Leeds LS9 .... 61 C1
Gipton Wood Ave. Leeds LS8 .... 61 B2
Gipton Wood Cres. Leeds LS8 ...... 61 B2
Gipton Wood Pl. Leeds LS8 .... 61 B2
Gipton Wood Prim Sch. Leeds 61 B3
Gipton Wood Rd. Leeds LS8 .... 61 B3
Girlington Prim Sch. Brad 74 A6
Girlington Rd. Brad BD8 .... 55 A1

Ginnhill Inf Sch. Feath 145 C4
Girnhill Inf Sch. Feath 145 C4
Gisbourne Rd. Hud HD2 .... 136 E5
Gisburn Ave. Wake WF1 .... 142 F8
Gisburn St. Keigh BD21 .... 35 B8
Gissing Rd. Wake WF2 .... 141 D4
Glade The. Pudsey LS28 .... 57 A2
Glade The. Scar LS14 .... 45 B7
Gladstonbury Ave. Wake WF1 ..... 121 F1
Gladstone Cres. Bacup OL13 ...... 106 A2
Gladstone Cres. Yeadon LS19 .... 40 B5
Gladstone Ct. Dew WF13 .... 118 A1
Gladstone Rd. Hali HX1 .... 113 A7
Gladstone Rd. Yeadon LS19 .... 40 B4
Gladstone St. Bacup OL13 .... 106 A2
Gladstone St. Bing BD16 .... 36 F2
Gladstone St. Brad BD15 .... 54 B1
Gladstone St. Brad BD3 .... 75 A7
Gladstone St. Cleck BD19 .... 116 D7
Gladstone St. Elland HX4 .... 134 A3
Gladstone St. Feath WF7 .... 145 D7
Gladstone St. Keigh BD21 .... 35 B6
Gladstone St. Nor WF6 .... 123 C3
Gladstone St. Pudsey LS28 .... 57 D1
Gladstone St. Queen BD13 .... 72 F1
Gladstone St. Tod OL14 .... 86 B10
Gladstone Terr. Castle WF10 ...... 124 E8
Gladstone Terr. Morley LS27 .... 98 A4
Gladstone Terr. Pudsey LS28 .... 57 F2
Gladstone View. Hali HX3 .... 113 E3
Gladwin St. Batley WF17 .... 118 B4
Glaisdale Cl. Sil BD20 .... 17 E8
Glaisdale Ct. Brad BD15 .... 54 A3
Glaisdale Gr. Brig HX3 .... 114 D7
Glamis Cl. Gar LS25 .... 83 B8
Glanville Terr. Roth LS26 .... 100 E6
Glasshouse St. Leeds LS10 .... 79 C5
Glasshouse View. Leeds LS10 .... 99 B4
Glastonbury Dr. Hud HD3 .... 153 C5
Glazier Rd. Queen BD13 .... 72 C2
Gleanings Ave. Hali HX2 .... 112 C7
Gleanings Dr. Hali HX2 .... 112 C7
Glebe Ave. Leeds LS15 .... 105 E8
Glebe Cl. Emley HD8 .... 175 D7
Glebe Field Chase. Weth LS22 ...... 13 D6
Glebe Field Cl. Weth LS22 .... 13 D6
Glebe Field Croft. Weth LS22 .... 13 D6
Glebe Field Dr. Weth LS22 .... 13 D6
Glebe Field Garth. Weth LS22 ...... 13 D6
Glebe Field Holt. Weth LS22 .... 13 D6
Glebe Gdns. Gar LS25 .... 83 A7
Glebe La. Weth LS22 .... 13 E6
Glebe Mount. Pudsey LS28 .... 76 E6
Glebe Pl. Leeds LS5 .... 59 A4
Glebe St. Castle WF10 .... 124 D7
Glebe St. Pudsey LS28 .... 76 E6
Glebe Terr. Leeds LS16 .... 59 D7
Gledcliffe. Hali HX3 .... 92 A2
Gledcliffe Rd. Hali HX3 .... 92 A2
Gledden Terr. Leeds LS15 .... 80 D8
Gledhow Grange View. Leeds LS8 .. 60 F2
Gledhow Ct. Leeds LS7 .... 60 E2
Gledhow La. Leeds LS8, LS7 .... 60 E2
Gledhow Mount. Leeds LS8 .... 61 A1
Gledhow Park Ave. Leeds LS7 .... 60 E1
Gledhow Park Cres. Leeds LS7 ...... 60 E1
Gledhow Park Dr. Leeds LS7 .... 60 E1
Gledhow Park Gr. Leeds LS7 .... 60 E1
Gledhow Park Rd. Leeds LS7 .... 60 E1
Gledhow Park View. Leeds LS7 ..... 60 E1
Gledhow Primary Sch. Leeds 61 A2
Gledhow Rd. Leeds LS8 .... 61 A1
Gledhow Terr. Leeds LS8 .... 61 A1
Gledhow Towers. Leeds LS8 .... 60 F2 1
Gledhow Valley Rd. Leeds LS7,
LS7, LS8 .... 60 E7
Gledhow Wood Ave. Leeds LS8 ..... 61 B2
Gledhow Wood Cl. Leeds LS8 .... 61 B2
Gledhow Wood Ct. Leeds LS8 ...... 61 A5
Gledhow Wood Gr. Leeds LS8 ...... 61 B2
Gledhow Wood Rd. Leeds LS8 ...... 61 B3
Glen Ave. Batley WF17 .... 118 C6
Glen Dale. Ship BD18 .... 53 F7
Glen Dene. Men LS29 .... 22 B4
Glen Field Ave. Hud HD2 .... 136 D5
Glen Gr. Morley LS27 .... 98 B4
Glen Lea Leigh. Bard LS17 .... 28 C6
Glen Mount. Cot BD13 .... 90 B6
Glen Mount. Men LS29 .... 22 B3
Glen Mount. Ship BD16 .... 54 A7
Glen Rd. Bail BD17 .... 37 D4
Glen Rd. Leeds LS16 .... 59 C7
Glen Rd. Morley LS27 .... 98 C3
Glen Rise. Ship BD16 .... 54 A7
Glen Side. Ship BD16 .... 54 A7
Glen View. Harden BD16 .... 36 B1
Glen View. Hebden HX7 .... 89 A3
Glen View Rd. Bing BD16 .... 37 A3
Glen View Rd. Shelf HX3 .... 117 D7
Glen View. Sow Br HX6 .... 112 C5
Glen View. Wils BD15 .... 53 B5
Glen Way. Harden BD16 .... 36 B1
Glenaire Dr. Ship BD17 .... 55 A8
Glenaire. Ship BD18 .... 54 F8
Glenbrook Dr. Brad BD7 .... 74 A4
Glencoe Cres. Gar LS25 .... 82 F6
Glencoe Gdns. Kippax LS25 .... 82 F6
Glencoe Rd. Castle WF10 .... 124 E6
Glencoe Terr. Kippax LS25 .... 82 F6
Glencoe View. Leeds LS9 .... 79 F6

Glendale Ave. Gar LS25 .... 82 F6
Glendale Cl. Brad BD6 .... 94 A7
Glendale Dr. Brad BD6 .... 94 A7
Glendale. Hor WF4 .... 140 F1
Glendare Ave. Brad BD7 .... 73 F6
Glendare Rd. Brad BD7 .... 73 F6
Glendower Pk. Hors LS16 .... 42 D2
Gleneagles Rd. Feath WF7 .... 124 D1
Gleneagles Rd. Leeds LS17 .... 43 B4
Gleneagles Way. Hud HD2 .... 135 F3
Glenfield Ave. Brad BD6 .... 94 A8
Glenfield. Ship BD18 .... 54 D8
Glenfield Ave. Weth LS22 .... 13 F4
Glenfield Mount. Brad BD6 .... 94 D8 8
Glenfields Cl. Crig WF4 .... 159 F4
Glenholm Cl. Neth WF4 .... 158 D5
Glenholm Rd. W Bail BD17 .... 38 C3
Glenholme Heath. Hali HX1 .... 112 E7
Glenholme Rd. Brad BD8 .... 55 B1
Glenholme Rd. Pudsey LS28 .... 57 C2
Glenholme. Ship BD18 .... 38 E1
Glenholme Terr. Ossett WF5 ...... 119 C1
Glenhurst Ave. Keigh BD21 .... 35 C5
Glenhurst. Brad BD4 .... 75 D1
Glenhurst Dr. Keigh BD21 .... 35 D5
Glenhurst Rd. Ship BD18 .... 54 E8
Glenlea Cl. Leeds LS28 .... 58 A3
Glenlea Gdns. Leeds LS28 .... 58 A3
Glenlee Rd. Brad BD7 .... 73 F7
Glenlyon Ave. Keigh BD20 .... 18 A1
Glenlyon Dr. Keigh BD20 .... 18 A1
Glenmere Mount. Yeadon LS19 .... 40 D7
Glenmore Cl. Brad BD2 .... 56 C1
Glenmore Ct. Bramha LS16 .... 24 E3
Glenmore Dr. Brad BD7 .... 73 E6
Glenmore Rd. Wake WF2 .... 160 C6
Glenroyd Ave. Brad BD6 .... 94 D7
Glenroyd Cl. Pudsey LS28 .... 76 C7
Glenroyd. Mars HD7 .... 168 F4
Glenroyd. Ship BD18 .... 38 E1
Glensdale Gr. Leeds LS9 .... 79 F7
Glensdale Mount. Leeds LS9 .... 79 F7
Glensdale Rd. Leeds LS9 .... 79 F7
Glensdale St. Leeds LS9 .... 79 F7
Glensdale Terr. Leeds LS9 .... 80 A7
Glenside Ave. Ship BD18 .... 54 E8
Glenside Cl. Hud HD3 .... 153 D8
Glenside Rd. Ship BD18 .... 54 E8
Glenstone Gr. Brad BD7 .... 73 F7
Glenthorpe Ave. Leeds LS9 .... 80 A8
Glenthorpe Cres. Leeds LS9 .... 80 A8
Glenthorpe Terr. Leeds LS9 .... 80 A8
Glenton Sq. Brad BD9 .... 55 A2
Glenview Ave. Brad BD9 .... 54 E3
Glenview Cl. Ship BD18 .... 54 C7
Glenview Dr. Ship BD18 .... 54 C7
Glenview Gr. Ship BD18 .... 54 C7
Glenview Rd. Ship BD18 .... 54 C7
Glenview Terr. Ship BD18 .... 54 C7
Glenwood Ave. Bail BD17 .... 37 E1
Global Ave. Leeds LS11 .... 78 E1
Globe Ct. Liver WF15 .... 117 B4
Globe Fold. Brad BD8 .... 74 C8
Glossop Gr. Leeds LS6 .... 60 A4
Glossop Mount. Leeds LS6 .... 60 A4
Glossop St. Leeds LS6 .... 60 A4
Glossop View. Leeds LS6 .... 60 A4
Gloucester Ave. Brad BD3 .... 56 D1
Gloucester Ave. Sil BD20 .... 5 C1
Gloucester Cres. Leeds LS12 .... 78 E8
Gloucester Gr. Wake WF2 .... 141 D5
Gloucester Pl. Wake WF2 .... 141 D5
Gloucester Rd. Bing BD16 .... 37 A2
Gloucester Rd. Leeds LS12 .... 78 E8
Gloucester Terr. Leeds LS12 .... 78 E7
Glover Ct. Brad BD5 .... 74 D3
Glover Way. Leeds LS11 .... 98 F8
Gloverfield. Bard LS17 .... 28 E7
Gloverfield. Kex S75 .... 177 C3
Glovershaw La. Bail BD16 .... 37 F5
Glusburn Cty Prim Sch. Glu 16 C6
Glydegate. Brad BD5 .... 74 D6
Glyndon Ct. Brig HD6 .... 136 B8
Glynn Terr. Brad BD8 .... 73 F8
Godfrey Rd. Hali HX3 .... 113 C3
Godfrey St. Brad BD8 .... 73 D7
Godley Branch Rd. Hali HX3 .... 92 E1
Godley Gdns. Northo HX3 .... 92 F1
Godley La. Hali HX3 .... 113 A8
Godley La. Hali HX3 .... 92 F1
Godley Rd. Hali HX3 .... 113 D8
Godly La. Hali HX3 .... 92 F1
Godwin St. Brad BD1 .... 74 D7
Goff Well La. Keigh BD21 .... 35 C2
Gog Hill. Elland HX5 .... 134 F7
Goit Side. Brad BD1 .... 74 D6
Goit Stock Cotts. Harden BD16 ..... 53 A8
Goit Stock La. Harden BD16 .... 53 B8
Goit Stock Terr. Harden BD16 ...... 53 A8
Golcar Brow Rd. Melt HD7 .... 170 C2
Golcar City Jun & Inf Schs. Hud .. 152 D4
Gold St. Leeds LS11 .... 98 F8
Golden Acre Cnr. Bramha LS16 .... 24 A1
Golden Acre Pk. Eccup 42 D8
Golden Butts Rd. Ilkley LS29 .... 8 D4
Golden Sq. Hor WF4 .... 141 A1
Golden Ter. Leeds LS12 .... 77 F6
Golden View Dr. Keigh BD21 .... 35 D4
Goldfields Ave. Elland HX4 .... 134 B8 2
Goldfields Cl. Elland HX4 .... 134 B8 1
Goldfields Way. Elland HX4 .... 134 B8
Goldfields View. Elland HX4 .... 134 B8
Golding View. Hud HD3 .... 153 B8
Goldington Ave. Hud HD3 .... 153 A8
Goldington Dr. Hud HD3 .... 153 A8
Golf Cres. Hali HX2 .... 91 F7

Goodrick La. Eccup LS17 .... 43 B7
Goodwin House. Queen BD13 .... 72 E1 5
Goodwin Pl. Hud HD2 .... 136 F5
Goodwin Rd. Leeds LS12 .... 78 C6
Goodwood Ave. Kippax LS25 .... 83 A2
Goodwood. Ilkley LS29 .... 7 F6
Goody Cross La. Swill LS26 .... 82 C2
Goody Cross. Swil LS26 .... 82 C2
Goose Cote La. Haw BD22 .... 34 E2
Goose Cote La. Haw BD22 .... 34 E2
Goose Cote Way. Haw BD22 .... 34 E3
Goose Eye. Keigh BD22 .... 34 B6
Goose Gn. Holmfi HD7 .... 189 A5
Goose Hill. Batley WF16 .... 117 D4
Goose La. Guise LS20 .... 21 C1
Goose West La. Sow Br HX6 .... 112 B2
Gooseacre Ave. Dearne S63 .... 194 C1
Goosefield Rise. Gar LS25 .... 82 C6
Goosehill La. Crof WF1 .... 143 E7
Goosehill Rd. Nor WF6 .... 144 A8
Gooshole La. S Elm WF9 .... 183 B1
Gordale Cl. Batley WF17 .... 118 B5
Gordale Cl. Brad BD4 .... 75 F3
Gordon Ave. Brad BD3 .... 56 A1
Gordon Ct. Leeds LS6 .... 59 D6
Gordon. Ossett WF5 .... 140 D6
Gordon Dr. Leeds LS6 .... 59 D6
Gordon Pl. Leeds LS6 .... 59 F6 5
Gordon Pl. S Elm WF9 .... 182 F2
Gordon Rd. Brad BD4 .... 75 B4 7
Gordon St. Brig HD6 .... 114 D4
Gordon St. Cleck BD19 .... 116 E8
Gordon St. Elland HX5 .... 134 F6
Gordon St. Feath WF7 .... 145 C7
Gordon St. Hali HX3 .... 92 B2
Gordon St. Keigh BD21 .... 35 E8 10
Gordon St. Leeds LS9 .... 8 C4
Gordon St. Shel HD8 .... 191 E4
Gordon St. Slai HD7 .... 170 A8
Gordon St. Sow Br HX6 .... 112 A3
Gordon St. Tod OL14 .... 108 C5 10
Gordon St. Wake WF1 .... 142 F2
Gordon Terr. Brad BD10 .... 39 B1
Gordon Terr. Knot WF11 .... 127 B3
Gordon Terr. Leeds LS6 .... 59 F6
Gordon Terr. Slai HD7 .... 152 D2
Gordon View. Leeds LS6 .... 59 F6
Gordonsfield. Ack M T WF7 .... 163 F5
Goring Park Ave. Ossett WF5 ...... 141 A4
Gorple Rd. Worst BB10 .... 66 A5
Gorse Ave. Bail BD17 .... 37 E1
Gorse Lea. Midd LS10 .... 99 D8 5
Gorse Rd. Hud HD3 .... 153 C6
Gorse St. Hem WF9 .... 163 B1
Gosling La. Rip HX6 .... 132 A3
Gosport Cl. Elland HX4 .... 152 A8
Gosport La. Elland HX4 .... 133 F1
Gosport La. Ripp HX4 .... 152 A8
Gothic Mount. Hali HX1 .... 145 A8
Gothic St. Queen BD13 .... 72 E1
Gott St. Haw BD22 .... 51 F8
Gott's Terr. Keigh BD20 .... 18 E1
Gotts Park Ave. Leeds LS12 .... 58 F1
Gotts Park View. Leeds LS12 .... 58 F1
Gotts Park Cres. Leeds LS12 .... 59 B1
Gotts Pk. Leeds 58 F2
Gotts Rd. Leeds LS12 .... 78 F7
Gough La. Rip HX6 .... 132 B7
Goulbourne St. Keigh BD21 .... 35 B6
Governor's Yd. Wake WF1 .... 142 D7
Gower St. Brad BD5 .... 74 E4
Gower St. Leeds LS2 .... 79 C8
Grace Leather La. Batley WF17 .. 118 C5
Grace St. Keigh BD21 .... 35 D7
Gracechurch St. Brad BD8 .... 74 D8
Gracey La. Brad BD6 .... 73 F1
Grafton Cl. Bail BD17 .... 37 F2
Grafton Pl. Hali HX3 .... 92 A3
Grafton Rd. Keigh BD21 .... 35 E8
Grafton St. Batley WF17 .... 118 D3
Grafton St. Leeds LS7 .... 79 C7
Grafton St. Keigh BD21 .... 35 E8
Grafton Villas. Leeds LS15 .... 62 D2
Graham Ave. Leeds LS4 .... 59 C3
Graham Ave. Upton WF9 .... 183 D8
Graham Gr. Leeds LS4 .... 59 C3
Graham Mount. Leeds LS4 .... 59 C3
Graham Rd. Men LS29 .... 22 A4
Graham St. Brad BD9 .... 55 A3
Graham St. Leeds LS4 .... 59 C3
Graham Terr. Leeds LS4 .... 59 D3
Graham View. Leeds LS4 .... 59 C3
Graham Wlk. Gild LS27 .... 77 C7
Grain St. Brad BD5 .... 74 B2
Grammar School St. Brad BD1 ...... 55 F1
Grampian Ave. Wake WF2 .... 141 E4
Grampian Cl. Shep HD8 .... 173 F3
Granary Ct. Hali HX3 .... 113 B4 5
Granby Ave. Leeds LS6 .... 59 D6
Granby Dr. Keigh BD20 .... 19 B5
Granby Gr. Leeds LS6 .... 59 D6
Granby La. Keigh BD20 .... 19 D5
Granby Mount. Leeds LS6 .... 59 D5 7
Granby Pl. Leeds LS6 .... 59 D6
Granby Rd. Brad BD6 .... 93 E8
Granby St. Brad BD4 .... 75 B4
Granby St. Keigh BD21 .... 35 D8
Granby St. Queen BD13 .... 72 E1
Grand Arc. Leeds LS1 .... 79 D1 2
Grand Cross Rd. Hud HD5 .... 154 D5
Grand Stand. Slai HD7 .... 152 B6
Grand View. Keigh BD22 .... 35 A4
Grandage Terr. Brad BD8 .... 74 B8
Grandsmere Pl. Hali HX3 .... 113 B4 5
Grane St. Brad BD8 .... 74 A8
Grange Ave. Bacup OL13 .... 106 A3
Grange Ave. Bir V WF16 .... 25 B4
Grange Ave. Brad BD15 .... 54 C1
Grange Ave. Feath WF7 .... 124 C1
Grange Ave. Hal E BD23 .... 1 D4
Grange Ave. Ilkley LS29 .... 8 E4
Grange Ave. Leeds LS7 .... 60 D6
Grange Ave. Men LS29 .... 21 F5
Grange Ave. Men LS29 .... 22 A5
Grange Ave. Mirf WF14 .... 138 A6
Grange Ave. Shep HD8 .... 174 A2
Grange Ave. Thorn BD13 .... 72 E6
Grange Ave. Yeadon LS19 .... 40 C6

Grange Bank Cl. Hud HD5 .... 154 D7
Grange Bank. Shelf HX3 .... 93 C6
Grange Castle. Yeadon LS19 ...... 40 D6
Grange Cl. Bad WF9 .... 164 E2
Grange Cl. Bard LS17 .... 28 D4
Grange Cl. Bri S72 .... 180 F3
Grange Cl. Elland HD3 .... 152 A8
Grange Cl. Hors LS18 .... 57 F8
Grange Cl. Ilkley LS29 .... 8 D4
Grange Cl. Knot WF11 .... 126 D4
Grange Cl. Leeds LS10 .... 79 D4
Grange Cotts. Mars HD7 .... 169 A4
Grange Cres. Baorse S63 .... 194 E1
Grange Cres. Keigh BD20 .... 18 E2
Grange Cres. Leeds LS7 .... 60 E4
Grange Cres. Yeadon LS19 .... 40 C6
Grange Croft. Leeds LS17 .... 43 C5
Grange Ct. B in Elm LS15 .... 62 F6
Grange Ct. Bad WF9 .... 164 E2
Grange Ct. Hali WF3 .... 114 A4
Grange Ct. Leeds LS15 .... 62 F6
Grange Ct. Leeds LS6 .... 59 F5
Grange Ct. Ship BD16 .... 54 A7
Grange Dr. Brad BD15 .... 73 C8
Grange Dr. Emley HD8 .... 175 D8
Grange Dr. Hud HD7 .... 152 A6
Grange Dr. Ossett WF5 .... 140 F3
Grange Est. Ilkley LS29 .... 8 D4
Grange Farm Prim Sch. Leeds 61 F6
Grange Fields Mount. Midd LS10 .. 99 F7
Grange Fields Rd. Midd LS10 ...... 99 F6
Grange Fields Way. Midd LS10 .... 99 F6
Grange Gr. Brad BD3 .... 75 F8
Grange Gr. Keigh BD20 .... 18 E1
Grange Holt. Leeds LS17 .... 43 C5
Grange House. Bri S72 .... 180 F3
Grange La. Brig HD6 .... 115 E2
Grange La. Burg DN6 .... 184 F3
Grange La. Floc WF4 .... 157 D4
Grange La. Haw BD22 .... 33 F3
Grange La. Kippax LS25 .... 83 B2
Grange La. Kirkb HD8 .... 173 D3
Grange Mid Sch. Keigh 18 E2
Grange Mount. Yeadon LS19 ...... 40 C6
Grange Park Ave. Leeds LS8 ...... 61 D5
Grange Park Cl. Kippax WF10 .... 103 A5
Grange Park Cl. Leeds LS8 .... 61 D5
Grange Park Cres. Leeds LS8 .... 61 D5
Grange Park Dr. Morley LS27 .... 98 B7
Grange Park Dr. Ship BD16 .... 54 B6
Grange Park Gr. Leeds LS8 .... 61 D5
Grange Park Mews. Leeds LS8 .... 61 D5
Grange Park Mews. Morley LS27 .. 98 B7 10
Grange Park Pl. Leeds LS8 .... 61 E5
Grange Park Rd. Leeds LS8 .... 61 D5
Grange Park Rd. Ship BD16 .... 54 A7
Grange Park Rise. Leeds LS8 ...... 61 D5
Grange Park Terr. Leeds LS8 ...... 61 E5
Grange Park Way. Morley LS27 .... 98 B7
Grange Pk. Leeds LS8 .... 61 E5
Grange Pk. Bail BD17 .... 38 E3
Grange Pl. Hali HX1 .... 113 A3
Grange Rd. Batley WF17 .... 118 A3
Grange Rd. Batley WF17 .... 118 F4
Grange Rd. Brig WF3 .... 119 F8
Grange Rd. Brad BD5 .... 73 C8
Grange Rd. Bri S72 .... 180 F2
Grange Rd. Bur in W LS29 .... 9 F1
Grange Rd. Castle WF10 .... 104 E1
Grange Rd. Clec BD19 .... 116 C8
Grange Rd. Dearne BD20 .... 4 D1
Grange Rd. Fst Sch. Brad 74 B5
Grange Rd. H Chap BB10 .... 85 A3
Grange Rd. Hud HD7 .... 152 E6
Grange Rd. Keigh BD20 .... 18 E1
Grange Rd. Roy S71 .... 179 B3
Grange Rd. Stee BD20 .... 17 A5
Grange Rise. Yeadon LS19 .... 40 C6
Grange St. Hali HX3 .... 92 A1
Grange St. Keigh BD21 .... 35 C8
Grange St. Wake WF2 .... 142 A5
Grange Terr. Leeds LS7 .... 73 C8
Grange Terr. Leeds LS7 .... 60 D4
Grange Terr. Mars HD7 .... 169 A4
Grange Terr. Morley LS27 .... 98 B7 8
Grange Terr. Pudsey LS28 .... 76 E8
Grange Terr. Ship BD18 .... 55 B6
Grange View. Leeds LS22 .... 13 E7
Grange Upper Sch. Brad 74 B2
Grange View. Brad BD3 .... 75 F8
Grange View. Dew WF12 .... 139 D1
Grange View. Leeds LS27 .... 44 F1
Grange View. Hem WF9 .... 181 D6
Grange View. Leeds LS7 .... 60 E4
Grange View. Ossett WF5 .... 140 F3
Grange View. Stee BD20 .... 76 E8
Grange View. Stee BD20 .... 17 A5
Grangefield Ave. Batley WF17 .... 118 B3
Grangefield Ave. Bur in W LS29 .. 9 F1
Grangefield Ind. Est. Pudsey 57 C1
Grangefield Rd. Pudsey LS28 .... 57 C1
Grangefields. Hud HD2 .... 135 E1
Grangeway. Hem WF9 .... 181 D6
Grangewood Ct. Hors LS16 .... 42 B1
Grangewood Ct. Loft G WF1 ...... 121 D5
Grangewood Gdns. Hors LS16 .... 42 B1
Grangewood Gdns. Leeds LS16 .. 58 C2
Granny Ave. Morley LS27 .... 98 C8
Granny Hall Dr. Brig HD6 .... 114 F2
Granny Hall La. Brig HD6 .... 114 F3
Granny Hall Pk. Brig HD6 .... 114 F4
Granny La. Leeds LS12 .... 78 A5
Granny La. Mir WF14 .... 138 B3
Grant Ave. Leeds LS7 .... 60 F8
Grant St. Brad BD3 .... 75 A7
Grant St. Keigh BD21 .... 35 A7
Grant St. Ox Oxen BD22 .... 51 C2
Grantham Pl. Brad BD7 .... 74 C5
Grantham Rd. Brad BD7 .... 74 C5
Grantham Rd. Hali HX3 .... 92 B2
Grantham Rd. Brad BD7 .... 74 C5
Grantham Terr. Brad BD7 .... 74 C5
Grantham Towers. Leeds LS9 .... 212 C1
Grantley Pl. Hud HD7 .... 152 D6
Grantley Pl. Hud HD7 .... 136 D5
Grantley St. Wake WF1 .... 142 D6
Grantley Way. Wake WF1 .... 142 D6
Granton St. Brad BD3 .... 75 C7

Granville Ave. Pont WF8 .... 146 C8 10
Granville Mount. Otley LS21 ...... 22 F7
Granville Pl. Brad BD15 .... 54 B1
Granville Pl. Otley LS21 .... 22 F7
Granville Rd. Leeds LS9 .... 60 E1
Granville Rd. Ship BD18 .... 55 C5
Granville St. Brad BD14 .... 73 C5
Granville St. Castle WF10 .... 124 C5
Granville St. Dew WF13 .... 139 B8
Granville St. Elland HX5 .... 134 F6 6
Granville St. Feath WF7 .... 145 C4
Granville St. Keigh BD21 .... 35 B7
Granville St. Liver WF15 .... 117 B3
Granville St. Nor WF6 .... 123 B2
Granville St. Pudsey LS28 .... 57 F2
Granville St. Pudsey LS28 .... 76 C8
Granville St. Tod OL14 .... 108 A1 2
Granville Terr. Guise LS20 .... 22 F2
Granville Terr. Guise LS20 .... 22 F2
Granville Terr. Hud HD1 .... 153 E5
Granville Terr. Otley LS21 .... 22 F7
Granville Terr. Ship BD18 .... 55 B5
Granville Terr. Yeadon LS19 ...... 40 C7
Grape St. Brad BD15 .... 54 C1
Grape St. Hali HX1 .... 113 B7
Grape St. Keigh BD21 .... 35 E8
Grasleigh Ave. Brad BD15 .... 54 A3
Grasleigh Way. Brad BD15 .... 53 F2
Grasmere Ave. Weth LS22 .... 13 C5
Grasmere Cl. Castle WF10 .... 104 E1
Grasmere Cres. Mapp S75 .... 178 A1
Grasmere Dr. Elland HX5 .... 135 B7
Grasmere Dr. Weth LS22 .... 13 C5
Grasmere Rd. Batley WF12 .... 118 E2
Grasmere Rd. Brad BD2 .... 56 A3
Grasmere Rd. Brig BD12 .... 94 E1
Grasmere Rd. Knot WF11 .... 126 E2
Grasmere Rd. Leeds LS12 .... 78 D6
Grasmere Rd. Mel HD7 .... 170 E1
Grasmere Rd. Wake WF2 .... 141 E7
Grasscroft Ave. Honley HD7 ...... 171 F4
Grasscroft. Hud HD5 .... 154 F7
Grasscroft Rd. Honley HD7 .... 171 E4
Grasscroft Rd. Hud HD1 .... 153 E7
Grasmere Rd. Hud HD1 .... 153 E7
Grassmoor Fold. Honley HD7 .... 172 A3
Gratrix La. Hali HX6 .... 112 C5
Grattan Rd. Brad BD1 .... 74 D3
Graveleythorpe Rd. Leeds LS15 .. 62 B1
Graveleythorpe Rise. Leeds LS15 .. 62 B1 2
Gray Ave. Ship BD18 .... 55 E5
Gray Cl. Leeds LS15 .... 81 D8
Gray Hall Cl. Elland HX4 .... 133 F3
Gray St. Liver WF15 .... 116 E4
Gray's Rd. Roy S71 .... 179 C1
Grayrigg Cl. Leeds LS15 .... 80 E7
Grayrigg Ct. Leeds LS15 .... 80 D7
Grayshon St. Birk BD11 .... 96 B5
Grayson Crest. Leeds LS4 .... 59 B3
Grayson Hts. Leeds LS4 .... 59 B3
Grayswood Cres. Brad BD4 .... 75 D3
Grayswood Dr. Brad BD4 .... 75 D3
Great Albion St. Hali HX1 .... 113 C7
Great Ben La. Slai HD7 .... 151 B4
Great Cross St. Brad BD1 .... 74 F6 1
Great Edge Rd. Hali HX2 .... 111 F6
Great George St. Leeds LS1 ...... 79 B4 8
Great George St. Leeds LS1, LS2 .. 79 B8
Great Horton Mid Sch. Brad 74 A4
Great Horton Rd. Brad BD7 .... 74 A3
Great Horton Rd. Brad BD7 .... 74 B5
Great House La. Rip HX6 .... 132 A3
Great House Rd. Tod OL14 .... 108 F8
Great & Little Preston CE Inf Sch.
  Swil 102 E7
Great & Little Preston Jun Sch.
  Swil 102 E7
Great Northern Rd. M'field LS25 .. 84 A6
Great Northern St. Hud HD1 ...... 154 B7
Great Northern St. Keigh BD21 .... 35 C5
Great Pasture. Bur in W LS29 .... 9 F2
Great Pond St. Dew WF13 .... 138 F5
Great Russell Ct. Brad BD7 .... 74 C7
Great Russell St. Brad BD7 .... 74 C7
Great Wilson St. Leeds LS11 ...... 211 E1
Great Wood St. Batley WF17 ...... 118 C4
Greatfield Cl. Ossett WF5 .... 140 E6
Greatfield Gdns. Ossett WF5 ...... 140 E6
Greatfield Rd. Ossett WF5 .... 140 E6
Greave Cl. Hud HD2 .... 136 F4
Greave Clough Cl. Bacup OL13 .. 106 B3 2
Greave Clough Dr. Bacup OL13 .. 106 B3 2
Greave House Fields. Hali HX2 .. 111 E8
Greave House La. Lepton HD8 .... 155 D3
Greave House Terr. Hali HX2 ...... 111 E8
Greave Rd. Bacup OL13 .... 106 A3
Greave Rd. Rip HX6 .... 131 E6
Greave St. Tod OL14 .... 108 B6
Greave. Wake WF4 .... 159 E4
Greaves Croft. Lepton HD8 .... 155 D3
Greaves Rd. Dew WF13 .... 138 D5
Greaves St. Brad BD5 .... 74 D3
Greaves St. Castle WF10 .... 124 D8
Greek St. Castle WF10 .... 124 C7
Greek St. Leeds LS1 .... 79 B8
Green Abbey. Holmfi HD7 .... 199 B7
Green Acre Cl. Bail BD17 .... 38 D3
Green Acre Cl. Emley HD8 .... 175 C6
Green Acres. Crig WF4 .... 160 A7
Green Acres. Feath WF7 .... 145 E3
Green Ave. Batley WF16 .... 117 E4
Green Ave. Sil BD20 .... 5 D2
Green Balk La. Lepton HD8 .... 155 F2
Green Bank. Bail BD17 .... 38 B1
Green Chase. Leeds LS6 .... 59 E7 2
Green Cl. Batley WF17 .... 118 C6
Green Cl. Brad BD8 .... 55 C1
Green Cl. Dew WF13 .... 118 A8
Green Cl. L Brad BD20 .... 4 C6
Green Cl. Wake WF2 .... 142 A6
Green Cliff. Honley HD7 .... 171 F5
Green Cres. Leeds LS6 .... 59 E7
Green Croft. Hem WF9 .... 163 B2
Green Ct. B in Elm LS15 .... 62 F7
Green Ct. Brad BD7 .... 73 F5
Green Ct. Brig BD19 .... 115 F8

Green Edge. Hud HD7 .... 152 C6
Green End. Brad BD14 .... 73 B4
Green End. Brig HD6 .... 115 A1
Green End. Bacup OL13 .... 106 A3 8
Green End La. Wake WF2 .... 142 C3
Green End Rd. Brad BD6 .... 94 B8
Green End Rd. Keigh BD20 .... 19 E2
Green Gate La. Mel HD7 .... 170 A5
Green Gate Rd. Holmfi HD7 .... 188 A4
Green Gdns. Hud HD7 .... 152 E5
Green Hall Pk. Shelf HX3 .... 93 D5
Green Head Ave. Keigh BD20 .... 18 A2
Green Head Dr. Keigh BD20 ...... 18 A2
Green Head La. Keigh BD20 ...... 18 A2
Green Hill Cl. Leeds LS12 .... 58 F1
Green Hill Croft. Leeds LS12 ...... 78 B6
Green Hill Dr. Leeds LS13 .... 58 E1
Green Hill Gdns. Leeds LS12 .... 78 B6
Green Hill. Hali HX2 .... 112 B6
Green Hill La. Leeds LS12 .... 78 B5
Green Hill Mount. Leeds LS12 .... 78 B6
Green Hill Pl. Leeds LS12 .... 78 B6
Green Hill Rd. Bacup OL13 .... 106 A1 8
Green Hill Rd. Leeds LS12, LS13 .. 58 E1
Green Hill Way. Leeds LS13 ...... 58 E1
Green Hill. Wake WF4 .... 144 C4
Green House. Kirkb HD8 .... 174 C4
Green House La. Shep HD8 .... 174 F7
Green La. Ack M T WF7 .... 163 D6
Green La. Ad Le S DN6 .... 184 E3
Green La. Add LS29 .... 2 E1
Green La. B Spa LS23 .... 30 F6
Green La. Bail BD17 .... 38 A4
Green La. Brad BD8 .... 55 C1
Green La. Brad BD8 .... 56 C8
Green La. Brad BD10 .... 56 C8
Green La. Brad BD12 .... 94 C2
Green La. Brad BD12 .... 94 C8
Green La. Brig HD6 .... 114 E5
Green La. Brig HD6 .... 115 F2
Green La. Bur in W LS29 .... 9 E3
Green La. Castle WF10 .... 103 F1
Green La. Castle WF10 .... 124 C5
Green La. Dew WF13 .... 118 A1
Green La. Elland HX4 .... 133 F1
Green La. Feath WF7 .... 145 D6
Green La. Gar LS25 .... 83 A7
Green La. Glu BD20 .... 16 B7
Green La. Hal E BD23 .... 1 A1
Green La. Hali HX2 .... 90 D1
Green La. Hali HX3 .... 113 A6
Green La. Hali HX3 .... 113 B6
Green La. Hew DD22 .... 33 F4
Green La. Hep HX7 .... 88 D2
Green La. Holmfi HD7 .... 189 A2
Green La. Holmfi HD7 .... 199 B7
Green La. Hors LS18 .... 41 A5
Green La. Kippax LS25 .... 83 A6
Green La. Kippax LS25 .... 82 B7
Green La. L Brad BD20 .... 5 A6
Green La. Ledst WF10 .... 103 E6
Green La. Leeds LS11 .... 62 B3 1
Green La. Leeds LS13 .... 58 B3
Green La. Leeds LS15 .... 78 B6
Green La. Leeds LS15 .... 63 A6
Green La. Liver WF15 .... 116 C3
Green La. M'town LS26 .... 102 F2
Green La. Mars HD7 .... 169 A6
Green La. Mel HD7 .... 170 C1
Green La. Men LS29 .... 21 F5
Green La. Neth WF4 .... 157 F6
Green La. Neth WF4 .... 158 F5
Green La. Otley LS21 .... 10 F1
Green La. Pont WF8 .... 146 A6
Green La. Pudsey LS28 .... 76 D6
Green La. Queen BD13 .... 72 D2
Green La. Rip HX4 .... 150 F8
Green La. S Kirk WF9 .... 182 B2
Green La. Shelf HX3 .... 93 B7
Green La. Thorn BD13 .... 72 C6
Green La. Upton WF9 .... 183 A7
Green La. Wake WF2 .... 142 A6
Green La. Yeadon LS19 .... 40 B5
Green Lane Mills (Ind Units). Hud .. 153 F6
Green Lea Rd. Hud HD5 .... 155 A6
Green Lea. M'town LS26 .... 102 F2
Green Lea. Neth WF4 .... 158 A6
Green Mdws. Hali HX2 .... 90 D1
Green Mount. Bail BD17 .... 38 B2
Green Mount. Bail BD17 .... 38 B2
Green Mount. Hud HD7 .... 152 E6
Green Mount La. Brig HD6 .... 115 F8
Green Mount Rd. Brig HD6 ...... 115 F8
Green Mount. Thorn BD13 .... 72 E6

Green St. Brad BD1 .... 74 F7 13
Green St. Brad BD12 .... 95 B5
Green St. Castle WF10 .... 103 D1
Green St. Elland HX4 .... 134 B4 3
Green St. Haw BD22 .... 51 C6
Green St. Hud HD1 .... 154 A7
Green St. Mel HD7 .... 170 D2
Green St. Oxen BD22 .... 51 C2 4
Green Sykes Rd. Keigh BD22 .... 34 A7
Green Terr. Dew WF13 .... 118 A2
Green Terr. Guise LS20 .... 39 E8
Green Terr. Leeds LS11 .... 79 C3
Green Terr. Wake WF14 .... 137 F6
Green Terrace Sq. Hali HX1 ...... 113 A5
Green The. Batley WF17 .... 96 F2
Green The. Bing BD16 .... 36 E7
Green The. Bing BD16 .... 37 A6
Green The. Bing BD16 .... 37 D3
Green The. Bing BD16 .... 37 D6
Green The. Birk BD4 .... 95 F7
Green The. Brad BD10 .... 56 B8
Green The. Castle WF10 .... 125 D8
Green The. Crof WF4 .... 144 C2
Green The. Feath WF7 .... 145 E4
Green The. Gar LS25 .... 83 A7
Green The. Guise LS20 .... 39 E8
Green The. Hors LS18 .... 58 A8
Green The. Hud HD2 .... 136 D5
Green The. Kippax LS25 .... 83 A1 1
Green The. Kirkb HD4 .... 172 F2
Green The. Leeds LS17 .... 43 E2
Green The. Leeds LS6 .... 58 E7
Green The. Mars HD7 .... 168 F4
Green The. Mir WF14 .... 137 E6
Green The. Ossett WF5 .... 140 E4
Green The. Otley LS21 .... 10 F1
Green The. Pudsey LS28 .... 57 D4
Green The. Roy S71 .... 179 C3
Green The. S Kirk WF9 .... 182 B3
Green The. Wake WF2 .... 120 E2
Green The. Wake WF2 .... 120 F3
Green The. Wool WF4 .... 178 A4
Green Top Gdns. Leeds LS12 .... 78 B5
Green Top. Leeds LS12 .... 78 B5
Green Top St. Brad BD8 .... 73 F7
Green View. Leeds LS6 .... 59 E7
Green View. Scar LS14 .... 45 C8
Green View The. Shaf S72 .... 180 C4
Green Way. Glu BD20 .... 16 C6
Green Way. Scar LS14 .... 45 C8
Green Wood Pk. Leeds LS6 .... 59 F7
Green's Sq. Hali HX2 .... 112 D8 3
Green's Sq. Kippax LS25 .... 83 B1
Greenacre Ave. Brad BD12 .... 94 D2 1
Greenacre Cl. Brad BD12 .... 94 D2 1
Greenacre Dr. D Dale HD8 .... 191 B5
Greenacre Park Ave. Yead LS19 .. 40 B5
Greenacre Park Mews. Yeadon
  LS19 .... 40 C5 1
Greenacre Park Rise. Yeadon 40 B5
Greenacre Pk. Upton WF9 .... 183 A7
Greenacre Rd. Upton WF9 .... 183 A7
Greenacre Wlk. Upton WF9 ...... 183 A7
Greenacres Ave. Shelf HX3 .... 93 D6
Greenacres Dr. Batley WF17 ...... 97 A2
Greenacres Dr. Shelf HX3 .... 93 D6
Greenacres Gr. Shelf HX3 .... 93 D6
Greenacres. Rip HX6 .... 132 E4
Greenacres. Shelf HX3 .... 93 D6
Greenbank Rd. Brad BD15 .... 73 B7
Greenbank Rd. Hud HD4 .... 153 A1
Greenbanks Ave. Hors LS18 ...... 41 C2
Greenbanks Cl. Hors LS18 .... 41 C2
Greenbanks Dr. Hors LS18 .... 41 C2
Greencliffe Ave. Bail BD17 .... 38 C2
Greencroft Ave. Northo HX3 ...... 93 B3
Greendale Ct. Honley HD7 .... 171 D4
Greenfell Cl. Leeds LS12 .... 78 A4
Greenfield Ave. Gar LS25 .... 83 A6
Greenfield Ave. Guise LS20 ...... 22 F1
Greenfield Cl. D Dale HD8 .... 191 F1
Greenfield Cl. Elland HX4 .... 133 F2
Greenfield Cl. Kippax LS25 ...... 82 F1
Greenfield Cl. Northo HX3 .... 93 A3
Greenfield Cl. Wool WF4 .... 178 A6
Greenfield Cres. Cull BD13 ...... 52 D6
Greenfield Ct. Hud HD2 .... 136 E5
Greenfield Dr. Brig BD19 .... 115 F8 6
Greenfield Dr. Gild LS27 .... 97 D7
Greenfield Garth. Kippax LS25 .. 83 A2
Greenfield Gdns. Stee BD20 ...... 16 D4
Greenfield La. Brad BD7 .... 73 F3
Greenfield La. Hal E BD23 .... 1 A2
Greenfield Mount. Wake WF2 .... 120 F2
Greenfield Pl. Brad BD8 .... 74 D8
Greenfield Rd. Leeds LS9 .... 80 A7
Greenfield Rd. Mir WF14 .... 138 A6
Greenfield. Roth LS26 .... 101 C6
Greenfield. Sil BD20 .... 5 D2

Greengates Ave. Brad BD12 ...... 94 C1 3
Greengates Fst Sch. Brad 56 E7
Greenhead Ave. Hud HD5 .... 154 F5
Greenhead Coll. Hud 153 F6
Greenhead Gram Sch. Hud 153 E7
Greenhead Grammar Sch. Keigh .. 18 B2
Greenhead La. Brig HD6 .... 135 E6
Greenhead La. Hud HD5 .... 154 E6
Greenhead La. Hud HD5 .... 153 F6
Greenhead Rd. Leeds LS16 .... 59 B8
Greenhill Ave. Pont WF8 .... 146 E6
Greenhill Bank Rd. Holmfi HD7 .. 189 C5
Greenhill Cty Prim Sch. Leeds .. 77 E7
Greenhill Cres. Leeds LS12 .... 78 C6
Greenhill Dr. Brig BD16 .... 36 F6
Greenhill End. Heb Br 110 F8
Greenhill La. Brad BD10 .... 56 F6
Greenhill La. Brad BD3 .... 75 C7
Greenhill Mid Sch. Leeds 77 D8
Greenhill Mount. Pont WF8 .... 146 E6
Greenhill Rd. Wake WF1 .... 142 D7
Greenhill St. Brad BD3 .... 75 C7
Greenhills. Yeadon LS19 .... 40 C3
Greenholme Ct. Brad BD4 .... 75 F2
Greenholme Trad Est. Bur in W .. 9 F2
Greenhouse Rd. Hud HD2 .... 136 A1
Greenhow Cl. Leeds LS4 .... 59 D2
Greenhow Gdns. Leeds LS4 .... 59 D2
Greenhow Pk. Bur in W LS29 .... 9 D1
Greenhow Rd. Leeds LS4 .... 59 D2
Greenhow Wlk. Leeds LS4 .... 59 D2
Greenland Ave. Queen BD13 ...... 92 E8
Greenland Villas. Queen BD13 .... 92 E8
Greenlea Cl. Yeadon LS19 .... 39 F6
Greenlea Cl. Holmfi HD7 .... 188 D5
Greenlea Ave. Yeadon LS19 ...... 39 F6
Greenlea Fold. Yeadon LS19 ...... 39 F5
Greenlea Mount. Yeadon LS19 .. 39 F6
Greenlea Rd. Yeadon LS19 .... 39 F5
Greenmoor Ave. Roth WF3 .... 100 C1
Greenmoor Cl. Roth WF3 .... 100 D1
Greenmoor Cres. Roth WF3 ...... 100 D1
Greenmount Ct. Leeds LS11 ...... 79 B3
Greenmount La. Leeds LS11 ...... 79 B3
Greenmount Pl. Leeds LS11 ...... 79 B3
Greenmount St. Leeds LS11 ...... 79 B3
Greenmount Terr. Leeds LS11 .... 79 B3
Greenock Pl. Leeds LS12 .... 78 A8 10
Greenock Rd. Leeds LS12 .... 78 A8
Greenock St. Leeds LS12 .... 78 A8 9
Greenock Terr. Leeds LS12 .... 78 A8

Greenroyd Ave. Clec BD19 .... 95 D1
Greenroyd Ave. Hali HX3 .... 113 B3
Greenroyd Cl. Hali HX3 .... 113 B3
Greenroyd Croft. Hud HD2 .... 135 E1
Greenroyd Ct. Dar WF8 .... 147 C5
Greenroyd Gr. S in Cra BD20 .... 16 D4
Greenroyd La. Hali HX2 .... 91 E1
Greens La. Bacup OL13 .... 106 A3
Greenside. Bar L DN5 .... 206 B1
Greenside Ave. Leeds LS16 .... 42 A2
Greenside. Brad BD12 .... 95 A4
Greenside. Clec BD19 .... 116 E7
Greenside Cl. Inf Sch. Hud 154 A5
Greenside Ct. Gild LS27 .... 97 D7
Greenside. D Dale HD8 .... 191 E4
Greenside Dr. Leeds LS16 .... 42 A2
Greenside Gr. Pudsey LS28 .... 76 E6
Greenside. Leeds LS12 .... 78 A4
Greenside. Liver WF16 .... 117 C1
Greenside. Mapp S75 .... 178 C1
Greenside Rd. Leeds LS12 .... 78 A4
Greenside Terr. Leeds LS12 .... 78 A4
Greensnook La. Bacup OL13 ...... 106 A3 1
Greensnook Terr. Bacup OL13 .... 106 A3
Greensway. Gar LS25 .... 83 A7
Greenthorpe Hill. Leeds LS13 .... 77 F7
Greenthorpe Mount. Leeds LS13 .. 77 F8
Greenthorpe Rd. Leeds LS13 .... 77 F7
Greenthorpe St. Leeds LS13 ...... 77 F7
Greenthorpe Wlk. Leeds LS13 .. 77 F7
Greenton Ave. Brig BD19 .... 94 E1
Greenton Cres. Queen BD13 ...... 72 D6
Greentrees. Brad BD6 .... 94 B6 1
Greenups Terr. Hali HX6 .... 112 B4
Greenview Cl. Leeds LS9 .... 61 D1
Greenville Ave. Leeds LS12 ...... 210 A2
Greenville Dr. Brad BD12 .... 94 E6
Greenville Gdns. Leeds LS12 .... 210 A2
Greenway. Brad BD15 .... 54 A4
Greenwood House. Wake WF2 .... 142 C6 24
Greenwood Mount. Leeds LS6 .... 59 E7

Greenwood Prim Sch. Leeds 79 C4
Greenwood Rd. Bail BD17 ..... 38 B1
Greenwood Rd. E Ard WF3 ..... 119 F7
Greenwood Rd. Wake WF1 ..... 142 E7
Greenwood Row. Pudsey LS28 ..... 76 F7
Greenwood St. Dew WF12, WF13 . 139 B8
Greenwood St. Dew WF12 ..... 139 C6
Greenwood St. Heb Br HX7 ..... 89 A3 5
Greenwood St. Hud HD4 ..... 154 A4
Greetland Ave & 3rf Sch. Elland 134 B7
Greetland Rd. Rip HX4 ..... 133 B6
Gregory Cres. Brad BD7 ..... 73 E2
Gregory Dr. Brad BD17 ..... 73 C4 1
Gregory Dr. Kirkb HD8 ..... 173 F7
Gregory La. Lepton WF14 ..... 156 A7
Gregory Rd. Castle WF10 ..... 124 E5
Gregory Springs La. Mir WF14 ..... 138 B3
Gregory Springs Mount. Mir WF14 138 B2
Gregory Springs Rd. Mir WF14 ..... 138 B3
Gregory St. Batley WF17 ..... 118 E5
Grenfell Dr. Brad BD3 ..... 75 D8
Grenfell Rd. Brad BD3 ..... 75 D8
Grenfell Terr. Brad BD3 ..... 75 D8
Grenley St. Knot WF11 ..... 127 A4
Grenville Wlk. Crig WF4 ..... 159 F3
Gresham Ave. Brad BD2 ..... 55 C7
Gresley Road. Ingb BD21 ..... 35 C7
Gresley Road 2nd Ed. Keigh 35 C7
Grey Cl. Loft G WF1 ..... 121 B3
Grey Ct. Loft G WF1 ..... 121 B3
Grey Gables. Neth WF4 ..... 158 E6
Grey Hall. Elland HX4 ..... 133 F3
Gray Scar Ct. Haw BD22 ..... 34 B7
Grey Scar Rd. Haw BD22 ..... 34 B7
Grey St. Loft G WF1 ..... 121 B3
Grey Stone La. Tod OL14 ..... 108 F8
Grey Stones La. Wad H HX7 ..... 69 B8
Greycourt Cl. Brad BD10 ..... 56 A6
Greycourt Cl. Hali HX1 ..... 113 A5
Greyfriar Wlk. Brad BD7 ..... 73 E3
Greyfrars Ave. Hud HD2 ..... 136 E4
Greysheils Ave. Leeds LS6 ..... 59 C4
Greyshiels Cl. Leeds LS6 ..... 59 C4
Greyshon Dr. Brad BD4 ..... 74 C1
Greystone Ave. Elland HX5 ..... 134 E5
Greystone Cl. B Spa LS23 ..... 30 C7
Greystone Cres. Brad BD10 ..... 56 C6
Greystone Ct. Brig HD6 ..... 136 A7
Greystone Mount. Leeds LS15 ..... 80 E7
Greystone Pk. Aber LS25 ..... 47 E1
Greystones Cl. Aber LS25 ..... 47 E1
Greystones Ct. B Spa BD22 ..... 34 F3
Greystones Dr. Ossett WF5 ..... 140 E3
Greystones La. Haw BD22 ..... 33 D7
Greystones Mount. Keigh BD22 ..... 34 F2
Greystones Rise. Keigh BD22 ..... 34 F3
Griff House La. E Ard WF3 ..... 120 B8
Griffe Dr. Brad BD12 ..... 94 C2
Griffe Gdns. Haw BD22 ..... 51 C6
Griffe Head Cres. Brad BD12 ..... 94 C2 2
Griffe Head Rd. Brad BD12 ..... 94 C2
Griffe Rd. Brad BD12 ..... 94 C2
Griffe Rd. Haw BD22 ..... 50 D8
Griffe View. Haw BD22 ..... 34 B2
Grime La. Crof WF4 ..... 144 B2
Grime La. Wth Com HD7 ..... 200 D6
Grimes Dyke Prim Sch. Leeds 62 D6
Grimescar Meadows. Hud HD2 ..... 135 D2
Grimescar Rd. Hud HD2 ..... 135 D3
Grimethorpe St. S Elm WF9 ..... 182 F2 1
Grimscar Ave. Hud HD2 ..... 135 F1
Grimthorpe Ave. Leeds LS6 ..... 59 C5
Grimthorpe Pl. Leeds LS6 ..... 59 C5
Grimthorpe St. Leeds LS6 ..... 59 D5
Grindlestone Bank. Hali HX2 ..... 91 C4
Grisedale Ave. Hud HD2 ..... 136 A5
Grizedale Cl. Holft LS25 ..... 13 B6
Grosmont Pl. Leeds LS13 ..... 58 C3
Grosmont Rd. Leeds LS13 ..... 58 C3
Grosmont Terr. Leeds LS13 ..... 58 C3
Grosvenor Ave. Lepton HD8 ..... 155 E3
Grosvenor Ave. Hem WF9 ..... 181 D7
Grosvenor Ave. Shop LS18 ..... 41 D8
Grosvenor Ave. Upton WF9 ..... 183 A7
Grosvenor Mews. Yeadon LS19 ..... 40 A4
Grosvenor Mount. Leeds LS6 ..... 59 F4
Grosvenor Park Gdns. Leeds LS6 . 59 F4
Grosvenor Pk. Leeds LS6 ..... 60 C7
Grosvenor Rd. Batley WF17 ..... 118 D6
Grosvenor Rd. Leeds LS6 ..... 59 F4
Grosvenor Rd. Shop BD18 ..... 54 F6
Grosvenor St. Batley WF16 ..... 117 D5 2
Grosvenor St. Brad BD8 ..... 55 D1
Grosvenor St. Dew WF12 ..... 139 C7
Grosvenor St. Wake WF1 ..... 142 F3
Grosvenor Terr. Batley WF16 ..... 117 D4 1
Grosvenor Terr. Brad BD8 ..... 55 D1
Grosvenor Terr. Leeds LS6 ..... 59 F4
Grosvenor Terr. Otley LS21 ..... 23 B8
Grouse Moor La. Queen BD13 ..... 72 C2
Grouse St. Keigh BD21 ..... 35 D8 8
Grove Ave. Hali HX3 ..... 92 A3
Grove Ave. Hem WF9 ..... 181 D7
Grove Ave. Leeds LS6 ..... 59 F6
Grove Ave. Pudsey LS28 ..... 76 D7
Grove Ave. S Kirk WF9 ..... 182 C2
Grove Ave. Shop BD18 ..... 55 C5
Grove Cl. Clec BD19 ..... 96 B1
Grove Convalescent Hospl The.
  Ilkley 8 B3
Grove Cotts. Brig HD6 ..... 114 E8
Grove Cres. B Spa LS23 ..... 30 E7
Grove Cres. Hali HX3 ..... 113 C2
Grove Cres. B. B Spa LS23 ..... 30 E7
Grove Cres. Walton WF2 ..... 161 A2
Grove Croft. Hali HX3 ..... 91 F2
Grove Ct. Hali HX3 ..... 92 A3
Grove Ct. Leeds LS6 ..... 59 F6
Grove Ct. Pudsey LS28 ..... 76 D7
Grove Dr. Hali HX3 ..... 91 F3

Grove Dr. S Kirk WF9 ..... 182 B2
Grove Edge. Hali HX3 ..... 91 F2
Grove Farm Cl. Hors LS16 ..... 41 F4
Grove Farm Cres. Hors LS16 ..... 41 E4
Grove Farm Croft. Hors LS16 ..... 41 E4
Grove Farm Dr. Hors LS16 ..... 41 E4
Grove Gdns. B Spa LS23 ..... 30 F7
Grove Gdns. Dew WF12 ..... 140 A8
Grove Gdns. Hali HX3 ..... 92 A3
Grove Gdns. Leeds LS6 ..... 59 F6
Grove Hall Park Homes. Dar WF8 . 147 D8
Grove Head. S Kirk WF9 ..... 182 B2
Grove House Dr. Brad BD2 ..... 56 A3
Grove House Dr. Brad BD2 ..... 56 A3
Grove House Fst Sch. Brad 56 A4
Grove House Rd. Brad BD2 ..... 56 A3
Grove La. Bad WF9 ..... 164 E3
Grove La. Clec BD19 ..... 96 B1
Grove La. Hem WF9 ..... 181 E6
Grove La. Knot WF11 ..... 126 E4
Grove La. Leeds LS6 ..... 59 E6
Grove La. S Kirk WF9 ..... 182 B2
Grove Lea Cl. Hem WF9 ..... 181 E6
Grove Lea Cres. Pont WF8 ..... 146 E7
Grove Lea Wlk. Pont WF8 ..... 146 E7
Grove Mill La. Hali HX2 ..... 112 A7
Grove Mount. Pont WF8 ..... 146 E8
Grove Mount. S Kirk WF9 ..... 182 B2
Grove Pk. Crig WF4 ..... 159 F6
Grove Pl. Hali HX3 ..... 92 A3
Grove Pl. B Spa LS23 ..... 30 E7
Grove Pl. Hem WF9 ..... 181 E6
Grove Rd. Batley WF16 ..... 117 E3
Grove Rd. Elland HX5 ..... 135 B7
Grove Rd. Heb Br HX7 ..... 89 A4
Grove Rd. Hem WF9 ..... 181 E6
Grove Rd. Hors LS18 ..... 58 C8
Grove Rd. Hud HD1 ..... 154 B7
Grove Rd. Ilkley LS29 ..... 7 E4
Grove Rd. Leeds LS6 ..... 59 E5
Grove Rd. Leeds LS10 ..... 79 E3
Grove Rd. Leeds LS15 ..... 81 A7
Grove Rd. Mapp S75 ..... 178 A1
Grove Rd. Men LS29 ..... 22 A4
Grove Rd. Pont WF8 ..... 146 E8
Grove Rd. Pudsey LS28 ..... 76 D7
Grove Rise. Leeds LS17 ..... 42 F5
Grove Rd. Wake WF1 ..... 142 D5
Grove Rise. Pont WF8 ..... 146 E8
Grove Royd. Hali HX3 ..... 92 A3
Grove Sq. Clec BD19 ..... 96 B1
Grove St. Hali HX6 ..... 91 F2
Grove St. Bacup OL13 ..... 106 A3
Grove St. Batley WF15 ..... 117 C2
Grove St. Batley WF17 ..... 117 E4
Grove St. Brig HD6 ..... 115 B2
Grove St. Dew WF13 ..... 139 C8
Grove St. Hali HX2 ..... 91 F3
Grove St. Hali HX6 ..... 112 D4
Grove St. Keigh BD21 ..... 35 B6
Grove St. Mir WF14 ..... 138 B6
Grove St. Ossett WF5 ..... 140 D5
Grove St. Pudsey LS28 ..... 57 E2
Grove St. S Hali HX1 ..... 112 F7
Grove St. S Kirk WF9 ..... 182 B2
Grove St. Slai HD7 ..... 151 F1
Grove St. Wake WF1 ..... 142 D5
Grove Terr. B Spa LS23 ..... 30 E7
Grove Terr. Birk BD11 ..... 96 A6
Grove Terr. Brad BD7 ..... 74 D6
Grove Terr. Brig HD6 ..... 114 E8
Grove Terr. Heb Br HX7 ..... 110 E8
Grove Terr. Ossett WF5 ..... 140 D5
Grove Terr. Pudsey LS28 ..... 57 E2 4
Grove The. Bail BD17 ..... 38 C4
Grove The. Batley WF17 ..... 118 A6
Grove The. Brig BD16 ..... 36 E6
Grove The. Brad BD10 ..... 56 B8
Grove The. Brig HX3 ..... 114 D8
Grove The. C ard S72 ..... 180 B1
Grove The. E Kes LS17 ..... 28 B6
Grove The. Hors LS18 ..... 41 B1
Grove The. Hud HD2 ..... 136 B2
Grove The. Ilkley LS29 ..... 8 A4
Grove The. Kippax LS25 ..... 83 B1
Grove The. Leeds LS17 ..... 42 F5
Grove The. Nor WF6 ..... 123 B2
Grove The. Pudsey LS28 ..... 76 D7
Grove The. Queen BD13 ..... 72 D1 7
Grove The. Ryhill WF4 ..... 162 C1
Grove The. Shelf HX3 ..... 93 C6
Grove The. Swil LS26 ..... 82 B2
Grove The. Walton WF2 ..... 161 A3
Grove The. Yeadon LS19 ..... 40 B6
Grove Way. S Kirk WF9 ..... 182 B2
Grovehall Ave. Leeds LS11 ..... 214 A1
Grovehall Dr. Leeds LS11 ..... 214 A1
Grovehall Par. Leeds LS11 ..... 214 A1
Grovehall Rd. Leeds LS11 ..... 78 F1
Grovelands. Brad BD2 ..... 56 B2
Groveville. Brig HX3 ..... 93 C1
Groves Hall Rd. Dew WF13 ..... 118 B1
Grunberg Pl. Leeds LS6 ..... 59 F5
Grunberg Rd. Leeds LS6 ..... 59 F5
Grunberg St. Leeds LS6 ..... 59 D5 6
Guard House Ave. Keigh BD22 ..... 35 A7
Guard House Dr. Keigh BD22 ..... 35 A7
Guard House Fst Sch. Keigh 35 A7
Guard House Gr. Keigh BD22 ..... 34 F7
Guard House Rd. Keigh BD22 ..... 34 F7
Guernsey Rd. Batley WF12 ..... 118 F2
Guild Way. Hali HX2 ..... 112 D7
Guildford Ave. Hud HD3 ..... 153 A5
Guildford Rd. Hud HD3 ..... 153 A5
Guildford St. Heb Br HX7 ..... 89 A4
Guildford St. Keigh BD21 ..... 35 C7
Guillemot App. Morley LS27 ..... 98 D3
Guiseley Dr. Guise LS20 ..... 22 E1
Guiseley Inf Sch. Guise 22 D1
Guiseley Sch. Guise 22 C2
Guiseley Sta. Guise 22 E1 3
Guiseley Queensway Jun & Inf Sch.
  Yeadon 40 A8
Gulley Rd. Leeds LS6 ..... 59 D5
Gulley Terr. Holmfi HD7 ..... 189 A7
Gully The. Holmfi HD7 ..... 190 C5
Gunter Rd. Weth LS22 ..... 14 A5
Gunthwaite La. Ingb S30 ..... 192 B2

Gunthwaite Top. D Dale HD8 ..... 191 F3
Gurbax Ct. Brad BD3 ..... 75 E7
Gurney Cl. Brad BD5 ..... 74 D3
Guy St. Brad BD4 ..... 74 F6 5
Guycroft. Otley LS21 ..... 22 F7
Gwynne Ave. Brad BD3 ..... 56 E1
Gynn Halley. Hud HD7 ..... 172 B5
Gypsy Ct. Castle WF10 ..... 125 C6
Gypsy La. Castle WF10 ..... 125 C5
Gypsy Wood Cl. Leeds LS15 ..... 81 D7
Gypsy Wood Crest. Leeds LS15 ..... 81 D7

Hacking La. S Elm WF9 ..... 183 B3
Hadassah St. Hali HX3 ..... 113 D4
Haddingley La. Holmfi HD7 ..... 190 D4
Haddon Ave. Hali HX1 ..... 202 A1
Haddon Ave. Leeds LS4 ..... 59 C2
Haddon Cl. Dew WF13 ..... 117 B8
Haddon Cl. S Elm WF9 ..... 183 A5
Haddon Pl. Leeds LS4 ..... 59 C2
Haddon Rd. Leeds LS4 ..... 59 E6
Hade Edge Sch. Holmfi 199 B8
Hadfield Hosue. Brad BD6 ..... 93 E8 3
Hadleigh Ct. Leeds LS17 ..... 43 D2
Hadleigh Rise. Pont WF8 ..... 146 D5
Hadrian Cl. Castle WF10 ..... 104 C1
Hadrian Cl. Th Aud WF8 ..... 165 A5
Hag Farm Rd. Bur in W LS29 ..... 21 E7
Hag Farm Rd. Men LS29 ..... 21 E7
Hag Hill. Emley HD8 ..... 175 E6
Hag Hill La. Emley HD8 ..... 175 E6
Hag La. Hali HX3 ..... 92 D3
Hagg La. Wr F LS24 ..... 48 A1
Hagg Hill Rd. Ossett WF5 ..... 141 A5
Haggs La. Wake WF2 ..... 141 C5
Haggroyd La. Honley HD7 ..... 171 E5
Haigh Ave. Roth LS26 ..... 100 C7
Haigh Beck View. Brad BD10 ..... 56 D7
Haigh Cnr. Brad BD10 ..... 56 D7
Haigh Croft. Roy S71 ..... 179 B4
Haigh Fold. Brad BD2 ..... 56 C5
Haigh Gdns. Roth LS26 ..... 100 C7
Haigh Hall. Brad BD10 ..... 56 D7
Haigh Hall Rd. Brad BD10 ..... 56 D7
Haigh. Wool S75, WF4 ..... 177 C6
Haigh House Hill. Elland HD3 ..... 134 A3
Haigh La. Floc WF4 ..... 157 A2
Haigh La. Hali HX3 ..... 93 B4
Haigh Moor Ave. E Ard WF3 ..... 119 E6
Haigh Moor Cres. E Ard WF3 ..... 119 E6
Haigh Moor View. E Ard WF3 ..... 119 E6
Haigh Park Rd. Leeds LS10 ..... 80 B2
Haigh Rd. Roth LS26 ..... 100 F6
Haigh Road Sch. Roth 100 E6
Haigh St. Brad BD4 ..... 75 B3
Haigh St. Brig HD6 ..... 115 A3 16
Haigh St. Elland HX4 ..... 134 C7
Haigh Terr. Roth LS26 ..... 100 C7
Haigh Wood Cres. Hors LS16 ..... 41 D2
Haigh Wood Gn. Hors LS16 ..... 41 D2
Haigh Wood Rd. Hors LS16 ..... 41 D2
Haigh's Sq. Hud HD5 ..... 154 D7
Haighside. Roth LS26 ..... 100 C6
Haighside Cl. Roth LS26 ..... 100 C6
Haighside Way. Roth LS26 ..... 100 C6
Haighside Dr. Roth LS26 ..... 100 C6
Haihead Dr. Pont WF8 ..... 125 F1
Haincliffe Pl. Keigh BD21 ..... 35 B4 11
Haincliffe Rd. Keigh BD21 ..... 35 B4
Haines Pk. Leeds 60 D7
Hainsworth Moor Cres. Queen
  BD13 ..... 92 D8 5
Hainsworth Moor Garth. Queen
  BD13 ..... 92 D8 4
Hainsworth Moor Mid Sch. Queen 92 D8
Hainsworth Moor View. Queen
  BD13 ..... 92 D8
Hainsworth Rd. Sil BD20 ..... 17 F8
Hainsworth Sq. Pudsey LS28 ..... 57 D3 7
Hainsworth St. Leeds LS12 ..... 210 A1
Hainsworth St. Roth LS26 ..... 100 D7
Hainworth Crag Rd. Keigh BD21 . 35 A2
Hainworth La. Keigh BD21 ..... 35 B3
Hainworth Rd. Keigh BD21 ..... 35 B4
Hainworth Wood Rd. Keigh BD21 . 35 B4
Hainworth Wood Rd N. Keigh BD21 35 B5
Haise Mount. Mapp S75 ..... 178 A1
Halcyon Hill. Leeds LS7 ..... 60 B6
Halcyon Way. Brad BD5 ..... 74 D2
Haldane Cl. Wake WF2 ..... 142 F1
Haldane Cres. Wake WF2 ..... 142 F1
Hales Rd. Leeds LS12 ..... 209 E2
Halesworth Cres. Brad BD4 ..... 75 F2
Haley Hill. Hali HX3 ..... 203 F4
Haley's Yd. Leeds LS13 ..... 58 A2
Half Acre Rd. Denh BD13 ..... 52 E1
Half Acres Fst & Mid Schs. Castle 124 C7
Half House La. Rip HX6 ..... 114 D5
Half Mile. Pudsey LS28 ..... 57 F5
Half Mile Cl. Pudsey LS28 ..... 57 F5
Half Mile Gdns. Pudsey LS28 ..... 57 F5
Half Mile Gn. Pudsey LS28 ..... 57 F5
Half Mile La. Leeds LS13 ..... 57 F5
Half Mile La. Pudsey LS28 ..... 57 F5
Half Moon La. Crof WF4 ..... 143 F1
Halfpenny La. Pont WF8 ..... 146 C5
Halfpenny La. Th Aud WF8 ..... 165 B5
Halifax Catholic High Sch. Hali 92 B1
Halifax General Hospl. Hali 113 B7
Halifax Ind Ctr The. Hali 71 B1
Halifax High Sch The. Hali 113 A4

Halifax Rd. Brig HD6 ..... 114 E5
Halifax Rd. Brig HD6 ..... 115 E7
Halifax Rd. Clec WF15 ..... 116 C5
Halifax Rd. Cull BD13 ..... 52 A5
Halifax Rd. Cull BD13 ..... 52 D6
Halifax Rd. Denh BD13 ..... 71 E5
Halifax Rd. Denh BD13 ..... 71 E7
Halifax Rd. Dew WF13 ..... 138 B7
Halifax Rd. Dew WF13 ..... 139 D8
Halifax Rd. Elland HX5 ..... 134 E8
Halifax Rd. Hali HX3, HX5 ..... 134 E8
Halifax Rd. Hud HD2 ..... 88 C2
Halifax Rd. Keigh BD21, BD22 ..... 35 A3
Halifax Rd. Litt HX6 ..... 148 A7
Halifax Rd. Northo HX3 ..... 93 B4
Halifax Rd. Queen BD13 ..... 92 C7
Halifax Rd. Rip HX6 ..... 132 E6
Halifax Rd. Slai HD7 ..... 152 B5
Halifax Rd. Tod OL14 ..... 108 D6
Halifax Sta. Hali 113 D6
Hall Ave. Hud HD1 ..... 153 F5
Hall Ave. S Elm WF9 ..... 163 C4
Hall Bank Dr. Bing BD16 ..... 36 F4
Hall Bank La. Heb Br HX7 ..... 110 E8
Hall Bank La. Mir WF14 ..... 138 A3
Hall Bower La. Hud HD4 ..... 154 B1
Hall Bury. Clay DN5 ..... 194 C4
Hall Cl. B Spa LS23 ..... 30 E7
Hall Cl. Bramho LS16 ..... 24 E3
Hall Cl. Bur in W LS29 ..... 9 D1
Hall Cl. Liver WF15 ..... 117 B2
Hall Cl. S in Cra BD20 ..... 16 D4
Hall Cl. Ossett WF5 ..... 119 D1
Hall Cliffe Cres. Hor WF4 ..... 141 A2
Hall Cliffe Ct. Hor WF4 ..... 141 A2
Hall Cliffe Gr. Hor WF4 ..... 141 A2
Hall Cliffe Rise. Hor WF4 ..... 141 A2
Hall Cliffe Rd. Hor WF4 ..... 141 A2
Hall Croft. Neth WF4 ..... 158 E6
Hall Cross Gr. Hud HD5 ..... 154 D3
Hall Cross Rd. Hud HD5 ..... 154 D3
Hall Dr. Bur in W LS29 ..... 9 D1
Hall Dr. Leeds LS16 ..... 24 E3
Hall Dr. Liver WF15 ..... 117 B2
Hall Gdns. Farnh BD20 ..... 4 E1
Hall Gr. Leeds LS6 ..... 59 F2
Hall Gr. Mapp S75 ..... 178 C1
Hall Green La. Rip HX6 ..... 150 D8
Hall Ing La. Honley HD7 ..... 172 C5
Hall Ing Rd. Honley HD4 ..... 172 E3
Hall Ing Rd. Kirkhe HD4 ..... 172 E3
Hall Ings. Brad BD1 ..... 201 C2
Hall Ings. Brad BD1 ..... 74 D6
Hall La. Ask LS21 ..... 9 D8 1
Hall La. Dew WF12 ..... 139 F7
Hall La. Hor WF4 ..... 141 A2
Hall La. Leeds LS12 ..... 210 A4
Hall La. Leeds LS12 ..... 59 A1
Hall La. Ledst WF10 ..... 103 E6
Hall La. Leeds LS17 ..... 43 A6
Hall La. Leeds LS7 ..... 60 D4
Hall La. Leeds LS11 ..... 211 E1
Hall La. Leeds LS13 ..... 58 D3
Hall La. Leeds LS17 ..... 43 A6
Hall La. Northo HX3 ..... 92 F2
Hall La. S Elm WF9 ..... 182 F4
Hall La. S in Cra BD20 ..... 16 D4
Hall La. S in Elm LS25 ..... 84 F4
Hall La. Ship BD18 ..... 55 B6
Hall Orchards Ave. Weth LS22 ..... 14 A6
Hall Park Ave. Crof WF4 ..... 143 F2
Hall Park Ave. Hors LS18 ..... 41 A1
Hall Park Ave. Liver WF15 ..... 117 A2
Hall Park Cl. Hors LS18 ..... 41 A1
Hall Park Croft. Kippax LS25 ..... 103 B8
Hall Park Garth. Kippax LS25 ..... 103 B8
Hall Park Meadows. Kippax LS25 . 103 B8
Hall Park Mount. Hors LS18 ..... 41 A1
Hall Park Orch. Kippax LS25 ..... 103 B8
Hall Park Rd. Th Arch LS23 ..... 15 A5
Hall Park Rise. Hors LS18 ..... 41 A1
Hall Park Rise. Kippax LS25 ..... 83 B1
Hall Pl. Leeds LS9 ..... 212 C2
Hall Rd. Brad BD2 ..... 55 E4
Hall Rd. Leeds LS12 ..... 209 E3
Hall Rd. Wake WF2 ..... 141 D4
Hall Rise. Bramho LS16 ..... 24 E3
Hall Rise. Bur in W LS29 ..... 9 D1
Hall Rise Cl. Bramho LS16 ..... 24 E3
Hall Rise Croft. Bramho LS16 ..... 24 E3
Hall Royd. Ship BD18 ..... 55 B6
Hall St. Batley WF17 ..... 96 F1
Hall St. Brig HD6 ..... 115 B1
Hall St. Castle WF10 ..... 124 D7
Hall St. Haw BD22 ..... 51 C6
Hall St. Hud HD1 ..... 153 E7
Hall St. Keigh BD21 ..... 35 C6
Hall St. Queen BD13 ..... 72 E1
Hall St S. Brad BD7 ..... 74 C6
Hall St. Shep BD18 ..... 55 A8
Hall Terr. Otley LS21 ..... 23 B8
Hall View. Otley LS21 ..... 23 B8
Hallamshire Mews. Wake WF2 ..... 141 C4
Hallas La. Cull BD13 ..... 52 C5
Hallas La. Leeds LS29 ..... 7 B8
Hallas Rd. Kirkb HD8 ..... 173 F7
Hallbank Cl. Brad BD5 ..... 74 C2
Hallcliffe. Bail BD17 ..... 38 C3
Hallcroft Dr. Add LS29 ..... 7 A8
Hallcroft Cl. Weth LS22 ..... 13 E6
Hallcroft La. Weth LS22 ..... 13 E6
Hallfield Dr. Bail BD17 ..... 38 B1
Hallfield La. Weth LS22 ..... 13 E5

Halfield Rd. Brad BD1 ..... 74 D7
Hallfield St. Brad BD1 ..... 74 E8
Hallfield Terr. M'field LS25 ..... 83 F7
Hallgate. Brad BD1 ..... 74 E8
Halliday Ave. Leeds LS12 ..... 78 A8
Halliday Dr. Leeds LS12 ..... 78 A8 16
Halliday Gr. Leeds LS12 ..... 78 A8
Halliday Mount. Leeds LS12 ..... 78 A8
Halliday Pl. Leeds LS12 ..... 78 A8
Halliday Rd. Gar LS25 ..... 82 E7
Halliday Rd. Leeds LS12 ..... 78 A8 18
Halliday St. Pudsey LS28 ..... 76 E8
Halliley Gdns. Dew WF13 ..... 139 C8 2
Halliley St. Dew WF13 ..... 139 B8
Halling Pl. Tod OL14 ..... 108 A1
Hallowes Gr. Cull BD13 ..... 52 D5
Hallowes Park Rd. Cull BD13 ..... 52 D6
Hallows Rd. Keigh BD21 ..... 18 E1
Hallows The. Keigh BD20 ..... 35 A8
Hallroyd Cres. Tod OL14 ..... 108 C5
Hallroyd Pl. Tod OL14 ..... 108 C5
Hallroyd Rd. Tod OL14 ..... 108 C5
Hallwood Gn. Brad BD10 ..... 56 E5
Halstead Dr. Men LS29 ..... 22 A5
Halstead Gr. Mapp S75 ..... 178 A2
Halsteads Way. Stee BD20 ..... 17 C6
Halton Cl. Hud HD5 ..... 154 F4
Halton Dr. Leeds LS15 ..... 81 A8
Halton Moor Ave. Leeds LS9 ..... 80 D7
Halton Moor Rd. Leeds LS15, LS9 . 80 D6
Halton Pl. Brad BD5 ..... 74 B3
Halton St. Wake WF1 ..... 142 F8
Halton St. Hud HD1 ..... 153 E7
Haltons Ct. Feath WF7 ..... 145 D7
Hambleton Ave. Knot RF4 ..... 95 B8
Hambleton Ave. Hali HX2 ..... 170 F1
Hambleton Bank. Hali HX2 ..... 91 B6
Hambleton Cotts. D Abby BD23 ..... 2 B8
Hambleton Cres. Hali HX2 ..... 91 B5
Hambleton Dr. Hali HX2 ..... 91 B5
Hambleton St. Wake WF1 ..... 142 C7 6
Hame The. Elland HX4 ..... 134 B8
Hamel Rise. Hem WF9 ..... 181 D6
Hamilton Ave. Leeds LS7 ..... 60 E4
Hamilton Cl. Nor WF6 ..... 123 C1
Hamilton Gdns. Leeds LS7 ..... 60 E3
Hamilton House. Brad BD15 ..... 73 B8 5
Hamilton Pl. Leeds LS7 ..... 60 E3
Hamilton Prin Sch. Leeds 60 E4
Hamilton Rd. Brad BD3 ..... 74 D8
Hamilton Terr. Leeds LS7 ..... 60 E4
Hamilton Terr. Otley LS21 ..... 23 B8
Hamilton View. Leeds LS7 ..... 60 E4
Hamm Strasse. Brad BD1 ..... 74 E8
Hammer La. Crof WF4 ..... 144 B4
Hammerstones Leach La. Elland
  HX5 ..... 134 D5
Hammerton Gr. Pudsey LS28 ..... 57 F4
Hammerton Gr. Pudsey LS28 ..... 76 F7 4
Hammerton Rd. Hud HD2 ..... 136 A2
Hammerton St. Brad BD3 ..... 75 A6
Hammerton St. Pudsey LS28 ..... 76 F7
Hammerton Terr. Tod OL14 ..... 108 B6 5
Hammond Cres. Birk BD11 ..... 96 E7
Hammond Pl. Brad BD9 ..... 55 A3
Hammond Rd. Wake WF1 ..... 142 F1
Hammond Sq. Brad BD9 ..... 126 D3
Hammond St. Hali HX1 ..... 112 F6
Hammond St. Northo HX3 ..... 92 F1
Hampden Cl. Knot WF11 ..... 126 E8
Hampden Pl. Brad BD5 ..... 74 D3
Hampden Pl. Hali HX2 ..... 91 F7
Hampden St. Leeds LS11 ..... 211 E1
Hampole Balk. La E Le DN6 ..... 184 E1
Hampshire Cl. Ilkley LS29 ..... 8 F4
Hampshire St. Hud HD4 ..... 154 C4
Hampson St. Batley WF17 ..... 118 C3
Hampton Pl. Brad BD10 ..... 55 F1
Hampton Pl. Leeds LS9 ..... 80 A7
Hampton St. Hali HX1 ..... 112 F5 6
Hampton Terr. Leeds LS9 ..... 80 A7
Hamworth Dr. Brad BD22 ..... 34 D2
Hanby Ave. Nor WF6 ..... 123 B1
Hand Bank La. Mir WF14 ..... 138 B4
Hand Carr La. Sow Br HX2 ..... 111 A6
Handel St. Brad BD7 ..... 74 C7
Handel Terr. Hud HD5 ..... 154 C6
Handel St. Leeds LS6 ..... 60 A4
Handel Terr. Hud HD5 ..... 154 D6 2
Hanging Heaton CE Sch. Batley 118 B3
Hanging Gate La. Oxen BD22 ..... 51 B5
Hanging Royd. Hali HX7 ..... 88 F5
Hanging Stone Rd. Hud HD4 ..... 153 C2
Hanging Stones La. Rip HX6 ..... 132 F5
Hangingroyd Cl. Heb Br HX7 ..... 89 A3 5 3
Hangingroyd La. Heb Br HX7 ..... 89 A3
Hangingroyd Rd. Heb Br HX7 ..... 89 A3 A36
Hangram St. Bing BD16 ..... 37 A3
Hanley Rd. Morley LS27 ..... 98 A3
Hannah Ct. Brad BD12 ..... 94 C3
Hanover Cl. Brad BD8 ..... 74 A8
Hanover Ct. Bac DN6 ..... 183 E5
Hanover Ct. Bac 106 A3
Hanover Gdns. Bur in W LS29 ..... 21 D8
Hanover La. Leeds LS3 ..... 211 E4
Hanover Mount. Leeds LS3 ..... 205 E1
Hanover Sq. Brad BD1 ..... 74 C7 4
Hanover Sq. Leeds LS3 ..... 211 E4
Hanover St. Batley WF17 ..... 118 C5
Hanover St. Brig HD6 ..... 115 B1
Hanover St. Hali HX1 ..... 203 D3
Hanover St. Keigh BD21 ..... 35 B6
Hanover Way. Bur in W LS29 ..... 21 D8
Hanover Way. Leeds LS3 ..... 211 E4
Hansby Ave. Leeds LS14 ..... 62 C5
Hansby Bank. Leeds LS14 ..... 62 C5
Hansby Cl. Leeds LS14 ..... 62 D5
Hansby Dr. Leeds LS14 ..... 62 C5
Hansby Gate. Leeds LS14 ..... 62 C5

Hansby Gdns. Leeds LS14 62 B4
Hansby Grange. Leeds LS14 62 B5 10
Hansby Pl. Leeds LS14 62 B5
Hanson Ave. Nor WF6 123 B1
Hanson Ct. Brad BD12 94 B2
Hanson Fold. Brad BD12 94 C3 8
Hanson La. Hali HX1 113 A7
Hanson La. Hud HD4 153 E2
Hanson Mount. Brad BD12 94 C2
Hanson Pl. Brad BD12 94 C3 7
Hanson Rd. Brig HD6 135 E8
Hanson Rd. Mel HD7 170 C1
Hanson Sch. Brad 56 A4
Hanworth Rd. Brad BD12 94 D6
Harbeck Dr. Harden BD16 36 B1
Harbour Cres. Brad BD6 94 A8
Harbour Pk. Brad BD6 93 F8 2
Harbour Rd. Brad BD6 94 A8
Harclo Rd. Keigh BD21 35 E8
Harcourt Ave. Thorn BD13 72 D7
Harcourt Dr. Add LS29 2 F1
Harcourt Pl. Leeds LS1 79 A8
Harcourt St. Brad BD4 75 B3
Harcourt St. Wake WF2 141 F5
Hard Ings Rd. Keigh BD21 18 C1
Hard Nese La. Oxen BD22 50 F1
Hard Nese La. Oxen BD22 51 B2
Hard Platts La. Elland HX4 133 F2
Hardaker La. Bail BD17 38 A2
Hardaker St. Brad BD8 74 D8
Hardaker's La. Ack M T WF7 163 E6
Hardakers App. Ack M T WF7 163 F5
Hardcastle Ave. Pont WF8 125 C1
Hardcastle Crags. Wad M 68 C1
Hardcastle La. Floc WF4 157 E4
Hardcastle La. Neth WF4 157 E4
Harden Brow La. Harden BD16 36 A1
Harden Fst Sch. Harden 36 B1
Harden Gr. Brad BD10 56 E3
Harden Gr. Keigh BD21 35 E5
Harden Hill Rd. Mel HD7 187 E8
Harden La. Harden BD15 53 B7
Harden La. Wils BD15 53 B7
Harden Moss Rd. Holmfi HD7 187 E4
Harden Moss Rd. Mel HD7 187 E7
Harden Rd. Harden BD16 36 D2
Harden Rd. Keigh BD21 35 F5
Hardgate La. Haw BD22 51 F7
Hardie Rd. Ryhill WF4 162 C1
Harding Houses. Glu BD20 16 E7
Hardings La. Glu BD20 16 F7
Hardings La. H Hill LS29 8 A8
Hardings La. Ilkley LS29 8 A7
Hardistry Dr. Pont WF8 146 B8
Hardknot Cl. Brad BD7 73 E3
Hardrow Gn. Leeds LS12 78 D5
Hardrow Gr. Leeds LS12 78 D5
Hardrow Rd. Leeds LS12 78 D5
Hardrow Terr. Leeds LS12 78 D5
Hardwick Cres. Pont WF8 146 D5
Hardwick Croft. Leeds LS7 60 D6
Hardwick Ct. Pont WF8 146 C7
Hardwick La. W Har WF4 145 B1
Hardwick Rd. Dar WF7, WF8 146 F3
Hardwick Rd. Feath WF7 145 C4
Hardwick Rd. Pont WF7, WF8 146 D5
Hardwick St. Keigh BD21 35 A6 8
Hardy Ave. Brad BD6 94 C8
Hardy Ave. Morley LS27 98 C8
Hardy Croft. Wake WF1 142 D6 5
Hardy Ct. Morley LS27 98 B4
Hardy Gr. Leeds LS11 79 A3 8
Hardy Pl. Brig HD6 114 E5
Hardy St. Brad BD6 74 C1
Hardy St. Brad BD4 74 F6
Hardy St. Brig HD6 115 B3
Hardy St. Leeds LS11 79 A3
Hardy St. Morley LS27 98 B4
Hardy Terr. Leeds LS11 79 B3 8
Hardy View. Leeds LS11 79 A3 7
Hare Farm Ave. Leeds LS12 77 D7
Hare Farm Cl. Leeds LS12 77 D7
Hare La. Pudsey LS28 76 F4
Hare Park Ave. Clec WF15 116 C4
Hare Park Cl. Clec WF15 116 C4
Hare Park La. Clec WF15 116 C4
Hare Park La. Crof WF4 161 F8
Hare Park Mount. Leeds LS12 77 D7
Hare Park View. Crof WF4 161 F8
Hare St. Hali HX1 113 A6 1
Harecroft Rd. Otley LS21 11 A1
Haredon Cl. Mapp S75 178 A2
Harefield Cl. Stee BD20 17 A5
Harefield Dr. Batley WF17 97 A1
Harefield E. Leeds LS15 80 E7
Harefield Rd. Pont WF8 146 F8 2
Harefield W. Leeds LS15 80 E8
Harehill Ave. Tod OL14 108 A6
Harehill Cl. Brad BD10 39 B1
Harehill Rd. Brad BD10 39 B1
Harehill St. Tod OL14 108 A6
Harehills Ave. Leeds LS7, LS8 60 F4
Harehills La. Haw BD22 33 D1
Harehills La. Leeds LS7, LS8, LS9 61 B1
Harehills Mid Sch. Leeds 60 F3
Harehills Park Ave. Leeds LS9 61 B2 15
Harehills Park Rd. Leeds LS9 61 B2 16
Harehills Park Terr. Leeds LS9 61 B2 17
Harehills Park View. Leeds LS9 61 B2 13
Harehills Pl. Leeds LS8 60 F3
Harehills Prim Sch. Leeds 61 A3
Harehills Rd. Leeds LS8 60 F3
Harepark Dr. Clec WF15 116 C4
Hares Ave. Leeds LS8 60 F4 6
Hares Mount. Leeds LS8 60 E4
Hares Rd. Leeds LS8 60 F4 4
Hares Terr. Leeds LS8 60 F4
Hares View. Leeds LS8 60 F4 5
Harewood Ave. Batley WF16 117 E3
Harewood Ave. Hali HX2 112 D8
Harewood Ave. Hare LS17 27 D7
Harewood Ave. Nor WF6 123 C3
Harewood Ave. Pont WF8 146 E8
Harewood Ave. Stee BD20 17 A5
Harewood CE Prim Sch. Hare 27 A7
Harewood Cl. Knot WF11 126 C4
Harewood Cres. Haw BD22 34 E2
Harewood Ct. Leeds LS17 43 D1
Harewood Ct. Leeds LS14 62 A4
Harewood Gate. Hare LS17 27 A7
Harewood Gr. Batley WF16 117 E3
Harewood House. Hare 26 E6
Harewood La. Upton WF9 183 D8
Harewood Lane Fst Sch. Upton 183 E8
Harewood Mews. Hare LS17 27 A7
Harewood Mount. Mel HD7 170 F2
Harewood Mount. Pont WF8 146 E8
Harewood Pl. Hali HX2 112 E6
Harewood Rd. Coll LS17 28 C7
Harewood Rd. E Kes LS17 28 C7
Harewood Rd. Keigh BD22 34 F3
Harewood Rd. Wake WF1 142 F8
Harewood Rise. Keigh BD22 34 F3
Harewood St. Brad BD3 75 B7
Harewood St. Leeds LS2 79 C8
Harewood View. Pont WF8 146 E8
Harewood Way. Pudsey LS13 77 B8
Hargrave Cres. Men LS29 21 F4
Hargreaves Ave. Loft G WF3 121 E5
Hargreaves St. Glu BD20 16 E6
Harker Rd. Brad BD12 94 C7
Harker St. Knot WF11 127 B4
Harker St. S in Cra BD20 16 E5
Harker Terr. Pudsey LS28 57 D1 1
Harland Cl. Brad BD2 55 E2
Harland Sq. Leeds LS2 60 A3
Harlech Ave. Leeds LS11 79 B2
Harlech Cres. Leeds LS11 79 B2
Harlech Gr. Leeds LS11 79 B2
Harlech Mount. Leeds LS11 79 B2
Harlech Rd. Leeds LS11 79 B2
Harlech St. Leeds LS11 79 B2
Harlech Terr. Leeds LS11 79 B2
Harlech Way. Gar LS25 83 B7
Harley Cl. Pudsey LS13 77 A8
Harley Ct. Pudsey LS13 77 A8
Harley Dr. Pudsey LS13 77 A8
Harley Gdns. Pudsey LS13 77 A8
Harley Gn. Pudsey LS13 77 A8
Harley Pl. Brig HD6 115 A1
Harley Rd. Pudsey LS13 77 A8
Harley Rise. Pudsey LS13 77 A8
Harley St. Brig HD6 115 A1 7
Harley St. Tod OL14 108 B6
Harley Terr. Pudsey LS13 77 B8
Harley View. Pudsey LS13 77 A8
Harley Wlk. Pudsey LS13 77 A8
Harley Wood. Tod OL14 107 E8
Harlington Ct. Morley LS27 98 A2 3
Harlington Rd. Morley LS27 98 A2
Harlock St. Wake WF1 142 E2
Harlow Ct. Leeds LS8 61 C7
Harlow Rd. Brad BD7 74 A5
Harmby Cl. Ad Le S DN6 184 F2
Harmon Cl. Brad BD4 95 C8
Harold Ave. Leeds LS6 59 E2
Harold Gr. Leeds LS6 59 E2
Harold Mount. Leeds LS6 59 E2
Harold Pl. Leeds LS6 59 E2
Harold Pl. Ship BD18 54 F8 13
Harold Rd. Leeds LS6 59 E2
Harold Sq. Leeds LS6 59 E2
Harold St. Bing BD16 36 E4
Harold St. Leeds LS6 59 E2
Harold Terr. Leeds LS6 59 E2
Harold View. Leeds LS6 59 E2
Harold Wilson House. Nor WF6 123 A1
Harold Wlk. Leeds LS6 59 E2
Harp Rd. Hud HD3 153 B5
Harpe Inge. Hud HD5 154 E7
Harper Ave. Brad BD10 39 B1
Harper Cres. Brad BD10 39 C1
Harper Gr. Brad BD10 39 B1
Harper Gr. S in Cra BD20 16 D4
Harper La. Yeadon LS19 40 B6
Harper Pl. Leeds LS2 79 D8
Harper Rock. Yeadon LS19 40 B6
Harper Royd La. Sow Br HX6 112 C2
Harper St. Leeds LS2 79 D7
Harper Terr. Yeadon LS19 40 B6 8
Harpers Sq. S in Cra BD20 16 D4
Harrap St. Wake WF2 141 D7
Harrier Cl. Brad BD8 73 B7
Harrier Way. Morley LS27 98 D4
Harriet St. Brad BD8 74 B8
Harriet St. Brig HD6 115 A4
Harriet St. Leeds LS7 60 D3
Harrington Ct. Mel HD7 170 F1
Harris Ct. Brad BD7 74 A4
Harris St. Bing BD16 37 A2 3
Harris St. Brad BD1 75 A7
Harrison and Potter Trust Homes
The. Leeds LS2 60 A3 6
Harrison and Potter Trust Homes
The. Leeds LS7 60 C1
Harrison Cres. Leeds LS9 61 D1
Harrison La. Mel HD7 170 E5
Harrison Pl. Glu BD20 16 B6
Harrison Rd. Crof WF4 143 F1
Harrison Rd. Hali HX1 113 C6
Harrison St. Bing BD16 37 A2
Harrison St. Leeds LS1 79 C8
Harrison St. Tod OL14 86 B1
Harrisons Ave. Pudsey LS28 57 F2 5
Harrogate Ave. Brad BD3 56 A2
Harrogate Pl. Brad BD3 56 A2
Harrogate Rd. Brad BD10, BD2 56 D5
Harrogate Rd. E Carl LS16 23 F2
Harrogate Rd. Hare LS17 27 A4
Harrogate Rd. Leeds LS17 43 E3
Harrogate Rd. Spoff LS22 13 B7
Harrogate Rd. Yeadon LS19 40 C5
Harrogate St. Brad BD3 56 A2
Harrogate Terr. Brad BD3 56 A2
Harrogate View. Leeds LS17 44 C5
Harrop Ave. Morley LS27 98 B2
Harrop Gr. Morley LS27 98 B2
Harrop La. Wils BD15 53 B3
Harrop Terr. Morley LS27 98 B2
Harrop Well La. Pont WF8 146 D8 12
Harrow St. Hali HX1 112 F7
Harrow St. S Elm WF9 182 E3
Harrowby Cres. Leeds LS16 59 B7
Harrowby Rd. Leeds LS16 59 B7
Harry La. Brad BD14 73 B4
Harry La. Oxen BD22 51 C2
Harry St. Brad BD4 75 C3
Hart St. Brad BD7 74 B4
Hart St. Hud HD4 154 A2
Hart's Hole. Slai HD7 152 A5
Harthill Ave. Gild LS27 97 D7
Harthill Cl. Gild LS27 97 D7
Harthill. Gild LS27 97 D7
Harthill La. Gild LS27 97 D8
Harthill Par. Gild LS27 97 D7
Harthill Rise. Gild LS27 97 D7
Hartington Mid Sch. Haw 51 C7
Hartington St. Batley WF17 118 C3
Hartington St. Keigh BD21 35 C8 9
Hartington Terr. Brad BD7 74 A5
Hartland Rd. Brad BD4 75 E4
Hartley Ave. Leeds LS6 60 B4
Hartley Cl. S Elm WF9 183 A4
Hartley Cres. Leeds LS6 60 B4
Hartley Gdns. Leeds LS6 60 B4
Hartley Gr. Dew WF13 118 C1
Hartley Gr. Leeds LS6 60 A4
Hartley Hill. Leeds LS2 60 C1
Hartley Park Ave. Pont WF8 146 B8
Hartley Park View. Pont WF8 146 B8
Hartley Pl. Morley LS27 98 B3 3
Hartley St. Brad BD4 75 B5
Hartley St. Castle WF10 124 C7
Hartley St. Dew WF13 118 C1
Hartley St. Glu BD20 16 A6
Hartley St. Hali HX1 113 A8
Hartley St. Morley LS27 98 B7
Hartley St. Morley LS27 98 C4
Hartley Terr. Feath WF7 145 C4
Hartley's Bldgs. Morley LS27 98 B3 6
Hartley's Sq. Keigh BD20 19 D1
Hartlington Ct. Bail BD17 38 E3
Hartman Pl. Brad BD9 54 F2
Hartshead Hall La. Liver WF15 116 D1
Hartshead Jun Mix & Inf Sch.
Liver 116 C2
Hartshead La. Liver WF15 116 C2
Hartshead Moor Sch. Clec 116 A6
Hartwell Rd. Leeds LS6 59 E2
Harvelin Pk. Tod OL14 109 A5
Harvest Croft. Bur in W LS29 9 D1
Harvey Royd. Hud HD5 155 A4
Harvey St. Wake WF1 142 E3
Harwill App. Morley LS27 98 C7
Harwill Ave. Morley LS27 98 C7
Harwill Croft. Morley LS27 98 C7
Harwill Gr. Morley LS27 98 C7
Harwill Rd. Morley LS27 98 C7
Harwill Rise. Morley LS27 98 C7
Harwood Cl. Hud HD5 154 F5
Harwood Cl. Wake WF2 142 E1
Haselden Cres. Wake WF2 141 E5
Haselden Rd. Wake WF2 141 E5
Haslam Cl. Brad BD3 75 A8
Haslam Gr. Ship BD18 55 E6
Haslemere Cl. Brad BD4 75 D3
Haslewood Cl. Leeds LS9 79 E8
Haslewood Ct. Leeds LS9 79 F8 1
Haslewood Dene. Leeds LS9 79 F8
Haslewood Dr. Leeds LS9 79 F8 2
Haslewood Gn. Leeds LS9 79 F8
Haslewood Mews. Leeds LS9 79 F8
Haslewood Pl. Leeds LS9 79 F8
Haslewood Sq. Leeds LS9 79 F8
Hasley Rd. Bur in W LS29 21 F8
Haslingden Dr. Brad BD9 54 F2
Hassocks La. Honley HD7 171 D4
Hassocks Rd. Mel HD7 170 C3
Haste St. Castle WF10 124 B8
Hastings Ave. Brad BD5 74 D2
Hastings Ave. Wake WF2 142 D2
Hastings Cres. Castle WF10 125 B7
Hastings Ct. Coll LS22 29 B8
Hastings Ct. Nor WF6 122 E4
Hastings Ct. Thorner LS17 44 E4
Hastings Gr. Wake WF2 142 D2
Hastings Pl. Brad BD5 74 D3
Hastings St. Brad BD5 74 D2
Hastings Terr. Brad BD5 74 D2
Hastings Way. Coll LS22 28 F8
Hastings Wlk. Castle WF10 125 B7
Hatchet La. Brad BD12 95 A4
Hatfield Gdns. Roy S71 179 B4
Hatfield Pl. Ryhill WF4 162 D2
Hatfield Rd. Brad BD2 56 B2
Hatfield St. Wake WF1 142 C7
Hathaway Ave. Brad BD9 54 D3
Hathaway Dr. Leeds LS14 45 B1
Hathaway La. Leeds LS14 62 B8
Hathaway Mews. Leeds LS14 45 B1
Hathaway Wlk. Leeds LS14 62 B8 1
Hathershelf La. Heb Br HX7 111 A7
Hatton Cl. Brad BD6 94 D8
Haugh End La. Sow Br HX6 112 A3
Haugh Rd. Tod OL14 108 E6
Haugh Shaw Croft. Hali HX1 113 A5 16
Haugh Shaw Jun & Inf Sch. Hali 113 A5
Haugh Shaw Rd. Hali HX1 113 A5
Haugh Shaw Rd W. Hali HX1 112 F5 24
Haugh Shaw Sec Sch. Hali 113 A5
Haughs La. Hud HD3 153 A7
Haughs Rd. Hud HD3 153 A7
Hauxley Ct. Ilkley LS29 8 D5
Hauxwell Cl. Ad Le S DN6 184 F2
Hauxwell Dr. Yeadon LS19 40 B6
Havelock Sq. Thorn BD13 72 E6 2
Havelock St. Brad BD7 74 A4
Havelock St. Dew WF13 138 E5
Havelock St. Thorn BD13 72 E6
Haven Chase. Hors LS16 41 E3
Haven Croft. Hors LS16 41 F3
Haven Ct. Hors LS16 41 F3
Haven Ct. Pont WF8 146 B5
Haven Garth. Hors LS16 41 E3
Haven Gdns. Hors LS16 41 E3
Haven Gn. Hors LS16 41 E3
Haven La. Heb Br HX7 110 B8
Haven Mount. Hors LS16 41 E3
Haven Rise. Hors LS16 41 E3
Haven St. Tod OL14 108 C5 15
Haven The. Brad BD10 56 C6
Haven The. Leeds LS15 81 D8
Haven View. Hors LS16 41 E3
Havercroft Cty Inf Sch. Ryhill 180 B8
Havercroft La. Dar WF8 147 E5
Havercroft. Ossett WF5 140 E5
Havercroft Rise. S Hie S72 180 E6
Havercroft Way. Batley WF17 117 F5
Haverdale Rd. Ryhill WF4 162 C1
Haveroid La. Crig WF4 159 F4
Haveroid Way. Crig WF4 159 F5
Haverthwaites Dr. Aber LS25 47 E1
Havertop La. Feath WF6 123 F2
Haw Ave. Yeadon LS19 40 C8
Haw Cliff La. Kirkb HD4 172 F1
Haw Hill View. Nor WF6 123 C3
Haw La. Yeadon LS19 40 B8
Haw Park La. Ryhill WF4 161 F3
Haw Park La. Walton WF2 161 B2
Haw View. Yeadon LS19 40 C8
Hawber Cote Dr. Sil BD20 5 F2
Hawber Cote La. Sil BD20 5 F2
Hawber La. Sil BD20 5 F1
Hawes Ave. Brad BD5 74 C2
Hawes Ave. Hud HD3 153 B6
Hawes Cl. Castle WF10 125 B8
Hawes Cres. Brad BD5 74 C2
Hawes Dr. Brad BD5 74 C2
Hawes Gr. Brad BD5 74 C2
Hawes Mount. Brad BD5 74 C2
Hawes Rd. Brad BD5 74 C2
Hawes Terr. Brad BD5 74 C2
Haweswater Cl. Weth LS22 13 B5
Haweswater Pl. Knot WF11 126 E1
Hawk St. Keigh BD21 35 D8 4
Hawk's Nest Gdns E. Leeds LS17 43 D4
Hawk's Nest Gdns S. Leeds LS17 43 D4
Hawk's Nest Gdns W. Leeds LS17 43 D4
Hawk's Nest Rise. Leeds LS17 43 D4
Hawkcliffe View. Sil BD20 5 C1
Hawke Ave. Batley WF16 117 E4
Hawke Way. Brad BD12 94 E6
Hawkesworth La. Guise LS20 39 B7
Hawkhill Ave. Guise LS20 39 D8
Hawkhill Ave. Leeds LS15 62 B2
Hawkhill Dr. Leeds LS15 62 B2
Hawkhill Gdns. Leeds LS15 62 B2
Hawkhills. Leeds LS7 60 E7
Hawkhurst Rd. Leeds LS12 78 C6
Hawkingcroft Rd. Hor WF4 140 F1
Hawkins Dr. Leeds LS7 60 C2
Hawkins Way. Litt OL15 129 C1
Hawkroyd Bank Rd. Hud HD4 171 E6
Hawksbridge La. Oxen BD22 51 A3
Hawkshead Cl. Brad BD5 74 E5
Hawkshead Cres. Leeds LS14 62 A3
Hawkshead Dr. Brad BD5 74 E5
Hawkshead Way. Brad BD5 74 E5 5
Hawkshead Wlk. Brad BD5 74 E5 6
Hawkstone Ave. Guise LS20 39 C7
Hawkstone Dr. Keigh BD20 18 A1
Hawkstone View. Guise LS20 39 D7
Hawkswood Ave. Brad BD9 54 F3
Hawkswood Ave. Leeds LS5 58 E7
Hawkswood Cres. Leeds LS5 58 E7
Hawkswood Gr. Leeds LS5 58 E7
Hawkswood Mount. Leeds LS5 58 E7
Hawkswood Pl. Leeds LS5 58 F6
Hawkswood St. Leeds LS5 58 F6
Hawkswood Terr. Leeds LS5 58 F6
Hawkswood View. Leeds LS5 58 E7
Hawksworth Ave. Guise LS20 39 D8
Hawksworth CE Prim Sch. Guise 38 F8
Hawksworth Cl. Men LS29 22 A3
Hawksworth Cty Prim Sch. Leeds 58 E7
Hawksworth Dr. Guise LS20 39 D7
Hawksworth Dr. Men LS29 22 A4
Hawksworth Gr. Leeds LS5 58 D6
Hawksworth Hall Sch. Guise 38 F8
Hawksworth Mid Sch. Leeds 58 E7
Hawksworth Rd. Bail BD17 38 C6
Hawksworth Rd. Hors LS18 58 D7
Hawksworth St. Ilkley LS29 8 B4
Hawley Cl. Morley LS27 97 F2
Hawley Terr. Brad BD10 56 E4
Hawley Way. Morley LS27 97 F2
Haworth Cl. Mir WF14 137 F6
Haworth Fst Sch. Haw 51 C7
Haworth Gr. Brad BD9 54 E3
Haworth La. Yeadon LS19 40 B7
Haworth Rd. Batley WF17 96 F2
Haworth Rd. Brad BD9 54 C4
Haworth Rd. Haw BD22 51 E8
Haworth Rd. Wils BD15 53 C4
Haworth Sta. Haw 51 C7
Hawthorn Ave. Batley WF17 118 A3
Hawthorn Ave. Brad BD3 75 E8
Hawthorn Ave. Crof WF4 143 E1
Hawthorn Ave. Knot WF11 126 E3
Hawthorn Ave. Yeadon LS19 40 C7
Hawthorn Cl. Brig HD6 115 C3
Hawthorn Cl. Wake WF2 120 B3
Hawthorn Cres. Bail BD17 38 D3
Hawthorn Cres. Leeds LS7 60 D7 4
Hawthorn Cres. Yeadon LS19 40 B7
Hawthorn Ct. Crof S65 143 E1
Hawthorn Dr. Brad BD10 56 C7
Hawthorn Dr. Pudsey LS13 57 D6
Hawthorn Dr. Yeadon LS19 40 C8
Hawthorn Gr. Ack M T WF7 163 F5
Hawthorn Gr. Bur in W LS29 21 F8
Hawthorn Gr. Pudsey LS13 57 D5
Hawthorn Gr. Roth LS26 100 F4
Hawthorn Gr. Silk S75 193 F1
Hawthorn La. Leeds LS7 60 D7 6
Hawthorn Mill. Leeds LS12 78 A4 5
Hawthorn Mount. Leeds LS7 60 D7 3
Hawthorn Pl. Tod OL14 108 B6 9
Hawthorn Rd. Bacup OL13 106 A2
Hawthorn Rd. Leeds LS7 60 D7
Hawthorn Rd. Slai HD7 151 F1
Hawthorn Rd. Yeadon LS19 40 C7
Hawthorn St. Brad BD3 75 E8
Hawthorn St. Brig HX3 114 D8
Hawthorn St. Hali HX1 113 A5 6
Hawthorn Terr. Hali HX1 113 A5 7
Hawthorn Terr. Hud HD1 154 B8
Hawthorn Terr. Ossett WF5 140 E3
Hawthorn Vale. Leeds LS7 60 D7 7
Hawthorn View. Bail BD17 38 E3
Hawthorn View. Leeds LS7 60 D7 5
Hawthorne Ave. Castle WF10 125 B6
Hawthorne Ave. Feath WF7 145 C4
Hawthorne Ave. Hem WF9 181 D6
Hawthorne Ave. Ship BD18 55 D8
Hawthorne Ave. Weth LS22 13 D7
Hawthorne Cl. Floc WF4 157 D3
Hawthorne Cl. Lepton HD8 155 D3
Hawthorne Cres. Hem WF9 181 C6
Hawthorne Flats. Dearne S63 194 D1
Hawthorne Gr. Wake WF2 141 E7
Hawthorne Mount. Nor WF6 144 B7
Hawthorne Rise. Leeds LS14 62 C8
Hawthorne St. Shaf S72 180 C3
Hawthorne St. Sil BD20 5 D1
Hawthorne Terr. Hud HD4 153 C4
Hawthorne Terr. Swil LS25 82 C5
Hawthorne Terr. Wake WF2 141 E7
Hawthorne Way. Keigh BD20 36 E8
Hawthorne Way. Shaf S72 180 C3
Hawthorne Way. Shep HD8 173 F3
Hawthorns The. Glu BD20 16 C6
Hawthorns The. Loft G WF1 121 D5
Hawthorns The. Ossett WF5 140 E3
Hawtop La. Wool WF4 177 F5
Hayburn Gdns. Batley WF17 118 B5
Hayburn Rd. Batley WF17 118 A5
Haycliffe Ave. Brad BD7 74 A2
Haycliffe Dr. Brad BD7 73 F2
Haycliffe Gr. Brad BD7 74 A2
Haycliffe Hill Rd. Brad BD5 74 B3
Haycliffe La. Brad BD5, BD6 74 B2
Haycliffe Rd. Brad BD5 74 B3
Haycliffe Terr. Brad BD5 74 B3
Hayclose Mead. Brad BD6 94 A6
Hayden St. Brad BD3 75 B6
Haydn Ave. Loft G WF3 121 E6
Haydn's Terr. Pudsey LS28 57 E2
Hayfield Ave. B Spa LS23 30 C8
Hayfield Ave. Hud HD3 153 A7
Hayfield Cl. Bail BD17 38 E4
Hayfield Cl. Holmfi HD7 189 D4
Hayfield Terr. Leeds LS12 78 C6
Hayfields The. Haw BD22 51 C8
Haygill Nook. Sil BD23 1 E1
Hayhills La. Sil BD20 5 D4
Hayhills Rd. Sil BD20 5 E2
Hayleigh Ave. Leeds LS13 58 C3 9
Hayleigh Mount. Leeds LS13 58 C3
Hayleigh St. Leeds LS13 58 C3 8
Hayleigh Terr. Leeds LS13 58 C3 7
Hayley Ct. Hali HX3 113 C8 4
Hayne La. Neth WF4 157 E5
Haynes St. Keigh BD21 35 D6
Hays La. Hali HX2 91 C7
Hayson Cl. Dew WF12 118 F1
Haythorns Ave. Sil BD20 5 D1
Haythorns Mount. Sil BD20 5 D1
Hayton Dr. Weth LS22 13 F4
Hayton Wood View. Aber LS25 64 E8
Haywain The. Ilkley LS29 8 D3
Haywood Ave. Hud HD3 153 C7
Hazebrouck Dr. Bail BD17 38 B4
Hazel Ave. Dew WF12 140 B7
Hazel Ave. Leeds LS14 62 C8
Hazel Beck. Ship BD16 54 A8
Hazel Cl. Birk BD11 96 A6
Hazel Cl. Dew WF12 140 B7
Hazel Cres. Dew WF12 140 B7
Hazel Croft. Ship BD18 55 D7
Hazel Ct. Roth LS26 100 F4
Hazel Ct. Wake WF2 142 A8
Hazel Dr. Dew WF12 140 B7
Hazel Gdns. Castle WF10 125 D6
Hazel Gr. Bacup OL13 106 B3
Hazel Gr. Batley WF17 118 A4
Hazel Gr. Brig HX3 115 A7
Hazel Gr. Floc WF4 157 D3
Hazel Gr. Hud HD2 136 B5
Hazel Gr. Hud HD7 152 F2
Hazel Gr. S in Cra BD20 16 C5
Hazel Grove Rd. S in Cra BD20 16 C5
Hazel Hurst Gr. Queen BD13 92 D7
Hazel Hurst Rd. Queen BD13 92 D7
Hazel La. Ham DN6 184 A2
Hazel Mount. Ship BD18 55 C7
Hazel Rd. Knot WF11 126 E2
Hazel Rise. M'town LS26 102 C1
Hazel Wlk. Brad BD9 54 D2
Hazelcroft. Brad BD2 56 D4
Hazeldene Cotts. Sickl LS22 12 C5
Hazeldene. Queen BD13 92 D8
Hazelheads. Bail BD17 38 C5
Hazelhurst Ave. Ship BD16 37 A1 1
Hazelhurst Brow. Brad BD9 54 D2
Hazelhurst Ct. Brad BD9 54 D2
Hazelhurst Ct. Brad BD9 75 C7
Hazelhurst Ct. Pudsey LS28 76 F7
Hazelhurst Rd. Brad BD9 54 D2
Hazelhurst Terr. Brad BD9 54 D2
Hazelmere Ave. Ship BD16 54 A8
Hazelwood Ave. Gar LS25 83 A5
Hazelwood Ave. Keigh BD20 18 F1
Hazelwood Ct. Loft G WF1 121 D5
Hazelwood Rd. Brad BD9 54 C3
Hazelwood Rd. Hem WF9 163 B1
Hazelwood Rd. Loft G WF1 121 D5
Hazelwood St. Tod OL14 108 B5
Hazledene Cres. Shaf S72 180 D1
Hazledene Rd. Shaf S72 180 D1
Headfield CE Middle Schs. Dew 139 C5
Headfield La. Dew WF12 139 C5
Headfield Rd. Dew WF12 139 D5
Headfield Rd. Hud HD4 154 A3
Headfield View. Dew WF12 139 D4
Headingley Ave. Leeds LS6 59 C5
Headingley Cres. Leeds LS6 59 D4
Headingley Ct. Leeds LS6 59 F4
Headingley Golf Course. Eccup 42 D6
Headingley Grounds (Cricket &
Rugby League). Leeds 59 D4
Headingley La. Leeds LS6 59 E4
Headingley Mount. Leeds LS6 59 C5
Headingley Prim Sch. Leeds 59 D5
Headingley Sta. Leeds 59 B4
Headingley View. Leeds LS6 59 D4
Headland Gr. Brad BD6 73 F1
Headland La. Dew WF12 139 F6
Headlands Ave. Ossett WF5 140 C5
Headlands CE (C) Jun & Inf Sch.
Liver 117 A4
Headlands Cl. Liver WF15 117 B3
Headlands Gr. Ossett WF5 140 C5
Headlands La. Knot WF11 126 E4
Headlands La. Pont WF8 125 D1
Headlands Pk. Ossett WF5 140 C5
Headlands Rd. Hud HD1 154 A7
Headlands Rd. Liver WF15 117 A4
Headlands Rd. Ossett WF5 140 C5
Headlands St. Liver WF15 117 A3
Headlands The. Liver WF15 117 A3
Headlands Wlk. Ossett WF5 140 C5
Headley Cotts. Bramham LS24 48 A8
Headley Golf Course. Thorn 72 D5
Headley La. Bramham LS23 30 E1
Headley La. Thorn BD13 72 D5
Headrow The. Leeds LS1 79 C8
Headwall Gn. Slai HD7 152 B3
Heald La. Bacup OL13 106 A8
Heald St. Castle WF10 124 F8
Heald Terr. Rip HX4 133 A5
Healdfield Rd. Castle WF10 124 F8
Healds Ave. Liver WF15 117 B4
Healds Rd. Dew WF13 118 A2
Healdwood Cl. Castle WF10 125 A8
Healdwood Rd. Castle WF10 125 A8
Healey Ave. Bing BD16 37 A2
Healey Cl. Batley WF17 117 F5
Healey Cres. Ossett WF5 140 D3
Healey Croft La. E Ard WF3 120 B7
Healey Dr. Ossett WF5 140 D4
Healey Green La. Lepton WF14 155 F7
Healey Jun Inf Sch. Batley 117 F5
Healey La. Batley WF17 117 F5
Healey La. Batley WF17 118 B5
Healey La. Bing BD16 37 A2 2
Healey La. Dew WF12 157 A7
Healey Rd. Ossett WF5 140 D3
Healey St. Batley WF17 117 F5
Healey Wood Cres. Brig HD6 115 A1
Healey Wood Gdns. Brig HD6 136 B8
Healey Wood Gr. Brig HD6 136 B8

Healey Wood Rd. Brig HD6 ...... 115 B1
Heap La. Brad BD3 .... 75 A8
Heap St. Brad BD1 .... 75 A7
Heath Av. Hali HX3 .... 92 C2
Heath Ave. Mel HD4 .... 113 B4
Heath Cl. Dew WF12 .... 140 B8
Heath Cl. Slai HD7 .... 170 E7
Heath Cres. Leeds LS11 .... 78 C2
Heath Cres. Leeds LS11 .... 4 C6
Heath Dr. B Spa LS23 .... 30 B7
Heath Dr. L Brad BD20 .... 4 C6
Heath Gdns. Hali HX3 .... 113 C4
Heath Gr. Keigh BD20 .... 36 D8
Heath Gr. Leeds LS11 .... 78 E3
Heath Gr. Pudsey LS28 .... 76 C6
Heath Hall Ave. Brad BD4 ..... 75 A1
Heath Hall. Hali HX1 .... 113 C5
Heath Hill Rd. Hali HX1 ...... 91 A2
Heath House La. Slai HD7 ..... 152 B4
Heath La. Hali HX3 .... 113 C4
Heath Lea. Hali HX1 .... 91 F1
Heath Mount. Brig HD6 .... 136 A8
Heath Park Ave. Hali HX1 ..... 113 C5
Heath Pk. Ilkley LS29 .... 7 F3
Heath Pl. Leeds LS11 .... 78 E3
Heath Rd. Brad BD2 .... 56 B1
Heath Rd. Dew WF12 .... 140 B8
Heath Rd. Hali HX1, HX3 ...... 113 C5
Heath Rd. Hud HD7 .... 152 F1
Heath Rd. Leeds LS11 .... 78 E3
Heath Rise. Leeds LS11 .... 78 E2
Heath Royd. Hali HX3 .... 113 C4
Heath St. Bing BD16 .... 37 A3
Heath St. Brad BD3 .... 75 C7
Heath St. Hali HX3 .... 113 C4
Heath St. Liver WF15 .... 117 B2
Heath Terr. Brad BD3 .... 75 C7
Heath Trng & Dev Ctr (Coll). Hali .. 113 C4
Heath View St. Hali HX1 ...... 113 C5
Heath Villas. Hali HX1 .... 113 C4
Heath Wlk. Dew WF12 .... 140 B8
Heathcliff. Haw BD22 .... 51 B7
Heathcliffe Cl. Batley WF17 .. 96 F3
Heathcote Ave. Thorner LS14 .. 45 F5
Heathcroft Bank. Leeds LS11 .. 78 E2
Heathcroft Cres. Leeds LS11 .. 78 E2
Heathcroft Dr. Leeds LS11 .... 78 E2
Heathcroft Lawn. Leeds LS11 .. 78 E2
Heathcroft Rise. Leeds LS11 .. 78 E2
Heathcroft Vale. Leeds LS11 .. 78 E2
Heathdale Ave. Hud HD2 .... 135 F1
Heather Ave. Mel HD4 .... 170 E1
Heather Bank. Cull BD13 ...... 52 D5
Heather Bank. Tod OL14 .... 108 B1
Heather Cl. Loft G WF1 .... 121 C5
Heather Cl. Scis WF5 .... 140 F3
Heather Cl. S Kirk WF9 .... 182 D3
Heather Cl. Batley WF17 ...... 96 E2
Heather Ct. Bing BD16 .... 37 A5
Heather Gdns. Leeds LS13 ..... 77 E8
Heather Gr. Burn in W LS29 ... 21 F8
Heather Gr. Hud HD2 .... 136 F5
Heather Gro. Leeds LS13 ...... 77 E8
Heather Rise. Bur in W LS29 .. 21 F8
Heather Side. Bail BD17 ...... 38 C3
Heather Vale. Scar LS14 ...... 45 B7
Heather View. Heb HD6 .... 37 D5
Heather View. Ossett WF5 ..... 140 D5
Heatherbank Ave. Keigh BD22 .. 34 F4
Heathercroft. Leeds LS7 ...... 60 E6
Heatherdale Ct. E ard WF3 .... 119 E8
Heatherdale Dr. E ard WF3 .... 119 E8
Heatherdale Rd. E ard WF3 .... 119 E8
Heatherfield Cres. Hud HD1 ... 153 D6
Heatherfield Rd. Hud HD1 ..... 153 D6
Heathergrove Fold. Hud HD5 ... 154 D7
Heatherlands Ave. Denth BD13 . 52 D2
Heatherstones. Hali HX3 ...... 113 B4 3
Heathfield Ave. Elland HX5 ... 135 B7
Heathfield Cl. Bing BD16 ..... 37 A4
Heathfield Cl. E Ard WF3 ..... 119 F8
Heathfield Gr. Brad BD7 ...... 73 E4
Heathfield La. B Spa LS23 .... 14 C1
Heathfield. Hors LS16 .... 42 B4
Heathfield Terr. Leeds LS6 ... 59 D6
Heathfield Wlk. Hors LS16 .... 42 A5
Heathmoor Cl. Brad BD10 ...... 56 E8
Heathmoor Mount. Hali HX2 .... 91 E8
Heathmoor Park Rd. Hali HX2 .. 91 E8
Heathmoor Way. Hali HX2 ...... 91 E8
Heathness Rd. Add LS29 .... 2 D1
Heathrow Inf Sch. Wake 142 D7
Heathrow La. Ryhill WF4 ...... 162 C2
Heathrow Pl. Hali HX2 .... 92 A5
Heathy Ave. Hali HX2 .... 91 F7
Heathy La. Hali HX2 .... 91 F7
Heaton Ave. Cleck BD19 .... 116 C7
Heaton Ave. Dew WF12 .... 139 E8
Heaton Ave. Keigh BD20 .... 36 C7
Heaton Ave. Kirkhe HD5 .... 137 C1
Heaton Ave. Rothw LS26 .... 101 C7
Heaton Cl. Bail BD17 .... 38 B4
Heaton Cl. Bing BD16 .... 37 B4
Heaton Dr. Bail BD17 .... 38 A4
Heaton Dr. Bing BD16 .... 37 B4
Heaton Fold. Keigh BD20 ...... 36 B7
Heaton Gr. Brad BD9 .... 55 B4
Heaton Gr. Ship BD18 .... 55 C7
Heaton Hill. Brad BD6 .... 93 E7

Heaton Mid Sch. Brad 54 D4
Heaton Moor Rd. Kirkhe HD5 ... 137 C1
Heaton Park Rd. Brad BD9 ..... 54 F3
Heaton Rd. Brad BD4 .... 54 F3
Heaton Rd. Brad BD8, BD9 ..... 54 F3
Heaton Rd. Batley WF17 .... 118 C7
Heaton Rd. Brad BD8, BD9 ..... 55 B2
Heaton Rd. Hud HD1 .... 153 D6
Heaton Royds. Ship BD18 ...... 54 D5
Heaton Royds La. Ship BD9 .... 54 D5
Heaton Royds Sch. Ship 55 A5
Heaton St. Ack M T WF7 .... 163 E5
Heaton St. Brad BD4 .... 75 A5
Heaton St. Brig HD6 .... 115 A2 4
Heaton St. Clec BD19 .... 116 D8
Heaton's Ct. Leeds LS1 .... 79 C7
Hebb View. Brad BD6 .... 73 E2
Hebble Cl. Hali HX2 .... 91 D4
Hebble Dean. Hali HX2 .... 91 F1
Hebble Dr. Holmfi HD7 .... 189 A7
Hebble End. Heb Br HX7 .... 88 F3
Hebble La. Hali HX2 .... 91 E1
Hebble La. Hali HX3 .... 91 F1
Hebble La. Mel HD7 .... 187 D8
Hebble Mount. Mel HD7 .... 170 E1
Hebble Row. Haw BD22 .... 34 C1
Hebble St. Dew WF13 .... 138 F5
Hebble St. Hud HD1 .... 154 B8 4
Hebble Vale Dr. Hali HX2 ..... 91 F1
Hebden App. Leeds LS14 .... 62 A5
Hebden Bridge Rd. Oxen BD22 .. 51 B1
Hebden Bridge Sta. Heb Br 89 B2
Hebden Chase. Leeds LS14 ..... 62 A5
Hebden Cl. Leeds LS14 .... 62 B6
Hebden Gdns. Leeds LS14 ...... 62 A6
Hebden Gn. Leeds LS14 .... 62 B6
Hebden Pl. Leeds LS14 .... 62 B6
Hebden Rd. Haw BD22 .... 51 D6
Hebden Rd. Wake WF1 .... 142 E8
Hebden Royd C of E Jun & Inf Sch.
  Heb Br 88 E3
Hebden Terr. Wad M HX7 .... 89 B8
Hebden Wlk. Leeds LS14 .... 62 B6
Heber Cl. Sil BD20 .... 17 F8
Heber St. Keigh BD21 .... 35 B6
Heber's Ghyll Dr. Ilkley LS29 7 F3
Heber's Gr. Ilkley LS29 ...... 7 E4
Heckmondwike Cty Prim Sch.
  Batley 117 C4
Heckmondwike Cty Sec Sch.
  Batley 117 E6
Heckmondwike Gram Sch.
  Batley 117 D4
Heckmondwike Rd. Batley WF13 . 117 F1
Heckmondwike Rd. Dew WF13 .... 138 F8
Heckmondwike The Royds Inf Sch.
  Batley 117 D5
Hector Cl. Brad BD6 .... 74 C1 7
Heddon Cl. Brad BD5 .... 74 F5
Heddon Gr. Brad BD5 .... 74 E5
Heddon St. Leeds LS6 .... 59 E6
Heddon Wlk. Brad BD5 .... 74 E5 4
Hedge Cl. Brad BD8 .... 54 D1
Hedge Top La. Northo HX3 ..... 93 B2
Hedge Way. Brad BD8 .... 54 E1
Hedley Chase. Leeds LS12 ..... 78 B4
Hedley Cres. Loft G WF1 ...... 121 B3
Hedley Gn. Leeds LS12 .... 78 B4
Heeley Rd. Wake WF2 .... 160 A4
Heidelberg Rd. Brad BD9 ...... 55 B3
Height Gn. Hali HX6 .... 112 B4
Height La. Draug BD23 .... 1 D1
Height La. Oxen BD22 .... 51 D2
Height Rd. Heb Br HX7 .... 88 F5
Height Rd. Heb Br HX7 .... 90 A2
Heights Bank. Leeds LS12 ..... 77 F7
Heights Cl. Leeds LS12 .... 77 F7
Heights Dr. Slai HD7 .... 170 D8
Heights E. The. Leeds LS12 ... 77 F7
Heights Garth. Leeds LS12 .... 77 F7
Heights La. Batley WF17 ...... 117 E3
Heights La. Bing BD16 .... 37 B6
Heights La. Brad BD9 .... 54 D3
Heights La. Leeds LS12 .... 77 F7
Heights Par. Leeds LS12 ...... 77 F7
Heights The. Holmfi HD7 ...... 189 A7
Heights W The. Leeds LS12 .... 77 F7
Heights Wlk. Leeds LS12 ...... 77 F7
Helena Cl. E Ard WF3 .... 120 C8
Helena St. Brad BD20 .... 5 B4
Hell La. Crof WF4 .... 143 E4
Hellewell St. Brad BD6 .... 93 F7 4
Hellewell's Rd. Hor WF5 ...... 140 D1
Hellwood La. Scar LS14 .... 45 D7
Helm La. Mir WF14 .... 137 D5
Helm La. Sow Br HX6 .... 132 C1
Helme CE (Aided) Jun & Inf Sch.
  Mel 170 A4
Helme La. Mel HD7 .... 170 A4
Helmet La. Mel HD7 .... 170 D2
Helmsley Dr. Leeds LS16 ...... 59 B7
Helmsley Rd. B Spa LS23 ...... 30 C7
Helmsley Rd. Leeds LS16 ...... 59 B7
Helmsley St. Brad BD4 .... 75 C5
Helston Croft. Midd LS10 ..... 99 A5
Helston Gn. Midd LS10 .... 99 A5
Helston Pl. Midd LS10 .... 99 A5
Helston Rd. Midd LS10 .... 99 A5
Helston St. Midd LS10 .... 99 B5
Helston Way. Midd LS10 .... 99 A5
Helston Wlk. Midd LS10 .... 99 A5
Hemingway Cl. Leeds LS10 ..... 79 F3
Hemingway Gn. Leeds LS10 ..... 79 F3
Hemingway Garth. Leeds LS10 .. 79 F3
Hemingway Rd. Castle WF10 .... 124 C6
Hemsby Rd. Keigh BD21 .... 35 B6
Hemsby St. Keigh BD21 .... 35 B6
Hemsworth Archbishop Holgate
  CE Fst Sch. Hem 181 D8
Hemsworth Grove Lea Fst Sch.
  Hem 181 E7

Hemsworth High Sch. Hem 181 E7
Hemsworth Hollygarth Sch. Hem 181 D7
Hemsworth Kinsley Fst Sch. Hem 163 A5
Hemsworth Kinsley Mid Sch. Hem 163 B3
Hemsworth La. Ryhill WF4 ..... 162 A3
Hemsworth S Kirk WF9 .... 181 F4
Hemsworth St Helens CE (Aided)
  Mid Sch. Hem 181 C6
Hemsworth Water Pk. Hem 163 D1
Hemsworth West End Mid Sch.
  Hem 181 C7
Hen Holme La. Sil BD20 .... 17 E7
Henacrewood Ct. Queen BD13 ... 92 E7
Henbury St. Queen BD13 .... 72 D10
Henbury St. Leeds LS7 .... 60 D1
Henconner Ave. Leeds LS7 ..... 60 C6
Henconner Cres. Leeds LS7 .... 60 C6
Henconner Dr. Leeds LS7 ...... 60 C6
Henconner Garth. Leeds LS7 ... 60 C6
Henconner Gr. Leeds LS7 ...... 60 C6
Henconner La. Leeds LS13 ..... 58 A3
Henconner La. Leeds LS7 ...... 60 C6
Henconner La. Leeds LS7 ...... 77 B8
Henconner Rd. Leeds LS7 ...... 60 C6
Hendal La. Wake WF2 .... 160 E5
Henderson Av. Nor WF6 .... 144 B8
Henderson Glen. Roy S71 ...... 179 A3
Henderson Pl. Brad BD6 .... 74 C1 8
Hendford Dr. Brad BD3 .... 75 B8
Henley Ave. Brad BD5 .... 74 D4
Henley Ave. Dew WF12 .... 139 E2
Henley Ave. Leeds LS13 .... 58 C2 1
Henley Ave. Yeadon LS19 ...... 40 D3
Henley Cl. Yeadon LS19 .... 40 D3
Henley Cres. Leeds LS13 ...... 58 C2
Henley Cres. Yeadon LS19 ..... 40 D3
Henley Croft. Hud HD5 .... 154 C6
Henley Ct. Brad BD5 .... 74 F2
Henley Dr. Yeadon LS19 .... 40 D3
Henley Gr. Brad BD5 .... 74 D4
Henley Gr. Leeds LS13 .... 58 C2
Henley Mount. Yeadon LS19 .... 40 D3
Henley Pl. Leeds LS13 .... 58 C2
Henley Rd. Brad BD5 .... 74 D4
Henley Rd. Leeds LS13 .... 58 C2
Henley Terr. Leeds LS13 ...... 58 C2
Henley View. Leeds LS13 ...... 58 C2
Henrietta St. Batley WF17 .... 118 C5 2
Henry Ave. Ryhill WF4 .... 162 C1
Henry Cl. Shaf S72 .... 180 C3
Henry Frederick Ave. Hud HD4 . 171 C6
Henry Moore Ct. Castle WF10 .. 125 B7
Henry Price Bldg. Leeds LS2 .. 206 B1
Henry Ralph Ave. Hud HD4 ..... 153 C1
Henry St. Batley WF17 .... 118 C2
Henry St. Brad BD14 .... 73 C4
Henry St. Brig HD6 .... 115 A3
Henry St. Hali HX1 .... 203 E3
Henry St. Hud HD1 .... 154 A6
Henry St. Keigh BD21 .... 35 C7
Henry St. Thorn BD13 .... 72 D6
Henry St. Wake WF2 .... 142 A6
Henry Terr. Yeadon LS19 ...... 39 F7
Henshaw Ave. Yeadon LS19 ..... 40 B6
Henshaw Cres. Yeadon LS19 .... 40 B6
Henshaw La. Yeadon LS19 ...... 40 B6
Henshaw Oval. Yeadon LS19 .... 40 B6
Henshaw Rd. Tod OL14 .... 108 B1
Henson Gr. Castle WF10 .... 125 B8
Hepton Ct. Leeds LS9 .... 61 B1
Hepton Dr. Hep HX7 .... 88 F5
Heptonstall Jun & Inf Sch. Hep 88 F5
Hepworth Ave. Morley LS27 .... 98 B8
Hepworth Cl. Mir WF14 .... 138 B6
Hepworth Cres. Holmfi HD7 .... 189 D3
Hepworth Cres. Morley LS27 ... 98 B8
Hepworth Dr. Mir WF14 .... 138 B6
Hepworth Rd. Holmfi HD7 ...... 189 F1
Hepworth St. Castle WF10 ..... 103 F1
Hepworths Bldgs. Hud HD2 ..... 136 D4
Herbalist St. Leeds LS12 ..... 78 B4
Herbert St. Brad BD2 .... 75 D8
Herbert St. Bing BD16 .... 37 A3
Herbert St. Brad BD14 .... 73 C3
Herbert St. Castle WF10 ...... 103 F6
Herbert St. Hali HX1 .... 112 F6
Herbert St. Ship BD18 .... 37 F1
Herbert Terr. Ship BD18 ...... 38 B1
Hereford Cl. Wake WF4 .... 159 F4
Hereford St. Leeds LS12 ...... 210 A2
Heritage Rd. Batley WF17 ..... 118 C3
Heritage Way. Haw BD22 .... 34 C2
Hermit St. Keigh BD21 .... 35 A8
Hermitage Pk. Lepton HD8 ..... 155 E2
Hermon Ave. Hali HX1 .... 113 A5
Hermon Rd. Leeds LS15 .... 62 B1
Hermon St. Leeds LS15 .... 62 B1
Heron Cl. Leeds LS17 .... 43 F4
Heron Cl. Queen BD13 .... 72 C8
Heron Dr. Wake WF2 .... 160 C5
Heron Gr. Leeds LS17 .... 43 F4
Herschel Rd. Brad BD8 .... 74 A8
Hertford Chase. Leeds LS15 ... 81 D6
Hertford Cl. Leeds LS15 ...... 81 D6
Hertford Croft. Leeds LS15 ... 81 D6
Hertford Fold. Leeds LS15 .... 81 D6
Hertford Lawn. Leeds LS15 .... 81 D6
Hesketh Ave. Leeds LS5 .... 59 A5
Hesketh La. E Ard WF3 .... 119 D8
Hesketh Mount. Leeds LS5 ..... 59 A5
Hesketh Pl. Leeds LS5 .... 59 A5
Hesketh Rd. Leeds LS5 .... 59 A5
Hesketh Terr. Leeds LS5 ...... 59 A5
Hesley Rd. S Elm WF9 .... 183 A4
Hessle Ave. Leeds LS6 .... 59 E3
Hessle Mount. Leeds LS6 ...... 59 E3
Hessle Pl. Leeds LS6 .... 59 E3 17
Hessle Rd. Leeds LS6 .... 59 E3
Hessle St. Leeds LS6 .... 59 E3
Hessle Terr. Leeds LS6 .... 59 E3
Hessle View. Leeds LS6 .... 59 E3
Hessle Wlk. Leeds LS6 .... 59 E3

Hetchell View. Bard LS17 ..... 28 D2
Hetton Rd. Leeds LS8 .... 61 B4
Heulwaine Ave. Weth LS22 ..... 13 F4
Hew Clews. Brad BD7 .... 73 E3
Hexham Gn. Hud HD3 .... 152 F5
Hey Beck La. E Ard WF12 ...... 119 C3
Hey Cres. Mel HD7 .... 170 D2
Hey Head La. Litt OL14 .... 129 A1
Hey Head La. Tod OL14 .... 108 D7
Hey La. Hud HD5 .... 154 D3
Hey La. Kirkb HD7 .... 172 B7
Hey La. Kirkb HD7 .... 171 F1
Hey Slack La. Wh Com HD7 ..... 190 C2
Hey St. Brad BD7 .... 74 D7
Hey St. Brig HD6 .... 115 B4
Hey St. Tod OL14 .... 108 C5 1
Hey's Bldgs. Nor WF6 .... 122 F4
Heybeck Wlk. Brad BD4 .... 75 F2
Heycliffe Rd. Holmfi HD7 ..... 189 B5
Heyford Ct. Brad BD2 .... 55 D3
Heygate Cl. Bail BD17 .... 38 D4
Heygate La. Bramham LS23 ..... 30 F3
Heygate La. Bramham LS23 ..... 31 A5
Heys Ave. Thorn BD13 .... 72 F6
Heys Cres. Thorn BD13 .... 72 F6
Heys Gdns. Holmfi HD7 .... 189 C8
Heys La. Hali HX2 .... 90 B6
Heys La. Rip HX6 .... 132 C3
Heys La. Slai HD7 .... 151 D2
Heys Rd. Holmfi HD7 .... 189 C8
Heys The. Mel HD7 .... 170 E4
Heywood Dr. Brad BD4 .... 75 F3
Heywood Cl. Northo HX3 .... 93 A2
Heywood Rd. Mel HD7 .... 187 A8
Heywood St. Hali HX1 .... 203 E3
Hick La. Batley WF17 .... 118 D5
Hick St. Brad BD1 .... 201 C3
Hicks La. M'town LS26 .... 102 D3
Hicks Memorial Sch. M'field .. 84 A7
Higgin Chamber. Sow Br HX2 ... 111 C5
Higgin La. Hali HX3 .... 113 E5
High Ash Ave. Clay W HD8 ..... 176 A2
High Ash Ave. Leeds LS17 ..... 43 F3
High Ash Cl. Notton WF4 ...... 178 F7
High Ash Cres. Leeds LS17 .... 43 E3
High Ash Dr. Leeds LS17 ...... 43 E3
High Ash Mount. Leeds LS17 ... 43 F3
High Ash Pk. Brad BD15 .... 55 E7
High Bank App. Leeds LS15 .... 81 D7
High Bank Cl. Leeds LS15 ..... 81 D8
High Bank Gate. Leeds LS15 ... 81 D7
High Bank Gdns. Leeds LS15 ... 81 E7
High Bank La. Ship BD18 ...... 54 E8
High Bank Pl. Leeds LS15 ..... 81 D7
High Bank. Skelm WF9 .... 182 E3
High Bank. Leeds LS15 .... 81 D7
High Bank Way. Leeds LS15 .... 81 E7
High Banks Cl. Keigh BD20 .... 18 F2
High Brook Fall. Loft G WF3 .. 121 F5
High Busy La. Brad BD10 ...... 56 A6
High Busy La. Ship BD18 ...... 55 B6
High Cl. Guise LS20 .... 39 B8
High Cl. Hud HD5 .... 154 E3
High Cl. Kex S75 .... 177 D1
High Cl. Slai HD7 .... 170 E8
High Cliffe Cl. Thorn BD13 ... 80 D6
High Cliffe. Leeds LS4 .... 59 D3
High Cote Farm. Riddl BD20 ... 18 B1
High Cote. Keigh BD20 .... 18 B1
High Court La. Leeds LS2 ..... 79 D7
High Crags Fst Sch. Ship 55 C6
High Crest. Hud HD7 .... 152 E2
High Croft Cl. Pudsey LS28 ... 76 E7
High Croft Cres. Hud HD5 ..... 154 F3
High Croft. Queen BD13 .... 72 E1
High Croft Rd. Tod OL14 ...... 86 A1
High Croft. Yarm BD20 .... 5 D1
High Cross La. Shelf HX3 ..... 93 B7
High Cl. Hep HX7 .... 88 B8
High End. Guise BD17 .... 39 B4
High Fernley Ct. Brad BD12 ... 94 C4 10
High Fernley First Sch. Brad . 94 B3
High Fernley Rd. Brad BD12 ... 94 B3
High Field La. Haw BD22 ...... 34 C6
High Field La. Rip HX6 .... 132 D6
High Fold. Bail BD17 .... 38 E4
High Fold La. Keigh BD20 ..... 19 E1
High Fold. Keigh BD20 .... 18 C1
High Gate. Brad BD9 .... 55 B4
High Grange Rd. Brad BD2 ..... 55 F3
High Green Ct. Brad BD2 ...... 55 E3
High Green La. Brig HD6 ...... 115 E5
High Green Rd. Nor WF6 .... 123 A2
High Grove La. Brig HX3 ...... 114 D6
High House Ave. Brad BD2 ..... 56 B5
High House La. Hali HX2 ...... 111 C5
High House La. Oxen HX7 ...... 88 A6
High House Rd. Brad BD2 ...... 56 B5
High Hoyland La. Hi Hoy S75 .. 193 B8
High La. Cowl BD22 .... 32 A8
High La. Hali HX2 .... 112 A8
High La. Heb Br HX7 .... 89 E8
High La. Holmfi HD7 .... 189 B3
High La. Hud HD4 .... 154 A1
High La. Mars HD7 .... 168 F4
High La. Wilsd BD15 .... 53 D4
High Lea. Holmfi HD7 .... 189 A5
High Meadow. Keigh BD20 ...... 18 A1
High Meadows. Dew WF12 .... 139 E1
High Meadows. Weth WF2 .... 161 B6
High Mill La. Add LS29 .... 2 F1
High Moor Ave. Leeds LS17 .... 43 D4
High Moor Cl. Leeds LS17 ..... 43 D4
High Moor Cres. Leeds LS17 ... 43 D3
High Moor Ct. Leeds LS17 ..... 43 D4
High Moor Gr. Leeds LS17 ..... 43 D3
High Park Cres. Brad BD9 ..... 54 C4
High Park Dr. Brad BD9 .... 54 C4
High Park Gr. Brad BD9 .... 54 C3
High Poplars. Brad BD2 .... 56 A5
High Ridge Ave. Roth LS26 .... 100 F6

High Ridge Ct. Roth LS26 ..... 100 E6
High Ridge. Neth WF4 .... 158 E6
High Ridge Pk. Roth LS26 ..... 100 F6
High Ridge Way. Bramle LS16 .. 24 F2
High Royds Dr. Guise LS29 .... 22 B3
High Royds Hospl. Guise 22 B2
High Spirit Sch. Batley 96 B7
High Spring Gardens La. Keigh
  .... 35 A8
High Spring Rd. Keigh BD21 ... 35 F6
High St. B Spa LS23 .... 30 D8
High St. Batley WF17 .... 96 E1
High St. Batley WF16 .... 117 E4
High St. Batley WF12 .... 118 F3
High St. Brad BD10 .... 56 B8
High St. Brig BD19 .... 115 B5
High St. Castle WF10 .... 124 C7
High St. Clay W HD8 .... 175 F2
High St. Clec BD19 .... 116 D8
High St. Crig WF4 .... 159 F5
High St. Crof WF4 .... 144 B5
High St. Dew WF13 .... 139 C1
High St. Elland HX4 .... 133 F3
High St. Elland HX4 .... 134 D7 8
High St. Hali HX1 .... 90 E1
High St. Heb Br HX7 .... 88 C1
High St. Heb Br HX7 .... 89 B5 5
High St. Hor WF4 .... 141 A1
High St. Hud HD1 .... 153 E5
High St. Hud HD1 .... 154 A6
High St. Keigh BD21 .... 35 B7
High St. Kippax LS25 .... 83 B1
High St. Knot WF11 .... 126 C5
High St. Mapp S75 .... 178 A2
High St. Morley LS27 .... 98 B3
High St. Morley LS27 .... 98 F8
High St. Ossett WF5 .... 119 C8
High St. Pudsey LS28 .... 57 D3
High St. Queen BD13 .... 72 E1
High St. Roy S71 .... 179 C3
High St. S Elm LS25 .... 83 A3
High St. S Hie S72 .... 180 E5
High St. S in Cra BD20 .... 16 D4
High St. Shep HD8 .... 190 E8
High St. Slai HD7 .... 152 A8
High St. Stee BD20 .... 17 C5
High St. Thorn BD13 .... 72 D6
High St. Uptont WF9 .... 183 B7
High St. Wool WF4 .... 178 A7
High Stones Rd. Heb Br HX7 ... 110 E3
High Street Pl. Brad BD10 .... 56 B8
High Sunderland La. Hali HX3 . 92 D1
High. Top. B Head HX7 .... 88 B8
High Trees La. Ell Hard HX4 .. 133 E6
High Trees Sch. B Spa 30 E6
High View. Crig WF4 .... 159 F5
High View. Roy S71 .... 179 B3
High Weardley La. Hare LS17 .. 26 A6
High Well Hill La. S Hie S72 . 180 C7
High Wheatley. Ilkley LS29 ... 8 E3
High Wicken Cl. Thorn BD13 ... 72 D6
High Wood Ct. Leeds LS6 ...... 59 E5
High Wood. Ilkley LS29 .... 8 E3
High Wood La. Kirkb HD8 ...... 174 B6
High Woodlands. E Ard WF3 .... 119 E8
Higham and Dob La. Sow Br HX6 111 C3
Higham La. Skel HD8 .... 175 C1
Highbridge Terr. Brad BD5 .... 74 E3
Highbury CE (C) Fst Sch. Kirkb 173 E8
Highbury Cl. Leeds LS6 .... 59 E6
Highbury La. Leeds LS6 .... 59 E6
Highbury Mount. Leeds LS6 .... 59 E6
Highbury Pl. Leeds LS6 .... 59 E6
Highbury Pl. Pudsey LS13 ..... 77 A8
Highbury Rd. Brad BD4 .... 75 C6
Highbury Rd. Leeds LS6 .... 59 E6
Highbury St. Leeds LS6 .... 59 E6
Highbury Terr. Dew WF12 ...... 139 E8 9
Highbury Terr. Leeds LS6 ..... 59 E6
Highcliff Dr. Hali HX2 .... 111 E8
Highcliffe Ave. Elland HX4 ... 134 B7
Highcliffe Ct. Leeds LS28 .... 57 A7
Highcliffe Ind Est. Morley ... 97 F3
Highcliffe Rd. Morley LS27 ... 97 F4
Highcliffe Rd. Batley WF17 ... 118 C3
Highcroft. Batley WF17 .... 118 C5
Highcroft. Coll LS22 .... 29 A8
Highcroft Gdns. Keigh BD21 ... 35 F6
Highcroft. Holmfi HD7 .... 188 E5
Highdale. Batley WF17 .... 118 E2
Highfield Ave. Brad BD10 ..... 56 B8
Highfield Ave. Gar LS25 ...... 82 F6

Highfield Cres. Leeds LS12 ... 78 D6
Highfield Cres. Mel HD7 ... 170 D3
Highfield Cres. Neth WF4 ... 157 F6
Highfield Cres. Pudsey LS28 ... 76 D6
Highfield Cres. Roth LS26 ... 101 C7
Highfield Ct. Castle WF10 ... 124 D6
Highfield Ct. Ltw BD22 ... 34 C7
Highfield Ct. Shep HD8 ... 190 E6
Highfield Ctr. Hem WF9 ... 181 D6
Highfield Dr. Batley WF17 ... 96 E2
Highfield Dr. Brad BD7 ... 54 E4
Highfield Dr. Gar LS25 ... 82 F5
Highfield Dr. Gild LS27 ... 97 D7
Highfield Dr. Hali HX2 ... 111 E8
Highfield Dr. Kippax LS26 ... 102 F5
Highfield Dr. Liver FW15 ... 116 E4
Highfield Dr. Wake WF2 ... 141 E8
Highfield Dr. Yeadon LS19 ... 40 C3
Highfield. E Ard WF3 ... 98 D1
Highfield Garth. Leeds LS12 ... 78 D5
Highfield Gdns. Brad BD9 ... 54 D4
Highfield Gdns. Dew WF12 ... 139 D3
Highfield Gdns. Gild LS27 ... 97 D7
Highfield Gdns. Leeds LS12 ... 78 D5
Highfield Gn. Kippax WF10 ... 102 F6
Highfield Gn. Pudsey LS28 ... 76 D8
Highfield Gr. Brad BD10 ... 56 A6
Highfield Gr. Hali HX5 ... 134 E8
Highfield Gr. Kippax WF10 ... 102 F6
Highfield La. B in Elm LS15 ... 63 E5
Highfield La. Batley WF13 ... 117 F4
Highfield La. Keigh BD21 ... 35 B8
Highfield La. Lepton HD8 ... 155 D5
Highfield La. Mel HD7 ... 170 C3
Highfield La. Roth LS26 ... 101 C7
Highfield La. S in Elm LS25 ... 84 D5
Highfield La. Sil BD20 ... 5 E2
Highfield Mews. Bail BD17 ... 38 C4 1
Highfield Mews. Keigh BD20 ... 19 D8
Highfield Mid Sch. Keigh ... 35 B7
Highfield Mount. Dew WF12 ... 139 E1
Highfield Mount. Roth LS26 ... 101 D6
Highfield Pl. Brad BD8 ... 55 C1
Highfield Pl. Hali HX1 ... 112 F6
Highfield Pl. Hem WF9 ... 181 C6
Highfield Pl. Kippax WF10 ... 103 A6
Highfield Pl. Morley LS27 ... 98 B3
Highfield Rd. Aber LS25 ... 64 E8
Highfield Rd. Brad BD2, BD10 ... 56 B7
Highfield Rd. Brig HD6 ... 133 E8
Highfield Rd. Clec BD19 ... 116 C7
Highfield Rd. Elland HX5 ... 134 F6
Highfield Rd. Hali HX3 ... 111 F8
Highfield Rd. Hem WF9 ... 181 D6
Highfield Rd. Hor WF4 ... 141 A1
Highfield Rd. Keigh BD21 ... 35 A8
Highfield Rd. Kirkb HD8 ... 173 F7
Highfield Rd. Leeds LS13 ... 58 D2
Highfield Rd. Mel HD7 ... 170 D3
Highfield Rd. Neth WF4 ... 158 A5
Highfield Rd. Pont WF8 ... 146 C6
Highfield Rd. Pudsey LS28 ... 76 D8
Highfield Rd. Ship BD9 ... 55 C5
Highfield Rd. Slai HD7 ... 151 F4
Highfield Rise. Wake WF2 ... 141 E8
Highfield. Shelf HX3 ... 93 C5
Highfield St. Keigh BD21 ... 35 B7
Highfield St. Leeds LS13 ... 58 D2
Highfield St. Pudsey LS28 ... 76 C8
Highfield Terr. Pudsey LS28 ... 76 D8
Highfield Terr. Queen BD13 ... 72 E1
Highfield Terr. Rip HX6 ... 132 E6
Highfield Terr. Ship BD18 ... 54 E8
Highfield Terr. Yeadon LS19 ... 40 C3
Highfield View. Gild LS27 ... 97 E7
Highfields. Hud HD1 ... 153 F7
Highfields Rd. Hud HD3 ... 153 F7
Highfields. Ryhill WF4 ... 162 D2
Highfields Sch. Hud ... 153 F7
Highfield. Yearlin I S19 ... 40 A5
Highgate Ave. Lepton HD8 ... 155 F3
Highgate. Brad BD9 ... 54 F4
Highgate Dr. Brad BD13 ... 73 C3
Highgate Dr. Lepton HD8 ... 155 F3
Highgate. Glu BD20 ... 16 C7
Highgate Gr. Brad BD13 ... 73 C3
Highgate La. Kirkhe HD5 ... 137 D1
Highgate La. Lepton HD8 ... 155 E3
Highgate Rd. Brad BD13 ... 73 B2
Highgate Rd. Dew WF12 ... 139 D3
Highgate St. Batley WF12 ... 118 D2
Highgate Terr. Dew WF12 ... D810
Highgate Wlk. Lepton HD8 ... 155 F3
Highland Ct. Roth LS26 ... 100 F3
Highland Ville. Brig HX3 ... 114 D8
Highlands Ave. Hud HD5 ... 154 F4
Highlands Cl. Brad BD7 ... 73 E1
Highlands Cl. Midd LS10 ... 99 F8
Highlands Cl. Midd LS10 ... 99 F8
Highlands Gr. Brad BD7 ... 73 E1
Highlands Gr. Midd LS10 ... 99 F8
Highlands Grammar Sch. Hali ... 91 F6
Highlands La. Hali HX2 ... 91 F6
Highlands The. Clec WF15 ... 116 D5
Highlands Wlk. Midd LS10 ... 99 F8
Highley Cl. Yeadon LS19 ... 39 F5
Highley La. Rip HX6 ... 150 F6
Highley Hall Croft. Brig HD6 ... 115 C3
Highley Pk. Brig HD6 ... 115 C3
Highmoor. Bail BD17 ... 38 A3
Highmoor Cres. Brig HD6 ... 115 C1
Highmoor La. Brig HD6 ... 115 C2
Highmoor La. Clec HD6 ... 116 A4
Highmoor Wlk. Bail BD17 ... 38 A3
Highroad Well La. Hali HX2 ... 154 D5 1
Highroyd Cres. Hud HD5 ... 154 F3
Highroyd La. Hud HD5 ... 154 F4
Highroyd. Lepton HD8 ... 155 F3
Highthorne Ave. Brad BD3 ... 56 E1
Highthorne Ct. Leeds LS17 ... 43 C1
Highthorne Dr. Leeds LS17 ... 44 A1
Highthorne Gr. Leeds LS17 ... 44 A1
Highthorne Mount. Leeds LS17 ... 43 F4
Highthorne St. Leeds LS12 ... 78 A8
Highthorne View. Leeds LS12 ... 78 A8 14
Highthorne View. Leeds LS12 ... 78 A8
Hightown Fst Sch. Clec ... 116 C5
Hightown La. Holmfi HD7 ... 189 A5
Hightown Rd. Clec WF15 ... 116 D5
Highway. Guise LS20 ... 22 E6
Highway. Leeds LS14 ... 61 E1
Highwood Ave. Leeds LS17 ... 43 C3

Highwood Cres. Leeds LS17 ... 43 C3
Highwood Gr. Batley WF17 ... 118 D5
Hilda St. Ossett WF5 ... 140 E4
Hilda St. Sower Bg BD9 ... 55 A4
Hill Brow Cl. Brad BD15 ... 54 A1
Hill Cl. Bail BD17 ... 38 B2
Hill Cl. Hud HD3 ... 134 F1
Hill Cl. Pont WF8 ... 146 D7
Hill Clough Gr. Keigh BD22 ... 34 D7
Hill Cres. Bail BD17 ... 38 C4
Hill Cres. Bur in W LS29 ... 21 F7
Hill Cres. Hali HX3 ... 113 F5
Hill Cres. Yeadon LS19 ... 40 C5
Hill Crest. Gar LS25 ... 83 A6
Hill Crest & Le D SN6 ... 184 E1
Hill Crest Ave. Denh BD13 ... 52 E1
Hill Crest Ave. Hali HX6 ... 112 B5 3
Hill Crest. Coll LS22 ... 29 E8
Hill Crest Dr. Denh BD13 ... 52 D1
Hill Crest. Hali HX6 ... 112 B5 1
Hill Crest Mount. Denh BD13 ... 52 D1
Hill Crest Rd. Dew WF12 ... 139 C5
Hill Crest Rd. Thorn BD13 ... 72 D7
Hill Crest. Ryhill WF4 ... 162 C1
Hill Crest. Swil LS26 ... 82 A1
Hill Crest View. Denh BD13 ... 52 D1
Hill Croft Cl. Dar WF8 ... 147 D5
Hill Croft. Rip HX6 ... 132 C1
Hill Croft. Thorn BD13 ... 72 E7
Hill Dr. Ack M T WF7 ... 164 A8
Hill End Cl. Brig HX4 ... 94 A2
Hill End Cl. Leeds LS12 ... 77 F8
Hill End Cres. Leeds LS12 ... 77 F8
Hill End Dr. Batley WF13 ... 139 E8
Hill End Gr. Brad BD7 ... 73 E3
Hill End La. Cull BD13 ... 52 F8
Hill End La. Harden BD16 ... 36 A1
Hill End La. Queen BD13 ... 92 D8
Hill End La. Sower LS12 ... 77 F8
Hill Estate. Upton WF9 ... 183 B7
Hill Foot. Ship BD18 ... 54 E7
Hill Gr. Hud HD3 ... 134 F1
Hill Gr S. Midd LS10 ... 99 F7
Hill Green Ct. Birk BD4 ... 76 E2
Hill Grove Lea. Hud HD3 ... 134 F1
Hill House Edge La. Oxen HX7 ... 70 B8
Hill House La. Denh BD13 ... 188 E2
Hill House La. Holmfi HD7 ... 188 E2
Hill House Rd. Holmfi HD7 ... 188 E2
Hill La. Holmfi HD7 ... 188 D8
Hill Lands. Brad BD12 ... 94 E5
Hill Park Ave. Hali HX3 ... 91 F1
Hill Rd. Castle WF10 ... 124 F6
Hill Rise Ave. Leeds LS13 ... 58 C4
Hill Rise Gr. Leeds LS13 ... 58 C4
Hill Side Ave. Holmfi HD7 ... 189 E2
Hill Side Mount. Pudsey LS28 ... 57 E2
Hill Side Rd. Brad BD3 ... 75 A7
Hill Side Terr. Brad BD3 ... 75 A7
Hill St. Brad BD6 ... 74 A1
Hill St. Brad BD4 ... 75 A7
Hill St. Clec BD19 ... 116 C7
Hill St. Hali HX1 ... 113 B6
Hill St. Haw BD22 ... 51 C6
Hill St. Holmfi HD7 ... 189 C5
Hill St. Leeds LS9 ... 60 E1
Hill St. Leeds LS9 ... 213 B3
Hill Top Ave. Barn S71 ... 178 E1
Hill Top Ave. Leeds LS8 ... 55 B4
Hill Top Ave. Leeds LS8 ... 44 A1
Hill Top. Brig HX3 ... 114 C7
Hill Top. Bur in W LS29 ... 9 E1
Hill Top Cct Fst Sch. Brad ... 94 D6
Hill Top. Castle WF10 ... 123 F7
Hill Top. Caw S75 ... 193 E5
Hill Top Cl. E Ard WF3 ... 119 E6
Hill Top Cl. Wren WF9 ... 163 A3
Hill Top Ct. Leeds I S17 ... 77 F8
Hill Top Cotts. Brad BD9 ... 54 F1
Hill Top Cres. Wor WF4 ... 159 F1
Hill Top Ct. E Ard WF3 ... 119 E6
Hill Top Dr. Hud HD3 ... 153 A8
Hill Top Gdns. E Ard WF3 ... 119 E6
Hill Top Fold. Slai HD7 ... 151 F1
Hill Top Gdns. E Ard WF3 ... 119 E6
Hill Top Gn. E Ard WF3 ... 119 E6
Hill Top. Hali HX2 ... 112 E5
Hill Top La. Bing BD16 ... 37 B3
Hill Top La. Haw BD22 ... 34 C1
Hill Top La. E Ard WF3 ... 119 E6
Hill Top La. Hali HX2 ... 111 F8
Hill Top Mews. Knot WF11 ... 126 F4
Hill Top Mount. Leeds LS8 ... 60 F4
Hill Top Pl. Leeds LS6 ... 59 F4
Hill Top Pl. Leeds LS8 ... 60 F4 15
Hill Top Rd. Floc WF4 ... 157 D3
Hill Top Rd. Hali HX2 ... 112 C5
Hill Top. Rd. Holmfi HD7 ... 188 F1
Hill Top Rd. Keigh BD21 ... 35 E8
Hill Top Rd. Leeds LS6 ... 59 F4
Hill Top Rd. Leeds LS12 ... 77 F8
Hill Top Rd. Slai HD7 ... 152 A3
Hill Top Rd. Thorn BD13 ... 72 C7
Hill Top Rd. Wake WF2, WF4 ... 160 D7
Hill Top Sch. Castle ... 125 C7
Hill Top. Slai HD7 ... 151 F1
Hill Top. Stee BD20 ... 17 C5
Hill Top View. Hud HD3 ... 144 A7
Hill Top View. Nor WF6 ... 144 A7
Hill Top Way. Keigh BD22 ... 34 F7
Hill Top. Wake WF2 ... 141 D8
Hill View. Bail BD15 ... 37 A6
Hill View Ave. Leeds LS7 ... 60 D7 1
Hill View Gdns. Leeds LS7 ... 60 D7 1
Hill View Mount. Leeds LS7 ... 60 D7 3
Hill View Pl. Leeds LS7 ... 60 D7 1
Hill View Terr. Leeds LS7 ... 60 D7 4
Hillam La. B Sal LS25 ... 105 E5
Hillam La. Hillam LS25 ... 105 E5
Hillary Pl. Leeds LS2 ... 60 B8
Hillary Rd. Ship BD18 ... 55 B5
Hillary St. Brad BD5 ... 74 E3
Hillary St. Leeds LS2 ... 206 A1
Hillary St. Batley WF13 ... 117 F3 2

Hillbrook Rise. Ilkley LS29 ... 7 F3
Hillcote Dr. Brad BD5 ... 74 E2
Hillcourt Ave. Leeds LS13 ... 58 C4
Hillcourt Croft. Leeds LS13 ... 58 C4
Hillcourt Dr. Leeds LS13 ... 58 C4
Hillcourt Gr. Leeds LS13 ... 58 C4
Hillcrest Ave. Batley WF17 ... 118 A5
Hillcrest Ave. Castle WF10 ... 125 D6
Hillcrest Ave. Feath WF7 ... 145 C5
Hillcrest Ave. Leeds LS7 ... 60 E4
Hillcrest Ave. Ossett WF5 ... 140 C8
Hillcrest Ave. Queen BD13 ... 92 F8
Hillcrest Ave. Sil BD20 ... 5 D1
Hillcrest Cl. Swil LS26 ... 81 F1
Hillcrest Dr. Castle WF10 ... 125 E6
Hillcrest Dr. Queen BD13 ... 92 F8
Hillcrest Mount. Brig BD19 ... 115 F7
Hillcrest Mount. Castle WF10 ... 125 E6
Hillcrest Mount. Mons LS16 ... 41 E4
Hillcrest. Nor WF6 ... 122 E4
Hillcrest Pl. Leeds LS7 ... 60 E4
Hillcrest Rd. Castle WF10 ... 125 E7
Hillcrest Rd. Queen BD13 ... 92 F8
Hillcrest Rise. Leeds LS16 ... 41 E4
Hillcrest View. Leeds LS7 ... 60 E4
Hillcrest Rd. Batley WF17 ... 118 A5
Hillesley Rd. Batley WF17 ... 119 A3
Hillfold. S Elm WF9 ... 183 B3
Hillfoot Ave. Pudsey LS28 ... 76 B8
Hillfoot Cres. Pudsey LS28 ... 76 B8
Hillfoot Dr. Pudsey LS28 ... 76 B8
Hillfoot Rise. Pudsey LS28 ... 76 B8
Hillgarth. Dew WF12 ... 139 D3
Hillgarth. Knot WF11 ... 126 E3
Hillhead Dr. Batley WF17 ... 97 A1
Hillhouse La. Hud HD1 ... 154 B8
Hillidge Sq. Leeds LS10 ... 79 D4
Hillingdon Way. Leeds LS17 ... 43 B6
Hillings La. Guise LS20, LS29 ... 21 E3
Hillings La. Men LS29 ... 21 E3
Hillside Ave. Guise LS20 ... 22 D3
Hillside Ave. Hali HX2 ... 111 D7
Hillside Ave. Haw BD22 ... 34 B2
Hillside. Bur in W LS29 ... 9 E1
Hillside Cl. Sil LS29 ... 6 E8
Hillside. Clay DL13 ... 103 D3
Hillside Cres. Bau.uy DL13 ... 106 A7
Hillside Cres. Bri S72 ... 180 A2
Hillside Cres. Hud HD4 ... 154 B7
Hillside Ct. Men LS29 ... 21 F4
Hillside. D Dale HD8 ... 192 A6
Hillside. Gar LS25 ... 82 E6
Hillside Gr. Bri S72 ... 181 A2
Hillside Gr. Haw BD22 ... 34 B2
Hillside Gr. Pudsey LS28 ... 76 E6
Hillside. Gr. Pudsey LS28 ... 77 A7
Hillside Mid Sch. Leeds ... 79 B4
Hillside Mount. Bri S72 ... 181 A2
Hillside Mount. Pont WF8 ... 146 D6
Hillside. Pool LS21 ... 24 D7
Hillside Rd. Ack M I WF7 ... 164 A6
Hillside Rd. Leeds LS7 ... 60 E6
Hillside Rd. Pont WF8 ... 146 D5
Hillside. Rise. Guise LS20 ... 22 D3
Hillside. Liver. Liver WF15 ... 117 B3
Hillside Special Sch. Brig ... 135 E7
Hillside Terr. Bail BD17 ... 38 C3
Hillside View. Hali HX6 ... 112 D5
Hillside View. Pudsey LS28 ... 76 E5
Hillside Works Ind Est. Clec ... 95 B3
Hilltop. Bri S72 ... 180 F3
Hilltop Est. S Kirk WF9 ... 182 C1
Hillview Gdns. Northo HX3 ... 93 A1
Hillway. Guise LS20 ... 22 D3
Hillway. Guise. Wen WF9 ... 181 F5
Hilton Dr. Ship BD18 ... 55 C5
Hilton Gr. Brad BD7 ... 74 B6
Hilton Gr. Keigh BD21 ... 35 B6
Hilton Gr. Leeds LS8 ... 207 F4
Hilton La. Feath WF7 ... 146 A8
Hilton Mt. Leeds LS8 ... 207 F4
Hilton Pl. Leeds LS8 ... 207 F4
Hilton Rd. Brad BD7 ... 74 B6
Hilton Rd. Keigh BD21 ... 35 B6
Hilton Rd. Leeds LS8 ... 207 F4
Hilton Grange Sch. Bramho ... 24 E4
Hilton St. Leeds LS8 ... 207 F4
Hilton Terr. Leeds LS8 ... 207 F4

Hive St. Keigh BD22 ... 35 A6
HMS Ceres Communication Trng Ctr.
  E Carl ... 23 E1
Hoads The. Brig HD6 ... 135 F7
Hob La. Haw BD22 ... 50 C7
Hob La. Hali HX2 ... 112 A3
Hob La. Rip HX6 ... 132 C5
Hob La. Sow Br HX6 ... 112 B1
Hobart Bldgs. Heb Br HX7 ... 89 D1
Hobart Rd. Castle WF10 ... 125 D8
Hobart Rd. Dew WF12 ... 118 F1
Hobb Nook La. Ask LS21 ... 10 A7
Hobberley La. Thorner LS17 ... 44 F3
Hobson Fold. Brad BD12 ... 94 D2
Hockney Rd. Brad BD8 ... 74 B8
Hodge La. K Smea WF8 ... 166 C6
Hodgewood La. Dar WF8 ... 147 D6
Hodgson Ave. Brad BD3 ... 56 D1
Hodgson Ave. Leeds LS17 ... 44 A3
Hodgson Cres. Leeds LS17 ... 44 A3
Hodgson La. Birk BD11 ... 96 C6
Hodgson Pl. Morley LS27 ... 98 B7
Hodgson St. Morley LS27 ... 98 C1
Hodgson St. Wake WF1 ... 142 B7
Hodgson Terr. Dew WF12 ... 139 D6
Hodroyd Cotts. W Hard ... 180 D1
Hodroyd Cl. Shaf S72 ... 180 D1
Hoffman St. Hud HD3 ... 153 A4
Hog Close La. Wh Com HD7 ... 200 C8
Hogley La. Holmfi HD7 ... 188 C4
Holays. Hud HD5 ... 154 E7
Holbeck La. Leeds LS11 ... 78 F6
Holbeck Moor Rd. Leeds LS11 ... 79 A5
Holbeck Towers. Leeds LS11 ... 79 A5 5
Holborn Appr. Leeds LS6 ... 60 A3
Holborn Ct. Brad BD2 ... 94 C6
Holborn Gdns. Leeds LS6 ... 60 A3 4
Holborn Gn. Leeds LS6 ... 60 A3
Holborn La. Leeds LS6 ... 60 B3
Holborn Terr. Leeds LS6 ... 60 B3
Holborn Towers. Leeds LS6 ... 60 B3 10
Holborn View. Leeds LS6 ... 60 A3
Holborn Wlk. Leeds LS6 ... 60 A3
Holden Ing Way. Batley WF17 ... 97 A4
Holden La. Bail BD17 ... 38 D4
Holden La. Sil BD20 ... 18 C6
Holden Rd. Brad BD8 ... 73 F8
Holden Rd. Brad BD8 ... 73 F8 1
Holdcn St. Keigh BD21 ... 35 C7
Holderness Rd. Hud WF11 ... 126 E4
Holderness St. Tod OL14 ... 108 C5 14
Holdforth Cl. Leeds LS12 ... 78 E7
Holdforth Gdns. Leeds LS12 ... 78 E7
Holdforth Gn. Leeds LS12 ... 78 E7
Holdforth Pl. Leeds LS12 ... 78 E7
Holdsworth Ave. Batley WF12 ... 117 F7
Holdsworth Ct. Clec BD19 ... 116 D7 6
Holdsworth Rd. Hali HX3 ... 92 A3
Holdsworth Sq. Brad BD2 ... 56 D4
Holdsworth St. Brad BD1 ... 74 D8
Holdsworth St. Brad BD1 ... 74 E8
Holdsworth St. Clec BD19 ... 116 D8
Holdsworth St. Ship BD18 ... 55 B7
Holdsworth Terr. Hali HX3 ... 113 D5
Hole Bottom Rd. Tod OL14 ... 108 B7
Hole La. Sil BD20 ... 18 C6
Holes La. Knot WF11 ... 126 E4
Holgate Ave. Hem WF9 ... 163 B3
Holgate. Hem WF9 ... 181 C7
Holgate Gdns. Hem WF9 ... 181 C7
Holgate Hospital. Hem WF9 ... 181 C8
Holgate Rd. Brad BD7 ... 73 E4
Holgate Terr. Hem WF9 ... 163 B3
Holgate. Wire. Bri S72 ... 181 C7
Holker St. Brad BD8 ... 74 D8
Holker St. Brad BD8 ... 74 B8
Holland St. Brad BD4 ... 75 B4
Holland Rd. Kippax LS25 ... 83 C2
Holland St. Brad BD4 ... 118 D5
Hollas La. Sow Br HX6 ... 111 F4
Hollas La. Sow Br HX6 ... 112 A4
Hollerton La. E Ard WF3 ... 119 F7
Hollin Ave. Hud HD3 ... 153 D7
Hollin Brigg La. Holmfi HD7 ... 188 E8
Hollin Close La. Brad BD2 ... 55 E3
Hollin Cres. Leeds LS16 ... 59 E7
Hollin Dr. Crig WF4 ... 159 F5
Hollin Dr. Leeds LS16 ... 59 E7
Hollin Edge. D Dale HD8 ... 192 A6
Hollin Gate. Otley LS21 ... 10 D2
Hollin Gdns. Leeds LS16 ... 59 E7
Hollin Greaves La. Hali HX3 ... 92 D1
Hollin Hall Rd. Ilkley LS29 ... 7 E3
Hollin Hall. Hud HD7 ... 152 C5
Hollin Hall Rd. Brad BD7 ... 74 B4
Hollin Head. Bail BD17 ... 38 F4
Hollin Hill Dr. Leeds LS8 ... 61 C5
Hollin Hill La. Leeds LS8 ... 61 C5
Hollin House La. Clay W HD8 ... 193 A8
Hollin House La. Holmfi HD7 ... 189 F5
Hollin La. Crig WF4 ... 159 D2
Hollin La. Leeds LS16 ... 59 E7
Hollin La. Sow Br HX6 ... 112 A1
Hollin Mews. Leeds LS16 ... 59 D7
Hollin Mount. Leeds LS16 ... 59 E6
Hollin Park Ave. Leeds LS8 ... 61 C6
Hollin Park Cres. Leeds LS8 ... 61 C6
Hollin Park Ct. Pudsey LS28 ... 57 A6
Hollin Park Dr. Leeds LS8 ... 61 C6
Hollin Park Par. Leeds LS8 ... 61 C5
Hollin Park Pl. Leeds LS8 ... 61 C6
Hollin Park Rd. Leeds LS8 ... 61 C6
Hollin Park Rd. Pudsey LS28 ... 57 A6
Hollin Park Terr. Leeds LS8 ... 61 C5
Hollin Rd. Brad BD2 ... 55 E3
Hollin Rd. Leeds LS16 ... 59 E6
Hollingbourne Rd. Leeds LS15 ... 62 D3
Hollings La. Mir WF14 ... 138 A6
Hollings Rd. Brad BD8 ... 55 B1
Hollings Sq. Brad BD8 ... 55 B1
Hollings St. Brad BD8 ... 55 B1
Hollings The. M'town LS26 ... 102 B3
Hollingthorpe Ave. Crig WF4 ... 159 F3

Hollingthorpe Ct. Crig WF4 ... 159 F2
Hollingthorpe Gr. Crig WF4 ... 159 E3
Hollingthorpe La. Crig WF4 ... 159 E3
Hollingthorpe Rd. Crig WF4 ... 159 E2
Hollingwood Ave. Brad BD7 ... 73 F4
Hollingwood Ct. Brad BD7 ... 73 E3
Hollingwood Dr. Brad BD7 ... 73 E3
Hollingwood Fst Sch. Brad ... 73 F3
Hollingwood Gate. Ilkley LS29 ... 7 E3
Hollingwood Gr. Brad BD7 ... 73 E3
Hollingwood Lane. Brad BD7 ... 73 E3
Hollingwood Mount. Brad BD7 ... 73 E3
Hollingwood Rise. Ilkley LS29 ... 7 D3
Hollingworth La. Knot WF11 ... 126 B8
Hollinhurst. Lead Tod OL14 ... 129 B8
Hollinhrst La. Neth WF4 ... 158 F6
Hollinhurst. Kippax WF10 ... 102 F6
Hollinroyd Rd. Dew WF12 ... 139 E8
Hollins Ave. Batley WF13 ... 117 F3
Hollins Bank. Hali HX6 ... 112 B4
Hollins Bank La. Stee BD20 ... 17 E4
Hollins Cl. Keigh BD20 ... 17 F2
Hollins Glen. Slai HD7 ... 170 A8
Hollins Gr. Kippax WF10 ... 102 F6
Hollins Hey Rd. Elland HX4 ... 134 A4
Hollins Hill. Guise BD17, LS20 ... 39 B6
Hollins La. Hali HX2 ... 91 C5
Hollins La. Hali HX6 ... 112 B5
Hollins La. Keigh BD20 ... 17 F2
Hollins La. Slai HD7 ... 169 E6
Hollins La. Sow Br HX6 ... 111 C5
Hollins Meadow. Tod OL14 ... 108 A1
Hollins Mill La. Hali HX6 ... 112 B4
Hollins Mount. Hem WF9 ... 181 C7
Hollins Pk. Kippax LS25 ... 83 A1
Hollins Pl. Tod OL14 ... 108 A113
Hollins Rd. Batley WF13 ... 117 F2 2
Hollins Rd. Tod OL14 ... 108 A1
Hollins Row. Slai HD7 ... 170 A8
Hollins Sow Br HX6 ... 111 C5
Hollins St. Tod OL14 ... 129 B8
Hollins The. Tod OL14 ... 108 B6
Hollinwood View. Keigh BD16 ... 36 D7
Hollow La. Hali HX4 ... 59 F1
Hollow Mill Hd7 ... 170 D2
Hollowfield Croft. Brad BD12 ... 95 B5
llalloygetc. holmfi HD7 ... 109 AG
Holly Ave. Hors LS16 ... 41 D3
Holly Bank. Brad BD10 ... 56 C5 14
Holly Bank Dr. Brig HX3 ... 114 C8
Holly Bank. Gar LS25 ... 83 B6
Holly Bank. Guise LS20 ... 39 D8
Holly Bank. Pk. Brig HD6 ... 135 F8
Holly Bank. Rd. B Spa LS23 ... 30 D7
Holly Bank. S in a BD20 ... 16 E5
Holly Bush Ct. B Spa LS23 ... 30 C6
Holly Cl. Crof WF4 ... 143 E1
Holly Cl. E Ard WF3 ... 119 E6
Holly Cl. Midd LS10 ... 99 B4
Holly Cres. Crof WF4 ... 143 D3
Holly Cres. Rip HX6 ... 132 C3
Holly Ct. E Ard WF3 ... 119 E6
Holly Ct. Guise LS20 ... 39 D8
Holly Ct. Wilf S75 ... 178 B1
Holly Dr. Hors LS16 ... 41 D3
Holly Gr. Batley WF17 ... 118 B3
Holly Gr. Hud HD4 ... 153 B2
Holly Hall La. Hud HD3 ... 153 A4
Holly Hall La. Hud HD3 ... 153 A4
Holly Hill. Hem WF9 ... 181 C7
Holly House. Castle WF10 ... 124 E6 7
Holly Park Dr. Brad BD7 ... 73 E3
Holly Pk. Rd. B Spa LS23 ... 30 D6
Holly St. Hem WF9 ... 181 C7
Holly St. Wake WF2 ... 141 F7
Holly Terr. Hud HD1 ... 154 B8
Hollybank Ave. Batley WF17 ... 118 C2
Hollybank Gdns. Brad BD7 ... 73 E3
Hollybank House. Brig HD6 ... 135 F8
Hollybank Rd. Brad BD7 ... 73 E3
Hollycroft Ave. Roy S71 ... 179 B3
Hollyfield Ave. Hud HD3 ... 153 A2
Hollyns Terr. Elland HX4 ... 134 C7 6
Hollynsmill. Elland HX4 ... 134 D7
Hollyshaw Cres. Leeds LS15 ... 81 C8
Hollyshaw Gr. Leeds LS15 ... 81 C8
Hollyshaw La. Leeds LS15 ... 81 C8
Hollyshaw St. Leeds LS15 ... 81 C8
Hollyshaw Terr. Leeds LS15 ... 81 C8
Hollyshaw Wlk. Leeds LS15 ... 62 C1 4
Hollyshaw Way. Leeds LS15 ... 58 B9
Holman Ave. Gar LS25 ... 82 F6
Holmbridge CE Sch. Holmfi ... 188 D2
Holmcliffe Ave. Hud HD4 ... 153 C2
Holmdale Cres. Holmfi HD7 ... 188 F8
Holmdene Dr. Mir WF14 ... 138 A4
Holme Ave. Hud HD5 ... 154 E5
Holme Cl. Floc WF4 ... 156 E4
Holme Cl. Glu BD20 ... 16 D6
Holme Ct. Sch. Holme ... 187 F1
Holme Farm La. Bad LS17 ... 28 C3
Holme Field. Ossett WF5 ... 140 E4
Holme Ghyll. Glu BD20 ... 16 D6
Holme Gr. Bur in W LS29 ... 21 F7
Holme House La. Hali HX2 ... 90 A1
Holme House La. Keigh BD22 ... 34 B6
Holme House Rd. Tod OL14 ... 108 A3
Holme House St. Litt OL15 ... 129 C1
Holme La. Brad BD4 ... 75 C2
Holme La. Holmfi HD7 ... 189 E3
Holme La. Holmfi HD7 ... 187 F1
Holme Lea. Roth LS26 ... 100 E5
Holme Mid Sch. Brad ... 75 C2
Holme Pk. Hud HD5 ... 154 E5
Holme Pl. Heb Br HX7 ... 89 A4

Holme Pl. Hud HD1 153 D7
Holme Rd. Hali HX2 112 B6
Holme St. Brad BD5 74 D4
Holme St. Brig HX3 115 A7
Holme St. Heb Br HX7 89 A3
Holme St. Liver WF15 117 B4
Holme St. Oxen BD22 51 C2
Holme St. Tod OL14 107 E7
Holme Styes La. Holme HD7 199 A8
Holme Terr. Litt OL15 129 D1
Holme Top La. Brad BD5 74 D4
Holme Top St. Brad BD5 74 D4
Holme Valley Bsns Ctr. Hud 171 E8
Holme Valley Memorial Hospl. Holmfi 189 A7
Holme View. Arth LS21 25 C6
Holme View Ave. Holmfi HD7 188 D5
Holme View Dr. Holmfi HD7 188 D5
Holme View Pk. Holmfi HD7 188 E5
Holme Villas. Mars HD7 169 C6
Holme Way. Ossett WF5 140 C7
Holme Well Rd. Midd LS10 99 E5
Holme Wood Rd. Brad BD4 75 D3
Holme Wood Rd. Keigh BD22 34 F6
Holme Woods La. Holme HD7 197 F6
Holme's Terr. Hali HX2 112 E8 9
Holmefield Fst Sch. Brad 75 E4
Holmefield Rd. Hud HD3 152 E6
Holmes Rd. Hali HX6 112 C4
Holmes St. Brad BD1 74 D8
Holmes St. Leeds LS11 79 C6
Holmeside Cl. Hud HD4 171 F8
Holmfield Ave. Clay W HD8 175 F2
Holmfield Ave. Wake WF2 142 B3
Holmfield Chase. Loft G WF3 122 B6
Holmfield Cl. Clay W HD8 175 F2
Holmfield Cl. Pont WF8 125 F4
Holmfield. Clay W HD8 175 F2
Holmfield Cotts. M'town LS26 102 E3
Holmfield Dr. Hud HD7 152 F5
Holmfield Dr. Leeds LS8 44 A1
Holmfield Gdns. Hali HX2 92 A5
Holmfield Gr. Wake WF2 142 B3
Holmfield Ind Est. Hali 92 A7
Holmfield La. Castle WF11, WF8 125 F5
Holmfield La. Wake WF2 142 B3
Holmfield Rd. Clay W HD8 175 F2
Holmfield Rd. S in Cra BD20 16 D5
Holmfield St. Brad BD1 74 D7
Holmfield Terr. Clay W HD8 175 F2
Holmfirth High Sch. Holmfi 189 C8
Holmfirth Jun & Inf Sch. Holmfi 189 A4
Holmfirth Rd. Diggle OL3 185 D1
Holmfirth Rd. Holmfi HD7 189 E7
Holmfirth Rd. Mel HD7 170 E1
Holmfirth Scholes Jun & Inf Sch. Holmfi 189 D3
Holmfirth Upperthong Jun Mix Sch. Holmfi 188 E4
Holmroyd Ave. Glu BD20 16 D6
Holmsley Ave. S Kirk WF9 182 A2
Holmsley Crest. Roth LS26 101 A6
Holmsley Field Ct. Roth LS26 101 C6
Holmsley Field La. Roth LS26 101 C6
Holmsley Garth. Roth LS26 101 B7
Holmsley Gr. S Kirk WF9 182 A2
Holmsley La. Roth LS26 101 B6
Holmsley La. S Kirk WF9 181 F2
Holmsley Mount. S Kirk WF9 182 A2
Holmsley Wlk. Roth LS26 101 B6
Holmwood Ave. Leeds LS6 59 E8
Holmwood Cl. Leeds LS6 59 F8
Holmwood Cres. Leeds LS6 59 F8
Holmwood Dr. Leeds LS6 59 F8
Holmwood Gr. Leeds LS6 59 F8
Holmwood Mount. Leeds LS6 59 F8
Holmwood View. Leeds LS6 59 E8
Holroyd Hill. Brad BD6 74 C1
Holroyd Sq. Elland HX4 133 F4
Holroyd St. Leeds LS7 60 D2
Holsworthy Rd. Brad BD4 75 E3
Holt Ave. Hors LS16 42 C5
Holt Ave. Hud HD2 136 C4
Holt Cl. Hors LS16 42 C4
Holt Cres. Hors LS16 41 F5
Holt Dr. Hors LS16 42 A5
Holt Farm Cl. Hors LS16 42 A5
Holt Farm Rise. Hors LS16 41 F5
Holt Garth. Hors LS16 42 A5
Holt Gdns. Brad BD10 55 F8
Holt Gdns. Hors LS16 42 C5
Holt Head Rd. Slai HD7 170 B6
Holt La. Holmfi HD7 188 F6
Holt La. Hors LS16 42 A5
Holt Lane Ct. Hors LS16 42 B4
Holt Park App. Hors LS16 42 A5
Holt Park Ave. Hors LS16 42 A5
Holt Park Cl. Hors LS16 42 A5
Holt Park District Ctr. Hors LS16 41 F5
Holt Park Dr. Hors LS16 42 A5
Holt Park Gate. Hors LS16 42 A5
Holt Park Gdns. Hors LS16 42 A5
Holt Park Gn. Hors LS16 42 A5
Holt Park Gr. Hors LS16 41 F5
Holt Park Grange. Hors LS16 42 A5
Holt Park La. Hors LS16 42 A5
Holt Park Mid Sch. Hors 42 A4
Holt Park Rd. Hors LS16 42 A5
Holt Park Rise. Hors LS16 42 A5
Holt Park Vale. Hors LS16 42 A5
Holt Park Way. Hors LS16 42 A5
Holt Rd. Hors LS16 42 A5
Holt Rise. Hors LS16 42 A5
Holt St. Litt OL15 129 D2
Holt The. Ship BD18 55 C8
Holt Vale. Hors LS16 42 A5
Holt View. Hors LS16 41 F5
Holt Way. Hors LS16 42 A5
Holt Wlk. Hors LS16 42 A5
Holtby Gr. Brig HX3 115 A7
Holtdale App. Hors LS16 41 F5
Holtdale Ave. Hors LS16 41 F5
Holtdale Cl. Hors LS16 41 F5
Holtdale Croft. Hors LS16 41 F5
Holtdale Dr. Hors LS16 41 F5
Holtdale Fold. Hors LS16 41 F5
Holtdale Garth. Hors LS16 41 F5
Holtdale Gdns. Hors LS16 41 F5
Holtdale Gn. Hors LS16 41 F5
Holtdale Gr. Hors LS16 41 F5
Holtdale Lawn. Hors LS16 41 F5
Holtdale Pl. Hors LS16 41 F5
Holtdale Rd. Hors LS16 41 F5
Holtdale View. Hors LS16 41 F5
Holtdale Way. Hors LS16 41 F5
Holts La. Brad BD14 73 B4
Holts La. Brad BD14 73 B5
Holts Terr. Hali HX3 113 D4
Holy Family RC Prim Sch. Leeds 78 D7
Holy Family Sch The. Keigh 18 B1
Holy Name Sch. Hors 42 A3
Holy Rood La. Ledsh LS25 104 E8
Holy Trinity CE (Aided) Sch. Hali 92 A6
Holy Trinity CE (Aided) Sch. Ossett 140 D6
Holy Trinity CE Fst Sch. Bing 37 A2
Holy Trinity CE Inf Sch. Hali 113 B6
Holy Trinity Jun Sch. Hali 113 B6
Holy Trinity Mid Sch. Hors 41 D5
Holybrook Ave. Brad BD10 56 D6
Holycroft Fst Sch. Keigh 35 B6
Holycroft St. Keigh BD21 35 B6
Holyoake Ave. Batley WF17 118 A5
Holyoake Ave. Bing BD16 36 F1
Holyoake St. Tod OL14 86 A1
Holyoake Terr. Hor WF4 140 E1
Holyoake Terr. Slai HD7 152 D1
Holyrood Cres. Nor WF6 122 F4
Holywell Ash La. Brad BD8 55 D1
Holywell Dene. Castle WF10 125 A6
Holywell Gdns. Castle WF10 125 A6
Holywell Gr. Castle WF10 125 A6
Holywell Green Jun & Inf Schs. Elland 134 B4
Holywell Halt. Skip 1 B7
Holywell La. Castle WF10 125 B6
Holywell La. Thorner LS17 44 D5
Holywell Mount. Castle WF10 125 B6
Home Farm Ct. H Pag DN5 195 D5
Home Lea Dr. Roth LS26 100 D6
Home Lea. Roth LS26 100 D7
Home View Terr. Brad BD8 55 B1
Homefield Ave. Morley LS27 98 A2
Homepaddock House. Weth LS22 13 F6
Homestead Dr. Wake WF2 141 F6
Homestead The. Batley WF16 117 E4
HomesThe. Hud HD2 136 F3
Honey Hole Cl. Tod OL14 108 B4
Honey Hole Rd. Tod OL14 108 B4
Honey Holme La. H Chap BB10 85 A7
Honley CE (C) Inf Sch. Honley 171 F5
Honley CE (C) Jun Sch. Honley 171 F4
Honley High Sch. Honley 172 A5
Honley Rd. Kirkb HD4 172 D6
Honley Sq. Hor WF4 141 A1
Honley Sta. Honley 172 B5
Honoria St. Hud HD1 136 A1
Hood St. Hud HD4 171 F8
Hood St. S Elm WF9 182 E1
Hooton Cres. Ryhill WF4 162 A1
Hooton Pagnell CE Fst & Mid Sch. H Pag 195 C5
Hooton Rd. Brod DN5 195 F4
Hoowood La. Holme HD7 187 E3
Hopbine Ave. Brad BD5 74 E2
Hopbine Rd. Brad BD5 74 E2
Hope Ave. Brad BD5 74 C2
Hope Ave. Ship BD18 55 D8
Hope Bldgs. Tod OL14 108 C5 11
Hope Hall St. Hali HX1 113 C6
Hope Hall Terr. Hali HX1 113 C6 13
Hope Hill View. Ship BD16 54 A7
Hope La. Bail BD17 38 B3
Hope Pl. Keigh BD21 35 B5
Hope Rd. Leeds LS9 79 D8
Hope St. Castle WF10 124 C2
Hope St. Dew WF13 118 C1
Hope St E. Castle WF10 124 D8 10
Hope St. Hali HX1 113 B7
Hope St. Heb Br HX7 89 A3 21
Hope St. Hud HD3 153 B5
Hope St. Hud HD3 154 A4
Hope St. Mapp S75 178 C1
Hope St. Morley LS27 98 A4
Hope St. Nor WF6 144 A8
Hope St. Ossett WF5 140 F3
Hope St. Ryhill WF4 180 C8
Hope St. Sow Br HX6 112 C3
Hope St W. Castle WF10 124 C7
Hope St. Wake WF1 142 C7
Hope Terr. Slai HD7 152 D3
Hope View. Ship BD18 55 D7
Hopefield Chase. Roth LS26 100 B4
Hopefield Cl. Roth LS26 100 B4
Hopefield Ct. E Ard WF3 120 C7
Hopefield Ct. Roth LS26 100 B4
Hopefield Dr. Roth LS26 100 B4
Hopefield Gdns. Roth LS26 100 B4
Hopefield Gn. Roth LS26 100 B4
Hopefield Gr. Roth LS26 100 B4
Hopefield Mews. Roth LS26 100 B4
Hopefield Way. Roth LS26 100 B4
Hopefield Wlk. Roth LS26 100 B4
Hopes Farm Mount. Midd LS10 99 F7 3
Hopes Farm Rd. Midd LS10 99 F7
Hopes Farm View. Midd LS10 100 A7
Hopetown Wlk. Nor WF6 123 C3
Hopewell Pl. Leeds LS6 59 E2 11
Hopewell St. Batley WF17 118 B6
Hopewell Terr. Kippax LS25 83 B1
Hopewell View. Midd LS10 99 D5
Hopewell Way. Crig WF4 159 E5
Hopkin St. Brad BD4 75 E1
Hopkinson Dr. Brad BD4 95 C8
Hopkinson Rd. Hud HD2 136 B4
Hopkinson St. Hali HX3 91 F3
Hopkinsons Bldgs. Hali HX3 91 F3
Hopps's Rd. Glu BD20 16 C7
Hopton Ave. Brad BD4 75 B1
Hopton Ave. Mir WF14 137 E2
Hopton Dr. Mir WF14 137 E2
Hopton Fst Sch. Mir 137 F4
Hopton Hall La. Mir WF14 137 F1
Hopton La. Mir WF14 137 F2
Hopton New Rd. Mir WF14 138 A3
Hopwood Bank. Hors LS18 41 C2
Hopwood Cl. Hors LS18 41 C2
Hopwood Gr. Castle WF10 125 B7
Hopwood La. Hali HX1 113 A6
Hopwood Rd. Hors LS18 41 C2
Horbury Bridge CE Jun & Inf Sch. Hor 140 E1
Horbury Fst Sch. Hor 141 C1
Horbury Rd. Ossett WF5 140 C4
Horbury Rd. Wake WF2 141 E3
Horbury Sch. Hor 141 C1
Horbury St Peter CE Sch. Hor 141 B1
Horley Green La. Hali HX3 92 E2
Horley Green Rd. Hali HX3 113 E8
Horn Cote La. Holmfi HD7 190 A6
Horn Croft. Caw S75 193 F5
Horn La. Holmfi HD7 190 A6
Horn La. Ingb S30 191 B1
Horn La. Sil BD20 5 C4
Hornbeam Ave. Wake WF2 142 A8
Hornbeam Gn. Pont WF8 125 F1
Hornbeam Way. Leeds LS14 62 C8
Hornby St. Hali HX1 112 F5
Horncastle St. Clec BD19 116 E7 2
Horncastle View. Ryhill WF4 162 D2
Horne St. Hali HX1 113 B7
Horne St. Wake WF2 142 C4
Horner Ave. Batley WF17 117 F6
Horner Cres. Batley WF17 117 F6
Hornes La. Mapp S75 178 C1
Hornsea Dr. Wils BD15 53 C4
Horse Croft La. Shep HD8 174 B3
Horse Fair Flats. Pont WF8 125 D1
Horse Fair. Pont WF8 125 D1
Horse Pond La. Slai HD3 152 A7
Horsefair. Weth LS22 13 E5
Horsehold La. Heb Br HX7 88 E2
Horsehold Rd. Heb Br HX7 88 E2
Horsfall St. Hali HX1 113 A5
Horsfall St. Morley LS27 97 F6
Horsfall St. Tod OL14 108 E6
Horsforth Featherbank Inf Sch. Hors 58 B7
Horsforth Golf Course. Yeadon 40 F5
Horsforth New Rd. Pudsey LS13 57 E6
Horsforth Sch & F Ed Ctr. Hors 41 B1
Horsforth St Margaret's CE Prim Sch. Hors 41 B1
Horsforth Sta. Hors 41 C3
Horsham Ct. Keigh BD22 34 E5
Horsham Rd. Brad BD4 75 E2
Horsley St. Brad BD6 74 C1 5
Horsman St. Brad BD4 75 F1
Horton Bank Top Fst Sch. Brad 73 E2
Horton Cl. Pudsey LS13 57 F4
Horton Garth. Pudsey LS13 57 F4
Horton Grange Rd. Brad BD7 74 B5
Horton Hall Cl. Brad BD5 74 D5
Horton Park Ave. Brad BD5, BD7 74 C5
Horton Pl. Hali HX2 91 F8
Horton Rise. Pudsey LS13 57 F4
Horton St. Batley WF16 117 D3
Horton St. Hali HX1 113 D6
Horton St. Ossett WF5 140 C6
Hospital La. Hors LS16 41 F3
Hospital Rd. Keigh BD20 19 A1
Hostingley La. Dew WF12 140 B2
Hothfield St. Sil BD20 5 D1
Hothfield Street Jun Sch. Sil 5 D1
Hough End Ave. Leeds LS13 58 D1
Hough End Cl. Leeds LS13 58 D1
Hough End Cres. Leeds LS13 58 C1
Hough End Ct. Leeds LS13 58 D1 1
Hough End Garth. Leeds LS13 58 C1
Hough End Gdns. Leeds LS13 58 D1 2
Hough End La. Leeds LS13 58 C1
Hough Gr. Leeds LS13 58 C2 16
Hough La. Leeds LS13 58 C2
Hough. Northo HX3 93 A1
Hough Side Cl. Pudsey LS28 77 B7
Hough Side High Sch. Pudsey 77 B8
Hough Side La. Pudsey LS28 77 A7
Hough Side Rd. Pudsey LS28 77 A7
Hough Terr. Leeds LS13 58 C2 17
Hough Top. Pudsey LS13 77 B8
Hough Tree Rd. Pudsey LS13 77 C8
Hough Tree Terr. Pudsey LS13 77 C8
Houghley Ave. Leeds LS12 58 F2
Houghley Cl. Leeds LS13 58 E2
Houghley Cres. Leeds LS12 58 F3
Houghley La. Leeds LS12, LS13 58 E1
Houghley Pl. Leeds LS12 58 F2
Houghley Rd. Leeds LS12 58 F2
Houghley Sq. Leeds LS12 58 F2
Houghton Ave. Knot WF11 126 B5
Houghton Pl. Brad BD1 74 D8
Houghton Rd. Dearne S63 194 A1
Houghton St. Brig HD6 115 B3
Houghton Twrs. Hali HX6 112 B4 10
Houghton's Almshouses. Hud HD5 154 F3 1
Hoults La. Elland HX4 134 C8
Houndhill La. Feath WF7 145 F5
House Grove Dr. Clay W HD8 175 E2
Hovingham Ave. Leeds LS8 61 A4
Hovingham Gr. Leeds LS8 61 A4
Hovingham Mount. Leeds LS8 61 A4 6
Hovingham Prim Sch. Leeds 61 A4
Hovingham Terr. Leeds LS8 61 A4 4
Howard Ave. Hud HD3 153 C7
Howard Ave. Leeds LS15 80 F7
Howard Cres. Crig WF4 159 E6
Howard Ct. Leeds LS15 80 F7
Howard Pk. Clec BD19 116 E7
Howard Pl. Batley WF17 118 C3
Howard Rd. Hud HD3 153 C7
Howard St. Batley WF17 118 C3
Howard St. Brad BD5 74 D6
Howard St. Hali HX1 113 A8
Howard St. Ossett WF5 140 D7
Howard St. Wake WF1 142 C7
Howard Villas. Clec BD19 116 E7
Howard Way. Litt OL15 129 C1
Howard Way. Mel HD7 170 E1
Howarth Ave. Brad BD2 56 A5
Howarth Cres. Brad BD2 56 A5
Howarth La. Hud HD1 153 E3
Howarth Pl. Leeds LS7 60 C1
Howarth Rd Fst Sch. Brad 54 D3
Howbeck Ave. Keigh BD20 19 A1
Howbeck Dr. Keigh BD20 36 A8
Howcans La. Hali HX3 92 B5
Howden Ave. Ad Le S DN6 184 E1
Howden Ave. Keigh BD20 18 A2
Howden Cl. Brad BD4 75 F1
Howden Cl. Hud HD4 152 F2
Howden Cl. Mapp S75 177 F1
Howden Clough High Sch. Batley 97 B1
Howden Clough Ind Est. Batley 97 C3
Howden Clough Rd. Batley LS27 97 D3
Howden Gdns. Leeds LS6 59 E2
Howden Pl. Leeds LS6 59 E2
Howden Rd. Sil BD20 5 F1
Howden Way. Wake WF1 142 E6
Howdenbrook. Shelf HX3 93 E7
Howell La. G Hou DN5 194 A4
Howell Wood Country Pk. S Kirk 194 A7
Howes La. Northo HX3 92 F2
Howgate. Brad BD10 56 C8
Howgate Rd. Slai HD7 169 F8
Howgill Gn. Brad BD6 94 A6
Howlett Cross. Roth LS26 100 B4
Howley Hall Golf Course. Batley 118 F8
Howley Mill La. Batley WF17 118 D7
Howley Park Cl. Morley LS27 97 F2
Howley Park Rd E. Morley LS27 98 A1
Howley Park Rd. Morley LS27 97 F2
Howley Park Trad Est. Morley 97 F2
Howley St. Batley WF17 118 D6
Howley Wlk. Batley WF17 118 E5
Howley Wlk. Batley WF17 118 E6
Howroyd La. Dew WF12 156 E7
Howroyd La. Rip HX4 133 B4
Howson Cl. Guise LS20 22 F1
Hoxton Mount. Leeds LS11 78 F3
Hoxton St. Brad BD8 74 A8
Hoylake Ave. Hud HD2 135 F3
Hoyland Rd. Wake WF2 160 B5
Hoyland Terr. S Kirk WF9 182 A2
Hoyle Court Ave. Bail BD17 38 E3
Hoyle Court Dr. Bail BD17 38 E3
Hoyle Court Fst Sch. Bail 38 E2
Hoyle Court Rd. Bail BD17 38 E3
Hoyle Fold. Keigh BD22 34 F5
Hoyle House Fold. Slai HD7 152 D1
Hoyle Ing Rd. Thorn BD13 72 F6
Hoyle Ing. Slai HD7 152 D1
Hoyle Mill Rd. Hem WF9 163 D2
Hubberton Green Rd. Sow Br HX6 111 C2
Hubert St. Brad BD3 75 B6
Hubert St. Hali HX2 112 D7
Hubert St. Hud HD3 134 E1
Hud Hill. Shelf HX3 93 B4
Huddersfield Coll of Ed. Hud 135 C1
Huddersfield Crem. Hud 136 A6
Huddersfield New Coll. Hud 152 F7
Huddersfield Rd. Batley WF17 117 E8
Huddersfield Rd. Brad BD12 94 C4
Huddersfield Rd. Brig HD6 136 B7
Huddersfield Rd. Densh OL3 167 A4
Huddersfield Rd. Dew WF13 138 D4
Huddersfield Rd. Dew WF13 139 B7
Huddersfield Rd. Elland HX5 135 A4
Huddersfield Rd. Hali HX3 113 C4
Huddersfield Rd. Holmfi HD7 189 A6
Huddersfield Rd. Holmfi HD7 189 E7
Huddersfield Rd. Honley HD7 172 A5
Huddersfield Rd. Hud HD3 135 A4
Huddersfield Rd. Ingb S30 191 E1
Huddersfield Rd. Kirkb HD8 174 A4
Huddersfield Rd. Mel HD7 171 A5
Huddersfield Rd. Shep HD8 174 A4
Huddersfield Rd. Skel HD8 174 D2
Huddersfield Rd. W Bret WF4 177 A6
Huddersfield Royal Infmy. Hud 153 C8
Huddersfield Sta. Hud 154 A6
Huddersfield Tech Coll. Hud 153 F2
Huddersfield Tech Coll. Hud 153 F5
Huddersfield Tech Coll. Hud 154 A6
Huddersfield Univ. Hud 154 B5
Huddleston Ct. Dew WF12 139 F8
Hudroyd. Hud HD5 154 F3
Hudson Ave. Brad BD7 74 B3
Hudson Ave. Notton WF4 179 B6
Hudson Cl. Brad BD7 74 B3 1
Hudson Cl. Weth LS22 13 E5
Hudson Cres. Brad BD7 74 B3
Hudson Gdns. Brad BD7 74 B4
Hudson Gr. Leeds LS9 61 A1
Hudson Mews. B Spa LS23 30 E7
Hudson Mill Rd. Hep HX7 88 C5
Hudson Pl. Leeds LS9 61 A1
Hudson Rd. Leeds LS9 61 A1
Hudson St. Brad BD3 75 D7
Hudson St. Leeds LS9 61 A1
Hudson St. Pudsey LS28 57 D1 2
Hudson St. Tod OL14 86 C1
Hudson The. Brad BD12 94 C3
Hudson's Terr. Yeadon LS19 40 C7 4
Hudswell Rd. Leeds LS10 79 D4
Hudswell St. Wake WF1 142 E3
Huggan Row. Pudsey LS28 76 F7 5
Hugh Gaitskell Mid Sch. Leeds 78 F2
Hugh St. Castle WF10 124 D7
Hughenden View. Morley LS27 98 A6
Hughendon Dr. Thorn BD13 73 A6
Hughendon Wlk. Thorn BD13 73 A6
Hugill St. Thorn BD13 72 D6
Hulbert Croft. Hud HD5 154 F4
Hulbert St. Bing BD16 37 A2
Hull St. Morley LS27 98 B4
Hullen Rd. Elland HX5 134 D6
Hullenedge Gdns. Elland HX5 134 D6
Hullenedge La. Elland HX5 134 D6
Hullenedge Rd. Elland HX5 134 E6
Hullett Cl. Heb Br HX7 89 F1
Hullett Dr. Heb Br HX7 89 F1
Hulme Sq. Castle WF10 104 D1
Hulme St. Sow Br HX6 112 B3
Humber Cl. Castle WF10 125 B8
Humber Cl. Slai HD7 152 D1
Humboldt St. Brad BD1 75 A7
Hume Crest. Batley WF17 118 C5 7
Humley Rd. Wake WF2 160 B5
Hundhill La. Dar WF8 146 D2
Hungate La. M'town LS26 122 E8
Hunger Hill. Hali HX1 113 C6
Hunger Hill. Ilkley LS29 8 C7
Hunger Hill. Morley LS27 98 A3
Hunger Hills Ave. Hors LS18 41 A1
Hunger Hills Dr. Hors LS18 41 A1
Hungerford Rd. Hud HD3 153 D8
Hunslet Bsns Pk. Leeds 79 E5
Hunslet Carr Prim Sch. Leeds 79 E2
Hunslet Green Way. Leeds LS10 79 D4
Hunslet Hall Rd. Leeds LS11 79 B4
Hunslet Hall Sh Ctr. Leeds 79 B4
Hunslet La. Leeds LS10 79 C6
Hunslet Moor Prim Sch. Leeds 79 C3
Hunslet Rd. Leeds LS10 79 C6
Hunslet Rd. Leeds LS10 79 D5
Hunslet St Mary's CE Prim Sch. Leeds 79 E3
Hunslet Trad Est. Leeds 79 F3
Hunston Ave. Hud HD3 153 B7
Hunsworth La. Birk BD19, BD4 95 E4
Hunsworth La. Clec BD19 95 E4
Hunt Ct. Wake WF2 141 E6
Hunt St. Castle WF10 103 D1
Hunt St. Castle WF10 124 B8
Hunt Yd. Brad BD7 74 A4 3
Hunter Hill Rd. Hali HX2 91 A5
Hunters Ct. Brad BD9 54 C4
Hunters La. Tod OL14 107 F6
Hunters Meadow. Sil BD20 5 E2
Hunters Park Ave. Brad BD14 73 E5
Hunters Wlk. Weth LS22 13 F7
Huntingdon Ave. Hud HD2 136 F4
Huntingdon Rd. Brig HD6 115 C1
Huntock Pl. Brig HD6 114 F5
Huntsman Fold. Wake WF2 141 D6
Huntsman's Cl. Hud HD4 171 D8
Huntsman's Way. Bad WF9 164 E2
Huntsmans Cl. Bing BD16 37 C5
Huntsmans Cl. Keigh BD20 35 A8
Huntwick Ave. Feath WF7 145 C4
Huntwick Cres. Feath WF7 145 B4
Huntwick Dr. Feath WF7 145 B4
Huntwick La. Feath WF7 145 A5
Huntwick La. W Har WF7 144 F3
Huntwick Rd. Feath WF7 145 C4
Hurst Knowle. Hud HD5 155 A4
Hurst La. Mir WF14 138 B4
Hurst Rd. Heb Br HX7 89 A4
Hurstville Ave. Birk BD4 95 F6
Hurstwood. Hud HD2 136 E4
Husler Gr. Leeds LS7 60 D3
Husler Pl. Leeds LS7 60 D3
Hustings The. Liver WF15 117 A4 3
Hustler St. Brad BD3 56 A1
Hustler's Row. Leeds LS6 59 D8
Hustlergate. Brad BD1 74 E7 7
Hutchinson La. Brig HD6 115 B2 1
Hutchinson's Pl. Leeds LS5 59 A3
Hutson St. Brad BD5 74 D4
Hutton Dr. Batley WF16 117 E4
Hutton Dr. S Elm WF9 183 A4
Hutton Mid Sch. Brad 56 C5
Hutton Rd. Brad BD5 74 C2
Hutton Terr. Brad BD2 56 D5
Hutton Terr. Pudsey LS28 76 E7
Hydale Ct. Brad BD12 94 C6
Hydale Ct. Keigh BD21 35 E5
Hyde Park Cl. Leeds LS6 59 F2
Hyde Park Cnr. Leeds LS6 59 F3 5
Hyde Park Pl. Leeds LS6 59 F3
Hyde Park Rd. Hali HX1 113 A5
Hyde Park Rd. Leeds LS6 59 F2
Hyde Park St. Hali HX1 113 A5
Hyde Park Terr. Leeds LS6 59 F3
Hyde Pk. Hali HX1 113 A6
Hyde Pk. Wake WF1 142 E6
Hyde Pl. Leeds LS2 60 A1
Hyde St. Brad BD10 39 B1
Hyde St. Leeds LS2 60 A1
Hyde Terr. Leeds LS2 60 A1
Hydro Cl. Ilkley LS29 8 F3
Hyman Wlk. S Elm WF9 183 A4
Hyne Ave. Brad BD4 75 C1
Hyrst Garth. Batley WF17 118 B2
Hyrst Wlk. Batley WF17 118 C3
Hyrstlands Rd. Batley WF17 118 C3
Hyrstmount Jun Sch. Batley 118 C3

Ibbetson Cl. Morley LS27 98 A7
Ibbetson Croft. Morley LS27 98 A7
Ibbetson Ct. Morley LS27 98 A7
Ibbetson Dr. Morley LS27 98 A7
Ibbetson Oval. Morley LS27 98 A7
Ibbetson Rd. Morley LS27 98 A7
Ibbetson Rise. Morley LS27 98 A7
Ibbotroyd Ave. Tod OL14 108 A7
Ibbotson Flats. Hud HD1 154 B6 6
Ibbottson St. Wake WF1 142 F3
Ida & Robert Arthington Hospl. Hors 41 F2
Ida St. Brad BD5 74 C3
Ida St. Leeds LS10 80 A2
Iddesleigh St. Brad BD4 75 D6
Ideal L Ctr. Brad 74 D1
Idle CE Fst Sch. Brad 39 B1
Idle Rd. Brad BD2 56 B3
Idlecroft Rd. Brad BD10 56 B8
Idlethorp Way. Brad BD10 56 C7
Ilbert Ave. Brad BD4 75 C1
Ilford St. Morley LS27 98 B4
Ilkley Golf Course. Nes 7 D6
Ilkley Grammar Sch. Ilkley 8 C3
Ilkley Hall Mews. Ilkley LS29 8 B3
Ilkley Hall Pk. Ilkley LS29 8 B3
Ilkley Mid Sch. Ilkley 8 E4
Ilkley Rd. Add LS29 7 B6
Ilkley Rd. Bur in W LS29 9 D3
Ilkley Rd. Keigh BD20 19 C5
Ilkley Rd. Otley LS21 22 F7
Ilkley Sta. Ilkley 8 B4
Illingworth Ave. Hali HX2 91 E7
Illingworth Ave. Nor WF6 122 E3
Illingworth Cl. Hali HX2 91 E7
Illingworth Cl. Yeadon LS19 40 C5
Illingworth Cres. Hali HX2 91 E7
Illingworth Dr. Hali HX2 91 E7
Illingworth Gdns. Hali HX2 91 E7
Illingworth Gr. Hali HX2 91 E7
Illingworth Rd. Brad BD12 94 F4
Illingworth Rd. Hali HX2 91 E7
Illingworth St. Ossett WF5 140 D5
Illingworth Way. Hali HX2 91 E7
Imperial Arc. Hud HD1 154 A6 23
Imperial Ave. Wake WF2 120 F2
Imperial Rd. Hud HD1, HD3 153 D7
Inchfield Rd. Tod OL14 129 A8
Incline The. Hali HX3 113 E8
Independent St. Brad BD5 74 C3
Industrial Ave. Batley WF17 96 D1
Industrial Rd. Hali HX6 112 B4
Industrial St. Bacup OL13 106 A2
Industrial St. Bing BD16 36 F3
Industrial St. Brig HD6 115 B3
Industrial St. Brig BD19 115 F8 13
Industrial St. Hor WF4 159 C8
Industrial St. Hud HD4 154 A4
Industrial St. Keigh BD22 35 A6
Industrial St. Leeds LS9 60 F1
Industrial St. Liver FW15 116 E4
Industrial St. Tod OL14 108 C5
Industrial St. Wake WF1 142 C7 4
Industrial Terr. Hali HX1 113 B5 2
Industrial Terr. Hud HD5 155 A5
Industry St. Thorn BD13 72 E6 3
Industry St. Tod OL14 108 A1
Infirmary St. Brad BD1 74 D7
Infirmary St. Leeds LS1 79 B8
Ing Field. Brad BD12 95 A4
Ing Head. Kirkb HD4 173 A2
Ing Head. Slai HD7 151 E1
Ing Head Terr. Shelf HX3 93 B4
Ing La. Hud HD4 154 A3
Ing St. Brad BD3 75 D7
Ingdale Dr. Holmfi HD7 189 B6
Ingfield Ave. Hud HD5 154 D6
Ingfield Ave. Ossett WF5 140 E6
Ingham Cl. Hali HX2 91 F8
Ingham Cl. Mir WF14 138 C4
Ingham Croft. Mir WF14 138 C4
Ingham Garth. Mir WF14 138 C5
Ingham La. Hali HX2 71 E1
Ingham Rd. Dew WF12 139 D3

Ingham St. Leeds LS10 79 D5
Ingham's Ave. Pudsey LS28 76 B8
Ingham's View. Pudsey LS28 76 B8
Inghams Ct. Hali HX3 92 A123
Inghams Terr. Pudsey LS28 76 B8
Inghead Gdns. Shelf HX3 93 B4
Ingle Ave. Morley LS27 97 F6
Ingle Cres. Morley LS27 98 A5
Ingle Dean. Heb Br HX7 88 D7
Ingle Gr. Morley LS27 98 A5
Ingle Row. Leeds LS7 60 D6
Ingleborough Dr. Morley LS27 98 C2
Ingleborough Dr. Morley LS27 98 C3
Ingleby Pl. Brad BD7 74 A6
Ingleby Rd. Brad BD7, BD8 74 A7
Ingleby St. Brad BD7 74 A7
Ingleby Way. Midd LS10 99 E7
Ingledew Cres. Leeds LS8 44 B2
Ingledew Ct. Leeds LS17 43 D4
Ingledew Dr. Leeds LS8 44 B2
Ingleton Cl. Leeds LS11 79 B310
Ingleton Ct. Leeds LS11 80 F7
Ingleton Gr. Leeds LS11 79 B311
Ingleton Pl. Leeds LS11 79 B3
Ingleton Rd. Hud HD4 154 B2
Ingleton St. Leeds LS11 79 B312
Inglewood App. Leeds LS14 62 B3
Inglewood Ave. Hud HD2 135 C1
Inglewood Dr. Leeds LS14 62 B3
Inglewood Dr. Otley LS21 27 F7
Inglewood. Mapp S75 178 A1
Inglewood Pl. Leeds LS14 62 B3
Ingram Cl. Leeds LS11 78 F5
Ingram Cres. Knot WF11 126 D3
Ingram Cres. Leeds LS11 78 F4
Ingram Ct. Leeds LS11 79 A5 1
Ingram Gdns. Leeds LS11 78 F5
Ingram Par. Buth LS26 100 E5
Ingram Rd. Leeds LS11 78 F5
Ingram Road Prim Sch. Leeds 78 F5
Ingram Row. Leeds LS11 79 B6
Ingram Sq. Hali HX1 113 A522
Ingram St. Hali HX1 113 A5
Ingram St. Keigh BD21 35 B6
Ingram View. Leeds LS11 78 F5 1
Ingrow Fst Sch. Keigh 35 A4
Ingrow La. Keigh BD21, BD22 35 A4
Ingrove Wess Bsa. Keigh 35 D4
Ings Ave. Guise LS20 22 D2
Ings Cl. Ryhill WF4 162 C1
Ings Ct. S Kirk WF9 182 D3
Ings Cres. Dew WF12 139 C2
Ings Cres. Leeds LS9 80 B7
Ings Cres. Liver WF15 117 B4
Ings Croft. Shelf HX3 93 C6
Ings Ct. Guise LS20 22 C1
Ings Dr. L Brad BD20 4 A4
Ings La. Dew WF12 139 C2
Ings La. Castle WF10 103 F2
Ings La. Con BD20 4 A4
Ings La. Dew WF12 139 C2
Ings La. Ledst WF10 103 E4
Ings La. Th Arch LS23 31 A8
Ings La. Wig LS24 31 F8
Ings Mere Ct. Far WF11 105 A4
Ings Mill Ave. Clay W HD8 175 F3
Ings Mill Dr. Clay W HD8 175 F2
Ings Mill Yd. Batley WF16 117 D4
Ings Rd. Batley WF17 118 A6
Ings Rd. Dew WF13 118 E1
Ings Rd. Hem WF9 163 B1
Ings Rd. Hud HD5 155 A4
Ings Rd. Leeds LS9 80 B8
Ings Rd. Liver WF15 117 B5
Ings Rd. Stee BD20 17 B7
Ings Rd. Wake WF1 142 C5
Ings The. Brig HD6 115 A6
Ings The. Clay W HD8 175 F3
Ings View. Castle WF10 125 B8
Ings View. M'town LS26 102 E3
Ings View. Stee BD20 17 C7
Ings Way. Ingb BD8, S30 191 D1
Ings Way. Lepton HD8 155 E3
Ings Way. Sil BD20 17 F8
Ings Way W. Lepton HD8 155 E3
Ings Wlk. S Kirk WF9 182 D3
Ingwell St. Wake WF1 142 C6 6
Ingwell Terr. Norton WF4 179 A7
Ingwell Dr. Notton WF4 178 F7
Ingwell Ct. Wake WF1 142 D6 6
Ingwell St. Wake WF1 116 E7
Ingwell Terr. Clec BD19 116 C7
Inholmes La. Th Arch LS24 15 C4
Inkerman Ct. D Dale HD8 192 A5
Inkerman St. Brad BD3 75 D4
Inkerman St. Brad BD4 54 D4
Inkerman St. Brad BD4 75 D4
Inkerman Way. D Dale HD8 192 A5
Inner Hey. Mars HD7 169 A4
Inner Hey Yd. Mars HD7 169 A4
Inner Ring Rd. Leeds LS1, LS2 60 C1
Institute Rd. Brad BD2 56 C5
Institute St. Glu BD20 16 C6
Intake Cl. Loft G WF3 121 F5
Intake Cl. Brad BD2 56 C2
Intake High Sch. Leeds 58 B8
Intake La. Hud HD4 152 E5
Intake La. Loft G WF3 121 F5
Intake La. Mel HD4 170 F5
Intake La. Ossett WF5 140 E6
Intake La. Pudsey LS13 57 F5
Intake La. Slai HD7 169 F4
Intake La. Wilsd BD15 53 B5
Intake Mt. Leeds LS10 99 E3
Intake La. Thorner LS14 45 D3
Intake La. Yeadon LS19 40 C7
Intake Mount. Midd LS10 99 E3
Intake Rd. Brad BD2 56 B2
Intake Sq. Midd LS10 99 E3
Intake Terr. Brad BD2 56 C2
Intake View. Midd LS10 99 E3
Intercity Way. Pudsey LS13 58 A1
Invargarry Cl. Gar LS25 83 B8
Inverness Rd. Gar LS25 83 B8
Invertrees Ave. Yeadon LS19 40 C4
Iona Pl. Hali HX3 92 C2 8
Iona St. Hali HX3 92 C1

Ireland Cres. Hors LS16 41 F3
Ireland St. Harden BD16 36 E3
Ireland Terr. Harden BD16 36 E3
Ireland Wood Cty Prim Sch. Hors 42 A4
Ireton St. Brad BD7 74 B6
Iron Row. Bur in W LS29 9 F1
Iron St. Clec BD19 116 C7
Ironwood App. Leeds LS14 62 A3
Ironwood Cres. Leeds LS14 62 A3
Ironwood View. Leeds LS14 62 A4
Irvin Terr. Castle WF10 124 C7
Irving St. Hali HX1 112 F5 2
Irving Terr. Brad BD7 73 C3
Irwell St. Brad BD4 75 A5
Irwin App. Leeds LS15 80 F7
Irwin Ave. Wake WF1 142 F7
Irwin Cres. Wake WF1 142 E7
Irwin St. Pudsey LS28 57 D2
Isaac St. Brad BD8 74 B8
Island The. Knot WF11 127 A5
Island View. Dew WF12 139 B6
Isles St. Brad BD8 73 F8
Ivanhoe Rd. Brad BD7 74 B5
Ive House La. Hali HX2 111 E8
Ivegate. Brad BD1 74 E7
Ivegate. Yeadon LS19 40 B7
Iveson App. Hors LS16 41 F2
Iveson Cl. Hors LS16 41 F2
Iveson Ct. Hors LS16 41 F2
Iveson Dr. Hors LS16 41 F2
Iveson Garth. Hors LS16 42 A2
Iveson Gdns. Hors LS16 41 F2
Iveson Gn. Hors LS16 41 F2
Iveson Gr. Hors LS16 41 F2
Iveson House Cty Prim Annexe. Hors 41 F2
Iveson Lawn. Hors LS16 42 A2
Iveson Lawn. Hors LS16 42 A2
Iveson Rd. Hors LS16 41 F2
Iveson Rise. Hors LS16 42 A2
Ivory St. Leeds LS10 79 C5
Ivy Ave. Leeds LS9 80 B8
Ivy Bank Ct. Bail BD17 38 D2 1
Ivy Bank La. Haw BD22 51 C6
Ivy Chase. Pudsey LS28 77 B7
Ivy Cl. Wake WF1 142 E8
Ivy Cotts. Roy S71 179 D4
Ivy Cres. Drig (HC) 114 C7
Ivy Cres. Leeds LS9 80 A7
Ivy Cres. Leeds LS9 80 A810
Ivy Ct. Leeds LS7 60 D6
Ivy Farm Cl. Roy S71 179 D1
Ivy Garth. Leeds LS7 60 D6
Ivy Gdns. Castle WF10 125 D5
Ivy Gr. Leeds LS9 80 B8
Ivy Gr. Ship BD18 54 E7
Ivy Gr. Wake WF1 142 E8
Ivy La. B Spa LS23 30 C7
Ivy La. Brad BD15 54 A1
Ivy La. Hali HX2 91 D6
Ivy La. Wake WF1 142 E8
Ivy Mount. Leeds LS9 80 A8
Ivy Mount. Slai HD7 151 F1
Ivy Pl. Glu BD20 16 C7
Ivy Pl. Leeds LS13 58 D4
Ivy Rd. Keigh BD21 35 E6
Ivy Rd. Leeds LS9 80 R8
Ivy Rd. Ship BD18 54 E7
Ivy St. Brig HD6 114 F3
Ivy St. Feath WF7 145 D6
Ivy St. Hali HX1 113 A5
Ivy St. Hud HD4 153 C4
Ivy St. Leeds LS9 80 A8
Ivy St. Mill HX3 113 A5
Ivy St S. Keigh BD21 35 B3
Ivy Terr. Brig HX3 114 F3
Ivy Terr. Keigh BD21 35 F6
Ivy View. Leeds LS9 80 A8 8

Jacinth Cl. Hud HD2 136 C2
Jack Bridge. B Head HX7 88 A5
Jack Close Orch. Roy S71 179 C4
Jack Field La. S in Cra BD20 16 A4
Jack Hill. Hud HD2 136 A1
Jack La. Lepton HD8 155 E3
Jack La. Leeds LS10, LS11 79 D5
Jack Royd. Hali HX3 91 F2
Jackdaw Cl. B Spa LS23 30 C8
Jackie Smart Ct. Leeds LS7 60 E3
Jackie Smart Rd. Brad BD5 74 E4 1
Jackman Dr. Hors LS18 58 B7
Jackroyd La. Hud HD4 154 A2
Jackroyd La. Mir WF14 137 E2
Jackson Ave. Leeds LS8 60 F7
Jackson Hill La. Queens BD13 92 F7
Jackson House. Hem WF9 181 D6
Jackson La. Rip HX4 133 A5
Jackson Meadows. Rip HX4 133 A5
Jackson Pl. S in Cra BD20 16 D4
Jackson St. S in Cra BD20 16 A8
Jackson's Well La. Wake WF1 142 D7
Jacques Gr. Sil BD20 5 D1
Jade Pl. Hud HD2 136 C2
Jaggar La. Honley HD7 171 F4
Jagger Green Dean. Elland HX4 134 A3
Jagger Green La. Elland HD3 134 B2
Jagger La. Emley HD8 174 F7
Jail Rd. Batley WF17 118 C5
Jakeman Cl. E Ard WF3 120 A8
Jakeman Ct. E Ard WF3 120 B8
Jakeman Dr. E Ard WF3 120 A8
James Ave. Leeds LS8 44 A3
James Ave. Stee BD20 17 C8
James Duggan Ave. Feath WF7 145 D6
James Gate. Brad BD1 74 D7

James Gibbs Cl. Feath WF7 145 D6
James La. Hud HD7 171 A6
James St. Batley WF17 118 B4
James St. Birk BD11 96 A6
James St. Brad BD15 54 C1
James St. Brad BD15 74 E7
James St. Brig HD6 115 A3
James St. Castle WF10 103 D1
James St. Dew WF13 118 B1
James St E. Keigh BD21 35 C6 8
James St. Elland HX5 134 B4
James St. Elland HX5 135 A6
James St. Glu BD20 16 D7
James St. Haw BD22 34 B2
James St. Heb Br HX7 89 A4
James St. Liver WF15 117 B3
James St. Mir WF14 138 A7
James St. S Hie S72 180 F6
James St. Mir WF14 137 F6
James St. Thorn BD13 72 D6
James St. Yeadon LS19 40 B4
James St. Wake WF1 142 D6
Jamie Hills. Ship BD17 55 A8
Jane St. Ship BD18 54 F8
Janeway. Kippax LS25 82 F7
Janet St. Haw BD22 51 B8
Jaques Cl. Leeds LS6 59 B4
Jardine Ave. Feath WF7 145 D6
Jardine St. Bing BD16 37 A310
Jarratt St. Brad BD8 55 B1
Jarratt St E. Brad BD8 55 B1
Jarrom Ct. Brad BD4 75 D2
Jarvis House. Brad BD6 93 E8 4
Jarvis Sq. Roth WF3 100 A3
Jarvis Wlk. Roth WF3 100 A3
Jasmin Terr. Brad BD8 74 C8
Jason Terr. Batley WF17 97 A2
Jasper St. Brad BD10 56 B8
Jasper St. Hali HX1 202 B1
Java Dr. E Ard WF3 119 E7
Jay House La. Brig HD6 115 D5
Jay St. Haw BD22 51 C8
JB Priestley Liby. Brad 74 C6
Jean Ave. Leeds LS15 81 A7
Jebb La. Caw S75 176 E3
Jebb La. H Hoy S75 176 F4
Jenkin Dr. Hor WF4 140 F1
Jenkin La. Hor WF4 140 F1
Jenkin Rd. Hor WF4 141 A1
Jenkinson Cl. Leeds LS11 79 A5
Jenkinson Lawn. Leeds LS11 79 A5
Jenkinson St. Batley WF17 118 C2
Jennetts Cres. Otley LS21 22 F7
Jennings Cl. Sil BD20 17 F8
Jennings Pl. Brad BD7 74 A4
Jennings St. Brad BD7 74 A4
Jenny La. Bail BD17 38 D4
Jenny La. Mir WF14 138 B7
Jepson La. Elland HX5 134 F7
Jeremy La. Brig HX3 115 B8
Jer La. Brad BD7 73 E2
Jermyn St. Brad BD1 74 F7 5
Jerry Clay Dr. Wake WF2 120 E2
Jerry Clay La. Wake WF2 120 E2
Jerry Fields Rd. Sow Br HX2 111 D6
Jerry La. Sow Br HX6 6 F1
Jerry La. Sow Br HX6 112 A3

John St. S Elm WF9 182 F2
John St. Ship BD18 55 A8
John St. Thorn BD13 72 D6
John St. Tod OL14 108 B5 4
John St W. Hali HX6 112 B4 2
John St. Wake WF1 142 D6
John St. Yeadon LS19 40 B4
John Street Mkt. Brad 74 D7
John William St. Clec BD19 116 D8 3
John William St. Elland HX5 134 F6 13
John William St. Hud HD1 154 A6
John William St. Liver WF15 117 B3 1
John William St. Liver WF15 117 C4
John's Cres. Wake WF2 120 E2
John's Gr. Otley LS21 23 A6
Johns Ave. Loft G WF3 121 C6
Johns La. Elland HX5 134 F4
Johnson St. Bing BD16 36 F3
Johnson St. Brad BD3 75 D7
Johnson St. Mir WF14 138 A3
Johnson Terr. Morley LS27 98 B4
Johnston St. Leeds LS6 142 D610
Jonathan Garth. Sil LS29 6 E8
Jons Ave. S Kirk WF9 182 A2
Jos La. Shep HD8 190 E8
Jos Way. Shep HD8 190 E8
Joseph Ave. Northo HX3 93 A2
Joseph Crossley's Almshouses. Hali HX1 113 A6
Joseph Priestley Coll. Roth 101 B7
Joseph Priestly Coll. Gild 97 E7
Joseph Priestly Inst of F Ed. Morley 98 B2
Joseph St. Brad BD4 75 A7
Joseph St. Brad BD4 75 E1
Joseph St. Leeds LS10 79 C6
Joseph Wright Ct. Brad BD10 39 A1
Josephine Rd. Hud HD4 153 A3
Joshua St. Tod OL14 108 B6 7
Jowett House La. Caw S75 193 B4
Jowett Park Cres. Brad BD10 39 A2
Jowett St. Brad BD1 74 C7
Jowett Terr. Morley LS27 98 A2 7
Jowett's La. Sil BD20 5 D8
Jubilee Ave. Loft G WF1 121 C4
Jubilee Ave. Nor WF4 144 A8
Jubilee Ave. Shep HD8 174 A8
Jubilee Bghes. Knot WF11 126 F4
Jubilee Cl. Ham WF9 191 F6
Jubilee Cres. Birk BD11 97 A7
Jubilee Cres. Loft G WF1 121 C4
Jubilee Cres. Pudsey LS28 57 D1
Jubilee Croft. Birk BD11 96 F7
Jubilee Ct. Hem WF9 163 A4
Jubilee Ct. Leeds LS11 79 B6 8
Jubilee Dr. Keigh BD21 35 A5 3
Jubilee Mount. Brig HD6 114 F2
Jubilee Pl. Morley LS27 98 B3
Jubilee Rd. Hali HX3 113 D3
Jubilee Rd. Hem WF9 181 D7
Jubilee Rd. Shep HD8 174 D1
Jubilee St. Brad BD1 74 D4
Jubilee St. Heb Br HX7 89 E1 9
Jubilee St. Leeds LS11 79 B6 1
Jubilee St N. Morley LS27 98 B4
Jubilee St. Crig WF4 159 F3
Jubilee St. Morley LS27 98 B3
Jubilee St N. Morley LS27 98 B4
Jubilee Terr. Hali HX3 113 D3
Jubilee Terr. Morley LS27 98 A3 2
Jubilee Terr. Ship BD18 55 D8
Judy Haigh La. Dew WF12 157 D8
Judy La. Hud HD2 136 B3
Julian Dr. Queens BD13 73 C1
Julie Ave. Crig WF4 159 F5
Jumb Beck Cl. Bur in W LS29 9 F8
Jumble Hole Rd. B Head OL14 88 B1
Jumble Wood. Caw S75 193 B4
Jumbles Ct. Roth WF3 100 C1
Jumbles La. Roth WF3 100 C1
Jumples Cl. Hali HX2 91 D4
Jumples Crag. Hali HX2 91 D4
Jumples Ct. Hali HX2 91 D4
Junction Row. Brad BD2 56 B4
Junction St. Leeds LS10 79 F4
Junction Terr. Brad BD2 56 B4
June St. Keigh BD21 35 D8
Juniper Ave. M'town LS26 102 E3
Juniper Cl. Brad BD8 74 B8
Juniper Grove. Hud HD4 171 E6
Juniper Pl. Leeds LS9 80 B8
Justin Way. Hud HD4 153 D1

Keelham La. Tod OL14 87 D1
Keenan Ave. S Elm WF9 182 E1
Keeper La. Birk BD4 76 E2
Keeper La. Notton WF4 178 D5
Keeton St. Leeds LS9 79 F8
Keighley Cl. Hali HX2 91 E6
Keighley Coll (Annex). Keigh 35 D7
Keighley Dr. Hali HX2 91 E4
Keighley Golf Course. Sil 18 A4
Keighley Ind Pk. Keigh 18 C1
Keighley Pl. Pudsey LS28 57 E2 6
Keighley Preparatory Sch. Keigh 18 C1
Keighley Rd. Bing BD16 36 E5
Keighley Rd. Brad BD8 55 C3
Keighley Rd. Cull BD13 52 C7
Keighley Rd. Denh BD13 52 D2
Keighley Rd. Hali HX2 16 E6
Keighley Rd. Hali HX2 91 E5
Keighley Rd. Harden BD16 36 A2
Keighley Rd. Haw BD22 34 E3
Keighley Rd. Heb BR HX7 89 A4
Keighley Rd. Ilkley LS29 7 F2
Keighley Rd. Keigh BD20 18 A4 5
Keighley Rd. Keigh BD21 35 C1
Keighley Rd. Ship BD20 51 D3
Keighley Rd. Ship BD9 55 C3
Keighley Rd. Sil BD20 5 F2
Keighley Rd. Stee BD20 17 E5
Keighley Rd. Wad M HX7 89 B8
Keighley Rd (Lidget). Haw BD22 34 D2
Keighley Sta. Keigh 35 D7
Keighley & Worth Valley Rly. Haw 34 F1
Kelburn Gr. Haw BD22 34 B3
Kelcliffe Ave. Guise LS20 22 E1
Kelcliffe La. Guise LS20 22 E1
Keldholme Cl. Pudsey LS13 57 F5
Keldholme Rd. Pudsey LS13 57 F5 2
Keldregate. Hud HD2 136 E4
Kell Beck. Otley LS21 10 F2
Kell La. Hali HX2 90 E6
Kell La. Northo HX3 92 F2
Kell St. Bing BD16 37 A3 6
Kellett Ave. Leeds LS12 78 C4
Kellett Cres. Leeds LS12 78 C4
Kellett Dr. Leeds LS12 78 C4
Kellett Gr. Leeds LS12 78 B5
Kellett La. Leeds LS12 78 B4
Kellett Mount. Leeds LS12 78 C4 2
Kellett Pl. Leeds LS12 78 C4
Kellett Rd. Leeds LS12 78 B5
Kellett Terr. Leeds LS12 78 C4 1
Kellett Wlk. Leeds LS12 78 C4
Kelloe St. Clec BD19 95 D1
Kelmore Gr. Brad BD6 93 E7
Kelmscott Ave. Leeds LS15 62 D3
Kelmscott Cres. Leeds LS15 62 D3
Kelmscott Garth. Leeds LS15 62 D3
Kelmscott Gdns. Leeds LS15 62 D3
Kelmscott Gn. Leeds LS15 62 D3
Kelmscott La. Leeds LS15 62 D3
Kelsall Ave. Leeds LS6 59 E2
Kelsall Gr. Leeds LS6 59 E2 E218
Kelsall Pl. Leeds LS6 59 E2
Kelsall Rd. Leeds LS6 59 E2 E217
Kelsall Terr. Leeds LS6 59 E2
Kelsey St. Hali HX1 77 F8 3
Kelso Gdns. Leeds LS2 59 F1
Kelso Gr. Hud HD5 155 A6
Kelso Pl. Leeds LS2 59 F1 2 3
Kelso Rd. Leeds LS2 59 F1
Kelso St. Leeds LS2 59 F1
Keltus Ave. Glu BD20 16 D7
Kelvin Ave. Hali HX2 91 D6
Kelvin Ave. Hud HD5 154 E6
Kelvin Cres. Hali HX2 91 D6
Kelvin Rd. Elland HX5 134 F5

Kemps Way. Honnth HD7 189 E3
Kempton Rd. Kippax LS25 83 A6
Kempsing Wlk. Leeds LS15 62 F2
Ken Churchill Dr. Ossett WF4 141 A3
Kendal Bank. Leeds LS3 59 F1
Kendal Carr. Leeds LS3 59 F1 8
Kendal Cl. Castle WF10 124 D6
Kendal Cl. Leeds LS3 59 F1
Kendal Croft. Castle WF10 125 E7
Kendal Dr. Castle WF10 124 D6
Kendal Dr. Leeds LS15 80 E7
Kendal Garth. Castle WF10 125 E7
Kendal Gr. Leeds LS3 59 F1 5
Kendal La. Leeds LS3 59 F1 6
Kendal Mellor Ct. Keigh BD21 35 B6 2
Kendal Rise. Castle WF10 124 D6
Kendal Rise. Walton WF2 161 A6
Kendal Rd. Leeds LS3 59 F1
Kendal Wlk. Leeds LS3 59 F1 4
Kendall Ave. Ship BD18 54 F8
Kendall St. Keigh BD21 35 B6
Kendell St. Leeds LS10 79 F7 3
Kenilworth Ave. Gild LS27 97 D6
Kenilworth Dr. Brad BD6 93 E7
Kenilworth Gdns. Gild LS27 97 D6
Kenilworth House. Brad BD15 73 B8 4
Kenilworth Rd. Gild LS12 77 F6
Kenilworth St. Leeds LS12 78 C4 1

Kenmore Cres. Birk BD11 96 B5
Kenmore Dr. Birk BD11 96 B4
Kenmore Dr. Brad BD6 93 E7
Kenmore Gr. Birk BD11 96 B5
Kenmore Gr. Brad BD6 93 E7
Kenmore Rd. Birk BD11 96 B5
Kenmore Rd. Hud HD3 153 A8
Kenmore View. Birk BD11 96 B5
Kenmore Wlk. Brad BD6 93 E7
Kenmore Way. Birk BD11 96 B5
Kennedy Ave. Hud HD3 135 A1
Kennedy Cl. Batley WF12 119 A3
Kennels La. Saxton LS24 65 E3
Kennerleigh Ave. Leeds LS15 62 D2
Kennerleigh Cres. Leeds LS15 62 D3

Laith Gdns. Hors LS16 42 A3
Laith Gn. Hors LS16 41 F3
Laith Rd. Hors LS16 41 F3
Laith Staid La. S in Elm LS25 65 F1
Laithe Ave. Holmfi HD7 188 C2
Laithe Bank Dr. Holmfi HD7 188 C2
Laithe Cl. Sil BD20 5 E2
Laithe Field. Elland HX4 133 D5
Laithe Gr. Brad BD6 74 B1
Laithe Rd. Brad BD6 74 B1
Laithecroft Rd. Batley WF17 118 E5
Laithes Croft. Dew WF12 139 E7
Laithes Dr. Wake WF2 141 D7
Lake Lock Dr. Loft G WF3 122 A6
Lake Lock Gr. Loft G WF3 122 A5
Lake Lock Rd. Loft G WF3 122 A5
Lake Row. Brad BD4 75 B5
Lake St. Brad BD4 75 B5
Lake St. Keigh BD21 18 E1
Lake Terr. Leeds LS10 79 D2
Lake View. Crig WF2 160 C4
Lake View. Hali HX3 113 B8
Lake View. Hud HD4 171 E8
Lake View. Pont WF8 125 C3
Lake Yd. Loft G WF3 122 A5
Lakeland Cres. Leeds LS17 43 A6
Lakeland Ct. Leeds LS15 80 D6
Lakeland Dr. Leeds LS17 43 B6
Lakeland Way. Walton WF2 161 A6
Lakeside Chase. Yeadon LS19 40 C4
Lakeside Cl. Ilkley LS29 8 B5
Lakeside Ct. Hud HD3 153 B8
Lakeside Ct. Leeds LS10 79 D2
Lakeside Est. Ryhill WF4 162 B2
Lakeside Gdns. Yeadon LS19 40 C4
Lakeside Ind Est. Leeds 77 E7
Lakeside Rd. Brad BD20 19 E2
Lakeside. Mars HD7 169 A4
Lakeside Rd. Leeds LS12 77 E6
Lakeside Terr. Yeadon LS19 40 C4
Lakeside View. Yeadon LS19 40 C4
Lakeside Wlk. Yeadon LS19 40 C4
Lakeview Ct. Leeds LS8 61 C8
Lamb Cote Rd. Hud HD2 136 D6
Lamb Hall Rd. Hud HD3 152 E8
Lamb Inn Rd. Knot WF11 127 A4
Lambe Flatt. Kex S75 177 C1
Lambert Ave. Leeds LS8 60 F6
Lambert Cl. Elland HX4 134 D7
Lambert Dr. Leeds LS8 60 F6
Lambert Pl. Brad BD2 56 B2
Lambert St. Elland HX4 134 D7 2
Lambert Terr. Hors LS18 41 E1
Lambourne Ave. Brad BD10 56 E5
Lambrigg Cres. Leeds LS14 62 A4
Lambton Gr. Leeds LS8 60 F4 27
Lambton Pl. Leeds LS8 60 F4 25
Lambton St. Leeds LS8 60 F4 23
Lambton Terr. Leeds LS8 60 F4 24
Lambton View. Leeds LS8 60 F4 26
Lamma Well Rd. Holmfi HD7 189 A2
Lampards Cl. Brad BD15 54 A2
Lamplands. Batley WF17 118 D6
Lanark Dr. Hors LS18 41 B4
Lanark Rise. Crof WF4 162 A8
Lancaster Cl. Pont WF8 146 D6
Lancaster Cres. Hud HD5 154 F4
Lancaster Ct. Keigh BD21 35 B
Lancaster La. Holmfi HD7 172 C
Lancaster St. Castle WF10 104 D
Lancaster St. Dearne S63 194 E
Lancastre Ave. Leeds LS5 58 F3
Lancastre Gr. Leeds LS5 58 F3
Land St. Pudsey LS28 57 D3
Land's Bldgs. Ossett WF5 140 D7
Landor St. Keigh BD21 35 D8
Lands Beck Way. Liver WF15 116 F4
Lands Head La. Northo HX3 93 A4
Lands La. Brad BD10 56 C5
Lands La. Guise LS20 22 E1
Lands La. Leeds LS1 79 C8
Landscove Ave. Brad BD4 75 F2
Landsdown Ave. S Kirk WF9 182 A1
Landseer Ave. E Ard WF3 119 E8
Landseer Ave. Leeds LS13 58 E3
Landseer Cl. Leeds LS13 58 D3
Landseer Cres. Leeds LS13 58 E3
Landseer Dr. Leeds LS13 58 E3
Landseer Gdns. Leeds LS13 58 E3
Landseer Gn. Leeds LS13 58 D3
Landseer Gr. Leeds LS13 58 E3
Landseer Mount. Leeds LS13 58 E3
Landseer Rd. Leeds LS13 58 D3
Landseer Rise. Leeds LS13 58 D3
Landseer Terr. Leeds LS13 58 E3
Landseer View. Leeds LS13 58 E3
Landseer Way. Leeds LS13 58 D3
Landseer Wlk. Leeds LS13 58 D3
Landsholme Ct. Brad BD4 75 F2
Landsmoor Gr. Bing BD16 37 C5
Lane and Dowry Rd. Slai HD7 169 F7
Lane Bottom. B Head HX7 87 F4
Lane Cotts. Roy S71 179 C3
Lane Court No 1. Brig HD6 115 B3 6
Lane Court No 2. Brig HD6 115 B3 7
Lane End. Bail BD17 38 C3
Lane End Croft. Leeds LS17 42 F5
Lane End Ct. Leeds LS17 42 F5
Lane End Fold. Pudsey LS28 76 F8
Lane End La. Bacup OL13 106 A1 2
Lane End Mount. Pudsey LS28 76 F8
Lane End Pl. Leeds LS11 79 B5
Lane End. Pudsey LS28 76 F8
Lane End Rd. Bacup OL13 106 A1
Lane End. Thorn BD13 72 D6
Lane Ends Cl. Brad BD8 73 F8
Lane Ends Cl. Hem WF9 163 A4
Lane Ends Gn. Brig HX3 114 C8
Lane Ends. Hali HX2, HX3 91 E2
Lane Ends La. Wad M HX7 89 C4
Lane Ends Terr. Brig HX3 114 C8
Lane Ends View. Loft G WF3 121 E5
Lane Fox Ct. Yeadon LS19 40 B6 7
Lane Hackings. D Dale HD8 191 E7
Lane Hackings Gn. D Dale HD8 191 E7
Lane Head Cl. Mapp S75 178 A2
Lane Head. Hep HX7 88 E5
Lane Head La. Hali HX2 91 D8
Lane Head La. Kirkb HD8 173 F6
Lane Head Rd. Caw S75 193 D3
Lane Head Rd. Rip HX6 132 C5
Lane Head Rd. Shep HD8 190 E7
Lane Head Rise. Mapp S75 178 A2
Lane House Gr. Hali HX2 111 E8
Lane Ings. Mars HD7 169 A4
Lane Side. Bacup OL13 106 A4
Lane Side Cl. Brad BD12 94 C4
Lane Side La. Kirkhe HD5 155 D7
Lane Side. Queen BD13 72 D3
Lane Side. Wils BD15 53 C4
Lane The. Leeds LS17 42 F5
Lane The. Leeds LS9 79 E7
Lane Top. Denh BD13 52 D2
Lane Top. Hud HD7 152 E1
Lanes The. Pudsey LS28 76 F8
Laneside Cl. Morley LS27 98 B7
Laneside. Elland HX4 134 A4
Laneside Fold. Morley LS27 98 B7 11
Laneside Gdns. Morley LS27 98 B7
Laneside. Kirkb HD8 174 A6
Laneside. Morley LS27 98 B7
Laneside St. Tod OL14 108 A4
Lang Kirk Cl. Farnh BD20 4 E1
Lang La. Ship BD2 55 D5
Langbar App. Leeds LS14 62 D6
Langbar Ave. Brad BD9 54 D3
Langbar Cl. Leeds LS14 62 D6
Langbar Garth. Leeds LS14 62 D6
Langbar Gdns. Leeds LS14 62 D5 2
Langbar Gn. Leeds LS14 62 D6
Langbar Gr. Leeds LS14 62 D5
Langbar Grange. Leeds LS14 62 D5 14
Langbar Pl. Leeds LS14 62 D6
Langbar Rd. Ilkley LS29 8 A6
Langbar Rd. Leeds LS14 62 D5
Langbar Sq. Leeds LS14 62 D5 1
Langbar Towers. Leeds LS14 62 D5 3
Langbar View. Leeds LS14 62 D6
Langcliffe Cl. Mapp S75 178 A2
Langdale Ave. Brad BD8 73 E8
Langdale Ave. Brig BD12 94 E1
Langdale Ave. Leeds LS6 59 C4
Langdale Ave. Loft G WF1 121 D5
Langdale Ave. Nor WF6 123 A4
Langdale Cl. Castle WF10 104 E2
Langdale Cl. Weth LS22 13 D6
Langdale Cres. Hali HX2 91 E1
Langdale Ct. Bing BD16 37 A4
Langdale Dr. Ack M T WF7 164 C7
Langdale Dr. Hud HD5 154 D7
Langdale Dr. Nor WF6 123 A4
Langdale Dr. Queen BD13 72 D1 2
Langdale Dr. Wake WF2 141 F6
Langdale Gdns. Leeds LS6 59 C4
Langdale Jun & Inf Sch. Roth 101 B7
Langdale Mews. Nor WF6 123 A4
Langdale Mount. Walton WF2 161 A6
Langdale Rd. Batley WF12 118 F2
Langdale Rd. Brad BD10 56 E4
Langdale Rd. Roth LS26 101 B6
Langdale Sq. Wake WF2 141 F6
Langdale St. Elland HX5 134 C4
Langdale Terr. Leeds LS6 59 C4
Langford Cl. Bur in W LS29 9 E1
Langford Ct. Bur in W LS29 9 E1
Langford La. Bur in W LS29 9 F1
Langford Mews. Bur in W LS29 9 E1
Langford Rd. Bur in W LS29 9 E1
Langford Ride. Bur in W LS29 9 F1
Langlands Rd. Ship BD16 54 A7
Langlea Terr. Brig HX3 114 C8
Langley Ave. Bing BD16
Langley Ave. Brad
La
La
Lar
Lan
Lang
Lang
Lang
Langw
Langw
Lansda
Lansdo
Lansdo
Lansdow
Lansdow
Lansdow
Lanshaw
Lanshaw
Lanshaw
Lanshaw C
Lanshaw Pl
Lanshaw Rd
Lanshaw Te
Lanshaw Vie
Lapage Mid S
Lapage St. Br
Lapage Terr. B
Lapwing Cl. Br
Larch Ave. Holn
Larch Cl. Batley
Larch Cl. Haw B
Larch Cl. Kirkhe
Larch Cl. Liver W
Larch Cl. Nor WF6
Larch Ct. Castle W
Larch Dale. Hud HD
Larch Dr. Brad BD6
Larch Gr. Bing BD16
Larch Hill. Brad BD6
Larch Hill Cres. Brad
Larch La. Gar LS25
Larch Rd. Hud HD1
Larch St. Keigh BD21
Larch Wood. Scar LS14
Larchfield Rd. Leeds LS
Larchmont. Brad BD14
Larchmont Fst Sch. Brad
Lark Hill Ave. Clec BD19
Lark Hill. Batley WF17
Lark Hill Cl. Clec BD19
Lark Hill Dr. Clec BD19
Lark St. Bing BD16
Lark St. Haw BD22
Lark St. Haw BD22 51 D7
Lark St. Keigh BD21 35 B7
Larkfield Ave. Yeadon LS19 40 C4
Larkfield Cres. Yeadon LS19 40 C4
Larkfield Dr. Yeadon LS19 40 C4
Larkfield Mount. Yeadon LS19 40 C4
Larkfield Rd. Pudsey LS28 76 E8
Larkfield Rd. Yeadon LS19 40 C4
Larkfield Terr. Keigh BD21 35 E6
Larkhill Cl. Leeds LS8 60 E8
Larkhill Gn. Leeds LS8 43 E1
Larkhill Rd. Leeds LS8 43 E1
Larkhill View. Leeds LS8 60 E8
Larkhill Way. Leeds LS8 43 E1
Larkhill Wlk. Leeds LS8 43 E1
Larks Hill. Pont WF8 146 B6
Larwood Ave. Brad BD10 56 E4
Lascelles Hall Rd. Kirkhe HD5 155 C6
Lascelles Mount. Leeds LS8 60 F3 7
Lascelles Pl. Leeds LS8 60 F3 5
Lascelles Rd. Batley WF16 117 E3
Lascelles Rd E. Leeds LS8 60 F3 8
Lascelles Rd W. Leeds LS8 60 F3 10
Lascelles St. Leeds LS8 60 F3 4
Lascelles Terr. Leeds LS8 60 F3 2
Lascelles View. Leeds LS8 60 F3 6
Lastingham Gn. Brad BD6 73 E1
Lastingham Rd. Pudsey LS13 57 F5
Latchmere Ave. Leeds LS16 58 F8
Latchmere Cl. Leeds LS16 59 A8
Latchmere Crest. Leeds LS16 58 F8 4
Latchmere Cross. Leeds LS16 58 F8 3
Latchmere Dr. Leeds LS16 58 F8
Latchmere Gdns. Leeds LS16 59 A8
Latchmere Gn. Leeds LS16 58 F8 5
Latchmere Rd. Leeds LS16 58 F8
Latchmere View. Leeds LS16 58 F8
Latchmere Wlk. Leeds LS16 59 A8 4
Latchmore Rd. Leeds LS12 78 E4
Latchmore Road Ind Est. Leeds 78 E4
Latham Ct. Clec BD19 96 B2
Latham La. Clec BD19 96 A2
Latham Lea. Clec BD19 96 A2
Latimer St. Brad BD3 75 D6
Launceston Dr. Brad BD4 75 E2
Laund Rd. Hud HD3 134 E1
Laund Rd. Mars HD7 151 C3
Laund Rd. Slai HD7 151 C3
Launton Way. Brad BD5 74 D4
Laura St. Brig HD6 115 A1 8
Laura St. Hali HX3 92 C1 4
Laura St. Leeds LS12 78 F6
Laurel Bank. Brig BD12 115 C8
Laurel Bank Cl. Hali HX2 92 A6
Laurel Bank Ct. Leeds LS6 59 C4
Laurel Bank. Hali HX1 113 A5 14
Laurel Cl. E Kes LS17 28 C5
Laurel Cl. Elland HX5 134 E6
Laurel Cl. Shelf HX3 93 C6
Laurel Cres. Hali HX2 91 F3
Laurel Cres. Keigh BD21 35 B8
Laurel Ct. Ossett WF5 140 C6
Laurel Dr. Batley WF17 118 A7
ds LS12 78 C7 8
WF17 117 F7
D16 36 E5
D21 35 B8
S12 78 C7
5 D1
ds LS15 81 D7
ds LS15 81 D7
ds LS15 81 D7
LS15 81 D7
s LS15 81 D7
LS15 81 D6
F10 124 E7 4
16 117 D4
113 A5 17
60 D5
76 E8
67 C4
78 C7
75 C6
113 A5
78 C7
133 F4
78 C7
76 E8
139 F7
60 F7
1 D7
9 F4
7 E4
1 D6
C5
F7
E2
C3 6
D5
E5
5
Lawns La. Loft G WF2 120 E6
Lawns Mount. Gild LS12 77 D3
Lawns Park Prim Sch. Leeds 77 E5
Lawns Sq. Gild LS12 77 D3
Lawns Terr. E Ard WF3 120 D7
Lawns Terr. Gild LS12 77 D3
Lawns The. Batley WF16 117 E4
Lawns The. Ilkley LS29 8 A4
Lawns The. Neth WF4 158 A6
Lawns View. Nor WF6 122 E4
Lawnswood Gdns. Hors LS16 42 B2
Lawnswood Rd. Keigh BD21 35 A5
Lawnswood Sch. Leeds 59 B8
Lawrence Ave. Leeds LS8 61 C4
Lawrence Cres. Batley WF16 117 D6
Lawrence Cres. Leeds LS8 61 C5
Lawrence Dr. Brad BD7 73 E2
Lawrence Gdns. Leeds LS8 61 C5
Lawrence Rd. Hali HX3 113 B3
Lawrence Rd. Hud HD1 153 E6
Lawrence Rd. Leeds LS8 61 C4
Lawrence St. Hali HX3 92 A1 14
Lawrence Wlk. Leeds LS8 61 C4
Lawson House. Brad BD6 93 E8 6
Lawson Rd. Brig HD6 115 B2
Lawson St. Brad BD3 74 F8 1
Lawson St. Leeds LS12 78 B7 2
Lawton St. Hud HD4 154 A3
Lay Garth Cl. Roth LS26 100 E5
Lay Garth Gdns. Roth LS26 100 E4
Lay Garth Gn. Roth LS26 100 E4
Lay Garth Mead. Roth LS26 100 E4
Lay Garth Pl. Roth LS26 100 E4
Lay Garth. Roth LS26 100 E5
Lay Garth Sq. Roth LS26 100 E4
Laycock Fst Sch. Keigh 34 C7
Laycock La. Keigh BD22 34 C7
Laycock Pl. Leeds LS7 60 D3
Laygarth Dr. Kirkhe HD5 155 C6
Laythorp Terr. Keigh BD20 19 D1
Laythorpe Ct. Pont WF8 147 A7
Layton Ave. Yeadon LS19 40 E3
Layton Cl. Yeadon LS19 40 E2
Layton Cres. Yeadon LS19 40 D3
Layton Dr. Yeadon LS19 40 E3
Layton La. Yeadon LS19 40 E3
Layton Mount. Yeadon LS19 40 D3
Layton Park Ave. Yeadon LS19 40 E2
Layton Park Cl. Yeadon LS19 40 D3
Layton Park Croft. Yeadon LS19 40 E2
Layton Park Dr. Yeadon LS19 40 E2
Layton Rd. Yeadon LS18, LS19 40 E3
Layton Rise. Yeadon LS18 40 F3
Lazenby Dr. Weth LS22 13 D6
Lazenby Fold. Weth LS22 13 D6
Le Marchant Ave. Hud HD3 153 C8
Lea Ave. Hali HX3 113 C3
Lea Cl. Brig HD6 115 A4
Lea Croft. B Spa LS23 30 D5
Lea Croft. Otley LS21 23 A7
Lea Ct. Brad BD7 73 E2
Lea Dr. Shep HD8 190 F8
Lea Farm Cres. Leeds LS5 58 F6
Lea Farm Dr. Leeds LS5 58 F6
Lea Farm Gr. Leeds LS5 58 F6
Lea Farm Mount. Leeds LS5 58 F7
Lea Farm Pl. Leeds LS5 58 F6
Lea Farm Rd. Leeds LS5 58 F6
Lea Farm Row. Leeds LS5 58 F6
Lea Farm Wlk. Leeds LS5 58 F7
Lea Gdns. Holmfi HD7 189 E4
Lea La. Feath WF7 145 E4
Lea La. Hud HD4 171 C6
Lea Mill Park Cl. Yeadon LS19 40 A7
Lea Mill Park Dr. Yeadon LS19 40 A7
Lea Park Cl. Midd LS10 99 F7
Lea Park Croft. Midd LS10 100 A7
Lea Park Dr. Midd LS10 99 F7
Lea Park Garth. Midd LS10 99 F7 2
Lea Park Gdns. Midd LS10 99 F7 1
Lea Park Gr. Midd LS10 99 F7
Lea Park Vale. Midd LS10 100 A7
Lea Rd. Batley WF17 117 F8
Lea Rise. Honley HD7 171 F3
Lea Side Gdns. Hud HD3 152 E7
Lea St. Hud HD3 135 C1
Lea St. Hud HD1 136 A1
Lea St. Hud HD1 154 A8
Lea The. Gar LS25 82 F5
Lea View. Batley WF17 117 F8
Leabank Ave. Gar LS25 83 A5
Leach Cres. Keigh BD20 18 E2
Leach Rd. Keigh BD20 18 D2
Leach Rise. Keigh BD20 18 E2
Leach Way. Keigh BD20 18 E2
Leadenhall St. Hali HX1 112 F5 17
Leadwell La. Roth LS26 100 C4
Leaf St. Castle WF10 124 C7
Leaf St. Haw BD22 51 E8 4
Leafield Ave. Brad BD2 56 C3
Leafield Ave. Hud HD3 152 E6
Leafield Bank. Hud HD3 152 E6
Leafield Cl. Hud HD2 136 D4
Leafield Cl. Leeds LS17 43 B2
Leafield Cres. Brad BD2 56 B3
Leafield Dr. Brad BD2 56 C4
Leafield Dr. Leeds LS17 43 B2
Leafield Dr. Pudsey LS28 76 F5 2
Leafield Gr. Brad BD2 56 C3
eafield Grange. Leeds LS17 43 B2
eafield Pl. Yeadon LS19 39 F7
afield Terr. Brad BD2 56 C3
field Way. Brad BD2 56 C3
and St. Hali HX1 113 A7
Pl. Leeds LS12 78 F6
all La. D Dale HD8 192 A6
ll Rd. D Dale HD8 191 F6
t. Castle WF10 124 E7
gton Dr. Brad BD10 56 C8
ton Rd. Ilkley LS29 8 C5
ton St. Brad BD9 55 B2
ton Terr. Dew WF12 139 D6
ton Terr. Ilkley LS29 8 C5
St. Hud HD1 154 B7
e. Holmfi HD7 188 F7
Dr. Thorn BD13 72 D7
e Ave. Leeds LS10 79 E2
we Cl. Leeds LS10 79 E2
owe Ct. Leeds LS10 79 E2 9
sowe Garth. Leeds LS10 79 E2
asowe Gdns. Leeds LS10 79 F2
easowe Rd. Leeds LS10 79 E2
Leatham Ave. Feath WF7 145 E4
Leatham Cres. Feath WF7 145 F4
Leatham Dr. Feath WF7 145 F4
Leatham Park Rd. Feath WF7 145 F4
Leather Bank. Bur in W LS29 9 E3
Leathley Ave. Men LS29 22 B4
Leathley Cres. Men LS29 22 B4
Leathley La. Leath LS21 24 B8
Leathley La. Men LS29 22 B4
Leathley Rd. Leeds LS10 79 D5
Leathley Rd. Men LS29 22 B4
Leathley St. Leeds LS10 79 D5
Leavens The. Brad BD10 56 D8
Leaventhorpe Ave. Brad BD8 73 D7
Leaventhorpe Cl. Brad BD8 73 D7
Leaventhorpe Gr. Brad BD13 73 C6
Leaventhorpe La. Brad BD13, BD8 73 C6
Leaventhorpe Mid Sch. Brad 73 B7
Leaventhorpe Way. Brad BD8 73 D7
Leaverholme Cl. H Chap BB10 85 A7
Leavington Cl. Brad BD6 94 B6
Leconfield Ct. Weth LS22 13 C6
Leconfield House. Brad BD10 56 C7
Ledbury Ave. Midd LS10 99 F4
Ledbury Cl. Midd LS10 99 F4 4
Ledbury Croft. Midd LS10 99 F4 3
Ledbury Dr. Midd LS10 99 F4
Ledbury Gn. Midd LS10 99 F4 1
Ledbury Gr. Midd LS10 99 F4 2
Ledgard Bridge Mills Ind Units. Mir 138 A3
Ledgard Dr. Crig WF4 159 F7
Ledgard Way. Leeds LS12 78 C8
Ledgate La. B Sal LS25 105 E4
Ledger La. Loft G WF1 121 B4
Ledger La. Roth WF3 100 C1
Ledger Pl. Loft G WF1 121 B4
Ledston Ave. Gar LS25 83 A5
Ledston Lady Elizabeth Hastings CE Sch. Ledst 103 E6
Ledston Luck Cotts. Ledst LS25 83 E2
Ledston Luck Enterprise Pk. Ledst 83 D2
Ledston Luck Villas. Ledst LS25 83 D2
Ledston Mill La. Ledst WF10 103 E4
Ledston Mill La. Ledst WF10 103 E7
Lee Bank. Hali HX3 92 B1
Lee Beck Gr. Loft G WF3 121 E8
Lee Bottom Rd. Tod OL14 109 A5
Lee Bridge. Hali HX3 113 B8
Lee Brig. Nor WF6 122 F3
Lee Cl. Wils BD15 53 C6
Lee Clough Dr. Heb Br HX7 89 F1
Lee Ct. Keigh BD21 35 F6
Lee Ct. Liver WF15 117 A5 10
Lee Ct. Ossett WF5 140 F4
Lee Gn. Mir WF14 138 A6
Lee Hall Rd. Hud HD3 135 C1
Lee Head. Hud HD2 153 F8
Lee La. Ack M T WF7 164 B8
Lee La E. Hors LS18 41 B2
Lee La. Hali HX3 92 D3
Lee La. Hors LS18 41 B2
Lee La. Kirkb HD8 173 E6
Lee La. Mapp S71 178 E2
Lee La. Roy S71 178 E2
Lee La. Tod OL14 108 F3
Lee La W. Hors LS18 41 A2
Lee La. Wh Com S30 200 F4
Lee La. Wils BD16 53 E6
Lee Mill Rd. Wad M HX7 89 A5
Lee Mills Ind Est. Hali 113 B8
Lee Moor La. Loft G WF3 121 E8
Lee Moor Rd. Loft G WF3 121 F6
Lee Mount Gdns. Hali HX3 92 A1 5
Lee Mount Inf Sch. Hali 92 A1
Lee Mount Jun & Inf Sch. Hali 92 A1
Lee Mount Rd. Hali HX3 92 A1
Lee Orchards. B Spa LS23 30 E8
Lee Rd. Dew WF13 138 D5
Lee St. Brad BD1 74 E6
Lee St. Brig HD6 115 A4
Lee St. Dew WF13 138 E6
Lee St. Liver WF15 117 A5
Lee St. Queen BD13 92 D8 7
Lee St. Wake WF1 142 C6
Lee Way. Kirkb HD8 173 E7
Lee Wood Rd. Hep HX7 88 F5
Leech La. Harden BD13 53 A8
Leeches Hill. Hud HD3 134 C1
Leeds 27 Ind Est. Morley 97 E5
Leeds and Bradford Rd. Leeds LS13 58 C4
Leeds & Bradford International Airport. Yeadon 40 F7
Leeds Bsns Pk. Morley 97 E4
Leeds Coll of Building. Leeds 60 D1
Leeds Coll of Building. Leeds 61 F4
Leeds Coll of Technology. Leeds 60 B1
Leeds Combined Court Ctr. Leeds 79 B8
Leeds Crem. Hors 42 B3
Leeds Girls' High Sch. Leeds 59 F4
Leeds Golf Ctr. Hare 44 B8
Leeds Grammar Sch (Jun). Leeds 59 F1
Leeds Grammar Sch. Leeds 59 F2
Leeds Jewish Day Sch. Leeds 43 D3
Leeds La. Swil LS26 82 B4
Leeds Metropolitan Univ. Leeds 59 B6
Leeds Metropolitan Univ. Leeds 60 B1
Leeds Old Rd. Batley WF16 117 D6
Leeds Old Rd. Brad BD3 75 E8
Leeds Polytechnic. Leeds 59 C6
Leeds Polytechnic. Leeds 60 C1
Leeds Rd. B in Elm LS15 63 B6
Leeds Rd. Batley WF17 97 B2
Leeds Rd. Brad BD10 39 B2
Leeds Rd. Brad BD2 56 B3
Leeds Rd. Brad BD2 56 C2
Leeds Rd. Brad BD1& BD3 75 C6
Leeds Rd. Bramho LS16 24 D4
Leeds Rd. Brig HX3 114 E8
Leeds Rd. Castle WF10 124 D5
Leeds Rd. Coll LS22 29 A8
Leeds Rd. Dew WF12 118 E1
Leeds Rd. E Ard WF12 119 B5
Leeds Rd. Guise LS20 39 E8
Leeds Rd. Hud HD2 136 F2
Leeds Rd. Ilkley LS29 8 D5
Leeds Rd. Kippax LS25 83 A2
Leeds Rd. Kippax WF10 103 A5
Leeds Rd. Liver WF16 117 C5
Leeds Rd. Loft G WF1 121 C5
Leeds Rd. Loft G WF3 121 C6
Leeds Rd. M'town LS26 102 B3
Leeds Rd. Northo HX3 114 A8
Leeds Rd. Ossett WF5 119 C1
Leeds Rd. Ossett WF5 140 C8
Leeds Rd. Otley LS21 23 D6
Leeds Rd. Pool LS16 24 D4
Leeds Rd. Roth LS26, WF3 100 B2
Leeds Rd. Roth LS26 100 F7

Long Gate. Rip HX6 ... 150 A8
Long Gate. S in Cra BD20 ... 33 B8
Long Grove Ave. Hud HD5 ... 154 C6
Long Hey La. Tod OL14 ... 108 C3
Long Heys. Elland HX4 ... 134 C6
Long Hill End. Cowl BD22 ... 32 D8
Long Hill Rd. Hud HD2 ... 136 C4
Long House Rd. Hain HD7 ... 91 C6
Long Ing Rd. Holmfi HD7 ... 199 A7
Long La. Ack M T WF7 ... 146 B1
Long La. B in Elm LS15 ... 63 E5
Long La. Brad BD15 ... 53 D1
Long La. Clay W HD8 ... 175 F3
Long La. Dew WF12 ... 139 F6
Long La. Floc WF4 ... 156 B1
Long La. Hali HX2, HX3 ... 91 E2
Long La. Hali HX3 ... 113 F6
Long La. Harden BD16 ... 36 A1
Long La. Heb Br HX7 ... 88 B8
Long La. Hud HD7 ... 109 D3
Long La. Hud HD5 ... 154 E7
Long La. K Smea WF8 ... 166 D3
Long La. Pont WF7, WF8 ... 146 F7
Long La. Queen BD13 ... 92 E7
Long La. Shep HD8 ... 173 E2
Long La. Ship BD9 ... 54 F5
Long La. Sower HX6 ... 112 A2
Long Lee Fst Sch. Keigh ... 35 F5
Long Lee La. Keigh BD21 ... 35 F5
Long Lover La. Hali HX1 ... 112 F8
Long Meadow Ct. Gar LS25 ... 83 A5
Long Meadow Gate. Gar LS25 ... 82 F5
Long Meadows. Brad BD2 ... 55 E4
Long Meadows. Bramho LS16 ... 24 F3
Long Meadows. Gar LS25 ... 82 F5
Long Moor La. Shep HD8 ... 174 B1
Long Reach. Hali HX2 ... 91 F1
Long Riddings. Add LS29 ... 2 E1
Long Ridge. Brig HD6 ... 136 A7
Long Row. Brad BD12 ... 94 C5
Long Row. Crof WF4 ... 144 A5
Long Row Ct. Brad BD5 ... 74 E3
Long Row. Hors LS18 ... 41 C2
Long Row. Thorn BD13 ... 72 C7
Long Royd Dr. Bail BD17 ... 38 E4
Long Royd La. Shep HD8 ... 191 B8
Long Royd Rd. Sow Br HX6 ... 112 C7
Long Shaw La. Tod OL14 ... 108 F4
Long St. Brad BD4 ... 75 B5
Long Thorpe La. Roth WF3 ... 100 B1
Long Tongue Scrog La. Kirkhe HD5 ... 155 E7
Long Tongue Scrog La. Lepton WF14 ... 155 F6
Long Wall. Elland HX5 ... 134 D6
Longacre. Castle WF10 ... 124 D6
Longbottom Ave. Sil BD20 ... 5 F1
Longbottom Ave. Sow Br HX6 ... 111 E3
Longbottom Terr. Hali HX3 ... 113 A4
Longcauseway. Dew WF12 ... 139 D7
Longclose Ind Est. Leeds ... 60 D2
Longcroft. Leeds LS6 ... 154 F2
Longcroft Jun Sch. Hud ... 154 F2
Longcroft. Keigh BD21 ... 35 C6
Longcroft Link. Brad BD1 ... 74 D7
Longcroft Pl. Brad BD1 ... 74 D7
Longcroft Rd. Ilkley LS29 ... 8 E3
Longdale Dr. S Elm WF9 ... 182 E4
Longden Ave. Hud HD4 ... 153 D2
Longdike Ct. Kippax LS25 ... 83 B1
Longdike Ct. Kippax LS25 ... 103 C8
Longdon Ave. Lepton HD8 ... 155 E3
Longdon Wk. Lepton HD8 ... 155 E3
Longfellow Gr. Loft WF3 ... 121 E6
Longfield Ave. Hud HD7 ... 152 E7
Longfield Ave. Pudsey LS28 ... 76 E6
Longfield Cl. Hud HD5 ... 154 D7
Longfield Ct. Mapp S75 ... 178 B1
Longfield Dr. Pudsey LS13 ... 57 F5
Longfield. Elland HX4 ... 134 C7
Longfield Garth. Pudsey LS13 ... 57 F5
Longfield Gr. Pudsey LS28 ... 76 F7
Longfield. Hud HD7 ... 152 E7
Longfield Rd. Tod OL14 ... 108 B3
Longfield Rd. Pudsey LS28 ... 76 E7
Longfield Terr. Pudsey LS28 ... 76 F7
Longfield Terr. Tod OL14 ... 108 B4
Longfield Terr. Wake WF2 ... 141 F7
Longfield Way. Tod OL14 ... 108 B4
Longford Terr. Brad BD7 ... 73 F5
Longhouse Dr. Denh BD13 ... 71 D8
Longhouse La. Denh BD13 ... 71 D8
Longlands Ave. Denh BD13 ... 52 D1
Longlands Dr. Haw BD22 ... 51 C6
Longlands Dr. Mapp S75 ... 178 B1
Longlands La. Sickl LS22 ... 12 D4
Longlands Rd. Batley WF13 ... 118 A2
Longlands Rd. Ossett WF5 ... 140 F6
Longlands Rd. Slai HD7 ... 151 E1
Longlands St. Brad BD1 ... 74 D7
Longlands Trad Est. Ossett ... 140 E6
Longley Edge La. Holmfi HD7 ... 189 B1
Longley Edge Rd. Holmfi HD7 ... 189 B1
Longley. Hud HD4 ... 154 A2
Longley La. Hud HD4 ... 154 A1
Longley La. Sow Br HX6 ... 111 F1
Longley Golf Course. Hud ... 154 C4
Longley Rd. Hud HD5 ... 154 D4
Longmeadow. Rip HX4 ... 133 D4
Longroyd Ave. Leeds LS11 ... 79 C3
Longroyd Cres. Leeds LS11 ... 79 C3
Longroyd Cres N. Leeds LS11 ... 79 C3
Longroyd Cres. Slai HD7 ... 152 A3
Longroyd Gr. Leeds LS11 ... 79 C3
Longroyd. Hud HD4 ... 153 D3
Longroyd Pl. Leeds LS11 ... 79 C3
Longroyd Pl. Hud HD4 ... 153 D3
Longroyd St. Leeds LS11 ... 79 C3
Longroyd St N. Leeds LS11 ... 79 C3
Longroyd Terr. Leeds LS11 ... 79 C3
Longroyd View. Leeds LS11 ... 79 C3
Longroyde Cl. Brig HD6 ... 114 F1
Longroyde Gr. Brig HD6 ... 114 F1
Longroyde Jun & Inf Sch. Brig ... 114 F1
Longroyde Rd. Brig HD6 ... 115 A1
Longside La. Brad BD7 ... 74 C6

Longsight Rd. Mapp S75 ... 178 A1
Longsight Terr. Hem WF9 ... 163 B1
Longwood Ave. Bing BD16 ... 36 E5
Longwood Cl. E Ard WF3 ... 119 D8
Longwood Cl. Leeds LS17 ... 44 B5
Longwood Cres. Leeds LS17 ... 44 B5
Longwood Ct. E Ard WF3 ... 119 E8
Longwood Edge Rd. Hud HD3 ... 152 E7
Longwood Fold. E Ard WF3 ... 119 E8
Longwood Garth. E Ard WF3 ... 119 E8
Longwood Gate. Hud HD3 ... 152 E6
Longwood House Rd. Hud HD2 ... 136 A3
Longwood Rd. E Ard WF3 ... 119 E8
Longwood Rd. Hud HD3 ... 153 C5
Longwood Vale. E Ard WF3 ... 119 E8
Longwood View. Bing BD16 ... 36 E5
Longwood Way. Leeds LS17 ... 44 B5
Longwoods Wlk. Knot WF11 ... 127 A5
Lonsbrough Ave. Batley WF16 ... 117 D5
Lonsbrough Flats. Hud HD1 ... 154 B7
Lonsdale Ave. Batley WF17 ... 117 F7
Lonsdale Meadows. B Spa LS23 ... 30 D7
Lonsdale Rd. E Ard WF3 ... 119 E8
Lonsdale Rise. E Ard WF3 ... 119 E8
Lonsdale St. Brad BD3 ... 75 B8
Lord La. Haw BD22 ... 33 E8
Lord St. Batley WF17 ... 117 F4
Lord St. Dew WF12 ... 140 B2
Lord St. Hali HX1 ... 113 C7
Lord St. Haw BD22 ... 51 D7
Lord St. Hud HD1 ... 154 B6
Lord St. Keigh BD21 ... 35 C7
Lord St. Leeds LS12 ... 78 B3
Lord St. Slai HD7 ... 151 F1
Lord St. Tod OL14 ... 108 A1
Lord St. Wake WF1 ... 142 F3
Lord Terr. Leeds LS12 ... 78 F6
Lord's Bldgs. Morley LS27 ... 98 A2
Lord's La. Brig HD6 ... 115 B1
Lordsfield Pl. Brad BD4 ... 95 C8
Loris St. Brad BD4 ... 75 D1
Lorne Fst Sch. Brad ... 75 B3
Lorne St. Brad BD4 ... 75 B3
Lorne St. Haw BD22 ... 51 F8
Lorne St. Keigh BD21 ... 35 E5
Lorry Bank. Leeds LS7 ... 60 C4
Lorry Ct. Leeds LS7 ... 60 C4
Loscoe La. Feath WF6, WF7 ... 124 A1
Loscoe La. Nor WF6 ... 123 E3
Lotherton Hall. Aber ... 65 B5
Lotherton La. Aber LS25 ... 65 B5
Lotherton Way. Gar LS25 ... 83 A8
Loughrigg St. Brad BD5 ... 74 E3
Louis Ave. Brad BD5 ... 74 C4
Louis Ct. Leeds LS7 ... 60 E3
Louis Gr. Leeds LS7 ... 60 E3
Louis Le Prince Ct. Leeds LS8 ... 60 F3
Louis St. Leeds LS7 ... 60 E3
Louisa St. Castle WF10 ... 124 C8
Lound La. H Pag DN5 ... 195 F5
Lovaine Gr. Wake WF2 ... 142 D1
Love La. Castle WF10 ... 124 D8
Love La. Hali HX1 ... 113 A2
Love La. Ossett WF5 ... 141 C6
Love La. Pont WF8 ... 146 B8
Love La. Wake WF2 ... 142 B5
Love Lane Terr. Pont WF8 ... 146 C8
Lovell Park Cl. Leeds LS7 ... 60 D1
Lovell Park Ct. Leeds LS7 ... 60 C1
Lovell Park Gr. Leeds LS7 ... 60 C1
Lovell Park Grange. Leeds LS7 ... 60 C1
Lovell Park Heights. Leeds LS7 ... 60 D1
Lovell Park Hts. Leeds LS7 ... 60 D1
Lovell Park Rd. Leeds LS7 ... 60 C1
Lovell Park Towers. Leeds LS7 ... 60 D1
Lovell Park View. Leeds LS7 ... 60 D1
Low Ash Ave. Ship BD18 ... 55 D7
Low Ash Cres. Ship BD18 ... 55 D7
Low Ash Dr. Ship BD18 ... 55 D7
Low Ash Gr. Ship BD18 ... 55 D7
Low Ash Rd. Ship BD18 ... 55 E7
Low Bank Dr. Haw BD22 ... 51 C6
Low Bank La. Oxen BD22 ... 51 B3
Low Bank Rd. Keigh BD21 ... 35 F6
Low Bank St. Pudsey LS28 ... 57 D3
Low Cl. Ilkley LS29 ... 8 D4
Low Cliff Wlk. Batley WF16 ... 117 E2
Low Close St. Leeds LS2 ... 60 A3
Low Farm La. Ack M T WF7 ... 164 C6
Low Farm La. Nor WF6 ... 123 A3
Low Farm La. Wool WF4 ... 177 F6
Low Farn La. Sil BD20 ... 5 F1
Low Fields Ave. Leeds LS11 ... 79 A6
Low Fields Rd. Leeds LS11 ... 78 E6
Low Fields Rd. Leeds LS12 ... 78 C6
Low Fields Way. Leeds LS11 ... 78 E4
Low Fold. Batley WF17 ... 96 F1
Low Fold. Bing BD16 ... 37 A2
Low Fold. Brad BD2 ... 56 C3
Low Fold. Denh BD13 ... 52 D2
Low Fold. Leeds LS19 ... 40 B4
Low Fold Rise. Brad BD2 ... 56 C3
Low Gate. Kirkb HD8 ... 173 F4
Low Gate La. Densh OL3 ... 183 A3
Low Gate. S Elm WF9 ... 183 A3
Low Gipton Cres. Leeds LS8 ... 61 C5
Low Grange. Ack M T WF7 ... 164 B5
Low Grange Cres. Midd LS10 ... 79 F1
Low Grange Rd. Dearne S63 ... 194 C1
Low Grange View. Midd LS10 ... 99 F8
Low Green. Brad BD7 ... 74 C6
Low Green Terr. Brad BD7 ... 74 C6
Low Hall Cl. Men LS29 ... 22 A4
Low Hall Pl. Leeds LS11 ... 79 A6
Low Hall Rd. Men LS29 ... 22 A4
Low Hall Rd. Yeadon LS18 ... 57 B8
Low Hill. Bail BD17 ... 37 F1
Low Hills La. Hud HD3 ... 153 B6
Low House Dr. Sil BD20 ... 17 C8
Low House Fold. Liver WF15 ... 116 F4
Low La. Brad BD14 ... 73 B5
Low La. Draug BD23 ... 1 E7
Low La. Embsay BD23 ... 1 E7
Low La. Hali HX3 ... 114 C5
Low La. Hors LS18 ... 41 D1
Low La. Neth WF4 ... 158 B8

Low La. Queen BD13 ... 72 C3
Low La. Sil BD20 ... 5 C5
Low La. Sil BD20 ... 18 A6
Low La. Thorn BD13 ... 73 A5
Low La. Wad M HX2 ... 90 A7
Low Laithes Golf Course. Wake ... 141 B7
Low Mill La. Add LS29 ... 7 B8
Low Mill La. Keigh BD21 ... 35 D7
Low Mill Rd. Ossett WF5 ... 140 C3
Low Mills Rd. Leeds LS12 ... 78 B4
Low Moor Cl. Brad ... 94 E6
Low Moor Fst Sch. Brad ... 94 E6
Low Moor La. Crig WF4 ... 159 E1
Low Moor Side La. Leeds LS12 ... 77 C2
Low Moor St. Brad BD12 ... 94 D6
Low Moor Terr. Hali HX2 ... 112 D7
Low Moorside Cl. Leeds LS12 ... 77 C3
Low Moorside Ct. Leeds LS12 ... 77 D3
Low Park Rd. Denton LS29 ... 9 B5
Low Platt La. Mars HD3 ... 150 C7
Low Rd. Dew WF13 ... 138 F8
Low Rd. Dew WF12 ... 139 C1
Low Rd. Leeds LS10 ... 80 A1
Low Road Prim Sch. Leeds ... 79 F3
Low Row. Mapp S75 ... 178 C1
Low Shops La. Roth LS26 ... 100 C6
Low Spring Rd. Keigh BD21 ... 35 F6
Low St. Broth WF11 ... 126 C7
Low St. E Ard WF3 ... 98 F1
Low St. St. E Ard WF13 ... 98 F1
Low Town. Kirkb HD8 ... 173 F4
Low Way. B Spa LS23 ... 30 D6
Low Way. Brarnham LS23 ... 30 D2
Low Well Rd. Brad BD5 ... 74 D3
Low Whitehouse Row. Leeds LS10 ... 80 A7
Low Wood Cl. Keigh BD20 ... 18 A3
Low Wood Rise. Ilkley LS29 ... 8 F3
Low Wood. Wils BD15 ... 53 D4
Lowcroft. Coll LS22 ... 29 A8
Lowdale. Batley WF12 ... 118 E2
Lowell Ave. Brad BD7 ... 73 F5
Lowell Gr. Pudsey LS13 ... 77 A8
Lowell Pl. Pudsey LS13 ... 77 A8
Lower Ashgrove. Brad BD5 ... 74 D6
Lower Back La. B Head HX7 ... 87 F4
Lower Bank House. Elland HX4 ... 134 A4
Lower Bankhouse. Pudsey LS28 ... 76 D4
Lower Basinghall St. Leeds LS1 ... 79 B7
Lower Bentley Royd. Hali HX6 ... 112 A4
Lower Bower La. Batley WF13 ... 117 F2
Lower Brockwell La. Sow Br HX6 ... 111 F2
Lower Brunswick St. Leeds LS2 ... 60 D1
Lower Calderbrook. Litt OL15 ... 129 C1
Lower Cambridge St. Castle WF10 ... 124 D7
Lower Clay Pits. Hali HX1 ... 112 F6
Lower Clifton St. Hali HX3 ... 113 B3
Lower Clyde St. Sow Br HX6 ... 112 C4
Lower Common La. Clay W HD8 ... 175 F5
Lower Constable Rd. Ilkley LS29 ... 8 F3
Lower Cross St. Dew WF13 ... 118 C1
Lower Cross St. Hali HX1 ... 113 B2
Lower Crow Nest Dr. Brig HX3 ... 115 B7
Lower Denby La. D Dale HD8 ... 192 B4
Lower Edge Rd. Brig HD5 ... 135 D7
Lower Edge Rd. Elland HX5 ... 135 C7
Lower Exley. Hali HX3 ... 113 D1
Lower Fields Mid Sch. Brad ... 75 C6
Lower Finkil St. Brig HD6 ... 114 F5
Lower Fitzwilliam St. Hud HD1 ... 154 B7
Lower Frid. Brig HD6 ... 114 F5
Lower Gate. Hud HD3 ... 153 C5
Lower George St. Brad BD6 ... 74 B1
Lower Grange Cl. Brad BD8 ... 73 C7
Lower Grange. Hud HD2 ... 136 C6
Lower Grattan Rd. Brad BD1 ... 74 D7
Lower Green. Bail BD17 ... 38 B2
Lower Hagg. Holmfi HD7 ... 172 B1
Lower Hall Cres. Kirkhe HD5 ... 155 C6
Lower Hall Dr. Liver WF15 ... 116 C4
Lower Hall La. Liver WF15 ... 116 C4
Lower Hall Mount. Liver WF15 ... 116 D4
Lower Hall Rd. Kirkhe HD5 ... 155 C6
Lower Haughs. Slai HD7 ... 152 B5
Lower Heights Rd. Thorn BD13 ... 72 B6
Lower Hey. Mel HD7 ... 170 D2
Lower Highfield. Hali HX3 ... 91 A3
Lower Holme. Bail BD17 ... 38 C1
Lower House La. Lepton HD8 ... 156 B2
Lower Kipping La. Thorn BD13 ... 72 D6
Lower Laith Ave. Tod OL14 ... 107 F8
Lower Lake St. Dew WF12 ... 139 E7
Lower Langwith. Coll LS22 ... 29 A8
Lower Lark Hill. Cleck BD19 ... 117 A8
Lower Maythorn La. Wm Com HD7 ... 200 D6
Lower Meadows. Holmfi HD7 ... 188 D5
Lower Mickletown. W'town LS26 ... 102 C3
Lower Mill Bank. Sow Br HX6 ... 132 A7
Lower Newlands. Brig HD6 ... 115 B3
Lower North St. Batley WF17 ... 118 B6
Lower Northcroft. S Elm WF9 ... 183 A3
Lower Northfield La. S Kirk WF9 ... 182 C3
Lower Oxford St. Castle WF10 ... 124 C7
Lower Park Grn. Sil BD20 ... 5 D1
Lower Park Royd. Rip HX6 ... 132 C4
Lower Peel St. Dew WF13 ... 118 C1
Lower Putting Mill. D Dale HD8 ... 191 E4
Lower Quarry Rd. Hud HD2 ... 136 E4
Lower Range. Hali HX3 ... 92 A1
Lower Rd. Mars HD3 ... 150 D6
Lower Reins. Honley HD7 ... 172 A5
Lower Rushton Rd. Brad BD3 ... 75 E7
Lower Sandhills. Thorner LS14 ... 46 E7
Lower Scholes. Haw BD22 ... 51 A8
Lower School St. Ship BD18 ... 55 B7
Lower Skircoat Gn. Hali HX3 ... 113 C1
Lower Smithy. B Head HX7 ... 88 A5
Lower Station Rd. Nor WF6 ... 123 A2

Lower Swift Pl. Rip HX6 ... 132 B2
Lower Taythes La. Pont WF8 ... 126 A1
Lower Top of Hill. Mars HD3 ... 150 F6
Lower Town End Rd. Holmfi HD7 ... 189 C7
Lower Town St. Leeds LS13 ... 58 D2
Lower Viaduct St. Hud HD1 ... 154 B7
Lower Warrengate. Wake WF1 ... 142 D6
Lower Wellgate. Elland HX4 ... 134 C7
Lower Wellhouse Rd. Slai HD7 ... 152 B3
Lower Wellington Rd. Ilkley LS29 ... 8 B4
Lower Westfield Rd. Brad BD9 ... 55 A1
Lower Wheat Royd. Hud HD5 ... 154 F3
Lower Whitegate Rd. Hud HD4 ... 154 B3
Lower Wormald. Rip HX6 ... 131 F1
Lower Wortley Prim Sch. Leeds ... 78 B5
Lower Wortley Rd. Leeds LS12 ... 78 B5
Lower Wyke Gn. Brig BD12 ... 115 B8
Lower Wyke La. Brig BD12 ... 115 C8
Lower York St. Wake WF1 ... 142 C7
Lowerhouses CE Inf Sch. Hud ... 154 D3
Lowerhouses. Hud HD7 ... 152 E2
Lowerhouses La. Hud HD5 ... 154 D3
Lowerhouses Rd. Hud HD5 ... 153 B6
Lowestwood Ave. Slai HD7 ... 152 B3
Lowestwood La. Slai HD7 ... 152 B3
Lowfield Cl. Knot WF11 ... 126 F2
Lowfield Cl. Brad BD12 ... 94 E5
Lowfield Cres. Hem WF9 ... 181 E7
Lowfield Cres. Sil BD20 ... 17 F8
Lowfield Dr. Gar LS25 ... 83 A6
Lowfield La. Beam BD23 ... 2 C5
Lowfield Rd. Dew WF13 ... 138 F8
Lowfields Way. Hali HX5 ... 135 A8
Lowlands Rd. Mir WF14 ... 138 B4
Lowood La. Batley WF17 ... 96 F3
Lowry Rd. E Ard WF3 ... 119 E8
Lowther Ave. Gar LS25 ... 82 F6
Lowther Cres. Swil LS26 ... 82 A2
Lowther Dr. Gar LS25 ... 82 E6
Lowther Dr. Swil LS26 ... 82 A2
Lowther Gr. Gar LS25 ... 82 E6
Lowther Rd. Gar LS25 ... 82 F6
Lowther St. Brad BD2 ... 56 B2
Lowther St. Leeds LS8 ... 207 C4
Lowther Terr. Swil LS15 ... 82 A6
Lowtown. Pudsey LS28 ... 76 F8
Loxley Gr. Wake WF2 ... 141 D8
Loxley St. Batley WF17 ... 118 A7
Lucas Ct. Leeds LS6 ... 60 C3
Lucas Pl. Leeds LS6 ... 60 C3
Lucas St. Leeds LS6 ... 60 B3
Luck La. Hud HD1, HD3 ... 153 D6
Lucy Ave. Leeds LS15 ... 80 E8
Lucy Hall Dr. Bail BD17 ... 37 F1
Lucy La. Lepton HD8 ... 155 E5
Lucy St. Hali HX3 ... 113 D8
Luddenden CE Inf Sch. Hali ... 111 D8
Luddenden La. Hali HX2 ... 111 D7
Luddenden La. Hali HX2 ... 111 D8
Luddendenfoot Jun & Inf Sch. Hali ... 111 F5
Luddington House. Liver WF15 ... 117 A5
Ludhill La. Honley HD7 ... 172 D5
Ludlow Ave. Leeds LS15 ... 62 D1
Ludlow St. Hali HX1 ... 113 B4
Ludolf Dr. Thorner LS17 ... 44 E4
Ludwell Cl. Dew WF12 ... 139 E7
Luke La. Holmfi HD7 ... 188 D4
Luke Rd. Brad BD5 ... 74 D4
Lulworth Ave. Leeds LS15 ... 62 E2
Lulworth Cl. Leeds LS15 ... 62 D2
Lulworth Cres. Leeds LS15 ... 62 E2
Lulworth Dr. Leeds LS15 ... 62 E2
Lulworth Gr. Brad BD4 ... 75 D2
Lulworth Gr. Leeds LS15 ... 62 E2
Lulworth View. Leeds LS15 ... 62 E2
Lulworth Wlk. Leeds LS15 ... 62 E2
Lumb Bottom. Dew WF12 ... 139 F3
Lumb Foot. Haw BD22 ... 50 F8
Lumb Gill La. Add LS29 ... 7 D8
Lumb La. Brad BD8 ... 74 D8
Lumb La. Hali HX2 ... 90 F6
Lumb La. Hali HX2 ... 91 B2
Lumb La. Hali HX3 ... 114 B8
Lumb La. Mir WF14 ... 138 B6
Lumb La. Tod OL14 ... 108 C5
Lumbfoot Rd. Haw BD22 ... 50 F8
Lumbrook Cl. Northo HX3 ... 93 C2
Lumbrook. Northo HX3 ... 93 C2
Lumby Cl. Pudsey LS28 ... 57 C3
Lumby La. Leeds LS8 ... 61 A6
Lumby La. Pudsey LS28 ... 57 C3
Lumby St. Brad BD10 ... 56 D7
Lumley Ave. Hud HD5 ... 154 E5
Lumley Ave. Leeds LS4 ... 59 C3
Lumley Gr. Leeds LS4 ... 59 C3
Lumley Mount. Castle WF10 ... 124 A6
Lumley Mount. Leeds LS4 ... 59 C3
Lumley Pl. Leeds LS4 ... 59 C3
Lumley Rd. Leeds LS4 ... 59 C3
Lumley St. Castle WF10 ... 124 A6
Lumley St. Leeds LS4 ... 59 C3
Lumley Terr. Leeds LS4 ... 59 C3
Lumley View. Leeds LS4 ... 59 C3
Lumley Wlk. Leeds LS4 ... 59 C3
Lunan Pl. Leeds LS8 ... 207 C4
Lunan Terr. Leeds LS8 ... 207 C4
Lund Dr. Batley WF17 ... 117 F4
Lund Hill La. Ryhill S71 ... 179 F4
Lund La. Keigh BD22 ... 34 C6
Lund St. Brad BD8 ... 55 B1
Lund St. Gild LS12 ... 77 D1
Lund St. Keigh BD21 ... 35 A7
Lund St. Keigh BD21 ... 35 B7

Luttrell Cl. Hors LS16 ... 42 A2
Luttrell Cres. Hors LS16 ... 42 A2
Luttrell Gdns. Hors LS16 ... 42 A2
Luttrell Pl. Hors LS16 ... 42 A2
Luttrell Rd. Hors LS16 ... 42 A2
Luxor Ave. Leeds LS8 ... 60 F4
Luxor Rd. Leeds LS8 ... 60 F4
Luxor St. Leeds LS8 ... 60 F4
Luxor View. Leeds LS8 ... 60 F4
Lydbrook Pk. Elland HX3 ... 113 A2
Lyddon Terr. Leeds LS2 ... 60 A2
Lydgate Cl. Holmfi HD7 ... 189 E8
Lydgate CE Prim Sch. Batley ... 118 F5
Lydgate Dr. Holmfi HD7 ... 189 D7
Lydgate Dr. Lepton HD8 ... 156 A3
Lydgate House. Brad BD5 ... 73 B7
Lydgate. Leeds LS9 ... 61 C1
Lydgate. Lepton HD8 ... 156 A3
Lydgate. Northo HX3 ... 93 A3
Lydgate Pk. Brig HX3 ... 114 E7
Lydgate Rd. Batley WF17 ... 118 F5
Lydgate St. Pudsey LS28 ... 57 A7
Lydgate Sch. Holmfi ... 189 D7
Lyme Chase. Leeds LS14 ... 61 F2
Lyme Terr. Ad le D DN6 ... 184 E1
Lymington Dr. Brad BD4 ... 75 E4
Lyncroft. Brad BD2 ... 56 A5
Lynda Gr. Ossett WF5 ... 141 A4
Lyndale Dr. Ship BD18 ... 55 E8
Lyndale Dr. Wake WF2 ... 141 E4
Lyndale Gr. Nor WF6 ... 123 C1
Lyndale. Kippax LS25 ... 103 A8
Lyndale Mews. Batley WF13 ... 117 F3
Lyndale Rd. Bing BD16 ... 37 C5
Lynden Ct. Brad BD6 ... 94 A7
Lyndhurst Ave. Brig HD6 ... 135 F8
Lyndhurst Cl. B in Elm LS15 ... 62 F7
Lyndhurst Cres. B in Elm LS15 ... 62 F7
Lyndhurst Gr. Brad BD15 ... 54 C1
Lyndhurst Grove Rd. Brig HD6 ... 136 A8
Lyndhurst Rd. B in Elm LS15 ... 62 F6
Lyndhurst Rd. Brig HD6 ... 136 A8
Lyndhurst. S in Cra BD20 ... 16 D5
Lyndhurst View. B in Elm LS15 ... 62 F6
Lyndon Ave. Bramham LS23 ... 30 D2
Lyndon Ave. B Spa LS23 ... 30 C8
Lyndon Cl. Bramham LS23 ... 30 D2
Lyndon Cres. Bramham LS23 ... 30 D3
Lyndon Rd. Bramham LS23 ... 30 D3
Lyndon Sq. Bramham LS23 ... 30 D3
Lyndon Terr. Bing BD16 ... 37 A3
Lyndon Way. Bramham LS23 ... 30 D2
Lynfield Dr. Brad BD9 ... 54 C1
Lynfield Mount. Ship BD18 ... 55 E8
Lynmouth Dr. Brad BD4 ... 95 F7
Lynn Ave. B Spa LS23 ... 30 C8
Lynnfield Gdns. B in Elm LS15 ... 63 D7
Lynthorne Rd. Brad BD9 ... 55 B4
Lynton Ave. Brad BD9 ... 55 A3
Lynton Ave. Wake WF2 ... 141 D5
Lynton Dr. Brad BD9 ... 55 A3
Lynton Dr. Ship BD18 ... 55 D5
Lynton Gr. Brad BD9 ... 55 A3
Lynton Gr. Sow Br HX6 ... 112 C5
Lynton Terr. Cleck BD19 ... 116 D8
Lynton Villas. Brad BD9 ... 55 A3
Lynwood Ave. Cleck BD19 ... 116 E8
Lynwood Ave. Leeds LS12 ... 78 A5
Lynwood Ave. Pont WF8 ... 146 C5
Lynwood Ave. Ship BD18 ... 54 E8
Lynwood Ave. Wake WF2 ... 120 D1
Lynwood Cl. Feath WF7 ... 144 E4
Lynwood Cres. Hali HX2 ... 112 F7
Lynwood Cres. Leeds LS12 ... 78 A5
Lynwood Cres. Pont WF8 ... 146 C5
Lynwood Cres. Roy S71 ... 179 C4
Lynwood Cres. Wake WF2 ... 120 D1
Lynwood Ct. Keigh BD21 ... 35 A7
Lynwood Dr. Mapp S75 ... 178 C1
Lynwood Garth. Leeds LS12 ... 78 A5
Lynwood Gr. Leeds LS12 ... 78 A5
Lynwood Gr. Nor WF6 ... 123 A1
Lynwood Mews. Brad BD4 ... 75 F2
Lynwood Mount. Leeds LS12 ... 78 A5
Lynwood Rd. Leeds LS12 ... 78 A5
Lynwood View. Leeds LS12 ... 78 A5
Lyon Rd. Pudsey LS28 ... 57 C2
Lyon St. Thorn BD13 ... 72 E6
Lytham Dr. Brad BD13 ... 72 E1
Lytham Gr. Leeds LS12 ... 78 A4
Lytham Pl. Leeds LS12 ... 78 A4
Lytham St. Sow Br HX6 ... 112 B3
Lytham Way. Hud HD3 ... 153 B8
Lytton Rd. Brad BD8 ... 74 C8
Lytton St. Hali HX3 ... 113 D1

Mabel Royd. Brad BD7 ... 73 F5
Mabel St. Heb Br HX7 ... 89 A4
Mabgate. Leeds LS9 ... 207 E3
Mabgate Gn. Leeds LS9 ... 207 E3
Macaulay Rd. Hud HD2 ... 136 F5
Macaulay St. Leeds LS9 ... 207 E4
Machen St. Hali HX1 ... 113 A4
Mackey Cres. Bri S72 ... 180 F1
Mackie Hill Cl. Crig WF4 ... 159 F5
Mackingstone Dr. Oldf BD22 ... 50 A5
Mackingstone La. Oxen BD22 ... 34 A1
Mackinnon Homes. Hali HX3 ... 113 A4
Macturk Gr. Brad BD8 ... 55 B1
Maddocks St. Ship BD18 ... 55 A7
Madeley Rd. Ryhill WF4 ... 162 C1
Madeley Sq. Castle WF10 ... 124 F6
Madgin La. Hud HD7 ... 171 A6
Madison Ave. Brad BD4 ... 75 E4

Madni Cl. Hali HX1 113 B7
Madri Muslim Girls Sch. Dew 139 D6
Mafeking Ave. Leeds LS11 79 A1
Mafeking Gr. Leeds LS11 79 A1
Mafeking Mount. Leeds LS11 79 A1
Magdalen Rd. Mel HD7 187 C6
Magdalene Cl. Hors LS16 42 A3
Magdalene Rd. Wake WF2 141 D5
Magistrates Ct. Brad 74 E6
Magna Gr. Wake WF2 142 E1
Magnolia Cl. Shaf S72 180 D2
Magnolia House. Castle WF10 124 E7 1
Magpie La. Morley LS27 98 C3
Maidstone St. Brad BD3 75 C7
Mail Cl. Leeds LS15 62 E3
Main Ave. Hud HD4 152 F3
Main Gate. Holmfi HD7 189 E2
Main Rd. Denh BD13 71 D8
Main Rd. Farnh BD20 16 E8
Main Rd. Keigh BD20 36 D8
Main Rd. Stee BD20 16 F6
Main St. Aber LS25 64 E7
Main St. Add LS29 7 A8
Main St. B in Elm LS15 62 F6
Main St. B in Elm LS15 63 D7
Main St. B Sal LS25 105 E3
Main St. Bad WF9 164 E2
Main St. Bing BD16 36 F3
Main St. Brad BD12 94 C4 2
Main St. Brad BD12 94 E6
Main St. Bur in W LS29 9 F1
Main St. Coll LS22 13 C2
Main St. Coll LS22 29 B8
Main St. Con BD20 4 A2
Main St. E Ard WF3 120 D7
Main St. E Kes LS17 28 C5
Main St. Farnh BD20 4 D2
Main St. Gar LS25 82 E7
Main St. Guise LS20 38 F8
Main St. Guise BD17 39 C5
Main St. Ham DN6 184 B1
Main St. Haw BD22 50 D7
Main St. Haw BD22 51 C7
Main St. K Smea WF8 166 D6
Main St. Kippax WF10 103 B4
Main St. L Brad BD20 4 C5
Main St. Ledst WF10 103 E6
Main St. M Fry LS25 105 F8
Main St. M'town LS26 102 D3
Main St. Men LS29 22 A4
Main St. Pool LS21 24 C7
Main St. Roth WF3 100 D3
Main St. S Hie S72 180 D6
Main St. S in Cra BD20 16 D5
Main St. Ship BD16 54 B6
Main St. Sickl LS22 12 C5
Main St. Sil LS29 6 E8
Main St. Tad LS24 31 E7
Main St. Th Arch LS23 15 A4
Main St. Thorner LS17 44 E4
Main St. Thorner LS14 45 F5
Main St. Upton WF9 183 D8
Main St. Wils BD15 53 C5
Mainspring Rd. Wils BD15 53 C5
Maitland Cl. Brad BD15 73 B7
Maitland Cl. Tod OL14 129 A8
Maitland Pl. Leeds LS11 79 A4
Maitland St. Tod OL14 129 A8
Maize St. Keigh BD21 35 A4 5
Maizebrook. Dew WF16 117 F1
Major St. Tod OL14 108 C5
Major St. Wake WF2 142 B3
Makin St. Wake WF2 142 A5
Malais La. S in Cra BD20 16 A5
Malham Ave. Brad BD9 54 C3
Malham Ave. Brig HD6 135 E8
Malham Cl. Leeds LS14 62 A4
Malham Cl. Shaf S72 180 C3
Malham Dr. Batley WF17 118 A5
Malham Dr. Liver WF15 116 F1
Malham Rd. Brig HD6 135 E7
Malham Rd. Wake WF1 142 F7
Malham Sq. Wake WF1 142 F7
Malin Rd. Batley WF12 118 F3
Mallard Ave. Wake WF2 160 C5
Mallard Cl. Brad BD10 56 C5
Mallard Cl. Midd LS10 99 F7
Mallard Ct. Brad BD8 73 C7 1
Mallard Rd. Castle WF10 124 C6
Mallard Way. Morley LS27 98 D4 3
Mallard Way. Slai HD7 169 F8
Mallinson St. Dew WF13 118 A1
Mallory Cl. Brad BD7 73 F6
Malmesbury Cl. Brad BD4 75 E1
Malmesbury Cl. Leeds LS12 78 C6 2
Malmesbury Gr. Leeds LS12 78 C6
Malmesbury Pl. Leeds LS12 78 C6
Malmesbury St. Leeds LS12 78 C6
Malmesbury Terr. Leeds LS12 78 C6
Malsis Cres. Keigh BD21 35 A6
Malsis Rd. Keigh BD21 35 B5
Malt Kiln Croft. Wake WF2 142 E1
Malt Kiln La. Kippax LS25 83 B1 2
Malt Kiln La. Thorn BD13 72 C5
Malt St. Keigh BD22 35 A4 8
Maltby Ct. Leeds LS15 81 D7
Malthouse Cl. Scar LS14 45 C8
Malting Cl. Roth WF3 100 B3
Malting Rise. Roth WF3 100 B3
Maltings Ct. Leeds LS11 79 C4 3
Maltings Rd. Hali HX2 91 D2
Maltings Rd. Leeds LS11 79 C3
Maltings The. Clec BD19 116 C8
Maltings The. Leeds LS6 59 E2
Maltings The. Mir WF14 137 F5
Maltings The. Pont WF8 125 D1
Maltings The. Roth WF3 100 B3
Maltkiln La. Castle WF10 124 E8
Maltkiln Dr. W Bret WF4 176 F8
Malton Rd. Upton WF9 183 D8
Malton St. Hali HX3 92 C2
Malton St. Hali HX6 112 B5 7
Malvern Brow. Brad BD9 54 D2
Malvern Cl. Castle WF10 123 F5
Malvern Cres. Keigh BD20 18 E3
Malvern Gr. Brad BD9 54 D1
Malvern Gr. Leeds LS11 79 B4
Malvern Rd. Brad BD9 54 D2
Malvern Rd. Dew WF12 118 F1
Malvern Rd. Hud HD4 154 B4
Malvern Rd. Knot WF11 126 E4
Malvern Rd. Leeds LS11 79 A4
Malvern Rise. Hud HD4 154 B3
Malvern Rise. Leeds LS11 79 A4
Malvern St. Brad BD3 75 A7
Malvern St. Leeds LS11 79 A4
Malvern View. Leeds LS11 79 A4 5
Manchester Rd. Brad BD5 74 D3
Manchester Rd. Hud HD4 153 D4
Manchester Rd. Mars HD7 168 B3
Manchester Rd Marsden. Mars HD7 168 E4
Manchester Rd (Slaithwaite). Slai HD7 170 A8
Manchester Road Clough Head. Mars HD7 168 C4
Manchester Road (Linthwaite). Slai HD7 152 D1
Manchester Sq. Otley LS21 23 A8
Manchester St. Hud HD4 153 C4
Mandale Gr. Brad BD6 93 D8
Mandale Mid Sch. Brad 93 D8
Mandale Rd. Brad BD6 73 D1
Mandarin Way. Midd LS10 99 F7
Mandela Ct. Leeds LS7 60 D5
Mandeville Cres. Brad BD6 93 F8
Mangrill La. B in Elm LS14 46 E6
Manitoba Pl. Leeds LS7 60 E6
Mankinholes Bank. Tod OL14 108 F3
Manley Ct. Gar LS25 82 F5
Manley Dr. Weth LS22 13 C6
Manley Gr. Ilkley LS29 8 D4
Manley Rd. Ilkley LS29 8 E4
Manley Rise. Ilkley LS29 8 D3
Manley St. Brig HD6 115 A3
Mann's Bldgs. Batley WF17 97 B2
Mannheim Rd. Brad BD9 55 A2
Manningham La. Brad BD1, BD8 55 D1
Manningham Mid Sch. Brad 55 D1
Mannville Gr. Keigh BD22 35 A6
Mannville Pl. Keigh BD22 35 A6 16
Mannville Rd. Keigh BD22 35 A6
Mannville St. Keigh BD22 35 A6 13
Mannville Terr. Brad BD7 74 D6
Mannville Way. Keigh BD22 35 A6 14
Mannville Wlk. Keigh BD22 35 A6 15
Manor Ave. Leeds LS6 59 E4
Manor Ave. Ossett WF5 140 F3
Manor Cl. Bad WF9 164 E2
Manor Cl. Brad BD8 73 D8
Manor Cl. Bramho LS16 24 D3
Manor Cl. Hali HX3 113 B4
Manor Cl. K Smea WF8 166 D5
Manor Cl. Notton WF4 178 F7
Manor Cl. Ossett WF5 140 F3
Manor Cl. Roth LS26 100 E6
Manor Cl. Yeadon LS19 40 B7
Manor Cres. Pool LS21 24 C7
Manor Cres. Roth LS26 100 D5
Manor Cres. Wake WF2 141 E4
Manor Cres. Walton WF2 161 A8
Manor Croft. Heb Br HX7 89 B3
Manor Croft. Leeds LS15 81 C7
Manor Croft. S Hie S72 180 D6
Manor Ct. Ossett WF5 140 F3
Manor Ct. Otley LS21 23 A8
Manor Ct. Ship BD16 54 A7 3
Manor Ct. Thorner LS17 44 F4
Manor Dr. Crof WF4 162 A7
Manor Dr. Feath WF7 124 C1
Manor Dr. Floc WF4 157 D3
Manor Dr. Hali HX3 113 B4
Manor Dr. Heb Br HX7 89 B3
Manor Dr. Leeds LS6 59 E4
Manor Dr. Mir WF14 137 D7
Manor Dr. Ossett WF5 140 F3
Manor Dr. Roy S71 179 B3
Manor Dr. S Hie S72 180 D6
Manor Dr. Ship BD16 54 B7
Manor Dr. Skel HD8 175 A1
Manor Farm. Bad WF9 164 E2
Manor Farm Cl. Midd LS10 99 D6
Manor Farm Cl. Ship BD16 54 B6
Manor Farm Cres. Morley LS27 98 C8
Manor Farm Ct. Crig WF4 159 E4
Manor Farm Dr. Batley WF17 118 F5
Manor Farm Dr. Midd LS10 99 D6
Manor Farm Dr. Morley LS27 98 C8
Manor Farm Est. S Elm WF9 183 A3
Manor Farm Gdns. Midd LS10 99 C6
Manor Farm Gn. Midd LS10 99 C6
Manor Farm Gr. Midd LS10 99 C6
Manor Farm Rd. Crig WF4 159 E4
Manor Farm Rd. Midd LS10 99 D6
Manor Farm Rise. Midd LS10 99 D6
Manor Farm Way. Midd LS10 99 C5
Manor Farm Wlk. Midd LS10 99 D6
Manor Fold. Ship BD16 54 B6 4
Manor Garth. Ledsh LS25 104 D8
Manor Garth. Leeds LS15 81 C7
Manor Garth Rd. Dew WF12 139 F7
Manor Garth Rd. Kippax LS25 83 B2
Manor Garth. Walton WF2 161 A8
Manor Gdns. Batley WF12 119 A2
Manor Gdns. Cull BD13 52 D5
Manor Gdns. Pool LS21 24 C7
Manor Gdns. Thorner LS14 46 A6
Manor Gr. Castle WF10 124 E5
Manor Gr. Keigh BD20 36 A8
Manor Gr. Leeds LS7 60 D6
Manor Gr. Ossett WF5 140 F3
Manor Gr. Roy S71 179 B3
Manor Gr. S Kirk WF9 182 A1
Manor Haigh Rd. Wake WF2 141 E4
Manor Heath Rd. Hali HX3 113 B4
Manor House Bglws. Knot WF11 126 F5
Manor House Croft. Hors LS16 42 D3
Manor House La. Hare LS17 43 F7
Manor House Mus & Art Gal. Ilkley 8 B4
Manor House Rd. Wils BD15 53 C6
Manor House St. Pudsey LS28 76 E7 5
Manor House. Wake WF1 142 D6 4
Manor Houses. Mel HD7 170 F2
Manor La. Ossett WF5 140 F3
Manor La. Ship BD18 55 B7
Manor Mill La. Leeds LS11 78 E1
Manor Occupation Rd. Roy S71 179 B4
Manor Park Ave. Kippax WF10 103 B5
Manor Park Ave. Pont WF8 125 F3
Manor Park Gdns. Birk BD19 96 B3
Manor Park Rise. Dar WF8 147 D4
Manor Park Way. Lepton HD8 155 D2
Manor Pk. Brad BD8 73 D8
Manor Pk. Dar WF8 147 D5
Manor Pk. Haw BD22 34 C2
Manor Pk. Mir WF14 137 C7
Manor Pk. Scar LS14 45 C7
Manor Pl. Hor WF4 141 A1 1
Manor Rd. Batley WF17 118 F5
Manor Rd. Beal DN14 127 F7
Manor Rd. Clay W HD8 176 A4
Manor Rd. Dearne S63 194 C1
Manor Rd. Dew WF13 139 B7
Manor Rd. Hor WF4 141 A1
Manor Rd. Hors LS18 58 A8
Manor Rd. Hud HD7 152 D4
Manor Rd. Keigh BD20 18 A2
Manor Rd. Kirkb HD4 172 F6
Manor Rd. Leeds LS11 79 B6
Manor Rd. Morley LS27 98 C8
Manor Rd. Ossett WF5 140 F4
Manor Rd. Roth LS26 100 D6
Manor Rd. Ship BD16 54 B7
Manor Rd. Wake WF2 141 F5
Manor Rd. Walton WF2 161 A7
Manor Rise. Hud HD4 154 B4
Manor Rise. Ilkley LS29 8 D4
Manor Rise. Skel HD8 175 A1
Manor Rise. Walton WF2 161 A8
Manor Row. Brad BD1 74 E7
Manor Row. Brad BD12 94 C7
Manor (Sports Ctr) The. Yeadon 40 B7
Manor Sq. Otley LS21 23 A8
Manor Sq. Yeadon LS19 40 B7 5
Manor St. Brad BD2 56 B3
Manor St. Brig BD19 115 F6
Manor St. Dew WF12 139 D8
Manor St. Hud HD4 154 B4
Manor St Ind Est. Leeds 60 E2
Manor St. Leeds LS7 60 D2
Manor St. Otley LS21 23 A8
Manor Terr. Brad BD2 56 B3
Manor Terr. Kippax LS25 83 B1
Manor Terr. Leeds LS6 59 E4
Manor View. Castle WF10 124 E5
Manor View. Leeds LS6 59 E4
Manor View. Pudsey LS28 76 E7
Manor View. Shaf S72 180 C2
Manor Way. Batley WF17 118 A4
Manor Way. S in Cra BD20 16 C4
Manorcroft. Nor WF6 123 B2
Manorfield Dr. Hor WF4 141 A2
Manorfield. Leeds LS11 78 F3
Manorfields Ave. Crof WF4 162 A8
Manorfields Ct. Crof WF4 162 A8
Manorley La. Brad BD6 93 E6
Manorstead. Skel HD8 175 A1
Manscombe Rd. Brad BD15 54 C1
Manse Cres. Bur in W LS29 9 E1
Manse Dr. Hud HD4 153 A3
Manse Rd. Bur in W LS29 9 E1
Manse St. Brad BD3 75 C7
Manse Way. Glu BD20 16 D6
Mansel Mews. Brad BD4 75 E2
Mansfield Ave. Bing BD16 37 C5
Mansfield Pl. Leeds LS6 59 D6
Mansfield Rd. Brad BD8 55 C2
Mansfield Rd. Bur in W LS29 9 E1
Mansion Gdns. Hud HD4 153 F1
Mansion La. Leeds LS8 44 B1
Manston App. Leeds LS15 62 C3
Manston Ave. Leeds LS15 62 C3
Manston Cres. Leeds LS15 62 C2
Manston Dr. Leeds LS15 62 C3
Manston Gdns. Leeds LS15 62 D3
Manston Gr. Leeds LS15 62 C3
Manston La. Leeds LS15 62 E2
Manston Prim Sch. Leeds 62 D3
Manston Rise. Leeds LS15 62 C3
Manston Terr. Leeds LS15 62 D3 5
Manston Towers. Leeds LS14 62 D4 3
Manston Way. Leeds LS15 62 C3
Manygates Ave. Wake WF1 142 D3
Manygates Cres. Wake WF1 142 D3
Manygates Ct. Wake WF1 142 D3
Manygates La. Wake WF1, WF2 142 D2
Manygates Pk. Wake WF1 142 D3
Manywells Brow. Cull BD13 52 C4
Manywells Cres. Cull BD13 52 D5
Manywells La. Cull BD13 52 C5
Maple Ave. Brad BD3 75 E8
Maple Ave. Haw BD22 34 D2
Maple Ave. Hud HD7 152 F5
Maple Ave. Pont WF8 146 C5
Maple Cl. Castle WF10 124 B5
Maple Cl. Kirkhe HD5 137 C1
Maple Croft. Leeds LS17 43 E3
Maple Croft. Leeds LS17 43 E3
Maple Croft. Leeds LS12 77 D5
Maple Ct. Leeds LS11 78 F2 2
Maple Dr. Leeds LS12 77 D5
Maple Dr. Pont WF8 146 D6
Maple Dr. Weth LS22 13 E7
Maple Fold. Leeds LS12 77 D5
Maple Gr. Clec BD19 96 A1
Maple Gr. Hud HD2 136 A5
Maple Gr. Keigh BD20 18 A1
Maple Gr. Nor WF6 144 A7
Maple Gr. Pont WF8 146 C5
Maple Rd. Dew WF12 140 B7
Maple Rd. Mapp S75 178 A1
Maple Rise. Roth LS26 100 F4
Maple St. Hali HX1 112 F5 14
Maple St. Hud HD5 154 C5
Maple St. Tod OL14 129 A7
Maple St. Wake WF2 141 F8
Maple Terr. Yeadon LS19 39 F7
Maple Way. Leeds LS14 62 C8
Maple Wlk. Dew WF12 140 B7
Maple Wlk. Knot WF11 126 E3
Maplin Ave. Hud HD3 134 F1
Maplin Dr. Hud HD3 134 F1 1
Mapplewell Cres. Ossett WF5 140 E5
Mapplewell Dr. Ossett WF5 140 E5
Mapplewell Inf Sch. Mapp 178 C1
Mapplewell Jun Mix Sch. Mapp 178 C1
Marbridge Ct. Brad BD6 74 B2
March Cote La. Ship BD16 54 A6
March St. Nor WF6 123 A1
Marchant St. Castle WF10 124 C8
Marchbank Rd. Brad BD3 75 C8
Marchwood Gr. Brad BD14 73 D5
Marcus Way. Hud HD3 134 D1
Mardale Cres. Leeds LS14 62 A3
Mardale Rd. Batley WF12 118 E2
Margaret Ave. Bard LS17 28 D4
Margaret Cl. Morley LS27 98 C6
Margaret St. Hali HX1 113 B7
Margaret St. Keigh BD21 35 A8
Margaret St. Loft G WF1 121 A4
Margaret St. Wake WF1 142 B7
Margate Rd. Brad BD4 75 A4
Margate. Roth LS26 101 C6 2
Margate St. Sow Br HX6 112 A3
Margerison Cres. Ilkley LS29 8 E3
Margerison Rd. Ilkley LS29 8 E3
Margetson Rd. Birk BD11 97 A5
Margram Bsns Ctr. Hali 113 B8
Margrove House. Brad BD15 73 B8 8
Maria St. Bur in W LS29 9 E2
Marian Gr. Leeds LS11 79 B3 16
Marian Rd. Leeds LS6 60 B3
Marian Terr. Leeds LS6 60 B3
Marie Cl. Kirkhe HD5 155 C6
Marina Cres. Morley LS27 97 F3
Marina Terr. Hud HD7 152 E5
Marine Villa Rd. Knot WF11 126 F4
Marion Ave. Wake WF2 141 D8
Marion Dr. Ship BD18 55 C7
Marion Gr. Wake WF2 141 D8
Marion St. Bing BD16 37 A3
Marion St. Brad BD7 74 C7
Marion St. Brig HD6 115 A3
Maris St. Leeds LS9 79 D7
Marizon Gr. Wake WF1 142 D7
Mark Bottoms La. Holmfi HD7 188 F6
Mark Cl. Brad BD10 56 C8
Mark La. Leeds LS2 79 C8
Mark La. Tod OL14 108 A7
Mark St. Brad BD5 74 E3
Mark St. Hud HD1 153 E5
Mark St. Liver WF15 117 B4
Mark St. Wake WF1 142 C4
Market Ave. Hud HD1 154 B6 9
Market Ct. Thorn BD13 72 E6 5
Market Pl. Clec BD19 116 E7 1
Market Pl. Dew WF13 139 D8
Market Pl. Hud HD1 154 A6
Market Pl. Keigh BD21 35 C7
Market Pl. Mars HD7 168 F4
Market Pl. Mel HD7 170 D2
Market Pl. Nor WF6 123 A2
Market Pl. Otley LS21 23 A8
Market Pl. Pont WF8 146 D8
Market Pl. Pudsey LS28 76 E7
Market Pl. Slai HD7 169 F8
Market Pl. Weth LS22 13 E5
Market Shops. Nor WF6 123 A2
Market Sq. Batley WF17 118 C5 5
Market Sq. Leeds LS14 62 B5 3
Market Sq. Ship BD18 55 B7
Market St. Batley WF17 96 E1
Market St. Batley WF16 117 D3
Market St. Bing BD16 36 F3
Market St. Brad BD6 74 C1 4
Market St. Brad BD1 74 E7
Market St. Brig HD6 115 B2
Market St. Clec BD19 116 E7
Market St. Dew WF13 139 D8 3
Market St. Feath WF7 145 C6
Market St. Hali HX1 113 C7
Market St. Heb Br HX7 89 A3
Market St. Hem WF9 181 D7
Market St. Holmfi HD7 189 A5
Market St. Hud HD3 153 B5
Market St. Hud HD1 153 E5
Market St. Hud HD1 154 A6
Market St. Keigh BD21 35 C7
Market St. Nor WF6 123 A2
Market St. Otley LS21 23 A8
Market St. Ship BD18 55 B7
Market St. Stee BD20 17 D5
Market St. Thorn BD13 72 E6
Market St. Tod OL14 108 A3
Market St. Wake WF1 142 C6
Market Wlk. Mars HD7 168 F4
Markfield Ave. Brad BD12 94 C5
Markfield Cl. Brad BD12 94 C5
Markfield Cres. Brad BD12 94 D5
Markfield Dr. Brad BD12 94 C5
Markham Ave. Leeds LS8 60 F4
Markham Ave. Yeadon LS19 40 C5
Markham Cres. Yeadon LS19 40 C5
Markham Croft. Yeadon LS19 40 C5
Markham St. Batley WF17 118 B4
Markham St. Wake WF2 142 A6
Marl Pit Hill. Pont WF8 146 A6
Marland Rd. Keigh BD21 35 E8
Marlbeck Cl. Honley HD7 171 F3
Marlborough Ave. Byram WF11 126 D7
Marlborough Ave. Hali HX3 113 B4 7
Marlborough Croft. S Elm WF9 182 F4
Marlborough Ct. Men LS29 22 B4
Marlborough Gdns. Dew WF13 118 B2
Marlborough Gdns. Leeds LS2 60 B2 7
Marlborough Gr. Ilkley LS29 8 D3
Marlborough Gr. Leeds LS2 60 B2 8
Marlborough Grange. Leeds LS1 79 A8 9
Marlborough House. Elland HX5 134 F7 9
Marlborough Rd. Brad BD8 55 C1
Marlborough Rd. Brad BD10 56 C8
Marlborough Rd. Heb Br HX7 89 A3
Marlborough Rd. Hud HD2 136 B5
Marlborough Rd. Ship BD18 55 A7
Marlborough Sq. Ilkley LS29 8 D3
Marlborough St. Keigh BD21 35 D8
Marlborough St. Leeds LS1 79 A8
Marlborough St. Ossett WF5 140 C5
Marlborough St. Wake WF2 142 A6
Marlborough Terr. Heb Br HX7 89 A3
Marlborough Towers. Leeds LS1 79 A8
Marlborough Villas. Men LS29 22 B4
Marlbro' Terr. Batley WF13 118 B2 5
Marldon Rd. Northo HX3 93 A1
Marley Cl. Brad BD8 73 E8
Marley Ct. Bing BD16 36 D7
Marley Gr. Leeds LS11 78 F3
Marley La. Queen BD13 72 E3
Marley Pl. Leeds LS11 78 F3
Marley Rd. Keigh BD21 35 F8
Marley St. Brad BD3 75 A7
Marley St. Keigh BD21 35 C6
Marley St. Leeds LS11 78 F3
Marley Terr. Leeds LS11 78 F3 5
Marley View. Bing BD16 36 D7
Marley View. Leeds LS11 78 F3
Marling Rd. Hud HD2 135 B3
Marlo Rd. Batley WF12 119 A2
Marlott Rd. Ship BD18 55 E8
Marlow Cl. Hud HD5 154 F6
Marlow St. Keigh BD21 35 E8
Marlowe Cl. Pudsey LS28 76 F5 3
Marlowe Ct. Gar LS25 82 F7
Marlowe Ct. Guise LS20 22 D1
Marlpit La. Dar WF8 147 B5
Marmion Ave. Brad BD8 73 C8
Marne Ave. Brad BD14 73 C3
Marne Cres. Brad BD10 56 B7
Marriner Rd. Keigh BD21 35 C6
Marriner's Dr. Ship BD9 55 B4
Marriner's Wlk. Keigh BD21 35 C5
Marriot Gr. Wake WF2 142 F1
Marsden Ave. Leeds LS11 79 A2
Marsden Ct. Pudsey LS28 57 D3 3
Marsden Gate. Elland HX4 151 E7
Marsden Golf Club. Mars 168 E1
Marsden Gr. Leeds LS11 79 A2
Marsden Inf Sch. Mars 169 A4
Marsden La. Mars HD7 169 A5
Marsden La. Mars HD7 169 B7
Marsden Mount. Leeds LS11 79 A2
Marsden Pl. Leeds LS11 79 A2
Marsden St. Skel HD8 175 A2
Marsden Sta. Mars 168 F4
Marsden View. Leeds LS11 79 A2
Marsett Way. Leeds LS14 62 B8
Marsh Croft. Broth WF11 126 C7
Marsh Delves. Hali HX3 113 F6
Marsh Delves La. Hali HX3 113 F6
Marsh End. Knot WF11 127 B5
Marsh Gdns. Honley HD7 171 F4
Marsh Gr. Brad BD5 74 C3
Marsh Grove Rd. Hud HD3 153 D8
Marsh Hall La. Kirkb HD4 172 F3
Marsh La. B Head HX7 88 B3
Marsh La. Birk BD11 96 A5
Marsh La. Byram WF11 126 F6
Marsh La. Hali HX3 113 F6
Marsh La. Knot WF11 127 B4
Marsh La. Leeds LS9 79 E8
Marsh La. Oxen BD22 51 B4
Marsh La. Shep HD8 190 D7
Marsh Lea Grove. Hem WF9 181 F7
Marsh Platt La. Honley HD7 172 A5
Marsh. Pudsey LS28 76 C7
Marsh Rd. Holmfi HD7 189 D3
Marsh St. Brad BD5 74 D3
Marsh St. Clec BD19 116 E6
Marsh St. Honley HD7 171 F4
Marsh St. Leeds LS6 60 A3
Marsh St. Roth LS26 100 F5
Marsh Terr. Pudsey LS28 76 C7
Marsh Vale. Leeds LS6 60 A3 3
Marsh Way. Wake WF1 142 D7
Marshall Ave. Crig WF4 159 F3
Marshall Ave. Leeds LS15 62 D2
Marshall Cres. Morley LS27 98 B2
Marshall Dr. S Elm WF9 182 F3
Marshall Mill Ct. Clay W HD8 175 E1
Marshall St. Keigh BD20 18 B1
Marshall St. Leeds LS15 62 C2
Marshall St. Leeds LS11 79 B6
Marshall St. Loft G WF3 121 F5
Marshall St. Mir WF14 138 A3
Marshall St. Morley LS27 98 B4
Marshall St. Yeadon LS19 40 B7
Marshall Terr. Leeds LS15 62 C2
Marsham Gr. Hud HD3 153 C7
Marshfield Fst Sch. Brad 74 C2
Marshfield Pl. Brad BD5 74 D3
Marshfield St. Brad BD5 74 D3
Marshway. Hali HX1 113 A8
Marsland Ave. Wake WF1 142 D6
Marsland Ct. Clec BD19 95 D2
Marsland Pl. Brad BD3 75 D7
Marsland Pl. Wake WF1 142 D6
Marsland St. Wake WF1 142 D6
Marsland Terr. Wake WF1 142 D6
Marston Ave. Morley LS27 98 A3
Marston Cl. Queen BD13 72 F1
Marston Ct. Castle WF10 124 A6
Marston Mount. Leeds LS9 60 E1
Marston Way. Weth LS22 13 C6
Marston Wlk. Nor WF6 122 E4
Marten Dr. Hud HD4 171 D7
Marten Gr. Hud HD4 171 E7
Marten Rd. Brad BD5 74 C3
Martin Ct. Leeds LS15 81 D8
Martin Frobisher Dr. Nor WF6 122 F3
Martin Gr. Wake WF2 160 E6
Martin Green La. Elland HX4 134 A7
Martin St. Batley WF17 96 E1
Martin St. Brig HD6 115 B3
Martin St. Nor WF6 144 A8
Martin Terr. Leeds LS4 59 C2
Martindale Dr. Leeds LS13 58 E1
Martlett Dr. Brad BD5 74 F2
Marton Ave. Hem WF9 181 C6
Marton Heights. Hali HX6 112 A5
Marwood Rd. Leeds LS13 77 E7
Mary Rose Ct. Feath WF7 145 C4
Mary St. Brad BD4 75 C5
Mary St. Brad BD12 94 C4
Mary St. Brig HD6 115 A4
Mary St. Denh BD13 52 E1
Mary St. E Ard WF3 120 E8
Mary St. Oxen BD22 51 C2 6
Mary St. Pudsey LS28 57 E4
Mary St. Ship BD18 54 F8
Mary St. Thorn BD13 72 D6 5
Maryfield Ave. Leeds LS15 62 A2
Maryfield Cl. Leeds LS15 62 A2
Maryfield Cres. Leeds LS15 62 B2
Maryfield Ct. Leeds LS15 62 B2 5
Maryfield Gdns. Leeds LS15 62 A2
Maryfield Gn. Leeds LS15 62 A2
Maryfield Mews. Leeds LS15 62 A2
Maryfield Vale. Leeds LS15 62 A2 1
Marygate. Wake WF1 142 C6 13
Maryville Ave. Brig HD6 114 E5
Masefield Ave. Brad BD9 54 C3
Masefield St. Guise LS20 39 F8
Masham Gr. Leeds LS12 78 D7
Masham Pl. Brad BD9 54 F2
Masham St. Leeds LS12 78 D7
Mason Sq. Hali HX2 91 F3
Mason St. Heb Br HX7 89 A3
Mason's Green. Hali HX2 91 E5
Masonic St. Hali HX1 112 E6
Master La. Hali HX2 112 F4
Matherville. Skel HD8 175 A1
Matlock St. Hali HX3 92 A1 9
Matlock St. Hud HD4 153 C4
Matterdale Cl. Batley WF12 118 E2
Matterdale Rd. Batley WF12 118 E2
Matthew Cl. Keigh BD20 18 F1
Matthew Gr. Mel HD7 170 C2
Matthew La. L Brad BD20 4 C5
Matthew La. Mel HD7 170 D2
Matthew La. Tod OL14 108 E7
Matthew Murray High Sch. Leeds 78 F4
Matty Marsden La. Ossett WF4 140 E2
Maud Ave. Leeds LS11 79 B2
Maud Pl. Leeds LS11 79 B3 14
Maud St. Brad BD3 75 B6
Maude Ave. Bail BD17 38 C2
Maude Cres. Sow Br HX6 111 E3
Maude La. Rip HX6 132 D4
Maude St. Elland HX4 134 D7
Maude St. Hali HX3 92 A3
Maude St. Leeds LS2 79 D7
Maudsley St. Brad BD3 75 B7

Maurice Ave. Brig HD6 ... 114 F4
Mavis Ave. Dew WF13 ... 139 A6
Mavis Ave. Hors LS16 ... 41 E6
Mavis Gr. Hors LS16 ... 41 E6
Mavis La. Hors LS16 ... 41 E6
Mavis Rd. Batley WF13 ... 117 F3
Mavis St. Brad BD3 ... 75 B7
Mavis St. Dew WF13 ... 139 A6
Maw St. Brad BD4 ... 75 F5
Mawcroft Cl. Yeadon LS19 ... 40 A5
Mawcroft Grange Dr. Yeadon LS19 . 40 A5
Mawcroft Dr. Brad BD1 ... 74 E7 16
Mawson St. Ship BD18 ... 54 F8 6
Maxwell Ave. Batley WF17 ... 118 C2
Maxwell Rd. Brad BD6 ... 93 F8
Maxwell Rd. Ilkley LS29 ... 8 D3
Maxwell St. Feath WF7 ... 145 C5
Maxwell St. Morley LS27 ... 97 F3
May Ave. Thorn BD13 ... 72 E6
May Bush Rd. Wake WF1 ... 142 E3
May St. Clec BD19 ... 95 D1
May St. Haw BD22 ... 51 D6
May St. Hud HD4 ... 153 C4
May St. Keigh BD21 ... 35 C8
May Terr. Leeds LS9 ... 79 F6
May Tree Cl. Brad BD14 ... 73 D5
Mayberry Dr. Silk S75 ... 193 F1
Maybrook Ind. Pk. Leeds ... 78 B8
Maybury Ave. Crig WF4 ... 160 A7
Mayfair Ave. Elland HX4 ... 133 F1
Mayfair. Brad BD5 ... 74 D4
Mayfair Pl. Hem WF9 ... 181 D7
Mayfair Way. Brad BD4 ... 75 D5
Mayfield Ave. Brad BD12 ... 94 D2
Mayfield Ave. Brig HD6 ... 115 B8
Mayfield Ave. Hali HX1 ... 113 A6
Mayfield Ave. Hud HD5 ... 154 F6
Mayfield Ave. ... 8 D4
Mayfield Cl. Glu BD20 ... 16 C6
Mayfield Cl. Ilkley LS29 ... 8 D4
Mayfield Ct. Ossett WF5 ... 140 E3
Mayfield Dr. Hali HX1 ... 113 A6
Mayfield Dr. Keigh BD20 ... 36 C8
Mayfield Gdns. Hali HX1 ... 112 D5
Mayfield Gdns. Hali HX1 ... 113 A6
Mayfield Gdns. Ilkley LS29 ... 8 D5
Mayfield Gr. Bail BD17 ... 38 D3
Mayfield Gr. Brig HD6 ... 115 B8
Mayfield Gr. Hali HX1 ... 113 A6
Mayfield Gr. Wilts BD15 ... 53 B6
Mayfield Mount. Hali HX1 ... 113 A6 3
Mayfield Rd. Heb Br HX7 ... 89 A4
Mayfield Rise. Leeds LS15 ... 81 B8
Mayfield Rise. Ryhill WF4 ... 162 A1
Mayfield St. Hali HX1 ... 113 A5 10
Mayfield Terr. Brad BD14 ... 73 C3
Mayfield Terr. Hali HX1 ... 113 A6 3
Mayfield Terr. S. Hali HX1 ... 113 A5 11
Mayfield View. Leeds LS15 ... 81 B8
Mayfields Way. S Kirk WF9 ... 182 B1
Mayflower St. Leeds LS10 ... 80 A3
Maylea Dr. Otley LS21 ... 22 D6
Mayman Cl. Batley WF17 ... 118 C5
Maynham St. Batley WF17 ... 118 C5
Maymes Cl. Dew WF12 ... 139 D2
Mayo Ave. Brad BD5 ... 74 E2
Mayo Cl. Leeds LS8 ... 61 D6
Mayo Cr. Brad BD5 ... 74 E1
Mayo Dr. Brad BD5 ... 74 E1
Mayo Rd. Brad BD5 ... 74 E1
Mayor's Walk Ave. Pont WF8 ... 146 D7
Mayor's Wlk. Pont WF8 ... 146 D7
Mayory Wlk. Castle WF10 ... 125 C7
Maypole Mews. B in Elm LS15 ... 63 D8
Maypole Rd. Hud HD2 ... 136 C4
Mayster Gr. Brig HD6 ... 135 F8
Mayster Rd. Brig HD6 ... 135 F8
Maythorne Ave. Batley WF17 ... 118 A4
Maythorne Cres. Brad BD14 ... 73 D4
Maythorne Dr. Brad BD14 ... 73 D4
Mayville Ave. Keigh BD20 ... 36 B8
Mayville Pl. Leeds LS6 ... 59 E3
Mayville Rd. Leeds LS6 ... 59 E3
Mayville St. Leeds LS6 ... 59 E3
Mayville Terr. Leeds LS6 ... 59 E3
Mazebrook Ave. Clec BD19 ... 95 E2
Mazebrook. Clec BD19 ... 95 E2
Mazebrook Cres. Clec BD19 ... 95 E2
McBride Way. Weth LS22 ... 13 E5
McBurney Cl. Hali HX3 ... 92 B2 2
McLaren Ave. Upton WF9 ... 183 D8
McMahon Dr. Brad BD13 ... 72 D1
McMillan Sch. Brad ... 39 C1
Mead Cl. Hud HD2 ... 136 A1
Mead View. Brad BD4 ... 95 C8
Mead Way. Kirkb HD8 ... 173 F6
Meadow Bank. Ack M T WF7 ... 146 A1
Meadow Bank Cres. Mir WF14 ... 137 E5
Meadow Bank. Dew WF13 ... 138 F8
Meadow Bank. Holmfi HD7 ... 189 C6
Meadow Bank. Ryhill WF4 ... 162 C1
Meadow Bank Bottom Rd. Tod OL14 ... 108 A1
Meadow Brook Chase. Nor WF6 ... 123 C1
Meadow Brook Cl. Nor WF6 ... 123 C1
Meadow Brook Ct. Nor WF6 ... 123 C1
Meadow Brook Gn. Nor WF6 ... 123 C1
Meadow Cl. B Spa LS23 ... 30 C8
Meadow Cl. Brad LS17 ... 28 E6
Meadow Cl. Con BD20 ... 4 A2
Meadow Cl. Harden BD16 ... 36 A1
Meadow Cl. Hem WF9 ... 181 C6
Meadow Cl. Liver WF15 ... 117 A4
Meadow Cl. Loft G WF1 ... 121 C5
Meadow Cl. Loft G WF1 ... 121 D5
Meadow Cl. Shelf HX3 ... 93 B6
Meadow Cres. Hali HX3 ... 113 B3
Meadow Cres. Roy S71 ... 179 D3
Meadow Croft. Birken LS15 ... 63 D8
Meadow Croft. Hud HD5 ... 137 C1
Meadow Croft. Leeds LS11 ... 79 B2
Meadow Croft. Loft G WF1 ... 121 D5
Meadow Croft. Roy S71 ... 179 D3
Meadow Ct. Castle WF10 ... 125 D6
Meadow Ct. Roy S71 ... 179 D3

Meadow Ct. S Elm WF9 ... 183 B3
Meadow Dr. Hali HX3 ... 113 B3
Meadow Dr. Liver WF15 ... 116 F1
Meadow Earth. Bramho LS16 ... 24 E2
Meadow Garth. Bramho LS16 ... 24 F1
Meadow Garth. Loft G WF1 ... 121 C5
Meadow Gn. Slai HD7 ... 170 D8
Meadow La. Con BD20 ... 4 A2
Meadow La. Dew WF13 ... 118 C8
Meadow La. Hali HX1 ... 91 E2
Meadow La. Leeds LS11 ... 79 C6
Meadow La. Liver WF15 ... 116 F1
Meadow La. Slai HD7 ... 151 F1
Meadow La. Wake WF2 ... 141 F7
Meadow Lea. Glu BD20 ... 16 C6
Meadow Park Cres. Pudsey LS28 ... 57 C2
Meadow Park Dr. Pudsey LS28 ... 57 B2
Meadow Pk. Kirkhe HD5 ... 137 B2
Meadow Rd. Brad BD10 ... 56 E8
Meadow Rd. Castle WF10 ... 124 B5
Meadow Rd. Gar LS25 ... 83 A7
Meadow Rd. Leeds LS11 ... 79 B5
Meadow Rd. Leeds LS7 ... 79 D3
Meadow Rd. Hud HD1 ... 153 D7
Meadow The. Nor WF6 ... 59 F7
Meadow Vale. Loft G WF1 ... 121 D5
Meadow Vale. Neth WF4 ... 158 D5
Meadow Valley. Leeds LS17 ... 43 B5
Meadow View. B in Elm LS15 ... 63 E8
Meadow View. Brad BD12 ... 94 C1
Meadow View. Haw BD22 ... 34 D2
Meadow View. Leeds LS6 ... 59 E3 13
Meadow View. Skelt HD8 ... 175 B8
Meadow Way. Ack M T WF7 ... 146 A1
Meadow Way. E Ard WF3 ... 120 D7
Meadow Way. Leeds LS17 ... 43 B5
Meadow Wlk. Bad WF9 ... 164 E3
Meadow Wlk. Hali HX3 ... 91 E2
Meadowbank Ave. Brad BD15 ... 54 B1
Meadowcroft Cl. Loft G WF1 ... 121 D5
Meadowcroft La. Rip HX6 ... 132 E5
Meadowcroft Mews. Leeds LS9 ... 79 E7
Meadowcroft Rd. Loft G WF1 ... 121 D5
Meadowcroft Rise. Brad BD4 ... 75 E2
Meadowfields Cl. Crof WF4 ... 162 A8
Meadowfields Dr. Crof WF4 ... 162 A8
Meadowfields Rd. Crof WF4 ... 162 A8
Meadowgate Croft. Roth WF3 ... 100 B2
Meadowgate Dr. Roth WF3 ... 100 B1
Meadowgate. Roth WF3 ... 100 C2
Meadowgate Vale. Roth WF3 ... 100 B1
Meadowhurst Gdns. Pudsey LS28 ... 76 D7
Meadowlands. Biring BD19 ... 96 E1
Meadows The. D Dale HD8 ... 191 F5
Meadows The. Hors LS16 ... 42 C3
Meadowside Rd. Bail BD17 ... 38 E4
Meadstead Dr. Roy S71 ... 179 B3
Meadway. Brad BD6 ... 93 F6
Meadway. Wrenf ... 144 C5
Meagill Rise. Otley LS21 ... 10 E2
Meal Hill La. Slai HD7 ... 151 F2
Meal Hill La. Holmfi HD7 ... 189 C7
Meal Hill. Slai HD7 ... 151 F2
Meal Hill Rd. Holme HD7 ... 187 F1
Mean La. Mel HD7 ... 170 E2
Meanwood CE Aided Prim Sch.
  Leeds ... 59 E7
Meanwood Cl. Leeds LS7 ... 60 B4
Meanwood Gr. Leeds LS6 ... 42 E1
Meanwood Park Hospl. Leeds ... 42 E1
Meanwood Rd. Leeds LS6, LS7 ... 60 B4
Meanwood Rd. Leeds LS6, LS7 ... 60 D7
Meanwood St. Leeds LS7 ... 60 D7
Meanwood Towers. Leeds LS6 ... 60 A8
Meanwood Valley Dr. Leeds LS7 ... 59 F6
Meanwood Valley Gn. Leeds LS7 ... 59 F6
Meanwood Valley Gr. Leeds LS7 ... 59 F6
Meanwood Valley Mount. Leeds
  LS7 ... 59 F6
Meanwood Valley Rd. Leeds LS7 ... 59 F6
Meanwood Valley Wlk. Leeds LS7 ... 59 F6
Mearhouse Bank. Holmfi HD7 ... 189 E4
Mearhouse Terr. Holmfi HD7 ... 189 E4
Medeway. Pudsey LS28 ... 57 C2
Medhurst Ave. Kippax LS25 ... 83 B2
Medley La. Nor/the HX3 ... 93 F7
Medley St. Castle WF10 ... 124 D7
Medlock Rd. Hor WF4 ... 141 A1
Medway Ave. Gar LS25 ... 83 B8
Medway. Kirkhe HD5 ... 137 B2
Meg La. Hud HD3 ... 153 B5
Meggison Gr. Brad BD5 ... 74 E4 3
Megnaway. Brad BD5 ... 74 E4 3
Melba Rd. Brad BD5 ... 74 C3
Melbourne Ave. Wake WF2 ... 120 F3
Melbourne Gr. Brad BD3 ... 75 B8
Melbourne Gr. Leeds LS13 ... 58 C2
Melbourne Mews. Wake WF2 ... 120 F4
Melbourne Pl. Brad BD5 ... 74 D4
Melbourne Rd. Tod OL14 ... 108 A1
Melbourne St. Hali HX1 ... 92 A1
Melbourne St. Leeds LS2 ... 79 E8
Melbourne St. Liver WF15 ... 117 B3 4
Melbourne St. Morley LS27 ... 98 B4
Melbourne St. Pudsey LS28 ... 57 D2 7
Melbourne St. Ship BD18 ... 55 B8
Melbourne Terr. Brad BD5 ... 74 D4
Melcombe Wlk. Brad BD4 ... 75 E2
Melford St. Brad BD4 ... 75 B3
Mellor Brook. Slai HD7 ... 151 F4
Mellor Mill La. Elland HX5 ... 134 F6
Mellor St. Brig HD6 ... 115 B1
Mellor St. Elland HX5 ... 134 F6
Mellor Terr. Hali HX1 ... 113 A7
Mellor's Bldgs. Dew WF4 ... 156 E5
Mellwood La. S Elm WF9 ... 182 F3
Melrose Dr. Bur in W LS29 ... 9 E1
Melrose Gr. Horb WF4 ... 141 A1 1
Melrose Pl. Horb WF4 ... 141 A1
Melrose Pl. Pudsey LS28 ... 76 D6
Melrose St. Brad BD7 ... 74 C6
Melrose St. Hali HX3 ... 92 A1

Melrose St. Hali HX3 ... 92 A1 26
Melrose Terr. Bacup OL13 ... 106 A7 9
Melrose Terr. Elland HX5 ... 134 F6
Melrose Wlk. Hors LS18 ... 58 E8
Meltham CE (C) Jun & Inf Sch. Mel ... 170 E1
Meltham House La. Holmfi HD7 ... 189 F4
Meltham Mills Ind Est. Mel HD7 ... 170 F2
Meltham Mills Rd. Mel HD7 ... 170 F2
Meltham Prim Sch. Mel ... 170 D1
Meltham Rd. Hud HD1, HD4 ... 153 F3
Meltham Rd. Mars HD7 ... 169 C5
Melton Ave. Midd LS10 ... 99 F4
Melton Cl. Midd LS10 ... 99 F4
Melton Cl. S Elm WF9 ... 183 A5
Melton Garth. Midd LS10 ... 99 F4
Melton Rd. Wake WF2 ... 160 A4
Melton St. Batley WF17 ... 118 B6
Melton Terr. Brad BD10 ... 56 E4
Melville Cl. Leeds LS6 ... 60 B3
Melville Gdns. Leeds LS6 ... 60 B3
Melville La. Ilkley LS29 ... 8 E4
Melville Pl. Leeds LS6 ... 60 B3
Melville Rd. Leeds LS6 ... 60 B3
Melville St. Brad BD7 ... 74 C7
Memorial Dr. Leeds LS6 ... 59 F7
Mendip Ave. Hud HD3 ... 135 A1
Mendip Cl. Gar LS25 ... 82 F5
Mendip Rd. Dew WF12 ... 118 F1
Menday Way. Brad BD12 ... 94 E5
Menin Dr. Bail BD17 ... 38 C5
Menston Inf Sch. Men ... 21 A4
Menston Dr. Guise LS29 ... 22 A3
Menston Old La. Men LS29 ... 21 F7
Menston Old La. Men LS29 ... 21 F7
Menston St. Brad BD7 ... 22 B5
Menstone St. Brad BD8 ... 74 C8 6
Mercer Cl. Hud HD4 ... 171 B6
Merchants Ct. Brad BD4 ... 75 A5
Mercia Way. Leeds LS15 ... 62 E2
Merequay Row. Otley LS21 ... 23 A7
Merewood Rd. Castle WF10 ... 123 F7
Meriden Ave. Gar LS25 ... 82 F5
Merlin Cl. Morley LS27 ... 98 C4
Merlin Gr. Brad BD8 ... 55 A1
Merlin Ct. Hud HD4 ... 171 E7
Merrion Ctr. Leeds LS2 ... 211 F4
Merlyn Rees High Sch. Midd ... 99 D4
Merrill Rd. Dearne S63 ... 194 C1
Merrion Cres. Hali HX3 ... 113 B5
Merrion Ct. Leeds ... 60 C8
Merrion St. Hali HX3 ... 113 B5
Merrion St. Leeds LS1, LS2 ... 59 F1
Merrion St. Leeds LS2 ... 211 F4
Merrion Way. Leeds LS2 ... 60 C1
Merry Bent La. Rip HX6 ... 132 A5
Merrybents St. Tod OL14 ... 108 D5
Mersey St. Tod OL14 ... 108 D5
Merseyside Ind Est. Dew ... 118 C8
Mersey St. Bacup OL13 ... 106 A1 4
Merton Ave. Pudsey LS28 ... 57 C2
Merton Dr. Pudsey LS28 ... 57 C2
Merton Fold. Brad BD5 ... 74 E4 6
Merton Gdns. Pudsey LS28 ... 57 C2
Merton Rd. Brad BD5 ... 74 E4 5
Merville Ave. Bail BD17 ... 37 F1
Metcalfe St. Brad BD4 ... 75 B4
Methley Dr. Leeds LS7 ... 60 C6
Methley Gr. Leeds LS7 ... 60 C6
Methley La. Leeds LS7 ... 60 C6
Methley La. Oult LS26 ... 101 F2
Methley Jun Sch. M'town ... 102 C3
Methley La. Leeds LS7 ... 60 C6
Methley Mount. Leeds LS7 ... 60 C6
Methley Pl. Leeds LS7 ... 60 C6
Methley Rd. Castle WF10 ... 124 B6
Methley Rd. Leeds LS7 ... 60 C6
Methley Terr. Leeds LS7 ... 60 C6
Methley View. Leeds LS7 ... 60 C6
Mews The. Nor WF6 ... 145 B3
Mexborough Ave. Leeds LS7 ... 60 C5
Mexborough Dr. Leeds LS7 ... 60 C5
Mexborough Gr. Leeds LS7 ... 60 C5
Mexborough Pl. Leeds LS7 ... 60 C5
Mexborough Rd. Leeds LS7 ... 60 C5
Mexborough Rd. Ship BD2 ... 55 D5
Mexborough St. Leeds LS7 ... 60 C5
Meynell Ave. Leeds LS26 ... 100 E5
Meynell Ct. Leeds LS15 ... 81 A8
Meynell Heights. Leeds LS11 ... 79 D4 6
Meynell Mount. Leeds LS26 ... 100 E5
Meynell Rd. Leeds LS15 ... 80 F8
Meynell Sq. Leeds LS11 ... 79 D4 5
Meynell Wlk. Leeds LS11 ... 79 D4 7
Meyrick Ave. Weth LS22 ... 14 A6
Miall St. Hali HX1 ... 113 A4
Michael Ave. Loft G WF3 ... 121 F5
Mickledore Cl. Brad BD7 ... 73 E2
Micklefield CE (C) Prim Sch. M'field 84 A7
Micklefield La. Yeadon LS19 ... 40 B4
Micklefield Rd. Yeadon LS19 ... 40 B4
Micklefield St. Yeadon LS19 ... 40 B4
Micklegate Sq. Pont WF8 ... 125 F1
Micklegate. Pont WF8 ... 146 D8
Micklethwaite Dr. Queen BD13 ... 92 D8
Micklethwaite Gr. Queen BD13 ... 92 C8
Micklethwaite La. Bing BD16 ... 37 E6
Micklethwaite View. Weth LS22 ... 14 A8
Mickley St. Leeds LS12 ... 59 D1
Mid Yorkshire Nuffield Hospl. Hors 58 B6
Middle Cl. Kex S75 ... 177 C1
Middle Cross St. Leeds LS12 ... 210 A2
Middle Dean St. Elland HX4 ... 134 B7
Middle Field La. Wool WF4 ... 177 F4
Middle Hall Cl. Liver WF15 ... 117 A5
Middle La. Brad BD14 ... 73 C4
Middle La. Dew WF12 ... 118 E1
Middle La. Dew WF12, WF13 ... 139 B8
Middle Oxford St. Castle WF10 ... 124 C8
Middle Rd. Dew WF12 ... 139 E8
Middle Rd. Leeds LS9 ... 80 A7
Middle Rd. Leeds LS9, LS10 ... 80 A5
Middle St. Brad BD1 ... 201 C3
Middle Way. Keigh BD21 ... 35 E7

Middlebrook Cl. Brad BD8 ... 73 C7
Middlebrook Cres. Brad BD8 ... 73 C7
Middlebrook Dr. Brad BD8 ... 73 D7
Middlebrook Hill. Brad BD8 ... 73 D7
Middlebrook Rise. Brad BD8 ... 73 C7
Middlebrook View. Brad BD8 ... 73 D7
Middlebrook Way. Brad BD8 ... 73 D7
Middlebrook Wlk. Brad BD8 ... 73 D7
Middlecliffe Dr. Wth Com S30 ... 200 D5
Middlecroft Cl. Midd LS10 ... 99 F8
Middlecroft Rd. Midd LS10 ... 99 F8
Middlefield La. K Sinea WF8 ... 166 A4
Middlegate. Batley WF17 ... 96 E1
Middlemoor. Leeds LS14 ... 62 B8
Middlethorne Mid Sch. Leeds ... 44 B5
Middleton Ave. Ilkley LS29 ... 8 B5
Middleton Ave. Leeds LS10 ... 99 F1
Middleton Ave. Leeds LS8 ... 61 A5
Middleton Ct. Morley LS27 ... 100 A5
Middleton Cres. Leeds LS11 ... 79 B2
Middleton Ct. Leeds LS11 ... 116 E4
Middleton District Ctr. Midd ... 99 D5
Middleton Gr. Leeds LS11 ... 79 B2
Middleton Gr. Morley LS27 ... 98 C4
Middleton La. Leeds LS10 ... 99 D3
Middleton La. M'field LS26 ... 101 A5
Middleton Park Ave. Midd LS10 ... 99 E4
Middleton Park Cres. Midd LS10 ... 99 C5
Middleton Park Ct. Midd LS10 ... 99 C5
Middleton Park Dr. Midd LS10 ... 99 B5
Middleton Park Gr. Midd LS10 ... 99 C5
Middleton Park High Sch. Midd ... 99 D4
Middleton Park Mount. Midd LS10 ... 99 B4
Middleton Park Rd. Midd LS10 ... 99 C5
Middleton Park Sq N. Midd LS10 ... 99 B4
Middleton Park Sq S. Midd LS10 ... 99 B4
Middleton Park Terr. Midd LS10 ... 99 C4
Middleton Prim Sch. Midd ... 99 C4
Middleton Railway. Leeds ... 80 B2
Middleton Rd. Ilkley LS29 ... 8 A4
Middleton Rd. Leeds LS10 ... 99 F8
Middleton Rd. Morley LS27 ... 98 C4
Middleton Rd. Wake ... 99 F7
Middleton St. Brad BD8 ... 55 B1
Middleton Terr. Morley LS27 ... 98 C4
Middleton Way. Knot WF11 ... 126 F4
Middleton Wlk. Knot WF11 ... 126 F3
Middleway. Sil BD20 ... 5 F1
Midge Hall Cl. Bur in W LS29 ... 9 F1
Midgeham Gr. Harden BD16 ... 36 A1
Midgehole La. Wad M HX7 ... 89 A6
Midgeley Rd. Bail BD17 ... 38 A3
Midgeley Rd. Bur in W LS29 ... 9 F1
Midgley Almshouses. Haw BD22 ... 51 E8 16
Midgley Cl. Loft G WF3 ... 100 A1
Midgley Pl. Leeds LS6 ... 59 E3 3
Midgley Rd. Bur in W LS29 ... 9 E1
Midgley Rd. Heb Br HX7 ... 89 F1
Midgley Terr. Leeds LS6 ... 59 E3 9
Midland Cl. Leeds LS10 ... 79 F3
Midland Garth. Leeds LS10 ... 79 F3
Midland Hill. Bing BD16 ... 36 F3
Midland Pas. Leeds LS6 ... 59 F3 1
Midland Pl. Leeds LS11 ... 79 A4
Midland Rd. Brad BD8 ... 55 C1
Midland Rd. Leeds LS10 ... 79 F3
Midland Rd. Leeds LS6 ... 59 F3
Midland Rd. Roy S71 ... 179 D4
Midland St. S in Cra BD20 ... 16 E6
Midland Terr. Leeds LS6 ... 59 F3
Midway. Hud HD4 ... 171 A6
Milan Rd. Leeds LS8 ... 61 A3
Milan St. Leeds LS9 ... 80 A8
Mildred Sylvester Way. Nor WF6 ... 123 B1
Mile Cross Gdns. Hali HX1 ... 112 F6
Mile Cross Pl. Hali HX1 ... 112 F6
Mile Cross Rd. Hali HX1 ... 112 F6
Mile Cross Terr. Hali HX1 ... 112 F6
Mile End. Mel HD7 ... 170 C2
Mile Thorn St. Hali HX1 ... 112 F7
Miles Garth. Bard LS17 ... 28 F5
Miles Hill Ave. Leeds LS7 ... 60 B5
Miles Hill Cres. Leeds LS7 ... 60 B6
Miles Hill Mount. Leeds LS7 ... 60 B6
Miles Hill Pl. Leeds LS7 ... 60 B6
Miles Hill Rd. Leeds LS7 ... 60 B5
Miles Hill Sq. Leeds LS7 ... 60 B5
Miles Hill St. Leeds LS7 ... 60 B5
Miles Hill Terr. Leeds LS7 ... 60 B5
Miles Hill View. Leeds LS7 ... 60 B5
Milestone Ct. Pudsey LS28 ... 57 F2
Milford Pl. Brad BD9 ... 55 B2
Milford Pl. Leeds LS4 ... 59 D1
Mill Bank. Bard LS17 ... 28 F5
Mill Bank Cl. Sow B HX6 ... 132 C2
Mill Bank Rd. Sow B HX6 ... 111 B1
Mill Bank Rd. Mel HD7 ... 170 D1
Mill Carr Hill Rd. Brad BD4, BD12 ... 94 F6
Mill Cl. S Kirk WF9 ... 182 B2
Mill Cl. Wake WF2 ... 141 F7
Mill Ct. Haw BD22 ... 51 F8
Mill Dam. K Sinea WF8 ... 166 E6
Mill Dam La. Pont WF8 ... 146 B7
Mill Forest Way. Batley WF17 ... 117 F5
Mill Garth. Leeds LS15 ... 81 B8
Mill Gate. Kirkhe HD5 ... 155 C7
Mill Green Cl. Leeds LS14 ... 62 C5
Mill Green Garth. Leeds LS14 ... 62 C5
Mill Green Rd. Leeds LS14 ... 62 C5
Mill Green View. Leeds LS14 ... 62 B5
Mill Hey. Haw BD22 ... 51 D7

Mill Hill. Ack M T WF7 ... 164 A8
Mill Hill Ave. Pont WF8 ... 146 C6
Mill Hill Cl. Dar WF8 ... 147 D5
Mill Hill Gn. Roth LS26 ... 100 E5
Mill Hill. Haw BD22 ... 51 C7
Mill Hill La. Brig HD6 ... 114 F4
Mill Hill La. Liver HD6 ... 115 F1
Mill Hill La. Liver HD6 ... 115 F1
Mill Hill. Leeds LS1 ... 79 C7
Mill Hill. Nor WF6 ... 123 A1
Mill Hill. Pudsey LS28 ... 76 F7
Mill Hill Rd. Pont WF8 ... 146 C7
Mill Hill. Roth LS26 ... 100 E5
Mill Hill Sq. Roth LS26 ... 100 E5
Mill La. Hap. Harden BD16 ... 53 B8
Mill La. Ack M T WF7 ... 164 A6
Mill La. Ad Le S DN6 ... 184 F2
Mill La. Bard LS17 ... 28 E4
Mill La. Batley WF17 ... 97 B2
Mill La. Batley WF17 ... 118 E3
Mill La. Birk BD11 ... 96 A6
Mill La. Birk BD11 ... 96 A6
Mill La. Brad BD4, BD5 ... 74 F5
Mill La. Brig HD6 ... 115 B2
Mill La. Castle WF10 ... 103 C1
Mill La. Clec BD19 ... 95 D3
Mill La. Dew WF12 ... 140 A7
Mill La. Elland HX4 ... 134 C4
Mill La. Feath WF7 ... 144 D6
Mill La. Floc WF4 ... 157 D2
Mill La. Gild LS27 ... 97 D2
Mill La. Guise LS20 ... 38 D8
Mill La. Hali HX2 ... 91 D7
Mill La. Hali HX3 ... 92 B2
Mill La. Haw BD22 ... 34 C2
Mill La. Hud HD5 ... 137 B5
Mill La. Leeds LS7 ... 206 B2
Mill La. Mapp S75 ... 177 E1
Mill La. Netter LS29 ... 10 F4
Mill La. Otley LS21 ... 10 E6
Mill La. Oxen BD22 ... 51 C3
Mill La. Pont WF8 ... 125 F3
Mill La. Queen BD13 ... 72 C2
Mill La. Ship BD17 ... 55 B5
Mill La. S Elm WF9 ... 183 B4
Mill La. Stee BD20 ... 17 C5
Mill La. Th Arch LS23 ... 30 E8
Mill Lane Cty Prim Sch. Batley ... 118 D3
Mill Moor Rd. Mel HD7 ... 170 C2
Mill Pit La. Roth LS26 ... 100 E4
Mill Pl. Mir WF14 ... 137 E2
Mill Rd. Dew WF13 ... 118 C2
Mill Row. Stee BD20 ... 16 F6
Mill Royd St. Brig HD6 ... 115 B2
Mill Shaw La. Holmfi HD7 ... 189 B8
Mill Shaw. Leeds LS11 ... 117 B8
Mill St. Bard LS17 ... 28 F5
Mill St. Brad BD1 ... 201 C2
Mill St. Brad BD7 ... 74 C5
Mill St. Castle WF10 ... 124 D8 6
Mill St. Cull BD13 ... 52 D6
Mill St. Elland HX5 ... 134 F7
Mill St. E Ard WF3 ... 120 D8
Mill St. Glu BD20 ... 16 C6
Mill St. Hud HD4 ... 153 E4
Mill St. Morley LS27 ... 98 B4
Mill St. S in Cra BD20 ... 16 E6
Mill St. Yeadon LS19 ... 40 C7
Mill View. Castle WF10 ... 124 D7
Mill View. Hem WF9 ... 181 C6
Mill View. Knot WF11 ... 126 C4
Millbank Cl. Pudsey LS28 ... 76 F6
Millbank Fold. Pudsey LS28 ... 76 F6
Millbank. Pudsey LS28 ... 76 F6
Millbeck Cl. Brad BD8 ... 73 C7
Millbeck Dr. Brad BD8 ... 73 C7
Millbeck Gn. Coll LS22 ... 29 A8
Millbridge Inf Sch. Liver ... 117 B4
Millbridge Upper Jun Mix Sch.
  Liver ... 117 B4
Millbrook Gdns. Tod OL14 ... 108 A1
Millcroft Est. Pont LS21 ... 24 D7
Miller Ave. Wake WF2 ... 141 F5
Miller Cl. Crig WF2 ... 160 A6
Miller Hill Bank. D Dale HD8 ... 192 A5
Miller Hill. D Dale HD8 ... 191 F5
Millers Ct. Liver WF15 ... 117 B4 14
Millersdale Cl. Brad BD4 ... 95 B8
Millfield Cl. Hud HD5 ... 154 D6
Millfield Gr. Hem WF9 ... 181 D7
Millfields. Sil BD20 ... 5 D1
Millgarth St. Leeds LS2 ... 79 B8
Millgarth St. Leeds LS2 ... 212 B3
Millgate. Brig HD6 ... 114 F3
Millgate. Elland HX5 ... 134 F7
Millmoor Cl. Brad BD6 ... 74 A1
Millshaw Park Ave. Leeds LS11 ... 98 F6
Millshaw Park La. Leeds LS11 ... 98 F6
Millshaw Park Way. Leeds LS11 ... 98 F6
Millshaw Mount. Leeds LS11 ... 98 E5
Millshaw Rd. Leeds LS11 ... 98 F6
Millshaw. Morley LS11 ... 98 E5
Millside. Shelf S72 ... 180 E3
Millside Wlk. Shelf S72 ... 180 E3
Millstone Rise. Liver WF15 ... 117 A3
Millward St. Ryhill WF4 ... 162 A1
Millwater Ave. Batley WF17 ... 118 B3
Millward St. Batley WF17 ... 117 F5
Millwood Rd. Hud HD3 ... 135 C1
Milne Ct. Leeds LS15 ... 81 E7
Milner Bank. Otley LS21 ... 22 D6
Milner Cl. Elland HX4 ... 134 C7

Milner Gdns. Leeds LS9 ... 79 F6
Milner Ing. Brad BD12 ... 94 C5
Milner La. Bard LS14 ... 28 F1
Milner La. Elland HX4 ... 134 C7
Milner La. Roth WF3 ... 100 A2
Milner La. Scar LS14 ... 45 F7
Milner La. Thorner LS14 ... 45 F7
Milner Rd. Brad BD3 ... 38 A1
Milner Royd La. Sow Br HX6 ... 112 E3
Milner St. Hali HX1 ... 113 B7
Milner St. Hud HD1 ... 153 E3
Milner St. Ossett WF5 ... 119 C1
Milner St. Queen WF3 ... 140 E6
Milner's La. Dar WF8 ... 147 D4
Milner's Rd. Yeadon LS19 ... 39 F7
Milnes Gr. Castle WF10 ... 125 B7
Milnes St. Leeds LS12 ... 78 E6
Milnsbridge Cty Sec Sch. Hud ... 153 A5
Milnthorpe Cl. Bramham LS23 ... 30 C3
Milnthorpe Cres. Wake WF2 ... 160 D7
Milnthorpe Dr. Wake WF2 ... 160 D8
Milnthorpe Garth. Bramham LS23 ... 30 C3
Milnthorpe Gdns. Bramham LS23 ... 30 C3
Milnthorpe La. Bramham LS23 ... 30 C3
Milnthorpe La. Wake WF2 ... 142 D2
Milnthorpe Way. Bramham LS23 ... 30 C3
Milroyd Cres. Batley WF17 ... 97 A2
Milton Ave. Hali HX6 ... 112 B5
Milton Ave. Liver WF15 ... 117 C3
Milton Cl. Crig WF4 ... 159 D6
Milton Cl. Liver WF15 ... 117 C3
Milton Cres. Wake WF2 ... 141 C4
Milton Dr. Loft G WF3 ... 121 F6
Milton Dr. B in Elm LS15 ... 62 F7
Milton Dr. Batley WF15 ... 117 C2
Milton Dr. Hem WF9 ... 163 B2
Milton Gdns. Batley WF15 ... 117 C2
Milton Gr. Batley WF17 ... 118 C2
Milton Pl. Hali HX1 ... 113 B7
Milton Pl. Ossett WF5 ... 140 D7
Milton Rd. Liver WF15 ... 117 C3
Milton Rd. Wake WF2 ... 141 D4
Milton St. Batley WF16 ... 117 D5 1
Milton St. Brad BD7 ... 74 C7
Milton St. Castle WF10 ... 124 C8
Milton St. Denh BD13 ... 71 E8
Milton St. Hali HX1 ... 112 B5 19
Milton St. Wake WF2 ... 142 A5
Milton Terr. Hali HX1 ... 113 B7
Milton Terr. Hem WF9 ... 181 C7
Milton Terr. Leeds LS15 ... 59 A4
Milton Terr. Yeadon LS19 ... 39 F7
Minden Cl. Pont WF8 ... 146 A7
Minden Way. Pont WF8 ... 146 A8
Minerva St. Hud HD4 ... 152 F3
Mini Market. Hud HD1 ... 154 C8 3
Minnie St. Haw BD22 ... 51 C6
Minnie St. Keigh BD21 ... 35 BA
Minor Roads. Mars HD7 ... 169 B8
Minorca Mount. Denh BD13 ... 52 D1
Minstead Ave. Brig HD6 ... 135 D7
Minsthorpe High Sch & Community
  Coll. S Elm ... 183 A5
Minsthorpe La. S Elm WF9 ... 182 E4
Minsthorpe La. S Kirk WF9 ... 182 E4
Minsthorpe Vale. S Elm WF9 ... 182 E4
Mint St. Brad BD2 ... 56 B2
Mint St. Hud HD1 ... 153 D7
Miramar. Hud HD2 ... 136 D5
Miry Butt La. Knot WF11 ... 126 B3
Mirey La. Sow Br HX6 ... 111 C3
Mirfield Ave. Brad BD2 ... 56 A5
Mirfield Free Gram Sch. Mir ... 137 F7
Mirfield Sports Ctr. Mir ... 137 F7
Mirfield Sta. Mir ... 138 A3
Miriam Lord Fst Sch. Brad ... 55 B1
Mirycarr La. Leeds LS ... 46 F1
Miry La. Clec WF15 ... 116 C5
Miry La. Heb Br HX7 ... 110 F6
Miry La. Holmfi HD7 ... 188 F8
Miry La. Holmfi HD7 ... 188 B8
Miry La. Yeadon LS19 ... 40 B7
Mission St. Brig HD6 ... 115 C1
Mistral Cl. Brad BD12 ... 94 E1
Mistral Gr. Brad BD12 ... 94 E1
Mistress La. Leeds LS12 ... 78 C8
Mitcham Dr. Brad BD9 ... 55 A2
Mitchell Ave. Dew WF13 ... 118 B2 3
Mitchell Ave. Hud HD5 ... 155 B5
Mitchell Cl. Brad BD10 ... 39 C1
Mitchell Cl. Brad BD10 ... 39 C1
Mitchell La. Sil BD20 ... 5 C1
Mitchell Sq. Brad BD5 ... 74 E4 8
Mitchell St. Hud HD6 ... 115 A3
Mitchell St. Hali HX6 ... 112 C4
Mitchell St. Heb Br HX7 ... 89 A2 6
Mitchell St. Tod OL14 ... 107 E8
Mitchell Terr. Bing BD16 ... 36 F2
Mitford Pl. Leeds LS12 ... 78 D7 2
Mitford Rd. Leeds LS12 ... 78 D7
Mitford Terr. Leeds LS12 ... 78 D7 1
Mitre Ct. Brad BD4 ... 75 D3
Mitre St. Dew WF13 ... 139 A8
Mitre St. Hud HD1 ... 153 C7
Mitton St. Ship BD16 ... 54 D8
Mixenden Cl. Hali HX2 ... 91 C5
Mixenden Ct. Hali HX2 ... 91 B6
Mixenden La. Hali HX2 ... 91 D6
Mixenden La. Hali HX2 ... 91 D6
Mixenden Rd. Hali HX2 ... 91 C6
Mixenden Stones. Hali HX2 ... 91 C6
Moad End. Thorner LS16 ... 45 F5
Moat Hill. Batley WF17 ... 97 A2
Moat Hill Farm Dr. Batley WF17 ... 97 A2
Modder Ave. Leeds LS12 ... 78 B7
Modder Pl. Leeds LS12 ... 78 B7
Model Ave. Leeds LS12 ... 78 D7
Model Rd. Leeds LS12 ... 78 D7
Model Terr. Leeds LS12 ... 78 D7
Moderna Bsns Pk. Heb Br ... 110 F8
Moffat Cl. Brad BD6 ... 93 F7
Moffatt Cl. Hali HX2 ... 91 F3
Moldgreen Cty Jun & Inf Sch. Hud ... 154 D6
Moles Head. Hud HD7 ... 170 A8
Molly Hurst La. Wool WF4 ... 177 F7
Mona St. Slai HD7 ... 151 F1
Mona St. Wake WF2 ... 160 B5
Mona's Terr. Tod OL14 ... 108 A1 1

Monckton Dr. Castle WF10 ... 125 C6
Monckton Rd. Wake WF2 ... 142 B2
Mond Ave. Brad BD3 ... 56 D1
Monk Barn Cl. Bing BD16 ... 37 A4
Monk Bridge Ave. Leeds LS6 ... 59 F6 11
Monk Bridge Dr. Leeds LS6 ... 59 F6 6
Monk Bridge Gr. Leeds LS6 ... 59 E6 2
Monk Bridge Mount. Leeds LS6 ... 59 F6 10
Monk Bridge Pl. Leeds LS6 ... 59 E6 1
Monk Bridge Rd. Leeds LS6 ... 59 E6
Monk Bridge St. Leeds LS6 ... 59 F6
Monk Bridge Terr. Leeds LS6 ... 59 F6
Monk Ings. Clec WF17 ... 96 C2
Monk Ings. Clec WF17 ... 96 D1
Monk St. Brad BD7 ... 74 C7
Monk St. Wake WF1 ... 142 D5
Monkfield. Mir WF14 ... 137 E6
Monkfield Ave. Pont WF8 ... 125 D2
Monkhill Dr. Pont WF8 ... 125 D2
Monkhill La. Pont WF8 ... 125 D3
Monkhill Mount. Pont WF8 ... 125 D3
Monkhill Sta. Pont ... 125 E2
Monkswood Ave. Leeds LS14 ... 61 F8
Monkswood Bank. Leeds LS14 ... 61 F8
Monkswood Cl. Leeds LS14 ... 61 F8
Monkswood Dr. Leeds LS14 ... 61 F8
Monkswood Gate. Leeds LS14 ... 62 A8 6
Monkswood Gn. Leeds LS14 ... 61 F8
Monkswood Hill. Leeds LS14 ... 61 F8
Monkswood Rise. Leeds LS14 ... 61 F8
Monkswood Wlk. Leeds LS14 ... 62 A8
Monkswood. Leeds LS5 ... 58 F8
Monkwood Rd. Loft G WF1 ... 121 B5
Mons Rd. Tod OL14 ... 107 F7
Monson Ave. Pudsey LS28 ... 57 B6
Mont Gr. Brad BD5 ... 74 D3 1
Montagu Ave. Leeds LS8 ... 61 C5
Montagu Cres. Leeds LS8 ... 61 C5
Montagu Ct. Leeds LS8 ... 61 B6
Montagu Dr. Leeds LS8 ... 61 B6
Montagu Gdns. Leeds LS8 ... 61 B5
Montagu Gr. Leeds LS8 ... 61 C5
Montagu Pl. Leeds LS8 ... 61 B5
Montagu Rd. Wyth LS22 ... 14 A6
Montagu Rise. Leeds LS8 ... 61 C4
Montagu View. Leeds LS8 ... 61 B5
Montague Cres. Gar LS25 ... 83 A7
Montague Pl. Gar LS25 ... 83 A7
Montague St. Brad BD5 ... 74 C3
Montague St. Sow Br HX6 ... 112 A3
Montague St. Wake WF1 ... 142 F2
Montcalm Cres. Leeds LS10 ... 79 E2
Montcalm Cres. Loft G WF3 ... 121 F3
Montfort Cl. Hors LS18 ... 41 A5
Montpelier Terr. Leeds LS6 ... 60 A3 3
Montreal Ave. Leeds LS7 ... 60 D6
Montreal St. Tod OL14 ... 108 A1 9
Montreal Terr. Pudsey LS13 ... 77 A8
Montrose Ave. Mapp S75 ... 177 F1
Montrose Pl. Queen BD13 ... 72 C2
Montrose Pl. Queen BD13 ... 72 C2 2
Montrose St. Ship BD2 ... 55 D4
Montserrat Rd. Brad BD4 ... 75 F1
Monument La. Pont WF8 ... 146 E7
Monument Mews. Pont WF8 ... 146 E7
Moody St. Brad BD4 ... 75 B4
Moor Allerton Ave. Leeds LS17 ... 43 E2
Moor Allerton Cty Prim Sch.
  Leeds ... 43 F1
Moor Allerton Cres. Leeds LS17 ... 43 E2
Moor Allerton Ctr. Leeds ... 43 D2
Moor Allerton Dr. Leeds LS17 ... 43 E2
Moor Allerton Gdns. Leeds LS17 ... 43 E2
Moor Allerton Way. Leeds LS17 ... 43 E2
Moor Ave. B Spa LS23 ... 30 D6
Moor Ave. Leeds LS15 ... 80 D7
Moor Bottom. Honley HD7 ... 171 F4
Moor Bottom La. Keigh BD21 ... 35 B3
Moor Bottom La. Keigh BD21 ... 37 B3
Moor Bottom La. Rip HX6 ... 132 F5
Moor Bottom Rd. Hali HX2 ... 91 D7
Moor Bottom Rd. Rip HX6 ... 132 F5
Moor Close Ave. Queen BD13 ... 72 C8
Moor Close Farm Mews. Queen
  BD13 ... 92 C8 2
Moor Close La. Queen BD13 ... 72 D1
Moor Close Par. Queen BD13 ... 72 C8
Moor Close Rd. Queen BD13 ... 72 C8
Moor Cottage Cl. Hud HD4 ... 171 E8
Moor Cres. Leeds LS11 ... 79 C3
Moor Crescent Chase. Leeds LS11 ... 79 C3
Moor Crest Rd. Hud HD4 ... 153 C3
Moor Croft. Bing BD16 ... 37 B5
Moor Croft. Hors LS16 ... 42 A4
Moor Dr. Haw BD22 ... 34 C1
Moor Dr. Leeds LS6 ... 59 E6
Moor Dr. Otley LS21 ... 22 D8
Moor Edge High Side. Harden BD16 ... 36 A3
Moor End Ave. Hali HX2 ... 91 F7
Moor End La. Batley WF13 ... 117 C2
Moor End La. Hali HX2 ... 91 F7
Moor End La. Sow Br HX6 ... 112 C1
Moor End Rd. Haw BD22 ... 33 B1
Moor End Rd. Hud HD4 ... 153 D3
Moor End Sec Sch. Hud ... 153 D3
Moor Farm Gdns. Leeds LS7 ... 60 C7
Moor Flatts Ave. Mido LS10 ... 99 C8
Moor Flatts Rd. Mido LS10 ... 99 C8
Moor Fold. Holmfi HD7 ... 189 E7
Moor Gr. Brad BD2 ... 55 F4
Moor Gr. Leeds LS6 ... 59 E6
Moor Gr. Pudsey LS28 ... 76 D6
Moor Grange Ct. Leeds LS16 ... 58 F7
Moor Grange Dr. Leeds LS16 ... 58 F7
Moor Grange Rise. Leeds LS16 ... 59 A7
Moor Grange View. Leeds LS16 ... 58 F7
Moor Haven Ct. Leeds LS17 ... 43 A4
Moor Hey La. Elland HX4 ... 134 F1
Moor Hey La. Elland HX4, HX4 ... 134 F1
Moor Hill Rd. Hud HD3 ... 152 E7
Moor House Ct. Leeds LS17 ... 44 A6
Moor Knoll Cl. E Ard WF3 ... 120 A8
Moor Knoll Dr. E Ard WF3 ... 120 A8
Moor Knoll La. E Ard WF3 ... 119 F8
Moor La. Add LS29 ... 2 C1
Moor La. Birk BD11 ... 96 E6
Moor La. Clift LS21 ... 10 C4

Moor La. Coll LS22 ... 29 F7
Moor La. Dar WF8 ... 147 A2
Moor La. E Kes LS17 ... 28 A5
Moor La. Guise LS20 ... 22 E2
Moor La. Hali HX2 ... 91 E4
Moor La. Hare LS17 ... 27 F6
Moor La. Holmfi HD7 ... 188 E8
Moor La. Hud HD4 ... 171 D7
Moor La. Kirkb HD4 ... 172 F5
Moor La. Kirkb HD8 ... 173 F7
Moor La. Men LS29 ... 21 E4
Moor La. Pont WF8 ... 146 E4
Moor La. Sil LS29 ... 6 D8
Moor La. Stut LS24 ... 48 F8
Moor La. Th Arch LS23 ... 14 D5
Moor La. Tod OL14 ... 108 B3
Moor Park Ave. Hud HD4 ... 153 C1
Moor Park Ave. Leeds LS6 ... 59 D6
Moor Park Cl. Brad BD3 ... 75 C8
Moor Park Cl. S Elm WF9 ... 183 A1
Moor Park Cres. Sil LS29 ... 6 D8
Moor Park Dr. Brad BD3 ... 75 D8
Moor Park Dr. Leeds LS6 ... 59 D6
Moor Park Dr. Sil LS29 ... 6 D8
Moor Park Gdns. Dew WF12 ... 118 E1
Moor Park Gr. Sil LS29 ... 6 D8
Moor Park La. Dew WF13 ... 118 E1 6
Moor Park Mews. Sil LS29 ... 6 D8
Moor Park Mount. Leeds LS6 ... 59 D6
Moor Park Villas. Leeds LS6 ... 59 D6
Moor Park Way. Sil LS29 ... 6 E8
Moor Rd. Bramho LS16 ... 24 D2
Moor Rd. Death WF7 ... 145 D5
Moor Rd. Ilkley LS29 ... 21 C7
Moor Rd. Leeds LS6 ... 59 D6
Moor Rd. Leeds LS10 ... 79 D2
Moor Rd. Loft G WF3 ... 121 C1
Moor Rd. Men LS29 ... 21 C7
Moor Royd. Honley HD7 ... 171 E3
Moor Side. B Spa LS23 ... 30 B7
Moor Side Cotts. Keigh BD20 ... 19 B3
Moor Side La. Oxen HD7 ... 200 C4
Moor Side La. Slai HD7 ... 151 D3
Moor Side La. Slai HD7 ... 170 E7
Moor Side Cotts. Heb Br HX7 ... 131 C8
Moor St. Oxen BD22 ... 51 C3
Moor St. Queen BD13 ... 72 E1 9
Moor Stone Pl. Shelf HX3 ... 93 C5
Moor Terr. Brad BD2 ... 56 C1
Moor Top. Birk BD11 ... 96 C5
Moor Top Ave. Kirkb HD4 ... 172 F2
Moor Top. Guise LS20 ... 22 E4
Moor Top. Guise LS20 ... 22 E4
Moor Top Gdns. Hali HX2 ... 91 D7
Moor Top. Hem WF9 ... 181 D5
Moor Top. Mytholm LS29 ... 9 F3
Moor Top. Otley LS21 ... 22 E4
Moor Top Rd. Hud HD4 ... 153 F2
Moor Top Rd. Kirkhe HD5 ... 137 C2
Moor Valley. Loft G WF3 ... 100 D3
Moor Valley Pk. Brad BD18 ... 55 A8
Moor View. Baci OL13 ... 106 A1
Moor View. Batley WF16 ... 117 D3
Moor View. C. Castle WF10 ... 124 F7
Moor View. Clec WF15 ... 116 C5
Moor View. Leeds LS11 ... 79 A5
Moor View. M'town LS26 ... 102 F3
Moor View. Mel HD7 ... 170 D2
Moor View. Pudsey LS28 ... 57 A1
Moor View Rise. Mel HD7 ... 170 D2
Moor View Terr. Batley WF17 ... 118 C5
Moor View. Haw BD22 ... 34 C1
Moorbottom Rd. Hud HD1 ... 153 D5
Moorbottom. Clec BD19 ... 116 F8
Moorcock Rd. B Head HX7 ... 128 C7
Moorcock Rd. B Head HX7 ... 129 A5
Moorcrest Rise. Mapp S75 ... 178 B2
Moorcroft Ave. Brad BD3 ... 56 D1
Moorcroft Avenues. Hud HD7 ... 152 D5
Moorcroft Dr. Dew WF13 ... 118 C1
Moorcroft Dr. Brad BD4 ... 75 F1
Moorcroft Rd. Brad BD4 ... 75 F1
Moorcroft Rd. Hud HD4 ... 153 A1
Moorcroft Terr. Brad BD4 ... 95 F8
Moordale Ave. Brad BD7 ... 73 E3
Moore Ave. Hud HD4 ... 153 C2
Moore Ave. Leeds LS11 ... 78 C1
Moore View. Brad BD7 ... 73 E3
Moored Edge La. Otley LS21 ... 10 B1
Moorend. Clec WF13 ... 117 F1
Moorend Gdns. Pudsey LS28 ... 57 A1
Moorfield Ave. Brad BD3 ... 56 D1
Moorfield Ave. Leeds LS12 ... 205 C2
Moorfield Ave. Mir WF14 ... 137 F6 1
Moorfield Bsns Pk. Yeadon ... 40 C8
Moorfield Cl. Leeds LS12 ... 205 D2
Moorfield Cl. Yeadon LS19 ... 40 C8
Moorfield Cres. Leeds LS12 ... 205 C2
Moorfield Cres. Pudsey LS28 ... 57 A2
Moorfield Cres. Yeadon LS19 ... 40 C8
Moorfield Croft. Yeadon LS19 ... 40 C8
Moorfield Ct. Yeadon LS19 ... 40 C8
Moorfield Dr. Bail BD17 ... 38 C4
Moorfield Dr. Haw BD22 ... 34 B2
Moorfield Dr. Yeadon LS19 ... 40 C8
Moorfield Gdns. Pudsey LS28 ... 57 A2
Moorfield Gr. Leeds LS12 ... 205 C2
Moorfield Gr. Mir WF14 ... 137 F6
Moorfield Gr. Pudsey LS28 ... 57 A2
Moorfield Pl. Brad BD10 ... 56 C7
Moorfield Pl. Tod OL14 ... 86 A1
Moorfield Rd. Bail BD17 ... 38 C4
Moorfield Rd. Leeds LS12 ... 205 C2
Moorfield Rd. Yeadon LS19 ... 40 C8
Moorfield St. Hali HX1 ... 113 A5
Moorfield St. Leeds LS12 ... 205 C2
Moorfield Terr. Yeadon LS19 ... 40 C8
Moorfield View. Liver WF15 ... 117 A4
Moorfield Way. Birk BD11 ... 96 B7
Moorfields. Leeds LS13 ... 58 C3
Moorgarth Ave. Brad BD3 ... 56 D1
Moorgate. Bail BD17 ... 38 C4

Moorgate Cl. Kippax LS25 ... 83 A2
Moorgate Dr. Kippax LS25 ... 83 B2
Moorgate Flats. Mel HD7 ... 170 D2
Moorgate Rd. Kippax LS25 ... 83 A3
Moorgate St. Hali HX1 ... 112 F5 16
Moorhead Cres. Ship BD18 ... 54 E7
Moorhead La. Ship BD18 ... 54 E7
Moorhead Terr. Ship BD18 ... 54 E7
Moorhouse Ave. Brad BD2 ... 56 A5
Moorhouse Ave. Leeds LS11 ... 79 F1
Moorhouse Ave. Wake WF2 ... 142 A6
Moorhouse Cl. Loft G WF3 ... 122 B6
Moorhouse Cl. Oxen BD22 ... 51 C3
Moorhouse Cres. Loft G WF3 ... 122 B6
Moorhouse Ct. Oxen BD22 ... 51 C3
Moorhouse Cres. S Elm WF9 ... 183 A1
Moorhouse Dr. Birk BD11 ... 96 F7
Moorhouse Gap. H Pag DN6 ... 183 F1
Moorhouse La. Hud HD4 ... 171 E1
Moorhouse La. Oxen BD22 ... 51 C4
Moorhouse La. Pont WF7 ... 164 A7
Moorhouse La. Ryhill WF4 ... 162 C4
Moorhouse Rd. Kls HD5 ... 137 C3
Moorhouse Rise La. Wool S75 ... 177 C5
Moorhouse View. Loft G WF3 ... 122 B6
Moorhouse View. S Elm WF9 ... 183 B2
Moorings The. Brad BD10 ... 56 D8
Moorings The. Leeds LS17 ... 43 E5
Moorings The. Mir WF14 ... 138 A4
Moorland Ave. Bail BD17 ... 38 D5
Moorland Ave. Gild LS27 ... 97 C8
Moorland Ave. Guise LS20 ... 22 C1
Moorland Ave. Leeds LS6 ... 59 F2
Moorland Ave. Mapp S75 ... 178 B2
Moorland Ave. Pudsey LS28 ... 76 D7
Moorland Cl. Gild LS27 ... 97 C8
Moorland Cl. Leeds LS6 ... 59 F2
Moorland Cl. Leeds LS17 ... 43 D1
Moorland Cl. Slai HD7 ... 170 D7
Moorland Cotts. Heb Br HX7 ... 131 C8
Moorland Cres. Bail BD17 ... 38 D5
Moorland Cres. Gild LS27 ... 97 C8
Moorland Cres. Guise LS20 ... 22 C2
Moorland Cres. Leeds LS6 ... 59 F2
Moorland Cres. Men LS29 ... 22 A5
Moorland Cres. Pudsey LS28 ... 76 D7
Moorland Dr. Bail BD17 ... 38 D5
Moorland Dr. Crig WF4 ... 159 F2
Moorland Dr. Guise LS20 ... 22 C2
Moorland Dr. Leeds LS17 ... 43 D1
Moorland Dr. Pudsey LS28 ... 57 A1
Moorland Garth. Leeds LS17 ... 43 C1
Moorland Gdns. Leeds LS17 ... 43 D1
Moorland Gr. Leeds LS17 ... 43 D1
Moorland Gr. Pudsey LS28 ... 76 D7
Moorland Ings. Leeds LS17 ... 43 D1
Moorland Leys. Leeds LS17 ... 43 D1
Moorland Mount. Clec BD19 ... 116 E7
Moorland Pl. Brad BD12 ... 94 E4 4
Moorland Rd. Brad BD12 ... 94 C1
Moorland Rd. Guise LS20 ... 22 C2
Moorland Rd. Leeds LS6 ... 205 D1
Moorland Rd. Pudsey LS28 ... 76 D6
Moorland Rise. Leeds LS17 ... 43 D1
Moorland Rise. Mapp S75 ... 178 B2
Moorland St. Oxen BD22 ... 51 C3
Moorland Terr. Gar LS25 ... 82 F7
Moorland Terr. Kexb S75 ... 180 A1
Moorland View. Brad BD12 ... 94 C1
Moorland View. Clec BD19 ... 116 F7
Moorland View. Hali HX2 ... 112 D7
Moorland View. Leeds LS7 ... 204 A2
Moorland View. Pudsey LS28 ... 76 D7
Moorland View. Roys S71 ... 179 D4
Moorland View. Wake WF2 ... 141 D8
Moorland View. Wren BD19 ... 95 D3
Moorland Wlk. Leeds LS17 ... 43 D1
Moorlands. B Spa LS23 ... 30 C8
Moorlands Ave. Batley WF17 ... 96 F1
Moorlands Ave. Brad BD3 ... 56 C1
Moorlands Ave. Dew WF13 ... 139 C8
Moorlands Ave. Gar LS25 ... 82 F7
Moorlands Ave. Oakwo LS8 ... 204 C4
Moorlands Ave. Yeadon LS19 ... 40 A7
Moorlands Cl. Mel HD7 ... 170 D2
Moorlands Ct. Gar LS25 ... 82 F6
Moorlands Dr. Oakwo LS8 ... 204 C4
Moorlands Dr. Yeadon LS19 ... 40 A7
Moorlands Pl. Hali HX3 ... 113 C4
Moorlands Rd. Brig HD6 ... 135 E7
Moorlands Rd. Dew WF13 ... 139 C8
Moorlands Rd. Mel HD7 ... 170 D2
Moorlands The. Wake WF2 ... 160 E5
Moorlands View. Hali HX3 ... 113 C3
Moorlea Dr. Bail BD17 ... 38 C2
Moorleigh Cl. Kippax LS25 ... 83 B1
Moorleigh Dr. Kippax LS25 ... 83 B1
Moormill La. Knot WF11 ... 127 A4
Moorside App. Birk BD11 ... 96 F6
Moorside Ave. Batley WF17 ... 117 F2
Moorside Ave. Brad BD11 ... 96 F6
Moorside Ave. Hud HD3 ... 135 A2
Moorside Ave. Ship BD18 ... 55 D8
Moorside Ave. Ship BD18 ... 55 D8
Moorside Cl. Brad BD11 ... 96 F6
Moorside Cl. Leeds LS13 ... 58 C4
Moorside Cres. Batley WF17 ... 117 F2
Moorside Croft. Brad BD2 ... 56 C5
Moorside Dr. Birk BD11 ... 96 F6

Moorside Dr. Leeds LS13 ... 58 C4
Moorside Dr. Batley WF13 ... 117 F2
Moorside Gdns. Birk BD11 ... 96 F5
Moorside Gdns. Leeds LS13 ... 58 C4
Moorside Gdns. Birk BD11 ... 96 F6
Moorside Gn. Birk BD11 ... 96 F6
Moorside Jun & Inf Sch. Hali ... 91 F4
Moorside La. Add LS29 ... 2 E4
Moorside La. Askw LS21 ... 10 A7
Moorside La. Brad BD3 ... 75 D7
Moorside La. Oxen BD22 ... 51 C6
Moorside Maltings. Leeds LS11 ... 79 C4
Moorside Mews. Brad BD2 ... 56 D3
Moorside Mount. Birk BD11 ... 96 E6
Moorside Paddock. Clec BD19 ... 116 B6
Moorside Par. Birk BD11 ... 96 F5
Moorside Pl. Batley WF13 ... 117 F2
Moorside Pl. Brad BD3 ... 56 C3
Moorside Rd. Birk BD11 ... 96 E5
Moorside Rd. Brad BD11 ... 96 F7
Moorside Rd. Brad BD2 ... 56 C5
Moorside Rd. Kirkhe HD5 ... 137 C1
Moorside Rd. Mars HD7 ... 168 F4
Moorside Rd. Wils BD13 ... 52 B2
Moorside Rd. Wils BD15 ... 53 C2
Moorside St. Brad BD12 ... 94 B6
Moorside St. Leeds LS13 ... 58 C4
Moorside Terr. Birk BD11 ... 96 F6
Moorside Terr. Brad BD2 ... 56 D2
Moorside Terr. Leeds LS13 ... 58 C4
Moorside Vale. Birk BD11 ... 96 F5
Moorside View. Birk BD11 ... 96 F5
Moorside Wlk. Birk BD11 ... 96 F5
Moorside. Birk BD11 ... 96 F6
Moorthorpe Ave. Brad BD3 ... 56 D1
Moorthorpe Sta. S Elm ... 182 E3
Moorthorpe Way. Birk BD11 ... 96 E6
Moorthorpe Way. Keigh BD20 ... 19 F1
Moortown Corner House. Leeds
  LS17 ... 43 D2
Moortown Cty Prim Sch. Leeds ... 43 D2
Moortown Golf Course. Leeds ... 43 B6
Moorview Ctr. Wils BD16 ... 53 E6
Moorview Cres. Wils BD16 ... 53 E6
Moorview Dr. Brad BD10 ... 39 A1
Moorview Dr. Ship BD18 ... 55 F7
Moorville Cl. Leeds LS11 ... 79 B4 3
Moorville Ct. Leeds LS11 ... 79 B4
Moorville Dr. Birk BD11 ... 96 A7
Moorville Gr. Leeds LS11 ... 79 A4
Moorville Rd. Leeds LS11 ... 79 B4
Moravian Pl. Brad BD5 ... 74 D4
Moresdale La. Leeds LS14 ... 62 A3
Moresdale La. Leeds LS14 ... 62 A3
Morley Ave. Brad BD3 ... 56 D1
Morley Carr Rd. Brad BD12 ... 94 C2
Morley Cl. Leeds LS9 ... 61 D1
Morley Fst & Mid Sch. Morley ... 97 F2
Morley Hall La. Sow Br HX6 ... 112 D4
Morley La. Hud HD3 ... 153 A4
Morley St. Brad BD7 ... 74 D7
Morley St. Keigh BD21 ... 35 C7
Morley St. Wake WF1 ... 142 F3
Morley Sta. Morley ... 98 A4
Morley Victoria Prim Sch. Morley ... 98 A5
Morley View. Hali HX3 ... 113 E3
Morning St. Keigh BD21 ... 35 B4 13
Morningside. Brad BD8 ... 55 A1
Morningside. Denh BD13 ... 52 A1
Mornington Rd. Bing BD16 ... 37 A3
Mornington St. Keigh BD21 ... 35 B7
Mornington Villas. Brad BD8 ... 55 C1
Morpeth Pl. Leeds LS9 ... 212 C3
Morpeth St. Brad BD7 ... 74 C6
Morpeth St. Queen BD13 ... 72 E1
Morphet Terr. Leeds LS7 ... 60 C5
Morrell Cres. Wake WF2 ... 120 F1
Morris Ave. Leeds LS5 ... 59 A5
Morris Cl. Hem WF9 ... 163 B2
Morris Gr. Leeds LS5 ... 59 A5
Morris La. Leeds LS5 ... 59 A5
Morris Mount. Leeds LS5 ... 59 A5
Morris Pl. Morley LS27 ... 98 A3
Morris View. Leeds LS5 ... 59 A4
Morrison St. Castle WF10 ... 124 D7
Morritt Ave. Leeds LS15 ... 62 B2
Morritt Dr. Leeds LS15 ... 80 F8
Morritt Gr. Leeds LS15 ... 80 F8
Mortec Pk. Leeds LS15 ... 81 E7
Mortimer Ave. Batley WF17 ... 118 D5
Mortimer Ave. Brad BD3 ... 56 C1
Mortimer Cl. Gar LS25 ... 82 D7
Mortimer Row. Batley WF17 ... 118 D5
Mortimer St. Batley WF17 ... 118 C5
Mortimer St. Brad BD8 ... 74 D8
Mortimer Terr. Batley WF17 ... 118 D5
Morton La. Keigh BD16 ... 36 C8
Morton La. Riddl BD16 ... 36 C8
Morton La. E Mor BD20 ... 19 E1
Morton La. Keigh BD20 ... 19 E1
Morton Terr. Guise LS20 ... 22 D1
Morton Terr. Guise LS20 ... 22 D1
Morton Vale. Keigh BD20 ... 19 E1
Morwick Gr. B in Elm LS15 ... 63 D7
Mossdale Ave. Brad BD9 ... 54 D4
Moseley Pl. Leeds LS6 ... 59 F4
Moseley Wood App. Leeds LS16 ... 41 E5
Moseley Wood Ave. Leeds LS16 ... 41 E6
Moseley Wood Bank. Leeds LS16 ... 41 E6
Moseley Wood Cl. Leeds LS16 ... 41 E5
Moseley Wood Cres. Leeds LS16 ... 41 D5
Moseley Wood Croft. Leeds LS16 ... 41 E5
Moseley Wood Dr. Leeds LS16 ... 41 E6
Moseley Wood Gdns. Leeds LS16 ... 41 E6
Moseley Wood Gn. Leeds LS16 ... 41 E6
Moseley Wood Gr. Leeds LS16 ... 41 E6
Moseley Wood La. Leeds LS16 ... 41 F6
Moseley Wood Rise. Leeds LS16 ... 41 E5
Moseley Wood View. Hors LS16 ... 41 E6
Moseley Wood View. Hors LS16 ... 41 E6

Moseley Wood Way. Hors LS16 .... 41 D6
Moseley Wood Wlk. Hors LS16 .... 41 D5
Moser Ave. Brad BD2 .... 56 A5
Moses Cres. Brad BD2 .... 56 A5
Moss Bridge Rd. Pudsey LS13 .... 57 F5
Moss Carr Ave. Keigh BD21 .... 35 F5
Moss Carr Gr. Keigh BD21 .... 35 F5
Moss Carr Rd. Keigh BD21 .... 35 F5
Moss Dr. Hali HX2 .... 91 E6
Moss Edge Rd. Holmfi HD7 .... 188 C1
Moss Gdns. Leeds LS17 .... 43 A5
Moss Hall La. B Head HX7 .... 87 E4
Moss La. Hali HX2 .... 91 E6
Moss La. Heb Br HX7 .... 89 A4
Moss Rise. Leeds LS17 .... 43 A5
Moss Rise. Holmfi HD7 .... 188 E5
Moss Rise. Leeds LS17 .... 43 A5
Moss Row. Wils BD15 .... 53 C8
Moss Side. Brad BD9 .... 54 E2
Moss St. Castle WF10 .... 124 C8
Moss St. Thorn BD13 .... 72 C7
Moss Syke. Scar LS14 .... 45 C8
Moss Valley. Leeds LS17 .... 43 A5
Mossdale Ave. Brad BD9 .... 54 C3
Mosstree Cl. Queen BD13 .... 72 C2
Mossy Bank Cl. Queen BD13 .... 72 E2
Mostyn Gr. Brad BD6 .... 94 A8
Mostyn Mount. Hali HX3 .... 92 A3
Mostyn Wlk. Crig WF4 .... 159 F2
Moulson Ct. Brad BD5 .... 201 B2
Moulson Ct. Brad BD5 .... 74 E3 1
Moulson Terr. Denh BD13 .... 71 D8
Mount Ave. Batley HX 117 E6
Mount Ave. Batley WF17 .... 118 D3 1
Mount Ave. Brad BD2 .... 56 C5
Mount Ave. Hali HX2 .... 112 C7
Mount Ave. Hem WF9 .... 181 D7
Mount Ave. Hud HD3 .... 134 D7
Mount Ave. Wake WF2 .... 120 F3
Mount Cres. Clec BD19 .... 116 D8
Mount Cres. H Chap BB10 .... 85 A8
Mount Cres. Hali HX2 .... 112 C7
Mount Cres. Wake WF2 .... 141 F3
Mount Dr. Leeds LS17 .... 43 B6
Mount Gdns. Clec BD19 .... 116 D8
Mount Gdns. Leeds LS17 .... 43 B6
Mount Gr. Brad BD2 .... 56 B5
Mount La. Brig HD6 .... 135 C6
Mount La. H Chap BB10 .... 85 A8
Mount La. Tod OL14 .... 86 C3
Mount Pellon Rd. Hali HX2 .... 112 E8
Mount Pisgah. Otley LS21 .... 23 B8
Mount Pl. Ship BD18 .... 55 B8
Mount Pleasant. Ack M T WF7 .... 163 F6
Mount Pleasant. Ack M T WF7 .... 164 A6
Mount Pleasant Ave. Hali HX1 .... 113 B6
Mount Pleasant Ave. Leeds LS8 .... 60 F5
Mount Pleasant. Brad BD6 .... 93 F7 1
Mount Pleasant. Brig HD6 .... 135 D6
Mount Pleasant. Castle WF10 .... 124 F6
Mount Pleasant. Denh BD13 .... 71 D8
Mount Pleasant. Dew WF12 .... 139 E7
Mount Pleasant Dr. Hem WF9 .... 164 E4
Mount Pleasant Gdns. Kippax LS25 .... 83 B1 5
Mount Pleasant. Glu BD20 .... 16 B6
Mount Pleasant. Guise LS20 .... 22 E2
Mount Pleasant. Hud HD1 .... 153 F5
Mount Pleasant. Ilkley LS29 .... 8 C3
Mount Pleasant Int Sch. Hud 153 F3
Mount Pleasant Jun Sch. Hud 153 F3
Mount Pleasant. K Smea WF8 .... 166 F6
Mount Pleasant. Keigh BD20 .... 20 C7
Mount Pleasant. Kippax LS25 .... 83 B1 4
Mount Pleasant La. Lepton HD8 .... 155 F2
Mount Pleasant. Men LS29 .... 21 F4
Mount Pleasant. Midd LS10 .... 99 C5
Mount Pleasant Rd. Pudsey LS28 .... 76 F8
Mount Pleasant. Rip HX6 .... 132 E4
Mount Pleasant. Sil LS29 .... 6 F8
Mount Pleasant Sports Ctr. Hud 153 F3
Mount Pleasant St. Feath WF7 .... 145 D6
Mount Pleasant St. Hud OL14 .... 108 D6 1
Mount Pleasant St. Pudsey LS28 .... 76 F8 2
Mount Pleasant St. Queen BD13 .... 72 E1
Mount Pleasant St. Tod OL14 .... 86 A1
Mount Pleasant View. Tod OL14 .... 86 B7
Mount Preston St. Leeds LS2 .... 60 A1
Mount Prim Sch. Hud HD1 .... 153 F3
Mount Rd. Brad BD2 .... 56 B5
Mount Rd. Brad BD6 .... 74 A1
Mount Rd. Hud HD1 .... 153 D7
Mount Rd. Loft G WF3 .... 121 F6
Mount Rd. Mars HD7 .... 168 E4
Mount Rise. Leeds LS17 .... 43 B6
Mount Royd. Brad BD8 .... 55 D2
Mount Scar View. Holmfi HD7 .... 189 D4
Mount St. Batley WF17 .... 118 D3
Mount St. Brad BD1 .... 56 B5
Mount St. Brad BD3, BD4 .... 75 B6
Mount St. Clec BD19 .... 116 D8
Mount St. Hali HX6 .... 112 B4
Mount St. Hali HX1 .... 113 C4
Mount St. Hud HD1, HD4 .... 153 F3
Mount St. Keigh BD21 .... 35 A7
Mount St Mary's High Sch. Leeds 79
Mount St W. Hali HX2 .... 112 B4
Mount Tabor Rd. Hali HX2 .... 91 A4
Mount Tabor St. Pudsey LS28 .... 76 C7
Mount Terr. Batley WF17 .... 118 D3
Mount Terr. Brad BD2 .... 56 B5
Mount The. B in Elm LS15 .... 63 D6
Mount The. Brad BD6 .... 94 C1
Mount The. Castle WF10 .... 125 C7
Mount The. Kippax LS25 .... 83 A1
Mount The. Leeds LS15 .... 61 B3
Mount The. Nor WF6 .... 123 A2
Mount The. Roth LS26 .... 100 F7
Mount The. Tod OL14 .... 108 A6
Mount The. Wake WF2 .... 141 F3
Mount View. Hali HX2 .... 91 F6
Mount Vernon Rd. Yeadon LS19 .... 40 C4
Mount View. Yead LS19 .... 40 C4
Mount Wlk. Castle WF10 .... 124 C5
Mount Zion Rd. Hud HD5 .... 154 D4
Mountain Cres. Dew WF12 .... 139 D2
Mountain Rd. Dew WF12 .... 139 D2

Mountain View. Ship BD18 .... 55 D6
Mountain View. Wyke BD12 .... 94 C3
Mountbatten Ave. Loft G WF1 .... 121 C5
Mountbatten Cres. Loft G WF1 .... 121 C5
Mountbatten Ct. Brad BD5 .... 74 E2 4
Mountbatten Gdns. Hud HD3 .... 153 B7
Mountbatten Gr. Loft G WF1 .... 121 C5
Mountcliffe View. Morley LS27 .... 98 B7
Mountfield Ave. Hud HD5 .... 155 B4
Mountfield Rd. Hud HD5 .... 155 B5
Mountfield Vils. S Kirk WF9 .... 182 B1
Mountfields. Brig HX3 .... 114 E8
Mountfields. Leeds LS3 .... 59 F1 3
Mountjoy Prep Sch. Hud 153 F7
Mountjoy Rd. Hud HD1 .... 153 F7
Mountleigh Cl. Brad BD4 .... 95 A7
Mouse Hole La. Mir WF14 .... 138 A6
Moverley Flatts. Pont WF8 .... 146 E7
Mowat Ct. Clec WF15 .... 116 B5
Mowbray Cl. Cull BD13 .... 52 C5
Mowbray Cres. Leeds LS14 .... 62 A3
Mowbray Ct. Leeds LS14 .... 62 A3
Mowbray Ct. Pont WF8 .... 146 D6
Moxon Gr. Loft G WF1 .... 121 B3
Moxon Pl. Wake WF2 .... 141 C5
Moxon Sq. Wake WF1 .... 142 D7
Moxon St. Loft G WF1 .... 121 C4
Moxon Way. Loft G WF1 .... 121 C4
Mozley Dr. Hali HX2 .... 91 F6
Mucky La. Elland HX5 .... 134 D4
Muddy La. Coll LS22 .... 13 B2
Muff St. Brad BD4 .... 75 B5
Muffit La. Batley BD19 .... 117 D8
Mug Mill La. Dew WF12 .... 157 E8
Mugup La. Holmfi HD7 .... 189 E1
Muirfield Ave. Feath WF7 .... 124 D1
Muirfield Cl. Cud S22 .... 180 C1
Muirfields The. Mapp S75 .... 178 A1
Muirhead Dr. Brad BD4 .... 75 E2
Muirlands The. Hud HD2 .... 136 E5
Mulberry Ave. Hors LS16 .... 42 D4
Mulberry Ave. Ryhill WF4 .... 162 B1
Mulberry Garth. Hors LS16 .... 42 D4
Mulberry Garth. Th Arch LS23 .... 14 E1
Mulberry House. Castle WF10 .... 124 E7 12
Mulberry Pl. Ryhill WF4 .... 162 B1
Mulberry Rise. Hors LS16 .... 42 D4
Mulberry St. Hud HD5 .... 154 C5
Mulberry St. Leeds LS10 .... 79 D5 08
Mulberry St. Pudsey LS28 .... 76 E7
Mulberry Terr. Hud HD1 .... 154 B8
Mulberry View. Hors LS16 .... 42 D3
Mulcture Hall Rd. Hali HX1 .... 113 D7
Mulehouse La. Elland HX3 .... 134 B1
Mulgrave St. Brad BD3 .... 75 B6
Mulberry Gdns. M'town LS26 .... 102 B2
Mullins Cl. Leeds LS9 .... 79 F7 6
Mumford St. Brad BD5 .... 74 E3
Munby St. Brad BD8 .... 73 F7
Muncaster Rd. Gar LS25 .... 83 A8
Mundhill La. Wake WF3 .... 99 F3 6
Murdoch St. Keigh BD21 .... 35 F8
Murdstone Ct. Brad BD5 .... 74 E3 5
Murgatroyd St. Ship BD17 .... 54 F1
Murgatroyd St. Ship BD17 .... 55 B8
Murray Rd. Hud HD2 .... 153 F8
Murray St. Brad BD5 .... 74 C3 3
Murton Cl. Leeds LS14 .... 62 A4
Museum Ct. Brad BD2 .... 56 D3
Museum St. Leeds LS9 .... 60 F1
Musgrave Bank. Leeds LS13 .... 58 E2
Musgrave Bldgs. Pudsey LS28 .... 76 F8 6
Musgrave Ct. Wake WF12 .... 141 D4
Musgrave Dr. Brad BD2 .... 56 C2
Musgrave Gr. Brad BD2 .... 56 C2
Musgrave Mount. Brad BD2 .... 56 C2
Musgrave Mount. Leeds LS13 .... 58 E2
Musgrave Rise. Leeds LS13 .... 58 E2
Musgrave St. Batley WF17 .... 96 E1 2
Musgrave View. Leeds LS13 .... 58 E2
Mushroom St. Leeds LS9 .... 60 E1
Musselburgh St. Brad BD7 .... 74 A4
Mutton La. Wils BD15 .... 53 D2
Myers Ave. Brad BD2 .... 56 C1
Myers Croft. Otley LS21 .... 23 A7
Myers La. Brad BD2 .... 56 C1
Myrtle Ave. Bgly BD16 .... 37 A2
Myrtle Ave. Dew WF13 .... 138 E5
Myrtle Ct. Bgly BD16 .... 37 A3
Myrtle Dr. Hali HX2 .... 91 E4
Myrtle Dr. Hem WF9 .... 181 C6
Myrtle Gdns. Hali HX2 .... 91 E4
Myrtle Gr. Bgly BD16 .... 36 F2
Myrtle Gr. Hali HX2 .... 91 E4
Myrtle Gr. Queen BD13 .... 72 C8 5
Myrtle Park Fst Sch. Bing 36 F2
Myrtle Pl. Bing BD16 .... 36 F3
Myrtle Pl. Hali HX2 .... 91 E4
Myrtle Rd. Dew WF13 .... 138 E5
Myrtle Rd. Elland HX5 .... 134 F6
Myrtle St. Bing BD16 .... 36 F3
Myrtle St. Brad BD3 .... 75 C6
Myrtle St. Brad BD4 .... 95 C8 1
Myrtle St. Hud HD1 .... 154 B7
Myrtle Terr. Haw BD22 .... 34 D2
Myrtle View. Haw BD22 .... 51 E8
Myson Ave. Pont WF8 .... 125 F3
Mytholm Cl. Heb Br HX7 .... 88 F3
Mytholm Ct. Heb Br HX7 .... 88 F3
Mytholm Steep. Heb Br HX7 .... 88 E3
Mytholmes. Haw BD22 .... 51 C7
Mytholmes La. Haw BD22 .... 51 C7
Mytholmes La. Haw BD22 .... 51 D8
Mytholmes Terr. Haw BD22 .... 51 C7
Mytholmroyd Sta. Heb Br 110 D8

Nab Cres. Mel HD7 .... 170 C2
Nab End La. Elland HX4 .... 133 F4
Nab La. Batley WF17 .... 96 F2
Nab La. Mir WF14 .... 137 F6
Nab La. Ship BD17 .... 55 B7
Nab The. Mir WF14 .... 138 A6
Nab The. Mir WF14 .... 138 D1
Nab Water La. Oxen HX7 .... 70 B6
Nab Wood Bank. Ship BD18 .... 54 E8
Nab Wood Cl. Ship BD18 .... 54 E8
Nab Wood Cres. Ship BD18 .... 54 E7
Nab Wood Dr. Ship BD18 .... 54 D8
Nab Wood Gdns. Ship BD18 .... 54 E7
Nab Wood Gr. Ship BD18 .... 54 E7
Nab Wood Grammar Sch. Ship 54 C7
Nab Wood Mid Sch. Ship 54 D7
Nab Wood Mount. Ship BD18 .... 54 D7
Nab Wood Pl. Ship BD18 .... 54 D7
Nab Wood Rd. Ship BD18 .... 54 D7
Nab Wood Rise. Ship BD18 .... 54 D7
Nab Wood Terr. Ship BD18 .... 54 D7
Nabbs La. Slai HD7 .... 151 F1
Nabgen La. Hud HD4 .... 153 D3
Nabcroft Rise. Hud HD4 .... 153 D4
Naburn App. Leeds LS14 .... 62 C8
Naburn Chase. Leeds LS14 .... 62 B7
Naburn Cl. Leeds LS14 .... 62 C7
Naburn Ct. Leeds LS14 .... 62 C8 3
Naburn Dr. Leeds LS14 .... 62 B7
Naburn Fold. Leeds LS14 .... 62 C7
Naburn Gdns. Leeds LS14 .... 62 B7
Naburn Gn. Leeds LS14 .... 62 B7
Naburn Pl. Leeds LS14 .... 62 B7
Naburn Rd. Leeds LS14 .... 62 B7
Naburn View. Leeds LS14 .... 62 C7
Naburn Wlk. Leeds LS14 .... 62 C7
Nairn Cl. Hud HD4 .... 153 C2
Nancroft Cres. Leeds LS12 .... 78 C7
Nancroft Mount. Leeds LS12 .... 78 C7
Nancroft Terr. Leeds LS12 .... 78 C7
Nanny Goat La. B in Elm LS25 .... 82 D8
Nansen Ave. Leeds LS13 .... 58 C2 9
Nansen Gr. Leeds LS13 .... 58 C2 10
Nansen Mount. Leeds LS13 .... 58 C2 11
Nansen Pl. Leeds LS13 .... 58 B2 1
Nansen St. Leeds LS13 .... 58 A2
Nansen Terr. Leeds LS13 .... 58 B2 3
Nansen View. Leeds LS13 .... 58 B2 2
Naomi Rd. Hud HD4 .... 154 A2
Napier House. Tod OL14 .... 129 A8
Napier Rd. Brad BD3 .... 75 D7
Napier Rd. Elland HX5 .... 134 E6
Napier St. Brad BD3 .... 75 D7
Napier St. Brad BD3 .... 75 D7
Naples St. Brad BD8 .... 55 B1
Nares St. Haw BD22 .... 51 E8 9
Nares St. Keigh BD21 .... 35 B7
Nares St Upper. Keigh BD21 .... 35 B7
Narrow Balk. H Pag DN5 .... 195 E5
Narrow La. Harden BD16 .... 36 B6
Narrows The. Harden BD16 .... 36 B1
Naseby Gdns. Leeds LS9 .... 60 E1
Naseby Gdns. Leeds LS9 .... 61 E8 5
Naseby Grange. Leeds LS9 .... 61 E8 9
Naseby Pl. Leeds LS9 .... 79 E8 3
Naseby Rise. Queen BD13 .... 72 F1
Naseby Terr. Leeds LS9 .... 79 E8
Naseby View. Leeds LS9 .... 79 E8
Naseby Wlk. Leeds LS9 .... 79 E8
Nashville Rd. Keigh BD22 .... 35 A6
Nashville St. Keigh BD22 .... 35 A6
Nashville Terr. Keigh BD22 .... 35 A6
Nassau Pl. Leeds LS7 .... 60 D7
Nat Mus of Photography & TV. Brad 74
Nathan La. Sow Br HX6 .... 132 C7
Nathaniel Waterhouse Homes.
  Hali HX1 .... 113 C6 8
National Pk. Leeds 79 E4
National School. Leeds LS10 .... 79 F4
Natty Fields Cl. Hali HX2 .... 91 E7
Natty La. Hali HX2 .... 91 E7
Navigation Gdns. Dew WF12 .... 139 B4
Navigation Rd. Castle WF10 .... 103 D1
Navigation Rd. Dew WF12 .... 139 B4
Navigation Rd. Hali HX3 .... 113 C8
Navigation Wlk. Leeds LS10 .... 79 C7
Navvy La. Ryhill S71 .... 179 B5
Naylor La. Hali HX2 .... 90 C1
Naylor St. Hali HX1 .... 118 F3 5
Naylor St. Ossett WF5 .... 140 C8
Naylor's Bldgs. Brig BD19 .... 115 F8
Naze View. Tod OL14 .... 107 F3
Neal Pl. Leeds LS5 .... 59 C4
Neal St. Brad BD5 .... 74 D5
Neale Rd. Hud HD1 .... 153 F5
Neale St. Heb Br HX7 .... 89 A2
Near Bank. Shep HD8 .... 174 B2
Nearcliffe Rd. Brad BD9 .... 55 A2
Neath Gdns. Leeds LS9 .... 61 D3
Necropolis Rd. Brad BD7 .... 74 A6
Ned Hill Rd. Hali HX2 .... 90 C3
Ned La. Brad BD4 .... 75 F3
Ned La. Slai HD7 .... 169 F8
Needless Inn La. Roth LS26 .... 101 C7
Nell Gap Ave. Neth WF4 .... 158 A5
Nell Gap Cres. Neth WF4 .... 158 A5
Nell Gap La. Neth WF4 .... 158 A5
Nelson Croft. Gar LS25 .... 82 F5
Nelson Ct. Morley LS27 .... 97 F3
Nelson Pl. Hali HX2 .... 112 D4 06
Nelson Pl. Morley LS27 .... 98 A5 1
Nelson Pl. Queen BD13 .... 72 E1
Nelson Rd. Ilkley LS29 .... 8 B4
Nelson St. Batley WF17 .... 118 C5
Nelson St. Birk WF15 .... 117 A4
Nelson St. Brad BD5 .... 74 D6
Nelson St. Brig HD6 .... 115 B1
Nelson St. Dew WF13 .... 139 C8
Nelson St. Gild LS27 .... 97 D7
Nelson St. Heb Br HX7 .... 88 F3
Nelson St. Leeds LS9 .... 80 A8
Nelson St. Liv WF15 .... 117 B2
Nelson St. Oss WF5 .... 140 F4
Nelson St. Otley LS21 .... 23 A8 2
Nelson St. S Hie S72 .... 180 E5
Nelson St. Tod OL14 .... 129 A8
Nene St. Brad BD5 .... 74 D3
Nepshaw La. Gild LS27 .... 97 D4
Nepshaw La N. Morley LS27 .... 97 E4
Nepshaw La S. Morley LS27 .... 97 E4
Neptune St. Leeds LS9 .... 212 C1
Nesfield Cl. Midd LS10 .... 99 F6
Nesfield Cres. Midd LS10 .... 99 F6
Nesfield Gdns. Midd LS10 .... 99 F6
Nesfield Gn. Midd LS10 .... 99 F6
Nesfield Rd. Ilkley LS29 .... 7 F5
Nesfield Rd. Midd LS10 .... 99 F6
Nesfield St. Brad BD1 .... 201 B4
Nesfield View. Ilkley LS29 .... 7 E5
Nesfield View. Midd LS10 .... 99 F6
Nesfield Wlk. Midd LS10 .... 99 F6
Nessfield Dr. Keigh BD22 .... 34 F5
Nessfield Gr. Keigh BD22 .... 34 F5

Nessfield Fst Sch. Keigh 34 F5
Nessfield Gr. Keigh BD22 .... 34 F5
Nessfield Rd. Keigh BD22 .... 34 F5
Nest Est. Heb Br HX7 .... 110 D8
Nestfield Cl. Pont WF8 .... 125 D3
Neston Way. Ossett WF5 .... 140 D1
Nether Cl. Hud HD5 .... 154 E8
Nether Cres. Hud HD5 .... 154 E8
Nether Hall Ave. Hud HD5 .... 154 E8
Nether La. Holme HD7 .... 187 C3
Nether Moor Rd. Hud HD4 .... 171 C8
Nether Moor View. Bing BD16 .... 37 A3 16
Netheracres Dr. Leeds LS17 .... 43 F3
Netheracres Hill. Leeds LS17 .... 43 F3
Netherby St. Brad BD3 .... 75 B7
Nethercliffe Cres. Guise LS20 .... 22 D2
Nethercliffe Rd. Guise LS20 .... 22 D2
Netherdale Ct. Weth LS22 .... 14 A6
Netherend Rd. Slai HD7 .... 151 F1
Netherfield Ave. Neth WF4 .... 158 D5
Netherfield Cl. Castle WF10 .... 123 F5
Netherfield Cl. Neth WF4 .... 173 F6
Netherfield Cl. Yeadon LS19 .... 40 B7
Netherfield Cres. Neth WF4 .... 158 D5
Netherfield Cl. Guise LS20 .... 22 D2
Netherfield Ct. Guise LS20 .... 22 D2
Netherfield Dr. Guise LS20 .... 22 D2
Netherfield Dr. Holmfi HD7 .... 189 A7
Netherfield Ind Pk. Dew 138 E5
Netherfield Pl. Clec BD19 .... 116 E7
Netherfield Pl. Neth WF4 .... 158 D6
Netherfield Rd. Dew WF13 .... 138 E5
Netherfield Rd. Guise LS20 .... 22 D1
Netherfield Rd. Guise LS20 .... 22 D1
Netherfield Rd. Neth WF4 .... 158 D6
Netherfields La. Hud HD5 .... 154 E8
Netherhall Ave. Halifax 94 C7
Netherlands Ave. Brad BD6 .... 94 C7
Netherlands Avenue Sch. Brad 94 D7
Netherlea Dr. Holmfi HD7 .... 188 F7
Netherlee Rd. Holmfi HD7 .... 188 F7
Netherley Dr. Mars HD7 .... 168 E2
Netherly Brow. Ossett WF5 .... 140 E3
Netherleigh Sch The. Brad 54 F3
Netherroyd Hill Rd. Hud HD2 .... 136 A3
Netherton Fd Inf Sch. Neth 158 D8
Netherton Fold. Hud HD4 .... 171 C6
Netherton Hall Gdns. Neth WF4 .... 158 E6
Netherton La. Neth WF4 .... 158 D7
Netherton Inf Sch. Hud 154 D8
Netherton Moor Rd. Hud HD4 .... 171 E6
Netherwood Cl. Hud HD2 .... 136 A3
Nettle Gr. Northo HX3 .... 93 A3
Nettleton Ave. Mir WF14 .... 137 F5
Nettleton Chase. Ossett WF5 .... 119 C1
Nettleton Ct. Leeds LS15 .... 62 B2 8
Nettleton Ct. Leeds LS15 .... 81 D8
Nettleton Hill Rd. Slai HD7 .... 152 B6
Nettleton House. Hem WF9 .... 181 D6
Nettleton Rd. Hud HD5 .... 155 B8
Nettleton St. Feath WF7 .... 145 D6
Nettleton St. Loft G WF3 .... 122 B6
Nettleton St. Ossett WF5 .... 140 C6
Nettleton Terr. Hud HD5 .... 155 A8
Nevill Gr. Brad BD9 .... 54 D3
Neville App. Leeds LS9 .... 80 C6
Neville Ave. Brad BD4 .... 75 B1
Neville Ave. Leeds LS9 .... 80 C6
Neville Cl. S Kirk WF9 .... 182 C3
Neville Cres. Leeds LS9 .... 80 C6
Neville Garth. Leeds LS9 .... 80 C6
Neville Gr. Gar LS25 .... 83 A7
Neville Gr. Leeds LS9 .... 80 C6
Neville Gr. Swil LS26 .... 82 A2
Neville Mount. Leeds LS9 .... 80 C6
Neville Par. Leeds LS9 .... 80 C6
Neville Pl. Leeds LS9 .... 80 D7
Neville Rd. Brad BD4 .... 75 B1
Neville Rd. Leeds LS9 .... 80 C6
Neville Rd. Otley LS21 .... 23 B7
Neville Row. Leeds LS9 .... 80 D6
Neville Sq. Leeds LS9 .... 80 D6
Neville St. Clec BD19 .... 116 E7
Neville St. Keigh BD21 .... 35 D8 12
Neville St. Leeds LS1 .... 79 B7
Neville St. Nor WF6 .... 123 B1
Neville St. S Elm WF9 .... 182 F1
Neville St. Wake WF1 .... 142 F4
Neville Terr. Leeds LS9 .... 80 C6
Neville Wlk. Leeds LS9 .... 80 C7
Nevins Rd. Dew WF13 .... 138 D6
Nevison Ave. Pont WF8 .... 125 E3
New Adel Ave. Hors LS16 .... 42 A3
New Adel Gdns. Hors LS16 .... 42 A3
New Adel La. Hors LS16 .... 42 A3
New Augustus St. Brad BD1 .... 74 F6
New Ave. Kirkhe HD5 .... 137 B1
New Bank. Hali HX3 .... 113 D8
New Bank St. Morley LS27 .... 98 B5
New Bond St. Hali HX1 .... 113 B7
New Bridge Rd. Mel HD7 .... 170 B2
New Briggate. Leeds LS1, LS2 .... 211 F4
New Brighton. Bgly BD16 .... 37 A4
New Brighton. D Dale HD8 .... 191 F3
New Brighton. Mir WF14 .... 138 A6
New Brook St. Ilkley LS29 .... 8 B4
New Brunswick St. Hali HX1 .... 113 B6
New Brunswick St. Wake WF1 .... 142 C5
New Cl. Hors LS18 .... 58 B8
New Cl. Mars HD7 .... 151 C1
New Clayton Terr. Cull BD13 .... 52 D5
New Close Ave. Sil BD20 .... 5 E1
New Close La. Mars HD7 .... 152 A4
New Close Rd. Ship BD18 .... 54 F7
New Craven Gate. Leeds LS11 .... 79 C4
New Cres. Hors LS18 .... 58 B8
New Cross St. Brad BD5 .... 74 F2
New Cross St. Brad BD12 .... 95 B5
New Dales La. Add LS29 .... 3 A1 4
New Delight. Heb Br HX7 .... 88 D4
New England Rd. Keigh BD21 .... 35 C5
New Fold. Brad BD6 .... 93 E7
New Fold. Ryhill WF4 .... 162 A1
New Grove Terr. Weth LS22 .... 13 F4
New Hall App. Neth WF4 .... 158 D5
New Hall Cl. Crig WF4 .... 159 F7
New Hall Croft. Crig WF4 .... 159 F7
New Hall La. Crig WF4 .... 159 E7
New Hall Way. Neth WF4 .... 157 F3

New Hey Moor Houses. Shep HD8 .... 173 F2
New Hey Rd. Brad BD4 .... 75 A4
New Hey Rd. Brig HD6 .... 135 D5
New Hey Rd. Elland HD3 .... 152 A8
New Hey Rd. Hud HD1, HD3 .... 135 D5
New Hey Rd. Hud HD2, HD3 .... 152 E8
New Hey Rd. Hud HD2, HD3 .... 153 C7
New Hey Rd. Mars HD3 .... 150 D2
New Hey Rd. Ship HD2, HD3, HD6 .... 151 D5
New Holme Rd. Haw BD22 .... 51 D6
New Holme. Hud HD7 .... 199 D7
New House La. Brad BD13 .... 73 B1
New House Rd. Hud HD2 .... 136 D4
New House. Slai HD7 .... 169 F7
New Inn Ct. Otley LS21 .... 23 A7
New Inn St. Leeds LS12 .... 78 A7
New John St. Brad BD1 .... 74 E7
New Kirkgate. Ship BD18 .... 55 B8
New La. B Head HX7 .... 88 D3
New La. B Spa LS25 .... 105 D3
New La. Birk BD4 .... 76 C2
New La. Brad BD4 .... 75 A6
New La. Castle WF10 .... 125 D5
New La. Clec BD19 .... 116 A6
New La. Crig WF4 .... 159 E7
New La. Elland HX4 .... 134 A6
New La. Farnh BD20 .... 4 F2
New La. Gild BD11 .... 97 B8
New La. Hali HX3 .... 113 B2
New La. Hali HX3 .... 113 D4
New La. Heb Br HX7 .... 110 D4
New La. Leeds LS11 .... 79 B6
New La. Mars HD3 .... 150 D4
New La. Midd LS10 .... 99 B5
New La. Skel HD8 .... 175 B1
New La. Slai HD7 .... 152 A3
New La. Slai HD7 .... 152 A6
New La. Sow Br HX7 .... 111 B5
New La. Upton WF9 .... 183 A7
New Laithe Cl. Hud HD4 .... 154 C2
New Laithe Hill. Hud HD4 .... 154 C2
New Laithe La. Holmfi HD7 .... 189 B5
New Laithe Rd. Brad BD6 .... 74 A1 3
New Laithe Rd. Haw BD22 .... 51 A6
New Laithe Rd. Hud HD4 .... 154 C2
New Laithes Jun Sch. Hors 58 A6
New Lane Cres. Upton WF9 .... 183 A8
New Leeds. Leeds LS13 .... 58 B5
New Line. Brad BD10 .... 56 E7
New Longley La. Sow Br HX6 .... 112 A1
New Longley. Sow Br HX6 .... 112 A1
New Market. Otley LS21 .... 23 A7
New Market Pl. Brad BD1 .... 74 E7 8
New Market St. Leeds LS1 .... 79 C7
New Mill La. B Spa LS23 .... 30 E5
New Mill Rd. Holmfi HD7 .... 172 C3
New Mill Rd. Honley HD7 .... 189 B7
New Mill Rd. Honley HD7 .... 172 C3
New North Par. Hud HD1 .... 154 A6
New North St. Hud HD1 .... 153 F7
New Occupation La. Pudsey LS28 .... 76 C6
New Otley Rd. Brad BD3 .... 75 A8
New Park Croft. Pudsey LS28 .... 57 E3
New Park Cl. Pudsey LS28 .... 57 E3
New Park La. Wake WF2 .... 141 B7
New Park Pl. Pudsey LS28 .... 57 E3
New Park Rd. Queen BD13 .... 71 D1
New Park St. Morley LS27 .... 97 F3
New Park Vale. Pudsey LS28 .... 57 E3
New Park View. Pudsey LS28 .... 57 E2
New Park Way. Pudsey LS28 .... 57 E3
New Popplewell La. Brig BD19 .... 115 F8
New Princess St. Leeds LS11 .... 79 B5
New Rd. B Head HX7 .... 87 F6
New Rd. Birstall BD11 .... 96 F5
New Rd. Bramham LS23 .... 30 D3
New Rd. Castle WF11 .... 126 A5
New Rd. Caw S75 .... 193 B5
New Rd. Denh BD13 .... 71 F8
New Rd. Elland HX4 .... 134 B6
New Rd. Elland HX3 .... 134 A8
New Rd. Feath WF7 .... 144 E7
New Rd. Heb Br HX7 .... 88 C3
New Rd. Heb Br HX7 .... 110 E8
New Rd. Hor W HD7 .... 178 E1
New Rd. Hud HX4 .... 133 A2
New Rd. Kirkhe HD5 .... 137 B2
New Rd. Ledsh LS25 .... 104 A6
New Rd. Mapp S75 .... 178 B1
New Rd. Neth WF4 .... 158 B7
New Rd. Pen S30 .... 192 A1
New Rd. Shep HD8 .... 173 F2
New Rd. Sils BD20 .... 5 D1
New Rd. Slai HD7 .... 151 F8
New Rd. Tod OL14 .... 86 C4
New Rd. Tod OL14 .... 108 A1
New Rd. Wilsden BD15 .... 53 C4
New Rd E. Hor W HD7 .... 178 E2
New Rd. W Har WF7 .... 145 C1
New Rd W. Hor W HD7 .... 178 B6
New Rd Side. Hors LS18 .... 57 F1
New Rd Side. Yeadon LS19 .... 40 A4
New Road Sq. Brig HD6 .... 115 B2
New Row. Brad BD10 .... 56 B8
New Row. Clec BD19 .... 116 C7
New Row. Dearne S63 .... 194 C1
New Row. Leeds LS15 .... 81 D7
New Row. Pudsey LS28 .... 57 A3
New Row. Ship BD16 .... 54 B8
New Scarbro' Rd. Leeds LS13 .... 58 D2 1
New St. Ack M T WF7 .... 163 E5
New St. Batley WF17 .... 118 C3
New St. Bing BD16 .... 37 A3
New St. Bing BD16 .... 36 F8
New St. Brad BD10 .... 56 B8
New St. Castle WF10 .... 103 F1
New St. Clec BD19 .... 116 E7
New St. Cull BD13 .... 52 D6
New St. D Dale HD8 .... 191 F3
New St. Dearne S63 .... 194 C1
New St. Delph OL3 .... 167 A1
New St. Dew WF12 .... 139 D7
New St. Elland HX4 .... 133 F3

New St. Elland HX4 .... 134 C7
New St. Elland HX5 .... 134 F7
New St. Farnh BD20 .... 4 D1
New St. Gild LS27 .... 97 C8
New St. Honley HD7 .... 172 B6
New St. Hud HX4 .... 133 F4
New St. Idle BD10 .... 56 E7
New St. Kippax LS25 .... 83 C1
New St. Mapp S75 .... 178 C1
New St. Mir WF14 .... 138 A5
New St. Pudsey LS28 .... 57 A1
New St. Pudsey LS28 .... 57 D1
New St. Pudsey LS28 .... 76 C7
New St. Roy S71 .... 179 C3
New St. S Elm WF9 .... 182 F2
New St. S Kirk WF9 .... 182 B3
New St. Slai HD7 .... 152 A3
New St. Thorn BD13 .... 72 E6
New St. Yeadon LS19 .... 40 C7
New St Cl. Pudsey LS28 .... 57 D1
New St Gdns. Pudsey LS28 .... 57 D1
New St Gr. Pudsey LS28 .... 57 D1
New Sturton La. Gar LS25 .... 83 A7
New Tanhouse. Mir WF14 .... 137 F5
New Temple Gate. Leeds LS15 .... 81 C7
New Toftshaw. Brad BD4 .... 95 D8
New Town Ct. Keigh BD21 .... 35 E8 6
New Village Way. Morley LS27 .... 97 F2
New Way. Guise LS20 .... 22 E1
New Wells. Wake WF1 .... 142 E3
New Wlk. Leeds LS8 .... 44 B2
New Windsor Dr. Roth LS26 .... 100 F6
New Wood Cl. Wyke BD12 .... 94 C3
New Works Rd. Low M BD12 .... 94 E6
New York Rd. Leeds LS2, LS9 .... 212 A4
New York St. Leeds LS2 .... 212 A3
Newall Ave. Otley LS21 .... 23 A8
Newall Carr Rd. Otley LS21 .... 10 E2
Newall Cl. Men LS29 .... 21 F5
Newall Cl. Otley LS21 .... 23 A8
Newall Croft. Otley LS21 .... 23 A8
Newall Hall Pk. Otley LS21 .... 23 B8
Newall Mount. Otley LS21 .... 23 A8
Newall St. Batley WF17 .... 118 C2
Newall St. Brad BD5 .... 74 E4
Newark Rd. Bgly BD16 .... 37 C5
Newark St. Brad BD4 .... 75 B4
Newark Vill. Wake WF1 .... 142 E3 7
Newbridge Ind Est. Pont 146 A5
Newbrook Terr. Sow Br HX6 .... 112 B3 1
Newby Rd. Hud HD1 .... 153 D6
Newby St. Brad BD5 .... 74 E2
Newclose La. S Elm WF9 .... 182 C3
Newcombe St. Elland HX5 .... 134 F7
Newfield Ave. Men LS29 .... 21 F5
Newfield Ave. Nor WF6 .... 123 A3
Newfield Cl. Brad BD4 .... 95 C8
Newfield Cres. Men LS29 .... 21 F5
Newfield Cres. Nor WF6 .... 123 A3
Newfield Ct. Nor WF6 .... 123 A3
Newfield Dr. Gar LS25 .... 82 F6
Newfield Dr. Men LS29 .... 21 F5
Newfield Gr. Nor WF6 .... 123 A3
Newfield La. Ledsh LS25 .... 104 E7
Newfields. B in Elm LS25 .... 63 C8
Newhall Bank. Midd LS10 .... 99 D6
Newhall Chase. Midd LS10 .... 99 D7
Newhall Cl. Midd LS10 .... 99 D6
Newhall Cres. Midd LS10 .... 99 D6
Newhall Croft. Midd LS10 .... 99 E7
Newhall Dr. Midd LS10 .... 99 E6
Newhall Garth. Midd LS10 .... 99 D5
Newhall Gdns. Midd LS10 .... 99 D6
Newhall Gn. Midd LS10 .... 99 D6
Newhall La. Midd LS10 .... 99 E7
Newhall Mount. Midd LS10 .... 99 D5
Newhall Mount. Wyke BD12 .... 94 B1
Newhall Rd. Brad BD4 .... 75 D2
Newhall Rd. Midd LS10 .... 99 E6
Newhall Wlk. Midd LS10 .... 99 E7
Newhaven Gdns. Hud HD4 .... 153 D3
Newhold. Gar LS25 .... 83 B8
Newhouse Pl. Hud HD3 .... 153 B4
Newhouses Terr. Denh BD13 .... 71 D8 4
Newi Cl. Brad BD6 .... 93 F8
Newland Ave. Hud HD5 .... 154 D6
Newland Ct. Wake WF1 .... 142 E2
Newland La. Nor WF6 .... 123 A1
Newland La. Ryhill WF4 .... 162 C5
Newland Rd. Hem WF9 .... 181 E7
Newland St. Wake WF1 .... 142 E3
Newlands. Bgly BD16 .... 37 A5
Newlands Ave. Bail BD17 .... 38 E4
Newlands Ave. Brad BD3 .... 56 E1
Newlands Ave. Hali HX3 .... 92 F2
Newlands Ave. Honley HD7 .... 172 A4
Newlands Ave. Yeadon LS19 .... 40 C4
Newlands Cl. Wake WF2 .... 141 D3
Newlands Cres. Morley LS27 .... 98 B2
Newlands Dr. Morley LS27 .... 98 B2
Newlands Dr. Nor WF6 .... 144 A8
Newlands Dr. Wake WF2 .... 141 D3
Newlands Dr. Wyke BD12 .... 94 C1
Newlands Gr. Morley LS27 .... 98 B2
Newlands La. Holmfi HD7 .... 199 A8
Newlands La. Mars HD7 .... 151 A4
Newlands Pl. Brad BD3 .... 56 E1
Newlands Rd. Hud HD2 .... 136 E3
Newlands Rise. Yeadon LS19 .... 40 C4
Newlands The. Upton WF9 .... 183 A8
Newlands Wlk. Wake WF2 .... 141 D3
Newlay Cl. Brad BD10 .... 56 C6
Newlay Gr. Hors LS18 .... 58 C7
Newlay La. Hors LS18 .... 58 C6
Newlay La. Leeds LS13 .... 58 C5
Newlay Lane Pl. Leeds LS13 .... 58 C5 1
Newlay Mount. Hors LS18 .... 58 C7
Newlay Wood Ave. Hors LS18 .... 58 D8
Newlay Wood Cl. Hors LS18 .... 58 D8
Newlay Wood Cres. Hors LS18 .... 58 D8
Newlay Wood Dr. Hors LS18 .... 58 D8
Newlay Wood Fold. Hors LS18 .... 58 D8 1
Newlay Wood Gdns. Hors LS18 .... 58 D8 2
Newlay Wood Rise. Hors LS18 .... 58 D8 3
Newlay Wood Rd. Hors LS18 .... 58 D8

236 New - Nor

New St. Hali HX2 112 E8
New St. Hali HX3 114 A4
New St. Haw BD22 34 D2
New St. Haw BD22 51 C6
New St. Hem WF9 163 C1
New St. Honley HD7 171 F4
New St. Hor WF4 141 B1
New St. Hors LS18 58 B8
New St. Hud HD7 152 E4
New St. Hud HD3 153 A4
New St. Hud HD1 153 E5
New St. Hud HD1 154 A5
New St. Hud HD4 171 C7
New St. Kippax LS25 83 B1
New St. Kirkhe HD5 155 C8
New St. Liver BD19 116 F6
New St. Mapp S75 178 B1
New St. Mel HD7 170 D2
New St. Ossett WF5 140 E5
New St. Pudsey LS28 57 D2
New St. Pudsey LS28 76 E6
New St. Roy S71 179 C3
New St. S Elm WF9 182 E3
New St. S Hie S72 180 D6
New St. Skel HD8 175 A2
New St. Slai HD7 152 A1
New Station St. Leeds LS1 79 B7
New Street Cl. Pudsey LS28 76 E6
New Street Gdns. Pudsey LS28 76 E6
New Street Gr. Pudsey LS28 76 E6
New Sturton La. Gar LS25 83 B7
New Tanhouse. Mir WF14 137 F5 6
New Temple Gate. Leeds LS15 81 A7
New Toftshaw. Brad BD4 95 D8
New Town Ct. Keigh BD21 35 A7 15
New Way. Batley WF17 118 C5
New Way. Guise LS20 22 C1
New Wellgate. Castle WF10 124 F6
New Wells. Wake WF1 142 C5
New Windsor Dr. Roth LS26 100 F6
New Wlk. Leeds LS8 44 B1
New Works Rd. Brad BD12 94 D5
New York La. Yeadon LS19 40 D2
New York Rd. Leeds LS2, LS9 79 D8
New York St. Leeds LS2 79 D7 1
Newall Ave. Otley LS21 10 F1
Newall Carr Rd. Clift LS21 10 F6
Newall Carr Rd. Otley LS21 10 F2
Newall Cl. Men LS29 22 B5
Newall Cl. Otley LS21 10 F1
Newall Cl. Otley LS21 22 F8
Newall Cres. Hem WF9 162 F3
Newall Fst Sch. Otley 11 A1
Newall Hall Pk. Otley LS21 11 A1
Newall Mount. Otley LS21 22 F8
Newall St. Brad BD5 74 D4
Newall St. Tod OL14 129 A8
Newark Cl. Mapp S75 178 B2
Newark Rd. Bing BD16 36 E5
Newark St. Brad BD4 75 B5
Newbridge La. Hal E BD23 1 D8
Newburn Rd. Brad BD7 74 B5
Newbury Dr. S Elm WF9 183 A5
Newbury Rd. Brig HD6 135 F7
Newbury Wlk. Kirkhe HD5 137 C1
Newby Fst Sch. Brad 74 D3
Newby Garth. Leeds LS17 44 B5
Newby Rd. Farnh BD20 16 E8
Newby St. Brad BD5 74 E4
Newby St. Glu BD20 16 D7
Newcastle Cl. Birk BD11 96 D5
Newcastle Farm Ct. Fair WF11 105 A4
Newcombe St. Elland HX5 135 A6
Newfield Ave. Castle WF10 124 E7
Newfield Ave. Nor WF6 123 C1
Newfield Cl. Nor WF6 123 C1
Newfield Cres. Nor WF6 123 C1
Newfield Ct. Nor WF6 123 C2
Newfield Dr. Gar LS25 83 B4
Newfield Dr. Men LS29 22 A5
Newfield La. Ledsh LS25 104 D8
Newforth Gr. Brad BD5 74 C2
Newgate La. Mel HD7 170 E2
Newgate. Mir WF14 138 A4
Newgate. Pont WF8 146 C8
Newgate St. Batley WF12 118 F3
Newhall Bank. Midd LS10 99 D5
Newhall Chase. Midd LS10 99 D6
Newhall Cl. Midd LS10 99 D6
Newhall Cres. Midd LS10 99 D6
Newhall Croft. Midd LS10 99 D7
Newhall Dr. Brad BD6 94 F8
Newhall Garth. Midd LS10 99 D5
Newhall Gate. Midd LS10 99 E7
Newhall Gdns. Midd LS10 99 D5
Newhall Gn. Midd LS10 99 D6
Newhall La. Mir WF14 138 B2
Newhall Mount. Brad BD6 94 F8
Newhall Mount. Midd LS10 99 D5
Newhall Rd. Brad BD4 75 B1
Newhall Rd. Midd LS10 99 D6
Newhill. S Kirk WF9 182 B1
Newhold. Gar LS25 83 A8
Newhouse Pl. Hud HD1 154 A7 2
Newill Cl. Brad BD5 75 A2
Newlaithes Cres. Nor WF6 123 D2
Newlaithes Garth. Hors LS18 58 A6
Newlaithes Gdns. Hors LS18 58 B7
Newlaithes Rd. Hors LS18 58 B6
Newland Ave. Hud HD2 135 F1
Newland Cres. Crig WF4 159 E7
Newland Ct. Wake WF1 142 E2
Newland La. Nor WF6 122 F1
Newland Rd. Hud HD5 155 B7
Newland St. Knot WF11 126 B5
Newland St. Wake WF1 142 E2
Newland View. Nor WF6 122 F3
Newlands Ave. Ad Le S DN6 184 F2
Newlands Ave. Brad BD3 56 D1
Newlands Ave. Clay W HD8 175 F2
Newlands Ave. Northo HX3 93 A3
Newlands Ave. Sow Br HX6 111 E3
Newlands Ave. Yeadon LS19 40 A7
Newlands Cl. Brig HD6 115 B1
Newlands Cres. Morley LS27 98 E4
Newlands Dr. Bing BD16 36 E6
Newlands Dr. Glu BD20 16 D7
Newlands Dr. Loft G WF3 121 E5
Newlands Dr. Morley LS27 98 D4
Newlands Dr. Northo HX3 93 A3
Newlands Gr. Northo HX3 93 A3
Newlands Jun Sch. Sow Br 111 E3
Newlands La. Holmfi HD7 188 C5
Newlands Pl. Brad BD3 56 B1
Newlands Prim Sch. Morley 98 D5
Newlands. Pudsey LS28 57 D2
Newlands Rd. Hali HX2 112 B7
Newlands Rise. Yeadon LS19 40 A7
Newlands The. Sow Br HX6 111 E2
Newlands Wlk. Loft G WF3 121 E5
Newlay Bridle Path. Hors LS18 58 C7 2
Newlay Cl. Brad BD10 56 E7
Newlay Gr. Hors LS18 58 B6
Newlay La. Hors LS18 58 B7
Newlay La. Leeds LS13 58 C4
Newlay Lane Pl. Leeds LS13 58 C4
Newlay Wood Ave. Hors LS18 58 C7
Newlay Wood Cl. Hors LS18 58 C7
Newlay Wood Cres. Hors LS18 58 C7
Newlay Wood Dr. Hors LS18 58 C7
Newlay Wood Fold. Hors LS18 58 B7 9
Newlay Wood Gdns. Hors LS18 58 C7 3
Newlay Wood Rd. Hors LS18 58 B7
Newlay Wood Rise. Hors LS18 58 C7
Newley Ave. Batley WF17 117 F8
Newley Mount. Hors LS18 58 B6
Newlyn Rd. Keigh BD20 19 A1
Newman Ave. Roy S71 179 C1
Newman St. Brad BD4 75 B2
Newmarket App. Leeds LS9 80 B6
Newmarket Gn. Leeds LS9 80 B6
Newmarket La. Leeds LS9 80 B6
Newmarket La. Loft G WF3 122 D8
Newmillerdam Country Park.
Notton 160 D2
Newport Ave. Leeds LS13 58 A2
Newport Cres. Leeds LS6 59 D3
Newport Gdns. Leeds LS6 59 D3
Newport Mount. Leeds LS6 59 D3
Newport Pl. Brad BD8 55 C1
Newport Rd. Brad BD8 55 C1
Newport Rd. Leeds LS6 59 D3
Newport St. Pont WF8 125 C1
Newport View. Leeds LS6 59 D3
Newroyd Rd. Brad BD5 74 E2
Newsam Ct. Leeds LS15 81 A7
Newsam Dr. Leeds LS15 80 E6
Newsam Green Rd. Swil LS26 81 E1
Newsholme La. Crig WF4 159 F7
Newsholme New Rd. Keigh BD22 34 B4
Newsome Ave. Hud HD4 154 A2
Newsome Jun Sch. Hud 154 A1
Newsome Rd. Hud HD4 154 B3
Newsome Rd S. Hud HD4 154 A1
Newsome Sec Sch. Hud 153 F1
Newsome St. Dew WF13 118 B1
Newsomes Row. Batley WF17 118 B4
Newstead Ave. Hali HX1 112 E7
Newstead Ave. Hem WF9 163 A3
Newstead Ave. Loft G WF1 121 A5
Newstead Cres. Hem WF9 163 A4
Newstead Dr. Hem WF9 163 A3
Newstead Gdns. Hali HX1 112 E7 8
Newstead Gr. Hali HX1 112 E7
Newstead Gr. Hem WF9 163 A3
Newstead Heath. Hali HX1 112 E7 5
Newstead La. Hem WF4, WF9 162 F3
Newstead Mount. Hem WF9 163 A3
Newstead Pl. Hali HX1 112 E7
Newstead Rd. Barn S71 178 E1
Newstead Rd. Otley LS21 23 B7
Newstead Rd. Wake WF1 142 B7
Newstead Terr. Hali HX1 112 E7
Newstead Terr. Hem WF9 163 A3
Newstead View. Hem WF9 163 A3
Newstead Wlk. Brad BD5 74 D4
Newton Ave. Loft G WF1 121 B2
Newton Cl. Loft G WF1 121 B1
Newton Cl. Roth LS26 100 B4
Newton Ct. Leeds LS8 61 C6
Newton Ct. Loft G WF1 121 B4
Newton Ct. Roth LS26 100 B4
Newton Dr. Castle WF10 125 B7
Newton Dr. H Chap BB10 85 A7
Newton Dr. Loft G WF1 121 C3
Newton Garth. Leeds LS7 60 E5
Newton Gn. Loft G WF1 121 B1
Newton Gr. Leeds LS7 60 E4
Newton Hill Rd. Leeds LS7 60 D5
Newton La. Fair WF11 104 C4
Newton La. Ledsh WF10 104 C4
Newton La. Ledst WF10 103 E4
Newton La. Loft G WF1 121 B4
Newton Lodge Cl. Leeds LS7 60 C5
Newton Lodge Dr. Leeds LS7 60 C5
Newton Par. Leeds LS7 60 D5
Newton Park Ct. Leeds LS7 60 E5
Newton Park Dr. Leeds LS7 60 E5
Newton Park View. Leeds LS7 60 E4
Newton Pk. Brig HD6 114 F6
Newton Pl. Brad BD5 74 E4
Newton Rd. Leeds LS7 60 E5
Newton Sq. Gild LS12 77 D3
Newton St. Brad BD5 74 E3
Newton St. Hali HX6 112 B4 9
Newton View. Leeds LS7 60 D5
Newton Way. Bail BD17 38 C4
Newton Wlk. Leeds LS7 60 E4
Newtown Ave. Roy S71 179 B4
Nibshaw La. Clec BD19 117 A8
Nibshaw Rd. Clec BD19 117 A8
Nice Ave. Leeds LS8 60 F4 16
Nice St. Leeds LS8 61 A4
Nice View. Leeds LS8 60 F4
Nicholas Cl. Brad BD7 73 F7
Nichols Cl. Weth LS22 13 C5
Nichols Way. Weth LS22 13 C5
Nicholson St. Castle WF10 124 C7
Nickleby Rd. Leeds LS9 80 A8
Nicolsons Pl. Sil BD20 5 E1
Nidd App. Weth LS22 13 D8
Nidd Ct. Sil BD20 5 E1
Nidd Dr. Castle WF10 125 B8
Nidd St. Brad BD3 75 B6
Nidderdale Cl. Gar LS25 83 B5
Nidderdale Wlk. Bail BD17 38 E4
Nields Cty Prim Sch. Slai 169 F8
Nields Rd. Slai HD7 169 F8
Nightingale Crest. Wake WF2 141 C4
Nightingale St. Keigh BD21 35 D8 3
Nile Cres. Keigh BD22 34 F6
Nile Rd. Ilkley LS29 8 B4
Nile St. Haw BD22 51 E8
Nile St. Hud HD1 153 F5
Nile St. Keigh BD22 34 F6
Nile St. Leeds LS2 79 D8
Nina Rd. Brad BD7 73 F3
Ninelands La. Gar LS25 83 A6
Ninelands Spur. Gar LS25 83 A6
Ninevah La. Bad WF9 164 E3
Ninevah La. Kippax WF10 102 F5
Nineveh Gdns. Leeds LS11 79 A5
Nineveh Par. Leeds LS11 79 A5
Nineveh Rd. Leeds LS11 79 A5
Ninth Ave. Clec WF15 116 B5
Nippet La. Leeds LS9 79 E8
Nixon Ave. Leeds LS9 80 B7
Nixon Cl. Dew WF12 139 F1
Noble Ct. Hud HD4 171 D6
Noble St. Brad BD7 74 B5
Nog La. Ship BD9 55 A4
Nook Gdns. B in Elm LS15 62 F8
Nook Gn. Dew WF12 139 D2
Nook La. Sow Br HX6 131 F8
Nook La. Wad M HX7 89 D4
Nook Rd. B in Elm LS15 62 F8
Nook The. Clec BD19 116 E8
Nook The. Cull BD13 52 D6
Nook The. E Ard WF3 119 E6
Nook The. Leeds LS17 43 D5
Nook Wlk. Dew WF13 138 F8
Nooking The. Wake WF2 120 B3
Nooks The. Gild LS27 97 D6
Noon Cl. Loft G WF3 121 E5
Nopper Rd. Hud HD4 170 F8
Nopper Rd. Mel HD7 170 F8
Nor Wood Rd. Hem WF9 181 D5
Nora Pl. Leeds LS13 58 A3
Nora Rd. Leeds LS13 58 A3
Nora Terr. Leeds LS13 58 A3
Norbeck Dr. Haw BD22 51 E8
Norbury Rd. Brad BD10 56 E4
Norcliffe La. Brig HX3 114 A7
Norcliffe La. Hali HX3 114 A7
Norcroft Brow. Brad BD7 74 D6
Norcroft Ind Est. Brad 74 C7
Norcroft La. Caw S75 193 F3
Norcroft St. Brad BD1, BD7 74 C7
Norcross Ave. Hud HD3 153 B7
Norfield. Hud HD2 136 A4
Norfolk Ave. Batley WF17 118 B3
Norfolk Cl. Broth WF11 126 C8
Norfolk Cl. Leeds LS7 60 D7
Norfolk Cl. Litt OL15 129 C1
Norfolk Cl. Roth LS26 101 D5
Norfolk Dr. Roth LS26 101 D5
Norfolk Gdns. Brad BD1 74 E6 1
Norfolk Gdns. Leeds LS7 60 D7
Norfolk Gn. Leeds LS7 60 D7
Norfolk House. Wake WF1 142 F3
Norfolk Mount. Leeds LS7 60 D7
Norfolk Pl. Hali HX1 113 A6
Norfolk Pl. Leeds LS7 60 D7
Norfolk St. Batley WF17 118 B4
Norfolk St. Bing BD16 37 A3 4
Norfolk St. Heb Br HX7 89 A2 3
Norfolk Terr. Leeds LS7 60 D7
Norfolk View. Leeds LS7 60 D7
Norfolk Wlk. Dew WF13 139 B8 5
Norfolk Wlk. Leeds LS7 60 D7
Norgarth Cl. Batley WF17 118 F5
Norham Gr. Brad BD12 94 D2
Norland CE (C) Jun & Inf Sch.
Sow Br 112 D2
Norland Rd. Sow Br HX6 112 C3
Norland Rd. Sow Br HX6 133 D8
Norland St. Brad BD7 73 F3
Norland Town Rd. Sow Br HX6 112 D2
Norland View. Hali HX6 112 D4
Norland View. Hali HX2 113 A4 6
Norman Ave. Brad BD2 56 B5
Norman Ave. Elland HX5 135 A6
Norman Cres. Brad BD2 56 B5
Norman Dr. Mir WF14 137 F6
Norman Gr. Brad BD2 56 B5
Norman Gr. Elland HX5 135 A6
Norman Gr. Leeds LS5 59 A4
Norman La. Brad BD2 56 B5
Norman Mount. Brad BD2 56 B5
Norman Mount. Leeds LS5 59 A4
Norman Pl. Hor WF4 141 B1 6
Norman Pl. Leeds LS8 44 A2
Norman Rae Playing Fields. Ship 54 F6
Norman Rd. D Dale HD8 191 F5
Norman Rd. Hud HD2 136 A1
Norman Rd. Mir WF14 137 F6
Norman Row. Leeds LS5 59 A4
Norman St. Bing BD16 37 A3
Norman St. Elland HX5 135 A6
Norman St. Hali HX1 112 F5 3
Norman St. Haw BD22 51 D7 14
Norman St. Leeds LS5 59 A4
Norman St. Ship BD18 55 D7
Norman Terr. Brad BD2 56 B5
Norman Terr. Elland HX5 135 A6
Norman Terr. Leeds LS8 44 A2
Norman View. Leeds LS5 59 A4
Normanon Pl. Leeds LS11 79 A4
Normans Way. Wake WF2 142 F1
Normanton C E (Aided) Fst Sch.
Nor 123 B2
Normanton Common Fst Sch.
Nor 123 D3
Normanton Cross St. Hor WF4 159 C8
Normanton Freeston High Sch.
Nor 123 B1
Normanton Gr. Leeds LS11 79 A4
Normanton Grammar Sch. Nor 123 A1
Normanton Ind Est. Nor 123 D3
Normanton Lee Brigg Fst Sch. Nor 122 E3
Normanton Martin Frobisher Fst
Sch. Nor 122 F4
Normanton Queen St Fst Sch. Nor 123 A2
Normanton St. Hor WF4 159 C8
Normanton Woodhouse Fst Sch.
Nor 123 A1
Normanton Woodlands Mid Sch.
Nor 144 A8
Norr Green Terr. Wils BD15 53 D6
Norridge Bottom. Holmfi HD7 189 A5
Norris Cl. Hud HD5 155 A4
Norristhorpe Ave. Liver WF15 117 A2
Norristhorpe La. Liver WF15 117 B2
Norristhorpe Sch. Liver 117 B2
North App. Stut LS24 48 A5
North Ave. Brad BD8 55 D2
North Ave. Castle WF10 123 F7
North Ave. Hor WF4 141 C1
North Ave. Otley LS21 23 A8
North Ave. Pont WF8 146 B7
North Ave. S Elm WF9 182 F2
North Ave. S in Cra BD20 16 D4
North Ave. Wake WF1 142 C8
North Baileygate. Pont WF8 125 E1
North Bank Rd. Batley WF17 118 A6
North Bank Rd. Hud HD2 135 F1
North Bank Rd. Ship BD16 54 B5
North Bolton. Hali HX2 91 E7
North Bridge. Hali HX1 113 C8 7
North Bridge L Ctr. Hali 113 C8
North Bridge St. Hali HX1 113 C8
North Broadgate La. Hors LS18 41 C1
North Brook St. Brad BD1, BD3 74 F8
North Byland. Hali HX2 91 E7
North Carr Croft. Hud HD5 154 E7
North Carr. Hud HD5 154 E7
North Cl. Feath WF7 124 C1
North Cl. Leeds LS8 61 D6
North Cl. Roy S71 179 C3
North Cliffe Ave. Thorn BD13 72 F6
North Cliffe Cl. Thorn BD13 72 E6 7
North Cliffe Dr. Thorn BD13 72 E6
North Cliffe Gr. Thorn BD13 72 E6 8
North Cliffe La. Thorn BD13 72 F6
North Cliffe. Sow Br HX6 112 B3
North Cres. S Elm WF9 183 B4
North Croft Grove Rd. Ilkley LS29 8 A4
North Cross Rd. Hud HD2 135 F2
North Ct. Leeds LS2 79 C8
North Cut. Brig HD6 114 F2
North Dean Ave. Keigh BD22 34 E7
North Dean Rd. Elland HX4 113 A1
North Dean Rd. Keigh BD22 34 F7
North Dene Rd. Sil BD20 5 E2
North Dr. Bramho LS16 24 F2
North Dr. Gar LS25 83 B4
North Dr. Hud HD7 152 E4
North East Wakefield Coll. Pont 125 B1
North Farm Rd. Leeds LS8, LS9 61 C3
North Featherstone Jun & Inf Sch.
Pont 145 E7
North Field La. Skel HD8 175 A2
North Field Rd. H Pag DN5 195 D7
North Fold. Brad BD10 56 B8
North Gate. Kirkhe WF14 137 E3
North Grange Mews. Leeds LS6 59 F4
North Grange Mount. Leeds LS6 59 F5
North Grange Rd. Leeds LS6 59 F4
North Grove App. Weth LS22 13 E7
North Grove Ave. Weth LS22 13 E7
North Grove Cl. Leeds LS8 61 D6
North Grove Cres. Weth LS22 13 E7
North Grove Ct. Weth LS22 13 E6
North Grove Dr. Leeds LS8 61 D6
North Grove Dr. Weth LS22 13 E7
North Grove Mount. Weth LS22 13 E7
North Grove Rd. Weth LS22 13 E7
North Grove Rise. Leeds LS8 61 D6
North Grove Way. Weth LS22 13 F6
North Hall Ave. Brad BD10 39 A2
North Hill Cl. Leeds LS8 61 C6
North Hill Ct. Leeds LS6 59 F5
North Hill Dr. Kirkhe HD5 155 C8
North Hill Rd. Leeds LS6 59 F4
North Hill. Scar LS14 28 D1
North Holme St. Brad BD1 74 E8
North Ives. Oxen BD22 51 C4
North John St. S Queen BD13 72 E1 3
North King St. Batley WF17 118 D4
North La. Caw S75 193 A2
North La. Leeds LS6 59 D5
North La. Leeds LS8 61 C6
North La. Roth LS26 101 C6
North La. Slai HD7 151 D1
North Lingwell Rd. Midd LS10 99 C5
North Lodge La. Dar WF8 147 F4
North Mead. Bramho LS16 24 F2
North Moor La. Kirkhe HD5 137 C2
North Ossett High Sch. Ossett 119 D1
North Par. Brad BD15 54 A2
North Par. Brad BD1 74 E7
North Par. Bur in W LS29 9 E2
North Par. Hali HX1 113 C7
North Par. Ilkley LS29 8 C4
North Par. Leeds LS16 59 A8
North Par. Otley LS21 23 A8
North Park Ave. Leeds LS8 44 A1
North Park Gr. Leeds LS8 44 A1
North Park Par. Leeds LS8 60 F8
North Park Rd. Brad BD9 55 B3
North Park Rd. Leeds LS8 61 A8
North Park St. Dew WF13 118 A1
North Park Terr. Brad BD9 55 C2
North Parkway. Leeds LS14 62 A6
North Pl. S in Cra BD20 16 C5
North Queen St. Keigh BD21 35 C7 1
North Rd. Brad BD6 74 B1
North Rd. Dew WF13 138 E6
North Rd. Fair WF11 105 A4
North Rd. Hors LS18 41 B3
North Rd. Kirkb HD8 173 E7
North Rd. Leeds LS15 62 C2
North Rd. Leeds LS9 80 D3
North Rd. Roy S71 179 D4
North Rd. S in Cra BD20 16 C5
North Rise. Hud HD2 136 C2
North Road Terr. Wake WF1 142 B7
North Row. S in Cra BD20 16 C5
North Row. Shep HD8 190 D8
North Royd. Rip HX4 133 B5
North Selby. Hali HX2 91 D7
North St. Add LS29 7 A8
North St. Batley WF16 117 D3
North St. Batley WF17 118 B6
North St. Brad BD10 39 B2
North St. Brad BD1 74 F7
North St. Brad BD12 95 A4
North St. Castle WF10 104 C3
North St. Castle WF10 124 C8
North St. Dew WF13 118 C1
North St. Elland HX4 134 B4
North St. Elland HX4 134 D7 4
North St. Glu BD20 16 E6
North St. Haw BD22 51 B7
North St. Hud HD1 153 D5
North St. Hud HD1 153 E3
North St. Keigh BD21 35 C7
North St. Leeds LS2, LS7 60 D1
North St. Mir WF14 137 F4
North St. Nor WF6 144 A8
North St. Otley LS21 23 A8
North St. Pudsey LS28 76 E8 9
North St. S in Cra BD20 16 D5
North St. S Kirk WF9 182 B3
North St. Sil BD20 5 E2
North St. Weth LS22 13 E5
North St. Yeadon LS19 40 B4
North Terr. Batley WF17 96 F1
North Terr. Leeds LS15 62 C2 3
North Terr. Yeadon LS19 40 B7
North View. Brad BD15 54 A1
North View. Bur in W LS29 9 F1
North View. Dew WF12 139 D6
North View. Hem WF9 163 A4
North View. Knot WF11 126 E4
North View. Men LS29 22 A3
North View Rd. Birk BD4 96 A7
North View Rd. Brad BD3 55 F2
North View. S in Cra BD20 16 D5
North View St. Keigh BD20 18 C1
North View St. Pudsey LS28 57 E2
North View. Stee BD20 16 F6
North View Terr. Dew WF13 117 F2 7
North View Terr. Dew WF13 118 B2 2
North View Terr. Haw BD22 51 C8
North View Terr. Pudsey LS28 57 E2 5
North View. Wils BD15 53 C5
North Way. Hud HD2 136 E4
North Way. Leeds LS8 61 D6
North West Rd. Leeds LS6 60 B3
North Wing. Brad BD3 74 F8
North Wlk. Harden BD16 36 A1
North Wlk. Hem WF9 181 D8
North's Pl. Mir WF14 138 A7
Northallerton Rd. Brad BD3 55 F1
Northampton St. Brad BD3 55 F1
Northbrook Pl. Leeds LS7 60 D7
Northbrook St. Leeds LS7 60 D7
Northcliffe Golf Course. Ship 54 E6
Northcliffe Rd. Ship BD18 55 B6
Northcote Cres. Leeds LS11 79 B4
Northcote Dr. Leeds LS11 79 B4
Northcote Fold. Coll LS22 13 B2
Northcote Gn. Leeds LS11 79 B4
Northcote. Ossett WF5 119 C1
Northcote Rd. Brad BD2 56 B2
Northcote St. Pudsey LS28 57 D2
Northcote Terr. Brad BD2 56 B1
Northcroft Ave. S Elm WF9 183 A4
Northcroft Rise. Brad BD8 54 E1
Northcroft. S Elm WF9 183 A3
Northdale Ave. Brad BD5 74 C2
Northdale Cres. Brad BD5 74 C2
Northdale Mount. Brad BD5 74 C2
Northdale Rd. Ship BD9 55 B5
Northedge La. Brig HX3 93 D1
Northedge Meadow. Brad BD10 56 B6
Northedge Pk. Brig HX3 93 D1
Northern Cl. Brad BD7 73 F2
Northern St. Leeds LS1 79 A7
Northfield Ave. Hud HD1 153 E4
Northfield Ave. Knot WF11 126 F3
Northfield Ave. Ossett WF5 140 D6
Northfield Ave. Roth LS26 100 C4
Northfield Ave. S Kirk WF9 182 C3
Northfield Ave. Weth LS22 13 E6
Northfield Cl. Elland HX5 134 F6 1
Northfield Cres. Ship BD16 54 A7
Northfield Dr. Pont WF8 125 F1
Northfield Gdns. Brad BD6 74 C1
Northfield Gr. Brad BD6 74 C1
Northfield Gr. Hud HD1 153 F3
Northfield Gr. S Kirk WF9 182 C3
Northfield La. Hor WF4 141 C1
Northfield La. Kirkb HD8 173 E8
Northfield La. S Kirk WF9 182 C3
Northfield Mid Sch. S Kirk 182 C3
Northfield Pl. Brad BD8 55 C1
Northfield Pl. Dew WF13 118 C1
Northfield Pl. Roth LS26 100 B4
Northfield Pl. Weth LS22 13 E6
Northfield Rd. Brad BD6 74 B1
Northfield Rd. Crof WF4 144 B3
Northfield Rd. Dew WF13 118 B1
Northfield Rd. Knot WF11 126 F3
Northfield Rd. Ossett WF5 140 D7
Northfield St. Dew WF13 118 C1
Northfield St. S Kirk WF9 182 B3
Northfield Terr. Queen BD13 73 A1
Northfield Terr. Slai HD7 152 A2
Northfields. Th Arch LS23 15 A3
Northgate. Bail BD17 38 C4
Northgate. Brad BD1 74 E7 1
Northgate Cl. Pont WF8 125 D1
Northgate. Clec BD19 116 D7
Northgate. Dew WF13 139 D8
Northgate. Elland HX5 134 F7
Northgate. Hali HX1 113 C8
Northgate. Hep HX7 88 F5
Northgate. Honley HD7 172 B6
Northgate. Hor WF4 141 A1
Northgate. Hud HD1 154 B7
Northgate. Hud HD1, HD5 154 F3
Northgate La. Coll LS22 13 A3
Northgate. Liver WF16 117 C4
Northgate Lodge. Pont WF8 125 D1
Northgate. Pont WF8 125 D1
Northgate Rise. Coll LS22 13 B2
Northgate. Roth LS26 101 C6 1
Northgate. S Hie S72 180 E6
Northgate. Wake WF1 142 C6 16
Northgate. Wake WF1 142 C7
Northgates. Weth LS22 13 E5
Northlands. Roy S71 179 C4
Northlea Ave. Brad BD10 39 B1
Northolme Ave. Leeds LS16 59 B7
Northolme Cres. Leeds LS16 59 B7
Northonthorpe Hall Sch. Clay W 175 D1
Northorpe La. Mir WF14 138 C7
Northowram Gn. Northo HX3 93 A3
Northowram Jun & Inf Sch. Northo 93 A3
Northrop Cl. Brad BD8 55 A1
Northside Ave. Brad BD7 74 A6
Northside Bsns Pk. Leeds 60 D2
Northside Rd. Brad BD7 74 A6
Northside Terr. Brad BD7 73 F6
Northstead. Dew WF13 138 D7
Northumberland St. Hud HD1 154 B6 1
Northway Cres. Mir WF14 137 F7
Northway Gdns. Mir WF14 137 F7
Northway. Mir WF14 137 F7
Northways Sch. B Spa 30 D5
Northwell Gate. Otley LS21 10 E2
Northwest Bsns Pk. Leeds 60 B3
Northwood Cl. Pudsey LS28 76 F5
Northwood Cl. Roth LS26 101 C7
Northwood Cres. Brad BD10 56 C6
Northwood Falls. Roth LS26 101 C7
Northwood Gdns. Leeds LS15 81 E7
Northwood Mount. Pudsey LS28 76 F5
Northwood Pk. Kirkb HD8 173 E7
Northwood Pk. Roth LS26 101 C7
Northwood View. Pudsey LS28 76 F5
Norton and Kirk Smeaton Rd.
Norton WF8 166 E4
Norton Cl. Elland HX5 134 F5
Norton Cl. Hali HX2 112 B7
Norton Dr. Hali HX2 112 B7
Norton Rd. Leeds LS8 44 A3
Norton Rd. Wake WF1 142 D7
Norton St. Elland HX5 134 F6
Norton St. Sil BD20 5 D1

Norton St. Wake WF1 ..... 142 E4
Norton Terr. Kirkb Hd4 ..... 173 C2
Nortonthorpe Ind Est. Clay W 175 D1
Norwich Ave. Leeds LS10 ..... 79 D2
Norwood Ave. Birk BD11 ..... 96 B4
Norwood Ave. Bur in W LS29 ..... 9 F1
Norwood Ave. Ship BD18 ..... 55 B6
Norwood Cl. Bur in W LS29 ..... 9 F1
Norwood Cres. Birk BD11 ..... 96 B4
Norwood Cres. Pudsey LS28 ..... 57 F2
Norwood Croft. Pudsey LS28 ..... 57 F2
Norwood Dar WF8 ..... 147 A5
Norwood Dr. Batley WF17 ..... 117 F8
Norwood Dr. Birk BD11 ..... 96 B4
Norwood Dr. Bri S72 ..... 181 A3
Norwood Dr. Birk BD11 ..... 96 B4
Norwood Gr. Leeds LS6 ..... 59 E3
Norwood Green Hill. Brig HX3 ..... 93 F2
Norwood Mount. Leeds LS6 ..... 59 E3
Norwood Pl. Hud HD2 ..... 135 D1
Norwood Pl. Leeds LS6 ..... 59 E3
Norwood Pl. Ship BD18 ..... 55 B6
Norwood Rd. Hud HD2 ..... 135 E2
Norwood Rd. Leeds LS6 ..... 59 E3
Norwood Rd. Ship BD18 ..... 55 B6
Norwood St. Brad BD5 ..... 74 D2
Norwood St. Ship BD18 ..... 55 B6
Norwood Terr. Bur in W LS29 ..... 9 F1
Norwood Terr. Leeds LS6 ..... 59 E3
Norwood Terr. Ship BD18 ..... 55 B6
Norwood View. Leeds LS6 ..... 59 E3
Nostell Cl. Brad BD8 ..... 74 D8
Nostell La. Ryhill WF4 ..... 162 B2
Noster Gr. Leeds LS11 ..... 78 F3
Noster Hill. Leeds LS11 ..... 78 F3
Noster Pl. Leeds LS11 ..... 78 F3
Noster Rd. Leeds LS11 ..... 78 F3
Noster St. Leeds LS11 ..... 78 F3
Noster Terr. Leeds LS11 ..... 79 A3
Noster View. Leeds LS11 ..... 78 F3
Notre Dame Sixth Form Coll. Leeds 60 B3
Nottingham St. Brad BD3 ..... 75 E7
Notton La. Notton WF4 ..... 179 B6
Nova La. Batley WF17 ..... 96 D2
Nowell App. Leeds LS9 ..... 61 B1
Nowell Ave. Leeds LS9 ..... 61 B1
Nowell Cl. Leeds LS9 ..... 61 B1 6
Nowell Cres. Leeds LS9 ..... 61 B1
Nowell End Row. Leeds LS9 ..... 61 B1
Nowell Gdns. Leeds LS9 ..... 61 B1 8
Nowell Gr. Leeds LS9 ..... 61 B1
Nowell La. Leeds LS9 ..... 61 B1
Nowell Mount Leeds LS9 ..... 61 B1
Nowell Par. Leeds LS9 ..... 61 B1
Nowell Pl. Hud HD5 ..... 154 F4
Nowell St. Leeds LS9 ..... 61 B1
Nowell St. Dew WF13 ..... 118 B1
Nowell Terr. Leeds LS9 ..... 61 B1
Nowell View. Leeds LS9 ..... 61 B1
Nowell Wlk. Leeds LS9 ..... 61 B1
Nowell's Yd. Dew WF13 ..... 139 B8
Nuffield Hospl. Hud 135 A1
Nunburnholme Wlk. Brad BD10 ..... 56 C6
Nunington Ave. Leeds LS12 ..... 28 C8 12
Nunington St. Leeds LS12 ..... 78 D8 1
Nunington Terr. Leeds LS12 ..... 78 C8 13
Nunington View. Leeds LS12 ..... 59 C1 4
Nunlea Royd. Brig HX3 ..... 115 A6
Nunn's Cl. Feath WF7 ..... 145 D4
Nunn's Croft. Feath WF7 ..... 145 D4
Nunn's Gn. Feath WF7 ..... 145 D4
Nunn's La. Feath WF7 ..... 145 D4
Nunnery La. Brig HX6 ..... 111 B6
Nunns Ave. Feath WF7 ..... 145 C4
Nunns Ct. Feath WF7 ..... 145 C3
Nunroyd Ave. Guise LS20 ..... 39 F8
Nunroyd Ave. Leeds LS17 ..... 43 D1
Nunroyd. Batley WF16 ..... 117 D5
Nunroyd Gr. Leeds LS17 ..... 43 D1
Nunroyd Lawn. Leeds LS17 ..... 43 D1
Nunroyd Rd. Leeds LS17 ..... 43 D1
Nunroyd St. Leeds LS17 ..... 43 D1
Nunroyd Terr. Leeds LS17 ..... 43 D1
Nunthorpe Rd. Pudsey LS13 ..... 93 F2
Nursar La. Brad BD5 ..... 74 C4
Nursery Ave. Hali HX3 ..... 91 F3
Nursery Cl. Bail BD17 ..... 37 E2
Nursery Cl. Hali HX3 ..... 91 F2
Nursery Cl. Keigh BD20 ..... 18 A3
Nursery Garth. Weth LS22 ..... 13 F6
Nursery Gr. Hali HX3 ..... 91 F3
Nursery La. Hali HX3 ..... 91 F3
Nursery La. Leeds LS17 ..... 43 C4
Nursery La. Rip HX6 ..... 132 B8
Nursery Mount. Midd LS10 ..... 79 F6
Nursery Mount Rd. Midd LS10 ..... 79 E2 12
Nursery Rd. Brad BD14 ..... 73 B4
Nursery Rd. Brad BD13 ..... 73 F2
Nursery Rd. Guise LS20 ..... 22 D3
Nursery St. Dew WF12 ..... 139 C4
Nursery St. Hud HD2 ..... 136 A1
Nursery Way. B Spa LS23 ..... 30 E7
Nursery Way. B Spa LS23 ..... 30 E7
Nursery Wood Rd. Batley WF17 ..... 118 D3
Nutclough. Heb HX7 ..... 89 B4
Nutclough Rd. Heb HX7 ..... 89 B4
Nutfield St. Tod OL14 ..... 108 B6 6
Nuthall Cl. Brad BD13 ..... 72 D6
Nuttall St. Bacup OL13 ..... 106 B3 3
Nutter La. Clec WF17 ..... 96 B1
Nutter St. Clec WF17 ..... 116 C8
Nutting Grove Terr. Leeds LS12 ..... 77 E5

O'Cot La. Mars HD3 ..... 151 B4
O'Grady Sq. Leeds LS9 ..... 79 F7 10
Oak Ave. Bing BD16 ..... 37 B4
Oak Ave. Brad BD8 ..... 73 C7
Oak Ave. Bur in W LS29 ..... 9 F1
Oak Ave. Hali HX6 ..... 112 A5
Oak Ave. Hud HD7 ..... 152 E5
Oak Ave. Leeds LS12 ..... 78 A4
Oak Ave. Loft S WF3 ..... 121 F4
Oak Ave. Mel HD7 ..... 170 C2
Oak Ave. Morley LS27 ..... 98 B3
Oak Ave. Nor WF6 ..... 144 A8
Oak Cl. Tod OL14 ..... 108 B4
Oak Cl. Bur in W LS29 ..... 9 F1
Oak Cres. Gar LS25 ..... 82 F7
Oak Cres. Leeds LS15 ..... 80 F7
Oak Dr. Gar LS25 ..... 82 F7
Oak Dr. Slai HD7 ..... 152 D3
Oak Gr. Brad BD8 ..... 73 C7
Oak Gr. Keigh BD21 ..... 35 A4
Oak Gr. Morley LS27 ..... 98 C3
Oak Half Pk. Crg WF4 ..... 159 C4
Oak Head Terr. Glu BD20 ..... 16 D8
Oak Hill. Sow Br HX6 ..... 115 B3
Oak Hill. Sow Br HX6 ..... 132 E8
Oak House. Castle WF10 ..... 124 E7 9
Oak La. Brad BD9 ..... 55 C2
Oak La. Hali HX1 ..... 113 A7 4
Oak La. Hali HX1 ..... 113 A7
Oak Leigh. Caw S75 ..... 193 E4
Oak Mount. Brad BD8 ..... 55 D2
Oak Mount. Tod OL14 ..... 108 B6
Oak Pl. Bail BD17 ..... 38 A4
Oak Pl. Brad BD8 ..... 55 C2
Oak Pl. Hali HX6 ..... 112 B5 10
Oak Pl. Hali HX1 ..... 113 A7
Oak Rd. Gar LS25 ..... 82 E7
Oak Rd. Leeds LS7 ..... 137 A5
Oak Rd. Leeds LS7 ..... 60 D5
Oak Rd. Leeds LS12 ..... 78 A4
Oak Rd. Leeds LS7 ..... 60 F7
Oak Rd. Morley LS27 ..... 97 F3
Oak Rd. Shaf S72 ..... 180 D2
Oak Ridge. Weth LS22 ..... 13 C5
Oak Rise. Clec BD19 ..... 95 D2
Oak Royd. Gar LS25 ..... 82 F7
Oak Scar La. Holmfi HD7 ..... 189 D3
Oak St. Batley WF16 ..... 117 D4
Oak St. Brad BD4 ..... 73 B4
Oak St. Crof WF4 ..... 162 A7
Oak St. Elland HX5 ..... 134 F6
Oak St. Hali HX6 ..... 112 B5 18
Oak St. Haw BD22 ..... 51 D7
Oak St. Heb br HX7 ..... 89 A4 9
Oak St. Leeds LS9 ..... 121 C4
Oak St. Morley LS27 ..... 98 B7
Oak St. Oxen BD22 ..... 51 C3
Oak St. Pudsey LS28 ..... 76 F8
Oak St. Elin WF9 ..... 182 F1
Oak St. Tod OL14 ..... 108 A4
Oak Terr. Elland HX4 ..... 134 A4
Oak Terr. Hali HX1 ..... 113 A7 2
Oak Terr. Hud HD2 ..... 136 B2
Oak Terr. Leeds LS15 ..... 62 D3 1
Oak Terr. Morley LS27 ..... 98 B7
Oak Tree Ave. Lepton HD8 ..... 155 D3
Oak Tree Bsns Pk. Leeds 62 A7
Oak Tree Cl. Leeds LS9 ..... 61 C3
Oak Tree Cres. Leeds LS9 ..... 61 C3
Oak Tree Ct. Leeds LS9 ..... 61 C3
Oak Tree Dr. Leeds LS8 ..... 61 C3
Oak Tree Gr. Leeds LS9 ..... 61 C3
Oak Tree Meadow. Walton WF2 ..... 161 A6
Oak Tree Mount. Leeds LS9 ..... 61 C3
Oak Tree Rd. Lepton HD8 ..... 155 D3
Oak Tree Terr. Lepton HD8 ..... 155 D3
Oak Tree Wlk. Leeds LS9 ..... 61 C3
Oak View. Sil BD20 ..... 5 E2
Oak View Terr. Batley WF17 ..... 117 F8 4
Oak Villas. Brad BD8 ..... 55 D2
Oak Wood Rd. Weth LS22 ..... 13 D7
Oakbank Ave. Keigh BD22 ..... 34 F5
Oakbank Broadway. Keigh BD22 ..... 34 F4
Oakbank Cres. Keigh BD22 ..... 34 F5
Oakbank Ct. Keigh BD22 ..... 34 F4
Oakbank Dr. Keigh BD22 ..... 34 F4
Oakbank Gr. Keigh BD22 ..... 34 F5
Oakbank Mount. Keigh BD22 ..... 34 F4
Oakbank Rech Ctr. Keigh 34 F4
Oakbank Sch. Keigh 34 F4
Oakburn Brf. Ilkley S77 ..... 8 A1
Oakdale Ave. Brad BD6 ..... 94 B8
Oakdale Ave. Ship BD18 ..... 55 D6
Oakdale. Bing BD16 ..... 37 A5
Oakdale Cl. Brad BD10 ..... 39 B1
Oakdale Cl. Hali HX3 ..... 92 A2
Oakdale Cl. Loft S WF3 ..... 121 B6
Oakdale Cres. Brad BD6 ..... 74 B1
Oakdale Cres. Hud HD3 ..... 153 A6
Oakdale Dr. Ship BD18 ..... 55 D6
Oakdale Fst Sch. Ship 55 E6
Oakdale Garth. Leeds LS14 ..... 45 B1
Oakdale Meadow. Leeds LS14 ..... 45 B1
Oakdale Pk. Pool LS21 ..... 24 D6
Oakdale Rd. Ship BD18 ..... 55 D6
Oakdene Cl. Pudsey LS28 ..... 76 F5
Oakdene Ct. Leeds LS17 ..... 44 A4
Oakdene Gdns. Leeds LS17 ..... 44 A4
Oakdene Vale. Leeds LS17 ..... 44 A4
Oakdene Way. Leeds LS17 ..... 44 A4
Oaken Bank Cres. Hud HD5 ..... 154 C4
Oaken Cl. Bacup OL13 ..... 106 B3
Oakenclough Rd. Bacup OL13 ..... 106 A3
Oakenshaw Cl. Brad BD19 ..... 95 A3
Oakenshaw Ct. Brad BD19 ..... 95 A3
Oakenshaw La. Crof WF4 ..... 143 F2
Oakenshaw La. Walton WF1, WF2 ..... 161 A8
Oakenshaw St. Wake WF1 ..... 142 E4
Oakes Ave. Honley HD7 ..... 172 C2
Oakes Gdns. Honley HD7 ..... 172 C2
Oakes Rd. Hud HD3 ..... 153 A8
Oakes Rd S. Hud HD3 ..... 153 A7
Oakes St. Wake WF2 ..... 141 D6
Oakfield Ave. Bing BD16 ..... 37 A3
Oakfield Ave. Roth LS26 ..... 100 D6
Oakfield. Bing BD16 ..... 37 A4
Oakfield Cl. Mapp S75 ..... 178 A1
Oakfield Cres. Knot WF11 ..... 126 C4
Oakfield Cres. Brad BD6 ..... 74 B1
Oakfield Dr. Bail BD17 ..... 38 E4
Oakfield Gr. Brad BD9 ..... 55 A3
Oakfield Gr. Skel HD8 ..... 175 A1
Oakfield. Leeds LS6 ..... 59 E6
Oakfield Pk. Pont WF8 ..... 146 B8
Oakfield Rd. Keigh BD21 ..... 35 C5
Oakfield Terr. Bing BD16 ..... 37 A3
Oakfield Terr. Hors LS18 ..... 58 C8
Oakfield Terr. Ship BD10 ..... 56 B6
Oakhall Rd. Batley WF17 ..... 118 A7
Oakhurst Ave. Leeds LS11 ..... 79 A1

Oakhurst Gr. Leeds LS11 ..... 78 F1
Oakhurst Mount. Leeds LS11 ..... 78 F1
Oakhurst Rd. Leeds LS11 ..... 79 A1
Oakhurst St. Leeds LS11 ..... 78 F1
Oakland Ct. Kirkb HD8 ..... 173 F7
Oakland Dr. Neth WF4 ..... 158 D5
Oakland Rd. Neth WF4 ..... 158 D5
Oakland St. Sil BD20 ..... 5 D1
Oaklands Ave. Northo HX3 ..... 93 B3
Oaklands Ave. Pudsey LS13 ..... 57 E5
Oaklands Cl. Holmfi HD7 ..... 189 A7
Oaklands Croft. Walton WF2 ..... 161 B6
Oaklands Dr. Hors LS16 ..... 41 E8
Oaklands Dr. Hud HD3 ..... 154 F5
Oaklands Fst. Pudsey LS13 ..... 57 E5
Oaklands. Ilkley LS29 ..... 8 A3
Oaklea Cl. Mapp S75 ..... 178 B2
Oaklea Gdns. Hors LS16 ..... 42 D2
Oaklea Rd. B in Elm LS15 ..... 62 F6
Oakleigh Ave. Brad BD14 ..... 73 B4
Oakleigh Ave. Wake WF2 ..... 141 E5
Oakleigh Cl. Brad BD14 ..... 73 B4
Oakleigh Gdns. Brad BD14 ..... 73 B4
Oakleigh Gr. Brad BD14 ..... 73 B4
Oakleigh Rd. Brad BD14 ..... 73 B4
Oakleigh Terr. Brad BD14 ..... 73 B4
Oakleigh View. Bail BD17 ..... 38 D4
Oakley Gr. Leeds LS11 ..... 79 C2
Oakley St. E Ard WF3 ..... 119 E1
Oakley Terr. Leeds LS11 ..... 79 C2
Oakley View. Leeds LS11 ..... 79 C2
Oakridge Ave. Men LS29 ..... 22 B4
Oakridge Ct. Bing BD16 ..... 37 A4
Oakroyd Ave. Brad BD6 ..... 74 C1
Oakroyd Cl. Birk BD11 ..... 96 A5
Oakroyd Ct. Bring HD6 ..... 115 B5
Oakroyd Dr. Bring HD6 ..... 115 B5
Oakroyd Dr. Birk BD11 ..... 96 A5
Oakroyd Fold. Morley LS27 ..... 98 C8
Oakroyd Mount. Morley LS27 ..... 98 C8
Oakroyd Rd. Brad BD6 ..... 74 C1
Oakroyd Terr. Bail BD17 ..... 38 C2
Oakroyd Terr. Brad BD8 ..... 55 C1 5
Oakroyd Terr. Morley LS27 ..... 98 C8
Oakroyd Villas. Brad BD8 ..... 55 C2
Oaks Dr. Brad BD15 ..... 73 C8
Oaks Farm Cl. Mapp S75 ..... 177 F1
Oaks Farm Dr. Mapp S75 ..... 177 F1
Oaks Fold. Brad BD5 ..... 74 E3
Oaks Gn Mount. Brig HD6 ..... 135 D7
Oaks Green Mount. Brig HD6 ..... 135 F7
Oaks La. B Spa LS23 ..... 30 B7
Oaks La. Brad BD15 ..... 73 C8
Oaks The. Guise LS20 ..... 22 E1
Oaks The. Leeds LS20 ..... 22 E1
Oaksfield. M'town LS26 ..... 102 D2
Oaktree La. Brad WF17 ..... 164 C5
Oakville Rd. B Head HX7 ..... 88 B2
Oakway. Birk BD11 ..... 96 B4
Oakwell Ave. Leeds LS8 ..... 61 A6
Oakwell Ave. Pont WF8 ..... 146 C6
Oakwell Cl. Birk BD11 ..... 97 A5
Oakwell Cl. Brad BD7 ..... 74 A4
Oakwell Ct. Heni WF9 ..... 163 A2
Oakwell Cres. Leeds LS8 ..... 61 A6
Oakwell Dr. Leeds LS8 ..... 61 A6
Oakwell Gdns. Leeds LS8 ..... 61 A6
Oakwell Gr. Pudsey LS13 ..... 58 A2
Oakwell Hall. Batley 96 E2
Oakwell Ind Est. Brad 74 B8
Oakwell Mews. Leeds LS8 ..... 61 A6
Oakwell Oval. Leeds LS8 ..... 61 A6
Oakwell Rd. Birk BD11 ..... 96 F5
Oakwell Terr. Pudsey LS13 ..... 58 A2
Oakwell Way. Birk WF17 ..... 97 A3
Oakwood Ave. Birk BD11 ..... 96 A4
Oakwood Ave. Leeds LS8 ..... 61 A6
Oakwood Ave. Roy S71 ..... 179 C4
Oakwood Boundary Rd. Leeds LS8 ..... 61 B6
Oakwood Cl. Nor WF6 ..... 122 F3
Oakwood Ct. Brad BD9 ..... 55 A2
Oakwood Ct. Leeds LS8 ..... 61 B6
Oakwood Dr. Bing BD16 ..... 37 A5
Oakwood Dr. Leeds LS8 ..... 61 A6
Oakwood Dr. Men WF9 ..... 181 B6
Oakwood Garth. Leeds LS8 ..... 61 B6
Oakwood Gdns. Leeds LS8 ..... 61 B6
Oakwood Gn. Leeds LS8 ..... 61 B6
Oakwood Gr. Brad BD8 ..... 55 C1
Oakwood Gr. Leeds LS8 ..... 61 A6
Oakwood La. Leeds LS8, LS9 ..... 61 B5
Oakwood Mount. Leeds LS8 ..... 61 A6
Oakwood Nook. Leeds LS8 ..... 61 A6
Oakwood Pk. Leeds LS8 ..... 61 B6
Oakwood Pl. Leeds LS8 ..... 61 A6
Oakwood Rd. Roy S71 ..... 179 C4
Oakwood Rise. Leeds LS8 ..... 61 B6
Oakworth Cl. Leeds LS8 ..... 61 B5
Oakworth Hall. Haw BD22 ..... 34 C2
Oakworth Terr. Haw BD22 ..... 34 C1
Oast House Croft. Wroth WF3 ..... 100 B3
Oastler Ave. Hud HD7 ..... 152 D4
Oastler Pl. Brad BD12 ..... 94 D6
Oastler Rd. Pudsey LS28 ..... 57 D4
Oastler Rd. Ship BD18 ..... 55 B8
Oates St. Dew WF13 ..... 139 B8
Oatland Cl. Leeds LS7 ..... 60 C2

Oatland Ct. Leeds LS7 ..... 60 C2
Oatland Dr. Leeds LS7 ..... 60 D2
Oatland Gdns. Leeds LS7 ..... 60 D2
Oatland Gn. Leeds LS7 ..... 60 C2
Oatland La. Leeds LS7 ..... 60 C2
Oatland Pl. Leeds LS7 ..... 60 C3
Oatland Rd. Leeds LS7 ..... 60 C2
Oatland Rd. Leeds LS7 ..... 60 C2
Oatlands Dr. Otley LS21 ..... 35 A4
Oats St. Keigh BD22 ..... 35 A4
Oban Cl. E Ard WF3 ..... 98 D1
Oban Pl. Leeds LS12 ..... 78 B8 6
Oban St. Leeds LS12 ..... 78 B8 8
Oban Terr. Leeds LS12 ..... 78 B8 7
Occupation La. Aber LS24 ..... 47 D4
Occupation La. Batley WF13 ..... 117 F3
Occupation La. Bramho LS16 ..... 24 B2
Occupation La. Hali HX2 ..... 91 F6
Occupation La. Holmfi HD7 ..... 189 F8
Occupation La. Keigh BD22 ..... 34 E4
Occupation La. Pudsey LS28 ..... 76 C7
Occupation Rd. Hud HD2 ..... 136 A4
Occupation Rd. Hud HD2, HD3 ..... 153 C8
Ochrewell Ave. Hud HD2 ..... 136 E3
Octagon Terr. Hali HX2 ..... 112 E4
Oddfellow St. Morley LS27 ..... 98 A4
Oddfellows Club Houses. Ack M T
Oddfellows' Ct. Brad BD1 ..... 74 E7
Oddfellows St. Brig HD6 ..... 115 B4 3
Oddfellows St. Brig BD19 ..... 115 F8
Oddfellows St. Mir WF14 ..... 138 A5
Oddy Pl. Brad BD6 ..... 74 B1 6
Oddy Pl. Leeds LS6 ..... 59 D6 4
Oddy St. Brad BD4 ..... 75 B1
Oddy's Fold. Leeds LS6 ..... 59 E8
Odsal Pl. Brad BD6 ..... 94 D8 9
Odsal Rd. Brad BD6 ..... 94 D8
Offley La. W Har WF9 ..... 163 B6
Ogden Cres. Denh BD13 ..... 52 D2
Ogden La. Brig HD6 ..... 135 F8
Ogden La. Denh BD13 ..... 52 D2
Ogden View Cl. Hali HX2 ..... 91 D7
Old Allen Rd. Wils BD13, BD15 ..... 53 B2
Old Arcade The. Hali HX1 ..... 123 C7 20
Old Bank Fst Sch. Mir 138 A7
Old Bank Fold. Hud HD5 ..... 154 D5 13
Old Bank. Hali HX3 ..... 113 D7
Old Bank. Leeds LS15 ..... 62 F6
Old Bank Rd. Mir WF14 ..... 138 A7
Old Bank. Rd HX6 ..... 132 E4
Old Barn Cl. Leeds LS17 ..... 43 A5
Old Bell Ct. Hali HX1 ..... 113 C6 9
Old Brandon La. Thorner LS17 ..... 44 F4
Old Bridge Rise. Ilkley LS29 ..... 8 A4
Old Canal Rd. Brad BD1 ..... 74 E8
Old Church St. Ossett WF5 ..... 140 D5
Old Cl. Morley LS11 ..... 98 D8
Old Cock Yd. Hali HX1 ..... 123 C7 18
Old Corn Mill La. Brad BD7 ..... 74 B4
Old Cross Stone Rd. Tod OL14 ..... 108 C5 17
Old Crown Rd. Wake WF2 ..... 141 D4
Old Crwy. Hali HX6 ..... 112 C4
Old Dalton La. Keigh BD21 ..... 35 D7
Old Earth. Elland HX5 ..... 135 A7
Old Earth Jun & Inf Sch. Elland 135 A7
Old Farm App. Leeds LS16 ..... 58 F8
Old Farm Cl. Leeds LS16 ..... 59 A8
Old Farm Cross. Leeds LS16 ..... 59 A8
Old Farm Dr. Leeds LS16 ..... 59 A8
Old Farm Garth. Leeds LS16 ..... 59 A8
Old Farm Par. Leeds LS16 ..... 59 A8
Old Farm Wlk. Leeds LS16 ..... 59 A8
Old Fieldhouse La. Hud HD2 ..... 136 D3
Old Fold. Pudsey LS28 ..... 57 D3 9
Old Garth Croft. Hart WF11 ..... 105 A8
Old Gate. Heb Br HX7 ..... 89 A3 24
Old Gate. Honley HD7 ..... 107 F7
Old Godley La. Northo HX3 ..... 92 F1
Old Great North Rd. Broth WF11 ..... 126 D8
Old Great North Rd. Knot WF11 ..... 127 A5
Old Ground. Mars HD7 ..... 169 A8
Old Guy Rd. Queen BD13 ..... 72 C1
Old Hall Cl. Glu BD20 ..... 16 D6
Old Hall Court Yd. Crof WF1 ..... 143 A6
Old Hall. Hali HX3 ..... 113 D4
Old Hall La. Emley HD8 ..... 175 F5
Old Hall Mews. Batley WF17 ..... 118 C7
Old Hall Rd. Batley WF17 ..... 118 D7
Old Hall Rd. Brad BD6 ..... 94 B7
Old Hall Rd. Glu BD20 ..... 16 B6
Old Hall. Shaf S72 ..... 180 C2
Old Hall View. Shaf S72 ..... 180 C2
Old Haworth La. Yeadon LS19 ..... 40 B7 6
Old Hollings Hill. Guise LS20, BD17 ..... 39 C6
Old Ivy St. Brad BD8 ..... 55 C1
Old La. Askw LS21 ..... 11 B5
Old La. Bramho LS16 ..... 24 E3
Old La. Brig HD6 ..... 115 B3
Old La. Brad BD5, BD7 ..... 74 D3
Old La. Cull BD13 ..... 52 D6
Old La. Hali HX3 ..... 92 B2
Old La. Hali HX3 ..... 92 C4
Old La. Holmfi HD7 ..... 189 E1
Old La. Ilkley LS29 ..... 7 D5
Old La. Leeds LS11 ..... 214 B4
Old La. Liver WF15 ..... 117 A4
Old La. Mel HD7 ..... 170 C8
Old Langley La. Bail BD17 ..... 38 F6
Old Lee Bank. Hali HX3 ..... 92 C1
Old Lees Rd. Heb Br HX7 ..... 88 F3
Old Lindley Rd. Holywell HD3 ..... 133 F2
Old Main St. Bing BD16 ..... 37 A3
Old Market. Hali HX1 ..... 123 D7
Old Marsh. Pudsey LS28 ..... 76 C7
Old Meadows Rd. Bacup OL13 ..... 106 A4
Old Mill Bsns Pk. Leeds 79 F4
Old Mill La. Castle WF10 ..... 104 C1
Old Mill La. Holmfi HD7 ..... 188 E4
Old Mill La. Leeds LS10 ..... 79 F6
Old Mill Rd. Ship BD17 ..... 55 B8
Old Mill The. Weth LS22 ..... 13 E5

Old Mill Yd. Ossett WF5 ..... 140 C3
Old Mill Rd. Honley HD7 ..... 171 E5
Old Mount Farm. Wool WF4 ..... 178 A6
Old Mount Rd. Mars HD7 ..... 168 E2
Old Oak Cl. Leeds LS16 ..... 59 A7
Old Oak Dr. Leeds LS16 ..... 59 A7
Old Oak Garth. Leeds LS16 ..... 58 F7
Old Orch The. Pool LS21 ..... 24 C7
Old Oxenhope La. Oxen BD22 ..... 51 B4
Old Park Rd. Brad BD10 ..... 56 C7
Old Park Rd. Leeds LS8 ..... 61 A8
Old Pool Bank. Bramho LS21 ..... 25 E8
Old Pool Bank. Pool LS21 ..... 24 B5
Old Popplewell La. Brig BD19 ..... 115 E8
Old Power Way. Hali HX5 ..... 135 A8
Old Rd. Brad BD7 ..... 73 E2
Old Rd. Denh BD13 ..... 71 D8
Old Rd. Holmfi HD7 ..... 188 D3
Old Rd. Morley LS27 ..... 98 C8
Old Rd. Neth HX4 ..... 133 D4
Old Rd. Pudsey LS28 ..... 57 D2
Old Rd. Thorn BD13 ..... 73 A6
Old Rd. Wadsw HX7 ..... 67 F2
Old Riding La. Hali HX2 ..... 90 F3
Old Robin. Clec BD19 ..... 116 D7 9
Old Run Rd. Leeds LS10 ..... 79 D1
Old Run Rd. Midd LS10 ..... 99 D8
Old Sawmills The. Rip HX6 ..... 132 C2
Old School Mews. Morley LS27 ..... 98 C8 4
Old Shaw La. B Head HX7 ..... 88 A4
Old Souls Way. Bing BD16 ..... 36 C6
Old South St. Hud HD1 ..... 154 A6
Old St. H Pag DH5 ..... 195 F7
Old St. Ham DN6 ..... 183 F1
Old Station Cotts. Ryhill S71 ..... 179 D7
Old Station Way. Sil LS29 ..... 6 F8
Old Town Jun & Inf Sch. Wad M 89 C5
Old Town Mill La. Wad M HX7 ..... 89 B5
Old Turnpike. Honley HD7 ..... 172 A4
Old Wakefield Rd. Hud HD5 ..... 154 D5 5
Old Water Mill The. Rip HX6 ..... 133 C2
Old Well Head. Hali HX1 ..... 113 C6
Old Westgate. Dew WF13 ..... 139 C8
Old Whack House La. Yeadon LS19 ..... 39 F6
Old Wood La. Guise BD16 ..... 37 C8
Oldfield Ave. Leeds LS12 ..... 78 C6
Oldfield Fst Sch. Haw 50 E4
Oldfield Gate. Haw BD22 ..... 51 A7
Oldfield. Honley HD7 ..... 171 F1
Oldfield La. Batley WF16 ..... 117 D3
Oldfield La. Haw BD22 ..... 50 E5
Oldfield La. Leeds LS12 ..... 78 C6
Oldfield La. Wilsd BD15 ..... 53 E7
Oldfield Rd. Hali HX3 ..... 92 A3
Oldfield St. Hali HX3 ..... 92 A3
Oldfield St. Hud HD4 ..... 154 B4
Oldgate. Hud HD1 ..... 154 B6
Oldham Rd. Rish HX6 ..... 150 C6
Oldroyd Cres. Leeds LS11 ..... 78 E2
Oldroyd Rd. Tod OL14 ..... 108 E4
Olicana Pk. Ilkley LS29 ..... 7 C6
Olive Gr. Brad BD8 ..... 73 E8
Olive St. Hud HD1 ..... 136 B1
Oliver Hill. Hors LS18 ..... 58 C7
Oliver St. Brad BD4 ..... 75 A5
Olivers Mount. Pont WF8 ..... 146 B8
Ollerdale Ave. Brad BD15 ..... 54 A3
Ollerdale Cl. Brad BD15 ..... 54 A3
Olney St. Slai HD7 ..... 152 A1
Olrika Ct. Leeds LS7 ..... 60 C5
Olympic Ct. Brad BD12 ..... 94 E5 6
Omar St. Liver WF15 ..... 117 A4
Onchan Dr. Bacup OL13 ..... 106 B1
One St. Brad BD1 ..... 74 D7
Onslow Cres. Brad BD4 ..... 75 D6
Ontario Pl. Leeds LS7 ..... 60 D6
Opal St. Keigh BD22 ..... 35 A4 10
Orange St. Brad BD3 ..... 74 E8
Orange St. Hali HX1 ..... 113 C8
Orange Tree Gr. E Ard WF3 ..... 120 C7
Orchard Cl. E Ard WF3 ..... 120 C7
Orchard Cl. Mapp S75 ..... 178 B1
Orchard Cl. Wake WF2 ..... 120 F3
Orchard Croft. Crof WF4 ..... 143 F1 8
Orchard Croft. Walton WF2 ..... 161 A7
Orchard Ct. Ack M T WF7 ..... 164 C5
Orchard Dr. Crof WF4 ..... 144 C4
Orchard Gdns. Crof WF4 ..... 143 F1
Orchard Gr. Bail BD17 ..... 37 F2
Orchard Gr. Men LS29 ..... 21 F5
Orchard Head Cres. Pont WF8 ..... 125 F3
Orchard Head Dr. Pont WF8 ..... 125 F2
Orchard Head Jun & Inf Sch. Pont 125 F3
Orchard Head La. Pont WF8 ..... 125 F2
Orchard La. Addi LS29 ..... 2 F1
Orchard La. Guise LS20 ..... 22 E1
Orchard Lea. Kirkhe HD5 ..... 155 C7
Orchard Mews. Wake WF2 ..... 120 F3
Orchard Rd. Kirkhe HD5 ..... 155 C8
Orchard Rise. Leeds LS15 ..... 62 C2
Orchard St. Heb Br HX7 ..... 89 A3
Orchard St. Tod OL14 ..... 108 B6
Orchard St W. Tod OL14 ..... 108 A7
Orchard Terr. Caw S75 ..... 193 E4
Orchard Terr. Hud HD4 ..... 154 B4
Orchard The. B Spa LS23 ..... 30 D8

Orchard The. Crof WF4 ... 144 A1
Orchard The. Elland HX4 ... 133 F3
Orchard The. Feath WF7 ... 124 D1
Orchard The. Mir WF14 ... 138 B2
Orchard The. Nor WF6 ... 123 B4
Orchard The. Ossett WF5 ... 140 D5
Orchard The. Wake WF2 ... 146 B5
Orchard The. Wake WF2, WF4 ... 120 F7
Orchard View. Broth WF11 ... 126 C8
Orchard Way. Guise LS20 ... 147 C5
Orchard View. Weth LS22 ... 13 E8
Orchard Way. Rob HD6 ... 115 A4
Orchard Wlk. Heb Br HX7 ... 89 F1
Orchards Cl. Bing BD16 ... 37 A5
Orchards Dr. Bier BD19 ... 117 C8
Orchards The. Leeds LS15 ... 62 C2
Orchards The. M'town LS26 ... 102 C2
Orchid Ct. Keth WF12 ... 100 B2
Oriental St. Leeds LS12 ... 78 C7 6
Orion Cres. Midd LS10 ... 99 E7
Orion Dr. Midd LS10 ... 99 E7
Orion Gdns. Midd LS10 ... 99 F7
Orion View. Midd LS10 ... 99 E7
Orion Wlk. Midd LS10 ... 99 F8
Orlando Cl. Mir WF14 ... 137 F7
Orleans St. Brad BD6 ... 93 F7
Ormond Rd. Brad BD6 ... 74 B1
Ormond St. Brad BD7 ... 74 A4
Ormonde Dr. Brad BD15 ... 73 A8
Ormonda Pl. Leeds LS7 ... 60 C3
Ormondroyd Ave. Brad BD6 ... 94 C6
Orville Gdns. Leeds LS6 ... 59 E4
Orwell Ct. Castle WF10 ... 125 D8
Osborne Ave. Hor WF4 ... 141 C2
Osborne Gr. Brig HX3 ... 114 D7
Osborne Pl. Tod OL14 ... 108 C5 3
Osborne St. Brad BD5 ... 74 E4
Osborne St. Hali HX1 ... 112 F8
Osborne St. Heb Br HX7 ... 89 A314
Osborne St. Hud HD5 ... 154 D15
Osborne Ct. Leeds LS12 ... 58 D8
Osmondthorpe Fst Sch. Leeds ... 80 D8
Osmondthorpe La. Leeds LS9 ... 80 D8
Osmondthorpe Med Sch. Leeds ... 80 D8
Osprey Cl. Leeds LS17 ... 43 A4
Osprey Ct. Brad BD8 ... 73 C7
Osprey Dr. Hud HD4 ... 171 E7
Osprey St. Hud HD5 ... 154 D15
Osprey Meadow. Morley LS27 ... 98 D4
Ossett Flushdyke Jun & Inf Sch.
 Ossett ... 140 E4
Ossett La. Dew WF12 ... 140 A6
Ossett South Parade Inf Sch.
 Ossett ... 140 E4
Ossett Southdale CE (C) Sch.
 Ossett ... 140 E4
Ossett Towngate Jun & Inf Sch.
 Ossett ... 140 F6
Osterley Gr. Brad BD10 ... 56 E5
Ostler Sch The. Hali ... 112 C8
Oswald St. Brad BD8 ... 55 C4
Oswald St. Ship BD18 ... 55 D7
Oswaldthorpe Ave. Brad BD3 ... 56 D1
Otley All Saints Fst Sch. Otley ... 23 B7
Otley Ashfield Fst Sch. Otley ... 10 E1
Otley Golf Course. Otley ... 22 C6
Otley La. Yeadon LS19 ... 40 B7
Otley Mount. Keigh BD20 ... 18 A1
Otley Old Rd. Bramho LS16 ... 24 B1
Otley Old Rd. E Carl LS16 ... 23 F3
Otley Old Rd. Hors LS16 ... 41 F4
Otley Rd. Brad BD10 ... 38 C2
Otley Rd. Bing BD16 ... 20 B1
Otley Rd. Bing BD16 ... 38 A6
Otley Rd. Bur in W LS29 ... 22 B8
Otley Rd. Guise LS20 ... 22 D1
Otley Rd. Hare LS17 ... 26 C7
Otley Rd. Hors LS18 ... 42 C5
Otley Rd. Keigh BD20 ... 19 F1
Otley Rd. Leeds LS16, LS6 ... 59 D6
Otley Rd. Shel BD17, BD18 ... 55 B7
Otley St. Hali HX1 ... 112 B7
Otley St. Keigh BD21 ... 35 B6
Otley Westgate Fst Sch. Otley ... 22 F7
Ottawa Pl. Leeds LS7 ... 60 D6
Otterburn Cl. Brad BD5 ... 74 E3 7
Otterburn Gdns. Hors LS16 ... 42 B3
Otterburn St. Keigh BD21 ... 35 C8
Otters Holt. Crig WF4 ... 159 F7
Otterwood Bank. Weth LS22 ... 168 F3
Ottiwells Terr. Mars HD7 ... 168 F2
Ouchthorpe Fold. Loft G WF1 ... 121 C4
Ouchthorpe La. Loft G WF1 ... 121 C2
Oueen's Ct. Leeds LS17 ... 43 C1
Oulton Dr. Roth LS26 ... 101 B6
Oulton Jun Sch. Roth ... 101 B6
Oulton Jun Sch. Roth ... 101 B6
Oulton La. Roth LS26 ... 101 B5
Oulton Terr. Brad BD7 ... 74 C6
Ounsworth St. Brad BD4 ... 75 B4
Our Lady of Good Counsel RC Sch.
 Leeds ... 62 A6
Our Lady of Lourdes RC Prim Sch.
 Hud ... 136 C1
Our Lady of Victories RC Prim Sch.
 Keigh ... 35 A2
Ouse Dr. Weth LS22 ... 13 B8
Ouse St. Weth LS22 ... 50 D7 2
Out Gang. Leeds LS13 ... 58 D3
Out La. Emley HD8 ... 175 C2
Out La. Holmfi HD7 ... 188 E7
Outcote Bank. Hud HD1 ... 154 A5
Outgang La. Leeds LS13 ... 58 C3
Outlane City Prim Sch. Hud ... 134 D1
Outlane Jun Sch. Brad BD2 ... 50 F2
Outwood Ave. Hors LS18 ... 58 C8
Outwood Grange Sch. Loft G WF1 ... 121 C5
Outwood La. Hors LS18 ... 58 C8
Outwood Ledger Lane Jun & Inf
 Sch. Loft G ... 121 B4
Outwood Park Ct. Loft G WF1 ... 121 A4
Outwood Wlk. Hors LS18 ... 58 C8
Ouzelewell La. Dew WF12 ... 139 A3
Ouzelwell La. Dew WF12 ... 139 A3
Ouzelwell Gdn. Roth WF3 ... 139 A3
Oval The. Bail BD17 ... 38 B2

Oval The. Beal DN14 ... 127 F5
Oval The. Bing BD16 ... 37 B2
Oval The. Brad BD8 ... 73 B8
Oval The. Guise LS20 ... 116 C5
Oval The. Gar LS25 ... 83 A7
Oval The. Guise LS20 ... 39 C8
Oval The. Holmfi HD7 ... 188 F7
Oval The. Leeds LS14 ... 61 F2
Oval The. Leeds LS10 ... 79 F4
Oval The. Notton WF4 ... 179 B6
Oval The. Otley LS21 ... 10 F1
Oval The. Roth LS26 ... 100 F5
Ovenden Ave. Hali HX3 ... 92 A1
Ovenden Cl. Hali HX3 ... 92 A1
Ovenden Cres. Hali HX3 ... 92 A2
Ovenden Ct. Hali HX3 ... 92 B2
Ovenden High Sch The. Hali ... 91 F3
Ovenden Park. Hali ... 91 F3
Ovenden Road Terr. Hali HX3 ... 92 A2 9
Ovenden Terr. Hali HX3 ... 92 A2
Ovenden Way. Hali HX3 ... 91 F3
Ovenden Wood Rd. Hali HX2 ... 91 D2
Over Hall Cl. Mir WF14 ... 138 B6
Over Hall Pk. Mir WF14 ... 138 B6
Over Hall Rd. Mir WF14 ... 138 B6
Over La. Yeadon LS19 ... 40 C3
Overburn Rd. S in Cra BD20 ... 16 D4
Overdale Ave. Leeds LS17 ... 44 A5
Overdale Ct. Weth LS22 ... 14 A4
Overdale Dr. Brad BD10, BD18 ... 38 F1
Overdale Mount. Hali HX6 ... 112 C5
Overdale Terr. Leeds LS15 ... 81 A8 4
Overend St. Brad BD6 ... 74 A1 6
Owerthorpe Ave. Dew WF17 ... 139 D1
Owerthorpe Rd. Dew WF12 ... 139 D3
Overton Dr. Brad BD6 ... 73 D2
Ovington Dr. Brad BD4 ... 75 E3
Ower's Cres. Honley HD7 ... 171 E3
Owl La. Batley WF12 ... 119 A2
Owl La. Batley WF17 ... 119 A3
Owl La. Dew WF12 ... 119 A2
Owl La. Leeds LS12 ... 78 B8
Owl News. Kirkhe HD5 ... 155 C6
Owl Ridge. Morley LS27 ... 98 C3
Owl St. Keigh BD21 ... 35 D6
Owlcotes Ct. Pudsey ... 57 D1
Owlcotes Dr. Pudsey LS28 ... 76 C8
Owlcotes Garth. Pudsey LS28 ... 76 C8
Owlcotes Gdns. Pudsey LS28 ... 76 C8
Owlcotes La. Pudsey LS28 ... 57 C1
Owlcotes La. Pudsey LS28 ... 76 C8
Owlcotes Rd. Pudsey LS28 ... 76 C8
Owlcotes Terr. Pudsey LS28 ... 76 D8
Owler Bars Rd. Mel HD7 ... 170 C2
Owler Ings Rd. Brig HD6 ... 115 A2
Owler La. Batley WF17 ... 96 F5
Owler Park Rd. Ilkley LS29 ... 7 F6
Owler's La. Brad WF9 ... 164 F4
Owlers Cl. Hud HD2 ... 136 B2
Owlet Grange. Ship BD18 ... 55 C5
Owlet Hurst La. Liver WF15 ... 117 B2
Owlet Rd. Ship BD18 ... 55 C7
Owlett Mead Cl. H Crof WF3 ... 99 F1
Owlett Mead. E Ard WF3 ... 99 E1
Ox Heys Meadow. Thorn BD13 ... 73 A6
Ox Lee La. Holmfi HD7 ... 199 B8
Oxenhope CE Aided Fst Sch. Oxen ... 51 C2
Oxenhope Sta. Oxen ... 52 C8
Oxfield Ct. Hud HD5 ... 155 A7
Oxford Ave. Guise LS20 ... 22 D1
Oxford Cl. Brad BD19 ... 117 B8
Oxford Cl. Queen BD13 ... 92 C8
Oxford Court Gdns. Castle WF10 ... 124 C7
Oxford Cres. Brad BD14 ... 73 B4
Oxford Cres. Hali HX1 ... 203 D2
Oxford Dr. Clec BD19 ... 117 B8
Oxford Dr. Kippax LS25 ... 83 A2
Oxford La. Hali HX3 ... 113 D3
Oxford Pl. Brad BD3 ... 74 F8
Oxford Pl. Hali HX1 ... 153 A3
Oxford Pl. Leeds LS1 ... 211 F4
Oxford Pl. Pudsey LS28 ... 57 E1
Oxford Rd. Brad BD2 ... 56 B2
Oxford Rd. Clec BD19 ... 96 B2
Oxford Rd. Gild LS27 ... 97 D7
Oxford Rd. Guise LS20 ... 22 D1
Oxford Rd. Hali HX1 ... 203 D2
Oxford Rd. Leeds LS7, LS8 ... 207 B2
Oxford Rd. Wake WF1 ... 142 E8
Oxford Row. Leeds LS1 ... 211 F4
Oxford St. Batley WF16 ... 117 D4
Oxford St. E ard WF3 ... 120 B8
Oxford St. Feath WF7 ... 145 C5
Oxford St. Guise LS20 ... 22 D1
Oxford St. Hali HX6 ... 112 B4
Oxford St. Heb Br HX7 ... 89 A3
Oxford St. Hud HD1 ... 154 B6
Oxford St. Morley LS27 ... 98 B4
Oxford St. Nor WF6 ... 123 B2
Oxford St. S Elm WF9 ... 182 F2
Oxford St. Tod OL14 ... 108 A1
Oxford St. Wake WF1 ... 142 E3
Oxford Terr. Baildon BD17 ... 38 C2
Oxford Terr. Bat WF17 ... 118 D6
Oxford Wlk. Clec BD19 ... 117 B8
Oxley Gdns. Brad BD12 ... 94 C7
Oxley Rd. Hud HD2 ... 136 C4
Oxley St. Brad BD8 ... 55 B1
Oxley St. Brad BD8 ... 79 F7
Oxley St. Leeds LS9 ... 212 C4
Oxton Gdns. Leeds LS9 ... 80 A7
Oxton Mount. Leeds LS9 ... 79 F8
Oxton Pl. Leeds LS9 ... 79 F8
Oxton Way. Leeds LS9 ... 79 F8
Oyster Cl. Wake WF2 ... 160 E8

Pacaholme Rd. Wake WF2 ... 141 D8
Pack Fold. Hud HD7 ... 152 E4
Pack Horse Ct. Clay W HD8 ... 176 A2
Pack Horse Ctr. Hud HD1 ... 154 B6
Pad Cote La. Cowl BD22 ... 32 A2
Padan St. Hali HX3 ... 113 D3
Paddock Cl. Brad BD12 ... 95 B5
Paddock Cl. Glar LS25 ... 83 A6
Paddock Cl. Mapp S75 ... 178 A1
Paddock Cl. S in Cra BD20 ... 16 D5
Paddock Dr. Birk BD11 ... 96 E5

Paddock Foot. Hud HD1 ... 153 E5
Paddock Gn. E Kes LS17 ... 28 C5
Paddock House La. Sickl LS22 ... 12 B3
Paddock Rd. Kirkb HD8 ... 173 F7
Paddock Rd. Kirkb HD8 ... 174 A7
Paddock Rd. Mapp S75 ... 178 C1
Paddock Rd. Northo HD8, S75 ... 92 E5
Paddock The. Brig HD6 ... 61 F2
Paddock The. Leeds LS14 ... 105 E3
Paddock The. Bail BD17 ... 38 F4
Paddock The. Brig BD19 ... 115 F8 12
Paddock The. Castle WF10 ... 125 C6
Paddock The. Cull BD13 ... 52 D6
Paddock The. Dew WF12 ... 139 F6
Paddock The. E Kes LS17 ... 28 C5
Paddock The. Kirkhe HD5 ... 155 C7
Paddock The. Knot WF11 ... 126 E8
Paddock The. Leeds LS6 ... 59 F7
Paddock The. Nor WF6 ... 123 A3
Paddock The. Roth LS26 ... 100 E5
Paddock The. Sil BD20 ... 5 E1
Paddock The. Thorner LS14 ... 45 F5
Paddock The. Wool WF4 ... 178 A7
Paddock View. Castle WF10 ... 125 D6
Paddy Bridge Rd. Heb Br HX7 ... 89 D1
Padgum. Bail BD17 ... 38 C4 12
Padma Cl. Brad BD7 ... 74 B8
Padmans La. B Spa LS23 ... 30 B8
Padstow Ave. Midd LS10 ... 99 A5
Padstow Gdns. Midd LS10 ... 99 A5
Padstow Pl. Midd LS10 ... 99 A4
Page Hill. Hali HX2 ... 91 B5
Page Wlk. Hud HD2 ... 154 B8
Paget Cres. Hud HD2 ... 135 D1
Paget St. Keigh BD21 ... 35 A8
Painthorpe House Country Club.
 Crig ... 159 E4
Painthorpe La. Crig WF4 ... 159 E4
Painthorpe Terr. Crig WF4 ... 159 E4
Paisley Gr. Leeds LS12 ... 78 B8 2
Paisley Pl. Leeds LS12 ... 78 B8 4
Paisley Rd. Leeds LS12 ... 78 A8
Paisley St. Leeds LS12 ... 78 B8 5
Paisley Terr. Leeds LS12 ... 78 B8 3
Paisley View. Leeds LS12 ... 78 A8 13
Pakington St. Brad BD5 ... 74 D4
Palace House Rd. Heb Br HX7 ... 89 A2
Paleside La. Ossett WF5 ... 140 D7
Palesides Ave. Ossett WF5 ... 140 D8
Palestine Rd. Heb Br HX7 ... 89 A4
Paley Rd. Brad BD4 ... 75 A4
Paley Terr. Brad BD4 ... 75 A4
Palin Ave. Brad BD3 ... 56 D1
Palin St. Hali HX3 ... 92 B2
Palm St. Hali HX3 ... 92 B2
Palma St. Tod OL14 ... 86 B1
Palmer Rd. Brad BD3 ... 75 B8
Palmer's Ave. S Elm WF9 ... 183 B2
Palmerston St. Brad BD2 ... 56 B2
Pangbourne Rd. Dearne S63 ... 194 C1
Pannal Ave. Wake WF1 ... 142 E8
Pannal St. Brad BD7 ... 74 B4
Panorama Dr. Ilkley LS29 ... 11 C4
Papyrus Villas. Tad LS24 ... 31 C6
Parade The. Brad BD4 ... 75 E3
Parade The. Leeds LS9 ... 77 E7
Parade The. Leeds LS9 ... 80 B1
Parade The. Yeadon LS19 ... 39 F6
Paradise. Stut LS24 ... 48 B5
Paradise Pl. Hors LS18 ... 58 C8
Paradise Rd. Brad BD9 ... 54 F4
Paradise St. Brad BD1 ... 201 A3
Paradise St. Hali HX1 ... 203 D3
Paradise St. Leeds LS11 ... 211 D3
Parish Ghyll La. Ilkley LS29 ... 7 F3
Parish Ghyll Rd. Ilkley LS29 ... 7 F3
Parish Ghyll Wlk. Ilkley LS29 ... 8 A3
Park Ave. Bing BD16 ... 36 F3
Park Ave. Brad BD8 ... 73 C7
Park Ave. Castle WF10 ... 124 F7
Park Ave. Crof WF4 ... 143 D7
Park Ave. Dar WF8 ... 147 C5
Park Ave. Elland HX5 ... 134 F6
Park Ave. Haw BD22 ... 34 D2
Park Ave. Hud HD1 ... 153 D6
Park Ave. Kippax WF10 ... 103 C5
Park Ave. Leeds LS8 ... 204 A4
Park Ave. Leeds LS12 ... 209 D3
Park Ave. Liver WF15 ... 117 B4
Park Ave. Mir WF14 ... 138 A5
Park Ave. Pont WF8 ... 125 D1
Park Ave. Roth LS26 ... 100 F5
Park Ave. S in Cra BD20 ... 16 D5
Park Ave. Shep HD8 ... 173 F1
Park Ave. Wake WF2 ... 141 D4
Park Ave. Yeadon LS19 ... 40 A7
Park Balk La. Bar E LS15 ... 63 B8
Park Cl. Brig HD6 ... 135 E7
Park Cl. Clec BD19 ... 116 E8
Park Cl. Crof WF4 ... 143 F3
Park Cl. Holmfi HD7 ... 189 E4
Park Cl. Kippax WF10 ... 103 C5
Park Cl. Queen BD13 ... 72 D1
Park Cl. Roy S71 ... 179 C4
Park Cl. Shep HD8 ... 173 F1
Park Cl. Steet BD20 ... 17 D6
Park Cres. Bing BD16 ... 37 B5
Park Cres. Gild LS27 ... 97 D6

Park Cres. Guise LS20 ... 39 C7
Park Cres. Hali HX3 ... 92 A1
Park Cres. Leeds LS8 ... 44 B1
Park Cres. Leeds LS12 ... 78 B8 13
Park Cres. Roth LS26 ... 101 A6
Park Cres. Roy S71 ... 179 D3
Park Cres. S in Cra BD20 ... 16 D5
Park Cross St. Leeds LS1 ... 79 B8
Park Ct. Brad BD9 ... 55 C2
Park Ct. Ossett WF5 ... 140 F4
Park Dale. Castle WF10 ... 104 C1
Park Dale. Men LS29 ... 22 B4
Park Dr. Bail BD17 ... 38 B5
Park Dr. Batley WF17 ... 118 A7
Park Dr. Bing BD16 ... 37 B5
Park Dr. Hors LS18 ... 58 A8
Park Dr. Hud HD1 ... 153 E7
Park Dr. Loft G WF1 ... 121 C7
Park Dr. Mir WF14 ... 138 B5
Park Dr. S. Hud HD1 ... 153 E6
Park Dr. S in Cra BD20 ... 16 D5
Park Dr. Shep HD8 ... 173 F3
Park Dr. Ship BD9 ... 55 B4
Park Dr. Swil LS26 ... 102 B8
Park Edge Cl. Leeds LS8 ... 61 C7
Park Est. S Kirk WF9 ... 182 C2
Park Farm Ind Est. Leeds ... 80 F1
Park Gate. Guise LS20 ... 22 A4
Park Gate Cl. Hors LS18 ... 58 A8
Park Gate Cres. Guise LS20 ... 39 D8
Park Gdns. Guise LS20 ... 171 F8
Park Gdns. Hali HX3 ... 92 A1
Park Gn. Nor WF6 ... 123 A1
Park Gr. Brad BD9 ... 54 F8
Park Gr. Ship BD9 ... 55 C4
Park Gr. Swil LS26 ... 102 B8
Park Grove Ct. Ship BD9 ... 55 C4
Park Grove Rd. Wake WF2 ... 142 A5
Park Head La. Dunbo HD8 ... 190 F5
Park Head La. Holmfi HD7 ... 188 E4
Park Hill. Brad BD8 ... 54 D1
Park Hill Cl. Brad BD8 ... 54 D1
Park Hill Dr. Wake WF1 ... 142 F6
Park Hill. Hud HD2 ... 136 F6
Park Hill. Kex S75 ... 177 B2
Park Hill La. Wake WF2 ... 141 F6
Park House Cres. Brad BD12 ... 94 E7
Park House Rd. Brad BD12 ... 94 E6
Park House. Stee BD20 ... 17 C6
Park La. Brad BD5 ... 201 A1
Park La. Castle WF10 ... 124 E8
Park La. D Dale HD8 ... 191 B5
Park La. Emley HD8 ... 175 C6
Park La. Gar LS25 ... 83 A8
Park La. Guise LS20 ... 39 C7
Park La. Hali HX3 ... 113 A4
Park La. Heb Br HX7 ... 110 C8
Park La. Hud HD4 ... 153 D3
Park La. Kippax WF10 ... 103 C5
Park La. Leeds LS3 ... 205 F1
Park La. Kippax LS25 ... 83 A8
Park La. Leeds LS3 ... 210 C4
Park La. Pont WF7, WF8 ... 124 E1
Park La. Queen BD13 ... 72 F1
Park La. Roy S71 ... 179 D4
Park La. Sickl LS22 ... 12 B5
Park La. S in Cra BD20 ... 16 D5
Park La. W Bret WF4 ... 176 F7
Park La. Wake WF2 ... 141 D4
Park Lane Coll. Leeds ... 210 C3
Park Lane Mews. Leeds LS17 ... 43 B2
Park Lea. Hud HD2 ... 136 F6
Park Lodge Cres. Wake WF1 ... 142 E6
Park Lodge Gr. Wake WF1 ... 142 F6
Park Lodge La. Wake WF1 ... 142 E5
Park Mead. Brad BD10 ... 39 B2
Park Mews. Pool LS21 ... 24 E6
Park Mount. Leeds LS12 ... 78 B8
Park Mount Ave. Bail BD17 ... 38 B4
Park Mount. Leeds LS5 ... 59 A4
Park Par. Dew WF13 ... 118 D1
Park Par. Leeds LS9 ... 80 B7
Park Par. Morley LS27 ... 97 F3
Park Pl. Brad BD10 ... 39 A7
Park Pl. Brig HX3 ... 114 A4
Park Pl. Hali HX1 ... 203 D3

Park Rd. Hud HD4 ... 153 E4
Park Rd. Leeds LS13 ... 58 C3
Park Rd. Leeds LS13 ... 78 A8
Park Rd. Leeds LS15 ... 81 D6
Park Rd. Men LS29 ... 22 A4
Park Rd. Pont WF8 ... 125 B2
Park Rd. Ship BD18 ... 55 C7
Park Rd. Tod OL14 ... 108 B6
Park Rd W. Hud HD4 ... 153 D4
Park Rd. Yeadon LS19 ... 40 A7
Park Rise. Castle WF10 ... 124 F7
Park Rise. Leeds LS13 ... 58 C4
Park Road Jun, Mid & Inf Sch.
 Batley ... 118 D5
Park Row. Brig HD6 ... 115 B2 6
Park Row. Bur in W LS29 ... 9 F2
Park Row. Leeds LS1 ... 211 F4
Park Row. Otley LS21 ... 23 B8
Park Row. Pudsey LS28 ... 57 B8
Park Side. Fioc WF4 ... 157 C3
Park Side. Holmfi HD7 ... 189 E4
Park Side. Hors LS18 ... 137 C1
Park Spring Gdns. Leeds LS13 ... 58 B1
Park Spring Prim Sch. Pudsey ... 77 B8
Park Spring Rise. Pudsey LS13 ... 58 B1
Park Sq. Brad BD6 ... 94 A8 1
Park Sq E. Leeds LS1 ... 79 B8
Park Sq. Loft G WF3 ... 121 C6
Park Sq N. Leeds LS1 ... 79 B8
Park Sq. Northo HX3 ... 93 A2
Park Sq. Ossett WF5 ... 140 F4
Park Sq. Pool LS21 ... 24 D6
Park Sq. Leeds LS1 ... 79 B8
Park Sq W. Leeds LS1 ... 79 B8
Park St. Batley WF17 ... 117 D4
Park St. Batley WF17 ... 117 C8
Park St. Brig HD6 ... 115 B2
Park St. Clec BD19 ... 117 C8
Park St. Dew WF13 ... 139 D1
Park St. Dew WF13 ... 118 D1
Park St. Haw BD22 ... 51 D7
Park St. Hali HX6 ... 112 D4
Park St. Hor WF4 ... 141 A1
Park St. Hud HD3 ... 153 A4
Park St. Leeds LS1 ... 211 F4
Park St. Leeds LS15 ... 81 B8
Park St. Morley LS27 ... 98 C8
Park St. Ossett WF5 ... 140 E4
Park St. S Elm WF9 ... 183 A8
Park St. Slai HD7 ... 152 C6
Park St. Wake WF1 ... 142 D3
Park Stone Rise. Shelf HX3 ... 93 B5
Park Terr. Brig HX3 ... 114 D7
Park Terr. Hali HX1 ... 113 A6
Park Terr. Keigh BD21 ... 35 F6
Park Terr. Otley LS21 ... 23 B8
Park Terr. Pool LS21 ... 24 A5
Park Top. Pudsey LS28 ... 57 C1
Park Top. Pudsey LS28 ... 76 C8
Park Top Cotts. Bing BD16 ... 37 B5
Park Towngate The. Hali HX3 ... 114 A4
Park View Ave. Haw BD22 ... 51 E8 13
Park View Ave. Leeds LS4 ... 59 A1
Park View Ave. Northo HX3 ... 93 A1
Park View. Cleck BD19 ... 116 C7
Park View. Castle WF10 ... 125 B6
Park View. Dar WF8 ... 147 D5
Park View. Elland HX4 ... 134 A1
Park View. Hali HX1 ... 113 A6
Park View. Leeds LS13 ... 58 B1
Park View. Leeds LS4 ... 59 A1
Park View. Roy S71 ... 179 D4
Park View. Shaf S72 ... 180 C2
Park View Cres. Leeds LS8 ... 44 B2
Park View. Hali HX1 ... 113 A6
Park View Rd. Brad BD9 ... 54 F2
Park View Rd. Leeds LS4 ... 59 A1
Park View Terr. Brad BD9 ... 54 F2
Park View Terr. Yeadon LS19 ... 40 A6
Park Villa Ct. Leeds LS8 ... 44 A1
Park Villas Dr. Pont WF8 ... 125 B1
Park Villas. Leeds LS8 ... 44 A1
Park Way. Bail BD17 ... 37 F1
Park Way. Steet BD20 ... 17 D6
Park West. Roth LS26 ... 100 F5
Park Wood Ave. Leeds LS11 ... 98 F8
Park Wood Cres. Leeds LS11 ... 98 F7
Park Wood Rd. Leeds LS11 ... 98 F8
Parkcroft. Dewsbury HX3 ... 93 C5
Parker Ave. Nor WF6 ... 123 C2
Parker La. Mir WF14 ... 138 A5
Parker Rd. E Ard WF3 ... 120 C8
Parker St. E Ard WF3 ... 120 D8
Parker St. S Elm WF9 ... 183 A3
Parker St. E Ard WF3 ... 120 C8
Parkfield Ave. Elland HX4 ... 134 D7
Parkfield Ave. Leeds LS11 ... 214 A3
Parkfield Cl. Pudsey LS28 ... 76 E8 7
Parkfield Cl. Kippax LS25 ... 83 A2
Parkfield Ct. Leeds LS14 ... 62 A3
Parkfield Dr. B Spa LS23 ... 30 C8
Parkfield Dr. Sow Br HX6 ... 112 A2

Parkfield Gr. Leeds LS11 79 A3
Parkfield La. Feath WF7 124 C2
Parkfield La. Sow Br HX6 112 D3
Parkfield Mount. Leeds LS11 79 A3
Parkfield Mount. Pudsey LS28 76 E7
Parkfield Pl. Leeds LS11 79 A3
Parkfield Rd. Brad BD8 55 D2
Parkfield Rd. Leeds LS11 79 A3 4
Parkfield Rd. Ship BD18 54 E8
Parkfield Row. Leeds LS11 79 A3
Parkfield St. Leeds LS11 79 C5
Parkfield Terr. Pudsey LS28 57 E1
Parkfield Terr. Pudsey LS28 76 E7
Parkfield View. Leeds LS11 79 A3
Parkfield View. Ossett WF5 141 A5
Parkfield Way. Leeds LS14 61 E3
Parkfield Way. Mir WF14 138 B4
Parkgate Ave. Wake WF1 142 E6
Parkgate. S Kirk WF9 182 B1
Parkhead Cl. Roy S71 179 A4
Parkhill Cres. Wake WF1 142 F6
Parkin Hall La. Sow Br HX6 111 B1
Parkin La. Brad BD10 56 F8
Parkin La. Tod OL14 107 E5
Parkin Sq. Slai HD7 152 B5
Parkin St. Clec WF15 116 C5
Parkin's Almshouses. Hud HD5 154 F3 2
Parkinson App. Gar LS25 82 F8
Parkinson Cl. Wake WF1 142 E6
Parkinson La. Hali HX1 112 F6
Parkinson Lane Jun & Inf Sch.
Hali 113 A6
Parkinson Rd. Denh BD13 71 E8
Parkinson St. Brad BD5 74 D4
Parkland Ave. Morley LS27 97 E3
Parkland Cres. Leeds LS6 43 A1
Parkland Dr. Brad BD10 56 C7
Parkland Dr. Leeds LS6 43 A1
Parkland Gdns. Leeds LS6 60 A8
Parkland Mid & Fst Schs. Brad 56 D7
Parkland Terr. Leeds LS6 60 A8
Parklands. Bing BD16 37 B5
Parklands. Bramho LS16 24 D3
Parklands. Castle WF10 124 E7
Parklands Cty Prim Sch. Leeds 62 A3
Parklands Cres. Bramho LS16 24 E3
Parklands Cres. Hor WF4 140 E1
Parklands Dr. Hor WF4 140 E1
Parklands Dr. Sow Br HX6 111 E1
Parklands Gate. Bramho LS16 24 E3
Parklands High Sch. Leeds 62 B4
Parklands. Ilkley LS29 8 D4
Parklands. Ossett WF5 140 F4
Parklands Wlk. Shep HD8 173 F3
Parkside Ave. Leeds LS6 59 F7
Parkside Ave. Queen BD13 72 D1
Parkside. Bing BD16 37 B4
Parkside Cl. Leeds LS6 59 F8
Parkside Cl. Tod OL14 86 B1
Parkside. Clec BD19 116 E7
Parkside Cres. Leeds LS6 59 F8
Parkside Ct. Haw BD22 51 E8
Parkside Gdns. Leeds LS6 59 F7
Parkside Gn. Leeds LS6 59 F7
Parkside Gr. Brad BD9 55 A3
Parkside Gr. Leeds LS11 79 A1
Parkside. Hali HX3 113 B4 10
Parkside Ind Est. Leeds 79 C2
Parkside La. Leeds LS11 79 C2
Parkside La. Loft G WF3 121 E2
Parkside Lawns. Leeds LS6 59 F7
Parkside Mount. Leeds LS11 79 A1
Parkside Par. Leeds LS11 79 A1
Parkside Pl. Leeds LS6 59 F8
Parkside Rd. Brad BD5 74 E2
Parkside Rd. Leeds LS16, LS6 59 E8
Parkside Rd. Pudsey LS28 57 D2
Parkside Rd. Tod OL14 86 B1
Parkside Row. Leeds LS11 79 A1
Parkside Terr. Cull BD13 52 E6
Parkside View. Leeds LS6 59 F8
Parkside Wlk. Pudsey LS28 57 E2
Parkstone Ave. Hors LS16 42 A1
Parkstone Dr. Brad BD10 56 C5
Parkstone Gn. Hors LS16 42 A1
Parkstone Gr. Hors LS16 42 A1
Parkstone. Hud HD2 136 F6
Parkstone Mount. Hors LS16 42 A1
Parkstone Pl. Hors LS16 42 A1
Parkview Ct. Leeds LS8 44 B2
Parkview Ct. Ship BD18 55 A7
Parkville Pl. Leeds LS13 58 C3
Parkville Rd. Leeds LS13 58 C3
Parkway. Brad BD5 74 F2
Parkway Cl. Leeds LS14 61 E4
Parkway. Crof WF4 143 F2
Parkway Ct. Leeds LS14 61 E3
Parkway. Gild LS27 97 D6
Parkway Grange. Leeds LS14 61 E3
Parkway. Keigh BD21 35 C5
Parkway Mews. Leeds LS14 62 B5
Parkway. Queen BD13 72 D1
Parkway. Stee BD20 17 B5
Parkway Towers. Leeds LS14 61 E4
Parkway Vale. Leeds LS14 61 F4
Parkway Vale. Leeds LS14 62 A4
Parkways Ave. Roth LS26 101 B5
Parkways Cl. Roth LS26 101 B6
Parkways Ct. Roth LS26 101 B6
Parkways Dr. Roth LS26 101 B6
Parkways Garth. Roth LS26 101 B5
Parkways Gr. Roth LS26 101 B6
Parkways. Roth LS26 101 B6
Parkwood Ave. Leeds LS8 61 A7
Parkwood Cl. Shep HD8 173 F3
Parkwood Fst Sch. Keigh 35 D6
Parkwood Gdns. Pudsey LS28 57 A6
Parkwood Rd. Hud HD3, HD7 152 E6
Parkwood Rd. Pudsey LS28 57 B6
Parkwood Rd. Ship BD18 54 F7
Parkwood Rise. Keigh BD21 35 C6
Parkwood St. Keigh BD21 35 D7
Parkwood Way. Leeds LS8 61 A7
Parliament Pl. Leeds LS12 78 D7
Parliament Rd. Leeds LS12 78 D7
Parliament St. Wake WF2 142 B6
Parlington Ct. B in Elm LS15 63 E7
Parlington Dr. Aber LS25 64 E7
Parlington House. Aber LS25 64 D7
Parlington La. Aber LS25 64 C4
Parlington Meadow. B in Elm LS15 63 E6
Parma St. Brad BD5 74 E5
Parnaby Ave. Midd LS10 79 F1
Parnaby Rd. Midd LS10 79 F1
Parnaby St. Midd LS10 79 F1
Parnaby Terr. Midd LS10 79 F1
Parratt Row. Brad BD3 75 D7
Parrock La. Wad M HX7 89 B6
Parrott St. Brad BD4 75 D1
Parry La. Brad BD4 75 C5
Parson La. Wool WF4 178 A8
Parson St. Keigh BD21 35 D8
Parson's La. Sil LS29 6 C8
Parsonage La. Brig HD6 115 A2
Parsonage Rd. Brad BD5 74 E3
Parsonage Rd. Brad BD4 75 D5
Parsonage Rd. M'town LS26 102 D3
Parsonage St. Hali S6 92 D1
Parsons Gn. Weth LS22 13 F5
Parsons Rd. Ship BD9 55 A4
Partons Pl. Loft G WF3 121 C6
Partridge Cl. Morley LS27 98 D4 5
Partridge Cres. Dew WF12 139 F1
Pasture Ave. Leeds LS7 60 D7
Pasture Cl. Brad BD14 73 E4
Pasture Cres. Leeds LS7 60 D7
Pasture Gr. Leeds LS7 60 D7
Pasture La. Brad BD14, BD7 73 D4
Pasture La. Leeds LS7 60 D7
Pasture Mount. Leeds LS12 78 B8
Pasture Par. Leeds LS7 60 D7
Pasture Pl. Leeds LS7 60 D7
Pasture Rd. Bail BD17 38 D2
Pasture Rd. Leeds LS8 60 F4
Pasture Rise. Brad BD14 73 D4
Pasture Side Terr E. Brad BD14 73 D4
Pasture Side Terr W. Brad BD14 73 C4 4
Pasture St. Leeds LS7 60 D7
Pasture Terr. Leeds LS7 60 D7
Pasture View. Leeds LS12 78 B8
Pasture View Rd. Roth LS26 100 E5
Pasture Wlk. Brad BD14 73 C4
Pastures Way. Hud HD7 152 D5
Pateley Cres. Hud HD2 136 A2
Patent St. Brad BD9 55 B2
Paternoster La. Brad BD7 74 A4 10
Paterson Ave. Wake WF2 142 A6
Patience La. Nor WF6 122 F3
Patterdale App. Weth LS22 13 B5
Patterdale Dr. Hud HD5 154 D6
Patterdale Rd. Batley WF12 118 E2
Patterson Ct. Wake WF2 120 F3
Pattie St. Keigh BD20 18 B1
Paul La. Kirkhe HD5 137 C4
Paul La. Lepton HD8 156 C2
Paul Row. Litt OL15 129 D1
Pauline Terr. Castle WF10 124 C7
Pavement La. Hali HX2 91 E8
Pavilion Cl. Bri S72 181 A3
Paw La. Queen BD13 92 F7
Pawson St. Brad BD4 75 D6
Pawson St. E Ard WF3 120 E8
Pawson St. Morley LS27 97 F3
Pawson St. Roth WF3 100 B2
Peabody St. Hali HX3 92 A1 6
Peace Hall Dr. Lepton HD8 155 C5
Peace St. Brad BD4 75 C5
Peach Tree Cl. Pont WF8 146 B6
Peach Wlk. Brad BD4 75 B4
Peacock Ave. Wake WF2 141 F7
Peacock Cl. Wake WF2 141 F7
Peacock Gn. Morley LS27 98 D3
Peacock Gr. Wake WF2 141 F7
Peak View. Batley WF13 117 F2
Pear Pl. Tod OL14 86 B1 3
Pear St. Hali HX1 112 F6
Pear St. Hud HD4 153 E4
Pear St. Keigh BD21 35 A3
Pear St. Oxen BD22 51 C2
Pear St. Tod OL14 86 B1 4
Pear Tree Acre. Th Arch LS23 14 E1
Pear Tree Cl. Pont WF8 146 B6
Pear Tree La. Hem WF9 181 D7
Pearl St. Batley WF17 118 A6
Pearl St.Keigh BD22 35 A4 12
Pearson Ave. Leeds LS6 59 E3 15
Pearson Fold. Brad BD12 94 F4
Pearson Gr. Leeds LS6 59 F3
Pearson La. Brad BD9 54 D1
Pearson Rd. Brad BD6, DN35 94 D8 11
Pearson Rd W. Brad BD6 94 D8 4
Pearson Row. Brad BD12 94 D3 3
Pearson St. Brad BD3 75 C6
Pearson St. Clec BD19 116 A6
Pearson St. Clec BD19 116 E6
Pearson St. Leeds LS10 79 D5
Pearson St. Nor WF6 123 A5
Pearson St. Pudsey LS28 57 B7
Pearson Terr. Leeds LS6 59 E3 14
Pearson's La. Dew WF12 156 F7
Pearsons Bldgs. Otley LS21 23 B7
Peartree Field La. Th Aud WF8 165 D5
Peas Acre. Bing BD16 36 F6
Peasborough View. Bur in W LS29 21 F8
Pease Cl. Pont WF8 146 D6
Peasehill Cl. Yeadon LS19 40 C4
Peasehill Pk. Yeadon LS19 40 C4
Peaseland Ave. Clec BD19 116 C7
Peaseland Cl. Clec BD19 116 D7
Peaseland Rd. Clec BD19 116 D7
Peaselands. Ship BD18 55 A7
Peat Ponds. Hud HD3 134 E1
Peckett Cl. Hud HD3 153 C7
Peckfield Bar. Gar LS25 83 D4
Peckover Dr. Pudsey LS28 76 A8
Peckover St. Brad BD1 74 F7
Peebles Cl. Hud HD3 135 B1
Peel Ave. Batley WF17 118 C5
Peel Cl. Brad BD4 75 E6
Peel Cl. Hor WF4 141 B1
Peel Cottage Rd. Tod OL14 108 A1
Peel Cottage St. Tod OL14 108 A1 5
Peel Ct. Brad BD2 56 A2
Peel Dr. Bacup OL13 106 B1
Peel House. Bing BD16 37 B2
Peel Park Dr. Brad BD2 56 B2
Peel Park Terr. Brad BD2 56 B2
Peel Park View. Brad BD3 56 A1
Peel Pk. Brad 55 F2
Peel Pl. Bur in W LS29 9 E2
Peel Row. Brad BD7 74 A4
Peel St. Bing BD16 37 B3
Peel St. Hali HX6 112 B4 8
Peel St. Hor WF4 141 B1
Peel St. Hud HD1 154 A5 5
Peel St. Liver WF16 117 C4
Peel St. Mars HD7 168 F4
Peel St. Mars HD7 169 A4
Peel St. Morley LS27 98 B4
Peel St. Queen BD13 72 F1
Peel St. Thorn BD13 72 D6
Peel St. Wils BD15 53 C4
Peel Street Prim Sch. Morley 98 B4
Peep Green Rd. Liver WF15 116 C2
Pegholme Dr. Otley LS21 22 D6
Pelham Ct. Brad BD2 56 B3
Pelham Pl. Leeds LS7 60 C7
Pelham Rd. Brad BD2 56 B3
Pell Ct. Holmfi HD7 189 C7
Pell La. Holmfi HD7 189 C7
Pellon La. Hali HX1 113 A8
Pellon New Rd. Hali HX1, HX2 112 F8
Pellon St. Tod OL14 108 A2
Pellon Terr. Brad BD10 39 B1
Pellon Wlk. Brad BD10 39 B1
Pemberton Dr. Brad BD7 74 D6
Pemberton Rd. Castle WF10 125 B8
Pembridge Ct. Roy S71 179 C4
Pembroke Cl. Morley LS27 97 F5
Pembroke Dr. Morley LS27 97 F5
Pembroke Dr. Pudsey LS28 76 E8 5
Pembroke Gdns. Leeds LS9 61 D2
Pembroke Rd. Pudsey LS28 76 E8
Pembroke Rise. Kippax LS25 83 C2
Pembroke St. Brad BD5 74 E4
Pembroke Towers. Leeds LS9 61 D3
Pembury Mount. Leeds LS15 62 F3
Penarth Ave. Upton WF9 183 A7
Penarth Rd. Leeds LS15 62 B2
Penarth Terr. Upton WF9 182 F7
Penda's Dr. Leeds LS15 62 D2
Penda's Gr. Leeds LS15 62 D3
Penda's Way. Leeds LS15 62 E3
Penda's Wlk. Leeds LS15 62 D2
Pendennis Ave. S Elm WF9 182 F4
Pendil Cl. Leeds LS15 81 C8
Pendle Ave. Bacup OL13 106 A3
Pendle Cl. Bacup OL13 106 A2
Pendle Rd. Bing BD16 37 B3
Pendragon. Brad BD2 56 A3
Pendragon La. Brad BD2 56 B3
Pendragon Terr. Guise LS20 39 D8
Penfield Gr. Brad BD14 73 C4
Penfield Rd. Birk BD11 96 F6
Pengarth. Bing BD16 37 C5
Penistone Hill Country Pk. Oxen 51 A6
Penistone La. Holmfi HD8 190 D6
Penistone Rd. D Dale HD7, HD8 191 C3
Penistone Rd. Holmfi HD7, HD8 190 C6
Penistone Rd. Holmfi HD7 199 D7
Penistone Rd. Hud HD8 155 C3
Penistone Rd. Kirkb HD8 173 E5
Penistone Rd. Lepton HD8 155 C3
Penistone Rd. Shep HD8 173 E5
Penistone Rd. Shep HD7, HD8 190 C6
Penlands Cres. Leeds LS15 81 D7
Penlands Lawn. Leeds LS15 81 D7
Penlands Wlk. Leeds LS15 81 D7
Penlington Cl. Hem WF9 181 D5
Penn Dr. Clec WF15 116 D6
Penn Gr. Clec WF15 116 D6
Penn St. Hali HX1 113 A8
Pennine Cl. Holmfi HD7 188 D5
Pennine Cl. Queen BD13 92 D7
Pennine Cl. Wake WF2 141 E3
Pennine Cres. Hud HD3 152 E8
Pennine Dr. Clay W HD8 175 D2
Pennine Gdns. Slai HD7 152 D1
Pennine Gr. Tod OL14 108 C6
Pennine Rd. Bacup OL13 106 A2
Pennine Rd. Dew WF12 139 E8
Pennine Rise. Clay W HD8 175 D2
Pennine View. B Head HX7 87 F4
Pennine View. Batley WF17 97 A2
Pennine View. Kirkhe HD5 137 C2
Pennine View. Mapp S75 178 A2
Pennine View. Slai HD7 152 D1
Pennine View. Upton WF9 183 A8
Pennine Way. Clay W HD8 175 D2
Pennine Way. Heb Br HX7 88 D1
Pennine Way. Hem WF9 181 F7
Pennine Way. Hep HX7 88 B6
Pennington Gr. Leeds LS6 60 A4 13
Pennington La. Roth LS26 101 B2
Pennington Pl. Leeds LS6 60 A3 1
Pennington St. Leeds LS6 60 A4
Pennington Terr. Brad BD5 74 C4
Pennington Terr. Leeds LS6 60 A4 12
Pennithorne Ave. Bail BD17 38 C4
Pennwell Croft. Leeds LS14 62 D5 6
Pennwell Dean. Leeds LS14 62 D5
Pennwell Fold. Leeds LS14 62 E5
Pennwell Garth. Leeds LS14 62 D5
Pennwell Gn. Leeds LS14 62 D5
Pennwell Lawn. Leeds LS14 62 E5
Penny Hill Ctr. Leeds 79 E4
Penny Hill Dr. Brad BD14 73 D4
Penny Lane Way. Leeds LS10 79 D4
Penny Spring. Hud HD5 154 E3
Pennyfield Sch. Leeds 42 F1
Pennygate. Bail BD16 37 D6
Penraevon Ave. Leeds LS7 60 C3
Penraevon Ind Est. Leeds 60 C3
Penrith Cres. Castle WF10 104 E1
Penrith Gr. Leeds LS12 78 C6
Penrose Beck Dr. Ack M T WF7 163 F5
Penrose Pl. Northo HX3 93 A2
Penryn Ave. Kirkhe HD5 155 C8
Pentland Ave. Brad BD14 73 C4
Pentland Ave. Knot WF11 126 E4
Pentland Cty Inf Sch. Dew 139 D6
Pentland Dr. Gar LS25 82 F5
Pentland Gr. Wake WF2 141 E3
Pentland Rd. Dew WF12 139 D6
Pentland Way. Morley LS27 98 A3 1
Pepper Gdns. Leeds LS13 58 E4
Pepper Hill. Shelf HX3 93 A6
Pepper Hills. Leeds LS17 43 E4
Pepper La. Leeds LS13 58 D4
Pepper La. Leeds LS10 79 E1
Pepper Rd. Leeds LS10 79 F2
Pepper Royd St. Dew WF13 118 D1
Per La. Hali HX2 91 D8
Percival St. Brad BD3 75 A7
Percival St. Hud HD3 152 F6
Percival St. Leeds LS2 60 B1
Percival Whitley Coll. Hali 113 A6
Percival Whitley Coll of F Ed. Brig 136 A8
Percy St. Bing BD16 37 A3
Percy St. Hud HD2 136 A1
Percy St. Keigh BD21 35 C4
Percy St. Leeds LS12 78 D6
Percy St. S Kirk WF9 182 B2
Peregrine Ave. Morley LS27 98 D4
Peregrine Ct. Hud HD4 171 E7
Peridot Fold. Hud HD2 136 C2
Permain Ct. Hud HD4 154 B4
Perry Cl. Keigh BD22 35 A4
Perserverance St. Pudsey LS28 76 C7
Perseverance La. Brad BD7 74 A4 12
Perseverance Rd. Hali BD13 72 A3
Perseverance Rd. Queen BD13 72 A3
Perseverance St. Bail BD17 38 D4
Perseverance St. Brad BD12 94 C4
Perseverance St. Castle WF10 124 D8 4
Perseverance St. Hali HX6 112 B5 13
Perseverance St. Hud HD4 154 A3
Perseverance Terr. Batley WF17 118 C3
Perseverance Terr. Hali HX1 113 A5
Perseverance Terr. Roth LS26 100 E4
Perseverence St. Hud HD4 153 A3
Perth Ave. Brad BD2 55 E3
Perth Dr. E Ard WF3 119 F8
Perth Mount. Hors LS18 41 B4
Peter Hill. Batley WF17 118 D2
Peter La. Hali HX2 112 B7
Peter La. Morley LS27 98 D4
Peterborough Pl. Brad BD2 56 B3
Peterborough Rd. Brad BD2 56 B2
Peterborough Terr. Brad BD2 56 B3
Petergate. Brad BD1 74 F7
Peterhouse Dr. Otley LS21 23 C7
Petersfield Ave. Midd LS10 99 E7
Petersgarth. Ship BD18 54 E8 5
Peterson Rd. Wake WF1 142 D6
Pether Hill. Elland HX4 133 F3
Petrie Cres. Pudsey LS13 57 D5
Petrie Gr. Brad BD3 75 E7
Petrie Rd. Brad BD3 75 E7
Petrie St. Pudsey LS13 57 D5
Petworth Croft. Roy S71 179 B4
Peverell Cl. Brad BD4 75 E3
Peveril Mount. Brad BD2 56 C3
Pexwood Rd. Tod OL14 107 F3
Pheasant Dr. Batley WF17 97 A3
Pheasant St. Keigh BD21 35 D8
Phil May Ct. Leeds LS12 78 E6 1
Philip Garth. Loft G WF1 121 C5
Philip's Gr. Loft G WF3 121 C6
Philip's La. Dar WF8 147 C5
Philippa Way. Leeds LS12 78 C3
Philips Rd. Bacup OL13 106 A7
Phillips St. Castle WF10 124 B8
Phoebe La. Hali HX3 113 D4
Phoebe Lane Ind Est. Hali 113 D4
Phoenix Ave. Emley HD8 175 D6
Phoenix Ct. Tod OL14 108 D6
Phoenix Ct. Wake WF2 142 A6
Phoenix St. Brig HD6 115 B2
Phoenix St. Tod OL14 108 D6
Phoenix Way. Brad BD4 75 E6
Phoenix Works. Brad 56 E1
Piccadilly. Brad BD1 74 E7
Piccadilly. Wake WF2 142 B6
Pick Hill Rd. Mel HD7 170 D3
Pickard Ct. Leeds LS15 81 C8
Pickard La. Sil BD20 5 E2
Picker St. Tod OL14 107 E8
Pickering Ave. Gar LS25 83 B8
Pickering Dr. Ossett WF5 119 C1
Pickering La. Ossett WF5 119 C1
Pickering Mount. Leeds LS12 78 D8
Pickering St. Leeds LS12 78 D8
Pickerings The. Queen BD13 92 E8
Pickersgill St. Ossett WF5 140 C8
Pickford St. Hud HD3 153 A4
Pickle Top. Slai HD7 151 E2
Pickles Ct. Tod OL14 108 B6 13
Pickles Hill. Haw BD22 33 E1
Pickles La. Brad BD7 73 F2
Pickles La. Skel HD8 175 B1
Pickles St. Batley WF17 118 B2
Pickles St. Keigh BD21 35 B5 13
Picklesfield. Batley WF17 118 B2
Pickthall Terr. Tod OL14 108 D5
Pickwood La. Sow Br HX6 112 E2
Picton St. Brad BD8 55 D1
Pictureville. Brad BD1 74 E6
Piece Hall Yd. Brad BD1 74 E7 6
Piece Wood Rd. Hors LS16 41 D3
Pigeon Cote Cl. Leeds LS14 62 A6
Pigeon Cote Rd. Leeds LS14 62 A6
Piggott St. Brig HD6 115 A3
Pighill Top La. Slai HD7 151 F2
Pike End Rd. Rip HX6 150 C7
Pike Law La. Slai HD7 152 B5
Pike Law Rd. Slai HD7 152 B5
Pike Law. Slai HD7 152 B5
Pildacre Brow. Ossett WF5 140 C6
Pildacre Croft. Ossett WF5 140 C6
Pildacre La. Ossett WF5 140 B6
Pilden La. E Ard WF3 120 C7
Pilgrim Ave. Dew WF13 138 F7
Pilgrim Cres. Dew WF13 138 F7
Pilgrim Dr. Dew WF13 138 F7
Pilkington St. Wake WF2 142 C4
Pill White La. Lindley LS21 11 F6
Pilling La. Skel HD8 175 C2
Pilling Top La. Kirkb HD8 174 C4
Pilmer Ct. Wake WF2 141 D4
Pilot St. Leeds LS9 60 E1
Pin Hill La. Hali HX2 90 D1
Pincheon St. Wake WF1 142 D6 11
Pinder Ave. Leeds LS12 77 F4
Pinder Gr. Leeds LS12 77 F4
Pinder St. Leeds LS12 77 F4
Pinder View. Leeds LS12 77 F4
Pinder's Gr. Wake WF1 142 E8
Pinderfields General Hospl. Wake 121 D1
Pinderfields Rd. Wake WF1 142 C7
Pinders Cres. Knot WF11 126 C5
Pinders Garth. Knot WF11 126 D5
Pinders Gn. M'town LS26 123 C8
Pinders Green Ct. M'town LS26 102 C1
Pinders Green Dr. M'town LS26 102 C1
Pinders Green Fold. M'town LS26 102 C1
Pine Cl. Castle WF10 124 E6
Pine Cl. Weth LS22 13 E7
Pine Court Mews. Hud HD4 171 D6
Pine Croft. Keigh BD20 18 A1
Pine Ct. Hud HD4 171 D6
Pine Ct. Leeds LS2 79 D7
Pine Gr. Batley WF17 118 B3
Pine Rd. Tod OL14 107 F7
Pine St. Bacup OL13 106 A1 7
Pine St. Brad BD1 74 F8
Pine St. Hali HX1 113 C6 10
Pine St. Haw BD22 51 C6
Pine St. Hud HD1 154 B7
Pine St. S Elm WF9 182 E1
Pine Tree Ave. B Spa LS23 30 E8
Pine Tree Ave. Pont WF8 146 B6
Pineapple Cotts. Crof WF1 143 E6
Pinedale. Bing BD16 36 F5
Pinehurst Ct. Hud HD3 135 B1
Pines Gdns. Ilkley LS29 7 F3
Pinewood Ave. Wake WF2 141 D6
Pinewood Cl. Ilkley LS29 8 A3
Pinewood Gdns. Elland HX4 134 B4
Pinewood Pl. Knot WF11 126 E3
Pinfold Cl. Dew WF12 139 E2
Pinfold Cl. Floc WF4 157 C2
Pinfold Cl. Knot WF11 126 C5
Pinfold Cl. Mir WF14 138 B5
Pinfold Cl. Rip HX4 133 A5
Pinfold Cross. K Smea WF8 166 D5
Pinfold Ct. Leeds LS15 81 B8
Pinfold Dr. Crof WF4 144 A1
Pinfold Gr. Leeds LS15 81 A8
Pinfold Gr. Wake WF2 142 E1
Pinfold Hill. Dew WF13 139 B7
Pinfold Hill. Leeds LS15 81 B8
Pinfold La. Brig HD6 135 D5
Pinfold La. Floc WF4 157 C2
Pinfold La. Gar LS25 82 F7
Pinfold La. Hors LS16 41 F7
Pinfold La. K Smea WF8 166 D5
Pinfold La. Leeds LS12 78 B7
Pinfold La. Leeds LS15 81 A8
Pinfold La. Lepton HD8 156 A3
Pinfold La. M'town LS26 102 E2
Pinfold La. Mars HD3 151 C5
Pinfold La. Mir WF14 138 C5
Pinfold La. Roy S71 179 C2
Pinfold La. Slai HD7 152 A4
Pinfold La. Sow Br HX6 111 E4
Pinfold La. Wake WF2 142 E1
Pinfold Mount. Leeds LS15 81 B7
Pinfold Rd. Leeds LS15 81 B7
Pinfold Rise. Aber LS25 64 E8
Pinfold Sq. Leeds LS15 81 A8
Pingle Rise. D Dale HD8 192 A7
Pink St. Haw BD22 51 C6
Pinnacle La. Heb Br HX7 109 E8
Pinnar Croft. Hali HX3 114 A4
Pinnar La. Hali HX3 113 F5
Pioneer St. Dew WF12 139 C4
Pioneer St. Tod OL14 129 A7
Pipe and Nook La. Leeds LS12 77 F7
Piper Hill. Fair WF11 105 A4
Piper La. Otley LS21 22 F7
Piper Well La. Shep HD8 190 E6
Pippins Green Ave. Wake WF2 120 B2
Pirie Cl. Brad BD2 55 F3
Pit Field Rd. Roth WF3 100 D2
Pit La. Batley WF13 117 F2
Pit La. Clec BD19 96 B2
Pit La. Denh BD13 52 C1
Pit La. M'Field LS25 83 F5
Pit La. M'town LS26 102 D4
Pit La. Queen BD13 72 C4
Pit La. Thorn BD13 72 C4
Pitcliffe Way. Brad BD5 74 F4
Pitfall St. Leeds LS1 79 C7
Pits La. Brig BD19 115 F6
Pitt Hill La. Rip HX4 133 D2
Pitt Row. Leeds LS1 79 C7
Pitt St. Keigh BD21 35 D7
Pitt St. Liver WF15 117 B2
Pitt St. Tod OL14 108 D5
Pitts St. Brad BD4 75 D4
Place's Rd. Leeds LS9 79 E7
Plaid Row. Leeds LS9 79 E8
Plain La. Sow Br HX6 111 C2
Plains La. Hali HX5 134 F8
Plains La. Mars HD7 169 A5
Plains. Mars HD7 169 A5
Plane Gn. Pont WF8 125 F1
Plane St. Hud HD4 154 B3
Plane St. Tod OL14 107 E7
Plane Tree Ave. Castle WF10 125 D5
Plane Tree Ave. Leeds LS17 43 F4
Plane Tree Cl. Leeds LS17 43 F4
Plane Tree Croft. Leeds LS17 43 F4
Plane Tree Gdns. Leeds LS17 43 F4
Plane Tree Gr. Yeadon LS19 40 D6
Plane Tree Nest. Hali HX2 112 E6
Plane Tree Nest La. Hali HX2 112 E5
Plane Tree Rd. Hali HX6 112 B5
Plane Tree Rise. Leeds LS17 43 F4
Plane Tree View. Leeds LS17 43 F4
Plane Trees Cl. Clec BD19 95 D3
Planetrees Rd. Brad BD4 75 C6
Planetrees St. Brad BD15 54 A1
Plantation Ave. Leeds LS17 44 A5
Plantation Ave. Leeds LS15 81 A7
Plantation Ave. Roy S71 179 D3
Plantation Dr. Hud HD4 154 A1
Plantation Gdns. Leeds LS17 44 B5
Plantation Pl. Brad BD4 75 C4
Plantation Way. Bail BD17 38 D3
Platt La. Slai HD7 152 A1
Platt Sq. Clec BD19 116 D7 7
Playfair Rd. Leeds LS10 79 D2
Playground. Gild LS12 77 D3
Pleasance The. Swil LS26 82 A1
Pleasant Ct. Leeds LS6 60 A3 2
Pleasant Mount. Leeds LS11 79 A5
Pleasant Pl. Leeds LS11 79 A5
Pleasant St. Brad BD7 74 A4
Pleasant St. Hali HX6 112 C4
Pleasant St. Leeds LS11 79 A5
Pleasant Terr. Leeds LS11 79 A5
Pleasant View. Loft G WF2 120 F7
Pledwick Cres. Wake WF2 160 D6
Pledwick Dr. Wake WF2 160 D5
Pledwick Gr. Wake WF2 160 C5
Pledwick La. Wake WF2 160 D5
Pledwick Rise. Wake WF2 160 D5
Plevna St. Leeds LS10 80 A2
Plevna Terr. Bing BD16 36 F4
Plimsoll St. Brad BD4 75 A4
Plimsoll St. Hem WF9 181 D7
Ploughcroft La. Hali HX3 92 C3
Ploughmans Croft. Brad BD2 55 E4
Plover Dr. Batley WF17 117 F5
Plover Rd. Hud HD3 153 B8
Plover St. Brad BD5 74 C3
Plover St. Keigh BD21 35 C8
Plover Way. Morley LS27 98 D3
Plum St. Hali HX1 112 F6
Plum St. Keigh BD21 35 A3
Plum Tree Cl. Pont WF8 146 B6
Plumpton Ave. Brad BD2 55 F6
Plumpton Cl. Brad BD2 56 A5
Plumpton Dr. Brad BD2 55 F6
Plumpton End. Brad BD2 56 A6
Plumpton Gdns. Brad BD2 55 F6
Plumpton Lea. Brad BD2 55 F6
Plumpton Mead. Brad BD2 55 F6
Plumpton Pl. Wake WF2 142 A6
Plumpton Rd. Wake WF2 142 A6

Plumpton St. Brad BD8 .... 74 A8
Plumpton St. Wake WF2 .... 142 A6
Plumpton Terr. Wake WF2 .... 142 A5
Plumpton Wlk. Brad BD2 .... 55 F6
Plymouth Gr. Hali HX1 .... 113 A8
Poet's Pl. Hors LS18 .... 41 C2
Pog Hall. Slai HD7 .... 170 C8
Pohlman St. Hali HX1 .... 112 F5
Pole Gate Branch. Slai HD7 .... 151 D4
Pole Gate. Slai HD7 .... 151 D4
Pole Rd. Keigh BD22 .... 33 F8
Pollard Ave. Bing BD16 .... 37 B5
Pollard Ave. Clec BD19 .... 96 B1
Pollard La. Brad BD2 .... 56 B4
Pollard La. Leeds LS13 .... 58 B3
Pollard La. Pudsey LS13 .... 58 C5
Pollard Park Mid Sch. Brad 75 B8
Pollard St. Brad BD4 .... 75 B2
Pollard St. Hud HD2 .... 136 B2
Pollard St. Loft G WF3 .... 121 C6
Pollard St. S Elm WF9 .... 183 B8
Pollard St. S Hud HD3 .... 153 B4
Pollard St. Tod OL14 .... 54 B6 1
Pollard St. Tod OL14 .... 107 E8
Pollard Way. Clec BD19 .... 96 B1
Pollit's Fields. Knot WF11 ...... 126 B5
Pollit Ave. Sow Br HX6 .... 111 F3
Polluns La. Fair WF11 .... 105 B6
Polperro Cl. Nor WF6 .... 123 B3
Pomfret Ct. Pont WF8 .... 147 A8
Pomfret Pl. Gar LS25 .... 83 B8
Pond Cl. Hud HD4 .... 153 F7
Pond La. Lepton HD8 .... 156 A2
Pond St. Keigh BD21 .... 35 C8
Ponden La. Haw BD22 .... 50 A7
Pondfields Cl. Kippax LS25 ..... 83 B2
Pondfields Crest. Kippax LS25 . 83 B2
Pondfields Dr. Kippax LS25 .... 83 B2
Pondfields Rise. Kippax LS25 .. 83 B2
Ponker La. Skel HD8 .... 174 E1
Ponker Nook La. Skel HD8 ...... 174 F1
Pontefract Carleton Jun & Inf Sch.
Pont 146 E6
Pontefract Cres. Pont 125 E1
Pontefract Cobbler's Lane Inf Sch.
Pont 126 A1
Pontefract Cobbler's Lane Jun Sch.
Pont 147 A8
Pontefract General Infmy. Pont . 146 D8
Pontefract H Fam & St Michaels
Prim Sch. Pont 126 A1
Pontefract Jun & Inf Sch. Pont . 125 D1
Pontefract Kings High Sch. Pont 146 C7
Pontefract La. Leeds LS9 .... 80 C5
Pontefract Lane Cl. Leeds LS9 . 79 F7
Pontefract Pk. Pont 125 A1
Pontefract Rd. Ack M T WF7 .... 146 A1
Pontefract Rd. Ack M T WF7 .... 164 A8
Pontefract Rd. Castle WF10 .... 124 C7
Pontefract Rd. Crof WF4 .... 144 A2
Pontefract Rd. Cud S72 .... 180 C1
Pontefract Rd. Feath WF7 ...... 145 E5
Pontefract Rd. Feath WF7 ...... 145 E6
Pontefract Rd. Knot WF11 ...... 126 B4
Pontefract Rd. Knot WF11 ...... 126 D4
Pontefract Rd. Leeds LS10, LS26 .. 80 B2
Pontefract Rd. Nor WF6 .... 123 D3
Pontefract St Giles CE Inf Sch.
Pont 125 D1
Pontefract St. Hem WF9 .... 181 E6
Pontefract Willow Park Jun Sch.
Pont 146 F8
Pontey Dr. Hud HD5 .... 155 A6
Pontey Mount. Hud HD5 .... 155 B5
Pool Bank Cl. Pool LS21 .... 24 D7
Pool Bank Ct. Pool LS21 .... 24 C7
Pool Bank New Rd. Bramho LS21 .. 24 C5
Pool Bank New Rd. Leath LS21 . 24 C5
Pool Comprehensive Sch. Pool . 24 D7
Pool Ct. Brad BD3 .... 75 A7
Pool Hill La. D Dale HD8 .... 192 D6
Pool in Wharfedale CE Prim Sch.
Pool 24 D7
Pool Rd. Leath LS21 .... 24 D7
Pool Rd. Otley LS21 .... 23 C8
Pool Sq. Keigh BD21 .... 18 E1
Poole Cres. Leeds LS15 .... 62 B1
Poole Mount. Leeds LS15 .... 62 B1
Poole Rd. Leeds LS15 .... 62 B1
Poole St. Leeds LS15 .... 62 B1
Pools La. Roy S71 .... 179 D3
Pope St. Keigh BD21 .... 35 D8
Popeley Rd. Batley WF16 .... 117 C6
Poplar Ave. Brad BD7 .... 73 F2
Poplar Ave. Castle WF10 .... 125 C7
Poplar Cres. Hali HX2 .... 91 F7
Poplar Ave. Hali HX6 .... 112 C5
Poplar Ave. Holmfi HD7 .... 172 C1
Poplar Ave. Leeds LS15 .... 62 C5
Poplar Ave. Ship S72 .... 180 C2
Poplar Ave. Tod OL14 .... 108 A7
Poplar Ave. Wake WF2 .... 141 E5
Poplar Cl. Bur in W LS29 .... 21 F8
Poplar Court. Leeds LS13 .... 58 C2
Poplar Cres. Hali HX2 .... 91 F7
Poplar Cres. Morley LS22 .... 98 C1
Poplar Cres. Ship BD18 .... 55 C5
Poplar Dr. Hors LS18 .... 57 F8
Poplar Dr. Hud HD1 .... 153 F5
Poplar Dr. Ship BD18 .... 55 C5
Poplar Dr. Wake WF1 .... 123 A5
Poplar Gdns. Leeds LS13 .... 77 E8
Poplar Garth. Leeds LS13 .... 77 E8
Poplar Gdns. Leeds LS13 .... 77 E8
Poplar Gdns. Pont WF8 .... 125 F1
Poplar Gr. Brad BD7 .... 73 F2
Poplar Gr. Harden BD16 .... 36 A1
Poplar Gr. Knot WF11 .... 126 E2
Poplar Mount. Leeds LS13 ...... 77 E8
Poplar Rd. Brad BD7 .... 74 A2
Poplar Rd. Ship BD18 .... 55 C6
Poplar Rise. Leeds LS13 .... 58 E1

Poplar Rise. Skel HD8 .... 175 B1
Poplar Sq. Pudsey LS28 .... 57 D213
Poplar St. Hali HX1 .... 113 C8
Poplar St. Hud HD2 .... 136 B1
Poplar St. Hud HD5 .... 154 D511
Poplar St. Loft G WF3 .... 121 C6
Poplar Terr. Hud HD5 .... 154 D517
Poplar Terr. Keigh BD21 .... 35 A714
Poplar Terr. Keigh BD20 .... 36 D7
Poplar Terr. Roy S71 .... 179 D4
Poplar Terr. S Elm WF9 .... 183 A2
Poplar View. Brad BD7 .... 73 F2
Poplar View. Brig HX3 .... 115 B6
Poplar View. Leeds LS13 .... 77 E8
Poplar Way. Leeds LS13 .... 77 E8
Poplars Farm Fst Sch. Brad 55 E4
Poplars Park Rd. Brad BD2 ..... 55 E4
Poplars The. Bramho LS16 ...... 24 F5
Poplars The. Guise LS20 .... 22 E2
Poplars The. Knot WF11 .... 127 B8
Poplars The. Leeds LS6 .... 59 E3
Poplars The. S in Cra BD20 ..... 16 C4
Poplars The. Leeds LS13 .... 58 C5
Poplars The. S in Cra BD20 ..... 16 C4
Popley Butts. Hud HD7 .... 170 C1
Popley Dr. Mel HD7 .... 170 C1
Popple Wells La. Hali HX2 .... 112 A7
Popples Dr. Hali HX2 .... 91 F7
Popples. Hali HX2 .... 91 F7
Poppleton Ct. E Ard WF3 .... 98 E1 1
Poppleton Dr. E Ard WF3 .... 98 E1
Poppleton Rd. E Ard WF3 .... 98 E1
Poppleton Rise. E Ard WF3 ..... 119 E8
Poppleton Way. E Ard WF3 ..... 119 E8
Porchester House. Hud HD5 .... 154 D6 4
Porritt St. Clec BD19 .... 75 D1
Portage Ave. Leeds LS15 .... 80 F7
Portage Cres. Leeds LS15 .... 80 F7
Portal Cres. Mir WF14 .... 138 A8
Portal Dr. Mir WF14 .... 138 A8
Portland Ave. Pont WF8 .... 125 B1
Portland Cl. Hud HD3 .... 153 C7
Portland Cres. Leeds LS1 .... 60 A1
Portland Ct. Keigh BD21 .... 35 B6
Portland Gate. Leeds LS1 .... 60 B1
Portland House. Elland HX5 .... 134 F714
Portland Pl. Bing BD16 .... 37 A2
Portland Pl. Hali HX1 .... 113 C6
Portland Pl. Upton WF9 .... 183 A7
Portland Rd. Hali HX3 .... 113 D8
Portland Rd. Leeds LS12 .... 78 B4
Portland St. Brad BD5 .... 74 E6
Portland St. Hali HX1 .... 113 C7 5
Portland St. Hem WF9 .... 181 C6
Portland St. Hud HD1 .... 153 F6
Portland St. Leeds LS1 .... 79 B8
Portland St. Pudsey LS28 .... 57 A7
Portland St. Wake WF1 .... 142 F3
Portland Way. Leeds LS1 .... 60 B1
Portman St. Pudsey LS28 .... 57 A6
Portobello Gr. Wake WF2 .... 142 D3
Portobello Rd. Wake WF1, WF2 . 142 D2
Portree House. Brad BD6 .... 93 F7 R 7
Portsmouth Ave. Brad BD3 ..... 75 C7
Portwood St. Brad BD9 .... 54 D2
Post Hill Ct. Leeds LS12 .... 77 D7
Post Office Rd. Brad BD2 .... 56 C5
Post Office Rd. Feath WF7 ...... 145 D5
Post Office St. Liver BD19 .... 116 F6
Pot La. Stee BD20 .... 17 C7
Pothouse Rd. Brad BD6 .... 94 B8
Potovens Cl. Loft G WF3 .... 100 B6
Potovens Ct. Loft G WF3 .... 121 B5
Potovens La. Loft G WF3 .... 121 B6
Potovens La. Wake WF1 .... 142 C5
Potter Ave. Wake WF2 .... 141 E4
Potter Brow Rd. Baid BD17 ..... 38 C7
Potternewton Ave. Leeds LS7 . 60 D6
Potternewton Cres. Leeds LS7 . 60 C6
Potternewton Ct. Leeds LS7 ... 60 D6
Potternewton Gdns. Leeds LS7 .. 60 D6
Potternewton Gr. Leeds LS7 ... 60 D6
Potternewton Heights. Leeds LS7 .. 60 D6
Potternewton La. Leeds LS7 ... 60 C6
Potternewton Lane Prim Sch. Leeds 60 D6
Potternewton Mansion Coll of F Ed.
Leeds 60 D6
Potternewton Mount. Leeds LS7 .. 60 C6
Potternewton View. Leeds LS7 . 60 D6
Potters Croft. Loft G WF3 .... 121 C6
Potters Gate. Wth Com HD8 ... 190 E1
Potters Wlk. Hud HD7 .... 152 E4
Potterton Ct. B in Elm LS15 ... 63 E8
Potterton La. B in Elm LS15 ... 63 E8
Potterton La. B in Elm LS15 ... 46 E2
Potterton La. Knot WF11 .... 126 E6
Potts Rd. Leeds LS10 .... 101 D7
Pottery St. Castle WF10 .... 124 D8
Pottery St. Hud HD1 .... 154 A5
Potts' Terr. Nor WF6 .... 144 B8
Poulton Pl. Leeds LS11 .... 79 D4
Poverty La. Sow Br HX7 .... 111 A1
Powell Ave. Brad BD5 .... 74 D4
Powell Rd. Bing BD16 .... 37 A3
Powell Rd. Ship BD18 .... 55 D5
Powell St. Batley WF16 .... 117 E3
Powell St. Hali HX1 .... 113 C6 13
Powell St. S Kirk WF9 .... 182 D3
Poxton Gr. S Elm WF9 .... 182 F1
Prail Cl. Pont WF8 .... 146 C8
Pratt La. Mir WF14 .... 138 A6
Pratt La. Ship BD18 .... 55 C6
Precinct The. Feath WF7 .... 145 C5
Premiere Pk. Ilkley LS29 .... 7 F3
Prescott St. Hali HX1 .... 113 C6
Prescott Terr. Brad BD15 .... 54 B1
Preston La. Hali HX2 .... 91 D7
Preston La. Hali HX2 .... 91 E7
Preston Par. Leeds LS11 .... 79 A2
Preston Pl. Hali HX1 .... 113 A7
Preston St. Batley WF16 .... 117 D4
Preston St. Brad BD7 .... 74 A3
Preston Terr. Bing BD16 .... 36 E6
Prestwich Ave. Hud HD3 .... 135 A1
Prestwich Dr. Hud HD2 .... 135 F3
Prestwick Cl. Otley LS21 .... 22 D6
Pretoria St. Castle WF10 .... 124 D7
Pretoria St. Feath WF7 .... 145 C4
Pretoria St. Slai HD7 .... 151 F1
Pretoria St. Slai HD7 .... 152 A1
Priest Bank Rd. S in Cra BD20 . 16 D5
Priest La. Rip HX6 .... 132 D4
Priesthorpe Ave. Pudsey LS28 . 57 D8
Priesthorpe Ct. Pudsey LS28 ... 57 D7

Priesthorpe High Sch. Pudsey . 57 B2
Priesthorpe La. Pudsey LS28 ... 57 B3
Priesthorpe Rd. Pudsey LS28 .. 57 B4
Priestley Ave. Batley WF16 ..... 117 D6
Priestley Ct. Brad BD6 .... 94 C8
Priestley Cl. Pudsey LS28 .... 76 F8
Priestley Dr. Pudsey LS28 .... 76 F8
Priestley Gdns. Pudsey LS28 ... 76 F8
Priestley Gn. Brig HX3 .... 93 F1
Priestley Gr. Hud HD4 .... 153 F1
Priestley Hill. Queen BD13 ..... 92 C6
Priestley Pl. Sow Br HX6 .... 112 A3
Priestley Sq. Batley WF17 .... 96 E2
Priestley St. Brad BD1 .... 74 F8 7
Priestley St. Thorn BD13 .... 72 D6
Priestley Terr. Brad BD6 .... 74 C1 1
Priestley View. Pudsey LS28 ... 76 F8
Priestley Wlk. Pudsey LS28 ..... 76 F8
Priestman St. Brad BD8 .... 55 B1
Priestthorpe Fst Sch. Bing 37 A3
Priestthorpe La. Bing BD16 .... 37 A3
Priestthorpe Rd. Bing BD16 .... 37 A4
Primitive St. Hud HD1 .... 154 B6 8
Primitive St. Wth WF3 .... 100 D3
Primley Gdns. Leeds LS17 .... 43 C4
Primley Park Ave. Leeds LS17 . 43 C4
Primley Park Cres. Leeds LS17 . 43 C4
Primley Park Ct. Leeds LS17 ... 43 C5
Primley Park Dr. Leeds LS17 ... 43 C5
Primley Park Garth. Leeds LS17 .. 43 D5
Primley Park Gn. Leeds LS17 ... 43 D5
Primley Park Gr. Leeds LS17 ... 43 C4
Primley Park La. Leeds LS17 ... 43 C5
Primley Park Mount. Leeds LS17 .. 43 C4
Primley Park Rd. Leeds LS17 ... 43 C4
Primley Park Rise. Leeds LS17 . 43 D4
Primley Park View. Leeds LS17 . 43 D5
Primley Park Way. Leeds LS17 . 43 C5
Primley Park Wlk. Leeds LS17 . 43 D5
Primrose Ave. Leeds LS15 ...... 81 A8
Primrose Ave. Swil LS26 .... 82 B1
Primrose Bank. Brig BD16 ...... 37 B2
Primrose Cl. Leeds LS15 .... 81 A8
Primrose Cl. Pont WF8 .... 146 D7
Primrose Cres. Leeds LS15 ..... 62 A1
Primrose Ct. Byram WF11 ...... 126 D7
Primrose Dene. Byram WF11 .. 126 D7
Primrose Dr. Castle WF10 ...... 125 C8
Primrose Dr. Leeds LS15 .... 81 A8
Primrose Garth. Leeds LS15 ... 81 A8 1
Primrose Gr. Keigh BD21 .... 35 E8
Primrose Gr. Leeds LS15 .... 81 A8
Primrose Hill Cl. Swil LS26 ..... 82 A1
Primrose Hill Dr. Swil LS26 ..... 82 B1
Primrose Hill Garth. Swil LS26 . 82 B1
Primrose Hill Gdns. Swil LS26 . 102 B8
Primrose Hill Gn. Swil LS26 .... 102 B8
Primrose Hill Gr. Swil LS26 ..... 102 B8
Primrose Hill. Pudsey LS28 ..... 57 E2
Primrose Hill Prim Sch. Leeds . 60 E2
Primrose Hill. Knot WF11 .... 127 A5
Primrose Hill. Swil LS26 .... 82 B1
Primrose La. B Spa LS23 .... 30 B6
Primrose La. Crig WF4 .... 159 F6
Primrose La. Hali HX3 .... 92 A3
Primrose La. Kirkb HD8 .... 173 E7
Primrose La. Leeds LS15 .... 81 A8
Primrose La. Pudsey LS28 ...... 57 E2
Primrose Rd. Leeds LS15 .... 81 A8
Primrose Row. Bail BD17 .... 38 F4
Primrose St. Brad BD3 .... 55 E1
Primrose St. Keigh BD21 .... 35 E8
Primrose St. Thorn BD13 .... 72 D6
Primrose Vale. Knot WF11 ...... 127 A5
Primrose Way. Shelf HX3 .... 93 D7
Primrose Wlk. Knot WF11 .... 127 A5
Prince Edward Gr. Leeds LS12 . 78 A4
Prince Edward Rd. Leeds LS12 . 78 A4
Prince Henry Rd. Otley LS21 ... 11 A1
Prince Henry's Gram Sch. Otley . 11 A1
Prince St. Brad BD4 .... 75 C2
Prince St. Hud HD1 .... 154 A6
Prince St. Keigh BD21 .... 35 D8
Prince's Ave. Wake WF2 .... 142 A6
Prince's Cres. Brad BD2 .... 56 B4
Prince's Ct. Leeds LS17 .... 43 C3
Prince's Gate. Hali HX3 .... 113 D3
Prince's St. Batley WF16 .... 117 D4
Prince's St. Brad BD6 .... 93 E7 4
Prince's Way. Brad BD1 .... 74 F6
Prince's Way. Wake WF2 .... 141 D6
Princes St. Batley WF14 .... 117 C4
Princess Alexandra Wlk. Hud HD1 154 B6 10
Princess Ave. Dew WF12 .... 140 A8
Princess Ave. Leeds LS17 .... 43 A4
Princess Cl. Dew WF12 .... 140 A8
Princess Cl. Dew WF12 .... 140 A8
Princess Cres. Dew WF13 .... 138 E1
Princess Fields. Dew WF12 .... 140 A8
Princess Gdns. Dew WF12 ...... 140 A8
Princess La. Leeds LS17 .... 43 A4
Princess Mary Cl. Wake WF2 .. 120 F3
Princess Rd. Ilkley LS29 .... 8 B4
Princess St. Clec BD19 .... 116 D6
Princess St. Clec BD19 .... 116 D8
Princess St. Elland HX5 .... 134 F7
Princess St. Elland HX4 .... 134 C7
Princess St. Hali HX1 .... 113 C7
Princess St. Hem WF9 .... 181 D7
Princess St. Keigh BD21 .... 35 A8
Princess St. Loft WF3 .... 121 C6
Princess St. Nor WF6 .... 123 B2
Princess St. Ossett WF5 .... 140 D4

Princess St. Wake WF1 .... 142 E2
Princess St. Yeadon LS19 .... 40 A4
Princeville Fst Sch. Brad 74 B6
Princeville Rd. Brad BD7 .... 74 B7
Princeville St. Brad BD7 .... 74 B6
Prior St. Keigh BD21 .... 35 D8
Prior's La. Hal E BD23 .... 1 E7
Priordale Rd. Feath WF7 .... 145 B4
Priory Ct. Bing BD16 .... 37 A4 7
Priory Cl. Mir WF14 .... 137 E6
Priory Cl. Nor WF6 .... 122 F4
Priory Ct. Ossett WF5 .... 140 D4
Priory Ct. S Elm WF9 .... 13 F6
Priory Croft. Ossett WF5 .... 140 D5
Priory Dr. Brad BD8 .... 74 C4
Priory Estate. S Elm WF9 .... 183 B2
Priory Gr. Bing BD16 .... 37 A4
Priory Grange. Pont WF8 .... 125 E2
Priory Mews. Loft G WF3 .... 121 C6
Priory Pl. Hud HD2 .... 136 F5
Priory Rd. Bing BD16 .... 37 A4
Priory Rd. Ossett WF5 .... 140 D5
Priory Sq. Walton WF2 .... 161 A7
Priory Way. Mir WF14 .... 137 E6
Privilege St. Leeds LS12 .... 78 D6
Prod La. Bail BD17 .... 37 E2
Progress Ave. Harden BD16 .... 36 A1
Prospect Ave. Hali HX2 .... 112 E4
Prospect Ave. Leeds LS13 ...... 58 C3
Prospect Ave. Nor WF6 .... 123 B3
Prospect Ave. Pudsey LS28 .... 76 D8
Prospect Ave. Ship BD18 .... 55 C7
Prospect Bank. Bramham LS23 . 30 E3
Prospect Cl. Hali HX2 .... 112 E4
Prospect Cotts. S Elm WF9 .... 182 E3
Prospect Cres. Keigh BD22 .... 34 E5
Prospect Cres. Leeds LS10 ..... 215 E6
Prospect Dr. Keigh BD22 .... 34 E5
Prospect Gdns. Leeds LS15 .... 81 B8 4
Prospect Gr. Pudsey LS28 ...... 76 D8
Prospect La. Birk BD11 .... 96 B5
Prospect Mount. Keigh BD22 . 34 E5
Prospect Mount. Ship BD18 ... 55 C7
Prospect Pl. Brad BD9 .... 54 F2
Prospect Pl. Brad BD7 .... 74 A4 6
Prospect Pl. Clec BD19 .... 116 D8 11
Prospect Pl. Glu BD20 .... 16 C6
Prospect Pl. Hali HX1 .... 113 B3
Prospect Pl. Leeds LS15 .... 81 B8
Prospect Pl. Pudsey LS28 .... 76 F7
Prospect Rd. Bur in W LS29 .... 21 F8
Prospect Rd. Clec BD19 .... 116 D7
Prospect Rd. Hud HD3 .... 152 F6
Prospect Rd. Liver WF15 .... 116 D2
Prospect Rd. Ship BD18 .... 55 C7
Prospect Row. Elland HX5 ...... 134 F7 18
Prospect Row. Men LS29 .... 21 C6
Prospect Sq. Pudsey LS28 ...... 57 D212
Prospect St. Batley WF17 .... 118 C5
Prospect St. Brad BD13 .... 73 B6
Prospect St. Brad BD4 .... 93 F7
Prospect St. Clec BD19 .... 116 D7 3N11
Prospect St. Glu BD20 .... 16 C6
Prospect St. Hud HD1 .... 154 B6 9
Prospect St. Keigh BD22 .... 34 F6
Prospect St. Leeds LS13 .... 58 C3
Prospect St. Pudsey LS28 .... 76 D8
Prospect St. Shep HD8 .... 190 D8
Prospect St. Thorn BD13 .... 72 E6
Prospect St. Yeadon LS19 .... 40 C4
Prospect Terr. Batley WF13 .... 117 F2 3
Prospect Terr. Leeds LS10 ...... 79 F4
Prospect Terr. Leeds LS15 ...... 81 B8 1
Prospect Terr. Liver WF15 ...... 116 D2
Prospect Terr. Pudsey LS28 .... 76 D8
Prospect View. Leeds LS13 ..... 58 C3
Prospect Villas. Weth LS22 ..... 13 E5 3
Prospect Wlk. Ship BD18 .... 55 C7
Prosper St. Leeds LS10 .... 79 F6
Providence Ave. Bail BD17 ..... 38 C4
Providence Ave. Leeds LS6 ..... 59 F5
Providence Bldgs. Hali HX3 .... 114 A4
Providence Cres. Haw BD22 ... 51 C6
Providence Cl. Morley LS27 .... 98 C5
Providence Cres. Haw BD22 ... 51 C6
Providence La. Haw BD22 .... 51 C6
Providence Pl. Bgly BD16 .... 36 F8 3
Providence Pl. Gar LS25 .... 83 A3
Providence Pl. Leeds LS2 .... 60 B1
Providence Pl. Kippax WF10 ... 103 C4
Providence Pl. Leeds LS11 ...... 79 A1
Providence Pl. Morley LS27 .... 97 F1
Providence Rd. Leeds LS6 .... 59 F5
Providence Row. Bail BD17 .... 38 C4
Providence Row. Byram WF11 . 126 D6
Providence St. Batley WF17 ... 118 C5
Providence St. Brad BD1 .... 74 D7
Providence St. Clec BD19 .... 116 D7
Providence St. Hali HX1 .... 113 C6
Providence St. Keigh BD21 ..... 35 C7
Providence St. Wake WF1 ...... 142 C7
Providence St. Wake WF2 ...... 141 D4
Provident St. Dew WF13 .... 139 D8 4
Prune Park La. Brad BD15 ...... 53 F2
Prune Park La. Brad BD15 ...... 54 A2
Pudding La. Tod OL14 .... 108 B6
Pudsey Bsns Ctr. Pudsey 76 F7
Pudsey Crawshaw Sch. Pudsey . 76 F7

Pudsey Grangefield Sch. Pudsey . 76 E8
Pudsey Greenside Prim Sch.
Pudsey 76 D6
Pudsey Primrose Hill Prim Sch.
Pudsey 57 D1
Pudsey Rd. Leeds LS12, LS13 ... 77 D8
Pudsey Rd. Pudsey LS12, LS13 . 77 B7
Pudsey Rd. Tod OL14 .... 86 E5
Pudsey Tyersal Prim Sch. Pudsey . 75 F6
Pudsey Waterloo Inf Sch. Pudsey . 76 C7
Pugneys Country Park. Crig 160 B8
Pugneys Rd. Wake WF2 .... 142 C2
Pullan Ave. Brad BD2 .... 56 C4
Pullan Dr. Brad BD2 .... 56 C4
Pullan Gr. Brad BD2 .... 56 C4
Pullan La. Guise BD17 .... 39 C5
Pullan St. Brad BD5 .... 74 D5
Pulman St. Brad BD4 .... 75 A4
Pumans Pl. Hali HX3 .... 113 C2
Pump La. Dew WF13 .... 138 F8
Pump La. E Ard WF13 .... 119 E5
Pump La. Kirkb HD8 .... 174 C7
Pump La. W Har WF4 .... 163 A8
Pump St. D Dale HD8 .... 191 B3
Pumphouse La. Mir WF14 .... 136 C8
Punch Bowl Rd. Brott WF11 ... 126 C8
Punch Bowl Yd. Clec BD19 ..... 116 D7
Pundles. Hali HX2 .... 91 E8
Purbeck Gr. Gar LS25 .... 82 F6
Purcell Dr. Sil BD20 .... 5 E2
Purley Wlk. Brad BD6 .... 94 B8
Purlwell Ave. Batley WF17 ..... 118 B3
Purlwell Cres. Batley WF17 .... 118 C4
Purlwell Hall Rd. Batley WF17 . 118 C4
Purlwell La. Batley WF17 .... 118 C4
Purprose La. Wad H HX7 .... 69 A1
Purston 1st Sch. Feath 145 D4
Purston La. Ack M T WF7 .... 145 F1
Purston Park Ct. Feath WF7 ... 145 D4
Purwell Inf Sch. Batley 118 B3
Pye Nest Ave. Hali HX2 .... 112 E5
Pye Nest Dr. Hali HX2 .... 112 E4
Pye Nest Gdns. Hali HX2 .... 112 E4
Pye Nest Gr. Hali HX2 .... 112 E5
Pye Nest Rd. Hali HX2 .... 112 E4
Pye Nest Rise. Hali HX2 .... 112 E4
Pyenot Ave. Clec BD19 .... 116 E6
Pyenot Dr. Clec BD19 .... 116 E6
Pyenot Gdns. Clec BD19 .... 116 E6
Pyenot Hall La. Clec BD19 ...... 116 E6
Pymroyd La. Hud HD4 .... 153 B3
Pynate Rd. Batley WF17 .... 96 D4
Pyrah Fold. Brad BD12 .... 94 D4
Pyrah Rd. Brad BD12 .... 94 D7
Pyrah St. Brad BD12 .... 94 D4
Pyrah St. Dew WF13 .... 118 C1

Quail St. Keigh BD21 .... 35 D8
Quaker House. Leeds LS2 .... 60 A3 9
Quaker La. Brad BD5 .... 74 B3
Quakes La. Clec BD19 .... 116 D6
Quakers La. Yeadon LS19 .... 40 B5
Quarmby Croft. Hud HD3 .... 153 A7
Quarmby Fold. Hud HD3 .... 153 A6
Quarmby Rd. Hud HD3 .... 153 A6
Quarrie Dene Ct. Leeds LS7 .... 60 C6
Quarry Ave. Hud WF4 .... 127 A3
Quarry Bank Ct. Leeds LS5 ..... 58 F6
Quarry Ct. Honley HD7 .... 171 C2
Quarry Dene Pk. Leeds LS16 ... 59 C8
Quarry Dr. Kirkhe HD5 .... 155 C5
Quarry Farm Rd. Pool LS21 .... 24 B5
Quarry Gdns. Leeds LS17 .... 43 A4
Quarry Hill. Ack M T WF7 .... 164 A8
Quarry Hill. Hud HD5 .... 155 B4
Quarry Hill. Leeds LS9 .... 79 B8
Quarry Hill. Let H WF10 .... 124 A6
Quarry Hill. Sow Br HX6 .... 112 B3
Quarry Hill. Wake WF1 .... 142 E5
Quarry La. Ard LS17 .... 11 A6
Quarry La. Batley WF17 .... 96 E1
Quarry La. Kirkhe HD5 .... 155 C5
Quarry La. Morley LS27 .... 98 B8
Quarry Mount. Leeds LS6 .... 60 A4 7
Quarry Mount Prim Sch. Leeds . 60 A4
Quarry Mount St. Leeds LS6 ... 60 A4 6
Quarry Mount Terr. Leeds LS6 . 60 A4 8
Quarry Pl. Brad BD5 .... 74 B3
Quarry Pl. Leeds LS6 .... 60 A3
Quarry Rd. Dew WF13 .... 117 F2
Quarry Rd. Brig HD6 .... 115 B7
Quarry Rd. Clec BD19 .... 117 B7
Quarry Rd. Dew WF12 .... 139 D7
Quarry Rd. Fair WF11 .... 105 A4
Quarry Rd. Holmfi HD7 .... 189 A8
Quarry St. Brad BD5 .... 74 B3
Quarry St. Hud HD1 .... 153 E4
Quarry St. Keigh BD21 .... 35 A8
Quarry St. Leeds LS6 .... 60 A4
Quarry View. Ack M T WF7 ..... 163 E6
Quarry Villas. Hali HX3 .... 114 D5
Quarryfield Terr. E Ard WF3 ... 120 C8
Quaryfield Terr. E Ard WF3 .... 120 C8
Quay St. Hud HD1 .... 154 B6
Quebec St. Brad BD1 .... 74 E7
Quebec St. Elland HX5 .... 134 F7
Quebec St. Keigh BD21 .... 35 B6
Quebec St. Leeds LS1 .... 79 B8
Queen Elizabeth Dr. Gar LS25 . 82 E6
Queen Elizabeth Gr. Gar LS25 . 82 E6
Queen Elizabeth Gdns. Hud HD1 . 153 F6
Queen Elizabeth Grammar Sch.
Wake 142 C7
Queen Margaret's Cl. Gar LS25 . 82 E5
Queen Margaret's Dr. Byram
WF11 .... 126 D8
Queen Margarets Ave. Byram
WF11 .... 126 D8

Queen Margarets Cl. Byram WF11 126 D8
Queen St. Bail BD17 38 C1
Queen St. Bing BD16 36 F3
Queen St. Brad BD10 56 D7
Queen St. Castle WF10 124 E8
Queen St. Clec BD19 96 B2
Queen St. Dew WF12 139 E7
Queen St. Dew WF13 138 E6
Queen St. Dew WF12 140 B7
Queen St. E Ard WF3 120 D8
Queen St. Elland HX4 134 C6
Queen St. Haw BD22 51 C6
Queen St. Heb Br HX7 110 E8
Queen St. Hor WF4 141 A1
Queen St. Hud HD1 154 B6/15
Queen St. Leeds LS1 79 A8
Queen St. Leeds LS10 80 A2
Queen St. Liver FW16 117 C3
Queen St. Loft G WF1 121 B4
Queen St. Mir WF14 138 A4
Queen St. Morley LS27 98 A5
Queen St. Nor WF6 123 E3
Queen St. Ossett WF5 140 D5
Queen St. Pont WF8 146 C8
Queen St. Roth WF3 100 D3
Queen St. S. Hud HD1 154 B5
Queen St. Sil BD20 5 E1
Queen St. Skel HD8 175 A2
Queen St. Sow Br HX6 111 E3
Queen St. Stee BD20 17 C5
Queen St. Swil LS26 102 E6
Queen St. Tod OL14 108 B5
Queen St. Wake WF1 142 C6
Queen St. Wils BD15 53 C4
Queen's Ave. Leeds LS19 40 A4
Queen Tap Yd. Hud HD1 154 A6/24
Queen Terr. Pont WF8 146 C8
Queen Victoria Cres. Northo HX3 93 B3
Queen Victoria St. Leeds LS1 79 C8
Queen's Ave. Leeds 79 C5
Queen's Ave. Brad BD2 55 F3
Queen's Ave. Pont WF8 146 A7
Queen's Ave. Pont WF8 144 C4
Queen's Cres. Ossett WF5 140 D5
Queen's Dr. Cud S72 180 C1
Queen's Dr. Ilkley LS29 7 F3
Queen's Drive La. Ilkley LS29 7 F3
Queen's Gate. Hali HX3 113 B4
Queen's Gdns. Ilkley LS29 8 A1
Queen's Gdns. Ossett WF5 140 D5
Queen's Gr. Morley LS27 97 F3
Queen's Park Dr. Castle WF10 125 B8
Queen's Prom. Morley LS27 98 A4
Queen's Rd. B Spa LS23 30 C8
Queen's Rd. Bing BD16 36 E6
Queen's Rd. Brad BD1, BD2, BD8 55 E2
Queen's Rd. Brig HX3 93 A3
Queen's Rd. Cud S72 180 C1
Queen's Rd. Hali HX1 112 F7
Queen's Rd. Hud HD2 153 E8
Queen's Rd. Ilkley LS29 8 A3
Queen's Rd. Keigh BD21 35 B5
Queen's Rd. Leeds 59 E2
Queen's Rd. Pont WF8 146 A7
Queen's Rise. Brad BD2 55 F3
Queen's Road Dr Prim Sch
 (Annexe). Leeds 59 E3
Queen's Sq. Pont WF8 146 A7
Queen's Sq. Leeds LS6 59 B6
Queen's Wlk. Ossett WF5 140 F5
Queens Cl. Bing BD16 37 B2
Queens Cl. Leeds LS7 60 C8
Queens Cl. Clec BD19 96 B2
Queens Ct. Leeds LS5 42 B3
Queens Ct. Morley LS27 98 A4
Queens Dr Cl. Ossett WF5 140 F5
Queens Dr. Hali HX3 114 A4
Queens Dr. Roth WF3 100 D3
Queens Dr. Wake WF2 120 E1
Queens Gr. Keigh BD21 35 B5
Queens Mill. Dew WF13 138 E5
Queens Mill Ind Est. Hud 154 A4
Queens Mill Rd. Hud HD1, HD4 154 A4
Queens Par. Leeds LS14 62 B5
Queens Park Cl. Castle WF10 125 B8
Queens Pl. Otley LS21 23 A7
Queens Pl. Ship BD18 54 F8
Queens Rd. Bing BD16 125 B7
Queens Rd. W. Hud HD4 153 B4
Queens Rd. Wake WF1 142 D6
Queens Terr. Heb Br HX7 88 F3
Queens Terr. Otley LS21 23 B7
Queens's Ct. Leeds LS1 79 C7
Queensbury Golf Course. Queen 91 F5
Queensbury Sch. Queen 92 E8
Queensbury Sq. Queen BD13 72 E1
Queensgate. Brad BD1 72 E1
Queensgate. Hud HD1 154 B6
Queenshill App. Leeds LS17 43 C2
Queenshill Ave. Leeds LS17 43 C2
Queenshill Cl. Leeds LS17 43 C2
Queenshill Cres. Leeds LS17 43 C3
Queenshill Cres. Leeds LS17 43 D3
Queenshill Dr. Leeds LS17 43 C2
Queenshill Garth. Leeds LS17 43 C2
Queenshill Gdns. Leeds LS17 43 C2
Queenshill Rd. Leeds LS17 43 C2
Queenshill View. Leeds LS17 43 C3
Queenshill Way. Leeds LS17 43 D2
Queenshill Wlk. Leeds LS17 43 C2
Queensthorpe Ave. Leeds LS13 77 F8
Queensthorpe Cl. Leeds LS13 77 F8
Queensthorpe Rise. Leeds LS13 77 D8
Queensway. Bing BD16 37 B2
Queensway. Gar LS25 82 D7
Queensway. Guise LS20 40 A6
Queensway. Hali HX1 112 F8
Queensway. Keigh BD21 35 C7
Queensway. Kirkb HD8 174 A5
Queensway. Leeds LS15 81 C8
Queensway. Morley LS27 98 A4
Queensway. Pont WF6 144 A1
Queensway. Pont WF8 125 F3
Queensway. Roth LS26 100 D6
Queensway. Sid. S71 179 C4
Queensway. Yeadon LS19 40 A8
Queenswood Cl. Leeds LS6 59 B4

Queenswood Ct. Leeds LS6 59 B4
Queenswood Dr. Leeds LS6 59 A5
Queenswood Gdns. Leeds LS6 59 C4
Queenswood Hts. Leeds LS6 59 C5
Queenswood Mount. Leeds LS6 59 B5
Queenswood Rd. Leeds LS6 59 B5
Queenswood Rise. Leeds LS6 59 B4
Quincy Cl. Brad BD2 56 C4

Raby Ave. Leeds LS7 60 D3
Raby Pk. Weth LS22 13 D6
Raby St. Leeds LS7 60 D3
Raby Terr. Leeds LS7 60 D3
Racca Ave. Knot WF11 127 B4
Racca Gn. Knot WF11 127 A4
Race Moor La. Haw BD22 34 C3
Rachael St. Hor WF4 140 F1
Racton St. Slai HD7 151 F1
Radcliffe Ave. Brad BD2 56 A5
Radcliffe Gdns. Pudsey LS28 76 E6
Radcliffe Gr. Pudsey LS28 76 E6
Radcliffe La. Pudsey LS28 76 E6
Radcliffe Pl. Wake WF1 142 C6
Radcliffe Rd. Hud HD3 153 B4
Radcliffe La. Pudsey LS28 76 E7
Radcliffe St. Slai HD7 152 B2
Radcliffe Terr. Pudsey LS28 76 E6
Radfield Rd. Brad BD6 74 E1
Radford Park Ave. S Kirk WF9 182 B1
Radnor St. Brad WF3 75 D7
Radnor St. Hud HD3 76 E8
Radwell Dr. Brad BD5 74 E5
Rae Ct. Loft G WF3 121 E5
Raeburn Dr. Brad BD6 94 A7
Rafborn Ave. Hud HD3 134 E1
Rafborn Gr. Hud HD3 134 E1
Raglan Ave. Keigh BD22 34 F6
Raglan Cl. Castle WF10 104 E1
Raglan Ct. Hali HX1 113 A7
Raglan Dr. Leeds 60 A3
Raglan Rd. Leeds LS2, LS6 60 A3
Raglan St. Brad BD3 75 B7
Raglan St. Hali HX1 113 A7
Raglan St. Keigh BD22 34 F6
Raglan St. Tod OL14 108 B5
Raglan Terr. Brad BD3 75 B7
Raikes La. Batley WF17 96 F2
Raikes La. Birk BD4 95 F7
Raikes La. Birk BD4 76 B2
Raikes Cl. Hali HX3 203 B2
Raikes Lane CE Inf Sch. Batley 96 E2
Raikes Wood Dr. Birk BD4 95 F7
Railes Cl. Hali HX2 91 C1
Railgate. Whit OL13 106 C1
Railway Cl. Brad BD17 38 C3
Railway St. Dew WF13 139 A6
Railway St. Dew WF12 139 D7
Railway St. Hud HD1 154 A6
Railway St. Leeds LS9 79 F7
Railway St. Liver WF16 117 D2
Railway Cutts. S Elm WF9 183 A4
Railway Cutts. B Abby BD23 2 C7
Railway Cutts. Dun Br S30 199 F7
Railway Cotts. Mfield LS25 84 B6
Railway Rd. Brad BD10 56 B8
Railway St. Brig HD6 115 B1
Railway St. Clec BD19 116 D7
Railway View. Castle WF10 124 B7
Railway View. Leeds LS9 81 D7
Railway View. Loft G WF1 121 B4

Ramshead Heights. Leeds LS14 62 A5
Ramshead Hill. Leeds LS14 62 A6
Ramshead Pl. Leeds LS14 62 A6
Ramshead Rd. Leeds LS14 62 A6
Rand St. Brad BD7 74 C5
Rand St. Brad BD7 74 C5
Randall Pl. Brad BD9 55 B5
Randall West St. Brad BD7 74 D6
Randolph St. Brad BD3 75 E8
Randolph St. Hud HX3 113 C8
Randolph St. Leeds LS13 58 A2
Random Cl. Keigh BD22 34 F5
Ranelagh Ave. Brad BD10 56 E5
Range Bank. Hali HX3 92 C1
Range Ct. Hali HX3 113 C8
Range Gdns. Hali HX3 92 C1
Range La. Hali HX3 92 C1
Range La. Hali HX3 92 C1
Ransdale Dr. Brad BD5 74 D3
Ransdale Gr. Brad BD5 74 D3
Ransdale Rd. Brad BD5 74 D3
Ranter's Fold. Hor WF4 141 A1
Raper View. Aber LS25 64 E8
Rapes Highway. Densh OL3 167 A5
Rashcliffe Hill Rd. Hud HD1 153 F4
Rastrick Comm. Brig HD6 136 A8
Rastrick High Sch. Brig 114 F1
Raspberry Pl. S in Cra BD20 16 D4
Rathlin Rd. Batley WF12 118 F3
Rathmell Rd. Leeds LS15 80 E7
Rathmell St. Brad BD5 74 D1
Ratten Row Rd. Sow Br HX6 111 C1
Raven La. Ryhil S72 180 A6
Raven La. Leeds LS9 59 E4
Raven St. Bing BD16 36 F3
Raven St. Hali HX1 112 F7
Raven St. Hud HD1 153 D5
Raven St. Keigh BD22 35 B7
Raven Terr. Brad BD8 73 C7
Ravens Ave. Dew WF13 139 A6
Ravens Ave. Hud HD5 154 E5
Ravens Cres. Dew WF13 139 A6
Ravens Croft. Dew WF13 139 A6
Ravens Gr. Dew WF13 139 A6
Ravens Lodge Terr. Dew WF13 139 A6
Ravens Way. Holmfi HD7 189 E4
Ravens Wlk. Dew WF13 139 A6
Ravenscar Ave. Leeds LS8 61 A6
Ravenscar Mount. Leeds LS8 61 A6
Ravenscar Pl. Leeds LS8 61 A6
Ravenscar Terr. Leeds LS8 61 A6
Ravenscar Wlk. Leeds LS8 61 A6
Ravenscliffe Ave. Brad BD10 56 E4
Ravenscliffe Fst Sch. Brad 56 E4
Ravenscliffe Rd. Pudsey LS28 76 F6
Ravenscourt. Hud HD1 153 D5
Ravenscroft Rd. Dew WF13 139 A6
Ravensfield Rd. Dew WF13 139 A6
Ravenshall Sch. Dew 139 A4
Ravenshouse Rd. Dew WF13 138 F7
Ravensthorpe Rd. Dew WF13 139 A5
Ravensthorpe CE Jun Sch. Dew 138 E5
Ravensthorpe Inf Sch. Dew 138 E5
Ravensthorpe Sce Ctr & Spec
 Care Unit. Dew 138 E5
Ravensthorpe Sta. Dew 138 F4
Ravensthorpe. Elland HX4 134 C6
Ravenstone Gdns. S in Cra BD20 16 E5
Ravenstone. Glu BD20 16 E6
Ravenswharf. Dew WF13 139 A6
Ravensworth Cl. Leeds LS15 62 F3
Ravensworth Way. Leeds LS15 62 F3
Raw End Rd. Hali HX2 112 A8
Raw Hill. Brig HD6 115 A1
Raw La. Hali HX2 91 D6
Raw La. Heb Br HX7 89 D3
Raw Nook Rd. Hud HD3 152 E8
Rawden Hill. Arth LS21 26 D2
Rawdon Cl. Prim Sch. Yeadon 40 D4
Rawdon Dr. Yeadon LS19 40 D3
Rawdon Golf Course. Yeadon 40 B3
Rawdon Littlemoor Jun & Inf Sch.
 Yeadon 40 C4
Rawdon Rd. Haw BD22 51 F8
Rawdon Rd. Yeadon LS19 40 D3
Rawdon St. Keigh BD21 35 A6
Rawfield La. Fair WF11 105 C6
Rawfolds Ave. Batley WF17 96 F2
Rawfolds Way. Liver BD19 116 F6
Rawgate Ave. Castle WF10 124 C7
Rawling St. Keigh BD21 35 B5
Rawling Way. Leeds LS6 59 E1
Rawnsley Ho. Brad BD5 201 B2
Rawroyds. Elland HX4 134 C5
Rawson Ave. Brad BD3 75 C6
Rawson Ave. Hali HX3 113 B3
Rawson Jun & Inf Sch. Hali 92 B2
Rawson Mkt. Brad 74 F7
Rawson Pl. Brad BD1 74 F7
Rawson Pl. Sow Br HX6 112 B3
Rawson Rd. Brad BD1 74 E8
Rawson Sq. Brad BD1 56 C1
Rawson St. Hali HX1 203 E3
Rawson St. Keigh BD21 35 B5
Rawson St. N. Hali HX3 92 B2
Rawson St. Brad BD13 72 E6
Rawthorpe CE Inf Sch. Hud 154 F4
Rawthorpe Cres. Hud HD5 154 F5
Rawthorpe High Sch. Hud 154 F4
Rawthorpe Jun Sch. Hud 154 E5
Rawthorpe La. Hud HD5 154 F6
Rawthorpe Terr. Hud HD5 155 A5
Rawtonstall Bank. B Head HX7 88 A4
Ray Gate. Holmfi HD7 189 D8
Ray Gate. Hud HD3 152 D8
Ray Gate. Wad W.H7 97 C3
Ray St. Hud HD1 154 A7
Ray Winfield Ind Est. Ack M.T 163 E3
Raygill Cl. Leeds LS17 44 B5
Raylands Cl. Midd LS10 99 F6
Raylands Ct. Midd LS10 99 F6
Raylands Fold. Midd LS10 99 F6
Raylands La. Midd LS10 99 F6
Raylands Pl. Midd LS10 99 F6
Raylands Rd. Midd LS10 99 F6
Raylands Way. Midd LS10 99 F6
Rayleigh St. Brad BD4 75 A4
Raymond Dr. Brad BD5 74 E2
Raymond St. Brad BD5 74 D3
Raymond St. Brad BD5 74 E3
Raynbron Cres. Brad BD5 74 E3
Raynel App. Hors LS16 42 A3

Raynel Cl. Hors LS16 42 A4
Raynel Dr. Hors LS16 42 A4
Raynel Garth. Hors LS16 42 A3
Raynel Gdns. Hors LS16 42 A4
Raynel Gn. Hors LS16 42 A3
Raynel Mount. Hors LS16 42 A3
Raynel Way. Hors LS16 41 F4
Rayner Ave. Batley WF16 117 D6
Rayner Ave. Brad BD8 54 F1
Rayner Dr. Hud HD5 154 D6
Rayner Gr. Yeadon LS19 39 F7
Rayner Mount. Brad BD15 73 A8
Rayner Rd. Brig HD6 115 A4
Rayner St. Hor WF4 141 A1
Rayner Terr. Pudsey LS28 76 F8
Rayners Ave. Clec WF15 116 C4
Raynham Cres. Keigh BD21 34 F8
Raynor Cl. Hud HD3 153 C7
Raynville App. Leeds LS13 58 E3
Raynville Ave. Leeds LS13 58 E3
Raynville Cl. Leeds LS13 58 E2
Raynville Cres. Leeds LS12 58 E2
Raynville Ct. Leeds LS13 58 E3
Raynville Dene. Leeds LS12 58 E3
Raynville Dr. Leeds LS13 58 E3
Raynville Gn. Leeds LS13 58 E2
Raynville Grange. Leeds LS13 58 E3
Raynville Mount. Leeds LS13 58 E3
Raynville Pl. Leeds LS13 58 E3
Raynville Prim Sch. Leeds 58 E2
Raynville Rd. Leeds LS12, LS13 58 E2
Raynville Rise. Leeds LS13 58 E2
Raynville St. Leeds LS13 58 E3
Raynville Terr. Leeds LS13 58 E3
Raynville Wlk. Leeds LS13 58 E2
Raynville Way. Leeds LS12 58 D3
Raywood Cl. Yeadon LS19 40 A8
Reap Hirst Rd. Hud HD2 135 D2
Rebecca St. Brad BD1 74 D7
Recreation Ave. Leeds LS11 79 A4
Recreation Cres. Leeds LS11 78 F4
Recreation Gr. Leeds LS11 79 A4
Recreation La. Elland HX5 134 E6
Recreation Mount. Leeds LS11 79 A4
Recreation Pl. Leeds LS11 79 A4
Recreation Rd. Hud HX6 112 F2
Recreation Rd. Leeds LS11 78 F4
Recreation Row. Leeds LS11 78 F4
Recreation St. Leeds LS11 79 A4
Recreation Terr. Leeds LS11 79 A4
Recreation View. Leeds LS11 79 A4
Rectory Ave. Castle WF10 124 D8
Rectory Cl. Gar LS25 83 A7
Rectory Cl. Mars HD7 168 F4
Rectory Cl. Roy S71 179 D1
Rectory Dr. Batley WF17 97 A1
Rectory Garden. Emley HD8 175 D7
Rectory Garth. Hem WF9 181 D7
Rectory La. Emley HD8 175 D8
Rectory Row. Keigh BD21 35 B7
Rectory St. Castle WF10 124 D8
Rectory St. Feath WF7 145 C5
Rectory St. Hali HX1 113 B6
Rectory St. Hem WF9 181 C7
Rectory St. Nor WF4 140 F2
Red Beck Rd. Northo HX3 92 F1
Red Beck Vale. Ship BD18 55 A5
Red Brink La. Sow Br HX6 132 C6
Red Deer Park La. Floc WF4 156 E5
Red Doles Ind Est. Hud 136 C1
Red Doles La. Hud HD2 136 C1
Red Doles Rd. Hud HD1, HD2 136 C1
Red Hall App. Leeds LS14 45 A1
Red Hall Ave. Leeds LS17 44 F1
Red Hall Chase. Leeds LS14 45 A1
Red Hall Cl. Leeds LS14 45 A1
Red Hall Cres. Leeds LS14 45 A1
Red Hall Ct. Leeds LS14 44 F1
Red Hall Dr. Leeds LS14 45 A1
Red Hall Gdns. Leeds LS17 44 F1
Red Hall Garth. Leeds LS14 45 A1
Red Hall Gn. Leeds LS14 45 A1
Red Hall La. Leeds LS14, LS17 44 F1
Red Hall La. Wake WF1 121 A1
Red Hall View. Leeds LS14 45 A1
Red Hall Way. Leeds LS14 45 A1
Red Hall Wlk. Leeds LS14 45 A1
Red House La. Clec 96 A3
Red House Mus. Clec 96 A3
Red La. Crof WF4 143 E5
Red La. Mel HD7 170 C5
Red Lees Rd. Burn BB10 85 A8
Red Lion Yd. Wake WF2 142 C5
Red Lodge Cl. Leeds LS8 61 C4
Redbeck Cotts. Yeadon LS19 57 E8
Redburn Ave. Ship BD18 55 A5
Redburn Dr. Ship BD18 55 A5
Redburn Rd. Ship BD18 55 A5
Redcar La. Leeds LS14 62 A4
Redcar Rd. Brad BD10 56 C6
Redcar St. Hali HX1 202 C3
Redcliffe Ave. Keigh BD21 35 A7
Redcliffe Gr. Keigh BD21 35 A7
Redcliffe St. Keigh BD21 35 A7
Redcote La. Leeds LS4, LS12 59 C2
Redcote La. Leeds LS12 59 C2
Reddisher Rd. Mars HD7 168 E4
Reddisham Scot Gate. Tod OL14 129 C5
Redesdale Gdns. Hors LS16 42 B3
Redhall Cres. Leeds LS11 78 E1
Redhall Gdns. Leeds LS11 78 E1
Redhill Ave. Castle WF10 125 A6
Redhill Ave. E Ard WF3 119 E5
Redhill Cl. Castle WF10 125 A6
Redhill Cl. E Ard WF3 119 E5
Redhill Cres. E Ard WF3 119 E5
Redhill Dr. Castle WF10 125 A6
Redhill Dr. E Ard WF3 119 E5
Redhill Fst Sch. Castle 125 A6
Redhill Gdns. Castle WF10 125 A6
Redhill Mount. Castle WF10 125 A6
Redhill Rd. Castle WF10 125 A6
Redhill View. Thorn BD13 72 D6
Redland Cres. Wake WF10 125 E4
Redland Dr. Kirkb HD8 173 F7
Redlands Cl. Netherl WF4 157 F4
Redman Cl. Brad BD15 54 B1
Redmayne Gr. Knot WF11 126 E2
Redmire Ct. Leeds LS14 62 A4
Redmire Dr. Leeds LS14 62 A4
Redmire St. Brad BD3 75 B7
Redmire View. Leeds LS14 62 A4
Redshaw Rd. Leeds LS12 78 D8
Redthorn Way. Shaf S72 180 C2
Redvers Cl. Hors LS16 42 A1

Redwood Ave. E Ard WF3 120 A8
Redwood Ave. Roy S71 179 C3
Redwood Cl. Keigh BD21 35 E5
Redwood Cl. Yeadon LS19 39 F7
Redwood Dr. Hud HD2 136 E5
Redwood Gr. Hud HD5 154 D6
Redwood Gr. Yeadon LS19 39 F7
Redwood Way. Yeadon LS19 39 F7
Reed Rd. Leeds LS12 78 C6
Reed St. Bacup OL13 106 A3
Reedham Rd. Hud HD2 153 F8
Reedling Dr. Morley LS27 98 C3
Reedsdale Ave. Gild LS27 97 C7
Reedsdale Dr. Gild LS27 97 C7
Reedsdale Gdns. Gild LS27 97 C7
Rees Way. Brad BD3 74 F8
Reeva Ave. Brad BD6 135 E8
Reeva Ave. Brad BD6 93 F8
Reevy Cres. Brad BD6 93 F8
Reevy Dr. Brad BD6 94 A8
Reevy Hill Fst Sch. Brad 73 F1
Reevy Rd. Brad BD6 94 B8
Reevy Rd. Brad BD6 93 E8
Reevy St. Brad BD6 94 A8
Reevylands Dr. Brad BD6 94 A8
Reform St. Clec BD19 96 B1
Regal Cl. Brig HX6 132 C1
Regal Dr. Brig HX6 132 E1
Regency Ct. Brad BD8 74 B8
Regency Ct. Leeds LS6 59 E4
Regency Park Dr. Pudsey LS28 76 E5
Regency Park Rd. Pudsey LS28 76 E5
Regency Rd. Mir WF14 138 A4
Regency View. Brad BD3 56 A2
Regent Ave. Hors LS18 58 C8
Regent Cl. Brig HD6 135 E6
Regent Cl. Hors LS18 58 C8
Regent Cres. Horb WF4 141 A8
Regent Cres. S Hiex S72 180 E5
Regent Ct. Leeds LS7 58 C7/10
Regent Ct. Wake WF1 216 C1
Regent House. Elland HX5 134 F7
Regent Park Ave. Leeds LS6 59 F4
Regent Park Cross Ave. Leeds LS6 59 F4
Regent Park Terr. Leeds LS6 59 F4
Regent Pl. Brad BD10 39 A1
Regent Pl. Hali HX6 112 B5/17
Regent Pl. Hali HX6 89 A4
Regent Rd. Hors LS18 58 C8
Regent Rd. Hud HD1 153 E7
Regent St. E Ilin WF9 182 F3
Regent St. Brad BD10 39 A1
Regent St. Castle WF10 124 C7
Regent St. Feath WF7 145 C5
Regent St. Hali HX1 113 B6
Regent St. Heb Br HX7 89 A4
Regent St. Hem WF9 181 C7
Regent St. Hor WF4 140 F2
Regent St. Leeds LS2, LS7 60 C7
Regent St. Leeds LS10 80 A4
Regent St. Liver FW16 117 C3
Regent St. Nor WF6 123 C4
Regent St. Queen BD13 72 F1
Regent St. S Elm WF9 182 E3
Regent St. S Hiex S72 180 E5
Regent St. Tod OL14 108 A1
Regent Terr. Hali HX6 89 A4
Regent Terr. Leeds LS6 60 C7
Reginald Mount. Leeds LS7 60 D8
Reginald Pl. Leeds LS7 60 D8
Reginald Row. Leeds LS7 60 D8
Reginald St. Brad BD5 74 D4
Reginald St. Leeds LS7 60 D8
Reginald Terr. Leeds LS7 60 D8
Reginald View. Leeds LS7 60 D8
Rein Cl. Aber LS25 64 E8
Rein Gdns. E Ard WF3 119 C8
Rein Mews. E Ard WF3 119 C8
Rein Rd. Hors LS18 58 B8
Rein Rd. Morley LS27 98 B8
Rein St. Morley LS27 98 C1
Rein The. Leeds LS14 61 F6
Reins Ave. Bail BD17 38 B1
Reins Rd. Brig HD6 135 E6
Reins Terr. Horb WF4 141 A8
Reinwood Ave. Hud HD3 153 B7
Reinwood Inf Sch. Hud 153 A7
Reinwood Jun Sch. Hud 153 A7
Reinwood Rd. Hud HD3 153 B7
Rembrandt Ave. E Ard WF3 119 F8
Renald Pl. Hud HD1 154 A7
Renshaw St. Brad BD10 39 B1
Renton Ave. Guise LS20 39 E8
Renton Dr. Guise LS20 39 D8
Renton Lea. Guise LS20 39 E8
Reservoir Pl. Hali HX2 111 D7
Reservoir Rd. Haw BD22 51 C7
Reservoir Rd. Hud HD3 152 F7
Reservoir St. Morley LS27 98 B4
Reservoir View. Thorn BD13 72 D7
Rest Farm Cl. Hud HD2 136 C5
Retford Pl. Brad BD7 74 B4
Reuben St. Liver WF15 117 A4
Reva Cl. Bing BD16 37 B4
Reva Syke Rd. Brad BD14 73 B4
Revel Garth. Q Dale HD8 173 F2
Revie Rd. Leeds LS11 78 F3
Reydon Wlk. Brad BD6 73 E1
Reyhill Gr. Brad BD5 75 A2
Reyner House Mews. Brad BD5 74 D4
Reynolds Ave. Brad BD7 73 F5
Rhine St. Brad BD4 75 B5
Rhode's Hill La. Bram LS23 30 E7
Rhodes Ave. Batley WF16 117 C6
Rhodes Cres. Pont WF8 146 D6

Rhodes Gdns. Loft G WF3 ... 121 C6
Rhodes La. B Spa LS23 ... 30 C6
Rhodes Pl. Ship BD17 ... 55 B8
Rhodes St. Castle WF10 ... 124 B7
Rhodes St. Castle WF10 ... 124 C8
Rhodes St. Hali HX1 ... 113 B7
Rhodes St. Liver FW15 ... 117 C4
Rhodes St. Ship BD18 ... 55 A8
Rhodes Terr. Brad BD2 ... 56 B4
Rhodes Terr. Leeds LS12 ... 78 E6
Rhodesia Ave. Brad BD15 ... 73 C8
Rhodesia Ave. Hali HX3 ... 113 C3
Rhodesia St. Glu BD20 ... 16 D6
Rhodesway. Brad BD8 ... 73 D8
Rhodesway Sch. Brad ... 73 C8
Rhondda Pl. Hali HX1 ... 112 E6
Rhum Cl. Brad BD6 ... 93 F6
Rhyddings Ave. Ack M T WF7 ... 163 F5
Rhyddings Dr. Ack M T WF7 ... 163 F5
Rhyddings Gdns. Ilkley LS29 ... 8 D4
Rhyl St. Feath WF7 ... 145 D6
Rhylstone Mount. Brad BD7 ... 73 F6
Ribble St. Keigh BD21 ... 35 E8
Ribblesdale Ave. Gar LS25 ... 83 B6
Ribbleton Gr. Brad BD3 ... 75 A8
Ribstone St. Heb Br HX7 ... 89 E1
Riccall Nook. Brad BD10 ... 56 D6
Rice St. Hud HD1 ... 154 B5 1
Rich Gate. Holmfi HD7 ... 189 B2
Richard Dunn Sports Ctr The. Brad . 74 D1
Richard Oastler Sch. Leeds ... 59 D2
Richard Pl. Brig HD6 ... 115 A4 4
Richard St. Bacup OL13 ... 106 A7 3
Richard St. Brad BD3 ... 75 A7
Richard St. Brig HD6 ... 115 A4
Richard St. Wake WF1 ... 142 C7 3
Richard Thorpe Ave. Mir WF14 ... 138 B5
Richardshaw Dr. Pudsey LS28 ... 57 E1
Richardshaw La. Pudsey LS28 ... 76 E8
Richardshaw Rd. Pudsey LS28 ... 57 F1
Richardson Ave. Brad BD6 ... 94 C8
Richardson Cres. Leeds LS9 ... 80 C7
Richardson Rd. Leeds LS9 ... 80 C7
Richardson Sq. Hud HD1 ... 154 A6 5
Richardson St. Brad BD12 ... 95 A4
Richmond Ave. Hud HD2 ... 136 A2
Richmond Ave. Knot WF11 ... 126 B5
Richmond Ave. Leeds LS6 ... 59 E4
Richmond Ave. Sow Br HX6 ... 111 F3
Richmond Cl. Hali HX1 ... 113 C8
Richmond Cl. Leeds LS13 ... 58 A2
Richmond Cl. Morley LS27 ... 98 A3 3
Richmond Cl. Roth LS26 ... 100 F6
Richmond Ct. Crof WF4 ... 162 A8
Richmond Ct. Hud HD4 ... 152 F3
Richmond Ct. Leeds LS9 ... 79 F7 1
Richmond Ct. Pont WF8 ... 125 D1
Richmond Ct. Roth LS26 ... 100 F6
Richmond Flats. Hud HD1 ... 154 B7 7
Richmond Garth. Ossett WF5 ... 140 F4
Richmond Gdns. Pudsey LS28 ... 77 A7
Richmond Gdns. Sow Br HX6 ... 111 F3
Richmond Green St. Leeds LS9 ... 79 E7
Richmond Hill App. Leeds LS9 ... 79 E7
Richmond Hill Cl. Leeds LS9 ... 79 E7
Richmond Hill Prim Sch. Leeds ... 79 F6
Richmond House Sch. Leeds ... 59 C7
Richmond Lea. Mir WF14 ... 138 A6
Richmond Mews. Ship BD18 ... 54 F8
Richmond Mount. Leeds LS6 ... 59 E4
Richmond Pl. Ilkley LS29 ... 8 C3
Richmond Pl. Ship BD18 ... 54 F8 16
Richmond Rd. Batley WF16 ... 117 E6
Richmond Rd. Batley WF17 ... 118 D2
Richmond Rd. Brad BD7 ... 74 D6
Richmond Rd. Hali HX1 ... 113 B8
Richmond Rd. Leeds LS6 ... 59 E4
Richmond Rd. Pudsey LS28 ... 57 C2
Richmond Rd. Ship BD18 ... 54 F8 17
Richmond Rd. Upton WF9 ... 183 A7
Richmond Rd. Wake WF1 ... 142 B8
Richmond St. Castle WF10 ... 124 D7
Richmond St. Clec BD19 ... 116 D7
Richmond St. Hali HX1 ... 113 B8
Richmond St. Keigh BD21 ... 35 B8
Richmond St. Leeds LS9 ... 79 E7
Richmond St. Tod OL14 ... 108 C5 8
Richmond Terr. Otley LS21 ... 22 F7
Richmond Terr. Pudsey LS28 ... 77 A7
Richmond Way. Gar LS25 ... 82 F5
Richmondfield Ave. B in Elm LS15 ... 63 E6
Richmondfield Cl. B in Elm LS15 ... 63 E6
Richmondfield Cres. B in Elm LS15 .. 63 E6
Richmondfield Cross. B in Elm LS15 63 E6
Richmondfield Dr. B in Elm LS15 ... 63 E6
Richmondfield Garth. B in Elm LS15 63 E7
Richmondfield Gr. B in Elm LS15 ... 63 E6
Richmondfield La. B in Elm LS15 ... 63 E6
Richmondfield Mount. B in Elm LS15 63 E6
Richmondfield Way. B in Elm LS15 .. 63 E6
Rickard St. Leeds LS12 ... 78 F6
Ridding Gate. Otley LS21 ... 10 E1
Riddings Cl. Hem WF9 ... 181 D5
Riddings Cl. Hud HD2 ... 136 D3
Riddings Rd. Hud HD2 ... 136 D3
Riddings Rd. Ilkley LS29 ... 8 B4
Riddings Rise. Hud HD2 ... 136 E3
Riddlesden CE Fst Sch. Keigh ... 18 F2
Riddlesden Golf Course. Sil ... 18 C4
Riddlesden St. Keigh BD20 ... 18 F1
Rider Rd. Leeds LS6 ... 60 B4
Rider St. Leeds LS9 ... 79 E8
Ridge Ave. Neth WF4 ... 158 A7
Ridge Bank. Tod OL14 ... 108 B5
Ridge Cl. Guise LS20 ... 39 C8
Ridge Cl. Hud HD4 ... 154 A3
Ridge Cl. Skel HD8 ... 175 A1
Ridge Cres. Neth WF4 ... 158 A6
Ridge Gr. Leeds LS7 ... 60 A5
Ridge Hill. Brig HD6 ... 114 E1
Ridge La. Sil BD20 ... 5 C7
Ridge Lea. Brig HD6 ... 114 F1
Ridge Mount. Leeds LS6 ... 60 A4
Ridge Rd. Kippax LS25 ... 83 D2
Ridge Rd. Leeds LS7 ... 60 B4
Ridge Rd. Neth WF4 ... 158 A6
Ridge Rd. Tod OL14 ... 108 B5
Ridge St. Hud HD4 ... 154 A3
Ridge Terr. Leeds LS6 ... 59 E5
Ridge The. Coll LS22 ... 13 C3
Ridge View. Elland HX5 ... 135 C6
Ridge View Gdns. Brad BD10 ... 56 C7
Ridge View. Pudsey LS13 ... 77 C8
Ridge View Rd. Brig HD6 ... 115 A1
Ridge Way. Leeds LS8 ... 60 F6
Ridgedale Mount. Pont WF8 ... 125 D4
Ridgefield St. Castle WF10 ... 124 D7
Ridgemount Rd. Keigh BD20 ... 18 E2
Ridgestone Ave. Hem WF9 ... 181 E7
Ridgeway Cl. Hud HD5 ... 154 E7
Ridgeway Cl. Leeds LS8 ... 60 F6
Ridgeway Cres. Roy S71 ... 179 C1
Ridgeway Dr. Batley WF17 ... 97 A1
Ridgeway Gdns. Brig HD6 ... 114 E5
Ridgeway. Guise LS20 ... 39 B8
Ridgeway. Hud HD5 ... 154 E7
Ridgeway Mount. Keigh BD22 ... 34 F5
Ridgeway. Queen BD13 ... 92 F8
Ridgeway. Ship BD18 ... 55 E6
Ridgeway Sq. Knot WF11 ... 126 F3
Ridgeway The. Knot WF11 ... 126 F3
Ridgeways The. Slai HD7 ... 170 D8
Ridgewood Cl. Bail BD17 ... 38 E3
Ridgley View. Castle WF10 ... 125 D5
Riding Head La. Hali HX2 ... 90 E1
Riding Hill. Shelf HX3 ... 93 E6
Riding La. Hali HX2 ... 91 D3
Riding St. Batley WF17 ... 117 E6
Ridings Cl. Loft G WF3 ... 121 B6
Ridings Ct. Loft G WF3 ... 121 B6
Ridings Fields. Honley HD7 ... 172 C3
Ridings Gdns. Loft G WF3 ... 121 B6
Ridings La. Holmfi HD7 ... 189 C7
Ridings La. Hud HD7 ... 152 C4
Ridings La. Loft G WF3 ... 121 B6
Ridings Mews. Loft G WF3 ... 121 B6
Ridings Rd. Dew WF13 ... 139 D8
Ridings Sh Ctr. Wake ... 142 C6
Ridings Way. Loft G WF3 ... 121 B6
Ridingwood Rise. Clay W HD8 ... 175 E2
Ridleys Fold. Sil LS29 ... 6 F8
Rievaulx Ave. Brad BD8 ... 74 C8
Rievaulx Cl. B Spa LS23 ... 30 C7
Rifle Fields. Hud HD1 ... 153 F6
Rifle St. Hud HD1 ... 154 B5
Rigg La. Ack M T WF7, WF8 ... 164 E7
Rightox Rd. Honley HD7 ... 172 C3
Rigton App. Leeds LS9 ... 79 E8
Rigton Bank. Bard LS17 ... 28 D4
Rigton Cl. Leeds LS9 ... 79 F8
Rigton Dr. Leeds LS9 ... 79 E8
Rigton Gn. Bard LS17 ... 28 E4
Rigton Gn. Leeds LS9 ... 79 E8
Rigton Lawn. Leeds LS9 ... 79 E8
Rigton Mews. Leeds LS9 ... 79 E8
Rigton St. Brad BD5 ... 74 D3
Riley La. Hali HX2 ... 91 F8
Riley La. Kirkb HD8 ... 173 E6
Riley Pk. Kirkb HD8 ... 173 F6
Riley St. Hud HD4 ... 154 B4
Rillbank La. Leeds LS3 ... 59 F1
Rillbank St. Leeds LS3 ... 59 F2
Rillington Mead. Brad BD10 ... 56 D6
Rills Mead. Otley LS21 ... 23 A7
Rillside. Shep HD8 ... 173 F1
Rilston St. Brad BD7 ... 74 B6
Rimswell Holt. Brad BD10 ... 56 E6
Ring O'Bells Yd. Hor WF4 ... 141 A1 9
Ring Rd Adel. Hors LS16 ... 42 D2
Ring Rd Beeston. Leeds LS12 ... 78 C3
Ring Rd Beeston Pk. Leeds LS11 ... 98 F7
Ring Rd Beeston Pk. Midd LS10 ... 99 A6
Ring Rd Cross Gates. Leeds LS15 ... 62 C3
Ring Rd Farsley. Pudsey LS28 ... 57 C4
Ring Rd Halton. Leeds LS15 ... 62 C1
Ring Rd (Horsforth). Hors LS18 ... 58 E8
Ring Rd Low Wortley. Leeds LS12 ... 78 B4
Ring Rd Meanwood. Leeds LS17 ... 42 F2
Ring Rd Middleton. Midd LS10 ... 99 F6
Ring Rd Moortown. Leeds LS17 ... 43 D3
Ring Rd Seacroft. Leeds LS14 ... 62 B6
Ring Rd Shadwell. Leeds LS17 ... 44 D2
Ring Rd Weetwood. Leeds LS16 ... 42 C1
Ring Rd West Pk. Leeds LS16 ... 42 A1
Ring Road Bramley. Pudsey LS13 ... 77 C8
Ring Road Farnley. Leeds LS12 ... 77 E7
Ringby La. Hali HX3 ... 92 B4
Ringstone Gr. Bri S72 ... 181 B3
Ringway. Gar LS25 ... 82 D6
Ringwood Ave. Leeds LS14 ... 62 A8
Ringwood Cres. Leeds LS14 ... 62 A8
Ringwood Ct. Loft G WF1 ... 121 D5
Ringwood Dr. Leeds LS14 ... 62 A8
Ringwood Edge. Elland HX5 ... 134 D6
Ringwood Gdns. Leeds LS14 ... 62 A8
Ringwood Mount. Leeds LS14 ... 62 A8 1
Ringwood Rd. Brad BD5 ... 74 C3
Ringwood Way. Hem WF9 ... 181 F7
Rink Par. Batley WF17 ... 118 D3 5
Rink St. Batley WF17 ... 118 D3
Rink Terr. Batley WF17 ... 118 D3 4
Ripley Cl. Nor WF6 ... 123 D2
Ripley Ct. Nor WF6 ... 144 B8
Ripley Dr. Nor WF6 ... 123 D3
Ripley La. Guise LS20 ... 22 E2
Ripley Rd. Brad BD4 ... 74 F4
Ripley Rd. Liver WF15 ... 116 F4
Ripley St. Brad BD15 ... 54 A2
Ripley St. Brad BD5 ... 74 E4
Ripley St. Brig HX3 ... 115 A7
Ripley St. Keigh BD20 ... 18 F1
Ripley Terr. Hali HX2 ... 111 D7
Ripon Ave. Hud HD2 ... 136 B2
Ripon House. Elland HX5 ... 134 F7 5
Ripon Rd. Dew WF12 ... 118 F1
Ripon St. Hali HX1 ... 112 E6
Ripon Terr. Hali HX3 ... 92 B1
Rippenden Stones Cty Jun Mix & Inf Sch. Rip ... 132 C2
Ripponden Jun & Inf School. Rip ... 132 E5
Ripponden New Bank. Rip HX6 ... 132 E4
Ripponden Old Bank. Rip HX6 ... 132 E4
Ripponden Old La. Rip HX6 ... 132 B3
Rise La. Tod OL14 ... 108 A5
Rise The. Broth WF11 ... 126 C8
Rise The. Kippax LS25 ... 83 A1
Rise The. Leeds LS5 ... 59 A5
Rise The. Northo HX3 ... 93 A2
Rise The. Pont WF8 ... 146 E7
Risedale Ave. Batley WF17 ... 97 B2
Risedale Cl. Batley WF17 ... 97 B2
Rishworth Ave. Emley HD8 ... 175 D6
Rishworth Hall Cl. Rip HX6 ... 132 B1
Rishworth Mill La. Rip HX6 ... 150 D8
Rishworth New Rd. Rip HX6 ... 132 B1
Rishworth Rd. Dew WF12 ... 139 D8
Rishworth Rd. Rip HX4 ... 133 A4
Rishworth Sch. Rip ... 132 C2
Rishworth St. Dew WF13 ... 139 D8
Rishworth St. Keigh BD22 ... 34 F6
Rishworth St. Wake WF1 ... 142 C7
Rishworthian Ct. Elland HX3 ... 113 A1
Ristone Fold. Leeds LS12 ... 78 C5
Rivadale View. Ilkley LS29 ... 8 B5
Rivelin Rd. Castle WF10 ... 124 C6
River Holme View. Honley HD7 ... 172 C2
River Pk. Honley HD7 ... 171 F5
River St. Brig HD6 ... 115 C1
River St. Haw BD22 ... 51 D7 6
River St. Keigh BD21 ... 18 E1
River St. Tod OL14 ... 108 C5
River Valley View. D Dale HD8 ... 192 A6
River View. B Spa LS23 ... 30 F7
River View. Castle WF10 ... 124 B8
River View. Ilkley LS29 ... 8 E5
River Wlk. Bing BD16 ... 36 F3
Riverdale Ave. Loft G WF3 ... 121 F2
Riverdale Cl. Loft G WF3 ... 121 F2
Riverdale Cres. Loft G WF3 ... 121 F2
Riverdale Dr. Loft G WF3 ... 121 F2
Riverdale Gdns. B Spa LS23 ... 30 F7
Riverdale Rd. Loft G WF3 ... 121 F2
Riverdale Rd. Otley LS21 ... 23 A8
Riverdale. Weth LS22 ... 13 F4
Rivermead. Wake WF2 ... 142 D3
Riverside Ave. Otley LS21 ... 11 B2
Riverside Cl. Otley LS21 ... 11 B1
Riverside. Clay W HD8 ... 175 E3
Riverside Cotts. Sil BD20 ... 17 D8
Riverside Cres. Otley LS21 ... 11 B1
Riverside Ct. Leeds LS1 ... 79 C7
Riverside Dr. Otley LS21 ... 11 B2
Riverside Est. Ship BD17 ... 55 B8
Riverside Ind Est. Dew ... 139 C7
Riverside Jun Sch. Heb Br ... 89 A3
Riverside. Keigh BD21 ... 35 F7
Riverside Pk. Otley LS21 ... 11 B1
Riverside Villas. Wake WF2 ... 142 D2
Riverside Way. Dew WF13 ... 138 E4
Riverside Wlk. Ilkley LS29 ... 7 F5
Riverwood Dr. Hali HX3 ... 113 B2
Riviera Gdns. Leeds LS7 ... 60 C6
Rivock Ave. Keigh BD20 ... 17 F3
Rivock Ave. Stee BD20 ... 17 D6
Rivock Gr. Keigh BD20 ... 17 F3
RM Grylls Mid Sch. Clec ... 116 B4
Roach Grange Ave. Kippax LS25 ... 83 A3
Road End. Elland HX4 ... 134 C7 4
Road Sides. Pont WF8 ... 146 D6
Roaine Dr. Holmfi HD7 ... 189 B4
Roans Brae. Brad BD10 ... 56 E6
Robb Ave. Leeds LS11 ... 79 A1
Robb St. Leeds LS11 ... 79 A1
Robbins Terr. Feath WF7 ... 145 D6
Roberson Terr. Clec BD19 ... 117 A8
Robert Ct. Liver WF15 ... 116 F3
Robert La. Holmfi HD7 ... 189 C7
Robert St. Brad BD3 ... 75 A6
Robert St. Hali HX3 ... 92 A2
Robert St. Haw BD22 ... 51 F8
Robert St N. Hali HX3 ... 92 C2 2
Robert's St. Clec BD19 ... 116 C7
Roberts Ave. Leeds LS9 ... 61 B2
Roberts Ct. Leeds LS9 ... 61 B2
Roberts Pl. Brad BD1 ... 74 D7
Roberts Pl. Leeds LS9 ... 61 C1
Roberts St. Keigh BD22 ... 34 C6
Roberts St. Pudsey LS28 ... 57 E1
Roberts St. Roth LS26 ... 101 C6 4
Roberts Way. Wake WF2 ... 142 F1
Robertsgate. Roth WF3 ... 100 B1
Robertshaw Rd. Heb Br HX7 ... 88 F3
Robertson Ave. Brig HD6 ... 136 A8
Roberttown CE (C) Jun Mix Sch. Liver ... 116 E2
Roberttown La. Liver WF15 ... 116 F2
Robin Chase. Pudsey LS28 ... 76 F7
Robin Cl. Brad BD2 ... 56 C4
Robin Cl. Pont WF8 ... 125 D3
Robin Dr. Brad BD2 ... 56 C4
Robin Hill. Batley WF17 ... 118 A8
Robin Hood Ave. Roy S71 ... 179 D4
Robin Hood Cres. Wake WF2 ... 141 E4
Robin Hood Gr. Hud HD2 ... 136 C4
Robin Hood Hill. Hud HD4 ... 171 F7
Robin Hood Jun & Inf Sch. Roth ... 100 B2
Robin Hood Rd. Hud HD2 ... 136 C4
Robin Hood St. Castle WF10 ... 124 E7 1
Robin Hood Way. Brig HD6 ... 115 E2
Robin La. Batley WF13 ... 117 F3
Robin La. Batley WF13 ... 118 B2
Robin La. Hem WF9 ... 181 A5
Robin La. Pudsey LS28 ... 76 E7
Robin La. Roy S71 ... 179 D4
Robin Rocks. Honley HD7 ... 172 C2
Robin Royd Ave. Mir WF14 ... 138 A8
Robin Royd Croft. Mir WF14 ... 138 A8
Robin Royd Dr. Mir WF14 ... 138 A8
Robin Royd Garth. Mir WF14 ... 138 A8
Robin Royd Gr. Mir WF14 ... 138 A8
Robin Royd La. Mir WF14 ... 138 A8
Robin St. Brad BD5 ... 74 C4
Robin St. Hud HD1 ... 153 D5
Robin Wlk. Ship BD18 ... 55 D6
Robin's Gr. Roth LS26 ... 100 F5
Robinia Wlk. Wake WF2 ... 142 A8
Robins The. Bur in W LS29 ... 21 E8
Robinson Ct. Brad BD7 ... 73 F6
Robinson La. Honley HD7 ... 172 B3
Robinson La. Kippax LS25 ... 83 B1
Robinson St. Hud HD1 ... 154 C5
Robinson St. Kippax WF10 ... 103 B4
Robinson St. Pont WF8 ... 125 D1
Robinwood Ct. Leeds LS8 ... 44 A1
Robinwood Jun & Inf Sch. Tod ... 107 E8
Robson Cl. Pont WF8 ... 146 D6
Robson's Rd. Wake WF1 ... 142 B6
Rochdale Rd. Bacup OL13 ... 106 A1
Rochdale Rd. Elland HX4 ... 134 B7
Rochdale Rd. Hali HX2, HX6 ... 112 D5
Rochdale Rd. Rip HX6 ... 131 C2
Rochdale Rd. Slai HD7 ... 151 F4
Rochdale Rd. Sow Br HX6 ... 111 F1
Rochdale Rd. Tod OL14 ... 108 A3
Rochdale Rd. Tod OL14 ... 129 B6
Rocheford Cl. Leeds LS10 ... 79 F3
Rocheford Ct. Leeds LS10 ... 79 F3
Rocheford Gdns. Leeds LS10 ... 79 F3
Rocheford Gr. Leeds LS10 ... 79 F3
Rocheford Wlk. Leeds LS10 ... 79 F3
Rochester Cl. Bacup OL13 ... 106 A7 2
Rochester Ct. Hor WF4 ... 141 C3
Rochester Dr. Hor WF4 ... 141 C2
Rochester Gdns. Pudsey LS13 ... 57 F4
Rochester House. Brad BD15 ... 54 B1
Rochester Pl. Elland HX5 ... 134 F6 5
Rochester Rd. Batley WF17 ... 96 F3
Rochester St. Brad BD3 ... 75 C7
Rochester St. Ship BD18 ... 55 C6
Rochester Terr. Leeds LS6 ... 59 D4
Rochester Wynd. Leeds LS17 ... 44 A4
Rock Cliffe Mount. Hali HX2 ... 111 D7
Rock Edge. Liver WF15 ... 117 A5
Rock Fold. Hud HD7 ... 152 D4
Rock Hill. Castle WF10 ... 125 A6
Rock House Dr. Dew WF13 ... 118 C2
Rock La. Leeds LS13 ... 58 B4
Rock La. Slai HD7 ... 152 A3
Rock La. Wils BD13 ... 72 C8
Rock Lea. Queen BD13 ... 72 F1 5
Rock Nook. Litt OL15 ... 129 D1
Rock Rd. Hud HD3 ... 135 B2
Rock St. Brig HD6 ... 115 A3 15
Rock St. Hud HD3 ... 152 E7
Rock Terr. Castle WF10 ... 125 A6
Rock Terr. Hud HD3 ... 135 B1
Rock Terr. Leeds LS15 ... 80 F8 2
Rock Terr. Morley LS27 ... 98 B5
Rock Terr. Thorn BD13 ... 72 D6
Rock Terr. Tod OL14 ... 108 A2
Rock The. Hud HD7 ... 152 E1
Rock View. Elland HX4 ... 134 C4
Rock View. Mars HD7 ... 168 F3
Rockcliffe Ave. Bail BD17 ... 38 C1
Rockery Croft. Hors LS18 ... 41 C2
Rockery Rd. Hors LS18 ... 41 C2
Rockfield Terr. Yeadon LS19 ... 40 C7
Rockhill Cl. Batley WF17 ... 96 F1
Rockhill La. Brad BD4 ... 95 A7
Rockingham Cl. Leeds LS15 ... 62 F3
Rockingham La. Bad WF9 ... 164 E4
Rockingham Rd. Leeds LS15 ... 62 F3
Rockingham St. Hem WF9 ... 163 B3
Rockingham Way. Leeds LS15 ... 62 F3
Rockland Cres. Brad BD7 ... 73 E5
Rocklands Ave. Bail BD17 ... 38 C4 2
Rocklands Pl. Bail BD17 ... 38 C4 3
Rockley Cl. Hud HD5 ... 154 E4
Rockley Dr. Wake WF2 ... 160 B6
Rockley Grange Gdns. Gar LS25 ... 82 D5
Rockley St. Dew WF13 ... 139 D8
Rockliffe La. Bacup OL13 ... 106 A1
Rockliffe Rd. Bacup OL13 ... 106 A1
Rockmill Rd. Honley HD7 ... 172 C2
Rocks La. Hali HX2 ... 71 D1
Rocks Rd. Hali HX3 ... 113 A4
Rocks View. Hali HX2 ... 113 A4 3
Rockville Terr. Hali HX1 ... 113 A5 19
Rockville Terr. Yeadon LS19 ... 40 C6
Rockwell La. Brad BD10 ... 56 C6
Rockwood Cl. Hud HD2 ... 136 E6
Rockwood Cl. Mapp S75 ... 177 F1
Rockwood Cres. Crig WF4 ... 159 D6
Rockwood Cres. Pudsey LS28 ... 57 A3
Rockwood Gr. Pudsey LS28 ... 57 B3
Rockwood Rd. Pudsey LS28 ... 57 A2
Rockwood Rise. D Dale HD8 ... 192 A7
Roderick St. Leeds LS12 ... 78 B7
Rodger La. Wake WF2 ... 120 F2
Rodillian Sch. Roth ... 100 B1
Rodin Ave. Brad BD8 ... 73 D7
Rodley La. Emley HD8 ... 175 D7
Rodley La. Leeds LS13 ... 58 A4
Rodley La. Pudsey LS28, LS13 ... 57 D6
Rodley Prim Sch. Pudsey ... 57 F5
Rodney Yd. Wake WF1 ... 142 C6
Rods Mills La. Morley LS27 ... 98 B3
Rods View. Morley LS27 ... 98 B3 4
Roe House. Bail BD17 ... 38 E2
Roebuck La. Clift LS21 ... 10 F4
Roebuck Memorial Homes. Hud HD5 ... 154 F6
Roebuck St. Batley WF17 ... 96 F1
Roebuck Terr. Clift LS21 ... 10 F4
Roeburn Cl. Mapp S75 ... 178 A2
Roger Ct. Brad BD2 ... 56 B2
Roger Dr. Wake WF2 ... 142 D1
Roger Fold. Kippax LS25 ... 83 B1 1
Roger Gate. Heb Br HX7 ... 89 C1
Roger La. Hud HD4 ... 154 C3
Rogers Ct. Loft G WF3 ... 121 F6
Rogers Pl. Pudsey LS28 ... 76 F8
Rogerson Sq. Brig HD6 ... 115 A3
Roils Head Rd. Hali HX2 ... 112 C7
Rokeby Gdns. Brad BD10 ... 56 E6
Rokeby Gdns. Leeds LS6 ... 59 C5
Roker La. Pudsey LS28 ... 77 A5
Roman Ave. Hud HD3 ... 134 D1
Roman Ave. Leeds LS8 ... 44 A3
Roman Cl. Hud HD3 ... 134 D1
Roman Cres. Leeds LS8 ... 44 B2
Roman Dr. Hud HD3 ... 134 D1
Roman Dr. Leeds LS8 ... 44 B2
Roman Gdns. Leeds LS8 ... 44 A2
Roman Gr. Leeds LS8 ... 44 B2
Roman Mount. Leeds LS8 ... 44 B2
Roman Pl. Leeds LS8 ... 44 B2
Roman Rd. Batley WF17 ... 117 F8 5
Roman Rise. Pont WF8 ... 146 C5
Roman St. Dearne S63 ... 194 E1
Roman Terr. Leeds LS8 ... 44 A2
Roman View. Leeds LS8 ... 44 B2
Romanby Shaw. Brad BD10 ... 56 D6
Rombald's View. Ilkley LS29 ... 8 D5
Rombalds Ave. Leeds LS12 ... 78 C8
Rombalds Cres. Leeds LS12 ... 59 C1
Rombalds Ct. Men LS29 ... 21 F4
Rombalds Dr. Bing BD16 ... 37 B3
Rombalds Gr. Leeds LS12 ... 78 C8
Rombalds La. Ilkley LS29 ... 8 E3
Rombalds Pl. Leeds LS12 ... 59 C1 1
Rombalds St. Leeds LS12 ... 59 C1
Rombalds Terr. Leeds LS12 ... 78 C8
Rombalds View. Leeds LS12 ... 59 C1
Rombalds View. Otley LS21 ... 10 D2
Romford Ave. Morley LS27 ... 98 A3
Romford Ct. Brad BD6 ... 93 F6
Romney Mount. Pudsey LS28 ... 77 A5
Romsey Cl. Hud HD3 ... 134 F1
Romsey Gdns. Brad BD4 ... 75 E3
Romsey Mews. Brad BD4 ... 75 D3
Ronald Dr. Brad BD7 ... 74 A7
Ronaldsway Cl. Bacup OL13 ... 106 B1
Roods La. Holmfi HD7 ... 188 B3
Rook La. Brad BD4 ... 75 C2
Rook St. Bing BD16 ... 36 F3
Rook St. Hud HD1 ... 154 A7
Rook's Nest Jun & Inf Sch. Loft G . 121 C4
Rook's Nest Rd. Loft G WF1 ... 121 D4
Rookery La. Hali HX3 ... 113 D3
Rookery The. Sil LS29 ... 6 F8
Rookes Ave. Brad BD6 ... 94 C8
Rookes La. Brig HX3 ... 94 A1
Rookhill Dr. Pont WF8 ... 146 E7
Rookhill Mount. Pont WF8 ... 146 F7
Rookhill Rd. Pont WF8 ... 146 F7
Rooks Ave. Clec BD19 ... 116 C8
Rooks Cl. Brig BD12 ... 94 D1
Rookwith Par. Brad BD10 ... 56 E6
Rookwood Ave. Kippax LS25 ... 103 A8
Rookwood Ave. Leeds LS9 ... 80 D8
Rookwood Cres. Leeds LS9 ... 80 C8
Rookwood Gdns. Leeds LS9 ... 80 C8
Rookwood Gr. Leeds LS9 ... 80 C8
Rookwood Hill. Leeds LS9 ... 80 C8
Rookwood Mount. Leeds LS9 ... 80 C8
Rookwood Par. Leeds LS9 ... 80 C8
Rookwood Pl. Leeds LS9 ... 80 C8
Rookwood Rd. Leeds LS9 ... 80 C8
Rookwood Sq. Leeds LS9 ... 80 D8
Rookwood St. Leeds LS9 ... 80 C7
Rookwood Terr. Leeds LS9 ... 80 C8
Rookwood Vale. Leeds LS9 ... 80 C7
Rookwood View. Leeds LS9 ... 80 C8
Rookwood Wlk. Leeds LS9 ... 80 C8
Rooley Ave. Brad BD6 ... 74 E1
Rooley Banks. Sow Br HX6 ... 111 E3
Rooley Cl. Brad BD5 ... 74 E1
Rooley Cres. Brad BD6 ... 94 E8
Rooley Ct. Sow Br HX6 ... 111 D3
Rooley Hts. Sow Br HX6 ... 111 D3
Rooley La. Brad BD4, BD5 ... 75 B1
Rooley La. Sow Br HX6 ... 111 D3
Roomfield Ct. Tod OL14 ... 108 B5 11
Roomfield St. Tod OL14 ... 108 B5
Rooms Fold. Morley LS27 ... 98 A6
Rooms La. Gild LS27 ... 98 A8
Rooms La. Morley LS27 ... 98 A6
Rope Wlk. Hali HX2 ... 90 F7
Rope Wlk. Knot WF11 ... 127 A4
Roper Ave. Leeds LS8 ... 60 F8
Roper Gdns. Hali HX2 ... 91 D4
Roper Gn. Hali HX2 ... 91 D4
Roper Gr. Leeds LS8 ... 60 F8
Roper La. Hali HX2 ... 91 F8
Roper La. Queen BD13 ... 72 B2
Roper St. Keigh BD21 ... 35 B7 11
Ropergate End. Pont WF8 ... 146 C8 8
Ropergate. Pont WF8 ... 146 C8
Ropergate Service Rd. Pont WF8 .. 146 C8 7
Rosary RC Prim Sch. Leeds ... 60 C2
Roscoe St. Leeds LS7 ... 60 D2
Rose Ave. Hors LS18 ... 58 B7
Rose Ave. Hud HD4 ... 152 F3
Rose Ave. Hud HD3 ... 153 C6
Rose Ave. Upton WF9 ... 183 A7
Rose Bank. Bur in W LS29 ... 21 E8
Rose Bank Pl. Brad BD8 ... 73 E7
Rose Bank Rd. Tod OL14 ... 108 A5
Rose Cl. Upton WF9 ... 183 A7
Rose Croft. E Kes LS17 ... 28 C6
Rose Ct. Gar LS25 ... 83 A7
Rose Farm App. Nor WF6 ... 122 F4
Rose Farm Cl. Nor WF6 ... 122 F5
Rose Farm Fold. Nor WF6 ... 122 F5
Rose Farm Rise. Nor WF6 ... 122 F5
Rose Garth. Crof WF4 ... 143 F1
Rose Garth. Men LS29 ... 21 C7
Rose Gr. Heb Br HX7 ... 89 A4 7
Rose Gr. Heb Br HX7 ... 110 E8
Rose Gr. Roth LS26 ... 100 D6
Rose Gr. Upton WF9 ... 183 A7
Rose Grove La. Hali HX2 ... 112 A5
Rose Heath. Hali HX2 ... 91 D7
Rose Hill Dr. Hud HD2 ... 135 E1
Rose La. Hem WF7 ... 163 D4
Rose Meadows. Keigh BD22 ... 34 E5
Rose Mount. Brad BD2 ... 56 A3
Rose Mount. Hud HD2 ... 135 D1
Rose Mount Pl. Leeds LS12 ... 78 D6
Rose Pl. Hali HX2 ... 111 E5
Rose St. Brad BD8 ... 55 B1
Rose St. Hali HX1 ... 112 F6
Rose St. Haw BD22 ... 51 C6
Rose St. Hors LS18 ... 58 B8
Rose St. Keigh BD21 ... 35 F7
Rose St. Tod OL14 ... 108 B5
Rose Terr. Add LS29 ... 6 F8
Rose Terr. Hali HX2 ... 113 A4 2
Rose Terr. Hali HX1 ... 113 A7 3
Rose Terr. Hors LS18 ... 58 A7
Rose Terr. Hud HD1 ... 154 B8
Rose Terr. L Brad BD20 ... 4 C5
Rosebank Cres. Leeds LS3 ... 59 F2
Rosebank Gdns. Leeds LS3 ... 59 F1
Rosebank Rd. Leeds LS3 ... 59 F1
Rosebank Row. Leeds LS3 ... 59 F1
Rosebank St. Batley WF17 ... 118 B6
Roseberry St. Haw BD22 ... 34 D2
Roseberry St. Tod OL14 ... 86 C1
Rosebery Ave. Hali HX3 ... 113 D4
Rosebery Ave. Ship BD18 ... 55 C7
Rosebery Mount. Ship BD18 ... 55 D7
Rosebery Rd. Brad BD8 ... 55 C2
Rosebery St. Elland HX5 ... 134 F6
Rosebery St. Hud HD2 ... 135 F1
Rosebery St. Pudsey LS28 ... 76 C8
Rosebery Terr. Hali HX1 ... 113 A8
Rosebery Terr. Pudsey LS28 ... 57 F2 3
Rosebud Wlk. Leeds LS8 ... 60 E2
Rosecliffe Mount. Leeds LS13 ... 58 C2
Rosecliffe Terr. Leeds LS13 ... 58 C2
Rosedale Ave. Brad BD15 ... 53 F2
Rosedale Ave. Hud HD5 ... 154 D5 16
Rosedale Ave. Liver WF15 ... 116 D2
Rosedale Ave. Wake WF2 ... 160 E8
Rosedale Bank. Midd LS10 ... 79 D1
Rosedale Cl. Bail BD17 ... 38 A2
Rosedale Cl. Upton WF9 ... 183 B7
Rosedale Gdns. Midd LS10 ... 79 D1
Rosedale Gn. Midd LS10 ... 79 D1
Rosedale Rise. B Spa LS23 ... 30 C7
Rosedale. Roth LS26 ... 100 F6
Rosedale Wlk. Midd LS10 ... 79 D1
Rosegarth Ave. Holmfi HD7 ... 189 C7
Rosehill Ave. Hem WF9 ... 181 C6
Rosehill Cres. Brad BD12 ... 94 C4
Roselee Cl. Hali HX3 ... 113 E3
Rosemary Cl. Brig HD6 ... 115 A1
Rosemary La. Brig HD6 ... 115 A1
Rosemary La. Hali HX3 ... 113 E3
Rosemont Ave. Leeds LS13 ... 58 C2 7
Rosemont Ave. Pudsey LS28 ... 76 F8 3
Rosemont. Bramho LS16 ... 24 E3
Rosemont Dr. Pudsey LS28 ... 76 F8
Rosemont Gr. Leeds LS13 ... 58 C2 8
Rosemont La. Bail BD17 ... 38 D2 2
Rosemont Pl. Leeds LS13 ... 58 C2
Rosemont Rd. Leeds LS13 ... 58 C2
Rosemont St. Leeds LS13 ... 58 C2
Rosemont St. Pudsey LS28 ... 76 F8 4
Rosemont Terr. Leeds LS13 ... 58 C2

Ros - St C 243

Rosemont Terr. Pudsey LS28 76 F8
Rosemont View. Leeds LS13 58 C2
Rosemont Wlk. Leeds LS13 58 C2 6
Rosemount Ave. Elland HX5 135 A6
Rosemount. Bacup OL13 106 A4
Rosemount Cl. Keigh BD21 35 B7 2
Rosemount Terr. Elland HX5 135 A6
Rosemount Wks. Elland 135 A5
Rosemount Wlk. Keigh BD21 35 B7 1
Rosendale Cl. Bacup OL13 106 B3 3
Rosendale Cres. Bacup OL13 106 B3
Roseneath Pl. Leeds LS12 78 D6
Roseneath St. Leeds LS12 78 D6
Roseneath Terr. Leeds LS12 78 D6
Rosetta Dr. Brad BD8 73 F8
Roseville Rd. Leeds LS8 60 E2
Roseville St. Leeds LS8 60 E2
Roseville Terr. Dew WF12 139 F8
Roseville Terr. Leeds LS15 62 D3 4
Roseville Way. Leeds LS8 60 E2
Rosewood Ave. Keigh BD20 18 F1
Rosewood Ave. Kippax LS25 82 F3
Rosewood Ct. Roth LS26 100 F7
Rosewood Gr. Brad BD4 75 D5
Rosewood Sq. S in Cra BD20 16 D4
Rosgill Dr. Leeds LS14 62 A5
Rosgill Wlk. Leeds LS14 61 F5
Rosley Mount. Brad BD6 93 F6
Roslyn Ave. Hud HD4 171 C7
Roslyn Pl. Brad BD7 74 B6
Ross Gr. Leeds LS13 58 B4
Ross Terr. Leeds LS13 58 A4
Rossall Gr. Leeds LS8 60 F4
Rossall Rd. Leeds LS8 60 F4
Rosse St. Brad BD8 74 A8
Rosse St. Ship BD18 55 B8
Rossefield App. Leeds LS13 58 D2
Rossefield Ave. Hud HD2 135 E1
Rossefield Ave. Leeds LS13 58 D2
Rossefield Chase. Leeds LS13 58 D2
Rossefield Cl. Leeds LS13 58 D2 3
Rossefield Dr. Leeds LS13 58 D2
Rossefield Gn. Leeds LS13 58 D2
Rossefield Gr. Leeds LS13 58 D2
Rossefield Lawn. Leeds LS13 58 D2
Rossefield Par. Leeds LS13 58 D2
Rossefield Pk. Ship BD9 55 B4
Rossefield Pl. Leeds LS13 58 D2
Rossefield Rd. Ship BD9 55 A4
Rossefield Sch. Ship 55 A4
Rossefield Terr. Leeds LS13 58 D2
Rossefield View. Leeds LS13 58 D2
Rossefield Way. Leeds LS13 58 C2
Rossefield Wlk. Leeds LS13 58 D2 5
Rossendale Pl. Ship BD18 55 A7
Rossington Gr. Leeds LS8 60 E4 2
Rossington Pl. Leeds LS8 60 E4 3
Rossington Rd. Leeds LS8 61 A5
Rossington St. Leeds LS2 79 B8
Rossiter Dr. Knot WF11 126 D3
Rosslyn Ave. Ack M T WF7 163 F5
Rosslyn Cl. Ack M T WF7 163 F5
Rosslyn Cl. Ack M T WF7 163 F5
Rosslyn Ct. Dew WF12 139 F7
Rosslyn Gr. Ack M T WF7 163 F5
Rosslyn Gr. Haw BD22 51 C6
Rossmore Dr. Brad BD15 54 C1
Rotcher La. Slai HD7 169 E8
Rotcher Rd. Holmfi HD7 189 A5
Rotcher. Slai HD7 169 E8
Rothbury Gdns. Hors LS16 42 B3
Rothesay Terr. Brad BD7 74 C6
Rothwell CE Sch. Roth 100 E6
Rothwell Dr. Hali HX1 113 B5
Rothwell Inf Sch. Roth 100 E4
Rothwell La. Roth LS26 101 B5
Rothwell Mount. Hali HX1 113 B5
Rothwell Rd. Hali HX1 113 B5
Rothwell Sports Ctr. Roth 101 C4
Rothwell St. Hud HD5 154 E6
Rothwell West Prim Sch. Roth 100 E4
Rough Hall La. Hali HX2 90 F5
Rough Side La. Tod OL14 108 C3
Round Close Rd. Holme HD7 199 B6
Round Hill Cl. Brad BD14 73 B2
Round Hill Cl. Hali HX2 91 F6
Round Hill. Hali HX2 91 F6
Round Hill La. Kirkhe HD5 137 B3
Round Ings Rd. Slai HD3 152 A6
Round St. Brad BD5 74 F3
Round St. Wake WF1 142 E4
Round Thorn Pl. Brad BD8 74 A8
Round Wood Ave. Hud HD5 155 A6
Roundell Ave. Brad BD4 95 B8
Roundhay Ave. Leeds LS8 60 F5
Roundhay CE Prim Sch. Leeds 61 D7
Roundhay Cres. Leeds LS8 60 F5
Roundhay Gdns. Leeds LS8 60 F5
Roundhay Gr. Leeds LS8 60 F5
Roundhay Hall Hospl. Leeds 61 A7
Roundhay High Sch. Leeds 61 A7
Roundhay Mount. Leeds LS8 60 F5
Roundhay Park La. Leeds LS17 44 B4
Roundhay Park. Leeds 61 B8
Roundhay Pl. Leeds LS8 60 F5
Roundhay Rd. Leeds LS7, LS8 60 F3
Roundhay Sch. Leeds 61 A7
Roundhay St John's CE Prim Sch.
Leeds 61 C6
Roundhay View. Leeds LS8 60 F5
Roundhead Fold. Brad BD10 56 E8
Roundhill Ave. Ship BD16 54 B7
Roundhill Mount. Ship BD16 54 B7
Roundhill Pl. Brad BD1 74 D7 6
Roundhill Rd. Castle WF10 124 D7
Roundhill St. Brad BD5 74 D4
Roundthorn Sch. Brad 74 E3
Roundway. Honley HD7 171 F4
Roundway. Honley HD7 172 A3
Roundway The. Morley LS27 97 F4
Roundwell Rd. Clec WF15 116 C5
Roundwood Ave. Bail BD17 38 F3
Roundwood Ave. Brad BD10 56 E4
Roundwood Cres. Wake WF2 141 C5
Roundwood Glen. Brad BD10 56 E6
Roundwood Hill Sch. Wake 141 D3
Roundwood Ind Est. Wake 141 B5
Roundwood Rd. Bail BD17 38 E4
Roundwood Rd. Ossett WF5 141 A4
Roundwood Rise. Wake WF2 141 D4
Roundwood. Ship BD18 54 F7
Roundwood View. Brad BD10 56 E6
Rouse Fold. Brad BD4 74 F5
Rouse Mill La. Batley WF17 118 D4
Rouse St. Liver WF15 117 A4 7
Row Gate. Shep HD8 190 D6
Row La. Mars HD7 169 C8
Row La. Sow Br HX6 111 D3
Row. Mars HD7 169 C8
Row St. Hud HD4 153 E4
Rowan Ave. Brad BD3 75 E7
Rowan Ave. Hud HD4 171 D6
Rowan Ave. Nor WF6 144 A7
Rowan Avenue Mews. Hud HD4 171 D6
Rowan Cl. Batley WF17 97 A2
Rowan Cl. Knot WF11 126 E2
Rowan Ct. Brad BD2 56 C1
Rowan Ct. Wake WF2 141 F8
Rowan Ct. Yeadon LS19 40 B5
Rowan Dr. Brig HD6 115 C3
Rowan Garth. Glu BD20 16 D6
Rowan Gn. Pont WF8 125 F1
Rowan Pl. Gar LS25 83 B6
Rowan St. Keigh BD20 18 A2
Rowanberry Cl. Brad BD2 56 B4
Rowans The. Bail BD17 37 F3
Rowans The. Bramho LS16 24 F2
Rowans The. Pudsey LS13 57 F3
Rowans The. Weth LS22 14 A6
Rowantree Ave. Bail BD17 38 B4
Rowantree Dr. Brad BD10 56 C6
Rowe Cl. S Elm WF9 183 A4
Rowgate. D Dale HD8 191 B6
Rowland La. Wad M HX7 89 C4
Rowland Pl. Leeds LS11 79 B3
Rowland Rd. Leeds LS11 79 B3
Rowland St. Roy S71 179 D4
Rowland Terr. Leeds LS11 79 C3 7
Rowlands Ave. Hud HD5 154 F6
Rowlands Ave. Upton WF9 183 A7
Rowlestone Rise. Brad BD10 56 E6
Rowley Dr. Ilkley LS29 8 F3
Rowley Dr. Lepton HD8 155 D3
Rowley La. Lepton HD8 155 E2
Rowley La. S Elm WF9 183 A2
Rowley Lea. Brad BD10 56 E5
Rowsley St. Keigh BD21 35 D7 1
Rowton Thorpe. Brad BD10 56 E6
Roxburgh Gr. Brad BD15 73 B8
Roxby Cl. Leeds LS9 60 E1
Roxby St. Brad BD5 74 D3
Roxholme Ave. Leeds LS7 60 E5
Roxholme Gr. Leeds LS7 60 E5
Roxholme Pl. Leeds LS7 60 E5
Roxholme Rd. Leeds LS7 60 E5
Roxholme Terr. Leeds LS7 60 E5
Roy Rd. Brad BD6 73 D1
Roy St. Tod OL14 86 A1
Royal Armouries Mus The. Leeds 79 D6
Royal Cl. Leeds LS10 79 D2
Royal Ct. Leeds LS10 79 D2
Royal Ct. Pont WF8 146 B5
Royal Dr. Leeds LS10 79 D2
Royal Gdns. Leeds LS10 79 D2
Royal Gr. Leeds LS10 79 D2
Royal Halifax Infmy. Hali 113 B5
Royal Park Ave. Leeds LS6 59 F3
Royal Park Gr. Leeds LS6 59 F3
Royal Park Mount. Leeds LS6 59 F3
Royal Park Prim Sch. Leeds 59 E2
Royal Park Rd. Leeds LS6 59 F2
Royal Park Terr. Leeds LS6 59 F3
Royal Park View. Leeds LS6 59 F3
Royal Pl. Leeds LS10 79 D2
Royal Terr. B Spa LS23 30 E8
Royal Terr. Hud HD3 153 A5
Royd Ave. Batley WF16 117 D6
Royd Ave. Bing BD16 37 C3
Royd Ave. Holmfi HD7 189 E6
Royd Ave. Hud HD3 135 A3
Royd Ave. Hud HD5 153 A5
Royd Ave. Mapp S75 178 B1
Royd Cl. Glu BD20 16 D6
Royd Cres. Hali HX1 112 F8 2
Royd Cres. Heb Br HX7 89 F1
Royd Croft. Hud HD3 153 B6
Royd Edge Sch. Mel 170 E1
Royd Head Farm. Ossett WF5 140 C3
Royd House Gr. Keigh BD21 35 E3
Royd House La. Slai HD7 152 D1
Royd House Rd. Keigh BD21 35 E5
Royd House Way. Keigh BD21 35 E5
Royd House Wlk. Keigh BD21 35 E5
Royd Ings Ave. Keigh BD21 18 D1
Royd La. Hali HX3 92 A3
Royd La. Holmfi HD7 188 E2
Royd La. Keigh BD20 18 B1
Royd La. Rip HX6 132 D4
Royd La. Tod OL14 108 B6
Royd Mill Bsns Pk. Brig 115 C2
Royd Moor La. Bad WF9 164 C1
Royd Mount. Hali HX3 92 C2 4
Royd Mount. Holmfi HD7 189 A5
Royd Mount Mid Sch. Thorn 72 C6
Royd Pl. Hali HX3 92 C2
Royd Rd. Mel HD7 187 E8
Royd Rd. Tod OL14 108 B7
Royd Sq. Heb Br HX7 89 A3 2
Royd St. Brad BD12 94 C4 3
Royd St. Hud HD3 153 A5
Royd St. Keigh BD20 18 B2
Royd St. Slai HD7 151 F1
Royd St. Thorn BD13 72 C6
Royd St. Tod OL14 108 A6
Royd St. Wils BD15 53 C5
Royd Terr. Heb Br HX7 89 A3
Royd Terr. Hud HD4 171 E8
Royd View. Heb Br HX7 89 E1
Royd Way. Keigh BD21 18 C1
Royd Wood. Clec BD19 116 D6
Royd Wood. Oxen BD22 51 D4
Roydfield St. Hud HD2 136 B2
Roydlands St. Brig HX3 114 D7
Roydon Gr. Brad BD9 55 A2
Royds Ave. Birk BD11 96 B5
Royds Ave. Brig HD6 115 B8
Royds Ave. Castle WF10 125 C8
Royds Ave. Holmfi HD7 189 D6
Royds Ave. Hud HD3 153 C5
Royds Ave. Ossett WF5 140 C8
Royds Ave. Slai HD7 152 D6
Royds Cl. Holmfi HD7 189 D6
Royds Cl. Leeds LS12 78 C4
Royds Cres. Brig HD6 115 B7
Royds Dr. Holmfi HD7 189 D6
Royds Farm Rd. Leeds LS12 78 C3
Royds Gr. Loft G WF1 121 C5
Royds Hall Ave. Brad BD6 94 C8
Royds Hall La. Brad BD6 94 A7
Royds Hall La. Brad BD12, BD6 94 B5
Royds Hall Rd. Leeds LS12 78 C4
Royds Hall Sch. Hud 153 C6
Royds La. Leeds LS12 78 C3
Royds La. Leeds LS12 78 C4
Royds La. Roth LS26 101 A3
Royds Park Cres. Brad BD12 94 D4
Royds Pk. D Dale HD8 192 A6
Royds Sch. Roth 101 B2
Royds St. Mars HD7 168 F3
Royds The. Clay W HD8 176 A3
Royds The. Holmfi HD7 189 A5
Royds View. Slai HD7 152 D1
Roydscliffe Dr. Brad BD9 54 F4
Roydscliffe Rd. Brad BD9 54 F4
Roydsdale Way. Brad BD4 95 A6
Roydstone Rd. Brad BD3 75 D8
Roydstone Terr. Brad BD3 75 D8
Roydwood Terr (Back). Cull BD13 52 D6
Roydwood Terr. Cull BD13 52 D6
Royle Fold. Batley WF16 117 D4
Royles Cl. S Kirk WF9 182 C2
Royles Head La. Hud HD3 152 E6
Royston CE Sch. Roy 179 C3
Royston Cl. E Ard WF3 120 D6
Royston Comprehensive Sch. Roy 179 C4
Royston Hill. E Ard WF3 120 D6
Royston Inf Sch. Roy 179 C3
Royston La. Roy S71 179 C2
Royston Medstead Jun & Inf Sch.
Roy 179 B3
Royston Rd. Cud S72 180 B1
Royston Summer Fields Jun & Inf Sch.
Roy 179 A4
Ruby St. Batley WF17 118 A7
Ruby St. Keigh BD22 35 A4 13
Ruby St. Leeds LS9 60 E1
Rud La. Heb Br HX7 110 A3
Rudby Haven. Brad BD10 56 E5
Rudd St. Brad BD7 74 A4 11
Rudding Ave. Brad BD15 54 A1
Rudding Cres. Brad BD15 54 A1
Rudding Dr. Batley WF17 117 F6
Rudding St. Hud HD4 153 D4
Rudgate HM Prison. Th Arch 15 A2
Rudgate Pk. Th Arch LS23 15 A3
Rudgate. Tad LS24 31 D4
Rudgate. Th Arch LS23, LS24 15 D5
Ruffield Side. Brad BD12 94 C5
Rufford Ave. Yeadon LS19 40 C6
Rufford Bank. Yeadon LS19 40 C6
Rufford Cl. Yeadon LS19 40 C6
Rufford Cres. Yeadon LS19 40 C6
Rufford Dr. Yeadon LS19 40 C6
Rufford Pl. Hali HX3 113 B4 2
Rufford Rd. Elland HX5 134 F6
Rufford Rd. Hali HX3 113 B4
Rufford Rd. Hud HD3 152 F5
Rufford Ridge. Yeadon LS19 40 C6
Rufford Rise. Yeadon LS19 40 B6
Rufford St. Brad BD3 75 C7
Rufford St. Wake WF2 141 F6
Rufford Villas. Hali HX3 113 B4 4
Rufus St. Brad BD5 74 B3
Rufus St. Keigh BD21 35 C8 6
Rugby Ave. Hali HX3 91 F3
Rugby Dr. Hali HX3 91 F3
Rugby Gdns. Hali HX3 91 F3
Rugby Mount. Hali HX3 91 F3
Rugby Pl. Brad BD7 74 B6
Rugby Terr. Hali HX3 91 F3
Rumble Rd. Dew WF12 118 F1
Rumbold Rd. Hud HD3 153 D7
Rumple Croft. Otley LS21 10 E2
Runnymeade Ct. Brad BD10 56 B7
Runswick Ave. Leeds LS11 78 F5 3
Runswick Gr. Brad BD5 74 D1
Runswick Pl. Leeds LS11 79 A5
Runswick St. Brad BD5 74 D1
Runswick St. Leeds LS11 79 A5
Runswick Terr. Brad BD5 74 D1
Runswick Terr. Leeds LS11 79 A5
Runtlings La. Ossett WF5 140 C4
Runtlings. Ossett WF5 140 C5
Runtlings The. Ossett WF5 140 B5
Rupert Rd. Ilkley LS29 8 A3
Rupert St. Haw BD22 51 F8
Rupert St. Keigh BD21 35 C8 5
Rushcroft Terr. Bail BD17 38 C3
Rushdene Ct. Brad BD12 94 C1
Rushfield Vale. Lepton HD8 155 C4
Rushmoor Rd. Brad BD4 75 D2
Rusholme Dr. Pudsey LS28 57 C3
Rushton Ave. Brad BD3 75 E8
Rushton Hill Cl. Hali HX2 91 C1
Rushton Rd. Brad BD3 75 E8
Rushton St. Hali HX1 112 F8 6
Rushton St. Pudsey LS28 57 B6
Rushton Terr. Brad BD3 75 E7
Rushworth St. Hali HX3 92 A1 16
Ruskin Ave. Brad BD9 54 D3
Ruskin Ave. Wake WF1 121 A3
Ruskin Cl. Castle WF10 125 B8
Ruskin Cres. Guise LS20 39 F8
Ruskin Ct. Wake WF2 120 F2
Ruskin Dr. Castle WF10 125 B8
Ruskin Gr. Hud HD2 136 D3
Ruskin Pl. Castle WF10 125 B8
Ruskin St. Pudsey LS28 57 C1
Ruskin Terr. Hali HX3 92 A1 24
Russel Ct. Bard LS17 28 D3
Russell Ave. Crig WF4 159 F3
Russell Ave. Queen BD13 92 E8
Russell Cl. Batley WF16 117 E3
Russell Cl. Batley WF17 118 C5
Russell Gr. Birk BD11 96 B5
Russell Hall Fst Sch. Queen 72 E1
Russell Hall La. Queen BD13 72 E1 15
Russell Rd. Queen BD13 92 D8
Russell St. Brad BD5 74 D5
Russell St. Dew WF13 118 A1
Russell St. Hali HX1 113 C7 21
Russell St. Keigh BD21 35 B7
Russell St. Leeds LS1 79 B8
Russell St. Queen BD13 72 E1
Russell St. Ship BD18 55 C5
Russell St. Tod OL14 108 C5
Russell St. Wake WF1 142 C4
Russets The. Wake WF2 160 E6
Russett Gr. Hud HD4 154 C3
Rustic Ave. Hali HX3 114 A4
Ruswarp Cres. Brad BD10 56 D6
Ruth St. Haw BD22 51 E8 15
Ruth St. Hud HD4 154 A2
Ruthven View. Leeds LS8 61 A3
Rutland Ave. Pont WF8 146 D5
Rutland Ave. Wake WF2 142 C2
Rutland Cl. Kippax LS25 83 A2
Rutland Cl. Roth LS26 101 D6 5
Rutland Ct. Pudsey LS28 76 E8 3
Rutland Dr. Crof WF4 143 C2
Rutland Dr. Kippax LS25 83 B2
Rutland House. Bing BD16 37 A3 5
Rutland Ind Est. Wake 142 D4
Rutland Mount. Leeds LS3 78 F8 2
Rutland Rd. Batley WF17 118 D6
Rutland Rd. Floc WF4 157 C3
Rutland Rd. Hud HD3 153 A5
Rutland St. Brad BD4 75 A5
Rutland St. Keigh BD21 35 B5 7
Rutland St. Leeds LS3 79 A8
Rutland Terr. Leeds S18 78 F8
Rutland Wlk. Dew WF13 139 B8 7
Ryan Gr. Keigh BD22 34 D8
Ryan Mid Sch. Brad 74 F3
Ryan St. Brad BD5 74 D3
Ryburn Golf Course. Sow Br 112 C2
Ryburn La. Rip HX6 132 E5
Ryburn Pl. Wake WF2 142 B5
Ryburn Rd. Hud HD3 153 B7
Ryburn St. Sow Br HX6 112 B3
Ryburn Terr. Hali HX1 112 F7 1
Ryburn Terr. Rip HX6 132 C1
Ryburn Valley High Sch. Sow Br 111 E3
Ryburn View. Rip HX6 132 C3
Rycroft Ave. Pudsey LS13 58 B1
Rycroft Ave. Ship BD16 54 A6
Rycroft Cl. Pudsey LS13 58 B1
Rycroft Ct. Pudsey LS13 58 B1 2
Rycroft Dr. Pudsey LS13 58 B1
Rycroft Gn. Pudsey LS13 58 B1 1
Rycroft Pl. Pudsey LS13 58 B1 3
Rycroft Sq. Pudsey LS13 58 B1
Rycroft St. Ship BD18 55 D5
Rycroft Towers. Pudsey LS13 58 A1
Rydal Ave. Bail BD17 37 E1
Rydal Ave. Gar LS25 82 F6
Rydal Ave. Ship BD9 55 C4
Rydal Cres. Morley LS27 98 D5
Rydal Cres. Wake WF2 141 E7
Rydal Dr. Hud HD5 154 D6
Rydal Dr. Morley LS27 98 D5
Rydal Dr. Wake WF2 141 E7
Rydal Gr. Liver WF15 117 A1
Rydal St. Castle WF10 125 D8
Rydal St. Keigh BD21 35 A6
Rydale Ct. Ossett WF5 140 D4
Rydall Pl. Leeds LS11 78 F5
Rydall St. Leeds LS11 78 F5
Rydall Terr. Leeds LS11 78 F5
Ryder Cl. Pont WF8 146 B8
Ryder Gdns. Leeds LS8 61 A7
Rydings Ave. Brig HD6 115 A3
Rydings Cl. Brig HD6 115 A3 11
Rydings Dr. Brig HD6 114 F3
Rydings Wlk. Brig HD6 114 F3
Rye Close La. Holme HD7 187 E4
Rye Croft. Hali HX2 91 F6
Rye Field La. Mars HD3 150 F6
Rye Field La W. Mars HD3 150 F6
Rye Garth. Weth LS22 13 D8
Rye La. Hali HX2 91 C1
Rye Pl. Leeds LS14 61 F1
Rye St. Keigh BD21 35 B4 9
Rye Way. Castle WF10 125 B8
Ryebank. Holmfi HD7 189 B4
Ryebread. Castle WF10 103 E1
Ryecroft Ave. Ryhill WF4 162 C2
Ryecroft Cl. Loft G WF1 121 C5
Ryecroft Cres. Hali HX2 91 D1
Ryecroft Dr. Hud HD3 135 B1
Ryecroft Fst Sch. Brad 75 F2
Ryecroft. Harden BD21 35 F1
Ryecroft La. Brig HD6 136 C8
Ryecroft La. Hali HX2 91 D1
Ryecroft La. Holmfi HD7 189 C3
Ryecroft Mid Sch. Leeds 77 E6
Ryecroft Rd. Cull BD21 35 E1
Ryecroft Rd. Glu BD20 16 B7
Ryecroft Rd. Harden BD16 36 A1
Ryecroft St. Ossett WF5 140 C7
Ryecroft Terr. Hali HX2 91 D1
Ryecroft Way. Glu BD20 16 C6
Ryedale Ave. Knot WF11 126 E2
Ryedale Ave. Leeds LS12 78 B4
Ryedale Cl. Nor WF6 123 A5
Ryedale Ct. Leeds LS14 61 F5
Ryedale Holt. Leeds LS12 78 C5
Ryedale. Kirkhe HD5 137 B2
Ryedale Pk. Ilkley LS29 8 D3
Ryedale Pl. Nor WF6 123 A5
Ryedale Way. Brad BD15 54 A2
Ryedale Way. E Ard WF3 119 E7
Ryefield Ave. Brad BD14 73 B5
Ryefields Ave. Hud HD3 153 A7
Ryefields. Holmfi HD7 189 D4
Ryefields Rd. Hud HD7 152 E4
Ryeland St. Glu BD20 16 D7
Ryelands Gr. Brad BD9 54 D4
Ryhill Fst Sch. Ryhill 162 B1
Ryhill Ind Est. Ryhill WF4 162 B1
Ryhill Pits La. Ryhill WF4 161 E1
Rylands Ave. Bing BD16 37 B3
Rylstone Gdns. Brad BD3 56 A1
Rylstone Gr. Wake WF1 142 F8
Rylstone Rd. Bail BD17 37 F2
Rylstone St. Keigh BD21 35 D8
Ryndleside. Hud HD3 134 F1 4
Ryshworth Ave. Bing BD16 36 D6
Ryshworth Bridge. Bing BD16 36 D6
Ryshworth Mid Sch. Bing 36 E7
Ryton Dale. Brad BD10 56 E6

Sable Crest. Brad BD2 55 F4
Sackup La. Mapp S75 177 F1
Sackup La. Mapp S75 178 A2
Sackville App. Leeds LS7 60 C3
Sackville Rd. Sil BD20 5 E2
Sackville St. Brad BD1 74 E7 17
Sackville St. Dew WF13 138 E6
Sackville St. Heb Br HX7 89 A4 10
Sackville St. Leeds LS7 60 C3
Sackville St. Tod OL14 108 C5
Sacred Heart RC Prim Sch. Ilkley 8 D4
Sacred Heart RC Prim Sch. Leeds 59 B3
Sacred Heart RC Prim Sch. Sow Br 112 A3
Saddler St. Brad BD12 94 C4 7
Saddler's La. Broth WF11 105 C1
Saddlers Croft. Castle WF10 125 B6
Saddleworth Rd. Elland HX4 134 C7
Saddleworth Rd. Mars HX4, HX5 150 E5
Saddleworth Rd. Rip HX4, HX5 133 C5
Sadler Cl. Hors LS16 42 C4
Sadler Copse. Hors LS16 42 C4
Sadler Way. Hors LS16 42 C4
Sadlers Wlk. Weth LS22 13 F6
Saffron Dr. Brad BD15 73 B8
Sagar La. Tod OL14 86 D3
Sagar Pl. Leeds LS6 59 D4
Sagar St. Castle WF10 124 D8
Sage St. Brad BD5 74 C4
Saint St. Brad BD7 74 A4 1
St Abbs Cl. Brad BD6 94 C7
St Abbs Dr. Brad BD6 94 C7
St Abbs Fold. Brad BD6 94 C7
St Abbs Gate. Brad BD6 94 C7
St Abbs Way. Brad BD6 94 C7
St Abbs Wlk. Brad BD6 94 C7
St Agnes Preparatory Sch. Leeds 59 D6
St Aidan's Rd. Bail BD17 38 D2
St Aidan's Sq. Bing BD16 36 E6
St Aidans Rd. Swil LS26 102 E8
St Aiden's Wlk. Ossett WF5 141 A4
St Alban App. Leeds LS9 61 C1
St Alban Cl. Leeds LS9 61 C1
St Alban Cres. Leeds LS9 61 C1
St Alban Gr. Leeds LS9 61 C1
St Alban Mount. Leeds LS9 61 C1
St Alban Rd. Leeds LS9 61 C1
St Alban View. Leeds LS9 61 C1
St Alban's Ave. Hali HX3 113 C3
St Alban's Ave. Hud HD3 135 A3
St Alban's Pl. Leeds LS2 60 C1
St Alban's Rd. Hali HX3 113 C3
St Albans Croft. Hali HX3 113 D4
St Aldon's CE (Aided) Fst Sch. Skel 175 A1
St Andrew's Ave. Morley LS27 97 F3
St Andrew's CE Fst Sch. Keigh 35 A7
St Andrew's CE Inf Sch. Brig 115 A4
St Andrew's Catholic Sch. Leeds 43 D1
St Andrew's CE Jun & Inf Sch. Brad 95 B4
St Andrew's Cl. Morley LS27 97 E3
St Andrew's Cl. Pudsey LS13 57 E5
St Andrew's Cres. Brad BD12 95 A4
St Andrew's Dr. Brig HD6 115 A4
St Andrew's Gr. Morley LS27 97 F3
St Andrew's Pl. Brad BD7 74 C6
St Andrew's Pl. Leeds LS3 78 F8 6
St Andrew's Rd. Castle HD1, S11,
S74 104 D1
St Andrew's Rd. Hud HD1 154 C7
St Andrew's St. Leeds LS3 78 F8 1
St Andrew's Terr. Glu BD20 16 D7
St Andrew's Villas. Brad BD7 74 C7
St Andrews CE Jun Sch. Brig 115 A3
St Andrews Cl. Hali HX2 92 A5
St Andrews Cl. Yeadon LS19 40 C7 1
St Andrews Croft. Leeds LS17 43 B4
St Andrews Dr. Feath WF7 124 D1
St Andrews Dr. Kirkhe HD5 155 C8
St Andrews Dr. Knot WF11 126 C5
St Andrews Dr. Leeds LS17 43 C4
St Andrews Dr. Mapp S75 178 A1
St Andrews Rd. Yeadon LS19 40 C8
St Andrews Wlk. Leeds LS17 43 C4
St Ann St. Leeds LS2 79 B8
St Ann's Ave. Leeds LS4 59 D2
St Ann's Cl. Leeds LS4 59 C4
St Ann's Gdns. Leeds LS4 59 C3
St Ann's La. Leeds LS4 59 C3
St Ann's Mount. Leeds LS4 59 D3
St Ann's Rise. Leeds LS4 59 C3
St Ann's Sq. Leeds LS4 59 C3
St Ann's Sq. Leeds LS9 79 E8
St Ann's Way. Leeds LS4 59 C3
St Anne's Ave. Hud HD3 135 A3
St Anne's Cl. Dew WF12 139 D4
St Anne's Dr. Leeds LS4 59 C4
St Anne's Gn. Leeds LS4 59 C4
St Anne's Pl. Elland HX4 133 E4
St Anne's RC Cath. Leeds 79 B8
St Anne's RC Sch. Keigh 35 B8
St Anne's Rd. Hali HX3 113 C2
St Anne's Rd. Leeds LS6 59 C5
St Anne's St. Ryhill WF4 162 B1
St Annes Villas. Pont WF8 125 E2
St Anns Sq. Hali HX6 112 C4
St Anthony's Dr. Leeds LS11 78 F2
St Anthony's R C Fst Sch. Brad 73 D5
St Anthony's RC Jun Sch. Ship 55 F8
St Anthony's RC Prim Sch. Leeds 78 F2
St Anthony's Rd. Leeds LS11 78 E2
St Augustine's C E Fst Sch. Brad 56 A1
St Augustine's Jun & Inf Sch. Hali 113 A8
St Augustine's Terr. Brad BD3 56 A1
St Augustine's Terr. Hali HX1 113 A8 6
St Augustines R C Prim Sch. Leeds 61 B3
St Austin's Catholic Inf Sch. Wake 142 D7
St Austin's Catholic Jun Sch. Wake 142 D7
St Barnabas Rd. Clec WF15 116 C5
St Barnabas Rd. Leeds LS11 79 B6
St Barnabas Sch. Ship 55 A4
St Bartholomew's CE Prim Sch.
Leeds 78 C7
St Bartholomews Cl. Leeds LS12 78 C7
St Bartholomews Ct. Wake WF2 141 C4
St Bede's Grammar Sch. Brad 55 A3
St Benedict's Sch. Gar 82 F7
St Benedicts RC Sec Sch. Leeds 58 E5
St Bernard's Ave. Pont WF8 146 B8
St Bevan's Rd. Hali HX3 113 C3
St Blaise Ct. Brad BD5 74 E5
St Blaise RC Sec Sch. Brad 75 B1
St Boltophs Cl. Knot WF11 127 A4
St Brendan's RC Sch. Brad 56 D6
St Catherine's Cres. Leeds LS13 58 D4
St Catherine's Dr. Leeds LS13 58 D4
St Catherine's Gn. Leeds LS13 58 D4
St Catherine's Hill. Leeds LS13 58 D4
St Catherine's St. Wake WF1 142 F3
St Catherine's Villas. Wake WF1 142 F3
St Catherine's Wlk. Leeds LS8 61 A6
St Chad's Ave. Brig HD6 114 E5
St Chad's Ave. Leeds LS6 59 D6
St Chad's CE Prim Sch. Leeds 59 B7
St Chad's CE (Aided) Jun & Inf Sch.
Brig 114 E5
St Chad's Dr. Leeds LS6 59 C6
St Chad's Gr. Leeds LS6 59 C6
St Chad's Rd. Brad BD8 55 B1
St Chad's Rd. Leeds LS16 59 D6
St Chad's Rise. Leeds LS6 59 C6
St Chad's View. Leeds LS6 59 C6
St Christopher's Ave. Roth LS26 100 F5
St Christophers Dr. Sil LS29 6 F8
St Clair Rd. Otley LS21 23 B7
St Clair St. Otley LS21 23 B8
St Clair St. Wake WF1 142 D6
St Clairs Terr. Otley LS21 23 B8
St Clare's Ave. Brad BD2 56 D2
St Clare's RC Fst Sch. Brad 56 D2
St Clements Ave. Roth LS26 100 E5
St Clements Cl. Roth LS26 100 D4

St Clements Rise. Roth LS26 .... 100 D5
St Columba's RC Fst Sch. Brad 75 D2
St Cuthbert & the Fst Martyrs RC Sch. Brad 55 A2
St Cuthbert's Cl. Ackm M T WF7 .... 146 A1
St Cuthbert's Cl. Ackm M T WF7 .... 146 A1
St Cuthbert's RC Inf Sch. Brad 55 B3
St Cyprians Gdns. Leeds LS9 .... 61 B212
St Davids Rd. Otley LS21 .... 10 B2
St Davids Sch. Hud 153 C6
St Dominic's RC Mid Sch. Leeds 60 D3
St Edmunds Hall Prep Sch. Leeds 44 D3
St Edmunds Cl. Castle WF10 .... 125 C8
St Edward's RC Prim Sch. B Spa 30 D7
St Edward's Terr. B Spa LS23 .... 30 D5
St Edwards Cl. Byram WF11 .... 126 E7
St Elmo Gr. Leeds LS9 .... 80 A8 6
St Eloi Ave. Bail BD17 .... 38 C4
St Enoch's Rd. Brad BD6 .... 74 B2
St Francis Pl. Leeds LS11 .... 79 B6
St Francis Prim Sch. Leeds 79 B3
St Francis' RC Fst Sch. Brad 56 A4
St George's RC Sch. Brad 55 A3
St George's Ave. Hud HD3 .... 135 A3
St George's Ave. Roth LS26 .... 100 C7
St George's Cres. Roth LS26 .... 100 C7
St George's Pl. Brad BD5 .... 74 E5 2
St George's Pl. Brad BD5 .... 75 B4
St George's Rd. Hali HX1 .... 203 A3
St George's Rd. Holmfl HD7 .... 189 D4
St George's Rd. Leeds LS10 .... 61 B1
St George's Rd. Wake WF2 .... 141 D3
St George's Sq. Eltand HD3 .... 152 B8
St George's Sq. Heb Br HX7 .... 89 A317
St George's Sq. Hud HD1 .... 154 A618
St George's St. Heb Br HX7 .... 89 A316
St George's St. Hud HD1 .... 154 A6
St Georges Ct. Ryhill WF4 .... 162 D2
St Georges Wlk. Wake WF2 .... 160 C6
St Giles Ave. Pont WF8 .... 146 B8
St Giles CE Jun Mix Sch. Pont 125 D1
St Giles Cl. Brig HD6 .... 114 E5
St Giles Garth. Bramho LS16 .... 24 E3
St Giles Rd. Brig HX3 .... 114 E7
St Giles' View. Pont WF8 .... 146 B8
St Gregory's RC Prim Sch. Leeds 62 D5
St Helen's Ave. Hem WF9 .... 181 C7
St Helen's Dr. M'field LS25 .... 83 F8
St Helen's Gate. Hud HD4 .... 155 A2
St Helen's Way. Wake WF2 .... 142 F1
St Helen's La. Hors LS16 .... 42 C3
St Helen's Way. Ilkley LS29 .... 8 D4
St Helena Rd. Brad BD6 .... 74 B1
St Helens Ave. Hors LS16 .... 42 C3
St Helens Cl. Hors LS16 .... 42 C3
St Helens Gr. Hors LS16 .... 42 C3
St Helens Rd. Hors LS16 .... 79 D5
St Helens Way. Hors LS16 .... 42 D3
St Helier Gr. Bail BD17 .... 38 C4
St Hilda's Ave. Leeds LS9 .... 79 F614
St Hilda's Cres. Leeds LS9 .... 79 F616
St Hilda's Gr. Leeds LS9 .... 79 F616
St Hilda's Mount. Leeds LS9 .... 79 F613
St Hilda's Pl. Leeds LS9 .... 79 F612
St Hilda's Rd. Leeds LS9 .... 79 F611
St Hilda's Sch. Hor 141 A2
St Hilda's Terr. Brad BD3 .... 75 F8
St Hildas Cl. Dearne S63 .... 194 E1
St Ians Croft. Sil LS29 .... 6 F7
St Ignatius Jun & Inf Sch. Ossett 140 A1
St Ive's Gdns. Hali HX3 .... 113 C3
St Ives Cl. Pont WF8 .... 125 D1
St Ives Gr. Harden BD16 .... 36 C2
St Ives Gr. Leeds LS12 .... 78 A820
St Ives Mount. Leeds LS12 .... 78 A8
St Ives Pl. Harden BD16 .... 36 C2
St Ives Rd. Harden BD16 .... 36 C2
St James App. Leeds LS14 .... 62 B4
St James Ave. Hors LS18 .... 74 F6
St James Bsns Pk. Brad 74 E6
St James CE (C) Fst Sch. Crig 159 F6
St James Cl. Leeds LS12 .... 78 D4
St James Cres. Pudsey LS28 .... 76 D6
St James Ct. Brig HD6 .... 115 B3
St James Ct. Hali HX1 .... 113 C7 2
St James Ryhill WF4 .... 162 C1
St James Manston CE Mid Sch. 62 D3
St James Pk. Wake WF2 .... 141 C4
St James Rd. Bail BD17 .... 38 F4
St James Rd. Bail BD17 .... 38 F4
St James Sq. Brad BD1 .... 74 C7
St James's. Mkt. Brad 75 A6
St James's. Pl. Wake WF1 .... 142 E6
St James's Univ Hospl. Leeds 62 D3
St John Fisher RC High Sch. Dew 118 B1
St John Par. Dew WF13 .... 139 B7
St John St. Dew WF13 .... 139 B7
St John the Evangelist Inf & Jun Sch. Brad 73 A1
St John Wlk. Dew WF13 .... 139 B7
St John's Ave. Batley WF17 .... 118 A8
St John's Ave. Hud HD4 .... 154 A2
St John's Ave. Kirkhe HD5 .... 137 C1
St John's Ave. Leeds LS6 .... 59 E1
St John's Ave. Ushett WF5 .... 141 A5
St John's Ave. Thorner LS14 .... 45 C5
St John's CE Fst Sch. Brad 75 D1
St John's Chase. Wake WF1 .... 142 B7
St John's Cl. Aber LS25 .... 47 A1
St John's Cl. Heb Br HX7 .... 89 A3
St John's Cl. Ossett WF5 .... 141 A5

St John's Cl. Rip HX6 .... 132 C1
St John's Cres. Hud HD1 .... 154 A8
St John's Cres. Hud HD1 .... 154 A8
St John's Cres. Nor WF6 .... 144 A7
St John's Cres. Ossett WF5 .... 141 A5
St John's Croft. Wake WF1 .... 142 B8
St John's Cross. Hali HX2 .... 91 FB
St John's Ct. Bail BD17 .... 38 E2
St John's Ct. Keigh BD20 .... 18 A8
St John's Ct. Leeds LS7 .... 60 D4
St John's Ct. Lepton HD8 .... 155 F3
St John's Ct. Thorner LS14 .... 45 F5
St John's Ct. Wake WF1 .... 142 B7
St John's Ct. Yeadon LS19 .... 40 A6
St John's Dr. Hud HD1 .... 154 A8
St John's Dr. Yeadon LS19 .... 40 A6
St John's Garth. Aber LS25 .... 64 E8
St John's La. Leeds LS6 .... 59 F2
St John's La. Wake WF1 .... 142 C8
St John's Hospital (Almshouses). Ledsh LS25 .... 104 D8
St John's Jun & Inf Sch. Rip 132 C1
St John's Jun & Inf Sch. Wake 142 B7
St John's La. Hali HX1 .... 113 C6
St John's Mount. Wake WF1 .... 142 B7
St John's N. Wake WF1 .... 142 B7
St John's Pl. Clec BD19 .... 117 E5
St John's Pl. Birk BD11 .... 96 A6
St John's RC Sch. Nor 123 C2
St John's Rd. B Spa LS23 .... 30 D7
St John's Rd. Hud HD1 .... 154 A8
St John's Rd. Ilkley LS29 .... 8 D4
St John's Rd. Keigh BD20 .... 18 A2
St John's Rd. Kirkhe HD5 .... 137 C1
St John's Rd. Leeds LS3 .... 59 F1
St John's Rd. Yeadon LS19 .... 40 A6
St John's Residential Sch for the Deaf. B Spa 30 D7
St John's Sq. Wake WF1 .... 142 B7
St John's St. Con BD20 .... 4 A2
St John's St. Nor WF4 .... 140 F1
St John's St. Oven BD13 .... 101 C5
St John's St. Sil BD20 .... 5 E1
St John's View. B Spa LS23 .... 30 C7
St John's View. Batley WF17 .... 118 A6
St John's Way. Yeadon LS19 .... 40 A6
St John's Wlk. Roy S71 .... 179 D4
St Johns Ave. Sil LS29 .... 6 F8
St Johns Church Sch. Hud 152 D5
St Johns Cl. Dew WF13 .... 116 E7
St Johns Cl. Dew WF13 .... 139 B8
St Johns Cl. Holmfl HD7 .... 188 F4
St Johns Mews. Wake WF1 .... 142 B8
St Johns Way. Keigh BD22 .... 34 D7
St Joseph's Catholic Prim Sch. Weth 13 E6
St Joseph's Coll. Brad 55 C3
St Joseph's RC Fst Sch. Brad 56 A4
St Joseph's Prim Sch. Batley 118 A2
St Joseph's RC Fst Sch. Bing 37 A3
St Joseph's RC Inf Sch. Brad 74 D4
St Joseph's RC Jun & Inf Sch. Pont 146 C8
St Joseph's RC Jun Sch. Otley 23 A8
St Jude's Pl. Brad BD1 .... 74 A8
St Jude's St. Brad BD8 .... 74 D8
St Jude's St. Hali HX1 .... 113 B5 4
St Julien's Mount. Caw S75 .... 193 E4
St Lawrence Cl. Ship BD2 .... 55 E5
St Lawrence Ct. Pudsey LS28 .... 76 C7
St Lawrence St. Leeds LS7 .... 60 D6
St Lawrence Terr. Pudsey LS28 .... 76 C7
St Leonard's Ct. Brad BD8 .... 54 F1 4
St Leonard's Gr. Brad BD8 .... 54 F1
St Leonards Cl. Sil LS29 .... 6 F7
St Luke's CE Fst Sch. Brad 55 D1
St Luke's Cl. Clec BD19 .... 116 D7
St Luke's Cres. Leeds LS11 .... 79 A4
St Luke's Cres. Leeds LS11 .... 79 A4
St Luke's Hospl. Brad 74 D4
St Luke's La. Leeds LS11 .... 79 A4
St Luke's Rd. Leeds LS11 .... 79 A4
St Luke's Terr. Clec BD19 .... 116 B7
St Luke's Terr. Keigh BD20 .... 18 A4
St Luke's Terr. Leeds LS11 .... 79 A4 6
St Lukes Cl. Batley WF17 .... 118 E4
St Malachy's RC Sch. Hali 91 E7

St Martins Ave. Otley LS21 .... 10 F2
St Martins Cl. Feath WF7 .... 145 C4
St Mary's St. Hali HX1 .... 113 B6
St Mary's Ave. Batley WF17 .... 118 B3
St Mary's Ave. Brad BD12 .... 94 B8
St Mary's Ave. Holmfl HD7 .... 188 F8
St Mary's Ave. Mir WF14 .... 138 C6
St Mary's Ave. Swil LS26 .... 82 A1
St Mary's CE Jun & Inf Sch. Wake 142 D6
St Mary's CE Jun & Inf Sch. Sow Br 132 .... C7
St Mary's Cl. Brad BD12 .... 94 B2
St Mary's Cl. E Ard WF3 .... 119 D7
St Mary's Cl. Gar LS25 .... 82 B6
St Mary's Cl. Ilkley LS29 .... 8 C4
St Mary's Cl. S Elm WF9 .... 183 A2
St Mary's Comp Sch. Guise 22 C3
St Mary's Cres. Brad BD12 .... 94 B2
St Mary's Cres. Holmfl HD7 .... 188 F8
St Mary's Ct. Kippax WF10 .... 103 B4
St Mary's Dr. Brad BD12 .... 94 C2
St Mary's Fold. Brad BD4 .... 75 D5
St Mary's Garth. E Kea LS17 .... 28 B5
St Mary's Gdns. Brad BD12 .... 94 C2
St Mary's Heights. Hali HX2 .... 91 D5
St Mary's Hospl. Leeds 77 F8
St Mary's La. Kirkhe HD5 .... 155 C2
St Mary's La. Leeds LS9 .... 79 E8
St Mary's Mews. Honley HD7 .... 171 F3
St Mary's Mount. Brad BD12 .... 94 B2
St Mary's Pl. Castle WF10 .... 124 D8 1
St Mary's Pl. Dew WF12 .... 139 D8
St Mary's RC Fst Sch. Brad 74 F7
St Mary's RC Inf Sch. Batley 118 B6
St Mary's RC Jun Mix & Inf Sch. Roth 100 F4
St Mary's RC Jun Sch. Batley 118 B6
St Mary's RC Prim Sch. Bacup 106 B1
St Mary's RC Prim Sch. Hali 113 B6
St Mary's Rd. Brad BD8 .... 55 C5
St Mary's Rd. Brad BD9 .... 54 F3
St Mary's Rd. Brad BD4 .... 75 D5
St Mary's Rd. Holmfl HD7 .... 188 F8
St Mary's Rd. Honley HD7 .... 171 F5
St Mary's Rd. Keigh BD20 .... 18 F2
St Mary's Rd. Leeds LS7 .... 60 D6
St Mary's Rd. Leeds LS9 .... 79 E8
St Mary's Sq. Brad BD8 .... 54 F1
St Mary's Sq. Honley HD7 .... 171 F5
St Mary's Sq. Leeds LS9 .... 79 D8
St Mary's St. B Spa LS23 .... 30 D8
St Mary's St. Brad BD8 .... 75 D5
St Mary's St. Holmfl HD7 .... 188 F8
St Mary's St. Leeds LS9 .... 79 D8
St Mary's Way. M'field LS25 .... 83 F7
St Mary's Wlk. Mir WF14 .... 138 C6
St Mary's Way. Holmfl HD7 .... 188 F8
St Mary's Wlk. Mir WF14 .... 138 C6
St Marys Pk App. Leeds LS12 .... 77 F8
St Marys Gate. Elland HX5 .... 134 F712
St Stephen's St. Elland HX3 .... 113 A2
St Stephen's Terr. Brad BD5 .... 80 A8
St Swithins CE Fst Sch. Brad 74 E1
St Swithins Dr. Loft G WF3 .... 121 F2
St Swithins Gr. Loft G WF3 .... 121 E2
St Theresa's RC Prim Sch. Leeds 62 C1
St Thomas à Beckett Catholic Comp Sch. Wake 142 A4
St Thomas CE Jun Sch. Feath 145 C5
St Thomas Rd. Feath WF7 .... 145 C5
St Thomas Row. Leeds LS2 .... 60 D1
St Thomas' Rd. Brad BD1 .... 74 D7 2
St Urban's RC Prim Sch. Leeds 59 D8
St Vincent Rd. Pudsey LS28 .... 57 F6
St Winefride's RC Sch. Brad 94 B8
St Winifred's Cl. Hali HX2 .... 91 D5
Sal Nook Cl. Brad BD12 .... 94 D6
Sal Royd Rd. Brad BD12 .... 94 D6
Salcombe Pl. Brad BD4 .... 75 A2
Salem Pl. Gar LS25 .... 82 E7
Salem Pl. Leeds LS10 .... 79 F7
Salem St. Brad BD1 .... 74 E7
Salem St. Queen BD13 .... 72 E1
Salem St. Heb Br HX7 .... 88 F8
Salendine Nook High Sch. Hud 152 F7
Salford. Oaken BD13 .... 52 D6
Salford Way. Tod OL14 .... 108 A4
Salisbury Ave. Bail BD17 .... 38 E3
Salisbury Ave. Leeds LS12 .... 78 B5
Salisbury Cl. Dew WF12 .... 139 E3
Salisbury Ct. Nor WF6 .... 123 A3
Salisbury Gr. Leeds LS12 .... 78 B5
Salisbury Mews. Hors LS18 .... 41 A4
Salisbury Pl. Pudsey LS28 .... 57 D1
Salisbury Rd. Brad BD15 .... 54 B1
Salisbury Rd. Castle WF10 .... 125 C6
Salisbury Rd. Hud HD1 .... 153 F8
Salisbury Rd. Leeds LS12 .... 78 B5
Salisbury St. Leeds LS19 .... 40 C6
Salisbury St. Pudsey LS28 .... 57 D1
Salisbury Terr. Hud HD1 .... 153 F8
Salisbury Terr. Leeds LS12 .... 78 B5
Salisbury View. Leeds LS12 .... 78 B5
Salisbury View. Hors LS18 .... 41 A4
Salkeld Cl. OL15 .... 129 C1
Sally St. Leeds LS11 79
Salmon Cres. Hors LS18 .... 41 C1
Salt Gram Sch. Ship
Salt St. Brad BD8 .... 55 A1
Saltaire Rd. Ship
Saltaire. Haw BD22 .... 51 F8 4

St Paul's St. Hud HD1 .... 154 B5 3
St Paul's St. Leeds LS1 .... 211 F3
St Paul's St. Morley LS27 .... 98 B3 1
St Paul's Terr. Mir WF14 .... 138 A4
St Paul's Wlk. Wake WF2 .... 141 D8
St Paulinus Cl. Dew WF13 .... 139 B8
St Paulinus' RC Jun & Inf Sch. Dew 139 .... A7
St Pauls Rd. Kirkhe HD5 .... 155 B8
St Pauls Rd. Ship BD18 .... 55 B7
St Peg Cl. Clec BD19 .... 116 E7
St Peg La. Clec BD19 .... 116 E7
St Peter Claver's Coll. Mir 137 E8
St Peter & Paul RC Mid Sch. Wake 99 E5
St Peter & St Pauls RC Prim Sch. Yeadon 39 F6
St Peter's Ave. Roth LS26 .... 100 F5
St Peter's Ave. Sow Br HX6 .... 111 F3
St Peter's CE Inf Sch. Morley 98 B6
St Peter's CE Mid Sch. Leeds 79 E8
St Peter's CE Prim Sch. Leeds 79 E8
St Peter's Cl. Batley WF17 .... 96 D1
St Peter's Cres. Loft G WF3 .... 122 B6
St Peter's Cres. Wake LS27 .... 98 A6
St Peter's Ct. Leeds LS13 .... 58 D3
St Peter's Garth. Thorner LS14 .... 46 A6
St Peter's Gate. Dearne S63 .... 194 D1
St Peter's Gate. Tod OL14 .... 129 B8
St Peter's Gdns. Leeds LS13 .... 58 C3
St Peter's Gr. Hor WF4 .... 141 B1
St Peter's Inf Sch. Sow Br 111 F3
St Peter's Mount. Leeds LS13 .... 58 D2
St Peter's Par. Dew WF12 .... 139 F7
St Peter's Pl. Leeds LS9 .... 79 D8
St Peter's Sq. Leeds LS9 .... 79 D8
St Peter's Sq. Hor WF4 .... 141 B1
St Peter's St. Hud HD1 .... 154 B6 2
St Peter's St. Leeds LS9 .... 212 C4
St Peter's Way. Men LS29 .... 21 F4
St Peters Cres. Kirkhe HD5 .... 155 B8
St Peters Cl. Leeds LS13 .... 58 D3
St Peters Ct. Sil LS29 .... 6 F8
St Peters Gate. Ossett WF5 .... 140 D7
St Philip's Ave. Midd LS10 .... 99 B5
St Philip's CE Fst Sch. Brad 55 A3
St Philip's Ct. Burl in W LS29 .... 9 F1
St Philip's Dr. Bur in W LS29 .... 21 F1
St Philip's La. Bur in W LS29 .... 21 F1
St Philips Ct. Hud HD3 .... 135 B2
St Richards Rd. Otley LS21 .... 10 F2
St Stephen's CE Fst Sch. Brad 74 E3
St Stephen's Cl. Stee BD20 .... 17 C6
St Stephen's Rd. Brad BD5 .... 74 F8
St Stephen's Rd. Hud HD3 .... 153 B4
St Stephen's Rd. Steeton BD20 .... 17 C5
St Stephen's St. Pudsey LS28 .... 57 C5
St Stephen's St. Stee BD20 .... 17 C5

Saltaire Rd. Bing BD16 .... 37 D5
Saltaire Rd. Ship BD18 .... 55 A8
Saltaire Sta. Ship 37 F1
Saltburn Pl. Brad BD9 .... 54 F2
Saltburn St. Hali HX1 .... 112 F7 8
Salter Rake Gate. Tod OL14 .... 129 B8
Salter Row. Pont WF8 .... 146 D8 1
Salter St. Batley WF17 .... 118 C3
Salterhebble Hill. Hali HX3 .... 113 D3
Salterhebble Jun & Inf Sch. Hali 113 D3
Saltersgate Ave. Hovel WF11 .... 126 E4
Saltonstall La. Hali HX2 .... 90 D5
Sampson St. Liver WF15 .... 117 B4
Samuel Dr. Loft G WF3 .... 121 E5
Samuel St. Hud HD1 .... 154 A6
Sand Beds. Queen BD13 .... 72 F1
Sand Hill La. Leeds LS17 .... 43 D3
Sand Hill Lawn. Leeds LS17 .... 43 D3
Sand Moor Golf Course. Leeds 43 C6
Sand St. Haw BD22 .... 51 C6
Sand St. Hud HD1 .... 154 B5
Sand St. Keigh BD21 .... 35 B8
Sandal Ave. Wake WF2 .... 142 E1
Sandal Ag & Sprig Sta. Wake 142 E2
Sandal Ave. Wake WF2 .... 142 E1
Sandal Cliff. Wake WF2 .... 142 E1
Sandal Fst Sch. Bail 38 C3
Sandal Hall La. Wake WF2 .... 142 F1
Sandal Hall Mews. Wake WF2 .... 142 E1
Sandal Magna Endowed CE Mid Sch. Wake 160 E8
Sandal Magna Fst Sch. Wake 142 E2
Sandal Rise. Th Hud WF8 .... 165 A5
Sandal Way. Batley WF17 .... 96 F3
Sandale Wlk. Brad BD6 .... 93 F7 5
Sandall Cl. Kippax LS25 .... 83 B2
Sandall Magna. Shelf HX3 .... 93 E7
Sandals Rd. Bail BD17 .... 38 C3
Sandbeck Ind Est. Weth 13 F7
Sandbeck La. Weth LS22 .... 14 B8
Sandbeck Way. Weth LS22 .... 13 F7
Sandbed Ct. Leeds LS15 .... 62 D3
Sandbed La. Leeds LS15 .... 62 D3
Sandbeds Cres. Hali HX2 .... 91 E1
Sandbeds. Honley HD7 .... 171 F6
Sandbeds Rd. Hali HX2 .... 91 E1
Sandbeds Terr. Hali HX2 .... 91 E1
Sandene Dr. Hud HD4 .... 153 C2
Sanderling Ct. Brad BD8 .... 73 C7 7
Sanderling Garth. Midd LS10 .... 99 D5
Sanderling Way. Midd LS10 .... 99 D5
Sanderson Ave. Brad BD6 .... 74 C1
Sanderson Ave. Nor WF6 .... 123 A1
Sanderson La. Loft G LS26 .... 122 B8
Sanderson La. Roth LS26 .... 101 B1
Sanderson St. Wake WF1 .... 142 D6
Sandfield Ave. Leeds LS6 .... 59 E6
Sandfield Garth. Leeds LS6 .... 59 E6
Sandford Rd. Bacup OL13 .... 106 B1
Sandford Rd. Brad BD3 .... 56 C1
Sandford Rd. Leeds LS5 .... 59 B3
Sandford Rd. S Elm WF9 .... 183 A5
Sandgate La. Kippax LS25 .... 83 C2
Sandgate La. Kippax LS25 .... 83 C2
Sandgate Rise. Kippax LS25 .... 83 B3
Sandgate Terr. Kippax LS25 .... 83 B2
Sandhall Cres. Hali HX2 .... 112 D8
Sandhall Dr. Hali HX2 .... 112 D8
Sandhall Green. Hali HX2 .... 112 D8
Sandhall La. Hali HX2 .... 112 D8 5
Sandhill Ct. Leeds LS17 .... 43 D4
Sandhill Cres. Leeds LS17 .... 43 E4
Sandhill Gr. Leeds LS17 .... 43 E4
Sandhill Lawn. Pont WF8 .... 146 C7
Sandhill Mount. Brad BD10 .... 56 D7
Sandhill Mount. Leeds LS17 .... 43 D4
Sandhill Oval. Leeds LS17 .... 43 E4
Sandholme Dr. Brad BD10 .... 56 C6
Sandholme Dr. Bur in W LS29 .... 21 F8
Sandholme Dr. Ossett WF5 .... 140 D5
Sandholme Fold. Brad HD3 .... 114 D7
Sandhurst Ave. Leeds LS8 .... 61 A5
Sandhurst Gr. Leeds LS8 .... 61 A3
Sandhurst Mount. Leeds LS8 .... 61 A4
Sandhurst Pl. Leeds LS8 .... 61 A4
Sandhurst Rd. Leeds LS8 .... 61 A4
Sandhurst St. Pudsey LS28 .... 76 F7
Sandhurst Terr. Leeds LS8 .... 61 A4
Sandiway Bank. Dew WF12 .... 139 D2
Sandlewood Cl. Leeds LS11 79
Sandlewood Green. Leeds LS11 79
Sandmead Cl. Brad BD4 75
Sandmead Cl. Morley LS27 98
Sandmead Croft. Morley LS27 .... 98 A6
Sandmead Way. Morley LS27 98
Sandmoor Ave. Leeds LS17 .... 43 D5
Sandmoor Chase. Leeds LS17 43
Sandmoor Cl. Leeds LS17 43
Sandmoor Cl. Thorn BD13 .... 72 E6 6
Sandmoor Dr. Leeds LS17 43
Sandmoor Garth. Brad BD10 56
Sandmoor Gdns. Hali HX3 93
Sandringham Cres. Leeds LS17 .... 43 D3
Sandringham Dr. Leeds LS17 .... 43 D3

Sandringham Gdns. Leeds LS17 .... 43 D3
Sandringham Gn. Leeds LS17 .... 43 E4
Sandringham Mount. Leeds LS17 .... 43 E3
Sandringham Rd. Brad BD14 .... 73 D5
Sandringham Rd. Byran WF11 .... 126 D7
Sandringham Rd. Weth LS22 .... 13 E6
Sandringham Way. Leeds LS17 .... 43 D3
Sandrick Rd. Pont WF8 .... 125 E2
Sands House La. Hud HD4 .... 153 B1
Sands La. Dew WF12 .... 139 E7
Sands La. Lepton WF14 .... 155 F6
Sands La. Mir WF14 .... 138 D3
Sands Rd. Dew WF12 .... 139 E6
Sandsend Cl. Brad BD9 .... 54 D3
Sandside Cl. Brad BD5 .... 74 E8
Sandstone Cl. Honley HD7 .... 171 F3
Sandway Gdns. Leeds LS15 .... 62 B2
Sandway Gr. Leeds LS15 .... 62 B2
Sandway La. Leeds LS15 .... 62 B2
Sandwell St. Slai HD7 .... 151 F1
Sandwich Cres. Hud HD2 .... 135 F3
Sandyacre Way. Roth LS26 .... 100 F6
Sandy Banks. Harden BD16 .... 53 B8
Sandy Beck. Brad BD15 .... 54 A2
Sandy Dyke La. Sow Br HX6 .... 132 E8
Sandy Gate. Hara LS17 .... 28 F3
Sandy Gate. Heb Br HX7 .... 89 B4
Sandy Gate. Holmfi HX7 .... 189 C4
Sandy Gate. Keigh BD20 .... 35 A8
Sandy Gate. Leeds LS14 .... 146 C3
Sandy Gate La. Wad M HX7 .... 89 C4
Sandy Gr. Roth LS26 .... 100 F6
Sandy La. Hud HD4 .... 158 C7
Sandy La. Neth WF4 .... 158 C7
Sandy Lane Est. Sow Br Brad 54 A4
Sandy Lobby. Pool LS21 .... 24 C6
Sandy Way. Feagon LS19 .... 40 B7
Sandy Wlk. Bramho LS16 .... 24 F2
Sandy Wlk. Wake WF1 .... 142 B7
Sandyacres Cres. Roth LS26 .... 100 F6
Sandyacres Dr. Roth LS26 .... 100 F6
Sandyacres. Roth LS26 .... 100 F6
Sandybridge La. Shaf S72 .... 180 B4
Sandyfield Terr. Batley WF17 .... 118 B6
Sandyfoot. Rip HX4 .... 133 A4
Sandygate La. Hem WF9 .... 181 C7
Sandygate Terr. Brad BD4 .... 75 D5
Sandygate. Glu BD20 .... 16 D7
Sandywood. Hud HD4 .... 171 D6
Sangster Way. Brad BD5 .... 75 A1
Sanquah Terr. Nor WF6 .... 123 A2
Santa Monica La. Brad BD10 .... 56 A7
Santa Monica Gr. Brad BD10 .... 56 A7
Santa Monica Rd. Brad BD10 .... 56 A7
Santingley La. Ryhill WF4 .... 162 A6
Sanworth St. Tod OL14 .... 108 A5
Sapgate La. Thorn BD13 .... 72 E6
Saplin St. Brad BD8 .... 55 B1
Sapphire Ct. Batley WF17 .... 98 A5
Sarah St. E Ard WF3 .... 120 D8
Sardinia St. Leeds LS10 .... 79 D5
Saunders Cl. Hud HD3 .... 153 C7
Saunters Way. Nor WF6 .... 123 A4
Savile Ave. Brad BD10 .... 56 C5
Savile Ave. Leeds LS7 .... 60 D4
Savile Cl. Brig HD6 .... 115 B2
Savile Cres. Hali HX1 .... 113 A4
Savile Dr. Hali HX1 .... 138 A6
Savile Dr. Leeds LS7 .... 60 D3
Savile Dr. Nor WF4 .... 141 A2
Savile Gn. Leeds LS7 .... 60 D3
Savile Glen. Hali HX1 .... 113 A4
Savile Gr. Dew WF12 .... 139 C7
Savile House. Elland HX5 .... 134 F7 7
Savile La. Brig HD6 .... 115 D3
Savile Lea. Hali HX1 .... 113 A4
Savile Mews. Dew WF12 .... 139 C5
Savile La. Leeds LS17 .... 60 D3
Savile Par. Hali HX1 .... 113 A4
Savile Park Gdns. Hali HX1 .... 113 B5
Savile Park Rd. Cleck BD19 .... 95 D3
Savile Park Rd. Hali HX1 .... 113 A4
Savile Park St. Hali HX1 .... 113 A4
Savile Park Terr. Hali HX1 .... 113 A5 21
Savile Pk. La. Dew WF12 .... 140 A6
Savile Rd. Castle WF10 .... 124 C8
Savile Rd. Dew WF12 .... 139 C6
Savile Rd. Elland HX5 .... 135 A5
Savile Rd. Hali HX1 .... 113 A4
Savile Rd. Heb Br HX7 .... 88 E3
Savile Rd. Hud HD3 .... 153 C8
Savile Rd. Leeds LS7 .... 60 D3
Savile Rd. M'town LS26 .... 102 D3
Savile Royd. Hali HX1 .... 113 B5
Savile St. Batley WF16 .... 117 D4
Savile St. Batley WF17 .... 118 A5
Savile St. Dew BD19 .... 95 D1
Savile St. Hud HD3 .... 153 A5
Savile Town Cl. Sch. Dew 139 D6
Savile Way. Hali HX5 .... 135 A8
Savile Wlk. Bri S72 .... 181 B3
Savile Wik. Dew WF13 .... 139 C8 6
Savile Entley HD8 .... 175 D1
Saville Cl. Roth WF3 .... 100 C1
Saville Cl. Otley LS21 .... 22 F7
Saville Gn. Leeds LS9 .... 79 F7
Saville Rd. Skel HD8 .... 175 D1
Saville St. Clay W HD8 .... 175 D1
Saville St. Elland HX5 .... 135 A8
Saville St. Ossett WF5 .... 140 E4
Saville St. Wake WF1 .... 142 E5
Savill. Sow Br HX6 .... 132 E8
Saw Mill Rd. Ossett WF5 .... 140 C7
Saw Yd. Wake WF1 .... 142 C6
Sawley Cl. Wake WF1 .... 142 E8
Sawley Keigh BD20 .... 35 B1
Sawood La. Oxen HX7 .... 70 D3
Sawrey Pl. Brad BD5 .... 74 D6
Sawyers Garth. Add LS29 .... 7 A8
Saxon Ave. S Kirk WF9 .... 181 F2
Saxon Cl. Emley HD8 .... 175 C6
Saxon Cl. Emley HD8 .... 175 C6
Saxon Ct. Gildr WF2 .... 183 E7
Saxon Ct. Leeds LS17 .... 43 A3
Saxon Gate. Leeds LS17 .... 43 A3
Saxon Gn. Leeds LS17 .... 43 A3
Saxon Gr. Leeds LS17 .... 43 A3
Saxon Gr. S Kirk WF9 .... 182 A1

Saxon Mount. Leeds LS17 .... 43 B3
Saxon Mount. S Kirk WF9 .... 181 F1
Saxon Rd. Leeds LS17 .... 43 A2
Saxon St. Brad BD8 .... 74 C8
Saxon St. Hali HX1 .... 112 F8
Saxon St. Tod OL14 .... 108 A10
Saxon Way. Castle WF10 .... 125 A8
Saxon Ave. Brad BD6 .... 73 F1
Saxton House. Yeadon LS19 .... 40 B6
Saxton La. Leeds LS9 .... 79 E7
Sayer Pl. Hud HD5 .... 155 A4
Sayers Cl. Leeds LS5 .... 58 E7
Sayle Ave. Brad BD4 .... 75 B1
Sayner La. Leeds LS10 .... 79 D4
Sayner Rd. Leeds LS10 .... 79 D6
Scaitcliffe View. Tod OL14 .... 107 F5
Scale Hill. Hud HD2 .... 136 A2
Scalebor Park Hospl. Bur in W 21 D8
Scaley St. Brad BD3 .... 75 D7
Scaly Gate. Holmfi HD7 .... 190 A5
Scammonden Rd. Rip HX4 .... 133 B3
Scammonden View. Hud HD7 .... 152 F4
Scapegoat Hill Jun & Inf Sch. Slai .. 152 B6
Scar Bottom La. Elland HX4 .... 133 F7
Scar Gap. Keigh BD22 .... 34 D5
Scar Head Rd. Sow Br HX6 .... 112 B3
Scar La. Elland HX4 .... 133 E4
Scar La. Holmfi HD7 .... 190 A3
Scar La. Hud HD3, HD7 .... 152 F8
Scar Top Cotts. Haw BD22 .... 50 B7
Scar Top. Hud HD7 .... 152 D4
Scar Top La. Hud HD4 .... 171 D6
Scarborough Gr. Ship BD18 .... 55 A7
Scarborough Rd. Otley LS21 .... 22 E7
Scarborough St. Dew WF12 .... 139 D6
Scarborough Terr. Dew WF12 .... 139 D6
Scarbro'. Junc. Leeds LS13 .... 58 D1
Scarbro Terr. Elland HX5 .... 134 F6
Scarcroft Ct. Scar LS14 .... 45 D8
Scarfold. Holmfi HD7 .... 189 A6
Scargill Cl. Leeds LS9 .... 80 A8
Scargill Grange. Leeds LS9 .... 79 F8
Scarhouse La. Hud HD7 .... 152 E4
Scarlet Hts. Queen BD13 .... 72 F1
Scarr Bottom. Hali HX2 .... 112 F4
Scarr End La. Batley WF13 .... 117 F2
Scarr End La. Dew WF12 .... 139 F8
Scarr End View. Batley WF13 .... 117 F2
Scarr Green Cl. Mel HD7 .... 170 E2
Scarsdale Ridge. Bard LS17 .... 28 E6
Scarsdale La. Leeds LS9 .... 61 A2 5
Scarth Terr. Loft & WF3 .... 122 B6
Scarwood Cl. Bing BD16 .... 37 A4
Scatcherd La. Morley LS27 .... 97 F4
Scawthorpe Cl. Pont WF8 .... 175 A6
Sceptone Gr. Shaf S72 .... 180 C3
Schofield La. Hud HD5 .... 154 D4
Schofield St. Lift OL15 .... 129 C2
Schofields Cir. Leeds 79 C8
Scholebrook La. Pudsey BD4 .... 76 C4
Scholemoor Ave. Brad BD7 .... 73 E3
Scholemoor La. Brad BD7 .... 73 F3
Scholemoor Rd. Brad BD7 .... 73 F4
Scholes (Elmete) Jun & Inf Sch.
    B in Elm 62 F6
Scholes First Sch. Brig 115 B8
Scholes La. B in Elm LS15 .... 62 F6
Scholes La. Haw BD22 .... 33 F1
Scholes Moor Rd. Holmfi HD7 .... 189 C2
Scholes Rd. Leeds LS15 .... 62 F4
Scholes. Huud HD7 .... 191 B3
Scholes. Rd. Huud HD7 .... 103 E3
Scholes Rd. Holmfi HD7 .... 191 B3
Scholes St. Brad BD5 .... 74 E4
Scholey Ave. Brig HD6 .... 136 A1
Scholey Head La. H Chap BB10 .... 85 A8
Scholey Rd. Brig HD6 .... 115 B1
Scholfield St. Tod OL14 .... 108 B6 11
Scholl Ave. Dew WF13 .... 117 F1
Scholl Cl. Crof WF4 .... 144 B4
School Ave. Dew WF13 .... 117 F1
School Cl. Gild LS12 .... 77 D7
School Cl. Rip HX6 .... 132 E4
School Cote Brow. Hali HX3 .... 92 B6
School Cote Terr. Hali HX3 .... 92 B6
School Cres. Hali HX3 .... 91 F3
School Cres. Wake WF2 .... 141 D4
School Croft. Bront WF11 .... 105 C8
School Croft. Roth LS26 .... 100 E6
School Dr. Knot WF11 .... 126 C5
School Gn. Brad BD13 .... 73 A6
School Gn. La. Thorn BD13 .... 73 A6
School Green La. Thorn BD13 .... 73 A6
School Green Ave. Thorn BD13 .... 72 F6
School Hill. Hud HD4 .... 173 F6
School Hill. Kirkb HD8 .... 173 F6
School La. Aber LS25 .... 64 E7
School La. Brad BD6 .... 93 F7
School La. Castle WF10 .... 124 F6
School La. Coll LS22 .... 29 B8
School La. Dari HD8 .... 192 A6
School La. Elland HX4 .... 134 B6
School La. Hali HX3 .... 91 F7
School La. Hali HX3 .... 114 C8
School La. Hud HD4 .... 153 F2
School La. Kippa LS25 .... 83 A5
School La. Leeds LS17 .... 44 B7
School La. Leeds LS6 .... 59 E5
School La. Leeds LS7 .... 60 E7
School La. Leeds LS7 .... 60 C6
School La. Middl LS10 .... 99 A5
School La. Roys S71 .... 179 C4
School La. Th Arch LS23 .... 14 F4
School La. Tod OL14 .... 108 B8
School La. Walton WF2 .... 161 A2
School Land La. Hep HX7 .... 87 F6

School Pl. Brad16 BD12 .... 94 C4
School Rd. Keigh BD22 .... 34 F7
School Rd. Pont WF8 .... 146 F7
School Rd. Slai HD7 .... 152 B6
School Rd. Wake WF2 .... 141 B7
School St. Weth LS22 .... 13 F6
School St. Batley WF17 .... 96 F1 7
School St. Brad BD14 .... 73 B4
School St. Brad BD4 .... 75 E8
School St. Brad BD4 .... 75 C3
School St. Brad BD12 .... 94 C6
School St. Liver WF15 .... 117 B4
School St. Castle WF10 .... 124 C8
School St. Castle WF10 .... 103 E1
School St. Clec BD19 .... 116 B7
School St. Cull BD13 .... 52 D6
School St. Dearne S63 .... 194 D1
School St. Dew WF13 .... 138 E5
School St. Dew WF12 .... 140 B8
School St. E Ard FW12 .... 119 D5
School St. Elland HX4 .... 134 B7
School St. Hali HX1 .... 113 D6
School St. Heb Br HX7 .... 89 A3
School St. Hud HD5 .... 154 D5
School St. Honley HD7 .... 171 F3
School St. Liver WF15 .... 116 F2
School St. Mapp S75 .... 177 E1
School St. Mapp S75 .... 178 C1
School St. Morley LS27 .... 98 B4
School St. Morley LS27 .... 98 A3
School St. Ossett WF5 .... 119 C1
School St. Pudsey LS28 .... 57 D3
School St. Pudsey LS28 .... 76 D6
School St. Shel BD20 .... 5 D1
School St. Stee BD20 .... 17 C5
School St. Upton WF9 .... 183 D8
School St. W Vits BD15 .... 53 C5
School Terr. Fair HX1 .... 105 A4
School Terr. Shep HD8 .... 174 A3
School View. Leeds LS6 .... 59 F5
School St. Morley LS27 .... 98 B4
Schreiber Bsns Pk. Wake 142 D4
Scissett CE (Aided) Fst Sch. Clay W 175 D8
Scoley La. Dew WF12 .... 156 E8
Sconce La. Bail BD16 .... 38 B7
Scopsley Gn. Dew WF12 .... 156 E8
Score Hill. Northo HX3 .... 93 A4
Score Hill. Northo HX3 .... 93 A4
Scoresby St. Brad BD1 .... 201 B4
Scotch Park Trad Est. Leeds 78 D8
Scotchman La. Batley LS27 .... 97 D1
Scotchman La. Morley LS27 .... 97 E1
Scotchman Mid Sch. Brad 55 A2
Scotchman Rd. Brad BD9 .... 55 A2
Scotgate Rd. Honley HD7 .... 171 E4
Scotland Cl. Hors LS18 .... 41 B4
Scotland La. Hors LS18 .... 41 B5
Scotland Mill La. Leeds LS16 .... 42 F1
Scotland St. Clec WF17 .... 96 C2
Scotland Way. Hors LS18 .... 41 B5
Scotland Wood Rd. Leeds LS17 .... 42 F3
Scott Ct. Birk BD11 .... 96 B5
Scott Cl. S in D BD20 .... 16 D5
Scott Cl. Swil LS26 .... 82 A1
Scott Green Cres. Gild LS27 .... 97 C8
Scott Green Dr. Gild LS27 .... 97 C8
Scott Green Gr. Gild LS27 .... 97 C8
Scott Green Mount. Gild LS27 .... 97 C8
Scott Green Wlk. Gild LS27 .... 97 C8
Scott Hall Ave. Leeds LS7 .... 60 C4
Scott Hall Cir. Mid Sch. Leeds 60 C4
Scott Hall Cres. Leeds LS7 .... 60 C4
Scott Hall Gn. Leeds LS7 .... 60 C4
Scott Hall Pl. Leeds LS7 .... 60 C4
Scott Hall Rd. Leeds LS17 .... 43 B1
Scott Hall Rd. Leeds LS6, LS7 ...... 60 C4
Scott Hall Row. Leeds LS7 .... 60 D4
Scott Hall Sq. Leeds LS7 .... 60 C4
Scott Hall St. Leeds LS7 .... 60 C4
Scott Hall Terr. Leeds LS7 .... 60 C4
Scott Hall Way. Leeds LS7 .... 60 D4
Scott La. Batley WF16 .... 117 D4
Scott La. Cleck BD19 .... 116 D7
Scott La. Keigh BD21 .... 35 D8
Scott La. Mars HD7 .... 168 F4
Scott La. W. Keigh BD20 .... 18 E1
Scott Vale. Hud HD2 .... 136 C4
Scott Wood La. Leeds LS7 .... 60 C5
Scotty Croft La. Brig HD6 .... 115 A3
Scotts Almhouses. Leeds LS7 .... 60 C5
Scott Hill. Gild HD6 .... 110 F8
Scott Hill Rd. Dew WF13 .... 139 A6
Scott Wells Wik. Leeds LS7 .... 60 D5
Scout Bottom La. Heb Br HX7 .... 88 D4
Scout Rd. Heb Br HX7 .... 88 E5
Scout Hill Terr. Dew WF13 .... 139 A6
Scout La. Mars HD7 .... 151 C8
Scout Rd. Heb Br HX7 .... 88 E6
Scout Road. Jun. Mid & Inf Sch.
    Heb Br 110 F8
Scrapers La. Tod OL14 .... 109 A5
Sculptor Pl. Brig HD6 .... 115 A6 7
Sea Croft Rd. Hem WF9 .... 163 A2
Seacroft Ave. Leeds LS14 .... 62 C5
Seacroft Chase. Leeds LS14 .... 62 C5
Seacroft Cres. Leeds LS14 .... 62 C5
Seacroft Gate. Leeds LS14 .... 62 C5
Seacroft Grange Cty Prim Sch.
    Leeds 61 E1
Seacroft Ind Est. Leeds 62 B7
Seacroft Park Mid Sch. Leeds 62 B6
Seaforth Ave. Leeds LS9 .... 61 A3

Seaforth Gr. Leeds LS9 .... 61 A3 17
Seaforth Mount. Leeds LS9 .... 61 A3 18
Seaforth Pl. Leeds LS9 .... 61 A3 19
Seaforth Rd. Leeds LS9 .... 61 B3
Seaforth Terr. Leeds LS9 .... 61 A3 21
Seagrave Rd. Hud HD4 .... 153 C3
Seaton St. Brad BD3 .... 75 B7
Seckar La. Wool WF4 .... 178 B8
Seckar Rd. Wake WF2 .... 142 B3
Second Ave. Bard LS17 .... 28 E5
Second Ave. Brad BD3 .... 56 C1
Second Ave. Clec WF15 .... 116 B4
Second Ave. Hali HX3 .... 113 B4
Second Ave. Hem WF9 .... 163 A4
Second Ave. Hud HD7 .... 152 D4
Second Ave. Hud HD5 .... 154 F7
Second Ave. Keigh BD21 .... 35 B6 2
Second Ave. Kirkha HD5 .... 137 C1
Second Ave. Leeds LS12 .... 78 E7
Second Ave. Loft & WF1 .... 121 B3
Second Ave. Weth LS22 .... 13 E8
Second Ave. Wrenth WF4 .... 183 A8
Second Ave. Weth LS22 .... 13 F5
Second Ave. Yeadon LS19 .... 40 C5
Second St. Brad BD12 .... 94 E6
Sedan St. Hali HX1 .... 113 C6 1
Sedbergh Cl. Leeds LS15 .... 80 D7
Sedbergh Dr. Ilkley LS29 .... 8 B3
Sedbergh Pk. Ilkley LS29 .... 8 B3
Sedbergh Rd. Leeds LS15 .... 80 D7
Sedge Gr. Haw BD22 .... 51 C8
Sedgewick St. Batley WF17 .... 96 E1 3
Sedgfield Terr. Brad BD1 .... 74 D7 1
Sedgwick Cl. Brad BD8 .... 55 D1
Seed Hill Terr. Hali HX2 .... 91 C6
Seed Hill Terr. Stee BD20 .... 17 C5
Seed Row. Brad BD4 .... 95 B8
Seed St. Brad BD12 .... 94 C6
Sefton Ave. Brig HD6 .... 114 F5
Sefton Ave. Leeds LS11 .... 79 A3
Sefton Cres. Brig HD6 .... 114 F5
Sefton Dr. Brig HD6 .... 114 F5
Sefton Dr. Ilkley LS29 .... 8 B3
Sefton Gr. Brad BD2 .... 56 B3
Sefton La. Mel HD7 .... 170 D2
Sefton Rd. Brig HD6 .... 114 F5
Sefton St. Hali HX1 .... 113 A8
Sefton St. Keigh BD21 .... 35 C8
Sefton St. Leeds LS11 .... 79 B3
Sefton Terr. Hali HX1 .... 113 A8
Sefton Terr. Leeds LS11 .... 79 A3
Selborne Gr. Keigh BD21 .... 35 B5
Selborne Gr. Brad BD9 .... 55 C2
Selborne Mount. Brad BD9 .... 55 C2
Selborne Terr. Brad BD9 .... 55 B2
Selborne Terr. Ship BD18 .... 55 C8
Selborne Villas. Brad BD9 .... 55 B8
Selborne Villas. Brad BD14 .... 73 C3
Selbourne Ave. Dew WF13 .... 138 D5
Selby Ave. Leeds LS9 .... 80 B7
Selby Hali HX2 .... 91 D6
Selby Rd. Gar LS25 .... 83 C4
Selby Rd. Ledsh LS25 .... 84 B4
Selby Rd. Leeds LS15 .... 81 A8
Selby Rd. S Mill LS25, LS25, LS9 .. 81 A8
Selby St. Wake WF1 .... 142 E3
Seldon St. Brad BD5 .... 74 D4
Sellars Fold. Brad BD7 .... 74 A4 4
Sellerdale Ave. Brad BD12 .... 94 D1
Sellerdale Dr. Brad BD12 .... 94 D1
Sellerdale Rise. Brad BD12 .... 94 D1
Sellerdale Way. Brad BD12 .... 94 D1
Selso Rd. Dew WF12 .... 118 F1
Semon Ave. Brad BD2 .... 56 C5
Senior St. Dew WF13 .... 118 D1
Senior Way. Brad BD5 .... 74 D6
Senior St. Dew WF13 .... 139 B7
Sentry. Honley HD7 .... 171 F5
Sergeantson St. Hud HD1 .... 154 A6 14
Serpentine Rd. Cleck BD19 .... 116 D7
Servia Dr. Leeds LS7 .... 60 D3
Servia Gdns. Leeds LS7 .... 60 D3
Servia Hill. Leeds LS6, LS7 .... 60 D3
Servia Rd. Leeds LS7 .... 60 D3
Sessions House Yd. Pont WF8 .... 125 C1
Seven Hills Prim Sch. Morley 98 B4
Sevenoaks Mead. Brad BD15 .... 54 A1
Seventh Ave. Leeds LS12 .... 78 E7
Seventh Ave. Roth LS26 .... 101 A7
Seventh Ave. Loft & WF1 .... 121 B3
Severn Dr. Gar LS25 .... 83 B6
Severn Rd. Brad BD2 .... 56 A3
Severn Rd. Hud HD3 .... 153 B8
Severn Rd. Leeds LS10 .... 79 F3
Severn Way. Leeds LS10 .... 79 F3
Sewage Works Rd. Leeds LS9 .... 80 D5
Sewell Rd. Brad BD3 .... 75 B6
Sewerbridge La. Feath WF7 .... 145 A8
Seymour St. Brad BD3 .... 75 B6
Seymour Wlk. Mel HD7 .... 142 C4
Seymour Wlk. Mel HD7 .... 170 D2
Shackleton Terr. Hal BD16 .... 37 A4
Shade Jun & Inf Sch. Tod 108 A3
Shade St. Tod OL14 .... 108 A3
Shadwell La. Leeds LS17 .... 44 A5
Shadwell La. Leeds LS17 .... 43 E3
Shadwell Park Ave. Leeds LS17 .... 44 B6
Shadwell Park Cl. Leeds LS17 .... 44 B5
Shadwell Park Ct. Leeds LS17 .... 44 B5
Shadwell Park Dr. Leeds LS17 .... 44 B5
Shadwell Park Gdns. Leeds LS17 .. 44 C5
Shadwell Primary Sch. Leeds 44 D5
Shadwell Wlk. Leeds LS17 .... 44 C5

Shaftesbury Ave. Brad BD9 .... 55 A2
Shaftesbury Ave. Ilkley LS29 .... 8 E3
Shaftesbury Ave. Leeds LS8 .... 44 B2
Shaftesbury Ave. Ship BD18 .... 55 C5
Shaftesbury Rd. Leeds LS8 .... 44 B2
Shaftesbury Rd. Pudsey LS28 .... 76 E6
Shafton Hall Dr. Shaf S72 .... 180 B3
Shafton La. Leeds LS11 .... 78 F5
Shafton Pl. Leeds LS11 .... 78 F5 2
Shafton St. Leeds LS11 .... 79 A5
Shafton Two Gates Fst Sch.
    Shaf 180 C2
Shafton View. Leeds LS11 .... 78 F5
Shakespeare App. Leeds LS9 .... 60 F1
Shakespeare Ave. Leeds LS9 .... 61 A1
Shakespeare Ave. Nor WF6 .... 144 A2
Shakespeare Ave. Tod OL14 .... 108 D6
Shakespeare Bldgs. Hud HD1 .... 153 D6
Shakespeare Cl. Guise LS20 .... 39 F8
Shakespeare Cl. Leeds LS9 .... 60 F1
Shakespeare Cl. Loft OL15 .... 129 C1
Shakespeare Cl. Leeds LS9 .... 61 A1
Shakespeare Cres. Leeds LS9 .... 60 F1
Shakespeare Gdns. Leeds LS9 .... 60 F1
Shakespeare Grange. Leeds LS9 ... 60 F1
Shakespeare Lawn. Leeds LS9 ...... 60 F1
Shakespeare Prim Sch. Leeds 61 A1
Shakespeare Rd. Guise LS20 .... 39 F8
Shakespeare St. Hali HX1 .... 113 C7
Shakespeare St. Leeds LS9 .... 60 F1
Shakespeare Towers. Leeds LS9 ... 60 F1
Shalimar St. Hali HX1 .... 112 F7
Shambles The. Weth LS22 .... 13 E5
Shambles The. Weth LS22 .... 134 B6 11
Shann Ave. Keigh BD21 .... 34 F8
Shann Cres. Keigh BD21 .... 34 F8
Shann La. Keigh BD20 .... 17 F1
Shann St. Ship BD2 .... 55 D4
Shannon Cl. Brig HD6 .... 135 E7
Shannon Ct. Ilkley LS29 .... 7 F3
Shannon Rd. Brig HD6 .... 135 E7
Shannon Rd. Leeds LS9 .... 79 E8
Shannon Rd. Leeds LS9 .... 79 E8
Share Hill. Slai HD7 .... 152 C3
Sharehill. Slai HD7 .... 152 C4
Sharleston Jun & Inf Sch. Crof 144 B4
Sharnaley Ct. Pont WF8 .... 147 A8
Sharneyford Cty Prim Sch. Bacup .. 106 C1
Sharon Cotts. Ossett WF5 .... 140 D7
Sharp Ave. Brad BD6 .... 94 D8
Sharp House Rd. Midd LS10 .... 99 F4
Sharp La. Hud HD4, HD5 .... 154 F2
Sharp La. Midd LS10, LS10 .... 99 F4
Sharp St. Brad BD6 .... 74 C11
Sharp St. Dew WF13 .... 118 D1
Sharp's Row. Pudsey LS28 .... 76 E6
Sharpe St. Batley WF16 .... 117 D3
Sharpe St. Brad BD6 .... 74 E6
Shaw Ave. Nor WF6 .... 123 C2
Shaw Barn Croft. Weth LS22 .... 13 C5
Shaw Barn La. Weth LS22 .... 13 C5
Shaw Booth La. Hali HX2 .... 90 F4
Shaw Cl. Elland HX4 .... 134 C4
Shaw Cl. Guise LS20 .... 39 F8
Shaw Cl. Nor WF6 .... 123 C2
Shaw Cl. S Elm WF9 .... 183 A4
Shaw Cl. Mytholm Hali HX2 .... 90 F4
Shaw Fold. Wake WF2 .... 142 E1
Shaw Gate. Slai HD7 .... 169 F6
Shaw Hill. Hali HX3 .... 113 D5
Shaw La. Cud S72 .... 179 E1
Shaw La. Elland HX5 .... 134 C4
Shaw La. Guise LS20 .... 22 F1
Shaw La. Keigh BD21 .... 35 D6
Shaw La. Leeds LS6 .... 59 C4
Shaw La. Leeds LS6 .... 59 D4
Shaw La. Leeds LS6 .... 59 E4
Shaw La. Mir WF14 .... 137 F3
Shaw La. Oxen BD22 .... 51 B2
Shaw La. Ryhill WF4 .... 162 C2
Shaw La. Shep HD8 .... 173 F3
Shaw La. Slai HD7 .... 169 F6
Shaw La. Stain BD20 .... 16 C6
Shaw La. B in Elm LS15 .... 63 C6
Shaw La. Nor WF6 .... 123 C2
Shawhead Cotts. Dew WF12 .... 140 A6
Shaw Rise. Nor WF6 .... 123 C2
Shaw Rise. Nor WF6 .... 123 C2
Shaw Royd. Yeadon LS19 .... 40 A8
Shaw Royd Ct. Yeadon LS19 .... 40 A8 4
Shaw St. Brad BD2 .... 55 F4
Shaw St. Elland HX4 .... 134 C4
Shaw St. Hali HX1 .... 112 F5
Shaw St. Heb Br HX7 .... 89 A3
Shaw Terr. Cud S72 .... 179 E1
Shaw Wood Ave. Tod OL14 .... 109 A6
Shaw's Terr. Mars HD7 .... 168 F4
Shawcross St. Batley WF13 .... 119 A3
Shawcross WF12 Dew 140 A6
Shawmount. Hali HX2 .... 111 E8
Shaws La. B in Elm LS15 .... 63 C6
Shay Cl. Leeds LS9 .... 61 A3
Shay Cres. Brad BD9 .... 54 E3
Shay Ct. Brad BD9 .... 54 E3
Shay Dr. Brad BD9 .... 54 E3
Shay Fold. Brad BD9 .... 54 E3
Shay Gap Rd. Keigh BD22 .... 33 A5
Shay Gr. Brad BD9 .... 54 E3
Shay Gr. Leeds LS6 .... 59 C7
Shay La. Brad BD9 .... 54 E3
Shay La. Crof WF4 .... 143 F1
Shay La. Hali HX2 .... 91 F6
Shay La. Holme HD7 .... 187 E5
Shay La. Pont WF7 .... 145 F5
Shay La. Wild BD15 .... 53 B2
Shay Syke. Hali HX1 .... 113 D6
Shay St. Leeds LS6 .... 59 F3
Shearbridge Pl. Brad BD7 .... 74 D6 7
Shearbridge Rd. Brad BD7 .... 74 D6
Shearbridge Terr. Brad BD7 .... 74 D6
Shearing Cross Gdns. Hud HD1 .... 153 D4 1
Sheepridge Gr. Hud HD2 .... 136 C4
Sheepridge Rd. Hud HD2 .... 136 C4
Sheepscar Gr. Leeds LS7 .... 60 D2
Sheepscar St N. Leeds LS7 .... 60 D2
Sheepscar St S. Leeds LS7 .... 60 D1
Sheepscar Way. Leeds LS7 .... 60 D3
Sheepwalk La. Kippa WF10 .... 103 D6
Sheepwalk La. Upton WF9 .... 183 D8
Sheerien Cl. Baro S71 .... 178 E1

Sheffield Rd. Holmfi HD7 .... 189 E3
Sheila Terr. Liver WF16 .... 117 C3
Sheldrake Ave. Brad BD8 .... 73 C7
Sheldrake Rd. Castle WF10 .... 124 D6
Shelf Hall La. Shelf HX3 .... 93 C5
Shelf Juin & Inf Sch. Shelf 93 B5
Shelf Moor Rd. Shelf HX3 .... 93 C6
Shelf Moor. Shelf HX3 .... 93 C7
Shelf Rd. Heb Br HX7 .... 88 F3
Shelf La. Pudsey LS28 .... 57 B5
Sheldrake Dr. Midd LS10 .... 99 D5
Shelley Ave. Batley WF16 .... 117 E2
Shelley Cres. Roth LS26 .... 101 C3
Shelley Dr. Knot WF11 .... 126 B4
Shelley Fst Sch. Shep 174 A3
Shelley Gr. Brad BD8 .... 73 E8
Shelley High Sch. Shep 174 E2
Shelley La. Kirkb HD8 .... 174 A5
Shelley Wlk. Loft G WF3 .... 121 F6
Shelley Woodhouse La. Shep HD8 . 174 D1
Shelley Woodhouse La. Skel HD8 . 174 D1
Shepcote Cl. Hors LS16 .... 41 F3
Shepcote Cres. Hors LS16 .... 41 F3
Shepherd St. Brad BD7 .... 74 B4
Shepherd Dr. Keigh BD22 .... 34 E5
Shepherd's La. Leeds LS7, LS8 .. 60 F4
Shepherd's Pl. Leeds LS16 .... 60 F4
Shepherds Gr. Hud HD2 .... 136 B4
Shepherds Thorn La. Hud HD2 .. 136 C5
Shepley Fst Sch. Shep 190 E8
Shepley Mount. Mir WF14 .... 138 B7
Shepley Rd. Kirkb HD4 .... 173 C2
Shepley St. Wake WF1 .... 142 D8
Shepley Sta. Shep 173 F1
Shepstye Rd. Hor WF4 .... 141 A1
Sherborne Dr. Keigh BD22 .... 34 E5
Sherborne Rd. Brad BD10 .... 39 B1
Sherborne Rd. Brad BD7 .... 74 D6
Sherborne Cl. Hud HD5 .... 154 D6
Sherburn App. Leeds LS15 .... 80 F7
Sherburn App. Leeds LS14 .... 62 C6
Sherburn Cl. Ad Le S DN6 .... 184 E2
Sherburn Cl. Birk BD11 .... 96 B6
Sherburn Ct. Leeds LS14 .... 62 C6 3
Sherburn Gr. Birk BD11 .... 96 B6
Sherburn Pl. Leeds LS14 .... 62 C6
Sherburn Rd. Brig HD6 .... 135 E8
Sherburn Rd. Leeds LS14 .... 62 C6
Sherburn Rd N. Leeds LS14 .... 62 B7
Sherburn Row. Leeds LS14 .... 62 C6
Sherburn Sq. Leeds LS14 .... 62 C7
Sherburn Wlk. Leeds LS14 .... 62 C6
Sheridan Cl. Pudsey LS28 .... 76 F6
Sheridan Ct. Pudsey LS28 .... 76 F6
Sheridan St. Brad BD4 .... 75 B4
Sheridan St. Loft G WF1 .... 121 C5
Sheridan Way. Pudsey LS28 .... 76 F6
Sheriff La. Bing BD16 .... 37 B4
Sherwell Gr. Brad BD15 .... 54 C1
Sherwell Rise. Brad BD15 .... 54 C1
Sherwood Ave. Clec BD19 .... 117 A8
Sherwood Ave. Hud HD2 .... 136 F5
Sherwood Cl. Batley WF13 .... 117 F3
Sherwood Cl. Wake WF2 .... 160 D5
Sherwood Dr. Clec BD19 .... 117 B8
Sherwood Dr. Ad Le S DN6 .... 184 E2
Sherwood Dr. Hud HD4 .... 171 C7
Sherwood Ind Est. Wake WF3 ... 100 A3
Sherwood Gr. Wake WF2 .... 141 E4
Sherwood Ind Est. Roth 100 B3
Sherwood Pl. Brad BD2 .... 56 B2
Sherwood Rd. Brig HD6 .... 115 C2
Sherwood Way. Cud S72 .... 180 A1
Shetcliffe La. Brad BD4 .... 75 F2
Shetcliffe Rd. Brad BD4 .... 95 B8
Shetland Cl. Brad BD2 .... 55 F4
Shibden Dr. Batley WF17 .... 118 F5
Shibden Garth. Hali HX3 .... 113 F6
Shibden Grange Dr. Northo HX3 .. 92 F1
Shibden Hall Croft. Hali HX3 .... 114 A8
Shibden Hall Rd. Brig HX3 .... 113 F8
Shibden Hall Rd. Hali HX3 .... 114 A8
Shibden Head Fst Sch. Queen BD13 92 D7
Shibden View. Queen BD13 .... 92 D7
Shield Cl. Leeds LS15 .... 62 D7
Shield Hall La. Sow Br HX6 .... 111 C4
Shill Bank Ave. Mir WF14 .... 138 D6
Shill Bank La. Mir WF14 .... 138 C6
Shillbank View. Mir WF14 .... 138 C6
Shilling St. Wake WF1 .... 142 D8
Shillinghill La. Pont WF8 .... 126 B1
Shinwell Dr. Upton WF9 .... 183 A8
Ship St. Brig HD6 .... 115 B2
Ship Yd. Wake WF1 .... 142 D5
Shipley CE Fst Sch. Ship 55 A6
Shipley Coll of F Ed. Ship 55 A8
Shipley College Mill Annexe. Ship 37 F1
Shipley Fields Rd. Ship BD18 .... 55 C5
Shipley Golf Course. Harden 36 E1
Shipley Sta. Ship 55 C7
Shipley Wychliffe CE Mid Sch. Ship 55 A8
Shipton Mews. Morley LS27 .... 98 B3
Shire Cl. Brad BD6 .... 93 E8
Shire Oak Rd. Leeds LS6 .... 59 E5
Shire Oak St. Leeds LS6 .... 59 E5
Shires Hill. Hud HD1 .... 153 E5
Shires Gr. Wake WF1 .... 121 F5
Shirley Ave. Brad BD17 .... 38 C3
Shirley Ave. Clec BD19 .... 117 B8
Shirley Cres. Brad BD12 .... 94 D1
Shirley Dr. Leeds LS13 .... 58 C4
Shirley Gr. Brig HD6 .... 135 C6
Shirley Gr. Clec BD19 .... 117 B8
Shirley Manor Prim Sch. Brad 94 C1
Shirley Mount. Clec BD19 .... 117 B8
Shirley Pl. Brad BD12 .... 94 D1
Shirley Rd. Brad BD12 .... 117 B8
Shirley Rd. Clec BD19 .... 117 B8
Shirley Sq. Clec BD19 .... 117 B8
Shirley St. Brad BD17 .... 38 C3
Shirley St. Haw BD22 .... 51 C6
Shirley Terr. Clec BD19 .... 117 B8
Shirley Wlk. Clec BD19 .... 117 B8
Shoe Market. Pont WF8 .... 146 D8 4

Shoebridge Ave. Stee BD20 .... 16 F6
Shoebroad La. Tod OL14 .... 108 B4
Sholebroke Ave. Leeds LS7 .... 60 D4
Sholebroke Mount. Leeds LS7 .... 60 D4
Sholebroke Pl. Leeds LS7 .... 60 D4
Sholebroke St. Leeds LS7 .... 60 D4
Sholebroke Terr. Leeds LS7 .... 60 D5
Sholebroke View. Leeds LS7 .... 60 D5
Shoolsboards La. Pont WF8 .... 146 F8 3
Shop La. Kirkhe HD5 .... 137 C1
Shop La. Kirkhe HD5 .... 155 C8
Shop La. Loft G WF3 .... 121 B8
Shore End La. Wad M HX2 .... 90 A7
Shore Gn. Tod OL14 .... 86 C2
Shore New Rd. Tod OL14 .... 86 C1
Shoreham Rd. Leeds LS12 .... 78 C6
Short Cl. Brad BD12 .... 94 B5
Short La. Leeds LS7 .... 60 C6
Short St. Dew WF12 .... 140 A7
Short St. Hali WF7 .... 145 C5
Short St. Tod OL14 .... 108 B5
Shortway. Pudsey LS28 .... 57 A1
Shortway. Thorn BD13 .... 72 E6
Shroggs Rd. Hali HX3 .... 113 C4
Shroggs Rd. Hali HX1 .... 113 C4
Shroggs Vue Terr. Hali HX1 .... 113 A8
Shutt The. Hor WF4 .... 159 B8
Shuttleworth La. Brad BD8 .... 73 E8
Shuttocks Cl. Kippax LS25 .... 83 A3
Shuttocks Fold. Kippax LS25 .... 83 B3
Shutts La. Brig HX3 .... 93 E2
Sickle St. Clec BD19 .... 116 E8
Sicklehome Ct. Hud HD2 .... 136 F5
Sicklinghall Cty Prim Sch. Sickl .. 12 B5
Sicklinghall Rd. Coll LS22 .... 13 A3
Siddal Gr. Hali HX3 .... 113 D4
Siddal Inf Sch. Hali 113 E3
Siddal Jun Sch. Hali 113 E3
Siddal St. Hali HX3 .... 113 E3
Siddal Top La. Hali HX3 .... 113 E3
Siddall St. Leeds LS11 .... 79 B6
Siddal View. Hali HX3 .... 113 E3
Siddon Dr. Hud HD5 .... 155 A3
Side Copse. Otley LS21 .... 23 B8
Side La. Hud HD3 .... 152 F6
Sidings The. Guise LS20 .... 22 D1
Sidings The. Ship BD18 .... 55 C8
Sigget La. Tod OL14 .... 107 F6
Sigott St. Hud HD3 .... 153 A6
Silk Cl. Kex S75 .... 177 D7
Sike La. Walton WF2 .... 161 B5
Sikes Cl. Hud HD5 .... 154 F4
Silcoates Ave. Wake WF2 .... 120 E1
Silcoates Dr. Wake WF2 .... 120 E1
Silcoates La. Wake WF2 .... 120 E1
Silcoates Sch. Wake 120 E1
Silcoates St. Wake WF2 .... 142 A7
Silk Mill App. Hors LS16 .... 41 C3
Silk Mill Ave. Hors LS16 .... 41 C4
Silk Mill Cl. Hors LS16 .... 41 D3
Silk Mill Dr. Hors LS16 .... 41 D3
Silk Mill Gdns. Hors LS16 .... 41 D3
Silk Mill Gn. Hors LS16 .... 41 D3
Silk Mill Rd. Hors LS16 .... 41 C3
Silk Mill Way. Hors LS16 .... 41 D3
Silk St. Brad BD9 .... 55 A2
Silkstone Cres. Nor WF6 .... 122 F4
Silkstone Cl. Hud HD5 .... 154 F4
Silkstone Ct. Leeds LS15 .... 62 C1
Silkstone La. Caw S75 .... 193 F3
Silsbridge St. Brad BD1 .... 74 D7
Silsden Golf Course. Sil 18 A8
Silsden Rd. Add LS29 .... 6 C7
Silsden Rd. Keigh BD20 .... 18 B6
Silsden Rd. J. Brad BD20 .... 4 F5
Silson La. Baild BD17 .... 38 E4
Silver Birch Ave. Brad BD12 .... 94 D2
Silver Birch Dr. Brad BD12 .... 94 D2
Silver Birch Gr. Brad BD12 .... 94 D2
Silver Court. Ind Est. Hud 136 F5
Silver Ct. Pudsey LS28 .... 57 F1
Silver La. Yeadon LS19 .... 40 B7
Silver Mill Hill. Otley LS21 .... 23 B6
Silver Royd Ave. Leeds LS12 .... 77 F6
Silver Royd Cl. Leeds LS12 .... 77 F6
Silver Royd Dr. Leeds LS12 .... 77 F6
Silver Royd Garth. Leeds LS12 .. 77 F6
Silver Royd Gr. Leeds LS12 .... 77 F6
Silver Royd Hill. Leeds LS12 .... 78 A6
Silver Royd Pl. Leeds LS12 .... 77 F6
Silver Royd Rd. Leeds LS12 .... 77 F6
Silver Royd St. Leeds LS12 .... 77 F6
Silver Royd Terr. Leeds LS12 .... 77 F6
Silver St. Brad BD8 .... 55 B1
Silver St. Dew WF13 .... 139 D8
Silver St. Fair WF11 .... 105 A4
Silver St. Hali HX1 .... 113 C6
Silver St. Hud HD5 .... 154 D5
Silver St. Loft G WF1 .... 121 C5
Silver St. S Hie S72 .... 180 E7
Silver St W. Wake WF1 .... 142 E3
Silverdale Ave. Guise LS20 .... 39 D8
Silverdale Ave. Keigh BD20 .... 18 E1
Silverdale Ave. Leeds LS17 .... 43 A4
Silverdale Cl. Guise LS20 .... 39 D8
Silverdale Cres. Guise LS20 .... 39 E8
Silverdale Dr. Guise LS20 .... 39 E8
Silverdale Gr. Guise LS20 .... 39 D8
Silverdale Mount. Guise LS20 .... 39 E8
Silverdale Rd. Brad BD5 .... 74 D3
Silverdale Rd. Guise LS20 .... 39 D8
Silverdale Terr. Elland HX4 .... 134 A6
Silverhill Ave. Brad BD3 .... 56 C1
Silverhill Dr. Brad BD3 .... 56 C1
Silverhill Rd. Brad BD3 .... 56 B1
Silverwood Ave. Hali HX2 .... 91 C1
Silverwood Wlk. Hali HX2 .... 91 C1
Sim Royd La. D Dale HD8 .... 192 C6
Simeon St. Tod OL14 .... 86 F3
Simes St. Brad BD1 .... 74 D7
Simm Carr La. Northo HX3 .... 92 D4

Simmonds La. Hali HX3 .... 113 D5
Simms Dene. Brad BD15 .... 54 A4
Simon Cl. Brad BD4 .... 75 F2
Simon Green Rd. Slai HD7 .... 152 B3
Simpson Gr. Brad BD10 .... 39 C1
Simpson Gr. Leeds LS12 .... 78 D7
Simpson St. Heb Br HX7 .... 110 D8
Simpson Rd. S Elm WF9 .... 183 B4
Simpson St. E Ard WF3 .... 120 E8
Simpson St. Keigh BD21 .... 35 A7
Simpson's Lane A Inf Sch.
    Knot 126 D3
Simpsons La. Knot WF11 .... 126 D3
Sinclair Garth. Wake WF2 .... 160 E8
Sinclair Rd. Brad BD2 .... 55 F6
Sinden Mews. Brad BD10 .... 39 B2
Singleton St. Brad BD1 .... 55 E1
Sion Hill. Hali HX3 .... 113 C4
Sir George Martin Dr. Hors LS16 .. 42 D4
Sir Isaac Holden Pl. Brad BD7 .... 74 C7
Sir Karl Cohen Sq. Leeds LS12 .... 78 B7
Sir Wilfred Pl. Brad BD10 .... 56 D8
Sisley La. Tod OL14 .... 109 A4
Sissons Ave. Midd LS10 .... 99 B4
Sissons Cres. Midd LS10 .... 99 B4
Sissons Dr. Midd LS10 .... 99 B4
Sissons Gn. Midd LS10 .... 99 B4
Sissons Gr. Midd LS10 .... 99 B4
Sissons Mount. Midd LS10 .... 99 A3
Sissons Pl. Midd LS10 .... 99 B4
Sissons Rd. Midd LS10 .... 99 A4
Sissons Row. Midd LS10 .... 99 B4
Sissons St. Midd LS10 .... 99 B4
Sissons Terr. Midd LS10 .... 99 A3
Sissons View. Midd LS10 .... 99 A3
Sitka Cl. Roy S71 .... 179 B2
Sitlington Middlestown Jun & Inf Sch.
    Neth 158 A6
Sitlington Netherton Jun & Inf Sch.
    Neth 158 E6
Sixward St. Hem HX7 .... 163 A4
Six Heights. Rip HX6 .... 132 E6
Sixrood La. Burg DN6 .... 184 F5
Sixth Ave. Brad BD3 .... 56 C1
Sixth Ave. Clec WF15 .... 116 A5
Sixth Ave. Roth LS26 .... 101 A6
Sixth St. Crof WF4 .... 162 B7
Sizers Ct. Yeadon LS19 .... 40 A5
Skelbrooke Dr. Pont WF8 .... 146 D6
Skelda Rise. Ilkley LS29 .... 7 F3
Skelkow Rd. Ad Le S DN6 .... 184 F1
Skelmanthorpe Bsns Pk. Skel 175 A2
Skelmanthorpe Fst Sch. Skel 175 B2
Skelton Ave. Leeds LS9 .... 80 B8
Skelton Cres. Hud HD4 .... 153 A3
Skelton Cres. Leeds LS9 .... 80 B8
Skelton Grange Rd. Leeds LS10 .. 80 B2
Skelton Mount. Leeds LS9 .... 80 B8
Skelton Pl. Leeds LS9 .... 80 B8
Skelton Rd. Leeds LS9 .... 80 B8
Skelton St. Leeds LS9 .... 80 B8
Skelton Terr. Leeds LS9 .... 80 B8
Skelton Wlk. Brad BD10 .... 56 E7
Skelwith Wlk. Leeds LS14 .... 61 F3
Skelwith App. Leeds LS14 .... 61 F3
Skinner La. Brad BD8 .... 74 D8
Skinner La. Leeds LS7 .... 60 C1
Skinner La. Pont WF8 .... 146 C6
Skinner St. Leeds LS1 .... 79 A8 11
Skipton Ave. Hud HD2 .... 136 B2
Skipton Rd. Add LS29 .... 2 E1
Skipton Rd. Farnh BD20 .... 16 D7
Skipton Rd. Glu BD20 .... 16 C5
Skipton Rd. Ilkley LS29 .... 7 E4
Skipton Rd. Keigh BD20 .... 18 C1
Skipton Rd. Keigh BD20 .... 35 A8
Skipton Rd. Sil BD20 .... 5 C2
Skipton St. Batley WF17 .... 118 C2
Sladburn Gn. Leeds LS13 .... 58 C2
Slack Bottom. Hep HX7 .... 88 B6
Slack Bottom Rd. Brad BD6 .... 93 E7
Slack House La. Wad M HX7 .... 69 A6
Slack La. Crof WF4 .... 144 A3
Slack La. Elland HD3 .... 152 A3
Slack La. Hali HX2 .... 90 B4
Slack La. Holmfi HD7 .... 189 D3
Slack La. Hors LS16 .... 41 C6
Slack La. Hors LS16 .... 42 A6
Slack La. Wake WF2, WF4 .... 160 D5
Slack La. Skel HD8 .... 175 A4
Slack Side. Brad BD6 .... 93 F7
Slack Top La. Wh Com HD7 .... 190 C4
Slack Top La. Tod OL14 .... 86 B1
Slade Cl. B Spa LS23 .... 30 C7
Slade House. Brad BD2 .... 56 B7
Slade La. Brad BD11 .... 96 E5
Slaid Hill Ct. Leeds LS17 .... 44 B5
Slant Gate. Kirkb HD4 .... 173 E7
Slant La. Tod OL14 .... 85 E2
Slant Gate. Kirkb HD4 .... 173 D7
Slates La. Ilkley LS29 .... 7 C7
Slaymaker La. Oxen BD22 .... 51 C3

Slead Cres. Brig HD6 .... 114 F4
Slead Gr. Brig HD6 .... 114 F4
Slead Royd. Brig HD6 .... 114 F4
Slead Syke. Brig HD6 .... 114 F4
Sledbrook Cres. Wh Com S30 .... 200 C6
Sledgate La. Slai HD7 .... 169 E5
Sledge Gate. Mars HD3 .... 151 A4
Sledmere Croft. Leeds LS14 .... 62 C6
Sledmere Garth. Leeds LS14 .... 62 C6
Sledmere Gn. Leeds LS14 .... 62 C6 9
Sledmere La. Leeds LS14 .... 62 C6
Sledmere Pl. Leeds LS14 .... 62 C6
Sledmere Sq. Leeds LS14 .... 62 C6
Sleep Hill La. Ham DN6 .... 184 B6
Sleep Hill La. Ham DN6 .... 184 B6
Sleights La. E Kei LS17 .... 27 B6
Sleningford Gr. Ship BD18 .... 54 E8
Sleningford Rd. Bing BD16 .... 36 E5
Sleningford Rd. Ship BD18 .... 54 E8
Sleningford Terr. Bing BD16 .... 36 E5
Slicer's Yd. Bing BD16 .... 36 F3
Slipper La. Mir WF14 .... 137 E7
Slippery Ford La. Haw BD22 .... 33 C6
Slippy La. Hali HX2 .... 91 C5
Sludgwell La. Wake WF4 .... 159 B8
Slutwell La. Pont WF8 .... 146 D8
Smalewell Cl. Pudsey LS28 .... 76 D6
Smalewell Dr. Pudsey LS28 .... 76 C6
Smalewell Gdns. Pudsey LS28 .... 76 C6
Smalewell Gn. Pudsey LS28 .... 76 D6
Smalewell Rd. Pudsey LS28 .... 76 C6
Small Cl. Liver WF15 .... 117 B1
Small La. Haw BD22 .... 51 A5
Small La. Oxen BD22 .... 51 A5
Small Lees Rd. Rip HX6 .... 132 D3
Small Page Fold. Queen BD13 .... 72 E1 7
Small Shaw La. Tod OL14 .... 86 D2
Smallpage Yd. Wake WF1 .... 142 C6 9
Smallwood Gdns. Batley WF12 ... 119 A2
Smallwood Rd. Batley WF12 .... 119 A2
Smawell La. Notton WF4 .... 179 B7
Smawthorne Ave. Castle WF10 ... 124 D7
Smawthorne Gr. Castle WF10 .... 124 D7
Smawthorne La. Castle WF10 .... 124 D7
Smeatley's La. K Smea WF8 .... 166 E7
Smeaton App. Leeds LS15 .... 62 F3
Smeaton Gr. Swil LS26 .... 82 A2
Smeaton Rd. Upton WF9 .... 183 A8
Smiddles La. Brad BD5 .... 74 D2
Smiddle's La. Brad BD4, BD5 .... 74 D2
Smiddy Hill. Th Arch LS23 .... 15 A4
Smirthwaite View. Nor WF6 .... 123 A1
Smirthwaite View. Nor WF6 .... 123 A1
Smith House Ave. Brig HD6 .... 115 A5
Smith House Cres. Brig HD6 .... 115 A5
Smith House La. Brig HD6 .... 115 A4
Smith La. Brad BD9 .... 54 E3
Smith Rd. Batley WF13 .... 117 F1
Smith Rd. Brad BD7 .... 74 A3
Smith St. Brad BD4 .... 95 B8
Smith St. Castle WF10 .... 103 F1
Smith St. Clec WF15 .... 116 B4
Smith St. Keigh BD21 .... 35 A8
Smith St. Liver WF16 .... 117 C4
Smith St. Wake WF1 .... 142 E4
Smith Wlk. S Elm WF9 .... 183 A2
Smith's Terr. Hali HX3 .... 92 A3
Smithfield Ave. Brig HX3 .... 114 F4
Smithies La. Batley WF17 .... 96 E1
Smithies Moor Cl. Batley WF17 .. 117 F8
Smithies Moor La. Batley WF17 .. 117 F8
Smithies Moor Rise. Batley WF17 . 117 F8
Smithson Ave. Castle WF10 .... 125 C5
Smithson St. Roth LS26 .... 100 F4
Smithville. Keigh BD21 .... 34 E5
Smithwell La. Heb Br HX7 .... 88 F3
Smithy Carr La. Brig HD6 .... 115 A3
Smithy Clough La. Ripp HX6 .... 132 B5
Smithy Greaves. Nes LS29 .... 7 C7
Smithy Hill. Denb BD13 .... 71 C6
Smithy Hill. Wible BD6 .... 93 F8
Smithy La. Burg HX6 .... 131 E2
Smithy La. Denton LS29 .... 9 B7
Smithy La. E Ard WF3 .... 119 E7
Smithy La. Hali HX2 .... 91 D6
Smithy La. Holmfi HD7 .... 188 D4
Smithy La. Hors LS16 .... 41 C6
Smithy La. Leeds LS16 .... 42 B4
Smithy La. Mel HD7 .... 170 C8
Smithy La. Oakw BD22 .... 34 B3
Smithy La. Ship BD16 .... 54 B6
Smithy Mills La. Leeds LS16 .... 42 E2
Smithy Nook. Tod OL14 .... 86 A1
Smithy Par. Baild BD17 .... 38 E4
Smithy Place La. Honley HD7 .... 172 A3
Smithy St. Hali HX1 .... 113 C7
Smithy Wlk. Dew WF12 .... 139 D2
Snape Dr. Brad BD7 .... 73 D2
Snape St. Keigh BD21 .... 35 B4
Snapethorpe Ave. Wake WF2 .... 141 E4
Snapethorpe Cres. Wake WF2 .... 141 E4
Snapethorpe Gate. Wake WF2 ... 141 E4
Snapethorpe Rd. Crig WF4 .... 159 E4
Snapethorpe Rd. Wake WF2 .... 141 E4
Snaygill Ind Est. Skip 4 A8
Snelsins La. Clec BD19 .... 116 D8
Snelsins Rd. Clec BD19 .... 116 D8
Snittle Rd. Holmfi HD7 .... 200 A8
Snow Hill. Wake WF1 .... 142 E8
Snow Hill Gdns. Wake WF1 .... 142 E8
Snow Hill Rise. Wake WF1 .... 142 E8
Snow Hill View. Wake WF1 .... 142 E8
Snow Lees. Liver WF15 .... 117 B2
Snowden App. Leeds LS13 .... 58 D2
Snowden Ave. Brad BD10 .... 56 D6
Snowden Cl. Leeds LS13 .... 58 D2
Snowden Cres. Leeds LS13 .... 58 D2
Snowden Crest. Leeds LS13 .... 58 D2
Snowden Fold. Leeds LS13 .... 58 D2
Snowden Gn. Leeds LS13 .... 58 D2
Snowden Gr. Leeds LS13 .... 58 D2
Snowden Lawn. Leeds LS13 .... 58 D2
Snowden Rd. Ship BD18 .... 55 A8
Snowden Royd. Leeds LS13 .... 58 D2
Snowden St. Brad BD1 .... 74 D7
Snowden Vale. Leeds LS13 .... 58 D2

Snowden Way. Leeds LS13 .... 58 D3
Snowden Wlk. Leeds LS13 .... 58 D2
Snowden Ave. Knot WF11 .... 126 C4
Snowden St. Batley WF17 .... 118 B4
Snug La. Holmfi HD7 .... 190 A1
Snydale Ave. Nor WF6 .... 123 C1
Snydale Cl. Nor WF6 .... 123 C1
Snydale Ct. Nor WF6 .... 123 C1
Snydale Gr. Nor WF6 .... 123 C1
Snydale Rd. Nor WF6 .... 123 C1
Soaper House La. Brig HX3 .... 93 D8
Soaper La. Brad BD6 .... 93 E8
Soaper La. Shelf HX3 .... 93 D8
Sod House Gn. Hali HX3 .... 92 A3
Soho St. Brad BD1 .... 74 E7
Soho St. Hali HX1 .... 112 F7
Solid. Hud HD4 .... 153 F7
Solomon Hill. Hali HX2 .... 90 D2
Solway Rd. Batley WF17 .... 118 F5
Somerdale Cl. Leeds LS13 .... 58 D1
Somerdale Gdns. Leeds LS13 .... 58 D1
Somerdale Gr. Leeds LS13 .... 58 D1
Somerdale Wlk. Leeds LS13 .... 58 D1
Somers Pl. Leeds LS1 .... 79 B8 5
Somerset Ave. Brig HD6 .... 136 A7
Somerset Ave. Leeds LS17 .... 43 C5
Somerset Rd. Hud HD5 .... 154 D4
Somerset Rd. Pudsey LS28 .... 76 D8
Somerton Dr. Brad BD4 .... 75 E2
Somerville Ave. Brad BD6 .... 94 A7
Somerville Ave. Leeds LS14 .... 61 F2
Somerville Dr. Leeds LS14 .... 61 F3
Somerville Gn. Leeds LS14 .... 61 F3
Somerville Gr. Leeds LS14 .... 61 F3
Somerville Mount. Leeds LS14 .... 62 A2
Somerville Pk. Brad BD6 .... 94 A7
Somerville Terr. Otley LS21 .... 11 F2
Somerville View. Leeds LS14 .... 61 F2
Sonning Rd. Brad BD15 .... 73 B8
Soothill La. Batley WF17 .... 118 E5
Soothill La. E Ard WF17 .... 119 A5
Sorbus Way. Leeds HD28 .... 155 E3
Sorrel Cl. Pont WF8 .... 146 D7
Sorrin Cl. Brad BD10 .... 56 E7
Sotheron Croft. Dar WF8 .... 147 C5
Sourceby Cross Way. Birk BD4 ... 96 A6
Sourhall Cotts. Tod OL14 .... 107 D6
South Accommodation Rd. Leeds
    LS10, LS9 .... 79 E5
South App. Bramham LS14 .... 46 F6
South App. Bramham LS23 .... 47 C6
South App. Stut LS25 .... 48 A3
South Ave. Castle WF10 .... 123 F7
South Ave. Hud WF4 .... 171 C7
South Ave. Hud HD4 .... 152 F3
South Ave. S Elm WF9 .... 182 F2
South Baileygate. Pont WF8 .... 125 E1
South Bank. E Kes LS17 .... 28 C6
South Bank. Lepton HD8 .... 155 D4
South Bank Rd. Batley WF17 .... 118 A6
South Bolton. Hali HX2 .... 91 E7
South Bradford Golf Course. Brad 94 F7
South Brook Terr. Brad BD7 .... 74 D5
South Cl. Guise LS20 .... 39 D8
South Cl. Roy S71 .... 179 C2
South Cliffe. Thorn BD13 .... 72 E6
South Clough Head. Hali HX2 .... 112 A8
South Craven Sch. Glu 16 D6
South Cres. S Elm WF9 .... 183 B4
South Croft Ave. Birk BD11 .... 96 A6
South Croft Dr. Birk BD11 .... 96 A6
South Croft Gate. Birk BD11 .... 96 A6
South Dr. Guise LS20 .... 39 D8
South Dr. Roy S71 .... 179 C2
South Edge. Keigh BD20 .... 35 A8
South Elmsall Ash Grove Fst Sch.
    S Elm 183 A4
South Elmsall Mid Sch. S Elm 182 F1
South Elmsall Sta. S Elm 183 A3
South End Gr. Leeds LS13 .... 58 E1
South End Mount. Leeds LS13 .... 58 E1
South End Terr. Leeds LS13 .... 58 E1 1
South Farm La. Leeds LS9 .... 61 C2
South Farm Rd. Leeds LS9 .... 61 C2
South Gr. Brig HD6 .... 114 D5
South Gr. Ship BD18 .... 54 D7
South Hawksworth St. Ilkley LS29 . 8 A4
South Hiendley Est Sch. S Hie 180 D6
South Hill Cl. Midd LS10 .... 99 D8
South Hill Croft. Midd LS10 .... 99 E8
South Hill Dr. Bard LS17 .... 28 E3
South Hill Gdns. Midd LS10 .... 99 E7
South Hill Gr. Midd LS10 .... 99 E8
South Hill Rise. Midd LS10 .... 99 E7
South Hill Way. Midd LS10 .... 99 E8
South Holme. Liver WF15 .... 117 C3
South Kirkby Common Road
    Prim & Nd Sch. S Kirk 182 A1
South Kirkby Moorthorpe
    Prim & Nd Sch. S Elm 182 A1
South Kirkby Stockingate Prim
    Sch. S Kirk 182 A1
South La. Elland HX5 .... 134 F4
South La. Holmfi HD7 .... 189 C1
South La. Shelf HX3 .... 93 C5
South Lee. Hali HX3 .... 92 B2
South Leeds Bsns Pk. Leeds 79 D3
South Leeds Golf Course. Midd .. 99 B4
South Leeds High Sch. Leeds 79 B8
South Leeds Stad. Leeds 79 D3
South Nelson St. Morley LS27 .... 98 B5
South Par. Clec BD19 .... 117 C8
South Par. Hali HX1 .... 113 C6
South Par. Ilkley LS29 .... 8 A4
South Par. Leeds LS1 .... 79 D8
South Par. Leeds LS1 .... 79 D8
South Par. Morley LS27 .... 98 B3

Stainbeck High Sch. Leeds 60 B8
Stainbeck La. Leeds LS7 ...... 60 B7
Stainbeck Preparatory Sch. Leeds . 60 B7
Stainbeck Rd. Leeds LS7 ...... 60 A7
Stainbeck St. Leeds LS7 ...... 60 C8
Stainbeck Wlk. Leeds LS7 .... 60 B7
Stainburn Ave. Leeds LS17 .. 125 A5
Stainburn Cres. Leeds LS17 .. 43 E1
Stainburn Dr. Leeds LS17 .... 43 D1
Stainburn Gdns. Leeds LS17 . 43 E1
Stainburn Mount. Leeds LS17 60 D8
Stainburn Rd. Leeds LS17 .... 60 D8
Stainburn Terr. Leeds LS17 .. 60 D8
Stainburn View. Leeds LS17 . 43 E1
Staincliffe Cl Jun Mix Sch. Batley . 118 A3
Staincliffe Cres. Batley WF13 117 F2 4
Staincliffe Ct. Sil BD20 .... 5 D1
Staincliffe Hall Rd. Batley WF13 118 A4
Staincliffe House. Brad BD15 . 73 B7 9
Staincliffe Rd. Dewe WF13 .. 118 A1
Staincross Comm. Mapp S75 178 E2
Stainecross Ave. Hud HD4 .. 153 C2
Staines Croft. Hud HD5 ...... 154 E6
Stainland Dean. Eland HX4 .. 133 B6
Stainland Rd. Eland HX4 .... 134 C6
Stainland Rd. Rip HX4 .... 133 B4
Stainmore Cl. Leeds LS14 .... 62 A3
Stainmore Pl. Leeds LS14 .... 62 A3
Stainton Cl. Brad BD6 .... 93 E8
Stainton La. Roth WF3 ...... 100 D3
Stair Foot La. Leeds LS16 .. 42 D5
Staircase La. Bramho LS16, LS21 24 D5
Stairfoot Cl. Hors LS16 ...... 42 D5
Stairfoot View. Hors LS16 .. 42 D5
Stairfoot Wlk. Hors LS16 .... 42 D5
Staithe Ave. Midd LS10 ...... 99 D5
Staithe Cl. Midd LS10 .... 99 D5
Staithe Gdns. Midd LS10 .... 99 D5 2
Staithgate La. Brad BD6 ...... 94 D7
Stake La. Heb Br HX7 .... 110 F7
Stake Lane Bank. Holmfi HD7 189 C4
Stakes Fold. Batley WF16 .... 117 E4
Stallabrass St. Brad BD8 .... 74 C8 4
Stalley Royd La. Holmfi HD7 189 F3
Stamford Ave. Castle WF10 . 124 A6
Stamford St. Brad BD4 ...... 75 B5
Stamford Way. Mapp S75 .. 178 B2
Stammergate La. Coll LS22 .. 13 C2
Stamp Hill Cl. Sil LS29 .... 6 E8
Stan Valley. K Smea WF8 .. 166 E6
Stanacre Pl. Brad BD3 .... 74 F8 3
Stanage La. Shelf HX3 .... 93 C7
Stanally St. Tod OL14 ...... 107 E8
Stanbury Fst Sch. Haw 50 D6
Stanbury Rd. Wake WF1 .... 142 E8
Stanbridge Garth. Crig WF4 159 F5
Standale Ave. Pudsey LS28 .. 76 D8
Standale Cres. Pudsey LS28 . 76 D8
Standale Rise. Pudsey LS28 . 76 D8
Standard Dr. Hud HD4 ...... 153 B2
Standard Ind Est. Brad 56 C3
Standbridge Cl. Wake WF2 160 A5
Standbridge Fst Sch. Wake .. 160 B6
Standbridge La. Wake WF2, WF4 160 B6
Standbridge La. Wake WF2 160 C2
Standiforth La. Hud HD5 .... 154 F6
Standiforth Pl. Hud HD5 .... 154 F6
Standiforth Rd. Hud HD5 .. 154 D6
Standish Cres. S Kirk WF9 .. 182 B1
Standsall Ave. Pudsey LS28 . 57 D1 3
Stanhope Ave. Caw S75 .... 193 F5
Stanhope Ave. Hors LS18 .. 41 C2
Stanhope Cl. Hors LS18 ...... 58 C8
Stanhope Dr. Hors LS18 .... 58 B8
Stanhope Gdns. E Ard WF3 . 99 E1
Stanhope Gr. Hud HD4 ...... 99 E1
Stanhope Rd. E Ard WF3 .... 99 E1
Stanhope St. Clay W HD8 .. 175 D1
Stanks App. Leeds LS14 .... 62 D4 1
Stanks Ave. Leeds LS14 .... 62 D4
Stanks Cl. Leeds LS14 .... 62 E4
Stanks Cross. Leeds LS14 .. 62 E4
Stanks Dr. Leeds LS14 ...... 62 D5
Stanks Gdns. Leeds LS14 .. 62 E4
Stanks Garth. Leeds LS14 .. 62 E4
Stanks Gn. Leeds LS14 ...... 62 D4
Stanks La N. Leeds LS14 .. 62 C5
Stanks La S. Leeds LS14 .... 62 D4
Stanks Par. Leeds LS14 ...... 62 D4
Stanks Rd. Leeds LS14 ...... 62 E4
Stanks Rise. Leeds LS14 .... 62 E4
Stanks Way. Leeds LS14 .... 62 D4
Stanley Ave. Leeds LS9 ...... 80 A8
Stanley Cotts. Hali WF6 ...... F2 10
Stanley Ct. Hali HX1 .... 112 F7 6
Stanley Dr. Leeds LS8 .... 44 B2
Stanley Gr. Gurse LS20 ...... 39 C8
Stanley Grove Jun & Inf Sch. Leeds LS9 ... 121 F3
Stanley La. Elland HX4 ...... 134 A3
Stanley La. Liver WF15 ...... 117 A5
Stanley Lofthouse Gate Jun & Inf Sch. Loft G .. 121 D1
Stanley Newton Mill Cty Prim Sch. Loft G .. 121 C2
Stanley Pl. Batley WF17 .... 118 D5
Stanley Pl. Hud HD7 .... 152 D4
Stanley Rd. Brad BD2 ...... 55 D4
Stanley Rd. Hali HX1 .... 112 F5
Stanley Rd. Hud HD3 ...... 135 C1
Stanley Rd. Keigh BD22 .... 35 A5
Stanley Rd. Leeds LS9 ...... 80 A8
Stanley Rd. Liver WF15 .... 117 A2
Stanley Rd. Ship BD2 ...... 55 D4
Stanley Rd. Wake WF1 .... 142 C6
Stanley Royd Hosp. Wake 142 D8
Stanley St. Brad BD1 .... 74 E8
Stanley St. Brad BD10 ...... 56 D7
Stanley St. Dewe WF13 .... 138 E6
Stanley St. Bing HX6 .... 115 B3
Stanley St. Castle WF10 .... 124 E8
Stanley St. Clec BD19 ...... 116 D8
Stanley St. Feath WF7 ...... 145 D7
Stanley St. Haw BD22 ...... 51 C6
Stanley St. Hud HD1 .... 153 E3
Stanley St. Keigh BD21 .... 35 B8

Stanley St N. Hali HX2 ...... 92 A5
Stanley St Peter's CE (C) Sch. Loft G .. 121 F5
Stanley St. Ship BD18 .... 55 C5
Stanley St. Wake WF1 ...... 142 D6
Stanley Terr. Leeds LS9 .... 61 A210
Stanley Terr. Leeds LS12 .. 78 C7
Stanley Terr. Leeds LS12 .. 78 C7
Stanley Wrenthorpe Inf Sch. Wake .. 120 F2
Stanley Wrenthorpe Jun Sch. Wake .. 120 F2
Stanmoor Dr. Loft G WF3 .. 121 E6
Stanmore Ave. Leeds LS4 .. 59 C3
Stanmore Cres. Leeds LS4 . 59 C3
Stanmore Gr. Leeds LS4 .... 59 C3
Stanmore Hill. Leeds LS4 .. 59 D3
Stanmore Mount. Leeds LS4 59 C3
Stanmore Pl. Brad BD7 ...... 74 A4
Stanmore Pl. Leeds LS4 .... 59 C3
Stanmore Pl. Leeds LS4 .... 59 C3
Stanmore Rd. Leeds LS4 .. 59 C3
Stanmore St. Leeds LS4 .... 59 C3
Stanmore Terr. Leeds LS4 .. 59 C3
Stanmore View. Leeds LS4 . 59 C3
Stannard Well Dr. Hor WF4 141 B2
Stannard Well La. Hor WF4 141 C2
Stannary Pl. Hali HX1 .... 113 B8
Stannery End La. Heb Br HX7 110 F7
Stanningley Ave. Hali HX2 .. 91 C5
Stanningley By-Pass. Leeds LS13 58 B1
Stanningley By-Pass. Pudsey LS13 58 B1
Stanningley Ct. Pudsey LS28 57 F2 4
Stanningley Field Cl. Leeds LS13 58 A1
Stanningley Green Jun Sch. Hali 91 B5
Stanningley Prim Sch. Pudsey 57 F2
Stanningley Rd. Hali HX2 .. 91 C5
Stanningley Rd. Leeds LS12, LS13 58 D1
Stanningley Rd. Pudsey LS28 57 F2
Stanningley Sch. Pudsey 57 F2
Stansfield Cl. Castle WF10 125 C8
Stansfield Cl. Hali HX1 ...... 113 A7
Stansfield Ct. Sow Br HX6 112 B3
Stansfield Dr. Castle WF10 125 C8
Stansfield Grange. Sow Br HX6 111 F1
Stansfield Hall. Litt LS15 .... 29 D8
Stansfield Hall Rd. Tod OL14 108 C6
Stansfield Mill La. Sow Br HX6 111 F1
Stansfield Pl. Brad BD10 .. 39 A1
Stansfield Rd. Castle WF10 125 B8
Stansfield St. Tod OL14 .... 108 B5
Stansfield St. Tod OL14 .... 108 B6 8
Stansfield Terr. Tod OL14 .. 86 B1 6
Stanwick House. Ship BD2 . 55 D4
Stapleton House. Ship BD2 55 D4
Stapper Gn. Wils BD15 ...... 53 B6
Star St. Brad BD5 .... 74 C3
Starbeck Rd. Wake WF1 .. 142 E8
Starkey La. Farnh BD20 ...... 4 E1
Starkie St. Keigh BD21 ...... 35 B6
Starling House. Hem WF9 181 D6
Starling Post. Brad BD10 .. 55 F7
Starwort Ct. Pont WF8 .... 146 D7
Station App. Bur in W LS29 21 E8
Station App. Gar LS25 ...... 82 F7
Station App. Leeds LS13 .. 108 B5
Station Cl. Gar LS25 .... 82 F7
Station Cotts. Tad LS24 .... 31 C6
Station Cres. Leeds LS12 .. 78 B7
Station Ct. Leeds LS15 ...... 81 F8
Station Fields. Gar LS25 .... 82 F7
Station Gdns. Wels LS22 .. 13 D5
Station Gr. Glu BD20 .... 16 D7
Station Gr. Leeds LS13 ...... 58 C212
Station Ind Est. Hali 111 D7
Station La. Birk BD11 ...... 96 B6
Station La. Castle WF10 .. 103 D4
Station La. E Ard WF3 ...... 98 E1
Station La. Feath WF7 ...... 145 C5
Station La. Hud HD7 .... 152 D3
Station La. Leeds LS14 .... 171 F8
Station La. Liver WF16 .... 117 C4
Station La. Pont WF8 ...... 146 E6
Station La. Roth LS26 ...... 101 D7
Station La. Shep HD8 ...... 173 F1
Station La. Thorner LS14 .. 45 F6
Station Mount. Leeds LS13 58 C2
Station Par. Leeds LS5 ...... 59 B4
Station Par. Tod OL14 ...... 108 A3
Station Pl. Leeds LS13 ...... 58 C2
Station Plaza. Ilkley LS29 .. 8 B4
Station Rd. Ack M T WF7 164 C7 10
Station Rd. Arth LS21 ...... 24 F6
Station Rd. B in Elm LS15, LS25 64 A7
Station Rd. Bail BD17 ...... 38 D3
Station Rd. Batley WF17 .. 118 D4
Station Rd. Birk BD11 ...... 96 B6
Station Rd. Brad BD1 ...... 55 E2
Station Rd. Brad BD14 .... 73 C4
Station Rd. Brad BD12 .... 94 B2
Station Rd. Brad BD13 .... 88 F5 5
Station Rd. Bur in W LS29 . 9 D1
Station Rd. Castle WF10 .. 124 C8
Station Rd. Clerk LS28 .... 58 E8
Station Rd. Cull BD13 ...... 52 D6
Station Rd. Denh BD13 .... 71 E8
Station Rd. Dew WF12 .... 139 C5
Station Rd. Dew WF12 .... 139 F6
Station Rd. Elland HX4 .... 140 A6
Station Rd. Elland HX4 .... 134 A8
Station Rd. Elland HX5 .... 134 F7
Station Rd. Glu BD20 ...... 16 D7
Station Rd. Gol HD7 .... 153 C7
Station Rd. Guise BD17 .. 38 D4
Station Rd. Hali HX3 .... 92 A5
Station Rd. Haw BD22 .... 51 C6
Station Rd. Holmfi HD7 .. 189 A5
Station Rd. Hud HD1 ...... 154 A6
Station Rd. Keigh BD21 .. 35 C8
Station Rd. Kip LS25 ...... 83 A1
Station Rd. Kirkh WF11 .. 127 B4
Station Rd. Knott WF11 .. 126 D4
Station Rd. Leeds LS12 .. 78 B7
Station Rd. Leeds LS15 .. 62 F3
Station Rd. Leeds LS13 .. 58 C2
Station Rd. Leeds LS14 .. 45 A8
Station Rd. Lept HD8 ...... 155 D3

Station Rd. Liver WF16 .... 117 D3
Station Rd. M'town LS26 102 C3
Station Rd. Mapp S75 ...... 177 E1
Station Rd. Men LS29 ...... 22 A4
Station Rd. Mir WF14 ...... 138 A4
Station Rd. Morley LS27 .. 98 B5
Station Rd. Nor WF6 ...... 122 F3
Station Rd. Ossett WF5 .. 140 E4
Station Rd. Otley LS21 .... 23 A7
Station Rd. Oxen BD22 .. 51 C3
Station Rd. Ryhill WF4 .... 162 A1
Station Rd. S Elm WF9 .. 183 A3
Station Rd. Ship BD18 .... 55 B7
Station Rd. Skel HD8 ...... 175 A2
Station Rd. Stee BD20 .... 17 D6
Station Rd. Tod OL14 ...... 86 C1
Station Rd. Wils BD13 .... 53 C4
Station Rd. Stee BD20 .... 17 D6
Station St. Tod OL14 ...... 86 A6
Station St. Hud HD1 ...... 154 A6
Station St. Mel HD7 ...... 170 D2
Station St. Pudsey LS28 .. 76 D6
Station St. Wake WF1 .... 142 E3
Station Terr. Kippax WF10 103 C4
Station Terr. Leeds LS13 .. 58 C2
Station Terr. Roy S71 ...... 179 E4
Station View. Leeds LS15 62 C1
Station View. Oxen BD22 51 C3
Station Way. Leeds LS12 209 C2
Station Wlk. Ossett WF5 .. 140 E5
Station Works Ind Pk. Keigh 35 E7
Staups La. Northo HX3 .... 92 F1
Staveley Cl. Bing BD16 .... 36 F4
Staveley Dr. Ship BD18 .. 54 D7
Staveley Gr. Keigh BD22 .. 35 A3
Staveley Rd. Bing BD16 .. 37 A4
Staveley Rd. Brad BD7 .... 74 B6
Staveley Rd. Keigh BD22 35 A4
Staveley Rd. Ship BD18 .. 54 D7
Stavely Mews. Bing BD16 37 A4 5
Staverton St. Hali HX2 .... 112 E7 1
Staybrite Ave. Bing BD16 54 A7
Staygate Gn. Brad BD6 .. 74 E1
Staynton Cres. Hud HD2 136 B5
Stead Gate. Shep HD8 .. 174 D2
Stead La. Kirkha HD5 .... 155 B8
Stead La. Rip HX6 .... 132 C2
Stead La. Thorner LS14 .. 45 F5
Stead Rd. Brad BD4 ...... 95 E8
Stead St. Hali HX1 .... 112 E7 1
Stead St. Ship BD17 ...... 55 B8
Stead's Yd. Hors LS18 .... 41 C1
Steadman St. Brad BD3 .. 75 B6
Steadman Terr. Brad BD3 75 B6
Steander. Leeds LS9 ...... 79 D7
Steander La. Leeds LS9 .. 79 D7
Steander. Leeds LS9 ...... 79 D7
Steele La. Rip HX4 .... 133 C1
Steep La. Sow Br HX6 .. 111 B4
Steep Banking. Honley HD7 172 C3
Steeplands. Hud HD4 .... 154 D2
Steeple Dr. Gar WF8 ...... 156 F4
Genton Gr. Stee BD20 .... 17 C6
Steeton Hall Gdns. Stee BD20 17 D6
Steeton Jun & Inf Sch. Stee 17 D5
Stell Hill. Skel S72 .... 180 A2
Stella Gdns. Pont WF8 .. 125 F2
Stephen Cl. Northo HX3 .. 93 A1
Stephen Cres. Brad BD2 55 E3
Stephen Rd. Brad BD6 .. 73 F2
Stephen Row. Northo HX3 93 A2
Stephen St. Heb B HX7 .. 89 A10
Stephenson Rd. Wils BD15 53 D2
Stephenson St. Brad BD4 83 B3 2
Stephenson Way. Gild LS12 77 D3
Stephensons Way. Ilkley LS29 8 B4
Steps La. Rip HX6 .... 132 A5
Sterling Ind Pk. Castle .. 124 F5
Sterne Hill. Hali HX2 ...... 112 A4
Stevenson Ave. Castle WF10 125 B5
Stewart Cl. Brad BD2 .... 56 C5
Stewart Pl. Leeds BD22 51 F8
Stewart St. Haw BD22 .. 51 E8
Sticker La. Brad BD4 .... 75 C4
Stile Common Inf Sch. Hud 154 A3
Stile Common Jun Sch. Hud 154 A3
Stile Common Rd. Hud HD4 154 A3
Stile Hill Way. Leeds LS15 81 D6
Stile Rd. Tod OL14 .... 108 A7
Stiles Rd. Tod OL14 ...... 108 A7
Stillington House. Brad BD3 75 B7
Stillwell Dr. Wake WF2 .. 160 E8
Stillwell Garth. Wake WF2 160 E8
Stillwell Gr. Wake WF2 .. 160 E8
Stirley Hill. Hud HD4 .... 172 B8
Stirling Cres. Brad BD4 .. 75 E4
Stirling Cres. Hors LS18 41 B4
Stirling Rd. Bur in W LS29 9 E1
Stirling Rd. Stan BD20 .... 5 D1
Stirling St. Hali HX1 ...... 113 B6
Stirling St. Keigh BD21 .. 35 B4
Stirling Way. Gar LS25 .. 82 F8
Stirton St. Brad BD5 ...... 74 D3 3
Stithy Rd. Tod OL14 ...... 129 C5
Stock Hey La. Tod OL14 107 C6
Stock La. Hali HX3 .... 92 C2
Stockeld La. Sick LS22 .. 12 D6
Stockeld Rd. Ilkley LS29 . 8 B4
Stockeld Way. Ilkley LS29 8 A5
Stockhill Rd. Brad BD10 56 D6
Stockhill St. Dewe WF13 138 E6
Stocking La. B in Elm LS15 63 F5
Stocking La. Knot WF11 127 E7
Stocking La. Aber LS25 .. 64 E7
Stocks App. Leeds LS14 62 A2
Stocks Ave. Heb B HX7 .. 88 E3
Stocks Bank Rd. Mir WF14 137 D6
Stocks Gdns. Tod OL14 108 A1
Stocks Hill. Hali HX3 ...... 203 F4
Stocks Hill. Leeds LS11 .. 211 D1
Stocks Hill. Men LS29 .... 21 F4

Stocks La. Batley WF17 .. 118 C5
Stocks La. Brad BD13 .... 73 B1
Stocks La. Hali HX2 .... 90 E2
Stocks La. Heb Br HX7 .. 110 D8
Stocks La. Kirkb HD4 .... 173 B1
Stocks La. Sow Br HX6 .. 111 E3
Stocks Lane East. Sch. Brad 73 B1
Stocks Moor Rd. Kirkb HD4 173 B2
Stocks Rd. Leeds LS14 .. 62 C4
Stocks Rise. Leeds LS14 62 B4
Stocks St. Leeds LS7 .... 60 C3
Stocks Way. Shep HD8 .. 190 D8
Stocks Wlk. Hud HD5 .... 154 F3
Stocksbank Dr. Mir WF14 137 D6
Stocksmoor Rd. Neth HX4 158 C2
Stocksmoor Sta. Kirkb .. 173 C2
Stockwell Dr. Batley WF17 118 D6
Stockwell La. Hud HD4 .. 171 F8
Stockwell Vale. Hud HD4 171 F8
Stod Fold. Hali HX2 ...... 91 C8
Stogden Hill. Brad BD13 73 B1
Stone Acre Ct. Brad BD5 74 E2 3
Stone Acre Hts. Mel HD7 170 F1
Stone Brig Gn. Roth LS26 100 D4
Stone Brig La. Roth LS26 100 D4
Stone Cliffe. Hali HX3 .... 113 A4 1
Stone Ct. Keigh BD20 .... 36 D8
Stone Ct. S Hie S72 .... 180 E5
Stone Dene. Bing BD16 37 A6
Stone Fold. Honley HD7 171 F4
Stone Gr. Stee BD20 ...... 17 C6
Stone Hall Rd. Brad BD2 56 B4
Stone Hill. Bing BD16 .... 37 B5
Stone La. Oxen BD22 .... 51 B2
Stone Pits La. Gild LS27 97 D5
Stone Rd. Brad BD13 .... 54 A3
Stone St. Brad BD1 .... 74 E7
Stone St. Clec BD19 ...... 116 C7
Stone St. Haw BD22 ...... 51 C6 3
Stone Wood La. Shep HD4, HD8 173 D1
Stonebridge App. Leeds LS12 77 E6
Stonebridge Gr. Leeds LS12 77 E6
Stonebridge La. Leeds LS12 77 E6
Stonebridge La. Leeds LS12 77 E6
Stonecliffe Bank. Leeds LS12 77 E6
Stonecliffe Cl. Leeds LS12 77 E6
Stonecliffe Cres. Leeds LS12 77 E6
Stonecliffe Dr. Leeds LS12 77 E6
Stonecliffe Dr. Neth WF4 158 B7
Stonecliffe Garth. Leeds LS12 77 E6
Stonecliffe Gdns. Leeds LS12 77 E6
Stonecliffe Gn. Leeds LS12 77 E6
Stonecliffe Lawn. Leeds LS12 77 E6
Stonecliffe Mount. Leeds LS12 77 E6
Stonecliffe Pl. Leeds LS12 77 E6
Stonecliffe Terr. Leeds LS12 77 E6
Stonecliffe View. Leeds LS12 77 E6
Stonecliffe Way. Leeds LS12 77 E5
Stonecliffe Wlk. Leeds LS12 77 E6
Stonecroft. Brad BD2 .... 56 B5
Stonecroft Gdns. Shep HD8 190 F8
Stonecroft. Loft G WF3 .. 121 E5
Stonefield Pl. Batley WF17 96 F1
Stonefield Cl. Brad BD2 56 B4
Stonefield Pl. Batley WF17 96 F1
Stonefield St. Clec BD19 116 A6
Stonefield Terr. Morley LS27 98 A4
Stonefield Terr. Morley LS27 98 A4
Stonegate App. Leeds LS7 59 F6
Stonegate Cl. Leeds LS7 43 D3
Stonegate Cres. Leeds LS7 59 F7
Stonegate Dr. Leeds LS7 60 A7
Stonegate Edge. Leeds LS7 60 A7
Stonegate Farm Cl. Leeds LS7 59 F7
Stonegate Gdns. Roy S71 179 D4
Stonegate Gr. Leeds LS7 59 F7
Stonegate La. Ack M T WF7 163 E5
Stonegate La. Leeds LS7 59 F6
Stonegate Mews. Leeds LS7 59 F7
Stonegate Rd. Leeds LS17 60 A7
Stonegate Rd. Leeds LS17 43 A2
Stonegate Rd. Leeds LS6 59 F6
Stonegate Wlk. Leeds LS7 60 A6
Stonehaven Ct. Keigh BD21 35 E5
Stonehurst. Leeds LS14 .. 62 C4
Stonehurst Rd. Mir WF14 138 A6
Stonenyrst App. Leeds LS14 62 D4
Stoneleigh. Queen BD13 72 F1 4
Stoneleigh Ct. Dew WF12 139 C3
Stoneleigh Gr. Ossett WF5 140 E5
Stoneleigh La. Oxen BD22 51 C3
Stoneleigh Way. Sil BD20 5 C1
Stones Dr. Rip HX4 .... 132 E1
Stones La. Slai HD7 ...... 170 B8
Stones La. Tod OL14 .... 107 F4
Stones Rd. Ripp HX6 .... 132 D2
Stoney Back La. Hud HD4 153 E3
Stoney Bank La. Holmfi HD7 189 A6
Stoney Bank St. Dewe WF13 138 F7
Stoney Battery. Hud HD1 153 D7
Stoney Butts La. Rip HX4 133 D5
Stoney Croft. Clec BD19 116 D7
Stoney Cross St. Hud HD4 153 F2
Stoney Garth. Crig WF4 159 F4
Stoney La. Batley WF17 97 B3
Stoney La. Brig HD6 ...... 115 D2

Stoney Ridge Rd. Ship BD16 54 C5
Stoney Rise. Hors LS18 .. 58 B8
Stoney Rock Ct. Leeds LS9 60 F1
Stoney Rock Gr. Leeds LS9 60 F1
Stoney Rock La. Leeds LS9 60 F1
Stoney Royd La. Tod OL14 107 F7
Stoney Royd Terr. Hali HX3 113 D4
Stoney St. Keigh BD20 .. 18 B2
Stoneybrook Ct. W Bret WF4 176 F8
Stoneycroft. Hors LS18 .. 58 B8 3
Stoneycroft La. Keigh BD20 19 A7
Stoneycroft. Hors LS18 .. 58 B8 2
Stoneythorpe. Hors LS18 58 B8
Stonlea Dr. Brig HD6 .... 135 F7
Stony Croft La. Rip HX4 133 B5
Stony Gate. Holmfi HD7 188 E2
Stony La. B Head HX7 .. 88 D2
Stony La. Brad BD15 .... 53 F2
Stony La. Brad BD2 ...... 56 C5
Stony La. Bing HX4 ...... 114 C4
Stony La. Elland HX4 .... 134 A8
Stony La. Honley BD22 171 F3
Stony La. Leeds LS8 .... 44 D3
Stony Royd La. Heb Br HX7 110 A4
Stony Royd. Pudsey LS28 57 C3
Stoodley Cl. Tod OL14 .. 109 A5
Stoodley Glen. Tod OL14 109 A5
Stoodley Grange. Tod OL14 109 B5
Stoodley La. Heb Br OL14 109 B7
Stoodley Terr. Hali HX2 112 E5
Stopford Ave. Wake WF2 160 E8
Stopford Garth. Wake WF2 160 E8
Storey Pl. Leeds LS14 .. 61 E1
Storie Cres. Wake WF2 141 E4
Storiths Ct. Adst LS29 .... 7 F7
Storiths La. Hazl BD23 .... 3 B8
Stormer Hill La. Sow Br HX6 112 D1
Storr Hill. Brad BD12 .... 94 D4
Storrs Hill Rd. Ossett WF5 140 E2
Storth Ave. Hud HD4 .... 152 F3
Storth Pl. Hud HD2 ...... 135 F1
Storthes Hall Hospl. Kirkb 173 B5
Storthes Hall La. Kirkb HD8 173 C6
Storths Rd. Hud HD2 .... 135 F1
Stotfold Rd. Clay DN5 .. 194 E3
Stott Hill. Brad BD1 ...... 74 F7
Stott Rd. Leeds LS6 ...... 59 E3
Stott St. Leeds LS12 .... 78 D7
Stotts Terr. Brad BD2 .. 56 D4
Stourton Rd. Ilkley LS29 7 F5
Stowe Gr. Leeds LS9 .... 80 C8
Stowell Mill St. Brad BD5 74 D4
Stradmore Rd. Denh BD13 71 E8
Straight La. Add LS29 .... 6 D5
Straight La. Hali HX3 .... 91 F1
Straight La. Ham DN6 .. 184 B4
Straightacres La. Brad BD10 56 D5
Straits. Bail BD17 .... 38 C4 7
Stralau St. Batley WF17 118 A5
Strands Ct. Neth WF4 .. 158 A5
Stranglands La. Castle WF11 126 B5
Stratford Ave. Leeds LS11 79 A2
Stratford Cl. Hud HD7 .. 152 E5
Stratford House. Brad BD15 73 B7
Stratford Rd. Brad BD7 74 B5
Stratford St. Leeds LS11 79 A3
Stratford Terr. Leeds LS11 79 B3
Strathallan Dr. Bail BD17 38 D3
Strathearn Rd. Wake WF2 142 A7
Strathmore Ave. Bail BD17 38 B3
Strathmore Ave. Leeds LS9 61 B3
Strathmore Cl. Bail BD17 38 B4
Strathmore Dr. Bail BD17 38 B4
Strathmore Dr. Leeds LS9 61 B3
Strathmore Gdns. S Elm WF9 183 A4
Strathmore Rd. Ilkley LS29 8 E4
Strathmore St. Leeds LS9 61 B2 1
Strathmore Terr. Leeds LS9 61 A2
Stratton Rd. Brig HD6 .. 115 C1
Stratton View. Brad BD4 75 E3
Strawberry Ave. Gar LS25 82 E6
Strawberry Ave. Liver WF15 117 A3
Strawberry Bank. Liver WF15 117 A3
Strawberry Fields. Keigh BD21 35 C8 4
Strawberry Gdns. S Elm WF9 183 A4
Strawberry La. Leeds LS12 210 A3
Strawberry Rd. Leeds LS12 210 A3
Strawberry Sq. Liver WF15 117 A3
Strawberry St. Keigh BD21 35 C8
Stray St. Leeds LS9 ...... 80 A7
Stream Head Rd. Wils BD13 53 D8
Streamside. Leeds LS6 .. 59 E5
Streamside La. Hud HD3 153 A8
Street 1. Th Arch LS23 .. 31 A6
Street 2. Th Arch LS23 .. 31 B8
Street 3. Th Arch LS23 .. 15 A1
Street 5. Th Arch LS23 .. 30 F8
Street 6. Th Arch LS23 .. 31 A8
Street 7. Th Arch LS23 .. 14 F1
Street 8. Th Arch LS23 .. 31 A7
Street Furlong La. Pont WF8 147 C7
Street Head La. Haw BD22 50 E8
Street La. Gild LS27 ...... 97 C6
Street La. H Pag DN5 .. 195 F3
Street La. Keigh BD20 .. 19 C2
Street La. Leeds LS17 .. 43 C2
Street La. Leeds LS8 .... 44 A3
Street The. Sil LS29 ...... 6 D8
Streethouse Sta. Feath 144 D5
Strensall Gn. Brad BD6 93 E8 11
Stretchgate La. Hali HX2 112 C5
Strickland Ave. Thorner LS17 45 A6
Strickland Cl. Thorner LS17 45 A6
Strickland Cres. Thorner LS17 44 F4
Strickland Cres. Thorner LS17 44 F4
Strike La. Shep HD8 .... 190 E8
Strikes La. S in Cra BD20 16 A3
Strines Moor Rd. Holmfi HD7 199 D8
Stringer Cl. Brad BD4 .. 75 E2
Stringer House La. Emley HD8 175 A7
Stringer La. Wyer WF4 141 B1 4
Strong Close Gr. Keigh BD21 35 E6
Strong Close Rd. Keigh BD21 35 E6
Strong Close Way. Keigh BD21 35 E6
Stuart Gr. Nor WF6 ...... 123 B2
Stuart Pl. Hud HD2 ...... 136 F5
Stuart Rd. Pont WF8 .... 125 E1
Stuart St. Castle WF10 124 D7
Stubbin La. D Dale HD8 191 E5
Stubbing La. Holmfi HD7 188 F8
Stubbin Rd. Mars HD7 .. 169 B5

Stubbing Brink. Heb Br HX7 — 88 E3
Stubbing Dr. Heb Br HX7 — 88 E3
Stubbing Holme Rd. Heb Br HX7 — 88 F3
Stubbing La. Elland HX4 — 133 E5
Stubbing La. Sow Br HX6 — 132 E8
Stubbing Way. Ship BD18 — 55 C6
Stubbings Cl. Heb Br HX7 — 110 E8
Stubbings Inf Sch. Heb Br — 89 A3
Stubbings Rd. Bail BD17 — 37 F2
Stubbings St. Heb Br HX7 — 110 E8
Stubbins. Sow Br HX6 — 132 E8
Stubbs La. E ard WF3 — 120 E7
Stubham Rise. Ilkley LS29 — 8 A5
Stubley Farm Rd. Batley WF16 — 117 D6
Stubley Holme. Tod OL14 — 86 A1
Stubley La. Tod OL14 — 86 B1
Stubley Rd. Batley WF16 — 117 C6
Stubley St. Wake WF1 — 142 B6
Studfold View. Leeds LS14 — 62 A2
Studio Rd. Leeds LS3 — 59 E1
Studleigh Terr. Brig HD6 — 114 E5
Studley Ave. Brad BD6 — 94 B7
Studley Cl. Keigh BD20 — 19 D1
Studley Cres. Bing BD16 — 37 B3
Studley Rd. Brad BD3 — 55 F2
Stumpcross Cl. Pont WF8 — 125 F3
Stumpcross Ct. Pont WF8 — 125 F3
Stumpcross La. Pont WF8 — 125 F3
Stumpcross Way. Pont WF8 — 125 F3
Stunsteds Rd. Clec BD19 — 116 D8
Sturges Gr. Brad BD2 — 56 B1
Sturton Ave. Gar LS25 — 83 A7
Sturton La. Hali HX2 — 91 E6
Sturton Grange La. Gar LS25 — 83 A7
Sturton La. Gar LS25 — 83 A8
Sturton La. Hali HX2 — 91 E7
Stutely Gr. Hud HD2 — 136 B5
Sty La. Bing BD16 — 36 F6
Styebank La. Roth LS26 — 100 F6
Styes La. Sow Br HX6 — 111 D4
Styveton Way. Shee BD20 — 17 B6
Sude Hill. Holmfi HD7 — 189 F6
Sude Hill Terr. Holmfi HD7 — 189 F6
Sudforth La. Beal DN14 — 127 F5
Suffolk Ave. Batley WF17 — 118 B3
Suffolk Cl. Ossett WF5 — 140 C4
Suffolk Ct. Yeadon LS19 — 40 B7
Suffolk House. Wake WF1 — 142 F3
Suffolk Pl. Brad BD2 — 55 F4
Suffolk St. Batley WF17 — 118 B4
Sufton St. Hud HD2 — 136 C3
Sugar Hill Ct. Roth LS26 — 101 C3
Sugar Hill. Sil LS29 — 6 F8
Sugar La. Dew WF12 — 139 E8
Sugar La. Wake WF1 — 147 E3
Sugar Well App. Leeds LS7 — 60 A5
Sugar Well Mount. Leeds LS7 — 60 A5
Sugar Well Rd. Leeds LS7 — 60 A5
Sugarwell Ct. Leeds LS7 — 60 B4
Sugden St. Brad BD1 — 74 C7
Sugden St. Brad BD12 — 94 F4
Sugden's Almshouses. Haw BD22 — 34 E3
Sulby Gr. Brad BD10 — 56 E8
Sullivan Cl. Hud HD4 — 153 D3
Sullivan Gr. S Kirk WF9 — 182 B2
Summer Hall Ing. Brad BD12 — 94 C4
Summer Hill Rd. M'town LS26 — 102 B2
Summer Hill St. Brad BD7 — 74 A5
Summer La. Emley HD8 — 175 D6
Summer La. Roy S71 — 179 B4
Summer Meadow. Pont WF8 — 146 C7
Summer Rd. Roy S71 — 179 B4
Summer St. Hud HD1, HD4 — 153 E4
Summer St. Hud HD4 — 171 D7
Summerbridge Cl. Batley WF17 — 118 A6
Summerbridge Cres. Brad BD10 — 56 E8
Summerbridge Cres. Clec BD19 — 96 C2
Summerbridge Dr. Brad BD10 — 56 D5
Summerdale. Clec BD19 — 96 B2
Summerfield Ave. Brth HD4 — 153 D5
Summerfield Ave. Leeds LS13 — 58 A3
Summerfield Cl. Bail BD17 — 38 B3
Summerfield Dr. Bail BD17 — 38 B3
Summerfield Dr. Byram WF11 — 126 E8
Summerfield Gdns. Leeds LS13 — 58 A3
Summerfield Gn. Bail BD17 — 38 B3
Summerfield Gn. Leeds LS13 — 58 A3
Summerfield Gr. Bail BD17 — 38 B3
Summerfield Pk. Lepton HD8 — 155 D2
Summerfield Pl. Leeds LS13 — 58 A3
Summerfield Prim Sch. Pudsey — 57 F3
Summerfield Rd. Brad BD10 — 56 C6
Summerfield Rd. Tod OL14 — 108 D5
Summerfield Rd W. Tod OL14 — 108 B8
Summergate Pl. Hali HX1 — 112 F6
Summergate St. Hali HX1 — 112 F6
Summerhill Ave. Keigh BD20 — 19 E1
Summerhill Dr. Stee BD20 — 17 D6
Summerhill Gdns. Leeds LS8 — 44 B2
Summerhill Gr. Gar LS25 — 82 D6
Summerhill La. Stee BD20 — 17 D6
Summerhill Pl. Leeds LS8 — 44 B2
Summerhill Rd. Gar LS25 — 83 D6
Summerlands Gr. Brad BD5 — 75 A2
Summerscale St. Hali HX1 — 113 A8 4
Summerseat Pl. Brad BD7 — 74 C5
Summerville. Holmfi HD7 — 189 A6
Summerville Rd. Brad BD7 — 74 A4
Summerville Rd. Pudsey LS28 — 57 C2
Summit St. Keigh BD21 — 35 B8
Sun Ct. Hebd WF7 — 145 C8
Sun Field. Pudsey LS28 — 57 C1
Sun Fold. Hali HX1 — 113 C6
Sun Hill Dr. Bail BD17 — 37 C1
Sun La. Bur in W LS29 — 9 C2
Sun La. Haw BD22 — 34 D7
Sun La. Wake WF2 — 142 A6
Sun St. Brad BD1 — 74 E8
Sun St. Haw BD22 — 51 C7
Sun St. Keigh BD20 — 18 C1
Sun St. Keigh BD21 — 35 C7
Sun St. Stee BD20 — 17 C5
Sun St. Tod OL14 — 108 A1
Sun Terr. Tod OL14 — 86 B1
Sun Vale Ave. Tod OL14 — 129 B7
Sun Way. Hali HX3 — 113 F5
Sun Wood Ave. Shelf HX3 — 93 B4
Sunbeam Ave. Leeds LS11 — 79 B1
Sunbeam Gr. Leeds LS11 — 79 B1 9
Sunbeam Pl. Leeds LS11 — 79 B1
Sunbeam Terr. Leeds LS11 — 79 B1

Sunbridge Rd. Brad BD1 — 74 D7
Sunbury Gr. Hud HD5 — 154 E6
Sunderland Ct. Brig HD6 — 115 A3 6
Sunderland Rd. Brad BD9 — 55 C2
Sunderland Rd. L Brad BD20 — 4 D5
Sunderland St. Hali HX1 — 113 B7 7
Sunderland St. Haw BD22 — 51 F8
Sunderland St. Keigh BD21 — 35 B6
Sundown Ave. Brad BD7 — 73 F4
Sunfield Cl. Pudsey LS28 — 57 D2
Sunfield Dr. Pudsey LS28 — 57 D2
Sunfield Gdns. Pudsey LS28 — 57 D2
Sunfield Pl. Pudsey LS28 — 57 D2
Sunfield Terr. Clec BD19 — 116 E7 11
Sunhurst Cl. Haw BD22 — 34 C2
Sunhurst Dr. Haw BD22 — 34 C2
Sunningdale Ave. Leeds LS17 — 43 A4
Sunningdale Ave. Mapp S75 — 178 A1
Sunningdale. Brad BD8 — 73 D8
Sunningdale Cl. Leeds LS17 — 43 A4
Sunningdale Cres. Gull BD13 — 52 E5
Sunningdale Ct. Hud HD2 — 135 F3
Sunningdale Dr. Leeds LS17 — 43 A4
Sunningdale Gn. Leeds LS17 — 43 A4
Sunningdale Rd. Hud HD2 — 135 F3
Sunningdale Way. Leeds LS17 — 43 A4
Sunningdale Wlk. Leeds LS17 — 43 A4
Sunny Ave. S Elm WF9 — 183 B2
Sunny Ave. Upton WF9 — 183 A7
Sunny Bank Ave. Brad BD5 — 74 D1
Sunny Bank Ave. Mir WF14 — 138 A8
Sunny Bank. Brad BD9 — 54 D2
Sunny Bank Cres. Leeds LS8 — 44 A2
Sunny Bank Dr. Hali HX6 — 112 C4
Sunny Bank Dr. Mir WF14 — 137 F8
Sunny Bank Gr. Leeds LS8 — 44 A2
Sunny Bank. Hem WF9 — 163 A3
Sunny Bank. Knot WF11 — 127 A4
Sunny Bank La. Batley WF17 — 118 D7
Sunny Bank La. Brig HX3 — 114 B6
Sunny Bank La. Heb Br HX7 — 110 C8
Sunny Bank. Leeds LS8 — 60 F5
Sunny Bank. Nor WF6 — 144 B7
Sunny Bank Par. Mir WF14 — 137 F8
Sunny Bank Rd. Batley WF17 — 118 D6
Sunny Bank Rd. Brad BD5 — 74 D1
Sunny Bank Rd. Brig HD6 — 115 A2
Sunny Bank Rd. Mel HD7 — 170 C2
Sunny Bank Rd. Mir WF14 — 137 F8
Sunny Brow. Hud HD4 — 171 F8
Sunny Brow La. Brad BD9 — 54 D2
Sunny Gr. Morley LS27 — 98 C8 5
Sunny Heys Rd. Mel HD7 — 170 D3
Sunny Heys W. Mel HD7 — 170 D3
Sunny Hill Ave. Keigh BD21 — 34 F5
Sunny Hill Gr. Keigh BD21 — 34 F5
Sunny Hill. Wake WF2 — 141 D6
Sunny Mead. Hud HD5 — 155 A6
Sunny Mount. Brig HX3 — 114 C7
Sunny Mount. Harden BD16 — 36 A6
Sunny Mount. Keigh BD21 — 35 B8
Sunny Mount. Keigh BD22 — 35 A3
Sunny Mount Terr. Tod OL14 — 86 C1
Sunny Row. Leeds LS8 — 60 F5
Sunny Vale Country Club. Brig — 114 C6
Sunny View Cres. Hud HD7 — 152
Sunny View Terr. Queen BD13 — 92 C7 4
Sunny View. Leeds LS12 — 78 B7
Sunnybank Ave. Brig HD6 — 136 A8
Sunnybank Ave. Leeds LS18 — 58 B7
Sunnybank. Brig BD19 — 115 F7
Sunnybank Cres. Elland HX4 — 134 A3
Sunnybank Cres. Yeadon LS19 — 40 B5
Sunnybank. D Dale HD8 — 191 F5
Sunnybank Dr. Elland HX4 — 134 A3
Sunnybank Grange. Brig HD6 — 114 F1 A2 1
Sunnybank La. Elland HX4 — 134 A3
Sunnybank. Mfield LS25 — 84 B6
Sunnybank Rd. Elland HX4 — 134 A3
Sunnybank Rd. Hors LS18 — 58 B7
Sunnybank Rd. Mfield LS25 — 84 B6
Sunnybank St. Ossett WF5 — 140 D5
Sunnybank Terr. Brig HD6 — 115 A3
Sunnybrae Cres. Bing BD16 — 37 A3
Sunnycliffe. Keigh BD22 — 35 A5
Sunnydale Ave. Brig HD6 — 136 A8
Sunnydale Cres. Otley LS21 — 22 D6
Sunnydale Croft. Ossett WF5 — 140 E4
Sunnydale Gr. Keigh BD21 — 35 F6
Sunnydale Pk. Keigh BD20 — 19 E2
Sunnydale Rd. Keigh BD20 — 19 E2
Sunnydale Ridge. Otley LS21 — 22 D6
Sunnydene. Leeds LS14 — 62 A5
Sunnyfield Dr. Hem WF9 — 163 A3
Sunnyhill Ave. Wake WF2 — 160 D5
Sunnyhill Cres. Wake WF2 — 160 D5
Sunnyhill Croft. Wake WF2 — 160 D5
Sunnylea. Mars HD7 — 169 A4
Sunnymead. Mir WF14 — 138 B4
Sunnyridge Ave. Pudsey LS28 — 76 B8
Sunnyside Ave. Clec BD19 — 116 E8
Sunnyside. Batley WF16 — 117 D2
Sunnyside La. Brad BD3 — 75 C8
Sunnyside La. E Ard WF3 — 120 A1
Sunnyside. Leeds LS15 — 62 F2
Sunnyside Rd. Dew WF13 — 139 A6
Sunnyside St. Keigh BD21 — 35 C4
Sunnyvale Mount. S Elm WF9 — 183 A3
Sunnyview Ave. Leeds LS11 — 78 E4
Sunnyview Gdns. Leeds LS11 — 78 E4
Sunnyview Gr. Leeds LS11 — 78 E4
Sunnyview Terr. Leeds LS11 — 78 E4
Sunroyd Ave. Hor WF4 — 141 B1
Sunroyd Hill. Hor WF4 — 141 B2

Sunset Ave. Leeds LS6 — 59 E8
Sunset Dr. Ilkley LS29 — 8 D5
Sunset Dr. Leeds LS6 — 59 E7 6
Sunset Hilltop. Leeds LS6 — 59 E8
Sunset Mount. Leeds LS6 — 59 E7 5
Sunset Rd. Leeds LS6 — 59 E7
Sunset Rise. Leeds LS6 — 59 E8
Sunset Terr. Ilkley LS29 — 8 D5
Sunset View. Leeds LS6 — 59 E8
Surat Rd. Slai HD7 — 151 F3
Suresnes Rd. Keigh BD21 — 35 B7
Surgery St. Haw BD22 — 51 D6
Surrey Gr. Brad BD5 — 74 E4
Surrey Gr. Pudsey LS28 — 76 E8
Surrey Rd. Pudsey LS28 — 76 E8
Surrey St. Batley WF17 — 118 D5
Surrey St. Hali HX1 — 112 F6
Surrey St. Keigh BD21 — 35 E8
Sussex App. Leeds LS10 — 79 F3
Sussex Ave. Hors LS18 — 41 C3
Sussex Ave. Leeds LS10 — 79 F3
Sussex Cl. Hem WF9 — 181 D8
Sussex Cres. Castle WF10 — 125 E8
Sussex Gdns. Leeds LS10 — 79 F3
Sussex Gn. Leeds LS10 — 79 F3
Sussex Pl. Leeds LS10 — 79 F3
Sussex St. Batley WF17 — 118 D5
Sussex St. Keigh BD21 — 35 E8
Sussex St. Leeds LS9 — 79 F7
Sussex Wlk. Dew WF13 — 139 B8 2
Sutcliffe Pl. Brad BD6 — 94 D8 6
Sutcliffe St. Hali HX2 — 112 E8
Sutcliffe Wood La. Brig HX3 — 114 C6
Sutherland Ave. Leeds LS8 — 44 A2
Sutherland Cres. Leeds LS8 — 44 A2
Sutherland Dr. Hud HD3 — 153 C2
Sutherland Mount. Leeds LS9 — 61 A2
Sutherland Rd. Brig HX3 — 114 E8
Sutherland St. Leeds LS12 — 78 C6
Sutherland Terr. Leeds LS9 — 61 A2
Sutton App. Leeds LS14 — 61 E1
Sutton Ave. Brad BD2 — 56 A4
Sutton Cres. Brad BD4 — 95 A8
Sutton Dr. Cull BD13 — 52 D5
Sutton Dr. Hud HD5 — 155 A8
Sutton Fields. Glu BD20 — 16 C6
Sutton Gr. Brad BD4 — 75 E5
Sutton Gr. Morley LS27 — 98 A3 3
Sutton La. S in Cra BD20 — 16 E6
Sutton Rd. Brad BD4 — 75 E5
Sutton St. Leeds LS12 — 78 F6
Sutton-in-Craven CE Prim Sch.
  S in Cra — 16 D5
Suzanne Cres. S Elm WF9 — 182 E3
Swaine Hill Cres. Yeadon LS19 — 40 A7
Swaine Hill St. Yeadon LS19 — 40 A7
Swaine Hill Terr. Yeadon LS19 — 40 A7
Swale Cres. Gar LS25 — 83 B8
Swale Ct. Sil BD20 — 17 E8
Swale Dr. Castle WF10 — 125 B8
Swale Rise. Wreth LS22 — 13 F6
Swales Moor Rd. Hali HX3 — 92 C4
Swales' Yd. Pont WF8 — 146 C8 5
Swallow Ave. Leeds LS12 — 78 A4
Swallow Cl. Leeds LS17 — 43 A4
Swallow Cl. Ossett WF5 — 140 E6
Swallow Cres. Leeds LS12 — 78 A4
Swallow Dr. Pont WF8 — 146 A8
Swallow Fold. Brad BD8 — 73 B7
Swallow Garth. Wake WF2 — 160 D6
Swallow Hill. Batley WF17 — 118 A8
Swallow La. Hud HD7 — 152 C5
Swallow La. Mel HD7 — 170 C2
Swallow Mount. Leeds LS12 — 78 A4
Swallow St. Hud HD1 — 154 A5 1
Swallow St. Keigh BD21 — 18 D1
Swallow Vale. Morley LS27 — 98 C4
Swallows The. Leeds LS14 — 62 C5
Swallows The. Wake WF2 — 160 D6
Swan Bank La. Holmfi HD7 — 189 A4
Swan Bank La. Brad BD4 — 111 B5
Swan La. Elland HX4 — 134 B5
Swan St. Brad BD5 — 74 E6
Swarcliffe App. Leeds LS14 — 62 C4
Swarcliffe Ave. Leeds LS14 — 62 C5
Swarcliffe Bank. Leeds LS14 — 62 C5
Swarcliffe Dr E. Leeds LS14 — 62 D4 2
Swarcliffe Dr. Leeds LS14 — 62 C4
Swarcliffe Gn. Leeds LS14 — 62 D4
Swarcliffe Prim Sch. Leeds — 62 C5
Swarcliffe Rd. Leeds LS14 — 62 C5
Swarcliffe Towers. Leeds LS14 — 62 D5
Swardale Gn. Leeds LS14 — 62 C4
Swardale Rd. Leeds LS14 — 62 C4
Swarland Gr. Brad BD5 — 74 E2
Swartha La. Add BD20 — 5 B2
Swears Yd. Mir WF14 — 138 A4
Sweet Cl. Leeds LS14 — 62 D5
Sweet St. Leeds LS11 — 79 E3
Sweet St W. Leeds LS11 — 210
Swift Dr. Ossett WF5 — 140 E6
Swift Way. Wake WF2 — 160 D5
Swift's Fold. Honley HD7 — 171 F5
Swillington La. Swil LS26 — 82 B1
Swillington Prim Sch. Swil — 82 A1
Swinburne Ave. Elland HX4 — 133 F3
Swincar Ave. Yeadon LS19 — 39 F7
Swincliffe Cl. Birk BD19 — 96 B6
Swincliffe Cres. Birk BD19 — 96 B6
Swincroft. Morley LS27 — 97 F3
Swindon Rd. Dew WF13 — 140 B5
Swine La. Keigh BD20 — 17 B4
Swine Market La. Heb Br HX7 — 89 A4
Swinegate. Leeds LS1 — 211
Swineshead Rd. Tod OL14 — 108 A1
Swinnow Ave. Leeds LS13 — 58 A1
Swinnow Cres. Pudsey LS28 — 58 A2
Swinnow Dr. Leeds LS13 — 58 A2
Swinnow Garth. Leeds LS13 — 58 A1
Swinnow Gdns. Leeds LS13 — 58 A1

Swinnow Gn. Pudsey LS28 — 77 A8
Swinnow Gr. Pudsey LS13 — 58 A1
Swinnow La. Leeds LS13 — 58 A1
Swinnow La. Leeds LS13, LS28 — 77 B8
Swinnow North Sch. Pudsey — 77 A8
Swinnow Pl. Pudsey LS13 — 58 A2
Swinnow Rd. Pudsey LS13 — 58 B1
Swinnow Rd. Leeds LS13 — 58 A1
Swinnow View. Leeds LS13 — 58 A1
Swinnow Wlk. Pudsey LS13 — 58 A1
Swinton St. Brad BD3 — 75 B8
Swinton Pl. Brad BD7 — 74 B5
Swinton Terr. Hali HX1 — 112 F5
Swire Smith Mid Sch. Keigh — 35 E6
Swires Rd. Brad BD2 — 56 C1
Swires Rd. Hali HX1 — 113 B6
Swires Terr. Hali HX1 — 113 B6
Swiss St. Castle WF10 — 103 E1
Swithen Hill. Kex S75 — 177 B3
Swithen's La. Roth LS26 — 100 D8
Swithen's St. Roth LS26 — 100 F4
Swithenbank Ave. Ossett WF5 — 140 D8
Swithenbank St. Ossett WF5 — 119 C1
Swithens Ct. Roth LS26 — 100 F4
Swithens Dr. Roth LS26 — 100 E4
Swithens Gr. Roth LS26 — 100 E4
Sycamore Ave. Bing BD16 — 36 F2
Sycamore Ave. Hud HD3 — 152 F5
Sycamore Ave. Kippax LS25 — 82 F2
Sycamore Ave. Leeds LS8 — 60 F5
Sycamore Ave. Leeds LS15 — 81 A8
Sycamore Ave. Mel HD7 — 170 D1
Sycamore Ave. Tod OL14 — 108 A7
Sycamore Ave. Wake WF2 — 160 D7
Sycamore Chase. Pudsey LS28 — 76 F7
Sycamore Cl. Brad BD3 — 75 A8
Sycamore Cl. Bramho LS16 — 24 F1
Sycamore Cl. Knot WF11 — 126 D2
Sycamore Cl. Leeds LS8 — 60 F8
Sycamore Cl. Lepton HD8 — 155 F3
Sycamore Copse. Wake WF2 — 141 F5
Sycamore Croft. Leeds LS11 — 79 B3
Sycamore Ct. Brad BD3 — 75 A8
Sycamore Ct. Hud HD8 — 152 F5
Sycamore Dr. Add LS29 — 6 A8
Sycamore Dr. Brig HX3 — 115 A6
Sycamore Dr. Elland HX5 — 134 D6
Sycamore Dr. Roy S71 — 179 A3
Sycamore Fold. Leeds LS11 — 79 B3
Sycamore Gn. Pont WF8 — 125 F1
Sycamore Gr. Nor WF6 — 144 A8
Sycamore House. Castle WF10 — 124 E7
Sycamore La. Leeds LS15 — 81 D7
Sycamore La. W Bret WF4 — 176 F8
Sycamore Row. Leeds LS13 — 58 A4
Sycamore St. Wake WF1 — 142 E4
Sycamore Terr. Honley HD7 — 171 E3
Sycamore View. Keigh BD20 — 19 C1
Sycamore Wlk. Ossett WF5 — 141 B5
Sycamore Wlk. Pudsey LS28 — 57 D2
Sycamore Wlk. Roth LS26 — 101 B6
Sydenham Pl. Brad BD3 — 75 B6
Sydenham Rd. Leeds LS11 — 79 A3
Sydenham St. Leeds LS11 — 78 F6
Sydney St. Brad BD10 — 56 D6
Sydney St. Clec BD19 — 116 E8
Sydney St. Roth LS26 — 100 D6
Syke Ave. Dew WF12 — 139 F8
Syke Ave. Shep HD8 — 173 F1
Syke Cl. E ard WF3 — 119 D2
Syke Gdns. E Ard WF3 — 119 D2
Syke Gn. Scarc LS14 — 45 C8
Syke Gr. Dew WF12 — 139 F8
Syke La. Earl WF12 — 140 A6
Syke La. Elland HX4 — 133 F2
Syke La. Hali HX2 — 91 E1
Syke La. Queen BD13 — 92 F7
Syke La. Scar LS14 — 45 B8
Syke Rd. Dew WF12 — 139 F8
Syke Rd. E Ard WF3 — 119 D2
Syke Rd. Keigh BD20 — 18 A1
Syke St. Clec BD19 — 119 F8
Syke View. Dew WF12 — 139 F8
Sykefield. Hud HD2 — 135 E4
Sykes Ave. Batley WF17 — 118 B6
Sykes Cl. Birk BD19 — 96 A3
Sykes La. Batley WF17 — 118 B6
Sykes La. Elland HX4 — 133 F2
Sykes La. Haw BD22 — 34 A6

Talbot Mount. Leeds LS4 — 59 C3
Talbot Rd. Leeds LS8 — 43 F1
Talbot Rise. Leeds LS17 — 43 F2
Talbot Row. Batley WF17 — 118 D5
Talbot St. Brad BD7 — 74 C7
Talbot St. Keigh BD21 — 35 A7 4
Talbot St. Nor WF6 — 123 A2
Talbot Terr. Leeds LS4 — 59 C3
Talbot Terr. Roth LS26 — 100 E4
Talbot View. Leeds LS4 — 59 C3
Talbot View. Mir WF14 — 138 A6
Tall Trees Dr. Fnath WF7 — 145 D8
Tamar St. Brad BD5 — 74 C4
Tammy Hall St. Wake WF1 — 142 C6 3
Tamworth St. Brad BD4 — 75 E6
Tan House Ct. Brad BD4 — 95 C8
Tan House La. Ack M T WF7 — 164 B7
Tan House La. Shelf HX3 — 93 A5
Tan House La. Wils BD15 — 53 B6
Tan La. Brad BD4 — 95 B6
Tan Pit Cl. Clay DN5 — 194 D4
Tandem Ind Est. Kirkhe — 155 B6
Tandem Way. Kirkhe HD5 — 155 B6
Tandy Trad Est The. Leeds — 59 C3
Tanfield Cl. Roy S71 — 179 A4
Tanfield Rd. Hud HD1 — 153 F8
Tanglewood Ct. Brad BD6 — 74 A1 2
Tanhouse Hill. Brig HX3 — 114 C7
Tanhouse Hill. Hors LS18 — 58 B8
Tanhouse La. Lepton WF14 — 156 B7
Tanhouse Pk. Brig HX3 — 114 C7
Tanner Cl. Brad BD3 — 56 B1
Tanner Hill Rd. Brad BD7 — 73 E3
Tanner St. Clec WF15 — 116 B5
Tanners. Slai HD7 — 169 F7
Tannett Gn. Brad BD5 — 74 F2
Tanpits. Heb Br HX7 — 89 A3 23
Tanshelf Dr. Pont WF8 — 146 C8
Tanshelf Est. Pont — 125 C1
Tanshelf Sta. Pont — 125 C1
Tansy Ind. Owen BD22 — 51 E2
Tanton Cres. Brad BD14 — 73 D4
Tanton Wlk. Brad BD14 — 73 D4
Tanyard Ave. Hud HD3 — 153 A7
Tanyard Fold. Crig WF4 — 160 A2
Tanyard Rd. Hud HD3 — 153 A4
Tanyard Rd. Hud HD3 — 153 B4
Tarn Cl. Castle WF10 — 104 E1
Tarn Ct. Keigh BD20 — 19 F8
Tarn Ct. Loft S WF1 — 44 E7
Tarn La. Barwi LS17 — 28 B7
Tarn La. Keigh BD22 — 34 B8
Tarn Rd. Fent WF7 — 145 E4
Tarn View Rd. Yeadon LS19 — 40 D7
Tarnhill Mews. Brad BD5 — 74 E3
Tarnside Dr. Leeds LS14 — 62 A3
Tate Naylor St. Dew WF13 — 118 B2
Tatefield Cl. Kippax LS25 — 83 A1
Tatefield Gr. Kippax LS25 — 83 A1
Tateley Cl. Ossett WF5 — 119 C1
Tatham Way. Leeds LS8 — 61 A6
Tatton St. Wake WF1 — 142 F3
Taunton House. Brad BD5 — 74 D4
Taunton St. Ship BD18 — 55 B8
Tavern St. Wake WF1 — 142 A6
Taverngate. Guise LS20 — 38 E8
Tavora St. Wake WF1 — 142 E4
Tawny Ct. Morley LS27 — 98 D4 1
Tay Ct. Brad BD2 — 56 D5
Taylor Cl. Ossett WF5 — 140 F4
Taylor Hall La. Mir WF14 — 137 F7
Taylor La. Bil in Elm LS15 — 63 B5
Taylor La. Hali BD13 — 72 A1
Taylor Rd. Brad BD6 — 94 D8 10
Taylor St. Batley WF16 — 117 C4
Taylor St. Clec BD19 — 116 C7
Taylor St. Hud HD7 — 152 D4
Taylor Wood Cotts. W Har WF4 — 163 B6
Taylor's Bldgs. Hud HD4 — 154 A2
Taylor's Cl. Leeds LS13 — 58 A2
Teal Cl. Castle WF10 — 124 D6
Teal Dr. Morley LS27 — 97 D4
Teal Mews. Midd LS10 — 99 D5
Tealbeck App. Otley LS21 — 23 B7
Tealbeck House. Otley LS21 — 23 B7
Teall Ct. Ossett WF5 — 140 F4
Teall St. Ossett WF5 — 141 A5
Teall St. Wake WF1 — 216
Teasdale St. Brad BD4 — 75 B4
Teasel Cl. Brad BD8 — 73 C7
Technology Dr. Batley WF17 — 118 C4
Teddington Ave. Hud HD5 — 154 F5
Tees Cl. Castle WF10 — 125 B8
Teesdale Pl. Knot WF11 — 126 E2
Telephone Pl. Leeds LS9 — 61
Telford Cl. Castle WF10 — 104
Telford Cl. Leeds LS10 — 80 A2
Telford Gdns. Leeds LS10 — 80 A2
Telford Pl. Leeds LS10 — 80 A2
Telford St. Leeds LS10 — 79 F2
Telford Terr. Leeds LS10 — 79 F2
Telford Wlk. Leeds LS10 — 80 A2
Telscombe Dr. Brad BD4 — 75 E2
Temperance Field. Brad BD12 — 94 C4
Temperance Fields. Brig BD19 — 115 E1
Tempest Pl. Leeds LS11 — 79
Tempest Rd. Leeds LS11 — 79
Tempest Rd. S Kirk WF9 — 182
Templar La. Leeds LS2 — 212
Templar La. Leeds LS15 — 81
Templar Pl. Leeds LS2 — 212
Templar St. Leeds LS2 — 212
Templar's Way. Brad BD8 — 73 C8
Templars Cl. Elland HX4 — 134 A7

Tong Wlk. Leeds LS12 77 D7
Tongue La. Leeds LS6 42 F1
Toot Hill La. Sow Br HX6 111 B2
Tootal St. Wake WF1 142 D5
Toothill Ave. Brig HD6 136 A7
Toothill Bank. Brig HD6 136 A7
Toothill La. Brig HD6 136 A7
Toothill La S. Brig HD6 135 F6
Top Fold. Fair WF11 105 A4
Top Headlands. Ossett WF5 140 C5
Top House Farm Mews. Fair WF11 105 A4
Top La. Clay DN5 194 C5
Top La. W Bret WF4 158 D1
Top Meadow. Mir WF14 137 F2
Top Moor Side. Leeds LS11 79 A5
Top o' Th' Bank. Honley HD7 172 E1
Top o' Th' Close Rd. Tod OL14 129 C6
Top o' Th' Hill Rd. Tod OL14 108 A1
Top o' th' Moor. Kirkb HD4 173 C2
Top o' The Hill. Slai HD7 169 E7
Top of Carr. Batley WF17 118 B2 1
Top of the Hill. Honley HD7 172 E1
Top Orch. Ryhill WF4 162 B1
Top Rd. D Dale HD8 191 E7
Top Row. Mapp S75 177 E3
Top St. Hem WF9 181 C7
Top St. Tod OL14 128 F7
Top Stone Cl. B Sal LS25 105 E3
Topaz Cl. Hud HD2 136 C2
Topcliffe Ave. Morley LS27 98 D4
Topcliffe Ct. Morley LS27 98 D4 8
Topcliffe Fold. Morley LS27 98 C2
Topcliffe Gn. Morley LS27 98 D4 7
Topcliffe Gr. Morley LS27 98 C2
Topcliffe La. Morley LS27 98 C2
Topcliffe La. Morley LS27 98 D2
Topcliffe Mead. Morley LS27 98 D4 6
Topcliffe Mews. Morley LS27 98 D4 9
Tor Ave. Brad BD12 94 C1
Tor View. Honley HD7 172 C2
Torcote Cres. Hud HD2 136 C5
Tordoff Ave. Brad BD7 73 E5
Tordoff Gn. Brad BD6 94 B8 4
Tordoff Pl. Leeds LS5 59 A4
Tordoff Rd. Brad BD12 94 E6 5
Tordoff Terr. Leeds LS5 59 A4
Toronto Pl. Leeds LS7 60 D6
Torre Cl. Leeds LS9 80 A8
Torre Cres. Brad BD6 73 D1
Torre Dr. Leeds LS9 61 A1
Torre Gdns. Leeds LS9 79 F8
Torre Gn. Leeds LS9 79 F8
Torre Gr. Brad BD6 73 D1
Torre Gr. Leeds LS9 61 A1
Torre Hill. Leeds LS9 61 B1
Torre La. Leeds LS9 80 B8
Torre Mount. Leeds LS9 61 A1
Torre Pl. Leeds LS9 80 A8
Torre Rd. Brad BD6 73 D1
Torre Rd. Leeds LS9 80 A8
Torre Sq. Leeds LS9 61 B1 7
Torre View. Leeds LS9 61 B1
Torre Wlk. Leeds LS9 61 B1
Torridon Cres. Brad BD6 93 E6
Torridon Rd. Batley WF12 118 E2
Totties La. Holmfi HD7 189 D5
Toulston La. Bramham LS23 30 F2
Tower Ave. Upton WF9 183 A8
Tower Bldgs. Batley WF16 117 D3 1
Tower Cswy. Tod OL14 107 B7
Tower Dr The. Pool LS21 24 E6
Tower Gdns. Hali HX2 112 F4 2
Tower Gr. Leeds LS12 78 A8
Tower Hill. Hali HX6 112 B4
Tower House St. Leeds LS2 60 C1
Tower La. Leeds LS12 77 F8
Tower La. Leeds LS12 78 A8
Tower Pl. Leeds LS12 77 F8
Tower Rd. Leeds LS9 80 D4
Tower Rd. Ship BD18 54 E8
Tower St. Brad BD2 50 D2
Tower St. Tod OL14 86 A1
Towers Cl. Crof WF4 162 A8
Towers La. Crof WF4 144 B1
Towers Sq. Leeds LS6 60 A8
Towers Way. Leeds LS6 60 A8
Towlerton La. Wake WF2 120 E2
Town Ave. Hud HD1 154 C8
Town Cl. Hors LS18 41 B1
Town Cres. Hud HD1 154 C8
Town End Ave. Ack M T WF7 164 C7
Town End Ave. Holmfi HD7 189 C6
Town End. Brad BD7 74 A4
Town End Cl. Glu BD20 16 D6
Town End Cl. Leeds LS13 58 E1
Town End Cres. Holmfi HD7 189 C7
Town End. Gar LS25 82 E8
Town End. Gild LS27 97 D7
Town End. Hud HD7 152 D4
Town End. Hud HD5 154 F4
Town End La. Lepton HD8 156 A3
Town End. Ossett WF5 140 D5
Town End Rd. Brad BD14 73 B5
Town End Rd. Holmfi HD7 189 B7
Town Fields Rd. Elland HX5 134 E6
Town Gate. Brad BD10 56 B8
Town Gate. Brad BD12 94 C3
Town Gate. Brig BD19 115 F8
Town Gate. Guise LS20 22 E1
Town Gate. Heb Br HX2 90 B1
Town Gate. Hep HX7 88 F5
Town Gate. Holmfi HD7 188 D5
Town Gate. Holmfi HD7 188 F8
Town Gate. Holmfi HD7 189 A5
Town Gate. Holmfi HD7 189 E2
Town Gate. Kirkb HD8 173 E8
Town Gate. Lepton HD8 156 A4
Town Gate. Mars HD7 168 F4
Town Gate. Northo HX3 93 A2
Town Gate. Pudsey LS28 57 B6
Town Gate. Sow Br HX6 111 E3
Town Gn. Dew WF12 139 E7
Town Hall Bldgs. Elland HX5 135 A6
Town Hall Sq. Yeadon LS19 40 B7 4
Town Hall St E. Hali HX1 113 C7 6
Town Hall St. Elland HX5 134 F6 4
Town Hall St. Hali HX6 112 B4
Town Hall St. Holmfi HD7 189 A5
Town Hall St. Keigh BD21 35 C7
Town Hall St. Mir WF14 138 A4
Town Hall Way. Dew WF12 139 D8
Town Head. Honley HD7 171 F5
Town Hill. Bramham LS23 30 D2
Town Hill St. Ship BD16 54 B6
Town La. Brad BD10 39 B1
Town Moor. Kirkb HD4 172 F2
Town Pl. Hud HD1 154 C8
Town Rd. Kirkhe HD5 137 C1
Town St. Batley WF17 118 C2
Town St. Birk BD11 96 A6
Town St. Dew WF12 139 F7
Town St. Gild LS27 97 D7
Town St. Guise LS20 22 E1
Town St. Hem WF9 181 C7
Town St. Hors LS18 41 B1
Town St. Leeds LS7 60 D7
Town St. Leeds LS12 78 B7
Town St. Leeds LS11 78 E2
Town St. Midd LS10 99 C5
Town St. Pudsey LS28 57 D3
Town St. Pudsey LS28 57 E2
Town St. Pudsey LS13 57 F5
Town St. Roth WF3 100 D2
Town St. Yeadon LS19 40 B7
Town St. Yeadon LS19 40 D3
Town Street Mews. Leeds LS7 60 D7
Town Street Wlk. Leeds LS7 60 D7 8
Town Terr. Hud HD1 154 C8
Town The. Dew WF12 139 D2
Town Top. Kirkhe HD5 137 C1
Town Wells Dr. Pudsey LS28 57 B6
Townend Pl. Glu BD20 16 C6
Townend Pl. Pudsey LS28 76 F8 8
Townend Rd. Leeds LS12 78 B5
Townfield La. Hep HX7 88 F5
Townfield. Wils BD15 53 C5
Townfold. Ossett WF5 140 E6
Towngate Ave. Brig HD6 115 D3
Towngate. Bail BD17 38 C4 8
Towngate. Brig HX3 114 C8
Towngate. Brig HD6 115 E2
Towngate Gr. Mir WF14 138 B5
Towngate. Hali HX3 114 A4
Towngate House. Elland HX5 134 F7 1
Towngate. Hud HD4 154 A2
Towngate. Keigh BD21 35 C7
Towngate. Mapp S75 178 B1
Towngate. Mir WF14 138 B6
Towngate. Ossett WF5 140 F6
Towngate Rd. Batley WF17 118 A5
Towngate. Ship BD18 55 D7
Townhead Fold. Sil LS29 6 E8
Townley Ave. Hali HX3 114 A4
Townley Rd. Wake WF2 141 D4
Townville Dr. Castle WF10 125 D5
Townville Fst Sch. Castle 125 C7
Towton Dr. Castle WF10 124 A6
Track Mount. Batley WF17 118 B2
Track Rd. Batley WF17 118 B3
Trafalgar Rd. Dew WF13 118 B1
Trafalgar Rd. Ilkley LS29 8 B4
Trafalgar Sq. Hali HX1 113 A5 4
Trafalgar St. Batley WF17 118 A4
Trafalgar St. Brad BD1 74 E8
Trafalgar St. Hali HX1 113 A5 5
Trafalgar St. Leeds LS2 79 D8
Trafford Ave. Leeds LS9 61 B2 4
Trafford Gr. Leeds LS9 61 B3
Trafford Terr. Leeds LS9 61 B2 2
Tranbeck Rd. Guise LS20 22 B1
Tranfield Ave. Guise LS20 22 C1
Tranfield Cl. Guise LS20 22 C1
Tranfield Ct. Guise LS20 22 C1
Tranfield Gdns. Guise LS20 22 C1
Tranmere Dr. Guise LS20 22 C1
Tranmere Park Jun & Inf Sch. Guise 39 C8
Tranquility Ave. Leeds LS15 62 C2
Tranquility Ct. Leeds LS15 62 C2 2
Tranquility. Leeds LS15 62 C2
Tranquility Wlk. Leeds LS15 62 C2 1
Transvaal Terr. Batley WF17 118 B7
Tranter Gr. Brad BD4 75 E5
Tranter Pl. Leeds LS15 80 E8
Travis House. Tod OL14 129 A7
Travis Lacey Terr. Dew WF13 139 B8 8
Tredgold Ave. Bramho LS16 24 F2
Tredgold Cl. Bramho LS16 24 E2
Tredgold Cres. Bramho LS16 24 E2
Tredgold Garth. Bramho LS16 24 E3
Tree La. Hali HX2 90 F5
Tree Top View. Queen BD13 72 C2
Treefield Ind Est. Gild 97 D6
Trees St. Brad BD8 55 C1
Trelawn Ave. Leeds LS6 59 D5
Trelawn Cres. Leeds LS6 59 D5 11
Trelawn Pl. Leeds LS6 59 D5
Trelawn St. Leeds LS6 59 D5
Trelawn Terr. Leeds LS6 59 D5
Tremont Gdns. Leeds LS10 79 E2
Trenam Park Dr. Brad BD10 39 A2
Trenance Dr. Ship BD18 54 F7
Trenance Gdns. Elland HX4 134 A7
Trenholme Ave. Brad BD6 94 B6
Trenic Cres. Leeds LS6 59 D3 7
Trenic Dr. Leeds LS6 59 D3 13
Trent Ave. Gar LS25 83 B6
Trent Ave. Nor WF6 123 A4
Trent Rd. Leeds LS9 61 A1
Trent St. Leeds LS11 79 B5
Trentham Ave. Leeds LS11 79 B2 8
Trentham Gr. Leeds LS11 79 B2 7
Trentham Pl. Leeds LS11 79 B2 9
Trentham Row. Leeds LS11 79 B2 6
Trentham St. Leeds LS11 79 B2
Trentham Terr. Leeds LS11 79 B3 29
Trenton Dr. Brad BD8 55 C1
Trenton Rd. Batley WF12 118 F3
Trescoe Ave. Leeds LS13 58 E1
Tresham Ct. Batley WF12 118 F2
Trevelyan Sq. Leeds LS1 79 C7
Trevelyan St. Brig HD6 115 A5
Trevelyan St. Hud HD5 154 D5 9
Trevor Terr. Loft G WF2 120 E6
Triangle Bsns Pk. Batley 97 A3
Triangle CE Inf & Jun Sch. Sow Br 111 E1
Triangle The. Hud HD1 153 E5
Triath Ct. Batley WF17 117 E6
Trilby St. Wake WF1 142 D7
Trimmingham La. Hali HX2 112 E6
Trimmingham Rd. Hali HX2 112 E6
Trinity & All Saints' Coll. Hors 41 A3
Trinity Bsns Ctr. Wake 142 D5
Trinity Church Gate. Wake WF1 142 D6
Trinity Ct. Honley HD7 171 F4
Trinity Dr. D Dale HD8 191 F5
Trinity Gr. Brig HD6 115 A4 2
Trinity House. Wake WF1 142 D6 3
Trinity Pl. Bing BD16 37 A2
Trinity Pl. Hali HX1 113 C6
Trinity Rd. Brad BD5 74 D5
Trinity Rd. Hali HX1 113 C6
Trinity Rise. Otley LS21 23 B7
Trinity St. Batley WF17 118 C2
Trinity St. Hali HX1 113 C6
Trinity St. Heb Br HX7 88 F3
Trinity St. Hud HD1 153 F7
Trinity St. Keigh BD21 35 C8
Trinity St. Mir WF14 138 A4
Trinity St. Pont WF8 125 D1
Trinity St. Wake WF1 142 F3
Trinity Street Arc. Leeds 79 C7
Trinity View. Brad BD12 94 E7
Trinity View. Hali HX3 113 D6
Trinity View. Ossett WF5 140 D7
Trinity Way. S Elm WF9 183 A4
Trinity Wlk. Brad BD12 94 E7
Trip Garth. Coll LS22 13 B2
Trip La. Coll LS22 13 A2
Tristram Ave. Brad BD5 75 A2
Troon Dr. Hud HD2 135 F3
Trooper La. Hali HX3 113 E5
Trooper Terr. Hali HX3 113 D6
Trough La. Cull BD13 52 A3
Trough La. Denh BD13 52 A3
Trough La. S Elm WF9 183 C3
Trough Well La. Wake WF2 120 E3
Troughton Pl. Pudsey LS28 76 F5
Troughton St. Pudsey LS28 76 F5
Troutbeck Ave. Bail BD17 37 E1
Troy Hill. Morley LS27 98 A5
Troy Rd. Hors LS18 41 C2
Troy Rd. Morley LS27 98 A5
Troy Rise. Morley LS27 98 B5
Troydale Gdns. Pudsey LS28 77 B5
Troydale Gr. Pudsey LS28 77 B5
Troydale La. Pudsey LS28 77 B5
Trueman Ave. Batley WF16 117 E5
Trueman Ct. Brad BD12 94 E6
Trueman Way. S Elm WF9 183 A4
Truncliffe. Brad BD5 74 D1
Trundles La. Knot WF11 127 B4
Truro Dr. Nor WF6 123 B3
Truro St. Leeds LS12 78 C8
Truro Wlk. Nor WF6 123 B3
Tubby La. Hud HD2 136 B1
Tudor Cl. Pont WF8 146 C5
Tudor Croft. Hud HD2 136 F5
Tudor Ct. Pudsey LS28 57 C2
Tudor Gdns. Leeds LS11 78 E2
Tudor House. Wake WF1 142 C6 23
Tudor Lawns. Leeds LS8 61 C7
Tudor Lawns. Loft G WF2 120 E5
Tudor St. Brad BD5 74 D4
Tudor St. Slai HD7 170 A8
Tudor Way. Castle WF10 125 B8
Tudor Way. Dew WF12 139 B3
Tuel La. Hali HX6 112 B4
Tuel Lane Inf Sch. Hali 112 B4
Tufton St. Sil BD20 5 E1
Tulip St. Haw BD22 51 C5
Tulip St. Leeds LS10 79 D3
Tumbling Cl. Ossett WF5 140 E6
Tumbling Hill. Dar WF8 147 A5
Tumbling Hill St. Brad BD7 74 D6
Tun La. S Hie S72 180 D7
Tunnacliffe Rd. Hud HD4 154 B3
Tunnel St. Denh BD13 71 D8
Tunnel St. Hud HD4 171 C7
Tunnicliffe Pl. Sil BD20 5 D1
Tunstall Gn. Brad BD4 75 E3
Tunstall Rd. Leeds LS11 79 C3
Tunwell La. Brad BD2 56 C4
Tunwell St. Brad BD2 56 C4
Tup La. Ryhill WF4 180 C8
Turbary Ave. Pudsey LS28 57 E2 2
Turbid La. Hud HD4 171 A6
Turbury La. Elland HX4 133 E8
Turbury La. Sow Br HX4 133 E8
Turf Ct. Cull BD13 52 C5
Turf La. Cull BD13 52 C5
Turgate La. Sow Br HX7 111 A1
Turkey Hill. Pudsey LS28 76 F6
Turley Cote La. Elland HX4 134 C2
Turn o' The Nook. Ossett WF5 140 C6
Turnberry Ave. Leeds LS17 43 B4
Turnberry Cl. Leeds LS17 43 B4
Turnberry Dr. Leeds LS17 43 B4
Turnberry Gr. Cud S72 180 C1
Turnberry Gr. Leeds LS17 43 B4
Turnberry Pl. Leeds LS17 43 B4
Turnberry Rise. Leeds LS17 43 B4
Turnberry View. Leeds LS17 43 B4
Turnbridge Rd. Hud HD1 154 C6
Turnbull Ct. Leeds LS8 61 D5
Turner Ave. Batley WF17 118 C5
Turner Ave. Brad BD7 73 F5
Turner Ave N. Hali HX2 91 D5
Turner Ave S. Hali HX2 91 E4
Turner Cl. E Ard WF3 119 E8
Turner Cres. Otley LS21 11 B1
Turner Dr. E Ard WF3 119 E8
Turner La. Hali HX3 92 D1
Turner La. Sil LS29 6 C6
Turner La. Sil LS29 6 D8
Turner Pl. Brad BD7 74 B5
Turner Pl. Hali HX2 91 E5
Turner St. Pudsey LS28 57 D3 5
Turner's Ct. Hali HX3 92 B2 1
Turners Yd. Pudsey LS28 57 D3
Turney St. Hali HX3 92 A2
Turnip La. Dew WF12 139 D2
Turnkey Park. Leeds 78 C4
Turnpike St. Elland HX5 135 A7
Turnshaw Rd. Haw BD22 33 F2
Turnshaw Rd. Kirkb HD8 174 A6
Turnshaws Ave. Kirkb HD8 174 A7
Turnshaws Cl. Kirkb HD8 174 A7
Turnshaws Special Sch. Kirkb 174 A7
Turnsteads Ave. Clec BD19 116 B8
Turnsteads Cl. Clec BD19 116 C8
Turnsteads Cres. Clec BD19 116 C8
Turnsteads Dr. Clec BD19 116 C8
Turnsteads Mount. Clec BD19 116 C8
Turnstone Ct. Midd LS10 99 D5 3
Turnways The. Leeds LS6 59 C4
Turret Hall Rd. B Head HX7 88 C2
Turret Royd Rd. B Head HX7 88 D2
Turton Gn. Gild LS27 97 D7
Turton St. Wake WF1 142 D6
Turton Vale. Gild LS27 97 D6
Turver's La. Beal WF11 127 F3
Turvin Rd. Litt HX6 130 D2
Turvin Rd. Rip HX6 130 D2
Twain Cres. Castle WF10 125 C6
Tweed Cl. Batley WF17 97 A1
Tweedale Gdns. Dew WF13 139 B8
Tweedale St. Dew WF13 139 B8 2
Tweedy St. Wils BD15 53 C5
Twelfth Ave. Clec WF15 116 B5
Twickenham Ct. Brad BD8 55 D2
Twitch Hill. Hor WF4 141 B1
Twivey St. Castle WF10 124 C7
Two Dales Sch. Guise 39 C8
Two Gates. Slai HD7 151 E1
Two Laws Rd. Haw BD22 49 D8
Tyas Gr. Leeds LS9 80 B7
Tyas La. Mars HD7 151 B2
Tyburn La. Emley HD8 175 C6
Tyersal Ave. Pudsey BD4 75 F6
Tyersal Cl. Pudsey BD4 75 F6
Tyersal Cres. Pudsey BD4 75 F6
Tyersal Ct. Pudsey BD4 75 F6
Tyersal Dr. Pudsey BD4 75 F6
Tyersal Fst Sch. Brad 75 D5
Tyersal Garth. Pudsey BD4 75 F6
Tyersal Gn. Pudsey BD4 75 F6
Tyersal Gr. Pudsey BD4 75 F6
Tyersal La. Brad BD4 75 F4
Tyersal La. Pudsey BD4, LS28 76 A5
Tyersal Pk. Pudsey BD4 75 F6
Tyersal Rd. Pudsey BD4 75 F6
Tyersal Terr. Pudsey BD4 75 F6
Tyersal View. Pudsey BD4 75 E6
Tyersal Wlk. Pudsey BD4 75 F6
Tyler Cl. Nor WF6 123 E2
Tyndale Ave. Hor WF4 141 C2
Tyndale Wlk. Batley WF16 117 E5
Tyne St. Brad BD3 74 F8
Tyne St. Haw BD22 51 D7 1
Tyne St. Keigh BD21 35 D7
Tynedale Ct. Leeds LS7 60 A6
Tynwald Cl. Leeds LS17 43 A2
Tynwald Dr. Leeds LS17 43 A2
Tynwald Gdns. Leeds LS17 43 A2
Tynwald Gn. Leeds LS17 43 A3
Tynwald Hill. Leeds LS17 43 A2
Tynwald Mount. Leeds LS17 43 A2
Tynwald Rd. Leeds LS17 43 A2
Tynwald Wlk. Leeds LS17 43 A3
Tyrrel St. Brad BD1 74 E7 9
Tyrrell Ct. Wake WF2 141 D7
Tyson St. Brad BD1 74 D8
Tyson St. Hali HX1 112 E6

Ullswater Ave. Batley WF12 118 E3
Ullswater Cl. Batley WF12 118 E2
Ullswater Cl. Knot WF11 126 E1
Ullswater Cres. Leeds LS15 80 E7
Ullswater Cres. Roth LS26 101 C6
Ullswater Dr. Brad BD6 93 F6
Ullswater Dr. Weth LS22 13 C6
Ullswater Rd. Batley WF12 118 E3
Ullswater Rise. Weth LS22 13 C5
Una Pl. Hud HD2 153 E8
Underbank Ave. B Head HX7 88 C1
Underbank Old Rd. Holmfi HD7 189 B4
Undercliffe Fst Sch. Brad 56 B1
Undercliffe La. Brad BD3 56 A1
Undercliffe Mid Sch. Brad 56 B1
Undercliffe Old Rd. Brad BD2 56 B1
Undercliffe Pl. Brig HX3 114 B7
Undercliffe Rd. Brad BD2 56 B3
Undercliffe Rise. Ilkley LS29 8 F2
Undercliffe St. Brad BD3 56 B1
Undercliffe Terr. Hali HX2 112 F4 1
Underwood Dr. Yeadon LS19 40 C1
Union Cross Yd. Hali HX1 113 C7
Union Gr. Liver WF15 117 B3
Union House La. Brad BD13 73 C2
Union La. Hali HX2 71 D1
Union Pl. Leeds LS11 79 B6
Union Rd. Brad BD7 74 B5
Union Rd. Brad BD12 94 C7
Union Rd. Liver WF15 117 B3
Union Sq. Wake WF1 142 D6
Union St. Bail BD17 38 E2
Union St. Batley WF17 96 F1 8
Union St. Bing BD16 36 E7
Union St. Castle WF10 124 B7
Union St. Dew WF13 139 D8
Union St. Elland HX4 134 B7 8
Union St. Hali HX6 112 C4
Union St. Hali HX1 113 C6
Union St. Hem WF9 181 E6
Union St. Hud HD3 153 B8
Union St. Hud HD1 154 B7 6
Union St. Leeds LS2 79 D8
Union St. Liver FW16 117 C3
Union St. Morley LS27 98 C8 1
Union St. Ossett WF5 140 D6
Union St. Otley LS21 22 F7
Union St. Queen BD13 72 E1 11
Union St S. Tod OL14 108 B5
Union St. Slai HD7 151 F1
Union St. Sow Br HX6 111 E1
Union St. Wake WF1 142 C7
Union Terr. Leeds LS7 60 C6
Union Yd. Brad BD10 56 B8
Unity Cl. Leeds LS6 60 B4
Unity St. Heb Br HX7 89 A4
Unity St. Keigh BD20 18 F2
Unity St N. Bing BD16 36 F2
Unity St. Roth WF3 100 D3
Unity St S. Bing BD16 36 F2
Unity St. Tod OL14 129 A8
Unity Terr. Hali HX1 112 E6
Univ of Bradford. Brad 74 D6
Univ of Bradford Management Ctr. Ship 55 B4
University Rd. Leeds LS2 60 A2
University St. Castle WF10 124 D7
Unna Way. Hud HD1 154 A7
Unwin Pl. Brad BD9 54 E2
Upland Cres. Leeds LS8 61 A5
Upland Gr. Leeds LS8 61 A5
Upland Rd. Leeds LS8 61 A4
Uplands Ave. Brad BD13 73 B2
Uplands Cl. Brad BD13 73 B2
Uplands Cres. Brad BD13 73 B2
Uplands Dr. Mir WF14 138 A6
Uplands Gr. Brad BD13 73 B2
Uplands. Keigh BD20 18 A1
Uplands The. Pont WF8 146 C7
Upper Accommodation Rd. Leeds LS9 79 E7
Upper Ada St. Ship BD18 54 F8 8
Upper Addison St. Brad BD4 74 F5
Upper Allerton La. Brad BD13 72 E8
Upper Armley CE Sch. Leeds 78 B8
Upper Ash Gr. S Elm WF9 183 B3
Upper Ashley La. Ship BD17 55 B8
Upper Bank End Rd. Holmfi HD7 189 B3
Upper Bank Hey Bottom. Rip HX6 132 E3
Upper Barker St. Liver WF15 117 A4
Upper Basinghall St. Leeds LS1 79 B8
Upper Batley La. Batley WF17 118 B8
Upper Batley Low La. Batley WF17 118 C8
Upper Battye St. Batley WF16 117 D4
Upper Bell Croft. Hali HX3 114 A4
Upper Bell Hall. Hali HX1 113 A5
Upper Bolton Brow. Hali HX6 112 D4
Upper Bonegate. Brig HD6 115 B3
Upper Brig Royd. Rip HX6 132 E4
Upper Brockholes. Hali HX2 91 D8
Upper Brow Rd. Hud HD1 153 D5
Upper Butts. Clec BD19 116 D7
Upper Calton St. Keigh BD21 35 B5
Upper Camroyd St. Dew WF13 118 D1
Upper Carr La. Pudsey LS28 57 A6
Upper Carr St. Liver WF15 117 A5
Upper Castle St. Brad BD5 74 F4
Upper Chelsea St. Keigh BD21 35 B5
Upper Clough Rd. Slai HD7 170 D7
Upper Commercial St. Batley WF17 118 C5
Upper Common La. Clay W HD8 192 F8
Upper Croft Rd. Batley WF17 118 B4
Upper Cross St. Dew WF13 118 C1 2
Upper Cumberworth CE Aided Fst Sch. D Dale 191 B6
Upper Ellistones La. Elland HX4 134 A7
Upper Exley. Hali HX3 113 E1
Upper Ferndown Gn. Brad BD15 54 A1
Upper Field House La. Sow Br HX6 111 D2
Upper Field La. H Hoy S75 176 E1
Upper Field La. Kex S75 176 E1
Upper Fountain St. Hali HX6 112 B4
Upper Fountaine St. Leeds LS2 79 C8
Upper Gate. Holmfi HD7 189 E2
Upper George St. Batley WF16 117 D4
Upper George St. Brad BD6 74 B1 4
Upper George St. Hud HD1 154 A6 3
Upper Grange Ave. Brad BD15 73 B8 3
Upper Green Ave. Brig BD19 115 F8 10
Upper Green Ave. E Ard WF3 119 D7
Upper Green. Bail BD17 38 B2
Upper Green. Brad BD7 74 A3 1
Upper Green La. Brig HD6 114 E5
Upper Green Way. E Ard WF3 119 D7
Upper Hagg Rd. Holmfi HD7 172 B2
Upper Hagg Rd. Honley HD7 172 B2
Upper Hatfield Pl. Ryhill WF4 162 D2
Upper Haugh Shaw. Hali HX1 113 A5 13
Upper Heaton La. Kirkhe HD5 137 B2
Upper Heights Rd. Thorn BD13 72 C8
Upper Hird St. Keigh BD21 35 A5
Upper Hirst. Hud HD3 152 D8
Upper Holme. Slai HD7 169 D8
Upper Hopton CE (C) 5-9 Sch. Mir 137 F1
Upper House La. Clec WF15 116 C4
Upper House Rd. Holmfi HD7 199 C8
Upper House St. Brad BD4 75 B5
Upper Kirkgate. Hali HX1 113 D7
Upper La. Clec BD19 117 B7
Upper La. Emley HD8 175 D6
Upper La. Neth WF4 158 D4
Upper La. Northo HX3 92 F3
Upper La. Tod OL14 87 D1
Upper Langwith. Coll LS22 28 E8
Upper Lombard St. Yeadon LS19 40 A4
Upper Lumb La. Heb Br HX7 110 C4
Upper Marsh. Hali HX3 113 F5
Upper Marsh La. Oxen BD22 51 A5
Upper Martin Gn. Elland HX4 134 A7
Upper Mary St. Ship BD18 54 F8 9
Upper Maythorn La. Wh Com HD7 200 D8
Upper Meadows. Holmfi HD7 188 D5
Upper Meadows. Queen BD13 92 E8
Upper Mill Row. Keigh BD20 19 E2
Upper Millergate. Brad BD1 74 E7 13
Upper Mosscar St. Brad BD3 75 A7
Upper Mount. Mel HD7 170 F1
Upper Mount St. Batley WF17 118 C3
Upper Mount St. Hud HD1 153 F4
Upper Nidd St. Brad BD3 75 D6
Upper Norcroft. Caw S75 193 F3
Upper North St. Batley WF17 118 B4
Upper North St. Leeds LS2 60 B1
Upper Parish Ghyll La. Ilkley LS29 7 F3
Upper Park Gate. Brad BD1 74 F7
Upper Peel St. Dew WF13 118 D1 1
Upper Piccadilly. Brad BD1 74 E7 2
Upper Quarry Rd. Hud HD2 137 A6
Upper Raglan St. Tod OL14 108 B6
Upper Rd. Batley WF17 118 B2
Upper Reins. Honley HD7 172 A5
Upper Rushton Rd. Brad BD3 56 D1
Upper Seymour St. Brad BD3 75 B7
Upper South St. Dew WF13 118 C1
Upper Station Rd. Batley WF17 118 D4
Upper Sutherland Rd. Brig HX3 114 E8
Upper Swain Royd Mews. Brad BD15 53 E4
Upper Town. Oxen BD22 51 C2
Upper Town St. Leeds LS13 58 C3
Upper Warrengate. Wake WF1 142 D6 12
Upper Washer La. Hali HX2 112 F5
Upper Wellhouse Rd. Slai HD7 152 C3
Upper West St. Batley WF17 118 E5
Upper Westlock Ave. Leeds LS9 61 A1
Upper Whitley Fst Sch. Floc 156 E5
Upper Willow Hall. Hali HX2 112 D6
Upper Woodlands Rd. Brad BD8 55 A1
Upper Woodview Pl. Leeds LS11 79 B2 16
Upper Wortley Dr. Leeds LS12 78 B7 1
Upper Wortley Prim Sch. Leeds 78 B6
Upper Wortley Rd. Leeds LS12 78 B7
Upper Wortley Recn Ctr. Leeds 77 F7
Upper York St. Wake WF1 142 C7
Upperfield Dr. Hud HD7 152 C4
Upperhead Row. Hud HD1 154 A6 11
Uppermoor Cl. Pudsey LS28 76 D6
Uppermoor. Pudsey LS28 76 D7
Upperthong La. Holmfi HD7 188 E5
Upton Mid Sch. Upton 182 F7
Upton St. Batley WF17 118 B6
Upwood La. Keigh BD20 19 D2
Upwood Pk. Oxen BD22 51 E3
Urban Terr. Floc WF4 156 E5
Ure Cres. Brad BD8 74 D8
Ure Gr. Weth LS22 13 D8
Usher St. Brad BD4 75 A5
Usher Street Fst Sch. Brad 75 A5
Utley Fst Sch. Keigh 18 A2
Uttley St. Hali HX3 92 B2 4

Vale Ave. Knot WF11 126 D4
Vale Ave. Leeds LS8 44 A3
Vale Cl. Hud HD5 154 F3
Vale Cres. Knot WF11 126 D4
Vale Crest. Knot WF11 126 D4

Ward Place La. Holmfi HD7 188 F3
Ward Sq. Hud HD1 154 A6 26
Ward St. Brad BD7 74 A3
Ward St. Dew WF13 118 D1
Ward St. Keigh BD21 35 B6
Ward St. Leeds LS13 79 D5
Ward's End. Hali HX1 113 C6
Wardman St. Keigh BD21 18 E1
Wards Hill. Batley WF17 118 C5
Wards Hill Ct. Batley WF17 118 C5
Wareham Cnr. Brad BD4 75 E2
Warehouse Hill Rd. Mars HD7 169 A4
Warehouse St. Batley WF17 118 D4
Waring Way. Dew WF12 118 E1
Warlands End Gate. Litt OL14 129 D5
Warlbeck. Ilkley LS29 7 F4
Warley Ave. Brad BD3 75 D8
Warley Dene. Hali HX2 112 B6
Warley Dr. Brad BD3 75 D8
Warley Edge La. Hali HX2 112 C7
Warley Gr. Brad BD3 75 D8
Warley Gr. Hali HX2 112 D7
Warley Rd. Hali HX1, HX2 112 E6
Warley Road Jun & Inf Sch. Hali 112 D6
Warley St. Hali HX1 113 A6
Warley Town Cty Prim Sch. Hali 112 B6
Warley Town La. Hali HX2 112 A6
Warley View. Hali HX2 112 D7
Warley Wood Ave. Hali HX2 111 F5
Warley Wood La. Hali HX2 111 F5
Warm La. Yeadon LS19 40 A5
Warmfield Heath Parochial Sch. Crof 143 B4
Warmfield La. Crof WF1 143 E7
Warmfield View. Wake WF1 142 F7
Warmliegh Pk. Queen BD13 72 B1
Warneford Ave. Ossett WF5 140 D7
Warneford Rd. Hud HD4 153 A3
Warneford Rise. Hud HD4 153 A3
Warnford Gr. Brad BD4 75 D3
Warrel's Ave. Leeds LS13 58 C3 4
Warrel's Ct. Leeds LS13 58 C2
Warrel's Gr. Leeds LS13 58 C2
Warrel's Mount. Leeds LS13 58 C2
Warrel's Pl. Leeds LS13 58 C2
Warrel's Row. Leeds LS13 58 C2 4
Warrel's St. Leeds LS13 58 C2
Warrel's Terr. Leeds LS13 58 C2 19
Warren Ave. Bing BD16 37 B5
Warren Ave. Wake WF2 141 C6
Warren Dr. Liver WF15 117 B2
Warren Cl. Roy S71 179 D5
Warren St. Wake WF1 142 D6
Warren Dr. Bing BD16 37 B4
Warren Dr. Feath WF7 145 A8
Warren House La. E Carl LS19 23 D1
Warren House La. Hud HD3 135 A3
Warren House. Wake WF1 142 C6 22
Warren La. Arth LS21 25 A7
Warren La. Bing BD16 37 B4
Warren La. Bramham LS24 31 A1
Warren La. Mapp S75 178 C4
Warren La. Wool S75 178 D4
Warren Park Cl. Brig HD6 114 E5
Warren Pk. Bing HD6 114 E6
Warren St. Dew WF12 139 D6
Warrens La. Clec WF17 96 D3
Warrenside. Hud HD2 136 B4
Warrenton Pl. Brad BD7 74 A4
Warrington Terr. Mars HD7 168 E4
Warsop Rd. Barn S71 178 E5
Warton Ave. Brad BD4 75 B1
Warwick Ave. Brad BD4 75 B2
Warwick Cl. Brad BD4 75 C1 3
Warwick Cl. Leeds LS9 58 C7 1
Warwick Dr. Brad BD4 75 B1
Warwick Rd. Hali HX3 113 B4 1
Warwick Rd. Battley WF17 118 D5
Warwick Road Jun & Inf Sch. Batley 118 C3
Warwick St. Wake WF1 142 F3
Wasdale Cres. Wake WF1 141 E7
Wasdale Rd. Wake WF1 141 E7
Washburn Cl. Sil BD20 5 D1
Washburn Ct. Weth LS22 13 D8
Washburn Dr. Leeds LS16 42 E3
Washer La. Hali HX2 112 E5
Washer Lane Ind Est. Hali 112 F4
Washfold Rd. Heb Brad WF7 131 B7
Washington Pl. Pudsey LS13 77 A8
Washington St. Brad BD8 54 F1
Washington St. Hali HX3 92 A1 20
Washington Terr. Pudsey LS13 77 A8
Washpit New Rd. Holmfi HD7 189 B3
Wasp Nest Rd. Hud HD1 154 A6
Waste La. Hud HD5 154 E4
Waste La. Mir WF14 137 F3
Waste La. Mir WF14 137 E1
Waste The. Mir WF14 137 F1
Wastwater Dr. Brad BD6 93 F6
Watchit Hole La. Th Aud WF8 165 A1
Watchley La. H Pag DN5 195 B3
Water Gn. Rip HX6 132 A6
Water Green La. Rip HX6 132 A6
Water La. Brad WF8 146 D2
Water La. Dar WF8 146 D2
Water La. Dew WF12 139 B6
Water La. Dew WF13 139 A6
Water La. Hali HX3 113 D4
Water La. K Smea WF8 166 E8
Water La. Keigh BD21 35 B6
Water La. Leeds LS12 79 F8
Water La. Leeds LS11 79 F8
Water La. Leeds LS11 211 D3
Water La. Mir WF14 138 A5
Water La. Pont WF8 125 F3
Water La. S Kirk WF9 181 F3
Water La. Shep HD8 174 A3
Water La. Wake WF1 158 D8
Water Lane Gr. Mir WF14 158 C8
Water Row. Holmfi HD7 189 D6

Water St. Brig HD6 115 B3
Water St. Clay W HD8 175 D1
Water St. Holmfi HD7 188 D3
Water St. Hud HD1, HD4 153 F3
Water St. Hud HD1 153 F3
Water St. Sow Br HX6 112 B3
Water St. Tod OL14 108 B5
Water Stalls Rd. Heb Br HX7 110 F2
Watercock St. Brad BD4 75 A5
Watercroft. Hud HD5 154 F3
Waterfall Cotts. Mars HD7 168 D5
Watergate. Brig HX3 114 C7
Watergate. Hud HD1 154 A6
Watergate. M'town LS26 102 B1
Watergate. Pont WF8 125 C1
Watergate Rd. Dew WF12 139 B7
Waterhouse Ct. Hors LS18 58 A7 8
Waterhouse Dr. E Ard WF3 120 B7
Waterhouse Gr. Wake WF2 141 D7
Waterhouse St. Hali HX1 113 C7
Waterhouse St. Keigh BD21 18 D7 8
Waterloo Cl. Castle WF10 123 F5
Waterloo Cres. Brad BD10 56 D7
Waterloo Cres. Leeds LS13 58 C2
Waterloo Fold. Brad BD12 94 D2 2
Waterloo La. Leeds LS13 58 C2
Waterloo Mount. Pudsey LS28 76 B8
Waterloo Rd. Bing BD16 37 A3
Waterloo Rd. Brig HD6 115 A3
Waterloo Rd. Hud HD5 155 A6
Waterloo Rd. Leeds LS10 215 E2
Waterloo Rd. Pudsey LS28 76 C7
Waterloo St. Wake WF1 142 D4
Waterloo Terr. Hali HX6 112 B5
Waterloo Way. Leeds LS13 58 B3
Waters Rd. Mars HD7 168 D5
Waterside. Bing BD16 36 D5
Waterside Fold. Heb Br HX7 89 A4
Waterside. Hali HX3 91 A1 D6
Waterside. Hud HD1 153 F2
Waterside Ind & Leis. Hud HD1 153 F2
Waterside Mill. Oxen BD22 51 E1
Waterside. Oxen BD22 51 C2
Waterside Ind Pk. Leeds 80 B2
Waterside. Sil BD20 5 E1
Watering Wlk. Kirkhe WF14 127 D5
Waterton La. Warm LS23 14 A4
Waterton Cl. S Kirk WF9 182 D3
Waterton Prim Sch. Wake 141 D4
Waterton Rd. Wake WF2 141 D4
Waterton St. Castle WF10 124 B7
Waterwood Cl. E Ard WF3 119 E7
Waterwood Gr. Wake WF1 142 C4
Watery La. Holme HD7 197 F8
Watford Ave. Brig HX3 93 F3
Watkinson Ave. Hali HX3 72 F6
Watkinson Dr. Hali HX2 91 F4
Watkinson Bglws. Hali HX2 91 F4
Watkinson Dr. Hali HX2 91 E4
Watkinson Rd. Hali HX2 91 F4
Watling Rd. Castle WF10 104 E1
Watmough St. Brad BD7 74 A3 2
Watroyd La. Slai HD7 152 A2
Watson Ave. Dew WF12 140 B8
Watson Cl. Oxen BD22 51 C2
Watson Cres. Wake WF1 142 F7
Watson Mill Rd. Sow Br HX6 112 A2
Watson Rd. Leeds LS15 81 A6
Watson St. Morley LS27 97 F3
Watson St. Wake WF1 123 A2
Watson's La. Tad LS24 31 D5
Watt St. Brad BD4 75 D6
Wattlesyke. Coll LS22 29 E8
Watts St. Brad BD7 74 A3
Watty Hall Ave. Brad BD6 74 A2
Watty Hall La. Brad BD6 74 A2
Watty Hall Rd. Brad BD6 74 A2
Watty Terr. Tod OL14 107 F3
Wauchope St. Wake WF2 141 E5
Wauds Gates. Bail BD17 38 C1
Waulkmill Cl. Upton WF9 183 A7
Wavell Garth. Wake WF2 160 F7
Wavell Gr. Wake WF2 160 F7
Waverley Ave. Brad BD7 74 B5
Waverley Ave. Keigh BD20 36 C8
Waverley Cres. Ave. Keigh BD20 36 D8
Waverley Garth. Leeds LS11 79 B4
Waverley Pl. Brad BD7 74 B5
Waverley Mill Sch. Brad 74 B5
Waverley Rd. Elland HX5 134 F6
Waverley Rd. Hud HD1 153 C5
Waverley St. Dew WF12 139 C7
Waverley St. Slai HD7 151 F1
Waverley Terr. Brig HX3 114 C8
Wayland Ct. Leeds LS16 42 D4
Wayland Dr. Leeds LS16 42 D4
Wayne Cl. Batley WF17 118 C6
Wayside Ave. Bard LS14 28 D1
Wayside Cres. Bard LS14 28 D1
Wayside Cres. Brad BD2 56 C2
Wayside Mount. Bard LS14 28 C1
Wayside Gdns. Bard LS14 28 C1
Weardley La. Hare LS17 26 B6
Weather Hill La. Heb Br HX7 110 F8
Weather Hill La. Holme HD7 198 D8
Weatherall Pl. Ad St S DN6 184 F1
Weatherhead Pl. Sil BD20 5 F1
Weatherhill Cres. Hud HD3 135 A1
Weatherhouse Terr. Hali HX2 91 D6
Weaver Cl. Brad BD8 73 E7
Weaver Gdns. Morley LS27 98 B2
Weavers Cotts. Oxen BD22 51 C2 1
Weavers Croft. Brad BD10 39 B2
Weavers Ct. Brad BD6 74 C1
Weavers Ct. Mel HD7 170 E2
Weavers St. Pudsey LS28 76 F1
Weavers Hill. Haw BD22 51 C6

Weavers Rd. Pont WF8 125 E1
Weavers Wlk. D Dale HD8 192 B7
Weavers Wlk. Brad BD4 75 A1
Webb Dr. Brad BD2 56 A2
Webb's Terr. Hali HX3 113 D3
Weber Ct. Brad BD3 75 B7
Webster Hill. Dew WF13 139 C8
Webster St. Brad BD3 75 B7
Webster St. Leeds LS9 212 A4
Webster Ave. Leeds LS12 78 B6
Webster Row. Leeds LS12 78 B6
Wedgewood Ct. Leeds LS8 44 A1
Wedgewood Dr. Leeds LS8 44 A1
Wedgewood Gr. Leeds LS8 44 A1
Wedgwood Sch. Brad 75 F2
Weeland Ave. Crof WF4 144 B3
Weeland Cres. Crof WF4 144 C3
Weeland Dr. Crof WF4 144 C3
Weeland Rd. Knot WF11 127 D8
Weet Shaw La. Cud S72 180 B1
Weetlands Cl. Kippax LS25 83 B2
Weetwood Cty Prim Sch. Leeds 59 D7
Weetwood Cres. Leeds LS16 59 C7
Weetwood Ct. Leeds LS16 59 D8
Weetwood Grange Gr. Leeds LS16 59 C8
Weetwood House Ct. Leeds LS16 59 D7
Weetwood La. Leeds LS16 59 D8
Weetwood Manor. Leeds LS16 59 C8
Weetwood Park Dr. Leeds LS16 59 B8
Weetwood Rd. Brad BD8 74 A8
Weetwood Rd. Leeds LS16 59 B8
Weetwood St. Brad BD8 73 F8
Weetwood Terr. Leeds LS16 59 C8
Weetworth Ave. Castle WF10 124 F6
Weetworth. Castle WF10 124 E6
Weir La. Bacup OL13 106 A7
Weir Side. Mars HD7 168 F4
Weir St. Tod OL14 108 B6
Welbeck Dr. Brad BD7 73 E4
Welbeck La. Wake WF1 143 B8
Welbeck Rd. Batley WF17 96 F7
Welbeck Rd. Leeds LS9 80 A7
Welbeck Rise. Brad BD7 73 E4
Welbeck St. Wake WF1 142 D3
Welburn Ave. Leeds LS16 59 C4
Welburn Ave. Leeds LS16 59 C4
Welburn Ct. Wake WF1 142 F1
Welburn Dr. Leeds LS16 59 C4
Welburn Gr. Leeds LS16 59 C4
Welbury Dr. Brad BD8 73 D8
Weldon Dr. Elland HD3 152 A8
Weldon Rd. Dew WF12 139 E7
Welham Wlk. Brad BD3 56 B1
Well Cl. Swil LS26 102 E8
Well Cl. Yeadon LS19 40 C3
Well Close Rise. Leeds LS7 60 D7
Well Close St. Brig HD6 115 B3
Well Croft. Shep BD18 55 B7
Well Garth Bank. Leeds LS15 62 C2
Well Garth Mount. Leeds LS15 62 C2
Well Garth. Leeds LS15 62 C2
Well Garth. Swil LS26 82 A1
Well Gr. Hud HD2 136 F5
Well Green La. Brig HD6 114 F5
Well Head Dr. Hali HX1 113 C6
Well Head La. Hali HX1 113 C5
Well Head La. S Hipp HX6 112 D3
Well Head La. Sow Br HX6 112 D3
Well Heads. Denth BD13 71 E5
Well Hill. Yeadon LS19 40 B7
Well Hill Gr. Roy S71 179 C4
Well Hill. Roy S71 179 C4
Well Hill. Yeadon LS19 40 B7
Well Holme Mead. Gild LS12 77 E3
Well House Ave. Leeds LS8 61 A5
Well House Ct. Leeds LS8 61 A5
Well House Dr. Leeds LS8 61 A5
Well House Gdns. Leeds LS8 61 A5
Well House Rd. Leeds LS8 61 A5
Well La. Batley WF17 118 D5
Well La. Brig HD6 115 A3
Well La. Guise LS20 22 E1
Well La. Hali HX1 113 D7
Well La. Kippax LS25 83 A1
Well La. Tod OL14 108 B5
Well La. Yeadon LS19 40 B7
Well Royd Ave. Hali HX2 112 C7
Well Royd Cl. Hali HX2 112 C7
Well St. Denh BD13 71 D6
Well St. Dew WF13 118 D1
Well St. S in Cra BD20 16 D5
Well St. Wils BD15 53 C4
Well St. Brad BD1 201 C3
Well St. Guise LS20 22 E1
Well St. Hor WF4 141 A1 6
Wellands La. Clec BD19 116 A7
Wellcroft. Guise LS20 22 E1
Wellcroft. Otley LS21 23 B7
Wellesley La. Wake WF2 141 E7
Wellesley St. Brad BD1 201 C4
Wellfield Cl. Floc WF4 156 E5
Wellfield Dr. Batley WF16 117 E4
Wellfield Terr. Clec BD19 116 D7
Wellgarth. Hali HX1 113 A7
Wellgate. Ackw WF7 163 F5
Wellgate. Elland HX4 134 A4
Wellgate. Mir WF14 138 A4
Wellgate. Slai HD7 152 A2
Wellhouse La. Mir WF14 138 B7
Wellholme Ave. Brig HD6 115 A4

Wellhouse La. Mir WF14 138 B7
Wellhouse Mid Sch. Mir 138 B7
Wellhouse. Mir WF14 138 B7
Wellington Arc. Brig 115 B2 7
Wellington Bridge St. Leeds LS12 78 F8
Wellington Bridge St. Leeds LS12 79 A7
Wellington Bsns Ctr. Elland 135 A7
Wellington Cres. Ship BD18 55 A7
Wellington Ct. Brig HD6 115 A6
Wellington Ct. Hali HX2 112 E8 4
Wellington Fst Sch. Brad 56 B3
Wellington Garth. Leeds LS13 58 D3
Wellington Gdns. Leeds LS13 58 D4
Wellington Gr. Brad BD2 56 B2
Wellington Gr. Leeds LS13 58 D3
Wellington Gr. Pudsey LS28 76 C7
Wellington Hill. Thorner LS14 45 A3
Wellington Mid Sch. Brad 56 B3
Wellington Mount. Leeds LS13 58 D4
Wellington Pl. Knot WF11 126 D4
Wellington Pl. Brad BD2 56 B3
Wellington Rd. Dew WF13 139 C8
Wellington Rd. Bing BD16 37 A3
Wellington Rd. Dew WF13 139 C8 10
Wellington Rd. Ikley LS29 8 B3
Wellington Rd. Keigh BD21 35 C6 4
Wellington Rd. Leeds LS12 78 F7 2
Wellington Rd. Tod OL14 108 B6
Wellington Rd. Wils BD15 53 C4
Wellington Rise. Leeds LS13 58 D4
Wellington St. Leeds LS1 211 D3
Wellington St. Dew WF13 139 C8 11
Wellington St. Liver WF15 117 B3 3
Wellington St. S Hali HX1 113 D6
Wellington St. Hud HD1 153 F6
Wellington St. Keigh BD21 35 B3
Wellington St. Leeds LS1 211 D3
Wellington St. Liver WF15 117 B3
Wellington St. Wils BD15 53 C4
Wellington St. W. Hali HX1 113 B6
Wellington St. Yeadon LS19 40 C7
Wellington St. Wils BD15 53 C4
Wellington Terr. Leeds LS13 58 D4
Wellington Terr. Mars HD7 169 A4
Wells Croft. Leeds LS6 59 F7
Wells Ct. Hali HX1 92 B1
Wells Ct. Ossett WF5 140 C5
Wells Gr. Guise LS20 22 E1
Wells Prom. Otley LS21 23 A7
Wells Rd. Guise LS20 22 E1
Wells Rd. Ilkley LS29 8 A4
Wells St. Morley LS27 98 B4
Wells Terr. Otley LS21 23 A8
Wells Wlk. Ilkley LS29 8 A4
Wellstone Ave. Pudsey LS13 77 B8
Wellstone Dr. Pudsey LS13 77 A8
Wellstone Garth. Pudsey LS13 58 B1
Wellstone Gdns. Pudsey LS13 77 B8
Wellstone Gn. Pudsey LS13 77 B8
Wellstone Rise. Pudsey LS13 77 B8
Wellstone Way. Pudsey LS13 77 B8
Welton Gr. Leeds LS6 59 E3
Welton Mount. Leeds LS6 59 E3
Welton Pl. Leeds LS6 59 E3
Welton Rd. Leeds LS6 59 E3
Welwyn Ave. Batley WF17 117 F6
Welwyn Ave. Ship BD18 55 A6
Welwyn Dr. Bail BD17 38 C3
Welwyn Dr. Ship BD18 55 A6
Welwyn Rd. Batley WF17 118 F3
Wembley Ave. Thorn BD13 72 E6
Wenborough La. Brad BD4 75 C2
Wendel Ave. B in Elm LS15 63 D7
Wenlock St. Brad BD3 75 A8
Wenning St. Keigh BD21 35 B8
Wensley Ave. Leeds LS7 60 C7
Wensley Ave. Ship BD18 55 A6
Wensley Bank Terr. Thorn BD13 72 C6
Wensley Bank. Thorn BD13 72 C6
Wensley Bank W. Thorn BD13 72 C6
Wensley Cres. Leeds LS7 60 C7
Wensley Dr. Leeds LS7 60 C7
Wensley Dr. Pont WF8 125 E2
Wensley Gn. Leeds LS7 60 C7
Wensley Gr. Leeds LS7 60 B7
Wensley Gr. Hud HD3 135 A1
Wensley Rd. Leeds LS7 60 B7
Wensley St. Dew WF13 139 C8
Wensley View. Leeds LS7 60 C7
Wensleydale Ave. Leeds LS12 77 D7
Wensleydale Cl. Leeds LS12 77 C7
Wensleydale Cres. Leeds LS12 77 D7
Wensleydale Ct. Leeds LS7 60 A6
Wensleydale Dr. Leeds LS12 77 C7
Wensleydale Mews. Leeds LS12 77 D7
Wensleydale Rd. Brad BD3 75 D8
Wensleydale Rise. Bail BD17 38 D4
Went Cl. Ackw WF7 146 F1
Went Croft. Pont WF8 146 C5
Went Edge Rd. Kbur WF9 182 A7
Went Edge Rd. Th Aud WF9 166 D1
Went Fold. Pont WF8 146 C5
Went Garth. Pont WF8 146 C5
Went Gr. S Elm WF9 182 F3
Went Hill Gdns. Kirk WF9 182 E3
Went La. Upton WF9 183 A8
Went Vale. Pont WF8 146 C5
Went View. Th Aud WF8 165 B1
Wentbridge La. Th Aud WF8 165 B3
Wentbridge Rd. Feath WF7 145 F6
Wentcliffe Rd. Knot WF11 127 B4
Wentdale. K Smea WF8 166 E6
Wentworth Ave. Emley HD8 175 C6

Wentworth Ave. Leeds LS17 43 C4
Wentworth Cl. Men LS29 22 A4
Wentworth Cl. Wool WF4 177 F7
Wentworth Cres. Leeds LS17 43 C4
Wentworth Ct. Brig HD6 135 F7
Wentworth Ct. Crof WF4 162 A8
Wentworth Dr. Emley HD8 175 C6
Wentworth Dr. Hali HX3 92 C1
Wentworth Gate. Weth LS22 13 B6
Wentworth Gr. Hali HX3 92 C1
Wentworth Park Roa. Dar WF8 147 D5
Wentworth Rd. Feath WF7 145 B4
Wentworth St. Hud HD1 153 F7
Wentworth St. Wake WF1 142 B7
Wentworth Terr. Horn WF1 142 B7
Wentworth Terr. Wake WF1 142 B7
Wentworth Terr. Yeadon LS19 40 C3
Wentworth Way. Leeds LS17 43 C4
Wentworth Way. Wake WF2 142 B1
Wepener Mount. Leeds LS9 61 B1
Wepener Pl. Leeds LS9 61 B1
Wesdale Cl. S Kirk WF9 182 C2
Wesley Ave. Brad BD12 94 C3 3
Wesley Ave S. Brad BD12 94 C6 3
Wesley Cl. Batley WF17 96 C1
Wesley Cl. Leeds LS11 78 F3
Wesley Cl. Leeds LS11 78 F3
Wesley Cl. Hali HX1 113 C2 7
Wesley Ct. Leeds LS11 60 A3
Wesley Ct. Leeds LS11 78 F2
Wesley Ct. Ossett WF5 140 C6
Wesley Dr. Brad BD12 94 E7
Wesley Garth. Leeds LS11 78 F3
Wesley Gr. Leeds LS11 78 F3
Wesley Hall Ct. Loft G WF3 121 F2 1
Wesley Pk. Leeds LS9 80 F8
Wesley Pl. Pen LS19 61 B1
Wesley Pl. Keigh BD21 35 B3
Wesley Pl. Leeds LS9 80 F8
Wesley Pl. Keigh BD21 35 B3
Wesley Pl. Sil BD20 5 E1
Wesley Rd. Leeds LS12 78 B4
Wesley Rd. Pudsey LS28 57 D2
Wesley Row. Pudsey LS28 76 E8 10
Wesley Sq. Pudsey LS28 76 E7 6
Wesley St. Castle WF10 124 C5
Wesley St. Clec BD19 116 D8
Wesley St. Dew WF13 139 C8
Wesley St. Leeds LS11 211 E1
Wesley St. Morley LS27 98 B3
Wesley St. Morley LS27 98 B4
Wesley St. Otley LS21 23 A8
Wesley St. Pudsey LS28 76 E8
Wesley St. Pudsey LS28 57 D2
Wesley St. Pudsey LS13 57 D2 7
Wesley St. S Elm WF9 182 F3
Wesley Terr. Bacup OL13 106 A7 1
Wesley Terr. D Dale HD8 191 F6
Wesley Terr. Leeds LS13 58 D1
Wesley Terr. Pudsey LS13 57 F5 1
Wesley Terr. Pudsey LS13 57 D2
Wesleyan Terr. Brad BD4 75 C3
Wesleyan Head Rd. Mel HD7 170 E1
Wessenden Rd. Mars HD7 169 B1
West Acres. Byram WF11 126 D7
West Ave. B Spa LS23 14 C1
West Ave. Bail BD17 38 C3
West Ave. Brig HX3 115 A7
West Ave. Hor WF4 141 C1
West Ave. Honley HD7 172 A7
West Ave. Hud HD2 136 C2
West Ave. Roy S71 179 D4
West Bank. S Elm WF9 183 B3
West Bank Cl. Keigh BD22 34 E4
West Bank Gr. Keigh BD20 18 E2
West Bank. Hali HX2 91 A4
West Bank. Keigh BD22 34 E4
West Bank Rd. Keigh BD22 34 E4
West Bank Rise. Keigh BD22 34 E4
West Bolton. Hali HX2 91 C7
West Bowling Golf Course. Brad 74 E3
West Bradford Golf Course. Brad 54 C2
West Brook Ct. Hali HX1 202 C4
West Busk La. Otley LS21 22 B6
West Byland. Hali HX2 91 C1
West Carr La. Mars HD3 150 E2
West Chevin Rd. Otley LS21 22 D3
West Chevin Rd. Otley LS21 22 D3
West Cl. Hor WF4 141 B1
West Cl. Hud HD2 136 B2
West Cliffe. Hali HX3 113 A6
West Cliffe Rd. Otley LS21 23 A8
West Cliffe Terr. Otley LS21 23 A8
West Cl. Leeds LS13 58 C1 6
West Dene. Keigh BD20 19 D1
West Dene. Leeds LS17 43 F4
West Dr. Oxen BD22 51 C2 4
West Dr. Swil LS26 82 F1
West End App. Morley LS27 97 F3
West End Ave. Bing BD16 37 A5
West End Ave. Roy S71 179 D4
West End Cl. Hor WF4 141 B1
West End Cl. Leeds LS18 41 C1
West End Cres. Roy S71 179 D4
West End Dr. Clec BD19 116 D7
West End Dr. Hor WF4 141 B1
West End Dr. Leeds LS18 41 C1
West End Gdns. Hali HX1 202 B3
West End Golf Course. Hali 112 B4
West End La. Hors LS18 41 B1
West End Jun & Inf Sch. Hors 41 C1
West End Mid Sch. Clec 116 D7

Whetley La. Brad BD8 — 74 A8
Whetley Mid Sch. Brad — 74 A8
Whetley Terr. Brad BD8 — 74 C8 1
Whewell St. Batley WF17 — 96 C6
Whimbrel Cl. Brad BD8 — 73 C7
Whin Cl. Hem WF9 — 181 D5
Whin Gdns. Dearne S63 — 194 D1
Whin Knoll Ave. Keigh BD21 — 34 F8
Whin Mount. Nor WF6 — 144 C8
Whin St. Keigh BD21 — 35 A7
Whin View Ct. Ryhill WF4 — 162 C1
Whinberry Pl. Batley WF17 — 96 F3
Whinbrook Cres. Leeds LS17 — 43 C1
Whinbrook Ct. Leeds LS17 — 43 C1
Whinbrook Gdns. Leeds LS17 — 43 C1
Whinbrook Gr. Leeds LS17 — 43 C1
Whinburn Sch. Keigh — 17 F2
Whincop Ave. Castle WF10 — 124 A4
Whincover Cl. Leeds LS12 — 77 F5
Whincover Cross. Leeds LS12 — 77 F5
Whincover Dr. Leeds LS12 — 77 F5
Whincover Gdns. Leeds LS12 — 77 F5
Whincover Gr. Leeds LS12 — 77 F5
Whincover Grange. Leeds LS12 — 77 F5
Whincover Hill. Leeds LS12 — 77 F5
Whincover Mount. Leeds LS12 — 77 F5
Whincover Rd. Leeds LS12 — 77 F5
Whincover View. Leeds LS12 — 77 F5
Whincup Gdns. Leeds LS10 — 79 E2 3
Whinfield Ave. Keigh BD22 — 34 F8
Whinfield Cl. Keigh BD22 — 34 F8
Whinfield Dr. Keigh BD22 — 34 F8
Whinfield. Hors LS16 — 42 A8
Whinfield Pl. Ossett WF5 — 141 B4
Whingate Ave. Leeds LS12 — 78 A7
Whingate Cl. Leeds LS12 — 78 A7
Whingate Gn. Leeds LS12 — 78 A7
Whingate Gr. Leeds LS12 — 78 A7
Whingate Jun Sch. Leeds — 78 A7
Whingate Rd. Leeds LS12 — 78 A7
Whingrove Ave. Mel HD7 — 170 D1
Whinmoor Cl. Silk S75 — 193 F1
Whinmoor Cres. Leeds LS14 — 45 A1
Whinmoor Ct. Leeds LS14 — 45 A1
Whinmoor Dr. Silk S75 — 193 F1
Whinmoor Gdns. Leeds LS14 — 45 A1
Whinmoor La. Thorner LS17 — 44 F3
Whinmoor Mid Sch. Leeds — 45 B1
Whinmoor View. Silk S75 — 193 F1
Whinmoor Way. Leeds LS14 — 45 A1
Whinmoor Way. Silk S75 — 193 F1
Whinmore Gdns. Clec BD19 — 117 C7
Whinney Ct. Pozth WF7 — 144 A5
Whinney Field. Hali HX3 — 113 C4
Whinney Hill Pk. Brig HD6 — 115 B5
Whinney Moor Ave. Wake WF2 — 141 E4
Whinney Royd La. Shelf HX3 — 93 A5
Whinny La. Feath WF7 — 144 D5
Whins La. Spoff HG3 — 2 C8
Whins La. Th Arch LS23 — 14 F1
Whins The. Keigh BD21 — 35 A4
Whinside Cres. Dearne S63 — 194 C1
Whirlaw Ave. Tod OL14 — 108 A7
Whirlaw La. Tod OL14 — 108 B8
Whiskers La. Northo HX3 — 92 E4
Whisperwood Cl. Loft G WF1 — 121 D5
Whisperwood Rd. Loft G WF1 — 121 D5
Whitacre Cl. Hud HD2 — 136 E3
Whitacre St. Hud HD2 — 136 E3
Whitaker Ave. Brad BD2 — 56 C3
Whitaker Cl. Brad BD2 — 56 C3
Whitaker St. Batley WF17 — 118 D7
Whitaker St. Pudsey LS28 — 57 D2
Whitby Ave. Hud HD2 — 136 D3
Whitby Cres. Dew WF12 — 139 F8
Whitby Rd. Brad BD8 — 55 A1
Whitcliffe Mount Sch. Clec — 116 B8
Whitcliffe Rd. Clec BD19 — 116 D8

Whitebeam Gn. Pont WF8 — 125 F1
Whitebeam La. Midd LS10 — 99 D8 6
Whitebeam Wlk. Brad BD2 — 56 B5
Whitebridge Ave. Leeds LS9 — 80 E8
Whitebridge Prim Sch. Leeds — 80 E7
Whitebridge Spur. Leeds LS9 — 61 E1
Whitechapel Cl. Leeds LS8 — 61 C6
Whitechapel Gr. Brig BD19 — 95 A1
Whitechapel Mid Sch. Clec — 116 C8
Whitechapel Rd. Brig BD19 — 116 A8
Whitechapel Rd. Clec BD19 — 116 C8
Whitechapel Way. Leeds LS8 — 61 B6
Whitecliffe Cres. Swil LS26 — 82 A2
Whitecliffe Dr. Swil LS26 — 82 A2
Whitecliffe Rise. Swil LS26 — 82 A2
Whitecote Prim Sch. Leeds — 58 D4
Whitecote Gdns. Leeds LS13 — 58 B4
Whitecote Hill. Leeds LS13 — 58 B4
Whitecote La. Leeds LS13 — 58 B4
Whitecote Rise. Leeds LS13 — 58 B4
Whitefield Pl. Brad BD8 — 74 A8
Whitegate Dr. Hali HX3 — 113 D4
Whitegate. E Kes LS17 — 28 C6
Whitegate. Hali HX3 — 113 D4
Whitegate Hill. Dar WF8 — 164 E8
Whitegate La. Ack M T WF8 — 164 E8
Whitegate Rd. Hali HX3 — 113 D4
Whitegate Rd. Hud HD4 — 154 D4
Whitegate Terr. Hali HX3 — 113 D4
Whitegate Top. Hali HX3 — 113 D5
Whitehall. Ripp LS21 — 11 A1
Whitegates Gr. Lepton HD8 — 155 D2
Whitehall Ave. Brad BD12 — 94 C1
Whitehall Ave. Mir WF14 — 138 A2
Whitehall Ave. Wake WF1 — 121 A1
Whitehall Cres. Wake WF1 — 121 A1
Whitehall Croft. Roth LS26 — 100 F5
Whitehall Ct. Hor WF4 — 141 B1 1
Whitehall Gr. Birk BD11 — 96 B5
Whitehall Gr. Birk BD11 — 96 D6
Whitehall Gr. Birk BD11 — 96 C6
Whitehall Ind Est. Brad BD2 — 94 C1
Whitehall Rd. Brig BD12 — 94 C1
Whitehall Rd. Clec BD19 — 95 D2
Whitehall Rd E. Birk BD11 — 96 B5
Whitehall Rd. Gild LS12 — 77 D2
Whitehall Rd. Leeds LS12 — 78 A4
Whitehall Rd. Leeds LS12 — 78 F6
Whitehall Rd. Leeds LS12 — 78 B6
Whitehall Rd. Leeds LS1, LS12 — 79 A7
Whitehall Rd. Leeds LS12 — 78 A6
Whitehall Rd W. Birk BD11 — 96 A4
Whitehall Rd W. Clec BD19 — 95 F3
Whitehall Rise. Wake WF1 — 121 A1
Whitehall St. Brig HX3 — 114 D8
Whitehaven Cl. Brad BD6 — 93 F7
Whitehead Gr. Brad BD2 — 56 C4
Whitehead La. Hud HD4 — 154 A3
Whitehead La. Mel HD4 — 170 F6
Whitehead St. Brad BD4 — 75 B6
Whitehead St. Brad BD3 — 75 B5
Whitehill Terr. Hali HX1 — 112 F7 3
Whitehill Cl. Jun & Inf Schs. Hali — 91 E6
Whitehill Cres. Hali HX2 — 91 E6
Whitehill La. Hali HX2 — 91 E6
Whitehill Gn. Hali HX2 — 91 F6
Whitehill Rd. Hali HX2 — 91 E6
Whitehills The. Bgly BD16 — 36 F3
Whitehouse Ave. Swil LS26 — 102 D8
Whitehouse Cres. Swil LS26 — 102 E8
Whitehouse Gn. Swil LS26 — 82 C8
Whitehouse La. Swil LS26 — 82 C2
Whitehouse La. Yeadon LS19 — 40 D8
Whitehouse St. Leeds LS10 — 79 D3
Whitelands. Cres. Brad BD17 — 38 D3
Whitelands. Pudsey LS28 — 76 F8 1
Whitelands Rd. Pud BD17 — 79 D2
Whiteley Ave. Sow Br HX6 — 111 F3
Whiteley Croft Cl. Otley LS21 — 23 A7
Whiteley Croft Garth. Otley LS21 — 23 A7
Whiteley Croft. Otley LS21 — 23 A7
Whiteley Croft Rd. Otley LS21 — 22 F7
Whiteley Croft Rise. Otley LS21 — 23 A7
Whiteley St. Feath WF7 — 145 C5
Whiteley Terr. Rip HX6 — 132 E5
Whitelock St. Leeds LS7 — 60 C1
Whiteoplatts St. Tod OL14 — 86 B12
Whiterose Mead. Gar LS25 — 82 F6
Whitestone Cres. Yeadon LS19 — 40 B7
Whitestone La. Hud HD1 — 154 B8 2
Whitewood Cl. Morl S71 — 179 B3
Whitfield Ave. Leeds LS10 — 79 E4
Whitfield Gdns. Leeds LS10 — 79 E4
Whitfield Pl. Leeds LS10 — 79 E4
Whitfield Sq. Leeds LS10 — 79 E4
Whitfield St. Clec BD19 — 116 D8 9
Whitford Freight Ctr. Nor — 123 D4
Whitham Cl. B Spa LS23 — 30 D8
Whitkirk Cl. Leeds LS15 — 81 E8
Whitkirk La. Leeds LS15 — 81 E8
Whitkirk Prim Sch. Leeds — 81 C7
Whitkirk St. Ship BD18
Whitley Gdns. Leeds LS8 — 207 F4
Whitley Grange Hospl. Dew — 138 F1
Whitley La. Holmfi HD7 — 189 E8
Whitley Pl. Knot WF11 — 126 F3
Whitley Rd. Dew WF12 — 139 F7
Whitley Rd. Wilsd WF15 — 115 A2
Whitley Rd. Wth Com S30 — 200 F7
Whitley Spring Cres. Ossett WF5 — 140 F5
Whitley Spring Rd. Ossett WF5 — 140 F6
Whitley St. Bgly BD16 — 37 A2
Whitley St. Brad BD3 — 75 A7
Whitley Terr. Wth Com S30 — 200 F7
Whitley Way. Flock WF4 — 157 B3
Whittle Cres. Brad BD14 — 73 B5
Whittle Croft Rd. Batley LS29 — 8 C4
Whitty Ave. Elland HX5 — 134 F7
Whitwell Ave. Elland HX5 — 135 A6
Whitwell Gr. Elland HX5 — 135 A6
Whitwell Green La. Elland HX5 — 135 B6
Whitwell St. Brad BD4 — 75 A5
Whitwood Common La. Castle WF10 — 123 E5

Whitworth Enterprise Pk. Nor — 123 B3
Whitwood Ho. Brig HD6 — 115 D7
Whitwood La. Castle WF10 — 123 E6
Whitwood Mining & Tech Coll (Annexe). Castle — 124 B8
Whitwood Mining & Tech Coll. Castle — 124 A6
Whitwood Terr. Castle WF10 — 123 E5
Whitworth Rd. Dew WF13 — 139 B7 1
Wholestone Gate. Hud HD7 — 152 B5
Whytecote End. Brad BD12 — 94 C4
Wibsey Fst Sch. Brad — 74 B1
Wibsey Mid Sch. Brad — 74 B1
Wibsey Park Ave. Brad BD6 — 94 A8
Wicken La. Thorn BD13 — 72 D7
Wicket. Pudsey LS28 — 57 B7
Wickets Cl. Brad BD6 — 94 D8
Wickets Dr. Brad BD6 — 94 D8
Wickets The. Leeds LS15 — 81 E7
Widdop Ave. B Spa LS23 — 30 C8
Wickham Ave. B Spa LS23 — 30 C8
Wickham Dr. B Spa LS23 — 30 C8
Wickham St. Brig BD19 — 94 F1
Wickham St. Leeds LS11 — 79 A3
Wickong La. Rip HX6 — 132 A8
Wickons La. Holmfi HD7 — 188 D6
Widdop Ave. Holmfi HD7 — 189 D3
Widdop Rd. Hep HX7 — 88 D6
Wide La. B Spa LS23 — 30 C8
Wide La. Morley LS27 — 98 D4
Wide La. Wake WF1 — 142 B8
Wigan St. Brad BD1 — 74 D7
Wiggan La. Hud HD2 — 136 D4
Wiggin Cross. Slai HD7 — 152 E1
Wighill La. Th Arch LS23 — 15 C2
Wighill La. B Spa LS23 — 15 C2
Wighill St. S in Cra BD20 — 16 C5
Wightman St. Brad BD3 — 56 A1
Wignall St. Keigh BD20 — 18 A1
Wigton Chase. Leeds LS17 — 44 A5
Wigton Gate. Leeds LS17 — 43 E6
Wigton Gn. Leeds LS17 — 43 F6
Wigton La. Leeds LS17 — 43 F6
Wigton Moor Prim Sch. Leeds — 43 F5
Wigton Park Cl. Leeds LS17 — 43 F6
Wike La. Bard LS17 — 28 B3
Wike Ridge Ave. Leeds LS17 — 44 B5
Wike Ridge Gr. Leeds LS17 — 44 A5
Wike Ridge La. Hare LS17 — 44 C7
Wike Ridge La. Leeds LS17 — 44 C7
Wike Ridge Mount. Leeds LS17 — 44 B5
Wilberlee Cfty Prim Sch. Slai — 151 D2
Wilby St. Clec BD19 — 116 D7
Wilcock La. Ryhill BD20 — 4 F5
Wild Gr. Pudsey LS28 — 76 A7
Wild's Yd. Wake WF1 — 142 D5
Wildcy Cl. Bing BD16 — 36 F6
Wildspur Gr. Holmfi HD7 — 189 E4
Wilford Rd. Barn S71 — 178 E1
Wilfred Ave. Leeds LS15 — 81 B8
Wilfred St. Brad BD14 — 73 C4
Wilfred St. Leeds LS15 — 81 B8 2
Wilfrid Terr. Leeds LS12 — 78 A4
Wilkin St. Keigh BD21 — 18 C1
Wilkinson Fold. Brad BD12 — 94 C3 9
Wilkinson Terr. Brad BD7 — 73 F6
Wilkinson Way. Otley LS21 — 10 E1
Willans Rd. Dew WF13 — 118 C1
Willans Ave. Roth LS26 — 100 F7
Willerton Cl. Batley WF12 — 119 B3
Willgutter La. Haw BD22 — 33 F1
Willgarth Ave. Leeds LS15 — 80 E8 2
William Henry Senth Sch The. Brig — 135 E8
William St. Brig HD6 — 115 A3 1
William Henry St. Brig HD6 — 58 F8 2
William Henry St. Leeds LS9 — 61 B2
William Horsfall St. Hud HD4 — 153 C3
William Prince Gr. Wake WF1 — 142 E3
William Rise. Leeds LS15 — 80 E8
William St. Birg HD6 — 115 A10
William St. Castle WF10 — 103 D1
William St. Castle WF10 — 104 C2
William St. Denh BD13 — 52 D1
William St. Dew WF13 — 139 C8
William St. Elland HX4 — 134 D6
William St. Elland HX4 — 134 B7
William St. Leeds LS7 — 59 F7
William St. Pudsey LS28 — 57 D1 8
William St. Pudsey LS28 — 57 F7
William Ct. Leeds LS7 — 61 D2
Williamson St. Hali HX1 — 203 F3
Willans Rd. Harden BD16 — 36 B1
Willoughby Terr. Leeds LS11 — 79 A3
Willow App. Leeds LS4 — 59 D1
Willow Ave. Bacup OL13 — 106 A3
Willow Ave. Brad BD2 — 56 A2
Willow Ave. Leeds LS4 — 59 E1
Willow Bank. Hali HX1 — 113 A5
Willow Bank. Tod OL14 — 108 B6
Willow Beck. Wake WF1 — 121 A7
Willow Cl. Brad BD6 — 94 C7
Willow Cl. Bur in W LS29 — 9 E1
Willow Cl. Guise LS20 — 22 D1
Willow Cl. Hali HX2 — 91 E4
Willow Cres. Bacup OL13 — 106 A3
Willow Cres. Leeds LS9 — 80 D8
Willow Dene Ave. Hali HX2 — 112 A6
Willow Dr. Brad BD6 — 94 C7
Willow Dr. Hem WF9 — 181 D5
Willow Dr. Leeds LS4 — 59 D1
Willow Garth Ave. Glu BD20 — 16 D7
Willow Garth Ave. Leeds LS14 — 62 B8

Willow Garth Cl. Leeds LS14 — 62 B8
Willow Garth. Crig WF4 — 159 F6
Willow Garth. Feath WF7 — 124 C1
Willow Garth. Leeds LS14 — 59 C1
Willow Gdns. Bing WF9 — 183 B2
Willow Gdns. Brad BD2 — 56 A6
Willow Gdns. Wake WF2 — 141 D7
Willow Gr. Clec BD19 — 22 E1
Willow Gdns. Guise LS20 — 22 E1
Willow Gr. Leeds LS4 — 59 D1
Willow Gr. Wake WF2 — 141 D7
Willow Glade. B Spa LS23 — 30 D5
Willow Gn. Loft G WF1 — 121 B3
Willow Gr. B Spa LS23 — 30 D6
Willow Gr. Brad BD2 — 56 A6
Willow Gr. Hud HD7 — 152 E5
Willow Gr. Keigh BD21 — 35 A6
Willow Gr. Kippax LS25 — 82 F3
Willow Gr. Ossett WF5 — 140 E3
Willow Gr. Leeds LS4 — 59 E1
Willow Hall Dr. Hali HX6 — 112 D5
Willow Hall La. Hali HX6 — 112 D5
Willow La. B Spa LS23 — 30 D5
Willow La. Crof WF1 — 143 D7
Willow La. E. Feath WF7 — 124 C1
Willow La. E. Hud HD1 — 154 B8
Willow La. Feath WF7 — 124 C1
Willow La. Hud HD1 — 154 A8
Willow La. Wake WF2 — 141 D7
Willow Park Dr. Shelf HX3 — 93 D6
Willow Pk. Loft G WF1 — 121 B2
Willow Pk. Pont WF8 — 146 F8
Willow Rd. Batley WF17 — 118 E4
Willow Rd. Castle WF10 — 125 C6
Willow Rd. Dearne S63 — 194 D1
Willow Rd. Knot WF11 — 127 A5
Willow Rd. Leeds LS4 — 59 E1
Willow Rd. Pudsey LS28 — 57 E2
Willow Rd. Wake WF2 — 141 D7
Willow Rise. Hali HX2 — 112 D6
Willow St. Bgly BD16 — 175 A8
Willow St. Clec BD19 — 95 B3
Willow St. Hali HX1 — 113 A6
Willow Terr. Batley WF17 — 118 E4
Willow Terr. Hali HX6 — 112 D5
Willow Terr Rd. Leeds LS1 — 60 B1
Willow Tree Cl. Keigh BD21 — 35 D5
Willow Tree Gdns. Bing BD16 — 37 C5
Willow Villas. Brad BD2 — 56 A6
Willow View. Hali HX6 — 112 C5
Willow Villas. Brad BD2 — 56 A6
Willow Way. S in Cra BD20 — 16 C4
Willow Wlk. Ingl LS15 — 80 B8
Willows The. Castle WF10 — 124 A6
Willowbank. Rd. Norton WF8 — 166 F5
Willowbrook. Ad Le S Sch. Leeds — 184 F2
Willowdene La. Pont WF8 — 125 D3
Willowfield Ave. Hali HX2 — 112 D5
Willowfield Cl. Hali HX2 — 112 D5
Willowfield Cres. Hali HX2 — 112 D5
Willowfield Dr. Hali HX2 — 112 C5
Willowfield Fst Sch. Brad — 56 A6
Willowfield Rd. Hali HX2 — 112 D5
Willowfield St. Brad BD7 — 74 B6
Willowfield Terr. Hali HX2 — 112 D6
Willowfield View. Hali HX2 — 112 D5
Willowgarth High Sch. Grim — 181 A1
Willowgarth Ave. Grim — 181 A1
Willround Ave. Wake WF1 — 121 E7
Willround Mount. Leeds LS15 — 81 C7
Willows The. Leeds LS17 — 43 C2
Willows The. Leeds LS17 — 43 C2
Willows The. Harden BD16 — 36 B1
Willows The. Leeds LS17 — 43 C2
Willows The. Nor WF6 — 144 B5
Wills Gill. Guise LS20 — 22 F1
Wilman Hill. Brad BD6 — 94 A7
Wilman Hill. Brad BD6 — 153 A1
Wilman Post. Ossett WF5 — 140 C6
Wilman Rd. Brad BD2 — 74 B1 3
Wilmar Dr. Ship BD9 — 55 A4
Wilmer Dr. Ship BD9 — 55 A4
Wilmer Rd. Brad BD9 — 55 B2
Wilmington Gr. Leeds LS7 — 60 D2
Wilmington St. Leeds LS7 — 60 D2
Wilmington Terr. Leeds LS7 — 60 D2
Wilmot Rd. Ilkley LS29 — 8 C4
Wilmour Mount. Hali HX2 — 111 D6
Wilsden First Sch. Wils — 53 C5
Wilsden Hill. Wils BD15 — 53 B5
Wilsden Old Rd. Harden BD16 — 36 B1
Wilsden Rd. Harden BD16 — 36 B1
Wilshaw Ct. Sch. Mel — 188 B4
Wilshaw Mill Rd. Mel HD7 — 187 F4
Wilshaw Rd. Mel HD7 — 188 B4
Wilson Ave. Mir WF14 — 137 F5
Wilson Ave. Ossett WF5 — 141 A4
Wilson Ave. Stee BD20 — 17 B6
Wilson Rd. Bing BD16 — 37 A4
Wilson Rd. Hali HX1 — 202 C4
Wilson Rd. Wash WF4 — 156 E6
Wilson St. Brad BD5 — 201 B2
Wilson St. Castle WF10 — 103 E5
Wilson St. Feath WF7 — 145 C5
Wilson St. S Elm WF9 — 183 B3
Wilson St. Wake WF2 — 142 A5

Windermere Rd. Brad BD7 — 73 E3
Windermere Rd. Castle WF10 — 125 D7
Windermere Rd. Mel HD7 — 170 E1
Windermere Ter. Wake WF7 — 141 F7
Windermere Ter. Brad BD7 — 73 E3 3
Wingate. Sil BD20 — 17 F8
Windhill Ave. Mapp S75 — 178 A3
Windhill CE Fst Sch. Ship — 55 E8
Windhill Cres. Mapp S75 — 178 A3
Windhill Cres. Wake WF1 — 142 E8
Windhill Dr. Wake WF1 — 142 F8
Windhill Mount. Mapp S75 — 178 A3
Windhill La. Mapp S75 — 178 A3
Windhill Mount. Mapp S75 — 178 A3
Windle Cl. Liver HD8 — 190 F2
Windle Edge. Dun Br S30 — 199 D1
Windle La. Con BD20 — 4 A2
Windle Royd La. Hali HX2 — 112 C7
Windmill App. Leeds LS10 — 99 E8
Windmill Chase. Roth LS26 — 100 E4
Windmill Cl. Leeds LS10 — 99 E7
Windmill Cres. Northo HX3 — 93 A2
Windmill Gdns. Mel HD8 — 175 B1
Windmill Ct. Leeds LS14 — 62 B6
Windmill Dr. Northo HX3 — 93 A2
Windmill Field Rd. Roth LS26 — 100 E4
Windmill Gdns. Gr. Roth LS26 — 100 E4
Windmill Gdns. Liver BD19 — 117 B6
Windmill Hill. Brad BD6 — 74 A1
Windmill Hill La. Emley HD8 — 174 F8
Windmill Hill La. Floc WF4 — 156 F1
Windmill La. Birk BD11 — 96 C6
Windmill La. Batley WF17 — 97 A1
Windmill La. Brad BD6 — 74 C1
Windmill La. Guise LS20 — 22 D4
Windmill La. Guise LS20 — 22 D4
Windmill La. Leeds LS14 — 62 B6
Windmill La. Loth HD7 — 190 D3
Windmill La. Yeadon LS19 — 40 C6
Windmill Prim Sch. Leeds — 99 E8
Windmill Rd. Branham LS23 — 30 E4
Windmill Rd. Midd LS10 — 99 E8
Windmill Rise. Aber LS25 — 64 E6
Windmill Rise. Leeds LS12 — 209 E1
Windmill View. Wake WF1 — 121 C7
Windross. Ct Mel HD4 — 123 A4
Windsor Ave. Ack M T WF7 — 164 C7
Windsor Ave. Leeds LS15 — 62 C3
Windsor Cl. Batley WF12 — 119 B2
Windsor Cl. Kippax LS25 — 83 A2
Windsor Cres. Hali HX2 — 91 E1
Windsor Cres. Roth LS26 — 100 E6
Windsor Cres. Leeds LS15 — 121 A1
Windsor Ct. Leeds LS15 — 62 C3
Windsor Ct. Morley LS27 — 98 A4
Windsor Ct. Roth Hud HD5 — 155 A6
Windsor Dr. Knot WF11 — 126 E5
Windsor Dr. Leeds LS15 — 117 B2
Windsor Gr. Gar LS25 — 83 B7
Windsor Dr. Skel HD8 — 175 B1
Windsor Gdns. Batley WF12 — 119 B2
Windsor Gn. Haw BD22 — 34 B2
Windsor Gr. Haw BD22 — 34 B2
Windsor Gr. Thorn BD13 — 72 D6
Windsor Mount. Leeds LS15 — 62 C3
Windsor Pl. Hud HD2 — 136 E5
Windsor Rd. Batley WF17 — 118 B2
Windsor Rd. Bing WF4 — 119 C7
Windsor Rd. Heb Br HX7 — 89 A4
Windsor Rd. Ship BD18 — 55 C6
Windsor Royd. Nor WF6 — 181 F6
Windsor St. Brad BD4 — 201 D1
Windsor St. S Elm WF9 — 183 A4 1
Windsor Terr. Batley WF12 — 119 B2
Windsor View. Heb Br HX7 — 89 A4 1
Windsor Wlk. Hud HD1 — 153 E5
Windy Bank La. Clec WF15 — 116 B4
Windy Bank La. Heb Br HX7 — 116 B4
Windy Bank La. Queen BD13 — 92 B6
Windy Gr. Wils BD15 — 53 D4
Windy Harbour La. Tod OL14 — 87 B1
Windy Ridge. Thorn BD13 — 72 D7
Windyridge. St Ossett WF5 — 140 C6
Wine St. Leeds LS1 — 207 B8
Wine Tavern La. Sow Br HX6 — 111 B1
Wine Tavern Rd. Sow Br HX6 — 111 B3
Winfield Dr. Brad BD6 — 74 C2
Winfield Gr. Leeds LS2 — 206 B2
Winfield Pl. Leeds LS2 — 206 B2
Winfield Terr. Leeds LS2 — 206 B2
Wingate Ave. Keigh BD22 — 34 F6
Wingate Gr. Keigh BD22 — 160 E4
Wingate Way. Keigh BD22 — 34 F6
Winget Ave. Hud HD4 — 153 F3
Wingfield Cl. Bing BD16 — 37 A4
Wingfield Mount. Brad BD3 — 75 B7
Wingfield St. Brad BD3 — 75 B7
Winning La. Flan WF7 — 145 A5
Winnard Ct. Nor S71 — 179 C1
Winnipeg Pl. Leeds LS7 — 60 D6
Winrose App. Leeds LS10 — 99 F6
Winrose Ave. Leeds LS10 — 99 E6
Winrose Cl. Brad BD12 — 94 C4
Winrose Cres. Leeds LS10 — 99 F6
Winrose Dr. Leeds LS10 — 99 E6
Winrose Garth. Leeds LS10 — 99 E6
Winrose Gr. Leeds LS10 — 99 F6
Winrose Hill. Leeds LS10 — 80 A1
Winslow Rd. Brad BD10 — 56 E7
Winstanley Terr. Leeds LS6 — 205 D4
Winston Gdns. Leeds LS6 — 59 C4
Winston Mount. Leeds LS6 — 59 C4
Winston Terr. Brad BD7 — 74 A5
Winter St. Hali HX1 — 202 B2
Winters La. Tod OL14 — 85 F7
Winter's Cotts. B Head HX7 — 88 C2
Winter's La. B Head HX7 — 88 C2

Winterbourne Ave. Morley LS27 .... 98 B6
Winterburn La. Hali HX2 .... 112 A6
Winterburn St. Keigh BD21 .... 35 C8 3
Winterbutlee Gr. Tod OL14 .... 108 A1 16
Winterbutlee Rd. Tod OL14 .... 108 A1
Winterneb. Hali HX2 .... 111 E5
Wintersett La. Ryhill WF4 .... 162 A5
Winterton Dr. Brad BD12 .... 94 C5
Winthorpe Ave. Midd WF3 .... 99 D2
Winthorpe Cres. Midd WF3 .... 99 D2
Winthorpe St. Leeds LS6 .... 59 F6
Winthorpe View. Midd WF3 .... 99 E2
Winton Gr. Brad BD6 .... 94 B6 2
Winton St. Hud HD1 .... 153 E3
Wintoun St. Leeds LS7 .... 60 D1
Wisbey Bank. Brad BD6 .... 74 D1
Wistons La. Elland HX5 .... 135 A7
Witchfield Hill. Shelf HX3 .... 93 D6
Witham Rd. Ship BD18 .... 54 E8
Witham Way. Gar LS25 .... 83 B6
Withens Cl. Mapps S75 .... 178 A1
Withens End La. Rip HX4 .... 150 E7
Withens Hill Croft. Hali HX2 ...... 91 E7
Withens La. Heb Br HX7 .... 109 E3
Withens La. Rip HX4 .... 150 F8
Withens New Rd. Hali HX2 .... 109 F3
Withens New Rd. Heb Br HX7 ..... 109 E3
Withens Rd. Batley WF17 .... 96 E2
Withens Rd. Hali HX2 .... 91 A7
Withen Fields. Hali HX3 .... 114 A4
Withins Cl. Brad BD5 .... 74 B3
Withyside. D Dale HD8 .... 192 A6
Witmore St. S Elm WF9 .... 183 A3
Witton St. Wake WF1 .... 142 D7
Woburn Dr. Hud HD5 .... 155 B6
Woburn Terr. Brad BD14 .... 73 B4 1
Wold Cl. Thorn BD13 .... 72 D6
Wolfstones Rd. Holmfi HD7 ...... 188 D6
Wolley Ave. Gild LS12 .... 77 D3
Wolley Ct. Gild LS12 .... 77 D3
Wolley Dr. Gild LS12 .... 77 D3
Wolley Gdns. Gild LS12 .... 77 D3
Wolseley Rd. Leeds LS4 .... 59 D2
Wolseley St. Brad BD14 .... 73 C5
Wolsey Ave. Pont WF8 .... 146 B8 2
Wolsley Terr. Hali HX1 .... 113 A7 1
Wolston Cl. Brad BD4 .... 75 E2
Womersley Pl. Pudsey LS28 ...... 76 D6 4
Womersley Rd. Knot WF11 .... 127 B2
Womersley St. Hali HX1 .... 112 F7 18
Wonder St. Wake WF1 .... 142 D5
Wood Ave. Batley WF16 .... 117 D5
Wood Bottom La. Brig HD6 .... 114 E4
Wood Bottom Rd. Honley HD4 .... 171 C5
Wood Cl. Bail BD17 .... 38 B2
Wood Cl. Hem WF9 .... 163 A2
Wood Cl. L Brad BD20 .... 4 C3
Wood Cl. Leeds LS7 .... 60 C7
Wood Cl. Nor WF6 .... 122 E3
Wood Cl. Roth LS26 .... 100 D6
Wood Cres. Roth LS26 .... 100 D6
Wood Croft. Brig HD6 .... 114 F1
Wood Croft. Sow Br HX6 .... 111 E3
Wood Dr. Roth LS26 .... 100 D6
Wood End Cotts. Mir WF14 .... 137 F3
Wood End Cres. Ship BD18 .... 55 D8
Wood End. Hud HD4 .... 153 F3
Wood End La. Rip HX4 .... 133 D6
Wood End La. Shep HD8 .... 190 C7
Wood End Rd. Hud HD4 .... 171 E8
Wood Farm La. Honley HD7 ...... 172 C2
Wood Gr. Castle WF10 .... 123 F5
Wood Gr. Leeds LS12 .... 77 D7
Wood Gr. Ossett WF5 .... 140 D8
Wood Hey La. Heb Br HX7 .... 89 B1
Wood Hill Ct. Hors LS16 .... 41 C3
Wood Hill Cres. Hors LS16 .... 41 C4
Wood Hill Garth. Hors LS16 ...... 41 C4
Wood Hill Gdns. Hors LS16 ...... 41 D4
Wood Hill Gr. Hors LS16 .... 41 D3
Wood Hill Rise. Hors LS16 .... 41 D4
Wood Hill Rd. Hors LS16 .... 41 C3
Wood La. B in LS15 .... 62 E6
Wood La. Bard LS17 .... 28 E3
Wood La. Batley WF17 .... 118 D3
Wood La. Brad BD2 .... 55 F5
Wood La. Brig HX3 .... 114 B8
Wood La. Castle WF10 .... 123 F5
Wood La. Crig WF4 .... 160 B3
Wood La. D Dale HD8 .... 191 E6
Wood La. Dew WF13 .... 118 D1
Wood La. Gild LS12 .... 77 C7
Wood La. Hali HX2, HX3 .... 91 E2
Wood La. Holmfi HD7 .... 189 A6
Wood La. Hors LS18 .... 58 D8
Wood La. Hud HD4 .... 154 C3
Wood La. Kirkb HD8 .... 173 C4
Wood La. Kirkhe WF14 .... 137 E4
Wood La. Leeds LS7 .... 60 C7
Wood La. Leeds LS12 .... 77 D7
Wood La. Leeds LS13 .... 58 B4
Wood La. Leeds LS6 .... 59 E5
Wood La. Mapp S71 .... 178 E2
Wood La. Neth WF4 .... 157 F7
Wood La. Roth LS26 .... 100 D6
Wood La. Roy S71 .... 179 C1
Wood La. Roy WF9 .... 164 F3
Wood La. Sow Br HX6 .... 111 E3
Wood La. Swil LS26 .... 102 B4
Wood La. Th Arch LS23 .... 14 E5
Wood La. W ad M HX2 .... 90 A5
Wood Lea. Byram WF11 .... 126 D8
Wood Lea. M'town LS26 .... 102 D3
Wood Moor Rd. Hem WF9 ...... 181 F7
Wood Mount. Neth WF4 .... 157 F6
Wood Nook La. Hali HX6 ...... 112 C5
Wood Nook La. Honley HD7 .... 171 D3
Wood Nook Terr. Pudsey LS28 .. 57 C1
Wood Rd. Brad BD6 .... 74 B4
Wood Rd. Leeds LS12 .... 77 D7
Wood Rise. Ship BD16 .... 54 C7
Wood Row. M'town LS26 ...... 102 B3
Wood Royd Hill La. Holmfi HD7 .. 200 B8
Wood St. Bail BD17 .... 38 C1
Wood St. Batley WF17 .... 118 C5

Wood St. Bing BD16 .... 36 E6
Wood St. Brad BD15 .... 54 C1
Wood St. Brad BD8 .... 74 C8
Wood St. Brig HD6 .... 115 B2
Wood St. Castle WF10 .... 124 C8
Wood St. Clay W HD8 .... 175 D1
Wood St. Clec BD19 .... 116 C7
Wood St. Dew OL14 .... 144 B3
Wood St. Dew WF13 .... 118 D1
Wood St. E Ard WF3 .... 120 D8
Wood St. Elland HX5 .... 135 A6
Wood St. Haw BD22 .... 51 C6 4
Wood St. Hors LS18 .... 41 C2
Wood St. Hud HD3 .... 153 A5
Wood St. Hud HD5 .... 154 D6
Wood St. Keigh BD21 .... 35 C6
Wood St. Morley LS27 ...... 97 F5
Wood St. N. Hali HX3 ...... 92 B2
Wood St. Ossett WF5 .... 140 D8
Wood St. S Hie S72 .... 180 F6
Wood St. Slai HD7 .... 174 F2
Wood St. Slai HD7 .... 151 F1
Wood St. Steet BD20 .... 17 C5
Wood St. Tod OL14 .... 108 B6
Wood St. Wake WF1 .... 142 C6
Wood St. Hud HX1 .... 113 B6
Woodhouse Ave. Hud HD2 ... 136 C2
Woodhouse CE(A) Jun Sch. Hud .. 136 C1
Woodhouse Cl. E Ard WF3 ... 120 B6
Woodhouse Cl. Keigh BD21 .. 35 C6
Woodhouse Cliffe. Leeds LS6 .. 60 A4
Woodhouse Cotts. Slai HD3 ... 151 D5
Woodhouse Cres. Nor WF6 ... 144 B8
Woodhouse Ct. Leeds LS2 ... 206 B3
Woodhouse. D Dale HD8 ..... 192 A6
Woodhouse Dr. Keigh BD21 .. 35 C6
Woodhouse Gdns. Brig HD6 .. 115 A3
Woodhouse Gr. Brig HD6 .... 115 A3
Woodhouse Gr. Hud HD2 .... 136 C2
Woodhouse Gr. Keigh BD21 .. 35 C5
Woodhouse Hall Rd. Hud HD2 .. 136 C2
Woodhouse Hill. Hali HX3 ... 114 C7
Woodhouse Hill Ave. Leeds LS10 .. 79 E2 7
Woodhouse Hill Gr. Leeds LS10 .. 79 E2
Woodhouse Hill. Hud HD2 ... 136 C2
Woodhouse Hill Pl. Leeds LS10 .. 79 E2 7
Woodhouse Hill Rd. Leeds LS10 .. 79 E2 7
Woodhouse Hill Terr. Leeds LS10 .. 79 E2 5
Woodhouse La. Brig HD6 .... 136 B8
Woodhouse La. Brad WF3 ... 120 B5
Woodhouse La. Emley HD8 .. 175 A7
Woodhouse La. Hali HX3 .... 113 A3
Woodhouse La. Leeds LS2 ... 206 B2
Woodhouse La. Leeds LS6 ... 206 A4
Woodhouse La. Mir WF14 .... 137 F5
Woodhouse La. Tod OL14 ... 108 E6
Woodhouse Rd. Keigh BD21 .. 35 C5
Woodhouse Rd. Tod OL14 ... 108 E6
Woodhouse Sq. Leeds LS3 ... 206 A1
Woodhouse St. Leeds LS6 ... 206 A4
Woodhouse Terr. Brad BD6 .. 74 B1
Woodhouse Way. Keigh BD21 .. 35 C5
Woodhouse Wlk. Keigh BD21 .. 35 C5
Woodkirk Ave. E Ard WF3 ... 120 A8
Woodkirk Gdns. Dew WF12 .. 119 D8
Woodkirk Gr. Brad BD12 .... 94 C1
Woodkirk Gr. E Ard WF3 ... 120 A8
Woodland App. Leeds LS14 .. 45 B1
Woodland Cl. Leeds LS15 ... 81 C8
Woodland Cres. Roth LS26 .. 101 D6
Woodland Cres. Brad BD9 ... 54 F2
Woodland Croft. Hors LS18 .. 41 A2
Woodland Cl. Crig WF4 ..... 159 F4
Woodland Dr. Crig WF4 ..... 159 F4
Woodland Dr. E Ard WF3 ... 120 A8
Woodland Dr. Hali HX2 ..... 112 E4
Woodland Dr. Honley HD7 ... 172 A4
Woodland Dr. Leeds LS7 ... 207 D4
Woodland Dr. Roth LS26 .... 100 D6
Woodland Dr. Swil LS26 .... 82 A1
Woodland Dr. Wake WF2 ... 141 D4
Woodland Gr. Leeds LS7 ... 207 D4
Woodland Gr. Roth LS26 .... 100 D6
Woodland Gr. Swil LS26 .... 82 A1
Woodland Hill. Leeds LS15 .. 81 C8
Woodland La. Leeds LS7 ... 207 D4
Woodland Mount. Leeds LS7 .. 207 D4
Woodland Park Rd. Leeds LS6 .. 59 F4
Woodland Pk. Roth LS26 .... 100 D6
Woodland Rise. Leeds LS15 .. 81 C8
Woodland Sq. Brig HD6 .... 114 F1
Woodland St. Brig HD6 ..... 114 F1
Woodland Terr. Leeds LS7 .. 207 D4
Woodland View. Gar LS25 .. 83 A7
Woodland View. Hali HX3 .. 92 C1
Woodland View. Leeds LS7 .. 207 D4
Woodland View. Pont WF8 .. 146 E6
Woodlands Ave. Hali HX3 ... 92 B2
Woodlands Ave. Wake WF2 .. 120 C2
Woodlands. Brad BD13 ..... 73 B1
Woodlands Cl. Brad BD13 .. 73 B1
Woodlands Cl. Hal WF8 .... 165 B4
Woodlands Cl. Mir WF14 ... 137 F3
Woodlands Cl. Morley LS27 .. 98 A6
Woodlands Cres. Batley WF17 .. 117 F4
Woodlands Cres. Sed Br HX6 .. 112 A3
Woodlands. D Dale HD8 .... 192 A7
Woodlands Dr. Gar LS25 ... 82 E7
Woodlands Dr. Mir WF14 ... 137 F3
Woodlands Dr. Morley LS27 .. 98 A6
Woodlands Fold. Birk BD11 .. 96 A7
Woodlands Gr. Bing BD16 ... 36 F2
Woodlands Gr. Hali HX3 ... 92 B2
Woodlands Gr. Kippax LS25 .. 102 E8
Woodlands Gr. Pudsey LS28 .. 76 F7
Woodlands La. Bing BD16 .. 36 D6
Woodlands Mount. Hali HX3 .. 92 B2
Woodlands Pk. Guis LS20 .. 39 C8
Woodlands Park Gr. Pudsey LS28 .. 76 D5

Woodhead Cl. Hud HD2 .... 136 C3
Woodhead La. Holme HD6 ..... 115 E2
Woodhead La. Gild LS27 ...... 97 C7
Woodhead Rd. Batley WF17 ... 97 B4
Woodhead Rd. Brad BD7 ...... 74 B6
Woodhead. Holmfi HD7 .... 188 B3
Woodhead Rd. Holmfi HD7 .... 172 B3
Woodhead Rd. Honley HD4 .... 172 B3
Woodhead Rd. Hud HD1 ...... 153 B6
Woodhead St. Clec BD19 ..... 116 E14
Woodhead Rd. Lepton HD8 ... 155 E3
Woodhill Cres. Leeds LS16 ... 41 D4
Woodhill Ct. Leeds LS16 ..... 41 C4
Woodhill Rise. Leeds LS16 ... 41 D4
Woodhill View. Wake WF2 ... 141 F6
Woodland Ave. Swil LS26 .... 82 A1
Woodland Ave. Crof WF1 .... 143 C7
Woodland Cl. E Ard WF3 ..... 120 B8
Woodland Cres. Crig WF4 .... 159 E4
Woodland Ct. Crig WF4 ...... 159 E4
Woodland Dell. Wake WF2 ... 159 E4
Woodland Gr. Crig WF4 ...... 159 E4
Woodland Pl. Crig WF4 ...... 159 F4
Woodland Rd. Crig WF4 ...... 159 F4
Woodland Terr. Crig WF4 .... 159 E4
Woodland View. Crig WF4 ... 159 E4
Woodland Way. Crig WF4 .... 159 E4
Woodlands Ave. Leeds LS16 .. 42 C3
Woodlands. B Spa LS23 ..... 30 D7
Woodlands. B Spa LS23 ..... 30 D7
Woodlands Ct. Leeds LS16 .. 42 B4
Woodlands Ct. Leeds LS16 .. 42 C3
Woodlands Dr. Hali HX2 .... 91 B2
Woodlands Gr. Leeds LS16 .. 42 C3
Woodlea Ave. Yeadon LS19 . 39 F5
Woodlea Chase. Yeadon LS19 . 39 F5
Woodlea Cl. Yeadon LS19 ... 39 F5
Woodlea Ct. Leeds LS11 .... 78 F3
Woodlea Ct. Yeadon LS19 ... 39 F5
Woodlea Dr. Leeds LS11 .... 78 F3
Woodlea Dr. Yeadon LS19 .. 39 F5
Woodlea Fold. Leeds LS11 .. 78 F3
Woodlea Fold. Yeadon LS19 . 39 F5
Woodlea Garth. Leeds LS11 . 78 F3
Woodlea Gdns. Leeds LS11 .. 78 F3
Woodlea Gn. Leeds LS11 .... 78 F3
Woodlea Gr. Leeds LS11 .... 78 F3
Woodlea Gr. Yeadon LS19 .. 39 F5
Woodlea Holt. Leeds LS11 .. 78 F3
Woodlea La. Leeds LS11 .... 78 F3
Woodlea Lawn. Yeadon LS19 . 39 F5
Woodlea Mount. Leeds LS11 . 78 F3
Woodlea Mount. Yeadon LS19 . 39 F6
Woodlea Pk. Leeds LS11 .... 78 F3
Woodlea Pl. Leeds LS11 .... 78 F3
Woodlea Rd. Yeadon LS19 .. 39 F5
Woodlea Sq. Leeds LS11 .... 78 F3
Woodlea St. Leeds LS11 .... 78 F3
Woodlea View. Yeadon LS19 . 39 F5
Woodleigh. Gar LS25 .... 82 F6
Woodleigh Ave. Gar LS25 ... 82 F6
Woodleigh Cres. Nor WF6 ... 123 A3
Woodliffe Cres. Leeds LS7 .. 60 C7
Woodliffe Ct. Leeds LS7 .... 60 C7
Woodliffe Dr. Leeds LS7 .... 60 C7
Woodman Ave. Elland HX5 .. 134 F6
Woodman Ave. Hud HD2 .... 136 C3
Woodman St. Leeds LS15 ... 62 C1
Woodmoor Cl. Crig WF4 .... 159 E4
Woodmoor Ct. Crig WF4 .... 159 E4
Woodmoor Rise. Crig WF4 .. 159 E4
Woodmoor Rd. Crig WF4 .... 159 E4
Woodnook Cl. Hors LS16 ... 41 D3
Woodnook Dr. Hors LS16 ... 41 D3
Woodnook Garth. Hors LS16 . 41 D3
Woodnook Rd. Hors LS16 ... 41 D3
Woodrow Cres. M'town LS26 . 102 D3
Woodrow Dr. Brad BD12 .... 94 E6
Woodroyd Ave. Brad BD5 ... 74 E3
Woodroyd Ave. Honley HD7 .. 172 B5
Woodroyd Dr. Hali HX3 .... 114 B8
Woodroyd Gdns. Ilkley LS29 . 8 F7
Woodroyd Gdns. Hali HX3 .. 111 F2
Woodroyd. Honley HD7 ..... 172 B5
Woodroyd Mid Sch. Brad ... 74 E2
Woodroyd Rd. Brad BD5 .... 74 E3
Woodroyd Terr. Brad BD5 ... 74 E3
Woods Ave. Mars HD7 ..... 169 A4
Woods Mount. Mars HD7 ... 169 A4
Woods Row. Pudsey LS28 .. 57 B7
Woodside. C of Swil WF4 ... 144 C2
Woodside Ave. Brad BD13 .. 73 A1
Woodside Ave. Hali HX3 ... 92 A2
Woodside Ave. Leeds LS4 .. 59 D2
Woodside Ave. Shep HD8 .. 190 D8
Woodside Cl. Morley LS27 .. 98 A6
Woodside Cres. Batley WF17 . 118 E2 8
Woodside Cres. Hali HX3 .. 92 A2
Woodside Ct. Hors LS16 ... 41 D4
Woodside Dr. Ackw WF7 ... 163 F6
Woodside. D Dale HD8 .... 192 A6
Woodside Gdns. Morley LS27 . 98 A6
Woodside Gr. Hali HX3 .... 92 A2
Woodside Gr. Kippax WF10 . 102 F6
Woodside Hill Cl. Hors LS18 . 41 D4
Woodside La. Hal WF8 .... 165 B4
Woodside La. Morley LS27 .. 98 A6
Woodside Mews. Leeds LS6 . 59 E5
Woodside Mount. Hali HX3 . 92 A1
Woodside Pk. Pont WF8 .... 146 D7
Woodside Pl. Hali HX3 .... 92 A2
Woodside Rd. Batley WF17 . 118 E2
Woodside Rd. Brad BD13 .. 73 A1
Woodside Rd. Brad BD12 .. 94 B5
Woodside Rd. Pont WF8 ... 146 D7
Woodside Rd. Shep HD8 ... 190 D8
Woodside St. Kippax WF10 . 102 F6
Woodside Terr. Brad BD13 . 73 A1
Woodside Terr. Hali HX3 .. 92 A2
Woodside Terr. Leeds LS4 . 59 D2
Woodside View. Batley WF17 . 118 E2
Woodside View. Bing BD16 . 37 A4
Woodside View. Hali HX3 . 92 A1
Woodside View. Leeds LS4 . 59 D2
Woodsley Gn. Leeds LS6 ... 205 F2
Woodsley Rd. Brad BD10 .. 56 C8
Woodsley Rd. Leeds LS2 ... 205 F2
Woodsley Rd. Leeds LS6 ... 59 F2
Woodsley Terr. Leeds LS2 .. 206 A2

Woodlands Park Rd. Pudsey LS28 .. 76 D5
Woodlands Rd. Batley WF17 ... 118 A8
Woodlands Rd. Bing BD16 ..... 37 C4
Woodlands Rd. Brad BD8 ...... 55 A1
Woodlands Rd. Brad BD13 .... 96 A1
Woodlands Rd. E. Lepton HD8 . 155 D3
Woodlands Rd. Hali HX5 ...... 134 F8
Woodlands Rd. Lepton HD8 ... 155 D3
Woodlands Rise. Haw BD22 ... 51 C6
Woodlands Rise. Ilkley LS29 .. 7 F4
Woodlands. Sow Br HX6 ..... 111 F3
Woodlands St. Brad BD8 ..... 74 C8
Woodlands Terr. Brad BD8 ... 55 A1
Woodlands Terr. Pudsey LS28 . 57 C1
Woodlands The. Pont WF8 ... 146 E6
Woodlands View. Hali HX3 ... 92 C1 8
Woodlands View. Hali HX3 ... 92 B2
Woodlands View. Heb Br HX7 . 89 A2
Woodlea App. Yeadon LS19 .. 39 F6
Woodlea Ave. Leeds LS11 ... 78 F3
Woodlea. E Elm WF9 .... 182 F2 6
Woodside Gr. Hali HX3 ..... 92 A2
Woodside Mews. Hud HD8 .. 175 A1
Woodside Mid Sch. Hali 92 A2
Woodside Pl. Hali HX3 ..... 92 A2
Woodside Pl. Leeds LS4 .... 59 D2
Woodside Rd. Hali HX3 .... 92 B2
Woodside Rd. Leeds LS4 ... 59 D2
Woodside St. Brad BD5 .... 74 D4
Woodsome Ave. Mir WF14 .. 138 A7
Woodsome Dr. Kirkb HD8 .. 173 F4
Woodsome Estate. Kirkb HD8 . 173 F5 8
Woodsome Hall La. Kirkb HD8 . 173 E5
Woodsome Lees La. Kirkb HD8 . 174 A4
Woodsome Rd. Kirkb HD8 .. 173 C1
Woodstock Cl. Leeds LS16 .. 42 E2
Woodstock Wlk. Brad BD5 .. 74 E5 3
Woodthorne Croft. Leeds LS17 . 44 A4
Woodthorpe Cl. Wake WF2 .. 160 E7
Woodthorpe Dr. Wake WF2 .. 160 E7
Woodthorpe Glades. Wake WF2 . 160 E7
Woodthorpe Mount. Wake WF2 . 160 E7
Woodthorpe Park Dr. Wake WF2 . 160 E7
Woodthorpe Terr. Hud HD1 .. 153 F5
Woodvale Cl. Brad BD16 .... 37 A5
Woodvale Cres. Bing BD16 .. 37 A5
Woodvale Gr. Brad BD7 .... 73 E5
Woodvale Rd. Brig HD6 .... 115 B3
Woodvale Way. Brad BD7 .. 73 E5
Woodview Ave. Bail BD17 .. 38 C4
Woodview. Bard LS17 ..... 28 D4
Woodview Cl. Bail BD17 ... 38 C4
Woodview Cl. Brad BD17 .. 38 C4
Woodview Mount. Leeds LS11 . 79 B2
Woodview Rd. Leeds LS11 .. 79 B2
Woodview St. Leeds LS11 .. 79 B2
Woodview Terr. Brad BD8 .. 55 D3
Woodview Terr. Leeds LS11 . 79 B2
Woodville Ave. Hors LS18 .. 58 D8 4
Woodville Cres. Hors LS18 . 58 D8 4
Woodville Ct. Leeds LS8 ... 44 A1
Woodville Gr. Hors LS18 ... 58 D8 7
Woodville Gr. Leeds LS10 .. 80 A1
Woodville Gr. Hali HX2 .... 91 C2
Woodville Pl. Brad BD9 ... 54 F4
Woodville Pl. Hors LS18 .. 58 D8
Woodville Rd. Hud HD1 ... 136 A1
Woodville Rd. Keigh BD20 . 35 B8
Woodville Sq. Midd LS10 .. 99 E5
Woodville St. Brad BD9 ... 54 F4
Woodville St. Hors LS18 .. 58 D8 3
Woodville St. Ship BD18 .. 55 D8
Woodville Terr. Haw BD22 . 51 F8 7
Woodville Terr. Hors LS18 . 58 D8 8
Woodward Ct. Mir WF14 .. 138 B7
Woodway. Dr. Hors LS18 .. 58 C7
Woodway. Hors LS18 ..... 58 C7
Woodworth Gr. Keigh BD21 . 35 B3
Wooler Ave. Leeds LS11 .. 79 A2
Wooler Dr. Leeds LS11 ... 79 A2
Wooler Gr. Leeds LS11 ... 79 A2
Wooler Pl. Leeds LS11 ... 79 A2
Wooler Rd. Leeds LS11 ... 79 A2
Wooler St. Leeds LS11 ... 79 A2
Woolford Way. Loft G WF3 . 121 D6
Woolgreaves Ave. Wake WF2 . 160 D6
Woolgreaves Croft. Wake WF2 . 160 D6
Woolgreaves Dr. Wake WF2 . 160 D6
Woolgreaves Garth. Wake WF2 . 160 D6
Woollin Ave. E Ard WF3 .. 119 E6
Woollin Cres. E Ard WF3 .. 119 E6
Woolpack's Yd. Wake WF1 . 142 D8 6
Woolrow La. Brig HD6 .... 115 D6
Woolshops. Sq. Hali HX1 .. 203 E3
Woolston Terr. Hud HX1 .. ...
Wootton St. Brad BD5 .... 74 E4
Worcester Ave. Midd LS10 . 99 F4
Worcester Cl. Midd LS10 .. 99 F4
Worcester Dr. Midd LS10 .. 99 F4
Worcester Gr. Hud HD4 ... 154 B3
Wordsworth App. Pont WF8 . 146 C7
Wordsworth Ct. Knot WF11 . 127 A4
Wordsworth Dr. Knot WF11 . 101 C3
Wordsworth Dr. Castle WF10 . 124 F7
Workhouse La. Elland HX4 . 134 A6
Workhouse La. Hali HX2 .. 112 A7
Wormald Row. Leeds LS2 .. 206 C2
Wormald St. Dew WF13 ... 139 C8
Wormald St. Liver WF15 .. 117 A4
Worrall Sq. Bus WF4 ..... 142 A3
Worsley Pl. Ad le S DN6 .. 184 F1 2
Worsnop Bldgs. Brad BD12 . 94 C4 15
Worstead Rd. Haw BD22 .. 51 F8
Worth Ave. Keigh BD21 ... 35 E8
Worth Bridge Rd. Keigh BD21 . 35 E8 1
Worth Valley Mid Sch. Keigh . 35 D6
Worth Way. Keigh BD21 ... 35 C6
Worth Way. Keigh BD21 ... 35 C6 3
Worthing Head Rd. Brad BD12 . 94 C3 2
Worthing St. Brad BD12 ... 94 C3
Worthing St. Brad BD12 ... 94 C3
Worthville Cl. Keigh BD21 . 35 D5
Wortley Heights. Leeds LS12 . 210 A3
Wortley La. Leeds LS12 ... 210 B2
Wortley Moor La. Leeds LS12 . 77 F3 14
Wortley Moor Rd. Leeds LS12 . 77 F4
Wortley Pk. Leeds LS12 ... 209 F3
Wortley Rd. Leeds LS12 ... 209 F4
Wortley St. Bing BD16 .... 37 A3
Wortley Towers. Leeds LS12 . 210 A3
Worts Hill La. Slai HD7 ... 151 D2
Worts Hill Side. Mars HD7 . 151 C1
Wrangbrook La. Upton WF9 . 183 D6
Wrangbrook Rd. Ad le S DN6 . 184 C2
Wrangbrook Rd. Upton WF9 . 184 A4
Wrangthorn Ave. Leeds LS6 . 205 F3
Wrangthorn Pl. Leeds LS6 .. 205 F3
Wrangthorn Terr. Leeds LS6 . 205 F3
Wray's Bldgs. Wake WF2 .. 141 D5
Wreakes La. Mapp S75 ... 178 B1
Wrelton Cl. Roy S71 ...... 179 B3
Wren Ave. Brad BD7 ..... 73 E2
Wren Croft. Pont WF8 .... 125 D3
Wren Dr. Morley LS27 .... 98 D3

Wren Garth. Wake WF2 ... 160 D5
Wren Hill. Batley WF17 ... 118 A8
Wren Nest Rd. Rip HX6 ... 132 A4
Wren St. Haw BD22 ... 51 D7 17
Wren St. Hud HD1 ... 153 D5
Wren St. Keigh BD21 ... 35 C8
Wrenbeck Ave. Otley LS21 ... 11 B2
Wrenbeck Cl. Otley LS21 ... 11 B2
Wrenbeck Dr. Otley LS21 ... 11 B2
Wrenbury Ave. Hors LS16 ... 41 D5
Wrenbury Cres. Hors LS16 ... 41 E5
Wrenbury Gr. Hors LS16 ... 41 E5
Wrenthorpe Jerry Clay La Jun & Inf
  Sch. Wake ... 120 E2
Wrenthorpe La. Wake WF2 ... 120 D1
Wrenthorpe La. Wake WF2 ... 120 E1
Wrenthorpe Rd. Wake WF2 ... 120 E2
Wrexhall Rd. Batley WF12 ... 118 E2
Wrexham Rd. Bur in W LS29 ... 9 D2
Wright Ave. Haw BD22 ... 34 D3
Wright St. Bacup OL13 ... 106 A7 5
Wright St. Haw BD22 ... 34 D2
Wright St. S in Cra BD20 ... 16 D5
Wrigley Ave. Brad BD4 ... 75 B1
Wrigley Hill. Hali HX2 ... 91 E5
Wroe Cres. Brad BD12 ... 94 C3
Wroe Pl. Brad BD12 ... 94 C3
Wroe St. Dew WF13 ... 117 F1
Wroe Terr. Brad BD12 ... 94 C3
Wrose Ave. Brad BD2 ... 56 A5
Wrose Ave. Ship BD18 ... 55 D6
Wrose Brow Rd. Ship BD18 ... 55 D8
Wrose Dr. Ship BD18 ... 55 D6
Wrose Gr. Ship BD18 ... 55 D6
Wrose Hill Pl. Ship BD2 ... 55 D5
Wrose Mount. Ship BD18 ... 55 E6
Wrose Rd. Brad BD2 ... 56 A6
Wrose Rd. Ship BD18 ... 55 E6
Wrose View. Bail BD17 ... 38 C3
Wrose View. Ship BD18 ... 55 D6
Wrosecliffe Gr. Ship BD10 ... 55 F8
Wycliffe Cl. Pudsey LS13 ... 57 D5
Wycliffe Dr. Leeds LS17 ... 43 D2
Wycliffe Gdns. Ship BD18 ... 55 A8
Wycliffe Rd. Pudsey LS13 ... 57 D5
Wycliffe Rd. Ship BD18 ... 55 A8

Wycliffe St. Ossett WF5 ... 140 D7
Wycoller Rd. Brad BD12 ... 94 C4
Wycombe Gn. Brad BD4 ... 75 E3
Wyebeck Ave. Leeds LS9 ... 80 D7
Wyke Cres. Brad BD12 ... 94 D2
Wyke La. Brad BD12 ... 94 E3
Wyke Manor Upper Sch. Brad ... 94 D3
Wyke Mid Sch. Brad ... 94 C3
Wyke Old La. Brig HD6 ... 115 B7
Wykebeck Ave. Leeds LS9 ... 80 D8
Wykebeck Cres. Leeds LS9 ... 80 D8
Wykebeck Gdns. Leeds LS9 ... 80 D8
Wykebeck Gr. Leeds LS9 ... 80 D8
Wykebeck Mount. Leeds LS9 ... 80 D8
Wykebeck Pl. Leeds LS9 ... 80 E8
Wykebeck Prim Sch. Leeds ... 61 D2
Wykebeck Rd. Leeds LS9 ... 80 D8
Wykebeck Sq. Leeds LS9 ... 80 D8
Wykebeck St. Leeds LS9 ... 80 D8
Wykebeck Terr. Leeds LS9 ... 80 D8
Wykebeck Valley Rd. Leeds LS9 ... 61 D2
Wykebeck View. Leeds LS9 ... 80 D8
Wykelea Cl. Brad BD12 ... 94 D3
Wycliffe Gdns. Leeds LS17 ... 43 D2
Wyncroft Gr. Bramho LS16 ... 24 F2
Wyncroft Rise. Ship BD18 ... 55 D5
Wyndham Ave. Brad BD2 ... 55 F3
Wynford Ave. Leeds LS16 ... 42 B1
Wynford Dr. S Elm WF9 ... 183 A3
Wynford Gr. Hors LS16 ... 42 B1
Wynford Mount. Hors LS16 ... 42 A1
Wynford Rise. Hors LS16 ... 42 B1
Wynford Terr. Hors LS16 ... 42 A1
Wynford Way. Brad BD12 ... 94 E7
Wynmore Ave. Bramho LS16 ... 24 F2
Wynmore Cres. Bramho LS16 ... 24 F2
Wynmore Dr. Bramho LS16 ... 24 F2
Wynmore Dr. Hud HD3 ... 134 F1
Wynne St. Brad BD1 ... 74 D8
Wynthorpe Rd. Hor WF4 ... 141 B1
Wynthorpe Rd. Hor WF4 ... 159 B8
Wynyard Dr. Morley LS27 ... 97 F4
Wyther Ave. Leeds LS5 ... 58 F3 2
Wyther La. Leeds LS5 ... 59 A3
Wyther Gn. Leeds LS5 ... 59 A3
Wyther La. Leeds LS5 ... 58 F3

Wyther Lane Ind Est. Leeds ... 58 F3
Wyther Park Ave. Leeds LS12 ... 58 F1
Wyther Park Cl. Leeds LS12 ... 58 F1 1
Wyther Park Cty Prim Sch. Leeds ... 58 F3
Wyther Park Cres. Leeds LS12 ... 58 F2
Wyther Park Gr. Leeds LS12 ... 58 F2
Wyther Park Hill. Leeds LS12 ... 58 F2
Wyther Park Mount. Leeds LS12 ... 58 F2
Wyther Park Pl. Leeds LS12 ... 58 F1
Wyther Park Rd. Leeds LS12 ... 58 F1
Wyther Park Sq. Leeds LS12 ... 58 E1
Wyther Park St. Leeds LS12 ... 58 F1
Wyther Park Terr. Leeds LS12 ... 58 F1
Wyther Park View. Leeds LS12 ... 58 F2
Wyvern Ave. Hud HD3 ... 153 C6
Wyvern Cl. Batley WF17 ... 118 C6
Wyvern Cl. Brad BD7 ... 73 F5
Wyvern Pl. Hali HX2 ... 112 E8
Wyvern Terr. Hali HX2 ... 112 E8 12
Wyverne Rd. Hud HD7 ... 152 E4
Wyvil Cres. Ilkley LS29 ... 8 E5
Wyvil Rd. Ilkley LS29 ... 8 E5

Yarborough Croft. Northo HX3 ... 93 A4
Yard No 1. Batley WF17 ... 118 A3
Yard No 3. Batley WF17 ... 118 A3
Yard No 4. Batley WF17 ... 117 F8 1
Yardley Way. Brad BD12 ... 94 E6
Yarn St. Leeds LS10 ... 79 E4
Yarwood Gr. Brad BD7 ... 73 E3 2
Yate La. Oxen BD22 ... 51 C3
Yates Flat. Ship BD18 ... 55 D6
Yates La. Hud HD3 ... 153 B4
Ye Farre Cl. Brig HD6 ... 115 A4 3
Yeadon Dr. Hali HX3 ... 114 A4
Yeadon House. S in Cra BD20 ... 16 C5
Yeadon Moor Rd. Yeadon LS19 ... 40 E6
Yeadon Moor Rd. Yeadon LS18 ... 41 A8
Yeadon Westfield Inf Sch. Yeadon ... 39 F6
Yeadon Westfield Jun Sch. Yeadon ... 39 F6
Yew Gr. Hud HD4 ... 152 F3
Yew Green Ave. Hud HD4 ... 153 E3
Yew Green Rd. Hud HD4 ... 153 E3
Yew La. Gar LS25 ... 83 B6
Yew Pk. Brig HD6 ... 114 E5
Yew St. Hud HD2 ... 136 A1

Yew Tree Ave. Brad BD8 ... 54 D1
Yew Tree Cl. L Brad BD20 ... 4 C6
Yew Tree Cres. Brad BD8 ... 54 E1
Yew Tree Ct. Liver WF15 ... 117 A5 6
Yew Tree Ct. Tod OL14 ... 129 A8
Yew Tree Gr. Brad BD8 ... 54 E1
Yew Tree La. Brad BD13 ... 72 E8
Yew Tree La. Holmfi HD7 ... 188 C3
Yew Tree La. Hud HD4, HD7 ... 152 F3
Yew Tree La. Slai HD7 ... 169 F7
Yew Tree Rd. Hud HD2, HD3 ... 135 B3
Yew Tree Rd. Shep HD8 ... 173 F1
Yew Tree. Slai HD7 ... 169 F7
Yew Tree St. Wake WF1 ... 142 E4
Yew Tree Wlk. Knot WF11 ... 126 E2
Yew Trees Ave. Northo HX3 ... 93 A3
Yew Trees Croft. Hali HX2 ... 90 C1
Yewbank Cl. Ilkley LS29 ... 8 A4
Yewbank Terr. Ilkley LS29 ... 8 A4
Yewdall Rd. Pudsey LS13 ... 57 E5
Yewdall Way. Brad BD10 ... 56 C6
Yews Hill Rd. Hud HD1, HD4 ... 153 E4
Yews Mount. Hud HD1 ... 153 F4
Yew Ave. Hud HD2 ... 136 A2
York Cl. S Elm WF9 ... 183 A4
York Cres. Bing BD16 ... 37 A2 1
York Dr. Batley WF16 ... 117 D6
York Dr. Clec BD19 ... 116 D8 8
York Pl. Leeds LS1 ... 79 B8
York Pl. Tod OL14 ... 108 B5 14
York Rd. Batley WF17 ... 118 C6
York Rd. Bick LS22 ... 14 D7
York Rd. Bur in W LS29 ... 9 F1
York Rd. Dew WF12 ... 139 F8
York Rd. Leeds LS14, LS15, LS9 ... 61 E1
York Rd. Leeds LS14, LS15 ... 62 C6
York Rd. Mir WF14 ... 137 F5

York Rd. Weth LS22 ... 14 D7
York Road Ind Est. Weth ... 13 F6
York St. Bing BD16 ... 37 A2
York St. Brad BD8 ... 73 E7
York St. Brig HD6 ... 115 A1
York St. Castle WF10 ... 124 E8
York St. Dearne S63 ... 194 F1
York St. Glu BD20 ... 16 D7
York St. Hali HX1 ... 113 B6
York St. Heb Br HX7 ... 89 A2 2
York St. Hem WF9 ... 181 E5
York St. Leeds LS9 ... 79 D7
York St. Nor WF6 ... 122 F3
York St. Queen BD13 ... 72 E1
York St. Tod OL14 ... 108 B6
York Terr. Hali HX3 ... 92 B1
York Villas. Nor WF6 ... 123 B2
Yorkshire Martyrs Collegiate Sch.
  Birk ... 96 A8
Yorkshire Sculpture Pk. W Bret ... 176 E7
Yorkshire TV Studios. Leeds ... 59 E1
Yorkshire Way. Brad BD7 ... 74 B3
Young St. Brad BD8 ... 73 F8
Young's Ct. Aber LS25 ... 64 E6

Zakaria Muslim Girls High Sch.
  Batley ... 118 D4
Zealand St. Brad BD4 ... 75 D4
Zermatt Gr. Leeds LS7 ... 60 C6
Zermatt Mount. Leeds LS7 ... 60 C6
Zermatt St. Leeds LS7 ... 60 D6
Zermatt Terr. Leeds LS7 ... 60 D6
Zetland Pl. Leeds LS8 ... 60 F3 1
Zetland St. Hud HD1 ... 154 B6 12
Zetland St. Wake WF1 ... 142 C6
Zion Cl. Hud HD3 ... 135 B1
Zion Dr. Mapp S75 ... 178 B1
Zion St. Bacup OL13 ... 106 A3
Zion St. Heb Br HX7 ... 89 E1
Zion St. Leeds LS9 ... 79 E6
Zion St. Ossett WF5 ... 119 C1
Zoar St. Morley LS27 ... 98 A4

Also available in various formats

- Berkshire
- Bristol and Avon
- Buckinghamshire
- Cardiff, Swansea and Glamorgan
- Cheshire
- Derbyshire
- Durham
- Edinburgh & East Central Scotland
- East Essex

- West Essex
- Glasgow & West Central Scotland
- North Hampshire
- South Hampshire
- Hertfordshire
- East Kent
- West Kent
- Lancashire
- Greater Manchester

- Merseyside
- Nottinghamshire
- Oxfordshire
- Staffordshire
- Surrey
- East Sussex
- West Sussex
- Tyne and Wear
- Warwickshire
- South Yorkshire

◆ Colour editions (Hardback, Spiral, Pocket) ◆ Black and white editions (Hardback, Softback, Pocket)

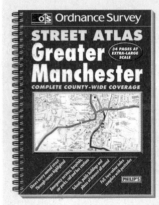

◆ Spiral

◆ Pocket

◆ Hardback